ST. THOMAS AQUINAS COLLEGE

3 6156 01019930 3

E 170.3 ENC
Encyclopedia of applied ethics

W9-AOD-325

REFERENCE ONLY

$625.00 (4 vols)

11-6-98

37779011

V4

ENCYCLOPEDIA OF APPLIED ETHICS

VOLUME 4

S–Z, INDEX

EDITOR-IN-CHIEF

RUTH CHADWICK

RESEARCH ASSISTANT ADAM HEDGECOE

CENTRE FOR PROFESSIONAL ETHICS
UNIVERSITY OF CENTRAL LANCASHIRE, UK

ADVISORY COUNCIL

DAN CALLAHAN
THE HASTINGS CENTER

PETER SINGER
MONASH UNIVERSITY

EXECUTIVE ADVISORY BOARD

TIMO AIRAKSINEN
University of Helsinki

BRENDA ALMOND
University of Hull

ANDREW BELSEY
University of Wales

ALASTAIR CAMPBELL
University of Otago

STEPHEN CLARK
University of Liverpool

ANNE DONCHIN
Indiana University

STRACHAN DONNELLEY
The Hastings Center

GERALD DWORKIN
University of Illinois

HETA HÄYRY
University of Helsinki

MATTI HÄYRY
University of Helsinki

JØRGEN HUSTED
University of Aarhus

RIHITO KIMURA
Georgetown University

JOHN KLEINIG
John Jay College

SUSAN MENDUS
The University of York

EMILIO MORDINI
Psychoanalytic Institute of Social Research

REN-ZONG QIU
Chinese Academy of Social Sciences

FREDERIC G. REAMER
Rhode Island College

JOHN J. SHEPHERD
University College of St. Martin

RUBEN SHER
National AIDS Training and Outreach Programme

ROBERT C. SOLOMON
University of Texas

RAY SPIER
University of Surrey

HENK TEN HAVE
Katholieke Universiteit Nijmegan

HENK J. L. VAN LUIJK
Nijenrode University

JOHN R. WILCOX
Manhattan College

ENCYCLOPEDIA OF APPLIED ETHICS

VOLUME 4
S–Z, INDEX

REFERENCE ONLY

ACADEMIC PRESS

SAN DIEGO   LONDON   BOSTON   NEW YORK   SYDNEY   TOKYO   TORONTO

ST. THOMAS AQUINAS COLLEGE
LOUGHEED LIBRARY
SPARKILL, NEW YORK 10976

This book is printed on acid-free paper. ∞

Copyright © 1998 by ACADEMIC PRESS

All Rights Reserved.
No part of this publication may be reproduced or transmitted in any form or by any
means, electronic or mechanical, including photocopy, recording, or any information
storage and retrieval system, without permission in writing from the publisher.

Academic Press
a division of Harcourt Brace & Company
525 B Street, Suite 1900, San Diego, California 92101-4495, USA
http://www.apnet.com

Academic Press Limited
24-28 Oval Road, London NW1 7DX, UK
http://www.hbuk.co.uk/ap/

Library of Congress Card Catalog Number: 97-074395

International Standard Book Number: 0-12-227065-7 (set)
International Standard Book Number: 0-12-227066-5 (v. 1)
International Standard Book Number: 0-12-227067-3 (v. 2)
International Standard Book Number: 0-12-227068-1 (v. 3)
International Standard Book Number: 0-12-227069-X (v. 4)

PRINTED IN THE UNITED STATES OF AMERICA
98 99 00 01 02 03 MM 9 8 7 6 5 4 3 2

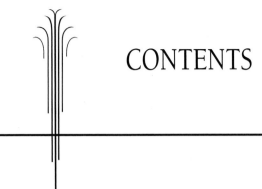

CONTENTS

CONTENTS OF OTHER VOLUMES

CONTENTS OF VOLUME 2

CONTENTS OF VOLUME 3

CONTENTS BY SUBJECT AREA

CONTRIBUTORS

G. JOHN M. ABBARNO
HOMELESSNESS
D'Youville College
Buffalo, New York

FRANCIS J. AGUILAR
CORPORATIONS, ETHICS IN
Harvard University
Cambridge, Massachusetts

WILLIAM AIKEN
CHILDREN'S RIGHTS
Chatham College
Chatham, New York

TIMO AIRAKSINEN
PROFESSIONAL ETHICS
University of Helsinki
Helsinki, Finland

LARRY ALEXANDER
FREEDOM OF SPEECH
University of San Diego
San Diego, California

ANDREW ALEXANDRA
EXECUTIVE COMPENSATION
Charles Sturt University
Bathurst, New South Wales, Australia

GARLAND E. ALLEN
GENETICS AND BEHAVIOR
NATURE VERSUS NURTURE
Washington University
St. Louis, Missouri

JONATHAN ALDRED
WILDLIFE CONSERVATION
Cambridge University
Cambridge, England, UK

DAVID ARCHARD
CHILD ABUSE
University of St. Andrews
Fife, Scotland, UK

MARY BETH ARMSTRONG
CONFIDENTIALITY, GENERAL ISSUES OF
California Polytechnic Institute
San Luis Obispo, California

RICHARD J. ARNESON
EQUALITY AND EGALITARIANISM
University of California, San Diego
San Diego, California

ROBERT L. ARRINGTON
ADVERTISING
Georgia State University
Atlanta, Georgia

RICHARD ASHCROFT
HUMAN RESEARCH SUBJECTS, SELECTION OF
University of Bristol
Bristol, England, UK

SUE ASHFORD
TERRORISM
University of Western Australia and Murdoch
University
Medina, Western Australia

ROBIN ATTFIELD
ENVIRONMENTAL ETHICS, OVERVIEW
University of Wales, Cardiff
Cardiff, Wales, UK

ROBERT D. BAIRD
HINDUISM
School of Religion, University of Iowa
Iowa City, Iowa

DOUGLAS BAKER
LAND USE ISSUES
University of Northern British Columbia
Prince George, British Columbia

NORMAN BARRY
WELFARE POLICIES
University of Buckingham
Buckingham, England, UK

BERNARD H. BAUMRIN
DIVORCE
    City University of New York
    New York, New York

JOHN D. BECKER
NATIONAL SECURITY ISSUES
WARFARE, STRATEGIES AND TACTICS
    United States Air Force Academy
    Colorado Springs, Colorado

HUGO ADAM BEDAU
CAPITAL PUNISHMENT
CIVIL DISOBEDIENCE
    Tufts University
    Medford, Massachusetts

RON L. P. BERGHMANS
COERCIVE TREATMENT IN PSYCHIATRY
    Institute for Bioethics
    Maastricht, The Netherlands

ROBERT H. BLANK
FETAL RESEARCH
    University of Canterbury
    Canterbury, England, UK

PAULA BODDINGTON
SELF-DECEPTION
    Australian National University
    Canberra, Australia

ANNIE BOOTH
LAND USE ISSUES
    University of Northern British Columbia
    Prince George, British Columbia

STEPHEN BOSTOCK
ZOOS AND ZOOLOGICAL PARKS
    Glasgow Zoo and University of Glasgow
    Glasgow, Scotland, UK

ANDREW BRENNAN
GAIA HYPOTHESIS
    The University of Western Australia
    Nedlands, Western Australia

ANDREW BRIEN
JURY CONDUCT
MERCY AND FORGIVENESS
    Australian National University
    Canberra, Australia

ROGER L. BURRITT
ENVIRONMENTAL COMPLIANCE BY INDUSTRY
    Australian National University
    Canberra, Australia

EDMUND F. BYRNE
PRIVACY
    Indiana University
    Indianapolis, Indiana

JOAN C. CALLAHAN
BIRTH-CONTROL ETHICS
    University of Kentucky
    Lexington, Kentucky

EAMONN CALLAN
PLURALISM IN EDUCATION
    University of Alberta
    Edmonton, Alberta

ARTHUR L. CAPLAN
INFORMED CONSENT
    University of Pennsylvania
    Philadelphia, Pennsylvania

ALEXANDER MORGAN CAPRON
DEATH, DEFINITION OF
    University of Southern California
    Los Angeles, California

ALAN CARLING
EXPLOITATION
    University of Bradford
    Bradford, England, UK

STANLEY R. CARPENTER
SUSTAINABILITY
    Georgia Institute of Technology
    Atlanta, Georgia

RUTH CHADWICK
GENETIC SCREENING
ORGAN TRANSPLANTS AND DONORS
    Centre for Professional Ethics
    University of Central Lancashire
    Preston, England, UK

TIMOTHY CHAPPELL
PLATONISM
THEORIES OF ETHICS, OVERVIEW
    University of Manchester
    Manchester, England, UK

VICHAI CHOKEVIVAT
AIDS IN THE DEVELOPING WORLD
    Thai Department of Health and Human Welfare

JOHN CHRISTMAN
PROPERTY RIGHTS
    Virginia Polytechnic Institute and State University
    Blacksburg, Virginia

JOHN P. CLARK
POLITICAL ECOLOGY
    Loyola University
    New Orleans, Louisiana

ANGUS CLARKE
GENETIC COUNSELING
    University of Wales College of Medicine
    Cardiff, Wales, UK

MARGARET COFFEY
BROADCAST JOURNALISM
    Australian Broadcasting Corporation
    Malvern, Australia

DAVID CONWAY
LIBERALISM
    Middlesex University
    London, England, UK

LINDSEY COOMBES
MENTAL HEALTH
    Oxford Brookes University
    Oxford, England, UK

WILLIAM COONEY
RIGHTS THEORY
    Briar Cliff College
    Sioux City, Iowa

PRESTON K. COVEY
GUN CONTROL
    Center for the Advancement of Applied Ethics
    Carnegie Mellon University
    Pittsburgh, Pennsylvania

CHRISTOPHER J. COWTON
SOCIALLY RESPONSIBLE INVESTMENT
    University of Huddersfield
    Queensgate, Huddersfield, England, UK

CHARLES CRITCHER
MEDIA DEPICTION OF ETHNIC MINORITIES
    Sheffield Hallam University
    Sheffield, England, UK

THOMAS CLOUGH DAFFERN
NATIVE AMERICAN CULTURES
    University of London
    London, England, UK

TIM DARE
APPLIED ETHICS, CHALLENGES TO
    The University of Auckland
    Auckland, New Zealand

MICHAEL DAVIS
CONFLICT OF INTEREST
    Illinois Institute of Technology
    Chicago, Illinois

ANGUS DAWSON
PSYCHOPHARMACOLOGY
    University of Liverpool
    Liverpool, England, UK

JUDITH WAGNER DECEW
WARFARE, CODES OF
    Clark University
    West Newton, Massachusetts

C. A. DEFANTI
BRAIN DEATH
    United Hospitals of Bergamo
    Bergamo, Italy

CARLOS DEL RIO
AIDS IN THE DEVELOPING WORLD
    Emory University

PHILIP E. DEVINE
HOMICIDE, CRIMINAL VERSUS JUSTIFIABLE
PUBLISH-OR-PERISH SYNDROME
    Providence College
    Providence, Rhode Island

BERNARD DICKENS
PATIENTS' RIGHTS
    University of Toronto Law School
    Toronto, Ontario

SUSAN DIMOCK
CRIME AND SOCIETY
JUVENILE CRIME
    York University
    North York, Ontario

SUSAN DODDS
SEX EQUALITY
    University of Wollongong
    Wollongong, Australia

STRACHAN DONNELLEY
HUMAN NATURE, VIEWS OF
    The Hastings Center
    Briarcliff Manor, New York

JUDE P. DOUGHERTY
THOMISM
    Catholic University of America
    Washington, DC

NIGEL DOWER
DEVELOPMENT ETHICS
DEVELOPMENT ISSUES, ENVIRONMENTAL
WORLD ETHICS
    University of Aberdeen
    Aberdeen, Scotland, UK

HEATHER DRAPER
EUTHANASIA
    University of Birmingham
    Birmingham, England, UK

DENIS DUTTON
PLAGIARISM AND FORGERY
    University of Canterbury
    Christchurch, New Zealand

SUSAN EASTON
PORNOGRAPHY
    Brunel University
    Uxbridge, England, UK

ANDREW EDGAR
QUALITY OF LIFE INDICATORS
SPORTS, ETHICS OF
    University of Wales
    Cardiff, Wales, UK

BENGT ERIK ERIKSSON
PREVENTIVE MEDICINE
    University of Linköping
    Linköping, Sweden

GAVIN FAIRBAIRN
SUICIDE
    North East Wales Institute of Higher Education
    Wrexham, Wales, UK

JOHN FENDER
ALTRUISM AND ECONOMICS
  University of Birmingham
  Birmingham, England, UK

DAVID E. W. FENNER
ARTS, THE
  University of North Florida
  Jacksonville, Florida

J. CARL FICARROTTA
MORAL RELATIVISM
  United States Air Force Academy
  Colorado Springs, Colorado

BETH A. FISCHER
SCIENTIFIC PUBLISHING
  University of Pittsburgh
  Pittsburgh, Pennsylvania

ANTHONY FISHER
CHRISTIAN ETHICS, ROMAN CATHOLIC
  Australian Catholic University
  Ascot Vale, Australia

CHARLES J. FOMBRUN
REPUTATION MANAGEMENT BY CORPORATIONS
  New York University
  New York, New York

NORMAN FORD
FETUS
  Caroline Chisholm Centre for Health Ethics
  East Melbourne, Australia

CLAIRE FOSTER
RESEARCH ETHICS COMMITTEES
  King's College
  London, England, UK

LESLIE PICKERING FRANCIS
RAPE
  University of Utah
  Salt Lake City, Utah

LUCY FRITH
REPRODUCTIVE TECHNOLOGIES
  University of Liverpool and University of Oxford
  England, UK

K. W. M. FULFORD
MENTAL ILLNESS, CONCEPT OF
  University of Warwick
  Coventry, England, UK

SUSANNE GIBSON
ABORTION
ACTS AND OMISSIONS
  University College of St. Martin
  Lancaster, England, UK

CHRISTOPHER GILL
GREEK ETHICS, OVERVIEW
  University of Exeter
  Exeter, England, UK

RAANAN GILLON
BIOETHICS, OVERVIEW
  Imperial College
  London University
  London, England, UK

ANDREW GILMAN
PERSONAL RELATIONSHIPS
  Andover Newton Theological School
  Stratham, New Hampshire

DONALD A. GRAFT
SPECIESISM
  Software Engineer Manager
  Pondicherry, India

WILLIAM GREY
PLAYING GOD
  University of Queensland
  Queensland, Australia

MATTHEW W. HALLGARTH
CONSEQUENTIALISM AND DEONTOLOGY
  United States Air Force Academy
  Colorado Springs, Colorado

JOCELYN Y. HATTAB
PSYCHIATRIC ETHICS
  Talbia Mental Health Center
  Hebrew University
  Jerusalem, Israel

HETA HÄYRY
GENETIC ENGINEERING
PATERNALISM
  University of Helsinki
  Helsinki, Finland

MATTI HÄYRY
GENETIC ENGINEERING
  University of Helsinki
  Helsinki, Finland

TIM HAYWARD
ANTHROPOCENTRISM
  University of Edinburgh
  Edinburgh, Scotland, UK

ADAM M. HEDGECOE
GENE THERAPY
GENOME ANALYSIS
  Centre for Professional Ethics
  University of Central Lancashire
  Preston, England, UK

ERIC HEINZE
VICTIMLESS CRIMES
  University of London
  London, England, UK

SIRKKU HELLSTEN
DISTRIBUTIVE JUSTICE, THEORIES OF
  University of Helsinki
  Helsinki, Finland

ALAN HOLLAND
ECOLOGICAL BALANCE
    Lancaster University
    Lancaster, England, UK

SØREN HOLM
AUTONOMY
EMBRYOLOGY, ETHICS OF
    University of Copenhagen
    Copenhagen, Denmark

TERRY HOPTON
POLITICAL OBLIGATION
    University of Central Lancashire
    Preston, England, UK

J. STUART HORNER
MEDICAL ETHICS, HISTORY OF
    University of Central Lancashire
    Preston, England, UK

GILLIAN HOWIE
GENDER ROLES
    University of Liverpool
    Liverpool, England, UK

RICHARD HUGMAN
ETHICS AND SOCIAL SERVICES, OVERVIEW
    Curtin University of Technology
    Perth, Australia

GEOFFREY HUNT
WHISTLE-BLOWING
    European Centre for Professional Ethics
    University of London
    London, England, UK

DOUGLAS N. HUSAK
DRUGS: MORAL AND LEGAL ISSUES
    Rutgers University
    New Brunswick, New Jersey

JENNIFER JACKSON
BUSINESS ETHICS, OVERVIEW
    University of Leeds
    Leeds, England, UK

MARJA JÄRVELÄ
ENVIRONMENTAL IMPACT ASSESSMENT
    The University of Jyväskylä
    Jyväskylä, Finland

MARGOT JEFFREYS
AGED PEOPLE, SOCIETAL ATTITUDES TOWARD
    Centre of Medical Law and Ethics
    King's College
    London, England, UK

MARIANNE M. JENNINGS
ELECTION STRATEGIES
    Arizona State University
    Tempe, Arizona

EDWARD JOHNSON
INTELLIGENCE TESTING
MEDIA OWNERSHIP
POLITICAL CORRECTNESS
    University of New Orleans
    New Orleans, Louisiana

JEFFERY L. JOHNSON
NUCLEAR DETERRENCE
    Eastern Oregon State College
    LaGrande, Oregon

PAULINE JOHNSON
SEXISM
    Macquarie University
    Sydney, Australia

TREVOR JONES
POLICE AND RACE RELATIONS
    Policy Studies Institute
    London, England, UK

RABINDRA N. KANUNGO
LEADERSHIP, ETHICS OF
    McGill University
    Montreal, Quebec

HELMUT F. KAPLAN
VEGETARIANISM
    University of Salzburg
    Salzburg, Austria

PAUL KELLY
CONTRACTARIAN ETHICS
    London School of Economics
    London, England, UK

DAMIEN KEOWN
BUDDHISM
    Goldsmiths College, University of London
    London, England, UK

JACINTA KERIN
SEXUAL ORIENTATION
    Monash University
    Toronto, Ontario

EDWARD W. KEYSERLINGK
MEDICAL CODES AND OATHS
    McGill University
    Montreal, Quebec

JUKKA KILPI
MERGERS AND ACQUISITIONS
    University of Helsinki
    Helsinki, Finland and Monash University
    Clayton, Victoria, Australia

DAHLIAN KIRBY
TRANSSEXUALISM
    University of Wales
    Cardiff, Wales, UK

STEPHEN KLAIDMAN
FREEDOM OF THE PRESS IN THE USA
    Georgetown University
    Washington, DC

JAMES W. KNIGHT
BIRTH-CONTROL TECHNOLOGY
    Virginia Polytechnic Institute and State University
    Blacksburg, Virginia

LORETTA M. KOPELMAN
FEMALE CIRCUMCISION AND GENITAL MUTILATION
MEDICAL FUTILITY
    East Carolina University School of Medicine
    Greenville, North Carolina

MARK KUCZEWSKI
CASUISTRY
    Medical College of Wisconsin

PAUL ALFRED KURZMAN
WORKPLACE ETHICS: ISSUES FOR HUMAN SERVICE
   PROFESSIONALS
    Hunter College, City University of New York
    New York, New York

KRISTIINA KUVAJA-PUUMALAINEN
ENVIRONMENTAL IMPACT ASSESSMENT
    Jyvaskyla University
    Jyvaskyla, Finland

WILL KYMLICKA
ETHNOCULTURAL MINORITY GROUPS, STATUS AND TREATMENT OF
    University of Ottawa
    Ottawa, Ontario

OLLI LAGERSPETZ
TRUST
    Abo Academy
    Abo, Finland
    and The University of Wales at Swansea

DAVID LAMB
DEATH, MEDICAL ASPECTS OF
    University of Birmingham
    Birmingham, England, UK

HAROLD Q. LANGENDERFER
ACCOUNTING AND BUSINESS ETHICS
    University of North Carolina
    Chapel Hill, North Carolina

DUNCAN LANGFORD
INTERNET PROTOCOL
    University of Kent
    Canterbury, England, UK

ROBERT LARMER
IMPROPER PAYMENTS AND GIFTS
    University of New Brunswick
    Fredericton, New Brunswick

OLIVER LEAMAN
JUDAISM
    Liverpool John Moores University
    Liverpool, England, UK

GRANT S. LEE
TAOISM
    Colorado State University
    Fort Collins, Colorado

KEEKOK LEE
BIODIVERSITY
    The University of Manchester
    Manchester, England, UK

STEVEN LEE
NUCLEAR TESTING
    Hobart and William Smith Colleges
    Geneva, New York

BURTON M. LEISER
CORPORAL PUNISHMENT
SLAVERY
    Pace University
    Briarcliff Manor, New York

A. CARL LEOPOLD
STEWARDSHIP
    Boyce Thompson Institute for Plant Research
    Cornell University
    Ithaca, New York

HARRY LESSER
AGEISM
    University of Manchester
    Manchester, England, UK

CAROL LEVINE
CUSTODY OF CHILDREN
    The Orphan Project
    New York, New York

MAIRI LEVITT
RELIGION IN SCHOOLS
    University of Central Lancashire
    Preston, England, UK

XIAORONG LI
WOMEN'S RIGHTS
    University of Maryland
    College Park, Maryland

JUDITH LICHTENBERG
OBJECTIVITY IN REPORTING
    University of Maryland
    College Park, Maryland

C. DAVID LISMAN
ETHICS EDUCATION IN SCHOOLS
    Community College of Aurora
    Aurora, Colorado

ANDROS LOIZOU
THEORIES OF JUSTICE: RAWLS
    University of Central Lancashire
    Preston, England, UK

VALERIE C. LORENZ
GAMBLING
Compulsive Gambling Center, Inc.
Baltimore, Maryland

ROBERT B. LOUDEN
VIRTUE ETHICS
Westfalische WIlhelms-Universitat
Munster, Germany

JOHN LYDEN
CHRISTIAN ETHICS, PROTESTANT
Dana College
Omaha, Nebraska

CHRIS MACDONALD
EVOLUTIONARY PERSPECTIVES ON ETHICS
University of British Columbia
Vancouver, British Columbia

CARLOS MAGIS
AIDS IN THE DEVELOPING WORLD
Conasida, Mexico

THOMAS MAGNELL
EPICUREANISM
Drew University
Madison, New Jersey

RUDOLPH J. MARCUS
GOVERNMENT FUNDING OF RESEARCH
Ethics Consultant
Sonoma, California

IAN MARKHAM
RELIGION AND ETHICS
Liverpool Hope University College
Liverpool, England, UK

GARY T. MARX
ELECTRONIC SURVEILLANCE
UNDERCOVER INVESTIGATIONS, ETHICS OF
Center for Advanced Study in the Behavioral
Sciences
Stanford, California

RICHARD O. MASON
GENETIC RESEARCH
INFORMATION MANAGEMENT
Southern Methodist University
Dallas, Texas

TODD MAY
POSTSTRUCTURALISM
Clemson University
Clemson, South Carolina

MARY ANN MCCLURE
INFERTILITY
John Jay College of Criminal Justice
New York, New York

PATRICIA E. MCCREIGHT
ENVIRONMENTAL COMPLIANCE BY INDUSTRY
Australian National University
Canberra, Australia

TONY MCGLEENAN
GENETIC TECHNOLOGY, LEGAL REGULATION OF
The Queen's University of Belfast
Belfast, Northern Ireland, UK

C. B. MEGONE
ARISTOTELIAN ETHICS
University of Leeds
Leeds, England, UK

GREGORY MELLEMA
COLLECTIVE GUILT
Calvin College
Grand Rapids, Michigan

MANUEL MENDONCA
LEADERSHIP, ETHICS OF
McGill University
Montreal, Quebec

MICHAEL A. MENLOWE
SAFETY LAWS
University of Edinburgh
Edinburgh, Scotland, UK

BEN MEPHAM
AGRICULTURAL ETHICS
University of Nottingham
Loughborough, England, UK

SEUMAS MILLER
TABLOID JOURNALISM
Charles Sturt University
Wagga Wagga, Australia

JEAN-NOËL MISSA
PSYCHOSURGERY AND PHYSICAL BRAIN MANIPULATION
Free University of Brussels
Brussels, Belgium

DARRELL MOELLENDORF
IMPERIALISM
University of Witwatersrand
Johannesburg, South Africa

PETER MOIZER
AUDITING PRACTICES
University of Leeds
Leeds, England, UK

DAVID WENDELL MOLLER
DEATH, SOCIETAL ATTITUDES TOWARD
Indiana University
Indianapolis, Indiana

J. DONALD MOON
COMMUNITARIANISM
Wesleyan University
Middletown, Connecticut

EMILIO MORDINI
SUGGESTION, ETHICS OF
Psychoanalytic Institute for Social Research
Rome, Italy

JONATHAN D. MORENO
INFORMED CONSENT
SUNY Health Science Center at Brooklyn
Brooklyn, New York

MAURIZIO MORI
LIFE, CONCEPT OF
Center for Research in Politics and Ethics
Milan, Italy

STEPHEN J. MORSE
INSANITY, LEGAL CONCEPT OF
University of Pennsylvania Law School
Philadelphia, Pennsylvania

PETER MUNZ
DARWINISM
Victoria University of Wellington
Wellington, New Zealand

TIMOTHY F. MURPHY
AIDS
University of Illinois College of Medicine
Chicago, Illinois

CHARLES R. MYERS
MILITARY CODES OF BEHAVIOR
United States Air Force Academy
Colorado Springs, Colorado

JAN NARVESON
CONSUMER RIGHTS
EGOISM AND ALTRUISM
STOICISM
University of Waterloo
Waterloo, Ontario

DEMETRIO NERI
EUGENICS
University of Messina
Messina, Italy

NINA NIKKU
PREVENTIVE MEDICINE
University of Linköping
Linköping, Sweden

RICHARD NORMAN
PACIFISM
University of Kent
Canterbury, England, UK

DAVID NOVITZ
LITERATURE AND ETHICS
University of Canterbury, New Zealand
Christchurch, New Zealand

KATHERINE O'DONOVAN
FEMINIST JURISPRUDENCE
Queen Mary's Westfield College
University of London
London, England, UK

JOHN O'NEILL
TRUTH TELLING AS CONSTITUTIVE OF JOURNALISM
Lancaster University
Lancaster, England, UK

GERALD M. OPPENHEIMER
HEALTH CARE FINANCING
Brooklyn College, City University of New York
Brooklyn, New York

R. WILLIAM OUTHWAITE
DISCOURSE ETHICS
University of Sussex
Sussex, England, UK

GUILLERMO OWEN
GAME THEORY
Naval Postgraduate School
Monterey, California

ROBERT A. PADGUG
HEALTH CARE FINANCING
Brooklyn College, City University of New York
Brooklyn, New York

GABRIEL PALMER-FERNÁNDEZ
CIVILIAN POPULATIONS IN WAR, TARGETING OF
Youngstown State University
Youngstown, Ohio

MARK PARASCANDOLA
ANIMAL RESEARCH
Smithsonian Fellow
Washington, D.C.

JENNETH PARKER
PRECAUTIONARY PRINCIPLE
Lecturer
Hastings, England, UK

MICHAEL PARKER
MORAL DEVELOPMENT
The Open University
Milton Keynes, England, UK

ELLEN FRANKEL PAUL
AFFIRMATIVE ACTION
SEXUAL HARASSMENT
Bowling Green State University
Bowling Green, Ohio

MICHEL PETHERAM
CONFIDENTIALITY OF SOURCES
The Open University
Milton Keynes, England, UK

JON PIKE
STRIKES
Glasgow University
Glasgow, Scotland, UK

EVELYN PLUHAR
ANIMAL RIGHTS
The Pennsylvania State University, Fayette Campus
Uniontown, Pennsylvania

GAYNOR POLLARD
RELIGION IN SCHOOLS
University College Chester
Chester, England, UK

NELSON POTTER
KANTIANISM
University of Nebraska-Lincoln
Lincoln, Nebraska

IGOR PRIMORATZ
PROSTITUTION
Hebrew University
Jerusalem, Israel

JANE PRITCHARD
CODES OF ETHICS
Centre for Professional Ethics
University of Central Lancashire
Preston, England, UK

ROBERT PROSSER
TOURISM
University of Birmingham
Birmingham, England, UK

LAURA M. PURDY
CHILDREN'S RIGHTS
Wells College
Aurora, New York

K. ANNE PYBURN
ARCHAEOLOGICAL ETHICS
Indiana University
Indianapolis, Indiana

MAUREEN RAMSAY
MACHIAVELLIANISM
University of Leeds
Leeds, England, UK

DOUGLAS B. RASMUSSEN
PERFECTIONISM
St. John's University
Jamaica, Queens, New York

KATE RAWLES
BIOCENTRISM
Lancaster University
Lancaster, England, UK

RUPERT READ
COURTROOM PROCEEDINGS, REPORTING OF
University of Manchester
Manchester, England, UK

FREDERIC G. REAMER
SOCIAL WORK
Rhode Island College
Providence, Rhode Island

MICHAEL REISS
BIOTECHNOLOGY
Homerton College, Cambridge
Cambridge, England, UK

TONY RILEY
HOMOSEXUALITY, SOCIETAL ATTITUDES TOWARD
Yale University School of Medicine
New Haven, Connecticut

SIMON ROGERSON
COMPUTER AND INFORMATION ETHICS
De Montfort University
Leicester, England, UK

BERNARD E. ROLLIN
VETERINARY ETHICS
Colorado State University
Fort Collins, Colorado

RICHARD D. RYDER
PAINISM
Tulane University
New Orleans, Louisiana

MARK SAGOFF
ENVIRONMENTAL ECONOMICS
University of Maryland
College Park, Maryland

HANS-MARTIN SASS
ADVANCE DIRECTIVES
Kennedy Institute of Ethics
Georgetown University
Washington, DC

GEOFFREY SCARRE
UTILITARIANISM
University of Durham
Durham, England, UK

UDO SCHÜKLENK
AIDS IN THE DEVELOPING WORLD
HOMOSEXUALITY, SOCIETAL ATTITUDES TOWARD
ORGAN TRANSPLANTS AND DONORS
SEXUAL ORIENTATION
Centre for Professional Ethics
University of Central Lancashire
Preston, England, UK

ADINA SCHWARTZ
PUBLIC DEFENDERS
John Jay College of Criminal Justice
City University of New York
New York, New York

ANNE SELLER
PACIFISM
University of Kent
Canterbury, England, UK

JOHN J. SHEPHERD
ISLAM
University College of St. Martin
Lancaster, England, UK

RUBEN SHER
AIDS TREATMENT AND BIOETHICS IN SOUTH AFRICA
National AIDS Training and Outreach Program
Johannesburg, South Africa

DARREN SHICKLE
PRIVACY VERSUS PUBLIC RIGHT TO KNOW
RESOURCE ALLOCATION
   University of Sheffield
   Sheffield, England, UK

KRISTIN SHRADER-FRECHETTE
HAZARDOUS AND TOXIC SUBSTANCES
NUCLEAR POWER
   University of South Florida
   Tampa, Florida

DEBORAH H. SIEGEL
ADOPTION
   School of Social Work
   Rhode Island College
   Providence, Rhode Island

ANITA SILVERS
DISABILITY RIGHTS
   San Francisco State University
   San Francisco, California

NIKKY-GUNINDER KAUR SINGH
SIKHISM
   Colby College
   Waterville, Maine

ANTHONY J. SKILLEN
RACISM
   University of Kent
   Canterbury, England, UK

JOHN SNAPPER
TRADE SECRETS AND PROPRIETARY INFORMATION
   Illinois Institute of Technology
   Chicago, Illinois

EUGENE SPAFFORD
COMPUTER SECURITY
   Purdue University
   West Lafayette, Indiana

CLIVE L. SPASH
WILDLIFE CONSERVATION
   Cambridge University
   Cambridge, England, UK

PAUL SPICKER
POVERTY
SOCIAL SECURITY
SOCIAL WELFARE: PROVISION AND FINANCE
   University of Dundee
   Dundee, Scotland, UK

R. E. SPIER
SCIENCE AND ENGINEERING ETHICS, OVERVIEW
   University of Surrey
   Guildford, England, UK

DEAN A. STEELE
HONOR CODES
   United States Air Force Academy
   Colorado Springs, Colorado

ELIZA STEELWATER
HUMANISM
   University of Illinois
   Champaign, Illinois

EDWARD STEIN
SEXUAL ORIENTATION
   Yale University
   New Haven, Connecticut

JON STEWART
EXISTENTIALISM
   Søren Kierkegaard Research Center
   University of Copenhagen
   Copenhagen, Denmark

TADEUSZ SZUBKA
FREUDIANISM
   University of Queensland
   Brisbane, Australia

WIN TADD
NURSES' ETHICS
   University of Wales
   Cardiff, Wales, UK

CARL TALBOT
DEEP ECOLOGY
ENVIRONMENTAL JUSTICE
   University of Wales, Cardiff
   Cardiff, Wales, UK

JULIA PO-WAH LAI TAO
CONFUCIANISM
   City University of Hong Kong
   Kowloon, Hong Kong

LAURENCE THOMAS
FRIENDSHIP
   Syracuse University
   Syracuse, New York

JOHN J. TILLEY
HEDONISM
   Indiana University/Purdue University
   Indianapolis, Indiana

G. E. TOMLINSON
GENETIC RESEARCH
   University of Texas
   Dallas, Texas

ROSEMARIE TONG
FEMINIST ETHICS
   Davidson College
   Davidson, North Carolina

MAX TRAVERS
COURTROOM PROCEEDINGS, REPORTING OF
   Buckinghamshire College

JOHN C. TULLOCH
VIOLENCE IN FILMS AND TELEVISION
   Charles Sturt University
   Bathurst, Australia

MARIAN I. TULLOCH
VIOLENCE IN FILMS AND TELEVISION
Charles Sturt University
Bathurst, Australia

RICHARD H. S. TUR
LEGAL ETHICS, OVERVIEW
Oriel College
Oxford, England, UK

ROBERT TWYCROSS
PALLIATIVE CARE
Oxford University and Churchill Hospital
Oxford, England, UK

CAROLE ULANOWSKY
FAMILY, THE
The Open University
Milton Keynes, England, UK

GREGORY UNGAR
ELECTRONIC SURVEILLANCE
University of Colorado
Boulder, Colorado

JORGE M. VALADEZ
INDIGENOUS RIGHTS
Marquette University
Milwaukee, Wisconsin

JOHANNES J. M. VAN DELDEN
DO-NOT-RESUSCITATE DECISIONS
Center for Bioethics and Health Law
Utrecht University
Utrecht, The Netherlands

WIBREN VAN DER BURG
SLIPPERY SLOPE ARGUMENTS
Tilburg University
Tilburg, The Netherlands

PAUL VIMINITZ
NUCLEAR WARFARE
University of Waterloo
Waterloo, Ontario

ANDREW VINCENT
MARX AND ETHICS
University of Wales, Cardiff
Cardiff, Wales, UK

ROBERT WACHBROIT
HEALTH AND DISEASE, CONCEPTS OF
Institute for Philosophy and Public Policy
University of Maryland
College Park, Maryland

NEIL WALKER
POLICE ACCOUNTABILITY
University of Aberdeen
Aberdeen, Scotland, UK

DANIEL WARNER
CITIZENSHIP
Graduate Institute of International Studies
Geneva, Switzerland

DAVID WASSERMAN
DISCRIMINATION, CONCEPT OF
Institute for Philosophy and Public Policy
University of Maryland
College Park, Maryland

JOHN WECKERT
SEXUAL CONTENT IN FILMS AND TELEVISION
Charles Sturt University
Bathurst, New South Wales, Australia

CHARLES WEIJER
RESEARCH METHODS AND POLICIES
Joint Centre for Bioethics
University of Toronto/Mount Sinai Hospital
Toronto, Ontario

D. DON WELCH
SOCIAL ETHICS, OVERVIEW
Vanderbilt University School of Law
Nashville, Tennessee

JOS V. M. WELIE
PLACEBO TREATMENT
Creighton University
Omaha, Nebraska

CELIA WELLS
CORPORATE RESPONSIBILITY
Cardiff Law School
University of Wales
Cardiff, Wales, UK

CAROLINE WHITBECK
RESEARCH ETHICS
Massachusetts Institute of Technology
Cambridge, Massachusetts

MARGARET WHITELEGG
ALTERNATIVE MEDICINE
University of Central Lancashire
Preston, England, UK

URBAN WIESING
MEDICAL ETHICS, USE OF HISTORICAL EVIDENCE IN
University of Münster
Münster, Germany

JOHN R. WILCOX
HIGHER EDUCATION, ETHICS OF
Manhattan College
Riverdale, Bronx, New York

RICHARD R. WILK
ARCHAEOLOGICAL ETHICS
Indiana University
Indianapolis, Indiana

BERNARD WILLIAMS
CENSORSHIP
University of California, Berkeley

CHRISTOPHER WINCH
AUTHORITY IN EDUCATION
  Nene College
  Northhampton, England, UK

EARL R. WINKLER
APPLIED ETHICS, OVERVIEW
  University of British Columbia
  Vancouver, British Columbia

CLARK WOLF
THEORIES OF JUSTICE: HUMAN NEEDS
  University of Colorado
  Boulder, Colorado

PAUL ROOT WOLPE
INFORMED CONSENT
  University of Pennsylvania
  Philadelphia, Pennsylvania

MICHAEL WREEN
PATENTS
  Marquette University
  Milwaukee, Wisconsin

MICHAEL J. ZIGMOND
SCIENTIFIC PUBLISHING
  University of Pittsburgh
  Pittsburgh, Pennsylvania

A GUIDE TO THE ENCYCLOPEDIA

The *Encyclopedia of Applied Ethics* is a complete source of information contained within the covers of a single unified work. It is the first reference book that addresses the relatively new discipline of applied ethics in a comprehensive manner; thus in effect it will provide the first general description of the components and boundaries of this challenging field.

The Encyclopedia consists of four volumes and includes 281 separate full-length articles on the whole range of applied ethics. It includes not only entries on the leading theories and concepts of ethics, but also a vast selection of entries on practical issues ranging from medical, scientific, and environmental ethics to the ethics of social relationships and social services. Each article provides a detailed overview of the selected topic to inform a broad spectrum of readers, from research professionals to students to the interested general public.

In order that you, the reader, will derive maximum benefit from your use of the *Encyclopedia of Applied Ethics,* we have provided this Guide. It explains how the Encyclopedia is organized and how the information within it can be located.

ORGANIZATION

The *Encyclopedia of Applied Ethics* is organized to provide the maximum ease of use for its readers. All of the articles are arranged in a single alphabetical sequence by title. Articles whose titles begin with the letters A to D are in Volume 1, articles with titles from E to I are in Volume 2, and those from J to R are in Volume 3. Volume 4 contains the articles from S to Z and also the Index.

So that they can be easily located, article titles generally begin with the key word or phrase indicating the topic, with any descriptive terms following. For example, "Distributive Justice, Theories of" is the article title

rather than "Theories of Distributive Justice" because the specific phrase *distributive justice* is the key term rather than the more general term *theories.* Similarly "Sports, Ethics of" is the article title rather than "Ethics of Sports" and "Human Nature, Views of" is the title rather than "Views of Human Nature."

TABLE OF CONTENTS

A complete alphabetical table of contents for the *Encyclopedia of Applied Ethics* appears at the front of each volume of the set, beginning on page *v* of the Introduction. This list includes not only the articles that appear in that particular volume but also those in the other three volumes.

The list of article titles represents topics that have been carefully selected by the Editor-in-Chief, Prof. Ruth Chadwick, Head of the Centre for Professional Ethics, University of Central Lancashire, UK, in collaboration with the members of the Editorial Board.

In addition to the alphabetical table of contents, the Encyclopedia also provides a second table of contents at the front of each volume, one that lists all the articles according to their subject area. The Encyclopedia provides coverage of 12 specific subject areas within the overall field of applied ethics, as indicated below:

- **Theories of Ethics**
- **Ethical Concepts**
- **Medical Ethics**
- **Scientific Ethics**
- **Environmental Ethics**
- **Legal Ethics**
- **Ethics in Education**
- **Ethics and Politics**
- **Business and Economic Ethics**
- **Media Ethics**
- **Ethics and Social Services**
- **Social Ethics**

ARTICLE FORMAT

Articles in the *Encyclopedia of Applied Ethics* are arranged in a single alphabetical list by title. Each new article begins at the top of a right-hand page, so that it may be quickly located. The author's name and affiliation are displayed at the beginning of the article. The article is organized according to a standard format, as follows:

- Title and Author
- Outline
- Glossary
- Defining Statement
- Main Body of the Article
- Cross-References
- Bibliography

OUTLINE

Each article in the Encyclopedia begins with an Outline that indicates the general content of the article. This outline serves two functions. First, it provides a brief preview of the article, so that the reader can get a sense of what is contained there without having to leaf through the pages. Second, it serves to highlight important subtopics that are discussed within the article. For example, the article "Genome Analysis" includes the subtopic "The Human Genome Project."

The Outline is intended as an overview and thus it lists only the major headings of the article. In addition, extensive second-level and third-level headings will be found within the article.

GLOSSARY

The Glossary contains terms that are important to an understanding of the article and that may be unfamiliar to the reader. Each term is defined in the context of the particular article in which it is used. Thus the same term may appear as a Glossary entry in two or more articles, with the details of the definition varying slightly from one article to another. The Encyclopedia includes more than 1,000 glossary entries.

The following example is a glossary entry that appears with the article "Precautionary Principle."

indicator species A particular species whose presence (or absence) is regarded as characteristic of a given environment, and whose ability or failure to thrive there is thus thought to be indicative of the overall ecological status of this environment.

DEFINING STATEMENT

The text of each article in the Encyclopedia begins with a single introductory paragraph that defines the topic under discussion and summarizes the content of the article. For example, the article "Biotechnology" begins with the following statement:

> *BIOTECHNOLOGY* is the application of biology for human ends. It involves using organisms to provide humans with food, clothes, medicines, and other products.

CROSS-REFERENCES

Nearly all of the articles in the Encyclopedia have cross-references to other articles. These cross-references appear at the end of the article, following the conclusion of the text. They indicate related articles that can be consulted for further information on the same topic, or for other information on a related topic. For example, the article "Biotechnology" contains cross-references to the articles "Agricultural Ethics," "Animal Research," "Eugenics," "Genetic Counseling," and "Genetic Engineering."

BIBLIOGRAPHY

The Bibliography appears as the last element in an article. It lists recent secondary sources to aid the reader in locating more detailed or technical information. Review articles and research papers that are important to an understanding of the topic are also listed.

The bibliographies in this Encyclopedia are for the benefit of the reader, to provide references for further reading or research on the given topic. Thus they typically consist of no more than ten to twelve entries. They are not intended to represent a complete listing of all the materials consulted by the author in preparing the article, as would be the case, for example, with a journal article.

INDEX

The Subject Index in Volume 4 contains more than 5000 entries. The entries are listed alphabetically and indicate the volume and page number where information on this topic will be found. Within the entry for a given topic, references to the coverage of the topic also appear alphabetically. The Index serves, along with the alphabetical Table of Contents, as the starting point for information on a subject of interest.

PREFACE

Applied Ethics has come to prominence as a field of study in the last 25 to 30 years, after a period in which the prevailing view among philosophers, at least, was that Philosophy could not usefully be applied to practical problems. The importance of Applied Ethics became obvious first in the medical context, where in the aftermath of World War II and the expanding interest in human rights, developments in technology gave rise to challenging ethical issues such as the use of transplant technology and the allocation of scarce resources such as kidney dialysis. Questions such as the extent to which health care professionals should intervene to extend life became extensively debated. Medical Ethics as a defined area became established, with principles such as autonomy being given central importance. In more recent times contested topics have included assisted reproduction and the advances in and implications of human genome analysis. The latter have led to controversy not only about the options concerning the applications of the technology in medical practice, but also about their wider social uses and even their implications for the meaning of what it is to be human.

Applied Ethics is, however, by no means confined to the medical context and to the social implications of technologies that have been developed for medical purposes or have clear medical applications. Ethical issues arise in any area of life where the interests of individuals or groups conflict, including the interests of different species. In compiling the Encyclopedia we became increasingly aware of the enormity of the task—the list of topics covered could have been expanded indefinitely. We chose to concentrate, however, on areas we regarded as central in contemporary society such as issues concerning the environment, law, politics, the media, science and engineering, education, economics, the family and personal relationships, mental health, social work, policing and punishment, minority rights.

In addition to these areas in which particular issues arise, it is essential for those engaged in Applied Ethics to reflect on what, if anything, is being applied. We therefore included a number of entries on ethical and philosophical approaches, both historical and contemporary, religious and secular. There are different models concerning what is involved in Applied Ethics—for example, whether it is a matter of "applying" a particular theory to a specific ethical dilemma; or whether phenomena, specific developments, particular cases, can affect the development of appropriate theory; whether there is room for a ëbottom-upí rather than a ëtop-downí approach. Some would argue that a central task of Applied Ethics, and one that is prior to the application of theory, is the very identification of the moral dimensions of a situation. Thus we have also included entries on Applied Ethics itself and on challenges to it.

Several disciplines may be involved in Applied Ethics; one branch of Applied Ethics, for example, Bioethics, is commonly explicated in terms of ethical, legal and social issues. In this Encyclopedia by no means all the entries are written by philosophers: some are written by practitioners in the particular field in question; other disciplines represented include law and economics. The Encyclopedia will be a reference work for use by a number of readerships, working in a variety of specialisms; but particularly for students in higher education studying on Applied Ethics courses, for which there is increasing demand. It also has much to offer the general reader interested in the ethical issues arising in contemporary social life.

The number of people who have enabled this enterprise to come to fruition is very large. I should like to thank, first, the members of the Editorial Board and Advisory Council, for participating in the project and for their expert advice on and help with the selection and reviewing of material; the reviewers of the articles, for their time in making the assessments of individual submissions; the University of Central Lancashire, for providing research assistance in the Centre for Professional Ethics—first Jane Pritchard and then Adam Hedgecoe, without whom I cannot imagine how the task would have been completed; and of course Academic Press, especially Scott Bentley and Naomi Henning, for their unfailing support throughout, but also their colleagues in the San Diego office who looked after me extremely well on my visit in 1996. All of my colleagues in the Centre for Professional Ethics have given their support to the project—some by writing entries themselves. Finally, the authors of the articles deserve a very large thank you, for contributing their expertise in their field and for working to very tight deadlines to produce the 281 entries in this Encyclopedia.

RUTH CHADWICK

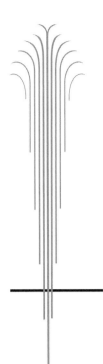

SAFETY LAWS

Michael A. Menlowe
University of Edinburgh

GLOSSARY

autonomy Self-rule; the freedom to determine one's own ends without interference.

hard paternalism The view that it is justifiable to prevent self-harming actions on the grounds of the subject's best interest even if the subject's self-harming action is fully voluntary.

legal paternalism The view that it is sometimes justifiable to use the law to prevent individuals causing harm to themselves.

paternalism The essence of paternalism is that one person (or group of persons) substitutes his judgment about the good of another person (or group of persons)—the subject—against that subject's will.

soft paternalism The view that it is justifiable to prevent self-harming actions only if the action is less than fully voluntary.

SAFETY LAWS prevent harm to others and prevent people from harming themselves. These two functions raise different philosophical issues. Safety legislation preventing harm to others aims to achieve a balance between the liberty of those who cause the harm and the rights of the harmed to protection. Safety laws that are designed to prevent harm to oneself are controversial because they are often believed to be paternalistic. Some safety laws that are often thought to be paternalistic can be justified on other grounds.

I. INTRODUCTION

Most current discussions of safety laws are shaped by John Stuart Mill's discussion in his essay "On Liberty." Mill distinguishes harm to others and harm to self and argues that, whereas it is sometimes appropriate for the law to intervene to prevent harm to others, it is never appropriate for the law to intervene to prevent harm to self.

> ... the only purpose for which power can be rightfully exercised over any member of a civilised community, against his will, is to prevent harm to others. His own good, either physical or moral, is not a sufficient warrant.... The only part of the conduct of any one, for which he is amenable to society, is that which concerns others. In the part which merely concerns himself, his indepen-

dence is, of right, absolute. Over himself, over his own body and mind, the individual is sovereign.

There are many examples of safety legislation designed to prevent harm to others. Most countries will have legislation in the following areas: ownership and use of weapons, road traffic, dangerous industrial practices, sanitation and pollution control, the licensing of professionals (such as doctors), and the safety of foods and medicines. The legislation can be either criminal or civil. In principle, there is no difficulty about the use of the law to prevent harm to others: that is simply the business of the criminal law and of the law of torts. Controversy centers on the relevant notion of harm and the extent to which the law is justified in preventing harm to others. Legislation preventing harm to others is often seen as striving for some balance between the liberty of those who cause the harm and the rights of the harmed to protection. Smoking in public places exemplifies the problem. Another example is legislation controlling industrial pollutants. Such legislation may adversely affect the liberty of industrialists to maximize profits. All safety legislation, and particularly legislation to prevent harm to others, is affected by the problem of how to assess the risks.

There are some cases of preventing harm to others that involve a decision other than one of balance. Many jurisdictions operate on the basis of the principle *volenti non fit injuria*; that is, individuals are permitted to consent to being harmed by others. However, there is an interesting kind of safety law designed to negate that principle. There are laws that deny individuals the legal capacity to consent to being harmed: for example, laws that prohibit individuals from contracting to do very hazardous work, to engage in dangerous activities such as prize fighting, or to consent to dangerous experimental medical or surgical treatments. Such safety laws are analogous to the rule in many jurisdictions that the victim cannot give valid consent to an assault.

Examples of legislation apparently designed to prevent persons harming themselves include laws requiring motorists to wear seatbelts and motorcyclists to wear helmets, laws proscribing or regulating the sale of dangerous substances (such as certain drugs and glue), some laws permitting authorities to treat against their will persons who are believed to be suffering from mental illnesses, laws that prohibit persons under a certain age from engaging in full-time employment or persons of any age from working an excessive number of hours or in a dangerous environment, and much consumer-protection legislation. Legislation of this second kind is usually much more controversial than that

of the first kind because it is, or is often believed to be, paternalistic.

Paternalism is controversial because it involves a conflict of very fundamental values. Legal paternalism is often justified on the grounds that the legislation serves the subject's best interests or the subject's good. The argument against paternalism relies on the claim that what is often called the subject's autonomy is more important than promoting what someone other than the subject thinks is the subject's good. The specific issue in the context of safety legislation is that such legislation prevents us from taking risks. The antipaternalist argues that a concern for the subject's autonomy is the reason to permit the subject to take risks. The essence of the paternalistic justification for safety legislation is that it is better for the subject if the subject is prevented from taking some risks. Frequently, but not always, paternalistic safety legislation is aimed at characteristics of the decision-making process like carelessness, impulsiveness, imprudence, thoughtlessness, and weakness of will. The smoker will come to wish that he had not smoked; the helmetless motorcyclist who has suffered brain damage will wish he had worn a helmet.

II. HARD PATERNALISTIC JUSTIFICATIONS

Writers on paternalism commonly distinguish between hard (or strong) and soft (or weak) paternalism. The hard paternalist emphasises the subject's good, rather than the voluntariness of the subject's action. A common illustration of hard paternalism is the prohibition against voluntarily selling oneself into slavery. The soft paternalist emphasises the voluntariness of the subject's action. The soft paternalist holds that if the subject can demonstrate that the action is fully voluntary then interference with the action is not justified. In this section, I will consider whether there is a hard paternalistic justification for safety legislation.

There are a number of arguments that attempt to justify preventing the subject doing what the subject wishes on hard paternalistic grounds. (1) There is the consequentialist argument that autonomy, construed here as the freedom to make any choice the subject likes, is only an instrumental value and its denial can be justified by appealing to some other good. (2) There is the argument that the subject's subsequent consent to the interference can be expected and would justify the interference. (3) There is the argument that interference can be justified by appealing to the subject's real will or to some hypothetical rational will. (4) There is John Kleinig's argument that justification can be given in terms of the subject's "personal integrity."

Of these four arguments, the argument from personal integrity seems to me the most convincing in the context of certain kinds of safety legislation. The main idea is that individuals have settled core projects, goals, and preferences which may be threatened by the kinds of defects in deliberation mentioned above:

> Where our conduct or choices place our more permanent, stable and central projects in jeopardy, and where what comes to expression in this conduct or these choices manifests aspects of our personality that do not rank highly in our constellation of desires, dispositions, etc., benevolent interference will constitute no violation of integrity. Indeed, if anything, it helps to preserve it. (Kleinig, J. (1983). *Paternalism,* p. 68. Manchester: Manchester University Press).

This is a strong argument in the context of some examples of safety legislation—for example, seatbelts and motorcycle helmets—directed at preventing some kinds of defects in decision-making mentioned above. Compared to the importance of our core projects or preferences, putting on a seatbelt is only a minor inconvenience. The argument may also justify some restrictions on workers in the workplace: the requirement to wear safety helmets and protective goggles, for example, However, the argument is limited. As Kleinig notes, the argument will not persuade the antipaternalist who believes that it is always wrong to coerce a mature subject's present choice for the sake of his own probable future good. Nor has it any force in a case in which the subject claims that the paternalist is trying to interfere with one of the subject's core projects. As Kleinig explains, we have to distinguish the risk that not wearing a seatbelt poses to one's career as a philosopher and the risk that mountain climbing does.

III. ASSESSING PATERNALISTIC JUSTIFICATIONS: SAFETY AT WORK

In this section, I will assess some paternalistic justifications, using safety at work as an illustration. Much safety legislation is concerned with the two risks: the risk of irremediable harm and the risks of harm through ignorance or mistake. There are many examples of the risk to workers of irremediable harm: working with asbestos or benzene (which can cause leukemia), women of child-bearing age working with lead (which can cause sterility), and workers using powerful agricultural chemicals. Also included here are those who work in dangerous environments, such as miners, and those who work with dangerous machinery, such as noisy aircraft engines. In many cases of irremediable harm, the workers know that there is a risk and apparently accept the risk. Paternalistic safety legislation would prevent or limit to some extent their power to consent to the risks. Many of these examples also illustrate the second problem of ignorance or mistake. Often, workers in danger do not know the harm, or cannot accurately assess the risk, or are mistaken about the harm and the risk. Soft paternalistic safety legislation aims to limit the worker's liberty to act when less than fully informed. Furthermore, in respect of both kinds of risks, workers may be imprudent, foolish, or lazy. Paternalistic safety legislation aims to protect workers from such defects in decision-making.

Some of the most important points about the risk of irremediable self-harm have already been made. The best hard paternalistic justification for safety laws that prohibit workers from running such risks is the justification based on personal integrity. But the antipaternalist will argue that such legislation may itself defeat the subject's most important ambitions. The subject wants to earn money, and perhaps employment opportunities for someone with the subject's skills are few. Some industrial processes require dangerous chemicals; or if the dangerous chemicals can be replaced, or more safely used, the production costs may be driven up to the point where the business becomes unprofitable or has to pay much lower wages. Paternalistic safety legislation could make the subject worse off. The antipaternalist will also argue that it may deprive some subjects of the opportunity of earning a large sum of money by taking a great risk. Moreover, because safety legislation has to be generally applicable, it cannot be sufficiently flexible to exclude from its scope those workers whose personal integrity is not threatened by the risk. Therefore, in respect of irremediable harm, a soft paternalistic justification for safety legislation looks more plausible than a hard paternalistic one. The soft paternalist will want to ensure that the subject's decision to take the risk is fully voluntary. But there are problems with soft paternalistic justifications that will now be discussed.

There are dangers in the workplace that most workers can assess for themselves. When the decision to take the risk is evidently fully voluntary, the soft paternalist and the antipaternalist will agree in permitting the worker to take the risk. But there are less obvious risks, and the worker will need information and perhaps advice in assessing these risks. These less obvious risks are created or increased by ignorance and factual mistake. Soft paternalists and antipaternalists will disagree about how to respond to these risks through ignorance or mistake. To put it roughly: the antipaternalist might argue that workers who work with dangerous substances (for example) should be warned only to the extent of a notice in the workplace; while the soft paternalist will argue that a much more extensive process of education and training is necessary. Ignorance and mistake are generally important in discussions of paternalism because they affect the voluntariness of the action. While ignorance and mistake raise different issues, they both raise the same crucial question for the soft paternalist; that is, when do ignorance and mistake so adversely affect voluntariness that the action becomes sufficiently nonvoluntary to justify paternalism?

The general point is illustrated by an example of someone proposing to cross a dangerous bridge. It should be uncontroversial that someone proposing to cross an unsafe bridge should be warned that it is dangerous. What is interesting is whether further interference with her liberty—such as physically restraining her—is justified on the grounds of the possibility of other factual mistakes. Suppose that the pedestrian does not believe the warning, or falsely believes that the padded clothing she is wearing will prevent injury if she falls, or falsely believes that the river under the bridge is deep enough to enable her to survive a drop into it. Are such factual mistakes sufficient to make her act less than fully voluntary?

While many antipaternalists will agree that gross ignorance of the risk of serious harm is a sufficient condition for at least temporary interference, they also argue that some mistakes are consistent with claiming that the subject's action is sufficiently voluntary to be immune from interference. If there is a sign warning that the bridge is dangerous and the pedestrian proceeds in the (false) belief that there is no good reason to heed the sign, then the action is sufficiently her own to make it immune from interference. But some soft paternalists argue that the mistakes make the action less than fully voluntary and therefore a candidate for paternalistic intervention. Feinberg, for example, argues that a necessary condition for that act being sufficiently voluntary is that the pedestrian chooses to cross the bridge under the description of choosing to be killed when the bridge collapses. The antipaternalist and soft paternalist agree that once the relevant standard of voluntariness is achieved, no further intervention is justified. The philo-

sophical disagreement is about whether some mistakes negate voluntariness. The practical effect of that disagreement is that the soft paternalist will be more willing to prevent certain conduct because it will be more difficult to satisfy him that the act is sufficiently voluntary. In the bridge case, the antipaternalist requires only that the pedestrian is warned; the soft paternalist may require that evidence that she intends to commit suicide before allowing her to proceed.

Similar practical differences will appear in the case of safety legislation of the kind under consideration. The antipaternalist may be satisfied with legal requirement for a warning of the dangers: a sign displayed in the workplace, for example. But for the soft paternalist, this may be insufficient. The soft paternalist may believe that workers are insufficiently knowledgeable about the dangers of the workplace and so would require them by law to undergo a process of education and training to ensure the required degree of voluntariness. This educational process could extend from compulsory viewing of graphic videos, to visits to persons who have suffered the harm, to attendance at classes to learn about the relevant scientific literature, to passing written examinations, to temporary permission to use dangerous substances or work in dangerous environments under strict supervision with the permission becoming permanent only after a long apprenticeship. At some point along this continuum of restriction, the soft paternalist will set the standard for voluntariness; that is, the point at which the presumption against voluntariness is rebutted. What is that point in the case of dangers in the workplace?

Feinberg ties voluntariness to the seriousness of the harm. For the moment, knowledge of fact is the only aspect of voluntariness that is relevant. His view seems to be if the possible harm is serious, certainty that the subject knows clearly the risk she is running will be required to rebut that presumption. Therefore, considerable interference with her freedom will be justified to rebut the presumption. However, even if we accept that the knowledge required for sufficient voluntariness is relative to harm, it is not clear in general how much knowledge even serious harm demands. So it is not therefore clear how much interference with liberty would be warranted.

The fact is that we permit people to risk serious dangers without ascertaining that their knowledge of the danger is very complete and accurate. Certain sports expose participants to the risk of serious harm. But must the athlete know exactly what physical injuries could result from playing in order for his participation to be sufficiently voluntary? Does the mountain climber need to know all the risks of climbing? We permit the smoker to smoke with only a brief warning. Arguably, all these risks are of dangers as serious as the dangers posed by dangerous bridges and dangerous workplaces. If the risks and harms are comparable, then the consistent soft paternalist should require the same educational process in respect of all.

Finally, it seems that the soft paternalist would want to extend considerably the scope of paternalism. We run risks of serious harm with aspects of our diet (cholesterol levels) and our life-style (stress). If the harm is serious, then the presumption against voluntariness must be high, and more extensive interference than anything we yet experience might be justified.

The soft paternalist has a number of choices. He might say that we should require some rigorous educational process to establish voluntariness in all these cases. But in that case ordinary life would become very difficult. Moreover, it would probably be practically very difficult (and certainly very costly) to establish the various programs. The result would be a level of interference far greater than anything most paternalists propose for these cases.

A different choice would be to make it very easy to rebut the presumption of nonvoluntariness; but in this case, the soft paternalist's view becomes indistinguishable from that of many antipaternalists. The third choice would be to set the standard somewhere in between— but where? If the seriousness of harm does not determine the standard of voluntariness, then the point at which the presumption of nonvoluntariness is held to be rebutted looks arbitrary.

So there is a general problem for the soft paternalist about when the presumption against voluntariness is rebutted. In the context of the kind of safety legislation under consideration, three further problems arise for the soft paternalist. First, voluntariness is affected by many factors in addition to the seriousness of harm. It is affected by real and perceived constraints on changing jobs and by conditions of employment, such as pension entitlements and other benefits. Second, the soft paternalist contemplating legislation will have to suppose that there is a generally acceptable level of risk in respect of a specific danger. Otherwise, voluntariness would have to be established for each individual—and this must surely be impracticable—or at least for different kinds of workers (e.g., the research scientist and the person who cleans the laboratory). But the assumption that there is a generally acceptable level of risk may itself be a paternalistic assumption in need of justification.

Third, there is the question who is to pay for what the soft paternalist requires. Industrial costs will be driven up in obvious ways with all the obvious adverse implications for the workers. But other costs will arise. The industry itself may have to bear the cost of the scientific research that the soft paternalist's strategy advises. I think it can be demonstrated that many countries have abandoned the kind of safety legislation the soft paternalist requires because it is believed to make industry uncompetitive. Moreover, to be effective, safety legislation may have to establish the workers' right to compel the industry to disclose the results of research affecting safety at work, the right to insist on inspection by an independent safety inspectorate, and some mechanism for resolving disputes between employers and employees. Because some employers claim the right to order workers to do hazardous work, safety legislation may need to provide workers with a right to refuse. So soft paternalistic justifications for safety legislation are inseparable from wider economic and political issues.

IV. NONPATERNALISTIC JUSTIFICATIONS FOR SAFETY LEGISLATION

Some antipaternalists have tried to deprive paternalists of clear examples of accepted and acceptable paternalistic legislation by arguing that some apparently paternalistic legislation is not. For example, laws that the majority use to bring about some state of affairs believed to be good against the wishes of the minority—such as fluoridation of the public water supply—are disputably paternalistic. It may appear in such cases that the majority is acting paternalistically in respect to the minority. However, some writers think that a more accurate antipaternalistic rationale is available; namely, that the majority is seeking a good for itself that cannot be obtained without compelling the participation of the minority. This rationale clearly applies to smoking in public places whenever these places are occupied by a nonsmoking majority who do not want to suffer the harm of passive smoking. Another illustration is provided by laws regulating safety in the workplace and the maximum number of hours of work. The majority of workers may want to regulate these but cannot do so if there is a minority willing to work without safe practices or for longer hours. One way in which the majority achieves its aim is through legislation. Such conduct may be unfair but it is not paternalistic.

Legislation requiring bicyclists and motorcyclists to wear helmets and laws requiring the occupants of motor cars to wear seatbelts raise a different issue. Paternalists cite these as examples of acceptable paternalistic legislation. However, antipaternalists think that these laws (and others) can be justified on the nonpaternalistic basis of preventing harm to others. Let us consider the case of requiring motorcyclists to wear helmets.

It was argued earlier that these laws may be justified on the basis of the hard paternalistic argument of personal integrity. There may also be a soft paternalistic justification for requiring helmets. The question for the soft paternalist is whether refusing to wear a helmet is sufficiently voluntary. The soft paternalist will require some educational process to rebut the strong presumption against voluntariness. There is no reason to deny that some process can be instituted, and that some subjects will satisfy the soft paternalist that they voluntarily risk the harm. At that point, the soft paternalist's options are to embrace hard paternalism for a limited range of cases, or to join the antipaternalist either in opposing a legal requirement to wear helmets or in arguing that the legal requirement is justified on the nonpaternalistic grounds of preventing harm to third parties.

One way to argue for the harm to others option is to point out that in many cases the medical costs of the harm to the helmetless rider fall on third parties and so constitute a harm to them. But that argument does not justify a legal requirement to wear a helmet. This harm could be reduced by adopting the nonpaternalistic policy of requiring motorcyclists to purchase additional medical insurance as a condition of obtaining a license. However that policy has a limitation.

Even if there is a legal requirement to purchase additional medical insurance, some riders will not do it and will ride helmetless. So third parties will be placed in the position of paying their medical costs. Even if third parties announce in advance that they will not pay for the consequences of helmetless riding, the third party has to bear what Gerald Dworkin calls the "psychic costs" of that policy; the costs of ignoring or abandoning people in distress or the burden of knowing that one caused harm or death to another. One only has to imagine that one is a car driver who nonnegligently causes the death of a helmetless motorcyclist.

So it seems that only legislation requiring helmets will reduce these psychic costs. The usual way of justifying liberty-limiting laws that prevent harm to others is to balance the loss of liberty and the harm prevented. But Dworkin thinks that it will not always be the case that the "psychic costs" to third parties will outweigh the loss of liberty to the rider. So he concludes that only a hard paternalistic justification is available for a

law requiring motorcycle helmets to be worn. However, I think he overlooks a nonpaternalistic remedy that may be as effective as the paternalistic requirement. The antipaternalist who is impressed by the "psychic costs" argument argues that the law should provide that third parties who suffer emotional harm are entitled to be compensated generously by the helmetless motorcyclist, and that there is a legal requirement that the motorcyclist's insurer covers that risk. The insurer will charge heavily for that cover. This will not prevent some motorcyclists riding without a helmet; but neither will the paternalistic prohibition. So, the antipaternalist may be able to provide a nonpaternalistic alternative to reducing some third party harm.

Similarly, the antipaternalist may be able to deal with the legal requirement that drivers of motorcars wear seatbelts on the basis of preventing harm to others. Passengers not wearing seatbelts pose different problems. Because passengers, unlike drivers, are not required to be insured, passengers whose injuries are a direct result of not wearing a seatbelt do impose medical costs on third parties that are not recoverable through the injured's insurance. That may be a sufficient antipaternalist justification for a legal requirement to wear a seatbelt. Passengers not wearing seatbelts may also impose psychic costs on drivers who injure them. It might be argued that these costs to the driver who caused the injury do not outweigh the passenger's loss of freedom, as in the helmet case. Supposing that were so, then a requirement for passengers to wear seatbelts could not be justified on the grounds of preventing these costs to the driver. However, the antipaternalist could again argue for a different remedy. Many jurisdictions accept that a passenger whose injuries are the result of not wearing a seatbelt is contributorily negligent. Contributory negligence reduces the quantum of compensation to which the passenger is entitled. It might be thought appropriate to allow the psychic costs of the driver who causes the injury to be set-off against the compensation to which the injured seatbeltless passenger is entitled.

V. CONCLUSION

This article has been mainly concerned with safety laws intended to prevent harm to oneself. It has been argued that, for a limited range of safety legislation, the hard paternalistic argument of preserving individual integrity has much to commend it. These are the cases in which it is implausible to deny that the legislation is actually promoting the subject's most important projects at the cost of minor inconvenience. The case of soft paternalism is more difficult to assess. Soft paternalism appears to be an attractive justification for some safety legislation, because it emphasizes the element of the voluntariness of the choice. However, there are problems with soft paternalism. Soft paternalism may be arbitrary, may justify very extensive paternalistic intervention, and may be impracticable in many ways, especially in terms of costs. Finally, even if it were thought that all paternalism is, in principle, objectionable, some safety legislation can be justified by nonpaternalistic arguments.

Also See the Following Articles

AUTONOMY • PATERNALISM

Bibliography

Anderson, E. (1988). Values, risks and market norms. *Philosophy and Public Affairs, 7*, 54–65.

Arenson, R. J. (1980). Mill versus paternalism. *Ethics,* 90, 470–489.

Carter, R. (1977). Justifying Paternalism. *Canadian Journal of Philosophy, 7,* 133–145.

Daniels, N. (1985). *Just health care.* Cambridge: Cambridge, University Press.

Dworkin, G. (1990). Paternalism: Some second thoughts. In Feinberg, J., and Gross, H. (Eds.), *Philosophy of Law* (4th ed.). Belmont, CA: Wadsworth.

Ezorsky, E. (Ed.) (1987). *Moral rights in the workplace.* Albany, NY: State University Press.

Faden, R. R., & Beauchamp, T. L. (1988). The right to risk information and the right to refuse health hazards in the workplace. In Beauchamp, T. L., and Bowie, N. E., *Ethical theory and business* (3rd ed.). Englewood Cliffs, NJ: Prentice Hall.

Feinberg, J. (1986). *The moral limits of the criminal law, Volume 3, Harm to self.* New York: Oxford University Press.

Fessenden-Raden, J., & Gert, B. (1988). A Philosophical approach to the management of occupational health hazards. In Beauchamp, T. L., and Bowie, N. E. *Ethical theory and business* (3rd ed.), pp. 218–226. Englewood Cliffs, NJ: Prentice Hall.

Goodin, R. E. (1989). *No smoking.* Chicago: University of Chicago Press.

Mill, J. S (1962). *On liberty.* In Warnock, M. (Ed.), *Utilitarianism.* London: William Collins and Son.

Nelken, D., & Brown, M. S. (1984). *Workers at risk.* Chicago: University of Chicago Press.

Sartorius, R. E. (1983). *Paternalism.* Minneapolis: University of Minnesota Press.

SCIENCE AND ENGINEERING ETHICS, OVERVIEW

R. E. Spier
University of Surrey

GLOSSARY

codes Bodies of text that delineate in general terms appropriate behavior.

engineering An activity that requires knowledge, practical skills, and the generation of significant novelty (as in a patent) with an objective of providing benefit for society.

ethical or moral conduct A way of behaving that is acceptable, good, or satisfies one or another ethical objective.

ethics A subject area equivalent to morals dealing with the way humans conduct their lives.

fabrication The construction and reporting of data that were not actually observed.

falsification The modification of observed data.

misappropriation The theft of the intellectual or physical property of another.

misconduct Acts by humans that are held to be unethical or immoral.

misrepresentation The deliberate misleading of another by the presentation of false or incomplete information.

noncompliance The disregarding of laws, codes, regulations, ordinances, and so on.

obstruction The deliberate prevention of the freedom of another to achieve her objectives.

peer review The examination of one's work or proposal by a group of people drawn from a background similar to one's own.

plagiarism The passing off of the work by another as one's own.

science Knowledge that has been tested to determine the level of confidence with which this knowledge may be held.

SCIENCE AND ENGINEERING ETHICS is concerned with the behavior of scientists and engineers with regard to the way they carry out their vocations coupled with the products of those vocations. Whereas it was thought that scientists could generate new knowledge without regard to the ethical implications of their actions, the burgeoning subject areas of biotechnology, computers, and nuclear physics have quickly brought to the attention of the perpetrators of those subjects that their actions have consequences beyond the mere compilation of new knowledge and capabilities. As our societies have increased their wealth, the citizens have determined that their environments and the biota that inhabit those locations can be considered to be integral to the determination of the quality of their lives. These events have occurred during a period when the research and development activities supported by the state have come under increasingly critical scrutiny. Members of the academic research community have been encouraged to compete; they have been urged to associate with industry; they have been rated, graded, reviewed, and evaluated. This has led directly to the action of governmental agencies to prevent misconduct by researchers enjoying state funding for their work. Such actions in turn have led to the emergence of this new area of science and engineering ethics.

I. A REVIEW OF THE PREDISPOSING SALIENT EVENTS

In contemporary Western societies there is a pervading sense that we have lost our way. Gone are the certainties on which constitutions and interpersonal interactions have been based. We are faced with a reexamination of traditional religions, with constitutions preventing beneficial social developments, and with democracies turning into dictatorships. Since the explosion of the atomic bomb at Hiroshima, the social engineering of the Final Solution holocaust, and the catastrophic failure of the nuclear power station at Chernobyl, we have become aware that the practice of science and engineering can lead to situations that threaten the continued existence of humans on planet Earth. These events have led to a resurgence of interest in the way we behave and the factors that control that behavior.

Naturally, this moves us into considerations of ethics. One such set of ethical issues pertains to the suite of activities that goes under the designation of doing "science and engineering." This article focuses on this area and begins by examining how the need to delineate this subject emerged. Once the requirement was set, there follows the necessary establishment of the boundary conditions used to define the field. From this platform we can look both backward at historic events, as well as forward as our contemporary situation melds into the future.

A. The Need to Achieve Accountability

The current political climate in the Western democracies seeks to decrease the pervasiveness of "government" and to return to individuals more control of the resources that they earn or acquire. In cutting public expenditures governments have sought to maintain the level and quality of services that they had supplied at the previous higher expenditure rates. To achieve this end they have become more assiduous in assessing the qualitative nature of publicly purchased services, including those in the education sector that involve science and engineering research in universities and in government research institutes. This development has led to an increase in the requirement for such institutions to demonstrate their responsible deployment of resources allocated to them from the public purse; it has led to the implementation of a greater degree of accountability.

The consequence of these efforts to reduce the public funding of research and development programs, while maintaining the quality and quantity of the output, has been a transformation of the way science and engineering research and development has progressed. By reducing education budgets by 3% per annum the government of the United Kingdom has sought to achieve increases in the efficiency of the production of graduates and research workers. Another way of seeking to promote improved performance with less funding has been the instigation of increased competitiveness both within and between institutions. This has been achieved by the operation of league tables and peer-reviewed assessment of research quality that has, again in the United Kingdom, important consequences on the level of future government funding. A third repercussion has been that universities have been encouraged to enter into active collaborations with the commercial/industrial worlds; this interaction is not without its special ethical problems (R. Spier, 1995).

The intensification of the pressure on university and government research laboratory personnel to perform and raise grant monies from both the public and private sectors on the basis of their research and publication activities has led to the sense that such researchers might act in a manner that was considered inconceivable prior to the application of these contemporary requirements. Issues of fraud, theft, and dissimulation have now become part of the vocabulary of active scientists. As such matters are not dealt with by the normal civil courts, because it is difficult if not impossible to ascertain the monetary value of the damages caused and the people involved do not, in the main, have the necessary monetary ability to mount a lawsuit, it has fallen to the institutes themselves to monitor and control the behavior of their employees. This movement has been augmented by the involvement of public bodies. Since the early 1990s it has become a requirement of the U.S. government agencies of the National Science Foundation (NSF) and National Institutes of Health (NIH) to require grantholders to have taken an approved course in science and engineering ethics prior to having a grant award made to them.

B. Pressing Universities and Industry Together

In efforts to increase the flow of inventions from "basic" scientists to industry and therefore to provide additional justification for the public funding of such investigations, scientists in universities have been cajoled into forming groups, consortia, and consultancies to generate such a flow of knowledge. Few have been successful (Stanford's capitalization on the patents taken out by Cohen and Boyer in 1975 on methods for genetic engineering have been outstandingly productive). However, in the inevitable scrapping around for contracts it is clear that compromises with what would have been considered approved behavior are made. There are numerous examples of such practices, some of which involve conflicts of interest (CoI), while others border on the edge of downright theft or fraud. So, those institutions whose members apply for publicly funded grants have to establish ethics committees and to acquire from putative grantholders any information that would indicate whether or not there would be a CoI were those grantholders to work with public monies in ways that would provide them or their immediate families with "insider benefits."

C. High Profile Cases

In the climate that has come to prevail in the last couple of decades, there have been some notable cases of questionable behavior, often by noted, well-respected and leading scientists. Paul Gallo and his laboratory colleague Mikulas Popovic have only recently had resolved the investigation of their behavior with regard to the discovery of the virus that causes the Acquired Immunodeficiency Disease Syndrome (AIDS) vis à vis the countervailing claims of Montagnier. Recently concluded is the case of Nobel Laureate David Baltimore's association with an unsubstantiated allegation of falsification of data before presentation perpetrated by the research worker, Imanishi-Kari. Other cases involving the painting of black spots on mice and the generating of irreproducible experiments that purport to demonstrate a "phosphate cascade" in the transmission of information between the exterior of the cell to the responding genes, have been well documented (W. Broad and N. Wade (1982). *Betrayers of the Truth*, p. 256. Simon & Schuster, New York). And there are cases where one scientist's work has been plagiarized by another as, for example, in the settled case of Heidi Weissman, whose published work was used, unacknowledged, by her senior.

There are also cases of whistle-blowing in industry. When the space shuttle *Challenger* failed spectacularly (January 28, 1986) on a widely televised launch, tragically killing the seven astronauts (including a teacher), the efforts of Roger Boisjoly to prevent the launch, when made public, raised an outcry as to how his warnings were not heeded (See C. E. Harris Jr., M. S. Pritchard, & M. J. Rabins (1995). *Engineering Ethics*, p. 1. Wadsworth Publishing Company, London. See also S. H. Unger (1994). *Controlling Technology, Ethics and the Responsible Engineer*. Wiley Interscience, New York). The crunch point in this event was when, during a telephone conversation to NASA about the impending launch, the senior vice-president of Morton Thiokol, Gerald Mason, asked the director of engineering, Robert Lund to ". . . take off your engineering hat and put on your management hat"; this made him change his decision from "do not launch" to "launch." There are other cases where the warnings of staff were taken up by management as in the case of J. Thomas Condie who asserted that his superior John Ninnemann misrepresented data.

All such events became headline news in recent times with a consequence that people began to ask about the training of people who occupy responsible positions in engineering and science. Such questionings were also instrumental in leading to the establishment of science and engineering ethics (SEE) courses in universities, the founding of a journal with the same name, and an increase in interest in this subject area by senior members of industry. This is evidenced by the establishment of the Ethics Officers Association as the appointment of individuals at such a level became a requirement for a company to tender for a large government contract.

D. Environmental Issues

Because fully loaded oil tankers have been breaking up in full view of the television cameras and the resulting pictures of dead and despoiled animals populating our littoral areas and riversides have been brought to viewers instantly, there has arisen a social mood that seeks to eliminate and prevent such happenings. Laws have been enacted. Authorities with powers to investigate and deter potential polluters of the environment have been established, and vigilante groups have been formed to police what they think is the boundary between acceptable (to them) and unacceptable behavior in this regard. At times of social difficulty (such as the depression of the 1930s) or war, environmental issues do not take preference over the need to do everything possible to maintain the existence of the society, even if that means creating a less than desirable environment for the local animals and plants. However, in times of relative plenty, environmental issues do become of increasing social importance and the inculcation of an ethic involving the objective of sustainability becomes necessary.

Industry may be said to be the largest problem in this area. Engineers and scientists working in a "for profit" organization are often presented with CoI issues on the basis of how they call a particular action, which may cause pollution outside the set and tolerated limits. In addition, such individuals may be seen to be working for many masters; their employer, the prevailing society and themselves and their families. Often, while well-meaning individuals can see that environmentally hazardous (or personally jeopardizing) activities may be in train, their notification to their supervising officer can either be ignored, can be denied, can be justified in the interests of the greater good of the company, or can be denigrated as being either irresponsible or naive.

E. Animals Have Become Eligible for Human(e) Treatment

Our use of animals to promote our survival has developed over the years from food source, sentinel early warning system, and toxic material test bed to their use in medical experimentation for new therapeutics and prophylactics, animal competitions for gambling, draft animals for work, and the use of animals to gratify emotional requirements that are not fulfilled by humans. In this process we have learned to rear animals efficiently and intensively. Also, as a corollary, the increased efficiency of our hunting activities has brought many animal species to the point of extinction or to unsustainable recovery from overfishing or hunting; examples abound; whales, boar, buffalo, great apes, manatees, eagles, wolves, and many others are, or have been, on the extinction point. Of course, in highlighting animals we must not overlook the changes to the plant and microbial communities. While these are more contingent to our well-being than the animal cohorts, we tend not to respond to their needs as emphatically, possibly due to our disinterest in anthropomorphizing them.

To investigate the "way animals function" (effected so that we can design improved medicaments for humans (and domestically useful animals)) we now have suites of rules and codes that determine what would be acceptable practices. In sum such regulations seek to decrease the numbers of animals used, to decrease the use of animals whose nearness to humans is evident

(even though this means that much research on the action of immunogenic agents in mice has to be completely redone in primates when it comes to justifying trials in humans), and to decrease the pain and suffering to the minimal levels held to be absolutely necessary. All such trials and their protocols have to be agreed in advance, and clear and available records must be kept. Nonetheless, in spite of the urgings of those who have set up "The Great Ape Project" of a "Homeland" with full sovereign rights for the great apes in some parts of Africa, we may not have to go quite that far. But we cannot deny the need to examine each such issue on its merits and to act accordingly.

F. Engineering with Cells and Genes

In the mid 1970s a suite of abilities was developed that enabled biochemical geneticists deliberately to introduce or delete genetically based characteristics into or from a wide range of micro- and macro-organisms. Such activities may be classified as falling into the purlieu of engineering as defined in Section II.D. The use and widespread distribution of such genetically altered organisms poses a number of ethical issues. There are two outstanding sources of concern. One is that researchers will construct organisms, which, in an uncontrollable manner, would damage our lives or environments. The second worry is that the functions or intentions of some deity will be abrogated and living beings will be created that might be regarded as personifications of the monsters or devils of ancient cultures. And finally there is a sense that genetically engineered organisms are unnatural. In many countries these anxieties have led to the establishment of committees to oversee and vet applications to make genetically engineered organisms. Such committees will examine issues, in addition to the ones mentioned, and from a list such as:

- How much genetic information can or should be passed on to insurance companies when they are asked to quote premiums for life insurance policies?
- Can we replace or modify genes that control human propensity to disease(s)?
  —aging;
  —intelligence (cognitive abilities);
  —height;
  —skin color;
  —sexual potency;
  —mood;
  —aggressiveness, and so on.

- Should such genes be modified on a somatic or gametic cell basis?
- In making animal models of human or animal diseases may we create new genotypes that are designed to experience the pain and suffering we associate with particular disease states, for example, the oncomouse?
- Can we change the balance of the species that occupy particular ecological niches?
- Can we use mood enhancing genes in the absence of the disease condition of depression, and so on?

Another biotechnological area that has generated ethical issues is that of the extra corporeal (*in vitro*) fertilization of human ova and the ability to form clones of animals, including the mammals. This, in the case of humans, has thrown up a set of questions such as:

- the rights of a viable human embryo held in a frozen state in the event that the natural parents disappear or die;
- the use of surrogate mothers to bring to maturity the embryos of others with or without compensation;
- the age of a mother at the time of implantation;
- the use of the sperm or the eggs of named donors who may be living or dead;
- the use of viable embryos for experimental purposes;
- the use of eggs from aborted fetuses or virgins;
- the development and promulgation of cloned humans.

The application of biotechnology can, and probably will, significantly alter the genetic and hence the phenotypic nature of the animals and plants that inhabit planet Earth. Such events will have major implications for our economic state, for the way we organize our societies and for the new value structures we establish. It is important therefore to obtain a view as to the direction such changes may take. This requires that we examine the objectives of our behavior, that is, our ethics, so we can take full advantage of these new and awesome capabilities.

G. Physicochemical/Engineering Issues

The world is in a state of alarm over the prospects of an ubridaled active nuclear confrontation. Visions of a fully robotized battle being fought with satellite information technology coupled with nuclear-tipped rockets and computerized battle logistics, which obviates the footsoldier in the field, are causes for deep concern. In addition to this we have a (relatively) peaceful takeover

of the way we conduct our lives by the pervasiveness of information technology systems, as manifested by the Internet and the World Wide Web, as well as the prevalence of closed circuit television cameras surveying our city centers and motor routes to capture on film or video the malefactors in the society. Notwithstanding these serious developments, we have a burgeoning private vehicular transportation system that, at great social expense, moves people to and from their work, shopping venues, and children's educational facilities. A tendency that increases with rising crime rates that, in part, results from engineering decisions made about the way we organize as a society. Machines that have revolutionized the way the routine tasks of the home are effected have enabled women to become an increasingly important section of the labor force, which has implications on the way children are raised and brought to morality. In short, engineered products have revolutionized the way we live; the ethical implications of these changes have yet to be fully appreciated.

H. Summary

In this introductory section I have outlined some of the contemporary factors and events that have brought ethical issues to the forefront of our attention. Such issues are the need for accountability, especially as this applies to the behavioral aspects of how scientists and engineers perform. The admixture of the universities with industry and the inculcation of a competitive ethos has also conspired to introduce practices that require ethical examination. As we have become richer as societies, we have been able to adopt a more involved and critical appraisal of the way we treat the environment with its human and animal populations. The occurrence of such events has conspired to cause the emergence of an area of active endeavor that is rapidly becoming a new discipline: that of science and engineering ethics.

II. TOWARD A DEFINITION OF SCIENCE AND ENGINEERING ETHICS

Words are only as useful as the meanings that are attributed to them. While it may seem that definitional issues can be dismissed as mere semantics, such concerns are yet the matter for the considerable, weighty, and labored deliberation of much of what is the daily activity of lawyers and jurists. Thus, words and their definitions are important and they do justify critical examination. Furthermore, while there are many books that have dealt with the substance of the nature of science, there is not an equivalent literature dealing with engineering matters. Ethics, of course, has been one of the prime areas of interest of humans as this affects the way they behave with repercussions on the decisions they make and, as a result, on their success or failure in themselves or their communities. In this section I offer the reader definitions of science and engineering that may be slightly at variance with traditional definitions. Yet, while the definition of ethics poses fewer problems, the manifestation of different ethical systems is often the source of socially disruptive conflict that saps the intellectual and social strengths of our modern societies. I will also spell out how I perceive the relationship between knowledge (science) and ethics. This is not a "hands-off" distancing exercise, but rather an intimate, connected, and direct interaction between the worlds of being and the worlds of obligation.

A. A Definition of Science

As a first order definition, science, deriving from the Latin *scientia*, translates directly into knowledge. This then requires us to look into the nature of knowledge as a second order consideration. When we translate the nature of the world outside of our minds (in this I take the mind and its thinking capability to be an activity of the nerve cells of the brain, and the exterior world to include the brain and the rest of our body) into thoughts, ideas, concepts, imaginings, guesses, or other products of an active mind we may be said to be creating or generating new knowledge. From that time, this knowledge has an existence independent of the exterior world and can be used without direct reference to it, as in situations when we reflect, think, or dream. As I hope to show, there are two additional qualifying characterizations of knowledge in the confines of our minds. The first characterizing tag is that of the degree of confidence we have in a new or old mental construct or idea. The second concerns the importance we assign to that knowledge—its value to us as we seek to survive.

It would seem from this definition that all knowledge is science and all science is knowledge. This is almost the case but not wholly. In 1840 Whewell defined science as knowledge acquired by scientists. Such individuals did not generally regard the images, conceptualizations, or constructs that exist as mental phenomena as knowledge. It was only those selfsame images, conceptualization, or constructs that survived a rigorous system of experimentation and testing that could legitimately be lodged in the mind as knowledge: and such knowledge was science. The method by which sense

data became knowledge became known as the scientific method and the people who practiced the scientific method were scientists. The scientific method was then described as:

- make repeated observations of the exterior world;
- make a hypothesis as to the relationship between these observations;
- test that relationship by further observations;
- if the additional observations do not require you to change your hypothesis then either continue with the testing or allow your hypothesis to become your knowledge;
- if after exhaustive, rigorous, and stringent testing the hypothesis is not found wanting then it may be considered a theory;
- theories describing particular relationships that have been extensively tested over long periods by many people may be said to have become laws.

This seemingly seamless rendition of the way observations become knowledge was rattled by K. Popper who, in 1934, asserted that it is impossible to *prove* that a hypothesis is true because there is always the possibility that someday an experiment will be effected that will require the modification of that hypothesis. However, he went on to declare that it is possible to prove that a hypothesis is wrong; for any experiment or test that refutes the hypothesis eliminates it for all time from what can be considered true.

I would add to what Popper has expounded, that it is also *not* possible to *prove* a hypothesis wrong. Even an experiment from which we have to infer that our hypothesis is wrong may itself be a flawed experiment. So if we cannot either prove that the hypothesis is right or that the hypothesis is wrong what can we say about it? What we can attribute to a hypothesis is not a determination of rightness or wrongness but rather *a level of confidence* in the knowledge that the hypothesis presents to the mind. Clearly, hypotheses that withstand the most stringent and exhaustive tests will acquire thereby a high level of confidence while those that fail will be accorded a low or even a vanishingly small level of confidence. As we proceed we continually test all our hypotheses and adjust the associated levels of confidence accordingly. (A similar process may be said to occur when we assign levels of value to each item of knowledge we lodge in our minds (Thomas Bayes 1702–1761)). Clearly, a hypothesis such as "the moon is made of green cheese," would not command a great deal of confidence, particularly because we have had the chance to examine moon rocks returned to earth, but we can argue that such rocks are unrepresentative or are forgeries or trick substitutions for the "real" moon materials, which means that we still have to allow a vanishingly small possibility for the original hypothesis to have some validity. To conclude this exposition; the knowledge or science that we store in our minds cannot be considered to be the truth, or something that is proven nor yet a statement of reality. It is but a guess (a less prosaic word than the equivalent word, hypothesis) at an external reality that we can believe to exist in truth; but we cannot know its nature exactly, or with absolute reliability. So the words truth, proof, fact, certainty, reality, exact, correct, right, and their synonyms cannot be used as qualifiers for the ideas and concepts we acquire, store, and manipulate in our minds.

B. Knowledge and Information

We can now relate knowledge to information. The latter may be said to be preliminary sense data that is on its way to becoming tested so as to obtain the status of knowledge. Are there mental constructs that may contain information that may not be considered to be knowledge? I would propose that information or knowledge that is given to use with an admonition that we must not seek to test this knowledge is therefore not to be considered as part of what we understand as knowledge or science as it has been denied examination by the scientific method as described in Section II.B. There are many important cases where this occurs. For example, the first premises of some religious systems require that the believer accepts, unquestioningly, the existence of a god and/or a holy spirit and/or the giving of the laws governing human conduct by God to Moses. But theology, as a study of gods, can be included in science; for it does not exclude questions. Similarly, the lore about ghosts, sprites, fairies, trolls, and the like who can allegedly effect activities that are not in accord with what we believe to be possible in a system where all effects are caused by the preexisting state of the physical/energetic universe, can be considered science. For such information can, in some circumstances, open itself to testing. (It does not last long in the area of high-level-of-confidence thoughts, except perhaps in the area where the tooth fairy regularly and reliably exchanges money for the milk teeth laid carefully under the pillows of our youngsters).

In concluding this section on the definition of science it is interesting to note that it is possible to discern a number of different types of science. For example, it is clear that those who test hypotheses in laboratories or by experiment in the wider horizons of societies, earthly phenomena, and space do so in a way that is markedly different from individuals who test hypotheses using the published literature deposited in libraries or in the attic of a departed savant. While we may wish to characterize these types of individuals as *laboratory* and *library* scientists, respectively, we can also identify another area where knowledge, guesses, or hypotheses are tested, and that is on the street. Conversations are probably the most common way of "doing science." We test our ideas in speaking with others. I would call this *street* science. Additionally, we test our ideas by relating them to other ideas we already have stored in our minds; surely this may be called *conscious* science. And we even test ideas subconsciously: *subconscious* science. This latter test system can be evidenced by the realization by each driver of a car who gets from A to B without having realized that she or he was both steering the car to keep it in its appropriate position on the road and flexing ankle and calf muscles to depress the accelerator peddle to a degree appropriate to the road conditions at the time, all without recourse to the conscious mind.

C. Constructed Science

The constructivist philosophical movement adds a social dimension to the first-order hypotheses we generate from our excited sense organs. While some have used this movement to denigrate science as "just another construction of reality" it actually extends our concept of what we perceive as it integrates it with aspects of the contemporary society. It should be noted that such social interpretations are themselves derived by a guess/ test method and may therefore be considered as part of the knowledge (science) derived by the use of the scientific method. In this sense such considerations might be regarded as a facet of *societal biology*, where the other biological areas are molecular, cellular, and organismal.

In summary, I identify five kinds of science: laboratory, library, street, conscious, and subconscious. The social construction of our knowledge is a special part of this activity where meanings are affected by the associated societal aspects. So, as everybody, including most animals, effects the scientific method, that is "they do science," I have to return to Whewell and define *scientists* as those individuals who, generally in exchange for a stipend, initiate and test guesses in areas that are difficult for most people. These areas may involve either the microscopic or the galactic scales; more detailed or more complex analyses or relating the phenomena of the external world to numerical descriptors.

D. Engineering Requires Genius and Morals

Having practiced as a microbial engineer, it was clear to me that there are four components to the activities that can be construed as engineering:

- engineers use existing and generate new knowledge (when creating and testing new knowledge, they become scientists, and they engage in an activity that is often referred to as engineering science);
- engineers generate products that may either be substantive or intellectual;
- engineers seek to, or intend to, inculcate significant novelty into their products; and
- engineers engage in a social contract that requires them, as their primary objective, to work for the benefit of society (however defined).

While the statements depicted above seem clear and straightforward, in practice they are anything but. For example, the need to define "significant novelty" is a tetchy requirement, as is a clear and agreed view of what is socially beneficial.

Readers may use the definitions of science and scientists as set out in Section II.B. to come to a realization of what an engineer does when addressing a new problem or project. But the issue of the nature of the product of an engineer's endeavors needs a little further elucidation. While it is customary to regard the product of the engineer's work as a bridge, road, ship, car, building, computer, power switch, antibiotic, plastic, and so on, it is not customary to include in such a category a painting, sculpture, musical score, or a propounded philosophy or even a work of literary fiction; yet I would contend that each of the latter items can be considered as the products of an engineering process, if there is a compliance with the conditions as presented above. It is clear that even in each of the latter categories a knowledge base is used or generated; a product is created; the intent of the author, sculptor, painter, philosopher, or composer is to create something that will benefit society in providing an outstandingly novel idea or message. Thus, it is only those individuals who set out with the *intent* of providing social benefit by the generation of something that is significantly novel who are to be included in the category of engineer.

As the word engineer contains the French word *genie*, which means clever or innovative (among other things), it behooves the engineer to express genius. For the purpose of defining engineering, I have taken this to mean the manifestation of *significant novelty*. Clearly,

everything everybody does each day is novel. But what distinguishes significant novelty from mere novelty is that the product is, for one, patentable. Second, something that is significantly novel should "surprise one, gifted in the relevant arts and working in the same field." A third test of significant novelty is that it is quite different from anything that has gone before. There may be additional criteria one can adduce to further categorize that which is purported to be significantly novel, but it is not my purpose here to develop this. Rather, having come to this juncture I can proceed to the more difficult issue of social benefit.

One way to determine the nature of social benefit is to discover a social concordance on what it regards as beneficial. This may not turn out to be the case even if agreement has been reached and a referendum or democratic process has been used to make the determination. For example, the subset of people who supported the Third Reich agreed to the elimination of the mentally impaired, gypsies, and Jews, and so they defined social benefit as that which achieved these objectives. In the long term, this determination may not have been beneficial for this society for it failed in war, lost a huge proportion of its intellectual elite, and has voluntarily held back the development of what is one of the hottest areas of pharmaceutical research, that of genetic engineering. So how can social benefit be determined? This requires us to affirm the aims that society seeks to achieve. These in turn are conditioned by the ethical principle that is adopted as the goal for all behavior; an area that is examined further below.

In concluding this section, I have to refer to another misused word, "technology," which can be translated as the "study of techniques"; a scientific endeavor. I would offer a definition of a technician as a person who effects techniques, albeit doing different or novel things at each turn of the activity, and who makes a product, beneficial to society, without seeking to incorporate anything that is "significantly novel." Such a definition includes most people who would not see themselves as engineers and also some people trained as engineers (with the paper qualifications and the practical experience) who do not seek to or intend to innovate in ways that can, for example, be patented. This means that there are people, often self-designated as inventors, who might actually be eligible for the qualification of engineer, but who have not studied for the normal paper qualifications. Institutions of professional engineers recognize such categories and are prepared, in exceptional cases, to give membership, and hence engineer status, to gifted inventors whose products have been thoroughly tested and have made a significant contribution to the well-being of the community (each year the Engineering Council of the United Kingdom examines for engineer status some 200 to 300 applicants who have not acquired formal qualifications).

E. Introducing Ethics

Ethics is about those aspects of our behavior we categorize as our duties or obligations, or what we consider right or wrong (of actions) or good or bad (of things); it covers much of what we do on a day-to-day basis and it may be equated with its latinized cousin: morals. Clearly our autonomic behavior such as coughing, sneezing, digesting, and breathing do not come under this heading. But those human activities that evoke guidelines for our nonautonomic behavior is the subject of this section. Clearly, in this regard the laws of the land, ordinances of the local community, codes of conduct of the professional institution, and the myriad of rules and regulations that fill the shelves of those who govern our behavior are all part of what we would define as ethics. There is yet another subset of rules that is not written down and whose violation does not immediately result in some compulsory penalty. Such rules might apply when we determine the way we eat, help the less fortunate, obey dress codes, and use language or gestures. In each of these areas, defined or not, we seek to behave so as to maximize some function or principle.

1. Ethical Systems

There are two levels at which the subject of ethics is discussed. The principles, rules, and guidelines that are used to directly control behavior are at the most applied level and are termed *normative ethics*. While the grounding, foundation, or basis for the adoption of such principles, rules, and so on, which is at a more theoretical level, form part of the subject of *metaethics*. In the following treatment, I examine the implications of both transcendental and nontranscendental bases for the determination of ethical principles. For this purpose, I define the transcendental as being a state of affairs that is outside the cause-and-effect system. The latter in turn is defined as those activities that are contingent solely on the interactions of material and energetic entities.

It is in the area of determining which particular principle or principles apply for each individual person where difficulties arise. This encyclopedia is replete with expositions of such principles. For my purpose it is necessary to recognize two sets of such principles. The one is based on what is held to be the wishes or commands of a transcendental entity; a god; a supernatural being; a being that can operate outside the cause-and-effect system. Such a being can appear or disappear at will, it can create material goods on the spot from nothing, it can talk to people while remaining invisible and controlling events and/or providing freedom from the cause-and-effect system, as that being chooses. Individuals who derive their ethical grounding from such transcendental entities may either make dogmatic statements based on the experience of voices, interpretations of that which is regarded as holy writ of deeply felt personal convictions (conscience); such ethics are also regarded as *absolute* ethics. Reason, logic, and common sense does not interfere with those who acquire from transcendental sources convictions of what is right or ethical. However, there is also a subset of people who, while holding to a belief in a transcendental entity, will engage in discourse with their fellow citizens and, providing their basic belief system is not impugned, will come to decisions about behavior that may be consonant with common sense.

The other set of principles is based on the acceptance of the determining nature of the cause-and-effect system. It looks to the observable and tangible events that are incorporated into our knowledge and science. It then moves to determinations of the guidelines for behavior. This scheme does not accept the ruling that is often leveled at such developments, which is that it is not possible to move rationally from statements about the world of being to statements about the world of duty, obligation, or ought. (This is a denial of the validity of the naturalistic fallacy.) It is important to realize that this system of *relative* ethics, where the situation of the world determines our duties and obligations, is itself subject to a number of variants. Many of these variants can be found in this volume (see also Singer, P. (1991). *A Companion to Ethics*, p. 565. Oxford: Blackwell). I summarize below some of the leading contenders for the provision of the principles whereby we decide how to behave:

- Golden Rulers who assert that you should do unto others as you would have others do to you or as Confucious would have it, "do not do to others that which you would not have done to yourself";
- utilitarians who assert that you should do what is most useful, (to you, to the community);
- eudaemonists who assert that you should do what makes you and or the community happiest;
- biological determinists/Darwinians might assert that you should do that which most promotes survival of yourself and/or your community and/or other communities and/or other biotic entities;

- Kantians assert that you should act in accordance with the Categorical Imperative, which requires you to "act only on the maxim through which you can at the same time will that it be a universal law";
- conformity ethics requires you to find out what is acceptable and effect that;
- traditionalists require that you behave in the manner in which your antecedents or progenitors behaved;
- theists hold that you behave in a way defined by the edicts or perceived intentions of a god or deity,
- practical ethicists require you to act naturally;
- contractualists hold that your actions be in accordance with your contract with the society you live in.

It is clear that there is a wide variety of principles from which to choose when making an ethical decision. There are, also, definite differences of emphasis in protecting and/or promoting the interests of the individual versus the interests of the society. While this may not matter when the outcome is the same, when the outcome is different there is a need to resolve the otherwise inevitable conflict. In view of the importance of this issue the section below focuses on how such dissonances may be, in some measure, reconciled.

2. When Ethical Principles Are in Conflict

There is a series of practices that can be put in place to aid the resolution of ethical (and other) issues where the protagonists seem to adopt irreconcilable positions. These reduce to a set of actions that can include one or more of the following:

- define the issue over which there is a dispute so that it is clear that both parties have the same view of the difference between them;
- make sure that what are stated to be the "facts" of the case are indeed the most reliable concepts of the situation at hand;
- by examination of the extreme views of the outcome that might be required by each protagonist it may be possible to move to some compromise position in the middle where neither protagonist obtains all that was originally desired;
- the method of *casuistry* requires that one of the two ends of the possible action spectrum be taken by a solution that is evidently right, while the other end is occupied by a solution that is evident to all to be wrong; we can then move to a solution by interpolating additional cases whose rightness or

wrongness are not quite as well defined but on which some agreement can be obtained so as to eventually bracket, contain, and resolve the test case that instigated the examination;
- find a technical solution which solves the ethical dilemma;
- spread the load so that others accept their share of any costs that are incurred as a result of, say, a newly perceived need to improve performance specifications;
- determine and define the dominant ethical issue and act on the basis of that teaching;
- do a calculation of the consequences of the outcomes of the alternative solutions in a common medium (money, lives, dignity) and agree on maximizing the level of this parameter in the solution;
- require each protagonist to attempt to stand outside the system and view it as if they were a member of an arbitration tribunal; compare results and move from this position rather than the *ab initio* situation,
- obtain the agreement of the disputants that the resolution of the difference will provide for both parties benefits that otherwise could not be obtained; once this has been ascertained, the examination of the issues may begin afresh;
- enclose the disputants in a confined space and exert physical pressure on them to resolve their differences (decrease the temperature, quality of the food and beverages, amount of space available, and so on, as per the procedures used for the selection of a new Pope);
- select an abiter (ombudsman) or seek the help of an arbitration service, ethics committee, and so on.

The most difficult disputes to solve are those that involve the lives of humans or animals. For some it is not enough to equate the value of a human life at £750,000 for a road user and £2,000,000 if a railway user, or the assessment of the courts when awarding damages in a civil trial of between £20,000 and £2,500,000 (based on a calculation of lifetime earnings foregone). Others will not, or cannot, put a price on a life saved. All lives are infinitely valuable including those of some (all) animals. Therefore, they would argue it is justified to spend all of our resources to save the life of one cat, canary, or child.

We clearly do not behave in this way. Each structure we build, each car or airplane we construct, or each bridge we design can fail under unforeseen conditions of weather, loading, or component defect. To guard against and to prevent all putative disaster scenarios would require infinite resources, and so compromises are made; risks are taken; and we value our lives in proportion to the level of risk to which we voluntarily expose ourselves. Thus, by an examination of extremes and the ways in which we actually live our lives it should be possible to reach an accommodation with even those absolutists, who assert that the deity made all his creatures of equal value, by asking some frank questions about how they would *actually* behave in particular situations as opposed to how they would *like to* behave were they the possessor of infinite resources.

F. Science and Engineering Ethics

From the definitions I have given above for science and engineering the reader will perceive that I have taken a wide approach to the subject area. I do not confine science to that which is effected in laboratories, nor do I confine engineering to the transformation of materials into products. Rather, I would take the position that teaching is adding value to students, that law makers engineer verbal statements to control our behavior in our best interests, and that jurists engineer verdicts by processes that are themselves the products of other engineering activities. While so engaged scientists and engineers are subjected to situations in which they may not act in accordance with one or another ethical principle. Recently, such aberrations of appropriate behavior have settled into a number of sections that I will elucidate below.

It is useful to further subdivide the area into four categories: (1) process issues in the generation of new knowledge or science; (2) product issues that apply to the use of the so generated knowledge; (3) process issues associated with the practice of engineering; and (4) product issues derived from the consequences of the deployment of material entities resulting from engineering processes.

1. Process Issues in Science

The intent of those engaged in the progression of science is to effect research which will "... extend human knowledge of the physical, biological, or social world beyond what is already known" (1995. *On Being a Scientist*, p. 27. Washington, DC: National Academy Press). In pursuing this goal mistakes are made, due care is not applied, or there are deliberate attempts to obtain personal advancement by the manipulation of observations and people. Some of the commoner forms of misconduct are delineated below. The depiction of these misdeeds should not, however, blind the reader to the hundreds of thousands of scientists who strive diligently to discover new knowledge of the world that they attempt to present to us all in a manner that will command our respect and confidence.

a. Fabrication of Data

Events have come to light wherein an individual has deliberately created data so as to be able to propound with greater conviction a particular hypothesis. Such data were made up and were not derived from empirical observation. Examples include the faking of skin transplants by Summerlin in 1974 and the origin of cancer experiments by Spector in 1980 and 1981.

b. Falsification of Data

Data manipulation or falsification occurs when figures are altered to fit in with a notional guess as to what they ought to have been. Sometimes a predetermined result is aimed at because a senior investigator has achieved such a result previously and a student is under pressure to repeat the supervisor's work in a purportedly analogous situation. (An example is the falsification of results on insulin receptors by Soman in the period from 1978 through 1980). In other cases a degree of acclaim is the objective from the presentation of data that provide evidence for a radically new approach to a subject area.

c. Plagiarism

This involves passing off as one's own work or ideas of others. Such events are used to acquire prestige or to win a grant application. Examples are the theft of authorship of the Bernoulli equation by the father from the work of the son in 1738, around 60 papers copied by Alsabati between 1977 and 1980, the case of Heidi Weismann, and that of Pamela Berge.

d. Data Selection, Manipulation, and Management

Experimenters generate masses of data or observations. Some of these observations are acquired before the experimenter has learned how to do the experiment in the most effective manner. It is clear that data derived from such "learning" experiments are not required in a final publication although they may be presented in a report to a supervisor or a granting agency. Similarly, some data that are generated in a fully established experimental system may just appear to be so wildly at variance with the flow of the data that the experimenter may choose not to include them in any report. For example, data taken from a culture that harbored a suspected contaminant might be wholly discarded. Or a suspect test tube might have been used in a sensitive enzyme action, with the result that an unknown contaminant was completely inhibited. Or more commonly still, an ingredient of the reaction was inadvertently missed and a second reaction container may have received a double dose. These are common occurrences and experimenters are familiar with handling the suspicious data that occur as a result.

There are other ways of manipulating data that rely more on presentation techniques than on making up new numbers. The choice of a statistical technique can be all important in the determination of the significance of an observation. Or a graphical presentation can be designed to magnify or diminish a particular effect. In such cases fraud is not an issue but the principle of *caveat emptor* might also apply to one's reception of data from the scientific literature.

Data management is a serious factor in the work of scientists. Sometimes the withholding of data from competing scientists may be justified on the basis of its preliminary nature and the situation that, without a number of repeat experiments, such data would be more misleading than helpful. Sometimes a research contract requires the noncommunication of data, and the potential commercial application of some piece of information may consign a piece of research to the part of the library that holds the undisclosable material. But when a scientist knows something with a high degree of confidence that would have materially helped a fellow scientist, albeit a competitor, it could be considered unethical for that individual to retain the information and not divulge it. An even worse situation results when deliberately misleading data are issued. In short, the management of data is often the only way an individual scientist may think it possible to preserve his or her position in a particular subject area. It is short-termism of the highest order. But in today's world with so many young scientists clutching at the straws that are supporting their careers it is to be expected that some practices as outlined above will occur.

e. Conflict of Interest

A conflict of interest applies in both the areas of science and engineering. It happens when an individual is driven by motives other than those that have been overtly declared but which do influence the way a project is effected and in a manner that was not intended and could be antithetical to the requirements of the organization that financed the work originally. An engineer in industry might have a conflict between his or her employers and the benefit of society. Examples are the Challenger incident related above and the conditions outlined in the paper of M. McDonald, "Ethics

and Conflicts of Interest" (this appears on the World Wide Web at http://www.ethics.ubc.ca/papers/conflict.html).

f. Authorship Issues

The improper assignation of authorship is akin to theft as when intellectual property is improperly allotted, assigned, or abrogated. To be an author one must have contributed to the intellectual content of the work described; it is not appropriate to become an author as a result of the gift of the actual author (courtesy authorship). Examples are the Baltimore case mentioned earlier and the parallel scandal of the Darsee case.

g. Mentoring Issues

It is inappropriate to take advantage of the teacher–student relationship so as to deprive the student of recognition and to abuse the education process in the interest of achieving a research success for the supervisor. An example is the way Lipmann dealt with his research worker in 1960, which lead to the need to withdraw a publication purporting to demonstrate another example of Lipman's original finding.

h. Harassment in the Workplace

In the necessarily close relationship between student and teacher in a research environment it is unethical for a teacher to take advantage of such a situation and, for example, make sexual advances or improper proposals. Examples were presented by Louise Fitzgerald and Myra Strober in a symposium organized by Stephannie J. Bird and Catherine J. Didion for the AAAS in 1994.

i. Discrimination in the Workplace

Discrimination on the basis of race, creed, or color is illegal, but it is clearly not possible to treat everybody in an identical manner. Indeed, we would all suffer were we to try to do so. Nevertheless, it is clear that to deliberately disadvantage an individual on the basis of some nonrelevant criterion should not be permitted. The magnitude of this problem varies in different parts of the world and there are even major differences in the different states in the United States. An example would be the activities of the National Research Council of Canada in allocating jobs and contracts.

j. Peer Review: Misconduct/Theft

Grants are given and papers are accepted for publication on the basis of the reviews of the peers of the proposer or putative author. When the competition for grants and recognition is fierce, the temptation to reject a grant application or steal the idea in such an application is a powerful motivator. It is also possible for a referee of a publication to delay issuing the review until that referee has had a chance to either submit his or her own application or to do extra work to maintain leadership in the field. All such cases are difficult to prove and generally do not get a public airing; yet all those engaged in the grant/publication process have a warchest of stories to justify such suspicions.

k. External Examination

This suffers from many of the potential problems of peer review, but the opportunities for self-benefit are less, and in general there is more than one examiner, which prevents most anomalous excesses.

l. Safety Issues

Scientists working at the laboratory bench find the practices imposed by safety committees, while obligatory, are irksome and are not seen to be preventing probable harm to research workers. Nevertheless, a significant industry has come into being to provide scientists and engineers the specialized equipment to dispense fluids in defined volumes that does not involve mouth pipetting. Centrifuges are fitted with interlocking lids and radioactive materials are controlled with great assiduity. The use of masks, eye protectors, gloves, and containment cabinets are and were *de rigueuer* before the imposition of the current suite of regulations under the banner of COSHH (Care of Substances Hazardous to Health) regulations in the United Kingdom.

2. Product Issues in Science

a. Information Ethics

Privacy is the right not to have published that which one wishes to keep to one's self or to selected others. Modern computers can process data bases that contain ever increasing amounts of information. It is clearly possible to link computer records involving the health of an individual with court records, with insurance claim records, and with a record of all the items one has bought using the credit card. Who may have access to this information cornucopia? How can it be policed so that individuals who do not have the right to access this data base can be detected and brought to justice? How can we protect individuals from incorrect data being used? These are examples of the kinds of questions that are being raised with regard to the use of information.

Other issues to be faced in the computer age involve the theft of information using the networks to transport such illicit information. The pirating of computer pro-

grams is one such case where an unscrupulous individual might purchase a program, inactivate the protective mechanism, and then make the program available at a price that is below the manufacturer's cost. Other issues involve the electronic scanning of articles in journals and the transmission of the resulting digital information via the Internet or the World Wide Web to whomever is interested in picking it up. An additional area is that of computer viruses. The design and implementation of a computer virus to attack the programs stored in a computer so that the owner of the infected computer must spend considerable amounts of time and money to sort the matter out is not something that is a joke or that can be taken lightly. Rather, we may consider the sources of such viruses as the individuals from whom society (or those infected) might be eligible for due recompense.

An additional issue that has stirred much interest is that of the encryption of messages. On the one hand governments are anxious that messages that promote illegal activities may be transmitted in a way that cannot be intercepted and understood by the authorities. On the other hand commercial and confidential transactions of a legal nature may be coded in a nondecipherable form during the normal course of business dealing. It has been mooted that a special encrypting chip (the clipper chip) made available by the U.S. government might cover the encryption of legal transactions, but users are not necessarily willing for outside observers to become aware of their activities. Indeed, encryption devices that cannot be decoded are available to serve this purpose. The resolution of this dilemma may be found in the way government surveillance of civilian activities is controlled. An open system, available for public scrutiny, under the authority of an individual who is also answerable to the democratically elected assemblies may be a part of the answer; but whichever way we turn the need for cascaded control systems (control systems to control, control systems, to control . . .) as occurs within organisms and within collections of organisms is needed.

The ability of computers to control robots to act in precise and defined ways has in some countries redefined the nature of the workplace. Japan and Southeast Asian countries have been actively installing robotic procedures to manufacture goods to a higher technical specification and at less cost than in other countries. This and the implementation of computers to handle the repetitive clerical work in government and industrial bureaucracies has led to a downsizing of such operations and the release of many thousands of "middle managers" and their staff onto the labor market. Job security is threatened across the board and society has yet to develop ways to handle such events with fairness and justice, again highlighting the need for a review of the ethics that we adopt.

b. Knowledge Issues

The traditional credo of the scientist has been that the knowledge generated as a result of the application of the scientific method is value free and is available for others to apply in the practical arena where good or bad effects may be engendered. However, modern science has generated sets of ideas that cause us to reevaluate the basis of the ethical systems which have worked for the last 2 or 3000 or so years. In particular, we now have knowledge about the nature, origin, and evolution of life in which we can place more confidence than the creation myths or stories provided by the ancient religions. Additionally, we can explain by using only our knowledge of material and energetic interactions such phenomena as lightning, thunder, volcanic activity, earthquakes, temporal cycles, infectious disease, and the way our bodies work and develop from a single-celled embryo. This knowledge has weakened our dependence on the books of holy writ that provided the most plausible explanations for these phenomena. Consequentially, it has impugned the link between deities and the provision of the rules for human behavior or conduct. In short, the manifestation of contemporary science has required us to rethink both the basis on which behavior should be founded and also the implications for our conduct on our acceptance of such a grounding. Therefore, we have to take the involvement of science in the realm of ethics to be a subject area for further study and development.

c. Clinical Trials

One knowledge area that is much abused is the area of clinical trials of pharmaceutical, food, and cosmetic products. Whereas the former (pharmaceutical) trials have to withstand the rigorous examinations of a Food and Drug Administration or a Committee of Safety of Medicinal Products, new foods and cosmetics are not as stringently regulated as to their value and safety. The financial implications of the trial results are significant, so product promoters are interested in obtaining as favorable a result as possible to be better able to promote their new product. This raises the profile of the double-blind clinical trial to a high level. Nevertheless, there are many reports of the fraudulent operation of such trials and the "unblinding" of the trial while it is yet in progress.

d. Scientific Predictions

Scientists are often asked questions about the future. Contemporaneously, there are questions as to the safety of British beef, the issue of global warming or cooling and what is responsible for any such change, the prediction of earthquakes, the path of tornadoes, and the eruption of volcanoes. We also have issues in the prevalence of infectious diseases, such as AIDS, tuberculosis, malaria, and others. Much of the information generated and tested by the application of the scientific method bears on such questions, but it is necessary for the lay public and the media to realize that answers to questions about the nature of the future must of necessity bear a probabilistic qualification. Scientists do not claim to make predictions with 100% certainty, although the assertion that the sun will rise tomorrow can be made with a confidence approaching that level. In other cases, such as the timing and location of earthquakes, the degree of certainty is much less, and it varies inversely with the degree of precision of the prediction.

The use of knowledge in making predictions, irrespective of the accuracy of the predictions, can lead to ethical problems. Secrecy is generally thought proper when the affairs of state or the profitability of a company are at risk. It would be less well thought of if antisocial events followed the withholding of information about what could transpire in the future.

3. Process Issues in Engineering

a. Whistle-blowing and Conflicts of Interest

As engineering can involve the generation of new knowledge, many of the process issues as discussed earlier pertain. However, the emphasis in engineering changes because the products of engineering appear in the marketplace. So the issues of whistle-blowing and conflicts of interest exist in a more potent and tangible form because the financial condition of a company and its personnel may depend on closing a particular deal, and the selection of the data and the manner of its presentation can be crucial to achieving such an end. Under such circumstances honesty and the presentation of all the relevant information is the ethic to be followed.

b. Safety

Furthermore, as engineers tend to work at larger and faster scales of operation, issues of safety in the workplace are more pressing than at the relatively benign environment of the laboratory bench. Indeed, the issue of product safety is a matter of concern for all engineers, for it is clear that there will be a legal liability as well as ethical opprobrium were a product resulting from a design that was inherently unsafe to be let into the marketplace.

c. Honesty and Confidentiality

Scientists adopt the view that the communication of research is a priority, whereas engineers working in industry, commerce, or in a political institution may be required to keep much of what they know and do in confidence. The breaching of such a confidence can have financial implications on the share price of a company or the popularity of a political party. Again the divulgence of information outside the preordained channels can constitute an illegal act and one that throws the perpetrator and the company into an ethically reprehensible light.

d. Codes of Practice

Finally, engineers accept that their actions and behavior will be governed by the code of practice set out by their qualifying institution or professional society. Examples of such codes may be obtained from the institutions/ societies. The policing of compliance with such a code is an issue that requires more attention. While in the medical, legal, architectural, and media areas there have been actions based on noncompliance with codes, the relationship between the professional, his or her institution, and the legal system is such that the further development of voluntariness in this area is of dubious value. It may be necessary to provide professional institutions with immunity from prosecution for effecting their duties by applying the codes in a legitimate fashion with appropriate sanctions. This would protect societies from litigation resulting from actions taken against a member of the society who felt aggrieved at the treatment received.

4. Product Issues in Engineering

a. Bioethics

The application of ethical principles to humans and animals is part of the general subject of science and engineering ethics as this is just another area where knowledge is generated and used for benefit. This not only applies in the way humans relate to animals and the way humans relate on a one-to-one basis with other humans, but also in cases when humans operate in the societal state. It is clearly a vast subject and is the matter of many learned tomes. (e.g., 1987. *Bioethics,* p. 620. edited by T. A. Hannon, Paulist Press).

Bioethics impinges on the promulgation of science in the use of humans and animals for experimental purposes. Such issues have been dealt with in great detail by bodies set up to monitor, regulate, and control such activities. Codes of behavior have been written and are widely distributed and used as exemplified by the Declaration of Helsinki: World Medical Association, revision of Hong Kong 1989.

Other bioethical issues concerning humans abound. Abortion, contraception, eugenics, euthanasia, homosexuality, infanticide, heroic medicine, prophylaxis versus therapy, informed consent, resource allocation, harassment, and discrimination are all issues that are under constant review in popular and specialist journals. In addition there are the issues referred to earlier dealing with our ability to manipulate genomes and cells where the latter can become human embryos.

b. Ethical Problems with Widgets

While the practice of engineering engenders many ethical issues that are similar to those thrown up in the area of science, there is a subset of problems that are more closely associated with the tangible products of the engineering activity. For example, there is a suite of engineering product issues:

- there are benefits and disbenefits resulting from the exploitation of nuclear energy;
- the mass production of the weapons of war can be an industry devoted to societal defense or an opportunity for profiteering and the instigation of needless conflicts between client states;
- the chemical and oil industries contribute to our well-being in numerous ways but they also provide us with toxic wastes and, in the event of oil tanker catastrophes, with environmental disasters;
- transportation by private or public means as a way to preserve energy, decrease pollution, and generate amenity;
- intensive rearing of animals for food purposes;
- the production of drugs and therapies where prophylactic measures would yield greater social benefit.

c. Ethical Issues in Social Engineering

Ingenuity may also be expressed in the creation and promotion of those cultural organs that control and determine the way we behave as social beings; examples of such activities are:

- the production, execution, and monitoring of laws;
- the criminal justice system;
- the management of an economy so that predefined social or ethical principles can be achieved;

- the operation of an educational system that fits in with the needs of the individual to be provided with an equal opportunity to develop his or her talents to the greatest degree coupled with the need to satisfy the requirement of society for educated individuals;
- the promulgation of eating and exercising habits that drain health care resources to the least amount.

Such issues are coming into focus with increasing clarity and intensity as our modern societies develop without the incursion of a major catastrophe such as a world war, a famine, a cosmic catastrophe (accident), or a universal and devastating plague.

III. A HISTORICAL PERSPECTIVE

A. Data Manipulation

As we do not, nor can we, know with complete certainty the nature of the world outside of ourselves we have to make guesses at what it might be, generally based on some observations or sensate data. Nevertheless, those who have sought to make some sense of what they perceived were on occasion somewhat cavalier with how they handled the raw data. For example, Newton used fudge or adjustment factors to enable his observations to marry to the relationships he devised; Dalton, the formulator of the modern version of the atomic theory, altered his basic data on the weights of the elements that combined with measured weights of other elements, so that he could present his results in the most convincing way. And Millikan, who showed that the charge on the electron was constant and that fractional charges did not exist, selected those experiments that "went right" in order to present his case effectively. (This author has done some similar experiments when investigating the relative charge on hydrated microcarriers and can vouch for the occurrence of the "odd-ball" observation.) It is also alleged that the data on which Gregor Mendel based the concept of genetics and genes were selected from his observations so that the patterns of heredity were clearly depicted in his reported figures. A similar massaging of the data may also have occurred in the presentation of the statistics regarding the inheritance of mental capabilities in identical and nonidentical twins by C. Burt. Forgery is also not uncommon in the area of paleontology, as evidenced by the Piltdown Skull believed to have been fabricated by C. Dawson and M. A. C. Hinton between 1908 and 1912.

There is little doubt that, in spite of the manipulation of the data by these investigators, the concepts that emanated from their endeavors were worthy and valuable to subsequent workers. It is important to realize that in testing guesses it may be of value to see the data or observations in the light of what they "ought" to be on the basis of some notion or theory of what is out there. While there are pressures to acquire the accolade of being the first individual to demonstrate such a theory or relationship, and that the presentation of data that fits "miraculously" with what one is purporting is a tempting thing to do, it may be more appropriate in the world in which we are increasingly brought to account for our actions to actually do the fudging openly with some comment to the effect that "my methods of making measurements were somewhat unreliable, but within the noisy data I collected, I can discern some relationships that I believe pertain in that reality out there, and these are...."

1. Data/Concept Misappropriation

Not only may data be molded to theories but data or ideas can be "borrowed without acknowledgment" from others. Claudius Ptolemy (2nd century CE) was able to convince the world for almost 1500 years, that this planet was the centre of the universe based on data which, it seems, he purloined from the observations of Hipparchus (who flourished between 146 and 127 B.C.E.). it is suggested that Charles Darwin first saw the ideas implicit in natural selection in the papers of Edward Blyth (of 1835 and 1837), whom he did not acknowledge, whereas he was most careful in giving credit to Malthus for sparking the idea that populations expand in excess of their food supplies, to Wallace for his concomitant realization of the nature of the process of natural selection, and to Spencer for the latter's concept of "survival of the fittest." It has also been suggested recently that, on occasion, Pasteur could be economical with the truth. For when he presented to the public his anthrax vaccine for sheep he told those who assembled to witness the experiment, that he had oxygen-attenuated the material, whereas his notebooks show that he had used the *antiseptic* potassium bichromate (an oxidizing agent). This was because he was reluctant to acknowledge the work of the veterinarian Toussaint who previously showed that organisms killed by the use of the *antiseptic,* phenol or carbolic acid, were effective in making anthrax and other vaccines.

IV. CONTEMPORARY ISSUES

A. Office of Research Integrity (ORI)

The field of science and engineering ethics became recognized as a major area of governmental interest in the United States during the 1980s, culminating in the 1992 formation of the Office of Research Integrity. This body deals with reports of misconduct allegations and oversees the way institutions in receipt of government research grants comply with the recommendations to prevent the occurrence of misconduct and conflicts of interest. Universities are learning to cope with these issues through the formation of the appropriate committees. Bioethics committees abound. Most countries as well as the European Community have bodies that deal with issues resulting from new developments in Medicine and Biotechnology. A recent report of the ORI, entitled "Integrity and Misconduct in Research" (1995. Published by the USDHHS/PHS) defines misconduct as fabrication falsification and plagiarism and includes misappropriation, interference, and misrepresentation as well as obstruction and noncompliance with codes.

B. Ethics Courses

To comply with the need to behave ethically, scientists and engineers in universities and industry have been offered educational courses covering many of the points discussed in this article. It is generally held in this field that the most effective way of purveying this information is by a variegated and structured approach to the subject area. This will include special classes dealing with ethical issues in their historical, operational, and case study aspects. The use of role-playing scenarios engages the involvement of the participants and onlookers, while the formats of seminars, discussions, and debates also serve to instruct. The fundamental problem faced in such interactions is that the proliferation of ethical systems means that some course leaders regard their function as merely showing the students (a) that there are problems and (b) that there are a variety of ways of approaching a solution. The ability to "close-out" a problematic issue is not taken as an objective of the exercise. This causes student dissatisfaction. It therefore becomes of increasing importance to emphasize, portray, and exemplify methods of conflict resolution as I have indicated above. In addition, it is important that ethical issues relevant to subjects that are expounded are brought up during that teaching period. This requires that teachers in all subject areas are famil-

iar with the ethical implications, problems, and pitfalls in their area of specialization, and that they are willing and capable of handling them in the didactic situation. The combination of the provision of the ethical tools coupled with the demonstration of the relevance of such considerations for each area is pivotal in the promotion of ethical thinking and behavior in students, teachers, and practitioners.

A further handle to the didactic situation is slowly coming to the fore. This deals with the efficacy of ethics courses in the subsequent thinking and behaviors of those who have been exposed to such experiences. In the work of Deni Elliot, et al., it is clear that the change in the way some people operate in areas they perceive as vital to their self-interest after having been subjected to a course in ethics is minimal, but measurable.

Although Plato in the Meno comes to the conclusion that virtue cannot be taught, K. D. Pimple and his colleagues at Indiana University have used definitions of the various stages of ethical development to determine the efficacy of ethics teaching practice. Such stages may be depicted as (1) being able to discern the possible actions and their implications when presented with an issue requiring a judgment; (2) the determination of the morally right (fair, just, or good) course of action; (3) such a determination should be above personal values if these militate against the course judged right; and (4) the person should be able to implement the morally correct decision in the face of forces militating against such an implementation.

This may become the paradigm for the future as more effective and relevant ethics courses come online and, perhaps what is more important, is that more people in the institution become conscious of ethics and provide examples of ethically appropriate behavior that become accepted as the norm while the ethically suspect behaviors receive general and public disapprobation. It will be of continuing interest to work out ways in which we can measure the efficacy of such courses by the way the participants live their lives subsequent to their exposure to such courses.

C. Whistle-blowing

There are other live issues. Whistle-blowers have been surveyed recently with the result that most of them have recorded that they either lost their jobs, were held back in the promotion stakes, or were held in low esteem and perceived as troublemakers by their colleagues. Of the people who responded to a recent survey, 69% said that they had experienced some negative consequences. It is clear that legislation has to be available to protect the reasonable interests of the whistle-blower. Notwithstanding such protection it should also be clear that deliberate, unjustified, and vindictive victimization of individuals by whistle-blowers should be treated with all due severity (the Hamurabi Code of *ca.* 1700 B.C.E. has it that, if you act as a false witness to a murder then you are subject to the punishment that would have accrued to that murderer).

D. Insurance Issues

As a result of our newly found abilities to effect genetic screening it is possible to determine in advance the propensity of an individual to a range of debilitating disease states. The ethical question at stake is whether such information should be made available to insurance companies who are providing life insurance coverage. This should be compared against an actuarially derived calculation based on the population as a whole rather than the probability of the insured individual making a claim. Such considerations also apply to those who are covered by health management organizations (HMOs). The issue is based on whether society or the individual is responsible for the health and well-being of the individual. One can ask the question as to whether those of us who are born with genes that do not give us a propensity to disease should support financially those who do have such a propensity. Our sense of society and the contract we each have with the body politic would indicate that we shoulder the burden communally; but some individuals would not wish to be part of this: hence the dilemma.

E. Gene Patenting

All the canons of patent law require that there be an inventive step by human intervention in the description of the item or process for which a patent is sought. It is clear that the determination of the sequence of bases in a gene by the application of well-tried-and-tested (often highly automated) procedures cannot be considered to be inventive. Nevertheless, companies, academies, and individuals persist in applying for patents for the sequences of the bases of genes whose function is often unknown. Clearly, such patents cannot be held to be inventions. However, there are situations in which genes are sequenced from particular individuals who may express different genetic properties that could be of benefit to others. Such genes may belong to an individual or a tribe as property and it could be expected that the exploitation of that property requires compensation. Were such gene sequences not patentable then

it would be difficult to effect the compensation. This need not be the case, as I may lend anybody some of my property for a fee without the need for patent protection. Where there are modifications to the genes that are not just "cosmetic," then it may be admissible to file for a patent. Or, indeed, if the product of gene expression is modified, formulated, produced, or delivered in a novel way it is also reasonable to expect patent protection of the invention that in this case will be a useful product.

It is possible to patent antibiotics, which are the products of bacterial and fungal organisms, as it requires ingenuity to grow the producing organism in culture in a manner that provides economic yields of the antibiotic. So, it is argued, it should be possible to patent genes that are natural products like antibiotics. Were this to be the case then each material generated by every organism can be patented; this is contrary to the intent of society, which is to strike a contract with an inventor so as to reward personal ingenuity by the granting of a patent monopoly in exchange for making the invention freely available to the public some 10 to 20 years after the granting of the patent. So it behooves the patenter of a gene to show how ingenuity or inventiveness has been expressed, bearing in mind that the sequencing of the gene is not enough.

F. Who Watches the Watchers? (*Quis custodiet custodies*)

When peers are asked to review manuscripts prior to publication or research grant applications or the quality of contribution of a department or unit to an area of research endeavor then the possibilities of deliberate wrongful judgments and theft of intellectual property are rife. People asked to effect reviews of their contemporaries work are bound by conventions and warnings, yet the public prosecution of any misdeeds is not evident. Nevertheless, there is considerable mistrust of what is held to be the least odious way of apportioning credits. Most people who do not achieve success attribute some of their failure to the misjudgments and intellectual thefts experienced at the hands of the members of reviewing boards. Were it possible to conjure such boards from people who do not have a vested interest in the outcome of the judgments and therefore do not suffer from *a priori* conflict of interest then a considerable service would have been rendered. Such people might be retirees or people from abroad, or groups of individuals, each of whom reviews all the documents before the board and makes a judgment on each document (see also *Science and Engineering Ethics*

(1997), Vol. 3, Issue 1, specializing in an examination of the subject of peer review).

G. Cloning and Chimeras

We are fascinated and horrified in turns with our growing capabilities to clone animals and plants. On the one hand we have the possibilities of the high yields of the monoculture, but on the other hand there is the possibility of disease eradicating the whole crop. Other problems pertain to animals. Experiments with ovines and bovines have demonstrated the two possibilities of cloning and chimera formation. From the latter the deified entities that were depicted as part beast, part man come closer to realization. There is little doubt that such developments open up possibilities for humans. While three are proscriptions against the continuance of such work, the myriad of possibilities it presents will probably be made available if, and when, we can be confident that the social and personal control systems we have implemented are worthy and reliable.

V. CONCLUSION

Ethics embraces the law. The law deals with all aspects of theft, fraud, misrepresentation, and injury, and, indeed, were any individual to believe they have cause to be aggrieved, they are free to bring a civil suit to court and claim damages proportional to the injury held to have been suffered. Such cases in the area of science and engineering, as defined above are not common. While civil courts have been involved with issues of plagiarism, for the most part the injuries suffered by scientists (and to a lesser extent by engineers) have just been tolerated. However, in recent times, the pressures on scientists and engineers to perform under a harsher employment regimen than heretofore has meant that officials in governments have been fearful that misconduct would ensue. So attention has been focused on the practices in laboratories with a view to preventing misconduct.

It is clear that there are many "gray" areas where recourse to the courts is futile and where codes can be ignored or "corners cut," yet where conduct can be improved:

- removal, sabotaging (by, for example, making a lense dirty, changing a setting, or jolting a mirror out of alignment), or monopolizing time on a crucial instrument can be done with the intent of depriving a potential competitor of a success;

- holding back seemingly trivial, yet crucial, oral or written information that could help an adversary is a mean but often practiced device;
- providing misleading information (dissimulation) is another stratagem to put a rival off the scent of one's true intentions;
- the use of ideas acquired, but not publicly acknowledged, from conversations, meetings, or reviewing of papers and grant applications is a form of theft that may be effected consciously or subconsciously;
- the abuse of the role of the supervisor in exploiting a research student's educational opportunity;
- the disregard for safety codes in order to work faster can affect not only the perpetrator but also the other members of the laboratory;
- the mistreatment of animals while seemingly complying with codes;
- the disruption of the spirit of collegiality to foster self-interest.

The perpetration of a competitive and financially restrictive environment by governmental agencies has promoted behaviors that are antithetical to the objectives and missions of science and engineering research establishments. It is therefore not surprising that the behavior of individuals will come under scrutiny. The study, development, and promotion of science and engineering ethics, as a subject discipline, will help us become aware of what we are about and hopefully, in spite of the harsh conditions, it will promote behaviors that will enable us to live together with mutual respect and with a view to what it is that we must do for communal as well as personal self-interest.

Also See the Following Articles

BIOETHICS, OVERVIEW • LEGAL ETHICS, OVERVIEW

Bibliography

Cohen, J. (1994). U.S.-French patent dispute heads for showdown. *Science,* **265,** 23–25.

Crossen, C. (1992). *Tainted truth,* p. 272. New York: Simon & Schuster.

Elliott, D., & Stern, J. E. (1996). Evaluating teaching and student's learning of academic research ethics. *Science and Engineering Ethics,* **2,** 345–366.

Gee, H. (1996). Box of bones 'clinches' identity of Piltdown palaeontology hoaxer. *Nature,* **381,** 261–262.

Geison, G. L. (1995). *The private science of Louis Pasteur.* Princeton: Princeton University Press.

Holden, C. (1994). Breaking the glass ceiling for $900,000. *Science,* **263,** 1688.

Jasanoff, S., Markle, G. E., Petersen, J. C., & Pinch, T. (1995). *Handbook of Science and Technology Studies,* p. 820. London: Sage Publications.

Kaiser, J., & Marshall, E. (1996). Imanishi-Kari ruling slams ORI. *Science, 272,* 1864–1865.

Poole, T., & Thomas, A. De. (1994). Primate vaccine evaluation network recommendations. Guidelines and information for biomedical research involving non-human primates with emphasis on health problems in developing countries. Pub. DGXII/B/4-SDME R2/105.

Marshall, E. (1995). Suit alleges misuse of peer review. *Science,* 270, 1912–1914.

Rest, J. R., Bebeau, M. J., & Volker, J. (1986). An overview of the psychology of morality. In J. R. Rest (Ed.), *Moral development: Advances in research and theory,* pp. 1–39. Boston: Prager Publishers.

Rhoades, L. J. (1996). Whistleblowing Consequences. *Science, 271,* 1345.

Spier, R. (1989). Ethical problem? Get a technical fix. *Vaccine,* 7, 381–382.

Spier, R. (1995). Ethical aspects of the university-industry interface, *Science and Engineering Ethics,* 1, 151–162.

Spier, R. E. (1995a). Science, engineering and ethics: Running definitions. *Science and Engineering Ethics,* 1, 5–10.

Spurgeon, D. (1992). Canadian research council found guilty of job bias. *Nature,* 359, 95.

Uehiro, E. (1974). Practical ethics for You. Tokyo: Rin-yu Publishing Co, Ltd.

SCIENTIFIC PUBLISHING

Beth A. Fischer and Michael J. Zigmond
University of Pittsburgh

GLOSSARY

editor The individual designated by the publisher to have overall responsibility for the content of a journal, including deciding which manuscripts are accepted for publication.

peer-review The evaluation of a manuscript by researchers knowledgeable about the field/content under discussion. These individuals must not be part of the editorial staff of the journal to which it was submitted.

research article "The first disclosure containing sufficient information to enable peers (1) to assess observations, (2) to repeat experiments, and (3) to evaluate intellectual processes; moreover, it must be susceptible to sensory perception, essentially permanent, available to the scientific community without restriction, and available for regular screening by one or more of the major recognized secondary services." (Council of Biology Editors definition.)

reviewers Individuals chosen by the editor of a journal to evaluate the quality and significance of the work reported in a manuscript submitted for publication. These persons generally are not paid for their services.

scientific journal A periodically issued compendium of technical articles intended for an audience of peers.

PEER-REVIEWED RESEARCH ARTICLES have long played a significant role in science—facilitating scientific progress by permitting the sharing of methods, results, and interpretations, and establishing a mechanism for judging the expertise and productivity of individual researchers. Perhaps because publications hold such value it should not be surprising that some individuals have sought to circumvent traditional publication practices so as to increase their standing in the field. The damage that can be inflicted on the researcher, their colleagues, and the scientific enterprise by such incidents has led some scientific societies and journals to develop guidelines outlining responsible conduct with regard to publishing research articles. This article outlines some of the major ethical concerns with regard to publication practices, describes some of the points at which a conflict in values or obligations may arise, and discusses some of the mechanisms that have been developed to minimize such conflicts and their impact on the discipline. Although we focus specifically on peer-reviewed research articles, many of the issues we discuss—for example, plagiarism, honorary author-

Encyclopedia of Applied Ethics, Volume 4
Copyright © 1998 by Academic Press. All rights of reproduction in any form reserved.

ship, and failure of scholarship—are equally relevant to other forms of publications, including abstracts, review articles, and monographs.

I. THE ROLE OF PUBLICATIONS IN SCIENCE

Peer-reviewed research articles serve several essential roles in the sciences: they enable individuals to benefit from the work of others, help to safeguard the integrity of the research process, and provide a mechanism for assessing a scientist's productivity. The first scientific journals were published in 1665; although much research had been done prior to that time, the results were not widely disseminated, in part because individual scientists had few reliable ways to establish priority or to ensure credit for their work. However, with the emergence of the first scientific journals and their dissemination to research laboratories and libraries, there evolved a generally available account of experiments performed, including the investigator's methods, results, and interpretations. It now became possible to make work public while at the same time guarding one's intellectual property rights.

The ability to disseminate information widely and have a permanent record of the knowledge gained was a tremendous advance. Investigators could now build on the foundation of work begun by previous researchers, as is reflected in statements such as that by Isaac Newton (1642–1727): "If I have seen farther [than Descartes] it is by standing on the shoulders of giants." Indeed, since the emergence of the first journals, scientific knowledge has accumulated at an increasingly rapid pace.

A standard structure for journal articles eventually emerged. Commonly referred to by its acronym "IMRAD," this format includes four principal sections: **In**troduction, **M**ethods and Materials, **R**esults, **A**nd **D**iscussion. An essential component of the IMRAD system is its separate methods section, which makes it easier for colleagues to evaluate and, if desired, replicate the work presented in the paper. The ability to replicate experiments is essential to the progress of science, as a finding usually is accepted only after it has been observed by other independent researchers. The IMRAD system also ensures that in standard-length research articles there is a formal separation of the data from the author's interpretation of those data. The former is presented in the results section, whereas the latter is included in the discussion section; this division helps to minimize any

ambiguity about what was observed versus what is being speculated. A variant of the IMRAD format is found in *short*, or *brief, communications*, a mechanism for reporting less-comprehensive studies. In this type of article, the results and discussion sections frequently are merged.

In addition to being a mechanism for disseminating information and providing a permanent record of the progress of science, peer-reviewed research articles have additional significance for members of the field. For scientists, authoring publications frequently represents the key to advancing in their career. The number and quality of peer-reviewed publications is used in evaluating the productivity of the scientist and consequently influences whether a given scientist will secure funding for their work, receive tenure, and be able to attract students of high caliber. Publications have thus emerged as part of the "currency" of science, through which scientists are rewarded for their ideas and productivity.

Research articles are so highly regarded that elaborate systems for measuring their impacts on the field have been devised. And in some countries, such data are even used to determine a scientist's salary. A major indexing service, The Institute for Scientific Information, compiles an annual "Science Citation Index," which includes data on the number of articles in which a given paper is cited, and the average citation rate for articles within a given journal. Presumably, these factors represent, respectively, the significance of the work reported, and the overall quality of the journal in which the work was published. However, these data might not be as telling as one might assume. Citation practices, including guidelines for how many articles should be cited in support of an idea, vary from field to field. Moreover, papers that contain incorrect results may be cited for that reason rather than because they have a positive impact. And, review articles are likely to be cited more frequently than are research articles, simply because the former may be used to support a greater number of statements. Thus, impact factors and other similar data should be considered only as rough estimates of impact rather than exact measurements.

II. ETHICAL ISSUES IN THE PUBLICATION OF RESEARCH

Given the importance of publications to the advancement of the field and individual scientists, it is not surprising that the values and obligations of the individuals and organizations involved sometimes conflict, leading to ethical dilemmas. Tensions may arise at multiple points in the publication process, and may involve any of the major players—authors, reviewers, and editors. In the following sections, some of the issues over which a conflict of values or interests is likely to occur are described, along with some of the checks that have been instituted to protect against such infractions.

A. Levels of Misconduct

Fabrication, falsification, and plagiarism are the major ethical issues pertaining to publishing and, as such, have been the center of attention for some time. *Fabrication* refers to the making up of data; *falsification*, the altering of data; and *plagiarism*, the use of someone else's data or ideas without attribution. Fabrication and falsification pollute the literature with fraudulent information, and in doing so, reduce the usefulness of the information that already exists. Plagiarism diminishes the reward system for disseminating the results of one's work.

Misconduct of these types can have far-reaching implications, as is illustrated by the following three examples: First, false information that is published may be used unwittingly by other investigators as the foundation upon which they base their experiments. Not only can this lead to a researcher spending a significant amount of time and resources pursuing lines of investigation that may have little chance of success, but for data that have clinical applications, fraudulent information may lead to patients being exposed to unnecessary risk. Second, scandals involving fabrication, falsification, or plagiarism can become the focus of media attention, undermining the trust that policy makers and the public have in science and scientists. Given that much of scientific research is made possible through grants funded with public moneys, maintaining this trust is essential to the continuing health of the research enterprise; just one major, well-publicized case of misconduct can significantly harm the scientific community. Third, although the effects of plagiarism are often less dramatic than those of fabrication or falsification, it can still inflict serious harm. Plagiarism robs the original authors of credit for their work and in so doing reduces the incentive for individuals in the field to make their work public.

Although the "high crimes" of fabrication, falsification, and plagiarism receive a great deal of attention, they are far from the only ethical concerns with regard to publishing. Moreover, it is the "misdemeanors" that most scientists will struggle with on a day-to-day basis.

These issues often are less obvious, and their designation as unethical sometimes derives from violating the conventions adopted by a field rather than values central to science. For example, it is a widely held proscription that research articles should be submitted to only one journal at a time. However, a novice to the field, unfamiliar with the conventions of science, might indeed think the reverse, that is, to facilitate publication, submit the manuscript to several different publishers and see where it is accepted first. Thus, in addition to respecting the values upon which the field operates, scientists must be aware of the conventions within their discipline and ensure that they follow them in their daily practice.

B. Roles and Responsibilities

Conflicts in values, obligations, and desires may occur at many junctures in the publication process. Authors, reviewers, and editors are each bound by certain ethical precepts. Their roles, responsibilities, and some of the tensions they may experience are discussed in the following sections.

1. Authors

a. Defining Authorship

Given the role of publications in the career of a scientist, the determination of authorship is a key issue. The word "author" comes from the Latin *auctor*, meaning "to create, or produce." The U.S. National Academy of Sciences, along with most other scientific organizations, considers three criterion when assessing whether an individual meets the requirements for authorship: authors should (1) have made a significant intellectual contribution to the work; (2) be able to defend the work presented in the paper, or in the case of a paper involving several highly specialized areas of research, that portion of the work for which the individual had primary responsibility; and (3) have approved the final version of the manuscript, including providing explicitly their assent to be designated as an author.

Depending on the field and even the individual laboratory, the order in which the authors are listed is sometimes significant. For example, in many biomedical fields, the first author is the individual who had primary responsibility for the research and writing, and the most senior author is listed last. In between these two positions, individuals are listed in order of relative contribution to the work. A recent variant of this practice is the designation via a footnote of two individuals as "first author," each having made equal major contributions to the work presented.

Researchers would be well-advised to make an initial determination of both authorship and the order of the authors before a new project is undertaken. Should the work lead in a different direction than originally anticipated, these decisions can be renegotiated, if necessary. However, it is often much easier to resolve disputes over relative contributions to the project before the work is begun.

b. Honorary Authorship

Authorship is generally not related to the position held by an individual. For example, the director of a lab would not be an author on a manuscript solely because of their role in acquiring the funding, laboratory space, or equipment necessary to conduct the research. Authorship based on such qualifications is generally regarded as "honorary," and is considered by many to be unethical. And, just as a position does not automatically qualify someone for authorship, neither does it exclude them from authorship; for example, a technician whose contribution met the criteria for authorship should be justly included as such.

Honorary authorship is a commonly encountered ethical issue, and it usually involves designating senior investigators as authors even though they have not met the standard criteria. Typically, honorary authorship is granted to increase the number of publications by the recipient of honorary authorship, to confer status to a junior researcher by linking their name with that of a better-known scientist, or to increase the probability that the manuscript will be accepted by the editor and subsequently be taken seriously by readers. However, each of these scenarios may bestow unearned benefits on the individuals involved, consequently providing them with an unfair advantage over their competition. Given the reliance of science on the values of trust and fairness, the community discourages this practice.

There are yet additional reasons to discourage honorary authorship. Authors have a responsibility for the work presented; indeed, some journals explicitly require that at least one author has responsibility for any material presented in the document. Unearned authorship places the honorary author at risk for associating themselves with fraudulent work. Should this occur, the situation can have significant repercussions not only for their future, but for the careers of everyone who has been associated with them through collaboration.

In addition to explicit statements against honorary authorship, some journals now require authors to sign a letter of consent to be listed as such. Presumably this is to guard against individuals being designated as an author on a paper without their agreement. Although an unethical investigator may have no reservations about signing an incorrect statement, this procedure does serve as a reminder of the severity of the ethical issues involved. Moreover, explicit policies on honorary authorship, as listed in a journal's instructions to authors or in a scientific society's code of ethics, may provide useful support for junior investigators who are being pressured by a more-senior individual to grant them honorary authorship.

A final argument against honorary authorship is that the allocation of credit associated with a publication is typically related to the number of authors on the paper. The more authors, the less credit that may be attributed to each of them, based on the assumption that increasing numbers of authors decreases the contribution made by any one individual. Thus, the addition of an individual to a list of authors diminishes the credit received by others who have legitimately earned it.

c. Acknowledgments

Many individuals make significant contributions to the work presented in papers yet do not meet the criteria for authorship. The acknowledgments section of a paper provides a mechanism for recognizing their efforts. However, anyone who is acknowledged should provide their consent, as readers may interpret the acknowledgment of an individual as an endorsement of the work or ideas in the paper. Yet, not everyone who offers advice may wish to be linked to the paper in this way. For example, a colleague who provides critical feedback on a draft of the manuscript may not agree with the conclusions of the authors, and consequently may prefer not to be formally associated with the manuscript.

d. Issues of Scholarship

So as not to plagiarize, authors are required to acknowledge the sources of their information, ideas, and any text they quote, unless the material is considered to be common knowledge within their discipline. Authors also have a responsibility to do so in a scholarly way: When possible, authors should reference the *originator* of the data or ideas by citing the first publication of such information rather than subsequent articles or secondary sources. Moreover, the authors should actually have consulted that primary source rather than depend on a secondary source for the reference. Only in these ways can one be assured that proper credit is provided.

Authors also need to be knowledgeable about the statistical tests they employ, understanding the assumptions underlying the procedures and confirming that the data sets meet those criteria. And authors have an obligation to make their tables and graphs clear and unambiguous. This includes taking care to ensure that the axes on graphs are properly labeled, and that any special graphical procedures, such as data transformations or axes that do not intersect at the origin, are properly noted. Science cannot operate on a "let the buyer beware" basis. Authors must accept responsibility for expressing themselves clearly so that readers are not misled.

e. The Obligation to Publish

Given the use of public moneys to fund the training of scientists and much of the research that they subsequently conduct, investigators have an *obligation* to publish their results so that other researchers, and consequently society as a whole, can benefit from it. Although certain types of research may preclude publication (as in the case of classified government research) or make it necessary to delay publication (for example, commercial works being patented), in general, scientists should publish their work in an expedient manner.

In addition to a responsibility to share their results with colleagues, there is an increasing sense among scientists that there is an obligation to convey the results and significance of their work to the lay public, as well. However, articles written for the lay public usually are not peer reviewed, and thus researchers have a special responsibility to ensure that their work meets the standards of their profession.

f. General Obligations

Scientists have a responsibility to conduct their research in accordance with any applicable regulations, particularly when the work involves human or animal subjects. In addition, many journals now require that authors explicitly state in a cover letter and/or the manuscript itself that all relevant guidelines were followed. And, journals may also request that authors disclose any potential conflicts of interest that could result from the publication of the manuscript.

When space limitations preclude the publication of all of the data necessary for understanding or replicating a study, for example in the case of gene sequences, journals may require that such data be deposited in one of the publicly accessible data banks and that an accession number be provided in the article. In addition, journals may also require that critical reagents that are not commercially sold be made available to knowledgeable colleagues, so that the work reported may be replicated or used as a foundation for further investigation.

g. Fragmented Publication

Just as it is possible to publish too few reports, it also is possible to publish too many. Encouraged by the benefits conferred by publications, practices such as dividing one's work into the "least publishable unit" have arisen through which an individual may artificially inflate their list of publications. Premature publication of research that does not yet make a significant contribution to the literature adds little more than noise to the system, and such practices may distract from truly significant findings. Moreover, fragmented publications may inadvertently conceal the significance of the phenomenon reported. Thus, many publishers and scientific societies generally discourage the practice.

h. Duplicate Publication

Most journals require that a manuscript being submitted for consideration as a peer-reviewed research article be an original work, neither previously published nor under simultaneous consideration as a peer-reviewed publication elsewhere. This holds for the manuscript as a whole, as well as every component of it down to the individual data points. This is an essential convention: Journal space and the reviewers' and publishers' time are precious resources and should be respected as such. Furthermore, the publication record serves as an indicator of the number of times a given phenomenon has been observed, and publishing the same data more than once in a peer-reviewed research article may mislead readers into thinking that a finding has been replicated more times than it has. For example, duplicate publication of a study in which the side effects of a drug are discussed may lead readers to think that the incidence of cases in which side effects of the drug have been experienced is much higher than it actually is.

There is an exception to this rule: Sometimes it is useful to include in a peer-reviewed research article a small amount of previously published data for the sake of comparison with a new data set. For example, one might wish to compare a previously published control value with a new, experimental value. In such cases, which occur infrequently, it is the obligation of the author to ensure that (1) the reader is aware that data are being republished; (2) the original source is clearly cited; and (3) permission to reprint the table, figure, or text has been provided in writing by the copyright holder. Moreover, although it is unethical to publish the same data twice in a peer-reviewed research article (with the infrequent exception cited above), it is perfectly acceptable to republish those data in a book, set of meeting proceedings, or review article, provided that copyright permissions have been obtained and the original publication is clearly cited. In this case, the data are not being presented as part of a research article, and therefore readers are not likely to mistake it for an independent replication of the work cited.

i. Electronic Publishing

The recent development of electronic publishing has brought additional considerations to bear, many of which are still being debated. Currently, one of the primary concerns relates to the issue of duplicate publication, specifically, defining what constitutes prior publication. For example, if a work is posted to a publicly accessible, non-peer-reviewed journal on the Internet, does that constitute prior publication and therefore preclude publishing the work in a print journal? If so, does the same hold true if only a portion of the article, perhaps one of the figures, has been posted on the Internet? Or, are these types of publications like preliminary presentations of data at scientific conferences, which publishers generally do not regard as prior publications? These questions are being actively discussed by many of the parties involved in the process. Our own perspective is that unless information has been reviewed and accepted by a peer-reviewed journal, it may be included in a manuscript being submitted for such review whether or not it has been presented at a scientific meeting, published in a non-peer-reviewed book chapter, *or placed in a non-peer-reviewed forum on the Internet.* However, this view is not universally held among journals; indeed it may be in the minority. Thus, although we think it an unfortunate incursion on the free exchange of scientific information, authors should proceed cautiously, as reporting a result on the Internet may preclude future publication in many scientific journals.

2. Reviewers

Peer review is regarded to be an essential part of ensuring the quality of the published literature. The concept of peer review emerged at about the same time as the first journals, often with the editor also serving as the reviewer. Indeed, the implementation of a formal process in which experts outside of the editorial staff of the journal served as reviewers was not routinely practiced until roughly 1950. At that time science was undergoing a rapid expansion, prompted (at least in the United States) by the federal government funneling large amounts of money into the research enterprise. Journals, lagging behind this expansion, now had to be much more selective in choosing works for publication and toward this end peer review was instituted widely.

Some individuals have criticized the peer-review system for suppressing novel ideas and innovations that contrast with current dogma. They may cite, for example, the initial rejection of the first manuscripts to describe the Kreb's cycle or human blood types, which now are generally regarded as landmark publications. However, despite the limitations of peer review, most critics admit few feasible alternatives for ensuring the publication of quality research.

a. The Review Process

All scientists ultimately benefit from the peer-review system. Not only is an individual author's work strengthened by the incorporation of feedback provided by a thoughtful reviewer, but science as a whole benefits from the resulting overall improvement in the quality of the journals. Thus, it is generally assumed that all individuals within a given field have a responsibility to do their share of reviewing. Indeed, some societies, such as the American Chemical Society, state this explicitly in their code of ethics. However, even without such directives many scientists are willing to serve as reviewers and do so in a collegial manner.

Journal editors are charged with the responsibility of identifying individuals with expertise of relevance to the research subject to provide an objective evaluation of manuscripts under consideration. Reviewers are asked to evaluate manuscripts based on criteria that center around the relevancy of the work to the needs of the journal's readership. Specific issues include the following: (1) Is the work that is reported significant and within the purview of the journal? (2) Is the work technically and scientifically sound? and (3) Is the article well written?

Reviewing practices vary. Within the biomedical sciences, manuscripts are generally not reviewed "blind"; that is, the reviewer knows the identity of the author. In contrast, in certain areas of social sciences and education, blind reviewing is common. The universal use of blind reviewing might seem more desirable, for it decreases the partiality of the reviewer. However, it is not often practical or even possible. Science has become so compartmentalized that the number of individuals specializing in a given line of research using a particular set of techniques is limited, thus often making it relatively easy to surmise the identity of the author. Moreover, because most scientists tend to focus on a given line of research, present work usually builds on previous work and therefore the references cited by the author would also provide clues as to the author's identity. Thus, blind reviewing is often not attainable. On the other hand, the relationship is not reciprocal; in most instances authors do not know who has reviewed their manuscript.

Individuals are selected as reviewers primarily because of their expert knowledge of the area of work reported on in the manuscript. However, therein lies the source of much tension: Often the individual who is most qualified to judge an author's research is working in the same area of investigation as the author—and frequently they are competitors. This situation engenders two types of ethical dilemmas: biased review and unauthorized use of privileged information.

b. General Obligations

Reviewers have a responsibility to submit their evaluation promptly. Whether intentional or not, delayed reviews can hinder the publication of the work at hand. Such actions are particularly suspect when the manuscript is that of a competitor. Reviewers also have an obligation to respect well-reasoned differences in opinion as these are essential to the advancement of the field. Moreover, when criticism is merited, reviewers have a responsibility to deliver their comments in a polite and professional manner; personal attacks are never justifiable. Finally, reviewers should provide the rationale behind their evaluation, so that the author will have an opportunity to address or correct the issues involved.

c. Biased Review

Reviewers have an obligation to actively guard against partiality in their evaluation. Biases in review range from barely perceptible to obvious. Often, biases result from preconceived ideas regarding the abilities of the authors, or a conflict of interest regarding the information contained in a manuscript. For example, reviewers commonly are more skeptical of work from individuals who are employed at less-prestigious institutions, and they may not be sufficiently skeptical of works from the labs of famous scientists. Likewise, reviewers may be biased by the gender or ethnicity of the author. They may also be prejudiced by work that contradicts or supports their hypothesis, or because they are in competition with the author or have a financial interest that could be affected by publication of the manuscript. When sent a manuscript for review, individuals with a potential conflict of interest are well-advised to return the document without reading it; at the very least, they should notify the editor and let that person decide whether under the circumstances they are an appropriate reviewer. Indeed, many journals now explicitly request that reviewers disclose potential conflicts of interest prior to accepting a manuscript for review.

d. Use of Privileged Information

By nature of their position, reviewers have access to privileged ideas, methods, and data unavailable to the rest of their colleagues. Use of this information is a violation of the trust in the frequently unspoken, but generally implied, conditions of review, and it can seriously harm the research enterprise. In a recent U.S. court case it was alleged that reviewers of a manuscript used the information contained therein to obtain patent rights to the substance under investigation. Although the case was settled out of court, it is likely that repercussions may lead to changes in the peer-review system—at the very least, more-explicit instructions regarding the ethics of the reviewer–author relationship.

Tensions frequently arise during the evaluation process if a reviewer's work is closely related to that described in the manuscript under consideration. Although the proscription not to use information contained in a manuscript under review seems to be a fairly straightforward idea, in practice it can be difficult to comply. For example, the origins of a new idea are often hard to trace—especially for someone who is immersed in the research, spending most of their time thinking about and reading about the problem discussed in the manuscript.

Even when it is known that the source of an idea was a manuscript under review, it still may be difficult not to make use of the information. For example, if a manuscript provides solid evidence that the line of research that the reviewer is pursuing is fruitless, must the reviewer continue the research? Clearly it would not be realistic to expect such behavior and, indeed, some scientific societies now explicitly allow an individual to *terminate* their research on the basis of privileged information. However, the converse is not true—it is generally understood that a reviewer is prohibited from *initiating* a project as a result of information gained in confidence.

It also is generally agreed that a reviewer should never share information gained from a manuscript under review unless this is done specifically to aid in the evaluation. Under such circumstances, the reviewer must act in accordance with guidelines of the journal; for example, it may be necessary to obtain the editor's permission and/or to disclose the name of the individual whose advice was obtained. Moreover, the initial reviewer is responsible for ensuring that the secondary reviewer understands and accepts the requirement of confidentiality. Finally, reviewers are usually expected to destroy any manuscripts once the review process is complete.

3. Editors

a. General Obligations

Journal editors have overall responsibility for the content of their journal. They set the standards for publication, choose individuals as reviewers, and make the final decision as to whether a manuscript will be accepted for publication. Editors are typically senior scientists who have agreed to perform these duties as part of their service to the scientific community. Editors have many of the same basic ethical obligations as the reviewers: to protect confidentiality, to provide a fair and timely evaluation, to disclose potential conflicts of interests, and to refrain from using privileged information. Even though editors usually must answer to an editorial board, external advisory committee, or the journal's owner, they are generally thought to wield much power within their field. Given that it is the editor who is supposed to guard the integrity of the publication process and be the arbiter of disputes, the responsibility to act ethically takes on an additional level of importance.

b. Selection of Reviewers

Because reviewers serve such an important role in the publication process, it is necessary that they be chosen with care. Editors have a responsibility to select as reviewers individuals who (1) have adequate knowledge of the area described in the manuscript, and (2) are prompt, fair, and justified in their evaluations. Occasionally, authors will request that their manuscript not be reviewed by certain individuals. This may be prompted by concerns over major philosophical differences, personal disputes, or competitiveness. In such cases, the editor must weigh their ability to honor the request with the need for adequate review of the work.

c. Mediating Disputes and Overseeing Investigations

Editors usually are responsible for mediating disputes between the authors and reviewers. It is essential for editors to be aware that reviewers are not automatically correct when they disagree with an author's methods, interpretations, or theories. Editors also are responsible for addressing allegations of misconduct involving manuscripts that have been published or are under consideration. Should an ethics investigation be necessary, it usually is the editor's role to oversee it, and particular care must be taken to avoid even the appearance of partiality.

d. Ensuring High Standards versus Censorship

Editors are traditionally seen as the gatekeepers. In general, this is viewed positively, for editors are charged with setting high standards for publication, and thereby protecting the scientific literature and encouraging the adoption of equally high standards for the work performed. However, such a role is not without negative implications. Given their relatively unlimited authority over decisions regarding which works are accepted for publication in their journal, they also have the capacity for excluding work on the basis of extrascientific considerations. For example, manuscripts might be accepted or rejected because the conclusions are inconsistent with current dogma in the scientific community or with existing norms in the lay community. We are not aware of any journals that currently have a written policy prohibiting the publication of politically sensitive work; nevertheless, we do not doubt that such decisions are occasionally part of the decision-making process.

e. Preferential Treatment

A final ethical issue involving editors is the practice of "fast-tracking" manuscripts. This involves the editor of a journal inviting a researcher—often quite a prominent individual—to write and submit a manuscript for publication that then will be given an expedited review and be rapidly accepted for publication. Critics of this practice raise concerns over the quality of the peer review (which may occur over a period of hours rather than days or weeks) and the favoritism shown to the individual, especially when no indication is provided to the reader that the manuscript received any special consideration.

III. RESPONDING TO ALLEGATIONS OF FRAUD

Regardless of the individuals involved, or whether it is a high crime or misdemeanor, misconduct in publishing is harmful to the research enterprise. Some individuals and organizations have concluded, therefore, that anyone who believes that they have evidence of misconduct *must* report it to the individual who is responsible for oversight. We agree with this position in theory; however, although the scientific community strives to protect them, individuals making allegations of misconduct often suffer at least as much as does the accused. Therefore, we believe that individuals must be apprised of the possible repercussions, and then decide for themselves whether or not to make a report.

Allegations of misconduct must be investigated in an objective and timely manner. And, just as the rights of the accuser must be protected, so must the rights of the accused. Finally, if misconduct has been determined, sanctions must be invoked against the perpetrator. Such penalties might range from a reprimand for honorary authorship to termination of funding and/or employment for fabrication of data. Likewise, should it be concluded that the accused is innocent, the community must take every measure possible to repair harm that may have come to that individual as a result of the accusation or investigation.

IV. MINIMIZING UNETHICAL BEHAVIOR

Misconduct—even investigations of misconduct—is costly for all parties involved. It is expensive, time consuming, and it diverts energies from the advancement of science. Allegations of fraud often impact negatively on all of the individuals involved, regardless of whether the individual is the accused, accuser, editor, publisher, or any individual or institution even remotely associated with the case. Moreover, the media attention given to such incidents reduces the public trust in both scientists and science. And even when conclusive evidence of misconduct exists, it is difficult to limit the use of the information that already exists in the literature. It is often hard to get authors and journal editors to publish corrections or retractions. Even when corrections or retractions are made, they are relatively ineffective because the original article itself as well as any publications that cite it will always remain in the literature. For all these reasons, we must focus on *prevention* rather than detection and correction.

Many institutions require training in the ethics of science. The U.S. government currently requires that anyone supported on a federal training grant must receive training in the responsible conduct of research, and it is likely that this requirement will soon be extended to cover *anyone* involved in federally sponsored research. Typically included in the topics to be covered with regard to publication are the high crimes—fabrication, falsification, and plagiarism. However, we encourage instruction in the misdemeanors, as well. Beyond providing formal training in ethical publication practices, much can be accomplished by raising the overall level of concern for ethics

in science. It seems likely that providing instruction in—and proper examples of—ethical behavior in any aspect of science will help to minimize the occurrence and severity of unethical behavior in other areas of the discipline.

V. SUMMARY

The development of a peer-reviewed journal system has greatly facilitated advances in science. This publication process relies on many of the same values that underlie the discipline itself—trust, honesty, and collegiality. Unethical publication practices can have widespread deleterious effects, reducing the incentive scientists receive for sharing the results of their work, lessening the value of the published literature, and disrupting the public trust in the scientific enterprise. For these reasons and more, the integrity of the publication process is a central ethical concern.

Multiple points in the publication process are vulnerable to misconduct and by and large most of the actors are on their honor to behave responsibly. Many scientific societies have developed codes of ethics that specifically address the many issues related to scientific publication. However, given the potential for abuse, providing instruction in responsible publication practices is widely encouraged. Although not all offenses are equal in their seriousness, it is worthwhile to address both the major and the less-serious offenses, as raising the overall attention to responsible conduct may contribute to a reduction in the occurrence of unethical behaviors. Not only the reputations of the scientists involved are at risk, but the health of the scientific enterprise, and the benefits that science brings to society, rests in the balance.

Acknowledgments

We thank Drs. Floyd E. Bloom and Marcel C. LaFollette for discussions regarding this article.

Also See the Following Articles

PUBLISH-OR-PERISH SYNDROME • RESEARCH ETHICS • RESEARCH METHODS AND POLICIES • SCIENCE AND ENGINEERING ETHICS, OVERVIEW

Bibliography

American Chemical Society. (1995). Ethical guidelines to the publication of chemical research. *Chemistry Review*, **95**, 11A–13A.

Day, R. A. (1994). *How to write and publish a scientific paper.* (4th ed.). Phoenix, AZ: Oryx Press.

Frank-Fox, M. (1994). Scientific misconduct and editorial and peer review processes. *Journal of Higher Education,* **63**:3, 298–309.

LaFollette, M. C. (1992). *Stealing into print: Fraud, plagiarism, and misconduct in scientific publishing.* Berkeley, CA: University of California Press.

Macrina, F. L. (1995). *Scientific integrity: An introductory text with cases.* Washington, DC: ASM Press.

National Academy of Sciences (1995). *On being a scientist* (2nd ed.). Washington, DC: National Academy Press.

National Academy of Sciences. (1993). *Responsible science: Ensuring the integrity of the research process.* (Volume 2). Washington, DC: National Academy Press.

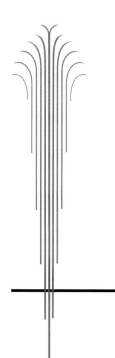

SELF-DECEPTION

Paula Boddington
Australian National University

GLOSSARY

bad faith (*mauvaise foi*) In Sartre's philosophy, a kind of self-deception in which the agent denies to him- or herself that he or she is free, in various ways.

integrity A state of wholeness or completeness of the self, which may be taken to imply honesty or purity.

other-deception The deception of another person; manipulating another's beliefs with the intention of hiding the truth.

repression In psychoanalytic terms, the keeping of a thought in the unconscious realm of the mind.

self-deception Literally, the deception of oneself; the motivated, irrational manipulation of one's own beliefs.

sub-belief state A mental state similar to belief but less strong or certain, such as conjecture or working hypothesis.

SELF-DECEPTION has aroused intense interest not only within philosophy and ethics, but also within fields such as psychology, literature, and religion. There is much dispute about how exactly self-deception should be understood, although it can be broadly characterized as some form of deliberate manipulation of one's own beliefs. There is even disagreement over whether there is actually any such phenomenon as self-deception, although most writers agree that it does exist, that it is widespread, or even that it is endemic to the human condition. Indeed, many thinkers see it as something of central concern to any understanding of human functioning.

Much of the philosophical literature on self-deception has in the past concerned itself with the problem of how self-deception can be possible, seeing it as an issue in epistemology (the theory of knowledge) and the philosophy of mind, with only scant reference to the moral or value issues which have long concerned writers in the fields of religion and literature. However, especially since the 1980s, more philosophers have addressed the question of self-deception and its relation to morality and have asked what, if anything, is wrong with self-deception. Some have tried to argue that in at least some circumstances, self-deception may be morally innocuous or even of some benefit. However, even those who argue such a line tend to see it as a failing in at least some cases, or as a partial failing, and there is a much stronger tradition that sees self-deception as a grave moral problem of one sort or another. It may be seen to be intrinsically wrong, for example, as a failure of integrity. Additionally or alternatively, it may be seen as a failing that has particular problems for how the self-deceiver makes moral judgments.

I. THE DEFINITION OF SELF-DECEPTION

A. The Paradoxes of Self-Deception

Much of the philosophical literature which has attempted to describe self-deception and show whether, and how, it is possible has been driven by responses to alleged paradoxes which arise when an attempt is made to model self-deception on other-deception. It will be necessary to understand these paradoxes fully to understand the nature of the strong connection of self-deception with ethics.

1. The Paradox of Being Self-Deceived

This has been called the "static paradox"—how could someone be in a state of self-deception? (A. Mele, 1987. "Recent Work in Self–Deception," *American Philosophical Quarterly,* **24,** 1–17). The self-deceiver (A) has a belief that he or she finds uncomfortable, such as "I have been cheating in my studies" (p). He or she, when self-deceived, also has an opposing belief such as "I have not really been cheating in my studies" (not-p). To attribute self-deception, then, we have to attribute to A at the same time that

A believes p & A believes not-p,

which has been thought to be problematic or even impossible. However, we may attribute such beliefs to people who are simply confused; but there is a deeper puzzle with self-deception.

2. The Paradox of Becoming Self-Deceived

This is a problem about how someone can enter the state of self-deception and has been called the "dynamic paradox (Mele, *ibid.*)." The self-deceiver A who comes to believe not-p enters a state of self-deception *because* of the uncomfortable belief p. In the words of J-P. Sartre, "I must know the truth very exactly *in order* to conceal it more carefully" (1956. *Being and nothingness* (trans. H. E. Barnes, p. 49). New York: Philosophical Library, emphases in original). The problem is then how the deception can succeed, because in ordinary cases of two-person deception, knowing that one is being deceived about p will mean that the deception will fail.

It is this paradox that distinguishes self-deception, a motivated irrationality, from simple accidental errors in belief due to faulty reasoning.

3. The Paradoxes of Self-Deception and Its Normative Assessment

It is important to note that, however the alleged paradoxes of self-deception are described, their problems arise because self-deception seems to involve irrationality that is motivated. It is precisely this charge of motivated irrationality that leads, in various ways according to different writers, to assessments of self-deception as wrong in some way, often as some kind of moral failing. The agent has helped him- or herself into this state of imperfection; some degree of responsibility and culpability then may be attributed.

B. Skeptical and Nonskeptical Accounts of Self-Deception

1. Skeptical Accounts of Self-Deception

Some argue that the paradoxes of self-deception are insurmountable and that, therefore, there is really no such thing. Rather, instances that may commonly seem to be self-deception are generally acknowledged to exist but are explained away as something else. For example, M. R. Haight argues that alleged instances of self-deception are really cases of lying, not to oneself, but to other people. The alleged self-deceiver really knows the truth, but wants others to think that he or she does not know it.

2. Nonskeptical Accounts of Self-Deception

Many have no such skepticism but argue that self-deception does actually occur in one form or another. Such an account may be argued for on the grounds that the paradoxes of self-deception can be overcome, or are misdescribed as overly paradoxical. Moreover, many argue that self-deception is so widespread, and such an important phenomenon for understanding the human condition, that some nonskeptical account of it must be possible. Most writers on the subject take such a view; some even take self-deception as a central feature of human beings.

There is a great variety of nonskeptical accounts. In general, these understand self-deception as having two main elements, one of belief states or sub-belief states (which may be states "lesser" than full belief, such as conjecture, acting as if p were true, and so on), and one of motivation or intention, to some degree. Self-deception, then, is some kind of motivated irrationality, or deliberate error in belief. It typically involves distortions of the evidence, forming beliefs in the face of contrary evidence, or beliefs which go beyond that which the evidence warrants. Certain strategies are generally adopted to achieve this, such as denial, rationalization, and avoidance.

Some writers attempt to model self-deception as closely as possible on the deception of other people, and these may be called accounts of "literal self-deception." Other accounts take a rather different tack, as for instance the influential account by Herbert Fingarette in *Self-Deception* which attempts to explain self-deception as a failure to adequately spell out to oneself one's engagements in the world. One important class of cases explains self-deception by positing some kind of split in the self; the deceived part of the self and the deceiving part are separated by the split or splits, thus enabling the deception to occur (D. Pears, 1984. *Motivated Irrationality*. Oxford University Press, Oxford). The splits in the self may be seen as a way of modeling self-deception on other deception.

C. Examples of Self-Deception in Various Fields

1. Literature

Self-deception is an extremely common theme in works of literature. Literature provides a very rich source for examples of self-deception, and for consideration of its morality, because in the course of an entire novel or play there is far more scope for displaying the necessary complexity and subtlety of the schemings, motivations, and manipulations of the self-deceiver than is possible in more purely philosophical texts. Literature often concerns itself with exploring how the self-deceiver may be judged as well as why someone might be led to self-deception and what outcomes it might have. Examples of works that have provided rich source material for philosophers and ethicists include Leo Tolstoy's *The Death of Ivan Illych*; Albert Camus's *The Fall*; Henrik Ibsen's *The Wild Duck*; Eugene O'Neill's *The Iceman Cometh*; and those of Stendhal and André Gide. Self-deception has also been treated in many films, such as *Mephisto* (1981).

2. Psychology

Psychology has concerned itself with self-deception in a large number of ways. Here just two, contrasting, examples are discussed (extremely) briefly along with their implications for the moral assessment of self-deception.

a. Freud and His Heirs

Sigmund Freud's work on psychoanalysis relied heavily on a notion of self-deception as pivotal to a picture of the human mind. For Freud, the unconscious is dynamic or active. Unwanted thoughts and wishes may be repressed and hence confined to the unconscious; that this repression is intentional makes this a form of self-deception. Some significant points to note here are, firstly, that the goal of psychoanalysis is to make the unconscious conscious, and hence to be rid of self-deception. This may not be presented as a *moral* goal as such, but it is an aim that is shared by many who have followed Freud and can be seen as a general goal of the personal growth or human potential movement. Secondly, this goal may be assisted by another, the analyst, without whom the agent may be incapable of unlocking his or her own unconscious mind and hence of escaping from self-deception.

b. Cognitive and Social Psychology

There is much work in psychology that can be construed as skeptical about the charge of self-deception as a "motivated irrationality." Psychology has paid much attention to the question of the nature and origin of beliefs, such as stereotypes and prejudices. Such beliefs may be considered to be irrational, and often motivated, since they are formed in a way that defends or enhances the ego—so-called "hot" cognitive errors.

However, it has been argued that an explanation of the empirical evidence does not demand motivational interpretations, and that nonmotivational factors account for most of the phenomena. Many such faulty beliefs are unmotivated, or simple "cold" cognitive errors (R. Nisbett and L. Ross (1980) *Human Interference: Strategies and Shortcomings of Social Judgment*. Prentice-Hall, Englewood, NJ.). Other work questions the very charge of irrationality itself in some cases. For example, much work has assumed that stereotyping involves distorted belief formation, but this has been subjected to the criticism that stereotypes are actually often useful for gaining accurate pictures of social reality (P. Oakes, S. A. Haslam, J. C. Turner (1994). Stereotyping and Social Reality. Blackwell, Oxford). If correct, such findings could in at least some cases obviate any account of self-deception and its corresponding moral appraisal.

3. Religion

Religious traditions have often focused on self-deception as a human failing that needs to be addressed in religious terms. Many religions place a premium on truth, or at least truth with regard to certain spiritual or moral matters, and may see self-deception as something that leads one into sin, or a faulty relationship with God. (See section II.C.) For example, in Christianity, something of the impact of self-deception is shown in the following well-used verses: "If we say we have no sin, we deceive ourselves and the truth is not in us. If we confess our sins, he is faithful and just, and will forgive our sins and cleanse us from all unrighteousness" (1 John 1:8–9). Within Buddhism, self-deception may be considered a universal human condition blocking self-understanding and ultimately spiritual progress to enlightenment (Trungpa, C. R. (1973). *Cutting Through Spiritual Materialism.* J. Bake and M. Casper (Eds.). Shambala, Boston.). That self-deception is given such widespread attention within religions again points to its importance for understanding human life.

II. FEATURES OF SELF-DECEPTION AND THEIR MORAL SIGNIFICANCE

Self-deception is a highly complex phenomenon, and moreover one which can take many forms, varying, for example, in the degree of disruption to beliefs, the type of motive, and the degree to which it is in the agent's control. This section examines some main features of self-deception and their relation to moral questions.

A. Self-Deception and Related Phenomena

An understanding of self-deception, and of its place in a normative assessment of human beings, may be deepened by seeing how it compares to other related phenomena.

1. *Wishful thinking* may be considered a "lesser" phenomenon than self-deception. The agent manipulates his or her belief states only mildly, perhaps imagining that p were true or daydreaming or fantasizing about p. Wishful thinking may be more fleeting and easier to escape from than self-deception. Self-deception is thus subject to more severe normative criticism.

2. *Delusion* may be considered a "deeper" phenomenon than self-deception. Irrational beliefs may be more widespread and depart from the evidence more wildly than in self-deception. The formation of these beliefs may be thought less in the agent's control, or indeed out of his or her control altogether. Hence, again, self-deception, where the agent is deemed to have more control, is subject to correspondingly more severe judgment.

3. Self-deception is often compared to *faith*, which some would accuse of being a form of self-deception in at least some instances. Faith may be seen similarly to disregard what normally may be counted as evidence, and may too be accused of being motivated by self-interest by those who view religion as some kind of "opium of the masses." Counters to these charges may give a different picture of the relation of faith to evidence, claiming, for instance, that it goes beyond evidence but not against it, or that different evidential standards apply in cases of faith. Faith too may be argued to be driven by respect for something higher than the self, rather than merely by the baseness of the self's sordid self-interest. An extensive exploration of the relationship between faith and paradox is found in the works of Søren Kierkegaard.

4. *Weakness of will* may be seen to be parallel to the motivated irrationality of self-deception in the area of action rather than of belief. In genuine cases of weakness of will, one knows what one ought to do, or what one judges best to do, all things considered, yet deliberately does something else. Attempts to understand weakness of will then often grapple with the same kinds of problems as attempts to understand self-deception.

As self-deception itself admits of varieties and degrees, so there may be no clear hard and fast borders between self-deception and weakness of will or delusion, and, some would say, faith.

B. The Subject Matter of Self-Deception

In any normative assessment of self-deception it is important to consider its subject matter. Self-deception is generally seen to concern itself with matters serious enough for the agent to have a strong motive for engaging in the difficult duplicitous task of self-deception. It is a truism that the belief that the self-deceiver tries to evade must be related to the self in some way. It is this reference to the self, however close, that provides the motive for the self-deception. Some have considered that self-deception especially relates to knowledge about the self, such as one's weaknesses, emotions, true motivations, self-definition, the true nature of one's projects in the world, and one's religious beliefs. All can have serious moral implications. Self-deception may also be seen to occur in other areas, such as the behavior and character of those close to oneself, the true nature of political regimes, and so on.

C. Self-Deception and Responsibility

There is much, although not universal, agreement that the self-deceiver is responsible in some way for his or her self-deception, but there are deep problems about how this is so. Many take it that to enter self-deception is to abrogate a responsibility toward oneself; other accounts focus also or exclusively on the effects on other people.

Insofar as self-deception is intentional, and the agent is him- or herself the deceiver, the agent may be held responsible for the self-deception, and hence for any negative consequences. However, many have argued there are difficulties with ascribing responsibility to the self-deceiver, since the agent is also the "innocent" victim of the deception. There are two standard excuses for inappropriate behavior: that one was ignorant, or that the actions were involuntary. Both may seem to apply to self-deception. It may be relatively easy to judge the responsibility of the deceiving part of the agent, and of the deceived part, but problematic what to say about the agent as a unity.

Some have adopted a "partial" model of responsibility in the face of this problem. However, it can still be difficult to spell out a coherent and apt account of responsibility. To say that the self-deceiver is somewhat responsible may be to draw an analogy with cases like attempting to do something that requires enormous effort or will power, so that any responsibility for failure is hence diminished. But self-deception seems more paradoxical than that. It could be said that as deceiver, the agent is wholly responsible, but as deceived, wholly innocent. The verdict is a mixed one, and this differs from simply being responsible to some extent.

It is important also to distinguish between responsibility and blame. Someone may be responsible for a choice of action, even one with bad outcomes, yet not be blameworthy, as when one chooses the lesser of two evils, or fails in the face of a superhuman task. Hence those who argue, for instance, that self-deception may be a way to maintain human functioning in the face of intolerable burdens, may see the self-deceiver as responsible for his or her condition, yet exonerated from blame. (See Section III.B.1.)

Judgments of responsibility for self-deception may also vary with different cases, in the following ways:

1. *The degree to which the self-deception is intentional*, which may vary from case to case; in general, the more intentional, the more the agent may be held responsible.

2. *The extent to which beliefs or sub-belief states are manipulated.* The more serious the disruption to one's belief states, the greater the fault in rationality and hence the greater the burden of responsibility. However, a limit to this may be found. Great irrationality may be thought to diminish agency, and hence responsibility. So where belief states are radically disrupted, the self-deception may be out of the agent's control and hence responsibility may be diminished.

3. *The motive for self-deception.* This may be more or less self-interested, or more or less honorable, and judgments of responsibility may vary accordingly. In some cases, the truth is so hard to bear, that some may excuse self-deception and lessen charges of responsibility. Motive is inextricably linked to the following:

4. *The subject matter of the deception*, with some subjects being perhaps more trivial than others. Some subjects are so important that any self-deception about them is a serious matter, while in other cases it may be that the subject matter of the self-deception is so painful that the agent may be excused, at least to an extent.

5. *The effects of self-deception.* The worse the effects, the more the self-deceiver has responsibility for. This judgment may apply to negative effects on the self, but may be aimed more especially at the effects on others.

6. *The degree to which self-deception is entrenched.* Self-deception may be a relatively fleeting and surface phenomenon, which the agent may escape from with comparative ease. At the other end of the spectrum, it may be deeply embedded and hard or practically impossible to overcome. To sustain the original self-deception it may frequently involve the agent in further self-deception and in habitual violations of rational belief formation. Paradoxically in such a case the agent may be seen as especially responsible for ending up in such a bad way, and/or less responsible, as it may look as if things have gone too far for the agent to control any more. In some instances there may be some similarity to ascriptions of responsibility in the case of acquired addictions. Here, the agent may be responsible for knowingly risking becoming addicted; having become so, it may be beyond his or her control to end the addiction. From one perspective then, the agent is acquitted of responsibility; from another, he or she still retains the responsibility for having knowingly acquired the addiction. Some self-deception may be viewed likewise.

For many of these aspects of responsibility for self-deception and moral assessment of it, it appears that "mild" cases may attract mild judgments, and "deeper" cases more serious judgment, whereas at the extreme, judgments of responsibility may begin to lessen.

D. Group Self-Deception

While most the philosophical literature focuses on the individual self-deceiver, it is also important to note that self-deception may be a social phenomenon interactively affecting two or more people to varying degrees. This may range from couples and families, to large numbers of self-deceived or deluded cult members. Indeed, in such cases the different parties may typically mutually reinforce their distorted beliefs. In the case of the lone self-deceiver, he or she may well be faced by others who manifestly do not share the deceptively formed belief(s); to maintain his or her state of self-deception the agent will have to counter any suggestions from others that he or she is mistaken or self-deceived. Where others with whom one mixes join in with one's duplicity, not only is there no challenge to one's beliefs, but the simple fact that others share them may in itself be used as evidence that they are true and hence help to support the self-deception.

Because of such factors, the individual may be looked on as having diminished responsibility to some extent. However, this does not by any means imply that such cases are morally innocuous. The group self-deception may be deliberately orchestrated by a leader, as may occur with certain cults. And by the nature of things, where an entire group of people are concerned, their self-deception can lead them, at worst, to the most appalling acts of destruction. An example of this may be the Jonestown massacre, where hundreds of cult followers of Jim Jones committed mass suicide in 1978. Some may also consider some element of mass self-deception lies behind the behavior of some supporters of various political regimes.

E. The Accusation of Self-Deception

Judgments of self-deception should be made with care, because not only is to judge that someone is in a state of self-deception very often to make a negative judgment of them, but it is also often hard to be certain that one is presented with a genuine case of self-deception. Various interpretations of people's actions and beliefs are always possible and never more so than here. To come to an assessment requires often long and careful study, and the typical careful schemings, rationalizations, evasions, and manipulations of the self-deceiver may make a judgment of self-deception hard to stick.

III. SELF-DECEPTION AS WRONG IN ITSELF

There are many kinds of answers to the question of what, if anything, is wrong with self-deception. If seen to be wrong, this may be understood explicitly as a moral failing, or, as a nonmoral wrong, a failing in human development perhaps. It may be seen to be wrong in itself, that is, wrong intrinsically. It may be seen to be wrong for extrinsic reasons; for example, it is commonly held to be wrong insofar as it leads one

into moral error. Some see it as necessarily a wrong; for others, it may or may not be wrong, depending on the facts of the particular case. This section considers claims that self-deception is intrinsically wrong, together with some arguments against such views, while Section IV goes on to consider its effects on making moral judgments. The claim that self-deception is intrinsically wrong may be based on religious reasons, moral reasons, accounts of human nature and ideals of the self, or on ideals of rationality.

A. The Ideals of Truth and Rationality

Self-deception may be considered a failing of the ideal of rationality. Any kind of irrationality may be held to undermine an ideal of rationality; insofar as it is deliberately attained irrationality, self-deception is a slap in the face of rationality. We need to ask both how it can be possible to believe against reason and what, if anything, is wrong with this. Note that it may be possible that quite different accounts may need to be given of what is wrong with irrationality *simpliciter* and of what is wrong with motivated irrationality.

To answer these questions we have firstly to ask to what extent rationality is an ideal. Why should humans strive for rationality at all times and in all contexts? For the creature so often defined as a "rational animal," the lure of truth and reason may seem blindingly obvious. In fact we may seem so dazzled by the light of reason that we find it hard to see and hence spell out exactly what is so good about it. But given the ubiquitous nature of self-deception, weakness of will, and simple stupidity and ignorance, humans could perhaps be dubbed the "irrational animal."

If we sometimes deliberately fail at rationality, does this simply mean it is not such an enduring value for us, or does it rather mean that we should not, in some way, evade rationality? We need also to ask, if it is an ideal, whether on some occasions there might be other ideals that would overrule it. Note that an ideal might be overturned by another in a way that means that the defeated ideal loses its attraction completely, or in a way that means that it retains its force, despite being buried beneath a stronger ideal. Answers to these questions will in turn affect answers to the questions of whether, and why, self-deception is wrong or is justified, and whether it is always wrong, always justified, or sometimes wrong and sometimes justified.

What is rationality? Slightly different accounts of it may be given. But in general, to have inconsistencies in one's beliefs is a form of irrationality, since in a set of inconsistent beliefs not all can possibly be true together.

Beliefs that are false, or beliefs that are held on too little evidence or against evidence, may all be held to be irrational. Rationality may incorporate the ideals of truth, of consistency, and of sound belief formation. And conceived of in different ways, rationality may have quite different requirements for us. There is a great deal of difference in practice between the aim of seeking truth and the aim of avoiding error (see W. James (1910). The Will to Believe and Other Essays in Popular Philosophy. Longmans Green and Co., New York).

Why do we have such ideals? Consistency may be valued because inconsistency guarantees that at least some of one's beliefs are false. Basing beliefs on sound evidence may be valued because it makes the truth of one's beliefs more likely. Further than this, it may be that truth and rationality represent ultimate values that cannot be cashed in other terms. Because it may seem hard to spell out why truth and rationality are valued, pragmatic accounts of rationality may have some appeal. These attempt to explain the value of truth in its use to us. Having a true picture of the world helps us get around it safely, and helps us to achieve our goals. The value of truth then can be cashed out in terms of these goals. One difficulty is then that self-deception may simply be seen as a case where one's goals are best served by distortions of the truth. Hence, any criticism of it on grounds of violations of ideals of truth or rationality may be empty, or else have to rely on arguing that the interests of others, or the long-term interest of the self, are not best served by this irrationality.

However, one thing that must be accounted for is the way that truth and rationality still seem to be ideals for the self-deceiver. This can be seen in the way the self-deceiver pays lip service to these ideals in his or her rationalizations, and in denial of self-deception. If truth did not have some appeal, one could simply adopt convenient irrational belief without much worry. The self-deceiver is in conflict, and therefore must feel the pull of rationality enough to have to devise strategies for overcoming it, and yet not feel the pull so much that he or she is incapable of violating canons of rationality where the motive is strong enough.

B. Self-Deception as a Character Fault: Integrity and Sincerity

The integrity of the self has been an enduring human preoccupation. It has been a concern of ancient religions, and is also a vital concern of the modern personal growth movement. It survives even moral skepticism and moral relativism in that even many of those who would refrain from praising or condemning this or that action as morally good or bad may still negatively judge the person who is inconsistent in actions and beliefs, or lacking in integrity or sincerity.

1. How Self-Deception May Undermine Integrity

Integrity may be understood in different ways but is generally seen as a wholeness or completeness of the self—a consistency within one's beliefs, ideals, and actions. It may be understood additionally as an ideal of honesty with the self, and hence with others: "This above all: to thine own self be true, And it must follow, as the night the day, Thou canst not then be false to any man" (Shakespeare, *Hamlet*). It may be seen as a state of the self, or as a process of moving toward this goal. Self-deception undermines integrity not only because it is an inconsistency within the self, but because this inconsistency is motivated and hence constitutes an assault on the process of moving toward integrity. It may then be seen as *the* way of corrupting integrity. Self-deception violates integrity to the extent that it corrupts our belief-forming process, and also because, especially in entrenched cases, it may undermine our agency. Any self-deceptive manipulation of our beliefs and goals may be seen as an assault on our autonomy. On some accounts, self-deceptive undermining of integrity may mar the agent's honesty toward some external value, such as one's relationship with God or acceptance of objective moral demands. On other accounts, such as that of Sartre, it is one's honesty with oneself which is the only thing at issue.

2. An Example of Lost Integrity—Sartrean Self-Deception: Bad Faith and Sincerity

Jean-Paul Sartre gives a particular account of self-deception understood as bad faith (*mauvaise foi*) where the nature of self-deception, and why it is a failing, must be understood in relation to Sartre's accounts of human freedom (Sartre, 1956, Part 1, chap. 2). For Sartre, humans are radically free in many ways. This includes freedom to make moral choices, which cannot be made for us by any "external" morality, and freedom to acknowledge facts about the world, oneself, and one's actions. Attempts to deny such freedoms are acts of bad faith. For Sartre, freedom is the basis for all other values; thus bad faith is an ultimate failing. But the enormous burden of our freedoms brings anguish, and so the temptation to bad faith is always with us. So, as Sartre tried to show in a famous example, the waiter who pretends to himself that all of his actions are dictated by his role, and that he is not at all times *choosing* to behave as is expected of a waiter, is in bad faith; he is imposing a fixed self-image on a radically free human nature. In another example, a woman who deliberately distracts her attention from the sexual overtones of a situation evades the responsibility of her freedom to choose how to respond to a man's advances.

Note that for Sartre, any claim that one is acting in accordance with the obligations of an imposed morality will always be an instance of bad faith. Not only is it to deny one's own freedom, but it may often lead one to attempt to deny or curtail the freedom of others. However, the picture of Sartrean gloom does not stop here, since he also claims that it is impossible for us ever to be rid of bad faith and be completely sincere. Attempts to strive for sincerity are doomed to failure, since they construe the self as being one way or another, and in this deny our radical freedom; hence the attempt can only lead to further bad faith. Criticisms of Sartre's notion of bad faith frequently take issue with his radical account of freedom, which many consider attributes humans with too much responsibility for things genuinely out of their control.

3. What Is Wrong with Self-Deceptive Attacks on Integrity?

Integrity is often presented as a goal of human agency, often strongly connected with religious, spiritual, personal, or moral ideals. To appreciate the worth of this goal may be the only way of making sense of many of humanity's struggles: the growth toward an integrated self may be portrayed as a major task of a worthwhile human life. To live without integrity may lead to living one's life by false or futile ideals; to avoiding spiritual or personal crises, hence missing out on the opportunity to grow in the resolution of crises; and to general errors of judgment and hence then, in particular, to moral errors. It may be seen to poison one's relationship with oneself, hampering the attractive goal of being able to feel completely at ease with oneself. It may be seen to poison one's relationships with others, leading to manipulation of others and to dishonest communications with them.

It is important to note that, in undermining integrity, self-deception may be seen to diminish the value of one's life quite apart from any further bad effects it may or may not produce: someone who refuses to face certain important truths is the poorer for it, even if his or her life is otherwise exemplary—even if, perhaps, facing up to these truths could lead to unresolved chaos or crisis. Remember too that some see the wrong of self-deception in terms of morality, whereas others see it as a nonmoral disvalue. The latter may be understood as a psychological

dysfunctioning that represents a failure to realize human potential. A mixed view is also possible.

4. How Self-Deception May Be Said to Support Integrity

Insofar as integrity admits of degrees, from the fully integrated down to the dysfunctionally disordered and incoherent, self-deception is often argued actually to support integrity at least to an extent. Self-deception may be thought necessary to make life bearable in the face of overly demanding challenges. Hence it may be a way of salvaging a level of integrity when otherwise the agent might simply collapse. The human condition may be considered such that self-deception is a necessarily common response. Within such an approach, there are two main attitudes to the valuation of self-deception. One is that integrity is simply too much to ask of human beings, and the limited integrity achieved by self-deception may then not only be permissible, but actually a good. Alternatively, it may be seen that, understandable as self-deception is in human terms, it is nonetheless always a violation of an ideal of integrity.

5. Can the Goal of Integrity Ever Be Achieved?

How one views the value of integrity, and hence the (dis)value of self-deception, will depend partially on which side one takes on the question of whether it is a goal that can ever be fully achieved. Firstly, this goal may be seen to be impossible in practice because the task is so huge. Secondly, it may be seen as impossible because consciously to adopt the goal of achieving integrity and overcoming self-deception may be seen as self-defeating. As already seen, Sartre argued that one cannot successfully aim for complete sincerity. One may call to mind here the self-defeating attempts Stendhal records to achieve perfect authenticity, as he makes manifestly self-conscious and stilted notes on his success (Stendhal, 1975. *Memoirs of an egotist* (trans. D. Ellis). London: Chatto & Windus).

Conversely, it may be set out as an ultimate, achievable goal. For example, it is clearly such within Buddhist thought, where enlightenment, requiring the absence of self-deception, is held up as possible (with the complications that Buddhist notions of self do not lend themselves easily to standard Western accounts of integrity, and that there are variations between different Buddhist traditions). However, it is also highly significant that here, in most Buddhist traditions, this ultimate goal is held to take many lifetimes to achieve; it is also significant that, having attained birth as a human, enlightenment is seen as possible, with the hard work of much diligent spiritual practice, within one *human* lifetime.

C. Self-Deception as Sin or the Ultimate Moral Failing

Those who hold such a position consider self-deception, or at least, certain varieties of it, especially bad, and always wrong. It thus may be seen as wrong in itself, and/or as wrong because always leading to further wrong, in wrong actions. A selection of examples follows.

1. Self-Deception and Sin—Augustine

Augustine identified self-deception with sin. God's standard is truth, man's is falsehood, and the Devil is the "father of lies." Every sin is a falsehood. The sinful self is a "house divided against itself" and tries to preserve an illusion of goodness or integrity. This clouding separates the individual from God. Augustine describes graphically how in a state of sin the mind is at odds with itself. "I had known it [my wickedness] all along but I had always pretended that it was something different. I had turned a blind eye and forgotten it" (St. Augustine, 1961. *Confessions* (trans. R. S. Pine-Coffin, p. 169). Harmondsworth: Penguin).

2. Self-Deception as the Greatest Moral Failing—Butler

Joseph Butler, in his "Sermon X 'Upon Self-Deceit'" describes self-deception as "in itself extreme guilt; the blinding of the inward eye" (1874. In *The works of the right reverend father in God Joseph Butler.* (vol. II), pp. 118–173. Oxford: Clarendon Press). His account depends on an understanding of wrongdoing as generally stemming from an overregard or partiality for ourselves. In self-deception, this partiality extends to the understanding and influences judgment. It is this warped understanding and judgment that is the source of our moral judgments. Self-deceit, then, "is therefore so far from extenuating guilt, that it is itself the greatest of all guilt in proportion to the degree it prevails; for it is a corruption of the whole moral character in its principle" (p.127).

3. Self-Knowledge as the First Requirement of Morality—Kant

Immanuel Kant's view is very similar to that of Butler. In his *Metaphysics of Morals* he states the "First Command of All Duties to Oneself" to be the command "*know* (scrutinize, fathom) *yourself*" (1991. *The Metaphysics of Morals* (trans. M. McGregor, p. 236). New

York: Cambridge Univ. Press, emphases in original). What is required is moral self-knowledge, and this is seen as the initial starting point of all human wisdom. By implication self-ignorance and self-deception on these matters will then be a primary failing. Note that Kant portrays the attaining of this self-knowledge as hard work: one "seeks to penetrate the depths (the abyss) of one's heart that are quite difficult to fathom" (p. 236). Self-deception here then could be expected to be unfortunately common.

4. Self-Deception and Evil

M. Scott Peck gives a contemporary account of a particular type of self-deception as evil in his book, *People of the Lie* (1988. London: Random House). He distinguishes between evil and sin. Evil is characterized by the subtle, persistent consistency of sinning, and by the evil person's constant attempts to hide and cover up their own evil nature, often through an outward display of goodness. In fact they are deceiving themselves about their own evil nature (as well as other people). They insist on affirming their sense of their own goodness, quite independently of any evidence. Evil people then display an "*absolute* refusal to tolerate the sense of their own sinfulness" (p. 79, emphasis in original). Their self-deception functions to avoid their own spiritual growth which would involve having to face their own failings. The self-deceptive refusal to acknowledge that one might be in the wrong means that evil is especially hard to overcome.

IV. SELF-DECEPTION AS A CAUSE OF POOR MORAL JUDGMENT

The self-deceiver has distorted beliefs; this irrationality affects judgments the agent makes and can be seen to be far more problematical than simple error or confusion in belief for three main reasons. Firstly, the irrationality is purposeful; the self-deceiver then is likely to show some resistance to having it pointed out, and typically engages in strategies such as denial or avoidance in order to maintain their deceptive state. Secondly, the irrationality is motivated by certain reasons, which means that it concerns matters of some importance to the agent. It can be expected that it is especially likely to affect moral judgments. For instance, it is likely to affect judgments that require understanding of one's own inner states, to affect the need for impartiality, to affect the making of judgments that might imply that the agent needs to examine painful issues or make certain sacrifices, and so on. Thirdly, for those moral theories that assess the state of mind of the agent as part and parcel of assessment of moral judgments, self-deceptively formed judgments may be reprehensible in a way that those based on simple ignorance or stupidity are not.

The following sections examine some aspects of how self-deception may affect moral judgments, by looking at a variety of different approaches in moral theory to how moral judgments are or should be formed. Self-deception is a concern both at the level of normative ethical theory, which aims to make substantive moral judgments, and at the level of metaethical theory, which considers the nature of moral judgments themselves. Self-deception can be seen to be at issue, in different ways, in all of the approaches to morality considered next.

A. Consequentialism

Consequentialism in its pure form measures the rightness or wrongness of an action by sole reference to the outcomes. For example, utilitarianism (of which there are many variants) may view the overall happiness and unhappiness for all affected as the only morally relevant consideration. It will be crucial that any assessment weighs the interests of all parties, including oneself, equally and impartially. Any judgment could have results that a consequentialist will deem significant, such as effects on total happiness or fulfillment of desires, so this section looks at how self-deception may distort general judgments as well as specifically moral judgments. A consequentialist would hold that whether the self-deceiver makes judgments with poor moral outcomes will depend on the particular circumstances and on a global assessment of all effects.

1. How Self-Deception May Interfere with Consequentialist Moral Judgments

For a consequentialist, such as a utilitarian, it is important that moral judgments are made with a sound appreciation of the facts and likely consequences, and in particular that all affected parties are treated equally. One obvious problem would be the discounting of the consequences of one's actions. This discounting of consequences may relate to simple factual matters, and also to emotional matters which may be especially vulnerable to the ravages of self-deception. For example, it may render one insensitive to the suffering of others, or blind to the fact that one's actions will have or are likely to have serious consequences for others. Frequently cited examples of this are of cases of self-deceptive

acquiescence to Nazi policies in Germany, such as that of a doctor who supplied SS storm troopers with large quantities of cyanide, "surprised" to find it had been used for exterminating people (quoted in Lineham, Elizabeth A. (1982). Ignorance, self-deception and moral accountability. *Journal of Value Inquiry* 16:101–115). However, for a consequentialist account of whether self-deception is morally reprehensible or not, it is necessary to examine individual cases.

2. The Consequences of Self-Deception May Be Good

A shipwrecked sailor deceives himself about his chances of swimming to shore, which gives him the courage to continue the effort. This belongs to a special group of examples where self-deception about one's own chances of success or one's own powers may enable one to achieve what otherwise is not possible. In a sense, the self-deception in these cases is a self-fulfilling prophesy. In other cases, self-deception may be seen to be a good if it enables the agent to carry on (with a worthwhile life or some particular worthwhile project) in the face of a truth which would otherwise be intolerable and lead to collapse. Much literature suggests that the maintenance of human relationships frequently requires self-deception on the part of one or both parties. Some may consider human life to be such that such self-deception is necessarily common (see Section III.B.5).

3. The Consequences of Self-Deception May Be Trivial

For example, having suspected something is afoot, one may deceive oneself about one's own surprise birthday party in order not to spoil the surprise (Foss, J. (1980). Rethinking self-deception. *American Philosophical Quarterly,* 17:237–243). However, most examples of self-deception seem to be motivated by more serious reasons than this. Furthermore, there may be systemic reasons why self-deception may seldom be limited to minor, trivial, or isolated instances (see IV.A.5).

4. The Consequences of Self-Deception May Be Bad

Examples of this are legion. Self-deception may lead to failure in relationships, failure in one's abilities to parent, limits to one's own growth as a person, corruption in business or government, and on and on. Self-deception may blind one to the facts, be they "hard" facts or appreciation of emotional states or assessments of the seriousness of suffering. In particular it may produce partiality to oneself or to those one cares about and hence corrupt a fair balance between all concerned.

5. Systemic Reasons Why the Consequences of Self-Deception May Be Bad

These may mean that even a consequentialist is likely to judge self-deception bad at least *prima facie*, or bad in most cases. Self-deception may be of an entrenched nature. In order to keep up the pretense to oneself, much else may be distorted to fit in with one's lie to oneself, and this may lead to general failings of judgment. This has been called the "rippling effect" of self-deception (Baron, M. (1988). What is wrong with self-deception? In B. P. McLaughlin & A. O. Rorty (Eds.) *Perspectives on Self-Deception*. University of California Press, Berkeley). Self-deception then may make one particularly prone to assess consequences poorly, especially where favors to oneself are concerned. It may also make one habitually insensitive to the needs and sufferings of others.

B. Deontological Theories

Deontological theories are those which understand morality in terms of rules which lay down certain types of behavior that are required or prohibited. Making moral judgments thus is a matter of deciding which rules are sound, whether certain actions do or do not comply with the rules, and further, what to do if there is a clash between different rules. Following rules can in theory help guard against the partiality and distorted thinking of the self-deceiver. Immanuel Kant exemplifies such a view in setting reason as the standard by which moral judgments are to be made. For Kant, reason sets its own, universal, agenda independently of the corrupting influence of particular human desires. In practice, however, in forming and following moral rules, much scope is left for self-deception to wreak its havoc. Some examples of how self-deception may affect these processes are given in the next sections. Furthermore, since a sound appreciation of the facts of the matter is always relevant to a moral decision, much of the preceding discussion in Section IV.A is relevant to a deontologist.

1. Fitting the Particular to the General

A classic instance of self-deception is to deny that a particular case falls under a general rule. Since applying rules always involves some kind of interpretation of the situation, and situations are generally complex, there may be ample scope for such denial, which generally involves some partiality whether to oneself or to someone or some group one favors. So, for example, one may believe in general that stealing is wrong, but justify one's own shoplifting to oneself by thoughts such as, "It isn't stealing to take what one needs," "It isn't stealing to take from large companies who themselves engage in dubious practices and make plenty of profit," or "I am being forced to shoplift by the government which refuses to fund higher education students properly." One difficult moral problem is to discriminate between cases of self-deceived rule bending and cases where a judgment that the rule does not apply is justified.

2. Taking Advantage of the Vagueness of Rules

Joseph Butler discusses this in his sermon "Upon Self-Deceit." This concerns those areas of morality where there are no exact, hard and fast rules but ones "whose bounds and degrees are not fixed" (1874, 125). (These then may be thought to show the boundaries of a strict deontological account.) Butler, with good reason, sees such as supplying great opportunity for self-deception to operate in distorting and rationalizing since there will be more scope for claiming that one's actions do not violate any moral code. An example he gives is that of oppression: a "detestable wickedness" (p. 126), yet one hard to define and hence easy to deny.

3. Self-Knowledge and Rule Following—The Doctrine of Double Effect

The very same physical movements can constitute different actions in different circumstances. The movements used in signing one's name may constitute signing a check, signing a marriage register, trying out a new pen, and so on. The intention with which one carries out certain physical movements may be crucial to what action is performed; knocking someone over may be an assault or an attempt to remove him or her from danger. In such cases, self-deception about one's own intentions may mean that one self-deceivingly performs a morally prohibited action, while telling oneself something quite different.

For example, the doctrine of the double effect states that, in certain circumstances, one may perform an action, X, with certain known bad side effects, Y, so long as the aim of one's actions was to achieve X and not Y. A case of this would be, given that direct killing of a human being is morally impermissible, the administration of certain drugs with the intention of relieving pain, even when a predicted side effect will be that the drugs will eventually kill the patient. A frequent criticism of this doctrine is that the intentions of the agent cannot be verified with certainty by others. A further danger is that the agent may be deceived about his or her own intentions, and really intend, in his or her heart, directly to kill the patient. Were this the case, the action would have been one of intentional killing and so the rule prohibiting killing would have been broken.

4. The Golden Rule as a Possible Way Out of Self-Deception

The Golden Rule states, "Do unto others as you would have them do unto you." In its various forms it is found throughout the world and throughout history. It can be taken as a global rule for working out what more specific rules or particular actions are permitted. It too can of course be vulnerable to the duplicity of the self-deceiver, who can pretend to him- or herself that he or she would welcome certain harsh treatment meted out to others.

However, it potentially can be used as a device for helping to overcome self-deception. Self-deception frequently involves some partiality to the self, or things close to the self, over others. The Golden Rule asks one to go through the exercise of putting oneself in another's place when thinking of actions that affect others; and of putting others in one's own place when thinking of actions affecting oneself. Carried out stringently, this could provide an opportunity to have one's self-deceptive bias laid bare to oneself in being confronted with inconsistent results between treatment of self and that of others. The more recalcitrant self-deceiver will, however, be resistant even to this attempted safeguard.

C. Virtue Ethics

Virtue ethics cashes out what the morally proper thing to do is in terms of what the morally virtuous agent would do. There are many accounts possible of what virtues such an agent possesses, but the virtue of integrity, which would include being free from self-deception, may be seen to be a key virtue. This is because of the devastating effects of self-deception on self-knowledge and one's functioning as an agent, and the way it may spread widely to infect the development of one's character. Freedom from self-deception may thus be a prerequisite for the complete development of all other virtues. (See Section III.B).

D. Ideal Observer Theories

An ideal observer (or impartial spectator) theory in ethics is one where moral judgments are made against the standard of what moral conclusions an ideal ob-

server would reach. The qualities of an ideal observer would generally include disinterest, rationality, integrity, complete appreciation of all the relevant facts, and understanding of all relevant moral considerations. In other words, the forming of moral judgments vitally relies on the qualities of mind possessed by the ideal observer. "Ordinary" moral judges can strive to attain these qualities as far as possible. It is obvious that on any such account, self-deception is incompatible with these qualities; and that one ought to strive to rid oneself of self-deception in moral decision making.

1. Rawls' Theory of Justice and Self-Deception

John Rawls's *A Theory of Justice* (1972. Oxford: Oxford Univ. Press) is a social contract theory which contains elements of an ideal observer theory in his account of justice as fairness. The principles of justice for a society are those made in the hypothetical situation of the Original Position, by free, rational, equal and mutually disinterested men (*sic*), each concerned to further his own interests. To ensure that agreements reached are fair, those in the Original Position have general knowledge about how societies work, but work behind a veil of ignorance, which means they are unaware of certain facts about themselves and their particular society. They do not know, for instance, their social or class status; their abilities, intelligence, or psychological attributes; or the state of advancement of their society. The purpose of this veil of ignorance is to render irrelevant anything which could place an individual at an advantage.

The rationality of the persons in the Original Position could be seen to preclude self-deception. Additionally, their ignorance of specific personal facts could be seen to work to nullify the grounds of self-deception, which is, in general terms, motivated by self-interest. The point of Rawls' theory is that individuals have no basis on which to judge where their self-interest lies. It also follows that for Rawls' account to work, those in the Original Position must additionally be free of the kind of self-deception or self-bias which deludedly supposes one's interest lies in this or in that, on the basis of inadequate knowledge or of more or less wild fantasy. Such wishful thinking is common enough that it needs to be guarded against.

E. Conscience Theories

On such accounts, an agent discovers what to do morally by examination of his or her own conscience. The conscience may, or may not, be specifically understood in religious terms as something deriving from God. It is also something that can be clouded or obscured. Coming to a moral judgment is thus an essentially private act of introspection, although an appreciation of the relevant facts will be needed and there may be recourse to prayer. Such an account of the origin of moral judgments shows them as especially vulnerable to self-deception. They require self-knowledge, of one's own conscience, and self-knowledge is especially prone to self-deception. Making moral judgments is also a very private affair which may then miss out on the critical and skeptical scrutiny of others which can be a valuable tool in combating self-deception.

V. CONCLUSION

It should be apparent from the preceding discussion that self-deception should be guarded against in the practice of and teaching of applied ethics. Particular points to note include the following: the ways in which self-knowledge (or its lack) may interfere in making moral judgments; the many opportunities for self-deceptive distortion of judgments; how the moral goal of impartiality may be lost to self-deception; how vital emotional knowledge of the self is for avoiding distortion and partiality; and how a third party may be needed in order to assist the agent in overcoming self-deception (notwithstanding the possibility of joint or group self-deception). The practice of applied ethics then can be argued to require stringent self-scrutiny and to benefit greatly from free and open discussion with others.

Also See the Following Articles

ARISTOTELIAN ETHICS • CONTRACTARIAN ETHICS • EXISTENTIALISM • FREUDIANISM • KANTIANISM • PSYCHIATRIC ETHICS • SUGGESTION, ETHICS OF • VIRTUE ETHICS

Bibliography

Butler, B. J. (1874). Sermon X "Upon Self-Deceit." *Sermons*. In *The works of the right reverend father in God Joseph Butler* (vol. II), pp. 118–133. Oxford: Clarendon Press.

Fingarette, H. (1969). *Self-deception*. London: Routledge & Kegan Paul.

Haight, M. R. (1980). *A study of self-deception*. Sussex: Harvester.

Kant, I. (1948). *The moral law* (trans. H. J. Paton). London: Hutchinson. Originally published as *Groundwork for the metaphysics of morals*.

Kierkegaard, S. (1941). *Fear and trembling* (trans. W. Lowrie). Princeton, NJ: Princeton Univ. Press.

Martin, Mike W. (1986). *Self-Deception & Morality*, Univ. Press of Kansas, Lawrence.

McLaughlin, B. P., and Rorty, A. O. (Eds.) (1988). *Perspectives on Self-Deception*. Univ. of California Press, Berkeley.

Peck, M. S. (1988). *People of the lie: The hope for healing human evil*. London: Random House.

Rawls, J. (1972). *A theory of justice*. Oxford: Oxford Univ. Press.

Sartre, J-P. (1956). *Being and nothingness* (trans. H. E. Barnes). New York: Philosophical Library.

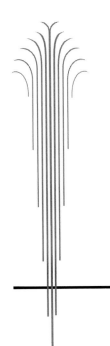

SEX EQUALITY

Susan Dodds
University of Wollongong

GLOSSARY

affirmative action/equal opportunity/equity in employment opportunities A set of policies to promote greater participation in employment, education, and civic life of relatively disadvantaged groups (e.g., people with disabilities, women, indigenous peoples, members of identifiable racial or ethnic groups) through practices that take salient differences into account or practices that promote opportunities for members of these groups to develop the skills and qualifications required for participation in all areas of society. Affirmative action practices often include preferential hiring or selection systems. In some contexts these terms are used interchangeably; in others they are given more specific meanings tied to employment practices.

antidiscrimination legislation Laws designed to protect people against unfair discrimination on the basis of sex, race, ethnicity, religion, sexuality, and so on.

femininity The characteristics (capacities, skills, interests, and pursuits) associated with the meaning of the category Woman in particular cultural contexts.

gender The meanings given to sex differences as they are manifested in particular cultural contexts.

masculinity The characteristics (capacities, skills, interests, and pursuits) associated with the meaning of the category Man in particular cultural contexts.

psychological androgyny (from the Greek: *andros*, man and *gyne*, woman) The view that the full array of desirable gender characteristics, skills and interests ought to be equally encouraged for both men and women, and that no human capacities should be understood as particularly appropriate (or inappropriate) to men as a group or to women as a group.

public/private distinction The distinction between people's activities in their private "domestic" lives and their activities in the public "civic" world. Often reflected in the view that laws, employers and the state should be concerned solely with the public or civic life or citizens or employees.

sex or gender roles The set of activities, projects and skills thought to be socially appropriate for men and women in a particular culture, because of their gender.

SEX EQUALITY addresses the different interpretations that are given to the claim that men and women are equal or ought to be treated equally. This essay examines some of those interpretations. Sex equality raises a number of issues in applied ethics, feminist thought, and political theory. Because of its concern with equality and equal rights, discussion of sex equality is of particular concern to liberal political philosophy and ethics. Liberal theory views justice, or "treating equals equally" as a central concern; sex equality, then, involves discussion of just treatment. Sex equality is contrasted with sex discrimination. Discussion of sex equality is often linked with arguments against other forms of discrimination including race, class, religious, or ethnic discrimination. In particular, in arguments advocating equality of opportunity and preferential hiring schemes, policies directed at ending sexual discrimination are grounded in the same conception of justice as those aimed at ending racial discrimination. One concern in contemporary ethical and political discussion of sex equality is the underrepresentation of women in many high-status, economically rewarding professions and their overrepresentation in undervalued low-paid jobs, relative to men.

Debate about the merits of preferential employment as a means of redressing this inequality has been prevalent in Western industrial countries since the 1970s. Two issues are central to the debate: on the one hand the effects of historical unjust discrimination against women are visible in the continuing relative social disadvantage of women as a group; and, on the other, preferential treatment does not redress the injustice done to specific women in the past. The men discriminated against through affirmative action policies were not the perpetrators of the historic discrimination, nor are most of the women who are advantaged by preferential treatment likely to have been subject to sex bias by employers. Because of the apparent tension between the justice or otherwise of treatment toward individuals and that toward groups, women, like members of the other groups identified as beneficiaries of preferential treatment, have been ambivalent in their response to these practices. While explicit discrimination against women may be readily decried, many women are concerned that preferential selection or advancement practices will render the genuine skills and capacities of women invisible. Some women are concerned that the community as group will assume that any woman in a sought-after position has been selected primarily because of preferential treatment, and not on her merits.

The issues surrounding sex equality are not simply matters of equality in employment, however. Equality of the sexes raises deeper conceptual questions about human nature; whether men and women share a single "human" nature or whether they have different, complimentary natures; about the significance (metaphysical or moral) of biological sexual differences; and about the current structure of social institutions. While most policy makers and employers publicly embrace antidiscrimination policies, it is not clear that equalizing employment opportunities between the sexes is sufficient for genuine equality between men and women.

The following section identifies three different meanings that have been given to the term "sex equality." Section II examines the historical approaches to sex equality that have given rise to these different interpretations of sex equality, focusing on liberal theory. In the third section sex equality understood as equal treatment is examined in conjunction with antidiscrimination and affirmative action policies. The fourth section discusses some contemporary feminist critiques of sex equality as an ideal.

I. THE MEANINGS OF SEX EQUALITY

A. Equality

Whenever things are said to be equal, there must be some measurable property of the things in respect to which they are equal: number, size, merit, and so on. Equality requires commensurability. In ethical and political arguments about sex equality, there is an implication that there are some respects in which men and women are equal—that there is some feature, or set of features, in virtue of which men and women are equal, despite sex and gender differences (e.g., rational capacities or capacities for virtue).

The term sex equality is used in three ways. Sex equality has been taken to mean: (i) that men and women are the same in all relevant characteristics and capacities; (ii) that the distinct capacities and characteristics of men and women are equally valuable; and (iii) that men and women merit equal treatment—that sex difference alone does not justify differential treatment. These different understandings of sex equality reflect different ethical responses to claims of inequality or discrimination on the basis of gender.

B. Three Different Senses

1. Men and Women Are the Same

An early expression of the view that men and women have the same capacities is found in Book V of Plato's *Republic*, where Plato has Socrates argue that the ruling, guardian class of the ideal republic should be composed of both men and women. Men and women are to receive the same training as guardians, and women will fight side by side with men, except during pregnancy. Socrates claims that there are no specifically female biological or psychological characteristics that would preclude women from engaging in all the activities of guardians. He states that natural capacities are distributed alike among both men and women, although women as a group are weaker in the exercise of human capacities than men as a group. Socrates argues both that women and men have the same basic nature (although Man's is more perfected) and that pregnancy and child-rearing do not necessarily interfere with women's ability to engage in training and the responsibilities of guardians.

In the time since Plato, debate about the relative natural competencies and character traits of men and women has continued. At different points in history men and women were found to share different characteristics and the same characteristic might at one time be thought "manly" while at another "feminine." In the 1970s, some feminist theorists argued for a conception of sexual equality as psychological androgyny. Starting with the claim that the capacities, skills, and interests of human persons are shared equally by men and women, they argued that all valuable human capacities, pursuits and interests ought to be equally encouraged in both biological males and females. This view of androgyny goes beyond Plato's vision in the *Republic* as it includes characteristics that have been associated particularly with the "feminine" among those human characteristics that are to be valued and encouraged.

2. Equally Valuable

The second sense of sex or gender equality accepts that there are significant differences between masculine and feminine characteristics, and claims that those characteristics associated with femininity should be valued equally with those associated with masculinity. This view of sex equality challenges the assumption that the distinctive skills, interests, and capacities that are associated with women are less valuable than those associated with men and hence that the different capacities of men and women justify treating women as subordinate to men.

In advocating that the distinctive characteristics of women should be valued equally to those of men, this approach requires a systematic reevaluation of the attributes of femininity, in order to resist the patriarchal assessment that what is associated with femininity is in some way less important or valuable than what is associated with masculinity. Sex equality understood as the equal value of gender traits requires a more sophisticated assessment of valuable traits than one that simply accepts either the male or female standard as ideally valuable. This becomes more difficult once it is acknowledged that what is taken to be an "objective" judgment that a trait is valuable may be influenced by biased cultural evaluations of gender traits.

3. Equal Treatment

The third sense of sex equality addresses procedural justice in the distribution of publicly valued benefits and burdens, including opportunities, within a society. Equal treatment between men and women requires that people with the same entitlement to some good be treated equally in access to that good, so bias based on gender is to be eliminated from determination of merit. For those who support this understanding of sex equality, the fact that men as a group perform statistically differently from women as a group on a wide array of activities is not relevant in assessing whether a particular woman or a particular man will be better at performing a specific task: each person is to be assessed on her or his individual capacity to perform the task.

In advocating sex equality as equal treatment, many writers recognize the difficulties inherent in overcoming a long history of unequal treatment and systematic discrimination. In order for women, or any other group that has suffered discrimination, to be able to participate equally in socially valued activities, a number of impediments must be overcome. First, those who have engaged in discriminatory practices in the past (e.g., employers, courts, educational institutions, social service providers) must recognize that women are able to perform the relevant activities as well as men. Second, women must have equal opportunities to men to develop the capacities required to compete equally with men. Third, women must be able to imagine themselves as able to strive and achieve in jobs, benefits, and positions of status previously reserved for men. A variety of affirmative action policies and practices aimed at enhancing women's ability to compete equally with men are often recommended as an aspect of equal treatment.

Some feminists have argued that sex equality, understood as equality of treatment, preserves the primacy of the male standard. In the activities associated with male public life (areas of employment, educational achievement, sporting or artistic skill, etc.), traditional (male) measures of success are simply applied to women as well, while some (morally irrelevant) impediments to women's success, on men's terms, are removed or neutralized.

These three different interpretations of sex equality are grounded in historical views about human nature, gender roles, and justice. These historical links are discussed in the following section.

II. HISTORICAL VIEWS ON HUMAN NATURE AND SEX ROLES

A. The Complementarity of Man and Woman

1. Men and Women Are Complimentary in Nature or Role

An account of the moral and political implications of the equality or inequality of the sexes must explain the ways in which men and women have been thought to differ naturally (e.g., biological differences, differences in reproductive roles, differences in strength) and the moral, social, and political significance of these differences. According to the complementarity thesis, women and men are different, but complimentary. Those who accept this view argue that although men and women share some characteristics (same species, equally the children of God, same capacity for rationality, etc.) there are some important respects in which they differ, but that these differences should not be interpreted as one sex being inferior to the other, nor that the different capacities and skills of one sex are inferior to those of the other. Where men and women come together and form a family, the differences between men and women compliment one another, insofar as both sets of attributes are valuable and, together, contribute to the well-being of the family. Jean-Jacques Rousseau (1712–1778) held the view that Man and Woman had different natures that compliment one another. Mary Wollstonecraft (1759–1797) argued that Man and Woman share the same nature (same capacity for reason and for virtue), but that because of Woman's (God-given) reproductive capacity, she should exercise her rationality and virtue in the "sphere" of domestic and child-rearing responsibility; thus that men and women are morally equal with complimentary roles.

2. Rousseau's Complimentarity of Nature

Rousseau argued that Woman's nature complimented Man's and that men and women could be guided through education to pursue a domestic and civic life in accord with human nature. According to Rousseau, the education of a boy should equip him to participate equally and dispassionately with other men in the life of the state among the fraternity of citizens and to rule and enjoy the intimacy of his home, his wife, and his children. Because of their biology, women are, according to Rousseau, closer to nature than men and less able to develop their capacity to engage in rationality, or to separate universal principles from socially mediated prejudices. Because of their nature, grounded in their biological difference from men, women are not equipped to be citizens. Girls are to be educated as good daughters and to become good wives and mothers. Their responses to social mores are to be trained to develop their sensitivity to social expectation as they are unable to rely on their own moral judgment. Women, through their modest deportment and through the values they inculcate in their children, are the protectors of morality as received from society, although they are not to critically challenge those moral dictates. Each girl's education is directed toward the development of a proper womanly character complimenting the independent, critical, rational life of men; to be adornments in the lives of men; to be obedient and to raise men's children.

3. Wollstonecraft—Complimentary roles of Men and Women

Wollstonecraft wrote *The Vindication of the Rights of Women* (1792) as a refutation of Rousseau's views on education (Wollstonecraft, M. (1994). *Political Writings*. Oxford: Oxford University Press). She argues that it is women's poor education, not a natural difference in rational capacity, that causes women to appear to be emotionally rather than rationally guided creatures. According to Wollstonecraft, women's capacities for rationality and virtue are equal to men's. Thus, if women's right to equal education were guaranteed, then women would display the same capacity for rationality as men. Women's disadvantaged status in society is due to the inferior education and intellectual opportunities open to women. While Wollstonecraft argues against the view that women ought to have different education and opportunities in virtue of the biological differences between men and women, women's reproductive capacities have assigned them to a different sphere of activity for the exercise of rationality and virtue

Wollstonecraft's religious conviction leads her to the view that women have the same rational and moral makeup as men; for men and women to be morally equal in the eyes of God they must have the same capacities for exercising reason and virtue in their action. That conviction also explains the different roles that women and men are to play in society. God created Man and Woman equal in moral and intellectual capacities, but different in reproductive capacities. Woman's role in the generation of children marks out her special role in the raising of children to be rational and virtuous adults. Women's rationality, then, is to be engaged in the raising and education of children. That role, Wollstonecraft argues, requires women to be well educated so they can inculcate, by example, independent rational thought in their children, rather than being guided by passion and social prejudice.

For Wollstonecraft, child raising is a socially significant activity because of its effects on the intellectual and moral character of children, who are to become answerable to God. She argues that the significance of the role should be treated more seriously and should be recognized, publicly, as valuable. Woman's domestic role of encouraging her children, and her husband, to be moved by reason, rather than passion, contributes to the well-being of society more generally. There should be no split in kind between the activities and concerns of the family and the activities and concerns of those participating as active citizens. While Rousseau saw home and family as the citizen's refuge from the demands of dispassionate, rational engagement or debate among equal citizens, Wollstonecraft views both home and state as properly ruled by rationality and directed to morality in all regards, including in the raising and educating of children. There is a clear tension in Wollstonecraft's argument, as she acknowledges the importance of independence in the development and exercise of reason and virtue, while consigning women to dependency in the domestic sphere.

4. Current Views on Complementarity

Although a number of contemporary feminists valorize differences between men and women, most feminists now reject the simple view that women have a complimentary nature to men. They also reject the view that women, in virtue of their child-bearing capacity have a different functional role, child rearing, which compliments men's role as "bread winners." A particular concern is that while Wollstonecraft enjoins men to recognize the value of women's domestic–reproductive role and activities she does not challenge the patriarchal values that assign superiority to men's activities and roles in any way that forces a general reconsideration of the value given to all roles and activities within society.

In the absence of any challenge to patriarchal assignments of value, the values associated with women's roles are, at best, concessionally "tacked on" to the dominant masculine values. On that patriarchal scale of values, the activities and roles associated with masculinity have already been identified as of greater value than those associated with femininity. In order to show that the set of characteristics, roles, or activities associated with women are equally valuable to those associated with men, there must be some means of measuring one against the other. Two things that are incommensurably different cannot be valued as equal. While some cultural feminists recommend that women should reject patriarchal evaluations and embrace those characteristics of women that have been disvalued by patriarchy, a consequence of doing so may be separatism, rather than greater equality, as there may remain no common ground for argument and debate.

One aspect of complementarity that has been developed more fully in recent years is the idea that there is an approach to ethical decision making more associated with women than with men. Carol Gilligan has developed the view that women are more "care oriented" in their ethical stance, while men are more "justice oriented" (Gilligan, C. (1993). *In a Different Voice.* Cambridge: Harvard University Press). In her psychological research, Gilligan found that while men tend to explain their responses to ethical problems in terms of impartial application of universal principles of justice, women are more likely to explain their responses in terms of relationships of care and dependence, seeking to protect and promote relationships between interdependent people. While Gilligan is careful to say that both men and women are able to take up either ethical "voice," the differences are principally grounded in the different experiences of men and women's lives. Impartial application of the principles of justice may be appropriate in meting out pay or grades, but is unlikely to be appropriate in responding to one's children or partner. Gilligan's work has thrown new light on the ethics of interdependent relationships, yet some feminists have been concerned that advocacy of "the ethic of care" may relegate women exclusively to caring roles in society. "Care" has been associated both with the women's traditional domestic–reproductive role and has been represented as natural or instinctual, rather than as a rational project. As such, there is a concern that adoption of an ethic of care may undermine feminist calls for equal respect for women and men.

B. Men and Women Have the Same Nature

1. Equal Capacities Merit Equal Treatment and Equal Rights

Contemporary liberal theory is grounded on the assumptions that persons have the capacity for independent rational thought and choice, that they are morally equal, and that each individual should be free to pursue her or his conception of the good life, constrained by the requirement that one's actions not cause harm to others. On the liberal view, given that men and women are equal in capacities and moral worth, they ought to be treated equally: a woman's capacities to pursue her own conception of the good life ought to be fostered by liberal political institutions just as a man's are so fostered. Two theorists who articulated this view were John Stuart Mill (1806–1873) and Harriet Taylor (later Mill) (1807–1858) (Mill, J. S., & Taylor, H. (1970). *Essays on Sex Equality*. A. Rossi (Ed.). Chicago and London: University of Chicago Press).

2. Millian Liberal Equality

Mill, a utilitarian, argued for treating women equal to men because the whole of society will benefit from women having equal rights to men. In particular, Mill challenged laws and practices of the time that served to exclude women from various opportunities. He challenged the exclusion of women from universities and colleges, from paid employment, from property ownership in marriage, and from inheritance. If women and men are treated equally, he argued, there is no need to fear that women of little talent will take occupations away from men. The result of equal treatment is that the best person, man or woman, will achieve positions of merit. There is no moral ground for holding women back from competing with men; those who lack skill or inclination will be judged equally unworthy of such positions, whether they be men or women. Mill's work shares with more recent liberal theorists a conception of equality that allows women to claim equality with men, rather than one that questions the assumption that the supposedly superior status that men enjoy is objectively valuable.

Mill wishes to limit the arbitrary power of husbands to physically abuse their wives or to constrain their freedom. While he assumes that most women *will* chose a domestic life of marriage and child rearing, he argues for placing the bonds of marriage on more equal terms: first that marriage should be a based on the free consent of equal friends; second, that the decision to marry ought to be postponed until both parties are sufficiently mature to avoid foolish matches; and, third, that divorce be available as a last recourse where the parties to marriage no longer agree to the marriage contract. For Mill, then, equal treatment under law for men and women is not directed to the goal of women's economic self-sufficiency, but to respect for women's autonomy, so that their choice to become wives and mothers is made sufficiently freely. Unlike Taylor, Mill's view of sexual equality is more formal than substantial.

Harriet Taylor took a more radical view than Mill to the subject of women's self-sufficiency and responsibility. In brief, her view was that women should not be made dependent on men and that they should take full responsibility for their own children. To protect women from the need to find a husband to ensure her material provision, Taylor argued that women should not only have equal opportunities to become educated, but they must also have opportunities to pursue gainful occupations. Thus, unlike Mill, Taylor was concerned with the positive conditions of women's liberty, not simply the absence of formal, legal constraint. If women take responsibility for their own children then women will take greater care to avoid having more children than they can provide for and, if a marriage breaks down, women would not have to chose between an intolerable marriage and the loss of their children.

By arguing for enhancing women's alternatives to marriage, their capacity for self-sufficiency and their responsibility for their children, Taylor explicitly articulates a view of women as having the potential to be full, liberal agents who choose whether to marry or seek other occupations on the basis of rational, free choice. More than other early liberal theorists, Taylor recognizes men and women as equals in their capacity for moral agency and enunciates what she takes to be required for women's role in reproduction to be accommodated by a conception of liberal sex equality.

As Genevieve Lloyd has argued, however, the very concept "reason" on which women's claim to equal moral agency is grounded, has been conceptualized in opposition to characteristics associated with "the feminine" (Lloyd, G. (1984). *The 'Man' of Reason*. London: Methuen). Women's engagement in reproduction and child rearing have been thought to immerse women more so than men in the realm of embodied nature, and emotion rather than the dispassionate exercise of abstract rationality. In this view of reason, unless the association of women's reproductive capacity with feminine irrationality is severed, women's moral agency will be limited and constrained by the demands of her body, her children, and her cares. In retaining the liberal conception of the rational moral agent as disembodied and dispassionate, Taylor's account does not challenge the apparent anomaly of a "rational mother." While women have the capacity to be men's equals, they may have to overcome special, socially constructed, barriers to exercise that capacity, because of the "interference" of their reproductive capacities.

3. Psychological Androgyny

Some feminist theorists, for example Alison Jagger and Susan Okin, have argued for a conception of sexual equality as psychological androgyny. Those valuable traits and activities culturally identified as "masculine" and those identified as "feminine" are to be severed from the assumption that they properly apply to biological males or females, respectively. Okin's work links the goal of psychological androgyny most explicitly with the liberal ideal of equal treatment and justice. Psychological androgyny is an ideal for human achievement, not a description of current human psychology

Psychological androgynists argue that a sharp distinction can be made between "sex" and "gender"; that sexual differences, while biologically given, are irrelevant to the development of valuable human capacities; and that what have been identified as gender characteristics are open to infinite change, irrespective of the physical features or cultural location of the person who bears them. This understanding of the mutability of the human character and the relative insignificance of biology or culture is very closely tied to the value placed on individual autonomy and individual freedom in liberal political theory. In many accounts of liberalism, persons are conceived of as equal individuals who have the capacity to choose, autonomously, the course of their lives. Biological difference is morally irrelevant for liberals, while socially imposed constraints on autonomous choice will only be justified where they protect more significant exercises of autonomy, or its development. Thus, liberal feminists view arbitrary assignment of gender roles as an illegitimate impediment to autonomy and freedom.

Those feminists arguing for the ideal of psychological androgyny question the conventional assignment of greater value to masculine characteristics compared with those thought to be feminine. These feminists aim to "envalue", or revalue, those characteristics associated with femininity so that possessing a feminine character trait can be of comparable value to possessing a masculine trait. Further, they argue that all genuinely valuable character traits, whether traditionally associated with men or with women, are valuable *human* character traits that should be valued equally regardless of who displays them. Unlike those who seek to embrace feminine characteristics as specific to women, androgynists reject the traditional assignment of particular characteristics according to gender, thus undermining any attributions of special traits to women or men.

III. EQUAL TREATMENT

A. Equal Rights as Citizens

Through the nineteenth and twentieth centuries in industrialized liberal democracies there has been an extension of equal rights of citizenship from propertied, adult, White men, to adult men and women of all classes and races. The movement for extending civic rights has included, in many places, measures ensuring that people are not discriminated against in access to public goods like education, health care, housing, and welfare benefits. More recently legislation has been enacted in various jurisdictions to protect people against discriminatory practices in some private institutions including places of employment. This movement towards greater equality of treatment, rights, and opportunities focuses on equal status within the state or equal access or opportunity to participate in publicly valued activities, where those activities pursued by White, propertied men are taken to be of higher value than those undertaken by subordinated members of society.

The legislation in this area frequently treats matters of discrimination on the basis of sex together with discrimination on the basis of race, religion, ethnic identity, physical disability, and sexual orientation. It would be oversimplistic, however, to assume that "equal treatment" or "discriminatory practices" could be fully understood independent of the contexts that condone the specific form of unequal treatment or discrimination. To understand how discriminatory practices affect people, often it will be important to understand how a particular individual may be multiply discriminated against, when, for example she is an unemployed Muslim woman living in a secular but predominantly Christian state. While the following discussion addresses gender inequalities, it does not address, exhaustively, the kinds of discrimination that women experience.

Feminists disagree about the value of legislation to ensure that women are treated equally with men in employment. Liberal feminists, with their focus on individualism, justice and rights are most clearly in favor of legislation ensuring women equal treatment. However, socialist feminists, feminists influenced by poststructuralism, and cultural feminists question the narrow focus of some antidiscrimination legislation that appears to assume that inequalities in domestic and child-rearing responsibilities are not salient inequalities, nor that they affect women's opportunities to compete on equal terms with men. Many also question the value of the male-dominated activities that women are "enabled" to participate in under the legislation. Feminists outside the liberal paradigm question the focus on inequality in employment opportunities that does nothing to question the primacy of public or civic life over the private or domestic realm.

B. Equal Rights and Liberal Feminism

Liberal feminists argue that women have been disadvantaged historically by laws and practices that discriminate against women or that give women fewer options for choice in their lives than men, as a group, have had. Liberal feminists have been vocal in demanding changes in laws to remove arbitrary barriers to women's participation in the public sphere and in demanding the enactment of laws protecting women against discrimination on the grounds of sex, marital status, pregnancy, or parental responsibilities. The policies sought by liberal feminists have been argued on the grounds of justice: treating similars equally.

In demanding nondiscriminatory policies, liberal feminists have sought to give women access equal with men to participation in the socially valued public realm of paid employment, education, and public office and to de-emphasize the differences between women and men. In doing so, liberal feminists have been accused, by both feminists and antifeminists, of forcing women to "become like men" in seeking publicly recognized status. Some of the legislation initially enacted was charged by cultural feminists with being "gender blind" insofar as it encourages the society to focus on conformity, rather than acknowledging salient differences (in ability, opportunity, values, responsibility, cultural background, etc.) in the lived experiences of men and women within a particular society.

An example of the debate within feminism is found in the 1985 United States antidiscrimination case *EEOC v Sears, Roebuck and Co.* The Sears case involved, in part, the claim that differences in the pay among sales staff between men and women, where men tended to cluster in higher-paid commissioned sales, was discriminatory. On one side of the debate was the argument that the different distribution of men and women in areas of sales reflected the natural outcome of differences between the genders in interests and capacities, thus the differences in pay were not discriminatory. Differences in self-conception as a result of socialization were as irrelevant as other differences in preference, if women chose to work in less financially rewarding areas, that was an expression of their autonomy. The other side challenged the "naturalness" of the distribution of higher paid work and the view that it is unjust to use antidiscrimination legislation to redress imbalances between groups as a result of cultural forces, as well as to redress discrimination against individuals. The differences in self-conception, interests, and ambitions of women and men were taken, by these writers, to be an effect of cultural subordination of femininity, not an expression of women's (genuine) autonomous choice. In this view the pay differentials of men and women reflect women's continued subordination, rather than just recognition of different interests and preferences.

Within feminist jurisprudence, writers like Catherine Mackinnon and Martha Minnow have argued that one way around the tension between sameness and difference is to understand sex equality in terms of the relative social standing of men and women. Catherine Mackinnon argues that once sex equality is understood in terms of social standing and it is appreciated how current norms are covertly male-biased, then it will be seen that sex equality and antidiscrimination is fundamentally about redressing the subordination of women to men and not about sameness or difference (Mackinnon, C. (1987). Difference and Dominance: Two Theories of Sex Discrimination. In *Feminism Unmodified.* Cambridge, MA: Harvard University Press).

C. Antidiscrimination Legislation

Attempts to legislate sex equality provisions have a long history. In 1921, United States suffragist Alice Paul drafted the Equal Rights Amendment (ERA) to the U.S. Constitution, which provides that "equality of rights under the law shall not be denied or abridged by the United States or any state on account of sex" and gives Congress the power to enforce the provisions of the Amendment. Proponents argue that the amendment provides more explicit protection against sex discrimination than the equal protection clause of the Fourteenth Amendment of the Constitution. It has been introduced in Congress at every session since 1923 and passed Congress in 1972, but failed to be ratified by the required 38 states by the deadline in July 1982; 35 states had ratified the amendment.

Starting in the mid-1970s countries like the United States, the United Kingdom, Canada, New Zealand, and Australia passed antidiscrimination legislation, to ensure that women were treated the same as men in areas such as: employment, education, and in access to social services. Each jurisdiction has produced different legislation, reflecting the different histories, social context, and political institutions of each nation, and including different groups of people under the protection of antidiscrimination legislation. Often there are both federal and provincial or state legislation covering aspects of antidiscrimination.

Over time antidiscrimination legislation has moved away from a simplistic opposition between sameness and difference. Antidiscrimination legislation has given women grounds for complaint where practices discriminate on the basis of sex, marital status, pregnancy, or other arbitrary criteria for employment like height, weight or other criteria for which many fewer women than men are likely to be able to comply. More recent legislation and judicial findings have been more comprehensive in identifying areas of discrimination and grounds for complaint. For example, legislation in the United Kingdom has been more broadly interpreted in light of legislation binding on the United Kingdom through its membership in the European Union in a manner that benefits women. Some of the most recent legislation explicitly recognizes that equality in employment may require difference in treatment; legislation for equality while recognizing salient differences, for example the Australian Sex Discrimination Act 1984, which allows for complaints on the grounds of discrimination based on potential pregnancy, pregnancy and dismissal on the grounds of family responsibilities.

D. Equality of Employment Opportunity and Affirmative Action

Once antidiscrimination legislation had been enacted, some people were disappointed to find that although individual women were now less likely to face discriminatory employment practices, women were still underrepresented in many areas of employment, particularly in more senior positions in the work force. Women as a group were still disadvantaged relative to men as a group. In order to redress the disadvantage that women experience, some employers and educational institutions have been encouraged to adopt affirmative action and equal employment opportunity (EEO) practices designed to diversify the workplace by enhancing women's (and other targeted groups') appointment and promotion opportunities. Among the practices used to meet this goal are: targeting of positions for women; providing women with workplace training and professional development schemes; formal recognition of previous career levels where a person's work history has been interrupted by parental responsibilities; giving preference in employment to women over men where job applicants are equal on other criteria; and setting employment or promotion quotas or goals. Affirmative action and employment equity policies go beyond the similar treatment of equals demanded by antidiscrimination legislation. These policies require that some employment procedures explicitly recognize salient differences (member-ship of a disadvantaged group) and treat individuals differently in virtue of those differences.

Some applied ethicists have rejected affirmative action and EEO policies on the ground that they are not "sex blind" but discriminate on the basis of sex. Reverse discrimination (discriminating in favor of women, for example) is thought to be as unjust as the earlier discriminatory practices that excluded women. In both cases a distinction between people is made on the basis of a characteristic that is irrelevant to performing the occupation; thus the discrimination is arbitrary. Proponents of affirmative action and EEO policies argue that, in focusing on individuals rather than groups, the liberal position ignores those features of the social context of the history of sex discrimination that continue to affect women's opportunities to participate in employment and education. It is only by recognizing the effects of discrimination on community attitudes, on quality of education and material well-being prior to entering the work force, and on individual expectations that a full understanding of women's continued relative underrepresentation can be gained.

Because affirmative action and EEO policies require an explanation of the historic causes of group-based disadvantages that extend beyond identifying specific cases of discrimination, legislators have tended to resist moves to legislate in favor of these measures. Western liberal democracies still emphasize the similarities of citizens over their differences, although those countries that describe themselves as multicultural (rather than assimilationist) have been quicker to consider employment equity and affirmative action legislation.

The federal legislatures of Australia and Canada have passed affirmative action or employment equity legislation. The Australian federal Affirmative Action (Equal Employment Opportunity For Women) Act 1986 requires organizations to establish affirmative action programs for women. The Canadian Employment Equity Act had not come into force at the time of writing, but was assented to by the Canadian parliament in December 1995. The Act extends the provisions of the Canadian Human Rights Act that encourage affirmative action and employment equity programs. It places responsibilities on most private and public sector employers who have 100 or more employees, and unions and their representatives to provide positive mechanisms to reduce barriers to employment opportunities and to enhance opportunities for participation by members of designated groups. The groups identified to benefit from this legislation are women, aboriginal people, persons with disabilities, and members of visible minorities.

IV. CRITICISMS OF SEX EQUALITY AS AN IDEAL

This section provides an overview of some contemporary feminist criticisms of various interpretations of sex equality. The following subsections discuss: socialist feminist criticism of the focus on equality in employment; feminist critiques of the exclusion of the family from liberal discussions of sex equality; and challenges to sex equality posed by difference feminists.

A. Socialist Feminist Critiques

Socialist feminists have long found the argument for equal rights to be hollow so long as women lack the economic means to enjoy greater equality. According to socialist feminists, the liberal feminist focus on individual rights of equality in civic and employment opportunities draws attention away from two key areas of oppression that directly disadvantage women: capitalism and the patriarchal nuclear family. For socialist feminists, women's engagement in the paid workforce, under capitalism, like that of working-class men, is alienated and oppressive as workers do not control the means of production and receive less than the value of their labor power in exchange for their alienated work. Women's overrepresentation in poorly paid jobs and in subordinate positions to men reinforces the oppressive features of capitalism. The sexual division of labor means that women (whether or not they are in paid employment) are often saddled with the burden of unpaid and unrecognized domestic labor and child care responsibilities. While equal pay and equal rights legislation may limit some of the workplace discrimination women experience, it does nothing to challenge capitalism fundamentally and it continues patriarchal capitalism's shrouding of domestic labor from public recognition.

B. Critiques of the Liberal Focus on the Public Sphere

The liberal focus on equal rights in civic life renders invisible the role that women play in patriarchal societies in reproduction and child rearing. Feminist political theorists have argued that liberal political theory is founded on the view that political institutions are designed to regulate public office, property rights, and contracts made between (male) citizens. The state's authority, under liberalism, does not extend into the private domestic affairs of the citizens. A clear distinction is made between the democratic authority of the state

in regulating the public or civic interactions of citizens and the despotic power of the patriarchal head of household. Similarly, feminist critics of John Rawls' theory of justice have argued that liberal conceptions of justice and of the just state have not envisaged marriage and the family as spheres for the application of principles of justice. If, as radical and socialist feminists argue, women's role in reproduction and domestic labor under patriarchy is a key source of women's oppression, then attempts at achieving sexual equality that do not directly interrogate the social construction, meaning, and institutions that perpetuate those roles is unlikely to have substantial (rather than formal) success. While equality of men and women before the law in the areas covered by antidiscrimination legislation is valuable and few feminists would wish to lose that equality, there are limits to the value of sex equality as an ideal.

For many feminists, equality between the sexes as a goal in itself is problematic for at least three reasons: first, there are significant differences between men and women in reproductive capacity and so some difference in treatment, even if only immediately concerning pregnancy and childbirth, will inevitably occur; second, the meaning of sex differences is interpreted in and through culture, so the lived experiences of two individuals identified as of different genders will be significantly different, even if they are treated in law as full equals; and third, the survival and development of human children requires that some adults provide for the needs of those children fully outside the realm of liberal contract theory.

In a patriarchal culture women's capacity to bear a child is associated with responsibilities for caring for children: even if a particular women never bears a child, the fact that she is viewed as having the capacity to bear children often means that she is treated as if she will have child-rearing responsibilities that impede her ability to act in socially valuable roles. A man, lacking the capacity to gestate a child, is not interpreted as being denied the opportunity to bear and raise children; rather he is understood as having full capacities to participate in the central activities of social existence and having the capacity to provide for this family through his voluntary labors. On many accounts of sexual equality, for women and men to be sexual equals, women must overcome the special burdens placed on them by their role in reproduction and become like men engaged fully in civic life. Those accounts do not then explain how child-rearing responsibilities are to be adequately met. This is not to say that child rearing cannot be separated from pregnancy, but rather that assignment of child-rearing responsibilities simply does not fit into a model based on free choice, contract, and justice.

C. Sex Equality versus Sex Differences

In challenging sex equality as an ideal, many feminists, explicitly or implicitly, seek to challenge the view that Man is to be understood both as the norm of human existence and as the ideal of human attainment. Rather than understanding women as anomalous participants in humanity, these feminists wish to reaffirm women's lived experience as full members of humanity. To do so in a way that neither relegates women to being men's compliments, nor as very like, but inferior, to men requires the possibility of women articulating their lives and experiences *as women* rather than in comparison with men.

French feminist writings on language and discourse simultaneously demonstrate patriarchal dominance of language and meaning and indicate ways in which the interstices between meanings in language can be used to create a new feminine discourse that "writes" women's existence. Iris Young, drawing on phenomenology and de Beauvoir's account of oppression, has developed an approach to understanding lived experience through women's bodies that recognizes the cultural meaning and significance attributed to female bodies, the affects of those meanings on the subjectivity of women, and the experiences specific to subjectivity as a woman in a patriarchal culture (de Beauvoir, S. (1975). *The Second Sex.* Harmondsworth: Penguin). Yet other feminists have moved toward a relational conception of persons that, rather than viewing persons paradigmatically as individuals, attends to the importance of social forces and relationships in the development of a person's identity and knowledge. Each of these developments adds to a richer understanding of the experiences of women and the significance of culture in the constitution of persons.

V. CONCLUSIONS: BEYOND SAMENESS AND DIFFERENCE

While the ideal of sex equality has been important in promoting women's interests and changing women's lives over the past 30 years, it cannot be thought of continuing value without a critical reexamination of the differences between the lives and experiences of men and women and a critical reevaluation of those characteristics, institutions, and practices thought to be valuable for human social existence. The relationship between theoretic developments in feminist theory and social institutions should be dynamic as the cultural contexts within which women and men experience their lives are constantly changing, in response to legislative change, revised theoretical explanations, and historical events. To assume that, with the right legislation and practices, we could ensure stable equality between the sexes is to misunderstand human social existence.

Also See the Following Articles

AFFIRMATIVE ACTION • DISCRIMINATION, CONCEPT OF • EQUALITY AND EGALITARIANISM • FAMILY, THE • FEMINIST ETHICS • GENDER ROLES • HUMAN NATURE, VIEWS OF • SEXISM • WOMEN'S RIGHTS

Bibliography

Bacchi, C. L. (1990). *Same difference: Feminism and sexual difference.* Sydney: Allen & Unwin.

Fraser, N. (1994). After the family wage: Gender equity and the welfare state. *Political Theory, 22,* 4:591–618.

Held, V. (1993). *Feminist morality: Transforming culture, society and politics.* Chicago: University of Chicago Press.

McKay, N. Y. (1993). Acknowledging differences: Can women find unity through diversity? In S. M. James and A. P. A. Busa (Eds.), *Theorizing black feminisms: The visionary pragmatism of black women.* New York: Routledge.

Minnow, M. (1990). *Making all the difference.* Ithaca: Cornell University Press.

Okin, S. M. (1989). *Justice, gender and the family.* New York: Basic Books.

Okin, S. M. (1994). Gender inequality and cultural differences. *Political Theory 22,* 1:5–24.

Rhode, D. L. (1989). *Justice and gender: Sex discrimination and the law.* Cambridge: Harvard University Press.

Young, I. M. (1991). *Justice and the politics of difference.* Princeton: Princeton University Press.

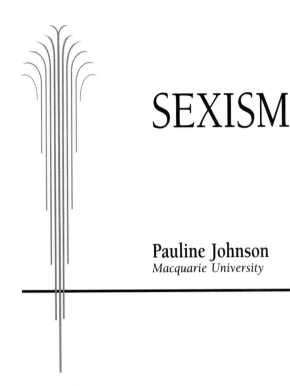

SEXISM

Pauline Johnson
Macquarie University

GLOSSARY

affirmative action policies Policies designed to disclose and counter informal processes and descriptions of merit seen to discriminate against the equal access of women into a range of occupations. Such policies may also involve legislation that prescribe targets for appropriate gender balance within specific occupations.

equal opportunity policies Policies designed to lift formal constraints upon the equal participation of women in a range of social institutions.

first wave feminism Protests in the latter part of the nineteenth century against legal and political limitations on the rights of women.

modern humanism The conviction that identity is no longer to be "received" as a taken-for-granted place in a community and social hierarchy. For modern humanism, each individual must be recognized as a unique, potentially autonomous being, creating their own destiny, making themselves.

second wave feminism Widespread protest movements against sex discrimination that emerged from the late 1960s.

SEXISM denotes forms of behavior, institutionalized practices, and ideologies in which individuals are ascribed dispositions and capacities simply by virtue of their sex. This kind of prejudgment typically involves a denigration of femininity seen as a marker for various sorts of incapacities and unenviable character traits. As such, sexism as ideology tends to legitimate and mask patterns of constraints and inhibitions applied to the life chances of modern women. Sexism is a concept that operates within certain cultural boundaries. It denotes a discriminatory breach of a modern humanist conviction that all individuals ought to be recognized as unique personalities and permitted the free discovery and self-development of their potentials and capacities.

I. TWO PARADIGMS

The critique of the sexism of key institutions and entrenched forms of behavior in the Western world has grown apace since the emergence of a "second wave" of feminism in the late 1960s. The flowering of feminism in the late twentieth century has been a follow up to the vigorous campaigns of the suffragettes in the latter part of the nineteenth century (first wave feminism). The expanding presence of feminism in the Western world (in 1970 the National Organization of Women, the major American feminist body, had a membership of 3000 compared to its current membership of 250,000) has been accompanied by a diversification of the terms in which the critique of sexism has been conceived. While significant common ground remains, contemporary feminism has developed at least two main ways of understanding the character and significance of sexism.

A. The Liberal View

This is a construction of sexism that condemns practices and attitudes seen to discriminate against women by denying them the realization of their full human potential. The classic exponents of this interpretation of sexism are the nineteenth-century British liberals John Stuart Mill and Harriet Taylor. Guided by the liberal principle that individuals must be permitted to find their own objectives and allowed to realize them in their own way, this critique of sexism condemns all those attitudes and behaviors that seek to deny the extension of this principle to women. For the liberal critique, sexist practices are discovered in all those attitudes and practices that attribute to women natural dispositions that suggest that they are either disinclined to or incapable of the pursuit of autonomous self-development. Sexist practices may appear, for example, as those attitudes and behaviors that confer a naturalness on the confinement of women in modern Western societies to the private, domestic sphere. Such attitudes serve the function of disciplining and controlling women; confining them to the presumed naturalness of their role in the home—servants to the needs of their husbands and children. The liberal critique often points to the hostility and at times violence that may meet attempts by women to break out of the constraints of their ascribed social function.

B. Gender Difference

An alternative to the liberal critique of sexism has emerged since the 1980s. The liberal paradigm discovers sexism in all those ideas and practices that inhibit the extension of the principle of autonomous self-definition to women. Some feminists have argued, however, that this understanding of sexism does not itself fully escape the traps of sexist ideas. They suggest that the ways in which the ideas of self-determining autonomy have been formulated by liberalism typically reflect and celebrate the achievements of men. The logic of the liberal critique of sexism is, accordingly, found to perpetuate a sexist ideology that upholds the socially ascribed attributes and priorities of men as the human characteristics to which a femininity that is presumed to be deficient ought to aspire. On this account, liberal feminism has come to be associated with the idea that the pursuit of individual self-realization requires women to project ambitions and objectives in terms established by men.

In contrast to the liberal view, the standpoint of gender difference proposes that we can continue to talk in terms of gendered priorities and ways of doing things without necessarily reproducing sexist attitudes. The standpoint of gender difference suggests that the recognition of gender-typical responses and approaches to tasks is guilty of sexism only in those cases in which difference is seen to be a matter of natural indisposition rather than a positive acquisition of behaviors through socialisation processes. Difference is construed as inferiority only in the context of a presumption that an equalization of the status of the sexes requires a quest for sameness. From the perspective of gender difference, sexist ideologies appear in the guise of one gendered set of priorities seeking to claim for itself the status of a prescriptive standard by which all alternative priorities, sets of behaviors, and dispositions might appear as mere incapacity.

II. ISSUES IN THE INTERPRETATION OF SEXISM

A. Gender Difference and the Moral Divide

Sexist ideas and behaviors frequently work through the ascription of inferior capacities to women simply on the basis of their sex. This supposed inferiority may involve a denigration of the intellectual capacities and physical dispositions of women. It may also involve a derogatory attitude toward the capacity of women for exercising moral judgment. Some recognized scales for measuring the moral development of individuals suggest a ranking that might be understood as a devaluation of feminine capacities for moral judgment. In this case, a capacity for moral reasoning that approaches its task as a matter for the impartial application of abstract principles is frequently associated with masculine judgment. Women, by contrast, tend to be associated with a supposed immature capacity for moral reflection that considers all questions of justice in terms of the competing rights and needs at play in particular, concrete situations. The supposed inferiority and immaturity of a feminine capacity for moral judgment is seen to rest with the presumed incapacity of women to appreciate that all questions of justice require the disinterested application of universal principles that display no prejudical interest in the special, concrete circumstances of particular individuals.

An ideology of the moral incapacity of women was used to legitimate delaying the extension to women of such basic civil rights as the right to vote until the early decades of this century. (Women only won the right to vote in 1902 in Australia, 1919 in West Germany, 1920 in the United States, 1928 in the United Kingdom, and 1971 in Switzerland). Seen to be enmeshed in their own privatistic concerns, women were supposed incapable of achieving that impartiality of judgment assumed vital to the responsible exercise of voting rights. The sexism of this attribution of incompetence to the moral reasoning capacities of women has provoked the ire of many feminists determined to dispute its descriptive accuracy. The suffragettes did not attempt to challenge dominant descriptions of those attitudes deemed appropriate to the fully entitled citizen but, in the main, sought to establish the capacity of educated women to conform with these norms.

A competing feminist response has suggested that there might well be some validity to the claim that men and women approach the task of moral reasoning from different perspectives. On this viewpoint, the attribution of a moral divide between the sexes appears sexist only when gender difference is scaled in terms of an apparent contrast between supposedly weak and nominally strong appreciations of the principles of justice. This kind of ranking of the significance of gendered difference in processes of moral reasoning has been contested by, in particular, American feminist Carol Gilligan. On the basis of her 1982 study of the patterns of moral reasoning exhibited by American male and female college students, Gilligan suggests that there might be grounds for supposing that the sexes are encouraged to weigh differently considerations relevant to the formation of moral judgment. She argues, then, that the sexist character of the thesis of a moral divide does not lie in the mere attribution of difference itself. Rather, the sexism of the description of moral difference is seen to lie in the supposition that a supposed typically feminine interest in the well-being of particular individuals renders them incapable of due respect for the cause of universal justice. Gilligan's claim is that a supposed typically feminine interest in the lived conditions of particular individuals ought not be seen as a rival commitment to the idea of universal, impartial justice. On the contrary, this "feminine" perspective might be understood as a peculiar recognition that the principles of universal justice can best be applied in a fair, nondiscriminatory, fashion in the context of a "feminine" sen-

sitivity to the specific contexts and circumstances that might condition the bahaviors and shape the options of affected parties. All morally motivated decisions need to be informed by the observance of such universalistic principles as a commitment to the right to life of all humans. Yet, in any given concrete situation a fair application of such moral norms might be seen to a require a (supposedly feminine) sensitivity to the competing claims of, particular, differently placed individuals.

B. Sexism in the Measurement of Success

One measure of the continuing influence of sexist ideologies that describe women in terms of their supposed incapacities is the rate of inclusion of women into the decision-making structures of government and the corporate sector. The advancement of women here has been slow. In most countries few women have achieved high office in government and in the corporate sector there are very few women at the top—rarely more than 1 or 2% of senior management postions. Women continue to be in the minority in administrative and management jobs overall, although their participation increased in almost every region from 1980 to 1990 (See Fig. 1).

A range of distinct explanations for this slow progress has been advanced. The "glass ceiling" refers to those informal barriers that serve to frustrate the efforts of women to rise from middle ranking to the highest positions of authority in bureacratic institutions. These informal barriers can be seen to include the entrenched sexist culture of the institutions themselves. The employees of large organizations learn to constitute themselves as a club united by shared experience and traditional affiliations. The club will tend to seek to reproduce itself, throwing up, in the process, various obstacles to and failing to recognize the merits of aspiring outsiders. Responsibility too has been attributed to the supposed inhibiting role that a "culture of women" has played in their career advancement as a group. Women, it has been supposed, are not yet fully persuaded to the desireability of forefiting family ties to embrace the rigorous demands of an executive career. The constraints the "executive culture" and the "culture of women" are sometimes cited as twin factors in the inhibition of the rise of women to positions of power and influence.

Those interpretations that target a culture of women as an inhibition to career advancement have come from two directions. On one argument, women have been acculturated into a "fear of success"; their gender-role expectations have socialized them into a culture

ST. THOMAS AQUINAS COLLEGE
LOUGHEED LIBRARY
SPARKILL, NEW YORK 10976

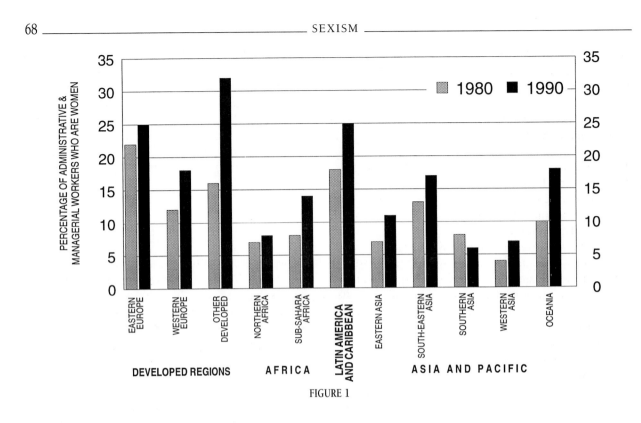

FIGURE 1

of "success avoidance" perceived as an unwillingness to assume positions of substantial power and authority. A rival explanation draws upon the idea of a "women's culture" to quite different effect. Women, on this account, do not simply "fear" success but have been acculturated into a particular understanding of the character of achievement that is relatively autonomous from dominant, market-driven, constructions of the "successful life." The argument here is that a reluctance among women to pursue the "high-flying" positions in modern bureaucracies might well be attributed not merely to "success avoidance" but to an allegiance to an alternative set of ideas in the measurement of achievement. Maria Markus's studies suggest a trend among women to evaluate their achievements less in terms of career advancement than on the basis of the quality of personal (not functional) relations with others and in accordance with the value of the work well done for its own sake.

In large modern bureaucracies it becomes increasingly difficult to measure individual performance and, hence, the evaluation of "performing capacity" has to be accomplished symbolically. It is increasingly based on "extrafunctional" attitudes and ascriptive criteria of various sorts rather than on any effective achievement. (Markus, M. (1987). Women, success, and civil society: Submission to or subversion of, the achievement principle. In S. Benhabib and D. Cornell (Eds.), *Feminism as Critique.* Cambridge: Polity Press.) Such extrafunctional attitudes are seen to involve a wide range of institutional loyalties and the ascriptive criteria are usually based on the "natural" categories of sex, race, or ethnic background and on external "institutional links" of various kinds. On this diagnosis, an attempt to combat the influence of sexist imperatives in the workplace requires widespread affirmative action policies. These policies seek to unmask and to redress the discriminatory processes whereby individuals achieve career advancement on the basis, not of an assessment of their effective achievements, but in response to their conformity to symbolic indices to presumptive capacity.

C. Attitudes toward Women's Bodies

A liberal approach, which sees sexism in the discriminatory denial to women of a life aimed at the many-sided development of their human potentials, discovers a sexist representation of women's bodies at the base of major institutions in the modern world. Rape, prostitution, pornography, sexual harassment in the workplace, and the activities of the advertising industry have all been targeted by feminist protests. It is, specifically, the production and reproduction of the idea of women's bodies as property that is taken as the substance of a sexist construction. The sexist representation of the body establishes it as a passive body; a body that is required to surrender to the will, to the active appropriation, of another. This exploitation of the body as an object, possession, or commodity suggests a continuum in the sexist treatment of women's bodies that can be traced through from rape, sexual violence, prostitution, pornography, and forms of advertising. In each case, an attempt is made to treat the body as an item separable from the whole person, which can be made over into the property of another.

Dispute as to whether, and in what sense, the issue of consent should enter into an evaluation of the sexist character of the representation of the body remains a significant feature of both legal and feminist discussions on this topic. In the case of adult prostitution, for example, it may be argued that the prostitute enters into a contractual relationship with a client and is, thereby, not engaged in a sexually exploitative process. A contrary view here has maintained that the act of prostitution itself—the contracting out of one's body for the gratification of another—is a practice that is only possible in the context of a general culture that tends to take for granted the sexist treatment of the body. It is this taken-for-granted background culture that obscures recognition of the fact that prostitution is a major site of the enactment and reproduction of the sexist construction of the female body.

Given a culture in which women's bodies are routinely represented in reference to the uses and pleasures of others, it has, some suggest, become increasingly difficult to conceptualize a nonsexist representation of the female body. A woman's body, seen as an object, as property to be assessed by and appropriated for the use of others comes to be experienced by the woman herself as an object; as an alien body. On this account, the sexist construction of the female body is not simply construed as a matter of a discriminatory denial to women of their full human potentialities by a culture desirious of reducing women to their sex. The sexist construction of the female body is seen, rather, as a matter of a culture that seeks to efface any positive description of women's bodily difference from men. The bodies of women are described and constructed by the medical establishment, the media, and by the various institutions of the sex industry in terms of their relationships to an appropriative masculinity.

The sexist construction of women's bodies means that women inhabit bodies whose sexual pleasures have been described from the standpoint of others. There has in the last few decades been some significant attempts to redress this situation, redescribing the bodies of women in terms that might establish them as specific bodies with pleasures and sensual qualities different, in a positive sense, from the bodies and pleasures of men. The hope here is that, together with legal sanctions, concerted efforts made by feminists to redescribe the feminine body as an inhabited body might begin to present an obstacle to the ideology of the body as property that appears at the base of sexist construction of the bodies of women.

D. Masculinity

Sexism is a term usually associated with the denigration of women; with the ascription of characteristics and qualities to them simply by virtue of their sex. It might seem that this same process occurs quite systematically with the social description of masculinity also. Men are attributed with certains sorts of psychological dispositions; with gender-specific kinds of behavior simply on the basis of their sex. Recent studies point to the ascriptive character of a culture of masculinity that valorizes and rewards physically aggressive, competitive, task-focused, achievement-oriented attitudes and behaviors in men. Although recognition of the ascribed character of a set of masculine dispositions is now fairly commonplace, there is rather less agreement on the terms in which these gendered descriptions might be seen to be oppressive. For some, it appears that the ascribed character of masculine character traits do not function in terms that parallel the ascription of characteristics to women. In the case of women, the ascription of gendered attributes, typically seen to involve a diminishing of their capacities and trivialization of achievements, assumes a clearly oppressive, sexist role. The gendered characteristics attributed to men however, are, not seen to perform the same kind of belittling function. While not disputing that men too have certain more or less rigidly ascribed psychologies to negotiate, it is argued that the oppressive character of an ascribed masculinity is essentially asymmetrical to the sexist loading of an imposed femininity. Admittedly, a sexist culture does not confer power in equal measure on all men. It constructs hegemonic images of masculinity—a psychology that valorizes the competitive, emotionally reserved, achievement-oriented personality—which must be reproduced if masculine power is to renew its legitimacy.

An alternative viewpoint stresses that sexist attitudes toward men are every bit as debilitating as is sexism directed towards women. This latter assessment, which claims a parity in the sexism experienced by both genders, holds that masculinity is achieved at the cost of the well-being of most men. Here masculinity appears as an ascribed condition that requires competitive relations with others, a driving ambition for recognition and that penalizes any expression of vulnerability and dependency. Men, victims of a sexist ideology that ascribes emotional self-sufficiency and self-control as appropriate masculine traits, are said to be deprived of a rich emotional life and to fail to develop a capacity for sympathetic relations with others.

Some commentators have highlighted cultural trends suggestive of changes in the character of masculinity. The appearance throughout the 1980s of nonsexist men's groups in the metropolitan regions of many Western cities has supported this perception of the changing character of norms of masculinity. However, developments here have had a very uneven impact. Some commentators have suggested that the social expectations and psychological burdens placed on men have proven even more rigid, less amendable to conscious change, than have the ideologies of femininity. There is some evidence to suggest, moreover, that for those who suffer a structural denial of that set of behaviors and responsibilities deemed masculine, masculinity is increasingly experienced as an oppressive ideology. According to some studies, the burdens of masculinity are increasingly felt during periods of high unemployment giving rise to the phenomenon of "breadwinner suicides" suggesting that many men cannot see the erosion of their "breadwinner" role without serious damage to themselves.

E. Political Representation

In democratic countries women have achieved formal equality with men in many areas. They have attained the right to vote, to stand in elections, and to compete for political office. However, there has been a low participation rate for women in both national and local politics. With the exception of the Nordic countries, women figure in national politics at something between 2 and 10%; in Britain and the United States, women have found it difficult to break the 5% barrier. Only 24 women have been elected heads of state or government, half since 1990 (Table I).

A liberal critique of the underrepresentation of women in government insists that the expansion of numbers of women into the higher echelons of political power is an equal opportunity issue. The history of exclusion of women from political power appears as the same sort of problem as the barriers encountered by women as they seek career advancement in the arenas of corporate power. A liberal critique of sexism resists all attempts to view the problem of underrepresentation in terms other than an equal-employment issue. Traditionally, liberalism has insisted that the processes of political decision-making must maintain a relative autonomy with respect to sectarian, private interests. Political decision-making is seen to be properly a matter for the exercise of impartial judgment steered by a view to the general interests of the nation state as a whole. Hence, for classical liberalism, the person of the political representant ought, from the standpoint of the constituent, to be considered immaterial.

Against this liberal construction of the character of the problem of underrepresentation, conceived as an equal-opportunity issue, there has been a growing trend to view the problem more broadly, as matter of concern for the well-being and vigor of liberal democratic institutions themselves. The interests of women have, it is argued, been neglected and overlooked by political institutions in which the major decision-making functions have been monopolized by men. On this point of view, the domination of political decision-making processes by men is seen to have itself promoted a systematic betrayal of the responsibility of government to exercise its authority on behalf of the well-being of the community as a whole. In particular, a history of male-dominated government has, it is argued, skewed the definition of those issues deemed politically relevant in narrow, sectarian terms; in terms seen to reflect the acquired priorities and perspectives of a certain class of privileged men.

The twentieth century has seen a progressive shift of issues, such as housing and welfare and sexual relations, formerly deemed social questions, into the domain of politics. The climate of economic rationalism that presently grips many Western democracies has suggested to some the fragility of this only lately achieved expansion of the scope of politically relevant concerns. Women, it is argued, have a specific vested interest in actively seeking to arrest this return to a narrow conception of the political. Seen as particular beneficiaries of a broader conception of politically relevant issues—one that assumes jurisdiction over formerly "social questions" (women have, for example, benefited from the introduction of legislation designed to outlaw violence in marriage) women appear as central stakeholders in those vigorous struggles underway in many liberal democratic countries over the question of the character and the scope of politics.

The underrepresentation of women in parliament has been perceived not merely in terms of a problem of equal opportunity and not simply in terms of the

TABLE I

Women Elected Heads of State or Government in the Twentieth Century
(as of December 31, 1994).

Presidents		
Argentina	Isabel Martinez der Peron	1974–1976
Bolivia	Lidia Gueiler	1979–1980
Haiti	Ertha Pascal-Trouillot	1991
Iceland	Vigdis Finnbogadottir	1980–
Ireland	Mary Robinson	1990–
Nicaragua	Violeta Chamorro	1990–
Philippines	Corazon Aquino	1986–1992
Sri Lanka	Chandrika Bandaranaike Kumaratunga	1994–
Yogoslavia	Milka Planinc	1982–1986
Prime Ministers		
Bangladesh	Khaleda Zia Rahman	1991–
Burundi	Sylvie Kinigi	1993
Canada	Kim Campbell	1993
Dominica	Eugenia Charles	1980–
France	Edith Cresson	1991–1992
India	Indira Gandhi	1966–1977
Israel	Golda Meir	1969–1974
Norway	Gro Harlem Brundtland	1981, 1986–1989, 1990–
Pakistan	Benazie Bhutto	1988–1990, 1993
Poland	Hanna Suchocka	1992–1993
Portugal	Maria de Lourdes Pintasilgo	1981–1985
Rwanda	Agathe Uwilingiyimana	1993–1994
Sri Lanka	Siramovo Bandaranaike	1970–1977, 1994–
Turkey	Tamsu Ciller	1993–
United Kingdom of Great Britain and Northern Ireland	Margaret Thatcher	1979–1990

Source: Division for the Advancement of Women of the United Nations Secretariat.

supposed peculiar investments of women in protecting a broad conception of the scope of politics; a case has been made also that women might change for the better the culture of political decision-making processes itself. The argument here is that, while the inclusion of individual women into government may have no evident impact on the culture of politics, a recruitment of women into processes of political decision-making in sufficient numbers may succeed in bringing about substantial change in the conduct of political decision-making processes. The hope is that women, as a group, might bring a different style of argumentation to the political process; a style that is less combative, more receptive to the force of the better argument and less influenced by the claims of personal interests. Several major parties within liberal democratic countries (including the federal Australian Labour Party, the British Labour Party and the Swedish Social Democrats) have now introduced quota systems designed to help redress the gender imbalance in the elected representatives in their national assemblies.

F. Education

Arguments traditionally used to prevent women from obtaining formal schooling indicate a seeming fear that education for women may foster ambitions that would render them unfit for their traditionally ascribed roles. Jean-Jacques Rousseau, one of the founding fathers of modern education, believed that the education of women should not provoke in them aspirations that might render women dissatisfied with their destiny of subjection to the judgment and will of men. It was only in the nineteenth century that Western societies began to lift formal restrictions on the education of women who were for the first time permitted into the universities.

On a global perspective, women continue to suffer significant educational disadvantages. United Nations studies suggest that, although literacy rates for women have increased in the last few decades across the globe, in countries with high illiteracy overall, the illiteracy rate among women aged 15 to 24 is at least 25 percentage points higher than among young men. Basic education gives women access to the knowledge, skills, and technologies that improve their opportunities. The United Nations has, accordingly, targeted education as an urgent priority in its efforts to improve the lot of the world's women. "Priority action should include education programs for women and girls designed to eliminate the social and cultural barriers that have discouraged or even excluded them from the benefits of regular education programs, and to promote equal opportunities in all aspects of their lives" (*The World's Women 1990–1995 Trends and Statistics* (1996). United Nations Department of International Economic and Social Affairs Statistical Office Centre for Social Development and Humanitarian Affairs).

In this century many girls and women in Western societies have grasped the opportunities for entry into an education system from which they were formerly barred. Ideologies that condemn the pursuit of higher education for women have, however, not entirely disappeared. The trend now is to emphasize the sacrifice that the pursuit of higher education and tertiary training might seem to exact from women themselves. The much vaunted idea of the "superwomen," the professional who, unrealistically, it is supposed, seeks to "have it all" higher education, career, and family, has more than a descriptive sociological function. The ideology of the superwoman assumes, also, a disciplinary role. This image appears as an accusation directed at the supposed romantic folly of the "liberated woman" herself. In this case the entrenched sexism of those social institutions that offer no material support to the aspirations of women to the full realization of their diverse potentials are exempted from all serious criticism.

The feminist critique of the system of education has increasingly targeted the sexist bias of those various institutions to which women are now formally admitted. In particular, the curricula of many traditional education establishments is said to be itself gender-biased. This critique suggests that the process of education always involves, in some degree, an induction into a certain worldview and, it is supposed, unless these are deliberately prodded into self-consciousness, systems of formal education will continue to mirror and legiti-

mate the socially ascribed superiority attributed to professions and ways of doing things traditionally deemed masculine. A gender bias is found then to exist in curricula that privileges in "hard" sciences over the humanities. Gender bias is discovered also in the neglect in historical and sociological studies of issues and phenomena of particular relevance to the experience of women. Some commentators have supposed that traditional modes of delivering such subjects has rendered them unattractive to girls as career options. The motivation for this feminist critique of sexist bias built into the education system is not necessarily a desire to return to gender-specific curricula. The challenge to the gendered priorities built into norms and entrenched practices of institutions of formal learning, is, rather, frequently inspired by a concern to broaden the base of human experience deemed relevant to the education process. In promoting reflection upon the ideologies embedded in the curricula and modes of delivery adopted by traditional schooling, the critique also seeks to facilitate the practical implementation of officially recognized charters of equal opportunity.

III. RENEGOTIATING COMMON IDEALS

The concept of sexism suggests patterns of behavior and ideologies that ascribe a difference to women interpreted as discriminatory. It is, then, a judgment that calls upon, and is bounded by, certain cultural norms and value ideas through which the significance of an ascribed gender difference is interpreted. In particular, the concept of sexism is informed by a background allegiance to the value ideas of modern humanism. Modern humanism insists that identity is no longer to be "received" as a taken-for-granted place in a community and social hierarchy and determines that each individual be recognized as a unique, potentially autonomous being, creating their own destiny, making themselves. The idea of sexism denotes, then, a judgment upon those ideologies about and behaviors toward women that indicate the illegitimate revival of an imposed "naturalized" identity description.

The concept of sexism suggests a humanity divided by practices and ideologies of discrimination. Sexism denotes behaviors and ideas that seek to legitimate the power of men over women by attributing inferiority to the capacities, abilities, and dispositions of women. Sexism does not, however, suggest any immediate ties of solidarity between women united by shared oppression.

The experience of sexism is always mediated by the contingencies of particular circumstance. Against the ideology of a "sisterhood" of women that used to characterize the politics of early second wave feminism, it is now frequently stressed that sexism is encountered by lesbian and heterosexual, and by Black and White women in such distinctive terms as to discredit any suggestion of an immediate unity of experience.

The divisions connoted by the concept of sexism run deep. Yet, this concept, which suggests a protest at the patterns of discrimination it describes, is also indicative of an on-going recognition of the injustice of sexist ideologies and practices in modern liberal democracies. It is this recognition that must be constantly reproduced, clarified, and rendered more subtle if we are to continue to invest hope in the amelioration of the seeming intractability of a sexist culture. The concept of sexism provides us with a way of identifying ideologies and behaviors seen to constitute a betrayal of the values and principles of modern humanism. It is thereby a concept that presupposes a common currency of such value ideas that might act as the medium through which its critical consciousness might be communicated. At the same time, the concept of sexism suggests a renewal and a specific intepretation of modern humanism; par-ticipating in the constant expansion of the legitimate juridiction of these great, constantly embattled, pattern of values ideas and principles.

Also See the Following Articles

AFFIRMATIVE ACTION • FEMINIST ETHICS • FEMINIST JURISPRUDENCE • GENDER ROLES • SEX EQUALITY • WOMEN'S RIGHTS

Bibliography

Barrett, M., & Phillips, A. (Eds.). (1992). *Destabilizing theory*. Cambridge: Polity Press.
Faludi, S. (1991). *Backlash: The undeclared war against American women*. New York: Crown Publishers Inc.
Gilligan, C. (1982). *In a different voice*. Cambridge, MA, and London: Harvard University Press.
Johnson, P. (1994). *Feminism as radical humanism*. Sydney: Allen and Unwin.
Norris, P., & Lovenduski, J. (Eds.). (1994). *Different roles. different voices: Women and politics in the United States and Europe*. New York: HarperCollins.
Pietlia, H., & Vickers, J. (1990). *Making women matter: The role of the United Nations*. London: Zed Books.
Wearing, B. (1996). *Gender: The pleasure and pain of difference*. Victoria: Longman.

SEXUAL CONTENT IN FILMS AND TELEVISION

John Weckert
Charles Sturt University

GLOSSARY

conceptual structure The knowledge, beliefs, and attitudes that form the framework within which a person acts and perceives.
eroticism Material intended to stimulate sexual desire.
freedom of expression In John Stuart Mill, the position that people should be able to live their lives and express themselves as they wish, providing that no harm is caused to others.
pornography Sometimes not distinguished from eroticism, but more often considered as sexual material of a violent, degrading, and exploitative nature.
sexual content *Explicit* sexual content comprises material such as human copulation. *Indirect* or *implicit* sexual content is implied or suggested, and is often "in the eye of the beholder."

SEXUAL CONTENT IN FILMS AND TELEVISION is not easy to define. While there are core examples, in many instances whether or not something counts as sexual depends on the context and on the beliefs and attitudes of the viewer. The chief moral issues raised by sexual material concern pornography, particularly in films, the portrayal of women in television commercials, the protection of children and the formation of moral attitudes in educational programs, and privacy and victimization in news bulletins. Finally, there are questions regarding the restriction of sexual material, which raises the issues of freedom of expression.

I. SEXUAL CONTENT: WHAT IS IT?

The title of this article probably evoked images or thoughts of humans engaged in explicit sexual activity, and perhaps of material that would typically be called pornographic or erotic. When considered more carefully, however, it becomes unclear just what constitutes sexual content in film and television, and what is morally interesting. While the pollination of pumpkins and the courtship of peacocks are undoubtedly sexual, and films or television programs about these would undoubtedly have sexual content, it is difficult to see any interesting moral issues here, so the discussion will be restricted primarily to human sexual activity.

The most obvious sexual content is human copulation depicted or discussed explicitly and in detail. It might be pornographic or erotic, or perhaps neither, perhaps factual. Such content could be in a film or an educational program, but probably not in a news bulletin, a sitcom, or a soap opera. Sexual content also comprises references, perhaps oblique, to sexual activity, language involving certain innuendos, as well as scenes that infer sexual activity. For example, the statement, "Last night I went back to Bill's place and we did it" is clearly sexual in the context of a sitcom about very attractive people in their twenties whose lives revolve around relationships with members of the opposite sex. Similarly, a couple walking up the stairs can, in the right context, imply immanent sexual enjoyment, and so counts as sexual content. These examples however raise an interesting question. Where the sexual reference or scene is not explicit, to what extent is sexual content "in the eye of the beholder"? We will return to this shortly.

Sexual content can form part of the artistic or the entertainment content of films (including sitcoms and soap operas), where there would normally be some intent to portray a level of sexuality. But it is not all like this. In educational programs, news bulletins, and documentaries it could be just factual, and there may even be an intention to downplay the sexuality in some scene or discussion. This could and should be the case in news reports of, for example, rape, pedophilia, and litigation for sexual harassment, and in educational programs dealing with sexual, particularly human, reproduction.

Finally, a comment on television commercials, which frequently have, or so it is claimed, sexual content. This is rarely explicit. It is much more likely to be in the form of young and attractive people, perhaps wearing seductive clothes or in seductive poses, or using sexually suggestive language. The impression often given is that the purchaser of the relevant product will be as sexually attractive as the person or people in the advertisement.

The sexual content of commercials is usually implicit rather than explicit, which takes us back to the question raised a moment ago regarding this content being "in the eye of the beholder." What does it mean to say this? It means, generally, that sexual "content" is in the mind of the viewer and not in the material itself. In Wittgenstienian terms we might say that the viewer *sees* the material *as* sexual (Wittgenstein 1968: 193–194). Another viewer might not see it in this way. While care must be taken in claiming that we *see as* rather than just see, we can and do see things differently depending both on the context in which things are couched, and on our own knowledge and beliefs (our conceptual structure) and perhaps on what is uppermost in our minds at the time of viewing.

This issue of seeing material in a sexual way makes it very difficult to specify just what constitutes sexual content. Explicit scenes of human copulation are obviously sexual, but what about fondling, hugging, kissing, and sexually suggestive language? It clearly depends on the context and on the viewers. But once it is conceded that context and viewers are important it is difficult to know where to stop. A meal scene in the well-known *Tom Jones* movie is said to be highly sexual, presumably because it excites the imagination in some way. Young schoolboys might fall down laughing at a shot of a banana, or someone might look lustfully at a preacher extolling the virtues of celibacy. Do these constitute sexual content? Perhaps not, but consider a different case. Suppose that a group of people brought up with public nudity see a film containing scenes of people frolicking nude in a swimming pool. These viewers might see nothing at all sexual in this, although another group probably would. If sexual content is that which evokes images or thoughts of sexual activity, then the scenes of the banana and of the preacher are as sexual as the nude frolickers. If it cannot be extended to this type of material, the latter should not be included either. Clearly, apart from the core examples, sexual content can only be defined in terms of the context of the scene and the conceptual structures of the audience.

II. THE MORAL ISSUES

Given the importance of sexual activity for sexually reproducing organisms, it is something of a wonder that the sexual content in films and television is worth discussing in an ethical context. It is as vital for the survival of many species as is eating, and this is certainly true in the case of humans. While there may be some ethical discussion of gluttony, there is not much of eating in general. In the case of human sexual activity, however, it is not just overindulgence that is thought to raise ethical issues; it is the activity as such. Furthermore, it is not only those activities that engender debate, it is also their portrayal in film, in television, and in the written and spoken word. Why is sexual activity considered so much more important ethically than eating when both are common, and indeed must be if the species is to survive? Perhaps, because everyone must eat to survive while sexual activity is not essential for the survival of an individual. Perhaps, too, it is partly because of the difficulty of always separating this activity from emotional bonds that it can promote and enrich. This leads to what is probably the most important point. Sexual activity normally involves another person, and possibly the creation of more. It is social, usually, and as such is essentially ethical. The rights of both, or all, the participants must be considered.

Although sexual activity itself may necessarily involve ethics, it does not follow that its portrayal necessarily does. The ethical questions in this sphere arise because of the harm or supposed harm caused by some sexual material, and the offense it gives to some people. It could be argued that sexual material is immoral in itself regardless of its consequences. This view would normally be closely associated with particular religious beliefs, and nothing much of significance can be said about this without an examination of those beliefs. In any case, holders of this position would probably be offended by sexual material, so to some extent it will be covered by offense. We will first consider what the moral issues might be in films, and then in television.

A. Films

Most discussion of what is wrong with sexual material in films, whether shown in theaters or on television, concerns pornography. It is not easy, however, to say what pornography is. First, definitions vary widely. The most moderate define it as sexual content of a film, or whatever, that is designed to arouse sexual desires, or perhaps to satisfy sexual desire. Other accounts make it anything but innocuous. It is sexual content that is combined with one or more of violence, abuse, degradation, dominance and conquest. Second, to what content do these definitions refer? Does the first refer to something that was designed to arouse sexual desire but regularly fails to, because it was done so badly? And what about scenes that were not designed for this purpose, but that regularly do? The second definition does not fare much better. While physical violence and abuse are not too difficult to describe, degradation, for example, can take many forms, and what one person sees as degrading another may not.

These criticisms of the definitions do not show that the word "pornography" is too vague to be useful. What they show is that care must be taken when discussing it. There is little point in merely saying that pornographic films should be censored. There may be a lot of point in saying this once a clear statement of what is meant by pornography is given.

Some writers distinguish between the pornographic and the erotic, while others claim that there is no difference. A middle position is that eroticism is a weaker form of pornography. A useful way to differentiate the two is to use "pornography" in the second sense above, where it is linked to violence abuse, dominance, coercion, inequality, and the like, and to use "eroticism" for sexual content that concerns sexual desire but that is free from any violence, dominance, and so on.

Not all sexual content is necessarily pornographic or erotic. Some is simply for artistic purposes (eroticism, of course, could be artistic). The film is better with it than without it. Just what constitutes art, or what distinguishes art from nonart is not easy to say; nevertheless, importance is placed on this distinction. It is much less common for sexual material to be condemned if it is considered artistic than if it is not.

The most controversial sexual content is the pornographic, in the sense where it is distinguished from the erotic. The main reasons advanced for the wrongness of this material are that it causes harm, both to individuals and to society, that it is degrading, particularly to women, that it is exploitative, and that it is offensive.

1. Harm

It is argued sometimes that there is a causal link between pornographic material in films, and rape and other violence, against women in particular. While there is some anecdotal evidence for this, the hard evidence is more ambiguous. It appears that so far no strong case has been established for a causal link, or for the lack of one. On the other side, there is also some evidence, again inconclusive, that watching pornographic films can have a beneficial effect on some, by reducing aggressive and violent behaviour.

The more general claim that pornographic and erotic material weaken society is even more difficult to substantiate, partly because it is essentially ideological. The claim often is that this material encourages promiscuity, weakens marriage and the family, etc. Even if a causal link were established, more argument would be required to show that that is undesirable.

2. Degradation

It is difficult to make a case that erotica is degrading to anyone, but it is plausible to say that pornography is. There is a sense in which it is degrading to all participants, including the viewers, but it is especially so to the individuals or groups who are the recipients of violence or who are subservient, usually women. It seems equally degrading to the victims in pornography if they suffer violence or other indignities against their will, or if they play the parts willingly.

3. Exploitation

Another common criticism of pornography is that some of the participants, namely, those playing the subservient roles, are exploited. Undoubtedly in many instances this is true. However, where women, and in some cases men, willingly participate, it is difficult to see where the exploitation lies. It might be argued that nobody would willingly play those roles, but this is demeaning to those who do. It implies that any people who willingly and without any coercion decide to play subservient roles, are not really acting freely, and are deluding themselves if they think that they are. Many, of course, who are not coerced, may only "voluntarily" participate because they are so poor that they see no other alternative to escape poverty. Their participation is therefore hardly voluntary. However, there could be cases where there is no such necessity. In any event, this sort of exploitation could be eliminated now with the use of current computer simulation techniques and image manipulation. It may be that some consumers would not find this material as enjoyable if they knew that there were no real people involved in the activities that they were watching, but that is another matter.

4. Offense

Sexual material of any sort, but particularly pornography, is sometimes condemned on the grounds that it is offensive. Because of the perceived importance of this objection in relation to anything sexual, and because the nature of offence is seldom discussed in any detail, we will return to it in Section III.

B. Television

In this section we will concentrate on the nonfilm component of television, in particular on commercials, educational programs, and news bulletins. Here pornography is not particularly important, and neither is erotica, except to a limited extent in commercials. The moral issues raised therefore will be slightly different from those discussed previously, although there is some overlap.

1. Commercials

Advertisers want to sell products, so generally will try to avoid material offensive to their target audience. As already mentioned, the sexual content is likely to be inferred rather than explicit, therefore it could be argued that the content itself is not sexual. But this, as we have also seen, is a dubious claim. What are the moral issues in this context? In commercials, sexual material is almost always unnecessary, and therefore, perhaps, has more potential to portray people, usually women, as sexual objects, even where there is nothing very significant about the content if it were in another context. As is often the case in popular quiz shows, the women involved are little more than decorations—they

look attractive and perhaps stimulate the imagination, but they do little that is necessary. The moral issues here revolve around whether this portrayal harms women, and whether it is offensive. One argument is that it helps perpetuate the view that women are not capable of much beyond looking good and giving pleasure to men. This reinforces typical male attitudes and the male dominance of society. As such, this material is offensive to many. Counterarguments to this might be first, that such material cannot be offensive to too many, because "sex sells"—the commercials work, and second, that the material does not, or cannot, harm women in the way suggested because is must be seen in a certain way to be classed as sexual. It is not sexual in itself. The first response clearly must be rejected. Something is not morally right simply because it works. Ends do not always justify means. Neither does the fact that these commercials work show that nobody is justifiably offended by them. The second response is too glib. Certain material can count as genuine sexual content even though it must be seen in a certain way, and it could still be harmful.

2. Educational Programs

Educational programs can be aimed at people of any age, but the main moral concerns tend to be over whether certain material is appropriate for children of certain ages, and whether the material is dealt with in a proper manner. Should, for example, homosexuality be portrayed as acceptable? Even in moderately tolerant societies, this question generates heat. Some see an affirmative answer as obvious, while others believe that portrayal will help lead to the undermining of traditional family and other religious values. A similar issue is whether sexual activity should be shown as an end in itself, or whether it should always be shown as part of a loving relationship. Another question is to what extent are children upset or psychologically damaged by nonviolent explicit sexual material?

There appear to be two main moral issues here: first, how much should we protect children for their own good, and second, to what extent should we try to stop children acquiring "false," or "morally bad," values? Adults certainly do have an obligation to protect children from harm, and the issues here are what material is harmful, and how long this protection should last. The second main moral issue will always be a problem in any society in which a wide variety of moral values are tolerated. Almost nobody in a civilized society would want children to believe that violence is acceptable in sexual relationships (or in any other), but it is not so obvious what "false" or "morally bad" beliefs are with respect to nonviolent and consensual sexual activity.

3. News Bulletins

The sexual content of television news bulletins raises some moral issues that are different from those discussed so far, because news items are, supposedly, of real events. People usually become the subjects of these news items through misfortune, with no intent of making their private lives public; therefore, the most important moral issues concern privacy and victimization. And it is frequently not only a victim of, for example, rape or sexual harassment who should be taken into account. Anyone close to the victim, say a child or parent, should also have their privacy respected. This respect for privacy should also extend to close associates of accused persons, even if and when they are convicted. There will frequently be conflicts between society's right to know and an individual's right to privacy, but society does not have a right to all details, and journalists do not have the right to victimize people in order to get details.

III. OFFENSE

Because sexual material is undoubtedly offensive to many, it is worth looking more carefully at giving and taking offense. Offense is a sort of unhappiness, mental distress, or some other sort of suffering. An offended person has his or her feelings hurt in some way. An important point is that something will only offend someone if that person *takes* offense. Offense is closely related to beliefs, attitudes, feelings, and so on.

Two questions emerge: (1) What, if anything, is wrong with giving offense? and (2) Why do people take offense? In answer to (1), one may be inclined to say that there is nothing really wrong with giving offense. After all, if people are so silly or sensitive that they become hurt at something said or seen, so much the worse for them. While this contains an element of truth, it is a bit hard, but we will return to this after a brief look at (2).

Obviously, offense is taken for different reasons by different people and over a wide range of areas, but here our only interest is in sexual material in films and on television. Part of the explanation for the offense taken clearly has to do with upbringing and socialization. But this is not a complete explanation. There might be anger where something is not liked because it is thought that it will have harmful consequences. For example, it will lead to rape or to the lowering of moral

standards. Offense, however, seems to involve something more than this. If I find something offensive I take it personally in some way. I am *hurt*, not just angered. A reasonable explanation of why I am hurt is that I identify closely with beliefs that this sort of behavior is wrong, and in a way I feel violated. If you expose me to these things that you know I do not like, then you are not showing me the respect that I deserve as a person. Even if it was not directed at me in particular, I may feel that people like me are not respected enough. In both cases we may feel devalued as persons.

A related point is that material that denigrates a particular group or in some way portrays that group to be inferior can offend because one has no choice in belonging to that group. A relevant example is the portrayal of women in pornography and in some television commercials. There is a real sense here in which our self-image and self-respect can suffer. Offense will more often be bound up with self-respect.

We find that there is a close connection between the taking of offense and self-respect or self-esteem. When someone displays material that we find offensive, we feel that we are not being respected as humans. Our self-respect may be lessened to some extent. Too many of these comments can cause us to see ourselves as people of little worth. If something that is an integral part of me is ridiculed, say my gender or my moral or religious beliefs, this is evidence that others do not value me as a person. They are not showing me the respect that I deserve as a person. Perhaps what is wrong with giving offense in general is that it is showing a lack of respect for others and that it may cause them to lose some of their self-respect.

This account shows that the giving of offense needs to be taken seriously. It can be more than a matter of few oversensitive or old-fashioned people having their sensibilities attacked. The problem, of course, is that almost any sexual material will be offensive to some, so if all offense is taken as a reason for restriction, almost nothing of a sexual nature could be portrayed. Offense must be taken seriously in the sense that it ought not be brushed aside as irrelevant in all cases. A plausible argument might be that material that is generally offensive to a group whose members have no alternative but to belong to that group, say women or any racial group, could be restricted in some way, but that material found offensive in other situations should not. There seems to be a relevant difference between material that is offensive to women because it degrades them as a group, and material that is offensive to some people simply because they find it embarrassing or they do not like it for some other reason.

IV. RESTRICTING SEXUAL CONTENT

Restrictions of various kinds are often placed on material of a sexual nature. It might be banned altogether, or it might just be given a code to indicate its content or the kind of audience for which it is intended. Such codes warn audiences of what they might expect to see or hear. If they do not heed the warnings, they have little cause to complain if they find the material offensive. It is easily avoidable. In the case of television programs, there might also be restrictions placed on when they are allowed to be shown. Programs containing explicit sex scenes might only be allowed to be shown late at night when young children are less likely to see them.

The arguments against restrictions tend to revolve around freedom of expression. Some of the best-known come from J. S. Mill. Mill's conception of a good human life is one in which we think, reflect, and rationally choose for ourselves from different beliefs and life-styles according to what seems most true or meaningful to us. This is shown in his arguments for the freedom of expression. His central tenet here is that people ought to be allowed to express their individuality as they please "so long as it is at their own risk and peril" (Mill 1975: 53). The basic argument is that the diversity created has many benefits. One is that "the human faculties of perception, judgement, discriminative feeling, mental activity, and even moral preference, are exercised only in making a choice" (Mill 1975: 55). And exercising this choice makes it less likely that we will be under the sway of the "despotism of custom" (Mill 1975: 66). If there is this diversity, each human will be more aware of the various options available, and so more competent to make informed choices in lifestyle and self-expression. We will be able to lead happier and more fulfilled lives.

This and other such arguments for freedom of expression do support the claims for lack of restrictions and control of sexual material in films and on television. However the support is qualified, because one person's right to freedom of expression can impinge on another's rights, and can clash with other goods. There is little sense in the idea of complete freedom of expression for all. So the issue now becomes one of where to draw the lines for this freedom. Common criteria are harm to others and the giving of offense. Mill places particular emphasis on the former. We should be able to express ourselves more or less as we like providing that others are not harmed by our actions.

While many arguments concerning sexual content commonly revolve around pornography and obscenity, others involve the protection of children even from material much more benign. Viewing that might not be detrimental to adults, might be to children. Or perhaps it might instile in them undesirable values. In this context, television is more important. Not only are films on television more accessible to children, but sexual material can also be found in educational programs, news broadcasts, and documentaries. Of concern here are not so much the pornographic and erotic, but more "harmless" sexual material, perhaps nudity in general, and open discussion of sexual issues, and perhaps even the mating behavior of the high mammals. Mill, it should be noted, did not include children in his argument, chiefly because they could not, according to him, be improved by free and rational discussion.

V. CONCLUSION

This article has concentrated on problems of deciding what constitutes sexual content in films and television, on what the main moral issues are, and on questions concerning restriction or control of sexual material. Sexual content is not easy to define, largely because much is not explicit but rather depends on the context and on the viewer. In films the chief concern is pornographic material, although there is disagreement about what pornography is, and why it is objectionable, if it is. The central arguments against it are based on harm, degradation, exploitation, and offense. Offense, while it cannot be an overriding consideration, does deserve serious consideration. In the nonfilm component of television, the important moral issues arise in commercials, educational programs, and news bulletins. In commercials the primary concern is the portrayal of women, and in educational programs, the type of sexual material to which children ought to be exposed, and its effect on them. Because news bulletins deal with real events, privacy and victimization of victims of sex crimes are of paramount importance. Finally, there are strong reasons for allowing freedom of expression, even where the material is of a sexual nature.

Also See the Following Articles

CENSORSHIP • PORNOGRAPHY • VIOLENCE IN FILMS AND TELEVISION

Bibliography

Baird, R. M., & Rosenbaum, S. E. (Eds.). (1991). *Pornography: Private right or public menace?* Buffalo, NY: Prometheus Books.

Baker, R., & Elliston, F. (Eds.). (1984). *Philosophy and sex* (New Revised Edition). Buffalo, NY: Prometheus Books.

Belliotti, R. A. (1993). *Good sex: Perspectives on sexual ethics.* Lawrence: The University Press of Kansas.

Christensen, F. M. (1990). *Pornography: The other side.* New York: Praeger.

Davies, S. (1991). *Definitions of art.* Ithaca, NY: Cornell University Press.

Dines, G., & Humez, J. M. (Eds.). (1995). *Gender, race and class in media: A text reader.* Thousand Oaks, CA: Sage Publications.

Feinberg, J. (1985). *The moral limits of the criminal law. Vol. Two: Offense to others.* Oxford: Oxford University Press.

Fink, C. C. (1988). *Media ethics: In the newsroom and beyond.* New York: McGraw-Hill.

MacKinnon, C. A. (1989). *Toward a feminist theory of the state.* Cambridge: Harvard University Press.

Mill, J. S. (1975). *John Stuart Mill On Liberty: Annotated Text, sources and background criticism,* Spitz, D. (Ed.). New York: W. W. Norton & Company.

Oshima, N. (1992). *Cinema, censorship, and the state: The Writings of Nagisa Oshima 1956–1978.* Edited and with an introduction by Annette Michelson. Translated by Dawn Lawson. Cambridge: MIT Press.

Russell, D. E. H. (Ed.). (1993). *Making violence sexy: Feminist views on pornography.* Buckingham: Open University Press.

Steinem, G. (1978, November). Erotica and pornography: A clear and present difference. *Ms* magazine. Reprinted in Baurd and Rosenbaum (1991), 51–55.

West, M. I. (1988). *Children, culture and controversy.* Hamden, CT: Archon Books.

Williams, B. (1981). *Obscenity and film censorship: An abridgement of the Williams report.* Cambridge: Cambridge University Press.

Wittgenstein, L. (1968). *Philosophical Investigations.* (G. E. M. Anscombe, Trans.) Oxford: Basil Blackwell.

SEXUAL HARASSMENT

Ellen Frankel Paul
Social Philosophy and Policy Center
Bowling Green State University

GLOSSARY

civil case A case brought to remedy a wrong or enforce a right (e.g., a right to property) by one private person against another or against a company. Civil cases, thus, are distinguished from criminal proceedings. All sexual harassment cases—whether brought under Title VII or various state tort theories—are civil actions.

Civil Rights Act of 1964 The most significant civil rights legislation since Reconstruction (1865–1877) this act banned discrimination in the workplace as well as in places of public accommodation and in programs receiving federal funds.

compensatory damages Award of money in a civil, tort suit designed to recompense the victim for actual injury or harm sustained as a result of the act, omission, or negligence of the defendant.

Equal Employment Opportunity Commission (EEOC) The agency created by the Civil Rights Act of 1964 to implement, interpret, and enforce its proscription against workplace discrimination. The EEOC issued influential *Guidelines* defining discrimination by sex as including a ban on sexual harassment. This regulatory agency receives complaints of sexual harassment from employees, investigates such complaints, and attempts to resolve those it deems meritorious by conciliation or, selectively, litigation.

feminism A movement directed at achieving equality for women. Earlier in the twentieth century, feminists predominantly argued for equality of rights, and their greatest accomplishment was securing the vote for women by the passage of the Nineteenth Amendment to the United States Constitution in 1920, and by parliamentary vote in Great Britain in 1928. Beginning in the late 1960s, feminism was reinvigorated, and gradually a division emerged between equal rights feminists of the old school and a more radical branch that makes the case for women's oppression by men in a patriarchal society. Feminists are divided, also, over the issue of differences between men and women, with one faction contending that women are different and should be provided with certain dispensations as a result, and the other faction parrying that any differences are irrelevant to how society ought to treat women.

First Amendment Part of the Bill of Rights to the United States Constitution. It prohibits Congress from interfering with freedom of speech, among other prohibitions. Courts have extended the ban from just covering Congress to all federal govern-

Encyclopedia of Applied Ethics, Volume 4
Copyright © 1998 by Academic Press. All rights of reproduction in any form reserved.

ment activities and to the states, localities, and state agencies (such as state-supported universities).

Hostile environment sexual harassment Harassing conduct of a sexual nature by a supervisor or co-workers that impairs a person's job performance or emotional well-being by creating a hostile or intimidating work environment.

prima facie case The initial evidence that a plaintiff must produce that would enable him or her to prevail until refuted by the defendant. If this burden of building a prima facie case is not met, then the defendant is exculpated. If the burden is met, then the case proceeds, and the defendant must try to rebut the charges.

punitive damages Awards to victorious plaintiffs in civil, tort cases in which the defendant's behavior was egregious, malicious, fraudulent, or violent. The rationale for granting such damages above compensation for the actual loss or harm is that doing so will set an example to discourage others from engaging in similar behavior, to punish the defendant, or to compensate the plaintiff for psychic wounds.

quid pro quo sexual harassment The typical *quid pro quo* scenario involves a male supervisor who attempts to extort sexual favors from a female subordinate in exchange for employment, promotion, retention, salary enhancement, or other job benefit, and retaliates if the woman objects.

sexual harassment Unwelcome sexual advances, propositions, or conduct that is made a condition of employment, or that unreasonably interferes with a person's performance of his or her job or education, or that causes mental anguish.

strict liability In a product liability case the manufacturer of a defective, inherently dangerous product that injures a consumer is held strictly liable. Negligence need not be demonstrated. By analogy, for *quid pro quo* sexual harassment, strict liability means that an employer is held liable for the behavior of its supervisor, regardless of whether the employer knew or should have known of his (or more rarely, her) transgressions.

strict constructionist A judge or legal commentator who argues that the Constitution should be interpreted as the framers intended (including the various framers of the Bill of Rights and the later amendments). Liberal jurists, in contrast, conceive the Constitution as a living, malleable document that each generation must interpret for itself.

Title VII The section of the Civil Rights Act of 1964 that prohibits discrimination in employment based on race, color, religion, sex, or national origin. The "sex" element of this prohibition has been (since the late-1970s) interpreted by the federal courts to include a ban on sexual harassment.

Tort A civil, not criminal, wrong against person or property. A wronged individual or company may sue another person or company to recover damages for an injury or harm to person or property (other than a breach of contract). Common tort cases arise from incidents of medical malpractice, defective products that cause injury, trespass, automobile accidents, wrongful death.

SEXUAL HARASSMENT can be defined in one of two ways: the narrower definition is gender neutral, while the broader, more radical definition incorporates the concept of male domination and female subjugation. The gender neutral version is the one preferred by the Equal Employment Opportunity Commission (EEOC) in its *Guidelines on Discrimination Because of Sex* (29 C.F.R. § 1604.11 (1980)), a formulation that was destined to have great influence over the judicial development of sexual harassment theory. The EEOC defined sexual harassment as "Unwelcome sexual advances, requests for sexual favors, and other verbal or physical conduct of a sexual nature" when that conduct affects an individual's employment, or the conditions of employment, or unreasonably interferes with work performance, or creates "an intimidating, hostile, or offensive working environment." The more radical definition, one preferred by many feminists, incorporates the notion of male hegemony over women in society, and the use of that power by men in a sexual guise in the workplace to subjugate women employees. On this latter view, preserving male position and privilege is the ultimate objective, while imposing sexual conditions or abuse is the means.

I. INCUBATION PERIOD

A. Women Transform the Workplace

With the great influx of women into the workforce that began in the 1960s and continued in the decades that followed, the nature of the workplace underwent dramatic changes. While women still were vastly overrepresented in the traditionally female service occupations of nurse, secretary, and teacher, women branched out into formerly male bastions of the executive suite, the professions, the boardroom, and the factory floor.

This vast transformation in social roles and expectations occurred over a relatively short period by historical standards, and with relatively little overt confrontation. This peaceful social revolution was due in some measure to the antidiscrimination provisions of the Civil Rights Act of 1964, to the rampant inflation and the high tax regimen of the period that made a middle-class life-style all but unattainable on a one-earner paycheck, to the social dissolution of the family through divorce and illegitimacy that left single mothers the heads of households of children, and to the rise of feminism that encouraged women to seek fulfillment outside the home.

Women of the 1960s and 1970s were the trailblazers. Frequently, they were the "firsts": the "firsts" in their class at elite professional or graduate schools; the "firsts" on the municipal police force or firefighting division; the "firsts" in the coal mines or assembly lines; the "firsts" on the board of directors of a Fortune 500 corporation; the "firsts" to make partner in a Wall Street law firm; or the "firsts" to head a department at a major medical school. It was not that women had never entered these fields, for a few had, but that this new breed of women expected to exercise power, have "equal opportunity" with their male peers, and bring waves of their sisters in their wake.

Sexual harassment is also a concern in countries other than the United States, in which it was first recognized in the law. In a study on the problem published in 1993 and conducted in 23 industrialized countries, the International Labor Organization (ILO) found that 7 countries—Australia, Canada, France, New Zealand, Spain, Sweden, and the Unites States—had laws directly aimed at combating sexual harassment in the workplace, while the other countries dealt with it indirectly through statutes on unfair dismissal. Surveys from the countries, which varied in technique and definition of the term, found that women in varying numbers said that they had experienced sexual harassment, ranging from a high of 74% in Great Britain to a low of 21% in France. The ILO expects that future studies in developing countries will find more serious problems than those found in the industrialized nations.

B. Early Feminists Identify Sexual Harassment

Gradually, it became increasingly unfashionable for men to express overt opposition to women's employment and advancement, and any such expression became potentially costly should a disappointed female applicant or disgruntled employee bring suit for sex discrimination. It was, perhaps, inevitable that the tensions inherent in this social change would take on a more reclusive, insidious form. By the mid-1970s feminists began writing about sexual harassment in the workplace and the university, two conspicuous arenas in which men and women met each other on an unequal battlefield, where males felt their power ebbing, and where opportunities for sexual predation were ever more abundant.

Three influential books helped shape the future debate over sexual harassment, both in public discourse and in the courts. The first, written by law professor Catharine A. MacKinnon (1979), *Sexual Harassment of Working Women: A Case of Sex Discrimination*, vigorously argued for a novel position: that sexual harassment should be incorporated into the Civil Rights Act of 1964's Title VII that prohibited sex discrimination in the workplace. Heretofore, that prohibition had been understood to mean that the same criteria of selection, advancement, compensation, and benefits must be applied to female workers as to their male counterparts. MacKinnon's approach came with a good deal of ideological accouterments, for she viewed sexual harassment as a metaphor for a capitalist system rife with exploitation. "Economic power is to sexual harassment as physical force is to rape," she declared. The class conflict that drove traditional Marxian analyses of the defects of capitalism mutated in MacKinnon's writings into clashing male and female sexes, with men imposing a "group injury" of sexual harassment on women, because they are women and not because of their individual and unique qualities. Men control women's sexuality and capital controls women's employment, and the two are intertwined. "Prostitution and marriage as well as sexual harassment in different ways institutionalize this arrangement," and women throughout history have been forced to exchange sexual favors for material survival, according to MacKinnon. The core of MacKinnon's argument—that a woman fired for refusing sexual favors is really fired because she is a woman, not because of her particular sexual allure—would soon receive judicial recognition and acceptance.

Although MacKinnon's work was the most influential, two other books of the period also contributed to the fashioning of sexual harassment as a key element of feminist philosophy: L. Farley's (1978) *Sexual Shakedown: The Sexual Harassment of Women on the Job*, and B. W. Dziech and L. Weiner's (1984) *The Lecherous Professor: Sexual Harassment on Campus*.

C. Sexual Harassment's Defining Moment

Sexual harassment would have been just one of many feminist issues—like date rape, pornography, or comparable worth—had it not been for a seminal event in 1991 that galvanized the media and the public in a way that some commentators analogized to the Salem witch trials of the late 1600s. Surely, women had publicly complained of sexual harassment prior to 1991, had filed complaints with the EEOC, and had brought suit in the courts, but nothing that had transpired compared to the spotlight placed on the issue by the nomination of Clarence Thomas to the Supreme Court. Nominations to the federal bench by Republican presidents had previously been highly controversial, dating back to the Nixon Administration. During the second term of the Reagan Administration Judge Robert Bork's nomination to the high Court had met with fierce opposition and ultimate defeat on the floor of the Senate. Other strict-constructionist nominees to lower federal courts had also succumbed. Yet, nothing that preceded the Clarence Thomas hearings before the Democratically controlled Senate Judiciary Committee would forewarn President Bush of the maelstrom that his nominee would face. The Senate's constitutionally mandated advise and consent power would take on bizarre dimensions when a Republican administration's conservative nominee triggered the worst ideological fears of a Senate controlled by liberal Democrats.

Thomas had recently been confirmed by the Senate for a judgeship on the District of Columbia Appeals Court, and the hearings on that nomination had not garnered liberal opposition of the sort that had accompanied other conservative nominees. The stakes, however, were much higher when the prize was a crucial seat on a Supreme Court riven by ideological division. With the resignation of associate justice Thurgood Marshall, a Black civil rights leader before his elevation to the Court and a strong liberal voice once on the bench, pressure mounted on the president to select a minority candidate to fill Marshall's shoes. Immediately upon Thomas's selection, leading Democrats in the Senate, their staffs, and liberal interest groups—all of whom had been clamoring for a minority appointee—went on the attack. Although Thomas is an African American, they discerned in him none of the ideological commitments that they found so appealing in Justice Marshall. Thomas had served as assistant secretary for civil rights in the Department of Education and chairman of the EEOC during the Reagan years, and was now sitting on the most influential of the federal appeals courts. In each of these capacities he had not endeared himself to liberal opinion makers.

Thomas's qualifications for ascension to the Supreme Court were scrutinized by media pundits, and found wanting. Character issues were raised, including trivial ones, such as his alleged penchant for attending pornographic movies while a Yale law student. The coalition of activist groups that had come together to defeat the Bork nomination were less effective at the outset against Thomas because of the initial reluctance by some civil rights groups to oppose a Black nominee. Nevertheless, a loosely knit coalition—comprised of women's groups (such as the National Organization of Women and the National Abortion Rights Action League), broadly based liberal activist groups (People for the American Way), and some civil rights organizations (the National Leadership Conference on Civil Rights, the Alliance for Justice, and later the National Association of Colored People)—did coalesce in opposition.

During eight days of hearings before the Senate Judiciary Committee, Judge Thomas attempted to palliate his conservative image, fearful perhaps of repeating Bork's supposed mistake of cantankerously defending all of his discordant views. Waffling on such "hot-button" issues as abortion, Thomas denied that he had ever discussed the issue or held a firm position on it, a tactic met with skepticism or derision by his opponents. On other contentious issues and Court cases, Thomas reverted to the pre-Bork tradition of simply refusing to comment on the grounds that the issues might confront him as a Supreme Court justice, and he must not prejudge such matters.

Despite this less than stellar performance, one that managed to both dishearten his enthusiasts for lack of a vigorous defense and infuriate his detractors, the committee on a tie vote along party lines (with Democratic Chairman Biden voting with the Republicans) passed the nomination to the full Senate without recommendation. The Senate deliberated on October 3, and a vote was scheduled for five days later. Expectations were that the vote would be a squeaker, but that Thomas would be confirmed.

A grenade was about to be launched that would explode this prediction and embarrass the nominee, the Senate Judiciary Committee, and the White House. Unbeknownst to all but a few key Senate leaders and committee members, a little-known University of Oklahoma law professor, who had worked with Thomas as a special assistant at the Department of Education and then followed him to the EEOC, had lodged a confidential complaint to the committee months before, alleging that Thomas had sexually harassed her. On October 6, just two days before the final Senate vote was scheduled, reporters for *Newsday* and National Public Radio's "Weekend Edition" broke the story. Professor Anita Hill held a news conference the following day, in which she aired her allegations against Judge Thomas. She avowed that during her tenure with Thomas, he had made numerous sexually explicit comments to her about X-rated movies and had asked her repeatedly for dates, despite her refusals. Skeptics found it implausible that the very man who as chairman of the EEOC had promulgated expansive guidelines on sexual harassment and had urged a reluctant Reagan Administration to support them before the Supreme Court, would commit just such ribald behavior.

Public disclosure of Hill's confidential complaint caused such consternation in the Senate, among the activist groups opposing Thomas's nomination, and in the media that the nominee requested a delay in the vote, and the Judiciary Committee was granted by the Senate another week to investigate the charges. Three days of public hearings ensued, and the nation was riveted to its television screens for what became a "teach-in" on sexual harassment. Judge Thomas denied all of Professor Hill's charges, maintaining that he was tormented and mystified by them. Their interactions, on Thomas's account, had been strictly professional, a mentoring relationship in which he had often acted to promote her career. Hill's testimony followed, filled with salacious and lurid details, imperturbably recounted. On one occasion, she claimed, Thomas queried her about "Who had put pubic hair on my Coke," on other occasions he referred to his larger-than-normal penis and to the pleasures of oral sex, and on still others he commented on the pornographic movie star Long Dong Silver.

In an evening coda to the first day's hearings, Judge Thomas reappeared to again deny all charges. He startled the committee and the nation by declaring that he had not bothered to listen to Hill's testimony. Taking the initiative, in a stratagem that opponents would later denounce as playing the "race card," he compared the proceedings to a "high-tech lynching for uppity blacks who in any way deign to think for themselves. . . ." The next day Thomas returned for six hours of grilling by the committee, and Hill countered that she would be taking a lie detector test the following day, but the tide had turned in Thomas's favor, with public support running for him 2 to 1. When the dust settled in the early hours of October 14—after all of the testimonials to Thomas's sterling character by his former female underlings, and after Hill's friends' attempts at hearsay support for her charges—neither side had provided witnesses to the alleged events, decisive proof, or a "smoking gun."

Elite opinion fervently supported Hill, condemning American society as riddled with harassment of women and sexual exploitation. Public opinion at the time seemed extraordinarily impervious to media instruction, but polls a year after the hearings showed that public perceptions had shifted, with Hill reaching parity or slightly ahead of Thomas in believability. Commentators attributed the shift to the continued barrage of support for Hill in the media. In the immediate aftermath of the hearings, Thomas was confirmed to the high Court on a 52–48 Senate vote, historically the slimmest margin of victory.

Sexual harassment for the near future is destined to be associated in the public consciousness with the Hill–Thomas hearings. Although a striking departure from the prototypical sexual harassment allegation that might lead to an EEOC complaint or a lawsuit—because the incidents transpired a decade before Hill's charges were aired, and the venue was a Senate committee hearing televised throughout the nation—the drama heightened awareness of the issue. After the hearings, grievances filed with the EEOC in 1992 on sexual harassment grounds mushroomed by 50%. The workplace seemed preternaturally plagued by sexual predators.

In Section II, we will examine the legal framework for sexual harassment, and it will be apparent just how extraordinary the Hill affair was. Yet despite these aberrations, the Hill–Thomas proceedings do display in a most striking way problems that are endemic to the typical charge of sexual harassment. Often witnesses to the alleged events are nonexistent: because of the very nature of the act, it is likely to occur behind closed doors, especially when a supervisor is the perpetrator. Without eyewitnesses to the harassment, the accuser may try to establish a pattern of sexual harassment of other women (as the Hill contingent unsuccessfully attempted when a disgruntled female former employee declined to testify). The accused must then demonstrate that no such pattern existed (as Thomas and his female witnesses maintained). Usually, the accused vociferously denies that the incidents ever transpired, or at most concedes that they occurred but were misinterpreted or blown out of proportion by the female employee. Frequently, the tables are turned and the character of the accuser is made the issue, much as the Republican senators on the Judiciary Committee scrutinized Hill's background, and inconsistencies in her story, in an attempt to discredit her. Likewise, the possible motives of the woman for bringing such charges are frequently probed, just as Hill's Republican interrogators suggested, variously, that she might have been a disgruntled would-be lover, that she perhaps took offense at Thomas's selection of a White woman as his wife, or that Hill might have been pursuing a political agenda in league with Democratic staffers and interest-group liberals.

More globally, critics of Hill suggested that the Senate Judiciary Committee farce was a good barometer of just how expansive the notion of sexual harassment had become under the tutelage of feminist activists. These challengers suggest that even if Hill's allegations against Thomas were true, they amounted to little more than social obtuseness in repeatedly importuning a reluctant female for dates, and to a propensity to tell off-color jokes. Thomas did not stand accused of extorting sexual favors for promotion, nor did he retaliate in any way when his overtures were rebuffed—the classical scenario for the most flagrant form of sexual harassment. Nor, apparently, did Thomas's actions amount to the other form of sexual harassment recognized in the law: for he did not create such an oppressive environment that Hill's working conditions were made unbearable, since she followed him on his ascending career path to the EEOC. Critics condemn the trend in the courts and society to expand the definition of sexual harassment to cover complaints of Hill's sort. Thus, they find the Hill–Thomas hearings exceedingly disturbing.

D. The Aftermath of the Hill–Thomas Imbroglio

The Hill–Thomas hearings proved to be the defining moment for sexual harassment, and in the afterglow Congress passed the Civil Rights Act of 1991, and President Bush signed it a mere five weeks after Hill's charges were aired. The act made available for the first time full compensatory damages and punitive damages (although capped) to successful plaintiffs in federal sexual harassment suits. Perhaps, fickle public opinion would have rapidly moved on to other mesmerizing issues, but several scandals ensued in rapid succession to keep the embers red-hot. In June 1992, a female Navy lieutenant, Paula Coughlin, went to the press with revelations of a rowdy "gauntlet" of drunken, groping airmen that she was forced to pass through when she made a wrong turn down a hallway at the Tailhook Association's September 1991 convention in a Las Vegas hotel. Claiming that the Navy had ignored her complaint, Coughlin's charges, augmented by similar allegations from other female attendees, reverberated through the media for two years.

Ultimately, the failure to properly investigate the charges would cost the Secretary of the Navy and several admirals their jobs. A federal jury would later award the lieutenant $1.7 million in compensatory damages and $5 million in punitive damages for inadequate security from the hotel that hosted the convention. In a pretrial settlement, she also received $400,000 from the Tailhook Association. On appeal, the hotel succeeded in reducing its liability to $1.3 million in compensatory and $3.9 million in punitive damages.

Sexual harassment complaints against three United States senators also stirred the embers. Republican Senator Packwood of Oregon, a long-standing supporter of "women's issues" and ally of women's activist groups, was forced to resign for "groping" several former female employees. To cap off the trend of charges of sexual harassment against politicians, President Clinton was accused of sexually harassing a female Arkansas state employee at a business convention while he served as governor.

The philanthropic world was not immune from sexual harassment charges, either. The minister who headed the National Association for the Advancement of Colored People (NAACP) was forced to resign over a 1993 incident. His female former deputy of a month's duration threatened to sue him for sexual harassment, and he used NAACP funds of over $300,000 to persuade her to desist. These national scandals were augmented by localized ones throughout the nation.

Another sexual harassment charge that garnered much media attention came in April of 1996, when Mitsubishi Motor Manufacturing of America became the target of an EEOC lawsuit. The EEOC charged that Mitsubishi's Japanese managers had failed to remedy and had contributed to a sexually infused *hostile environment* endured by some 500 female employees. The EEOC's announcement of its huge class-action suit met with unaccustomed opposition from the company and many Mitsubishi employees, including women. Not all women took the atmosphere at the plant in Illinois so lightly, and a group of 30 women later filed a separate suit against the company, complaining of degrading comments, grabbing, fondling, dirty tricks, sexual graffiti, nude photographs, demands for sexual acts, and management training that included trips to Japan where managers were entertained at "audience participation bars." In an unusual and highly visible move, the company initially encouraged its workers to organize a day of protest against the charges, a show of resistance rarely displayed by corporations under fire from the EEOC, and short-lived.

II. THE LEGAL BACKGROUND

A. Sexual Harassment as Sex Discrimination: The Early Quid Pro Quo Cases

In the federal courts, sexual harassment suits are now an accepted cause of action under Title VII of the Civil Rights Act of 1964's prohibition against employment discrimination on the basis of sex. Although initially, back in the mid-1970s, federal judges were reluctant to include sexual harassment charges as a legitimate component of this ban, this view rapidly succumbed to changing times and attitudes. Judges who heard the early cases found even the typical quid pro quo scenario—in which someone holding a supervisory role over an employee attempts to exact or actually exacts sexual favors in return for hiring, promotion, or other job-related benefits—suspect as a Title VII transgression. They recalled that the element of sex discrimination itself was added to Title VII in a peculiar way. It was appended as an amendment to the 1964 Civil Rights Act on the proposal of a Southern congressman who was more interested in sabotaging the whole piece of legislation as racial engineering than in promoting the equality of women. The congressman hoped that adding sex to the list of attributes that could no longer count in employment decisions would serve as a "poison pill," felling the bill. Thus, enlarging the sex discrimination component by reading into it a further ban on harassment on the basis of sex seemed fairly remote from legislative intent, something judges try to discern from the language of an act or from its legislative history. In this instance, the language was cryptic, and expressions of legislative intent nonexistent. If nothing of substance had been provided by Congress to assist the courts in interpreting Title VII's sex discrimination proscription, surely legislators had not intended to have it interpreted as making a federal offense out of sexual excesses in the workplace.

The early judges were troubled, too, by the structure of liability built into Title VII— which required that employers be held responsible for the transgressions of their supervisory employees. Holding employers liable for the sexual peccadilloes of managers just did not seem appropriate, since these judges viewed harassing overtures as essentially personal matters, which should be litigated if at all by the victims suing the perpetrators, not their employers. A case decided in 1975, *Corne v. Bausch & Lomb* (390 F. Supp. 161 (D. Ariz.)), is representative of the initial cases. The plaintiffs were two women who claimed that they had been forced to resign when their supervisor's sexual propositions became unbearable. The presiding judge reflected on previous Title VII sex discrimination cases that had raised issues of objectionable employment practices that "arose out of company policies": job assignments; fringe benefits; pregnancy restrictions; bans on the employment of married women. This novel complaint differed, he argued, because the "conduct appears to be nothing more than a personal proclivity, peculiarity or mannerism...." Rather than the company having benefited in any way from an employment policy, the employer itself "can only be damaged by the very nature of the acts complained of." Furthermore, a supervisor could in theory direct sexual advances equally against men and women, and then gender would not be a relevant factor, and the offensive acts would not be sex discrimination under Title VII. Other judges would echo this refrain, finding the gender of the parties "incidental to the claim of abuse."

The *Corne* judge evinced irritation with the complaints of the two women, writing that it was "ludicrous" to assume that Title VII was designed to cover such incidents. Another judge, as late as 1984, would remark that the inclusion of sex discrimination itself in Title VII was a "joke." With such views persisting, it is not surprising that the first judges who heard sexual harassment cases were not sympathetic to enlarging Title VII with claims of a personal nature. They thought such claims should more properly be treated as state court torts (i.e., claims for compensation for personal injury). In all of these initial cases, the presiding judges feared that if they decided to recognize sexual harassment as a component of Title VII sex discrimination, the floodgates would be opened. The federal bench would be inundated with frivolous claims every time someone was offended by a maladroit sexual advance.

The wall of rejection of sexual harassment claims was breached for the first time in 1976, the year after *Corne* was decided. *Williams v. Saxbe* (413 F. Supp. 654 (D.D.C.)) found a district court judge in the nation's capital sympathetic to the plight of a woman who was fired after she declined the sexual overtures of a supervisor. Contradicting *Corne*, the judge contended that sexual harassment was indeed gender-related, since it created an employment "rule" in the nature of an artificial barrier to the employment of one gender but not the other. Rejected, also, was the *Corne* claim that the offensive behavior was not a policy of the employer, but merely the personal peccadillo of one supervisor: "If this was a policy or practice of plaintiff's supervisor, then it was the agency's policy or practice, which is prohibited by Title VII."

Williams adumbrated the new course that other courts would speedily emulate. In short order, it became accepted doctrine that quid pro quo sexual harassment is indeed an element of Title VII's proscribed sexual discrimination in the workplace. Charges are litigated under what is called the "disparate treatment" model for employment discrimination suits. "Disparate treatment" is one prong of a two-pronged approach that the federal courts have adopted for assessing Title VII employment discrimination claims. Plaintiffs lodging "disparate treatment" claims must show that an employer, through its stated policies or its practices, *intentionally* discriminated against them. A plaintiff must first establish a prima facie case by showing that she is a woman, that she was subject to unwelcome sexual harassment, that this harassment was based on her sex, that it affected a term or condition of employment, and that her employer is liable. If this burden is met, then the employer proceeds to rebut the charges. Typically, in rebutting a sexual harassment charge, the employer claims that the employee was dismissed, passed over for a promotion, or denied a raise not for refusing sexual overtures, but for work-related deficiencies. Finally, the employee is given the opportunity to refute the employer's justification. Courts follow the EEOC *Guidelines* in holding employers strictly liable for quid pro quo sexual harassment, of a worker by a supervisor. Strict liability means that no negligence on the part of the employer need be proved, nor must it be shown that the employer knew of the harassing behavior. (The other prong of Title VII employment discrimination analysis, not relevant here, is called "disparate impact," and it is aimed at ferreting out practices and policies that seem fair on their face, but in actual operation serve to discriminate against women or minorities: e.g., employment tests; high school graduation requirements; pregnancy leave rules.)

B. Hostile Environment Sexual Harassment Finds Acceptance

When the courts would later come to accept another variant of sexual harassment, *hostile environment*, as falling within the purview of Title VII sex discrimination, it too would be scrutinized under the "disparate treatment" mechanism. A 1981 case, *Bundy v. Jackson* (640 F. 2d 934 (D.C. Cir.)), was the first to recognize the legitimacy of hostile environment sexual harassment, analogizing it to the racial hostile environment model first articulated a decade earlier by the Fifth Circuit appeals court. In cases of both sorts, courts find that psychological and emotional aspects of the work environment can be tainted by harassment and amount to Title VII race or sex discrimination. Hostile environment sexual harassment covers circumstances in which either a supervisor or co-worker(s) makes the victim's working environment so traumatic that she (or rarely, he) suffers ill effects or resigns. If perpetrated by a supervisor, the hostile environment claim does not require the extortion of sexual favors for job benefits. The supervisor, or the co-worker(s), might have besieged the woman with unwelcome sexual advances, teasing, salacious jokes, flaunting of male bodily parts, or even displays of pinups. The harassment complained of must reach a threshold of being "sufficiently pervasive," so that not just the occasional off-color jest qualifies.

Employers are offered a bit more protection in hostile environment, co-worker cases than in their quid pro quo cousins, in that strict liability is not imposed in the former as it is in the latter. Rather, a knowledge standard is utilized for liability to arise, so that the employer must have been informed of the harassing conduct and must have failed to take adequate remedial action, or the conduct must have been so pervasive that the employer is presumed to have known of it. The legal landscape is still a bit unsettled on which standard should be applied to employers when their supervisors commit hostile environment offenses, whether the strict liability standard from quid pro quo or the looser knowledge standard applied to co-workers who create a hostile environment. This uncertainty persists, despite the Supreme Court's first and belated foray into sexual harassment adjudication. In *Meritor Savings Bank v. Vinson* (477 U.S. 57 (1986)), the Court sanctified the results of years of lower court creativity by agreeing that hostile environment sexual harassment is sex discrimination under Title VII when it is "sufficiently severe or pervasive 'to alter conditions of employment and create an abusive working environment." The *Meritor* Court declined to settle the liability dispute over the proper standard for supervisors who create hostile environments, for they found the facts in the case too inconclusive to propound a "definitive rule." The EEOC's *Guidelines* for hostile environment sexual harassment, however, impose a strict liability standard for supervisors and a knowledge or constructive knowledge (i.e., should have known) standard for co-workers.

C. Summary

As judges created sexual harassment as an element of Title VII's prohibited sex discrimination, they distinguished between two types of offensive behavior: (1) quid pro quo—that of supervisors who extort sexual favors from female (or occasionally male) employees in return for job security or benefits, retaliate if spurned, and cause the victim economic hardship; and (2) hostile environment—that of supervisors or co-workers who through their sex-tinged behavior offend the victim and cause her (or occasionally him) psychological, physical, or emotional damage. Employers in quid pro quo scenarios are held liable for the offenses of their supervisors on a strict liability standard; employers are held to a knowledge or constructive knowledge standard for co-workers who create a hostile environment; and employers of supervisors who commit hostile environment offenses are held to either a strict liability or a knowledge/constructive knowledge standard, depending upon the jurisdiction. In Section III.C, several of the most controversial elements in this sexual harassment paradigm will be discussed.

III. CONTROVERSIES: THE SOCIAL, LEGAL, AND PHILOSOPHICAL ISSUES

A. The Critics' Concerns

Sexual harassment, after quickly overcoming initial skepticism, rapidly gained acceptance in the legal community as a Title VII breach. Yet academic critics persist in raising most of the same issues that the early judges found questionable when they doubted that sexual harassment fell within the purview of Title VII sex discrimination. Beyond legal disputations, social critics raise doubts of a wider scope, fearing that a too zealous passion for ferreting out offensive sexual conduct in the workplace, university, and other venues might stifle healthy and perfectly harmless flirtations or flattery that make life enjoyable. They fear, too, that in our efforts to extirpate obnoxious behavior, but behavior that falls short of the extortionist, quid pro quo type, feminists and those they influence may have gone too far, with the result that innocent behavior has come to be seen as aberrant and culpable. Especially troubling to these critics were two separate incidents in late 1996 in which a six-year-old and a seven-year-old were punished by their school districts for committing sexual harassment when they kissed female classmates.

It should be noted that critics of both the legal paradigm and the social effects of an activist pursuit of sexual harassment agree that there really is such a thing as sexual harassment, that it ought to be considered reprehensible, and that it should be legally actionable in clear-cut cases. The sorts of behavior that they include in their narrower conception is of the archetypical quid pro quo variety, that is, when a supervisor in the workplace or a professor in the university uses his (or her) position of authority to extort sexual favors under threat of reprisal for obstinacy. Critics are usually willing to concede, in addition, that a workplace that is so infused with sexual threats or abusive behavior that it makes an individual's work environment genuinely intolerable should fall within the framework of sexual harassment. Beyond this, however, they display deep skepticism.

Critics of both types are dubious about polls that purport to demonstrate that a large percentage of women (and a smaller but measurable percentage of men) experience sexual harassment on the job as a regular occurrence. Such studies, they contend, fail to define sexual harassment, leaving it to the imagination of the respondents to interpret it in any manner from an off-color jest, to an offensive look, to a pinup, to a promise of promotion at the price of sexual intercourse, and even to rape. This broadbrush approach produces inflated and, hence, meaningless statistics. Thus, cynicism is their reaction to studies like the one conducted in 1994 among federal government employees by the United States Merit Systems Protection Board (*Sexual Harassment in the Federal Workplace: Trends, Progress, Continuing Challenges.* Washington, DC: U.S. Government Printing Office). The board found that despite 87% of supervisors and 77% of government workers having received training in the recognition and prevention of sexual harassment, and the promulgation of policies prohibiting sexual harassment by all federal agencies, no significant decrease had occurred since 1987. Still in 1994, 44% of women claimed victim status, as did 14% of their male colleagues. Polls conducted by other organizations have discerned harassment levels as high as 80% among female workers, and wide disparities between the results attained in different studies is the norm. With such extreme variability in results, critics wonder exactly what is being measured, and they speculate that activists are finding exactly what they need as ammunition to promote their cause.

We shall now turn to the views of the social critics who demur from current trends in the extirpation of sexual harassment, and then to the critics of the legal framework, and finally to the philosophical critics. Occasionally, responses from supporters are presented, but their concerns will be discussed more fully in Section IV.

B. Social Criticisms

Anita Hill's charges against Clarence Thomas, as examined in Section I.C, personify the social critics' forebodings of what society might look like if ferreting out sexual harassment becomes an all-consuming pursuit. Undocumented charges, unwitnessed by others, and emerging from someone's distant past at his most public and vulnerable moment, are for them a frightening prospect. Where feminists see in the Hill–Thomas spectacle justice at least attempted, if hardly vindicated, the critics see ideological excess run amuck and a dignified and courageous man's reputation irreparably sullied.

1. Sexual Harassment Charges after the Hill–Thomas Hearings

Beyond the Hill–Thomas imbroglio, critics focus upon other recent instances in which men were charged with behavior that critics might characterize as churlish or socially inept, but not deserving of career termination or legal action. In a 1995 federal district court case in Kansas, the court upheld the firing of two managers, one for purchasing and presenting, and the other for making lewd remarks about, a dildo presented to a female employee as a gag gift at the suggestion of another woman co-worker. The recipient did not complain to Boeing Co., their employer, but a third manager did. The two managers were fired, the manager who informed was disciplined, as were the two women. The court was unsympathetic to the two managers' complaint of reverse discrimination for being treated more harshly than the others. The two managers had, just two months before, attended a sexual harassment seminar, stressing that managers must not tolerate sexually explicit material in the workplace. The firing, the court outcome, and the necessity to bring the issue before a federal court in the first place, is seen by the critics as overkill.

The university setting has been a fertile field for charges of sexual harassment, dismissals, and countersuits by disciplined or discharged professors, and the critics find much to be concerned by in several incidents that occurred in the mid-1990s. Much of the impetus for combating sexual harassment on campus comes from Title IX of the Education Act Amendments of 1972. Title IX includes a ban on sex discrimination akin to the one in the Civil Rights Act's Title VII. Litigation under Title IX has been less abundant and interpretation less developed than under Title VII, but courts have applied similar standards. With the growing influence of feminists on American campuses, it is not surprising that awareness of and sometimes near panic about sexual harassment has gripped many universities. Critics lament the misfortunes of several male professors who have fallen victim to this heightened scrutiny. J. Donald Silva, a tenured professor of creative writing at a branch of the University of New Hampshire, was suspended from teaching and instructed to undergo psychiatric counseling for a classroom incident that triggered complaints from a handful of female students. Professor Silva made two remarks to his class: one involving belly dancing and Jell-O and the other, sex and writing. Explaining similes to his students, the professor offered as an example: "Belly dancing is like Jell-O on a plate—with a vibrator under the plate"; explaining the idea of focus in writing, he said, "Focus is like sex....You move from side to side....You and the subject become one." In a 1993 suit filed by the professor seeking vindication, the university agreed that the remarks were not profane or intimidating, and that they served an educational purpose. The university contended, nevertheless, that they created a "hostile environment." Freedom of speech, the professor's lawyers responded, was jeopardized by the university's harsh reprisals against the professor for speech that ought to be within the protection of the First Amendment.

Another case that achieved notoriety emanated from Cornell University in 1994, when a popular psychology professor of 31 years' service, and documentary film maker, James B. Maas, was charged by four former students with sexual harassment. The charges came a year after Maas had been named by the student newspaper as the best professor at the university. The women, all of whom had graduated, complained of events six or seven years earlier: two claimed that he had made sexually suggestive comments and kissed them; one maintained that he had given her expensive gifts; and the fourth claimed that he had grabbed her breast on a film trip. Professor Maas contended that he had merely behaved in a friendly fashion, as was his customary manner of social interaction. The women either assisted Maas on his film crews, in his labs, or as a nanny for his children. The professor, by all accounts, was an affectionate person who lavished personal attention and small gifts on many students and acquaintances. Some of the alleged incidents occurred in front of his wife and family. A law professor who aided Maas likened the faculty panel that disciplined him to "a Massachusetts witch trial." The panel recommended that the university rescind a $25,000 award for teaching excellence and fire him if he were found guilty of the same offense in the future. The university decided to freeze his salary for one year. The Center for Individual Rights, a civil libertarian group that represented both Maas and Silva, brought suit. The Center complained: that the charges were handled in a prejudicial manner; that the professor who reviewed the complaints pronounced Maas guilty before the hearing; that his "friendly advisor," permitted by the university's rules, was barred from speaking during the hearings; and that Maas was banished from the room when his accusers testified and he was not permitted to question them. The American Association of University Professors raised similar concerns about lack of academic due process in the way the charges were handled, and the university has since changed its procedures by placing responsibility for investigating complaints with administrators rather than faculty. A New York State judge, in September 1996, dismissed six of the eight counts brought by Maas in his $1.5 million suit against the university, but allowed two of the charges relating to the university's alleged negligence in handling the case.

2. Poisoned Social Atmosphere

Social critics discern in cases such as those of Professors Silva and Maas a chilling effect on normal human relationships. They fear that men must self-censor themselves or face potential ruin for the slightest remark, the merest "My, don't you look nice today." Even the most discreet male, who never violates the new "politically correct" social norms, could still fall prey to sexual harassment charges brought by a disgruntled female associate denied promotion or a vengeful former employee fired for work-related cause. The seemingly unrestricted "statute of limitations" on sexual harassment complaints lodged with university tribunals, the failure to accord rudimentary due process rights to the accused, the vagueness of the charges, the leaks to the press that undermine confidentiality, and the fact that the accused were never informed by their accusers that their actions were offensive at the time they occurred, are all features of the Maas, Silva, and other episodes that the critics find extremely distressing.

3. Heightened Monetary Awards and the Proliferation of Sexual Harassment Complaints

Critics suspect that much of the increase in sexual harassment complaints to the EEOC and the courts since 1991 is due to avariciousness, rather than to an explosion in harassing behavior. Substantial monetary rewards are now available for those whose sexual harassment charges are vindicated in the courts, especially since the Civil Rights Act of 1991 expanded remedies available under federal civil rights law. No longer are victorious plaintiffs restricted to receiving just back pay, reinstatement, or promotion. Recovery now includes compensatory damages and, more importantly, punitive damages (see Glossary for explanations of these terms). Although capped at a maximum of $300,000 for the largest employers, with the addition of state charges under various tort theories or state laws, the final figure can be quite substantial. For example, the FBI in January 1995 settled for $297,500 a sexual harassment suit brought against it by a female special agent, exceeding two earlier settlements the previous May for $192,500 and $155,000. In another well-publicized case brought by a legal secretary against the largest law firm in the country and one of its partners, a jury awarded the victorious plaintiff $6.9 million in punitive damages from the firm and $225,000 from its partner. Later, a California Superior Court reduced the $6.9 million amount to $3.5 million, finding that the jury's award of punitive damages at a rate 138 times compensatory damages of $50,000 was excessive. The woman had charged that the partner grabbed her breast and put M & M's in her shirt pocket, and then held her arms behind her back and demanded to know which of her breasts was larger. In yet another California state court case, Chevron Corporation agreed in February 1995 to settle, in the amount of $2.2 million, plus court costs and attorneys' fees, a sexual harassment charge brought by four women employees. Such large awards are still atypical. "Nuisance suits" are often settled for a lot less, in the $25,000 range, when employers decide that it is less costly and time consuming to settle rather than incur the large and unpredictable costs of lengthy litigation. Critics wonder whether those who suffer slight injuries might not be tempted to pursue their claims with the prospect of "hitting the jackpot," or at worst picking up the $25,000 consolation prize.

According to a study of EEOC records by the Center for Women in Government at the State University of New York at Albany (Spring 1994, "Women in Public Service" bulletin), between 1992 and 1993 total awards in sexual harassment cases handled by the EEOC doubled. Monetary damages of $25.2 million were won by 1546 individuals. The researchers attributed the increase in the number of complaints filed with the EEOC and the money awarded to two factors: the publicity surrounding Anita Hill's charges against Judge Thomas; and the enhanced recovery options introduced by the Civil Rights Act of 1991. Charges filed with the EEOC on sexual harassment grounds increased 112% between 1989 and 1993.

C. Critics of the Legal Framework

1. Title VII: A Poor Fit

Critics of the current Title VII paradigm for treating sexual harassment as an element of the banned sex discrimination in employment find many defects in the model. The analysis given by Judge Robert Bork, when he served on the Court of Appeals for the District of Columbia, in a dissent in *Vinson v. Taylor* (760 F. 2d 1330 (D. C. Circuit 1985) is representative. Judge Bork favored the line of argumentation propounded in the earliest sexual harassment cases. "Congress was not thinking of individual harassment at all," he wrote, "but of discrimination in conditions of employment because of gender," when it legislated Title VII. Classification of sexual overtures as discrimination seemed an awkward fit to him, particularly when he contemplated two previous cases in which his court had remarked that Title VII does not bar sexual harassment by a bisexual supervisor if that person demands sexual services from both males and females. It seemed anomalous to him that a predator who preys upon men and women equally would be beyond Title VII, yet one who preferred victims of one sex or the other would fall afoul of the law. Conceding that sexual harassment is objectionable, he nevertheless concluded that "Title VII was passed to outlaw discriminatory behavior and not simply behavior of which we strongly disapprove."

2. Homosexual Sexual Harassment and the Meaning of Discrimination

While same-sex sexual harassment may be well settled as a Title VII offense in the D.C. circuit, it is still controversial in the federal bench at large, with the courts divided over whether such harassment falls under the purview of Title VII sex discrimination. The trend seems to be in the direction of accepting the subsumption. Courts that find suspect the inclusion of homosexual propositions or a hostile environment due to homosexual teasing or advances, typically focus on the absence of "discriminatory hostility." To prevail on a hostile environment claim, employees would have to show that they perceived the workplace as hostile because they were men or women, not just because they were uncomfortable with homosexuality or with displays of homosexual pictures. Other courts have taken a different view, accepting the argument that homosexual harassment is harassment on the basis of sex, and thus subsumable under Title VII. A federal district court in Tennessee took precisely this view, arguing that but for the male victim's sex he would not have been the recipient of harassment by his homosexual supervisor, and in May 1995 a jury awarded the male employee $1.6 million in punitive damages and $75,000 in compensatory damages.

At the state level, too, some state courts have accepted this argument, and they have included homosexual advances under state law. In California, for example, the courts have entertained such litigation under the California Fair Employment and Housing Act, which bans discrimination on the basis of sex in the workplace and the housing market.

Critics, naturally, find the arguments of the judges who demur on homosexual harassment as sex discrimination to be most compelling. The arguments of these judges crystallize for the skeptics one of their main objections to treating sexual harassment as a Title VII offense: demanding sexual favors in exchange for job perks or tormenting co-workers with sexual innuendoes just does not seem to them close enough to discrimination. By "discrimination" they understand the sorts of racial practices that barred African Americans from the lunch counters of the segregationist South, that made them sit in the back of the bus, and that denied them the ballot. By "sex discrimination," in particular, they recall practices that prevented women from entering certain occupations by licensure laws, that excluded women from elite graduate schools, and that paid women less than men for performing the same job. Preying on women for sexual favors in the workplace is not an employment policy of an employer, they reason, and thus, it is not the sort of thing that Title VII was designed to remedy. (For a detailed philosophical analysis of the arguments for and against subsuming sexual harassment under sex discrimination see: Le Moncheck, L., & Hajdin, M. (1997), *Sexual Harassment: A Debate*. Totowa, NJ: Rowman & Littlefield). Of course, supporters of the Title VII paradigm have a ready response: that because women in overwhelming numbers are the victims of sexual predation, Title VII can be logically extended to encompass such job impediments.

3. Remedying the Defects in the Title VII Paradigm

For the reasons adumbrated above and others, critics have suggested various approaches for remedying the defects in the current Title VII paradigm. I have argued elsewhere (Sexual Harassment as Sex Discrimination: A Defective Paradigm. *Yale Law & Policy Review*, Volume 8, Number 2, 1990) that a state court tort remedy designed specifically for sexual harassment could avoid many of the troubling aspects of our current method of federalizing such offenses under Title VII. I found it particularly troubling that Title VII's target is the employer, rather than the supervisor or co-worker(s) who actually perpetrated the harassment. Employer liability makes a great deal of sense when the discrimination that the federal government wishes to extirpate is of the traditional variety—treating people differently and worse because of their race or sex. In most instances the problem could be traced back directly to discriminatory policies or practices of the employer itself, rather than to a rogue supervisor. With the offensive sexual overtures, propositions, or teasing that characterizes sexual harassment, punishing the employer makes far less sense, because the employer is in effect an ancillary victim to the offense. When a supervisor takes time out of the business day to threaten a woman with firing or denies her a raise unless she agrees to have sexual intercourse with him, the supervisor is sexually harassing the woman, but he is also cheating his employer who pays him to manage workers, not to waste time harassing women, and not to wreak havoc among his underlings with sexual threats. Thus, it seems unfair to make the employer pay twice: once for the lost productivity the harasser causes; and again for legal costs and Title VII damages. Just because employers have "deep pockets" does not mean that they should always be easy targets for plaintiffs—despite trends in other areas of the law.

In recent times, victims of sexual harassment have appended various tort claims to their Title VII suits, and federal courts have exercised what is termed "pendant jurisdiction" in order to deliberate on these tort grievances that are normally aired in state courts. Tort theories have included claims for wrongful discharge, interference with contract, invasion of the right to privacy, interference with a contractual relationship, and intentional infliction of emotional distress. If Title VII is a clumsy fit for sexual harassment charges, and if an alternative is desirable, it would be better, I argued, to craft a new tort—a tort of sexual harassment—rather than cobbling together another ill-fitting solution by embracing a bevy of existing torts. Such a tort would focus on the individual harm to the victim and the individual liability of the harasser. It would also have the advantage of covering sexual harassment wherever it occurs under a single theoretical umbrella, while Title VII only covers such offenses in the workplace.

By patterning a new tort of sexual harassment on an old one—intentional infliction of emotional distress—innovation in the law can be kept to a minimum. The new tort, like the old, would stress that offensive behavior must rise above mere annoyance or petty oppression, and must be so egregious that a reasonable person should not be expected to endure it. It would cover both quid pro quo and hostile environment sexual harassment, with the former requiring that an unwelcome sexual proposition be accompanied by an overt or implicit threat of reprisal, and with the latter requiring that the offensive behavior be so persistent and offensive that a reasonable person would find it extreme and outrageous. The harasser, to be held liable, must have acted either intentionally or recklessly, and the victim as a result must have suffered economic detriment and/or extreme emotional distress. For an employer to be held liable, the employer must have been informed of the conduct and failed to engage in a good faith effort to prevent future occurrences. Employers could also be held liable if they did not provide an appropriate complaint mechanism, thus precluding the victim from informing the company of the harassment. In addition to the benefits already mentioned—in providing greater theoretical consistency, in placing blame where blame belongs, in identifying undesirable conduct outside of the workplace as well as inside—this tort approach would discourage frivolous suits by setting a high threshold of "extreme and outrageous behavior."

D. Philosophical Criticisms and Responses

1. Group Discrimination versus Individual Rights

Philosophical criticism in many ways echoes the complaints of the social and legal critics, but there are some novel issues that we have not yet explored. Of deep concern to the philosophical critics is the group-rights perspective that permeated the issue of sexual harassment from the outset, when Catharine MacKinnon and other feminists first urged its proscription by law. MacKinnon undoubtedly would find unsatisfactory a tort approach of the sort outlined above (in Section III.C.3). That tort proposal relies on an individual-rights perspective by focusing on the perpetrator and the victim, and ignoring larger social forces. In her 1979 book on sexual harassment she argued that by "treating the incidents as if they are outrages particular to an individual woman, rather than integral to her social status as a woman worker, the personal approach on the legal level fails to analyze the relevant dimensions of the problem." A more recent commentator in the *Harvard Law Review* (Note. (1994). Sexual Harassment Claims of Abusive Work Environment under Title VII, Vol. 97, p. 1463) also found an individualistic approach unappealing. A tort law approach would trivialize the problem as a mere affront to a single individual, ignoring the larger picture: that "sexual harassment injures a discrete and identifiable group by subjecting its victims to demeaning treatment and relegating them to inferior status in the workplace."

Anita M. Superson is especially vigorous in propounding the group-rights position. For her, sexual harassment is a form of sexism; it is "about domination, in particular, the domination of the group of men over the group of women." Men have power and they use it to oppress women. When a man sexually harasses a woman "the comment or behavior is really directed at the group of all women, not just a particular woman," an understanding not captured even by the current legal paradigm. (Superson (1993, Spring). A Feminist Definition of Sexual Harassment. *Journal of Social Philosophy*, Vol 24, No. 1, pp. 46–64; see also, John C. Hughes and Larry May (1980, Fall). Sexual Harassment. *Social Theory and Practice*, Vol. 6, No. 3.)

Thus, there is a fundamental, philosophical dispute concerning the essential unit of social analysis between critics and supporters of the current Title VII paradigm. Is that unit the individual, or the group?

2. A Fundamental Right: Freedom of Speech

Fundamental liberties, some philosophers argue, are also put in jeopardy by the pursuit of sexual harassers, particularly the freedoms of speech and privacy. Mane Hajdin, in his half of *Sexual Harassment: A Debate*, contends that both freedoms are jeopardized in the current, highly charged legal and social atmosphere.

Hajdin views the legal landscape on sexual harassment as impinging on freedom of speech because the state proscribes one kind of speech while leaving blameless the opposite point of view. A man who makes disparaging remarks in a police station to the effect that women are not fit to serve as police officers, if he says it truculently and persistently enough, can be accused of hostile environment sexual harassment under current law, Hajdin contends, while another person expressing the opposite viewpoint would be blameless. [It should be noted that his example is hyperbolic, since current law does not punish the mere expression of a viewpoint. The expression in this example would have to be so offensive and persistent that it would rise above what we would normally consider an expression of an opinion. But with cases like *Robinson v. Jacksonville Shipyards*, 760 F. Supp. 1486 (M.D. Fla., 1991), Hajdin's concern becomes more plausible. Here, a district court empathized with a female welder's complaint of nude pinups, obscene graffiti, and catcalls of "honey" and "babe."]

Furthermore, Hajdin argues, since the EEOC *Guidelines* direct that "verbal. . .conduct" can be sexual harassment, it is difficult for a person to know beforehand whether a statement he makes is going to be offensive to listeners. Thus, the pursuit of sexual harassers curbs free expression and harms—through self-censorship—even those whom it does not catch in its net. A sexual joke may be amusing to some and sexual harassment to others, but the net result is that speech is inhibited by government action, a clear violation in Hajdin's mind of the First Amendment and the fundamental right to freedom of speech. F. M. Christensen, a philosopher at the University of Alberta and a wholesale critic of the sexual harassment concept, states this position emphatically: "The notion of 'sexual harassment' has. . .become a major source of injustice in this society. And it represents the greatest violation of freedom of speech to emerge in decades." Men's careers are being threatened because they act as men, the traditional and biological instigators of sexual overtures, and because of the highly charged atmosphere surrounding sex in society. It would be a similar injustice if society were to punish women for stating feminist views in the presence of others who might take offense ((1994, January). "Sexual Harassment" Must Be Eliminated. *Public Affairs Quarterly*, Vol. 8, No. 1).

Curiously, Nadine Strossen, as president of the American Civil Liberties Union (ACLU), the organization dedicated to an "absolutist view of the First Amendment," argues a contrasting position ((1995). The Tensions Between Regulating Workplace Harassment and the First Amendment: No Trump. *Chicago Kent Law Review*, Vol. 71, No. 2, pp. 701, 727). She maintains that protecting freedom of speech can be compatible with protecting people from racial or sexual harassment. Freedom of expression must be distinguished, she points out, from "targeted individual harassment in the form of expression." Even an absolutist viewpoint on the First Amendment does not mean that public universities, for example, cannot prohibit "harassment, intimidation, and invasion of privacy." Sexist expression in the workplace, however, should be tolerated, since it may provoke thought and have the opposite reaction to that desired by the speaker. Here, she shares the concern expressed by Hajdin: such speech ought to be protected, "unless it constitutes intentional incitement to imminent illegal discrimination or violence."

3. Another Fundamental Right: Privacy

Mane Hajdin identifies another fundamental right that the pursuit of sexual harassers vitiates: the right to privacy. He offers an example of two co-workers engaged in pleasurable and consensual sexual relations. If a third employee reports the relationship to their employer, suspecting that it might involve sexual harassment, the employer is obliged to investigate or risk being left defenseless if a lawsuit ensues. Thus, "two people who are pursuing a perfectly happy sexual affair may find the privacy of their interaction invaded by the sexual harassment bureaucracy, if someone else, who is for whatever reason upset by their affair, chooses to complain." Furthermore, he fears that employers and co-workers in the future will have even more legal incentive to "monitor" the behavior of their fellows, because any consensual dating situation can readily "turn into a case of sexual harassment." Since it is difficult to distinguish between sexual harassment and an innocuous office flirtation, he thinks that "monitoring" will amount to nothing less than spying.

Advocates of the battle against sexual harassment have argued, contrary to Hajdin, that sexual harassment itself is a "form of invasive communication that violates a victim's privacy rights" (Edmund Wall. (1991, October). "The Definition of Sexual Harassment." *Public Affairs Quarterly*, Vol. 5, No. 4). Philosopher Vaughana Macy Feary concurs, arguing that sexual matters are irrelevant to the assessment of job performance, and managers must forebear from probing into employees' sexual lives beyond the workplace, just as they must "discourage sexual conversations within it" ((1994). Sexual Harassment: Why the Corporate World Still Doesn't "Get It." *Journal of Business Ethics*, 13, pp. 649–662). She sees moral offensiveness and rights violations in the acts of the harassers, rather than in the activities of those who seek to eradicate sexual harassment. Such harassment harms women psychologically: it can trigger "sexual harassment trauma syndrome," she believes. It even has a far more dire potential to harm women physically: a sexually infused workplace can encourage rape or physical assault. Harassment can also deny a woman the "liberty right" to work, if she is forced to resign in the face of abuse, and it can deny her "rights to fair equality of opportunity," by undermining her authority in the workplace.

E. Summary

Sexual harassment, in its social, legal, and philosophical aspects, has been examined from a critical perspective in Section III. We have explored the major concerns of the critics, including qualms about: the expansivity of the offense and its indeterminacy; the propensity of advocates to utilize possibly inflated polling results; the danger to careers and reputations as an immediate result

of a charge; the tendency of ever-increasing damage awards to promote meretricious suits; poisoned social relations between male and female colleagues due to shifting mores and self-censorship; Title VII as an inappropriate mechanism for litigating sexual harassment claims; sexual harassment charges impinging upon the fundamental, individual rights of freedom of speech and privacy. We also examined some of the responses to these criticisms, and in Section IV we will explore the remaining concerns of those who have advocated the largely successful campaign to raise public awareness of sexual harassment and to expand legal remedies.

IV. THE ADVOCATES' AGENDA FOR THE FUTURE

A. Success and Frustration

Those who, back in the 1970s, wrote about and agitated for the incorporation of sexual harassment under Title VII's ban on sex discrimination in the workplace, and under Title IX of the Education Act Amendment's similar ban on sex discrimination in the academy, have achieved their initial goals. Yet, sexual harassment is still a problem for women in education and in the workplace. Victory is partial and bittersweet. While the advocates of expunging sexual harassment have succeeded amazingly well in dramatizing their cause, in garnering media attention, and in heightening awareness throughout society on this issue, they remain frustrated by the results. Critics might debunk the poll numbers that the enthusiasts trumpet in their public appearances and writings, but whatever a truly scientific study might reveal, it is indisputable that sexual extortionists prey upon the economic vulnerability of female subordinates. It is indisputable, too, that women suffer this indignity at rates far exceeding those for male workers. Even the skeptics find this quid pro quo harassment reprehensible. Most skeptics go further, conceding that hostile environment harassment of the most egregious sort ought to be socially disparaged at the least, and a legal wrong at most.

Advocates remain unsatisfied with this "half-a-loaf" victory. They are pleased that the Hill-Thomas affair permitted them to air their views before a captivated, although highly polarized audience. Early promoters, such as Catharine MacKinnon, appeared as expert network commentators throughout the proceedings, and their views for the first time reached the public unfiltered by journalists. While the resolution of the affair— with Thomas's ascension to the high Court and Hill's brief celebrity on the lecture circuit—was less than satisfying for the advocates, the proliferation of sexual harassment charges to the EEOC and the heightened media attention to charges by aggrieved women throughout the country, was some consolation. The hearings underscored one of the advocates' persistent complaints: that women are terribly vulnerable when they charge men for various sorts of sexual transgressions, from rape to sexual harassment. Often, the tables are turned, and the woman and her reputation become the focal point of an investigation or trial, rather than the behavior of the man. After Anita Hill, many more women were willing to undergo this scrutiny, rather than just putting up with the offensive behavior or resigning their positions. For the advocates, this state of affairs is still highly unsatisfactory, but an improvement nevertheless.

B. Unfulfilled Agenda

For the advocates, the battle to extirpate sexual harassment has been joined, but not yet won. Their major unfulfilled goals fall into three categories: education; the expansion of legal remedies; and encouraging more sexual harassment complaints.

1. Education

After the Hill–Thomas confrontation, businesses throughout the nation realized as never before that they were exposed to potentially large damage judgments if found liable for sexual harassment. The only way of minimizing exposure was to educate their workforces about what sexual harassment is and how it can be prevented, by promulgating sexual harassment guidelines if they had not already done so, and by establishing internal and independent complaint resolution mechanisms. With the complexity of the issue and the uncertainty of evolving legal criteria, companies perceived a need for expert advice, both from lawyers who could help them with their written policies and complaint vehicles, and from consultants who could bring to their offices and factories training manuals, films, workbooks, and lectures that could sensitize their employees to this issue. The demand for consultants exploded, as did their numbers. Not all of the advice was deft, nor all of the students receptive—as illustrated by our previous discussion of the case of two recently trained managers who nevertheless participated in a birthday gift of a dildo to a female employee. Much, then, remains to be accomplished, the advocates emphasize.

2. Expansion of Legal Remedies

Proponents focus most of their attention on refining and expanding legal remedies for victims of sexual ha-

rassment. Here, too, the results have been mixed, but by and large, encouraging. In its second foray into the sexual harassment arena, the Supreme Court, in a 1993 case, *Harris v. Forklift Systems, Inc.* (510 U.S. 17 (1993)), made it a bit clearer that plaintiffs in Title VII hostile environment suits could prevail without having to show economic detriment or adverse effects on job performance. Harris quit her job as a manager at Forklift after its president made repeated derogatory statements about women directed at her, uttered sexual innuendoes that undercut her authority, and engaged in other salacious behavior. Two lower federal courts had found this to be a close case, but not enough to make out a claim for hostile environment sexual harassment. Reaffirming and elaborating on its earlier decision in *Meritor Savings Bank v. Vinson*, the unanimous Supreme Court stated that the lower courts had misunderstood the criteria for making out such a case. Harm, in the form of economic or tangible discrimination, need not be shown; it is enough if the plaintiff can demonstrate that the workplace was permeated with "discriminatory intimidation, ridicule, and insult...that is sufficiently severe or pervasive to alter the conditions of the victim's employment and create an abusive working environment." Justice O'Connor, writing for the Court, understood this as a middle path between making "merely offensive" conduct actionable and requiring a showing of "tangible psychological injury." Conduct not "severe or pervasive enough to create an *objectively* hostile or abusive work environment—an environment that a *reasonable person* would find hostile or abusive—is beyond Title VII's purview" (emphasis added). Similarly, she continued, if the victim does not perceive the environment as hostile, then no Title VII violation occurs. In other words, "Title VII comes into play before the harassing conduct leads to a nervous breakdown." The Court concluded that there cannot be a "mathematically precise test," and listed several criteria that ought to be considered, but insisted that no single factor, such as psychological harm, need be proven. These factors include: "the frequency of the discriminatory conduct; its severity; whether it is physically threatening or humiliating, or a mere offensive utterance; and whether it unreasonably interferes with an employee's work performance."

Some advocates find this apparent loosening of the standard of proof for hostile environment sexual harassment still far from ideal. The "objective" perspective of the "reasonable person," many argue, ought to be replaced by a "reasonable woman" or a "reasonable victim" standard, since the "reasonable person" is a holdover from negligence law's traditional "reasonable man" standard. Its provenance renders it suspect to the advocates because of its male cast. What should matter is how a typical woman would feel in such circumstances, not how a male or a degendered, archetypical person might feel, since male sensitivity to such behavior as sexist jokes, sexual overtures, teasing, and groping are notoriously different from that of the typical woman. Advocates want the focus exclusively on the woman's viewpoint. (See: Deborah L. Wells and Beverly J. Kracher. (1993, June). Justice, Sexual Harassment, and the Reasonable Victim Standard. *Journal of Business Ethics*, Vol. 12, No. 6).

Other, more extreme advocates would go further, aiming to completely eliminate the objective element from the test. If a woman *is* offended, that should be enough, and they do not see why it is relevant how others—whether women or "persons"—would react in similar circumstances. While it is unlikely that courts will go this far—because then a charge of sexual harassment, seemingly, would be sufficient in itself for victory—several have already embraced a "reasonable woman" standard, but with the objective component of the test intact.

Ramona L. Paetzold, a business, public policy, and law professor at Texas A&M, offers another variant on this argument. She rejects the "reasonable person" or even the "reasonable woman" standard, not on the basis of the "person" or "woman" component, but on the basis of the "reasonableness" element. Reason is male; it is part of patriarchal male oppression, and it should be extirpated from sexual harassment law, she urges. "'Reasonableness' preserves male privilege in law in a manner parallel to the way sexual harassment preserves male privilege in the workplace." She would excise "reasonableness" from the elements of proof in hostile environment cases, replacing it with a focus on creating organizational cultures to foster "equal opportunity for all employees" and eliminating behavior with a detrimental effect on individual women. (It is not clear from her argument how these substitutes would fit into the structure of Title VII; see Paetzold and Bill Shaw. (1994). A Postmodern Feminist View of "Reasonableness" in Hostile Environment Sexual Harassment. *Journal of Business Ethics*, Vol. 13, pp. 681–689; Shaw offers a contrasting viewpoint.)

3. Encouraging More Sexual Harassment Charges

Beyond the legal arena, activists would take this objective/subjective dispute one step further. Arguing that since women have been conditioned by society to accept boorish social behavior of a sexual nature,
women might not recognize sexual harassment when they are truly the victims of it. In the counseling setting, on university campuses especially, they urge that women ought to be encouraged to think of sexual teasing, grabbing, and pornographic pictures as sexual harassment, and file complaints.

V. CONCLUSION: FUTURE PROSPECTS

The current trend toward expanding the concept of hostile environment sexual harassment—beyond oppressive taunts, groping, and offensive displays of body parts to encompass, for example, hanging a pinup calender on a dockyard or reading *Playboy* in a firehouse—is likely to continue. The advocates will press vigorously for further reform in the law, more educational workshops conducted by sympathetic consultants, and the encouragement of young women to see themselves as victims of male oppression. Although there are some academics who question this trend, and some resistance by judges to the further loosening of legal standards, energy and passion reside with the advocates. As with most controversial issues, it is difficult to avoid polarization, but it should be recognized, too, that there is much agreement between the camps, particularly on the desirability of expunging sexual harassment of the extortionist, quid pro quo variety. In addition, most critics agree with the advocates that hostile environment sexual harassment, when truly egregious, is intolerable in a business or educational setting, and should be in some way legally actionable if an employer ignores pleas for relief. On the more extreme ideological trappings and the more zealous interpretations of the law, critics and supporters do part company. Perhaps, with the passage of time—as women supervisors, professionals, coal miners, and police officers become less of a novelty—a new set of rules for workplace interaction between the sexes will be imbibed by future generations, and much of the present tension will be alleviated.

Also See the Following Articles

Bibliography

Brant, C. (1994). *Rethinking sexual harassment.* (Yun Lee Too, Ed.). London: Pluto Press.

Buss, D. N., & Malamuth, N. M. (Eds.). (1996). *Sex, power, conflict: Evolutionary and feminist perspectives*. New York: Oxford University Press

Conte, A. (1990). *Sexual harassment in the workplace: Law and practice*. New York: John Wiley and Sons, Inc.

Dziech, B. W., & Weiner, L. (1990). *The lecherous professor: Sexual harassment on campus* (2nd ed.). Urbana: University of Illinois Press.

Farley, L. (1978). *Sexual shakedown: The sexual harassment of women on the job*. New York: McGraw-Hill.

Francis, L. P. (1997). *Sexual harassment in academe: The ethical issues*. Totowa, NJ: Rowman & Littlefield.

Leone, B., Szumski, B., Wekesser, C., & Swisher, K. L. (1992). *Sexual harassment*. San Diego, CA: Greenhaven Press.

Mackinnon, C. A. (1979). *Sexual harassment of working women: A case of sex discrimination*. New Haven: Yale University Press.

Paludi, M. A. (1996). *Sexual harassment on college campuses: Abusing the ivory power*. Albany, NY: State University of New York Press.

Smitherman, G. (ed.). (1995). *African American women speak out on Anita Hill-Clarence Thomas*. Detroit, MI: Wayne State University Press.

Wall, E. (Ed.). (1992). *Sexual harassment: Confrontations and decisions*. Buffalo: Prometheus Books.

SEXUAL ORIENTATION

Edward Stein,* Jacinta Kerin,† Udo Schüklenk‡
*Yale University, †Monash University, ‡University of Central Lancashire

I. A Survey of Scientific Research on
   Sexual Orientations
II. Positive Ethical Implications
III. Negative Ethical Implications
IV. Freedom of Scientific Research
V. Conclusion

GLOSSARY

female feticide The selective elimination of female fetuses.
heritability The proportion of total variation among
individuals of the same species that can be attributed
to genetic variation.
homophobia Fear and/or hatred of homosexuals, and
the discriminatory attitudes and behaviors to which
such sentiments lead.
naturalistic fallacy The mistake of reasoning from the
way things in fact are to the way they ought to be.

SCIENTIFIC RESEARCH ON SEXUAL ORIENTATION
has been conducted ever since the emergence of the idea
that people have sexual orientations, which occurred in
the 19th century. For as long as such research has been
carried out, people have pondered its ethical implications. Some have argued that such research has the
potential to improve the conditions of lesbians, gay

men, and other sexual minorities, while others have
warned of its negative effects on these same groups.
Contemporary research on why a person has the sexual
orientation that she or he does (much of which has
focused on the sexual orientation of homosexual men)
has garnered unprecedented attention outside the scientific community; the research of scientists who claim
to have discovered a biological basis for homosexuality
has received the most attention recently. Many activists
and scientists tout the liberatory potential of scientific
research; some argue that the scientific research is irrelevant to ethical and political questions; and some claim
that such research is dangerous, especially in the context of homophobic societies. These ethical claims are
especially relevant in light of developments in genetic
technology, whether actual or merely purported.

I. A SURVEY OF SCIENTIFIC RESEARCH ON SEXUAL ORIENTATIONS

Scientific research on sexual orientation has taken many
forms. One early idea was to find evidence of a person's
sexual orientation in such bodily features as amount of
facial hair, size of external genitalia, and the ratio of
shoulder width to hip width. Today's more sophisticated morphological research looks instead at neuroan-
atomical structures (S. LeVay, 1991. *Science* **253**, 1034–
1037). Such research usually assumes that sexual

orientation is a trait with two forms, one typically associated with males and the other typically associated with females. Researchers who accept this assumption expect particular aspects of an individual's brain or physiology to conform to either a male type that causes sexual attraction to women (shared by heterosexual men and lesbians) or a female type that causes sexual attraction to men (shared by heterosexual women and gay men). This assumption is scientifically unsupported, and there are alternatives to it.

Another early idea was to find evidence of a person's sexual orientation in his or her endocrine system. The idea was that gay men would have more female-typical sex hormones than heterosexual men and that lesbians would have more male-typical sex hormones than heterosexual women. However, an overwhelming majority of studies failed to demonstrate any correlation between sexual orientation and adult hormonal constitution (for a survey, see H. F. L. Meyer-Bahlburg, 1984. *Prog. Brain Res.* **71**, 375–397). Current hormonal theories of sexual orientation claim that lesbians and gay men were exposed to atypical hormone levels early in their development. Such theories draw heavily on the observation that, in rodents, hormonal exposure in early development exerts organizational influences on the brain that determine the balance between male and female patterns of mating behaviors in adulthood. Extrapolating from behaviors in rodents to psychological phenomena in humans is, however, quite problematic. In rodents, a male who allows himself to be mounted by another male is counted as homosexual, while a male that mounts another male is considered heterosexual. Such theories define sexual orientation in terms of specific postures. In the human case, sexual orientation is defined by one's pattern of erotic responsiveness and the sex of one's preferred sex partner, not by the "position" one takes in sexual intercourse.

Early sex researchers also claimed that sexual orientation runs in families. Recent studies seem to confirm this claim with respect to male homosexuality, but they are not helpful in distinguishing between genetic and environmental influences, because most related individuals share both genes and environmental variables. Further disentanglement of genetic and environmental influences requires adoption studies. One study of male homosexuality (J. M. Bailey and R. C. Pillard, 1991. *Arch. General Psychiatry* **48**, 1089–1096) has included an adoption component. This study suggests a significant environmental contribution to the development of sexual orientation in men in addition to a moderate genetic influence. The study assessed sexual orientation in identical and fraternal twins, nontwin biological brothers, and unrelated adopted brothers of gay men. If there were no environmental effect on sexual orientation, then the rate of homosexuality among adopted brothers should be equal to the base rate of homosexuality in the population, which recent studies place at somewhere between 2 and 5%. The fact that the observed concordance rate was 11% suggests a major environmental contribution, especially when compared to the 9% rate of homosexuality among nontwin biological brothers.

The concordance rate for identical twins (52%) was, however, much higher than the rate for fraternal twins (22%). The higher concordance rate in identical twins is consistent with a genetic effect, because identical twins share all of their genes while fraternal twins, on average, share only half. Nevertheless, the increased concordance rate in identical twins cannot be attributed entirely to increased gene sharing. When considered together, the data from the twins and the adopted brothers suggest that the increased concordance in identical twins is due to the combination of both genetic and environmental influences. Further, the combined effect of genetic and environmental influences might not simply be their sum; these factors could interact in a nonadditive or synergistic manner. The most interesting and consistent finding of the recent heritability studies is that, despite sharing both their genes and familial environments, approximately half of the monozygotic twins were nonetheless discordant for sexual orientation. This finding, which has been consistent across studies, underscores how little is known about the origins of sexual orientation.

Of all the recent biological studies, the most conceptually complex was a genetic linkage study (D. Hamer, H. Stella, V. Magnuson, N. Hu, and A. Pattatucci, 1993. *Science* **261**, 321–327). This study presents statistical evidence that genes influencing sexual orientation may reside in the q28 region of the X chromosome. Females have two X chromosomes, but they pass a copy of only one to a son. The theoretical probability of two sons receiving a copy of the same Xq28 from their mother is thus 50%. This study reports that of 40 pairs of gay siblings, 33 instead of the expected 20 had received the same Xq28 region from their mother. This finding is often misinterpreted as showing that all 66 men from these 33 pairs shared the same Xq28 sequence. In fact, all it shows is that each member of the 33 concordant pairs shared his Xq28 region with his brother, but not with any of the other 64 men. No single specific Xq28 sequence was common to all 66 men.

There are several problems with this study. First, another research team was unable to duplicate the finding using a comparable experimental design. Second, the study was confined to the X chromosome on the basis of family interviews that revealed a disproportionately high number of male homosexuals on the mothers' side of the family. It has been suggested, however, that women might be more likely to know details of family medical history, rendering these interviews less than objective in terms of directing experimental design. Third, there is some question about whether the results, correctly interpreted, are statistically significant. The conclusions rest on the assumption that the base rate of homosexuality is 2%. If the base rate is actually 4% or higher, then the results are not statistically significant; in fact, the data reported by Hamer's group support the 4% estimate (N. Risch, E. Squires-Wheeler, and B. Keats, 1993. *Science* **262**, 2063–2065).

While scientists and others have speculated about the existence of "gay genes," genes in themselves cannot directly specify any behavior or psychological phenomenon. Instead, genes direct a particular pattern of RNA synthesis that in turn specifies the production of a particular protein that may influence behavior. There are necessarily many intervening pathways between a gene and a specific behavior, and even more between a gene and a pattern that involves both thinking and behaving. The term "gay gene" is, therefore, without meaning, unless one proposes that a particular gene, perhaps through a hormonal mechanism, organizes the brain specifically to support the desire to have sex with people of the same sex. No one has, however, presented evidence in support of such a simple and direct link between genes and sexual orientation.

Importantly, "gay genes" are not required for homosexuality to be heritable. This is because heritability has a precise technical meaning: it refers to the ratio of genetic variation to total (i.e., phenotypic) variation. As such, heritability merely reflects the degree to which a given outcome is linked to genetic factors; it says nothing about the nature of those factors nor about their mechanism of action. Homosexuality would be heritable even if genes worked through a very indirect mechanism. For example, if genes act on temperamental or personality variables that influence how we perceive and interact with our environment, then temperament or personality could play an important role from the moment of birth in shaping the relationships and experiences that influence how sexual orientation develops. A particular genetically influenced temperamental variant could predispose to homosexuality in one environment, while making no contribution to sexual orientation in other environments. The moral for heritability studies of sexual orientation is that any genetic influence on sexual orientation might prove to be very indirect. In general, there is no convincing evidence for the claim that differences in sexual orientation are biologically based.

II. POSITIVE ETHICAL IMPLICATIONS

A. The Immutability Argument

Some people believe that scientific research on sexual orientation will have positive ethical implications. Various scholars and lesbian and gay activists (most of them in the United States) have argued that establishing a biological basis for sexual orientation will provide an incontrovertible basis upon which to argue for the elimination of discrimination against lesbians and gay men. Underlying such arguments is the idea that one does not choose one's sexual orientation if it is biologically based. If people do not choose their sexual orientations, the argument goes, they ought not to be discriminated against because of them.

An example of such an argument focuses on the specifics of U.S. legislation. The idea is that scientific evidence will establish the immutability of sexual orientation, which, according to an interpretation of the Equal Protection Clause of the 14th Amendment of the U.S. Constitution, is one of the three criteria required for a classification to evoke special judicial scrutiny. In this context, the attempts of certain scientists to show that homosexuality is as innate a characteristic as skin pigmentation are thought to have political force. United States-centered arguments, such as this one, have been criticized as ethically irresponsible in global terms: since the results of scientific research are available to the global community, justifications that go beyond U.S. legislation are required. Such critiques emphasize the political climates in which scientific information is likely to be received: some countries are less tolerant of homosexuality than the United States; in these countries, scientific information might be used for agendas other than securing antidiscrimination laws.

There are deeper flaws, however, with arguments which seek to show that finding biological bases for characteristics render them nonvoluntary. Such efforts depend on a deterministic view of genetics, according to which genes cause behavioral traits. This is overly simplistic. Both scientists and nonscientists alike have criticized this sort of genetic theory, emphasizing instead the interactive, mutually responsive nature of genes and environmental factors. Moreover, because of the general tendency to consider genetic factors to be more deterministic and immutable than social factors, biological factors are pursued with an intensity that reflects a neglect of the importance of societal factors in determining behavior. Social factors, too, can be determining of one's behavior, and yet not "chosen." Many socially acquired characteristics are neither "chosen" nor "genetic," for example, one's native language. The discovery of either biological or societal factors does not necessarily indicate that a trait is voluntary. It follows that sexual orientation does not need to be genetically determined to be impervious to change.

Perhaps the most problematic aspect of the immutability argument is the implicit assumption that choosing one's sexual orientation places one in a position where discrimination on the basis of choice is justifiable. The implication here seems to be that if you can choose, and you fail to choose what most people choose, then you are deserving of discrimination. It is not clear why this should be the case; further arguments need to be constructed to support this position. But why is it that people wish to find a biological basis for behavior in the first place? Recourse to the realm of biology usually involves the ideas that what is biological is "natural," and that what is "natural" is more acceptable than what is consciously created.

B. "Natural" and "Normal"

Some people argue that scientific research has positive ethical implications because it can provide answers to century-old questions concerning whether or not homosexuality is natural or normal. This question of normality is considered important because of the persistent conflation of "natural" with "good," the common mistake of deriving an "ought" from an "is" that philosophers call the "naturalistic fallacy." If the results of empirical scientific research indicated that homosexuality was natural or normal, then it would be an instance of the naturalistic fallacy to derive normative assumptions on the basis of empirical information regarding the normality of homosexuality. There is, in this context, an even more fundamental question over whether what is natural or normal can ever be the legitimate subject of empirical inquiry in the first place. It seems clear that empirical research can provide the answers to questions of normality defined in a descriptive sense as a statistical average. This sense of normal is irrelevant to an ethical evaluation of homosexuality. Many human traits and behaviors are abnormal in a statistical sense, but this does not provide grounds for ethical evaluation. When people invoke the notions of what is natural and normal to provide prescriptions about what is good and bad, they are using them as words that are normative concepts. Normative concepts cannot be the subject of empirical inquiry; thus science cannot tell us what is natural or normal in anything other than a statistical sense.

This leads to the question of why is there a dispute as to whether homosexuality is natural or normal. Many people seem to think that nature has a prescriptive normative force such that what is deemed natural or normal is necessarily good and therefore ought to be. Everything that falls outside these terms is seen as unnatural and abnormal, and it has been argued that this relegation alone constitutes sufficient reason to consider homosexuality worth avoiding. Positions holding the view that homosexuality is unnatural, and therefore wrong, inevitably develop incoherencies. They fail to explicate the basis upon which the line between natural and unnatural is drawn. More importantly, they fail to explain why we should consider all human-made or artificial things as immoral or wrong. These views are usually firmly based in a nonempirical, *prescriptive* interpretation of nature rather than a scientific *descriptive* approach. They define arbitrarily what is natural and have to import other normative assumptions and premises to build a basis for their conclusions. For instance, they often claim that a god or a God-like figure has declared homosexuality to be unnatural and sinful.

C. Historical Evidence

Historical evidence is cited by both supporters and opponents of the claim that scientific research into sexual orientation has positive implications. Opponents of such research claim that, historically, all of the etiological research into sexual orientation has operated, directly or indirectly, to serve homophobic agendas. They therefore infer that current research is likely to be used to the detriment of homosexuals. To counter this claim, some supporters refer to instances of past research that have not been used to the detriment of homosexuals. The general idea is that current sexual orientation research is likely to have positive consequences, because, historically, similar research has also had such consequences. In order for this reply to be effective, however, the past research that is invoked must be analogous to present-day research in ethically significant ways. It is important to identify which sorts of historical events can be considered relevant to the debate concerning the implications and applications of research on sexual orientation.

Others who think that scientific research has positive ethical implications use historical examples of sexual orientation research that has been dangerous for homosexuals in order to characterize a type of research as problematic. For example, in order to defend genetic research on sexual orientation, Simon LeVay claims that such research has been less dangerous than psychological and sociological research. He gives the example of the Nazis, who, he claims, supported psychological and psychiatric research on sexual orientation, but did not advocate genetic research. This is historically incorrect, since the Nazis were supportive of any research which might eliminate homosexuality. Further, it is a mistake to claim that one sort of research is legitimate because some other research is ethically problematic; rather, acknowledging that some research into the origins of sexual orientation is problematic only provides further reason to question the entire enterprise of which they are both a part.

III. NEGATIVE ETHICAL IMPLICATIONS

A. The History of "Treatment" of Homosexuals

Many people are more circumspect in their assessment of research into sexual orientation. Some are not content to stop at countering predictions of positive ethical implications because they believe that such scientific research has negative ethical implications. For example, the professional sex research societies in Germany have called for a moratorium on such research in order to draw attention to the potential for abuse of the results of sexual orientation research, especially in homophobic societies. Such a stance is supported by the disturbing history of the use of scientific research into sexual orientation.

Historically, almost every investigation into the causes of homosexuality has aimed at its elimination. This has been reflected in the many and varied attempts to "cure" healthy people, including electroshock treatment, hormone therapies, genital mutilation, and brain surgery. Some "patients" were forced to undergo such "treatment," while others volunteered, presumably in response to overt societal homophobia. Even in contemporary societies, lesbians, gay men, and bisexuals are subject to widespread discrimination and social disapprobation. Against this background, the development of theories of the origins of sexual orientations are likely to lead to further attempts at conversion therapies. This is happening in some parts of the fields of psychoanalysis and psychiatry (for an example, see Friedman,

R. C. (1988). "Male Homosexuality: A Contemporary Psychoanalytic Perspective." Yale University Press. New Haven), and there is no reason to think that the "hard" sciences will not be employed to serve similar strategies. History strongly suggests that current genetic research will have negative effects on lesbians and gay men, particularly in homophobic societies and especially when it is done by homophobic researchers. There is, in fact, some evidence that genetic screening would be used against homosexuality. For instance, in Singapore, where homosexual sex acts are a criminal offense (the Singapore Penal Code, sections 377 and 377A, threatens sentences ranging from 2 years to life imprisonment for homosexual people engaging in same-sex acts), a National University of Singapore psychiatrist, in a recently published article, asked whether "pre-symptomatic testing for homosexuality should be offered in the absence of treatment" (L. C. C. Lim, 1995. *Ann. Acad. Med. Singapore* **24**, 759–763), thereby accepting the idea that homosexuality is something in need of a cure.

B. Homophobia in Contemporary Research

Various commentators have pointed to ways in which contemporary research on sexual orientation is homophobic. The language in which contemporary scientific research on homosexuality is framed is often cited as underscoring an institutionalized tendency toward its pathologization. Scientific literature contains descriptions of homosexuality as a "disease," "dysfunction," and "abnormal brain development" (G. Dörner, 1989. *Exp. Clin. Endocrinol.* **94**, 4–22). It is argued that the persistent use of such language reflects entrenched homophobia, regardless of whether or not individuals admit to such biases. Furthermore, "treatment" continues to be discussed, in terms of "optimizing" "natural conditions" or by "correcting abnormal concentrations" (Dörner, 1989). Critics point out that this current wish for "treatment" indicates a modern-day version of what was previously attempted with electroshock therapy.

A further example of the homophobia of contemporary research on sexual orientation involves children with "gender identity disorder" (the term officially approved by most psychiatric associations to refer to children who behave in ways that are atypical for children of their sex). Such children are assumed to be at risk of becoming homosexuals; they are thus subject to extreme forms of medical and psychiatric interventions. The assumption of such "treatment" is that adult homosexuality is a condition worth avoiding at great costs to children.

Research conducted within a homophobic framework is likely to have negative effects on homosexuals for a number of reasons. So long as homosexuality is seen as a dysfunction, "prevention" and "treatments" therapies are more likely to be pursued. While it is generally admitted that not all researchers interested in the origins of sexual orientation are necessarily homophobic, it is emphasized that good or neutral intentions do not prevent negative use of results, especially when scientific research is received by homophobic societies.

C. Genetic Screening

Others have worried that scientific progress will enable the development of tests that could be used to screen fetuses for sexual orientation. Such tests might operate by detecting genes or hormone levels that are thought to correlate with sexual orientation. The concern is that such "orientation selection" techniques would enable prospective parents to selectively abort "prehomosexual" fetuses (fetuses that seem to be predisposed to same-sex orientation). Proponents of these concerns are not necessarily opposed to abortion or other selection techniques per se, but are worried about their use insofar as they could enable further discrimination against gay men and lesbians. The thought is that the availability of orientation-selection techniques would have ramifications for existing homosexuals in a number of ways. In broad terms, it would both engender and perpetuate homophobic attitudes, such as that homosexual people are, at best, less valuable than heterosexuals and, at worst, not worthy of living.

It has been argued that orientation-selection techniques will fail to work because one's sexual orientation is not determined before birth. The implication here is that a technique must work for it to have significant consumer interest. To assume that something has to work to be utilized is naive. One only has to consider the dramatic demand for *in vitro* fertilization programs in developed countries, even though their success rate is quite low. Demand for technologies is often created and sustained through ideology. A homophobic society might be more concerned with maximizing the probability of heterosexual outcome at whatever the cost, rather than considering the limited predictive abilities of any biological test. A related argument suggests that the medical profession will not advocate such tests if they do not work and, therefore, few prospective parents will make use of them. Not only does this argument ignore homophobia within medicine, it also assumes that public demand for genetic testing varies predominantly according to medical advice. Should such a test become available, however, it seems quite likely that the media hype surrounding its market arrival would render its existence common knowledge. This factor, when coupled with the fact that most parents desire heterosexual children, would likely create a strong demand for the test irrespective of its efficacy.

Further attempts to defend the development of "orientation-selection" techniques rely on the claim that they would be too infrequently used to warrant serious ethical concern. For example, it has been claimed that orientation selection will not become commonplace because diagnostic genetic testing is not currently in great demand. While this may indeed be true in certain countries, this may have far more to do with the types of tests currently offered than with a reluctance on the part of either the medical profession or the reproducing public to partake of such technology. For example, the types of tests available are diagnostic for diseases and are offered on the basis of family history or specific risk factors. The possibility of tests that purport to be predictive of behavioral traits opens genetic technology to a far greater population than those with a family history of genetically determined disease.

Perhaps the most striking case against the development of "orientation-selection" techniques, however, is provided by the case of techniques to select the sex of children. Arguments that remain ignorant of this link are Eurocentric, insofar as sex selection is in great demand in a number of non-Western countries where sex discrimination is particularly overt and pervasive. A great deal of feminist analysis has been devoted to this topic, and many of the arguments pertaining to sex selection are directly relevant to those concerning orientation selection (H. Baequart-Holmes, 1985. In *Biomedical Ethics Review* (J. Humber and R. Almeder, Eds.), pp. 39–71. Humana, Clifton, NJ). Perhaps the most crucial point is that sex selection provides an example of how genetic screening has already been used to reduce the frequency of a socially undesirable trait. In certain parts of India, for example, abortion on the basis of female sex (female feticide) is commonplace, irrespective of its legality. The case of sex selection suggests that we have good reason to believe that many people will make use of any selection techniques to avoid a discriminated-against characteristic.

While some have argued that orientation selection would be used infrequently, others have worried that such screening might become mandatory, and that intervention might be either required or strongly recommended if a "pre-homosexual" fetus was identified. In response to this, it has been pointed out that such mandatory screening would be unlikely, especially in places where discrimination against homosexual people is illegal. This response, however, offers little comfort to those living in political climates where legal antigay discrimination is widespread. Thus, if the concerns of homosexuals in diverse political circumstances are taken seriously, the antidiscrimination laws of certain countries can not be used to assuage fears of state-regulated screening.

Finally, in response to claims that the use of orientation-selection techniques is inherently discriminatory, it has been argued that homosexual people themselves might make use of such technology. However, just as the fact that homosexual people conduct scientific research on sexual orientation does not show that it is ethically justifiable, the fact that some homosexuals might use such techniques would not prove that the technology does not serve to discriminate. For women living in India, there are many practical reasons why male children might be preferable. In a society in which routine discrimination against women is common, it is problematic to condemn women who use sex selection to ensure they will bear sons. This is not to say that sex selection is ethically acceptable. Rather, the point is to acknowledge that people's choices are constrained by the society in which they live. The fact that women sometimes seek abortions for the purpose of having male offspring shows the degree to which sexism operates. Similarly, in societies where homophobia is entrenched, there are good reasons for preferring a heterosexual child. Some of these reasons might be most salient to homosexual people themselves, given their direct experiences of discrimination. The use of a technology by people against whom it may discriminate does not, however, prove its neutrality. It does highlight the pervasive biases within a given society that should be addressed directly rather than be fostered with enabling technology.

IV. FREEDOM OF SCIENTIFIC RESEARCH

In response to those who call for the prohibition of scientific research on sexual orientation, it has been suggested that such action would be incompatible with the freedom of intellectual and academic inquiry. This reason alone, it is argued, provides sufficient grounds upon which to reject such regulation. The idea that people should be free to undertake whatever kind of research they like is based predominantly on two arguments: first, that accumulation of knowledge of any kind is good for its own sake, and second, that undue outside pressure compromises impartial scientific endeavor to an undesirable degree. The first argument does not seem to survive philosophical scrutiny if one considers that there is no "realm of pure knowledge" that stands unsullied by political interests: even science is a social enterprise. The results of scientific research are always used for some purpose, whether they be enjoyed or suffered. Thus the value of research is always context relative, and, as such, needs to be balanced against other values. The second argument is a consequentialist argument that sees the overall impact of "restricted" research as negative. As such, it is especially susceptible to consequentialist counterarguments. Such arguments would be structured to balance the likelihood and magnitude of possible benefits against the likelihood and magnitude of possible harms resulting from a particular practice. If, in balance, the harms outweighed the benefits, it would be unethical to proceed with a given practice. For example, one might argue that permitting sexual orientation researchers to continue their work could lead to harmful consequences similar to those which have occurred in the case of sex selection. Such harmful consequences could, then, outweigh the benefits of developing such a technology in the first place.

The German Constitution might provide an example of a code which would support such an approach to scientific research. It links the freedom of academic research to the responsible behavior of those conducting the research. If the people in question are found to act unethically, the Constitution allows for intervention. This seems sensible, since unless the potential harms are considered as possible limiting factors to scientific research, there might be no basis to prevent the sort of experiments that were undertaken in German concentration camps.

V. CONCLUSION

Homosexual people have, in the past, suffered greatly from societal discrimination against their lifestyle. Historically, the results of biological research on sexual orientation have been routinely used against homosexual people. The arguments that claim such research will have positive ethical implications or will no longer have negative ones fail to survive philosophical scrutiny. In some countries in Scandinavia, North

America, and most parts of Western Europe, the legal situation of homosexual people has improved. Thus, despite the existence of homophobia in large parts of these liberal democratic societies, homosexual people would have the means to act against possible abuses of the results of etiological research on sexual orientation. However, an ethical analysis of the implications of this research has ramifications beyond Europe and the western world, where the legal situation is less protective against discrimination and harm. Sexual orientation researchers must take into account the global implications of their work, and must not ignore the very real prospect that the mere existence of their research could harm homosexual people in countries other than their own. It is difficult to imagine any good that could come from scientific research on sexual orientation in homophobic societies. There are strong arguments that such research should not be undertaken where homophobia persists. These concerns about this scientific research may not hold in a world without homophobia. In such a world, however, scientific research on human sexual desires would surely take a dramatically different form.

Also See the Following Articles

FETAL RESEARCH • GENDER ROLES • GENETIC RESEARCH • GENETIC SCREENING • HOMOSEXUALITY, SOCIETAL ATTITUDES TOWARD • RESEARCH ETHICS

Bibliography

Bullough, V. (1994). "Science in the Bedroom: The History of Sex Research." Basic Books, New York.

Byne, W., and Stein, E. (1997). Ethical implications of scientific research on the causes of sexual orientation. *Health Care Anal.* 5, 136–148.

Halley, J. (1994). Sexual orientation and the politics of biology: A critique of the new argument from immutability. *Stanford Law Rev.* 46, 503–568.

LeVay, S. (1996). "Queer Science: The Use and Abuse of Research in Homosexuality." MIT Press, Cambridge, MA.

Murphy, T. (1995). Abortion and the ethics of genetic sexual orientation research. *Cambridge Quart. Healthcare Ethics* 4, 340–350.

Ruse, M. (1988). "Homosexuality: A Philosophical Inquiry." Blackwell, New York.

Schüklenk, U., and Ristow, M. (1996). The ethics of research into the causes of homosexuality. *J. Homosexuality* 31, 5–30.

Stein, E. (in press). "Sexual Desires: Science, Theory and Ethics." Oxford Univ. Press, New York.

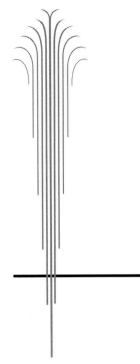

SIKHISM

Nikky-Guninder Kaur Singh
Colby College

GLOSSARY

amrit The ceremonial nectar of immortality.
Dharam Moral duty; the first stage of the spiritual journey.
Guru Granth The sacred text of the Sikhs. Also known as the Adi Granth.
Gurudwara A Sikh place of worship.
gurmukh One drawn to the guru; seeker of enlightenment.
haumai Pride and arrogance; selfish motivations.
jivanmukt One who attains liberation while living on earth.
Khalsa Literally "pure ones." The fellowship of Sikhs founded by Guru Gobind Singh, the Tenth Guru, on Baisakhi in 1699.
langar A community meal.
manmukh One drawn to the self; a selfish egotist.
rahit Conduct.
sangat Gathering or congregation.
seva Deeds of love and service.

CONCERNING SIKHISM, in a lecture to his English audience, the renowned scholar Max Arthur Macauliffe remarked that it "embraces an ethical system such as has never been excelled." It is not just for the generous claim that Macauliffe should be credited, but also for the very appropriate visual image that he evokes. Ethics in this Indian religious tradition does not operate on the theoretical and scientific level; here moral life is not propounded in a thematic or rigid format. Instead, Sikhism warmly and intimately "embraces" metaphysical ideals, individual actions, emotions, virtues, and social interactions. The Western separation of aesthetics, ethics, and religion as Kierkegaard prescribed does not come into play. The Sikh religion is grounded in an aesthetic savoring of the Infinite Reality—concretized in relationship with fellow beings. The overall pattern of Sikh ethics is the integral unity between the individual, society, and the Transcendent.

I. ORIGINS

The foundation of Sikh ethics can be traced to the life and vision of Guru Nanak. He was born on April 15,

1469, in Talwandi, a small village in north India which is now part of Pakistan. He was named after his older sister, Nanaki. His father was an accountant for the local Muslim landlord. His mother, Tripta, is remembered in Sikh history as a pious woman. Nanak was born in an upper caste Hindu family, but from a young age, he refused to go through any of the traditional rituals. The substitution of ethical conduct for elaborate ceremonies was central to his worldview. The Janamsakhis (see Section II) tell us that when Nanak was asked to wear the customary *janeu* (symbolic of the twice-born castes), he urged that the thread be replaced with compassion, contentment, and truth. Nanak grew up in a philosophically and culturally vibrant milieu, one in which he freely met and conversed with Hindus, Muslims, Buddhists, and Jains.

In this diverse and pluralistic context Nanak had revelation of the One Reality. He articulated his experience of the infinite and singular reality as *Ikk Oan Kar*, which is the quintessential formula of Sikh metaphysics and ethics. In Ikk Oan Kar (One Being Is), Ikk or I, literally stands for the numeral one; Oan or Om from the Sanskrit Aum refers to the Ultimate unity; and Kar ("is") celebrates the existence of the One. This insight into the Divine marked the beginning of Guru Nanak's mission. Thereafter for 24 years Guru Nanak traveled throughout India and beyond spreading his message of absolute Unity. He was accompanied during most of his travels by his Muslim companion Mardana who played on the rebec while Guru Nanak sang songs of intense love addressing the Ultimate One.

From the early narratives of his life we learn that Guru Nanak was dressed in combined elements of Hindu and Muslim garb as he set out on his journeys. His dress was symbolic of his common message for all peoples. The rich but simple style of Guru Nanak's teaching drew people from different religious, cultural, and social backgrounds. Wherever Guru Nanak went, people began to follow him, calling themselves Sikhs, a Punjabi word which means disciple. "Sikh" can be traced to the Sanskrit *shishya* or the Pali *sekka*. Bhai Gurdas, the first Sikh historian and theologian, called Sikhism *gaadi raaha*—the grand highway—for showing the path through moral precepts. He viewed this new faith as "a needle which sews materials that are ripped asunder, bringing harmony to the torn and conflicting groups" (*Varan Bhai Gurdas* 33:4).

At the end of his travels, Guru Nanak settled in Kartarpur, a Punjabi village he had founded on the bank of the river Ravi. A community of disciples grew around him there. It was not a monastic order of any kind, but a fellowship of men and women engaged in the ordinary occupations of life. The daily routine and the moral ideals fostered in this first Sikh community constitute the core of Sikh ethics. It was here that the Sikh institutions of *seva*, *langar*, and *sangat*, had their genesis. The distinctive Sikh way of life originated with Guru Nanak's establishment of the community at Kartarpur.

Before he passed away in 1539, Guru Nanak appointed Angad, his disciple, as his successor. Guru Nanak also bequeathed his inspired poetry to the second Sikh guru. Guru Angad continued the tradition of sacred poetry, which he felt was important for the beauty it brought to human life as well as for the knowledge it transmitted. The transference of guruship from Nanak to Angad was repeated successively through the installation of the Tenth Guru, Gobind Singh, in 1675. For the Sikhs the same light is reflected in 10 different bodies, and the same voice speaks through all 10. Before his death in 1708, the Tenth Guru ended the line of personal gurus by passing the succession not to another person but to the Guru Granth, the holy book of the Sikhs. The Guru Granth opens with Ikk Oan Kar, and its 1430 pages can be read as a poetic and sublime commentary on Guru Nanak's statement. Thus the message and the mission begun by Guru Nanak continued through nine more gurus and reached culmination in the Guru Granth.

II. TEXTUAL SOURCES

Guru Granth, also called the Adi (primal) Granth, is the primary text for Sikh ethics. It was compiled in 1604 by the Fifth Guru, Arjan. It contains the verse of the Sikh gurus, as well as that of Hindu and Muslim saints. Whatever was in harmony with Guru Nanak's vision of the Divine, Guru Arjan included in his edition. He also organized most of the collection into 31 sections according to their raga, or melodic pattern. These 31 ragas belong to the Indian musical tradition, each with its own distinctive intervals, rhythms, and timing, and its association with a particular season of the year.

The aesthetic partaking of the Word was vital to Guru Arjan's compilation of the Sikh sacred volume. The Guru Granth does not delineate any obligatory rituals; it does not draw up a list of prescriptions and proscriptions. It is a collection of spiritually exalted poetry carrying only intimations. Yet we discover here a comprehensive ethical model sustained vigorously. Throughout the text, the reader is entreated to translate the metaphysical oneness into the everyday life. It sums up Sikhs ethics as applied spirituality.

Dasam Granth is the book of the Tenth Guru, Gobind Singh, compiled some time after his death in 1708. Although the Guru Granth forms the center of Sikh worship, the poetry of Guru Gobind Singh is highly esteemed by the Sikhs, and also forms part of their daily prayers. Guru Nanak's moral ideals receive in Guru Gobind Singh's verse a heroic diction and energetic meter. His "Jaap," with which opens the Dasam Granth (analogous to the "Jap" of Guru Nanak, the opening of the Guru Granth), is one of the morning prayers of the Sikhs. It is also one of the hymns recited as part of the Sikh initiation ceremony. It consists of 199 stanzas saluting the Infinite One through vigorous metaphors and rhythm.

Guru Gobind Singh's "Akal Ustat," which occupies 28 pages of the Dasam Granth, focuses upon the unity of humanity. It proclaims, "Hindus and Mulsims are one. The same Being is creator and nourisher of all. Recognize no difference between them. The Hindu temple and the Muslim mosque are the same. . . . All humanity is one." Guru Gobind Singh's poetry empowers readers with the vision of the Transcendent One, and incites them to fight against social, political, and economic exploitations.

Bhai Gurdas (1551–1636) is known as the first formulator of Sikh *rahit*, or way of life. His long life span made him the contemporary of five Sikh gurus—Guru Angad through Guru Hargobind. The first recension of the Guru Granth was transcribed by him at the invitation of Guru Arjan. Bhai Gurdas' *Vars*, or ballads, in the Punjabi language are extremely popular as they present Sikh ideals, morals, and society in a simple, bold, and urgent manner. Guru Arjan called them the key (*kunji*) to the Guru Granth. The ethical precepts and values of the Sikh holy text are artistically interpreted by Bhai Gurdas. He tellingly illustrates vice and virtue through vibrant images and metaphors from the Punjabi landscape.

Janamsakhis are the contemporary stories (*sakhis*) of Guru Nanak's life (*janam*) and teachings. They are collected out of an assortment of oral traditions, the popular among them being the *Puratan, Bala,* and *Meharban*. They convey morals of altruism and social interactions. It is through Janamsakhis that children get their first introduction to Sikh morality. From a very early age, children are familiarized with these stories often through brightly illustrated editions. The narratives portray the divine dispensation of their founder and his concern for kindness, social cohesiveness, and divine unity. And they poignantly illustrate Guru Nanak's rejection of empty ritual. We see him, for example, sprinkling water from a jug across the village. Nanak's criticism was that if water sprinkled by priests could reach the dead ancestors, surely his would reach the fields down the road. These stories about their first guru continue to nurture Sikhs throughout their lives.

Rahitnamas, or codes of conduct (*rahit*), were formulated after Guru Gobind Singh's inauguration of the Khalsa order in 1699. Their compilers, such as Chaupa Singh, Nand Lal, Bhai Desa Singh, and others, drew upon the Guru Granth to reinforce the devotional discipline for the consolidation of the Sikh community. However, in seeking to describe the Sikh way of life at its best, the manuals present confusing views and stringent rules and injunctions that go against the open and inclusive spirit of the Guru Granth.

Gurbilas, or "Splendor (*bilas*) of the Guru," is narrative poetry exalting the heroism of the gurus in their fight for justice and equality. This style of literature was developed during the 18th and early 19th centuries. Its aim was to restore righteousness and destroy evil by means of the sword. It focuses on the great warrier gurus and their skill in battle—Guru Hargobind (Nanak 6) and Guru Gobind Singh (Nanak 10). Works in this genre include *Gur Sobha*, attributed to the poet Sainapati; *Gurbilas Dasvin Patshahi* to Sukha Singh; *Gurbilas Patshahi 10* to Koer Singh; and *Gurbilas Chhevin Patshahi* to Sohan.

The Singh Sabha was a renaissance movement that began in 1872. With Maharaja Ranjit Singh (1780–1839) there was political ascendancy for the Sikhs but a lapse in their ideals and values. The dynamic protagonists of the Singh Sabha were committed to reviving the guidelines and moral preferences issuing from the Sikh gurus and the Guru Granth. A variety of literary forms such as tract, commentary, poetry, drama, novel, and epic were utilized to bring out the central aspects of Sikh ethical thought. Bhai Vir Singh, the most prolific and inspiring Singh Sabha author, created vivid female characters like Sundari, Rani Raj Kaur, and Subhag Kaur as paradigms for Sikh morality enshrined in the Guru Granth.

Sikh Rahit Maryada is the Sikh code of conduct published by the Shiromani Gurdwara Prabandhak Committee (SGPC) in 1950. It is accepted as an authoritative statement of Sikh conduct. This booklet of 37 pages is the result of many years of deliberation. In 1931 a meeting was held at the Akal Takht in Amritsar with the goal to draw up a code to regulate individual and corporate life. Teja Singh was the convener of the meeting. Several other eminent Sikhs within India and abroad were engaged in drafting the manual. Jodh Singh, Sher Singh, Bhai Kahan Singh, Bhai Vir Singh, and Ganga Singh were consulted locally, and so were

Sikhs in the USA, Burma, and Malaya. On 3 February 1945 the Rahit Maryada was approved by the SGPC and subsequently published. It is used as the standard guide by Sikhs in their performance of personal (*shakhsi*) and organizational (*panthak*) duties.

The *Sikh Rahit Maryada* defines a Sikh as a person who has belief in the Timeless Being (Akal Purakh), without allegiance to any gods or goddesses. A Sikh should regard only the Ten Gurus and their teachings as the medium for liberation. A Sikh should not practice caste, untouchability, magical rites, or superstitions. (Injunctions from the *Sikh Rahit Maryada* are also discussed in later sections.)

III. TELEOLOGY

The goal of Sikh moral life is union with the Ultimate Reality. This union of humans with the Ultimate liberates them from the cycle of birth and death. As their founder Guru Nanak articulated, the Ultimate for the Sikhs is the all-pervasive singular transcendent One named Truth. When individuals merge with this spaceless and timeless Reality, they become infinite themselves. Thus all confinements are shattered and the person never returns to any finite form. The entry into the realm of Truth is the goal of every Sikh. However, this metaphysical ideal is not apart or separate from their everyday life; rather, the deeper the awareness of the Transcendent, the more vibrant is participation in Sikh daily life. From this teleological framework emerge the following characteristics of Sikh ethics.

A. Integration of Religious Rituals and Daily Routine

Sikh scripture loudly affirms that ultimate freedom is attained in active engagement in our daily tasks. Elaborate forms of worship, rituals, and ceremonies are rejected. Guru Nanak denounced external actions and rites that were empty and oppressive, and all kinds of austere and ascetic practices. A hymn by the Fifth Guru categorically states that "liberation is attained while laughing, playing, dressing up, and eating (Guru Granth, p. 522). The artistic images that express union with the Divine in Sikh scripture therefore emerge from everyday chores. Dyeing fabrics and stitching them, acts of dressing up and applying makeup, and working in a smithy or churning butter at home symbolize complete devotion and single-minded attachment with the One. The immutability of Truth is not rendered through

some ceremonial formulation but through the mundane task of sewing: "Truth is eternal; once sewn, It never gets ripped asunder" (Guru Granth, p. 955). In Sikh life, normal activities are validated; each and every routine action is imbued with spiritual significance.

Reading their sacred verse, hearing it, singing it, or sitting in its presence constitutes the core of Sikh ritual. The Guru Granth is the sole visual and aural icon and main source of their daily prayers. All rites of passage take place in the sound and sight of this text: the newborn baby is named in its presence, the marriage ceremony entails walking around it four times, and death in a home is followed by a reading, often continuous, of its 1430 pages.

The everyday routine (*nit nem*) of the Sikh involves the recitation of several hymns. They may recite or read them alone, with their families, or with congregation in Gurudwaras (Sikh shrines). Morning prayers reverberate through a Sikh home as family members go about their activities. Mothers recite stanzas from the Jap as they prepare breakfast or comb their children's hair. Fathers pray while picking up bedding, cleaning, or gardening. If their home is large enough for a separate worship room, a family may gather there in the morning to recite hymns together. Some Sikhs visit a neighborhood shrine, thus combining devotions with a morning walk. Sacred poetry resonates within the Sikhs as they continue to perform their daily tasks. The morning and evening communion with the Transcendent provides them with a richer and fuller encounter with their family, friends, and colleagues.

B. Stress on Praxis

Guru Nanak's statement that the Divine is Truth is soon followed by his question, "How to become Truth? How to break the walls of falsity?" (Guru Ganth, p. 1). The transition from Truth to True living is immediate and spontaneous, underscoring the experiential dimension of Reality. Sikhism does not hold on to an abstract view of Truth. Truthful mode of existence takes precedence over the conception of Truth: "Higher than everything is Truth but higher still is True living" (Guru Granth, p. 62). In his Sukhmani, Guru Arjan vividly expresses how a person acts, lives, feels, speaks, sees, and speaks truthfully with the recognition of Truth: "Truth is in their hearts, Truth is on their lips, Truth is in their sight, truth their form, truth is their way, Truth their revelation. They who discern the Transcendent as Truth, says Nanak, they themselves merge with Truth" (Guru Granth, p. 283). The goal of Truth becomes the path itself. For the Sikhs then, ethics and religion are a singular venture, a life fully lived with the knowledge and experience of the Divine.

C. Proximity of the Transcendent

Jap, the first hymn of the Guru Granth, presents five stages (Dharam, meaning duty; Gyan, knowledge; Saram, aesthetics; Karam, grace; and Sach, truth) which lead human beings to the Ultimate Reality. The destination of the Sikh mystical journey is Sach Khand, the realm of Truth. It is the union with the One, and an end of the transmigratory cycle. But the articulation of the ineffable and infinite locale of Sach Khand is instantaneously juxtaposed to a scene in a smithy. With its anvil, bellows, and hammers, the 38th stanza of the Jap quickly shifts to the phenomenal world:

> Let continence be your smithy, and patience your
>   goldsmith;
> Let wisdom be your anvil, and knowledge your
>   hammer;
> Let awe be the bellows, and inner control the
>   blazing fire;
> In the crucible of love, let the ambrosia flow;
> In this true mint, forge the Word.
> Such fulfillment comes to those blessed with the
>   Gaze;
> Says Nanak, happy are they who are gazed upon.

The scene of the smithy constitutes an intersection of the complex stages of the entire spiritual journey: performing action with patience and love (Dharam); using knowledge and wisdom (Gyan); refining artistic sensibilities, for after all, it is the gold-like divine Name that is being forged (Saram); receiving the benevolent glance (Nadar); and enjoying the fulfillment (Sach). The juxtaposition of stanza 37 with its description of Sach Khand to stanza 38 with its common, everyday working scene illustrates the proximity of the two spaces. The very familiar and ordinary workshop is a metaphor for the spiritual ideal, a smithy in which the goldsmith forges the divine Name on the crucible of love. This motion (phora) across (meta) the physical and the metaphysical, noumenon and the phenomena, spirtual and the practical, is the quintessence of Sikh ethics.

D. Social Equality

The Sikh gurus repeatedly claimed that Dharam, the ordained duties, were the same for people of all races, classes, and ages. Although the term Dharam retains its Sanskrit meaning (what holds together), Sikh gurus did not specify any duties in accordance with injunctions of the traditional Hindu scriptures. In Sikhism, Dharam does not prescribe the customary fourfold division of Hindu society into Brahmins, Kshatriyas, Vaishyas, and Shudras, nor does it institute a division of the stages of life into that of brahmacarin, grahastha, vanaprastha, and sanyasin (varna-ashrama-dharma). In contrast to the fourfold societal hierarchy and its corresponding privileges, duties, and responsibilities, there is in Sikh ethics an emphasis on equality. Everyone is equally impelled to perform their ethical duty throughout their entire life.

In fact the first stage in the spiritual voyage is Dharam Khand—our life as active agents on earth. Our foremost duty is that we human beings coexist harmoniously and ethically with all beings on earth. Time is a major factor in Dharam Khand, which is described as a region made up of nights, seasons, dates, and days. All the elements—air, water, fire, and earth—and all the compounds produced from them are a part of this physical universe, with the earth as the axis, uniting all species. According to Guru Nanak, "In it are colourful beings and lifestyles/Infinite are their names and infinite their forms" (Guru Granth, p. 7). Although plurality and multiplicity are accepted, everyone is interconnected, and there is no implication of any disjunctions or divisions of gender, race, and class in this organic earth. All are provided with an equal opportunity to act ethically and purposefully. No action is singled out or reserved for anyone. But whatever we do has an effect, for, as we sow, so do we reap. The sense of morality is developed in Dharam Khand.

The Guru Granth affirms that all the four castes possess the one and same Order: "khatri brahman sud vais, updes cahu varna ko sajha"—be they Kshatriyas, Brahmins, Shudras or Vaishyas, the Message is shared by people of all complexions (Guru Granth, p. 747). This Message, according to Guru Arjan, is shared not just by people of the four castes, but includes people of all complexions. Rejecting distinctions and restrictions, the Guru Granth declares that Dharam succeeds when the entire earth becomes equal, literally one color: "sristi sabh ikk varan hoi" (Guru Granth, p. 663). The Fifth Guru describes the enlightened as "those who view everyone equally, like the air touching king and beggar alike" (Guru Granth, p. 272). Guru Gobind Singh urges his people to recognize the single caste of humanity. His verse, "manas ki jat sabhe eke janbo," is popularly recited by the Sikhs throughout the world.

There is a saying in Sikhism that a Sikh should be a Brahmin in piety, a Kshatriya in defense of truth and the oppressed, a Vaishya in business ventures and professional drive, and a Shudra in serving humanity. Thus a Sikh should share in the virtue of each caste but belong to none.

E. From Self to Others

The individual in search of liberation has a natural desire to reach out to family and friends, and guide others in their search. A selfish motivation is overridden by mutuality and relationships. "Those who remember the Name earn true success. Their faces shine, and they take many with them to liberation" (Guru Granth, p. 8). The paradigmatic figure of Sikh ethics lives freely in the world without any bonds or limitations. Such a person may be variously known as a *jivanmukt* (free in life), *brahmgyani* (enlightened), or *sant* (saint), but he or she invariably enjoys serving others. Guru Tegh Bahadur describes how an individual becomes free by abandoning attachment, greed, passion, and pride, and how in turn the same person becomes a channel for the liberation of others (Guru Granth, p. 1427). Recognition of the Singular Creator is manifested in acts of love toward all fellow beings. What we find here is the importance of the companionship of the good, and a reiteration of the nexus between self and others.

F. Moksha Becomes a Political Ideology

Moksha, the Sikh ideal of spiritual liberation (an end to entry into any finite form), extends to an egalitarian and free model of being here and now. The free world beyond entails a life without political, sexual, racial, and caste oppressions on earth. Along with their spiritual goal of moksha, the Sikh gurus tried to formulate new possibilities for the weak and the degraded within their society. Their poetic articulations seek a radical transformation of the life of the oppressed, especially that of women and the low caste.

The Sikh gurus tried to give women status and dignity. Guru Nanak and his successors were deeply conscious of women's victimization prevalent in their society. Customs like *sati* (a widow having to jump on the funeral pyre of her husband) and *purdah* (veiling), and such beliefs as menstrual pollution, which denigrated women in their milieu, were loudly denounced. There is no priesthood in Sikhism, and the sacred text stresses the equality of men and women in their search for the Divine. Celibacy is rejected; wives are regarded as essential partners for moral and spiritual development. Rules of conduct and religious duties are the same for both men and women. Both have identical status, and

as early as Guru Amar Das (Nanak 3), women were appointed as religious leaders along with men.

In 1699 Guru Gobind Singh fulfilled his aspiration for freedom and equality through his inauguration of the Khalsa, the Order of the Pure. It was a casteless and self-abnegating body of Sikhs ready to take up arms to fight against injustice and tryanny. Chanting verses from the Guru Granth, Guru Gobind Singh began the new initiation into the Khalsa by churning water, poured into a steel bowl, with a double-edged sword. His wife, Mata Sahib Kaur, came forward and dropped sugar crystals into the vessel. Sweetness through the feminine hand was thus mingled with the alchemy of iron. The occasion marked a dramatic departure from the past. The drink (*amrita*) was sipped from the same bowl, sealing the pledge of equality and faithfulness.

The amrita initiation is open to both men and women, and both are to wear the emblems of the Khalsa, popularly known as the five K's. Men are given the surname of Singh, meaning lion, and the women, Kaur, meaning princess. Their rebirth into the Order represents an annihilation of their family (caste) lineage, their confinement to a heredity occupation, and all their stifling beliefs and rituals. In the egalitarian structure established by Guru Gobind Singh, women were liberated from tracing their lineage to their father or adopting a husband's name after marriage. As Singh and Kaur, Sikh men and women are enjoined to help the weak and fight the oppressor.

Guru Gobind Singh reiterated the First Guru's message to have faith in the One, and consider all human beings equal, irrespective of caste and religion. He also composed heroic and martial poetry to inspire bravery, dispel cowardice, and infuse the hearts of men and women with confidence and courage. Within half a century of their Tenth Guru's death (1708), Sikhs became a major political force, and they established a state of their own in another 40 years. Guru Nanak's vision to affirm and celebrate the oneness of Ultimate Reality and the oneness of humanity was given a practical form by Guru Gobind Singh. The sword that his followers carry is a metaphor for the triumph of knowledge over nescience, a symbol to fight for the protection of the oppressed and the cause of liberty. It is, however, to be undertaken as a last resort, as it should only be used in defense.

Nir bhau (without fear) and *nir vair* (without enmity), the characteristics attributed to the Divine by Guru Nanak (at the very beginning of the Japji), have come to define Sikh character. Sikhs are to fight valiantly against subjugation and tyranny, but they are to have enmity toward no one. A just cause must be the motive for battle, not revenge or greed.

IV. VICE AND VIRTUE

Kam, krodha, lobh, moh, and *ahankar*—lust, anger, greed, attachment, and pride, respectively—are the five vices. Sikh scripture speaks of them as thieves and robbers that reside in us, for they steal the preciousness with which we are all endowed (Guru Granth, p. 600). These five are the psychological and inner propensities that are harmful. While splitting the individual from the Transcendent core, they are also antisocial elements that detach us from one another. Lust, anger, greed, attachment, and pride put a person out of joint, and each of these emotions hurts a person psychologically and physiologically. But each of them also puts social cohesion and integration into jeopardy. They rob the individual of the underlying unity of humanity and brutally destroy social relations. From the Sikh perspective, then, the individual and the society are interrelated, and the psychological balance of an individual constitutes the good of society at large.

Haumai, literally, "I myself," is regarded as the root cause of human suffering. It means investing oneself with pride and arrogance. By constantly centering on "I", "me", and "mine," the self is circumscribed as a particular person, away from the universal source. In the Jap, Guru Nanak provides the image of a wall; just as a wall constructs barriers, so does haumai. By building up the ego, the individual is divided from the One Reality. Duality (*dubida*) comes into play. The selfish ego sees itself in opposition to others—in opposition to the cosmos. The divine spark within remains obstructed. The singular harmony is broken. Such an existence is measured through competition, malice, ill-will toward others, and a craving for power. Blinded, the individual lives for himself or herself alone. The selfish person is called *manmukh,* "turned toward the *me*," in contrast with one who remains in harmony with the divine Word and is called *gurmukh,* "turned toward the guru."

How are the five thieves caught? How is the wall of egotism broken? Sikh ethical injunctions reiterate that pilgrimages, fasts, and ascetic practices are of no avail. Physical torture or any form of extreme measure cannot get rid of vice. "One removes vice with virtue, for virtue is our only true friend and sibling" (Guru Granth p. 595). Metaphors that integrate us with family and friends are used to express the importance of living virtuously. Balance and equipoise, and a very natural

rhythm of daily routine, are the way to attain ultimate liberation. To this end, Guru Nanak provides a simple formula: *sunia, mania, manu kita bhau.*

Sunia literally signifies hearing, and it means hearkening to the divine Word. It is the first step toward awakening to the transcendent core of the universe. Hearing is the sense that most directly connects the conscious and the unconscious realms. According to Guru Nanak, by listening to the melodious Name, one fathoms the oceans of virtue. Stanzas 8–11 of the Jap explain the vital role of listening. Through listening one gains the faculties of all the gods, one gains knowledge of all the continents, one acquires the import of all the ancient texts, one learns all the techniques of meditation, one masters the experience of all the sages of Hinduism and Islam (and by implication all religions), and all suffering and distress are annulled. By hearing the divine Name the ultimate objective is achieved: one becomes immortal and is freed from the finitude of death. The refrain in these stanzas acknowledges that the devotees who hear the Name of the True One enjoy eternal bliss.

Mania means remembering the One—keeping the One constantly in our mind. This process is not purely intellectual for it has connotations of trust and faith. It is the second step, for it is only after something is heard that it can enter the mind. By keeping the Divine in our mind, we are liberated from the constant bondage of birth and death, and we also assist in liberating family and friends.

Manu kita bhau means to be full of love for the Divine. This state of devotion is the third step, one that goes beyond hearing the Name and keeping the Name in mind. For those who attain this state, "every thread of their being is drenched in love." It is the highest form of action. Love is passionate and takes lovers to depths of richness and fullness where there is freedom from all kinds of limitations of the self. Cleansing through love and devotion is the starting point of Sikh ethics. Again and again in the Guru Granth, love is applauded as the supreme virtue: "Pure, pure, utterly pure are they, Says Nanak, who recite the Name with love" (Guru Granth, p. 279). Love empowers us; its strength dispels all vice, claims Guru Arjan. The response of love regarded as the path to liberation by the first Sikh guru is reiterated throughout the Guru Granth. It is also encapsulated by the Tenth Guru:

I tell the Truth, do listen to me
  they alone who live, find the Beloved

(Savayye no. 9)

V. SIKH INSTITUTIONS

A. Seva

The highest ideal in Sikh ethics is seva, which is voluntary manual labor in the service of the community. Beginning with Guru Nanak, it is seen as an essential condition of spiritual discipline. Through seva, Sikh believers cultivate humility, overcome ego, and purify their body and mind. Over the centuries, seva has become an essential part of Sikh life. It may take the form of attending to the holy book, sweeping and dusting Sikh shrines, preparing and serving food, or looking after and even cleaning the shoes of the worshippers. The young and old, and the rich and poor, each takes on and performs the different tasks. Seva also includes serving the community at large by helping them to build schools, hospitals, orphanages, and charity homes. A leprosarium was established by Guru Nanak at Taran Taran, and medical work and the care of the needy have always been regarded as important forms of seva. The attachment of medical clinics to Sikh shrines is traced to Guru Har Rai's interest in medicine.

Seva goes beyond serving fellow Sikhs. It is to be extended to all, friend and enemy alike. One Sikh account tells the story of a Sikh soldier named Ghanaya in the army of Guru Gobind Singh. His fellow soldiers saw him giving water to fallen enemies and reported him to the Guru. Ghanaya was called in and questioned. He responded that as he moved about the battlefield, he had seen neither friend nor foe but only the Guru's face. According to this account, Guru Gobind Singh gave him medicines and bandages and sent him back to help the wounded. Sikhs point to these actions as an example of nonpartisan, humanitarian aid to the victims of war that predates the Red Cross and the Red Crescent by centuries. Most Sikh shrines include lodging houses where pilgrims and travelers may stay.

B. Langar

Langar is both the community meal and the kitchen in which it is prepared. It is a central practice of Sikhism. It testifies to the social equality and familyhood of all people. This fundamental institution involves the process of preparing meals together as well as eating together. The food used at langar is vegetarian. Both men and women engage in preparation and cleanup— chopping vegetables, kneading and rolling out dough, and cleaning utensils. Then they sit in pangat, or a long row, without regard to caste, race, or religion, and they eat the meal that they have prepared together.

In Guru Nanak's time, the idea of different castes eating together was bold and revolutionary. Yet the first Guru understood the importance of a shared meal in creating a feeling of belonging and fellowship. Like a Thanksgiving feast or Christmas dinner, like the Jewish Seder or other traditional meals, all of which are shared with close ones, langar creates a feeling of family. It extends the concept of the family meal as a step toward bonding human beings regardless of race, gender, caste, and class.

No idea of pollution is to be associated with langar. As an instrument of social change, langar continued to gain importance under the leadership of the successive gurus. In Guru Angad's day, his wife, Mata Khivi, was known for the rich and delicious meals she served. The Third Guru, Amar Das, insisted that visitors first enjoy langar with the community before meeting with him. "First pangat, then meeting with the guru," he decreed.

Sikhs consider langar to be a way of earning merit toward rebirth and their next life. Whether in Amritsar, London, Paris, or Toronto, Sikhs stress the community meal. So long as they observe the basic guidelines, non-Sikhs and foreigners are welcomed too. Often, langar extends beyond the Gurudwaras. During certain celebrations, such as the birthday of a guru, the celebration of an important historical event, or the martyrdom of a Sikh hero, langar is everywhere, even on the Indian highways and byways. Sikhs of all ages arrange themselves in rows to block the road or they lay tree trunks across it to stop the flow of traffic. They stop the speeding buses, cars, and trucks, the slow-going bullock-carts, rickshaws, and pedestrians, and they enthusiastically serve langar including tea, chappatis, dal, and vegetables to the drivers and passengers.

C. Sangat

Sangat is the Sikh gathering, or local community. It is a democratic community without priests or ordained ministers. Sikhs prize comradeship and company with others, and the fellowship of the sangat is of primary importance in their religious practice. The tradition of an active and fruitful involvement with the community comes from Guru Nanak himself, and Sikhs see community participation as an essential part of their faith. According to a popular Sikh saying, "One disciple is a single Sikh, two form a holy association, but where there are five present, there is the Ultimate Reality Itself."

Like langar, sangat is open to all. Members of Sikh congregation sit on the floor, singing hymns, listening to readings from the holy text, reciting verses, and praying with no restrictions as to gender, race, creed, or caste. The inclusive nature of sangat dates to the time of Guru Nanak, who welcomed everyone who wished to follow his teachings. Sangat is a mode of both spiritual and moral inspiration. According to Guru Nanak, "Through sangat, one obtains the treasure of the Divine Name.... Just as iron rubbed against the philosopher's stone turns into gold, so does dark ignorance transform into brilliant light in company of the good." Participation with others becomes a force for inspiring the spiritual quest.

VI. POPULAR MORALITY

At the everyday level, Sikh morality is best summed up in the maxim, *Kirat karni, vand chhakna, te nam japna*—to labor for one's keep, to share with others, and to practice the repetition of the Divine Name.

Kirat karni is one of the basics of Sikh ethics. In Punjabi kirat means "the labor of one's hands." It is manual work—honest, upright work in pursuit of one's living. The term underscores the dignity of all labor. Sikhs understand it to mean that not to work if one is able is an offense to the faith. Honest work and its satisfactions create a positive attitude toward life. Sikhs reject withdrawal from society. Home and family are the rule.

Vand chhakna is the sharing of money and goods before using them oneself. The phrase comes from vand, distribution or sharing, and chhakna, to eat. It is based on mutual respect and sharing among equals, not on charity. Just as members of a family share their earnings and goods with one another for the benefit of the whole, so Sikhs try to act in the larger family of the community for its well-being. This principle of sharing is basic to the institutions of sangat and langar, which have been primary factors in shaping Sikh conduct.

Nam japna is to remember the Divine Name. Nam literally means name, and japna to repeat or meditate on. Constantly to repeat the name of the One is a great virtue in Sikh religion. Name is more important spirtually than other traditionally religious actions: "superior to all acts of piety, charity, and austerity is nam." Nam does not take the place of other acts, but it is the source from which all ethical action emerges.

VII. DEONTOLOGY

A. Daily Prayers

As the *Sikh Rahit Maryada* decrees, a Sikh should rise early, take a bath, and then meditate on the One True Reality. A recitation, reading, or hearing of five hymns forms a part of the daily Sikh schedule. Guru Nanak's Japji along with Guru Gobind Singh's Jap Sahib and Ten Swayyai constitute the morning prayers. Sodar Rahiras is to be recited in the evening and Kirtan Sohila before going to bed. The Almighty One and major figures of Sikh history are remembered during the course of the day through Ardas, the prayer recited while standing up. In the aural or visual presence of the sacred verse, heads of both men and women are covered. In the presence of the Guru Granth, the shoes are also taken off.

B. The Five K's

Since 1699, both Sikh men and women have maintained their identity through five external signs, all beginning with the letter "k":

1. *Kesha*, or uncut hair, denoting the way of nature
2. *Kangha*, a comb tucked into the kesha to keep it tidy in contrast with the recluses who keep it matted as a token of their having renounced the world
3. *Kara*, a steel bracelet worn on the right arm, the steel representing spiritual courage and strength, and its circular form the unity of the Ultimate One, with no beginning or end
4. *Kaccha*, short breeches worn by the soldiers at the time of the Tenth Guru, stand for chastity and moral restraint
5. *Kirpan*, a sword symbolizing self-defense and the fight against injustice

Sikh men are easily recognized with their untrimmed beards and colorful turbans wrapped around their heads. The turban is the most notable feature of Sikh men's clothing. Other men of India may wear the turban, often a feature of Muslim dress, but it is particularly associated with Sikhs, who wear it as a religious symbol. Such a visible symbol has sometimes been a problem. Britain had to pass special laws to exempt turbaned Sikhs from a law requiring them to wear motorcycle helmets. In America, a court case brought by a Sikh has led the U.S. Army to consider whether its Sikhs may be permitted to wear the turban with their uniforms.

Women and girls refrain from cutting their hair as well. Young girls wear long braids, and women tie up their hair in a variety of styles. Sikh women dress in a particular style and can be identified by their clothing—loose trousers (salvar), a shirt that reaches to the knees (kameez), and a long, sheer scarf wound around the neck or over the head (dupatta).

C. Rules Regarding Women in the *Sikh Rahit Maryada*

In its attempt to formalize the message of the Ten Gurus, the *Sikh Rahit Maryada* developed several rules that would combat female oppression.

Twice it makes the point that Sikh women should not veil their faces. It prohibits infanticide, and even association with people who would pratice it. It allows for widow remarriage, and it underscores that the ceremony be the same as that of the first marriage—a marked difference from the custom where the widow was shamefully wrapped in a sheet and carried away to a brother of the dead husband.

Sikhs should be free of all superstitions, and not refuse to eat at the home of their married daughter. The assumption underlying this injunction most likely is that daughters should not be treated like an object or piece of property passed away to her husband and his family.

Dowry is prohibited. Neither a girl nor a boy should be married for money. Child marriages are not permitted. A girl should marry only when she has attained physical and mental maturity.

There is no prohibition against abortion.

D. Negative Imperatives

The *Sikh Rahit Marayada* specifically prohibits the following four acts:

1. Cutting or trimming hair for both men and women
2. Eating of meat put through the slow purification rite (*halal*); Sikhs may eat meat but only that from an animal slaughtered in one stroke (*jhatka*)
3. Adultery
4. Use of narcotics

Sikhs should not take intoxicants and narcotics, such as hemp, opium, spirits, and tobacco, as they harm the mind.

In the case of a violation of these imperatives, the person may appear before any religious congregation of the Sikhs, seek their punishment, perform it cheerfully, and be reinitiated into Khalsahood. Even if the people at fault be Granthis (official attendants to the Guru Granth), they must present themselves before a congregation of Sikhs and go through the same process.

VIII. CONCLUSION

Overall, Sikh ethics harmonizes very well with the modern world. Sikhs see the message of Guru Nanak as a response to contemporary problems of racism, gender, caste, and class. The particular ethical structure of Sikhism is based on recognizing a Universal Reality that can be experienced by people of all races and creeds. The Sikh ideal of unity in diversity offers a hopeful direction for the world of the future.

See Also the Following Article

RELIGION AND ETHICS

Bibliography

Cole, W. O., & Sambhi, P. S. (1978). *The Sikhs, their beliefs, and practices.* London: Routledge & Kegan Paul.
McLeod, W. H. (1989). *Who is a Sikh?* Oxford: Clarendon Press.
Singh, A. (1970). *The ethics of the Sikhs.* Patiala: Punjabi Univ.
Singh, N. (1990). *Sikh moral tradition.* New Delhi: Manohar.
Singh, N.-G. K. (1993). Sundari: The paradigm of Sikh ethics. In *The feminine principle in the Sikh vision of the transcendent* (pp. 188–204). Cambridge: Cambridge Univ. Press.

SLAVERY

Burton M. Leiser
Pace University

GLOSSARY

concubine A girl or woman who is required to serve a man although she is not married to him, and who has the duty to permit him to have sexual intercourse with her. Concubinage is different from prostitution in that it is usually an exclusive, continuing relationship that is not necessarily dependent upon the concubine's willingness to participate in it.

emancipation The freeing of a slave.

Helot A slave employed in agriculture, especially in ancient Sparta.

manumission The act of freeing a slave, conferring independence and freedom upon him or her.

servitude A kind of slavery, in which one person is forced, against his or her will, to act in accordance with the demands of another.

SLAVERY is an involuntary form of human servitude. Although there are many forms of slavery, the predominant form involves absolute control of the slave by his or her master, in which the master owns the slave, who is regarded as a possession or piece of property, in the same sense as one might own a cow, an acre of land, or a piece of furniture. Thus, slaves may be bought or sold, given by one person to another as gifts, and transmitted from one generation to another by way of inheritance. They may also be pledged as security for loans, so that if the loan is not paid on time, they may be taken away and ownership in them transferred to the lender. They may be required to do any kind of work or perform any kind of service for their masters, without limitation, and their masters have virtually absolute control over them.

I. TYPES OF SLAVERY

A number of forms of slavery that have existed are still recognized by leading authorities, including the United Nations, which adopted a Convention on Slavery and the Slave Trade and Institutions Similar to Slavery in 1956. Each of these forms of slavery existed somewhere in the world when the Convention was adopted, and there is evidence that all of them continue to exist in various places.

The UN Convention distinguished the following forms of slavery:

- *Debt bondage:* A form of slavery or servitude that arises when a person pledges himself or herself or the services of another person over whom he or she has control. The pledge is open-ended, so that the individual must do any kind of work that is demanded, for any length of time, up to and including his or her lifetime, and can never buy out of the arrangement because no monetary value is assigned to the bargain.

- *Serfdom.* A condition in which a person lives on land belonging to another, and must work for the landowner without being able to move away or to change his or her status.
- *Exploitation of children.* This consists of any practice whereby a person under the age of 18 is delivered by a parent or guardian to another person, with or without payment. The individual who receives control of the child is then permitted to use the child for his or her own purposes, sexual or otherwise, and to exploit the child's labor.
- *Servile forms of marriage.* This condition arises when a girl or a woman is promised or given in marriage without her consent to a man who pays for the right to marry her. Power over her may then be transferred to another person, or if her husband dies, she may be inherited by another person as if she were property belonging to her husband's estate.

In addition, there is absolute slavery, as it has been practiced from time immemorial in many parts of the world, and as it existed in the United States until it was abolished by the Emancipation Proclamation and the Civil War Amendments (i.e., Amendments Thirteen, Fourteen, and Fifteen) to the United States Constitution. This is the form of slavery described in the definition at the head of this article. Such a slave was regarded as the absolute property of his or her master. The master could buy or sell his slaves. He could beat them. He could treat them as well or as badly as he pleased. He could exploit them sexually. Any children they bore were also his property, and he could either sell them or keep them, as he wished, to raise them to perform specific kinds of work. A slave owner who killed his slave, either directly or by starving or mistreating him, was usually subject to no punishment. The slave was in all respects like a pet dog or horse. If the owner concluded that one of his farm animals or one of his slaves was not worth keeping, he could dispose of either of them in any way he chose.

II. SLAVERY IN ANCIENT TIMES

Evidence from various parts of the world, including texts that have been preserved in stone and on papyrus,

suggests that everywhere throughout much of mankind's history, slavery in one form or another has been practiced.

A. The Middle East

1. Babylonia

Ancient legal codes, such as the Code of Hammurabi and other codes from the ancient Near East, refer frequently to laws and regulations governing slave ownership. Carvings, sculptures, and paintings from Babylonia, Assyria, Egypt, and other countries depict slaves performing a variety of tasks under the watchful eyes of their taskmasters.

Most people who became slaves were captured during the many wars that raged through the world. It was taken for granted that the conquering armies had the right to loot and pillage the enemy's territory, to rape any women they found, and to kill anyone they pleased. Those who were spared would be placed in chains and would be forced to march with the conquering army to fulfill its desires for sex and other services. If the army was continuing its military campaign, some of the vanquished men, women, and children might die on the way, or they might be traded or sold to merchants who usually followed in the wake of such armies. If the army was heading home, the captives would either be sold or distributed among the members of the brigade as their own property.

Most slaves probably were employed in heavy labor, such as road building, construction, and mining. Some, who were skilled artisans, would have been put to work at their trades. Female slaves might be employed as singers, dancers, and prostitutes, or, more often, put to work as household servants.

2. Ancient Israel

In ancient Israel, according to the Bible, the institution of slavery existed, but in greatly modified form. People could become slaves for a variety of reasons: because they were captured in war, because they had committed certain serious crimes, or because they were in debt and sold themselves into servitude in order to pay off their debts.

In ancient Israel, slaves did not lose all of their personal rights. For example, a slave who was seriously injured by his master was automatically entitled to be set free. A debtor who had sold himself into slavery in order to pay off his debt was either set free in the sabbatical year (one of these occurred every 7 years) or could be "redeemed," or bought out of the condition of slavery, by payment of the remainder of his debt.

Slave holders were not permitted to mistreat their slaves, but were obliged to treat them humanely. If a slave was a professional or practiced some skilled craft, his master was obliged to find a suitable occupation for him, so that he would not be reduced to doing menial work. Thus, a physician would continue to practice medicine, a teacher would continue to teach, and a carpenter would practice his trade. Although they were expected to work, their workload was not to exceed their physical abilities. They were permitted to enjoy and to observe the religious holidays and to have a day off each week on the Sabbath. They were entitled to own property of their own, and were thus able to accumulate enough wealth to redeem themselves.

Special rules applied to female slaves: When they became physically mature (that is, when they entered puberty), their masters were obliged either to marry them or to set them free.

Hebrew slaves could be held in bondage for no more than 6 years. Every 7th year was a "sabbatical" year during which all debts were forgiven and all slaves were set free. When a slave was set free (a process called "manumission"), it was strictly forbidden to let him or her go without enough to live on. A slave who insisted on remaining in a condition of bondage, either because he had developed a slave mentality, preferring dependency over liberty, or because he had developed some affection for his master and the conditions under which he was living, was permitted to do so. However, such a person, giving up his chance for freedom, was indelibly marked with a hole drilled in his ear. Later commentators suggested that this was to indicate that one who had heard the declaration of individual liberty and responsibility that was revealed in the Ten Commandments at Mount Sinai after the exodus from Egyptian slavery was disgraced by having chosen eternal bondage instead.

The people of Israel were constantly reminded in the Torah (the Hebrew Bible) that they were obliged to treat slaves and strangers with kindness and compassion, for they (or more properly, their ancestors) had once been strangers and then slaves in Egypt, where they were treated very badly indeed.

B. Ancient Greece and Rome

Although there were some differences in detail, and some developments that changed particular practices over time, the main outlines of slavery in the Mediterranean world during the long periods when it was dominated by the Greek and Roman empires were very similar.

Slavery was a major source of labor in the ancient world. Although we do not know exactly how many people were slaves, the best estimates are that on average, every household in Athens had about four slaves. Far more were at work on farms, in the mines, and tending animals, as well as in textile production and other enterprises.

The Greeks of the ancient world drew a rigid distinction between themselves and people of other nations, and so, later on, did the Romans. They were prepared to concede that other people were human beings; but they were barbarians, somewhat lower intellectually, spiritually, and socially than those who were native born. The word *barbarian* is probably derived from *barbar,* what a person who is jabbering a foreign language must have sounded like to the Greeks. The Greeks appear to have thought that people who talked in such an outlandish way must have been inferior intellectually to themselves, for they simply made no sense. Slaves, who were foreigners or "barbarians," for the most part, may have been human beings, but they were just barely above animals in the scale of Greek and Roman values. There was therefore no reason why they should not become someone's property, just as domestic animals were, and thus subject to the will of their owners. Their own wishes were quite irrelevant. They had no right to own property. Even if a slave's master allowed him to amass some wealth, the slave could not spend it or otherwise dispose of it without the master's permission, since after all, the slave himself was the master's possession. His family, if he was allowed to have one at all, was not his own. The members of a slave's family could be dispersed whenever the master decided to sell them off or trade them for other valuables. A slave's name appeared in no official register except the inventory of his owner's possessions. For all practical purposes, therefore, he was virtually a nonperson. He was cut off from his own cultural roots, he had no right to practice his own religious rites or even to speak his native tongue, unless he happened to be Greek by birth.

As far as the law was concerned, slave owners had virtually total control over their slaves and could do almost anything they wanted with them. If a slave owner was so inclined, he was legally entitled to castrate his male slaves. Such practices were discouraged on the ground that they set bad precedents for the treatment of free men, but there was no legal prohibition against them. Castration was practiced until quite recently, and may still be practiced in societies where slavery continues to exist, as a means of protecting female slaves and others against possible sexual relations with male slaves. Incidentally, in some Christian countries, boys who were particularly good singers were castrated so that their voices would not change at puberty. These men (called *castrati*) were particularly prized because their voices were so unique and added a special musical flavor to church choirs and opera companies.

Because they had no legal standing, slaves had to be represented in court by free men, and their testimony was accepted only if it was extracted under torture. It was believed that people with the mentality of slaves could not be counted on to tell the truth, but under torture, and with the threat of even greater pain to come, they would give more reliable testimony.

Any damage caused by a slave to the property of another person had to be paid for by the slave's master. It was a crime to murder a slave, but the charge of murdering a slave was strictly a private matter, brought by the slave's master, and the penalty was a fine, rather than death, unless the perpetrator was a slave himself. Since a trial for a slave's murder had to be brought by the slave's owner, it was virtually impossible for a slaveholder to be tried for having murdered one of his own slaves. No matter how harshly he had been abused, a slave could not defend himself against a free man, and the plea of self-defense was invalid if it was invoked by a slave.

A father whose daughter committed adultery had the right to sell her into slavery. Abandoned infants could be raised by anyone who found them and would be the slaves of those who cared for them as a kind of payment for the services rendered in saving their lives.

Some slaves were acquired through capture during war. Others were sold by the rulers of kingdoms that were getting overcrowded and needed some population relief. Many slaves were imported from Africa, but it appears that for many centuries, most of them came from the Baltic area. A substantial number seems to have fallen into the hands of Greeks through piracy and brigandage: Pirates roamed the seas, seizing vessels of all kinds and capturing crews and passengers, who were then sold into slavery at the most convenient port. Brigands, who spread across the countryside robbing and stealing, often kidnapped vulnerable individuals and either held them for ransom or sold them into slavery. At the conclusion of major battles, the entire population of large cities would be enslaved. Alexander the Great, for example, captured and enslaved all of the people of Thebes after he conquered it.

Slave merchants tagged along after Greek and Roman armies and bought the people who were captured by them. These unfortunate people would then be shipped off to a suitable slave market, usually far away so that they would not be found by relatives or neighbors who

might want to rescue them. There they would be displayed, usually stark naked, so that they could be carefully inspected by potential buyers, and they would then be sold at auction to the highest bidder. It was common for slaves to be branded, just as western ranchers used to brand their cattle and sheep, so that they might easily be traced to their proper owners if they were lost or attempted to escape.

The conditions in which some slaves worked were simply horrifying. Those who were consigned to the mines were exposed to highly toxic substances, and frequently ended up stunted, maimed, or blind. Their infirmities did not excuse them from their work, which continued, no matter how sick they were, until they were too feeble to get up from their beds. They were then left to die. The camps in which they lived were very much like what we would today call concentration camps—wretched places with inadequate housing facilities, no sanitation, and barely enough water and food. They were heavily guarded to prevent them from escaping.

It was generally accepted that both male and female slaves could be sexually exploited in any way that pleased their owners.

In Sparta, young boys used to hide in the fields, lying in wait for helots, publicly owned slaves who were forced to work in agriculture. When an unsuspecting helot came by, the boys would leap out and stab him to death for sport. This was regarded as perfectly natural by the boys' parents and by the authorities, who said, in effect, "Boys will be boys." In addition to such brutal murders, helots were whipped once every year to remind them that they were slaves and that they were expected to be obedient. In order to humiliate them still further, they were made to get drunk and put on public display.

Female slaves who were forced into prostitution led particularly wretched lives, although some, who became courtesans, lived in somewhat better circumstances, at least as long as they appealed physically to their masters.

Slaves were in most respects treated more or less as if they were animals. They were expected to learn obedience by being punished when they disobeyed and rewarded when they obeyed. Experts who taught the art of owning and properly managing slaves explained that masters should never joke with their slaves or spoil them by acting as if they were free men and women. They were to issue simple commands that even the most ignorant slave could understand.

Just as merchants and manufacturers are now expected to inform the buyers of their merchandise of any defects and to warranty them against any serious malfunctions for a reasonable period of time, slave merchants were expected to reveal any hidden defects in their slave merchandise, such as disease or mental or physical disability that might not be immediately obvious to the buyer. If a serious problem arose, the purchaser had the right to demand his money back within 6 months after the sale was concluded.

Natural increase, or slave farming, was another important source of slaves. If a free man, including the master of a slave, impregnated a slave woman, the child resulting from the pregnancy would have the status of its mother, and would thus be a slave and could be raised for that purpose.

III. SLAVERY IN CHRISTIAN AND ISLAMIC NATIONS

A. Shifting Attitudes toward Black Africans

In none of the sacred writings of the major Western religions—Judaism, Christianity, and Islam—is there any suggestion that race or color is a sign of inferiority, or that Blacks, in particular, are more suited to be slaves than other people. In fact, in some of them (e.g., the Biblical Song of Songs), being black is equated with being beautiful. Judaism and Islam both considered manumission (ransoming or freeing of slaves) to be most pious and meritorious, and Islamic religious authorities specifically condemned the enslavement of other Muslims, although they permitted non-Muslims to be enslaved. Among the Muslims of the Middle Ages, there was never any doubt as to the human status of slaves. They were always regarded in religious and official literature as human, and were entitled to be treated as such. However, the ideals of religious thinkers and the reality of practice did not always coincide. Moreover, as time passed, Islamic writers, like Christian writers, were thinking of black skin as being a mark of inferiority, and used the word "black" and its synonyms to signify evil and wickedness. Black Africans were depicted as savages who went about naked and practiced cannibalism, living more like animals than like human beings. Some writers suggested that apes were more intelligent and more easily trained than black Africans. It was just a short step from the premise that Blacks were animal-like to the conclusion that like animals, they could be captured and domesticated for the benefit of those who got possession and ownership of them.

We should not assume, however, that either Christians or Muslims believed that Blacks were the only people suited for slavery. On the contrary, they were quite prepared to enslave White people as well. Muslims were officially opposed to the enslavement of fellow Muslims or of Christians or Jews who lived in Islamic lands under the "protection" of Islamic authorities. However, they were very happy indeed when pirates stationed in North Africa captured ships with Christian passengers. Christians were especially valuable slaves and fetched high prices in the markets for concubines, servants, soldiers, and oarsmen on galleys. The Crusades helped to increase the bitter hatred that Muslims and Christians had for one another, and enhanced the prices that were paid in Islamic lands for Christian slaves. The converse was true in the Christian territories of Europe, where Muslim slaves were bought and sold.

B. The International Trade in Slaves

A thriving business developed in ransoming slaves. Jewish communities were especially hard hit, since they would spare no effort and no expense to ransom Jews who were captured by slavers. Christian emissaries brought large sums of money with them on their missions to ransom Christians who had been captured and faced a lifetime of slavery, and pirates and slave merchants made fortunes by dealing with such people. Christianity, which inherited the Roman Empire and many of the laws and customs of Rome, embraced slavery for many centuries.

The great trading cities of Italy, which did a thriving business importing and exporting goods to and from all parts of Asia and Africa, became involved in the slave trade quite early—centuries before Columbus's voyages to the New World. The merchants of Genoa in particular sold thousands of Christian slaves from the Balkans, Greece, and the area around the Black Sea to Muslims in Syria, Egypt, and other Islamic lands. The various popes issued edicts condemning such practices, but the Genoese traders seemed to be unfazed by them. As long as money was to be made, and their chief competitors in Venice were still in the business, they were unlikely to be deterred by papers issued by religious leaders in Rome. For many centuries, slavery had been an accepted practice in southern Italy, Sicily, Spain, and other parts of Europe along the Mediterranean. The people who were profiting from the trade in slaves were not about to give up this lucrative source of income. They simply saw no rational justification for doing so. So far as they were concerned, buying and selling human beings was not significantly different from buying and selling cattle or tropical birds.

C. The Introduction of Slavery into the New World

The Spanish and Portuguese invaders of the New World had no compunctions about enslaving the Indians they encountered. The Spanish conquistadors who overpowered the Inca kingdom of Peru in the late fifteenth and early sixteenth centuries used extraordinarily brutal methods to force the Indians to work for them. They placed iron collars around their necks and chained them together in work gangs, compelling them to descend into dark, smoky mines where they dug for gold and silver. Working with mercury to purify the precious metals for shipment back to Spain, the Indian slaves suffered from mercury poisoning, and within a very short time, the population began a dramatic tailspin. Deaths from disease, overwork, and malnutrition decimated the once-proud people; and the terrible working conditions were so unendurable that the men lost interest in their women, so that the birth rate fell precipitously. In the rest of Latin America and throughout the Caribbean, the same pattern was repeated. Before long, the entire populations of some of the islands disappeared into history, a campaign of genocide—the extinction of entire nations and races—that compares to some of the worst in history.

As the excitement over the New World spread throughout Europe, and other European nations sent their ships to explore and colonize North and South America and the Caribbean, they followed the example set by the Spanish and Portuguese in establishing work forces to exploit the natural resources of the lands they were conquering. England, the Netherlands, France, Germany, and others eagerly established sugar, cotton, and tobacco plantations and forced the native peoples into bondage in order to work them. It soon became evident, however, that the Indians would not survive long in captivity. Because they knew the territory, they were inclined to try to escape, and often did so successfully. In the end, however, their numbers were decimated by disease, malnutrition, and despair. In order to replenish their work forces, they turned to Black Africa, where a thriving business was going on. The Europeans preferred Blacks from Africa over other potential sources of slaves because they believed that Blacks were stronger and more suited to the kind of physical labor that needed to be done and that they were more likely to be able to tolerate the tropical climate of the Caribbean than others.

1. The African Slave Trade

As the demand for Black slaves increased, Black tribal leaders in Africa found that they could benefit greatly by supplying the European slave traders with the commodities that they wanted—their own people. They rounded up men and women from their own tribes and sold them to the European traders with whom they were doing business. They also sent raiding parties into neighboring territories to capture people from other tribes for sale to the Europeans. They were an important link in the slave trade that thrived for several centuries. The European traders themselves raided African villages, captured as many of the inhabitants as they could, and sent them off in chains to the ports from which they were shipped to Europe and the Americas. The shipmasters soon discovered that they could make a handy profit by following a triangular route. Starting in Europe, they would sail to Africa and pick up a cargo of newly acquired slaves. They would cross the Atlantic and trade the slaves for sugar, rum, gold, silver, and other commodities that were being produced in the Americas. These would then be brought to Europe, where they were eagerly snapped up at a tidy profit for the shippers, and the cycle would begin anew.

D. Slavery in the United States

The colonies that ultimately became the United States of America introduced slavery almost from the very beginning of their existence. Relatively few of the early colonists saw anything wrong with the institution of slavery, and they shared the views of their European brothers that it was normal and natural for some people to be slaves. Slavery continued to exist throughout most of Europe well into the nineteenth century. It was not surprising that Frenchmen, Englishmen, Dutchmen, Spaniards, Portuguese, and others who had possessed slaves in their homelands would transplant the practice to their new homes—especially when the people they enslaved seemed to be primitive and uncivilized and appeared to have so little in common with their masters.

It is often assumed that slavery was confined to the southern part of the United States. That assumption is incorrect. Residents of New York, Philadelphia, and Boston kept slaves and enjoyed the services they provided. In New York City, for example, black slaves constituted 21% of the population in the 1740s, and in Kings County (which is Brooklyn today), they were over 34% of the population. Even Virginia, Jamaica, and Antigua, all major slave-holding centers, had fewer slaves per capita.

In the South, however, slavery became a way of life, and from the White population's perspective, it was absolutely vital that it be maintained. Sugar, cotton, and tobacco, the main ingredients of the southern economy, could not be raised successfully without an enormous force to work the fields. Even if the farmers could have found free men and women willing to do the back-breaking labor, they could not have afforded to pay them what it would have taken to keep the plantations running profitably.

Slavery in the American South was about the same as it was in the slave-holding societies described above. Some southern planters moved a few of their slaves out of the fields and into household chores—cooking, cleaning, child care, and the like—but however warm personal relationships might have become, the psychological distance remained: a slave always remained a slave, a piece of property listed on the master's inventory like any farm implement or animal, incapable of winning his or her own freedom except through an unlikely act of grace and charity on the part of the master, subject to sale at a moment's notice, lacking even the most elementary human rights—other than those the master chose to recognize, but subject to losing them on the master's momentary whim.

An immense body of literature exists that reveals clearly the extent to which African American slaves were excluded from enjoying even the most elementary human rights, even after the Declaration of Independence declared that all men are created equal. The Constitution provided that a state's representatives would be apportioned by a census in which every free person would be counted as one person, but "all others," obviously meaning slaves, would count as three-fifths of a person.

1. The Dred Scott Decision

The hopelessness of the Black slave's plight was perhaps most dramatically exposed in the *Dred Scott* decision, in which the United States Supreme Court declared that a slave who traveled with his master from Missouri, where slavery was legal, to Illinois, where it was not, remained a slave throughout that time, and could not claim to have become a free man by virtue of his having been in a state where slavery was outlawed.

Chief Justice Taney argued that Congress had no right to decree that slaves or any other form of property could be taken from their owners in any territory that was under the jurisdiction of the United States, because the Constitution conferred no such right. Even though slavery was illegal in Illinois, the slave remained his owner's property throughout their visit to that State. Justice Daniel wrote:

> The African negro race never have been acknowledged as belonging to the family of nations; ... amongst them there never has been known or recognized by the inhabitants of other countries anything partaking of the character of nationality, or civil or political polity; ... this race has been regarded by all the nations of Europe as subjects of capture or purchase; as subjects of commerce or traffic; ... the introduction of that race into every section of this country was not as members of civil or political society, but as slaves, as property in the strictest sense of the term.

In Justice Daniel's opinion, a slave is strictly a piece of property, "to be used in subserviency to the interests, the convenience, or the will, of his owner." Slaves have no civil or political rights and cannot be citizens. And those disabilities do not disappear, even if a slave's master chooses to free him. He believed that the collapse of the Roman Empire was caused by Rome's "abasement" of the "proud title of Roman citizen" by the government's failure to keep "inferior classes" in their place. He implied, therefore, that allowing Blacks to become citizens or to have civil or political rights would set the United States on a path leading ultimately to its own destruction.

Slavery was finally brought to an end in the United States, not by a voluntary act on the part of southern slaveholders, but by a decree issued by President Lincoln (the Emancipation Proclamation) during the Civil War, and by some Constitutional amendments that outlawed slavery and involuntary servitude throughout the United States, conferred upon everyone born or naturalized in the United States the privileges and immunities of American citizenship, did away with the fractional counting of Black persons, and gave every citizen, including former slaves, the right to vote.

E. Slavery in the Twentieth Century

Slavery has existed in some parts of the world throughout the twentieth century. Frequent reports from reliable sources indicate that various types of slavery exist in some parts of the world as this article is being written. In some parts of Africa, for example, tribal religious leaders are given the young daughters of men who have committed adultery as a means of atonement for the fathers. The girls are slaves to the priests, who use them for household chores as well as sexual gratification as long as they wish. If a young woman ceases to please her master, he may return her to her father and demand another in her place.

In 1962, Prince Faisal of Saudi Arabia ordered importations of Black slaves from West Africa to be suspended. In the Persian Gulf emirates of Muscat and Oman, slavery officially ended in 1970. However, there is substantial evidence that slavery continues to exist in all of those places. Occasionally, there are court cases in England in which evidence is presented that Arab diplomats and residents have Indian and Sri Lankan slaves whose passports are confiscated so that they cannot flee. They are forbidden to leave the house, are fed irregularly, and are otherwise subjected to serious abuse. In 1984, testimony given to a UN working group alleged that there were about a quarter of a million female slaves in the hands of nomadic tribes in the Sahel. A questionnaire sent by the UN to all member states was answered by Chad as follows:

Does slavery exist in your country? Yes.

What are the causes or reasons for its existence? Tradition.

What steps has your government taken or contemplated for its elimination? None.

Mauritania, which has been one of the major collecting points for black slaves who were captured in various parts of Africa for centuries, is reported to be actively engaged in the slave trade to this day. In 1982, an English observer gave testimony about a slave woman who had refused to go to a new master after she had been sold. Her old master took her back, but in retaliation, dragged the slave woman's mother around by a rope attached to her neck, and beat her daughter so severely that she lost an eye. The woman went to court, but the case was dismissed when her master claimed that she was his wife. She escaped and learned later that her mother had been thrown into a rubbish dump and died because of lack of food and water.

F. Nazi Slave Camps

During the 1930s and 1940s, the Nazi government of Germany, acting upon a theory of racial and genetic inferiority, abolished all rights of persons belonging to certain "inferior" races, including particularly Jews and Gypsies, and systematically proceeded to enslave them and murder them.

The unique aspect of the Nazi form of slavery was its total disregard for the health and well-being of its slaves. In most other societies, although slave owners might have behaved cruelly toward their slaves and deprived them of all rights, they nevertheless considered them to be valuable property, and therefore made some effort to preserve their health and their lives. The Germans, however, had no interest at all in keeping their slaves alive. On the contrary, their policy was explicitly designed to annihilate every Jew. Thus, although Jewish men, women, and children were temporarily converted into slaves, the conditions of their existence were deliberately and systematically designed in such a way as to assure their ultimate destruction. In some camps, hundreds or thousands of people were gassed and burned in a kind of conveyor belt of human slaughter. In others, they were systematically overworked and starved, with death being the ultimate goal, but useful work expected of them as long as they were able to survive in the inhuman conditions into which they had been thrust. Those who became ill were disposed of rather than treated. Their labor was needed, both to further the Nazis' aim to conquer and dominate all of Europe and to complete the slaves' own destruction.

In every slaveholding society, the slaves were considered to be inferior to the slave owners, and were denied their civil and political rights. In Nazi Germany and the lands it occupied, those who employed slave labor were unique in the annals of history, for in the end, although they profited from the labor of their slaves, that was secondary to their ultimate goal of destroying every trace of the slaves themselves.

IV. JUSTIFICATIONS FOR SLAVERY AND ARGUMENTS AGAINST IT

Many Greeks believed that people from other parts of the world were feeble, either physically or mentally, because of such environmental conditions as the climate where they lived. They concluded, therefore, that they were not fit to live the lives of free men, and that they were suited by nature to be slaves. Aristotle, one of the two most renowned philosophers of ancient Greece (the other being Plato), concluded that some people are naturally fit to be free, while others are more suited, by nature, to be slaves. (*Politics* 1327B). Because it is natural for some people to be slaves, Aristotle concluded, it must also be beneficial for them to be slaves, perfectly just for civilized people like the Greeks to own them, and no violation of a slave's rights that he has become someone else's property.

Aristotle and many other philosophers after him believed that barbarians were morally deficient and lacked the full use of reason. Greeks, on the other hand, were assumed to be endowed by nature with a higher moral character and were therefore much more inclined to use reason and to live by it. It followed, according to their logic, that some people were meant to be slaves.

Moreover, they believed that slavery was necessary. Free time did not mean time off from work. It was time spent in the cultivation of the mind, which was essential for a civilized existence. People who are preoccupied with drudgery cannot cultivate their minds. They must be free of such demands on their valuable time so that they can make the most of the time they have to improve their minds. Slaves, who have no real use for free time because their minds are not suited to the life of reason anyway, ought to do the drudge work in order to enable those who can make the fullest use of their most precious asset—their intellects—to educate others and to become more enlightened themselves. In order to cultivate reason, people had to be well educated, and it was essential that they be in good physical shape as well. Slavery was therefore essential for any civilized people, for the slaves left them completely free to engage in sports, music, philosophy, and politics.

The Roman Catholic Church supported the institution of slavery for many centuries, justifying it on grounds similar to those put forward by Aristotle. In fact, the Church did not finally renounce its support of slavery until 1965, in the deliberations known as Vatican II.

Some of the most respected thinkers of modern times did not see slavery as a fundamentally immoral institution, even when they opposed it. Some of them, like Benjamin Franklin, David Hume, and Adam Smith simply believed that slavery was an inherently inefficient, expensive way to produce goods and services. In their view, slave societies inhibited population growth and therefore industrial progress and the scientific advances that industry brings in its wake. Because industry is essential to the production of wealth, societies that permit slavery were in their opinion more likely to be slower in accumulating wealth than those that relied on a free labor force.

Some Christian thinkers believed that slavery was gradually abolished because of an imperceptible improvement in the souls of men who were influenced by the Christian ethic. Some abolitionists believed that slavery was worse for the slaveholders than for the slaves, for it was a contagion that "poisoned the moral springs of the mind." Like the Jews of old, they cited Isaiah's cry, "Proclaim liberty throughout the land!"

Nevertheless, the idea that Blacks were an inferior breed, or possibly even an inferior species, held on. David Hume, the greatest of the British empiricist school of philosophers, expressed his suspicion that blacks were "naturally inferior to whites." When he was told of a Jamaican Negro who was supposedly very learned, he expressed his view that he was probably "admired for very slender accomplishments, like a parrot, who speaks a few words plainly." The debate was carried into the *Encyclopedia Britannica*, which reported the latest scientific conclusions on the nature of the Black person in its 1797 edition:

Vices the most notorious seem to be the portion of this unhappy race: idleness, treachery, revenge, cruelty, impudence, stealing, lying, profanity, debauchery, nastiness, and intemperance, are said to have extinguished the principles of natural law, and to have silenced the reproofs of conscience. They are strangers to every sentiment of compassion, and are an awful example of the corruption of man when left to himself.

Others argued that such characteristics were not part of the Black's nature, but were the natural result of centuries of tyranny, superstition, and degradation. Once emancipated, it was believed, those unhappy flaws would disappear, just as they do in all free and enlightened people. In any event, there was ample evidence that they were intellectually well endowed. West Indian craftsmen produced wonderful products with ingenious designs, proving that "God, who made the world, hath made of one blood all nations of men, and animated them with minds equally rational."

During the nineteenth century, the growing abolitionist movement placed considerable emphasis on what its adherents believed to be the religious foundations of their campaign to free the slaves. They were convinced that their movement flowed directly out of the fundamental principles of Christianity, and that as one of the movement's leaders put it, it was "the spirit of Jesus, who was sent 'to bind up the brokenhearted, to proclaim liberty to the captives, and the opening of the prison to them that are bound.'"

The essential ingredients for the abolition of slavery were the belief that Blacks were fully human beings possessing the faculty of reason; that they were therefore entitled to the natural rights of life, liberty, and the pursuit of happiness that had been celebrated in the American and French revolutions; that slavery was inherently evil, corrupting the master as much as the slave; that the evil of slavery was incompatible with fundamental moral as well as religious principles; and that consequently, no person had the right to ownership of another.

Once these principles were accepted, it was only a matter of time before the pressure of public opinion and political and economic events would bring about the full emancipation of the slaves. That emancipation took place first in Europe and not long afterward in the United States. It was hastened to a large degree by slave uprisings and rebellions, especially in the Caribbean. Once the Europeans learned of the degree to which the slaves were able to arm and organize themselves, and the ruthlessness with which they turned upon their masters when they had the opportunity to do so, they were no longer able to accept the old dogmas about the lack of reason among Blacks and their need—as if they were like children—to be guided and directed by men and women who were supposedly more capable than they of rational thought. Once that concept took hold, the demise of institutionalized slavery in the West was inevitable. It took longer in some places than in others, in part because of the innate conservatism of the societies that sanctioned slave ownership, and in part because of economic factors that left slave states feeling that their prosperity was doomed if their slaves were set free. Equally important, in a way, was their feeling that valuable property was being confiscated from them without just compensation. And there was also deep resentment against what was perceived to be an intrusion by a distant government into the sovereign affairs of their own government. In the case of the United States, it took a bloody civil war to resolve that conflict.

Bibliography

Davis, D. B. (1984). *Slavery and human progress*. Oxford and New York: Oxford University Press.

Finley, M. I. (1980). *Ancient slavery and modern ideology*. New York: Viking.

Garlan, Y. (1988). *Slavery in ancient Greece*. (Janet Lloyd, Trans.). Ithaca, NY: Cornell University Press.

Klein, H. S. (1967). *Slavery in the Americas: A comparative study of Cuba and Virginia*. Chicago: University of Chicago Press.

Patterson, O. (1982). *Slavery and social death*. Cambridge, MA: Harvard University Press.

Sawyer, R. (1986). *Slavery in the twentieth century*. London and New York: Routledge and Kegan Paul.

United Nations Sub-Commission on Prevention of Discrimination and Protection of Minorities (1984). *Slavery*. New York: United Nations.

SLIPPERY SLOPE ARGUMENTS

Wibren van der Burg
Tilburg University

GLOSSARY

argument from added authority An argument often (but in my view incorrectly) considered a slippery slope, holding that someone should not be given a certain authority or responsibility because he will probably abuse it.

empirical slippery slope argument A version of the slippery slope argument that argues that doing A will, as the result of social and psychological processes, ultimately cause B.

full slippery slope argument A version of the slippery slope argument that combines various other versions in one complex structure, together with an appeal to a social climate of public opinion.

L_1, or first logical version of the slippery slope argument A version of the slippery slope argument holding either that there is no relevant conceptual difference between A and B, or that the justification for A also applies to B, and therefore acceptance of A will logically imply acceptance of B.

L_2, or second logical version of the slippery slope argument A version of the slippery slope argument holding that there is a difference between A and B, but that there is no such difference between A and M, M and N, ..., Y and Z, Z and B, and that, therefore, allowing A will in the end imply the acceptance of B. (M, N, Y, and Z are intermediate steps on the slope.)

slippery slope argument An argument of the following form: if you take a first step A, as a result of a sticky sequence of similar actions by either yourself or by other actors that are relevantly similar to you, action B will necessarily or very likely follow. B is morally not acceptable. Therefore you must not take step A.

sorites (or paradox of the heap) This is an argument holding that if one grain is not a heap and one more grain cannot make the difference between a heap and not a heap, we can never speak of a heap.

SLIPPERY SLOPE ARGUMENTS hold that one should not take some action (which in itself may be innocuous or even laudable) in order to prevent one from being dragged down a slope toward some clearly undesirable situation. Their typical purpose is to prevent changes in the status quo, and, therefore, they are most common in those fields that are characterized by rapid developments. Slippery slope arguments are easily confused

Encyclopedia of Applied Ethics, Volume 4
Copyright © 1998 by Academic Press. All rights of reproduction in any form reserved.

with other types of arguments, like arguments that merely point to long-term effects in general or to side effects. Often they are not so much rational arguments, but expressions of feelings of unease about general trends in society. In such cases, we had better address those underlying worries directly rather than discuss them in their disguise as slope arguments.

There are various types of slippery slope arguments, and they should be carefully distinguished because the conditions under which they are convincing arguments differ. There are an empirical version and two logical versions, and there is a full or combined version. A second distinction can be made with regard to the contexts in which the slope is supposed to exist. The mechanisms of social dynamics and the role of logic differ in each of these contexts. The conclusion can be that they are only seldom convincing arguments; their most important role is in institutionalized contexts like law. Nevertheless, they are very popular in practical debates. To understand their popularity, we are to address their rhetorical role. The main reason why they are so hard to attack (and to substantiate) is that they are based on controversial interpretations of reality and of future developments, interpretations that are strongly influenced by underlying attitudes, different backgrounds and emotions.

I. INTRODUCTION

Case 1: "Perhaps, in some extreme cases, voluntary euthanasia may be morally justified. Yet, we should never do it, let alone make it legal, because this would be the first step on the slippery slope toward an inhumane society. Further steps could be the killing of severely handicapped newborns and then the killing of persons with a mental handicap, until we finally kill the useless elderly against their will."

Arguments like this are very common in applied ethics. They have the general following form: If we do (or accept) A, which in itself may not be morally wrong, we will start a process which will lead us to a clearly unacceptable result B. In order to avoid B, we must refrain from A.

Slippery slope arguments are frequently encountered in biomedical ethics. Their typical purpose is to prevent undesirable changes, and, therefore, they are most common in those fields that are characterized by rapid developments, like biomedicine. They can, however, be found in all fields of applied ethics. Consider the following examples:

Case 2: "Once public officials cross the line of accepting seemingly innocent gifts like bottles of wine, there is no stopping and the road to corruption is open."

Case 3: "If we allow the Communists to take over Vietnam, they will successively take over each of the countries of southeast Asia."

Case 4: "If we prohibit a meeting of a Nazi party, we will end up with prohibitions of fully democratic organizations."

More examples can easily be found (for a wealth of case material, see D. Walton, 1992. *Slippery slope arguments.* Oxford: Clarendon Press). The most common name nowadays for this type of argument is the slippery slope argument, but it has many synonyms. Various poetic titles have been used, like "the thin end of the wedge," "letting the camel's nose in the tent," "this could snowball," and "the domino theory."

Slippery slope arguments have dubious standing in philosophy; they have often been treated as mere fallacies. But this characterization does not really do justice to them, even though, as I will argue, they are only seldom convincing arguments. Not only do they often have great rhetoric power, but they usually also have a certain intuitive appeal and an initial plausibility, which means that they cannot simply be dismissed as always fallacious. Arguments of this kind can be brought forward against almost every change in the status quo: there is always a possible risk that this action starts an uncontrollable process leading to undesirable consequences. This makes them a strong rhetoric tool in the hands of conservatives. But this broad scope is also the central problem, because the argument is not discriminating enough. It could forestall almost every action and we clearly cannot avoid all the changes in the world we live in, even if we wanted to.

Therefore, the basic question of evaluation should not be, is the slippery slope argument valid and plausible? General answers to this question are impossible. The question should rather be, under what conditions are which types of slippery slope arguments acceptable arguments?

II. DEFINITION

The basic idea of a slippery slope argument may be easy to grasp, yet it is difficult to construe a precise definition. As a starting point, we might begin with a provisional one:

A slippery slope argument is an argument of the following form: if you take a first step A, as a result of a sticky sequence of events, step B will necessarily or very likely follow. B is clearly not acceptable. Therefore you must not take step A.

(For A and B we can fill in any type of action or omission. In fact, A and B may refer to an action taken by the actor himself or to an action taken by someone else, which the actor allows, accepts, or prohibits. For reasons of style, I will simply talk of doing, allowing, or accepting A.)

This formulation (which is essentially equal to most definitions found in the older literature) is still much too broad. Some further qualifications should be made, because it covers almost all the arguments that refer to possible negative consequences of a suggested action.

The most common suggestion is to add the requirement that A is in itself morally neutral or even justifiable. This does not seem a useful qualification to me. Often the question is precisely whether A is justifiable, because the proposed principles that seem to justify A would justify B as well and might, therefore, not be sound after all. Moreover, the parties in a practical debate often do not agree on the question of whether A is justifiable in itself, and in such situations the opponent of A might use the slippery slope argument as a second line of defense to convince the proponent that A should not be done after all. Consider Case 1: many opponents of legalizing euthanasia consider even voluntary euthanasia (=A) morally wrong as such. They use the risk of a slippery slope as an additional argument in discussions with those who disagree on that point to convince them that, nevertheless, all forms of euthanasia should be legally prohibited in order to prevent terrible consequences.

We should look elsewhere for useful qualifications of the provisional definition. Studying some concrete examples may show which modifications should be made.

Case 5: "The Supreme Court should not assume authority to evaluate the aspects of public policy involved in this case of affirmative action. Though the exercise of this authority is innocuous (perhaps even beneficial) in this specific case, the Court might later abuse it."

Case 6: "The government should not allow a manufacturer to dump PCB-contaminated waste into this small stream, because the PCBs will run into a downstream river. The PCBs would kill the fish and wildlife in that river and pollute the drinking water for those downstream who use the river for that purpose."

Case 7: "You should not use this pesticide to kill mosquitoes, because it will also kill many useful insects."

Case 8: "A grocery shop should not lower its prices in order to attract more customers, because the bakery around the corner will probably respond with a similar action. The resulting price war may lead to a situation in which both lose out."

Under the previous broad definition, each of these four cases would qualify as a slippery slope argument. There are, however, good reasons to exclude at least the first three and, depending on the perspective, perhaps the fourth as well.

Case 5 exemplifies the type of arguments that Walton (1992) and F. Schauer (1985. *Harvard Law Review,* **99,** 361–383) label the argument from added authority. It certainly can be a valid argument, as it draws our attention to the risk of abuse of power—but it is not a slippery slope argument. There is only one relevant action here: the action by which the Supreme Court implicitly or explicitly assumes authority with respect to a certain type of question. Further actions by the Court are of a completely different type: the exercise of that authority, presumably of an increasingly dubious nature.

If we would call this sequence of events a slippery slope, the category would include the warning for abuse against every action which transfers authority or responsibility to a person or institution. It would include lending a car to a potentially dangerous driver, selling a monumental house to a commercial firm, or even granting parental authority to any parents, simply because we know no parent is perfect. It does not seem useful to include this broad category of arguments from added authority or added responsibility under the heading of slippery slopes. In my opinion, it is essential that the first step and the next steps are somehow of a comparable nature. A first additional requirement for calling an argument a slippery slope argument can be distilled from this: sequential events leading from A to B should be of a relevantly similar type.

Case 6 (like case 5 inspired by Walton (1992), who regards both as slippery slopes) exemplifies what I would label a long causal chain argument. It argues that, through a series of events, action A will necessarily result in B. There is, however, apart from allowing the dump, no further action involved. It is perfectly natural to say that dumping such waste causes the death of fish and wildlife and causes the pullution of drinking water, even if the causal chain is quite long and complex. If we would qualify this type of argument as a slippery slope, we would have to include every argument that points to long-term consequences of actions. We may distill a further requirement from this analysis: a mere sequence of events is not enough, there should be a sequence of actions.

Case 7 points to the side effects of an action. These are, like the long-term effects, clearly relevant for evaluating an action. If the prohibition of abortion were to lead to a rise in the number of deaths among pregnant women as the result of illegal abortion practices, this is certainly a strong argument against it. But it is not a typical slippery slope argument. In practical debates, however, arguments referring to side effects are often intertwined with real slippery slope arguments, and careful analysis is needed to disentangle them, because the method of evaluation of both types is different. In fact, the distinction is implicit in the provisional definition if we realize that A and B should be different actions and not merely different descriptions of the same action.

Case 8, finally, is of a more ambiguous nature. It is what we could call a spiraling-down argument. Action A might trigger a downward spiraling movement through a process of action and reaction. From one point of view, this is not a slippery slope. The reaction is not by the grocery, but by a different actor—the bakery need not react in that way. A criterion for calling something a slippery slope could be that the actions should all be by the same person, group, or institution. Such a criterion would also be relevant in a complete analysis of Case 5, if we reformulate it as, "We should not let the Court assume authority...." Most of the examples mentioned in the discussion of that case, like lending a car to someone, also have to do with the fact that the actor conferring the authority is someone other than the actor exercising the authority.

From a different perspective, however, we might argue that the grocery and the bakery are relevantly similar and belong, in a sense, to the same group of actors, that of bread-selling shops. In this sense, we could say that the grocery does start on a slippery slope, just as an individual judge may take the first step, even though he is not involved in further steps taken by other judges.

This analysis indicates a further requirement. Not only should A start a series of further relevantly similar actions leading to B, but these actions should also be actions taken by the same person, institution, or group, or they should be the actions taken by persons, groups, and institutions that are relevantly similar. What counts

as similar both with respect to the actors and to the actions can, as this example illustrates, be a matter of controversy and will sometimes depend on the perspective taken, but we should at least stick to the criterion.

With the help of these four further requirements, we can now formulate a final definition as follows:

A slippery slope argument is an argument of the following form: if you take a first step A, as a result of a sticky sequence of similar actions by either yourself or by other actors that are relevantly similar to you, action B will necessarily or very likely follow. B is morally not acceptable. Therefore you must not take step A.

III. TYPES OF SLIPPERY SLOPE ARGUMENTS

There are various types of slippery slope arguments. A standard distinction is that between the logical (or conceptual) and the empirical (or psychological or causal) version. The logical form of the argument holds that we are logically committed to accept B once we have accepted A. We can further subdivide the logical version with the help of the criterion of whether there is a relevant difference between A and B or not. The empirical form tells us that the effect of accepting A will be that, as a result of psychological and social processes, we sooner or later will accept B.

In the literature, we find many further distinctions; some of them are, in fact, based on distinctions in the context of application (see the next section) rather than the form of the argument itself. A framework of three basic types (one empirical and two logical ones) and a combined version, as suggested below, will usually be sufficient for practical analysis.

A. The First Logical Slippery Slope Argument, L_1

The first logical version—I will call it L_1—states either that there is no relevant conceptual difference between A and B, or that the justification for A also applies to B, and, therefore, acceptance of A will logically imply acceptance of B. A and B need not be identical, but the differences are not relevant from a normative point of view. If L_1 is correct, this is a very strong argument. The moral demand of universalizability (which, according to many ethical theories, is central to morality) or the more general demand of consistency requires us to treat A and B in a similar way. If there is no relevant difference between A and B, and if B is clearly unacceptable, we should regard A as unacceptable as well. If, in Case 2, accepting a bottle of wine and accepting a $100,000 gift are not essentially different, as they are both to be seen as forms of corruption, and if accepting the larger bribe is clearly morally wrong, we should also refuse the bottle of wine.

Because the argumentative power of L_1 is primarily based on universalizability, one might refuse to call it a proper slippery slope argument and regard it as merely a slippery slope argument in disguise (a position I once took). Yet, there are good grounds to call it a slippery slope argument. Only after careful analysis, only when the debate is over, one can sometimes conclude that the argument boils down to an appeal to universalizability. At the start of the debate or the analysis, however, it is often difficult to say so, because the question of whether there is any relevant conceptual difference between A and B is yet unclear. In that phase of the discussion, it is often not (yet) possible to distinguish the two logical versions. Perhaps it will even be only after we have fully gone down the slope that we will finally be convinced that, after all, there was no relevant difference between A and B or that there was a distinction which we only noticed when we were beyond it. Though, theoretically, the distinguishing criterion between L_1 and L_2 is simple, in practical debates it is not always so.

B. The Second Logical Slippery Slope Argument, L_2

The second logical version holds that there is a difference between A and B, but that there is no such difference between A and M, M and N, ..., Y and Z, or Z and B, and that, therefore, allowing A will in the end imply the acceptance of B. (M, N, Y, and Z are intermediate steps on the slope.) There may seem to be a clear distinction between aborting a 3-month-old fetus and killing a newborn child, but this distinction collapses as soon as we realize there is no such distinction between a 3-month-old fetus and a 3-month-and-one-day-old fetus, and so forth. This version is the practical analogue of the sorites problem in logic: if one hair less cannot make a man bald, how can we ever call a man bald?

The crux in L_2 is that there is a gray zone. We know A is black and B is white, but we cannot tell where A stops and B begins. Some men are clearly bald and some are clearly not, and there is an intermediate category that we might as well call bald as not-bald. In this gray zone, there is no nonarbitrary cutoff point, but the need

to set a cutoff point somewhere is not arbitrary. This means that, if we are able, somehow arbitrarily but authoritatively, to set a cutoff point, any point will do. "Driving too fast" is a vague concept, but if we can authoritatively make it more concrete by stating that 30 mph is too fast on this specific road, this may be a reasonable solution. It is reasonable simply because a line has to be drawn somewhere in the gray zone. If it has been arbitrarily set too low, for instance, at 5 mph, it would have been unreasonable, because it would have been in the white zone. This nonarbitrary setting of an arbitrary cutoff point is not always possible, however.

The gray zone in L_2 is usually the result of both semantic indeterminacy and epistemic indeterminacy (R. C. Koons, 1994. *Mind,* **103,** 439–449). It is partly the result of the vagueness of our language. This can sometimes be countered by using more precise language, like in the case of speed limits. But it is also partly the result of a deficiency in our knowledge, both empirical and moral (I assume that we can speak of moral knowledge, if only metaphorically). We simply do not know in advance what the safe dose of a new drug will be for human beings, or what general criteria to set for a bargain in order for it to be considered "unfair." Making language more precise to counter this epistemic indeterminacy would only be an apparent solution and often be counterproductive.

The L_2 version (and the L_1 version as well) can usually be applied in two directions: as an argument both for and against a certain position. If we start from the intuitive idea that killing a newborn baby is clearly wrong, and then go backward by small steps, we will end up proving that killing an embryo is equally wrong. If we start from the intuitive idea that killing an embryo *in vitro* is not wrong, because an embryo is not yet a human person, we can go forward and defend that killing an older fetus is not the killing of a person and therefore not objectionable either. One line of argument thus leads to a prohibition of abortion at all stages of fetal development, and the other to a defense of legal abortion at all stages.

C. The Empirical Slippery Slope Argument

The empirical version argues that doing A will, as the result of social and psychological processes, ultimately cause B. The causal processes suggested vary from changes in the attitude toward killing held by physicians practicing euthanasia to a general shift in the ethos of a society. One could further subdivide this category by distinguishing the various causal mechanisms, but this does not seem very useful, because usually the various processes are connected.

D. The Full Slippery Slope Argument

The full or combined version combines various versions in one complex structure, together with an appeal to a social climate of public opinion. Walton (1992) demonstrates that in many actual debates slippery slope arguments have this complex nature. Usually the various constitutive elements are not made explicit, so that it remains unclear which versions precisely are combined and how they drive social practice along the various steps of the slippery slope.

The full version is, precisely because of its complexity, hard to evaluate. Especially the vague reference to public opinion makes it a difficult argument both to attack and to defend. The central question, to which we will return in Section V, is whether, and if so how, the combination of the various versions adds to its strength, or whether it is merely an argumentative chain that is as strong as its weakest link. In order to evaluate it, we must carefully disentangle the various subarguments and analyze them separately.

E. The Apocalyptic Slippery Slope Argument

A last type of slippery slope, only mentioned to be discarded again, is the Apocalyptic or Doomsday argument. A horrible situation is sketched that is so highly speculative that the cogency of the argument—insofar as it exists—depends more upon horror than upon its likelihood. Though it is frequent in public debates and has high demagogical power, it has no merits of its own. Insofar as it seems to embody an argument that should be taken seriously, it can better be reformulated as one of the other versions.

IV. CONTEXTS OF APPLICATION

A second important distinction is to be made with regard to the contexts in which the slope is supposed to exist and—in connection with this—the actors that take the first step. Is it the judge who takes the first step on a legal slope when, in an extreme case, he acquits the physician who practiced euthanasia? Is it society at large that, in its social practice, becomes more lenient toward dodging taxes? Or is it perhaps the individual official who accepts small presents from business relations as a small slide in her personal morality?

There are two reasons why this context of application is important. First, the mechanisms of social dynamics and the role of logic differ in each of these contexts. Second, for a slippery slope argument it is essential to discern the distinctive step A that leads us on to the slope; some contexts have more easily identifiable actions of identifiable actors that may count as the first step, like the passing of a bill by the legislature.

Usually, slippery slope arguments are vague about the precise context, or refer to a combination of contexts. We should make this explicit and analyze which contexts could be relevant and how plausible the various versions of slippery slopes are in those specific contexts, given the role of logic and social mechanisms in each of them. Case-by-case decision making in courts is, for instance, highly vulnerable to the L_2 version, because every judicial decision sets a new precedent. This new precedent in turn may be a good reason for taking further decisions that would not have been justified without the precedent. Legislation, on the other hand, is itself not vulnerable to L_2, but it may facilitate a slope of the L_2 version in judicial practice, if the language used in a statute is vague and leaves broad discretion to the judiciary. The opposite possibility is that legislation prevents a slippery slope by setting clear limits and standards, like 50 mph or the strict prohibition of experiments with embryos beyond 14 days after conception.

If various actors and contexts are combined, this will sometimes mean that it is their joined force that irresistibly drags society as a whole down the slope. (In such cases, we should, however, doubt that if all these actors and contexts have the same tendency, we really could avoid taking the first step at all.) The combination, then, is a negative factor. But the combination may also result in a careful social process, which helps us develop new standards that are more acceptable than the old ones and that constitute a sound guarantee against slides down the slope.

Thus, the interaction between the judiciary and the legislative (in connection with a broader public debate) can, in favorable circumstances, lead to defensible new lines. The judiciary may, through its case-by-case method that can take full account of all the relevant details of concrete situations, fulfill an important role in the careful exploration of new territory, e.g., by dealing with euthanasia cases and gradually developing criteria for cases in which euthanasia can be considered acceptable. This judicial "experimentation" might engender a broad public debate that may sometimes lead to refinement and retraction by the judiciary, and sometimes to further steps. Once this course of judicial experimentation and public debate has led to a broader consensus on some clearer standards, legislation may more strictly formulate these new standards as authoritative. (To make my point somewhat clearer, I would hold that the Dutch developments on euthanasia have largely, though not completely, followed this model.)

The second reason why the distinction between contexts and actors is relevant, is that we must be able to discern step A as a separate action for which we can freely choose. If A is not thus discernible, we are probably either already on the slope (there is no free choice) or A is not so much a separate step as part of a more general process. Then, we had better take a more general level of analysis and discuss that broader process to see whether it can be checked. Orientation of the discussion on A will then probably be a useless effort to fight this process at the wrong place. Only if A is a separate action that might as well not be taken does it make sense to discuss slippery slope arguments as an argument against A.

In some contexts, there are very clearly discernible steps that are a matter of free choice. They are usually actions where only one actor is involved (taking the first cigarette) or where the process of decision making is institutionalized, like in law. It makes perfect sense to say that the legislature made the first step toward the restriction of free speech when it accepted a statute prohibiting hate speech, or that the Supreme Court made the first step toward an inhumane society when it ruled in *Roe v. Wade*. (To avoid misunderstanding, I should add that, though these arguments make sense, they need not be valid or plausible.) With respect to a personal morality, a first step on the slope is usually also easily identifiable, for instance, when a public official accepts the first gift of a business relation. It is much more difficult to discern such a step when we discuss the social practice and positive morality of society at large.

How far should we go in distinguishing various types of contexts? In theory, the number of contexts is endless, because no context is completely identical, but the rough categorization below seems to be adequate for most practical purposes:

1. Personal morality, the morality actually accepted and practiced by an individual
2. Positive social morality, the morality actually shared and practiced by a social group or society
3. Critical morality, the general moral principles or ethical theory used in the criticism of actual social institutions including positive morality and law
4. Adjudication, the case-by-case decision making by both courts and other institutions like mediators

5. Legislation and regulation, the production of general rules by legislators both at the level of parliament and at other levels
6. Other institutionalized practices, like public policy making or managing a commercial company
7. Combinations of the former contexts, including other contexts, like practices based on prudence

V. EVALUATING VALIDITY AND PLAUSIBILITY

After these analytical exercises, we are now equipped to deal with the central question: When are slippery slope arguments good arguments? There are no general answers to this question. The only way to deal with them is careful analysis, to distinguish the versions of the argument involved and the contexts in which they are thought to apply, and then evaluate each of the versions in each of the relevant contexts. And even if after this analysis the conclusion is that the argument is not strictly invalid, it is seldom a fully conclusive argument but only a probabilistic argument, which should be considered more or less plausible and which can be overruled by other arguments. Nevertheless, some more general remarks are possible, and I will deal with them in the order of the four versions of the argument. I will not discuss all contexts but only those where some significant conclusions are possible.

A. The First Logical Slippery Slope Argument, L_1

As was noted in Section III.A, it is often not clear at the outset whether an argument is of the L_1 or L_2 version, because we do not know whether there is a relevant conceptual distinction between A and B or not. In many cases, close analysis will then show that an argument is a complex argument consisting of various versions. But sometimes, even after such an analysis, it remains unclear because we cannot oversee whether there is a reasonable distinction in a field of new phenomena that we do not yet fully understand. Our normative theories may simply not yet be adequate to deal with certain new phenomena. Should an embryo be considered a person or not? Is an obligatory HIV test morally different from an obligatory genetic test? Perhaps years of further study will result in an acceptable answer but, at the moment the decision has to be made, we just do not have adequate insight. In such cases, it seems to be wise to treat the case as one in which both the L_1 and the L_2 argument might hold.

An interesting problem is posed in the situation where there is a relevant conceptual difference on a line somewhere between A and B, but this difference is not so important that it can bear the whole weight of the presumed distinction between A and B. An example is the line of viability in the continuous development from conceptus to person. Surely, it is relevant and it is a reason for some difference in treatment, like a prohibition of abortion beyond that line. Yet, I would hold that the difference between viable and nonviable is not fundamental enough to constitute the basic line that completely marks the switch from an entity that, either legally or morally, is not worthy of protection to an entity that is. It seems to me that this is a gradual process.

When discussing experiments with embryos, viability is—in my view—not the fundamental line; protection against experiments should start much earlier. (If the reader does not agree with me on this example, he may invent other ones with similar characteristics.) This shows that the same line may in some respects be relevant and reasonable, e.g., concerning the question of whether abortion should be allowed, but not in other respects, e.g., concerning the question of whether experiments with embryos should be allowed. Then the conclusion must be that, only with respect to the abortion problem, we have a clear line and a relevant difference between A and B, so that accepting abortion before viability does not logically commit us to infanticide.

But, in my opinion, we do not (yet) have such a clear line with respect to other issues, like experiments with embryos, so that we cannot exclude that accepting those experiments with embryos would logically commit us to accepting similar experiments with babies. This means that both the L_1 argument and the L_2 argument can be countered when we discuss allowing abortion of 3-month-old embryos, but that it would be possible that they cannot be countered with respect to allowing experiments with 3-month-old embryos. It would well be that the point of no return with respect to embryo experiments is somewhere before the 3 months.

If the analysis shows that we can find no reasonable distinction between A and B, the L_1 argument can be a valid argument against A. (We can, however, also avoid this conclusion by arguing that B was not so wrong after all.) Moreover, in certain contexts this might be a very strong, if not conclusive, argument against A; if B is clearly unacceptable, we should consider A unacceptable as well. This will especially be the case in those contexts where consistency and universalizability are important ideals, like in critical morality, because most ethical theories consider universalizability an essential characteristic.

In the context of law, consistency is also an important requirement, but we should note that it has more force in the context of adjudication than in that of legislation. Legislation (and in some respects public policy making as well) can more easily set arbitrary limits than the judiciary, whose integrity is more strongly connected with consistency. A governmental or legislative decision declaring that only the first 10 applicants will get a grant (because financial means are insufficient to allow more grants) can be justified as a matter of public policy and can be laid down in legislation. But a judicial decision, without such a legal basis, stating that only the first 10 applicants will get asylum would be unacceptable.

The conclusion is that it depends on the context of application what force the L_1 argument will have. In debates on critical morality, it can be a valid and highly relevant argument. In institutionalized contexts, and especially in adjudication, it may have some force as well.

B. The Second Logical Slippery Slope Argument, L_2

The L_2 argument is not valid in the context of critical morality. L_2 holds that there is a difference between A and B but there is no nonarbitrary cutoff point on the continuum between them. As long as we are, in a reflective discussion, able to determine where the gray zone begins and ends (these limits need not be a point, but can also be gray zones themselves), we can make a decision to set an arbitrary line somewhere in that zone—every line will be justified. The fact that we do not know what speed exactly (50 or 55 mph?) should be considered too dangerous is no argument for not even allowing a speed of 45 mph.

The L_2 argument may have some force in positive morality, but then only in combination with the empirical version. As long as we can (like in critical morality) not only draw a line in the gray zone in our theoretical discussions but can also effectively uphold that line in our moral practice, there is no problem. Only if empirical factors result in the fact that we cannot effectively uphold the line, the slope becomes a real danger. But this means that the primary force in this case is the empirical slippery slope; so it is better to discuss it in Section V.C.

The most interesting context for the L_2 argument is law. It has a completely different role in legislation and adjudication: adjudication is highly vulnerable to this argument, whereas statutes may even form an explicit and safe barrier against it. In adjudication, the risk is real that through a series of small steps by different judges, each of them almost nonobjectional in the light of existing case law, but each adding a new precedent, we will end up with B. On the other hand, legislation can often effectively counteract such slippery slopes by setting clear limits like prohibiting driving at 50 mph rather than driving dangerously.

For example, in my view, nowhere on the continuum between conceptus and newborn is there a nonarbitrary cutoff point for the question of allowing experimentation. If the judiciary (or ethics review boards, which are in this respect comparable to the judiciary) were to develop standards case-by-case for situations in which experimentation is acceptable, the risk of the L_2 argument driving us too far might be real. Once the legislature has set a clear line, however, for example, by enacting a prohibition on experiments beyond 7 or 14 days after conception, even if this line is itself an arbitrary one, this may effectively forestall a slide down the slope.

C. The Empirical Slippery Slope Argument

The empirical slippery slope argument can be valid in almost all contexts. Only in the context of critical morality is its validity doubtful, depending upon the type of ethical theory used. It is hard to imagine how the general principles of utilitarianism or Kantianism could change as a result of an empirical process. But those ethical theories that recognize the importance of moral experience or intuitions as relevant in the formation of theories, like reflective equilibrium theories or neo-Aristotelianism, seem more vulnerable to the empirical slope. If our moral experiences change as a result of social processes, we might come to accept what we now think unacceptable. But for a neointuitionist this is not really an objection, precisely because she will accept that our current intuitions are fallible and, therefore, may be wrong. A hundred years ago, it would probably have been a good slippery slope argument against theories that defended votes for women, that this might lead to a female prime minister or president. But nowadays we do no longer have a strong moral intuition that this would be a bad result. Therefore, we can conclude that the empirical slippery slope argument does not apply to the context of critical morality.

In the other contexts, the empirical version may be valid in theory, but it is usually hard to judge whether it is plausible. A starting point for our analysis may be the discussion of two (partly overlapping) situations in which the argument is sometimes used, but in which it must be considered an invalid argument against the acceptance of A.

The first situation is when the acceptance of A is merely a symptom of a broad social process of which the acceptance of B might be the outcome. A is in fact a result of that process as well, without being itself a causal factor in the process leading to the acceptance of B. Attacking the symptom will not stop the process then, and will probably result in an ineffective symbolic campaign. Therefore, it is not a good argument against accepting A to say that, in the end, the same process will lead to accepting B, because not accepting A will not stop the process.

The second situation in which the empirical slippery slope argument is used is when accepting A, though not merely a symptom but part of the social process itself, is seen as a symbol of the process. Though in itself it may appear to be morally neutral or relatively harmless, it should not be allowed because it is part of that broad process which might ultimately lead to B. I think this is too easy a conclusion, for we could say so only if we are sure that all the constitutive and derivative elements of this social process are wrong in themselves. When we look at social processes in history, however, we find that these are always mixtures of good and bad elements. The French Revolution resulted in much violence but also in great reforms (we need only recall the great Napoleonic codifications).

The growing emphasis on autonomy, symbolized in the increasing acceptance of abortion, might lead to more than only growing tolerance of infanticide upon parental request, as some of the opponents of abortion argue. (For the sake of the argument, I assume with some opponents of abortion that it might do so, but I doubt whether this is an empirically sound assumption.) It might also lead to a strengthening of the norm of informed consent in medical treatment. We should not protest against the acceptance of informed consent only because it is part of the process that might lead to infanticide. The simple fact that acceptance of A is part of a social process leading to B can, as such, never be an argument against accepting A.

By allowing A in those situations, we do not step on the slippery slope; we are already on the slope. We only take a next step, but this step must be evaluated as an act or a process in its own right, for we cannot say a priori in which direction it will go. It may be a neutral step sideward. (For example, the acceptance of informed consent might be seen that way if we use only one criterion of the direction we take: Does it lead to infanticide or not?) Or it may even be a step upward. (If we strengthen the norm of informed consent, it might even form an extra barrier to infanticide.) Therefore, we need something more than the simple fact that the acceptance of A is part of a process toward B to establish a sound slippery slope argument.

Sometimes, however, there is some further evidence. Allowing A is a major factor in the process leading to the acceptance of B, or at least a necessary condition. The acceptance that abortion may sometimes be morally justified is a necessary condition for the acceptance of an abortion program based on eugenic purposes. The line between the status quo and A is a clear and effective one (for example, a general prohibition against killing or abortion), but there are no such lines between A and B. Allowing A will then remove a social barrier without instituting a new barrier. Factor A may not be the only factor, and it may not even be the main factor in the process leading to B. But sometimes it is the only factor we can influence, or it is simply the factor that is most easily influenced.

The distinction Bernard Williams makes between a reasonable and an effective distinction may be helpful here (1985. In M. Lockwood, Ed., *Moral dilemmas in modern medicine* (pp. 126–137). Oxford: Oxford Univ. Press). A reasonable distinction is one for which there is a decent argument, while an effective distinction is one that, as a matter of social or psychological fact, can be effectively defended. A reasonable distinction need not be an effective one, and vice versa.

The argument here is not that there is no reasonable distinction; the argument is that, though there may be a reasonable distinction between A and B, it is not enough. What is missing is an effective barrier against accepting B in the way the existing prohibition serves as an effective barrier. The prohibition against killing is effective against involuntary euthanasia, but once we have accepted voluntary euthanasia, there will be no more barriers. The old standard rule against killing is thus weakened, and the new rule that includes the exception for voluntary euthanasia will not be a defensible new barrier—or so the opponent of legalizing voluntary euthanasia might argue.

This is, in a sense, the empirical transformation of the logical versions. If there is no reasonable distinction, then we have the empirical analogue of L_1. If there is a reasonable distinction that is not effective, it is the empirical analogue of L_2. Once we accept A, we will be driven by long strides or by unnoticeable small steps toward B, without any possibility to stop. The reasons that there is no such effective barrier may differ—

maybe there is no consensus about the further distinctions to be drawn, or maybe the concepts used in defending A are so vague and ambiguous that the gray zone can easily be made to encompass B.

This version of the empirical argument cannot be dismissed a priori. It is obvious that it may hold, and it has some intuitive appeal. Whether in a discussion it may be considered a sound argument largely depends upon the facts of the case. Some general criteria will be helpful to judge whether the risk of a slope is really a good argument.

1. One has to make plausible that the expected short-term consequences are clear, negative, and probable, and that these follow from or directly have to do with the proposed act or policy
2. The long-term consequences should result from the short-term consequences and be clear and negative as well, but need not be inevitable
3. It must be plausible that while we can stop now, we will not have that same possibility further down the slope
4. There must be an acceptable alternative action that is less susceptible to the slippery slope

These requirements place a heavy burden of proof on the proponent of the slippery slope. Therefore, though it cannot be ruled out a priori, it will only seldom be a really convincing argument, especially not in those situations where we consider A in itself a morally recommendable action. Only when we do not have very strong opinions about the moral quality of A does the empirical version sometimes have enough plausibility to prevent us from doing it.

D. The Full Slippery Slope Argument

The full version depends for its strength on the constituent elements, the various versions out of which it is built. So we have to evaluate each of them separately first, but that does not mean that we should judge them in isolation. The power of the combined version is that to go from A to B one argument need not go the full way. Arguments of consistency may lead the judges from A to M, social processes may then lead society further from M to P, a move later codified in legislation using vague language and then again the judiciary, interpreting that vague language, may lead us from P to B. Each of the mechanisms may result in some steps. Moreover, sometimes the combination of different types of slopes in different contexts may reinforce one another. The step from A to M taken by the judiciary may be supported by similar arguments in ethical and public debates.

Even if combination and mutual reinforcement is possible, the argument is still as strong as its weakest chain. We have to consider whether each of the steps is likely in itself. Is it, for instance, really probable that in the codification of the move from M to P, Parliament will introduce vague legislation? It may as well create clear lines, for instance, by setting a definite standard of conditions under which euthanasia will be permitted. If this intervention is probable, a further slide down the slope could be prevented.

If on any of the steps between A and B such a stop is possible and not unlikely, it may well be the most effective use of our energy to try to establish an effective new barrier at that point rather than, probably without success, trying to prevent any moves to A at all. If A is in itself morally unobjectionable or even recommendable (as legalizing certain forms of euthanasia is, in my view), and finds support in both critical morality and social morality, it can be counterproductive to try to stop A. Probably there will then be a continuous effort by groups in our society to get A accepted and the arguments against it are then not very strong. Efforts to establish a new reasonable and effective barrier between A and B will then probably be more fruitful.

This shows how important a careful analysis of the slippery slope argument can be. If we try, impressed by the rhetoric of the argument, to stop a development at the wrong point, we will not only lose the battle on that point, but will perhaps also be unable to stop it at the point where it should and could have been stopped, simply because we have misdirected available energies. This is a good warning against too easy and uncritical use of the argument; it will sometimes only result in a short-term Pyrrhic victory that has disastrous consequences in the long run.

VI. THE RHETORICAL DIMENSION: PRACTICAL DEBATES

The conclusion of Section V is that slippery slope arguments are usually hard to substantiate, though in some contexts they may be valid and plausible. However, they are the most common types of arguments in practical debates. To understand this popularity, we have to address other dimensions of the use of these arguments.

One reason why the slippery slope is so frequent in practical debates is its emotional appeal. This makes it very useful for those who, rather than convince their opponents, simply want to win. "A Socialist government will be the first step towards Communist dictatorship" and similar phrases have sometimes been powerful arguments to win the electorate. Especially in political debates, the effectiveness of slippery slope arguments is often reversely correlated to their plausibility. Because of the emotional appeal, rebuttal is usually difficult—rational criticism only seldom can correct the emotions the argument has produced.

A second reason is that, even in rational practical debates, there is usually no fully conclusive argument that may decide the case. The decision is taken on the basis of a combination of various arguments, some of them stronger and others weaker. Especially more institutionalized debates, like court proceedings, have the character of a continuous shifting of the burden of proof to the opponent. As Walton (1992) has shown, the slippery slope precisely does that in many cases because when it has some initial plausibility, even far from being conclusive, it can shift the burden of proof to the proponent of a policy. Countertactics in a debate, correspondingly, need not always consist of a full critical analysis along the lines of the last section, but can have a more modest goal: to reshift the burden of proof to the other party. Thus, rather than trying to prove that the slope is highly unlikely, one might stress the positive consequences of A or argue that not doing A would have even worse consequences.

A third reason for their frequent use is that often appeals to slippery slopes express some underlying uneasiness about the rapid transformation of society. The slippery slope is then not really a specific argument against policy A, which is probably only the symptom or symbol of these changes. Yet, it can be a signal that there is something more fundamentally wrong about developments in society and we should try to find ways to address this signal. If a vague public distrust of new technology is the real motive behind the fear for a slippery slope, this distrust should be brought to the open, rather than being "rationalized away" by dismissing the appeal to a slippery slope as an invalid argument.

VII. THE SOCIOLOGICAL AND PSYCHOLOGICAL DIMENSIONS: PERCEIVING REALITY

The major factor that makes slippery slope arguments so problematic still has to be addressed. Slippery slope arguments are based on interpretations of social reality and especially of the likelihood of future devel-

opments. These interpretations are inherently controversial, and arguments for one interpretation over
another are always inconclusive. Is it likely that
legalizing early abortions will lead to the gradual
acceptance of later and later abortions, and in the
end to the acceptance of infanticide? Or is it rather
likely that strict enforcement of the abortion law will
lead to substantive suffering and the death of many
pregnant women as a result of illegal abortion practices? Both speculations have some initial plausibility,
but it is hard to tell which is better.

Moreover, even if the facts are clear, it is not always
certain that the presupposed causal relationships are
inevitable. An illustration is offered by the "Stepping
Stone" theory with respect to drugs.

Case 9: "In most Western countries, a large proportion of those using soft drugs like marijuana will
end up as addicts of hard drugs like heroin. We
should therefore prevent the use of soft drugs like
marijuana, even if in themselves they are much less
dangerous than accepted drugs like alcohol or nico-
tine, to prevent further steps to the more dangerous
and addictive drugs."

This is a very nice example of an empirical slippery
slope argument, in which the normative conclusion
seems to follow almost naturally from the empirical
facts. Dutch drug policies since the seventies, however,
have been based on the hypothesis that these "drugs
careers" were largely the result of the contingent fact
that both types of drugs were sold in the same illegal
subculture. If it were possible to separate the subculture
of soft drugs from that of hard drugs, it might be possible to prevent individual users of soft drugs from
switching to hard drugs.

Here again, there is no uncontroversial interpretation
of the facts, not even in hindsight. According to most
Dutch drug experts (and my impression is that they
are correct), this element of Dutch drug policies has
worked, resulting in relatively low numbers of hard-
drug addicts (though it is difficult to uphold the separation between the two subcultures, especially as the production and distribution of soft drugs remains illegal).
Nowadays, a much smaller proportion of those who
use soft drugs on a regular basis take the step to hard
drugs. But according to many opponents, especially
politicians from other countries, the effects of the Dutch
drug policy (especially the toleration of the use of soft
drugs) are disastrous. They do not believe that this is
a way to prevent the slippery slope; they even consider
the Dutch tolerance of soft drugs as the first step on a
different slippery slope (if only because they do not
want to distinguish between more and less harmful
drugs).

This controversy shows that even appeals to "objective" facts are not sufficient to decide the question of
whether there have been slides down the slope. Evaluative and ideological stances seem to color the observations by both parties in the debate (though, in my
opinion, not in equal proportions). When this is so
with regard to interpreting reality, it will be even more
so with regard to interpreting the future. The basic
difference between the optimist and the pessimist regarding the question of whether the glass is half full or
half empty is even more strongly reflected with respect
to the future danger of a slippery slope. Someone with a
pessimistic outlook, who believes "everything is getting
worse," will interpret the facts in a negative way and
will see every new technique as a further step in the
wrong direction. The optimist, on the other hand, will
interpret new developments as steps in the right direction; the more negative aspects will be seen as accidental
and correctable. These outlooks are also reflected in
attitudes toward the question of whether one thinks
things can be stopped. Someone who is highly critical
toward the existing political and legal order will have
less confidence in the possibility of stopping future
developments than someone with a strong trust in our
democratic institutions.

Thus we have an entanglement of, on the one hand,
controversial interpretations of social reality and unde-
cidable predictions regarding the future, and, on the
other hand, personal emotional, psychological, and
moral attitudes, and fundamental outlooks. The entanglement makes discussions of slippery slopes often futile, because parties do not talk about the same facts
and predictions.

VIII. A CASE STUDY: EUTHANASIA IN THE NETHERLANDS

I think the last section can best be illustrated by an
extensive discussion of what seems currently the most
controversial example of a suggested slippery slope:
Dutch euthanasia practice. I have the impression that
most physicians, lawyers, and ethicists in the United
States believe in something like the following story:

Case 10A: "In 1973, the Dutch took the first step on
the slippery slope. They tolerated active voluntary

euthanasia on request in a case where death was near and where there was unbearable suffering. Subsequently, however, they abandoned each of these criteria by small steps. Now they are even discussing 'euthanasia' without request in cases of comatose patients, psychiatric patients, and severely handicapped newborns. There seems to be no end to this sequence: we may expect them to go further down the slippery slope yet."

On the other hand, most Dutch physicians, lawyers, and ethicists seem to perceive the Dutch history on euthanasia quite differently, somewhat like the following story:

Case 10B: "In the late sixties, we began to realize that modern medical technology is not always beneficial. Life is not always worth living and sometimes suffering is so unbearable or the quality of life so poor that prolongation of life is itself an evil. Over the last 30 years, Dutch society as a whole has been involved in the process of this general discussion on medicine and health care, including topics like medical decisions concerning the end of life. This broad and intense discussion has been long and difficult, but gradually we have been moving toward some general agreement. The consensus started with the relatively easy cases: euthanasia in cases where there is a clear request and unbearable suffering, and where the end of life is near. We went on to discuss the more difficult cases and we are still struggling with them. Examples of the most challenging cases are psychiatric patients who request euthanasia, comatose patients, and handicapped newborns. Discussion is continuing on these cases."

This perception of the Dutch story is not one of a slippery slope, but that of a long and winding road. For many years, the Dutch have been trying to convince their U.S. colleagues of their—and what seems to me the correct—interpretation of the story, though usually (at least until recently) in vain.

Here we have an interesting problem which seems characteristic of many slippery slope arguments: the same reality is perceived in completely different ways. If opinions differ so strongly about the interpretation of a historical process, the differences will be even larger when discussing future developments. For instance, consider the recent initiatives in various U.S. states which would have allowed certain forms of euthanasia or physician-assisted suicide. If discussions about inter-

preting the Dutch situation have been in vain, how can we expect agreement on the assessment of the risks involved in following these initiatives? To answer this type of question, we cannot exclude psychological and emotional factors. We need to address these factors directly, because ultimately they seem to determine whether some person or group believes in the slippery slope or not.

In the Dutch euthanasia example, these factors may be quite complex. One explanation is that many Americans simply condemn every form of active euthanasia; every step will then clearly be perceived as a step down the slippery slope. A second explanation is that whether one perceives a development as a slippery slope largely depends on basic attitudes of trust in other persons and in society in general. In the United States, there seems to be much more distrust of physicians, lawyers, politicians, and fellow citizens (like family members) than in the Netherlands. The Dutch practice heavily leans on trusting physicians, because legal control of medical euthanasia practice is extremely difficult. Physicians trust fellow physicians, patients trust physicians, and the legal system entrusts physicians with these decisions. If someone with a basic attitude of distrust looks at this situation, he will see an extreme danger of abuse.

A third explanation is that implicitly one always interprets a development in the light of familiar facts and values. In the Netherlands, there is almost equal access to health care and almost no one will have to pay extremely high hospital bills; euthanasia is usually performed in the context of a long-standing physician–patient relationship, and there has been a long, intense, and broad discussion on euthanasia. These facts are essential to understand why the risk of a slippery slope is perceived as minimal in Dutch society. If one lives in a society where the facts are different, one will more easily perceive the risk of a slippery slope.

IX. CONCLUSION

Cases 10A and 10B illustrate nicely many of the problems surrounding slippery slope arguments. The facts do not await us in objective descriptions, nor are they neatly classified; the future is uncertain; and personal attitudes, backgrounds, and emotions strongly influence our perceptions. Slippery slope arguments are often not so much rational arguments as expressions of an underlying feeling of concern about general trends in society. If so, they have to be taken seriously by trying to reformulate them and bringing the underlying concerns into the open public debate.

In those cases where they are proper slippery slope arguments rather than other arguments in disguise, close analysis of the precise versions involved and the contexts in which they are thought to apply is necessary. Even if they are rarely valid and plausible, there may be situations in which some specific versions are convincing, especially in institutionalized contexts like law.

Also See the Following Articles

Acknowledgment

Portions of this article have been reproduced from: "The slippery slope argument," *Ethics*, 102, pp. 42–65 (October). Copyright 1991 by The University of Chicago Press. All rights reserved; And from "Critical study of 'Slippery Slope Arguments,'" *Informal Logic, XV*, pp. 221–229 (Fall).

Bibliography

Burgess, J. A. (1993). The great slippery slope argument. *Journal of Medical Ethics,* **19**, 169–174.

Holtug, N. (1993). Human gene therapy: Down the slippery slope? *Bioethics,* 7(5), 402–419.

Lamb, D. (1988). *Down the slippery slope. Arguing in applied ethics.* New York: Croom Helm.

Van der Burg, W. (1991). The slippery slope argument. *Ethics,* **102**, 42–65.

Walton, D. (1993). Critical study of "Slippery Slope Arguments." *Informal Logic,* XV, pp. 221–229.

Whitman, J. P. (1994). The many guises of the slippery slope argument. *Social Theory and Practice,* **20**, 85–97.

SOCIAL ETHICS, OVERVIEW

D. Don Welch
Vanderbilt University

I. The Ethics of Social Institutions
II. The Ethics of Social Selves
III. Value Theory and Social Moral Discourse

GLOSSARY

act utilitarianism The position that moral choices should be made by calculating which action will produce the greatest net good.

deontology A nonconsequentialist approach to ethics that evaluates actions on the basis of features of the acts other than their results.

descriptive ethics An analysis of the existing moral values and behavior of individuals and groups.

normative ethics A prescription of the moral values and actions that individuals and groups should choose.

rule utilitarianism The position that moral choices should be made by following the rules that produce the greatest net good.

teleology An approach to ethics that evaluates actions on basis of the consequences of those acts (utilitarianism is one kind of telelogical ethic).

SOCIAL ETHICS is the systematic reflection on the moral dimensions of social structures, systems, issues, and communities. Social ethics can be thought of as a branch of "applied ethics," the application of ethical reasoning to social problems. A typical list of the kinds of issues addressed under the rubric of social ethics includes poverty, research on human subjects, animal rights, euthanasia, abortion, discrimination and affirmative action, crime and punishment, and war and peace. Social ethicists, however, do not mechanically apply general theory to particular social problems. Their tasks, rather, are to: (1) examine social conditions, determining which of them are problematic in light of norms of what is good or right or fair; (2) analyze possible actions that could alter those conditions that have been found to be problematic; and (3) to prescribe solutions based on the examination of the problem and the analysis of the options for action. Each of these three steps is a thoroughly value-laden activity.

The subject matter of social ethics has been conceived of in two different ways. The first approach is one that draws a distinction between the moral choices each individual must make and the corporate decisions reached and actions taken by such collective bodies as corporations, municipalities, and nations. Characterized in this way, social ethics focuses on the policies and practices that social institutions should follow. The second view of social ethics is rooted in the notion that all ethics are, in a sense, social because they are socially constituted, embedded in a social matrix. This view focuses on the way in which individual moralities are shaped by social contexts and the way individual moral choices, in turn, shape social contexts. This overview will look at each of these two approaches. The distinction between the two approaches can become blurred in discussions about whether responsible agents are collective institutions or the individuals responsible for institutional policy and behavior.

I. THE ETHICS OF SOCIAL INSTITUTIONS

A. Descriptive and Normative Ethics

Humans are social beings whose existence is organized in and by communities. The behavior of large institutions has a great impact on the quality of life of all members of a society. Ethicists, those interested in the well-being of humans (and, in most cases, in that of members of other species), thus are inevitably involved in both describing the actions of collective bodies and prescribing policies and practices that should guide the future actions of such bodies.

Descriptively, social ethics includes an analysis of the social conditions that might call for corrective or ameliorative response, an examination of socially shared patterns of moral judgment and behavior, and a study of the actions of major societal institutions. In each case, the task is one of descriptive analysis, seeking to develop knowledge of the factual situation and to understand the organization of human communities and the shaping of social policies. The emphasis is on those matters that concern groups of people, as distinct from ethical inquiries that focus more on such individual matters as personal integrity or character.

Normative social ethics, in this traditional dichotomy between "personal" and "social" ethics, assumes the responsibility of going beyond an understanding of social institutions to prescribing what these institutions should be doing—what actions they should undertake in response to the understanding that has developed in the descriptive task. This normative responsibility is pursued on the basis of a set of values about the nature of the common good (a benchmark by which to judge a current state of affairs and to fashion remedies where needed), the purposes institutions are to serve in society, and the appropriate way for institutions to pursue those purposes. A current state of affairs is deemed to be a problem only when the judgment is made that that particular set of circumstances differs from what *ought* to be the case—from what *should* be going on. And any statements about what should be going on, about what kind of society we ought to have, are based on a set of values about what is good and right.

Ethical reflection examines and evaluates the kinds of reasons people give to support and justify the moral positions they take. While contemporary ethical thought exhibits a wide variety of options for assessing moral positions, the kinds of moral arguments that undergird such judgments have historically been divided into the two great classical traditions of teleology and deontology.

B. Teleology

A teleological (from *telos*, Greek for "goal") approach to ethics judges human action by the consequences that an act produces. Within this frame of reference, the appeal is to the value of the ends that result from a particular choice. Questions of morality are largely questions of results. The focus is on the good (and bad) consequences that flow from actual or contemplated decisions, especially as those results are compared to those of other available alternatives. The dictum that "the ends justify the means" is an expression of this perspective on morality. Many moral theorists focus on this future-directed, purposive character of human action and differ among themselves only in the ends that should be pursued: e.g., material well-being, happiness, power, self-actualization, freedom, and peace. Differences also arise concerning whose well-being is properly within the scope of ethical consideration with some ethicists, for example, moving beyond assessing consequences for humans and including those for animals or the earth. But in each case, the worth of an act—or of a social policy—lies in the results it produces.

1. Utilitarianism

Utilitarianism is probably the most widely practiced form of consequentialism, especially in the realm of social ethics. According to the utilitarian standard, an act is right if it produces the greatest possible balance of good consequences compared to bad consequences. The goal is to maximize benefits and minimize harm. For John Stuart Mill, the best known of the early utilitarians, the principle of utility identified happiness with benefit, and pain with harm, so that actions were judged by the net happiness or pleasure they produced.

Not all utilitarians have agreed with Mill that happiness or pleasure is the ultimate good that should inform our ethical calculations. Others have suggested that health, wisdom, and friendship, for example, are also goods that should be valued in this way. The lack of consensus about the content of benefit has led many present-day utilitarians to use the standard of personal preferences. In this preference-based utilitarianism, benefit is defined to be whatever people want. Maximizing the beneficial consequences for a person means acting so as to give her the most of what she desires. While this approach avoids the interminable debates about what is truly good or beneficial, it introduces a new debate about those preferences that many would think should not be honored because they seem to be immoral or unjust, such as a majoritarian desire to enslave or exterminate a minority group.

Utilitarians are often divided into act utilitarians and rule utilitarians. An act utilitarian argues that an actor should perform the act that leads to the greatest good in each and every situation. An act utilitarian considers rules such as "You ought to keep promises" as little more than summaries of decisions made in the past. Therefore, he would feel obligated to violate such a guideline in any set of circumstances in which he thought that the greatest good for the greatest number would result from breaking a promise. In each and every case, the decision maker is obligated to make a fresh calculation about whether such moral norms that might have been valid in the past have any weight in the new situation.

Rule utilitarians, on the other hand, believe that rules such as "You ought to keep promises" have more moral weight. An element of universalizability is added to utility by asking the question, "What would happen if everyone were to act in a particular way in such cases?" The rules that guide moral action are valid if they are the rules that produce the greatest good for the greatest number when they are consistently followed (as compared to other rules that could be followed or to the consequences of not following any rules). Thus, a utilitarian justification exists for the rule. For rule utilitarians, the willingness of act utilitarians to violate such rules in particular cases destroys the effectiveness of the rules, leading to a less beneficial future in the long run. The overall benefit for the greatest number is seen as being served by constant adherence to these valid rules.

The argument between act utilitarians and rule utilitarians turns on the issue of which approach would actually produce the most net benefit when all of the consequences for all of the affected parties are taken into consideration. The rule utilitarian wins if the case-by-case exceptions to moral rules advocated by the act utilitarian would, in fact, lead to a breakdown in the effectiveness of moral systems, or if authorizing such personal deviations would lead to individuals making more errors in calculating net benefit than would have been the case if the rules had been followed. The act utilitarian wins if individual judgment in particular cases would produce the greatest good as the result of personal sensitivities to the uniqueness of each situation that cannot be incorporated into general rules.

2. Benefit and Effectiveness

A teleological concern in social ethics is embodied in such principles as benefit and effectiveness. A concern for ends looks to benefits produced or harms avoided to justify moral decisions. The issue of defining what is beneficial can be a complex one, especially in pluralistic societies in which different persons have different views about the nature of a good society. Often a tension is created between the judgments of experts concerning societal benefit and the preferences expressed by individuals whose lives are actually affected by societal decisions.

A full consideration of ends looks not only at the direct product of decisions—the harms that are avoided or the benefits that are secured—but also at the costs (or risks of costs) entailed in avoiding those harms or securing those benefits. Cost–benefit analysis, cost-effectiveness analysis, and risk assessment are primary tools used by policy analysts that combine these principles of benefit and effectiveness in an effort to assess how well a policy or proposed policy provides the desired results. These assessments inevitably raise questions about the valuing of various costs and benefits, as well as about which costs and benefits should be included in the evaluation.

Concerns for effectiveness range beyond a straightforward cost–benefit analysis, including such questions as, Does the policy, in fact, provide the benefit or the solution to the problem it was intended to provide? How should we handle the uncertainty of projections of costs and benefits for proposed policies? Does the policy create other problems that should be weighed in the balance? Is there a better, more effective way, of solving this problem? Is there a relatively more effective way of using the resources required by one policy for solving other problems elsewhere in the community?

Cost–benefit analysis is a technique often employed to answer such questions. In its pure form, this method requires the assignment of value, measured in dollars (or some other currency), to all of the costs and benefits associated with a potential course of action. Assigning such monetary value is a difficult, if not impossible, task. How do we value a human life? How do we measure the benefit of a childhood free from small pox, a 20% reduction in respiratory disease due to a reduction in pollution, an education enriched by music and art classes, or the dignity that comes with protection from discrimination? At the heart of the effectiveness inquiry lies a trade-off between seemingly incommensurable benefits and costs.

Such trade-offs are more easily made when a course of action being considered is one in which all affected parties would be made better off. The concept of Pareto Efficiency is used to denote a situation in which it is not possible to make anyone better off without making another person worse off. Thus, to meet this standard, social changes should be made (and should only be made) as long as they result in a net benefit for someone and a net loss for no one. In the real world, social institutions rarely are presented with such opportunities. More often, social policies are evaluated by the Kador–Hicks (or potential Pareto) criterion which requires that those who gain from an action could fully compensate the losers and still be better off. This standard requires a net benefit but, because the compensation does not actually take place, the issue of the distribution of costs and benefits is not addressed.

In fact, critics of teleology most often fault this approach to ethics on two grounds: (1) it does not adequately take into account how benefits are distributed and costs are allocated, and (2) it does not adequately recognize moral obligations that arise in the relationships among persons as they make promises, enter into contracts, or otherwise incur responsibilities to others.

C. Deontology

Historically, the primary competitor of consequentialist ethics is deontology (from the Greek *deon*, "duty"). For the deontologist, there are considerations that should govern moral choice other than the goodness or badness of the consequences of possible actions. Morality is not a matter of producing right results, but of meeting obligations that relate to features of acts themselves rather than their results. For a deontologist it is possible for an action to be morally right or obligatory even if it does not produce the greatest possible net balance of good (or, in some cases, may not produce good consequences at all).

1. Kant's Categorical Imperative

The writing of Immanuel Kant, the 18th century philosopher, presents a consistent deontological ethic. Kant attempted to describe moral principles that can determine whether actions are right or wrong irrespective of calculations of consequences in particular circumstances. For him, such moral rules could be known, and could be known to be valid, only through the exercise of reason.

The fundamental principle for Kant was his Categorical Imperative: We should always act in such a way that we can will that the maxim of the act (the principle that directs the act) should become a universal law. This principle is categorical—in that it admits of no exceptions regardless of other considerations—and it is an imperative—in that it commands certain moral action. Kant uses the following example to explain: Could a person will that making a false promise to advance her own interest become a universal practice? He concludes that one could not will such a thing because if everyone lied, no one would make promises and the rule would destroy itself. Thus, such a rule would be contradictory and self-defeating.

The first statement of the Categorical Imperative is a generalization at a fairly abstract level. Kant provides two other formulations of the Categorical Imperative that provide more substance to this concept. A second formulation is that rational beings should always be treated as ends in themselves and never only as means to ends. This formulation, which appears often in modern discussions of social ethics, demands that persons never be treated purely as a means to achieving the purposes of others. Recognizing that her own worth results from the possession of rationality, no person would ever wish to be used as an instrument that had worth only as the means to an end.

A third formulation of the Categorical Imperative states that a rule is valid if all rational beings, thinking rationally, would accept the actions directed by the rule regardless of whether they would be the doers or the receivers of the action. In assessing the validity of moral rules, persons must consider the acts from the perspectives of both the actors and the persons being acted upon. Examples Kant gives to illustrate the significance of his Categorical Imperative, in addition to the maxim that one should not make false promises, are the principles that one should help others in distress and that one should not commit suicide.

Not all deontologists are Kantians. Some deontologists focus on considerations that recognize obligations that flow from, for example, agreeing to a contract, incurring a debt, or having children. Others ground their ethical decisions in divine commands that are found in a particular religious heritage. Still others rely on natural rights traditions that mediate truths that may even be claimed to be "self-evident." In addition, not all deontologists believe in imperatives that are categorical. Many follow the lead of W. D. Ross who argues that there are several types of duty, all of which create *prima facie* obligations—i.e., obligations we should honor unless they are overridden by obligations created by a greater duty. Which obligations are greater is a matter that may well depend on the conditions in a specific context.

2. Fairness

The feature common to all of these types of nonconsequentialism is that matters of right and wrong are assessed through reference to standards other than the results that are produced by certain decisions and actions. In each case there is something about the character of a choice or behavior, other than its consequences, that provides a basis for ethical evaluation. In particular, this notion of treating persons with respect, as ends and not merely means, moves beyond the single-minded pursuit of maximizing benefits by calling attention to the distribution of benefits and burdens and the processes by which they are allocated. The principle of fairness reflects the conviction that persons should get what they deserve, that goods and services should be justly distributed, and that particular individuals and groups should not bear an unfair burden in the pursuit of the social good. Such standards focus not on aggregate results but the way results are distributed among various persons and constituencies (including, in some cases, nonhuman constituencies).

A number of competing concepts of justice and fairness exist that provide different bases for deciding what people deserve or what they are entitled to. Among these approaches are those that would distribute benefits according to an individual's need, effort, societal contribution, production, or an equal division among all recipients. A different approach to fairness is one that focuses on equal opportunity or just procedures, an approach that is more concerned with fair processes than with particular schemes for distributing goods and services. All of these concepts are based in a fundamental belief that we should pay attention to the way in which a society distributes goods and services, and risks and burdens, but the differing guidelines for distribution yield differing results.

One of the most well-known efforts to develop an appropriate standard of justice for social ethics is that presented by John Rawls in *A Theory of Justice*. His goal is to settle on the meaning of fairness by contemplating the decisions parties would make in situations in which they would be rational and disinterested. Toward this end, he describes an "original position" in which the decision maker is totally unaffected by the contingencies of a particular social location. This original position is a hypothetical condition in which all persons are without knowledge of the contingencies of their lives—e.g., age, social status,

race, and gender. It is from behind such a veil of ignorance that an individual could develop a set of fair principles because no one would be able to design principles that favor his or her particular position. The basic conclusion Rawls reaches as a result of this mental experiment is that social groups would choose to distribute social goods and services equally except in those cases in which an unequal distribution would work to everyone's advantage—especially to the benefit of the worst off in society.

3. Integrity

The principle of integrity can be used to identify another set of deontological concerns. While the concept of integrity often relates to virtue or character in many ethical systems, it can be used to refer to a different set of concerns in a social ethic. Deontologists will often support rules such as "Don't break promises," or "Don't lie." Whether rooted in respect for persons, individual autonomy, or personal dignity, these strictures are concerned that social institutions observe moral limitations in their dealings with individuals. Such ethical guidelines are rooted in the conviction that it is important in the delivery of benefits that commitments are honored, contracts are adhered to, and promises are kept. Honesty can be a significant feature of this inquiry in the belief that people should not be lied to or otherwise deceived. In each case these particular concerns can be related to the Kantian notion that persons be treated as ends and not merely as means.

Deontological positions have not gone unchallenged. Given the fact that there are differing, conflicting versions of nonconsequentialist rules that we should follow, what basis other than welfare criteria do we have for choosing among them? How do we decide among the competing sources of obligation such as reason, intuition, tradition, and divine revelation? Are not result-oriented considerations covertly at the base of even the most rigidly deontological systems, such as Kant's? Take the example of the false promise. True enough, if everyone made false promises as a matter of course the institution of promising would self-destruct. But is that a "reasonable" grounding of the maxim prohibiting false promises, or does it not ultimately rely on the judgment that the consequence, the creation of a world without reliable promises, is a consequence we want to avoid? Finally, which approach best fits our moral experience? Particularly in the arena of social ethics, do we aspire to a morality based on such rules or do we aspire to a public morality that has public benefit as its focus?

Many ethics scholars have rejected the either–or choice of a thoroughgoing teleology or a traditional Kantian deontology, and the contemporary debate is no longer a two-party affair between utilitarians and deontologists. In the last half of the 20th century a variety of other approaches have been developed that combine elements of the two classical traditions, or that offer new approaches to envisioning the discipline. Among these have been ethics of virtue (which emphasizes an evaluation of the character of the person making choices and performing actions in terms of morally desirable virtues), casuistry (which stresses practical decision making in particular cases based on a thorough understanding of specific situations and analogous cases), ethics of responsibility (fashioning appropriate responses in relation to the contexts in which one acts), communitarian ethics (which focuses on communal values, social tradition and views of the common good, and the creation and maintenance of communities that preserve such values), and ethics of care (acting out of an emotional commitment on behalf of those with whom a person has significant relationships). The differences among these various theories and their meaning for social ethics are often more a matter of emphasis or focus than of mutually exclusive, incompatible principles. This wealth of alternative ways of conceptualizing the nature of ethics illustrates the richness of the human experience that is both the grounding for and the subject of ethical reflection.

D. Public Policy and Legitimacy

In recent years, discussions of social ethics have increasingly focused on public policy issues, with government—local, state, and national—becoming almost exclusively the institutional actor being analyzed. The concept of a "civil sphere" has been developed to identify an arena of social activity that is distinct from governmental activity, and a variety of institutions are important agents of social policy in this arena. In the case of public policy, however, a defining feature of those discussions is the social institution being asked to act: government. The appropriate response for a family, church, or corporation may not constitute an appropriate response for a state or municipality. Legitimacy is a principle grounded in the assumption that there are some moral values that government should enforce and there are other moral values that government should not enforce. The task is to determine when a problem is an appropriate

subject for the making of public policy, a judgment that rests on value-laden views about the proper nature of the state and a moral assessment of human nature. Discussions of legitimacy bring into focus the value of liberty, the belief that a respect for persons entails limitations on the extent to which the actions of social institutions should be allowed to interfere with personal freedoms and privacy. At times the demands of fairness or the prospects of general benefit are great enough to warrant such interference, but the case should be a compelling one.

II. THE ETHICS OF SOCIAL SELVES

All ethics are social in one sense because human beings are by nature social animals. Thus any bright-line boundaries between social ethics and what might be called personal or individual ethics is artificial—although such artificial divisions can be useful for analytic purposes. If it is understood that there is no dimension of ethics that is truly nonsocial, then "social ethics" can denote a valuable focus on the way in which personal moral values are formed by social context, and the way in which acting on those values in turn affects that context. This second way of conceptualizing social ethics incorporates reflection on the ways individual moral decisions and actions relate to social issues in addition to the effect they have in directing the actions of social institutions.

Individuals are creations of social contexts. The self is fundamentally social in the sense that it knows itself only in relationship to other selves and exists only in those relationships. A person's identity and values are formed in the context of and in response to the social world in which he or she is immersed. Thus, one of the primary tasks for this approach to social ethics is to examine the interdependence of self and society—persons and communities—in an attempt to understand how social contexts shape moral selves, the values they hold, and the decisions they make. This kind of investigation analyzes the values and responsibilities individuals inherit from various communities: religious, civic, cultural, and tribal. This dimension of social ethics is concerned with issues specific to a time and place, analyzing social organizations and the norms that are embedded in them and passed on to individuals. Personal perspectives and moral obligations are matters of particular social locations. Each person views the world from a standpoint (constituted by such factors as class, race, and gender) that shapes her values and the way she sees the world.

Beyond that, social location includes particular positions individuals have assumed—or into which they have been placed. The holder of a role or office has special responsibilities that accompany that specific role or office. Whether the role is that of parent, president, or priest (to mention three examples), the nature of one's moral responsibilities is a product of that role. Not only do individuals internalize the values of the social institutions they inhabit, but they are subject to moral claims inherent in the social roles they play. Each person assumes responsibilities peculiar to the social positions he or she occupies, creating moral obligations that might not otherwise exist. Social ethics entails the examination of the nature of moral responsibilities created in such social contexts.

Second, social ethics concerns itself with the way individuals' actions affect others as they respond to social institutions and processes. This normative aspect of social ethics entails a move from a descriptive account of social conditions to an evaluative discernment of appropriate responses to those conditions. As is the case with the ethics of social institutions, ethical theories such as teleology and deontology are relevant to this inquiry, as are such principles as benefit, effectiveness, fairness, integrity, and legitimacy. Assessments of personal morality, however, often focus on features of morality such as motive and character. For example, Kant insisted that an individual should act not only in accord with one's duty, but only for the sake of duty. For him, a person's motive for acting, and only that motive, provided the basis for evaluating that action. There is a continuing debate about whether such features of individual agents apply to collective agents, i.e., whether it is meaningful to speak of institutional character or intentionality.

Such an emphasis on the motive for acting, to the exclusion of the consequences of the action, is rarely a feature of the assessment of institutional actions. Few contemporary approaches to ethics are as internally focused as Kant's. Especially in the area of social ethics, moral analysis most often focuses on evaluating the choices and actions of individuals in terms of their relations with others: whether benefits are provided, whether costs and burdens are appropriately shared, whether processes are fair, and whether promises and commitments are honored. Such standards provide ways to more directly measure the health of the body politic, which is the first concern of social ethics.

III. VALUE THEORY AND SOCIAL MORAL DISCOURSE

A. Objective Value Theory

By its nature, social ethics, particularly in its normative dimensions, involves ethical discourse and deliberation among a large number of people. As such, this style of ethics raises issues in different ways than is the case in more personalized, privatized conversations about right and wrong. Just as there are different forms that ethical argumentation may take, so are there different views about the nature of ethics, which, in turn, suggests different purposes to be served by discourse in the arena of social ethics. If there is, in some sense, objective moral reality, then moral judgments can be objectively true or false. Within this view of the nature of ethics, ethical arguments are used to demonstrate, even "prove," that a particular social choice is the right one.

Objective value theory assumes that moral choices can be demonstrated or proven to be correct or incorrect. This approach to ethics is grounded in the belief that there are moral absolutes, operating on the premise that there are certain values that exist as objective realities. The assumption is that the ethical task is to discover what is right or good and then apply it to social problems. The act required is one of discovery, because standards for conduct already exist whether they are rooted in natural rights, human reason, or divine law. According to this view, objective assessments can be made through reference to these immutable standards of right and wrong, good and evil. The purpose of ethics, therefore, is to apply these objective standards to the options being examined in order to prove that a particular solution to a social problem is the correct one.

This type of ethical discourse appears to be especially effective in a setting in which there is agreement about the nature of the fixed standards, or at least agreement about deferring to an authority that will state what those fixed standards are. This understanding of the nature of ethical discourse may describe the purpose moral argument serves in a homogeneous community with universally agreed upon values, or in a tightly knit subgroup that functions with a high degree of consensus about fundamental truths and values. In a modern, pluralistic, diverse society there are obviously limitations on the conduct of social ethical discourse for this purpose, since mutually agreed upon ethical principles are few and very general in character, and their meanings are so often matters of contention among different groups.

B. Subjective Value Theory

Another view is that morality is subjective, meaning that one person's moral judgment is as good as another's. Thus ethical argumentation is seen as being little more than an expression of the opinions or feelings of an individual or group. The purpose that ethical argument can serve in the social arena is to do little more than to provide an aura of legitimacy for choices that are the result of simple exertion of power. In a pluralist community with diverse groups competing for power, subjective value theory offers an alternative to the absolute truth approach to ethical discourse. The proponents of this approach discount the validity of obligations incurred from values because such values are seen as relative to particular societies or even particular individuals. One understanding of ethical discourse is that it is composed simply of speech that reveals the personal preferences of each of the speakers or groups participating in the conversation. This kind of relativism is fed by comparative cultural studies that have led to the conclusion that since what is right differs dramatically from one society to another, right has no power at all: value is simply the summary of what a particular group or person prefers. There are no fixed standards to ground the demonstration of a choice to be the right choice. Rather, choice is a personal matter not amenable to objective evaluation.

Following this approach to ethics, a speaker making a moral argument could not be demonstrating that her choice was the right choice, and implementing that choice could certainly not depend on such a proof of moral correctness. Rather the choice is implemented if those for whom this choice is personally preferable have the power to implement it. The purpose of social moral discourse could be little more than providing moral "window dressing" for those constituencies for whom such considerations are important. A subjectivist who believes that values have no independent standing apart from the personal preferences of each individual is concerned neither with distinguishing between might and right, nor with the possibility that invoking moral principle is simply manipulating people.

C. Relational Value Theory

Some moralists have sought to avoid the two polar opposites and to develop a synthesis combining features of objectivisim and subjectivism. One understands that the ethical task is not to demonstrate the truth of one's position, but to develop an argument for that position that is convincing. In a pluralistic community, the ideas of the perfectibility, eternality, or objectivity of moral truth often give way to an understanding of truth as situated and partial if a meaningful debate on social policy is to take place. Viewed within this relational value theory, value is objective in the sense that value relations are understood to be independent of the feelings of particular observers, but not in the sense that value is itself some kind of objective reality. Values, truth, and knowledge emerge in particular relationships as persons encounter persons. Discussions about what is right and wrong have meaning only in relation to the individuals asking the question.

A distinction between verification and validation is pivotal in understanding this approach to ethical discourse. When one is arguing for a public policy position, she must attempt to establish her argument as the stronger. Her argument is a rhetorical one—in the best meaning of rhetoric—connecting her argument to the concerns, biases, values, and interests of the audience. Social ethical argumentation is not a matter of finding and applying authoritative rules or of logically deducing conclusions from established principles, but of persuading an audience that the position being advocated is appropriate in the particular context.

In the arena of social ethics, this kind of ethical discourse provides a communal forum for competing groups and individuals to engage in the formulation, airing, and advocacy of moral proposals. In the absence of a universal concurrence about a method for resolving differences in moral perspectives, these moral proposals are appeals for support for positions that may be in competition with a variety of ethical offerings. When a significant issue of any complexity is addressed, an ethical analysis calls for the assessing and weighing of contrary and conflicting norms—such as economic, political, and personal liberty; equality; equity; privacy; procedural fairness; general utility; civility; acceptance of risk; and the interests of future generations and of outsiders. The most powerful ethical arguments will be those that resonate with the community's sense of what is appropriate—that construct a convincing case and present it in a persuasive way.

Relational value theory is unsatisfying for those who believe there must be some source for ethical appeal that transcends specific communities. It is argued that if some universal values do not ground moral reasoning (human rights is often offered as a candidate), a reversion to subjective value theory is inevitable.

Bibliography

Almond, B., and Hill, D. (1991). *"Applied Philosophy: Morals and Metaphysics in Contemporary Debate"*. Routledge, London.

Howie, J., and Scheduler, G. (1995). *"Ethical Issues in Contemporary Society."* Southern Illinois Univ. Press, Carbondale.

Singer, P. (1993). *"Practical Ethics,"* 2nd ed. Cambridge Univ. Press, Cambridge.

Sterba, J., *et. al.* (1995). *"Morality and Social Justice: Point/Counterpoint."* Rowan & Littlefield, Lanham, MD.

Welch, D. D. (1994). *"Conflicting Agendas: Personal Morality in Institutional Settings."* Pilgrim, Cleveland.

Weston, A. (1992). *"Toward Better Problems: New Perspectives on Abortion, Animal Rights, the Environment, and Justice."* Temple Univ. Press, Philadelphia.

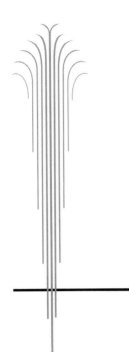

SOCIAL SECURITY

Paul Spicker
University of Dundee

I. Social Insurance
II. Income Maintenance
III. The Neoliberal Critique of Social Security
IV. Universality and Selectivity
V. Social Security and Social Policy

GLOSSARY

discretion Decisions that are not governed by specified rules.

income maintenance The provision of benefits, in cash or kind, as a means of providing or supplementing the resources of individuals or households.

means testing The distribution of benefits on the basis of and assessment of income or assets.

noncontributory benefits Benefits supplied without the condition of contribution; generally the term is limited to benefits that are not means tested.

poverty trap A problem of perverse incentives that occurs because increases in income reduce entitlements to benefit.

redistribution The process of transferring resources from some people to others.

selectivity A policy that targets resources for those most in need; sometimes equated with means testing.

social assistance The provision to the poor of cash benefits on the basis of need. In some countries, this is coupled with social work support.

social insurance An institutional arrangement for covering certain contingencies in which benefits are contingent on contributions.

social security Systems of social insurance or income maintenance.

universal benefits Benefits delivered on a categorical and unconditional basis to demographic groups.

SOCIAL SECURITY refers in different countries to a range of different aspects of social welfare provision. In the United States, Social Security refers primarily to a specific system of government-sponsored social insurance available to cover contingencies such as retirement and sickness. In France, social security is understood to cover the old-age pensions and the provision of health care, and some aspects of personal social service, such as social work, which are provided under the scheme, but not the system of unemployment insurance, which has a different institutional base. In Germany, the term sometimes refers to social insurance, but it also refers to a range of benefits, some welfare provision and some issues in industrial relations. In the United Kingdom social security describes a range of cash benefits.

The term "social security" is used in two main senses. *Social insurance* is an institutional arrangement for covering certain social contingencies. Social insurance is generally characterized by the requirement for contributions to be made as a condition of benefit receipt.

Encyclopedia of Applied Ethics, Volume 4
Copyright © 1998 by Academic Press. All rights of reproduction in any form reserved.

Income maintenance is a method of providing benefits, in cash or kind, as a means of providing or supplementing the resources of an individual or household. This usage extends beyond the scope of social insurance to include social assistance and noncontributory benefits.

I. SOCIAL INSURANCE

A. Bismarckian and Beveridgean Schemes

Social insurance developed historically through two main routes: the development of systems of mutual aid by trades unions, guilds, and professional groups, and the action of governments. There are still countries (e.g., Denmark and Israel) in which the provision of insurance benefits is within the province of trade unions. Bismarck's social insurance scheme in Germany, which was the first national scheme, based its national system on a system of independent funds under national tutelage. Contributions and benefits were geared to income and occupational status. This became the dominant pattern in central Europe. The British national system, first introduced in 1911 to cover health and unemployment, aimed for more comprehensive coverage, using levels of contribution and benefit based on what was economically and politically feasible rather than any actuarial foundation; this was continued in the Beveridge scheme of 1942.

The primary distinction in patterns of social insurance is still commonly represented in terms of Bismarckian and Beveridgean schemes. Bismarckian systems offer individualized, earnings-related benefits based on occupational status and are administered by independent (or quasi-autonomous) funds. The Beveridge scheme has been represented as comprehensive, offering uniform benefits from a unified administration (though a detailed examination of the scheme would raise doubts about these points).

Membership of social insurance schemes is often compulsory, though there may be some choice as to which scheme one joins. Mancur Olson, in *The Logic of Collective Action* (1971), analyzes the argument for compulsion in an economic framework, considering the benefits of entry to a mutual aid scheme, and consequent pooling of risks, in relation to each individual. He argues that an individual governed by rational self-interest will not contribute to a common fund beyond a certain point, and will attempt to avoid payment. Where the possibility exists for individuals to become free riders—receiving benefits without contributing—

the system may become unviable. Compulsion is necessary, then, for collective action to be undertaken. There are, however, national systems in which compulsion has not been deemed necessary: Denmark, Sweden, and Finland have voluntary schemes for unemployment insurance, and Bismarckian systems exempt people on higher incomes from the requirement to join. For many countries which have introduced compulsory provision, it has been a means of extending the coverage of such schemes and offering to the disadvantaged the same privileges enjoyed voluntarily by others.

B. The Contributory Principle

The central characteristic of social insurance is the contributory principle: benefits are paid for. Beveridge based his scheme on the belief that people wished to pay for their rights, rather than be given them. The basis for this belief might be seen as contractual—that people receive benefits they have paid for. Equally, it may be justified in terms of the norm of reciprocity, a basic social mechanism which accepts as legitimate actions which are undertaken in return for others. Social security systems tend to work on a mechanism of generalized reciprocity in which the people who receive are not the same as the people who contribute. Pensions, in general, are not usually funded from contributions which have been saved but rather are paid for not by pensioners but by the succeeding generation, as their pensions will be paid for by those who succeed them. The contributory principle seems to be a means of translating this moral stance into practical terms. However, there is little empirical support for the contention that people feel, or have ever felt, that rights are earned as a consequence of contributions. The concept of contribution seems to be based more on a generalized notion of life history and work record than on any specific mechanism linking benefits to contributions.

The contributory principle has been retained in practice primarily because it provides an effective, and widely accepted, means of raising revenue; although there are examples of tax-based systems replacing contributory schemes, there are equally cases in which contributory schemes have been introduced to replaced tax-financed benefits. There are two main limitations. The first is that pooling of risks works effectively when the contingencies being covered do not exceed the capacity of the contributory or membership base to meet them. This implies either that the contingencies themselves must be limited—the basis of the "assumptions" in the Beveridge report (1942) of full employment policy and a National Health Service for his scheme to be viable—or that the membership must be limited to lower risks. Where the contributory base shrinks, there may also be difficulties. The payment of pensions has mainly been achieved through a system of generalized reciprocity, whereby current contributions are used to pay current pensions, and future pensions will be paid for, not by saving, but by future contributions. In France, there has been a problem in maintaining the position of certain arrangements for pensions where the industrial base has shrunk and which thus lack the contributors to pay for current pensions. The problem is mainly addressed by intervention to transfer resources between professional funds.

The second main limitation of social insurance systems is their potential for exclusion. Because a contribution is required, those who are unable to contribute cannot in principle be covered. This principle may be stretched in practice; some systems have elements which disguise the nonpayment of contribution (the Beveridge scheme, for example, arranged for schoolchildren to be "credited" with contributions) or which seek to extend the coverage of the insurance scheme to those who would not otherwise be entitled (the French *allocation de solidarité spécifique*). It remains true, however, that an insurance system which does not have some test of contributions ceases to be insurance in any meaningful sense of the term, and in consequence it becomes more like a general system of income maintenance.

II. INCOME MAINTENANCE

A. The Nature of Income Maintenance

Income maintenance policies involve redistribution of income, or transfer payment, between groups. Redistribution is generally referred to as vertical (between richer and poorer people) or horizontal (between groups of people with different characteristics—for example, from people without children to those with children, or from younger to older people). Another perspective has recently been propounded by economists reviewing the effect of social security as a form of compulsory saving: Barr suggests that a principal feature of income maintenance systems is "income smoothing," in which income is redistributed across the life cycle of an individual.

The emphasis within this on financial resources links income maintenance inextricably with distribution in a market system. Cash transfers implicitly favor the distribution of welfare through the private

sector, in the sense that people are generally given money to spend rather than goods or services (like health and education). There are, however, aspects of social security schemes which limit the payment of cash to individuals. *Aide Sociale* in France makes payments to third parties for services, like residential or nursing care, while the U.S. Food Stamp program, for example, is based in the (economically illusory) belief that the payments will only be traded for food. The basic arguments are those for public versus private provision (considered elsewhere). In general, any support for items which would normally be paid for (like food, housing, or health insurance) can be seen as a supplement to income, releasing resources for expenditure elsewhere.

B. Social Security Benefits

Understood as income maintenance, social security covers a much wider range of action than social insurance. It is provided in the form of a range of benefits, adapted to different contingencies, and delivered through a range of mechanisms. There are five main types of social security payment: insurance benefits, means-tested benefits, noncontributory benefits based on a test of need, universal benefits, and discretionary payments.

Insurance benefits have already been discussed in principle. Because insurance benefits necessarily exclude a proportion of the potential recipient population, insurance is invariably part of a broader system of income maintenance.

Means-tested benefits are benefits delivered on the basis of a test of resources—usually income, though sometimes capital or other assets will be taken into account. Means-tested benefits tend to be used as a residual, or safety net, provision, though there are some countries in which means tests have a very extensive remit—for example, Australia, which has a basic means-tested rather than insurance-based old age pension. Means tests have two intrinsic disadvantages. The first is their administrative complexity. The second is the "poverty trap," a problem of perverse incentives which occurs because increases in income reduce entitlements to benefit. This may lead to circumstances in which people who attempt to improve their circumstances through working will find themselves little better off, and perhaps worse off, than they were before they started.

Noncontributory benefits is a broad term which can be used for any noninsurance benefit, but which tends to be used for specifically for non-means-tested benefits. Noncontributory benefits based on a test of need are used, for example, for people with physical disabilities as a form of compensation for severe disability or as a means of meeting special needs (such as a need for social care). The existence of a test means that the benefits are often administratively complex—in the case of disability benefits, they often require medical examination—and although they avoid a poverty trap in the strict sense, there are continuing problems of policing the borderlines and the potential to penalize people whose circumstances improve.

Universal benefits (or "demogrants") are benefits given to whole categories of a population, like children or old people, without other tests. The benefits are administratively simple, but their wide coverage tends to make them expensive. The principle of universal benefits, first put by Tom Paine, has been taken as the foundation for a different type of social security system, a Basic Income, which would be tax-financed and unconditional. Its proponents argue that it would be simpler and fairer, and would protect those in need more effectively than current systems. Opponents argue that it would be expensive and undermine incentives to work, and that its apparent simplicity would prove illusory when special circumstances arose.

Discretionary benefits are benefits given not as a right but at the discretion of officials or the judgment of professionals. Because some needs are unpredictable, many social assistance schemes have some kind of discretionary element to deal with urgent or exceptional needs; where social assistance is tied to social work, discretionary payments may also be used as a means of encouraging and directing appropriate patterns of behavior. Some provision for discretionary benefits is generally seen as a necessity, but in circumstances where other benefits are inadequate to meet basic needs, they are liable to be called on more frequently than is appropriate administratively, and frequent use makes the process of claiming an act of personal supplication. Discretion has been seen as driving out rights, because where an administrator can legitimately decide not to provide a service, no entitlement exists. On that basis, there have been attempts in some systems (including the United Kingdom, and some parts of the United States) to reduce the role of social workers, who exercise professional discretion, in social security administration. The existence of discretion does not, however, preclude the possibility of redress of grievances, and discretion may be subject to the sanctions which are requisite to positive rights.

C. Principles of Redistribution

Benefits are distributed in accordance with a wide range of principles. In Germany, three different principles are identified: the *Leistungsprinzip*, or principle of performance, a contributory principle which relates benefits to work record; the *Versorgungsprinzip*, or principle of provision, by which people have a legal right to tax-financed benefits; and the *Fürsorgeprinzip*, or principle of charity, which is the basis of social assistance. The principles of distribution include

• *Social protection.* Benefits are used to protect people against a range of hazards or contingencies, and in particular against the interruption, reduction, or loss of earnings. This is a primary characteristic of insurance benefits, though it is also an important justification for noncontributory benefits like schemes for industrial injury.

• *Financial need.* Benefits can be used to supplement or guarantee income where people have no resources. The main example is means-tested benefits, but other benefits (such as old age pensions) are often justified in these terms.

• *Special needs.* People who have identifiable personal needs may receive payment to meet those needs, even though they may be better off than others who do not have such needs. Examples are benefits for the special expenses available for disability.

• *Compensation.* Benefits for disabled people are also sometimes used as a form of compensation for disability. The compensation may be substantive (calculated to compensate for loss or expense) or symbolic (unrelated to losses or expenses).

• *Desert or contribution to society.* Some benefits, like war pensions, are used to reward people for services rendered.

• *Rehabilitation or social integration.* Some benefits are used to integrate people into society. The French *Revenu Minimum d'Insertion* is issued subject to the condition that recipients sign a "contract of insertion" which will facilitate their social integration, and recipients may be offered training or special facilities to achieve the ends agreed to in the contract.

• *Rights.* Universal benefits are delivered to citizens as of right; the same argument has been made for insurance benefits, and even the means-tested social assistance benefits may be considered a right by those who receive them.

• *Incentives or disincentives.* Social security may be used as a means of rewarding socially valued behavior (like raising children—natalism, or encouraging births, is an important basis for benefit provision in France) or deterring undesirable behavior (like failing to support one's family in the United Kingdom or United States).

The diversity of income maintenance provisions makes the arguments referring to it complex; a full account would need to consider each of these principles in detail. The sections which follow consider only the broader issues.

III. THE NEOLIBERAL CRITIQUE OF SOCIAL SECURITY

In political terms, the most important criticisms of social security have been made by the "new right." They have argued that social security involves states in a range of activities which are beyond their legitimate scope, and that it has undesirable economic and social effects.

The most basic objection, from libertarians, is that redistribution is illegitimate: individuals have rights to their property, and redistribution through taxation cannot be justified. There are two basic responses to this position. The primary response is that property is not produced by individuals who act in isolation from each other; goods and services are produced in a social context, and their value is socially determined. Property rights are conventional, not a matter of indisputable eternal truth; earnings and property reflect not the product of individuals but a complex set of social conventions, of which taxation and redistributive mechanisms are part. A secondary response is that the argument misrepresents the nature of social security provision. The assumption that redistribution through social security is the product of compulsory state intervention can be applied only to part of the range of benefits. In several countries, the pooling of risk and redistribution of resources which takes place through social security is voluntary, and does not take place directly under the auspices of the state. In countries where it has become compulsory, it has often been developed on the basis of previously existing voluntary arrangements. Where benefits are based in compulsory redistribution, there are several potential reasons and justifications for their existence, including principles like compensation, recognition of desert, or the rights of recipients; they have to be judged accordingly. Property rights are only one set of principles and have to be balanced against others.

In relation to economics, the main criticism of social security has been that it is too expensive for industrial states to support, and the effect of the substantial commitment to income maintenance has a limiting effect on economic growth. This argument has been pursued by neo-Marxists, who predict the collapse of capitalism, as well as by the new right. However, the general trend is for nations with the most successful economies to have the most developed social security systems (the prime exceptions are the United States and Japan). In *The Welfare State and Economic Performance* (1995), Atkinson examines the results of several studies. Within the developed countries there are as many with successful records of growth and extensive social security provision as there are unsuccessful, and there is no clear association between social security expenditure and economic success or failure.

The principal social criticism has been that social security creates a dependency culture in which the thrift and willingness of individuals to work are undermined. This has been used to explain the apparent persistence of poverty despite endeavors to alleviate or remove it. The proposition can be divided in two parts. The evidence on incentives to work, reviewed by Atkinson and Mogenson in *Welfare and Work Incentives* (1993), is equivocal. Some individual effects have been demonstrated, most markedly on women whose partners are not working. However, the structure of incentives depends as much on the structure of the labor market as on the benefits system, and aggregate figures do not show any association between benefits and participation in the labor market. Because unemployment is primarily related to economic activity rather than social security benefits, there is no relationship apparent between the relative generosity of benefit systems and the levels of unemployment prevailing over time.

The second part of the argument is that the persistence of individual dependent poverty, in the form of an underclass, can be attributed to the provision of social security. This argument has recurred in policy debates over the course of the last 250 years; it was made, for example, by Benjamin Franklin and Herbert Spencer. The proposition is not consistent with the available empirical evidence, because poverty has not persisted in the way that critics have supposed. Work on the dynamics of welfare, for example, in G. Room's *Beyond the Threshold* (1995), has shown that individual dependency is generally periodic, and the constitution of the dependent population below retirement age is not stable. Lydia Morris, in *Dangerous Classes* (1994), found that the population which forms the "underclass" is constantly changing. The apparent "persistence of poverty" does not describe continuing poverty among a constant group of people.

IV. UNIVERSALITY AND SELECTIVITY

A. Targeting the Poor

Social security is not reserved for the poor; much of it is not intended for, and does not reach, poor people. Family benefits and income maintenance during short-term sickness are primarily directed at the working population, and social insurance is generally conditional on work record. In Bismarckian systems, the impact of earnings-related benefits is to favor people who have enjoyed high incomes, and provision is not necessarily made for people who have been unable to contribute. Even in social assistance systems, which involve means tests, the practice in modern economies is generally not to insist on proof of destitution (the test under the Poor Laws of the 19th century), but rather to accept that interruption of earnings is itself a sufficient basis for social protection. If, for example, a person who owns a house and car becomes unemployed, the purpose of social protection is to make sure that income is replaced so that the person will not have to sell the house and car.

The debate about whether benefits should be reserved for the poorest is commonly characterized as a debate between selectivity, or targeting, and universality. These terms are used ambiguously, because selectivity can refer to a test of need rather than a test of means; some writers in consequence see noncontributory benefits for disabled people as selective, while others do not.

B. Selectivity

The basic argument for selectivity is that it is an efficient means of relief for the poor, offering maximum benefit at the least cost. Offering benefits to people who are not poor is seen as wasteful. The other main argument is that it is a limited approach in a context in which state intervention is held in some distrust; selectivity makes it possible to hold social security to the necessary minimum for the relief of extremes of deprivation, which links the approach with a general ideological attempt to hold state intervention to a residual level.

There are five main arguments against selectivity.

• *Cost.* Selectivity is administratively costly, which calls into question its efficiency. The process of testing claimants is liable to be cumbersome and complex. In the context of developing countries, the World Bank has argued that the most efficient means of distribution is not to target individuals, but to target whole sectors of a population.

• *The poverty trap.* Selectivity relies on a distinction

being made between those who are entitled and those who are not. There are problems of equity and in dealing with the boundaries between those who are entitled to benefit and those who are not. When circumstances change, so must entitlement to benefits, and the loss of benefits limits the potential of individuals to improve their circumstances. The problem is mainly associated with means testing, but also applies in relation to other benefits (for example, return to work after sickness, or rehabilitation of people with disabilities).

• *Incentives.* Means testing penalizes people who have made private or independent provision and those who have been thrifty—behavior which many advocates of means testing would wish to encourage.

• *Stigma.* The problems of stigma arise both because the benefits are dealing with stigmatized groups, like the poor or single parents, and because the operation of benefits is often humiliating or degrading.

• *Takeup.* Selectivity is not effective in directing resources to the poor. Many potential recipients fail to receive benefits to which they are entitled. The central problems are ignorance about benefits, about both their existence and the terms on which they are available; the complexity of the benefits system, which acts as a deterrent to claiming; and the problem of stigma. The argument is most usually made in relation to means testing, though arguments about ignorance of entitlement, administrative complexity, and degrading treatment can be applied equally to other benefits.

C. Universality

The arguments for universality are

• *Basic rights.* Universal benefits offer all citizens a guarantee of resources, without stigma, as a matter of right. Universal benefits are seen as minimally intrusive and in consequence are less likely to infringe liberty than benefits to which conditions are attached.

• *Simplicity.* Universal benefits can be simpler than selective benefits, with the attendant advantages in comprehensibility and administrative cost.

• *Effectiveness.* Proponents claim a virtually full takeup of benefit.

The central criticism of universal benefits is that they are costly. Arguments for a more extensive use of universality, offering a basic income, have also been criticized on three further grounds. The first is *limited flexibility.* Universal benefits cannot be adapted to individual need without ceasing to be universal; they are limited in their scope. This does not matter when universal benefits constitute only a small part of a benefits system; in relation to the argument that they can supplant other systems, the argument becomes increasingly important. The second criticism involves *incentives to work*. The delivery of benefit unconditionally would make it possible in theory for someone to live without having to earn a wage or agree to take part-time work in place of full-time work. Incentives depend necessarily on the structure of alternatives, including the marginal rewards of labor; this makes the argument difficult to judge in isolation. The third is *equity*. Benefits are distributed on a range of different principles, including financial need and rights, compensation, and reward for merit. Attempts to develop benefits based on one principle alter the balance relative to others. Richard Titmuss argued that any comprehensive system of social security would need in practice to combine aspects of universal benefits with selective systems designed to complement the basic measures and to meet individual needs.

V. SOCIAL SECURITY AND SOCIAL POLICY

Social security is an intrinsic part of social welfare provision, and redistribution is a characteristic of all social welfare policies. It is difficult to distinguish policies clearly from social policy in general. Redistribution may promote the interests and welfare of the individuals who receive it. Equally, it might be seen as relating to wider social or economic interests. This is presented schematically, with some simplification, in Table I.

Many of these functions are directed toward the individuals who receive the benefits. Provision for needs is most commonly associated with the relief of poverty, either directly through the use of income transfers on the basis of low income or indirectly through the protection of people against contingencies (like unemployment) in which they are liable to be vulnerable to poverty. Disadvantage may be remedied through compensatory payments for disability, which are not necessarily related to income, or sickness. Individual potential may be developed through training allowances or educational grants. Social protection is discrete; it is aimed at changes in individual circumstances, including the interruption of earnings.

The inclusion of mechanisms for changing behavior, and for producing disadvantage, refer to aspects of social security which may have a detrimental as well as a positive effect on individual welfare. The detrimental

TABLE I

The Role of Social Security in Social Policy

Functions	Focus	
	Individual	Collective
Provision for needs	Humanitarian	The welfare of society; economic development
Remedying disadvantage	Compensation; cure	Equality; social justice
Maintenance of social circumstances	Protection	Reproduction of society
The production of disadvantage	Punishment	Social division
Changing behavior	Rewards; incentives; treatment	Social control
Development of potential	Development of individual capacities	Solidarity; integration

Source: P. Spicker, 1993. *Poverty and social security* (p. 104). London: Routledge.

aspects of social security have to be considered in any schema; without them, increases in benefits would be treated as associated with the aims of policy while decreases in benefits would not. Social security benefits are used as both positive and negative incentives— carrots and sticks. Examples of carrots include special dispensations for people undertaking permitted forms of work, rehabilitation allowances. Examples of sticks include sanctions taken within benefit systems against people unwilling to work or to support their family.

Social security is not only intended to serve the individuals who receive it; it may be employed in furtherance of social aims. Social security for medical care helps to maintain a healthy workforce. Social security for unemployment can be seen as an economic regulator, helping to maintain demand when an economy is depressed and reducing expenditure when the economy is healthy (though the effect is disputed). Transfer payments may be used to decrease inequality, or to increase it. One of the principal arguments in Europe for social security is that it helps to promote social cohesion or integration. In France and northern Spain, the principle of a minimum integration income has put reciprocal obligations on claimants to participate in society as a prerequisite for receiving benefit. Social security may help the reproduction of society by promoting (or at least supporting) the care of children, the training of workers, and the movement of people into and out of the labor market. And it may be used, as before, in a negative sense, to control undesirable elements in society—one of the explicit purposes of the Poor Laws—or to maintain social division, which was part of the justification for policies in Nazi Germany.

The basic arguments for social security are that redistribution protects the welfare of citizens and provides for people's needs; that income maintenance acts as a form of collective social protection, equivalent in principle to insurance; and that redistribution helps to meet a range of social objectives, including social cohesion and economic stability.

The large potential of social security as an instrument of social policy also indicates its potential for its misuse: social security can be used to limit freedom, to control behavior, and to create inequity and disadvantage. The dominance of the neoliberal critique, which declares all intervention to be illegitimate, has regrettably meant that the distinction between legitimate and illegitimate forms of intervention is too little examined.

Also See the Following Articles

ETHICS AND SOCIAL SERVICES, OVERVIEW • HEALTH CARE FINANCING • POVERTY • RESOURCE ALLOCATION • SOCIAL WELFARE, PROVISION AND FINANCE • WELFARE POLICIES

Bibliography

Barr, N. (1993). *The economics of the welfare state*. London: Weidenfeld and Nicolson.
Spicker, P. (1993). *Poverty and social security*. London: Routledge.
Van Oorschot, W. (1995). *Realizing rights*. Aldershot, UK: Avebury.
Van Parijs, P. (Ed.) (1992). *Arguing for basic income*. London: Verso.

SOCIAL WELFARE, PROVISION AND FINANCE

Paul Spicker
University of Dundee

GLOSSARY

corporatism A model in which the state assigns functions to autonomous agencies, thereby incorporating them into its policy.

institutional welfare A model in which the provision of welfare is accepted as a normal part of social life.

mutual aid Not-for-profit organizations that exist to further the interests of members or subscribers.

residual welfare A welfare policy by which the state provides welfare as a last resort when other options have failed.

social division of welfare The relationship between the division of labor between different sectors of welfare and modes of operation, and the inequalities in the distribution of resources which results.

subsidiarity A principle that limits the intervention of higher authorities in the legitimate activities of lower bodies.

welfare pluralism The relationship of multiple agencies and providers in the provision of welfare.

welfare state A term used descriptively to refer to the provision of welfare services by the state, and norma-tively to indicate a model in which welfare is provided comprehensively to all citizens as of right.

DISCUSSION OF SOCIAL WELFARE and the welfare state in different countries often seems to be predicated on the assumption that the welfare state is equivalent to state welfare. Welfare in practice is delivered through a number of different channels, generally described as "sectors" of welfare, and the role of state intervention has to be understood in relation to the operation of these sectors. An emphasis on the extent of the public sector alone fails to capture the extent of the state's influence, while arguments for limits on state intervention may fail to recognize the extent to which existing networks of services are interdependent.

I. STATE INTERVENTION AND THE PROVISION OF WELFARE

Government, Edmund Burke wrote, is a contrivance of human wisdom to provide for human wants. Although few commentators would argue that the state has no legitimate role in relation to the welfare of its citizens, the extent of the state's responsibility is contentious. Seven main positions might be identified, covering a spectrum from the least to the most interventionist.

1. *The minimal state.* The minimal state is a "night watchman," in which the role of the state is limited to a range of functions, including policing and defense. The primary justification for this position is liberal: the state cannot legitimately intervene without jeopardizing the freedom or rights of its citizens.

2. *The "residual" state.* In this model, welfare is primarily the responsibility of individuals and families, and the state acts to provide welfare only as a safety net when other means have failed. The state holds its own direct activity to a minimum. This tends to mean that services focus on the poor, because people with resources are able to make alternative forms of provision. The state retains the role of legal regulation (establishing the framework, such as laws on charity), within which independent services operate, and there is an argument that says that the state may provide social services as an extension of its control functions.

3. *Subsidiarity.* The third model is a concept in which the state acts to increase the welfare of its citizens, but such activity is subject to restraints in principle. The Catholic principle of subsidiarity argues for limitations on the actions of higher bodies like the state, and for priority to decisions taken at the lowest possible levels of society—the individual, the family, and the locality. Although this is similar to residualism, there is an important distinction: the recognition that a state can legitimately act to aid lesser social bodies. This duty is expressed in Catholic social teaching in terms of solidarity. Duties are primarily founded in personal and communal relationships, but wider social networks can be developed in order to meet different kinds of responsibility. The combination of social responsibility with limitation on state activity has been a central tenet of Christian Democratic parties in Europe.

4. *Pragmatic or functional intervention.* A pragmatic approach to intervention judges the merits of intervention by the added value it offers, and so to the extent to which it offers benefits in excess of costs, whether for individuals or for society as a whole. The argument that welfare can be functional for the economy or for social integration is closely related to this. Intervention in education, for example, can be justified by its importance in socializing young people and the social benefit of a trained workforce; the provision of social insurance by the state acts to compensate and protect individuals while smoothing the impact of adjustments in the economy. The German Sozialstaat, although strongly identified with the principle of subsidiarity, justifies intervention primarily on the basis of the benefits of social provision to the economy.

5. *The welfare society.* The model of "institutional" welfare, a term proposed by Wilensky and Lebeaux, is one in which certain needs, like old age and sickness, are accepted (or "institutionalized") as a normal part of social life, and so where provision is identified as a collective social responsibility. The idea of the welfare society emphasizes the distribution of welfare through a range of different types of provision. The state acts to plan, regulate, and provide in order to foster a comprehensive range of social services, without being committed to controlling the services itself. In the Netherlands, this developed through the traditional "pillarization" of services, in which religious associations (Catholic and Protestant) provided welfare services within their own sphere, with state support, while the state simultaneously promoted activity within a secular pillar. In France, the aim of government policy has been progressively to extend the scope of solidaristic social networks, focusing in particular on those who were "excluded" from the process and attempting to "insert" them into society. This model has a considerable influence in the social policy of the European Union.

6. *The welfare state.* In a 1961 essay, historian Asa Briggs represented the postwar British welfare state as offering a guaranteed minimum income; social protection against contingencies like unemployment, sickness, and old age; and universal provision at the best standard possible. The third criterion, described by T. H. Marshall in terms of "citizenship" and the extension of social rights, most clearly distinguishes the ideal welfare state from the provision of welfare in most countries. The implementation of these principles, the emphasis on universal access and unified administration, and the vesting of responsibility in government led in practice to a strong association of the idea of the welfare state with public sector provision, though the link is not a necessary one.

7. *"Socialist" welfare.* The formerly communist states of eastern Europe claimed to be implementing a different kind of socialist welfare policy, in which state intervention was an intrinsic part of social activity and all citizens shared in the welfare of the society as members of a collective group. Lenin described the redistribution of income in terms of the division of a common social product, with parts being divided between wages, benefits, and services and the activities of the state. Socialist welfare is distinguished from the universal welfare state first in its rejection of the principles of market distribution, and second in its pursuit of equality as a primary social goal.

This does not constitute a comprehensive taxonomy of state welfare; it is aligned along a single dimension (the extent of state intervention), and does not take account of different patterns of service organization and delivery. Provision in some countries is underdeveloped; in some it is haphazard. There is no evident reason why measures have to follow a single, consistent criterion. French health care policy couples active intervention and redistribution with a commitment to liberal principles, while the Swedish welfare state, often identified with egalitarian solidarity, is also heavily geared to occupational status.

The emphasis on state intervention is basic to many of the arguments which fall between public and private. As the preceding models indicate, it is possible for a state to accept responsibility for welfare without providing the social services itself, and the private market has an identifiable role in six of the seven models. There is, in virtually all developed societies, some interplay between the role of the state and different providers of welfare.

II. THE SECTORS OF WELFARE

A. The Public Sector

The public sector generally refers to social services which are financed and administered by the state. Arguments for public sector provision are dependent on more general arguments for state intervention, but the specific question of whether provision should be made by the public sector, rather than by other means, is more limited: if the principle of state intervention has been accepted, the question remains whether the state should itself provide rather than delegating tasks or purchasing provision from independent providers.

There are four main arguments for public sector provision.

• *Universal standards.* The first is that the state is uniquely able to impose a general regime, and so can ensure uniform or minimum standards. The basic argument for uniformity is an argument for consistency: that people should not be treated differently unless there are relevant differences between them. Minimum standards may be considered requisite for individual rights, freedom, or social justice, and may be justified in those terms; an example is the introduction of universal elementary education for children.

• *Social control.* Some functions require some form of compulsion or control. The state may be seen as having a monopoly on the legitimate use of force; whether or not this is true, allowing independent agencies the use of compulsion is potentially problematic. Control may be appropriate where one person has to be controlled to protect the rights of another, which is the case in relation to the protection of children from abuse; because the person for whom provision is being made is subject to control, as in the care of prisoners; or as a means of promoting autonomy, which is an important element of arguments for the compulsory detention of mental patients and compulsory education.

• *Economic benefit.* The state may be able to perform the action more efficiently or cost effectively than is the case elsewhere; there may be economies of scale. The UK National Health Service has proved to be substantially more economical than many liberal systems; Italy's introduction of a national system was prompted in part by the desire to achieve similar economies.

• *Residual provision.* The state may be required to act as a safety net in circumstances where other sectors do not provide. The commercial sector has a strong incentive for "cream skimming" and adverse selection, which involve at different levels the exclusion of some people from provision on the basis that they are more expensive or difficult to deal with.

The arguments against provision by the state oppose it in terms of principle, method, and outcomes. In principle, there are general libertarian arguments, which believe state intervention is illegitimate. Hayek's argument in *The Road to Serfdom* is that any state-run activity, no matter how well intentioned, is liable to create a pattern of intervention which must infringe individual liberty. As a method, state intervention is believed to be inefficient, because there are insufficient constraints on cost. In relation to outcomes, the public sector is seen as liable to abuse: intervention may be paternalistic or promote clientelism (the "pork-barrel," in which politicians use their control of public services to buy support or favor their political supporters).

B. The Private Sector

The private sector is sometimes defined as if it were equivalent to provision beyond the state, but this covers a range of disparate activities. The private sector includes commercial activity (for profit), the provision of occupational welfare (for the benefit of employees or others), and the work of mutual aid and voluntary organizations (not for profit). (Confusingly, commercial and voluntary work are also sometimes referred to, in the context of health care, as the voluntary sector.)

Because the motivations and modes of operation are different, they require to be considered separately.

The commercial sector is distinguished primarily through its operation in an economic market, in which the price system conveys the information necessary to the production, distribution, and exchange of goods and services. Economic liberals, like Milton Friedman, argue that the market is the best means of organizing the provision of welfare. The market system is held out as offering informed choice to the consumer, responsiveness to individual needs, and efficient production (because competition disciplines the producers); further, unlike state welfare, it educates people about the costs and implications of their choices.

The first objection to provision through the market is that it distributes goods and services by inappropriate criteria. One problem is that it reflects the ability to pay, rather than need, desert, rights, or any other relevant criterion for distribution. Another is that social preferences are not necessarily the same as the aggregate of individual preferences. A risk of 1 in 10,000 is very small for any individual, and it would be reasonable to accept it; in a society with 200 million people, it would affect 20,000 people, and might be seen as a major social problem. There may, too, be social priorities distinct from individual priorities; there are public goods, like roads, parks, or public cleansing, which are unlikely to be provided on the basis of individual preferences. And the location of services relates to effective competition for customers rather than the best interests of the population served; there is a tendency for resources provided in the market to be geographically concentrated.

Second, the market does not guarantee a structure of services necessary to the population. The constraints of the market encourage firms to be efficient (producing units at minimum average cost) rather than cost effective (achieving social goals at minimum cost). The difference between the two is generally characterized by a process of selection and exclusion of cases which are less viable economically, whether this is because of the poverty of the potential clientele, the depth of their need, or special costs involved in providing for them. The coverage of social protection systems is limited because of adverse selection—the exclusion of bad risks—and the problem of moral hazard, where people are able to control the circumstances which lead to claims. The most basic problem is that many of the people most in need are unable to contribute, and so cannot be covered. In the case of health care, for example, the most expensive groups are elderly people (who represent a large proportion of the total cost of health care), poor people (because they are more likely to be ill), and people with chronic problems requiring residential care (such as mental illness). In the supposedly "private" system of the United States, these costs have often had to be met in practice by government (through Medicare, Medicaid, or state-run psychiatric care).

Third, whatever the theory, the market in practice is often costly and inefficient. Medical care in the private sector, the paradigmatic example, offers inferior coverage for a population, but it is also much more expensive than a national health service. Financial administration (like marketing and billing) has to be paid for, facilities are duplicated, and the separation of purchase from consumption, which is a necessary part of insurance, provides inadequate cost constraints. It is important to note that this does not apply with equal force to every kind of welfare service; the appropriateness of market provision depends strongly on the context in which it operates, and on the issues to which it is being addressed.

C. Occupational Welfare

Occupational welfare is provided, and partially financed, by employers. The criteria for distribution may be governed by the market—some provision made for employees is effectively a part of the contract of employment, and as such would be considered as part of the employee's remuneration—but equally it may be decided on other principles. Maintaining the welfare and health of the labor force may be seen as a form of investment; provisions like housing or crèches for workers can be justified in terms of enlightened self-interest. Another approach is the view of employment as a cooperative activity (characterized, for example, by Owenism), or a paternalistic one; in postfeudal times, an employer would still have a duty to protect ancient workers. The Japanese system of occupational welfare has elements which link it with feudal traditions.

The main limitation of occupational welfare is precisely that it is linked to the labor market; the effect of insecurity of employment is to create insecure social protection.

D. Mutual Aid

Mutual aid organizations, or mutualities, have been particularly important in the provision of insurance services and the finance of housing. Historically, many European welfare systems developed from the mutual aid arrangements established by trade unions, professional associations, and friendly societies; in a number of countries these associations have effectively become responsible for the provision of social insurance. The Israeli Histadruth, which is the general trades union organization, was primarily responsible for the development of health and social services, and most of the population still subscribes to the health care fund it established.

Mutual organizations are distinguished primarily by their voluntary nature, in which individuals subscribe or contribute to become members of the organization and receive in return coverage. The nature of the contribution varies; probably the most common pattern has been the payment of a subscription. In some organizations (like self-build housing cooperatives) it has called for people to give their labor.

Although mutualist organizations have been developed as the basis of national systems, they suffer from two important limitations in this respect. The first is that the ability of the organization to support its members is often inversely proportional to their needs. Organizations whose members are older, more frail, or poorer may find it difficult to maintain financial viability. In France, there has been a problem in maintaining the position of certain arrangements for pensions where the industrial base has shrunk; the problem is mainly addressed by intervention to transfer resources between professional funds. The second is that the mutual aid organizations have tended to exclude those who are unable to make an effective contribution.

E. Voluntary Social Services

The voluntary sector consists largely of nonprofit organizations which are formed for social purposes (though the term "voluntary" can in different contexts be extended to include any nonstatutory activity). There is a wide range of activities, ranging from small local societies to large, professional agencies. The term can refer to religious groups, social clubs, and arts groups as much as to fundraising groups, campaigning organizations, or community service.

Although in the United States the term "voluntary sector" is used to refer mainly to autonomous nongovernmental organizations, which may engage in commercial activity, in other countries the guiding principle is the use of voluntary or unpaid work. This does not preclude the existence of paid staff (a voluntary organization may be characterized by the presence of a voluntary committee or the efforts of volunteers coordinated by paid workers), and voluntary work can take place under the auspices of state organizations. Unpaid work which takes place outside a formal organizational con-

text is, however, considered to fall within the scope of the informal sector.

The role of the voluntary sector is determined through the motivation and behavior of those who undertake voluntary roles, rather than the needs of the population which is served. This has led to criticisms that voluntary effort is sometimes misdirected, sometimes tied to ancient causes rather than modern problems, and often not available where it is most needed. Voluntary sector effort has been criticized for producing undesirable social effects (for example, the monasteries in the Reformation, or "indiscriminate charity" in the 19th century, were criticized for supporting and encouraging vagrants).

By the same token, the primary justification for voluntary activity has been rooted in the position of those who give, rather than those who receive. Richard Titmuss, in *The Gift Relationship* (1970), argued that people have a need to give. This was a study of the distribution of blood products; it is one of the most important critiques of the private market. Voluntary donation, Titmuss argued, was not only morally superior, it produced greater quantities of blood, and blood that was less likely to be infected than blood which had been sold.

F. The Informal Sector

The informal sector consists of communities, friends, neighbors, and kin. Referring to welfare as a social responsibility tends to suggest that the role of families is relatively marginal. In practice, however, the comprehensive welfare state has often failed to make notable inroads into the burden of care experienced by families with members who are severely dependent. Michael Bayley's *Mental Handicap and Community Care* (1973) had a seminal influence. Bayley made the argument that most care was not being provided by the statutory services, but by informal carers. He argued that the role of the state is, realistically, to supplement, relieve, or reinforce the care given by others. State services had to be "interwoven" within the existing framework of provision, an idea subsequently developed as the selection of a package of services for dependent people.

With the discharge of people from institutions, the maintenance of individuals in the community, and the increasing stress on "normalization," there has been a growing emphasis on the role of carers. This approach has received support across the political spectrum. On the political right, conservatives have emphasized the pluralistic nature of welfare; traditional conservatism stresses an "organic view" of society, as a series of interconnecting relationships, and the role of family and duty. On the left, informal care is linked to a welfare society and social solidarity.

The emphasis on informal care has, however, led to a range of criticisms. From the perspective of carers, concern has been expressed about the physical and emotional burden of care, and the cost (in terms both of expenses and of income foregone). Feminist writers have criticized the burden imposed on women, and the expectation that where a woman is present she will have to incur the extra responsibility of care. From the perspective of dependent people, there are further problems. Carers may, like volunteers, be well meaning, but they will not necessarily offer adequate care from the perspective of people in need. The interests of carers may conflict with the interests of the people they are caring for, and in cases where dependent people have difficulty expressing their needs (for example, learning disability or dementia), there is a risk that the dependent person will be overlooked.

III. WELFARE PLURALISM

A. The Role of the State

The pattern of services is very much more complex than the simple identification of welfare states with state welfare suggests. The situation has been described variously as welfare pluralism, the welfare mix, or a mixed economy of welfare. Many services which are produced by one means may draw on finance from others. Voluntary social services often draw on state or commercial subvention; mutualist services may make some charges on a commercial basis; private sector activities may solicit voluntary donations; and states may delegate functions, or subvent, commercial or voluntary activity. Because the services have developed simultaneously, they are intertwined.

The state has the capacity not only to provide welfare services itself, but to affect the conduct of the other sectors. The basic approaches include regulation, finance, and planning. Regulation refers to the rules and settings under which services operate, including the legal framework. Financial intervention includes the use of subsidy, the creation of incentives or disincentives through taxation, and the purchase of services. The regulatory and financial processes make important sanctions available to the agencies of the state, and this is the basis of the planning role. Planning implies direction, but the planning role is more typically one of bargaining and negotiation in order to achieve intended goals, and the state has considerable bargaining power.

The dominant model of welfare provision in western Europe is corporatist, in the sense that the state delegates the principal welfare functions to autonomous agencies and supports them financially in part. In political terms, corporatism can be seen both as a system of interest group representation and as a mechanism for the exercise of hierarchical control over lower levels of activity. Although in principle this approach may involve a high degree of state intervention, it is fully compatible with limits on state activity, and on that basis it has a wide political appeal in Europe.

B. The Social Division of Welfare

Welfare pluralism has the direct implication that the outcomes of welfare policy have to be understood in terms of the interaction of different sectors of welfare, rather than the public sector alone. In the 1950s, Richard Titmuss introduced the concept of the social division of welfare as a means of identifying the distributive implications of different social services. He initially pointed to three main channels through which welfare might be distributed: social welfare, or the social services; fiscal welfare, or reliefs and subsidies through the tax system; and occupational welfare, social protection available under the auspices of employers. The range of mechanisms which might be identified could also include the legal system, mutual aid, and the voluntary and informal sectors.

The importance of Titmuss's classification is in his argument for a different understanding of the effect of state intervention in its social context. In order to examine the effectiveness of any social policy, it is necessary to examine the range of services which is being offered—the package—and the outcomes of that intervention. This approach has been particularly influential in the examination both of community care, where attempts are made to tailor the range of services to individual needs, and of social security, where the concept of an income package has been used to compare the impact of policies in different countries. Since the distributive outcomes of policy are fundamental to a range of policy objectives, including the relief of poverty, the formation of a structure of opportunity, and the development of incentives, the social division of welfare has been a key concept in the analysis of social policy.

IV. WELFARE REGIMES

Gøsta Esping-Andersen has argued that too much emphasis on expenditure or distributive outcomes is liable to disguise the character of the intervention undertaken, and has sought to analyze intervention in different terms. He classifies welfare regimes on the basis of the mechanisms which are used and the criteria on which provision is made, rather than on the level or nature of activity undertaken. Among the criteria he applies are the degree of corporatism, the extent of social security provision by the state, and the relative importance of the private sector. On the basis of his analysis, he distinguishes three principal types of welfare regime in modern societies.

Liberal regimes seek to minimize the commitment to state welfare, limiting state activity while depending strongly on the economic market to promote personal welfare. The welfare state is focused principally on the working class and the poor. The liberal regimes are often Anglo-Saxon countries, including the United States and Australia.

Corporatist regimes are characterized by state control of provision rather than by the provision of services by the state. The progressive extension of welfare services has tended to crowd out the market, but this has taken place within the context of conservative policies emphasizing the promotion of the economy. This model has been central to the development of provision in western Europe, including France and Germany.

Social democratic regimes had the fullest commitment to public expenditure on welfare, and developed universal rights. With this, the welfare state came to include extensive provision for the middle classes, to the point where some commentators have suggested that welfare state has been "hijacked" for the benefit of the middle classes. Esping-Andersen's main examples are Scandinavian welfare states.

Although this classification is clearly related to the continuum of state intervention, there are important differences; for example, the emphasis on method leads Esping-Andersen to characterize Australia, which makes extensive use of income tests for social security benefits, as liberal, when assessment in terms of coverage and distributive outcomes might lead to a different view. The liberal states are distinguished from social democratic ones not so much by the level of expenditure or involvement in welfare, but by what that expenditure is directed toward. Esping-Andersen's approach has been influential in the study of comparative social policy, but it has also been subject to criticism. The principal problem relates to the difficulty of identifying clear relationships between ideology and political practice; most countries have a mix of principles, often exercised inconsistently, and it is possible to classify welfare regimes in different ways depending on the criteria and indicators which are selected.

Also See the Following Articles

ETHICS AND SOCIAL SERVICES, OVERVIEW • HEALTH CARE FINANCING • POVERTY • RESOURCE ALLOCATION • SOCIAL SECURITY • WELFARE POLICIES

Bibliography

Esping-Andersen, G. (1990). *The three worlds of welfare capitalism.* Cambridge: Polity.

Gilbert, N., Specht, H., & Terrell, P. (1993). *Dimensions of social welfare policy.* Englewood Cliffs, NJ: Prentice Hall.

Legrand, J., Propper, C., & Robinson, R. (1992). *Economics of social problems* (3rd ed.). London: Macmillan.

Spicker, P. (1995). *Social policy: Themes and approaches.* New York: Prentice Hall.

Titmuss, R. (1987). *The philosophy of welfare.* London: Allen & Unwin.

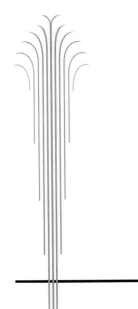

SOCIAL WORK

Frederic G. Reamer
Rhode Island College

GLOSSARY

confidentiality An ethical principle prohibiting social workers from disclosing to others information about a client without the client's consent.

direct practice Social work interventions with individual clients, couples, families, and small groups.

distributive justice The fair allocation of resources.

divided loyalties Instances when social workers feel caught between their simultaneous obligations to clients and to a third party, such as an employer or society at large.

dual relationships Instances when social workers relate to clients in more than one relationship, whether social, sexual, or business.

ethical dilemma Circumstances requiring a choice between competing ethical duties or obligations.

ethics committee A committee formed to provide case consultation, policy review, and/or education on ethical issues.

indirect practice Social work intervention involving administration, community organizing, social planning, and social policy.

paternalism Interfering with clients' right to self-determination for their own good.

professional boundaries A social work principle that requires practitioners to avoid social, sexual, and business relationships with clients.

self-determination An ethical principle in social work, according to which practitioners should respect clients' right to choose and help clients pursue their goals.

social work A profession in which the primary mission is to enhance human well-being and to help people meet basic human needs, with particular attention to the needs of people who are vulnerable, oppressed, and living in poverty.

whistle-blowing Disclosure of wrongdoing to people in positions of authority.

SOCIAL WORK is a profession in which the primary mission is to enhance human well-being and to help people meet basic human needs, with particular attention to the needs of people who are vulnerable, oppressed, and living in poverty. Social workers assist individuals, couples, families, groups, organizations, and communities. Key to social work's mission is its simultaneous focus on individual well-being in a social context and the well-being of the broader society. One of social work's hallmarks is the attention that the profession's practitioners pay to the environmental forces that create, contribute to, and address problems in liv-

Encyclopedia of Applied Ethics, Volume 4
Copyright © 1998 by Academic Press. All rights of reproduction in any form reserved.

ing. Social work activities may include counseling and clinical work with individuals, couples, families, and groups; community organizing; agency administration; consultation; advocacy; social and political action; policy development and implementation; education; and research and evaluation.

I. SOCIAL WORK: AN OVERVIEW

Social work began as a formal profession in the late 19th century. It grew out of a wide range of efforts to assist people experiencing problems in living. These efforts included work by "friendly visitors" in the early 1800s, primarily middle- and upper-class women who volunteered to help indigent families; charity organization societies, begun in the 19th century in Europe and the United States to provide services to the "worthy" poor and disabled; and settlement houses, also begun in the 19th century in Europe and the United States, in which the staff lived in the communities where they worked, devoting much of their effort to problems related to housing, health care, employment and working conditions, and sanitation. Prominent settlement houses included London's Toynbee Hall and Chicago's Hull House.

From these early attempts to help poor and vulnerable people, which have their historical roots in the English Poor Laws enacted between 1601 and 1834, social work has matured into a full-fledged profession with rigorous education, fields and methods of practice, and ethical standards. The first formal social work education program began in 1898, in the form of a 6-week summer training program sponsored by the New York Charity Organization Society. Six years later, the New York School of Philanthropy, which ultimately became the Columbia University School of Social Work, was formed to offer a 1-year educational curriculum.

Contemporary social work is practiced in a wide range of public- and private-sector settings, such as schools, prisons, hospitals, psychiatric facilities, nursing homes, senior citizen centers, rehabilitation centers, mental health clinics, private practice offices, community agencies, welfare agencies, child-welfare and human-service departments, policy offices in government agencies, and residential programs for children and adolescents with emotional and behavioral problems, people with disabilities, and people with substance abuse problems. Many social workers provide clinical services to people, such as individual, family, or group counseling. However, a significant portion of the profession is involved in activities such as agency administration, community organizing, social and political action, and research and evaluation.

II. THE EMERGENCE OF ETHICAL ISSUES

Social work has always been concerned with ethical issues. This stems in part from social work's early commitment to a core set of values. Throughout the profession's history, social workers have embraced values related to individual worth and dignity, social justice, confidentiality, individuals' capacity to change, respect for diversity and nondiscrimination, and professional integrity.

As in all professions, the nature of social work's concern about ethical issues has changed over time. During the profession's earliest period, many practitioners focused on the morality of their clients. Reinforced especially by the practices and perspectives of the charity organization society movement, many social workers sought to enhance the morality of clients whose rectitude and character seemed weak. During the Great Depression, social workers paid much more attention to issues of social injustice and they became champions of the poor and vulnerable. Prominent social workers lobbied in an effort to persuade both public- and private-sector organizations and institutions to meet their ethical obligation to care for society's most vulnerable citizens. Although this passionate agenda weakened during the 1940s and 1950s, in part because of the profession's understandable preoccupation with World War II and its aftermath, in the 1960s social work rejuvenated its concern about society's ethical obligations to poor and otherwise vulnerable people.

It was not until the 1970s, however, that social work focused explicit attention on the subject of professional ethics, beginning especially with Charles Levy's 1976 book, *Social Work Ethics*. Although the profession's literature contains a smattering of writings on ethics-related matters published prior to this period (for example, on subjects such as social work's values, client self-determination, and confidentiality), the bulk of social workers' efforts related to professional ethics has occurred since the late 1970s and early 1980s. This is evidenced by the proliferation of conference presentations, course offerings, and publications since 1980; in fact, about 75% of social work's literature on ethics has been published since 1980.

There are a number of reasons why social workers' interest in professional ethics has burgeoned in recent years. First, a variety of technological innovations has presented social workers with exceedingly complex ethical issues. For example, the advent of technology that enables organ transplantation has created difficult ethical choices for family members who must decide, perhaps with a hospital-based social worker's assistance, whether to donate the organs of a relative who has died suddenly. Technological advances in the computer industry (for example, the widespread computerization of mental health records and the use of the Internet to convey confidential information about clients) and the telephone industry (for example, social workers' use of cellular and cordless telephones) have produced ethical concerns about social workers' protection of clients' privacy.

In addition, the relatively recent enactment of various laws and public regulations has also created novel ethical issues. Two prominent examples involving social workers are the passage of mandatory reporting laws for the protection of children who appear to be at risk of abuse and neglect, and laws that require social workers to disclose confidential information about clients, perhaps without clients' permission, in order to protect third parties from harm. Mandatory reporting laws require that social workers who suspect that a child has been abused or neglected notify child-welfare officials, even if this means disclosing confidential information without clients' consent. Although social workers are generally supportive of mandatory reporting laws and recognize their value and importance, many clinical social workers have encountered situations where they believe that notifying child-welfare officials may be counterproductive and ultimately more damaging. Typical situations are those where social workers believe that notifying child-welfare officials will cause clients who have been making significant progress in treatment to feel betrayed and, as a result, to flee treatment. In these instances social workers sometimes claim that the risk of future abuse or neglect is most likely to be reduced if social workers do not breach clients' confidentiality by notifying child-welfare officials and continue to work with the clients themselves. But to do so means deliberately violating a law, and that entails an ethical choice.

Similar ethical challenges arise as a result of what are generally known as "duty to protect" or "duty to warn" statutes. These laws require social workers to disclose confidential information to a third party, preferably with but possibly without clients' permission, when social workers believe that a client has threatened to seriously harm that individual and the threat is imminent and foreseeable. Social workers sometimes face "gray area" cases where they must make a daunting ethical choice between respecting a client's confidentiality and disclosing confidential information over a client's strenuous objection in order to protect a third party from harm.

The legacy of the 1960s also inspired social workers' interest in ethical issues. Today many social workers are keenly interested in issues related to welfare rights, patients' rights, and prisoners' rights. Social workers are concerned about the rights poor people have to welfare assistance or to subsidized shelter, the rights that psychiatric patients have to refuse medication that has serious side effects, and the rights that prison inmates have to receive adequate health care. Many of these and other related concerns have their origins in the 1960s, when social workers and many other activists lobbied legislatures and other public bodies, sometimes in a militant fashion, to address people's rights in various social arenas.

Further, social work as a profession is much more aware of ethical issues because of publicized scandals involving colleagues, members of other professions, and other public figures. Sadly, social workers, and members of all other professions, have become much more aware of the ways in which colleagues and public figures behave unethically, in part because of the media's growing interest in the phenomenon. For example, social workers are much more knowledgeable about the relatively small group of colleagues who have been disciplined or sanctioned for their sexual involvement with clients, exploitation of clients, inappropriate disclosure of confidential information concerning clients, or other unethical behavior. Professional publications and the general media now report such matters regularly, in contrast to earlier periods in social work's history, thus creating increased concern among the profession's members about colleagues' ethical conduct.

Finally, social workers' increased interest in ethical issues also reflects the profession's own maturation. As in most professions, social work's earliest years were focused on the development of the profession's "technical" proficiency (the Greek root of the word technical is *technikos*, meaning art and craft). Understandably, a profession's earliest practitioners are primarily interested in establishing a firm technical foundation based on the best available knowledge. In fact, it took all of the major and minor professions decades to begin paying serious attention to pertinent ethical issues, dilemmas, and decision-making.

III. ETHICAL ISSUES AND DILEMMAS

Ethical issues and dilemmas in social work can be placed into three major groups, consisting of those involving (1) the delivery of services to individuals, couples, families, and groups, (2) agency administration, community organizing, and social policy, and (3) relationships among practitioners.

A. Services to Individuals, Couples, Families, and Groups

Social workers who provide services to individuals, couples, families, and groups (known in the profession as "direct" practice)—such as counseling, casework services, and concrete services such as housing and food—encounter a wide variety of ethical issues and dilemmas. Among the most common are related to confidentiality and privacy, client self-determination, professional paternalism, divided loyalties, professional boundaries, and professional and personal values.

1. Confidentiality and Privacy

Confidentiality and privacy are key concepts in social work, particularly for those practitioners who provide clinical and mental health services. Clients who seek social workers' services need reassurance that social workers will respect their right to confidentiality and privacy. Inappropriate violations of clients' rights to confidentiality and privacy undermine clients' trust and, ultimately, the profession's integrity.

Social workers recognize, however, that, like members of other mental health professions, extreme circumstances may require them to breach clients' confidentiality. For example, laws may require social workers to notify public officials when they suspect that a client has neglected or abused a child, or when social workers have substantial reason to believe that a client intends to harm an identifiable third party (such as an estranged spouse or partner).

2. Client Self-Determination and Professional Paternalism

Social workers have a deep-seated respect for clients' right to set and pursue their own goals. One of social work's hallmarks is practitioners' willingness, and even determination, to help clients chart the course of their own lives without undue influence from social workers or other parties. Social workers typically view their role as helping clients identify and think through options and realistic courses of action, related, for example,

to the handling of stressful relationships, self-esteem issues, clinical depression, substance abuse treatment, employment decisions, and caring for a disabled relative.

It is not unusual, however, for social workers to encounter circumstances when they question clients' judgment and the choices clients have made, or plan to make, for themselves. For instance, clients may decide not to end an intimate relationship with a spouse who is physically abusive, leave a nursing home against medical advice, stop taking psychotropic medication prescribed by their psychiatrist, continue using illegal substances, or end their lives by committing suicide.

Among the greatest ethical challenges facing social workers are those where they must decide to what extent clients' choices to engage in apparently self-destructive behavior should be respected. This circumstance raises questions about the extent to which there are or ought to be limits to clients' right to self-determination, and whether professional paternalism is sometimes appropriate.

Professional paternalism entails interfering with clients' right to self-determination (what philosophers call people's liberty interests) *for their own good*. Examples of professional paternalism include interfering with clients physically (examples: forcing a homeless person to sleep in a shelter, against his wishes, because the weather is brutally cold and dangerous, or involuntarily committing an individual with serious mental health problems to a psychiatric facility), withholding information from clients when that information may be deeply disturbing to clients or may lead clients to harm themselves (examples: not telling a hospital patient who has been critically injured in an automobile accident that her child was killed in the accident, or not telling an emotionally unstable client that her long-term prognosis is poor), and providing clients with inaccurate or misleading information (examples: telling an elderly client with dementia that he is going to a nursing home "only for a short stay," when the truth is that his stay will be long-term, or informing a vulnerable client that his mental health symptoms are improving, when they are not, in order to avoid distressing him).

Social workers need to be especially careful to avoid what is known in the social work literature as "pseudo-paternalism," where the concept of paternalism is used as camouflage to justify interfering with clients' right to self-determination against their wishes. In these instances, social workers may claim that they are interfering with clients physically, withholding information from them, or lying to them for the clients' own good, when in reality the paternalism is for the social worker's or someone else's convenience or benefit. For example, a social worker in a mental health treatment program may withhold information from a client alleging that it is for the client's own good, when, in fact, the social worker simply does not want to have to deal with a distraught and volatile client who may have difficulty coping with the information. Or, a social worker may initiate involuntary commitment of a client to a psychiatric hospital, alleging that the hospitalization is for the client's own good, when, in fact, the social worker is tired of dealing with the client's difficult behavior in the community.

3. Divided Loyalties

Ordinarily, social workers protect clients' interests. That is, when clients' interests conflict with others' interests, social workers are duty-bound to protect clients' interests. Client loyalty is a key ingredient in the profession's value base.

On occasion, however, social workers find that they are caught between two sets of competing interests, both of which demand their loyalty. For example, social workers may provide counseling to two or more parties who have relationships with each other, as in marriage counseling. Ethical dilemmas may arise when one the couple decide to divorce and the social worker is subpoenaed by one spouse to testify against the other in a child custody dispute. Or, one spouse may disclose information about the other spouse to the social worker, in confidence, (for example, concerning the second spouse's plan to commit a serious crime), and the social worker may be required by law to disclose that information to public officials.

4. Professional Boundaries

Social workers are trained to maintain clear and strict boundaries in their relationships with clients. For instance, a social worker functioning as a psychotherapist should not enter into a sexual or business relationship with a client. Social workers understand how clients may be harmed when social workers engage in such "dual or multiple relationships." Clients who are confused about the nature of their relationship with social workers may have difficulty benefiting from professional services.

There are situations, however, when it is difficult for social workers to maintain firm and clear boundaries. For example, social workers who practice in remote rural areas often find that dual or multiple relationships are unavoidable, such as when the one mental health professional in a small town, whose child is enrolled in the one second-grade at the town's only elementary school, is providing counseling services to the school's sole second-grade teacher, or when the one mental health professional in a small town is providing counseling services to her husband's boss.

5. Professional and Personal Values

Social workers usually find that their professional and personal values are compatible. For instance, social workers who actively lobby against racial discrimination or promote enhanced access to affordable housing and health care know that the profession's values support their efforts.

However, some social workers find that their own personal values conflict with the profession's. Some social workers, for example, oppose women's right to choose abortion, even though historically the social work profession has favored women's right to choose. Some social workers favor extensive cuts in welfare benefits, even though the social work profession has typically opposed cuts and/or lobbied for enhanced welfare benefits.

Social workers may also find that their personal values sometimes conflict with clients' values. This can occur when, for example, social workers who are deeply opposed to racism have clients who are racist, or when social workers who value marital fidelity work with clients who flaunt their extramarital affairs, apparently without compunction. In all of these instances social workers must reconcile these value conflicts in ways that do not compromise inviolable professional standards.

B. Agency Administration, Community Organizing, and Social Policy

Many social workers have administrative responsibilities or are involved in community organizing or the formulation and implementation of social policy—what social workers refer to as "indirect" practice. Prominent examples of ethical issues and dilemmas in this arena involve allocating limited resources, sorting out the responsibility of government and the private sector for social welfare programs, compliance with regulations and laws, labor–management disputes, and the use of deception.

1. Allocating Limited Resources

Social workers in administrative positions often face circumstances that require allocating scarce or limited resources. Directors of social service agencies whose budgets have been cut severely may have to decide which programs to scale back or which staff to release in order to avoid a budget deficit. Social workers who serve as legislators or on the staff of public officials may have to recommend what social services to fund in an annual budget, and what important services might need to be eliminated because of a shortfall in projected revenue.

Allocation decisions of this kind concern what philosophers call issues of distributive justice. Distributive justice concerns concepts and criteria used to allocate resources. Social workers, for example, may need to decide whether budgetary funds will be divided equally among various eligible categories, or whether certain services or populations will receive priority, perhaps based on the magnitude of the social need being addressed, affirmative action principles, or the ability of a particular program to generate additional revenue for the agency. Social workers need to understand that such allocation decisions involve more than administrative judgment; they also entail ethical considerations.

2. Government and Private-Sector Responsibility for Social Welfare

Throughout modern history social workers and others concerned about social welfare have debated the relative responsibilities of government and the private sector. One school of thought is that the public sector has a bottom-line duty to meet the basic needs of life's most vulnerable citizens. According to this perspective, government has an ethical obligation to use tax-generated revenue to finance services to the poor, disabled, unemployed, and so on.

In contrast, others argue that the public sector is ill equipped for this difficult task. From this point of view, government bodies are typically inefficient and intrusive, prone to meddling in private citizens' lives gratuitously and directing economic resources in wasteful directions. According to this ideological vantage point, the most productive way to address social needs is to minimize government involvement in people's lives and let market forces and conditions enhance employment and community wealth, which in turn will enhance the commonwealth's well-being. This socially and economically conservative perspective favors private charity and voluntary initiatives to help those in need. Its critics argue, however, that the private sector cannot be depended on to meet the needs of those who are most vulnerable, gaps in service and assistance are inevitable with this approach, and that, in the end, the public sector must assume responsibility for providing and maintaining society' safety net.

This ethical debate is critically important for social workers because of its implications for the profession's ability to offer programs and services to people in need. Historically, broad-based public-sector support for social welfare has strengthened social work's attempts to mount significant programs and policies. Diminished public-sector support, combined with greater reliance on the private sector, has ordinarily weakened social work's posture.

3. Compliance with Regulations and Laws

Social workers certainly understand the need to comply with laws and agency rules and regulations. After all, chaos would result if social workers felt no obligation to comply with, for example, child abuse and neglect mandatory reporting laws, informed consent procedures, agency intake or admission policies, and protection of human subjects guidelines governing research and evaluation.

Nonetheless, social workers sometimes face circumstances where they feel pressured to decide whether to comply with what appears to be an unjust, inhumane, or unreasonable law, regulation, or policy. For example, social workers in agencies that have strict income guidelines for determining prospective clients' eligibility for services may find it difficult to enforce these guidelines if they seem unduly strict and prevent the delivery of services to people in dire need. Social workers who are required by law to report cases of suspected or abuse of an elderly person may be tempted to violate the statute if they believe that reporting an incident to public officials would be counterproductive and would lead to an intrusive and disruptive investigation.

4. Labor–Management Disputes

Historically social workers have been "prolabor" and "prounion." Because of the profession's enduring concern about low-income, oppressed, exploited, and vulnerable people, social workers have been strong supporters of efforts to promote employment, workers' rights, decent working conditions, and so on. In general, social workers have respected workers' right to strike and to engage in job actions.

This commitment has also led to complex ethical choices for social workers employed in settings where job actions or strikes have been organized. Perhaps the prototypical example involves social workers employed in a hospital where the union has called a general strike of its members to protest a wage freeze and the hospital's failure to address certain issues related to working conditions. Social workers' participation in the strike would mean that critically important services would not be provided to patients, such as grief counseling, crisis intervention, and nursing home placement. Over the years social workers who function in a variety of capacities—line staff, supervisors, administrators—have debated the ethical implications of social workers' participation in job actions and strikes. Although the long-term impact of job actions and strikes may ultimately redound to clients' benefit, because of improved working conditions and morale among staff, the immediate consequences for clients may be severe.

5. The Use of Deception

Social workers understand how important veracity is in professional practice. In their clinical work with individuals, families, couples, and groups, social workers know that truthfulness and honesty are essential ingredients in their efforts to establish trusting relationships with clients. Similarly, truthfulness is key when social workers function as community organizers, administrators, and policy makers. Social workers who employ deceptive tactics in their work are not likely to be trusted or effective. Before long, colleagues, clients, and other constituents who sense that a social worker is deceptive will abandon their faith in the social worker's motives and methods.

There have been instances, however, when some social workers have concluded that some form of deception was ethically justifiable. Examples include embellishing agency statistics to impress funding sources, which could strengthen the agency's financial condition and ability to provide services, and providing misleading information to the public to avoid embarrassing staff who made an honest, but humiliating, mistake by releasing confidential information without proper authorization. Of course, whether such deception is ethically justifiable is questionable.

C. Relationships among Practitioners

On occasion social workers encounter ethical issues and dilemmas involving their colleagues. Most often these situations pertain to colleagues' ethical misconduct or impairment and the phenomenon of whistle-blowing.

1. Ethical Misconduct and Impairment

As in all professions, social workers sometimes encounter colleagues who have engaged in some form of ethical misconduct or who seem impaired. Social workers may discover colleagues who, for example, have had sexual contact with clients, defrauded insurance companies, misrepresented their professional credentials, or who

are experiencing serious mental health or substance abuse problems that are placing their clients at risk.

A key feature of a profession is its willingness and ability to regulate itself. One form of regulation involves practitioners' willingness to monitor colleagues' behavior and to confront unethical and unprofessional conduct. Despite professionals' widespread acceptance of this maxim in principle, many professionals are reluctant to confront colleagues about their unethical conduct or impairment. They may be reluctant to antagonize colleagues in a way that strains professional relationships, or they may be reluctant to involve themselves in a protracted series of inquiries, hearings, and other formal proceedings that often result when social workers raise concerns about colleagues. A practical consequence is that social workers sometimes face difficult ethical choices concerning their obligation to confront colleagues' ethical misconduct or impairment.

2. Whistle-Blowing

Social workers' ethical choices concerning colleagues' ethical misconduct or impairment often lead to ethical decisions related to whistle-blowing. Situations that cannot be handled satisfactorily among colleagues, as a private matter, may warrant some form of whistle-blowing, that is, disclosure to third parties who have responsibility for addressing such matters. Social workers may feel the need to bring their concerns about colleagues to agency supervisors, administrators, or members of the board of directors, or to bodies such as licensing boards, law enforcement officials, or professional associations that address ethical problems.

Whistle-blowing decisions can be among the most difficult ethical decisions social workers face. The potential risks and harms are enormous, given the possible consequences for colleagues' careers. Social workers who contemplate blowing the whistle on a colleague also have to consider the potential impact on their own careers, particularly because of questions that may be raised about their motives.

IV. ETHICAL DECISION-MAKING

Social workers, like all contemporary professionals, now have a wide range of resources to draw on when faced with ethical decisions. This has not always been the case. Before the late 1970s, the concept of applied and professional ethics was virtually nonexistent. Since then, nearly all professions have witnessed the burgeoning of a wide variety of concepts, literature, education and training programs, and consultation services to enhance the quality of ethical decision-making. A number of these significant developments originated outside of social work, in the context of the broader field of applied and professional ethics, and some have occurred within the profession itself.

Perhaps the most striking development has been the growth of the intellectual discipline of applied and professional ethics. There are two strains that have had an important impact on social work. First, the field of moral philosophy has been transformed in recent years, to include a widely recognized specialization focused on applied and professional ethics, supplementing the field's traditional preoccupation with largely theoretical issues related to metaethics (the theoretical study of ethical concepts and the derivation of ethical principles). Many philosophy departments in colleges and universities now offer graduate-level education in applied and professional ethics. Students in these programs must master classic philosophical history and theory, but their primary goal is the application of moral and other philosophical concepts to the practical ethical problems faced by professionals such as doctors, lawyers, social workers, nurses, psychiatrists, psychologists, engineers, dentists, accountants, law enforcement personnel, military officials, and business people. Consistent with this trend, most academic philosophy departments now offer formal courses on subjects related to applied and professional ethics.

The second strain includes professionals, most of whom do not have much, if any, formal education in moral philosophy, who have developed a keen interest in ethical issues. Every major profession now has a coterie of practitioners who specialize in ethical issues, but whose primary education is in their profession, not in moral philosophy or in the field of applied and professional ethics. The combination of these two strains has produced a rich collection of literature, constructive debate, education, and consultation resources that has enhanced professionals' ethical decision-making.

A. Ethical Theory

One of the by-products of the dramatic growth of the field of applied and professional ethics has been the deliberate application of ethical theory and concepts to ethical dilemmas encountered by social workers. Beginning in the late 1970s and early 1980s, a small group of social work scholars began exploring the relevance of moral theory and moral philosophy to contemporary social work. For the first time in the profession's history, scholars drew connections between traditional ethics concepts—such as metaethics, cognitivism, noncognitivism, normative ethics, deontology, teleology, consequentialism, act-and-rule utilitarianism, egoism, and distributive justice—and actual circumstances found in social work practice. By the mid-1980s, a significant number of publications on social work ethics, including several books, had been published drawing on ethical theory and concepts and applying them to social work practice. To varying degrees, these publications discussed how social workers could analyze ethical dilemmas using various ethical and moral concepts.

Today, a growing number of social workers are educated to understand how ethical and moral concepts can help them analyze ethical issues and dilemmas. Often this takes the form of applying ethical theory and concepts to case studies, in an effort to tease out the practical implications of different philosophical perspectives. For instance, social workers may speculate about the differences between a deontologist's and a utilitarian's approach to a case where a social worker is torn about complying with a law requiring mandatory reporting of suspected child abuse. Practitioners may explore the implications of a strict deontological or Kantian view that legitimately enacted laws ought to be obeyed, regardless of the consequences, and a teleological view that social workers ought to weigh the likely costs and benefits of different courses of action and pursue that which is likely to result in the greatest balance of "good" over "evil." Social workers may engage in a similar analysis with respect to many other ethical dilemmas, such as whether a practitioner should tell the truth to a client who, in the social worker's judgment, is likely to be harmed by a candid report, blow the whistle on an impaired colleague, engage in some kind of deception in an effort to uncover agency corruption, participate in a job action or strike, or force a homeless person to enter a shelter against his wishes. Social workers may also apply ethical and moral concepts in their analysis of a wide range of public policy issues related to, for example, allocating scarce or limited budgetary resources (distributive justice concepts), welfare rights, abortion rights, end-of-life decisions, and affirmative action.

B. Code of Ethics

Social work codes of ethics, another key tool in ethical decision-making, have also matured in recent years. They have moved from brief, superficial, and idealistic statements to lengthy, detailed, and conceptually sophisticated documents. For example, the first code of ethics enacted by the National Association of Social Workers, the largest professional social work organization in the world, consisted of a one-page statement of first-person principles, such as "I respect the privacy of the people I serve," and "I give precedence to my professional responsibility over my personal interests." However, soon after this code's adoption in 1960 a number of social workers expressed concern about its abstract nature and lack of practical usefulness. In 1979, NASW adopted a far more extensive and detailed code addressing issues related to social workers' ethical responsibilities to clients, colleagues, employers, employing organizations, the social work profession, and society.

In 1996 NASW enacted what is now the most ambitious code of ethics in the social work profession. The code includes four major sections: (1) a preamble, setting forth the social work profession's mission and core values, (2) a general overview of the code's main functions and a brief guide for dealing with ethical issues and dilemmas in social work practice, (3) a series of broad ethical principles, based on social work's core values, that inform social work practice, and (4) detailed ethical standards intended to guide social workers' conduct and provide a basis for adjudication.

Reflecting the dramatic growth of knowledge in recent years related to applied and professional ethics, the current NASW code of ethics includes many issues that were not broached in predecessor codes. In addition to the novel addition of a mission statement for the profession, which serves as the foundation for all of the code's principles and standards, the code addresses a variety of new issues concerning, for example, obtaining informed consent from clients who are not literate; social workers' obligation to be knowledgeable about client's culture and ethnicity; privacy and confidentiality of information transmitted by electronic mediums (computers, radios, and cellular telephones, for instance); disclosure of confidential information to protect third parties, during legal proceedings, and pertaining to deceased clients; sexual relationships with former clients and clients' relatives or close acquaintances; physical contact with clients; sexual harassment; sexual relationships with colleagues; bartering for services; addressing colleagues' incompetence; retention of client records; billing for services; continuing education; labor–management disputes; misrepresentation of professional qualifications, credentials, and affiliations; protection of human subjects involved in social work research or evaluation; and social workers' involvement in social and political action.

C. Ethics Education and Training

Consistent with the dramatic growth of interest in professional ethics, more and more social work education programs are including ethics content in their curricula. Some social work education programs, although relatively few, offer discrete courses on professional ethics. More often, social work educators devote portions of existing courses to ethical issues. For example, courses on clinical social work skills may include a section on informed consent procedures, the handling of confidential information, and issues of professional paternalism. Social welfare policy courses may include a section on ethical issues involved in the welfare rights debate, and courses on social work administration may address issues related to allocating scarce resources, labor–management disputes, or whistle-blowing. Research and evaluation courses may include a section on ethical issues involved in protecting the rights of clients who participate in research and evaluation studies.

Ideally, all social workers would receive comprehensive and thorough education concerning professional ethics. In fact, in 1992 the Council on Social Work Education greatly strengthened its requirement that accredited social work education programs offer explicit instruction on social work values, ethical dilemmas, and ethical decision-making. Unfortunately, not all social work education programs include this content in their curricula comprehensively. Many efforts to educate social workers about ethics are nascent at best, reflecting the relatively recent introduction of this topic, at least in its current ambitious form, into social work education.

Along with such efforts to educate students in colleges and universities, a growing number of social service agencies are providing staff with systematic training on social work ethics. This often involves inviting outside experts to conduct "in-service" training programs for staff. Agency administrators have been motivated to sponsor this training in part because of their enhanced awareness of ethical issues faced by their employees and in part because of their wish to prevent ethical misconduct and lawsuits that could result from such misconduct.

In addition, professional social work conferences, both national and local, are offering more and more ethics-related sessions. Especially since the early 1980s, there has been a steady increase in conference presentations on topics such as ethical issues and dilemmas, ethical decision-making, ethics consultation, ethical misconduct, and social work codes of ethics.

D. Ethics Committees

Many human service agencies have established ethics committees to help staff and clients who encounter complex ethical issues. The concept of ethics committees emerged in 1976, when the New Jersey Supreme Court ruled that Karen Anne Quinlan's family and physicians should consult an ethics committee in deciding whether to remove her from life-support systems. The court based its ruling on an important article that appeared in the *Baylor Law Review* in 1975, in which a pediatrician encouraged the use of ethics committees when health care professionals face difficult ethical decisions. Since that time, most major hospitals and some social service agencies have developed ethics committees. Social workers are often members of these committees.

Ethics committees carry out one or more of several functions. Most ethics committees serve as a "sounding board" for agency staff, and possibly clients and their families, who want some assistance in thinking through how to handle an ethical dilemma. For example, in health care settings, physicians, nurses, social workers, or clergy may ask an ethics committee to review the facts in a case where family members and medical staff disagree about initiating an aggressive course of treatment to prolong the life of a severely disabled patient. Or, family members may ask for ethics committee advice about terminating life support for a dying relative to enable the donation of his organs to another patient. In these instances, ethics committees, often with the involvement of a social worker, offer advice and counsel, rather than a binding decision.

Ethics committees may be used similarly in other human service settings, such as family service agencies and community mental health centers. In these settings, staff may use an ethics committee, or some agency committee with a different name but similar functions, to think through situations such as whether confidential information shared by a client should be disclosed to protect a third party, or whether a vulnerable client should be permitted to have access to her case record.

In addition to contemporaneous case consultation, ethics committees may also convene staff to review cases retrospectively, following an incident that raised complex ethical issues. For example, an agency may have dealt with a case where staff had to make a quick decision, without being able to convene colleagues for extensive discussion, concerning disclosure of confidential information without a client's permission or commitment of a client to a psychiatric facility against the client's wishes. Given the ethical and policy issues raised by the case, an agency's ethics committee might bring staff together to conduct an "ethics autopsy" in an effort to extract lessons from the experience.

Ethics committees might also focus staff members' attention on cases prospectively. That is, ethics committees might present hypothetical case material to help staff think through how they would handle such circumstances should they arise. The case material may include complicated ethical issues recently encountered in similar agencies.

In addition to providing case consultation, ethics committees may also organize and sponsor staff training. In many social service settings, ethics committees identify topics and issues about which staff want or need education and offer training sessions or engage outside experts to provide the training. Thus, ethics committees in mental health settings or family service agencies might sponsor sessions on topics such as confidentiality, informed consent, conflicts of interest, boundary issues, and the termination of services.

Ethics committees in some agencies, especially health care settings, sponsor ethics grand rounds, modeled after traditional hospital grand rounds, where staff gather to learn and consult about a particular patient's case. Ethics grand rounds usually feature the presentation of a case that raises complicated ethical issues that may have educational value for staff. Discussion usually focuses on the relevant ethical issues, a critique of actions taken to address the issues, other courses of action that might have been pursued, and implications for future practice.

Finally, ethics committees are sometimes charged with reviewing current ethics-related agency policies, recommending changes, and identifying areas where new policies need to be developed. Typical policies reviewed or developed by ethics committees concern confidentiality, informed consent, conflicts of interest, sexual harassment, sexual contact with current or former clients, physical contact with clients, protection of clients involved in evaluation or research studies, and termination of services.

V. ETHICAL MISCONDUCT

One of the unfortunate realities of professional life is that some practitioners violate prevailing ethical standards and engage in ethical misconduct. All professions have members, usually a very small minority, who misbehave or are negligent, and social work is no exception.

Most of the problems in social work stem from boundary violations. These cases involve social workers who, for example, develop social, business, or sexual relationships with clients or clients' relatives or close acquaintances. Other forms of misconduct or negligence involve issues such as inappropriate handling of confidential information (for example, failure to protect third parties or to comply with mandatory reporting laws, disclosure of confidential information without clients' permission), improper use of intervention techniques (for example, use of an experimental counseling technique that harms clients, failure to disclose risks associated with certain interventions, counseling clients outside of a social worker's area of expertise), defamation of clients' character (libel or slander), improper supervision of clients or staff, and fraud and deception (for example, submitting falsified or inflated bills for services rendered).

Social workers who engage in misconduct or are negligent may be sanctioned or disciplined in several different ways. First, disgruntled clients and concerned colleagues may file ethics complaints against social workers with professional associations to which social workers belong or with bodies responsible for licensing social workers. These organizations appoint committees to review such allegations, conduct hearings, and, when justified, impose sanctions against social workers found in violation of ethical standards. Standards contained in codes of ethics are often used as the basis for adjudication. Sanctions may include letters of reprimand or censure; requiring that a social worker obtain continuing education, consultation, or supervision; suspension of a license or professional membership; expulsion from a professional association; or revocation of a license.

Second, individuals who believe that they have been harmed by social workers' misconduct or negligence may file a lawsuit in court. Such lawsuits usually allege that one or more individuals have suffered injuries because of a social worker's negligence or failure to adhere to the profession's standards. For example, a disgruntled client may file a lawsuit alleging that she suffered emotional distress, lost wages, and the expense of psychiatric bills following her sexual involvement with a clinical social worker. Or, a client who claims that he was fired from his job because of a social worker's inappropriate release of information to his employer about the client's alcohol problem may file a lawsuit alleging breach of privacy. Most of these lawsuits are settled out of court, although some go to trial in civil court. Damages may be awarded to plaintiffs to compensate them for the injuries they have suffered (compensatory damages) or, occasionally, to punish the social worker

if there is evidence of reckless, wanton, or willful misconduct (punitive or exemplary damages).

Finally, in relatively rare instances social workers who engage in ethical misconduct will face criminal charges. Examples include social workers who are indicted for submitting falsified documents to a government agency or having sexual contact with clients who are minors.

VI. CONCLUSIONS

Social work, like all contemporary professions, has gained an increasingly mature grasp of ethical issues facing its practitioners. The profession has moved from its early preoccupation with clients' morality to its current concern with ethical dilemmas, ethical decision-making, and ethical misconduct. Social workers' appreciation of ethical dilemmas encountered in practice—especially related to the delivery of services to individuals, families, and small groups; agency administration, community organizing, and social policy; and relationships among colleagues—has deepened in recent years. The profession's literature now contains many discussions of ethical issues, social work education programs are more apt to include ethics-related content in their curricula, conference presentations and agency training on the subject are increasing, and agencies are making increased use of ethics committees and consultation.

In spite of these efforts, a relatively small number of social workers engage in ethical misconduct. Ethics complaints and lawsuits filed against social workers have increased in recent years, reflecting either an increase in ethical misconduct, a greater willingness or determination on the part of victims and concerned parties to confront social workers, or both. Fortunately, the profession has stepped up its efforts to educate both students and practitioners about forms of ethical misconduct and ways to prevent it.

In the future social workers will need to strengthen their efforts to address ethical issues. Both social work education programs and social service agencies need to intensify their educational and training offerings and provide them in a more systematic and comprehensive fashion. Social work administrators must be more assertive about identifying ethical issues in their agencies and appointing committees or task forces to address them. Social workers need to pay particular attention to the problem of practitioner impairment and they need to promote constructive strategies for addressing this problem.

Finally, social workers must recognize that the future is likely to produce ethical issues that today's practitioners can scarcely imagine. A significant number of the ethical issues that concern modern-day social workers (for example, the confidentiality of information transmitted by computers or cellular telephones, or the rights of people who are infected with the AIDS virus) would have been unimaginable to those social work pioneers who practiced in the early 20th century. Social workers should be both humbled by their inability to forecast the ethical issues that the future holds in store and vigilant in their efforts to identify and address these issues once they inevitably emerge.

Also See the Following Articles

CONFIDENTIALITY, GENERAL ISSUES OF • DISTRIBUTIVE JUSTICE, THEORIES OF • PROFESSIONAL ETHICS • SOCIAL ETHICS, OVERVIEW • WHISTLE-BLOWING

Bibliography

Levy, C. S. (1976). *Social work ethics*. New York: Human Sciences Press.

Loewenberg, F., and Dolgoff, R. (1992). *Ethical decisions for social work practice* (4th ed.). Itasca, IL: F. E. Peacock.

McDermott, F. E. (Ed.). (1975). *Self-determination in social work*. London: Routledge and Kegan Paul.

Pumphrey, M. W. (1959). *The teaching of values and ethics in social work*. New York: Council on Social Work Education.

Reamer, F. G. (1992). *Ethical dilemmas in social service* (2nd ed.). New York: Columbia University Press.

Reamer, F. G. (1994). *Social work malpractice and liability*. New York: Columbia University Press.

Reamer, F. G. (1995). *Social work values and ethics*. New York: Columbia University Press.

Reamer, F. G. and Abramson, M. (1982). *The teaching of social work ethics*. Hastings-on-Hudson, NY: The Hastings Center.

Reid, P. N. and Popple, P. R. (Eds.). (1992). *The moral purposes of social work*. Chicago: Nelson-Hall.

Rhodes, M. L. (1986). *Ethical dilemmas in social work practice*. London: Routledge and Kegan Paul.

SOCIALLY RESPONSIBLE INVESTMENT

Christopher J. Cowton
University of Huddersfield

I. Approaches to SRI
II. Implementation of SRI
III. The Ethics of SRI
IV. The Costs of SRI
V. Conclusions

GLOSSARY

green Eco-sensitive or environmentally friendly.
investment universe Set of available investment opportunities, especially stocks.
portfolio Set of investments held.
screen(ing) Process of evaluating possible investments against criteria.

SOCIALLY RESPONSIBLE INVESTMENT (SRI) can be taken to refer to a set of approaches which include social or ethical goals or constraints as well as more conventional financial criteria in decisions over whether to acquire, hold, or dispose of a particular investment. What helps to bind these various approaches together is their contrast with what might be termed *mainstream* investment, which focuses solely upon financial risk and return.

In SRI it is the nature of the source, and not just the size, of the financial return from an investment that is of concern. SRI can be carried out either by individual

"social investors"—personal or corporate (e.g., pension funds, religious organizations, universities)—or by professional fund managers acting on their behalf, perhaps via a suitably designed investment vehicle. Such vehicles are available in a number of countries, including the USA and United Kingdom, and have helped considerably to extend the practice of SRI and to make it more visible.

While the term *socially responsible investment* is well established, the following similar or related terms are also encountered, the first three being particularly common:

- Ethical
- Social
- Green
- Alternative
- Divergent (probably not complimentary)
- Targeted
- Creative
- Development
- Strategic

To some extent the use of different terms appears to be a matter of taste. For example, some people object to the use of the word "ethical" because it seems to imply that other, mainstream approaches to investment are "unethical"—but some would take that view, in any case. Such people often prefer the terms "social" or "socially responsible" investment, but fail to recognize that, following their own line of reasoning, such usage might imply that mainstream investing is "antisocial" or "irresponsible," which is not necessarily any less offensive to its practitioners than "unethical." Others appear to prefer *socially responsible* to *ethical* because they are uncomfortable about identifying the grounds for ethics or think that *ethical* carries religious or moralizing overtones. However, while different terms may be used to describe similar practices, there are a number of different approaches that can be taken.

I. APPROACHES TO SRI

A. Forms of Investment

Mainstream investment can take a variety of forms—stocks, bonds, property, bank deposits, equity investments in nontraded companies, etc. While some of these forms of investment will be regarded as inappropriate by some social investors (e.g., to a Muslim, a bank account offering a fixed rate of interest), in principle it should be possible to approach many of them, perhaps through suitable modifications, in such a way that they can become a valid element of a program of SRI. There will also be some forms of investment which, while not inconceivable for a mainstream investor, would be expected to be particularly attractive to many social investors. Co-operative ventures might be one example. And there are a number of initiatives that involve limiting expected financial return in order to achieve certain social aims. Social investors might, for example, lend money to a social bank or buy shares in certain organizations engaged in "fair trade" with the Third World. These are sometimes known as "alternative" investments, and some of them have a long tradition. However, the focus here will be upon stock-market-based equity investment, not least because of the economic importance of the entities concerned and the heightened significance being accorded to stock markets in economies around the world. Much of the discussion will be with the USA and United Kingdom in mind, because it is in those two countries that stock-market-based SRI is most firmly established, but it should be noted that it is beginning to take root in a number of other parts of the world too.

B. Avoidance Strategies

Perhaps the most common or basic approach to SRI involves the rejection of companies with characteristics regarded in a negative light. Such an approach might be termed an *avoidance* strategy. The negative character-istics can relate to the kinds of products or services that a firm provides, the way it conducts its business, or the location of its activities.

Under an avoidance strategy, "negative screening" is applied when stocks are being considered for purchase or when an existing portfolio is first being checked against ethical criteria, but subsequent regular monitoring also needs to be undertaken in order to check that the companies which have been invested in have not changed—through altered practices, development of their activities, or acquisition of another business—in such a way that they come to contravene the criteria. An avoidance strategy represents an attempt to cleanse an investment portfolio of companies with undesirable features.

There would appear to be two main types of possible error, analogous with the risks involved in statistical hypothesis testing, when carrying out an avoidance strategy. In a Type 1 error, a company is rejected on ethical grounds when it was really acceptable according to the investor's criteria. A Type 2 error occurs when a company is included in a portfolio when it should have been excluded. Such errors have different consequences. If a Type 1 error is discovered and the wasted investment opportunity concerned is known to have been financially attractive, some regret might be engendered. If the decision to exclude was accompanied by a critical statement to the company or some other party, embarrassment or worse might also be entailed. A Type 2 error means that the desired investment policy has not been properly carried out and thus the aims of the investor undermined, which can be particularly problematic where the investment portfolio is being managed by one party on behalf of another. In order to control the risk of potentially embarrassing error, some investors check their judgments with the companies concerned.

Perhaps Type 2 errors are inevitable though. Owing to the interconnectedness of the corporate sector, it has been questioned whether purity is a feasible goal. Investors who embark on this route have been described as "hopelessly naive," involving themselves in an endless series of illusions and arbitrary decisions. For such investors, it might be better not to invest at all, for it is virtually impossible to guarantee that the return they receive is "clean" money. In any case, a very long list of exclusions might leave a very restricted investment universe from which to select.

However, in practice many SRI policies do not use absolute standards, but instead employ more relaxed thresholds of acceptability or subjective cutoffs. This would appear to make an avoidance strategy more feasible, although there still exists the possibility of error in the composition of the investment portfolio. But whatever the practicalities of using thresholds, they do pose a problem in principle, or, to transpose an old saying, they may work in practice, but do they work in theory? The justification of arbitrary cutoff points rather than the imposition of an absolute embargo is a problem, because the use of thresholds explicitly condones the presence of certain avowedly undesirable attributes in the investment portfolio. Nevertheless, the use of thresholds is common among social investors and might be easier to justify where the investment policy involves an appreciation of corporations' virtues as well as their vices; which brings us to the notion of a supportive strategy.

C. Supportive Strategies

A bias toward the selection of shares of companies deemed to possess some approved and valued nonfinancial attribute or attributes may be described as a *supportive* strategy. Again, such positive features might relate to the kinds of products or services that a firm provides, the way it conducts its business, or the location of its activities.

Even if an explicit avoidance strategy is not in place, it is possible for one to be pursued by default when conducting a supportive strategy—if corporations that possess good attributes also tend not to have negative ones. Very often, though, a supportive strategy will be operated deliberately in tandem with an avoidance strategy.

D. Mixed Strategies

1. Two-Stage Approach

One way of explicitly combining avoidance and supportive approaches is to divide the selection process into two stages, beginning with the negative screening. The avoidance criteria can be viewed as constraints which determine the set of feasible or ethically acceptable investments. Positive criteria can then, if desired, be used in addition to financial criteria in the process of selecting the particular stocks to hold. In such a scenario, while the attempt to optimize the positive features of the portfolio (bearing in mind financial goals too) might seem to accord them considerable importance, it is in fact the negative criteria which are dominant, for the presence of some negative quality is deemed to outweigh any amount of positive features possessed by a particular company. Constraints are, in

effect, overriding goals. Such an approach, like a pure avoidance strategy, has the effect of imposing a blanket indictment on certain companies, even though their performance in some respects might be considered exemplary. This is the approach that tends to be favored by the social investment vehicles offered in the United Kingdom, many of which began life pursuing pure avoidance strategies.

2. Trade-Off Approach

An alternative to the two-stage assessment of the positive and negative features of corporations is to permit a trade-off between the two, perhaps calculating an overall score or rating for a company. Under this approach a portfolio might be considered "good" but not "clean," since investment in corporations with negative attributes is permitted if they exhibit sufficient positive features. Scoring is perhaps rather more common in the USA than in the United Kingdom.

E. Activism

An approach based on trade-offs does not imply that investors need passively accept the presence of negative attributes. Instead, while holding the share of a company that has some valued characteristics, they might engage in shareholder activism in an attempt to bring about change. In this they may find themselves allied with others who have become holders of stock precisely because of, not in spite of, its features deemed to be unacceptable. These lobbyists, who might own only a token shareholding, attempt to change corporate policy by actions such as asking questions at company meetings and formally proposing changes in corporate policy. It is in the USA that this practice has been most widespread, with high-profile examples such as Campaign GM, but there have also been notable cases elsewhere, such as the movement in the United Kingdom against bank loans to South Africa.

Admitting the possibility of engaging in at least some activism can place the constitution of a portfolio in a more ambiguous relation to an investor's ethics than a purely passive approach. Under a passive approach it can be assumed, barring errors, that none of the companies represented in the investment portfolio are subject to the investor's disapproval, whereas this cannot be assumed if the investor is also holding stock with a view to engaging in campaigning activities. However, it is likely that a serious investor will have to settle for at least a degree of passivity, since only a small proportion of a portfolio of companies can be lobbied effectively, given the time and other resources involved.

II. IMPLEMENTATION OF SRI

A. Issues

Having outlined the major varieties of SRI it is appropriate to examine the issues that have tended to concern its practitioners. Owing to the relatively small amount of empirical research that has been carried out, the varied ways in which it has been conducted, the different countries in which it has been done—chiefly the USA and United Kingdom—and the different dates at which it has taken place, it is impossible to state categorically what is of concern to a "typical" social investor. Moreover, the notion of a typical social investor may be misplaced, for we know enough from the research that has been carried out to date to realize that different social investors are concerned about different issues. However, there are a number of strong themes or strands in SRI. First, there is widespread avoidance, particularly on the part of church organziations, where many of the origins of SRI may be found, of the so-called "sin stocks" of alcohol, gambling, and tobacco. Second, corporate involvement in South Africa during the apartheid era was a major issue. Indeed, it would be fair to say that concern over South Africa was a massive stimulus to the development of the SRI movement in the United Kingdom. Third, the rise in environmentalism has been reflected in an increasingly sophisticated attempt to incorporate eco-relevant or "green" criteria into investment decision making. While this has been important in both the United Kingdom and the USA, where SRI is relatively well developed, it has been a particular feature of the recent emergence of SRI in continental European countries such as Germany. The decline in importance of involvement in South Africa as an investment issue following the changes there and the growth in concern for the environment serve to demonstrate that SRI is an evolving and dynamic field, reflecting trends in the wider social and political context.

Some writers attempt to distinguish green or environmental investment from other forms of SRI. If the investment strategy is concerned solely with making money out of the increase in environmental concern and regulation, it is sensible not to term it "ethical," not least because some of the companies that will be chosen will be far from green themselves, e.g., some waste management companies. But if the intention is to invest in a way that endorses, and does not merely exploit, the rise in environmentalism, then it seems sensible to view green investment as part of SRI. Environmental issues are, after all, important to many social investors, even if they are not the only concern for many.

A concern for the environment can be reflected in both avoidance and supportive strategies, since it can encompass a wide range of individual issues or elements. Other concerns tend to fall more naturally into one or the other. Thus, for example, a social investor is likely to be negative or neutral regarding tobacco, but it is unlikely in practice to feature in a supportive strategy. However, there are a few issues on which, rightly or wrongly, opinion can divide more sharply; trade with Israel is one such example.

Table I lists a number of issues that might be of concern to a social investor, and indicates whether they tend to feature positively in supportive strategies or negatively in avoidance strategies. This allocation is intended only as a judgment on the usual treatment of certain issues within SRI in practice, not on the rights and wrongs of particular questions. A few issues extend across both columns, as already explained. The issues are grouped according to whether they relate to the type of business the firm is in, the particular way in which it conducts that business, or the locations involved. The table is not intended to be definitive; different issues could have been cited, the ones included expressed or grouped in different ways, and there are overlaps between issues. Instead, the table is meant to be illustrative of the wide variety of concerns, both positive and negative, that have been featured in SRI policies.

Although Table I gives a flavor of what SRI is about, it does not indicate how it works in practice, for the raising of an issue in relation to investment does not usually, of itself, provide clear implications for the management of a portfolio. For ethical concerns to have an impact on investment portfolios necessitates the development of more specific criteria to guide decision making.

B. Criteria

A concern about a particular issue can generate a wide variety of possible criteria. For example, although there was a considerable degree of consensus among social investors that some form of avoidance was appropriate while apartheid was official policy in the Republic of South Africa, there were many different criteria in operation, some of them complementary and others mutu-

TABLE I

Examples of SRI Issues

Positive	Negative
Type of business	
Education	Alcoholic beverages
Housing	Gambling
Care for the elderly	Tobacco
Health care	Pornography
Healthy eating	Military contractor
Socially beneficial products	Hazardous products
Waste management	Mining and quarrying
Pollution control	Plantations
Safety and security	Animal-based products, e.g., fur
	Pesticides
	Military contracting
	Nuclear power
	Banking and finance
Conduct of business	
Charitable donations	Health and safety record
Good community relations	Polluter
Customer care	Multinational
Product quality	Company size
Recycling program	Animal testing
Product innovation and development	Improper or illegal business or political practices
	Advertising
	Treatment of employees
	Equal opportunities
	Labor relations
Location	
	Southern Africa
	Chile
	Repressive regimes
	Israel

ally exclusive. For example, did South Africa include Namibia? Should all operations and links be condemned, or only those in particular sectors? Or should the emphasis be not upon *that* a firm operated in South Africa, but *how* it did so; as indicated by its pay and promotion policies for nonwhites, for instance?

Perhaps the type of business that a firm is in appears, at first sight, to entail few judgments, although a choice between absolute avoidance and tolerance of some activity needs to be made, as indicated earlier. However, social investors can differ on the issue of which parts of the supply chain matter. A brewery clearly falls squarely into a category concerned with alcoholic beverages, but what about a grocery retailer for whom beer is but one product line? Some investors would choose to avoid the retailer while others would not. And what about a supplier of multipurpose raw materials or equipment to breweries?

Some differences of approach are evident in the published statements of SRI vehicles, even though they might not explicitly state any detailed criteria. Table II presents the statements made by a number of UK funds regarding defense or military contracting, which is an isssue of concern to many social investors.

From Table II it is apparent that some funds employ—or commit to—more stringent criteria than others. For example, two exclude only "substantial" or "significant" interests, which is not unusual. Many funds are imprecise about their thresholds, but at least

TABLE II

Examples of Avoidance of Military Contractors

Financial product	Stated armaments criterion
Abbey Life Ethical Trust	Armaments
Acorn Ethical Unit Trust	Manufacturing or distributing arms or armaments
Amity Fund	Manufacturing armaments
CIS Environ	Significant turnover in armament manufacture
Clerical Medical Evergreen Trust	The manufacture or provision of armaments
Ethical Investment Fund	Manufactures armaments of any description
Fellowship Trust	Known to be involved in the arms trade
Friends Provident Stewardship Trust	Involved in the arms trade
Medical Investments Health Fund	Manufacture, distribution, or sale of weapons
Merlin Jupiter Ecology Fund	Directly involved with armaments
NM Conscience Fund	The production and sale of armaments
Scottish Equitable Ethical Unit Trust	Manufactures armaments or nuclear weapons
Sovereign Ethical Fund	Manufactures or supplies armaments
Target Life Global Opportunities	Known to have substantial interests in the armaments industry

Source: Cowton, C. J. (1993). Peace dividends: The exclusion of military contractors from investment portfolios, J. Peace Res. **30**, 21–28.

prospective investors are put on notice that elements of the portfolio might have characteristics, in some degree, which they might prefer to avoid altogether. While the terms used lack precision, it is generally the case that there is more clarity regarding what funds avoid than what they support because avoidance is more easily described and monitored.

Funds also differ in the proportion of the supply chain considered. Some funds restrict their definition to the manufacture of armaments, while a number of others also refer to distribution, sales, or the arms trade. There are also differences in the range of products covered. Thus the use of words such as "arms," "armaments," or "weapons" might represent more than just choice of terminology, though they are clearly closely related terms. Some social investors might wish to go further and avoid companies which supply other goods and services to the military—for example, clothing, food, electronics, transportation equipment, or the construction of military installations.

It is also notable that some are careful to say that they *seek* to carry out their stated policies, or words to that effect, presumably in case they make a mistake. There is thus an indication of intention but no guarantee that a particular aspect of policy will be carried out. This should prevent intervention by the regulatory authorities, but might be considered unsatisfactory by investors who wish to rely upon the fund having certain ethical characteristics. However, this kind of qualification is less common with respect to military contracting than some other areas, which might suggest that fund managers are reasonably confident about their information sources.

C. Information

Whatever the criteria adopted in the pursuit of SRI goals, information is needed in order to establish how corporations measure up to them. Indeed, the availability of information is likely to influence the precise development of the criteria; it is no use setting a criterion which cannot be implemented. Since information is costly to obtain and process, a social investor will have to make decisions, not only about the investments to be held, but also about how to manage the information on which those investment decisions are to be based.

1. Do-It-Yourself

One possible information strategy for social investors is to gather it for themselves. The potential sources of data are many and varied. They are not restricted to financial statements or even corporate annual reports, but include press releases, newspaper articles, government statistics and regulatory reports, and material produced by lobby groups. Corporate annual reports are a useful starting point, but generally they contain only limited information on many matters that are likely to be of concern to social investors. They might be useful in framing questions, but they will tend to provide relatively few concrete answers. Referring back to the categories of issues used in Table I, annual reports are likely to be of more help in determining the business of a corporation than in judging how it conducts that business.

2. Information Services

The total informational needs of social investors are greater than those of mainstream investors, for information relevant to the SRI criteria is needed in addition to the normal financial information. Much of the information desired exclusively for the conduct of SRI is, depending on the concerns of the investor, likely to be hard to obtain, incomplete, difficult to interpret, or unreliable. Monitoring full compliance of all stocks held against all criteria might be particularly difficult during a period of merger and acquisition activity, and overseas companies tend to cause problems for many investors. Such informational difficulties add to the likelihood of errors in managing a portfolio. There might therefore be incentives, in terms of both cost and effectiveness of information use, to take advantage of another party's economies of scale and expertise in collecting and processing data. One possible avenue is to make use of the services of a specialist information intermediary. A number of such services have been established in the USA and United Kingdom. They may be able to provide information on individual companies, supply a report on an existing portfolio, or screen the market for stocks that meet certain criteria in order to generate a suitable investment universe.

3. Financial Products

The use of an information intermediary might still involve an investor in considerable effort, though, including on the financial side, which is why many mainstream investors prefer to invest in vehicles such as mutual funds or unit trusts. Investment vehicles oriented to the needs of social investors have existed in the USA for some time—Calvert Social Investment, Dreyfus Third Century, Pax World, New Alternatives, Parnassus, etc. The first British SRI unit trust—Friends Provident's Stewardship Trust—was not launched until 1984. It is still by far the market leader but it now has several competitors. It is the appearance of such funds which has presumably extended the practice of ethical investment beyond what it would otherwise have been. It has certainly made it more visible. While there are some commonalities, SRI vehicles do differ in the social investment criteria that they use, as Table II illustrates. They also offer different financial features.

From the point of view of the social investor, an SRI vehicle which follows certain social criteria in a sense has information "built in." The managers of investment funds can, like information intermediaries, be more expert and efficient than many individual social investors in the acquisition and use of information. Some of the sources of data, however, might lie beyond a fund manager's established expertise. Partly for reasons of acquiring extra expertise, some funds use a committee of reference to advise on ethical and social aspects of investment. And a fund manager might also elect to use a specialist information intermediary. Although professional fund managers might be charged more for the service than an individual would, from the individual investor's point of view this is likely to be a highly cost-effective way of tapping into the information intermediary's expertise because the fee is spread among a large number of people. However, the investor is also having to pay for fund management services that she might not require.

Another drawback is that, since the investment vehicle is a packaged product, it is unlikely to match precisely the criteria that the social investor would choose. Some compromise is almost certainly going to be necessary. However, to the extent that avoidance is desired, this is probably not as much of a problem as might appear to be the case. Suppose investor A wishes to avoid alcohol and tobacco, while investor B wishes to avoid tobacco and gambling. An investment vehicle which excludes alcohol, gambling, and tobacco stocks will satisfy their individual requirements—as long as neither is positively interested in investing in the "extra" dimension. Similarly, it is possible that a social investor would be satisfied with criteria tighter than she would independently have chosen.

III. THE ETHICS OF SRI

Having explained how it can be carried out—the approaches, issues, criteria, and information sources—attention will now be turned to the ethics of SRI.

A. Investor Integrity

The *prima facie* case for ethical considerations in investment decisions is that as an area of human activity it should not be immune from ethical considerations. There is, it is suggested, nothing special about investment in general that warrants its exclusion from the ethical considerations that are brought to bear on other areas of life.

From this perspective then, there is a sense in which mainstream investing with its exclusive concern with risk and return is, without some further qualification, unethical, notwithstanding the offended reaction of its practitioners to such an implication. At its most extreme would be those who, viewing the whole capitalist system as irredeemably tainted, refuse to invest consciously any money in the stock market. The middle ground, of participating but with explicit regard to the ethical dimensions of such action, is, as is so often the case, a rather more complex question.

What, then, is the ethical basis for SRI as described earlier? Two strands, woven together in some discussions of the ethics of investment, are discernible. The first, which follows naturally from the *prima facie* case already stated, seeks to ensure that consistent standards of behavior are applied in all areas of life. Thus, at a very basic level, it might be considered inappropriate for someone who practices and advocates teetotalism to hold shares in a distillery. Similarly, the British Medical Association was subject to criticism a number of years ago because, while it had an antismoking policy, it held shares in companies which had substantial tobacco interests. To many observers, passively holding a stock and making a return from it indicates some support for a particular activity. This is emphasized by some investment vehicles. "Invest for success with a clear conscience" and "Investing with an easy mind" are just two slogans that have been used by British unit trusts.

In this strand of argument, the integrity of the investor—or even "moral purity"—is the priority. An attempt is made to avoid the type of inconsistency which represents one of the central types of hypocrisy. A pure avoidance strategy might be the outcome of such a perspective. However, some commentators, preferring moral effectiveness to moral purity, are concerned more about the consequences of actions than about their conformance to principle.

B. Responsibility Toward Others

The second discernible perspective, which can complement the first, tends to emphasize the consequences of corporate actions upon others, perhaps conceived of as different groups of stakeholders such as employees, consumers, or local communities. This view is often reinforced by regarding stockholders not as speculators or even investors, but as owners who not only possess rights and privileges but also have responsibilities which entail a degree of involvement. If a duty not to impose damage or harm on other people is regarded as a minimum responsibility which runs through all morality, then it might be concluded that the avoidance of certain investments is appropriate, as under an "integrity" approach. However, a wider view of responsibilities is often taken which tends to justify supportive criteria or engagement in stockholder activism.

C. Points of Tension and Criticism

Proponents of the "investor responsibility" perspective are often critical of avoidance, pure and simple, as a strategy for the conduct of SRI. They suggest that, on its own, it entails two particular problems. First, it fails to identify positive areas which should be supported by investment; the "bad" has been isolated, but there is no further attempt to separate the "good" from the "indifferent" or neutral. Second, investors might feel that they have fulfilled their moral responsibility for the use of their capital, as suggested by some of the "clear conscience" slogans quoted earlier. This, it is contended, is particularly dubious in the case of investors who elect to dispose of shares they hold in ethically problematic companies. They are succeeding only in turning their backs on problems and controversy in pursuit of a clear conscience. This is not to say that divestment is never justified. In the case of a philanthropic organization, for example, divestment would be acceptable if not to do so would defeat the socially important purposes for which it was founded. But in many cases, particularly those concerned with how business is conducted, "quiet departure" is thought to be inappropriate as a first step because it has little or no impact on the corporation concerned. Investors who have already invested in a stock should do more.

It has to be admitted that attempts by small shareholders to influence corporate behavior would appear to offer little hope of success, and that the contribution of an individual small shareholder is negligible. Nevertheless, some would argue that they should still protest. Criticisms should be made explicit to the company, and shareholders are in a better position to do so than ordinary citizens, since they can gain information and can communicate by sponsoring and voting on resolutions. The prospect of immediate success might appear remote, but there might be some limited influence if enough small investors band together, use the media, or align themselves with consumer or community groups where possible.

Furthermore, it should not be forgotten that substantial shareholdings are held by some individuals, mutual funds (and the like), and institutions, whose opinions are likely to be listened to very carefully by corporate management, perhaps as part of a process of constructive dialogue during which both parties may learn from one another. However, it is very difficult to assess the effectiveness of such engagement. Even when something happens it is difficult to measure the impact of shareholder activism because both sides like to claim credit for any change that takes place. Certainly corporations tend to be reluctant to admit that they have bowed to external pressure. But the difficulty of claiming credit where it might be due is unlikely to deter social investors from pursuing their concerns.

However, notwithstanding the difficulty of establishing what effect shareholder activism is having, it can become clear when it is having *no* effect. If diligent efforts fail and appear doomed to failure in the future, even those whose views render them unsympathetic to divestment are likely to concede its appropriateness. It may not be very effective, but when coupled with suitable publicity it might achieve something, such as increasing public concern and helping to fuel a political climate which might affect lawmakers.

It is striking that in the literature on the ethics of SRI, writers have tended to concentrate on negative rather than positive approaches. Very little discussion of supportive strategies is evident. Moreover, the dominant question has been what to do when an existing shareholding arouses concern. In many cases, this reflects the question with which the writers were wrestling; namely, how to treat an existing portfolio if negative ethical criteria were introduced. But this does beg the question of the responsibility of nonowners. In other words, what is the responsibility, if any, to acquire a signficant (rather than token) stake and then lobby?

Of course, the discussion of the ethics of SRI tends to involve writers who are broadly sympathetic to it in one form of another. Others, however, take a somewhat more radical view. For some, any investment in a stock market is going to be unsuitable; they might prefer to focus on alternative investments, or might even prefer not to accumulate funds beyond what is needed for consumption purposes. On the other hand, many others view mainstream investment as essentially ethically unproblematic. However, while they might be unconvinced by any of the ethical arguments for SRI, being generally unsympathetic to corporate social responsibility too, they are likely to accept that investors at least have a general right to pursue SRI, holding or not holding stock as they wish, and participating in corporate affairs as active stockholders.

However, it has been questioned whether all investors do indeed have such a right. In particular, without explicit, legitimate authority, it is not clear that SRI is generally legal for pension funds or in other situations where there is a trust obligation involved. While it is difficult to come to firm conclusions for different jurisdictions in a general article of this length, discussions of the law in the USA and United Kingdom suggest that the possibility of sacrificing some financial performance would be a major impediment to SRI, running up against the "prudent man" rule. So, do social investors lose out?

IV. THE COSTS OF SRI

A. Financial Performance

Whether SRI does harm investment performance has been the subject of some discussion and investigation. For many "alternative" investments, the answer is straightforward, since the investor often accepts as a matter of policy the prospect of a lower financial return than would normally be the case for a project of similar financial risk. But whether SRI in the form of portfolios of stocks traded on developed stock exchanges involves significant sacrifice of financial performance is a moot point. In the slogans used to promote them, some of the SRI funds suggest the absence of conflict between financial and ethical concerns, for example,

- Profit doesn't have to be a dirty word
- Protecting your future and your ideals
- Profits with principles
- How to make money without selling your principles

Some commentators believe that SRI does not result in a financial sacrifice, and some go so far as to claim that it actually performs better than mainstream investment. However, the basis for such expressions of opinion is often suspect, being based on anecdotal or very limited evidence. It is certainly possible that a *particular* SRI policy over a *particular* period of time will outperform the market or some other relevant benchmark, but if there is a systematic positive effect, it requires some explanation. Suggestions include the possibility that social investors understand more about corporations because they have to research them in greater depth, or that they respond more quickly than mainstream

investors to emerging social trends that eventually become reflected in stock prices.

However, there are good reasons for questioning whether social investors are able to obtain as great a return as mainstream investors. As a general rule, it is more difficult to achieve a particular goal when other goals—whether in the form of actual goals or constraints—enter the equation. An SRI avoidance strategy, for example, excludes the possibility of investing in certain companies which might have been chosen on financial grounds, thus restricting the extent to which a portfolio can be managed to financial advantage. Put simply, social investors cannot do all that mainstream investors can do, but a mainstream investor can always construct the same portfolio as a social investor if it appears financially rewarding to do so. Thus some form of financial sacrifice as a result of SRI seems likely.

A more detailed assessment of the precise impact of constraints upon financial performance requires assumptions about the nature of stock markets. Based upon modern theories of portfolio management, a number of analyses have shown that the addition of avoidance criteria would be expected to leave a stock portfolio with higher risk and/or lower expected return than would otherwise have been the case. In fact, that is a foregone conclusion, given the nature of the models used. However, what is interesting is the suggestion that the impact is likely to be quite small. Unless the avoidance criteria are both wide-ranging in their scope and tight in their application, it seems that the remaining investment universe is still likely to be sufficient to permit the construction of a reasonably well diversified portfolio.

This conclusion based on abstract reasoning is mirrored in the results of empirical investigations of the performance of SRI portfolios, although the area is fraught with methodological challenges, including the choice of an appropriate benchmark portfolio against which to judge performance.

Thus it seems likely that there is some financial sacrifice involved with SRI, but even those who are most confident of this conclusion tend to indicate that it is not likely to be great. Most social investors are likely to suffer relatively little in terms of financial performance. However, account might also need to be taken of other costs associated with SRI, some of which are potentially important.

B. Portfolio Management Expenses

The other costs incurred in SRI derive from the demands that it places upon portfolio management. Reference has already been made to the extra information costs involved, whether related to the investor's research or fees paid to an information intermediary. Any significant lobbying activity will also incur costs. Both of these are continuing costs, but one category of costs is likely to prove particularly significant when an avoidance strategy is being imposed on an existing portfolio.

When an established portfolio is being purged of unwanted stocks, the trading activity is likely to lead to high transactions costs. The transactions cost penalty results not only from the process of divestment itself but also from any restructuring required to rebalance the portfolio to achieve the desired financial risk profile. Even after the portfolio has been ethically "corrected," the level of transactions may tend to be higher than that for a "normal" portfolio, *ceteris paribus*, as changes in firms' activities over time (e.g., from merger or acquisition) affect their standing against the SRI criteria. Thus in addition to activity resulting from the financial strategy of the investor, there will be a level of trading attributable solely to the presence of ethical criteria. This does not necessarily mean, though, that social investors will actually be relatively heavy traders, for there have been suggestions that they are, as a class, more inclined to be long-term holders of stocks, displaying greater loyalty than many.

These, and other costs, need not prevent SRI, but they should be borne in mind by an investor contemplating the introduction of ethical criteria, particularly as the precise criteria—their range and strictness—make a difference to the costs of running an investment portfolio and, possibly, its performance.

V. CONCLUSIONS

It is difficult, partly for definitional reasons, to estimate the extent of SRI, and hence figures which are published in the press from time to time should be treated with some caution. However, aided by financial products and information services which make its implementation increasingly feasible, it has clearly taken root in the USA and United Kingdom and is growing in a number of other countries too. It may not account for a major proportion of total stock market investment, but it is one way in which individuals can express their ethical values and a method whereby corporate investors, such as foundations, can seek to align their investment activities with their overall mission. While the precise way in which concerns enter into investment decision making can vary, this article has sought to delineate the major features of SRI and to cast light on the ethical and practical issues relating to its pursuit.

Bibliography

Anand, P., and Cowton, C. J. (1993). The ethical investor: Exploring dimensions of investment behaviour. *J. Econ. Psychol.* 14, 377–385.

Miller, A. J. (1991). "Socially Responsible Investing: How to Invest with Your Conscience." New York Institute of Finance, New York.

Sparkes, R. (1995). "The Ethical Investor." Harper Collins, London.

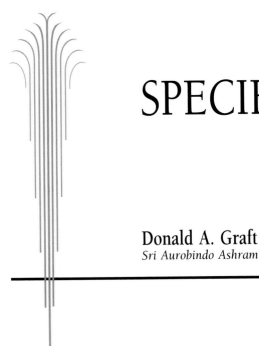

SPECIESISM

Donald A. Graft
Sri Aurobindo Ashram

GLOSSARY

argument from marginal cases A rejoinder to the argument that moral status derives from the possession of a given quality or capacity, for example, rationality. The argument asserts that because moral status is in practice accorded to individuals lacking the quality, the sole determinant of moral status cannot, in fact, be simply possession of that quality. For example, mentally retarded persons are granted full moral status despite being deficient in rationality.

biological species concept A doctrine that asserts that a "species" is a real entity in nature defined by reproductive isolation. For example, humans and rats are considered to be different species because they cannot interbreed.

moral individualism The doctrine that the moral status of an individual derives only from qualities and capacities of the individual, and not from considerations of the group memberships (e.g., sex, race, species, etc.) of that individual.

racism Discrimination based on consideration of race membership.

rationalism The doctrine that moral status derives from consideration of the extent of rationality exhibited by an individual or group.

sentience The capacity to experience sense perceptions, pleasure, and pain.

sentientism The doctrine that moral status derives from consideration of the sentience of an individual or group.

species A group of beings sharing essential common features and/or reproductively isolated from other groups of beings. Alternatively, a smudge in the space-time continuum of organisms, fuzzily delimited by an eclectic range of heuristic criteria.

speciesism The doctrine that moral status derives from consideration of species membership.

typism The doctrine that species can be adequately delimited through consideration of essential traits of individual beings.

utilitarianism The doctrine that the moral correctness of an act can be determined by considering the balance of good and bad that results from the act.

SPECIESISM is discrimination, prejudice, or differential treatment justified by consideration of species membership. A paradigmatic example of a speciesist practice is the use of nonhuman animals for food. Table 1 shows the numbers of animals slaughtered for food in the United States in 1995; the differential treatment of human versus nonhuman animals stands out starkly. The

TABLE I

Numbers of Animals Slaughtered for
Human Food Use in USA (1995)

Species	Number slaughtered
Cattle	36,900,000
Pigs	96,300,000
Sheeps	4,600,000
Chickens	7,528,100,000
Turkeys	280,600,000
Ducks	19,500,000
Humans	0

Source: National Agricultural Statistics Service, U.S. Dept. of Agriculture, 1996

term "speciesism," first used in a 1970 leaflet by Richard Ryder, is an awkward one, but it suggests parallels with racism, casteism, sexism, and so on, and it forces us to consider why these other "isms" are considered morally repugnant by society while speciesism is not.

Many people give no thought at all to the moral acceptability of speciesist practices. Others cite justifications for the practices, some facile and some quite well developed. Conversely, a growing number of people are now rejecting speciesism and offering moral systems that are species-blind. A substantial body of literature exists that attempts to ground these systems; several key references are given in the bibliography. Rather than repeat this material, we adopt a different approach. First, we present a prima facie case against speciesism, thereby throwing the burden of proof on the speciesist. Then we consider how several major speciesist philosophies stand up in their attempts to refute the prima facie case and to present a rigorous justification of speciesism.

A caveat regarding the term "species" is in order. We will shortly consider the notion that the species concept is arbitrary and therefore lacks coherence for use as the foundation of a moral system. Yet, the concept of "speciesism" itself seems to rely on a valid species concept. However, a heuristic species concept based on eclectic sources can give meaning to the notion of species, while denying its coherency for grounding a system of morality (we view "species" as denoting a smudge in the space–time continuum of organisms). We retain the option, therefore, to deny that "real species" exist, while still decrying speciesism.

Finally, we generally use "animal" to refer to a nonhuman. We are aware that humans are, in fact, animals, but the common usage is clear and less cumbersome than the alternatives.

I. SPECIESISM AS AN ANALOGY TO RACISM AND SEXISM

In 1789, in his book, *Introduction to the Principles of Morals and Legislation*, the utilitarian philosopher Jeremy Bentham forcefully asserted an argument in favor of a rejection of speciesism by analogy to racism:

The French have already discovered that the blackness of the skin is no reason why a human being should be abandoned without redress to the caprice of a tormentor. It may one day come to be recognized that the number of the legs, the villosity of the skin, or the termination of the *os sacrum* are reasons equally insufficient for abandoning a sensitive being to the same fate.

Bentham's theme is elaborated upon and illustrated with a number of provocative photographs in Marjorie Spiegel's 1988 book, *The Dreaded Comparison: Human and Animal Slavery*, and this theme forms an important part of many modern treatises on animal advocacy, including the popular works of Peter Singer (e.g., *Animal Liberation*).

Racism, prejudice based on race membership, is but one of a number of "isms" that are increasingly regarded as morally repugnant. Others include: *sexism*, prejudice based on sex membership (e.g., the denial of voting and other rights to women); *ageism*, prejudice based on age (e.g., the denial of employment to older workers); *sexualism*, prejudice based on sexual orientation (e.g., the denial of marriage and other privileges to homosexuals); and *casteism*, prejudice based on hereditary group membership (e.g., the denial of employment and other opportunities to members of certain social castes). Bentham *et. al.* would have us believe that speciesism is analogous to these other "isms" and should, therefore, be regarded as equally repugnant.

Caution must be observed when considering such an argument. First, not all "isms" are necessarily morally repugnant and one might as well argue that speciesism is analogous to those that are not. For example, some benign forms of nationalism may entail differences of treatment based upon an appeal to national citizenship (is it morally repugnant for a nation to allow only its citizens to vote?). Second, by their nature, arguments by analogy are not definitive but only suggestive. They rely upon an inference that if two things are alike in some respects, then they must be alike in other respects. But such inferences can be wrong; arguments by analogy can fail.

What, then, can we realistically expect from the argument by analogy to racism, sexism, and so on? It can form a prima facie case against speciesism, one that challenges us to explain why the analogy fails (if, indeed, it does fail). It can raise issues and dilemmas the resolution of which requires us to think deeply and rationally about the justification, if any, for our speciesist practices. Finally, a failure to adequately refute the argument will constitute a powerful augmentation of more definitive arguments that can be marshaled against speciesism. For these reasons, we pursue the argument in some detail, choosing racism as a paradigmatic morally repugnant form of prejudice. The approach taken is to try to explicate why racism is wrong, and to consider whether the reasons adduced can reasonably be applied to speciesism. Of course, more definitive arguments can be raised against speciesism, and the reader is encouraged to consult the bibliographic references in the light of the issues and dilemmas raised here.

Before considering why racism is wrong, it must be observed that not all acts that qualify as racist under our definition are necessarily wrong or repugnant, and that such acts serve as litmus tests for the reasons that we adduce. For example, consider the case of a movie about the life of Reverend Martin Luther King, Jr. The casting director would likely consider only Black actors for this role, and, certainly, that would constitute a case of prejudice by appeal to racial membership. Other, more controversial, differences of treatment based upon race membership are also not clearly morally repugnant: affirmative action, education assistance funds, clubs, and so on. Interestingly, and in support of the alleged analogy between speciesism and racism, there is a corresponding point to be made about speciesism. Consider the case of a modern-day Noah facing a new catastrophe on planet Earth. A spaceship will carry two members of each species to another planet. Thus far, two chimpanzees and one human have been admitted to the spaceship and now another chimpanzee and a human approach. Noah explains to the chimpanzee that he cannot be admitted *because he is a chimpanzee*. A clear speciesist act under our definition has been committed, yet it seems to us fair and above board. We will see, as we consider the reasons why many acts are considered wrong, whether the counterexamples cited can be encompassed.

A. Is the Underlying Concept Incoherent?

Many modern anthropologists and sociologists now regard the concept of race as an arbitrary classification. Typically, individuals are examined for possession of a set of traits held to be characteristic of a given race. For example, the "Negroid race" might be held to be characterized by dark skin, kinky hair, and broad noses. Yet, in examining populations, a continuous range can be found for each trait, leading us to ask what degree of expression of a trait justifies a classification; selection of any point along a continuum would be arbitrary. Furthermore, individuals may possess some of the traits but not others, for example, persons from south India may have very dark skin but quite straight hair. If racial classifications are, indeed, arbitrary, how can they form the basis for differences of treatment? Isn't it wrong to base important moral decisions on arbitrary criteria?

As we shall see later in this article, an identical objection can be raised against the concept of "species." If the notion is arbitrary, is it not then also wrong to base moral distinctions on the notion of species?

Consider now the "Black actor case" described above. Certainly, the casting director would be surprised if we argued that he shouldn't restrict the role to Blacks because the concept of "Black" is arbitrary. He might reply that he is quite able to distinguish a Black person from a White person. But how might he react when we produce our south Indian? It seems that the restriction he should have imposed is not that the actor should be Black, but that the actor should be credible in a portrayal of Reverend King. This might be best satisfied by a "real Black," or by a south Indian, or even by a superbly talented White actor wearing modern high-tech makeup.

The point to take away here is that if the notions of race and speciesism really are arbitrary, it is highly dubious and problematic to ground systems of morality on these concepts. Nevertheless, the lack of a nonarbitrary classification is not the definitive objection to racism or speciesism, because we can potentially agree on a given arbitrary classification yet still object to the prejudices based thereupon. We look, therefore, for further reasons to consider racism wrong.

B. Is the Practice Invidious?

It is sometimes asserted that the reason that racism is wrong is that it stigmatizes a group of people as inferior. But that cannot be the reason why racism is wrong, because it is *at least conceivable* that the group really is inferior in some regard. If a racist wishes to assert inferiority as the justification for his prejudice, we are required to show that his premise is faulty. It would be reversing his argument to say that his practices stigmatize the group as inferior, when, in fact, correctly or not, he is *deriving* his practices from the alleged inferiority.

More to the point might be to challenge the choice of traits and the justification for the claim that the selected traits are the morally relevant ones. For example, while the racist might assert that Blacks are inferior in intelligence, he may also believe that Whites are inferior in physical ability. Why is the trait of intelligence considered the crucial one for moral status? (Of course, such unsupported generalizations are themselves objectionable, as we shall see.)

Similar considerations arise for speciesism. Speciesists do not worry that their acts stigmatize animals as inferior; rather, many act as they do *because* they believe animals to be inferior (but we will also see other justifications for speciesist practices). Here again, the issue of trait selection arises, because while we may perhaps eat ducks because we consider them to be inferior to us in intelligence or some other trait, we do not acknowledge that they surpass us in the power of flight, and we do not explain why the former trait is crucial while the latter is irrelevant.

The assertion that racism is invidious really amounts to an assertion that the criterion used is not, in fact, solely race membership, but rather some other trait or traits that are asserted to correspond, perhaps causally, perhaps coincidentally, to race membership. We shall see later a reprise of this when we consider the forms of speciesism and, specifically, the distinction between strong and weak speciesism.

C. Does the Practice Constitute an Invalid Generalization?

Suppose that the racist produces compelling evidence that, *on average*, a given group is inferior in some regard. Suppose further that we accept that the trait is crucial. Still, we can object that when considering how to treat an individual, it is the traits of *that individual* that are relevant to a decision, not the group averages. Given individuals may, in fact, be superior in the crucial trait. Therefore, it is an invalid generalization to apply group averages to individuals and, furthermore, it is unfair to do so. This seems to be a decisive and convincing reason for asserting that racism is wrong. It also may pass the test posed by the Black actor case, because no obvious invalid generalization seems to be involved in the assertion that Whites would not be credible playing a Black.

Nevertheless, this reason is still vulnerable to the objection that a given racist system may be based upon a valid generalization. For example, if we believe that Blackness per se is inferior and crucial, then no invalid generalization is involved. Moreover, our objections to racism seem not to be based on the contingent fact of whether a given generalization is valid or not.

The application of this reason for considering racism wrong to speciesism is problematic, because the asserted inferiorities usually are actually true of all the individuals making up the group. For example, we may assert that ducks are inferior because they cannot speak with complex grammar. This is not an invalid generalization.

D. Is It Wrong to Rely on Traits Not Under an Individual's Control?

Ayn Rand has objected to racism on the grounds that one's race is not within the control of individuals, and that it is therefore unfair to treat them differently on that account. This seems problematic as a reason to object to racism for several reasons. First, many traits that are not within our control are now used to ground differences of treatment that we do not consider repugnant. For example, professional sports teams base their selection policies on skills that largely derive from genetic endowments; similarly, being born male or female is not within one's control, but one's eligibility for an Olympic event depends drastically upon it. Second, the reason to object fails the Black actor case, because while the rejected Whites had no control of their color, we do not therefore consider their rejection repugnant.

Animals, of course, have no control over their being animals. But the arguments above discourage us from arguing by analogy that speciesism is therefore wrong.

E. Are Irrelevant Criteria Used to Justify Differences of Treatment?

We might reasonably expect that differences in treatment should be justified by criteria that are not arbitrary, irrelevant, or trivial. This might be summed up by saying that the criteria should be *morally relevant*. Steve Sapontzis writes as follows (in *Morals, Reason, and Animals*):

> Racism is a prejudice because individuals' race is irrelevant to their ability to benefit from an education, to be informed voters, and otherwise

to enjoy and exercise many rights and responsibilities, yet they are denied these rights and responsibilities precisely on the basis of this irrelevant metaphysical condition.

Consider a concrete example. Suppose we decide to admit one candidate to medical school while denying another candidate. When asked to account for the denial, we respond by saying "We're sorry, but this candidate has freckles." Surely, all would acknowledge that we have used an irrelevant criterion. In the case of race, all would acknowledge, for example, that in granting the right to vote, the frizziness of a person's hair is an irrelevant criterion. Likewise, the Black actor case seems to be properly disposed of. In choosing an actor to play a person of a certain race, the race of the actor *is* relevant. If we chose to restrict acceptable actors to those people living on the south side of their street, *that* would be an irrelevant criterion.

It might be objected that race is not irrelevant to granting voting rights because it is believed that members of a race are less intelligent and therefore less capable of voting rationally. But then it turns out that the criterion really being used is intelligence and not race per se. Of course, one must then not make invalid generalizations, and one must consistently apply the criterion *across* racial boundaries, but the use of intelligence as a criterion for deciding voting rights is not outrageously implausible. (Serious theoretical and practical difficulties would arise; indeed, even in the case of animals, we cannot denounce animals as "less intelligent" without a rigorous statement of what intelligence is, and that is a highly controversial subject.)

We do have the problem of defining in a general way what are relevant criteria for given differences of treatment. James Rachels argues that this is not an insoluble problem, and that it need not be an obstacle to accepting the principle of moral relevancy as the definitive objection to speciesism and other "isms" (in *Created from Animals*).

The application of this principle to speciesism is highly provocative. Let us honestly consider whether the fact that a being happens to walk on all fours, or happens to be less intelligent (under some definition) than a human, is really a relevant criterion when considering whether we may stalk and brutally kill that being for "sport." Is speciesism to be regarded as a moral mistake as odious as racism or sexism, because it advocates differences of treatment grounded on morally irrelevant criteria?

F. Conclusion on the Argument by Analogy

The argument by analogy has served us well in bringing out issues and in leading us to a general principle for objecting to "isms": the principle of moral relevance. We now turn specifically to speciesism itself, and consider how the prima facie case may be refuted, and how well the refutations themselves stand up to scrutiny.

II. CAN SPECIESISM BE JUSTIFIED?

The previous section has demonstrated that a plausible prima facie case against speciesism can be made by analogy to racism, sexism, and so on. The burden is now on the speciesist to refute the argument by analogy and to present an affirmative defense of speciesist practices. A successful defense must contain two components. First, it must cite a morally relevant reason (or reasons) for adopting species-based discriminations. Second, it must provide an explicit calculus for deciding the extent of difference of treatment that is acceptable, given the justifying reasons.

A. What Reasons Can Justify Speciesism?

The reasons that have been adduced to justify speciesist practices are as varied as they are numerous. Box 1 presents many of these reasons (selected from a much longer list compiled by the author and available (at this writing) on the World Wide Web at http://www.envirolink.org/arrs/arguments.html). It is, of course, impossible to address each of these reasons in this article and, so, only a few major ones are selected for treatment here (most of these arguments are addressed in *Animal Rights Frequently Asked Questions*, also available (at this writing) on the World Wide Web at http://www.envirolink.org/arrs/faqtop.html).

Given the diverse range of possible differences of treatment that might be part of a speciesist regime (e.g., we eat animals, we experiment on animals, we use animals for entertainment, we hunt animals for sport, we decorate our residences with animal parts, etc.), one might be naturally cautious in accepting one single overriding reason in justification of all speciesist practices. Strangely, however, most often the defenders of speciesism *do* usually offer one reason that is held to be crucial. For example, for Immanuel Kant the key reason for withholding moral consideration from animals was that he held them to be incapable of reasoning.

Box 1	

Reasons Commonly Given to Justify Speciesism

Only humans can have rights.

Animals can't make claims.

Nobody suggests giving rights to plants (or insects or bacteria); so it's hypocritical to give them to animals.

Animals don't respect human rights.

There is no such thing as "natural rights"; we have to choose to confer them.

Morals are a human construction; it is thus irrational to try to apply them to animals.

Morality is subjective; the notion that animals have rights is just one opinion.

Morals is based on reciprocal agreements; because animals can't agree to anything, they can't be encompassed by morality.

Animals don't care about us so we need not care about them.

The law gives us the right to exploit animals.

The Bible gives humans dominion over animals.

Animals are raised to be eaten (or otherwise used).

Many animals wouldn't exist if we didn't raise them for our use.

We don't try to stop predators from killing, so we shouldn't be stopped.

Jobs, customs, and traditions would be lost if we stopped exploiting animals.

Humans are at the pinnacle of evolution; this gives them the right to exploit other species.

Humans are at the top of the food chain.

Animals are just machines.

Animals have no souls.

In nature animals kill and eat each other. The world is made up of predators and prey; we are just another predator.

Natural selection is at work and we shouldn't try to overcome it.

The animals are killed so fast they don't feel or know anything.

Evolution and natural selection justify a species-oriented approach to morality; as the human species, we have the right to exploit other species to benefit and safeguard our own.

Animals don't feel pain. Animals don't suffer. There's no adequate definition of suffering. Humans suffer more.

People are more important than animals.

Human lives have more potential than animal lives.

Just as mothers owe a special duty to their children, we owe a special duty to humans.

Animals are not rational.

Animals cannot talk.

In contrast, James Rachels argues that no single reason can ground all possible differences of treatment and that to suppose that it can is an unjustified simplification that, ironically, itself constitutes a major error of reasoning.

Another complication for the defenders of speciesism arises when a justifying reason appeals to a trait whose possession is not limited to humans, that is, where a difference of degree is involved. Consider the case of reasoning. Today, nobody seriously doubts that at least some animals are capable of quite sophisticated reasoning. A speciesist asserting the moral significance of reasoning must then offer both a relevant threshold for reasoning ability at which moral consideration comes into play and an objective measurement scheme by which performance to the threshold can be determined. Yet, such quantitative criteria are hardly ever offered by speciesists. Instead, the threshold is usually given in qualitative terms, for example, "as much reasoning as is required to understand reciprocal contracts." Of course, now we have the problem of quantifying this latter trait, but it is at least less nebulous than simple reasoning ability.

B. What Is the Calculus for Determining Allowable Differences of Treatment?

After providing a justifying reason or reasons, and quantifying them where necessary, the speciesist must explain and again quantify the calculus for determining *what kinds of* and *how much* difference of treatment is allowed by the given reason(s). Usually, however, speciesists just neglect this and assume that once a justifying reason is given, any and all differences of treatment are justified. Things are not so easy, however. In a discussion with a pharmaceutical researcher who uses animals to develop new drugs, this author attempted to elucidate the point. The researcher claimed to have "carefully balanced the concerns" and to have concluded that the suffering of animals was "outweighed" by suffering of humans. The author pressed him to explicitly present his calculus:

> I must enquire of you what your exact calculus for this process is. What are the relative values of concern for human suffering and animal suffering? How are these values changed when the postulated gain is merely a possibility, or just a gain in our knowledge? What is the inequality you use to make a decision in a specific case for whether the animal suffering is outweighed? Let me ask you this, and you can apply your calculus to provide the answer: Given a procedure that is guaranteed to allow one human to live who might otherwise die, how many chimpanzees would you "sacrifice" to bring that about? One? 10? 100? 1000? 1,000,000? *All of them*?

The researcher became uncomfortable and it became clear that he had no answer, belying his claim to have carefully weighed and balanced the concerns. Interestingly, he might have been further discomforted had he actually given an answer. Suppose he admitted that his calculus treated the suffering of one human as worth the suffering of 10 chimpanzees. He would then have to accept that it is morally correct to sacrifice one human if doing so would save 10 chimpanzees who might otherwise die! A refusal to work the calculus in reverse would constitute a retrenchment to a raw, indefensible form of speciesism.

We now turn to a consideration of several major and representative forms of speciesism. We classify them by considering the justifying reasons adduced, and we assess them by considering how satisfactory the justifying reasons are, and how well they translate into an explicit calculus for determining the types of, and extent of, differences of treatment that they entail.

III. FORMS OF SPECIESISM

We distinguish here three forms of speciesism: raw speciesism, strong speciesism, and weak speciesism. Raw speciesism appeals to justifying reasons that refer simply to species membership *and no more*. Strong speciesism, too, makes appeals to species membership but adds additional considerations with the intent to show why the species boundary is relevant. To qualify as a strong form, however, these additional considerations must not refer to traits that are only coincidentally, or contingently, correlated with the species boundary. Weak speciesism, in contrast, makes appeals to such traits. To make this distinction clearer, consider a doctrine that claims that moral status can be granted only to beings capable of sophisticated, grammatical language. It is contingently true that only humans qualify; therefore, to assess the status of a given being, it would be sufficient (unless conditions change due to future evolution!) to simply determine whether the being is a member of the human species. Yet, this is a form of weak speciesism, because the capability for language is only contingently correlated to species membership. We would more accurately refer to the doctrine as "languageism."

Consider now a time in the future when, we suppose, an additional 500 species have developed the capability for language. It now seems to be stretching things to think of the moral doctrine at hand as a form of speciesism. Furthermore, it is only because the trait is universally displayed (or not displayed) by all members of a given species that we can even think of applying the speciesism label. Suppose that one (or more) of the future species has evolved such that only a fraction of its individuals is capable of language. The species boundary is then not germane and the speciesism label cannot be attached.

So, in summary, weak speciesism makes appeals to contingent facts; strong speciesism does not. The following sections present specific examples.

A. Raw Speciesism

In a recent discussion on the Usenet newsgroup, *talk.politics.animals*, a poster stated "Whether one views humans as animals or not, the fact remains that nonhumans are, in fact, not human." While even a novice philosopher might immediately dismiss this as an empty tautology (and sophisticated philosophers might be inclined to laugh!), it is interesting to note that many people believe it to be sufficient to justify our speciesist practices. Other variants commonly heard are "but they are just animals" and "animals are animals, humans are humans." Perhaps those espousing such thoughts feel that the additional considerations are so obvious that they can go unsaid; however, in their absence, the thoughts deserve no credence. We might just as well say in justification of racism "but they are just Blacks" or "Whites are Whites and Blacks are Blacks." We might justify murder by saying "but he was him, and I am me."

Due to the total lack of plausible justifying reasons, the raw speciesist doctrine leaves us totally bereft of any means of determining how much difference of treatment is justified. The doctrine then looks more like an excuse for egregious practices than a rational philosophical position.

Raw (or bigoted) speciesism is thus totally indefensible. Peter Singer's famous assertion might be accurately qualified as "[raw speciesism], properly understood, is virtually never defended." Singer's original assertion, lacking the qualifier "raw," however, seems wrong regarding the strong and weak forms of speciesism, because there is a substantial body of literature propounding and defending them.

B. Strong Speciesism

We now consider several forms of strong speciesism. Of course, the labels "strong" and "weak" should not be taken as evaluative assessments of the strength of the arguments! They serve simply as names for the categories we have defined based on the presence or absence of appeals to contingent facts.

1. The Biological Argument

The biological argument augments the raw speciesist doctrine by adding additional considerations related to biological competition between species or genes. For example, it might be asserted that the human species has an inherent right to compete with and exploit other species to preserve and protect the human species. Moral status, given such a doctrine, is thus limited to members of the human species. It is possible to generalize this morality by asserting that other species also enjoy this right, leading us to say that moral status, *within a given species*, is limited to members of that species. For example, chimpanzees need only grant moral status to other chimpanzees.

The biological argument is addressed in detail in this author's paper, *Against Strong Speciesism*. Portions of the paper are used below and, in satisfaction of conditions for doing so, the author acknowledges that those portions have been previously published in the *Journal of Applied Philosophy*, and are copyrighted by the Society for Applied Philosophy.

Three main attacks on the strong speciesist position can be mounted: (1) The species concept itself can be shown to be incoherent in the context of morality; (2) it can be shown that "what is required" to ensure survival of a species is difficult to determine and may, in fact, place limits on the allowable exploitation—limits that are not typically observed by adherents of speciesist morality; and (3) it can be shown that the consequences of the strong speciesist position are unacceptable or absurd. Space allows us only to address in detail attack 1. Attack 2 is, in any case, not decisive, because although it might result in a scaling back of the exploitation that is considered permissible, it leaves the strong speciesist position essentially intact.

Many species concepts have been proposed by biologists and philosophers, and this fact alone suggests that "species" is a problematic concept. One might arrange these proposed concepts along a spectrum labeled at one end "conventionalism" and at the other end "realism." Further complicating this already untidy explication of "species" is the fact that many biologists embrace a pluralistic species concept, in effect combining several or all of the many species concepts explicated in the literature. As we shall see, the concepts aspire to greater objectivity and nonarbitrariness as they lie closer to the realism end of the spectrum, and these qualities would seem to be desirable to base a system of ethics. If variety, "race," and so on, are not to be as relevant to morality as "species," then a realistic species concept is required. Therefore, we address in detail here only the most realistic and arguably most "successful" of the species concepts (at least in terms of the number of adherents): the biological species concept. Before getting to it, however, we briefly address the special form of typism called genetic typism.

a. Genetic Typism

The classificatory line drawing problem typically faced by typism arises particularly vividly when the defender of type-based speciesism attempts to base his classification directly on the genotype, rather than on its phenotypic manifestations. In a recent posting to a Usenet newsgroup, a defender of speciesism happily claimed that the species concept could serve as a basis for morality because "unlike species, human individuals never differ by more than 2% of their genetic content." When asked whether the fact that bonobos and humans differ in genetic content by only 1.6% might affect his views, the poster chose instead to challenge the data. Unfortunately for him, the data is not in question. The technique used, DNA hybridization, is well known, respected, and in common use in the field of taxonomy, as well as in the better-known field of forensic DNA "fingerprinting."

These facts lead one to question whether the magnitude of the genetic difference between humans and chimpanzees is big enough to justify the type and moral distinctions drawn between the two. But there are other difficult questions to be answered. Which genes are the ones that confer moral status? If it is answered that it is just the ones that differ between humans and chimps, then we see that the argument is tautologous. After all, why should status be deserved solely on the basis of a certain sequence of genes? We also must ask, assuming that genetic content is relevant, why the relevant boundary is at the species level, rather than at the gene, individual, subspecies, order, phylum, or kingdom levels.

b. The Biological Species Concept

We learn in high school and college that the biological species concept is neat and tidy. If two animals cannot interbreed to produce viable offspring, then they are of different species. Unfortunately, the concept is not so tidy and, in fact, there is a strong case for asserting that the species concept is merely a fiction of the human mind and therefore unable to bear the moral weight that the speciesist wants to place upon it. Let us consider some of the factors leading to this conclusion.

Lions and tigers can interbreed to produce viable hybrids, yet they are reckoned to be of different species. Similarly, some groups of animals reckoned to be of the same species cannot interbreed. For example, the single species of owl monkey *Aotus trivergatus* contains several groups that cannot interbreed. Similarly, soldier termites are members of the same species as their fertile congenors, but they cannot interbreed. That the biological species concept admits of such exceptions (which are ubiquitous in nature) suggests that it may constitute nothing more than a theoretical construct.

It is well known that even where reproductive isolation is asserted, there is typically "leakage" of the isolating mechanism. So even the idea of isolation is not absolute and constitutes little more than a theoretical construct. "Isolation" ranges from complete interfertility to complete isolation and stating what constitutes a significant discontinuity is problematic. Furthermore, there is a serious ambiguity in the evolutionary literature over whether the interbreeding must be actual or potential and the distinction is not a fine point for one attempting to base a morality on the species concept.

We have left for last arguments based on continuums over time and space because they are the strongest and most embarrassing for the defender of strong speciesism. We will show that where the defender of speciesism wants nice clear boundaries, there are, in fact, continuums. These continuums lead to the conclusion that there should also be a continuum of morality. Dawkins describes a telling instance of a continuum (from the article "*Gaps in the Mind*," in *The Great Ape Project*):

The lawyer would be surprised and, I hope, intrigued by so-called "ring species." The best-known case is herring gull versus lesser black-backed gull. In Britain these are clearly distinct species, quite different in colour. Anybody can tell them apart. But if you follow the population of herring gulls westward round the North Pole to North America, then via Alaska across Siberia and back to Europe again, you will notice a curious fact. The "herring gulls" gradually become less and less like herring gulls and more and more like lesser black-backed gulls until it turns out that our European lesser black-backed gulls actually are the other end of a ring that started out as herring gulls. At every stage around the ring, the birds are sufficiently similar to their neighbours to interbreed with them. Until, that is, the ends of the continuum are reached, in Europe. At this point the herring gull and the lesser black-backed gull never interbreed, although they are linked by a continuous series of interbreeding colleagues all the way round the world.

Dawkins' example is a special instance of a clinal distribution: the cline wraps back upon itself. A cline is a distribution in which a trait varies across a spatially distributed group of organisms. Due to interbreeding across every point in the cline, there is gene flow from one end of the cline to the other. Yet, the variance along the cline may be sufficient that organisms at the two ends of the cline cannot interbreed. Such clinal distributions are common in nature. These clinal distributions present a problem for the species concept. Are the organisms at the two ends of the cline members of different species? If so, at what point along the cline does the species change? If they are regarded as still members of the same species, would it then be the loss of an intervening group of organisms that would complete speciation? How can such a loss have moral significance?

The question about where along the cline the species changes leads us to a key insight. A response is possible if we answer relative to a point on the cline, say, one end of the cline. We can then say the species changes at a point along the cline where the organisms at that point are no longer able to interbreed with the organisms at our reference end of the cline. This buys an answer at a great cost. First, the organisms adjacent to either side of the claimed boundary can interbreed, so it seems very wrong to assert that they are of different species. Second, selection of one point along a cline as the reference point is totally arbitrary.

Dawkins also describes a continuum in time that links humans back to their common ancestors with the chimpanzee. He shows that over time, just as with space, the concept of tidy, distinct species delimited by interbreeding capability cannot stand up to the realities of the natural world. Starting at humans and moving slowly along the gradation toward the ancestors, one never encounters a magic boundary at which organisms on either side cannot interbreed, and hence, at which one can say "moral consideration ceases here" (or, at which one can say "humanity starts here").

We see that an interbreeding boundary must be relative to a particular point in space and time. It is arbitrary to reference a given point as definitive of a species. Which point in space/time should be chosen as the baseline for "human"? That is, which individual or small group of individuals should we choose as our reference point for interbreeding?

Even if we agree upon a group of presently living individuals to serve as our reference for humanity, what happens when they die? Even more problematic is how to use this reference group in practice. We cannot attempt to interbreed it with all other individuals. Yet, if we do not, then we are unable to recognize the others as of the human species without assuming the boundary we are trying to test. Sokal and Crovello (Sokal, R. &

Crovello, T. (1970). *The biological species concept: A critical evaluation. American Naturalist*, 104, 127–153) put it this way: "Establishment of biological species from fertility characteristics is entirely quixotic."

Probably the most important rejoinder to the arguments given that undermine the species concept is the claim that they are irrelevant; it is argued that we *know* which creatures are human, and that the problems enumerated *do not apply* to the human species. Our reply involves two main points. First, it is not true that all the enumerated problems do not apply to humans; for example, the problem of the time continuum is definitely applicable. Even in space, we do not know whether a group of "humans" exists that may be reproductively isolated for one reason or another. But more significantly, it is merely a contingent fact that some of the known problems with the species concept may not currently apply to humans. Relative to evolutionary time scales, humans are virtually infants, having diverged only recently from our common ancestor with the chimpanzee. If humans manage to survive over evolutionarily significant time spans, increased variability will arise with the result that the problems described may become increasingly applicable.

Second, we must not lose sight of the fact that such a defense really amounts to an abandonment of the generalizable strong speciesist morality, because it asks us to look at the contingent facts surrounding one group of organisms, namely humans. The back-off from strong speciesism to contingent humanism (or "lionism," etc.) ties morality to a space/time frame, and the conditions pertaining therein. This defense transforms the generalizable strong speciesist morality into a form of weak speciesism. Shall we accept that our allegedly generalizable morality is applicable only to those groups that are fortunate enough to be delimited by spatial or other discontinuities?

The biological argument seems to offer a straightforward measure of what differences of treatment are acceptable: any difference of treatment that promotes the survival of the human species is acceptable. Of course, our survival depends on the survival of the biosphere as a whole, so it might be difficult in practice to determine whether a given speciesist act is actually justified, and it is likely that such considerations would result in a scaling back of many of our current speciesist practices.

2. The Importance Argument

It is not unusual for unsophisticated speciesists to appeal to the greater "importance" of human beings. They hold, for example, that it is allowable to experiment on primates because humans are "more important." We must, of course, ask some pressing questions of this metaphysical concept of importance. Is importance to be understood in an absolute or only a relative sense? If absolute, what is the definition and how is absolute importance assessed? If relative, can we say relative to whom without being arbitrary? Is there any real content in the assertion that humans are more important to humans, chimpanzees to chimpanzees, and so on? How is relative importance assessed? (Note that if a definition is advanced that appeals to *measurement* of some quality, then we should reclassify the importance argument as a form of weak speciesism, because the results of the measurements would be contingent facts. Because the argument is typically *not* accompanied by such a definition, we are content to consider it a strong form.)

We may also point out that, in practice, we do not *always* consider humans to be more important than animals. For example, humans in the United States spend billions of dollars per year on their pets, rather than on efforts to assist the millions of humans suffering throughout the world. Also, we voluntarily abridge our freedom to act toward animals with laws such as the Endangered Species Act. So, if the justification from importance breaks down in these cases, why does it not also break down in the cases of slaughter for food, experimentation, and so on?

Suppose we accept that our greater importance allows us to kill and eat animals. Should we then accept that the Albert Einsteins and Louis Pasteurs of this world, who by any objective measure are more important than the humble likes of everyday humans, should be free to kill and eat the less-important humans? Is there some threshold of difference of importance that is required? Clearly, the bare importance argument, devoid of definitions and measures, leaves us unable to derive the allowable differences of treatment.

If we respond to these points by equating importance to the utility that we derive from animals, we have bought a defense at great cost. First, we have in effect disavowed the defense of strong speciesism by resorting to a utilitarian ethics. Second, Peter Singer and others have shown that a fair and reasoned utilitarianism would encompass animals and require us to avoid many of the practices sought to be defended.

Given these considerations, the promoter of the importance argument is forced to either (a) retreat to raw speciesism, (b) disavow speciesism and embrace utilitarianism, or (c) assert another similar strong speciesist argument, the special relations argument, to which we now turn.

3. The Special Relations Argument

Gray argues in favor of speciesism by invoking what we here call the *special relations argument* (Gray, J. A. (1980). In defense of speciesism. *Behavioral and Brain Sciences*, Vol. 13, No. 1). Gray presents the example of a mother faced with the choice of saving one of two children from a fire, one of whom is her own child. He argues that no one would find it morally repugnant if the mother chose her own child to save. He further argues that even if some imbalance were involved, for example, the mother's child is retarded while the other child is not, that we would still not decry the mother's choice of her own child. There is, he asserts, *some* point at which the imbalance becomes great enough that we would decry the choice, but that we should not be surprised to find it to be rather large. Having established this premise, Gray then argues that similar considerations apply to the question of how we may treat animals. There is, he asserts, a special relation between humans, like that between the mother and the child, that justifies our choosing to benefit humans at the expense of animals. (A social-services worker known to the author recounts horrific tales of how some mothers treat their children—if those are special relations, perhaps we should prefer ordinary ones!)

Maclean strengthens the case by showing that relationships *are* important morally, and not just in choice situations (Maclean, A. (1993). *The elimination of morality*. London: Routledge). She discusses the case of a man, his banker, and his doctor. The banker would be morally innocent in asking for details of the man's finances; the doctor would be treading on morally questionable grounds by so prying. She generalizes as follows: "To say that some obligations are special is to say that *not all* obligations are general, not that *none* are."

Nagel refers to a tension between the personal and impartial standpoints (Nagel, T. (1991). *Equality and partiality*. New York: Oxford University Press). He views the reconciliation of these two standpoints as a central unsolved problem of moral theory and the core problem of political theory.

Even philosophers sympathetic to the plight of animals have acknowledged the soundness of the premise that special relations can overrule general, impersonal considerations. For example, Regan, well known for his case for animal rights, considers such relations one of several "special considerations" that can justifiably override his rights criteria (in *The Case for Animal Rights*). But he presents no explanation for how one is to balance the concerns. If this balancing is difficult for human/human interactions, how difficult must it be for human/animal ones?

The verdict is not unanimous, however. Utilitarian philosophers, such as Peter Singer, argue that consideration of special relations, while it may be commonly accepted, is wrong because it is irrational (!). Far from trying to find a moral theory that reconciles special relations with impartial considerations, we should, they argue, correct our moral thinking by repudiating all considerations of special relations. Maclean and Nagel counter that such a view is artificial and unconvincing, and stands in need of justification that the utilitarians do not offer.

If we can accept the moral relevance of special relations and its applicability to the problem of speciesism, we still must ask ourselves what differences of treatment it can justify. After all, an unrestrained special relations argument could be used to justify repugnant practices such as racism ("Whites have a special relationship with other Whites"). This is another way of asking what the imbalance is before we would decry an act as overly personally motivated and overly dismissive of the impartial standpoint, or, as Mary Midgley has put it, of determining the "inter-species exchange rate" (in *Animals and Why They Matter*). Midgley writes:

> The spectrum of animal use stretches right from the Eskimo defending himself, through pest control, medical research, roast lamb, fox-hunting, *pate de foie gras*, the use of sperm-whale oil when satisfactory substitutes are readily available, LD-50 [lethal dosage] testing, . . .and beyond that to further reaches too offensive to mention. The plea. . .is not going to hold much beyond the first four items, if so far.

Of course, animal rights proponents would argue that the exchange rate is pretty much even, that is, that the acts that the special relations argument would fail to justify in human/human situations should be essentially the same in human/animal situations. For example, if I cannot eat a stranger, despite having special relations with my family, why then, in virtue of having special relations with humans, can I eat a cow? There is no good answer to this telling question, because no general solution to the core problem of the role of special relations has yet been advanced.

Finally, we should point out that the tension we have been considering has application to the biological argument already considered. When we think that the human species is justified in doing whatever it thinks justified for its survival, are we in fact failing to acknowledge the tension between impartial and personal considerations? That is, is the personal standpoint the only

relevant one for the human species? Do we not also have competing obligations stemming from species impartiality? What is the exchange rate here?

4. The Divine Command Argument

Perhaps the most frequently encountered justification for our speciesist practices, but paradoxically the least well-founded (at least among objective philosophers!), is the view that the practices are morally acceptable because God says that they are. We will not consider this thesis in detail here for space reasons, but only mention it for completeness in our account of strong speciesist philosophies. We content ourselves with acknowledging the many philosophical problems with divine command arguments, even away from the sphere of animals, as evidenced by such accounts as that of Holmes (Holmes, R. L. (1993) *The divine command theory*. In *Basic moral philosophy*. Belmont, CA: (Wadsworth Publishing Company). And, after all, if the millions of animal-rights activists claim that their God tells them that we all must respect the rights of animals by not eating them, and so on, how can they be discredited? (How can *any* doctrine involving a leap of faith be discredited?)

C. Weak Speciesism

We have seen that weak speciesism involves an appeal to contingent facts regarding traits for its justification. For example, we might argue that a certain level of rationality is necessary for moral status, and that because animals do not have this level of rationality (the contingent fact), they do not merit moral status. The traits that have been used to ground weak speciesist doctrines are varied. Box 2 lists many of them.

The inclusion of ". . .be sentient" and ". . .be capable of experiencing pleasure and pain" may raise some eyebrows among supporters of animal rights, because these traits form the foundation of several major animal-rights philosophies, which are usually considered to be *antispeciesist*. However, rather than undermining the philosophies, this observation tends more to undermine the perjorative strength of the label "weak speciesism."

We might strictly argue that doctrines based on traits such as those in Box 2 are not speciesism per se, and thus are not a proper subject for this article. Nevertheless, as long as there is a perfect correlation between the crucial trait, rationality in our example, and species boundaries, then pragmatically the species boundary can be appealed to in justification of proposed differences of treatment. That the correlation must be perfect can be deduced from a consideration of our reaction

Box 2

Traits Commonly Used to Ground Weak Speciesist Doctrines

To merit moral status, a being must...

...have desires and preferences.

...be able to communicate symbolically.

...be able to speak with complex grammar.

...be self-aware.

...be able to make claims for its rights.

...be able to respect others' rights.

...be rational.

...be sentient.

...be capable of experiencing pleasure and pain.

...be autonomous.

...have a soul.

...have a mind.

...be able to participate in a social contract.

...be capable of forethought and planning.

---

to the possible contingency that (say) one in a hundred chimpanzees reaches the required level of rationality; we would need then to examine individual chimpanzees to ascertain their moral status instead of simply determining that they *are* chimpanzees.

Nevertheless, we shall consider one example of weak speciesism in some detail—the appeal to rationality—because the attacks on it are typically (but not universally) applicable to other forms of speciesism. We leave it as an exercise for the reader to determine whether the attacks are applicable to the weak speciesist doctrines that favor animals, such as sentientism.

1. The Appeal to Rationality

Our first question for a supporter of the appeal to rationality (hereafter the "rationality doctrine") is simply "why is rationality relevant to moral status?" We can acknowledge that humans exhibit rationality in greater measure than do animals (given a suitable definition of "rationality"). But chimpanzees, for example, are better climbers than humans; they are stronger than humans; they have nicer fur coats than humans. Why is the trait of rationality the crucial one for deserving moral status? Here, the response is usually that a high degree of rationality is required *to be a moral being*. For example,

it might be held that only humans are capable of performing the analyses required for Kantian determination of the moral correctness of an act—determining whether a maxim is capable of being universalized. After all, chimpanzees cannot even conceive of a maxim (or can they?). Or, it might be held that animals are not smart enough to comprehend the notion of rights, so it would be absurd to grant them any.

The rationality doctrine as explicated is subject to two related attacks that also attach to many other weak speciesist doctrines—the *moral agent/moral patient distinction* and the *argument from marginal cases*. Both allow us to question the assumption that a being must *be a moral being* to deserve moral status.

2. The Moral Agent/Moral Patient Distinction

Consider first the distinction between "moral agents" and "moral patients." A moral agent is an individual possessing the sophisticated conceptual ability to bring moral principles to bear in deciding what to do, and having made such a decision, having the free will to choose to act that way. By virtue of these abilities, it is fair to hold moral agents accountable for their acts. The paradigmatic moral agent is the normal adult human being. Moral patients, in contrast, lack the capacities of moral agents and thus cannot fairly be held accountable for their acts. They do, however, possess the capacity to suffer harm and to benefit from moral status and, therefore, are proper objects of consideration for moral agents. Human infants, young children, the mentally deficient or deranged, and animals are instances of moral patienthood. Given that animals *are* moral patients, it might be argued, they fall within the purview of moral consideration.

3. The Argument from Marginal Cases

The rationalists may, of course, respond that they accept that animals are moral patients, yet, nevertheless, they remain adamant in requiring moral agency for attribution of moral status. This response runs headlong into the argument from marginal cases, which can be articulated by making a simple substitution in the statement of the rationality doctrine: Infants, and so on, do not understand morals; therefore, they are not deserving of moral status (and we may eat them and perform experiments on them). Yet, our moral intuitions tell us that these moral patients *are* proper objects of moral consideration. We refrain from harming infants and children for the same reasons that we do so for adults. That they are incapable of conceptualizing a system of morals and its benefits surely is irrelevant. Mary Midgley has expressed this eloquently (in *Animals and Why They Matter*):

> In Kant's case, what is the reason involved in saying, "he does not fail in his duty to the dog, *for the dog cannot judge*"? This really seems to need explanation, because in a human case it would not work. Duties to babies, defectives and the senile, and to people too humble, confused or indecisive to be capable of judging whether they are wronged, are not cancelled by that incapacity. They are strengthened by it.

Several responses to the argument from marginal cases are possible, but none seems wholly satisfactory. One possibility is to simply reject the idea that we have any duties to moral patients; we *can* eat babies, defectives, senile people, and so on. Yet, this seems to be wildly at odds with our moral intuitions. A more promising rejoinder might involve appealing to the *potential* of babies to become true moral agents. This, however, neglects to account for our reticence in eating seniles, defectives, and so on, who have no real potential to become moral agents. There are many species that can reason in ways that we have to regard as superior to some human marginals. On what grounds do we privilege potentiality over actuality?

While it might be argued that science may one day restore human marginals to full moral agency, it could equally be argued that science may one day bestow full agency upon chimpanzees. The concept of potential, also, is fraught with other philosophical difficulties. For example, if we accept that potential is sufficient for attribution of status, need we then acknowledge that embryos (or even spermatozoa!) deserve full consideration due to their potential to become moral agents?

We might instead argue that marginals are *part of a group* the members of which normally are moral agents. But why group membership should be important is not clear and, worse, the argument seems to be irrational. Consider an analogy: "I will plant, water, and tend seeds that I know to be infertile because they are members of a group of seeds that are normally fertile." This is plainly irrational. It is the characteristics of the individual that merit a treatment; the distribution of the trait in a group is irrelevant.

It might be argued that our de facto duties to marginals derive from different and additional justifications than the ones used to ground moral status for moral agents. For example, we may hold that marginals are "covered" because harming them would offend or trouble some other moral agents. But are we to suppose

that we can eat a child because no one cares about it? And do we not need to acknowledge the offense taken by millions of animal-rights activists when animals are murdered for trivial reasons, such as a transient taste on the tongue? Or, we may hold that marginals are covered because we choose to "let them slide." But can we not also choose to "let animals slide."

Finally, Sapontzis argues that there is considerable evidence that many animals actually *are* moral agents (in *Morals, Reason, and Animals*). If that is accepted, our continued refusal to grant them at least some moral status would undermine the rationality doctrine, or constitute an additional appeal to a raw and, thus, indefensible, form of speciesism.

IV. CONCLUSION

We have considered, as part of our investigation of speciesism, diverse attempts to refute the prima facie case against speciesist practices by analogy to racism, sexism, and so on. None of these attempts can be considered to be wholly successful in meeting the two criteria that we advanced: (1) the justifying reasons adduced must be relevant and convincing, and (2) the reasons must translate into an explicit calculus for determining what differences of treatment are acceptable, given acceptance of the justifying reasons.

On the other hand, antispeciesist philosophies, such as Singer's utilitarianism, Regan's rights theory, and Ryder's sentientism, while offering accounts of our treatment of animals that appeal to criteria that are arguably more relevant than those presented by speciesists, are also subject to philosophical objections. Do these objections, however, succeed only in nibbling at the edges of our concern for animals, leaving intact the indictment of most of our current speciesist practices? The reader is invited to investigate these issues by reading the bibliographic references.

Perhaps, for all of us, the primary considerations lie before philosophy, or beyond philosophy, in the realm of pure compassion. To make this concrete, Figure 1 is offered. In parts of Africa, there is a growing problem of poaching of "bushmeat." The figure shows the leftovers from a meal made from a gorilla. How small a step it would seem for a human head to be occupying the bowl.

Also See the Following Articles

ANIMAL RIGHTS • ANTHROPOCENTRISM • PAINISM • RACISM • SEXISM • VEGETARIANISM

FIGURE 1   Bushmeat leftovers. (Photograph by Karl Amman; used with permission.)

Bibliography

Baird, R., & Rosenbaum, S. (Eds.), (1991). "Animal Experimentation: The Moral Issues," Buffalo, NY: Prometheus Books.

Cavalieri, P., & Singer, P. (Eds.), (1993). "The Great Ape Project: Equality Beyond Humanity," New York: St. Martin's Press.

Finsen, L., & Finsen, S. (1994). "The Animal Rights Movement in America: From Compassion to Respect," New York: Twayne Publishers.

Graft, D. (Ed.), (1994). "Animal Rights Frequently Asked Questions," Animal Rights Resource Site (ARRS) on the World-Wide Web, http://www.envirolink.org/arrs/faqtop.html.

Graft, D. (1997). "Against Strong Speciesism," *Journal of Applied Philosophy*, in press.

Midgley, M. (1984). "Animals and Why They Matter," Athens, GA: The University of Georgia Press.

Rachels, J. (1990). "Created from Animals: The Moral Implications of Darwinism," Oxford, UK: Oxford University Press.

Regan, T. (1983). "The Case for Animal Rights," Berkely and Los Angeles, CA: University of California Press.

Rollin, B. (1992). "Animal Rights and Human Morality," Revised Edition, Buffalo, NY: Prometheus Books.

Sapontzis, S. (1987). "Morals, Reason, and Animals," Philadelphia, PA: Temple University Press.

Singer, P. (1990). "Animal Liberation," Second Edition, New York, NY: Avon Books.

Spiegel, M. (1988). "The Dreaded Comparison: Human and Animal Slavery," New York, NY: Mirror Books.

SPORTS, ETHICS OF

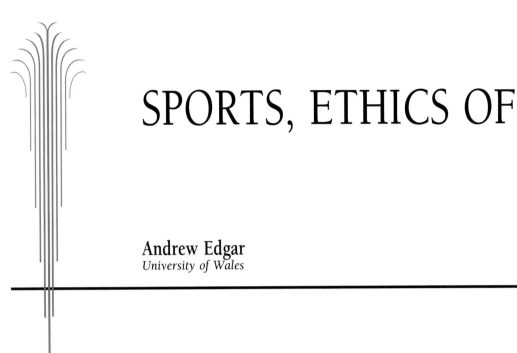

Andrew Edgar
University of Wales

GLOSSARY

athlete As used here, a competitor or participant in any sport (and will not be restricted to the usage of participants in track and field events), and thus as synonymous with sportsperson.

doping The intentional taking of pharmaceutical products (or, as in the case of "blood-doping," using other medical techniques) to improve an athlete's performance. The pharmaceutical products are thus referred to as performance-enhancing drugs.

fair play A central concept in the ethics of sport, typically expressing an athlete's respect for the spirit in which the sport is to be played, rather than mere observance of the rules. Its substance is typically defined negatively, as being opposed, for example, to all forms of cheating, time wasting, and lack of respect for opponents and officials.

gamesmanship Striving to win a game, strictly without cheating, but by cunning methods that exploit the letter of the rules of the sport.

professional foul A foul committed intentionally, as part of the strategy of the game, where the cost of being penalized for the foul is offset by the benefit of preventing the current run of play (i.e., the profes-

sional foul actually works to the advantage of the player or team committing the foul).

sportmanship/sportswomanship Quality of participating with due respect for the spirit of sport, or fair play.

WITTGENSTEIN famously used the concept of "game" to illustrate the point that many mundane and meaningful concepts are not open to precise definition. No single set of necessary and sufficient conditions can be given that will apply to all activities that we happily recognize as games. While any given game may share something in common with another game, and that with a third, common characteristics between the first and third may be few or nonexistent. The definition of "sport" proves, unsurprisingly, to be equally problematic. For example, while many sports are competitive, mountaineering and rock climbing are typically described as sports while not necessarily being played competitively, and many competitive activities (such as entrance exams and music competitions) are not understood to be sports. Similarly, while a play element may be important in sport, the sense in which many professional athletes "play" is unclear, and such playful activities as hopscotch and tag are not sports.

Bernard Suits has attempted to provide a definition of game and sport in terms of necessary and sufficient conditions. He proposes four elements that serve to constitute an activity as game-playing. His thesis is summarized thus: "To play a game is to attempt to achieve a specific state of affairs…, using only means permitted by rules, where the rules prohibit use of more efficient in favour of less efficient means…, and where such rules are accepted just because they make possible such activity." At least in the essay "The Elements of Sport," Suits argues that all sports are games, but that sports are characterized by a further set of four elements: "(1) that the game be a game of skill, (2) that the skill be physical, (3) that the game have a wide following, and (4) that the following achieve a certain level of stability" (Suits, Bernard. (1995, originally 1973). The Elements of Sport. In William J. Morgan & Klaus Meier (Eds.), *Philosophic inquiry in sport* (2nd ed.). Champaign IL: Human Kinetics, p. 11). Suits' elements explain why chess and the hula hoop are not sports (for the former does not entail the use of physical skill, and the latter lacks the institutional support, in terms of training, research, and the keeping of records, typical of a sport). Problem cases can still be suggested (such as piano competitions, and those activities, such as ballroom dancing, that either change status or lobby for a change of status). While the following account need not then be understood as accepting Suits' account in total, reflection on a number of the elements that he identifies (not least the significance of the rules of a sport) will be seen to be central to a consideration of the relationship of sport and ethics.

An alternative approach, responding to the Wittgensteinian insight, may be to suggest that problems of the definition of sport are akin to those found in the definition of art. What counts as art may change historically, and an adequate understanding of what art entails must embrace the historical and cultural traditions within which art is produced and consumed. Thus, what counts as sport may also be seen to change historically and culturally. Ballroom dancing becomes a sport when it is "baptized" as such by the Olympic Committee (just as a urinal becomes a work of art when it is accepted and displayed as such by artworld institutions). If the ethics of sport is to respond, as closely as possible, to ordinary-language usage of the word sport, then its scope is determined in part by historical contingency. On the one hand, the ethics of sport must be relevant to soccer, tennis, and now, ballroom dancing, but need not necessarily say anything of relevance to chess, piano competitions, or hopscotch. On the other hand, the inclusion of hunting and fishing as sports may simply be explained by the survival of the eighteenth-century use of the word sport, except that eighteenth-century intuitions as to what counts as fairness or a sporting chance continue to influence the broader twen-

tieth-century uses of sport and fair play. Again, the ethics of sport cannot afford to be insensitive to the historical nuances of its subject matter.

I. THE RELATIONSHIP OF SPORT AND MORALITY

A. The Evaluative Use of Sport

There is, for the present purposes, a further and telling parallel that may be drawn between the definition of sport and that of art. Both terms may have descriptive (or positive) and evaluative (or normative) uses. Just as "This is not art" may express the speaker's aesthetic condemnation of the art work, so "This is not sport" (or perhaps better "This is unsporting") may express moral condemnation of the manner in which the sport is being played. The evaluative use of the term sport is more plausibly defended than the equivalent use of art, and much of the ethics of sport will be seen to rest upon the thesis that sport is an inherently moral activity, embodying generally (or in the strongest version, universally) recognized moral values.

1. Sport as Challenge and as Practice

The evaluative use of sport suggests certain ways in which a working definition of sport may be developed, which is to say a definition that is of use to the ethics of sport. Two considerations may be proposed. Firstly, sport involves some form of challenge. Suits writes of the overcoming of unnecessary obstacles. Robert Sharpe suggests that for an activity to be sport there must be "the arbitrary selection of or creation of difficulties which it is our aim to overcome" (Sharpe, Robert. (1995). Sport. In Ted Honderich (Ed.), *The Oxford Companion to Philosophy*. Oxford: Oxford University Press). This challenge is more than merely an objective to be achieved (such as the defeat of an opponent, the climbing of a mountain, or the catching of a fish), for the achievement is prescribed in terms of exacting and at times inconvenient, if not downright bizarre, rules. The poacher has much more efficient methods for catching trout than those of the angler, and precisely because of this, poaching is unsporting. Sport may therefore be understood as a multilayered activity, such that the game may be broken down at numerous levels into sequences of intermediary or subordinate goals and activities, each of which will have their own intrinsic pleasures (and corresponding frustrations) (Skillen, Anthony. (1993). Sport: An historical phenomenology. *Philosophy, 68*, 343–368). The ultimate goal of the sport is pursued within the broader context of a set of rules, the mere observance of which is considered to be worthwhile.

This understanding of sport has been explicated along a number of important lines. The pursuit of goals may be understood in terms of the pursuit of excellence and self-discovery. To play a sport entails, typically, not merely playing according to the rules, but precisely insofar as the rules articulate intrinsically valuable subordinate goals, the use of those rules to test and to improve specific skills. There is satisfaction in a well-struck shot at goal, even if the shot is saved by the goalkeeper. From this it may be argued that the demands of the sport (and of worthy opposition) allow the athlete to develop in self-understanding. The precise nature (and indeed worth) of this self-understanding is perhaps undertheorized, but may initially be suggested to entail a recognition, not merely of one's capacity to develop and hone physical skills, but also of one's endurance, courage, and ability to perform under pressure. This analysis is given more depth by those who appeal to Alasdair MacIntyre's concept of "practice" as a necessary (although not sufficient) condition of an activity being a sport (Arnold, Peter J. (1992). Sport as a valued human practice: A basis for the consideration of some moral issues in sport. *Journal of Philosophy of Education* 26(2), 237–255). MacIntyre defines a practice as:

> any coherent and complex form of socially established co-operative human activity through which goals internal to that form of activity are realised in the course of trying to achieve those standards of excellence which are appropriate to, and partially definitive of, that form of activity, with the result that human powers to achieve excellence, and human conceptions of the goals and ends involved, are systematically extended (MacIntyre, Alasdair. (1981). *After virtue: A study in moral theory.* London: Duckworth).

He indeed gives "the game of football" as an example of a practice. Sport may therefore be understood as a practice insofar as it entails human cooperation in the achievement of intrinsic goals, and in having standards of excellence. Further, the individual participant subordinates him or herself to the authority of the practice, agreeing to be judged in terms of the standards that define the practice, and accepting condemnation (or here, sporting failure) as well as approval. Again, MacIntyre gives a sporting example: "If, on starting to play baseball, I do not accept that others know better than

I when to throw a fast ball and when not, I will never learn to appreciate good pitching let alone to pitch" (1981, p. 177).

Such an account may be complemented by Michael Oakeshott's analysis of the rules of a sport (Oakeshott, Michael. (1983). The rule of law. In his *On history and other essays.* Oxford: Blackwell, pp. 125–128). As has already been noted, the rules of a sport are not instrumental, even to the achievement of the objectives of the game. Thus, observance of the rules by a player cannot be explained instrumentally (although nonobservance, and especially the phenomenon of the professional foul, may be). Rather, observance can be justified only insofar as it constitutes the human agent as the player of a certain sport, placing him or her in a relationship of mutual recognition to other players, and acknowledging his or her acceptance of the authority of the rules of, and ideas of excellence within the sport. To acknowledge, during one's involvement in the sport, the authority of the rules of golf (and precisely insofar as those rules may include what may be understood as broadly moral prescriptions, one may be accepting a set of ethical values) is to be a golfer, or more precisely, it is to understand oneself as a golfer.

There are two implications to be drawn out here. First, Oakeshott's account implies that there is nothing else entailed in being a golfer other than acknowledging the rules of golf. The skill with which one plays the game is irrelevant. Second, self-understanding entails more than just the heightened awareness of certain physical, emotional, and mental capacities and potentials that one may possess, but is rather the understanding of oneself as a specific kind of person. This may be explained if it is accepted that one can question the rules of a sport (and thus the rules that ultimately constitute this self-understanding) only on very limited grounds. One cannot reject a rule because it is merely (instrumentally) inconvenient, nor add one that is convenient, but one might question the relevance of rules. That is to suggest that the rules of a sport are typically negotiated and changed through appeal to their role in facilitating the expression and practice of what it means to be a modern golfer, tennis player, or whatever. For example, the introduction of the penalty kick in soccer in 1891 was justified as a means to prevent defenders deliberately fouling opponents in order to prevent otherwise certain goals, which is to say that deliberate fouls are alien to what it means to play soccer. Players responded by claiming that it was an insult to them to assume that they intended to behave like cads, tripping, hacking, or pushing their opponents, declaring that "the lines marking the penalty area are a disgrace to the playing field of a public school" (C. B. Fry cited in McIntosh, Peter. (1979). *Fair play: Ethics in sport and education*. London: Heinemann, p. 80).

2. Sport as Unreal

The second consideration, emerging from the initial attempt to define sport, is that sport is unreal or purposeless. This follows from the peculiar nature of the challenges entailed in sport. Ignoring, for the moment, the commercial context within which much modern sport is played, and certain sociological considerations on the relationship between sport and society, the importance of sport may be suggested to lie in its marginal relevance to the concerns of everyday life. On the one hand, while certain sports, such as wrestling, the modern pentathlon, and archery, may have their historical roots in the training of skills necessary in other (here military) activities, these skills are typically no longer relevant, and the triple jump, synchronized swimming, and snow boarding (for example) appear to suggest no instrumental or extrinsic justification. Thus, to describe them as purposeless is to suggest that their purpose is wholly intrinsic, and cannot be further justified by appeals to activities and institutions that lie outside sport itself. On the other hand, to understand oneself as a tennis player will entail separating oneself from the "real" world, and the social relations that hold in that real world. For example, the tennis player should win because of his or her superior playing skills, and not because he or she commands greater economic or political power, or greater social status than does the other player in the real world. Ideally, the doctoral student should not let his or her supervisor win at squash, just because he or she is the supervisor (although it might be nice occasionally).

Sport's divorce from the mundane world, and thus its unreality, rests on its playfulness. (Philosophical reflection on play is relatively extensive, embracing figures such as Schiller, Sartre, and Eugene Fink, as well as historians, such as Johan Huizinga (1950 Homo ludens. London: Routledge and Kegan Paul). (See Morgan and Meier. (1995). *Philosophic inquiry in sports*. Champaign, IL: Human Kinetics, pp. 99–138.)) In sport, rules (and thus goals) that do not apply to everyday life are imposed, and rules that do apply in everyday life are suspended. While sport remains rule-governed and the rules are treated with all due seriousness (with this frequently being taken as the characteristic that distinguishes sport from mere play), the sporting rules are playful insofar as they cannot be justified by appeal to anything outside the sport. (To reiterate a point made above, the reason that tennis is played with a net

separating the two halves of the court is because that is what it means to play tennis. No other justification can be given.)

This begins to hint at the problematic moral status of sport. While sport allows the athlete to perform playful (and perhaps innocent) activities otherwise denied to him or her, such as running, jumping, rock climbing, and ball handling, and to leave behind the burdens of social position and responsibility, it also allows the performance of violent and otherwise illegal acts (be these within combat sports such as boxing, or in other contact sports such as the various codes of football). This has led support to the argument that sport is neither moral nor immoral, but is rather essentially amoral, insofar as the rules of a given sport serve to isolate a given set of activities from the moral judgments and sanctions that they would normally incur in everyday life. There is something bold and satisfying in such an argument, for it provides a simple and radical case for the unreality and purposelessness of sport. Sport would be radically divorced from even the moral concerns, values, and goals of the everyday world, let alone economic or other instrumental concerns.

The argument for sporting amorality can be questioned in that it ignores the complexity of the rules that govern sport. Boxing poses the most problematic case, for a legitimate goal of the boxer is the inflicting of brain injury (including concussion, and as an unavoidable consequence of blows to the head, the permanent damage of brain cells) to his or her opponent. Certain sports therefore appear to condone immoral acts. (Precisely for this reason, it may be argued that boxing is not a permissible activity, even as a sport.) Yet rules do govern boxing (and were in large part introduced to curb the extremes of prize fighting), and these rules foster diverse subordinate goals and activities, including dexterity, stamina, and self-discipline. Skillen thus describes sport in general as "a microcosm of life.... At any level, sporting activity involves the pursuit of quality, the struggle to do well, a 'technical' achievement requiring a measure of dedication, enterprise, attention to detail, capacity to relax, and self-subjection, not only to hard work, misfortune and defeat, but to criticism" (1993, p. 266). More pointedly, McIntosh notes the tension that exists between the individual as an athlete and the individual as person (or inhabitant of the real world) (1979, p. 117). Should a footballer punch an opponent, then he or she is judged as would be any other morally culpable person, and not simply as an athlete. The punch effectively marks the moment at which sport ceases, and reality is reimposed.

There are two positions here that may be untangled, and which in turn may throw light on the problematic relationship of sport and morality. On the one hand, McIntosh's example of the punch in football suggests that sport is ultimately subordinate to the morality of the wider society (or indeed, to avoid relativism, to universal moral standards). In 1995, the professional soccer player Duncan Ferguson was imprisoned for assault. The assault in question was against another professional player, and occurred in the normal run of a Scottish Premier Division match. The incident was judged to be so violent, by the Scottish Football Association, that it in effect violated the unreality of sport, and would thus not be adequately punished by sanctions merely internal to the sport (although Ferguson was sent off and was banned from playing in subsequent matches). The subordination of sport to a moral or legal reality may be taken further, to compromise the purposelessness of sport, by suggesting that its underlying purpose is one of moral education, or the rather vague and portentous "preparation for life." (Ferguson's punishment might therefore serve as a reprimand for the poor moral example he set.) Sport may therefore be justified, from this position, on the grounds that its practice necessarily entails the observance of universal moral (and legal) principles or values. Thus, again, the definition of sport would necessarily be evaluative.

On the other hand, Skillen explicitly rejects such reductionism. To emphasize the diversity of purposes and pleasures that exist within a sport serves to avoid the promotion of one purpose, even the moral purpose, above all others. To suggest that sport is a microcosm of society suggests, rather, that sport reflects the complexity, inconsistency, and contestability of social life. Sport is not then understood as being subordinated to a single set of moral values, but rather to present a unique series of situations and challenges in response to which moral characteristics may be tested, experienced, and expressed. (To act self-reflexively as a tennis player, mountaineer, or boxer may serve, in each case, to emphasize different facets of the ambient moral culture that are otherwise neglected or taken for granted.) It may thus be suggested that the very seriousness with which the playful and pointless objectives of sport are pursued allows sport to act as (among other things) a forum within which the complex, disputed, and seemingly contradictory moral concerns of everyday life are more or less safely articulated, challenged, and learned. In this light, what is perhaps most significant about the Ferguson case is the fact that the Football Association's decision to prosecute was widely criticized, and was taken to be indicative of its failure to control, or even

properly to understand the modern sport. Crucially, the boundary between sport and reality is therefore to be understood as continually under dispute, and the precise moral implications and interpretation of a given event within a sport are continually open to renegotiation, not least as a response to the shifting pressures and moral concerns that are current in the ambient (or real) world.

II. FAIR PLAY

A. A Moral Story about Golf

Many stories, both true and fictitious, are told about sport and its heroes and villains. The following intuits a commendable relationship between sport and the ethics of the real world.

In a U.S. Open golf championship in the 1920s, Bobby Jones (who was to become the great golfer of that period), played a shot into the rough. At that time, before the large galleries of the modern game, Jones went alone to his ball. He addressed the ball and, although he had not yet touched it, it moved. He had, therefore, by the rules of golf, incurred an extra stroke. No one except Jones had seen this happen. Jones, nonetheless, left the ball, and went to tell the match referee and his playing partner what had happened. He returned to the ball and continued with the round. As fate must have it, Jones lost the championship that year by a single stroke. When the press lauded Jones's honesty, he simply replied that they may as well praise a man for not robbing a bank.

B. Encoding Fair Play

1. Sporting Codes of Ethics

The idea that participation in sport presupposes a moral attitude, typically referred to as fair play (or sportsmanship/sportswomanship), is widely assumed. Thus, Baron de Coubertin, the founder of the modern Olympics, extolled the "serene and healthy philosophy" of the International Olympic Committee, that the "important thing in life is not victory, but struggle; the essential is not to have won but to have fought well." The struggle was presupposed to form a morally desirable character, typified by respect for one's opponents. The Declaration of Fair Play issued by the International Council of Sport and Physical Education in 1976, and endorsed by the IOC, thus includes the following sketch of the nature of fair play:

(a) honesty, straightforwardness and a firm and dignified attitude when others do not play fairly;
(b) respect for team colleagues;
(c) respect for opponents, given whether they are winning or losing, and with an awareness that an opponent is a necessary partner in sport, to whom one is bound by the companionship of sport;
(d) respect for the referee displayed through a positive attempt to collaborate with him at all times (cited in McIntosh, 1979, p. 127).

Such sentiments may be found in several other codes. The code of conduct issued by the English Schools Football Association details such points of fair play as, "[b]eat opponents by skill and not by unfair methods," "[d]o not appeal for throw-ins, off-sides, free kicks, etc.," and "[d]o not overact when your team scores a goal" (McIntosh, 1979, p. 120). In 1993, the Council of Europe published a code of sports ethics entitled "Fair play—the winning way." A brief review of this code is instructive, not least insofar as it strongly articulates the relationship between morality and sport in terms of moral education. While addressed to the coaching and participation of children and young people in sport, the code offers significant positive and negative definitions of what is expected in fair play, and thus what may lie at the kernel of an ethics of sport.

Fair play is taken to incorporate "the concept of friendship, respect for others and always playing in the right spirit," and is defined as "a way of thinking, not just a way of behaving." This concept thereby serves to justify sport itself, for fair sport does not merely promote "self-knowledge, self-expression and fulfilment," but "enriches society and the friendship between nations," and apart from leading to "enjoyment, good-health and well-being," certain sports "can help promote sensitivity to the environment." This suggests an intuition that what in the preceding section was theorized as the unreality or purposelessness of sport is being eroded by commercial and other pressures. (A key insight of the code is to highlight, as a moral issue, the influence that sports goods manufacturers may have on children and youths.) More precisely, perhaps, while the code does not go as far as to define sport evaluatively in terms of fair play, for it acknowledges and laments the possibility of unfair sport, it does rest heavily upon the assumption of an integral link between sport's playfulness and its morality.

The code seeks to defend the values of fair play (giving guidance and advice to governments and sports-related institutions as well as to individuals on the need to promote and reward fair play), and specifically to defend them against "the pressures in modern day society that appear to be undermining the traditional foundations of sport." The code's summary of these pressures provides an indication of what fair play is not. Thus, fair play is at odds with "cheating, gamesmanship, doping, violence (both physical and verbal), exploitation, unequal opportunities, excessive commercialisation and corruption." The implication, therefore, is that there is something inherently (and almost self-evidently) immoral, or at least potentially corrupting of morality, in all these pressures, and therefore that sport, ideally, should have nothing to do with them.

2. The Rules of Sport

Similar ideas are expressed within the rules of many sports. A brief review of some of these rules further serves to indicate the way in which the morality of sport is articulated by the athletes, or at least by their governing bodies. (The following examples are all taken from Pocock, T. (1995). *Official rules of sports and games, 1995–96*. London: Hamlyn).

In rugby union, "foul play" is defined as any action "which is contrary to the letter and spirit of the Game and includes obstruction, unfair play, misconduct, dangerous play, unsporting behaviour, retaliation and repeated infringements" (rule 26), with detailed descriptions of the first three of these actions being given. Typical examples of unfair play are noted, such as time wasting, violent play, and violation of the "spirit of good sportsmanship." Crucially, the emphasis may be seen to rest upon respecting a largely indefinable "spirit" that transcends the mere observance of rules.

In athletics (track and field), rule 22 covers misconduct, of which section (3) is the most telling: "Athletes or officials who shall knowingly conduct themselves in a manner which, in the opinion of the Council of the Federation, may bring discredit to the sport of athletics, shall be deemed to have committed an offence against the Federation, for which they shall be liable to suspension." Discredit, while receiving no further definition (for, as is necessarily the case for any quasi-legal code, its precise interpretation will depend upon its enactment, and thus any parallel case law), may be suggested to result from unfair play.

In boxing "fouls" are discussed principally under rule 19, and include passing reference to "unsportsmanlike" behavior. The details of this rule serve to reinforce the point made above, to the effect that the violent objective of boxing is constrained within an explicit moral discipline. A series of illegal punches, holds, and the failure to "break" are detailed, but so too are "[c]ompletely passive defence . . . intentionally failing to avoid a blow" (indicative of lack of courage), "[u]seless, aggressive, or offensive utterances during the round," aggressive behavior towards the referee, and "any other act the Referee may deem improper." Fouls may lead to cautions, warnings, and ultimately disqualification of the offender, and also the deduction of points by judges.

In association football (soccer), rule 12 covers "fouls and misconduct." A series of offenses are described, including striking, holding, and tripping an opponent, handling the ball, playing in a dangerous manner, intentionally obstructing an opponent and time wasting, that are to be penalized by either direct or indirect free kicks. In contrast, entering or leaving the game without the referee's permission, persistently infringing the laws of the game, showing dissent to the referee, or being "guilty of ungentlemanly conduct," will lead to a player being cautioned. (Two cautions in a single game lead to the player being sent off, with no substitution allowed.) Violent conduct, "serious foul play," and "foul or abusive language" are to be punished by sending off. Apart from the way in which this rule reflects ideas of fair play already encountered (e.g., in penalizing dissent and physical and verbal violence), two further points may be noted. First, a number of prima facie violent acts (such as striking and tripping) are given the same penalty as handling the ball (a direct free kick). While handling the ball clearly violates the meaning of association football, and may thus be described as a constitutive rule of soccer, morally it appears to be a relatively trivial offense alongside violent assaults (although it would be difficult to interpret intentional handling of the ball as anything other than a professional foul). These raise the problem, that can also be seen in ice hockey, that certain examples of foul play might be considered by players as a tactical option, if the benefits of the foul outweigh the costs of the resultant penalty (thus the professional foul). Secondly, it is noticeable that "ungentlemanly conduct" and indeed "violent conduct" are not defined by the rules. This partially closes the loophole of the professional foul, if it is generally agreed by the relevant officials that professional fouls are ungentlemanly. In effect, the spirit of the game is invoked, but acknowledging (perhaps realistically for a contact sport) that some violence is not simply within the letter of the law, but also within its spirit. Yet it also suggests that there is some appeal to moral standards that transcend those of the game itself, and that the precise interpretation of the spirit of the law depends (as was noted in a more extreme form with reference to the Ferguson case) upon the moral culture of the ambient (real) world.

By defining itself as a noncontact sport, basketball makes a distinction between "personal fouls," involving contact (rule 8), and "technical fouls" (rule 9) that do not involve contact. The sport recognizes that in practice a certain amount of contact is unavoidable, and should not be penalized (if it occurs through a bona fide attempt to play the ball, and that the opponent is not endangered). While accidental contact may still be penalized, an "unsportsmanlike" foul is defined in terms of contact that is committed deliberately (which again suggests that the intentional violation of a constitutive rule of the game typifies unfair play), but with advice being given to officials on the interpretation of such contact. Thus, the official is asked to judge whether the offender was making a legitimate attempt to play the ball, if there is excessive contact, or if there is hitting, holding, or pushing. Only in the second two cases is the contact judged unsporting. In contrast, technical fouls are concerned explicitly with unsporting conduct. Thus, article 51 (of rule 9) notes that "[b]oth teams are entitled to do their best to secure victory, but this must be done in a spirit of sportsmanship and fair play." Unfair play includes violence, disrespect to and disobedience of officials, offensive language, and time wasting. Crucially, emphasis is again placed upon the offender's intentions. Technical fouls cover not just players, but also coaches, substitutes, and team followers.

Golf and ice hockey provide a final contrast as to how sports define the scope of unfair play. The culture of golf places great emphasis on fair play. The rules of golf begin with "etiquette: courtesy on the course." While in part etiquette is concerned with the safety of players, the bulk of the regulations involve the respect that players should show to each other, expressed for example in order of play and the priority that one group of players may have over others, and the treatment of the course (e.g., replacing divots). What is perhaps most significant is that no penalty is indicated for the violation of the rules of etiquette. These are, seemingly, absolutes that cannot and will not be violated. The culture of ice hockey, in contrast, is typically taken in the ethics of sport literature to typify a high tolerance of aggressive behavior. The rules may be understood to reflect this, first in the detailed gradations of penalties allowed (centering on the temporary exclusion of a player from the ice), and second in detailing (as a major part of the "playing rules") various types of misconduct. The implication, similar to but perhaps more emphatic than that found in the rules of association football, is that, while foul play, including dissent, rough play, and "fisticuffs" is undesirable, it is inevitable, and is structurally incorporated within the rules of the sport.

Foul play is thus contained within the letter of the law, and the rules of ice hockey appear to make no reference to unfair, or unsportsmanlike play, or any equivalent concept. The sport therefore appears to accept certain forms of intentional violence and aggression as falling within its spirit. (As an aside, it may be noted that in 1975 the professional ice hockey player Dave Forbes, of the Boston Bruins, was brought to trial over an act of violence occurring during a game. A newspaper trial report commented that, "[p]erhaps the most revealing statement emerging from the trial was that of three of the seven men on the jury who announced that they would hold out 'a million years' against conviction" (cited in McIntosh, 1979, p. 103)).

As an initial conclusion to this review of the rules of sports, the degree of overlap that occurs in the interpretation of unfair play (so that themes of excessive violence, dissent, and abusive language recur, and fair play is set against unbridled competition and acknowledgment only of the letter of the rules) may be remarked. Yet so may the variation in interpretations. In part, the variation occurs because different sports necessarily have different rules that constitute their identity as sports (and the intentional violation of such rules is typically condemned). But sports also appear to have different moral cultures, which is to say that respect for the spirit of the law may involve wide substantive variations in the understanding of what is morally acceptable practice. A crucial problem then, and one to be addressed in the remainder of this section, is how calls for fair play can be and are justified in sport.

C. Acceptable and Unacceptable Advantages

1. The Unfairness of Sport

The emphasis placed upon fair play in sport may be understood against the background of the inherent unfairness of sport. It is seemingly in the nature of a sporting contest that it should be decided by skill. (One reason that justifies why a given activity, such as poker, is called a game rather than a sport may be the larger part that chance plays in determining its outcome.) For chance to spoil the athlete's opportunity to exercise his or her skill may therefore be considered unfair. To lose because one has been bested by one's more skilled or determined opponent is, clearly, part of the game. To lose because of an injury, or for a cricket team to fail to win because bad weather stopped play early, appears to fall outside of the meaning of the game.

Yet chance, in the form of events that lie outside the competitor's control and that may affect the result, cannot be eliminated from sport. Some sports incorporate specific moments of chance, as in the coin toss that determines the choice of ends or kickoff in football, and more crucially, the choice of batting or fielding first in cricket. It is, however, the unregulated chance events that provide the greatest test to an athlete's sense of fair play. In the Bobby Jones example cited above, the fact that Jones was not responsible for the ball's movement, and could have done nothing about it, might suggest that he had grounds for, or could at least have been excused for, playing on without reporting the incident. A round of golf is, however, full of such problems. The difference between a good shot and a bad one may be a matter of a few inches thanks to the gradient of the land, the positioning of a tree, or the extent of the rough. A good shot may be foiled by an unrepaired divot, or a poorly raked bunker. It may therefore be surmised that the reason that golf has such a demanding ethical code is not simply that it is one of the easiest sports at which to cheat, but also that the temptations to cheat, which is to say to compensate for the inherent arbitrariness of the game, are nearly overwhelming. Yet to "compensate" so would undermine the meaning of golf. More generally, this suggests that chance does not simply occur in sport in isolated and regulated moments (such as the coin toss), but is rather integral to many sports, so that the rules of the game acknowledge that while certain arbitrary or accidental events are to be eliminated from the game (hence, for example, the let in tennis) others (such as weather interrupting play in cricket) are part of the game, and thus something that athletes must deal with if they are to understand themselves in terms of that particular sport.

Apart from such accidents, a more thorough-going unfairness may appear to lie in the mere fact that some people are simply better than others at a particular (or indeed at any) sport. More precisely, sport does not obviously reward effort. However hard I practice and train, I will never become a county-class cricketer. Individual humans thus have inherent advantages and disadvantages that may be due to physiology, genetics, or environmental factors. (Great downhill skiers do not typically come from the Netherlands.) In the ethics of sport, this problem has been articulated (for example Gardner, Robert. (1995, originally 1989). On performance-enhancing substances and the unfair advantages argument. In William J. Morgan and Klaus Meier (Eds.), *Philosophic inquiry in sport* (2nd ed.). Champaign IL: Human Kinetics.) in terms of a distinction between acceptable and unacceptable unfair advantages. Involvement in most sports makes sense only if the athletes are testing biologically and culturally inherited, but also trained and practiced, abilities against each other. A crucial element in the ethos of fair play is therefore the acceptance of defeat, within the rules of the game. Thus, a player has an acceptable unfair advantage over her opponent if she is able to beat him according to the rules, whether victory is due to superior genetic endowment or to a lucky bounce. The advantage is unacceptable if the rules are bent or disregarded. Again, the rules of a particular sport may determine the precise scope of an acceptable advantage. Handicap systems in golf and polo allow inherently ill-matched opponents to compete on more or less equal terms, and boxing weight divisions keep ill-matched opponents apart. The Council of Europe's code of ethics, generalizing this point, emphasizes the need for "the structure of competition" to acknowledge "the special requirements of the young and growing child," and to provide "the opportunity for graded levels of involvement."

This still leaves an unresolved, and perhaps irresolvable, tension in sporting practice. On the one hand, the ethos of fair play suggests that each individual may find, and should be encouraged to find, his or her own level and source of enjoyment in sport. You may not be good enough to play county cricket, but there is always the village team. On the other hand, the understanding of sport as self-discovery may simply lead the athlete to discover, despite committed training, that he or she is not very good. While the ethos of fair play incorporates this in terms of articulating attitudes towards defeat, this is inadequate when the defeat may entail the discovery that you are not, or cannot become, the person that you long to be or imagine yourself to be. The commitment to the sport becomes simply wasted time. There is a bitter, and perhaps unpalatable, irony in being the best player in the minor league.

2. Cheating

Cheating in sport has been defined, by Gunther Lüschen, as "the act through which the manifestly or latently agreed upon conditions for winning such a contest are changed in favour of one side" (Lüschen, Gunther. (1976). Cheating in sport. In D. Landers (Ed.), *Social problems in athletics*. Urbana: University of Illinois Press, p. 67). To this may be added the relevance of intention on the part of the cheat. Cheating may therefore be summarized as the intentional taking of an unacceptable unfair advantage over an opponent. The precise nature of this advantage may be illustrated by comparing two forms of deception common in sport.

It is, on the one hand, acceptable to feign a pass in rugby, deceiving one's opponent into thinking that you will pass when you intend to run with the ball. On the other hand, it is unacceptable to feign injury in order to win a penalty, or to gain an unofficial time-out. The first example of deceit does not violate either the letter or the spirit of the laws of the sport, and the nature of the deceit is exposed as soon as the move has been made. The feigning of the injury is not, however, intended to be discovered. Thus does it fall outside of the spirit, and possibly the letter of the rules. Yet this may still raise doubts associated with the amoral account of sport. Certain sports, within their own rules and within their own code of fair play, seemingly encourage such prima facie immoral activities as deceiving another human being.

A distinction may be made between overt and covert cheating. The player feigning an injury is being covert, in that he or she does not intend to be found out. The player who commits a professional foul is acting overtly, insofar as he or she accepts the resultant penalty as being preferable to the run of play without the foul. Committing a professional foul may thus become part of the strategy of the particular game. As has been suggested in reference to the rules of soccer and ice hockey, it is conceivable that the culture of a sport could tolerate professional fouls, and Lüschen's definition of cheating refers to the "manifestly or latently agreed upon conditions" of the sport. This in turn raises the possibility that the most appropriate framework for understanding the ethics of sport may be a libertarian one. In effect, sport would then be understood as a contract into which players (and possibly officials and spectators) freely enter. If it is generally agreed that professional fouls, or other acts of prima facie unfair play are to be tolerated, then, if the autonomy of the participants is to be respected, this should not receive moral condemnation. A professional foul in a sport intolerant of such practice would still be cheating, and would be unfair, not the least insofar as it prevents opponents from freely using and benefiting from their skills. Yet, if the sport is tolerant of such practice, and precisely because it is done openly, the professional foul is not cheating. Perhaps the key issue here is not whether intolerance is universal, but rather how the supposed agreement on tolerance or intolerance is achieved.

The moral status of cheating may vary depending on the context of the sport and particular game. In refusing to cheat at golf, Bobby Jones was responsible ultimately only to himself. A distinction that Skillen draws from the ancient Olympics, between a prize and a reward, is relevant here (1993, pp. 350, 362). A reward was the material gain from winning, while the prize was the sacred honor of victory. As Skillen observes, a cheat, conceptually, can only win a reward (and such "winning" is akin to receiving an award because of mistaken identity). To win the prize one must compete according to the rules. Yet the athlete may have responsibilities to others than him- or herself. Even in the case of individual (as against team) competitions a responsibility to the sport may be considered. This is implied by the reference in the athletics code to bringing "discredit on the sport." While this may suggest that athletes should conduct themselves in a manner that conforms with the moral expectations of the ambient world, it may also serve to articulate something of the necessity to respect what it means to compete within this particular sport.

In team sports, the individual has responsibilities to the team, its coaches, and supporters. (Here, obligations to the sport may entail recognizing that one must respect not simply the wishes of one's own fans, but also of all followers of the sport. One's own fans may applaud a professional foul, while the neutral may simply see it as spoiling the game.) The following examples may highlight the ambiguities here. First, a soccer player accidentally handles the ball while playing in the middle of the pitch. If unnoticed by the officials, should he or she be expected to acknowledge this infringement? Second, the accidental handball occurs in the player's own penalty area, so that admission of the fault would incur a penalty kick and an almost certain goal. Strictly, in both cases the rules of the game have been knowingly violated, and yet, especially in the second case, admission may intuitively be regarded as at best naive. Again, the particular moral culture of the sport may be invoked, with different sports placing greater or lesser emphasis upon the players' honesty. The very presence of officials, for example, may suggest that one plays to the whistle, which is to say that if you accept the infringements that they do see (or imagine that they see), then equally you can get away with the ones that they do not. The precise nature of cheating may therefore be highly contestable.

3. Competition and Winning at All Costs

Sport may be regarded as an inherently immoral activity insofar as it entails competition. Competition here may be understood in terms of two agents (individuals or teams) pursuing an objective, knowing that its achievement by one will be at the expense of the other. Such an activity or manner of proceeding may be argued to entail working against others selfishly, and precisely insofar as selfishness is typically understood as the an-

tithesis of a morally desirable characteristic, competition, or any activity that encourages or condones competition, is itself morally undesirable. Further support to such conclusions may be given through consideration of the effect that failure has upon the competitor. This is a particularly important theme in the philosophy of education, and thus in consideration of the place of compulsory competitive sports within the school curriculum. The child who has no talent or interest in sport, and who is thus inevitably the loser in competition, suffers not simply the self-discovery that he or she is a sporting failure (which may not, on its own, be as damaging as the same discovery is to the dedicated athlete), but rather the social stigma that may accompany its public revelation in a competitively oriented social environment. In addition, a frequent theme within the sociology of sport (and particularly in its Marxist orientations) is that competition in sport reflects and ideologically serves to reproduce the competition that is characteristic of a capitalist economy. If competition in capitalism serves to alienate humanity from its true nature and inhibit the development of its true potential, so too will competition in sport.

In reply, a distinction is made between winning as one objective or pleasure of sport among others, and a mentality of "winning at all costs." The latter state of mind was famously attributed to the American football coach Vince Lombardi: "Winning is not the main thing, it's the only thing." The various expressions of fair play that have been reviewed pit themselves against this extreme (not least by emphasizing the taking part, and the way in which one plays). By promoting victory as the dominant goal of participation, at best one plays to the letter of the rules, disregarding the spirit, and even if one does not cheat (so that one still seeks to win the prize and not simply the reward), one proceeds with no obvious or necessary respect for one's opponents. Professional fouls, including violence and intimidation against opponents to prevent the exercise of their (superior) skills, would be permissible, albeit that one would expect to be penalized. Genuinely sporting competition (to use "sporting" in an evaluative sense that embraces fair play) is therefore argued to rest upon a bedrock of values that place victory alongside other goals (such as personal achievement, self-discovery and development), and that promote not merely team spirit and the good of cooperation within the team, but also respect for opponents. In this respect, Kretchmer (Kretchmer, R. Scott. (1983). Ethics and sport: An overview. *Journal of the Philosophy of Sport, 10*, 21–32) analyzes the nature of sport in terms of both the test that it provides, and the contest (understood through the Latin etymology of *con* and *testara*) of "witnessing together." A sporting contest is thus seen to entail a sharing of standards of excellence, and a mutual recognition that all competitors can be measured against the same standard. (It is noticeable that a custom remains in some sports for the teams to cheer their opponents, win or lose, at the end of a game. Equally, in professional association and American football the excessive or intimidatory celebration of a score can and increasingly will be penalized. The sharing of respect that is logically entailed in the contest is thereby kept somewhere to the fore of the competitors' consciousness.)

D. The Universality of Fair Play

The discussion above has frequently served to expose a tension in the understanding of sporting ethics. On the one hand, the appeal to fair play may be seen to articulate moral standards that do not merely transcend any individual sport, but typify morally desirable characteristics as such. On the other hand, the diversity of practices allowed in sports, linked to suspension of the moral rules of the ambient world during a sporting contest, allows sport to be interpreted as an essentially amoral activity, even if the participants within certain sports may choose to respect more widely accepted and more demanding moral standards.

It has been suggested above that the amoral view of sport might be interpreted in libertarian terms. At the core of such an ethics would be the presupposition of inalienable individual freedom. If competent adults consent, in full knowledge of the risks involved, to participate in violent sport (such as boxing), or to tolerate professional fouls in the course of play, that is merely an exercise of their rights. Any concept of fair play would be unnecessary in such an approach, for there would need to be no need to respect moral values that had not previously been agreed upon by the participants. Such an approach could still, however, proscribe certain activities. It may be held that certain Lockean rights, such as the right to life, are inalienable, so that not only can others not infringe upon them, but also the agent him- or herself is not free to relinquish them, and further that the agent needs to be protected against any inclinations so to do. The agent could not then be allowed to enter competitions with high risks of mortality (such as dueling). The exact point at which potentially hazardous sporting activities would begin to alienate such rights is, inevitably, debatable.

A more liberal view of human rights (open for example to positive welfare rights as well as to negative rights) may also be instructive. (Indeed, it has been noted that John Rawls's definition of society, as a cooperative venture for mutual advantage, may be taken to characterize important aspects of sport itself.) Thus, the reference in the Council of Europe code of fair play to "the rights of children and young people to participate and enjoy their involvement in sport" may readily be cashed out in terms of a more sophisticated rights theory. If rights are understood as protecting individuals' access to the resources and freedoms that allow them to develop valuable capacities that are characteristic of what it is to be human, then, to the degree that sport, or certain kinds of sport do this, a right to sport may be justified, as may obligations placed upon governments and others to protect and resource this right. Further implications of such an approach may also be sketched.

First, the issue of forced participation in sport against the agent's will might be clarified. A right to participate in sport does not, prima facie, appear to have the same status as a right to education (although forced participation in sport may typically occur within schools), for it is not clear that a failure to take advantage of sport by a child would damage his or her competence as an adult in the same way that failure to participate in other forms of education would. The Council of Europe code notes that "undue pressure" should not be placed upon a child which might impinge upon his or her rights "to choose to participate." The code emphasizes the pressure placed by parents and coaches on young, and potentially highly talented, competitors. A rights theory may therefore serve to articulate the grounds upon which a child or young person has the right to resist parental and other pressure.

Second, other relationships within sport may be considered in terms of rights and obligations. The competitor, especially in more highly organized competitions, acts not simply in relationship to other competitors, but also in relation to officials, coaches, and spectators. A case may indicate the issues involved. In 1996, in the United Kingdom, a rugby player who had his neck broken in a scrum (in a game in 1991, when the player was 17), sued the referee for damages on the grounds that the referee had failed in his duty to control the level of violence and aggression in the match, thereby subjecting the players to unnecessary risk. Regardless of the referee's legal liability, consideration of the officials' moral responsibility to players, and the precise nature of what would constitute an acceptable level of risk (in a violent contact sport) is instructive. On the one hand, it may be argued that all those who freely participate in rugby should be aware that they are exposing themselves to a small but nonetheless significant risk of serious injury. To be so injured is part of the (at times grave) unfairness of sport. On the other hand, it may be argued that the players implicitly contract with officials (and indeed with each other) to minimize this risk. Fair play might therefore be explicated in terms of the obligations (and correspondent rights) that participants must have to each other, not simply in order to facilitate a particular form of sport, but also to protect basic human capacities (such as health and mobility). In this particular case, the court found in favor of the player.

In summary, while liberalism and especially libertarianism superficially underpin an amoral approach, stressing the unreality of sport, these perspectives may, in fact, be appealed to in order to set limits upon the degree to which sport can suspend the moral values and principles of the ambient society. Sport is only then free within a framework of human rights. The scope of morally legitimate sporting activity depends upon the scope of the rights to which the theorist appeals.

An alternative approach to the justification of a universal concept of fair play comes from the application of virtue theory, and appeals to the definition of sport as practice outlined above. MacIntyre defines "virtue" thus:

> A virtue is an acquired human quality the possession and exercise of which tends to enable us to achieve those goals which are internal to practices and lack of which effectively prevents us from achieving any such goals (1981, p. 178).

Strictly, MacIntyre presents this as a "partial and tentative definition," but it serves to indicate the possibility that a virtue encodes the behavior and discipline that is necessary to achieve the objectives (and more specifically the prizes rather than the rewards) of a particular sport. Yet as such, this could still leave sport isolated from the rest of society. The aggression needed to succeed in ice hockey is seemingly a virtue at odds with those of most other social practices. MacIntyre in fact sees such fragmentation as a lamentable result of modern society, and his more exacting definition of virtue seeks a remedy.

> [A] virtue is not a disposition that makes for success only in some one particular type of situation. What are spoken of as the virtues of a good committee man or of a good administrator ... are professional skills professionally deployed in those situations where they can be effective, not virtues. Someone who genuinely possesses a virtue can be expected to manifest it in very different

types of situation.... Hector exhibited one and the same courage in his parting from Andromache and on the battlefield with Achilles (1981, p. 191).

A further appeal to the life of Bobby Jones may illustrate MacIntyre's definition as well as, if not better than, that of Hector. In later life Jones was afflicted by a muscular disease that eventually confined him to a wheelchair. He commented on his life with the disease, in contrast to his healthy and vigorous youth: "You play the ball where it lies."

McIntosh makes a point similar to MacIntyre's, when he separates two different contexts for the use of the word "good" in connection with a footballer. A good footballer may be such by virtue of his or her control of technical skills. In this case, "[w]e experience admiration but we do not aspire to his level of skill and only mildly identify with him." Conversely, if the footballer commits no fouls, or is never booked during his or her career, we may commend this behavior as good, and "we are commending acts within that class of acts showing whether or not a person is a good person, that is, a 'person to try to become like'" (McIntosh, 1979, p. 117). Fair play may therefore be suggested to be the manifestation of virtues applicable outside the special and unreal world of sport, and indeed implies that fair play should be of interest to all, regardless of their interest in this or any sport. All should admire Jones's sportsmanship in a fundamentally different way to which the golfer might admire the efficiency of his swing.

MacIntyre argues that certain virtues, such as courage, honesty, and friendship, will be common to all practices, and Arnold indicates that virtues of impartiality and respect for others are inherent to any sporting practice (p. 250). Yet MacIntyre acknowledges that these general concepts will be interpreted differently in different cultures. The exact scope, for example, of obligations to tell the truth, and the nature of the trade-off between truth-telling and sensitivity to anothers' feelings may vary historically and culturally. In relation to the virtues of sport, this raises the possibility that, even if fair play can be cashed out into Arnold's concepts of impartiality and respect, and that these may be broadly applied to all sports, different sports will interpret these terms differently and, more significantly, the historical development of sport will manifest an unfolding of (although by no means a uniform progress towards) contemporary concepts of fair play. Skillen demonstrates the ancient Greek sporting ethos did not typically entail anything but contempt for losers. Respect for losers, dependent upon the manner in which they competed, was more typical of Roman attitudes towards sport (1993, pp. 349, 357). McIntosh notes that the introduction of off-side rules into many sports served to transform "violent and brutish sports into games of grace and skill" (1979, p. 83). In effect, the introduction of off-side rules suggests a reinterpretation of the meaning of a sport, or more precisely, a recognition of the potential meaning that a sport may have. This suggests that "fair play" is a historically and culturally dynamic concept, dependent upon the interrelationship between sport and the ambient society, and the consequent interpretation and reinterpretation of what it means to be an athlete in general, and what it means to participate in a certain form of sport.

To return to the Bobby Jones stories, and so to indicate how this interrelationship may be understood, it may be suggested that morality is not merely manifest in the playing of a sport, but, possibly more significantly, is articulated in the stories that are told about it. Stories about Bobby Jones allow us to articulate ideas of fair play and, if scrutinized, a form of stoicism in his tolerance of morbidity. The stories are heart warming, but also nostalgic. They hark back to a golden age when athletes were uncorrupted by the temptations of modern life. (It is noticeable that a similar nostalgia is reflected in the Council of Europe code of fair play.) Yet moral tales of sport can also be more troubled. Contemporary, but equally valuable stories, are told about the problems of ambitious parents (and thus the values of a "genuine" childhood), or of struggles with drug addiction and other burdens of premature fame and glory. It may further be suggested that modern notions of fair play are in large part articulated in Victorian fiction (including Hughes's *Tom Brown's Schooldays*, and Horace Annesley Vachell's *The Hill* and *John Verney* (see Skillen, 1993, pp. 358f)), and in the use of sporting metaphor. During the Battle of the Somme, Captain D. P. Nevill enacted the metaphor by dribbling a football as he led his Surrey regiment towards the German trenches. He was killed in the action. The *Daily Mail* commented:

The fear of Death before them is but an empty name

True to the land that bore them the Surreys play the game.

It is not incidental (although perhaps ironic given standards of behavior in professional tennis) that Kipling's couplet,

If you can meet with Triumph and Disaster

And treat those two impostors just the same,

is inscribed over the entrance to the Centre Court at Wimbledon. ("If . . ." expresses much that typifies the idea of fair play.) Stories, be they true (as newspaper reports or match commentaries) or fictitious (including today movies such as *Chariots of Fire* and *Bull Durham*) may not be understood as a substitute for moral theory, but may provide a valuable focus of folk morality. It is perhaps in such story telling that sport's status as a microcosm of society has its full significance. The point is, then, not that fair play is simply more or less well manifest by an athlete's conduct, but rather that sport provides a basic material, through which the community may debate and articulate its moral values and moral concerns.

III. THREE MORAL ISSUES

A. Discrimination and Prejudice

Competitive sport, by its very nature, is discriminatory. A contest discriminates between competitors according to their ability (and perhaps luck) in being able to achieve the goals of the sport according to its exacting rules. (If the role of luck is to be removed from this account, then it may be suggested that competitive sports *in the long run* discriminate between competitors according to their ability, which is to say that, in a series of encounters the more talented player will win more frequently.) To discriminate between competitors because of factors or characteristics other than those demanded by the nature and meaning of the sport, is unfair. Thus, it has already been noted above that, played fairly, a social superior should not expect to be able to beat his or her social inferior, simply on the grounds of that extrasporting inequality. Arnold argues that an activity cannot properly be called a sport (at least according to his evaluative definition) if unjustifiable forms of discrimination are integral to it, for that would entail a failure on the part of its participants to respect each other simply as competitors. An activity that discriminates or segregates, say, White from Black competitors would therefore be contrary to the spirit and meaning of sport.

This case is, in fact, harder to argue than at first appears. While it may appear intuitively self-evident that to vary the rules for players of different racial, ethnic, or national background would be inherently unfair, most sports at least separate players according to gender, and if males and females are allowed to compete together, the rules are different for each. The tee for women golfers is, for example, set in front of the men's, shortening the length of the course for women. Gender discrimination is thus incorporated, explicitly, into the rules of sports. Age discrimination may also be applied, so that a 30-year-old cannot compete in an under-21 competition (although a 20-year-old could compete in adult competitions). In track events, handicaps (in terms of the distance behind or in front of the official start line one actually starts) can be introduced, according to age, to allow veterans to compete against younger athletes. Weight discrimination is applied in boxing, wrestling and various martial arts.

Discriminations in terms of age, weight, and gender can be justified in terms of bringing about a fairer contest. The exact meaning of fairness here is not clear-cut, for, as has already been argued, sport is inherently unfair. The handicaps, classifications and rule modifications serve to eliminate some of the inherent differences that exist between the competitors (although to eliminate all would make a nonsense of the competition, or at least turn the real sporting task into that of the handicapper). Boxing therefore entails that it is fairer to match competitors of more or less equal weights. Yet boxers are not classified according to their reach (when an extended reach will give a boxer a significant advantage over an opponent), let alone punching power or stamina. Similarly, it is not inconceivable that a contest akin to boxing could be devised, in which the power of the heavyweight is matched against the agility of the welterweight. While having different strengths and skills, these could be tailored, through appropriate rules, to balance each other, resulting in a "fair" contest. The privileging of weight over other physical characteristics, in the name of fairness, may thus be considered arbitrary, or more precisely, be part of the constitutive rules that determine what it means to be a boxer. (The separation of boxers by weight is justified in the same way as is the existence of the net in tennis.)

The handicaps introduced to allow different age groups or genders to compete together is, possibly, more clear-cut. The implication of the shorter women's golf course is that, for men not to win all golfing encounters with women, the women must be given some advantage that compensates for their inherent inferiority in achieving the objectives of golf. The competition is only worth playing if there is some doubt about the outcome, and for that doubt to be realized, the compensatory advantage must be in place. In the case of track athletics, statistical classifications can readily be drawn up that indicate the times that athletes of different ages and genders can be expected to obtain over a given distance. Such statistical differences can then be used in handicapping. The most obvious difference between golf and athletics is merely that athletics makes a more obvious use of scientific data. Underlying both is the assumption that there are differences in sporting ability

that are grounded in the natural (biological) constitution, not of the individual athlete, but rather of a normal or average human being. The individual in a handicap race therefore does not merely compete against his or her other individual competitors, but also against the statistical average that determined the handicap. The winner is better than that average. Discrimination is therefore allowed if it compensates for certain natural differences. (One might speculate on the possibility of cultural and environmental handicaps. For example, in order to allow them to compete on equal terms, could not say 20 seconds be deducted from the time of any Dutch skier in a grand slalom?) Racial discrimination is sport is therefore rejected on the grounds that there are no natural differences between racial, ethnic, or national groups that would require compensation in any sport.

The appeal to natural differences is problematic only insofar as it serves to conceal cultural differences. At its crudest, a spurious appeal to supposed biological facts may justify the exclusion of women from certain sports (including endurance and contact sports.) More subtly, it may be argued that if the male domination of a sport serves to deter female entrants to it, then any statistical data derived from the sample of women who did compete might be distorted. The data are derived from a smaller sample, and possibly potentially excellent athletes have not taken up the sport, so that either the average or best achievements are artificially lower. (The female competitor would, then, be competing against a more lenient statistical average than would the male.) The relative improvement in women's marathon running relative to men's may, for example, be due simply to increased female participation.

This interrelationship between biological and cultural factors may also be seen in the channeling of athletes of different ethnic and racial backgrounds into different sports, or into different specializations within a sport. Overt acts of discrimination, such as the barring of players of specific ethnic groups from certain sports does not occur in channeling. Rather, the talented athlete is more subtly directed towards activities that are regarded as more suitable for them, or more precisely to which they are perceived as being more naturally suited. Thus, the predominance of White quarterbacks in American football (set against the predominance of Black players in most other positions) is indicative of the stereotyping that underpins channeling, in the (possibly implicit and unacknowledged) presupposition that only Whites could take on tactical and leadership roles.

In summary, while the respect of natural difference in sport can lead to "fairer" contests, albeit within the arbitrary and unreal parameters of a given sport, an unreflective appeal to natural difference can conceal (and indeed, through the promotion of paradoxically successful role models, perpetuate) stereotyping and the resultant, unjustifiable discrimination.

B. The Commercialism of Sport

Commercialism is frequently presented, in the ethics of sport literature and elsewhere, as a threat to fair play and the true ethos of sport. Commercial influence serves to subordinate the true purposelessness of sport to the external and alien goal of profit maximization. This issue may be explored by theorizing it in terms of the influence of the spectator on sport. Skillen, through reference to ancient Greek and Roman sport, draws a distinction between:

> the background necessary for an audience of lesser mortals to constitute a champion's glory and the champion's being there only because there are people to applaud and financially maintain him. Similarly, there is a huge distinction between the privilege that an audience feels in being present at a great contest and the sense a crowd might have that it has a right to be impressed and entertained (1993, p. 355).

The implication here is that the commercialism of sport entails a shift in the status of the spectator, from one privileged to witness sporting prowess, to one who has an economic right, not merely to witness the event, but to be entertained by it. Robert Nozick's illustration of his libertarian philosophy, in *Anarchy, State and Utopia* (1974. Oxford: Blackwell, pp. 161–163), whereby the basketball player Wilt Chamberlain is imagined to contract freely for his cut of the gate money, beautifully and perhaps unwittingly expresses much of the issue of the commercialization of sport. Chamberlain prospers because he has a talent to entertain. But, to reward the athlete only for entertaining is to subordinate the complex and multileveled pleasures of sport to a single objective. It cannot be denied that a number of sports have changed under the influence of commercial and especially television influence. (The pace of professional American football is dictated by the need for commercial breaks in television coverage, and in the United Kingdom, rugby league football has been moved from a winter to a summer sport for the sake of television coverage.) Such changes are problematic if they serve to restrict the inherent and inherited richness of the sport, for example, by placing a premium on obvious spectacle rather than subtleties that require dedication or, more precisely, require disciplined subordination to the authority of the practice, even on the part of the spectator, to understand and appreciate. (The rules of first-class cricket constitute a game that is played over 3, 4, or 5 days. Such a game has scope for many fine nuances of physical, psychological, and tactical fortune. The rules of one-day cricket constitute a short and admittedly exciting game, that privilege only certain, rather obvious, characteristics of the longer game.)

The impact of commercialization on a sport can be seen in the recent professionalization of rugby union. By allowing not merely payments to be made to players, but also by giving increased scope for the marketing and television coverage of the game, and thus for making significant profits, the very nature of the rugby club is changed. An amateur club typically had a large membership of active players, who would have the opportunity to play at a level appropriate to their skill (and age). In principle, all could aspire to play in the first team. The initial impact of professionalization has been to separate the professional first team from the rest of the club. Not only do amateur players then find themselves increasingly denied access to the first team, but as the focus of the club increasingly shifts to the commercial exploitation of that first team, the club's non-profit-making amateur and youth teams are restricted or shed altogether. In effect, the professionalization of rugby union suggests the initial stages of the replacement of the active membership of an amateur club by the passive supporters of a professional club. The relationship of the club to its supporters is thereby changed fundamentally.

The above suggests that to understand the relationship between athlete and spectator as one of economic rights and obligations is to take too narrow a view of sport. The athlete also represents the spectator, or more precisely, a given athlete or team can represent a given community. The meaning of "representation" here is important, and the nature of representation will change under the impact of commercialization. Even in ancient Greece, an athlete was not required to represent only the city in which he was born. (Thus Astylus changed nationalities for the 480 Olympics.) Rather, as Skillen argues (p. 354), the athlete represents the community insofar as the community identifies with that athlete, and the athlete thereby becomes part of the self-understanding of the community. The athlete represents the community if the community acknowledges that representation. The nineteenth-century English public schools possibly provide the ground for modern relationships between athlete and community, in terms not merely of interschool but also of interhouse competitions. The success or failure of the individual constitutes the pride or shame of the community as a whole. The example of rugby union however suggests a further subtlety. In an amateur club the first team represents a wider and active membership, insofar as it was constituted out of the elite of that membership, and again, in principle, all members were elegible to compete for that elite status. (Similarly, the public-school house team represented the wider group as an elite.) In the professional club, while the same associations of pride and shame may hold, the team is no longer simply the sporting elite of that community, and by association, the individual supporter has an increased freedom of choice in the team that she takes as her representative. (Within the public school, the member of Greville house was never free to support the Brooke house XV.) The sense in which any given individual is represented by the professional team is thus less tightly defined. While the irrevocable nature of a supporter's psychological commitment to a particular team should not be underestimated, the associations that motivate one's commitment to a particular professional team may be diverse and elusive. The bonds of the school house, club membership and even communal or geographical association dissipate into something more akin to brand loyalty.

C. Performance-Enhancing Drugs

The Council of Europe code of fair play assumes, as self-evident, that "doping" is contrary to fair play, presumably independently of whether or not drug taking is explicitly prohibited by the rules of a particular sport. The moral problem of the use of performance-enhancing drugs is not that of whether or not individual athletes should take drugs when prohibited by the sport, for such an activity, if carried out covertly, is a straightforward case of cheating as intentional rule breaking, and if carried out overtly falls into the same category as the professional foul. (The penalties for drug taking in professional cycling may be considered to be relatively slight, allowing the cyclist to balance the risk of being found out and penalized against the benefits of drug use.) The issue of drug use is then whether or not the rules of a sport could, coherently, permit the open and general use of performance-enhancing drugs.

An important argument in favor of the use of performance-enhancing drugs appeals to a libertarian framework. Here, emphasis falls upon the risk that drug taking poses to the athlete. If the libertarian assumption that sport is constituted as a free contract between its participants, then, should the participants openly and freely choose to accept the risk of drug taking, then to prevent them is to deny their autonomy. The risks of many existing sports may be cited in parallel, including those of boxing, motor sport, rugby and American football, and cricket. One cannot choose to play cricket, for example, and exempt oneself from the risk of being hit by a fast moving and very hard ball. So, should the majority consent to it, the individual should not be able to choose to engage in body building, athletics or professional cycling, and not take the risk associated with the drug use necessary to compete at a reasonable level. (An important corollary of this argument suggests that, should drug taking be legalized in sport, pharmaceutical research can be openly carried out on developing genuinely effective, and as far as possible safe, drugs, and that these drugs would be administered under well-regulated regimes. This is to suggest that current levels of risk are in a significant part due to the illegality of drug use, not drug use as such.) In summary, the libertarian argument presents the individual athlete with a trade-off, between the (diverse) pleasures of the sport, and the risks inherent in drug use. Drug use would thus become contrary to the spirit of the sport at the point that the risks outweighed the pleasures (presumably for the majority of the potential participants).

The weakest argument posed against the use of drugs holds that they are, in some more or less well-articulated sense, against nature. This presupposes that sport is in some way inherently natural, or more plausibly (given the constitution of sports through cultural rules) that sport is a test of some inherent and biologically given capacity of the participants. The use of drugs would disrupt this innate capacity, allowing the athlete to perform beyond his or her natural potential. To be consistent, this argument would entail that all forms of coaching should also be banned, as would the application of the nutritional sciences, and possibly any medical intervention in the case of injury and illness. (It may be noted that an important theme of the movie *Chariots of Fire* was indeed the propriety of a gentleman athlete, Harold Abrahams, employing a professional coach to improve his performance.) In summary, while sport may test natural talent, that talent is honed, at least in the case of professional athletes but also for many amateur or occasional athletes, by scientifically informed training and coaching methods. The question then to be posed, is why should pharmaceutical sciences be excluded from, or prescribed in, the contribution they could make to this refinement?

The argument can be reworked, to suggest that sport tests character, not chemistry. Here the emphasis need not fall on innate talent alone, but may also stress the virtues that are displayed and refined in exercising and developing a sporting talent. The suggestion here is that the use of performance-enhancing drugs reduces the scope for character development, insofar as success is achieved with less effort and commitment. In this argument, and indeed in the previous one, the reply needs to recognize that a case is being made for all athletes to use drugs (or at least for all athletes to be free to use drugs). While it might be argued that effective performance-enhancing drugs could raise the capacity of a mediocre athlete to those of an elite athlete at relatively little effort (and so distort the order of nature, or disrupt one parameter of the unfairness that is essential to the meaning of the sport), if all athletes are taking drugs then, all other things being equal, the standards of the sport as a whole will rise, and the mediocre athlete will have to work as hard as before to compete with the elite. What might, conceivably, turn out to be unequal, is the responsiveness of individual athletes to drugs. The mediocre might benefit more than the elite. Yet even this is not obviously an unacceptable unfair advantage, for in this case, drug taking will have served to significantly change the nature of the sport and its inherent challenges (just as, for example, the allowing of metal shafted clubs did in golf, and the introduction of an off-side rule or a penalty kick did in soccer). In effect, if drug taking did not leave the competitors in the same order of success as before, then the issue of permitting drug use must be understood as a matter of whether or not to change the meaning of the sport.

Sports are historically dynamic practices, and so change is not to be resisted simply because it is change. Yet change might be resisted if it is considered to impoverish rather than to enrich the practice. If a suggested rule change were perceived to enrich the sport, by giving new scope to the development and exercise of human faculties and to the human body, then it is to be encouraged, for this (as MacIntyre argues) enriches the ambient community. For example, it might be argued that the use of drugs in body building may have served, positively, to redefine and challenge current understandings of the human body and, not least, stereotypes of bodily gender identity. If the change narrowed the focus of the sport, restricting the range of pleasures that its participants can enjoy, for example by placing undue emphasis on winning rather than competing and on spectacle rather than on participation, or even by transferring the skillful, strategic, and creative elements of the sport away from the players and to physiotherapists, nutritionists, and other technicians, then the change is to be resisted.

Bibliography

The material available on the philosophy and ethics of sport is relatively limited. The Philosophic Society for the Study of Sport has its own journal, *The Journal of the Philosophy of Sport,* and this is the major source of original articles in the field. Another important source of original material are journals published within the philosophy of education. Sadly, few essays on sport occur in mainstream philosophical journals.

Hyland, Drew A. (1990). *Philosophy of sport.* New York: Paragon Press.

Lapchick, Richard E. (Ed.) (1996). *Sport in society: Equal opportunity or business as usual.* London: Sage.

McIntosh, Peter. (1979). *Fair play: Ethics in sport and education.* London: Heinemann.

Morgan, William J., & Meier, Klaus (Eds.). (1988). *Philosophic inquiry in sport* (1st ed.). Champaign IL: Human Kinetics. (This is not completely superseded by the second edition.)

Morgan, William J., & Meier, Klaus (Eds.). (1995). *Philosophic inquiry in sport* (2nd ed.). Champaign IL: Human Kinetics. (The obvious starting point for any serious study of the philosophy of sport.)

Osterhoudt, Robert (Ed.). (1973). *The philosophy of sport: A collection of essays.* Springfield IL: Charles C. Thomas.

Simon, Robert L. (1985). *Sport and social values.* Englewood Cliffs, NJ: Prentice-Hall.

Suits, Bernard. (1978). *The grasshopper: Games, life and utopia,* Toronto: University of Toronto Press.

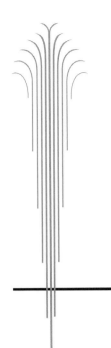

STEWARDSHIP

A. Carl Leopold
Boyce Thompson Institute for Plant Research at Cornell University

GLOSSARY

anthropocentrism A point of view focused strictly on human needs and preferences.

biosphere The entire biological system of the earth.

biotic community The assembled array of all living organisms in a given community, including their interactions.

chemical ecology The study of the chemistry of communication systems or other chemical functions utilized in interactions between living organisms.

deep ecology A viewpoint of ecological systems that attempts to avoid anthropocentric views of the world.

ecology The study of environmental systems, including interactions between organisms, between species, or between organisms and their environment.

entropy A measure of the randomness of energy within a system, as contrasted with the degree of organized complexity.

natural capital Natural resources as they provide the potential for materials useful to humans.

stewardship The custodianship of resources, as in the propitious management or caretaking of valuable materials.

A thing is right when it tends to preserve the integrity, stability, and beauty of the biotic community. It is wrong when it tends otherwise.

(ALDO LEOPOLD)

THE ETHIC OF STEWARDSHIP can be essentially delivered by means of these widely quoted words. While the terminology has varied over the years, stewardship can be taken to encompass such terms as conservation, environmentalism, sustainability, and the land ethic. Collectively, these ethical precepts are distinguished by a concern for more than social interactions of humans to one another. They each extend ethical concerns to orderly and sensible interactions between humans and the world they live in.

George Gaylord Simpson has declared that a demand for ethical standards is deeply ingrained in human psychology. The demand for standards in the relationship between humans and the environment has been discussed from biblical times, from religious, secular, scientific, and economic standpoints. The development of stewardship ideas over such a long period requires that this discussion be a very selective and limited review of an enormous literature.

I. EASTER ISLAND, A PARADIGM

Easter Island was once a bountiful place, isolated out in the Pacific Ocean, with rich forests, fertile soils, and a docile climate. The Polynesian people who settled there became rich in culture, knowledgeable about mathematics and science, and devoted to their religions. After an estimated 1500 years of habitation there, however, their forest resources became depleted, and their soils decreased in productivity. Their forest resources had been essential for their homes, for their fishing boats, and for the construction of their famous religious idols. Imagine the feelings of the persons who cut the very last of the trees; might they have had compunctions about completing the loss of this crucial resource? Or perhaps, instead, might they have felt that if they did not cut the last trees somebody else would? The lack of restraint toward the loss of these resources caused irrevocable damage. It was followed by the loss of their culture, their science, and their religion, and converted these gentle people into the savage cannibals cringing in caves that were discovered there by the Dutch explorers in the 18th century. Whatever the feelings of the last exploiters, the consequence of the lack of stewardship was catastrophe—the crumbling of their entire culture.

Humans living in communities know that effective communal living depends upon the acceptance of moral standards, or ethics. A functional feature of ethics is that the individual accepts certain restraints of actions, which allow then for a better functioning of the community. The "golden rule" and the Ten Commandments are obvious examples of such ethical restraints which allow for a better community. The lack of necessary restraint in utilization of resources has not been restricted to Easter Islanders; in fact it has wreaked damage to a long succession of cultures over millenia of time, from Babylon to Carthage, Greece, Rome, and Haiti, to mention only a few. And such a lack of restraint continues in most communities in the world today.

II. THE FOCUS OF ETHICAL CONCERNS

Instead of finding our place in the biosphere, we have behaved like shiftless pirates roaming the planet in search of ecological booty.

(V. B. WEIGEL)

As our social structure has become increasingly complex, the necessary rules for ethical behavior also have become increasingly complex. The range of subjects in this encyclopedia is evidence enough of such complexity. The titles cover such diverse areas as ethics in medicine, science, teaching, professional conduct between people, human health, social justice, and personal equity—all illustrate the complexity of ethics today.

It is vividly apparent, too, that ethical issues have been principally focused on social relations between humans. Interpersonal relations and professional behavior receive the most attention from ethicists. This anthropocentric focus reflects a priority for good-neighborliness.

But note the paucity of ethical concern for the resources that sustain us, and that are essential for the stability of our social system. One would have expected a strong priority for concerns for natural systems, especially since they underly the earth's ecological systems, underly the economics of social systems, and provide the substrate from which our civilization draws on for its sustenance. Did the Easter Islanders who cut the last trees from that island have no ethic of stewardship? And might an ethical requirement for the stewardship of their resources have averted the collapse of their culture?

III. STEWARDSHIP AND ECONOMICS

The part played by orthodox economists, whose common sense has been insufficient to check their faulty logic, has been disastrous to the latest act.

(J. M. KEYNES)

Perhaps a major cause of the anthropocentric focus of ethical concerns is related to the love affair of our society with economics. We have entrusted the management of large corporations almost exclusively to economists; the health of our economy is measured in econometric rubrics; and the effectiveness of corporate management is measured in terms of short-term economic profits. Each of these economic measures ignores the losses of irreplaceable natural resources or cultural values which are used up in order to achieve the corporate profits.

The concealment by classical economics of the crucial part played by natural capital—the resources supplied by nature—has led to serious misconceptions of the health of our financial community. A favorite economic measure, the Gross National Product, completely ignores natural capital. Further, it provides for no negative values when environmental damage is produced by production. Some economists take the amazing position that because of the growth of new technologies, the production of goods can be done with increasing independence from natural capital.

Two extreme statements of this debonair attitude toward natural resources may be noted here. Julian Simon, economic advisor to President Reagan, has asserted that resources are not a problem, for "they are not finite in any economic sense." Robert Solow, Nobel Prize winner in Economics, provides another frightening example, saying, "The world can, in effect, get along without natural resources." With such an inference of infinite resources and infinite substitutability, these economists reject the reality of limits on growth by natural resources (Prugh 1977).

Anyone who believes that we are not highly dependent on natural resources can easily test the belief by putting a clothespin on his nose and taping his mouth closed. This test will require less than a minute to produce an answer.

The role of economics in contemporary social functions has been demoted by the biologist G. Woodwell, who asserts that "the world is overpopulated and overdeveloped; the important problem now is ecology, not energy and not economics." This position has been stated in different terms by the economist Daly:

We need . . . to shift our emphasis toward ecological adaptation, that is, to accept matural limits to the size and dominion of the human household, to *concentrate on moral growth and qualitative improvement* rather than on the quantitative expansion of man's dominion.

A. Depletion of Resources

Because natural capital is the foundation upon which our ecological/economic house rests, there is nothing more prudent than ensuring its continuing soundness.

(T. PRUGH)

Returning to the position, then, that we have a keen dependency on our natural resources, an ethic of stewardship of these resources becomes a priority. And the priority should be expanded in view of the abundant evidence for the current depletion of major resources. Examples of such depletion include:

- *Petroleum*, a nonrenewable resource, is being used up at 3 billion tons per year
- *Water* use has increased fourfold since 1940, and critical shortages are developing, especially in the western United States
- *Minerals* are being depleted; e.g,. copper ores have declined in quality by 70% in 40 years
- *Fisheries* are declining worldwide; e.g., 107 species of salmon have become extinct in the last generation, and major oceanic fisheries have been depleted
- *Soils* are being eroded and depleted of nutrients; 2 billion hectares have become so eroded as to be useless for agriculture
- *Forests* are being destroyed worldwide; e.g., the losses of tropical rainforests are equal to an area the size of the state of Florida annually

An ethic of stewardship can be justified as well on the basis of the expanding environmental damages being incurred. Examples include:

- *Global warming*, confirmed as a real threat by the UN Commission on Climate Change
- *Ozone depletion* is progressing year by year, carrying new threats of damage to living systems
- *Species extinctions* are occurring at an estimated rate of 4000 species lost per year in the wet tropics alone
- *Chemical residues* are increasing in soils, in water supplies, and in the food chain
- *Loss of wetlands* is limiting access to clean water, and causing losses of marshland organisms

B. Entropy in Technological Progress

A theoretical basis for insisting on an ethic of stewardship can be found in the Laws of Thermodynamics. These physical laws state that matter and energy can flow only in one direction, and that energy cannot be lost. This directional stricture brings us to the concept of entropy, a measure of the cumulative randomness of matter or of energy. A famous contribution by N. Georgescu-Roegen brought this energy/entropy concept to light as a limit on economic development. As the complexity of technology increases, progress requires greater increases in energy consumption, and the resulting energy loss results in irrevocable increases in entropy. The more advanced economists are realizing that according to this Law, the manufacture of increasingly complicated products, which will use expanding amounts of both matter and energy, will lead to a point where the dissipation of waste and heat will exceed the energy built into the product. Therefore as our economy builds more products, and more complicated products, there will be increasing energy costs, increased entropy, and magnified costs associated with the need to dispose of the waste products and heat produced.

Ecomonic expansion characteristically is based on decreases in resources and exacerbates the environmental problems already listed. The magnitude of problems can be expected to increase in severity as proliferating economic expansion stimulates energy use worldwide. These problems of the costs of expanding energy production and of the consequent waste management already signal the need for a stewardship of resources and for sufficient moral (ethical) growth to maintain economic balance.

IV. THE CONCEPT OF STEWARDSHIP

The word stewardship has shifted through several different meanings. In feudal days, a steward was one who managed the realm while the king was away; there is clearly a component of "taking care" involved. It later came to mean tending to the needs of persons in a boat or airplane; again a "taking care" inference. In recent years it has taken on a new meaning: the custodianship of natural resources. In present-day usage, stewardship infers a protective restraint, a taking care of resources through nurturing and thrifty management of their use.

A. Is Stewardship Valuable?

A discussion of the ethics of stewardship immediately faces questions: what end does such a protective custodianship serve? Who will be served by restraint in the uses of resources? Some native American tribes held that resource uses should serve to preserve the needs for future generations. Today there are people who deny the alleged values of such restraint.

An example of such denial is the claim by M. Golding that future generations cannot be considered to be a part of our "moral community." He asserts that a social contract with such nonpersons is not possible. Since we cannot identify the participants, we cannot have a contract, and there would be no tangible reciprocity. Again, there could be neither a mutuality of benefits, nor a sense of altruistic or sympathetic impulses with nonpersons. R. E. Goodin also asserts that we have no obligation to future generations. He starts with the

assumption that future generations will be better off than present societies due to anticipated advances of science and technology. From this base, he asserts that resources should be used as needed now, without such regard. A denial from a slightly different position has been made by D. Parfit, who pointed out the paradox that future generations have no rights, since we cannot identify relevant persons receiving such rights. Therefore, the rights of such potential persons cannot be assigned, since many such potential persons may never be born. Yet another variation was introduced by James Watt, Secretary of the Interior in President Ronald Reagan's administration. He questioned the validity of conserving any resources, since his religion indicated that there would soon be a world cataclysm, with an expected judgment day, and restraint would then have been useless.

Somewhat more in line with current ideas of social justice are the arguments that present generations do in fact have obligations to the future. J. Rawls endorsed the idea that we need to take care not only of our own generation, but also of our immediate descendents. He suggested a "just savings principle" by which reasonable investments are made by the present generation to ensure protection for the next generation. This principle would deny the acceptability of pillaging resources, leaving none for the future. Extending that opinion, there is a stumbling block: what is the amount of any resource that should be left for the future? G. Kavka (1978) suggested that sufficient resources should be left as would be good for future generations. He also stressed the importance of not wasting resources. In another direction, R. Attfield (1983) dismissed such quantitative arguments and asserted that the most important needs of future generations will not change much from the needs we have—the need for clean air, clean water, a good diet, decent shelter, and a freedom from hazardous substances. He denied that basic needs would change very much with advances in science and technology. His goals for stewardship seem more definitive and rather more straightforward to achieve. Even more definitive are the needs defined by Wendell Berry, who focused more precisely on passing adequate agricultural resources and productive soils to future generations. And finally, E. B. Weiss assembled still more particular requirements, which she defined as the "patrimony of the planet." This included protecting the diversity of the resource base, passing on qualities of our environment equal to those we inherited, and conservation of access to the planet's resources. Her patrimony concept constituted a planetary ethic.

B. Stewardship and Biodiversity

In the decade of the 1980s, there developed an increased sensitivity to the potential values of species diversity. Associated with this sensitivity, chemical ecologists have expressed concern over the loss of genetic materials. Among the existing species of plants, animals, and microorganisms, there are unmeasured potentials for the development of medicinals. Among the medicinal products of the $60 billion pharmaceutical industry, approximately 40% originated from plant, animal, or microorganism sources. The present degradation of the tropical rainforests alone is causing enormous losses of species. For example, rainforest losses amount to an estimated 50,000 hectares per year, resulting in the loss of an estimated 4000 species per year. These represent irreversible losses of the chance to even search for useful medicinal materials in these species. The relatively new concepts of chemical prospecting and chemical ecology, then, have established an impressive argument for the stewardship of natural plant and animal communities. Aside from the inherent rights of species for continued existence, humans would do well to preserve them for their potential values to mankind.

C. Stewardship and Anthropocentrism

Enlightened *anthropocentrism calls for long-term survival of the human species [and] the long-term survival of species diversity.*

(V. POTTER)

In each of these arguments for or against stewardship of resources runs a clear line of anthropocentrism: each of them is focused on the needs and currency of resources directly or potentially useful to mankind. In addition to human needs, there is a need for stewardship simply to ensure the preservation of quality environments for the world's biota. There is reason to ask whether the planet is entirely at the disposal of humankind, or whether other species have rights for existence. For generations humans have nourished the mantra that they alone are the center of the universe, and the resources of the earth are there simply for humans to exploit. Not only is this opinion unrealistic, but by setting ourselves apart from nature, we create a wall separating us from the biological world which nurtures us, and which is essential for our own economy. By holding ourselves apart from the natural world, we become prisoners in ecological isolation from our primary necessities.

V. AN ETHIC OF STEWARDSHIP

In short, a land ethic changes the role of Homo sapiens *from conqueror of the land community to plain member and citizen of it.*

(ALDO LEOPOLD)

Rather than discussing the total historical progression of ideas relating to an ethic of stewardship, I will focus on the influences of three major contributors whose work collectively can be considered to form the major underpinnings of such an ethic. These three include Charles Darwin, Aldo Leopold, and Rachel Carson.

A. Evolution of an Ethic

A major step toward an environmental ethic (or morality) came when Charles Darwin's prolific researches led him to conclude that species originate through natural selection. His scientific findings established that organisms share their origins through a common process of natural selection. This meant that humans originated through natural selection and share a relationship with ancestral apes. He then placed mankind within the moral community of all living things. In his book, *The Descent of Man,* Darwin concluded, "The main conclusion arrived at in this work, namely, that man is descended from some lowly organized form, will, I regret to think, be highly distasteful to many" (1871, p. 643). Indeed there followed many fiery arguments denying that humans were descendants of apes.

The distasteful response of some to Darwin's revolutionary idea of evolution must have been heightened by the assertion by Thomas Hardy that

the most far-reaching consequence of the establishment of the common origin of all species is ethical.... (It) logically involved a readjustment of altruistic morals, by enlarging the ... application of what has been called "the Golden Rule" from the area of mere mankind to that of the whole animal kingdom. (Quoted in R. Nash, 1989, p. 43)

In subsequent decades there followed a gradual acceptance. Examples of such acceptance include a book by Edward Evans, who concluded that "Man is truly a part and product of Nature as any other animal, and (the) attempt to set him up on an isolated point outside of it is philosophically wrong and morally pernicious" (1897.). Likewise J. Howard Moore extended the ethical community to all living creatures. This included rodents, amphibians, insects, and fishes.

One generation later, Aldo Leopold proposed his land ethic. In a substantial divergence from the ethicists of earlier times, he called for an ethical responsibility for a completely different sector of the natural world: an ethical responsibility to biological communities, including the soils on which they grew. The inclusion of an ethical responsibility for natural resources made his "Land Ethic" a major step toward a comprehensive ethic of stewardship. Like Charles Darwin, Leopold spoke from the pulpit of science, using contemporary advances in plant and animal ecology as the underpinnings of his proposal. In his concern for the stewardship of natural resources, he expressed criticism of the misguided value assignments made by traditional economists.

A particularly impressive feature of the proposal by Aldo Leopold was his exceptional skill in perception, the beauty of his literary explanations of natural events, and his skill in transmitting the implications to be drawn.

In the first years after the publication of his book, *A Sand County Almanac*, the public gave little attention to his message, perhaps in part because of its call for a restructuring of current economic principles and a reconsideration of contemporary environmental exploitation. But the following 50 years have seen a continual growth in interest and an upwelling of dedication in young people to an ideology of stewardship toward the land and resources. Leopold's impact on environmental issues is yet to be measured, as his influence continues to increase and to mobilize new followers.

If Aldo Leopold was a subtle threat to economics and to industry's avid exploitation of resources, Rachel Carson's book, *Silent Spring*, was much more upsetting, especially to big-moneyed industrial interests. As a professional biologist and a writer of great sensitivity, she attacked the widespread use of DDT and other biocides, and lamented their effects in polluting the environment. For this she was viciously attacked from many sides—by executives of chemical firms, government officials, Time magazine, Nobel laureates, and even university researchers (some of whom were subsidized by grants from the chemical industries). She was villified as an hysterical woman, an old maid, "not a real scientist," and a communist. One government official called her a part of "the vociferous, misinformed group of nature-balancing organic gardening bird-loving unreasonable citizenry" (F. Stewart, 1995, p. 163).

In spite of the fierce attacks, Carson stood her ground. She challenged the unregulated freedom being given to the chemical industry and other special interests, taking them to task for regarding nature as a dumping ground for pesticides and biocides. She noted that

What is important is the relation of man to all life. This has never been so tragically overlooked as in our present age, when through our technology we are waging war against the natural world. It is a valid question whether any civilization can do this and retain the right to be called civilized. (1962)

Her book catalyzed a powerful mobilization of followers willing to put pressure on industries and governmental agencies for better environmental stewardship. Her emphasis on the dangers of a human-centered perspective of nature, which she saw as all-too prevalent, served to bring her ethical concerns directly into the realm of the politics of pollution.

By the 1960s, then, three main footings for the extension of ethics to include stewardship had been achieved. Darwin had clearly established the biological relatedness between animals, and inferred an ethical responsibility to living systems generally; Leopold had extended the ethical responsibility to include "the land," or all natural resources; and Carson had generated real public involvement, pitting stewardship against the immense damage to natural resources from the fouling of natural resources by polluters. A continuum had been completed for ethical concerns, from the scientific idea of relatedness, to the philosophical concern for the whole environment, to the practical issue of resisting chemical pollution of the planetary environment. In the course of this continuum, the exclusive concern with the needs and appetites of humans has at least come to be partially offset by concerns for sensible stewardship of the resources of our planet.

B. The Ethical Upshot

Preparing for future generations is an expression of the highest morality of which human beings are capable.

(E.O. WILSON)

Since Rachel Carson, the ethics of stewardship has become increasingly visible—at the philosophical level, the moralistic level, and even the political level. Professional societies of environmental ethics have been formed, journals of ethics published, and meetings and books dedicated to discussions of environmental ethics. Even laws about stewardship have been written using wording taken from the definition by Aldo Leopold that is cited at the beginning of this article.

Along with the philosophical expositions about the ethics of stewardship, a wealth of religious literature has been published which pins stewardship to religious morality. It is just possible that the religious embrace of an ethic of stewardship will have a greater impact on the public than the scientific or the philosophical writings.

An interesting upshot from the heightened concern about ecological stewardship has been the emergence of deep ecology. The philosophical underpinnings of this radical movement were defined by Arne Naess in his book, *Ecology, Community and Lifestyle*. He drew a distinction between "shallow ecology" as referring to an anthropocentric perception of the biosphere, and "deep ecology" as referring to an ecocentric perception in which self is submerged in a larger view of nature. The philosophy of deep ecology would subordinate the concept of self as a human-in-environment image—a view of self as an overseer of an environmental ethic—to a vision of the environment as a total-field image, with self being subordinated to larger environmental components. The precepts of deep ecology are rooted in almost a mystical acceptance of the importance of the biosphere. From this point of view, there is generated a strong repudiation of species extinction, class discrimination, resource depletion, pollution, and mercenary exploitation. It would embrace a biospherical egalitarianism and a symbiotic relationship between humans and other components of the biosphere rather than a managerial relationship.

But will the logic of an ethic for stewardship achieve acceptance and modify public behavior in the long run? Or, more specifically, are there specific pitfalls that can derail its acceptance? Four kinds of perturbations can short circuit even the most sensible stewardship of resources: (1) unbridled population explosion and the hardships resulting from it, (2) the tragedies of war, with the unspeakably damaging consequences which are possible with modern military technology, (3) extensive poverty, whether from a population explosion, warfare, or political crisis, and (4) the impoverishment and reckless exploitation of third-world countries—ordinarily carried out by international corporations.

The ethic of stewardship is faced with truly dreadful odds, when overpopulation and reckless power can and routinely do abolish sensible management of people and resources.

The need for acceptance of an ethic for stewardship is magnified by the increasingly intense damages to the biosphere occurring in contemporary times, by the burgeoning increases in population, and by the exponential increases in technological demands on the natural capital. As injuries to the biosphere mount, the urgency for acceptance of an effective and convincing ethic for stewardship increases.

Whether we seek an ethic for stewardship in the sense of ensuring a livelihood for future generations, or in the sense of assuring quality in the natural environment, the urgency for an acceptance of a sensible ethic of stewardship is enormous. The citizenry of the world needs an ethic which can provide sensible restrictions on resource depletion and wastage. With it, our civilization may avoid the kind of resource catastrophe which has overwhelmed civilizations, one after another, through the past two millenia.

Also See the Following Articles

ANTHROPOCENTRISM • BIODIVERSITY • DEEP ECOLOGY • ECOLOGICAL BALANCE • GAIA HYPOTHESIS • SUSTAINABILITY • WILDLIFE CONSERVATION

Bibliography

Attfield, R. (1983). "The Ethics of Environmental Concern." Columbia Univ. Press, New York.

Baker, B. (1996). A reverent approach to the natural world. *Bioscience* 46, 475–478.

Beatley, T. (1994). "Ethical Land Use." Johns Hopkins Univ. Press, Baltimore, MD.

Berry, W. (1977). "The Unsettling of America." Sierra Club Books, San Francisco.

Berry, W. (1981). "The Gift of Good Land." North Point, San Francisco.

Block, P. (1993). "Stewardship." Berrett-Koehler, San Francisco.

Brown, L. R. (Ed.) (1995). "Vital Signs." Worldwatch Institute, Washington, DC.

Carson, R. (1962). "Silent Spring." Houghton Mifflin, Boston.

Daly, H. E. (1991). "Steady-State Economics." Island, Washington, DC.

Darwin, C. (1871). "The Descent of Man." David McKay, Philadelphia.

Eisner, T. (1994). Chemical prospecting: A global imperative. *Proc. Am. Phil. Soc.*, 385–392.

Eisner, T., and Beiring, E. A. (1994). Biotic exploration fund—Protecting biodiversity through chemical prospecting. *Bioscience* 44, 95–98.

Evans, E. P. (1897). "Evolutional Ethics and Animal Psychology." New York.

Ferre, F., and Hartel, P. (1994). "Ethics and Environmental Policy." Univ. of Georgia Press, Athens.

Georgescu-Roegen, N. (1971). "The Entropy Law and the Economic Process." Harvard Univ. Press, Cambridge.

Golding, M. (1972). Obligations to future generations. *Monist* 56, 85–99.

Golley, P. B. (1994). Grounding environmental ethics in ecological science. In "Ethics and Environmental Policy" (F. Ferre and P. Hartel, Eds.). Univ. of Georgia Press, Athens.

Goodin, R. E. (1980). No moral nukes. *Ethics* 90, 417–490.

Hawken, P. (1995). Foreward to "Natural Capital and Human Economic Survival," by T. Prugh. International Society of Ecological Economics, Solomons, MD.

Kavka, G. (1978). The futurity problem. In "Obligations to Future Generations" (R. I. Sikora and B. Berry, Eds.). Temple Univ. Press, Philadelphia.

Leopold, A. (1949). "A Sand County Almanac." Oxford Univ. Press, New York.

Marx, K. (1978). "Economic and Philosophic Manuscripts." Norton, New York.

Myers, N. (1994). "Ultimate Security." Norton, New York.

Myers, N. (1995). The world's forests: Need for a policy appraised. *Science* 268, 823–824.

Naess, A. (1989). "Ecology, Community and Lifestyle." Cambridge Univ. Press, Cambridge.

Nash, R. (1987). Aldo Leopold and the limits of American liberalism. In "Aldo Leopold, the Man and His Legacy." Soil Conservation Society, Ankeny, IA.

Nash, R. (1989). "The Rights of Nature." Univ. of Wisconsin Press, Madison.

Oelschlager, M. (1995). "Postmodern Environmental Ethics." State Univ. of New York Press, Albany.

Parfit, D. (1984). "Reasons and Persons." Oxford Clarendon Press, Oxford.

Ponting, C. (1991). "A Green History of the World." Penguin, New York.

Potter, V. R. (1988). "Global Bioethics: Building on the Leopold Legacy." Michigan State Univ. Press, East Lansing.

Potter, Van R. (1995). Global bioethics: Linking genes to ethical behavior. *Perspect. Biol. Med.* 39, 118–131.

Prugh, T. (1995). "Natural Capital and Human Economic Survival." International Society of Ecological Economics, Solomons, MD.

Raven, P. H., and Wilson, E. O. (1992). A fifty-year plan for biodiversity surveys. *Science* 258, 1099–1100.

Rawls, J. (1971). "A Theory of Justice." Harvard Univ, Press, Cambridge.

Rifkin, J. (1980). "Entropy: A New World View." Bantam, New York.

Stewart, F. (1995). "A Natural History of Nature Writing." Island, Washington, DC.

Weigel, V. B. (1995). "Earth Cancer." Praeger, Westport.

Weiss, E. B. (1989). "In Fairness to Future Generations." Transnational, United Nations Univ., New York.

Westra, L. (1994). "An Environmental Proposal for Ethics." Rowman & Littlefield, Lanham, MD.

Wilson, E. O. (1984). "Biophilia." Harvard Univ. Press, Cambridge.

Wilson, E. O. (1992). "The Diversity of Life." Harvard Univ. Press, Cambridge.

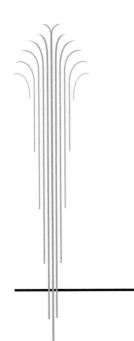

STOICISM

Jan Narveson
University of Waterloo

GLOSSARY

descriptive The status of laws of nature in our modern view; source of the impossibility of guidance from Stoic sources.

emotions Stoicism holds that we must master these if we are to be happy—not let them take control of us.

indifference The Stoic view that we should not be concerned about anything that is not strictly under our own control.

natural order The Stoic idea that world is organized in a rational way which can provide us with knowledge of how to live.

one's power (will) The center of the soul, practically speaking. Distinguishing what is and what is not strictly within our power is the primary principle of ethics for the Stoics.

STOICISM is a comprehensive system of philosophy dating to the ancient Greeks. A major part of that system was a set of ethical doctrines which the Stoic writers thought were integrally related to their more general metaphysical and logic views—it was they who first divided philosophy into logic, physics, and ethics. We will look briefly at their central ethical doctrines and the possible applications of those ideas to real life in contemporary society.

I. HISTORY

Stoicism has a very long history, dating back to such early Greeks as Zeno (ca. 333–261 B.C.); he lectured on the "Painted Porch" (Stoa Poikile) in Athens, from which the school takes its name. He and many others elaborated the basic idea that the universe is an orderly place, and thus (as he thought) that we are all subject to a "law of nature," and, in turn, that therefore the good life for man is life in accordance with nature, whereas bad lives deviate from what nature prescribes. This idea was taken in rather different directions by various thinkers, e.g., the "Cynics," who preached indifference to all worldly goods, notably those of their Roman conquerors or rulers.

Stoicism was immensely influential, and continued to be so in later times. Perhaps the most striking case is that of Spinoza (1632–1677), who taught that freedom is knowledge of necessity, so that the truly good man makes himself wholly at one with nature, specifically by bringing the emotions under rational control. Even among the more central moralists of the British tradition we may cite Joseph (Bishop) Butler (1692–1752), who teaches that what is right is what is conformable to our nature, and what is wrong out of accord with it. Even to this day, there are "self-realizationist" philosophies that proceed along recognizably similar lines.

However, what we especially associate with Stoicism are the doctrines of the later school, which flourished mostly in the 2nd century A.D. Above all, there is the exposition of the freed slave Epictetus (ca. 50–138 A.D.), who established a very influential school. Other influential members were the patrician Seneca (4 B.C.–65 A.D.) and the Emperor Marcus Aurelius (121–180 A.D.). It is a serendipitous irony of history that the acknowledged leader of this school stemmed from the bottom of society, while the comparatively less conceptually powerful were from the top—the emperor acknowledging the slave as his master in the world of ideas.

II. THE THEORY OF ULTIMATE RESPONSIBILITY

The slave upbringing of Epictetus—he was later freed—undoubtedly influenced his doctrines, which center around one very important idea: responsibility. According to Epictetus, the rational person must distinguish between that which is "his" and that which is not. We are only responsible for what is "ours," and not for what is due to someone else. What is ours is what is in our own power; what is not, just because it is not, is therefore something that a rational person should not worry about. This, he thought, had all kinds of important implications for the conduct of life. Perhaps most strikingly, Stoics are famous for preaching indifference to pain and suffering. Pain, after all, is not something we ourselves will or "do"—it is merely something that happens to us and is inflicted on us. Thus, concludes Epictetus, the thing to do is to ignore it! (Marcus Aurelius puts it succinctly: "Take away the complaint, 'I have been hurt,' and the hurt is gone" (*Meditation* IV.7).) This advice, needless to say, is harder for most people to follow than it apparently was for Epictetus. But if we cannot "ignore" it, at least we can perhaps learn to "endure" it, and that is a lesson strongly enjoined by the Stoics. Consistently, they also teach us not to be taken with pleasures, triumphs, accolades, and the like. (The Emperor Marcus Aurelius is especially good at this: "Whatever is in any way beautiful is beautiful in itself, and ... praise is no part of it" (*Meditation* IV.20).)

More disconcerting, perhaps, is Epictetus's doctrine regarding our emotional orientation toward others, including those we love. Here the Stoic teaching is that we must not let our emotions get the better of us, as it were: when contemplating a loved one's death or a friend's triumphs, we are always to remember that these are only emotions, not really "us," and comport ourselves with dignity, thinking that these things do not *really* matter. That is a very hard doctrine for most of us, nor is it entirely a clear one; but certainly it looks to us cold and even inhuman. (We get a warmer impression from Aurelius, who says, for instance, "the soul does violence to itself when it turns away from any man, or moves against him with the intention of harming him ...." (*Meditation* II.16).)

III. CRITICISM

The central thesis of Stoicism seems a strange, even bizarre, idea. When philosophers embrace such doctrines, we must ask whether they have really seen something that the rest of us have not—or is their vision perhaps narrowed by their own circumstances? Or have they made a mistake somewhere? In the case of Epictetus, it is easy to see how indifference to suffering could be useful for a slave, helping him to retain self-respect in a pretty demeaning situation. But we must be wary of doctrines suited only for special circumstances. The third possibility—of sheer philosophical mistake—seems likely, especially since, in Epictetus's case, the mistake can be pinpointed.

But we should also credit the Stoics with some important insights into human life, and some real wisdom in ways to deal with it. We can learn from great philosophers, even when their doctrines do not entirely add up. The adjective "stoical" has come to be regarded as nearly synonymous with "philosophical": to take things philosophically is to remain calm in the face of great adversity—to accept the inevitable without getting upset. Within limits, this is useful for anyone.

A. Stretching the Distinction of "Ours/Not Ours"

To see where the mistake lies in the Stoic argument, consider Epictetus's opening pronouncements in *The Enchiridion* to the effect that the only things *really* within our power are such things as "willing," "thinking," and "movement toward a thing." Everything else lies, strictly speaking, beyond the reach of our own selves—beyond our power. Evidently Epictetus's idea here is that a thing is either within our power or it is not. If it is, then it is *absolutely* so: you give the mental order, as it were, and the result follows with 100% certainty—it is a sure thing. Anything else, by contrast, is such that there might be a slip between cup and lip: you can order the muscle to move, but whether it will do so depends on the physical system being in working condition, as it might well not be, as when Epictetus's master had just broken his arm.

Two questions arise here. The first is whether Epictetus is right in thinking that even such inner things as he mentions are truly within our power. Take thought, for example. Is it genuinely certain that if I *will* to think a certain thing, than I necessarily *do* think it? A puzzling idea, in a way; but if what is meant is that one can will to solve Fermat's last theorem, then of course that is well beyond our powers—nobody can simply will to do such a thing. But even if I will to think of something I can think of, e.g., my daughter, is it certain that I will then do so? Even then, we must admit, the answer is no. Of course it is very *likely* we will do so—but in the sense Epictetus seems to have in mind, it seems we must reconcile ourselves to our fates: *nothing* is as certainly within our power as he seems to think.

The other question is whether he is right to think that the fact that something is "beyond our power" in his very extreme sense of that idea is sufficient reason to attach no importance to it, or to insist on not getting upset about it. Epictetus says that if one's friend or one's wife should die, well, that is the way people are built, after all, and it is beyond one's control, so we should not let ourselves get carried away. To which we might reasonably respond, "Well, why not?" We might even add, "My, you're a cold fish, aren't you?!"

The Stoic reaction may well strike us as inhuman. People as we know them do get involved, they have emotions, and the fact that they can do nothing about some of the situations that move them to a certain emotion strikes them as no reason at all why some emotion is not appropriate. Perhaps quite a lot of it, for that matter!

B. Psychology

That there is an important idea in Epictetus's way of looking at things is surely true. Maxims like, "Well, don't let it throw you!" and "Life goes on, after all!" certainly have their point, and perhaps it is really the very point Epictetus is trying to make, even if he makes

it in too extreme a fashion to be acceptable to most people. We need, somehow, to tone it down a bit.

How we go about "getting a grip on ourselves" is certainly a good question. What is this mysterious power to control our emotions that we all have to some degree and some, like Epictetus, to a quite extraordinary degree? While this is a very interesting and difficult question about human psychology, it is hard to see how a purely philosophical theory would be able to shed very much real light on the matter. In this case it is enough to recognize that it is obviously a very important thing to be able to control oneself, and very important to try to come up with a good account of just what principles can and ought to guide us in exercising such control.

C. Is Stoic Ethics Meaningful?

The stoics were very big on "virtue" and "duty," but not very helpful in explaining just what these things are, or, more importantly, exactly why they were important. Let us turn to their fundamental idea next to see whether the Stoic formulas actually have useful answers to these questions.

Stoics make much of the idea that we should "act according to our natures," and more generally according to Nature at large. This extremely influential idea, though, is also rather obscure. What makes it especially puzzling is the thought that, after all, such sense as we can readily attach to the expression "according to nature" is such that it is not at all clear what could be meant by *not* acting that way. Whatever anyone does, one might reasonably suppose, is something that is due to "one's nature," and must, necessarily, be "in accordance with" the *laws* of nature. And far from its being an open question of whether one will choose to act according to one's nature, the idea seems logically pleonastic, so that the idea of acting "against" it seems to be without sense.

The Stoics taught that nature is somehow "rational." If that meant, merely, "understandable," fair enough: our attempts to try to figure out the ways of nature have succeeded considerably, and we have good reason to hope for much further success. But if it is meant that nature has ideas about what we and everything ought to do, that seems animistic. Certainly modern science lends no support to the idea; the basic principles of physics, so far as we know them, just do not mention things like "rationality." Most importantly, they make no sense of the idea that something can be "against nature": nature simply is, and whatever happens in it happens in accordance with its "laws." All of this leaves the basic Stoic idea of living according to nature in serious trouble.

IV. STOICISM AND EXISTENTIALISM

Stoicism has, in this respect, some relation to the "existentialism" of European popularity in the postwar era. Existentialists held that choices make, or constitute, us: "Man is freedom," said Sartre. But we should note that it does not matter whether we are "free" or not in this supposed way: a person can be held to be constituted by the sequence of choices made in life, whether or not he had any "real" power to make them. The drug addict, the convict in chains, the hopeless neurotic—all are "constituted by their choices," in the circumstances. No matter what we choose, it will be true that we are thus constituted. Consequently, no advice at all, of any kind, can be given to anyone on this basis.

Likewise with Stoicism. If in choosing we "realize" our natures, that would seem to be true *no matter what* we choose. Again, then, the direction, "Always act in accordance with your nature!" seems to be without any real meaning—and therefore incapable of giving us any actual direction in life, for no matter what happens, it will be natural that stoicism fundamentally allows it: namely, that it happens in accordance with the regularities of natural law. As we now understand it, natural laws are descriptive; nothing in the world can "disobey" a natural law, because natural laws are not the sort of thing that tells anybody or anything to do anything, they simply tell us what fundamentally does happen. So anything that a human being does—literally anything, no matter what—will be an instance of some or other natural laws. There is no way to fail to "realize one's essence," and therefore no advice can be forthcoming from the advice to do so.

V. REINTERPRETING NATURALISM?

Other interpretive options might be thought possible. For example, we do sometimes say that this or that is "so natural," meaning something like that it goes easily or smoothly. But it is unclear that what is good must be like that—not to mention that resisting pain as the Stoics want us to is hardly going to be easy or smooth.

More fundamentally, it might be said that humans come equipped with certain desires and interests and that it is natural for them to act so as to achieve the objects of those desires or interests. But this turns out to be quite problematic, for in the first place, anything that we literally *do* must be something we somehow desired to do: we always act out of some kind of desire. So it would have to be added that what is "nataural" is to act out of certain desires and not others—say our more important ones. Our most basic desire might be to be happy, for instance. But then we should have to ask whether doing what you believe will make you happy is good because the desire to be happy is natural or whether, on the contrary, we suppose that happiness is natural because it is good.

Further pressing of this idea seems to get us back to the original idea that any action or desire is natural in that we do actually do it or have it; it is "in our nature." So if someone is thought to be acting against his happiness, on that account he is said to be acting "unnaturally." Yet however we characterize it, the supposedly unnatural desire is one he actually *has*. How can that be if the desire to be happy is natural? Or is it just that his idea of happiness is different from other people's, as shown by his behavior? But if happiness is getting whatever we desire, no matter what it is, we once again get no basic guidance from the idea of acting according to nature.

VI. APPLICATIONS

What has all this to do with "applied ethics"? The answer is, perhaps more than one might have supposed. The Stoic advice does not follow from its premises. We must therefore evaluate it in a different way from the one envisaged by its founders. That advice certainly has its place. Often enough we will do well to grin and bear it; often we will be well advised to "cool it," not to let our emotions get the better of us, and so on.

On the other hand, we must realize that the Stoic advice carries with it a serious danger. If it is known that Mr. B is a Stoic, how will Mr. A treat him? Is not the Stoic attitude virtually an invitation to inflict the very suffering or pain that the Stoic is so remarkable at enduring? Were Stoicism the prevailing attitude, those in a position to gain by making people suffer would, it seems, be encouraged to do so.

Epictetus did not think, in fact, that we should just allow people to get away with evil; but it is very difficult not to read some such implication into his doctrine. To adopt the Stoic attitude in a full-blooded way would, in contemporary circumstances, be a serious mistake. The disposition to complain about evils and do quite a lot to prevent them from being imposed by people in positions of power is probably more important to the average person now than it ever was. The Stoic view may, in short, encourage the agent to "cop out" regarding matters of serious importance to everyone. John Stuart Mill was surely right in suggesting that an active citizenry is essential to a genuinely working representative democracy. Stoicism *appears* to encourage just the reverse—the disposition simply to put up with whatever one's political masters have in store.

Does it actually do such things? That is difficult to tell, because there seems no fundamentally clear theory underlying the collection of maxims that have come down to us as stoicism. Yet consider these maxims of Epictetus: "Whoever, then, would be free, let him wish nothing, let him decline nothing, which depends on others, else he must necessarily be a slave" (*Enchiridion* no. 14), or, "For this is your business, to act well the character assigned you; to choose it is another's" (*Enchiridion* no. 17). Those sentiments are reiterated by other Stoics. Aurelius says, "Whenever in the morning you rise unwilling, let this thought be with you: I am rising to the work of a human being. Why then am I dissatisfied . . .?" (*Meditation* V.1).

While it is difficult to say just what believing those things really amounts to, it surely sounds as though they are recommending a way of life that accepts things as they are rather than trying to change them. But we should have our doubts about that. Perhaps things can be improved. Again, nothing in their fundamental ideas denies this, we could consider it our "appointed role" to get out there and man the barricades.

Still, Epictetus and other Stoics have a profound lesson to teach us. In holding that it is not the things themselves that are evil, but only our opinions about them, what they say has at least a grain of truth. Most of us could learn to put up with more pain than we think we can, and in some circumstances this will be very useful. We can prepare for trying situations by learning to put up with small pains, and then with greater ones. Having such abilities could well make life better in time of sickness or when we become old and incapable. To attain placidity of mind in such circumstances would be a very valuable thing—if we can do it. Epictetus says we can. And at least in some cases, he is right. Is he right in yours or mine? That is something we must learn for outselves.

Also See the Following Articles

ARISTOTELIAN ETHICS • EPICUREANISM • EXISTENTIALISM • PLATONISM

Bibliography

Campbell, K. (1986). *A Stoic philosophy of life.* Lanham, MD: University Press of America.

Erskine, A. (1990). *The Hellenistic stoa: Political thought and action.* London: Duckworth.

Long, A. A. (1986). *Hellenistic philosophy: Stoics, Epicureans, Sceptics* (2nd ed.). Berkeley, CA: Univ. of California Press.

Oates, W. J. (Ed.) (1940). *The Stoic and Epicurean philosophers.* New York: Random House, Modern Library Giant.

Rist, J. M. (1969). *Stoic philosophy.* Cambridge, UK: Cambridge Univ. Press.

Sandbach, F. H. (1975). *The Stoics.* London: Chatto & Windus.

Sherman, R. R. (1973). *Democracy, stoicism, and education; an essay in the history of freedom.* Gainesville, FL: Univ. of Florida Press.

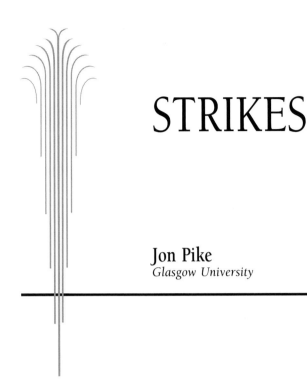

STRIKES

Jon Pike
Glasgow University

GLOSSARY

closed shop A workplace in which trade union membership is a requirement for a worker to be hired.

collective bargaining The practice of bargaining organized by workers' associations who bargain on behalf of all workers employed in a particular context (grade, workplace, etc.).

free riding The practice of gaining an advantage from a public good without contributing to it; the paradigm example is taking a free ride on public transportation systems.

general strike A strike by workers in all or most industries, with a view to securing a common goal.

independent arbitration The process in which an independent overseer examines a dispute and decides on the outcome, which may be a compromise position or agreement entirely with one party. Arbitration may be voluntary or binding.

labor contract The contract between the employer and the employee. It is contentious whether the contract is either suspended or broken by strike action and whether the contract is a written one or merely notional.

picketing The practice of demonstrating outside a struck workplace in order to dissuade, coerce, or block other workers, suppliers, or customers from entering it.

other forms of industrial action Actions that fall short of an outright strike include a *go slow*, in which workers deliberately slow down their work rate, a *work to rule*, in which employees work strictly according to the written terms of the contract (sometimes known as a withdrawal of good will) or an *overtime ban*. More informally, employees may express dissatisfaction with their conditions of work through absenteeism or poor time keeping.

protest strike A strike in which the employees' objection is not to the terms of employment themselves, but to an employers policies, perhaps on conscience or political grounds.

public sector A collective term for those employed by the government or governmental agencies work in the public sector and are funded indirectly out of tax receipts.

secondary strike A strike that is engaged in by a group of employees distinct from those engaged in the original dispute, and sometimes against a different employer.

trade or labor union A collective organization of workers designed to protect and further their interests.

union shop A workplace in which union membership is required after a grace period following the hire of a worker. In addition, in a union shop, discharge may result if loss of union membership results from a failure to pay dues.

wildcat strike A strike that is not endorsed by the apparatus of a labor union.

zero-sum game A game, typically involving two players, in which any gain by one player is simultaneously a loss to the other and the loss/gain sum is zero.

STRIKES are the collective withdrawal of labor from the person or body to which it has been contracted, normally designed to induce the employer into changing the conditions of work. A central assumption of strike action is that strikers have a legitimate claim over their jobs, and hence regard the employer taking on someone else to do the job as illegitimate. Strikers usually wish to alter the conditions of work, such as the hour worked or the rate of pay.

Some argue that confining the term "strike" to the withdrawal of labor is a mistake, because employers withdraw capital by closing down firms, instigating a lockout, or sometimes removing capital over national frontiers. Such "capital strikes" are often considered uncontroversial, because the employer is not held to owe any obligation to continue to employ her employees, while employees are considered to be obliged collectively to continue to work. Although capital strikes are a common feature of contemporary economic development, this article is confined to strikes of labor.

I. ORIGINS AND IMPORTANCE OF STRIKE ACTION

A. Origins of Strike Action

Strikes are a modern phenomenon, developing at first in small workplaces in tandem with the emergence of labor unions. Before the advent of universal suffrage they were often used as a means of securing wider political rights. Today, they differ widely in their form, from the small-scale actions of tens of workers who strike, perhaps for a matter of hours, to seek redress for a minor grievance, to earthshaking national events such as the French general strike of 1968. Strike incidence (Table 1) is relative to balances within the labor contract, welfare provision and the provision of trade union strike pay, the economic environment, as well as the legislative framework and the political culture on which this is based. In industrial societies of the

TABLE 1

Strikes and Lockouts: Workdays Not Worked (Thousands) in 1993

Australia	636
Denmark	114
France	511
Germany	84
Greece	1062
Italy	3411
Netherlands	45
New Zealand	24
Portugal	80
Spain	2141
United Kingdom	649
United States	3981
Canada	499

Source: *Yearbook of Labour Statistics* 1995 ILO (Geneva).

Western world there has recently been a decline in the numbers employed in manual labor and a shift to employment in the service sector, and strikes in the public sector and essential services have become a matter of pressing concern.

B. Strikes, Unions, and the Labor Contract

The contract between employer and employee that determines the conditions of work will always have elements that correspond to a zero-sum game, in which some interests are inevitably opposed. If employees secure a wage increase, this pushes up the costs for employers, and, other things being equal, their profits will fall. Attempts have recently been made to diminish this conflict, through the establishment of employee share ownership and profit-sharing schemes. Many employers, acting as managers for the owners of a firm, are at the same time employees, limiting the zero-sum nature of the relationship. However, it is not possible to reconcile employer and employee interests completely. Consequently, a balance has to be negotiated that aims to embody the claims of both parties. This tends to involve the techniques of collective bargaining, as a system of reciprocal power. Neopluralist writers such as Dahl and Lindblom have argued that the strike is an integral part of the machinery of collective bargaining that has developed with the eventual consent of Western state institutions. Labor unions have emerged as a countervailing power to the combination of control over the work place by the employer, and the impact of the price mechanism in the labor market, because the meshing of these two forms of control was felt to disadvantage workers systematically. The main source of power by which the workers institute bargaining as an alternative is the strike, because this gives them influence over the behavior of employers. When conditions have allowed, workers have refused to be taken advantage of, and have brought to public attention the need for a right to strike, and have used what power they have to help secure that right. Employers have tended to take the opposite view and have tried to secure legal constraints on strike activity.

II. ETHICS OF STRIKE ACTION

A. The Possibility of an Ethical Account of Strike Actions

Strikes are significant for the student of applied ethics, because they necessarily involve harm to an individual or individuals, and implicitly question the legitimacy and scope of some of the core social relations of contemporary society. They therefore seem to require justification in a way that purely self-regarding actions do not. However, such justifications are likely to be politically charged. Bitter strikes typically involve dramatically conflicting moral claims, as well as the potential on both sides for coercion, victimization, and violence. Strikes tend to polarize disagreements. Some theorists argue that the polarization is so strong that strikes cannot be discussed in a neutral way, because to conceive of them as a discrete object of moral inquiry is to comply with the constraints of a "bourgeois" morality that accepts the legitimacy of the labor contract as a free contract between equally placed individuals. But this view cuts both ways. It is also possible to deny, from the perspective of the employer, that moral judgments are applicable to public issues, which are simply a matter of power struggles; a strike is the result of a mistaken assessment of the strength of one's opponent. From a perspective far different from the Marxist condemnation of "bourgeois morality," a noticeably similar argument can be found: that strikes are not a question of morality at all, and questions of justice do not enter into a voluntary contract. If employers can fill the vacancy of strikers, there is no reason why they should not. Both these positions implicitly reject an extended right to strike, and its central assumption: that the striker has some claim or entitlement over the job,

while entering into negotiations over the conditions of labor.

The right to strike can be analyzed in terms of different versions of utilitarianism, from a Kantian viewpoint or through the prism of character ethics. A distinction can be drawn between ethical, legal, and political justifications of strikes. We can ask whether there is a *moral* case for workers and unions having a *legal* right to strike, or whether a strike is politically justified: whether it serves a wider political purpose with which one is in agreement. One variant of the latter is the Marxist view that strikes in general are an instrument to oppose exploitation, and the justification of strike action derives from the exploitative nature of the labor relation. From this point of view, all strikes are in principle justifiable, regardless of their immediate aims.

Much more restricted justifications work by analogy with discussion of just wars; strikes might be justified as a form of self-defense, or the defense of legitimate interests. Following Pope Leo XIII, Catholic teaching tends to recognize the liberty to strike in a just cause; people are justified in striking if, but only if, their cause is just. What often counts, in this line of argument, is whether the strike action is taken in response to an employer's attempt to cut back wages or alter conditions in a way that is detrimental to employees' interests. Strikes could be construed as a form of self-defense in which strikers defined their own legitimate interests as a form of self-preservation.

A utilitarian might also want to justify aggressive strike action taken by employees in order to advance their interests against employers. A straightforward utilitarian justification might be one in which a strike is justified as the lesser evil, if it secures increased overall utility. The usual problems faced by utilitarian arguments of calculation and distributive justice enter in here. Such calculations would need to factor in the risk of failure, and the possibility of failure, or of successful strike action that leads to overall utility losses, is clear. Another feature of such a justification is that it would have to take into account the damage caused to employers and their customers as well as the benefit to employees that flowed from the success of the strike. Philosophical utilitarianism prescribes maximizing the total utility of the community, but strikes, other than general strikes, aim only to promote a minority interest, and utilitarian considerations are often confined to that minority community. Strikes typically do not recognize the claim that this damage to the employer should be part of their calculation, simply because the interests of workers and employers are diametrically opposed in a zero-sum game.

III. THE RIGHT TO STRIKE

Simple utilitarian arguments are often wielded to show that particular strikes are justified but they cannot easily found a general "right to strike" if that right is a right to do X, whether or not X is itself justified. That is, they cannot found a right to strike, right or wrong. More sophisticated utilitarians appeal to the Rawlsian distinction between justifying a practice (striking) and justifying particular acts (particular strikes) that fall under it. Thus, one might try to justify the general practice of striking in utilitarian terms, by pointing to overall utility gains that have come from the general practice of striking in the past. So one could be in favor of strikes on the general basis of utility gains coming from a countervailing economic power to that of the employer. A second order question then, concerns not just the justification of particular strikes, but the grounds of a general right to strike. Because strike action itself is a historically emergent activity, it is difficult to found the right to strike as a fundamental natural right. Rather, it is seen as a historically emerent right based, like other rights, such as the right to health care, on particular interests. While some ingenious attempts have been made (such as by Smart) to found a general and universal right to strike, most theorists see the right to strike as a historically emergent and social right that arises from the interests of employees, opposed to those of employers.

A. The Nature of the Right to Strike

The nature of a right to strike is more complex than it appears. At its most minimal is the existence of a bare "liberty" right to strike: workers are free to strike and to take the consequences of their action. This account of the right to strike simply means that workers have no duty not to strike, and it carries no duty on the part of the employer not to dismiss. This right seems minimal, but it is precisely what is at stake in arguments over the right of health service employees to take strike action, because those who argue that no such right exists say that doctors do have a duty not to strike. A more extended right to strike would include immunities; against dismissal of strikers by the employer, against damages to employers and third parties. Finally, the right to strike might be said to involve a claim right against government for welfare benefits to dependents of strikers. In most disputes about the existence of the right to strike it is the second dimension—the right to take strike action without being sacked, that is in question.

The right to strike is an individual right in the sense that only individuals withdraw their labor. But the right to strike is also a collective right in the same sense that the right to vote, the right to freedom of discussion, assembly, and (often) worship are collective rights. The object of the right: voting, speaking out, worship, does not make sense unless others are engaged in the activity. In his respect, the right to strike is an individual right to engage in a collective activity. The right to strike can also be construed as a group right, in the sense that the group—usually the labor union—may be the subject of the immunity against claims for damages. Groups may be responsible (for good or ill) for strike action. So long as the right to strike is analyzed as sufficiently complex, all these different accounts of the right to strike are consistent.

B. Strikes and the Prisoners' Dilemma

A wider understanding of the ethics of strikes may be gained from looking at coerced cooperation as a response to prisoners' dilemmas. Strikes, as a distinctive form of collective action, exhibit the structure of the classical prisoners' dilemma: each worker as a rational, self-interested individual will tend to take the dominating option of cooperation with the employer rather than the dominated position of cooperating with his coworkers in strike action, because if the strike is unsuccessful, he will not have lost the pay that will be foregone by strikers during the strike, or have incurred the risk of losing his job entirely. If the strike is successful, however, then he will have lost nothing and will, by "free riding" receive the gains recorded to the whole work force, in improved terms of employment. This situation faces every individual worker conceived of as a rational and self-interested individual; its consequence is the failure to achieve the collective good of workers faced with these options. In his classic work, *The Logic of Collective Action,* Mancur Olson shows that "unless the number of individuals is quite small or unless there is coercion or some other special device to make individuals act in their common interest, rational self-interested individuals will not act to achieve their common or group interests" (Olson: *Logic of Collective Action,* p. 2). This means that no worker will strike and any possible gains from collective action against the employer will be forgone. When the dilemma is iterated, however, the loss of the potential collective gains may become clear to employees, who will tend to band together in order to secure them. Otherwise, the pursuit of these collective gains requires the use of "coercion or some other special device" to ensure that workers act in their collective interests. Such a special device is the organization of labor unions themselves and the historical articulation of fraternity, solidarity, and the principle that workers should not cross picket lines. These are moral norms that arise out of prisoners' dilemma situations. Once these norms are in place, a PD analysis is inapplicable, because the workers are no longer merely self-interested.

One important moral norm is the special nature of a strike vote—that it is binding on a minority who oppose strike action. The basis of this special obligation undertaken by those who take part in a ballot on strike action is that such a vote does not simply express an individual preference about the issue in question, but commits the member to recognizing the legitimacy of the outcome of the vote, and its binding nature. The scope of this obligation is disputed. Does it apply to all union members, or all those who voted, or all those who were able to vote? A wide account of this obligation is foregrounded by the PD structure of strikes, and the closed shop is designed to prevent unfair free riding by non-union members and nonstrikers on the backs of members or strikers. Closed and union shops are often justified by reference to principles such as Rawls' principle of fairness. Indeed, much of the rhetoric of labor unions is rational in the light of the PD structure of collective action. If cooperation is universal among a work force, perhaps because of a high level of organization, then coercion is unlikely to be necessary. If, however, it is not universal, as is often the case, some form of coerced cooperation is likely. So what is critical, for strikers, is how far the moral norms of union action have spread among a work force.

C. Consequences of Coerced Cooperation

The right of an individual to go to work directly conflicts with the right of a collective to strike effectively, because the activity of working itself undermines the strike. The two prima facie rights cannot be fully exercised at the same time. If this conflict arises, trade unionists are likely to attempt to "picket out" a workplace. The conflict between two sets of rights is exacerbated if the employer attempts to fill the jobs of strikers, by recruiting strike breakers. Among other factors, high unemployment makes this easier, whereas high rates of employment make union solidarity easier to enforce, because other workers are less willing or available to break the strike. A central concern of strikers is the notion that the employer is not entitled to hire and fire at will and that the strikers have some claim over the job. However, a claim over the job may be in conflict

with the right of other individuals to work. From this clash of prima facie rights, other problems arise. Where, for example, is the line to be drawn between coercion and persuasion on a picket line? Normally, pickets will be aiming to dissuade other workers, or customers of the employer from entering the workplace. If strikers are unsuccessful in their persuasion, are they entitled to block the way? Or to shout abuse? Or to punish strike breakers by ostracism? These sorts of issues are at the forefront of debate about legislative reform on picketing.

Gauthier argues that the norms that arise as a response to prisoners' dilemmas are distinctively moral, because such norms involve both prudence and self-sacrifice, and it is certainly reasonable to argue that some of the qualities exhibited in strike action such as tenacity, solidarity, sympathy, and mutual aid can be valued in themselves. A character ethicist might want to suggest that practices that encourage such traits are themselves to be valued, or place emphasis on vices encouraged by strike action, such as class enmity, and a willingness to resolve disputes by coercion. Marxists, who regard the labor contract as unjust, will also regard the traits that are conducive to strike action as essential for a further and more general struggle against exploitation, and therefore regard strike action as a valuable "school" for workers. Such considerations fold together in the argument over a general justification for the practice or institution of striking. But other commentators, such as Ullman-Margalit hold that, while some features of prisoners' dilemma norms may be necessary for moral actions, they are not sufficient; they point out that in the classical prisoners' dilemma situation, the prisoners are, in fact, robbers, and this gives an obvious reason for regarding their cooperation as morally condemnable. The robbers really ought to confess, on perhaps utilitarian or Kantian grounds. The fact of cooperation does not by itself, make the action moral; what matters is what the cooperation is *for*. This suggests that further justification of a right to strike is required, and if it is to be found, it is most likely to be rooted in the historical derivation of strike action as a form of countervailing power, and by recourse to thinking about a just or equal distribution of power.

D. Pragmatic Justification of the Right to Strike

There is, though, a further argument for respecting a right to strike that stems from the very contestability of particular strikes. If many strikes are justified but some are not, and people legitimately disagree about whether or not a strike in a certain cause is justified, they are entitled to act on their belief, even if they happen to have got it wrong. In the absence of a suitable authority, we ought to defer to people's entitlement to act on their own opinion. This is a justification of the practice of striking out of ignorance, as it were. Of course, someone could argue that the state or some sort of strikes ombudsman was a suitable authority to judge on competing moral claims, but this would involve states in doing something they have been fairly reluctant to do: judging the rights and wrongs of particular instances of industrial dispute. The political analogue of the right to strike from ignorance is the argument that the state ought to keep out of industrial disputes.

IV. HARD CASES

A. Strikes in the Public Sector and Essential Services

Particular ethical problems arise in the public sector. It is often argued that public sector strikes distort the democratic process, because they usurp the decision making of public representative bodies by imposing industrial muscle. Other problems are involved in strikes in the public sector and in essential services such as health care, the fire services, the armed services, and the police. Such strikes are likely to cause more, and more direct harm to individuals than those in the private sector. Services in these areas are "essential" to some degree, and employees in the areas are therefore argued to have special responsibilities that go beyond those of workers producing commodities in a competitive market in the private sector. Another way of putting this is to argue that these sectors of the economy are directed at the provision of human needs. The answer to the question "essential for what?" differs between the services provided by train drivers and those provided by doctors in an accident and emergency department. Often it is argued that strikes ought not to be pursued, or ought not to be allowed in such essential services. The issues are sharply focused if we look at the arguments presented against and in favor of the right of health care personnel to take strike action, but similar arguments apply to many strikes in areas that are considered essential, such as the fire service or the police.

B. The Case Against a Right to Strike for Health Care Personnel

Health care personnel ought not to take strike action, because they bear, as part of their job, a responsibility for the welfare and the lives of those they care for, and the lives of those they care for are put at risk by going on strike. The patients may suffer, or die. Doctors have special responsibilities, voluntarily undertaken, which make them unlike employees in nonessential services. The harm caused by the former striking is different in kind from the harm caused by the latter striking. If doctors strike, their patients suffer and may die, and their right to adequate health care is frustrated. If employees in nonessential services strike, then the goods or services that they produce are unavailable for the duration of the strike, but this causes inconvenience and not direct harm. While the special responsibilities of health care personnel have been undertaken voluntarily, once taken, they are binding. They arise from the right to health care that is the right of everyone in a developed society to necessary, basic treatment. However there is no corresponding "right" to a tin of baked beans, and therefore no special responsibility of workers in a baked bean factory not to strike. The case against a moral right to strike for health care personnel emphasizes the special nature of their work and the distinctive obligations carried with it. Often such opposition is based on a Kantian conception of overriding duty and the moral imperative on treating moral agents as ends in themselves. It is argued that using patients' suffering as a political weapon amounts to treating patients entirely as a means to an end rather than viewing them as an end in themselves, and so is morally impermissible. Other reasons for opposing a right to strike for health care personnel arise from matters of fact: senior doctors are often entrepreneurs rather than employees, and they normally have other mechanisms for the redress of grievances. Sometimes independent, binding arbitration is advocated in order to make up for the loss of a right that is available to others.

C. The Case for a Moral Right to Strike for Health Care Personnel

The case for a moral right to strike for health care personnel emphasizes the similarities between health care personnel and other employees. Interns, technicians, ambulance workers and manual staff are often comparatively low paid and work comparatively long hours. Indeed, public sector workers are sometimes held to be underpaid precisely because they are more vulnerable than workers in private industry to exploitation, because the employer is able to rely on their unwillingness to strike. But sometimes it is suggested that the responsibilities they bear are not just for current patients but for the welfare of actual and potential patients, including those who may be in need of medical care in the future. Hence, health care personnel have a responsibility to use their influence to ensure the highest provision of health care possible. The right to strike of health care personnel and the right to health care conflict, to be sure, but such rights are prima facie rather than absolute; they establish a presumption in favor of the permissibility of certain actions. When considering strike action, health care personnel may be fulfilling an obligation to themselves, couched in terms of their self-defense, and to the welfare of future patients, because strike action may be the only way in which to draw attention to the under provision in a hospital and to secure extra resources. Some suggest that the special responsibilities borne by health care personnel are also held by the agencies employing them.

An unsatisfactory attempt to downgrade the special responsibilities of health care personnel rests on the claim that the option of taking strike action is morally equivalent to the option of resigning one's job, and there is no reasonable objection to an employee resigning from her job. But this is not the case. Strike action takes place on the presumption that the striker's job ought not to be filled by someone willing to work under its current conditions of labor. But the opposite assumption applies to someone who resigns her job. They give up any claim to determine the conditions of work.

The doctrine that acts and omissions are morally on the same level, and the idea that potential patients and future patients ought to be accorded some moral weight are both brought into health care personnel's right to strike. If the moral symmetry of acts and omissions is rejected, and/or future generations are held to possess little moral weight, then the direct harm caused by strikes of health care personnel is likely to be the decisive factor. While advocates of the right to strike recognize that direct harm is likely to be caused, they also point out that harm and avoidable deaths are caused by all policy decisions that involve the distribution of scarce resources. It may be that not going on strike and hence remaining complicit in the existing levels of health care provision by overworked, error-prone, health care personnel itself entails harm, avoidable death, and suffering. Such calculations, which are like the calculations made by health resource allocators, are part of the special responsibilities that health care personnel possess, which are sometimes interpreted in line with the symmetry of acts and omissions as a responsibility not to provide inadequate health care. The utilitarian

tenor of the argument for a right to strike for health care personnel clearly confronts the Kantian tone of those who deny such a right.

Very often the key objection to strikes by health care personnel, that is, that they cause unnecessary suffering and possibly death, is partly undercut by the provision of emergency care throughout the duration of the strike (for example, during the 1990 ambulance workers' strike in the United Kingdom). Sometimes this is a legal obligation. Such cover is intended to ensure that patients suffer inconvenience but not serious harm. Threats have been made, however to close down cover in operating theaters on occasion, such as during the Ontario physicians strike in 1987, and the existence of this possibility is likely to create public apprehension. It is sometimes suggested that, however restricted the inconvenience caused to patients is, the act of striking breaks bonds of trust between health care personnel and their patients. Even if such strike action is unjustifiable, it is mistaken to slide from the impermissibility of strike action in such cases to the impermissibility of any strike action in essential services.

D. Secondary Action

In place of the term "secondary action" some favor the more positive terms sympathy or solidarity strike and argue that an effective strike generally requires such action. Some ambiguity is present when interpreting whether "employer" refers to the corporate identity concerned, or the individuals who actually own that identity; this problem arises from the practice of establishing separate corporate identities for the distribution part of an original firm that has been struck and then arguing that the action taken against it is secondary, illegitimate, and illegal. This was the strategy pursued by News International in the dispute that followed the dismissal of printworkers at Wapping in the United Kingdom in 1986. Some have argued that, faced with powerful transnational corporations, the only way to ensure that strike action is effective is for employees to encourage secondary action. In order to fill out a right to strike, it is felt necessary that strikers be able to act effectively and this is only possible if they are permitted to take secondary action. Against this is weighed the consideration that harm is caused to an employer not directly involved in the dispute, who is not only an innocent third party, but also has no power to change the terms and conditions of employment for those involved in the primary action.

E. Political and General Strikes

A political strike can be broadly defined as a strike directed at changing an aspect of public policy. However, while such analytical distinctions are clear enough as abstractions, they tend to break down if they are made the basis of classification. Public sector wage rates, for example, are a matter of public policy. Because strikes implicitly throw into question some key relationships of contemporary society, they are arguably always implicitly political. Strikes carried out for political ends raise wider ethical and political problems, particularly in democratic polities. They implicitly question the legitimacy of the standard procedures of decision making, and are very often illegal. What matters here is the availability of other avenues for employees to articulate their demands in an appropriate way. If such avenues are closed off, the right to strike can be seen as a democratic right. The openness of a society is in inverse proportion to the justification of a general strike for political change. Strikes that break the law take the ethics of strike action onto the terrain of state theory and raise questions about what kind of obligation is owed to a democratic state. It is commonly argued that political strikes distort the democratic process. Madison, following Rousseau, feared the influence of factions in democratic systems and it may be argued that trade unions use their power to overturn constitutionally established laws in order to promote their narrow sectional interests. More generally opposition to political strikes is based on the doctrine of the mandate; that when a government has a public mandate, the only justifiable form of protests is within the law, ultimately at an election.

Against this line of argument, the doctrine of the mandate might be rejected as a justification of any public policy at all. For, while it matters *how* the law is made, *what* law is made is also an ethically relevant consideration. Many rights theorists accept that the rights and interests of a group may not be undermined simply on the basis of a mandate to do so. The core of the principle of the mandate, the majority principle, appears to commit people to obeying a law that oppresses them. It gives the majority a warrant to impose any injustice on a minority. Hence, there might be a case for illegal action despite the existence of elections, because fundamental rights or interests are not respected.

Democratic political obligation is undermined by ideological disjuncture (disagreement over key values that underpin a democratic polity) and the structural privileging of the interests of capital over those of labor, reinforcing the excessive power of employers, which is determined by the structural arrangements of capitalist society. A further argument concerns the aims of a strike. Typically, democratic states are based on certain underlying relations of power, and it may be impossible to challenge those relations through the established forms of political debate and negotiation. As well as being a challenge to decision-making processes, widespread political strikes are an indication that at least a substantial number of the population of a polity regard the democratic consensus as having broken down, and they show a desire to renegotiate those underlying relations. Clearly, the judgment one reaches on political and general strikes will have a lot to do with the position taken on the ethics of civil disobedience, where such strikes are illegal, and the legitimacy or otherwise of the decision-making processes in place.

V. CONCLUSION

It is worthwhile questioning whether or not it is possible to establish the analytical independence of strikes from general perspectives on the nature of the work contract. Important social theorists Marx, Nozick, and Rawls all differ on the nature of that contract, and on the sort of rights that can be established as a result. It is plausible to argue that the right to strike is an essentially contested concept, and it is certainly politically contested, because of the contested nature of the work contract.

Strike action will remain a focus of ethical concern, particularly as shifting patterns of work mean a shrinking of manual work in the private sector and a shift of employment toward the public sector and essential services, just the areas where strike action is most contentious. The conflict between the right to strike and other responsibilities taken on by the providers of essential service will be one dynamic of future controversy. Other areas of ethical concern include the status and justifiability of wildcat strikes, and the widespread use of threats and bluffing that is often bound up in strike action.

Nevertheless, the acknowledgment of a bedrock right to strike is seen by many as one of the marks of a free society. There are two reasons for this. The first is that the right to strike is a barometer of the existence of other democratic and human rights that are thought to be important. The second is that by its nature the right to strike is instrumental in preserving and winning many other rights: bans on strikes can be defied, and strike action is a last resort method of protesting against an authoritarian regime and defending the rights of employees. While the consequences of strikes necessarily involve harm, the proscriptions on strike activity in the former Soviet Union ought to be persuasive arguments about the relationship between a right to strike and the democratic nature of a social system. Nevertheless, the justification of particular strikes will remain essentially contested.

Also See the Following Articles

ACTS AND OMISSIONS • CIVIL DISOBEDIENCE • GAME THEORY • KANTIANISM • MARX AND ETHICS • RIGHTS THEORY • UTILITARIANISM

Bibliography

Blanpain, R. (Ed.). (1994). *Employee rights and industrial justice.* Deventer: Kluwer.

Brecher, R. (1985). Striking responsibilities. *Journal of Medical Ethics,* **11,** 66–69.

Cullity, G. (1995). Moral free riding. *Philosophy and Public Affairs,* **24,** 1, 3–34.

Glick, S. M. (1985). Physicians strikes—a rejoinder. *Journal of Medical Ethics,* **11,** 196–197.

Locke, D. (1985). The right to strike. In A. Phillips Griffiths (Ed.), *Philosophy and practice.* Cambridge: Cambridge University Press.

Macfarlane, L. J. (1981). *The right to strike.* Harmondsworth: Penguin.

Malin, M. H. (1993). Public employees right to strike: Law and experience. *University of Michigan Journal of Law Reform,* **26,** 2, 313–401.

Meslin, Eric M. (1987, August). The moral costs of the Ontario physicians strike. *Hastings Center Report.*

Olson, M. (1965). *The logic of collective action.* Cambridge, MA: Harvard University Press.

Smart, B. (1985). The right to strike and the right to work. *Journal of Applied Philosophy,* **2,** 1.

Ullman-Margalit, E. A. (1976). *The emergence of norms.* Oxford: Oxford University Press.

SUGGESTION, ETHICS OF

Emilio Mordini
Psychoanalytic Institute for Social Research

GLOSSARY

altered states of consciousness (ASCs) Waking states that are characterized by a qualitative change in the consciousness that invariably includes dreamlike experiences. They include twilight states, mystical states, trancelike states, automatic behavior, hypnotic states, somnambulism, dissociative phenomena, and depersonalization. ASCs produced by means of drugs, meditation, yoga, hypnosis, and other techniques are indistinguishable from those occurring as a psychiatric symptom.

akrasia From ancient Greek, meaning a lack of self-control, or incontinence. The condition in which one does something different that what he or she knows to be his or her best because of a "weakness of will."

automatism The automatic performance of an act or acts; when the phenomenon occurs following hypnosis it is called *command automatism*, or *automatic obedience*.

autonomy/heteronomy Agents are autonomous (self-governing) if they have the *capacity* for self-government, namely, their will is free. They are heterono-

mous ("other governed") if their will is *under the control* of another.

dissociative disorders The class of psychiatric disorders apparently characterized by the subject's dissociation, that is, the subject's mental processes look *as if* they were performed by different subjects. They include symptomatic disturbances of memory (dissociative amnesia), of consciousness (dissociative fugue), and of personality (multiple personality disorder).

free will The belief that we are free agents. The reality of free will cannot be proved; moreover, the belief in free will appears to be in contrast to deterministic sciences (but some philosophers may contest this statement). Free will is, however, part of the everyday consciousness of ourselves and must be postulated to base moral reasoning.

hypnosis A distinctive waking state (the still common popular idea of hypnosis as a sleeplike condition is a misconception) in which a person is able to react to convenient suggestions by having alterations of perception, memory, or mood. The essential characteristic of the phenomenon is the subjective experience, because hypnosis cannot be neurophysiologically distinguished from other waking states in general. From the point of view of an external observer, hypnosis is characterized by the hypnotized subject's increased suggestibility and suspension of critical judgment.

posthypnotic suggestion Instructions supplied during a hypnotic session that the hypnotized subject fol-

Encyclopedia of Applied Ethics, Volume 4
Copyright © 1998 by Academic Press. All rights of reproduction in any form reserved.

lows afterward, that is, when he is out of the hypnotic trance. Hypnotic suggestions can drive persons to carry out complex actions because of a previous command while they attribute those activities to conscious intention.

self-deception A misunderstanding of facts due to an active and motivated believing in what is not true according to the subject's knowledge. The paradox is that the same agent, in the same moment, and regarding the same question is both the deceiver and the deceived *as if* he or she could simultaneously know and ignore something.

suggestion A mental process according to which an individual accepts a mental content or a conduct coming from other individuals, or institutions, or from himself (autosuggestion), without doing any rational verification.

—————————

SUGGESTION is the meeting point between many different disciplines (philosophy, psychology, anthropology, and psychiatry) as well as between many different problems that chiefly concern moral agency and responsibility. Generally speaking, suggestion is "the process of inducing someone to behave in a particular way, accept a particular opinion, or believe in something, by indirect methods" (Reber, A. S. (1985). *Dictionary of Psychology*. Penguin Books). This broad definition subsumes different kinds of suggestive influences on an agent's will. These influences appear to vary in intensity but not in quality. From a descriptive point of view, all suggestive influences seem to be associated with the induction of the suggested subject of any altered states of consciousness (ASCs) or like conditions. ASCs are not states of reduced conscience; in fact, they can even be states of increased awareness. Hypnosis is characterized by focusing on particular stimuli of which the subject becomes overly aware, until the point that she loses her awareness of other stimuli.

Many different stimuli may be suggestive—words, ritual music and chanting, meditation, drugs, and also specific techniques such as hypnosis. All of these stimuli are joined by the same capacity to induce, or provoke, or make use of, such alterations in the subject's conscience that she is no longer able to conduct a rational verification of suggested beliefs or conducts. An agent can also succeed in being both the subject and the object of the suggestion, namely in "suggesting herself." The philosophical paradox of *autosuggestion* is the same as that implied in the notions of *self-deception* and akrasia.

Suggestion obviously requires suggestibility, namely, the ability to respond to suggestion. Some persons are highly responsive to suggestions; others are less so. Suggestibility is a rather stable quality in adults, and it has nothing to do with compliance, conformity, or naiveté, but it is likely to be a basic human ability. This ability has an evolutionary meaning and it is already present in other mammals, especially in primates (e.g., yawn contagion, synchronization of gaze direction).

Several philosophical problems are raised by suggestion. By definition, suggestion is a process in which the subject's autonomy is overwhelmed and substituted by heteronomy. The mere existence of suggestive processes implies that one might be not responsible for her behavior. There is a basic experience that should be first be exposed to make clear the problem's frame: this experience is called "posthypnotic suggestion." During a hypnotic session we can give to the subject some instructions to be executed afterward; say, we can tell her to open the window as soon as she awakes. What is remarkable is not that the hypnotized subject obeys but that she invariably produces a rational explication to justify her gesture. Say, in our instance, if asked why she opened the window, she could answer: "It is too hot," or "The air is stale." In brief, she gives the same explications that any of us might give to explain any of our gestures. It then becomes clear why it has been argued that many normal daily activities can be conducted in a posthypnotic state; although most actions are attributed to conscious intention, they might, in fact, be carried out because of a previous suggestion. How can a suggestion be distinguished from a nonsuggestion? How can we be sure that we do not live under the effect of soft hypnosis, of suggestive influences, of unknown charms? This hypothesis may remind us of Descartes' evil genius and that indeed suggestion may deceive our senses, memories, and reasoning as that genius. Moreover, differently from the *malin génie*, suggestion does not leave us yet the possibility to ground a demon-proof point of certainty. If suggestion is ubiquitous, Descartes' solution, *cogito ergo sum*, is not valid any more; my thoughts could not be my thoughts, and their existence proves nothing but that there should be someone who has thought them (perhaps God as in Malebranche's theory). I might be just the recipient of "my" thoughts (admittedly it could be taken as a proof of my existence all the same). Suggestion is therefore a very subtle theme to be investigated because it directly regards our personal identity. The problem is whether free agency is a reality or just the result of an illusion. This is because the agent might not be free and, less obviously, because the mere existence of an agent might be illusory.

I. BIOLOGY

The biology of suggestion is largely unknown. One of the most important issues in research has been the nature of the relation between suggestion and the normal state of consciousness. The gap between these two conditions is bridged by "normal" automatic behaviors. Any definite distinction between conscious and unconscious mental processes, as well as between voluntary and involuntary behaviors, leaves out the important role played by automatic behaviors in everyday life: "The housewife staring vacantly over a cup of coffee, the student with a faraway look in his eyes during the middle of a lecture, and the driver who automatically reaches his destination with no memory of the details of his route, are all varieties of the common everyday trance" (Rossi, E. (1982) Hypnosis and ultradian cycles: A new state theory of hypnosis? *Am. J. Clin. Hypnosis,* **25**: 21–32, p.22). The notion of "common everyday trance" is quite crucial. Suggestibility and hypnotic susceptibility vary in degree of intensity during the day and appear in fact to be related to ultradian variations in wakefulness.

The brain is governed by different rhythms stimulated by several neural pacemakers. These rhythms are extremely sensitive, having an adaptive function in helping to synchronize the individual with her environment. Circadian rhythms organize bodily functions around the 24-hour day, while ultradian rhythms are recurrent rhythms of less than 24 hours. In humans there is evidence of an ultradian rhythm in vigilance, with changes in peripheral blood flow, respiratory amplitude, and visually evoked potential. There is also evidence of a parallel recurring cognitive and emotional cycle associated with an increase in daydream and fantasy. Subjects appear to repeat the cycle about 16 times per day, every 70 to 120 minutes. Neurologically, these cycles are likely to be the effect of an alternate change in hemispheric dominance. Ultradian rhythms of wakefulness seem therefore to constitute the source of automatic behaviors and common everyday trance, and they might explain the biological basis of suggestion.

II. ANTHROPOLOGY

Suggestive techniques have long been in use in religious, ceremonial, and healing practices. Trance and similar ASCs are universally recognized in all known cultures. While in literate culture the use of institutionalized ASCs is restricted to hypnosis, spiritual ceremonies, and some medical conditions, in preliterate societies, the use of ASCs is far more varied and typically involves a wide number of medical, religious, social, and psychological aspects.

In preliterate cultures various forms of ASCs (spontaneous trance or provoked by hallucinogens and other drugs) are used in a variety of way (music, chant, dance, poetry). They can be employed for physical healing or conflict arbitration, or for marking rites of passage. They are also important in defining social roles. In oral societies trance is frequently associated to particular social groups, for example, male homosexuals.

Suggestive and autosuggestive techniques were absolutely part of the poetic art, and the features of oral poetry were inherently hypnotic. Poetry was an important mnemonic and educational device for oral cultures. Memorization in a preliterate society is quite different from what we are used to, because there was no original text to memorize. What the oral poet memorizes is not a text but a certain number of themes and styles, a certain number of implicit linguistic patterns. These patterns become a sort of chant that "takes possession" of the poet by means of suggestive techniques. Medicine and religion (the identity between the two in preliterate societies has been widely discussed by many scholars) were other important fields where suggestive methods used to play an important role. Hypnotic techniques have been described in almost all ancient medical practices. We can find accurate descriptions of hypnoticlike procedures in one of the oldest Egyptians' medical document, the "Ebers Papyrus," and sleep healing at the temple of Asclepius in ancient Greece has been interpreted as a form of hypnosis. Moreover, trancelike states attributed to spirit, divine, or demoniac possession are part of the mystic traditions of Judaism, Islam, Christianity, and many other religions.

Actually, all of these situations (oral poetry, healing ceremonies, mystic rituals) are characterized by any form of possession. Possession is therefore the key concept for understanding suggestion in preliterate societies (see the classic description of this theme in the critical moment of the transition from oral to literate culture in Plato's *Phedro*). From an ethical and philosophical point of view, it seems particularly interesting to differentiate between two very different kinds of possession. Luc de Heusch (Heusch L. de (1971). *Pourquoi l'épouser et autres essais,* Paris; Gallimard) speaks of demonic, or "inauthentique," possession, and shamanic possession. The first one is due to some fault done by the subject who is invaded by an external power or spirit as a result of his ritual mistakes. The second kind of possession is the "holy possession," which takes the healer, the poet, or the priest and serves the community by storing collective memories, establishing a relationship with the god or healing maladies. The former kind of possession is the result of a breach of the moral order, while the latter puts the subject out of the moral order; in fact shamans, medicine men, and oracles all live in a moral world that is very different from that of ordinary people.

III. SUGGESTION AND HYPNOSIS

A. The Historical Background

The term "hypnosis" was coined by the Scottish surgeon James Braid in the 1840s. Braid believed that the hypnotic state was a sort of artificial somnambulism and called it υπνος, the Greek word for sleep.

The interest in hypnosis reached its peak in France toward the end of the nineteenth century with a famous controversy between the school of Nancy, led by Hippolyte Bernheim (1840–1919) and the school of Paris, led by Jean Martin Charcot (1825–1893). Bernheim claimed that hypnosis was a psychological phenomenon caused by suggestion. According to Bernheim, suggestion is a peculiar attitude that can be influenced by others, and that can be activated by emotions. Bernheim's model of suggestion is based on the sensorimotor reflex described by neurologists. He believed that suggestion can act as an idea that substitutes the direct sensory impulse in the reflex loop. He called this mechanism the ideomotor reflex. Charcot, on the other hand, thought that hypnosis was a pathological state of the nervous system that occurred in those who suffered from hysteria.

Charcot's works influenced one of the brightest scholars of this period, Pierre Janet (1859–1947). Janet was actually a philosopher. He followed a course given by Charcot and decided to give his doctoral dissertation on pathological psychology published in 1889 the title "L'automatisme psychologique." Janet first observed that hypnosis can cure some mental disorders by restoring to consciousness forgotten memories and that dissociative symptoms can be reproduced by the hypnosis. In particular, he observed that part of her mental life is unknown to the patient. This led Janet to formulate the notion of the "subconscious" (which had already been introduced in philosophy by Leibniz). Janet concluded that hypnosis and dissociation are both the result of the same element, which he called the *misère psychologique*. This *misère psychologique* is a pathological deficiency of the mental energy that should tie together the various mental activities. The consequence of this deficiency is that the various psychological operations can be dissociated, both spontaneously and as an effect of hypnosis.

Hypnosis was in fashion until the beginning of the twentieth century, when its application in therapy progressively declined. Only Janet, and some American psychiatrists, including M. Prince and B. Sidis, continued to employ it in a clinical setting.

After World War II, the American scholar Milton H. Erickson was the most influential clinician in the development of hypnotherapy. He advocated what he called a "naturalistic approach" to hypnosis. This concept is based on the idea that hypnosis is an extension of normal human experience, namely, the "common everyday trance." Erickson's influence extends beyond traditional hypnotherapy; for example, strategic family therapy owes a great deal to Erickson's technique.

B. Current Hypnotherapy

The past two decades have seen a renaissance of interest in suggestive methods in medicine and psychiatry, with a surge of systematic research; there has been a reevaluation of earlier concepts, such as dissociation, and better techniques for assessing hypnotic responsivity have been developed. Hypnosis is currently accepted as a therapeutic modality by the American Medical Association, the American Psychiatric Association, and the American Psychological Association, as well as by most medical and professional groups worldwide.

In medicine, hypnosis has been shown to be effective in controlling pain, ameliorating gastrointestinal and respiratory dysfunction, and it has been used as an adjunct in other disorders. Scientific literature has supported the value of hypnosis in analgesia, especially in treating headaches, cancer pain, musculoskeletal disorders, and labor pain. Pain reduction appears to be attributable not simply to the reduction of anxiety; however, mechanisms of hypnotic pain control remain poorly understood. It has also been suggested—and moral philosophers could be interested in it, for the puzzling problems that it may pose—that hypnosis could not induce true analgesia but can only block memory of the experienced pain by means of dissociative processes.

C. Ethics of Hypnotherapy

Hypnosis is rarely mentioned in psychological and psychiatric ethics codes. However, ethical concerns on hypnotherapy concern (i) safety of the method and risks of malpractice; (ii) respect for the patient's autonomy;

(iii) the use of hypnosis to block and unblock a patient's memories.

The induction of hypnosis in healthy persons is innocuous. In clinical context hypnosis poses the same ethical problems that are seen in psychotherapy. The risk of a patient's (economic, sexual, affective) exploitation does not appear to be any higher than in normal psychiatric practice. However, some risks of malpractice may surge when hypnotic methods are adopted by poorly trained therapists, even if they happen to be physicians. It has been said that hypnosis should never be used for a condition that a therapist is unprepared to treat.

As far as a patient's autonomy is concerned, the extent to which hypnotizable persons can be coerced into doing or saying things that are contrary to their values and beliefs remains highly controversial. Many persons view hypnosis as a method to control behavior, but research has failed to show that a person is any likelier to behave differently through hypnosis than by other means. Actually, hypnosis has failed in the long-term treatment of smoking, alcohol and drug abuse, and obesity. However, the suspension of critical judgment by the hypnotized patient makes it imperative for the therapist to examine the treatment goals carefully and to make them clear in the therapeutic contract.

The use of hypnosis to block and unblock memories is definitely controversial in a clinical setting and is not acceptable in a court of justice. Hypnosis should never be used to recover the memories of traumatic events for legal purposes, and doctors should refuse such a practice. In fact, confabulation and false memories, which very often occur, not only invalidate the procedure but they can also harm both the patients and their families.

IV. SOME PHILOSOPHICAL PROBLEMS

The chief philosophical problems raised by suggestion concern free agency and personal identity. In the standard philosophical account an action needs intention and an agent. To have done an action, one must have intended to do it under some description. Identifiable agents are still another central feature of action. If nobody acts, nobody is responsible. Both conditions are somehow threatened by the existence of suggestive phenomena.

A. Free Agency

Some scholars have argued that suggestion is a structural component of a normal mental life. In this view most behaviors might occur in hypnoticlike states. As a result, any behavior at any time can be attributed to suggestive influences. Desires, preferences, thoughts, and any mental content could be just ad hoc rationalizations that we construct a posteriori to justify what we have thought and done under suggestion. That is the reason these authors often argue that free agency is just an illusion. In the final analysis they all assume that autonomy can (almost) always be reduced to heteronomy. All of these aspects can be found in the Greek philosopher Gorgias of Leontini.

1. Gorgias of Leontini

In Western philosophy Gorgias of Leontini (ca. 483–376 B.C.) was the first to discuss the theme of suggestion. His speculation remains a paradigm for those theories that postulate that suggestion might play a major role in everyday life. Gorgias thinks the human mind is intrinsically passive. This passivity is manifested by two processes: the receptiveness to impressions coming from the senses and the openness to language. The language, however, can act only if the mind is put under a particular seduction, which Gorgias calls πειθω (often translated as "to persuade"), to suggest. But what does *suggesting* mean? Namely, which are the elements that constitute suggestion? According to Gorgias, suggestion is made by three elements: an external influence, which he calls *powerful speech*; an internal disposition, which he calls *opinion*; and the right moment, which he calls the *opportune time*. The ontological uncertainty is the real source of suggestion. Suggestibility comes from the fact that one's beliefs cannot be grounded on a true knowledge but they must be based on opinion. Opinion does not only mean "opinion," but it has a broader sense, indicating the human state of uncertainty that arises because reason cannot choose between different alternatives. Gorgias thinks that this condition is nothing but the constitutive human situation. As a consequence, humans are looking forward to achieving something with certainty. This something is, paradoxically, the *illusion* created by the persuasive speech, that Gorgias calls the *powerful speech*. This speech is not based on rational arguments or even on emotional appeals, but is a sort of charm, embodied in a tangle of words—almost a magic formula. According to Gorgias, theater, poetry, and rhetoric all originate from this mysterious, charming power that words may have. The powerful speech is definitely a sort of music (this theory probably comes from Pythagorean circles). However, uncertainty and powerful speech are not enough to explain suggestion. We need a third element, which Gorgias calls the time opportune. This concept is one of the most intriguing of the ancient Greek philosophy. This the time opportune in the sense of the word "timing," *tempo*, in music. The logic conception of the world, such as the principle of noncontradiction, is based on the postulate of linear time, where any moment is equal to any other, and one moment follows the other. What really exists must persist in linear time, and from this principle Plato derives that the True Being should be eternal. Gorgias refuses the conception according to which eternity is the truth of time. Gorgias believes that time is essentially discontinuous, made by right and wrong moments. Opportune time is the genius of the moment, and even if it is essential for political and military education, ethics is its real field of application. Gorgias' *Encomium of Helen* was the first clear treatment of the problem of free will, and the three elements that he enlightened (powerful speech, opinion, and opportune time) remain fundamental to understanding the debate on free agency and social context, including casuistry, contextualism, and feminist and situation ethics.

B. Personal Identity

Suggestion and related phenomena apply not only to our belief in free agency but they also weaken our everyday faith in the existence of the units of the self. Unity of the self, that is, of the person, has always been one of the most intriguing problems of philosophy. The elaboration of disparate psychological events into a coherent personality with a large measure of autonomy is a universal human experience. The problem arises when we try to understand whether the subjective experience of this coherent personality corresponds to any real object or is just a useful figment. Actually, the idea of one subject regarded as an agent, and as being aware of her own identity and of her role as subject and agent that survives through life's normal changes of experience, seems to be highly metaphysical.

The problem of personal identity was first debated in the modern era by Locke, who devoted an influential chapter to it in the *Essay Concerning Human Understanding*. Locke's solution is in the unity of the stream of consciousness, and particularly in the presence of memory of past actions. Some anticonventional thinkers have criticized the notion of personal identity. In antiquity it has been the case of Pyrrhonism, while in modern philosophy one should mention at least Hume's phenomenism and Taine's positivism. According to Hume and Taine, the self is nothing but an illusion without any substance. The only reality of the concept of "self" is just that of natural phenomena and their links deter-

mined by causal chains. As proposed by Hume, the bundle theory of the self (or of the mind) claims that we have no reason to think in terms of a single unified self that owns a variety of experiences or states. We only have access to the succession of states themselves. The enduring self is a fiction.

In the nineteenth century people were fascinated by double, alternate, and multiple personalities. Multiple personality disorder (MPD) and other forms of dissociation formed a central part of W. James' classic *Principles of Psychology*. James was intrigued by the implications of these disorders for the understanding of the relationship between memory and personal identity. James in fact described the mind as a "confederation of psychic entities," whose cohesion depends on memory. Memory is therefore the matrix of personal identity, and the sense of self is carried by memory through time. Alterations in memory (as seen in dissociative disorders) can lead to discontinuity in personal experience and in the sense of identity.

Modern reductionists have maintained that personal identity is nothing but the psychological continuity created by memory links. An excellent overview of the current debate on personal identity, memory, and mental phenomena can be found in the work of D. Parfit, who partly shares Locke's point.

Arguments on memory and personal identity have been raised in the current bioethical debate to address the issue of advance directives in Alzheimer's Disease and other dementing disorders. If catastrophic change in memory can dramatically modify personal identity, it implies that the subject who gave her advance directives does not exist any more, and we are not therefore entitled to apply her directives on the "new" subject, that is, on the "new mind" that is a consequence of the dementing disorder.

However, as far as suggestion is concerned, the main questions on personal identity are raised by akrasia, self-deception, multiple personality disorder, and other dissociative disorders.

1. Akrasia and Self-Deception

Self-deception and akrasia are in the limelight of the current debate among postmodern philosophers. This is not surprising, because they represent a good example of that deconstruction of the subject that characterizes this philosophical current. Actually, in postmodern accounts akrasia and self-deception are paradigms of the multiple self. When philosophers speak of the "problem of the weakness of will" and the "problem of self-deception" they usually pose the question of how these two phenomena are understandable given our notion of a unit self. Indeed, they both undermine our belief in a free, rational agent who is the subject of moral actions.

Akrasia, self-deception, and suggestion are actually strictly interlaced, and it has been proposed that suggestion could be one of the possible routes of the "akratic strategy." Akrasia is the "weakness of will," and it has been said that suggestion is nothing but a particular form of weakness of will, namely, the fact that one's will is not sufficient to withstand other wills, including different wills on the same subject.

Moral philosophers may be interested in knowing that prima facie obligations (pro tanto obligations) have been considered to be an example of akratic strategy, at least from a subjective point of view.

2. Multiple Personality Disorder and Other Dissociative Disorders

Multiple personality disorder (MPD) is a psychiatric disorder characterized by the spontaneous generation of an alternate version of self. The personalities have distinctive styles of expressing themselves and they often posses separate names, genders, ages, family histories, and life-styles. They may have different occupations, sets of friends, and social networks. Sometimes, the physiologic differences between the various MPD personalities can be really surprising: differences in IQ, handiness, handwriting style, visual acuity, and other features have been reported in the literature. Although personalities can be complementary to one other, very often one can distinguish an original personality from another personality that acts like a persecutor.

MPD is likely to occur as an attempt to integrate the consequences of traumatic experiences in individuals with high suggestibility. The exposure to a severe and emotionally overwhelming physical or mental trauma could somehow provoke dissociative disorders, as if the individual is unable to cope with the trauma of maintaining unit his own personality.

MPD is a controversial subject. Some scholars insist that it usually goes undetected; others have criticized the conception of childhood trauma. Actually, an explicit trauma may or may not be present. Trauma may also occur only in the internal, emotional world of the subject, without any detectable recognizable events is. This debate directly concerns the foundation of psychoanalysis.

MPD poses several puzzling problems for the theory of personal identity; this also holds true also for other dissociative disorders. Some patients are able to dissociate memories of single events (dissociative amnesia), or memories of complex behaviors, which they can accomplish in a trancelike state (dissociative fugue,

somnambulism, trance disorders). In the final analysis, dissociation appears to be an effort to repair models of self and others, namely, dissociative disorders show that we are constantly creating versions of ourselves and others, and these versions depend upon the social contexts and some inner capacities to select our memories both consciously and unconsciously.

Moral philosophers may be intrigued by this continuum, which begins with conscious fiction, passes through self-deception, akrasia, and autosuggestion, and arrives at dissociative disorders. Actually, there is a psychiatric syndrome that clearly enlightens all these aspects, called *Ganser's syndrome* (currently classified in DSM IV among *Dissociative Disorders not otherwise specified*). Ganserian patients are usually jailers who pretend to be mad. Their fictitious symptoms include bizarre delusions, amnesia, and confabulation. After a certain time Ganserian patients begin to believe more and more in their fiction until they develop a true "false psychosis," namely, dissociative disorders out of the control of their will that faithfully reproduce the original mental disturbance. From a legal and ethical perspective it is highly controversial whether Ganserian patients should be treated as if they are remarkable simulators or actual mentally disturbed people.

V. SUGGESTION AND ETHICS OF HEALTH CARE

There is no doubt that suggestion plays an important role in the doctor–patient relationship, especially in long-term care when the relation becomes a crucial element of the healing process. Facial expressions, prosodic elements of speech, vocal intonation, breathing, eye contact, and gestures are all bound together in an ongoing feedback system of nonverbal communication. These nonverbal messages shape the clinical setting, usually below the level of conscious awareness of both the patient and the doctor. Good physicians appear to synchronize their speech and gestures to those of their patients, and there is a strong positive correlation between patients' overall ratings of satisfaction and the individual physician's ability to respond nonverbally.

It has been argued that most bioethical debate on patient autonomy is marked by abstraction and does not take into account all of these aspects. The bioethicist's "ideal patient" is a single person in acute distress with well-defined options and choices, who is free to act and is fully rational, and who knows his own best interests and needs nothing except for technical information. This patient is clearly free of any suggestive influence, is not deceiving himself, and his will is not weak. This model adopted by the bioethics literature may work well enough for acute and time-limited medical conditions, but perhaps it moves too far from reality when the human interaction becomes an important element of the clinical context.

At least three subjects should be debated: Information; placebo effect; and suggestion and psychotherapies.

A. Information and Consent to Treatment

Informed consent is an important feature of bioethics theory. The standard bioethical account understands information as simply declarative: we "pass down" information to the patient. Against this standard bioethics view, it has been said that what we need is not plain, bare information but communication. Communication is not purely cognitive; it is not even just "in the head." It involves several elements: empathy, nonverbal messages, and unconscious reactions. Admittedly, even slight manipulations of voice tone may have a significant effect in changing the content of information given to the patient. As a consequence, suggestive messages may play an important role, both in passing the information and in negotiating the patient's consent. It is a common experience that nonverbal suggestions, combined with "neutral" and "irrelevant" comments, may dramatically alter the personal acceptance of a therapy. Scientific literature convincingly shows that doctors who do believe in the therapy that they are using can more easily achieve a patient's consent, while those who are doubtful are expected to have a higher rate of refusal (and failure in treatment).

The importance of nonverbal messages often has been underestimated both in therapy and in clinical trials. In 1985 an impressive article published in the *Journal of the American Medical Association* showed that about 70% of doctors and 80% of patients were perfectly aware of what substance (propranolol or placebo) was given in a large double-blind study (Byington R. P., Curb J. D., & Mattson M. E. Assessment of double-blindness at the conclusion of the beta-blocker heart attack trial. *JAMA* **253**: 1733–1736). The article ended by stating that true conditions of double-blindness are likely to be quite difficult to obtain. In brief, the net of unconscious messages that permeates the doctor–patient relationship should be always taken into account, especially if we aim to replace the too-formal notion of information with the more concrete concept of communication.

B. Placebo

The relationship between therapy and recovery can be explained in three ways. First, a treatment can be effective. Second, "nature" can heal the patient without any true causal relation between treatment and recovery (*vix medicatrix naturae*). Third, the medicament may work as a *placebo*. Placebo is a Latin word that means "I shall be loved." Any substance that acts independently from its pharmacological activity can be considered a placebo. The term was first used in the nineteenth century but the notion of placebo is as old as medicine. Generally speaking, a placebo works by means of suggestion. However, a convincing explanation and mechanism of action for placebo response have yet to be articulated. The substance used as a placebo can even have a biochemical activity (it is not required that it be inert) but the result of its administration is independent of its biochemical effects. In current medical practice, antibiotics and minor tranquilizers very often work as if they were placebos. It does not imply that they do not posses any pharmacological activity, but it may happen that this activity has nothing (or little) to do with their effectiveness in the clinical setting (e.g., an antibiotic may "cure" a flu even if flu is a viral disease, namely, a disease that is nonresponsive to antibiotics!). It should be also considered the notion of "nocebo," namely, of a negative placebo. One can speak of "nocebo effect" when effects of an active drug are reduced or even suppressed by a patient's negative reaction to the medicament.

The ethics of placebo treatment is a delicate issue. One should distinguish two very different situations: (i) when the placebo is knowingly used by the doctor; (ii) when both patient and doctor ignore the existence of a placebo effect. While the latter case does not pose ethical problems, the former does. Placebo implies that a doctor may consciously decide to deceive her patient. Is this ethically tenable? That is a very difficult question. Apart from clinical trials, doctors may sometimes have a need to deceive their patients. Suppose that a patient who is suffering from chronic pain due to an osteoarthritis is also suffering from a gastric ulcer. All known anti-inflammatory agents cannot be used on a peptic ulcer because they could dramatically impair it, while the medical literature convincingly shows that joint pain can be ameliorated by a placebo. In this case should the doctor be entitled to deceive her patient, namely to give him an inert medication, pretending that it is a powerful anti-inflammatory? If it works (and it may really work), is this deception ethically acceptable? Of course, it is very uncommon to have bald alternatives in clinical practice. Very often doctors may choose among different options, with only a few implying the use of deceptive methods. Nevertheless, the problem remains, at least theoretically.

C. Psychoanalysis and Other Psychotherapies

Suggestion appears in the Freud's works from two different perspectives. The first is related to therapy. Freud was not obsessed by the refusal of suggestive methods, and he accepted that suggestion can be useful in psychotherapy, even if he always stated that "pure" psychoanalysis should avoid using it. Actually, Freud believed that psychoanalysis should renounce deceptive methods because of an ethical exigency. At the end of his life he wrote: "One must not forget that the relationship between analyst and patient is based on a love of truth, that is, acknowledgment of reality, and that it precludes any kind of sham or deceit" (Freud S. (1939) Analysis terminable and interminable. In *The Complete Psychological Works of S. Freud* (Vol. 23), p. 248. London: Hogart Press, 1964).

From a more theoretical point of view, it is well known that the birth of psychoanalysis was marked by Freud's refusal to take advantage of the notion of suggestion. Freud has always criticized the use of suggestion as a mere expedient to produce ad hoc explanations of mental phenomena. He believes that the term "suggestion" denotes, somehow masking it, a particular kind of fusional love. The role of this peculiar love relationship in the construction of the human mind is limited to some archaic functions, used in the early stages of development, and that can be reactivated both by hypnosis and mass phenomena.

Suggestion was not discussed by other first-generation psychoanalysts, with the important exception of Sandor Ferenczi. According to Ferenczi the hypnotic state, such as any other suggestive state, is a transference phenomenon, in which he who suggests temporarily acquires the authority of a parent, some techniques being paternal, others maternal. Ferenczi's point was that the mere self-awareness obtained thanks to psychoanalytic interpretation often failed to recover patients. In 1924 he published a book he wrote with Otto Rank in which they sustained the idea that suggestive methods were the final point of development of the psychoanalytic technique. According to Ferenczi and Rank only by repeating whole fragments of their evolution, fragments that are very often inaccessible to the memory, can patients really recover.

After being ignored for years, Ferenczi's work has been recently revalued. It has been said the Ferenczi was the most modern among psychoanalysts of the Freudian circle. Indeed, Ferenczi posed basic questions about the essence of the "talking cure." Namely, he posed the crucial question about the nature of the mutative change agents in psychotherapy. This appears to be a technical question, but in fact it is a real theoretical conundrum that tends to dissolve any distinctions between different psychotherapies. As a matter of fact psychotherapies can work, but sometimes it seems that they work for reasons that are very different from those given by their theorists.

Two contemporary European scholars have recently discussed the theme of suggestion in psychotherapy. The French psychoanalyst, Jacques Lacan, stigmatized any use of suggestive methods in psychoanalysis, and he blamed the same notion of psychotherapy. Yet Lacan's theory is surprisingly very close to Gorgias. Lacan stated that the truth is nothing but the illusion created by speech, and, according to Lacan, words do not serve to communicate but rather to evocate. Even the importance given to the psychological dimension of time (*l'instant du regard*, the moment of the glance) has definitely played the same role as what Gorgias called the time opportune in Lacan's theory.

The Italian psychoanalyst Sandro Gindro has argued that suggestion is a primary and constitutive modality of mental life, which is interlaced with attachment mechanisms. As a consequence Gindro accepts that suggestive methods can also be used in dynamic psychotherapies. Yet he believes that, from an ethical point of view, any suggestive technique should be revealed to the patient as soon as it becomes possible, namely, when the disclosure of the truth cannot impair the treatment and harm the patient any more.

Nondynamic psychotherapies, especially family therapies, make broad use of suggestive methods. Conscious deceit (as in paradoxical injunction, and prescribing of the symptom) and intervention outside of the patient's awareness are good examples of these. Arguments that ethically justify these techniques can drift easily into manipulation, which is not respectful of the patient's autonomy, nor of the truth itself. Moreover, suggestive and deceiving methods have posed several problems for the issue of patient's informed consent. Most authors have argued that the patient's consent concerns the treatment as a whole and does not concern each single therapeutic act. However, this is against current trends in the ethics of informed consent that emphasize the need to achieve the consent for each passage of the treatment and that deny any validity to consent given in a generic way. It has been also proposed an ethical code for suggestive psychotherapies to protect patient's autonomy has also been proposed. All these issues have been debated widely in current psychiatric ethics.

Also See the Following Articles

AUTONOMY • FREUDIANISM • INFORMED CONSENT • PATIENTS' RIGHTS • PLACEBO TREATMENTS • PSYCHIATRIC ETHICS • SELF-DECEPTION

Bibliography

Collins, S. (1982). *Selfless persons.* Cambridge: Cambridge University Press.

Ellenberger, H. (1970). *The discovery of the unconscious.* New York: Basic Books.

Elster, J. (Ed.). (1979). *Ulysses and the sirens.* Cambridge: Cambridge University Press.

Elster, J. (Ed.). (1985). *The multiple self.* Cambridge: Cambridge University Press.

Karasu, T. B. (1995). Psychoanalysis and psychoanalytic psychotherapy. In Kaplan, H. I., & Sadock, B. J. (Eds.), *Comprehensive textbook of psychiatry* (6th ed.) New York: Williams & Wilkins.

Karasu, T. B. (1990). Ethical aspects of psychotherapy. In Bloch, S., & Chodoff, P. (Eds.), *Psychiatric ethics* (2nd ed.). Oxford: Oxford University Press.

McIntyre, N., & Popper, K. (1985). The critical attitude in medicine. *Br. Med. J.* 287: 1919–1923.

Mischyel, T. (Ed.). (1977). *The self: Psychological and philosophical issues.* Oxford: Blackwell.

Montefiore, A. (Ed.). (1973). *Philosophy and personal relations.* London: Routledge.

Orne, M. T., Dinges, D. F., & Bloom, P. B. (1995). Hypnosis. In Kaplan, H. I., & Sadock, B. J. (Eds.), *Comprehensive textbook of psychiatry* (6th ed.). New York: Williams & Wilkins.

Parfit, D. (1973). *Reasons and persons.* Oxford: Oxford University Press.

Prins, H. (1990). *Bizzare behaviors: Boundaries of psychiatric disorders.* London: Routledge.

Radden, J. (1996). *Divided minds and successive selves.* Cambridge: The MIT Press.

Rorty, A. O. (Ed.). (1976). *The identities of persons.* Berkeley: University of California Press.

Skrabenek, P., & McCormick, J. (1989). *Follies and fallacies in medicine.* Glasgow: Taragon Press.

Wolf, S. (1950). Effects of suggestions and conditioning on the action of chemical agents in human subjects—the pharmacology of placebo. *J. Clin. Invest.* 29, 100–109

Wolman, B., & Ullman, M. (1986). *Handbook of altered states of consciousness.* New York: Van Nostrand.

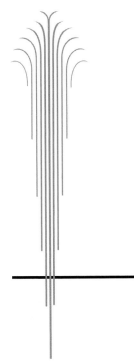

SUICIDE

Gavin Fairbairn
North East Wales Institute of Higher Education

GLOSSARY

assisted suicide An act or omission when a person knowingly assists another to suicide.

cosmic roulette An act by which the protagonist intends to gamble with his life and by which he does not intend unequivocally to end with either life or death; cosmic roulette may, but need not, involve actual self-harm.

extreme suicide conservative A person who believes that intervention in the suicidal acts of others is always morally permissible. This belief is founded on one of two prior beliefs—either that suicide is morally wrong or that since killing oneself is not something that a rational person could wish to achieve, it is always in a person's best interests to prevent his death.

extreme suicide liberal A person who believes that intervention in suicide is morally impermissible.

This belief is founded on the prior belief that since autonomous individuals have the right to direct their own lives, each person has the right to end his life if he wishes to do so.

gestured suicide A feigned act of suicide (which may, but need not, involve self-harm) at the end of which the protagonist wishes, intends, and expects to be alive.

nonfatal/failed suicide An act of suicide that ends in life rather than death.

physician-assisted suicide A label for an act by which a physician knowingly assists a patient to achieve his or her death. Where the individual is suffering pain or distress as a consequence of a terminal illness it might be more usual (and correct) to refer to such an act as voluntary and requested euthanasia.

suicide (as applied to acts) Suicide is an act, whether of commission or omission, and whether performed by himself or by others, by means of which an individual autonomously intends and wishes to bring about his death because he wants to be dead or wants to die the death he enacts. **suicide** (as applied to people) A person is a suicide if he imitiates a suicide act. **suicide** (as a verb) To suicide: to perform an act of suicide.

SUICIDE is most often used in referring to self harming acts intended to end in death, when the outcome is fatal. When the outcome falls short of death, such acts are usually referred to as "attempted suicide" to indicate that the individual was aiming at death but failed to achieve it. The problem is in knowing whether a particular instance of self-harm was both intentional and aimed at death, because only when both are true is it valid to refer to a person's act as suicide or, in the case of suicide that falls short of death, as attempted suicide.

Deciding whether a person was intent on death when he acted is practically important both in cases where he ends up dead and in cases where he lives through his brush with death. If he ends up dead, it is important in order that those who knew him may know how he died; it is also important for decisions in relation to practical matters such as insurance policies covering his life. If on the other hand the suicidal individual ends up alive, it is important in order that helpful decisions may be taken about ways of treating and interacting with him.

So suicide throws up many practical problems. But it also raises philosophical questions; indeed many of the practical problems referred to are underpinned by such questions. This article explores some of the more interesting and important conceptual and ethical questions that suicide raises. It begins with conceptual and linguistic questions and ends with ethical ones— moving, roughly speaking, from questions about what suicide is and how it relates to other phenomena to questions about whether it is OK and about whether it is OK to intervene in the suicidal actions of others.

I. INTRODUCTION

Suicide is devastating. It is an assault on our ideas of what living is about. It challenges us to consider the meaning not only of life but of death. It raises questions about the responsibilities we have to one another and about the extent to which we are and should be free to direct our lives (and our deaths).

People suicide in many different ways and for many different reasons, and acts of suicide could be classified according to the means used—for example, as suicide by drowning, by overdosing, or by jumping from a high place. More usefully, perhaps, a classification of suicide might refer to the motivation that underpins acts of deliberate self-destruction. Such a classification might contain categories such as judicial suicide for those whose suicide resulted from their belief that they should die as a punishment for real or imagined crimes; altruistic suicide for those who wish to end their lives in order to free others of the burden of caring for, or even just living with, them; political or ideological suicide for those whose sui-

cides are driven, for example, by the desire to change the world and who believe their dying might be one way of achieving such change; and existential suicide for those whose suicide acts result from the feeling that in the end, life is not worth the anxiety that it causes.

It is because suicide raises questions about the nature and value of human life and relationships that it has been an ongoing concern not only for practitioners of professions such as psychiatry, nursing, social work, and counseling—who may at times face the problem of deciding how it would be best to act toward those who are said to have attempted or threatened suicide, or to be "at risk" of suicide—but also for social scientists, philosophers, and literary writers. Suicide has also inspired cross-disciplinary studies, among which Alvarez's classic discussion, *The Savage God* (1972. London: Weidenfeld and Nicolson), is particularly noteworthy. Literature, including the work of, for example, Virginia Woolf, Sylvia Plath, and Leo Tolstoy, provides a rich source for teaching both about the psychology of suicide and about the ways in which we should think about it.

Philosophers have shown a great deal of interest both in problems of definition and in the ethical problems that it raises. Among the many collections of philosophical articles focusing on suicide and related phenomena, *Death, Dying and Euthanasia* (D. J. Horan & D. Mall, Eds., (1980. Frederick, MD: Altheia) and *Suicide: The Philosophical Issues* (M. P. Battin & D. J. Mayo, Eds., 1981. London: Peter Owen) contain work that is particularly useful. Camus was probably somewhat overstating the matter when, in *The Myth of Sisyphus*, he suggested that suicide is the only truly serious philosophical problem. However, suicide does raise countless questions of both a conceptual and an ethical kind, some of which will be discussed here.

II. WHAT IS SUICIDE?

The language and concepts that we possess influence the stories we tell about people who harm themselves and hence the ways that we act toward them. Language has the power to change both the ways in which we think and the ways in which we act. Of course this is true in all areas of human experience and endeavor. Connoisseurs can understand and appreciate an area of human experience in which they have expertise better than those who are not connoisseurs of that area, because they have access to its meanings through their knowledge of its specialized language. So, for example, a connoisseur of fine wine, English furniture, art, or music is likely to be able to convey his opinion of a glass of Chablis, a Chippendale chair, a painting by Chagall, or a Charpentier Chorale more succinctly and more clearly than someone whose acquaintance with these things is more slight.

Eskimos are connoisseurs of frozen water whose language and conceptual apparatus have developed to allow a discrimination between different varieties of ice and snow. On the other hand, unless say, we are skiing or winter climbing enthusiasts, we think about snow relatively simply. In a similar way since discriminating between different varieties of life-endangering self-harm does not have a high priority for most people, our language for discussing such acts is rather impoverished, and as a result we are limited in the ways in which we can speak and think about suicide, and about its relationship to other similar phenomena. This is why we will begin our discussion of suicide by addressing the question, "What is suicide and how does it relate to other human phenomena?" It is why we will then look slowly and carefully at the relationship between suicide and other acts of self-harm before addressing some of the ethical problems that it raises.

One way in which philosophers have thought about the nature of suicide is by cross examining deaths that may, from at least some points of view, be thought suicidal, teasing out differences between circumstances in which they should be thought of as suicide and others in which they should not. They have done this as a prelude to a discussion of ethical problems. For example, like many others who have wrestled with saying what suicide is, R. Holland's famous article (1969. In G. Vesey, Ed., *Talk of God.* London: Macmillan) talks both about the much discussed death of Socrates, who drank hemlock shortly before it was administered to him for allegedly "corrupting the young," and about the death of Lawrence Oates, whose last words to his colleagues before he left the tent during Scott's last Antarctic expedition are said to have been that he was "just going outside" and that he may be "some time."

The problem for philosophers as for anyone else in coming to a conclusion about the nature of such celebrated deaths is that however much philosophical or psychological archaeology is carried out, however detailed the postmortem examination of the recorded facts, it is never possible to know what was going on inside the head of an individual who acts in a way that may be suicidal. And since we can never know his intentions the most that can ever be said is that if he acted with the intention of bringing about his death because he wanted to die and he did not change his mind, then he was a suicide. This, at any rate, is the common view of suicide—an act by which an individual who wishes to be dead achieves

death. It is the view with which we shall begin, though as we proceed a new way of thinking will be introduced which places more emphasis on intention than on external facts, and in which the intentions that underpin an individual's acts and the meanings they have for him are more important than his success or otherwise in achieving his intended goal.

III. HOW MIGHT SUICIDE BE ATTEMPTED AND ACHIEVED?

Though the most common conception of suicide is of an action of his own by which an individual intentionally and directly brings about his death, suicide need not result from the direct action of the protagonist. It can also be performed by his omission to act, or by either the actions or the omissions of others, and as will be pointed out later, it is possible to think of some acts that are aimed at death as suicide even when the individual does not die. For the moment let us think about the range of ways in which suicide might be attempted and achieved.

A. Suicide by Actions of the Protagonist

A person may suicide by direct actions such as hanging, jumping from a high place, deliberately putting himself in the way of a vehicle such as a car or train, ingesting poison or an overdose of drugs, inhaling noxious gas, blowing his brains out with a high-powered gun, or slitting his throat. A person might also suicide less directly by putting himself in the way of a natural event that he expects and intends to kill him. So, for example, he might suicide by walking, inadequately clothed and with inadequate provisions, into the mountains on a winter's day when a storm was forecast. Though a person who died in such circumstances will have died because of something that he did, some people might doubt that he was a suicide because his actions will not have killed him. Of course, the natural description of such an event would be that the storm, in the way of which he has put himself, has killed him. However, it killed him because he wanted it to do so and arranged that it would; this is why he will have suicided rather than having died as the result of a misfortune.

Something similar is, of course, true of at least some of the other methods of suicide I have mentioned, including for example, the use of firearms in relation to which some people might wish, in a far-fetched kind of way, to claim that it was not the individual's act in pulling the trigger that kills him but the bullet that pierces his body. Equally odd would be the claim that a man who puts his head in a gas oven, or steps in front of a juggernaut, dies as the result, not of his action, but of the gas that poisons him or the vehicle that breaks his body. The difference is that in all of these cases, provided that protagonist takes good aim, ensures that he is not disturbed, or times things correctly, his death is ensured, whereas in the case of the storm things are left more to chance and the whim of the weather. This is why some people might prefer to think of the act of a man who dies during such an apparently ill-prepared expedition as a cosmic gamble rather than suicide.

B. Suicide by Omissions of the Protagonist

In addition to suicides that might be brought about by the direct actions of the suicidal individual, there are at least two distinctive ways in which an individual might suicide by his own omission. Both utilize perils to which he might be or become subject and they are distinguished by whether the peril in question is internal or external in origin. An example of the first— suicide by exposure to an internal peril—would be where an individual aimed at achieving his death by refraining from eating, drinking, or carrying out some regular life-preserving procedure such as injecting insulin. An example of the second would be where he aimed at achieving his death by refraining from acting so as to avoid an external peril to which he had become exposed. For example, a man contemplating the best way to end his miserable life might go to sea in a beautiful but small pea-green boat on a lovely summer's day and find, as the result of good fortune, that he was able to arrange his death by failing to return to shore when a storm unexpectedly appeared on the horizon.

C. Suicide by the Actions of Another

There are many ways in which a person might suicide via the actions of another. For example, he might suicide by persuading his friend or his wife or his lover, or perhaps in some countries his physician, to help him to suicide by shooting him in the head, holding a pillow over his face, or more humanely and elegantly, injecting him with a lethal dose of a drug. Such an act would most often be construed as assisted suicide in which the assisting person's involvement extended to deliv-

ering the death blow. Nevertheless, even though it was another's hand and not his that pulled the trigger, or administered the injection, or held the pillow over his face, the suicide would still be the agent of his own death, since he would have commissioned the other to perform the fatal act. Provided that she had benevolent intentions, a person who administered a fatal hurt to another who wished to die might be viewed simply as an extension of the suiciding individual—as the instrument rather than as the agent of his death. On the other hand, if she had entertained murderous wishes toward the protagonist before he asked for her assistance in suiciding, her act, at the same time as comprising suicide for him, could from her point of view be murder.

In recent years there has been a tendency to discuss suicide and euthanasia in the same breath as if the two were always closely related. And certainly many people would prefer to think of a situation in which a person who was sick and in interminable pain planned to suicide through another person's actions as euthanasia rather than as suicide, particularly where it involved the use of drugs, though in the case of psychological pain it is less likely that such an act would be viewed in this way. But while some acts of suicide are clearly closely related to acts of "voluntary and requested euthanasia"—in which death is chosen and directed by the individual who dies—suicide is always to be distinguished from the use of euthanasia to refer to acts in which a person is killed because others decide that his life is or will be so awful that he is better off dead than alive. Indeed some writers would wish to limit the use of the expression euthanasia to deaths that are directed by the person who dies; in this case the expression "voluntary euthanasia" would cease to have meaning since all euthanasia would be self-directed.

Even where suicide and euthanasia are closely related, these two species of self-directed death arguably differ in virtue of the reason that underpins the individual's desire for death, which in the case of suicide is about the wish to avoid living, while in euthanasia it is most often about avoiding a particular death. And so whether a death that is intentionally brought about is rightly thought of as suicide or euthanasia arguably depends not upon who delivers the blow that kills, but on the reason that death is sought and brought about. We might characterize the difference by saying that whereas in suicide an individual arranges his death (by his own hand or that of another) because he wants to avoid living the life he is living, in euthanasia an individual arranges his death in order to avoid a death he does not wish to die. Though this distinction depends on limiting the range of acts covered by the term euthanasia to acts that are directed by dying individuals, it could take account of deaths arranged in advance via a living will or advance directive.

The blurring of the boundaries between suicide and euthanasia has been influenced by discussions of assisted suicide, and in particular, of so-called "physician-assisted suicide" in the case of people who are terminally ill. Debates about the morality of allowing dying people to choose the time of their death are often couched as much in terms of assisted suicide as they are in terms of euthanasia. For example, in the Netherlands, some states of the USA, and the Northern Territories of Australia, limited acceptance of the idea that euthanasia might be legally allowed has begun to be acted out in practice, and in both the USA and Australia devices have been invented that allow some distance to be placed between physicians who wish to assist in the deaths of their patients and those whose deaths they arrange. For example, in the USA Dr. Jack Kevorkian has developed a machine called the Mercitron which allows a person to arrange for the delivery of a lethal dose after certain checks, and Dr. Philip Nitschke of Australia has developed a computer-based Deliverance device designed for the same purpose. One argument for such devices is that they allow a humane end to be provided for those who choose to die rather than living with their illness until they die more naturally. Some people might argue against this, that a death in which a machine delivers the death blow is far from humane.

The examples that have been given so far of suicide by the actions of another person have all involved that other as an active and willing partner in the protagonist's suicide. However, a suicide could also use another person's direct actions to achieve his purpose without that other being aware of what was going on. For example, he could stand up on a firing range between a shooter and her target just as she was letting off a round of rapid fire. In such a case it would be true to say that the shooter was causally responsible for the death of the suicide. However, it would not make sense to hold her morally responsible for his death unless some negligence on her part, for example, her failure to observe caution on the firing range, was a contributory factor. In such circumstances, given the suicide's intention to end his life, and regardless of legal decisions made by, for example, a coroner, the shooter would be the means by which he procured his death.

D. Suicide by the Omissions of Another

Suicide by the omission of another person may take two forms. First, an individual could suicide through another's omission to administer life-preserving treatment. For example, he could suicide by asking, begging, coercing, or ordering this other to refrain from injecting him with insulin or transfusing him with blood. Many people would assume that a decision to refuse life-saving treatment must result from irrationality and would hence refuse to believe that a person could suicide in this way because they believe that to count as suicide an act of deliberate self harm must be rationally intended. However, it is easy to imagine circumstances in which rational suicide was possible by such means—consider, for example, a situation in which, as the result of illness or accident, say, a person who had been planning to take his life found himself (fortunately from his point of view) in a situation where death was suddenly easy to procure.

As well as situations in which a previously suicidal person might achieve his wish by refusing treatment that had become necessary, there are at least two distinctive situations in which a person who had become suicidal as the result of a change in his circumstances might decide to end his life by refusing life-prolonging treatment. In both of these situations the individual would have carried out a cost–benefit analysis (however sketchy and hypothetical) in relation to his treatment and likely prognosis, and decided that the benefits did not justify the cost. For example, he might refuse painful treatment even when it would give him a good chance of survival with a high quality of life, because he did not value the prospect of continued life sufficiently to justify the pain he would have to endure in order to procure it. Again in such circumstances many people would believe that a person refusing treatment must be irrational. However, it is possible that a person would choose to die now rather than suffer to gain a prize in the future, even when the prize was continued and healthy life. In another, related scenario, the individual might decide against treatment to preserve his life following an accident because he would rather be dead than live the kind of life he would face in the future. Such a person may be viewed as forfeiting life in order to avoid pain and/or the torment that he knew would inevitably follow survival with severely limited capacities.

The second and less likely way in which a person might suicide through the omissions of another would involve his arranging that others failed to prevent his being harmed by an external source, though examples of this are more difficult to think of. A possible, though far-fetched, example would be where the would-be suicide happened (luckily from his perspective) to be in a building when it caught fire; if he begged the firemen to leave him to burn because he would rather be dead anyway, and they complied with his wish, then we could say that he had suicided by their omission to save him from the fire. Another, perhaps more plausible example might arise in a situation where a mountaineer, dreadfully injured after a fall and terrified of the indolent life he would necessarily face in the future given his injuries, begged his fellow climbers to return to base camp without him so that he could end his days as a mountaineer rather than confined to a wheelchair.

IV. DECIDING WHETHER AN ACT WAS SUICIDE

We have given some thought to possible means a person might use in suiciding, making clear that he can suicide as easily through the actions of another, or through his own omissions to act, as through his own direct actions. What is important, in most definitions of suicide, is that the individual wished to die and acted so as to procure his death. This allows us to say that if a person dies as the result of an act aimed at his death, he is a suicide who was successful in what he intended, while one who aimed at death but ends up alive was unsuccessful. The question of whether a person who unsuccessfully acts to procure his death should be considered a suicide, is a philosophical rather than a practical question and will be addressed later when we think about the term "nonfatal" suicide. For the moment let us think about the practical problem of deciding whether an act was a suicide.

No matter how clear our definition, it does not guarantee that we will be able to say unequivocally whether a particular act was suicide or not. So much depends upon what we cannot know—what was going on in the head of the individual when he acted. No one can be sure whether a person who has survived serious self-inflicted harm intended to live or to die. Deciding what kind of act an apparent suicide or nonfatal suicide represents necessitates complex detective work which will involve asking questions about the individual's past, about events leading up to the suicidal act, and about the act itself—from those who knew him and witnesses to the act if there are any, as well as gathering together empirical evidence from the scene. Where a suicidal act has not led to death we may also directly ask the protagonist about his intentions, though there is no guarantee that self-testimony is truthful.

The methods a person chooses, or at any rate the actions in which he engages or seems to engage are sometimes thought to be crucial in deciding whether

he was a suicide. Some actions—jumping from heights, the use of firearms, the swallowing of poisons, and the like, are so dangerous that they are often thought to offer conclusive proof that an individual was genuinely intent on ending his life. As a result others are likely to judge those who die as the result of such actions as having succeeded in what they set out to do—to achieve their death by dreadful means. By contrast those who engage in self-harming actions from which rescue is more probable, such as overdosing on prescribed medication, are more likely to be thought of as play acting, gesturing, crying for help, gambling, or submitting themselves to trial by ordeal; and where death results they are more likely to be thought of as having died as the result of a tragic accident or mistake.

However, though there may be some correlation between what a person does and his intention—for example, a man does not ingest a large quantity of sleeping pills, slit his wrists, and leap from a cliff or a skyscraper with the idea in mind that he may be saved—a simple correlation cannot be made between method and intention. Even if he acts in a way that is very likely to end with him dead, a self-harmer who dies may not have intended to die. He may, for example, die as the result of an accident while threatening or gesturing suicide. Consider, for example, a man who falls accidentally from a cliff while threatening to do so, or a man who, intent on scaring a loved one into submission following a major dispute, intentionally closes his finger on the trigger of a loaded gun that he believed to be empty, or accidentally closes it on the trigger of a gun that he knows to be loaded. On the other hand, a death that appears to be the result of an accident might have resulted from the intention to suicide; for example, a person who is apparently the victim of accidental electrocution when he plugs his portable CD player into the power point in his hotel room may have made sure both that his hands were wet and that he had removed his thick rubber soled shoes before doing so.

Just as the fact that a person engages in actions that are likely to end with death does not necessarily mean that he intended to die, so the fact that he acts in a way that is unlikely to end with his death does not necessarily mean that he did not have death in mind. For example, a person could take a massive overdose of vitamin pills sincerely intending that he should die.

In thinking about the way in which decisions might be made about whether a person is or is not a suicide, it is worth reflecting on the emphasis that is often placed on the presence of a suicide note as evidence in support of the decision that a person who has died and who may have intended to take his life actually wished to die. Here it is important to note the possibility that a person who wishes to persuade others of his intention to die, while ensuring that he lives, might write a note as part of an elaborate gesture at suicide, before taking action which through miscalculation or accident ended in his death.

Finally, let us consider the problems that arise for decisions about whether an individual who dies intended to kill himself, when we consider the possibility that in suicide, as in other areas of human activity, intentions and wishes may change. Imagine a man who wishes to die and intends to procure his death, who buys a stout chain and several strong padlocks, goes down to the railway where he used to work as driver, and chains himself to the line 10 min before a high-speed train arrives. He throws the keys for the padlocks into the shrubbery by the line and awaits his fate. Imagine that even as he is waiting for the means of his deliverance to arrive he begins reassessing his life—both his life to date and his future. Imagine that even as the train is approaching he changes his mind about what he is doing. In vain he calls to a partially deaf person cutting flowers in her garden adjacent to the railway line. The train driver does not see him until it is too late. His actions in chaining himself to the line and the note he left at home seem to indicate that he was a suicide. But do we, as philosophical observers, believe that he is a suicide when he dies? Granted he dies as the result of actions intended to take his life, but does that mean that he dies a suicide? I think not.

This person is no more a suicide than an individual who one evening takes an overdose of paracetamol or some equally deadly drug earnestly wishing to die, wakes the next morning in a different mood, goes to the hospital for help, and dies 10 days later despite the valiant efforts of the medical team to save him. We cannot know how often (and using which methods of suicide) individuals who act with the intention of dying change their minds about wanting to be dead but are unable to change the course of events so that they die when they want to live. However, evidence from those who do survive not only drug overdoses, but even more dramatic suicide acts such as jumping from heights, suggests that suicides do sometimes change their minds after acting, even at the last minute.

V. SUICIDAL ACTS THAT FALL SHORT OF DEATH

The language available to discuss suicide and other varieties of self-harm is sparse, consisting mainly of the umbrella concept "suicide" and a few variants including parasuicide and attempted suicide, along with terms like "cry for help." One result of the impoverished nature of suicide talk is that we are unable to distinguish with sufficient subtlety between acts that are aimed at death but fail to procure it and acts that are intended to look as if they are aimed at death when actually their aim is life with certain changes. Acts that end with the protagonist alive but may have been intended to end with him dead are most often referred to as either attempted suicide or as parasuicide even where others are unconvinced that he had the aim and intention of procuring his death.

A. Attempted Suicide and Parasuicide

Taken literally, the term "attempted suicide" implies that an act was intended to end in death, and thus that the agent failed to achieve his aim. However, it is often misleadingly and unhelpfully used whenever a person has been harmed as the result of actions that may have been intended to achieve death. Many people whose acts are labeled or thought of as suicide attempts have no intention of dying, and the loose use of the term attempted suicide may lead to inappropriate and unhelpful mistreatment of people whose intention was not about ending their lives but about changing them. For example, treating such people as if they really intended to die when they did not, might encourage repeat attempts whenever alternative and less dramatic means of communicating with others fail. It is because attempted suicide is such a weak and misleading term that many people think its use should be abandoned.

Like attempted suicide, parasuicide is used to refer to acts which resemble suicide but in which the individual ends up alive. Its definition refers only to behavior and makes no reference to whether the individual intended to live or die. Parasuicide is, roughly, a nonfatal act of deliberate self-injury, or a deliberate act in which a person ingests a substance in a quantity larger than any generally recognized therapeutic dosage. However, like attempted suicide, parasuicide is rather loosely used and may be attached to individuals whose brush with death has come about in a whole range of different ways. Thus, for example, some people would refer to anyone who is admitted to a hospital accident and emergency unit following a drug overdose as a parasuicide, even if the individual may have taken the overdose accidentally. Like attempted suicide, parasuicide is arguably well past its "sell by" date though it is still in daily clinical use.

There are, fortunately, other terms that may be more useful for describing suicide acts that fall short of death and for describing acts that, while they resemble suicide, have something other than death as their unequivocal aim. Two that may be used in relation to suicides that fall short of death are failed suicide and nonfatal suicide.

B. Failed and Nonfatal Suicide

The term "failed suicide" is less common than "attempted suicide," with which it tends to be used interchangeably. The intention of the failed suicide is the same as that of the (successful) suicide and different from that of those who self-harm but do so without the expectation and hope that they will die. Another way of labeling acts by which a person intent on suicide has failed to achieve his death might be to use the expression nonfatal suicide. A fatal suicide would be one that resulted in death; a nonfatal suicide would be one that did not.

This might seem an odd idea—suicide that does not lead to death—because for most people suicide is about killing oneself. However, the use of the term nonfatal suicide would allow us clearly to acknowledge that a person who fails in an earnest attempt to procure his death performs the same act as an individual who succeeds in his attempt to die—an act which is distinct, for example, from acts aimed at feigning suicide while ensuring that the individual remains alive. Consider, for example, a man who jumps from a high place, intent on achieving his death and unaware that even as he was preparing his death a marquee was being erected below so that rather than crashing to the ground, his fall is broken and he survives intact. The fact that he fails in his bid for death has nothing to do with his intention or with the nature of his act and everything to do with his luck (or lack of it) when he acted with death in mind. That is why he was a suicide when he jumped; it is why his act was suicide even though he lived.

The idea that some suicides can be nonfatal depends on the adoption of a definition of acts of suicide such as that given in the glossary at the beginning of this article, in which what is important is not external facts—for example, the presence or absence of a corpse following an apparently suicidal act—but internal facts—the presence of the intention and wish to die, in an individual who acts or commissions the acts of others with the intention of ending his life.

VI. DISTINGUISHING BETWEEN SUICIDE AND OTHER ACTS

Actions that look similar can mean quite different things. For example, a student who raises her hand in class may be indicating that she wishes to ask a question, volunteering an answer, pointing at an alarming hole in the ceiling, or merely stretching the tiredness out of her body.

Self-harming actions that look similar can also mean different things. Consider, for example, two people, each of whom has climbed onto a window ledge outside his apartment on the 20th floor of a block. Each has told everyone who has tried to reason with him that he intends to throw himself off the building because he wishes to die and that there is thus no point in trying to persuade him to change his mind because it is made up.

Imagine that each of these ledge standers falls to his death. From the point of view of observers each, having announced his intention to throw himself from the building, has done so. Given certain other evidence, for example, a letter on the kitchen table expressing his intention to die that night, or evidence about his state of mind, it is likely that the conclusion will be drawn in relation to each that suicide was his intention and that he succeeded in his attempt to arrange his death.

But imagine that we know, as only philosophical observers of human behavior can, that whereas one of these individuals (let's call him ledge stander 1) jumped (as he said he would) and died (as he intended) when he hit the ground, the other, ledge stander 2, never intended to die but only to apply pressure on his estranged wife to come back to him. Imagine further that we are aware that it was even as he was reflecting on the relative merit of "changing his mind" as the result of the cajoling he had been subjected to since he climbed out onto his ledge, or of waiting for some interfering busybody to effect his rescue, that ledge stander 2 slipped and fell to his death. As philosophical observers we are thus in possession of privileged information which allows us to say that whereas ledge stander 1 was a suicide because he wished to die, intended to die, and acted so as to achieve his death, ledge stander 2 was not—he died feigning the preparations for suicide, as the result of an accident.

The stories of these two ledge standers and the ways in which their deaths will be viewed by observers who do not have the benefit of a philosophical vantage point and the inside information we have shared about their motivations and intentions serve to illustrate the way in which people may be thought to have done the same thing when really they have done very different things.

Harré and Secord distinguish between the actions that a person performs and the act that the performance of these actions represents (R. Harré & P. Secord, 1972. *The explanation of social behaviour.* Oxford: Basil Blackwell). When I write my name on a piece of paper, the sequence of actions that I perform can constitute a variety of different acts depending both on the context in which I am writing and on the piece of paper on which I write. For example, I may be paying a bill, making a contract, or sending greetings to a sick friend. In a similar way the action or sequence of actions that a person performs in causing himself serious harm can constitute a variety of acts. Using this distinction we can say that although the actions performed by both ledge standers in climbing on to their respective ledges, their stated intentions, and the context in which they took place were the same, the act each performed was different. Whereas ledge stander 1 performed an act of suicide, ledge stander 2 did not.

In any consideration of suicide, whether practical or philosophical, it is important to distinguish between self-harming acts that are intended to end in death, which are suicide, and those that have some other aim, which are not. Two species of self-harming which will often be viewed as suicide, perhaps especially, though not only, when they result in death, are cosmic roulette and gestured suicide.

A. Cosmic Roulette

Suicide is to be distinguished from potentially self-destructive acts in which rather than setting out to die, some people intend to gamble with their lives. Such activities may usefully be referred to using the family name cosmic roulette. Of course, except in cases where death will almost certainly follow the suicidal act, whether a suicide lives or dies is to some extent a matter of luck. However, in cosmic roulette a person intentionally self-harms or creates a situation in which self-harm might come about, but does not do so whole-heartedly intending either that he should live or that he should die. As a result of his act, the cosmic gambler may die and bring an end to the troubles that precipitated the gamble; or he may survive, when the payoff is likely to be lots of attention, sympathy, and help. Whereas in suicide death is aimed at and the gamble is a risk created by the means one uses, in cosmic roulette the gamble is what is aimed at, and death is one of the possible outcomes.

B. Gestured Suicide

Perhaps more common than cosmic gambles are suicide gestures—acts that resemble suicide but are performed with the intention of ending with the individual alive rather than dead. Suicide gestures may involve intentional self-harm but they need not. Consider, for example, a person who claims to have washed a bottle of sleeping pills down his gullet, when actually he has flushed them down the toilet. In suicide a person wishes, intends, and expects to be dead after his suicidal act and acts so as to achieve his death; by contrast the person who gestures at suicide wishes and expects to be alive afterward and acts with the intention of arranging that he is.

A suicide gesturer may intend to punish another person or persons by his feigned suicide, or he may intend to induce some emotion such as guilt, anxiety, or fear in them, and most suicide gestures are at least arguably about the attempt to control others. Like an actor in a one-man play, the individual who gestures suicide stages, directs, and performs in an enactment of his death. In the theatrical performances that we call plays, actors intend to move and produce emotional reactions in the audience; in a suicide gesture, the actor—the suicide gesturer—also intends, by his performance, to move and produce emotional reactions in others. The suicide gesturer does not ask for help but demands it; those from whom help is demanded do not, if they are decent people, have any choice about helping a person who has self-harmed and with whom they come in contact. They must help or be care-less and insensitive. So whether or not they act to help the suicide gesturer, he has an effect on them; if he does not change their behavior or feelings, he changes their character.

VII. MORALISTIC OVERTONES OF THE LANGUAGE OF SUICIDE

Most of this entry so far has been devoted to a discussion of the language in terms of which we discuss suicide and related acts. In beginning now to address moral questions that suicide raises, we turn first to a brief consideration of some ways in which language may influence our beliefs about the morality of suicide. One of these concerns the use of the term "self-murder" to refer to suicide. Since murder is killing from bad intentions, this clearly begs the question of whether it is morally wrong, and for that reason unless we have other reasons for believing it to be wrong, it is probably best to think of suicide as intentional self-killing.

The second and probably more significant influence of language arises from the practice of referring to suicide as an act "committed." Since most acts that are committed are criminal—consider, for example, robbery, murder, rape, and fraud—it is at least arguable that this way of speaking is likely to shape our thinking to some extent by associating suicide and crime, again begging the question of whether suicide is wrong. Some people try substituting the phrase "to kill oneself" in the hope that the neutrality of this term will avoid the moral overtones carried by talk of individuals "committing suicide." But this cannot solve the problem because it is inaccurate; after all, a person can kill himself without being a suicide. A man who pours himself a glass of paraquat, mistakenly thinking it to be gin, will probably die when he drinks it, and if he does he will have killed himself. But although his actions in pouring the paraquat and in drinking it will have been intentional, he will neither have intended to drink paraquat nor to arrange his death, and so his act will not have been the act he intended; and it will not have been suicide. Talking of "intentionally killing oneself" instead of "killing oneself" would rid us of the problem caused by the use of the loaded expression "to commit suicide," but it would lead to convoluted language in an area where, as we have seen, language already causes problems.

Another strategy by which we might try to avoid begging the question of whether suicide is right or wrong merely by the language that we use might be to use the verb "to suicide." Doing so cannot in itself exorcise the idea that suicide is akin to, if not actually, a crime, but removing the evaluative "to commit" has the advantage that it leaves open the question of how a particular act of suicide is to be judged. To say of a person that "he suicided" is simply to describe him as having acted so as to achieve his death because he wished to be dead; it says nothing about the reasons that he had for doing so, or the effects that his doing so might have had on others, and it does not imply that his act was criminal.

VIII. IS SUICIDE PERMISSIBLE?

In most societies killing a person or arranging his death is thought to be wrong because life is a good, and depriving a person of a good is generally thought to harm him. Or rather it is thought to be wrong unless it takes place in a range of closely prescribed circumstances—such as war, self-defense, or less commonly,

capital punishment. Of course, death could be good for an individual, and killing a caring thing to do. Consider, for example, a person who has enjoyed a full and vigorous life, but for whom as the result of an incurable and painful terminal illness, it has become an intolerable burden. Such a person might decide that however much he loves life, enough is enough. In such circumstances death might be a blessing; killing might be both desirable for him and an act of kindness on the part of one who cares for him. This is why many people believe that voluntary euthanasia is morally acceptable or even morally required in certain circumstances. And it is why some people believe that at least some suicides are not only rational but morally right.

Is suicide the same, morally speaking, as other kinds of killing? Is it sometimes OK and sometimes not? Or is it always morally wrong? In suicide, as in (voluntary) euthanasia, the person who is killed is also the person who kills, or arranges the killing, though as we have already seen, the usual view of suicide is of a death that is self-imposed while euthanasia is usually thought of as death brought by another. And whereas, as we have seen, euthanasia is usually seen as a solution to a death that a person wants to avoid, suicide is usually viewed as a solution to a life that a person wants to avoid. This is why some people believe that whereas at times euthanasia is OK, suicide, which is a negation of life and hence an attack on human existence, never is. In contrast to this some people believe that at least some suicides—those that are designed to end a life that has been lived to the fullest before it declines to a level that the suicide considers would be a life not worth living—are a celebration of life.

A. The Right to Suicide

Any discussion of the morality of suicide will have to address questions about the rights we have over our own lives and about ways in which these rights are to be balanced against both the responsibilities we have to particular others and the responsibilities that we have for the effects that our actions have on others in general. It will have to take account of the importance for human beings of autonomy and self-determination. Suicide is a judgment on life and hence on those who live it. It is an assault on our notions of our place in the world. In trying to tease out the moral nature of suicide, three possible conclusions might be reached: that suicide is always morally wrong in itself, that it is wrong in certain circumstances (and right, perhaps even laudable, in others), or that it is always morally right. If we opt for the second of these possibilities we might find that in deciding on the morality of any particular suicide we have to consider the motives that underpin it and the spirit in which it was undertaken. Was it, for example, a revengeful suicide, one through which the protagonist said to others, "I'll show you, you bastards"? Was it, perhaps, a courageous and self-sacrificial suicide, one in which the individual gave up his life for the good (as he saw it) of others? In such a case even if those others suffered more than they benefited from his death, we might be inclined, if intentions rather than consequences are what concern us most, to believe that the suicide was morally OK.

What arguments are there in favor of a right to suicide? And what arguments are there against such a right? Is suicide always morally wrong? Or is it sometimes or always morally right?

Views of suicide and its moral acceptability have varied through time. In classical Greece and Rome, the view of Stoic philosophy was that suicide was not only to be permitted, but in some circumstances even encouraged—for example, in the case of ill health or poverty. In the late 20th century arguments in favor of the right to suicide draw on discussions about the importance of autonomy, which is widely thought to be an important feature of human beings. Autonomy is the ability and freedom to be in control of one's life; it is associated with a wide range of other ideas including individual liberty, self-determination, freedom of choice, and accepting responsibility for one's acts and moral choices. Each person, so the argument goes, has the right to decide what happens to her and should thus be permitted to make decisions about whether she lives or dies, unfettered either by the actions of others or by rules prohibiting her from doing so. This is a view with which large numbers of people would probably agree nowadays, provided that it was tempered by some reference to the fact that the liberty of individuals depends upon a degree of reciprocity—of respect and care for others—on the need, for example, to avoid imposing on others or harming them as the means to pursuing one's right to self-determination. That is why, for most people, activities such as theft, murder, rape, fraud, torture, and so on are frowned upon and why they are generally illegal.

So, where, as in most western societies, autonomy is considered a primary good, suicide is likely to be considered morally acceptable and possibly a right possessed by everyone. But for those who accept that autonomy needs to have some restrictions placed upon it, it seems clear that suicide will only be morally acceptable in certain circumstances, for example, where it does not cause significant harm to others.

B. Religious Arguments against Suicide

The ways in which we think about the morality of self-killing and self-harm that falls short of death are influenced by a number of factors including religious and cultural context. For example, for a traditionally raised Japanese person, self-killing is required in certain circumstances, while many people of a religious persuasion believe that suicide is always morally wrong because only God, who is the author of life, has the right to decide when we should die. This view has been subjected to many objections which have not only come from those who do not believe in the authority of God. For example, in his celebrated essay "Of Suicide," the Scottish enlightenment philosopher David Hume points out that if it is wrong to suicide on the grounds that human life is so important that only God has the right to dispose of it, it would be just as wrong of us to preserve our lives. So, to take an illustration from the 20th rather than the 18th century, if it is wrong to suicide, it is just as wrong to take antibiotics or aspirin, or for that matter to jump out of the way of an oncoming truck or to eat a bowl of muesli, because all of these will tend to preserve life.

Another common religious argument against suicide is that since life is the gift of God, it is wrong to abandon it intentionally. Clearly this could not convince those who do not believe in God that suicide is morally wrong. But even those who believe that life is a God-given gift might not accept it as an argument against suicide. For example, they might argue that even if life is God given, gifts which are freely given can be given away. The argument might proceed that even if God has the right to expect of us that we should live our lives as well as we can, to use them well, and to give them up gracefully when the time comes, it is arguably too much to expect that we should hold onto life when it is harming us to do so.

C. Suicide and Harm to Others

Arguments against suicide that have a religious underpinning clearly have a narrower sphere of relevance than those that do not, particularly when they derive from a particular body of religious doctrine. Perhaps the most important arguments against suicide are those that refer to the effects that suicide will have on others. Granting both that for the suicide death will be a good thing and that there is a right to suicide, those who argue thus would claim that considerations about the harm that it might do to others will most often be enough to override an individual's right to suicide. And so, in most circumstances, suicide will be morally wrong. The idea that suicide is morally wrong because of the effects it has on others has a long pedigree. For example, both Aristotle and Plato before him argued that suicide damages not the individual who dies—who does so voluntarily—but the state which as the result of his death loses the benefits he could bring, e.g., from the work he does. But more significant than injury to the state is arguably the harm that suicide does to those who knew the individual personally.

Suicide harms others. Those with whom a suicide had close contact, including members of the caring professions and neighbors as well as relatives and friends, are likely to be shocked and upset by his death. Those who loved or cared for someone who suicides will have to adjust their lives to take account of the fact not only that he has died, but also of the fact that he intended to die. They may feel not only grief but guilt because they find themselves wondering what they have done wrong—in driving him to take his life, or in failing to prevent him doing so. They will often suffer grief and guilt for a long time and sometimes forever. Retelling the story of their last encounters with a person who has killed himself and looking for clues that they missed is a common experience among survivors of suicide, as is retelling and reliving the real or imagined death of those who have suicided, particularly where death was achieved using violent means.

The emotional pain felt by survivors of suicide is significant, but it is not the only way in which they may be harmed by his act. Families may suffer financially if he was a significant source of income. Children may be deprived not only of the emotional bond that a dead parent provided but of all the other goods that a parent can give. Families may also suffer as a result of real or imagined ostracism about the suicide of a family member, because even in countries where suicide is not a crime, it is often frowned upon.

But it is not just those to whom he was in some way close that a suicide can harm by his death and its aftermath. Suicide usually involves other people to some extent—those who witness the fatal event or are directly involved in it. In some forms of suicide the protagonist will intentionally, though perhaps thoughtlessly, involve others in his bid to die—for example, the driver of the car or train in front of which he throws himself. Others will inevitably be involved in the aftermath of most suicides including, for example, those who discover the corpse or have to deal with the family or friends of the dead person. Imagine the psychological effects on a police officer who is charged with removing the decaying body of a suicide from the air conditioning system into which he has crawled to die peaceably and in private after taking an overdose; on the passersby who witness a suicide's self-immolation in a shopping mall after he douses himself in gasoline and sets himself alight; or on those who witness his body falling from a high building or see it broken to pieces on the sidewalk. Particularly in the case of violent suicides, those who are wittingly or unwittingly involved may suffer trauma as a result of the incident by which, directly or indirectly, the suicide (however unintentionally) assaulted them.

So even if suicide is morally acceptable in itself, it is arguably morally wrong in most circumstances because of the adverse effects it has. The extent to which a particular suicide is harmful to others and the extent to which it was intended to harm might thus be thought to suggest how morally acceptable it is. However, it might be argued that even if no one is actually affected, suicide is wrong because those who enact it aim to achieve (and perhaps do achieve) their own ambition for death at the risk that others will be harmed as a result.

Following this line of thought a suicide might be compared to a man who drives home successfully after a party at which he has consumed sufficient alcohol to render him unsafe as a driver. Such a person has been morally lucky that he did not meet either an unwary pedestrian or a tricky situation that caused him to crash, injuring others in the process. But the fact that he has not killed or injured others does not make him less immoral for driving under the influence of alcohol, though his moral luck means that he will not be charged with manslaughter or even with drunk driving. Those who drink and drive demonstrate that they are more concerned with gratifying their desire to drink without the inconvenience of finding some other means of transport than they are with the welfare of those they might meet when they are behind the wheel. And those who aim to procure death for themselves demonstrate that they are more concerned with gratifying their wish to be rid of life than they are with the possibility that others might suffer as a result.

The number of cases in which an individual could kill himself without affecting others is likely to be small, especially for those who meet with others on a daily basis and will hence be missed. An example would be a person who has no contact with others, even of a trivial and passing kind, so that no one will be upset simply by his ceasing to exist. Such a person could suicide without involving and hence harming others, provided he took careful steps to ensure that he was not found. He might do this by killing himself somewhere

where he is unlikely ever to be found—for example, deep in the furthest recesses of an unexplored cave. If he acted like this such an individual could not, unless he was very unlucky, be the cause of upset to anyone and could thus suicide without moral qualms. But for most people, modern life is such that dying in a way and in a place that will not affect others is likely to be difficult to achieve.

A problem might arise for those whose objections to suicide are grounded in the harm that it can cause to others, in cases where the distress and suffering experienced by a prospective suicide is so great as to make the distress others will suffer if he suicides seem trivial by comparison. In such a case anyone whose objection to suicide was based solely on the avoidance of the harm others would suffer as the result of suicide would have to concede that this was a morally acceptable suicide, or at least they would have to do so if their objections were founded on the idea that harm to people is to be avoided where possible.

IX. INTERVENTION IN SUICIDE

Some of the most difficult ethical questions in relation to suicide arise when we consider the question of what one should do when faced with a situation in which another has acted, or apparently acted, in a suicidal way. Should we intervene or should we refrain from intervention? Answers to this question will vary according to the position an individual occupies on a spectrum from what might be called the *extreme liberal view of suicide* to what might be called the *extreme conservative view*.

Extreme suicide liberals believe that since autonomy is centrally important to being a human person, we each have a right to do what we will with our lives, including ending them if we wish, and that thus those who have entered on a suicidal course of action should not be disturbed. In contrast, extreme suicide conservatives believe that intervention in suicide is always called for, either because suicide is morally wrong and should be stopped or because it can never be in a person's interests to suicide; that suicide is likely to arise from psychological disturbance; and therefore that it is always in the interests of a suicide for others to intervene and save his life.

There is another group of likely suicide interveners who may be either conservative or liberal on the question of whether individuals have a right to end their lives which we should note before examining the liberal and conservative positions in detail. Regard-

less of their beliefs about the morality of suicide in itself and regardless of their beliefs about whether autnomous individuals have a right to kill themselves, those who fall into this group will believe that intervention in most instances is justified in order to protect themselves or others from the harm that the suicide will cause them if it is allowed to proceed unhindered.

Between the two extremes of suicide liberalism and conservatism there will be a continuum of positions, with those who are drawn toward the liberal view asking themselves, "When is it permissible (i.e., morally right) to intervene in another's attempt to end his life?" while those who are drawn toward the conservative view ask, "When is it permissible (i.e., morally right) not to intervene in another's attempt to end his life?" Both those with liberal and those with conservative leanings will have difficulty in answering these questions. For example, suicide conservatives might consider that in certain circumstances—say where an individual's attempt on his life arose as a result of terminal illness—suicide, while undesirable, was understandable and even laudable if it was associated with a desire to spare family members the trauma of living with them until they died. They might find it particularly easy to feel sympathetic where the individual was a devoutly religious person who had talked of making peace with God before taking the final step. Their problems might arise both from nagging doubts about whether the individual was truly rational in his decision and from their inability to put aside the hope for a miraculous recovery.

The problems faced by suicide liberals will to some extent be similar. The aversion that they are likely to feel toward the possibility of acting paternalistically may, for example, be overcome by a desire (which they share with suicide conservatives) to make sure that the suicidal individual is autonomous in his decision—that is, that he really does want to die. Thus a suicide liberal may be willing to intervene, to interrupt the suicidal process, just to ensure that the decision to suicide was well thought out, thinking that having done so she will, if necessary, be able to allow the suicide to proceed as it was before she intervened. A problem for one who believes that autonomy in this as in all things is centrally important, is that even a highly skilled counselor or psychotherapist is likely to have difficulty in determining whether or not a person was acting autonomously and thinking rationally. For most people without this degree of skill, doing so will be even more difficult— perhaps especially if they have a leaning either toward the liberal view that suicide is generally to be accepted as an expression of autonomous human choice, or toward the conservative view that suicide is rarely a proper choice for people.

Another problem that arises for the concerned suicide liberal is that of deciding on the nature of the "suicide" upon which he stumbles. Is it a suicide? Or is it some other species of apparently suicidal act? Is it perhaps a suicide gesture or a cosmic gamble? Even if it is possible to determine whether the protagonist is autonomous, this does not guarantee that it will be possible to determine what he intended by his act. In any case it will most often be difficult to determine whether the individual is autonomous without doing something more significant than simply interrupting the suicidal process, which can then be allowed to continue if autonomy is established. Not only that, but there is the additional problem that most often suicidal and pseudo-suicidal acts that are chanced upon will be difficult acts in which to intervene in a temporary way. The individual may, for example, be unconscious or bleeding profusely, and hence intervention to determine autonomy will involve stopping rather than merely interrupting the act.

As a result of the problems that we have discussed, suicide liberals who truly value autonomy, and have reflected on the possibility that not all apparently suicidal acts that they come across may be intended to end in death, may end up acting in ways that do not accord with their liberal views. Consider, for example a suicide liberal who comes upon the following situation:

> Stuart is sitting in his car outside the house in which his wife is living with her new lover. He has pinned a note to his chest which speaks of his undying love for his wife, and of the fact that she has destroyed his life which is now no longer worth living. The engine of Stuart's car is running and a piece of hosepipe, which is rather crudely attached to the exhaust pipe, has been fed through the back window of the car.

Imagine that our suicide liberal, thoroughly convinced about the importance of autonomy in the life of women (and men) looks in through the window of Stuart's car and thinks, "Aha, a man who is attempting to arrange his death. What a pity that the fellow does not wish to live any longer. Nevertheless he is entitled to take his life if he wants and so I should go away and allow him to die because that is his wish." What is she to do? Well given her view of the importance of autonomy and her judgement both that Stuart has decided to take his life and that he has the right to do so, it is clear that our suicide liberal should turn round and walk away, leaving Stuart to die.

But now imagine that our suicide liberal has recently read an article entitled, "On Distinguishing Suicide from Other Related Phenomena." Imagine then that before leaving Stuart to die she reflects on the possibility that perhaps what she is looking at might be not a suicide but a suicide gesture or perhaps a cosmic gamble. Imagine that she reflects on the possibility that Stuart's note might not be intended to announce his death but rather to exert influence on his wife to come back to the marital home. Imagine then that our suicide liberal smashes the window of Stuart's car and effects his rescue.

Suicide liberals, as we have seen, have a strong belief in the importance of autonomy which underpins their belief in the idea that we each have the right to take our own lives if we wish. However, reflecting, as our suicide liberal did when she was confronted with Stuart's manipulative act of despair, on the possibility that what looks like a suicide might not be suicide, should lead most suicide liberals to intervene in suicides they come across. And what is more, they will do so in the name of autonomy because they will realize that except in cases where the protagonist has persuaded them that they are rational and both intend and wish to die, they will never be able to be sure that death was the autonomous wish of a suicide whose act they encounter. The actions of thoughtful suicide liberals in relation to most suicides and apparent suicides across which they come and their reactions to most suicides or apparent suicides about which they hear are thus likely to be similar to those of most people who lean toward suicide conservatism. And so regardless of our intuitions about suicide, and regardless of our moral instincts and religious and cultural upbringing, if we think about suicide and its nature carefully, our actions toward it and beliefs about it are likely to converge.

Also See the Following Articles

AUTONOMY • EUTHANASIA • HOMICIDE, CRIMINAL VERSUS JUSTIFIABLE

Bibliography

Battin, M. P. (1994). *Ethical issues in suicide* (2nd ed.). Englewood Cliffs, NJ: Prentice Hall.

Campbell, R., & Collinson, D. (1988). *Ending lives.* Oxford: Basil Blackwell.

Donnelly, J. (Ed.) (1990). *Suicide: Right or wrong?* Buffalo, NY: Prometheus.

Fairbairn, G. J. (1995). *Contemplating suicide: The language and ethics of self harm.* London: Routledge.

Hill, K. (1995). *The long sleep: Young people and suicide.* London: Virago.

Kupfer, J. (1990). Suicide: Its nature and moral evaluation. *Journal of Value Inquiry, 24*(1), 67–81.

Pritchard, C. (1995). *Suicide: The ultimate rejection?* Buckingham: Open Univ. Press.

SUSTAINABILITY

Stanley R. Carpenter
Georgia Institute of Technology

GLOSSARY

bequest package The material legacy of one generation to the next.

bequest package—structured Legacy to future generations that differentiates between natural, humanly created, and investment capital.

bequest package—unstructured Legacy to future generations that does not differentiate between natural, humanly created, and investment capital.

biosphere The area of water, soil, and air that surrounds the globe and provides the habitat for all terrestrial life.

capital, human Human skills and knowledge.

capital, humanly created Human production systems of manufacturing.

capital, investment Money that earns interest.

capital, natural Renewable and nonrenewable resources.

common patrimony A principle rooted in international law and derived from world philosophies, religions, and legal traditions that each generation is a legatee of the planet and its trustee for future generations.

discounting the future An evaluation presuming that some resource, perhaps a forest or a pool of oil, that might be worth, say, $1000 in 100 years, assuming a 5% interest rate, would have a net present value of $7.

economics, macro General aspects of national economies such as income, investments, and trade policies.

economics, micro Behavior of individual consumers aimed at maximizing preferences (utility), and of individual firms in terms of profits and losses.

fungibility The assumption that all resources, natural and humanly created, are intersubstitutable.

great primal contract The burkean conception of the interconnection between all creatures past, present, and future.

net primary product (NPP) The total food resource on Earth.

precautionary principle The principle that where there is risk of irreversible or serious damage to the environment, lack of full scientific certainty shall not constitute a reason to postpone preventative or ameliorative action.

photosynthesis The process by which living systems concentrate simple dispersed chemicals and use them to synthesize the most complex substances known, the source of all renewable resources.

regenerative technology Technology that provides for continuous replacement, through its own functional processes, of the energy and materials used in its operation.

resources, renewable Resources created by solar photosynthesis in short time with respect to human lifetimes.

resources, nonrenewable Minerals and metals created in long time with respect to human lifetimes.

save minimum standard (SMS) A concept based on game theory that calls for avoidance of extinction unless the social costs are unacceptably large. The level at which costs become excessive is a matter of intergenerational distribution.

sustainability, aboriginal The necessary condition of the human species prior to significant development of technologies powered by nonrenewable energy sources.

sustainability, strong economic The doctrine or policy enabling future generations to be as well off as the present by means of a structured bequest package that disaggregates natural capital into preserved renewable resources, conserved nonrenewable resources, and supplemental investment capital.

sustainability, weak economic The doctrine or policy of enabling future generations to be as well off as the present one by means of an unstructured bequest package.

technometabolism Inputs and outputs of materials and energy for human organisms culturally generated by technological processes that supplement the biometabolic inputs of food, water, oxygen, and the discharge of wastes.

two-tier decision procedure. A mixed resources use criterion involving economic utility theory at tier one and conservation ethics at tier two.

THE SUSTAINABILITY of human populations involves the persistence through time of the diversity of human communities and ethical ideals of human flourishing, the dynamically balanced development of economic enterprise, and the preservation and regeneration of ecological systems and resources that sustain that development.

I. INTRODUCTION: ETHICS AND SUSTAINABILITY

A. The Dimensions of Sustainability Discussions

The sustainability of human populations involves the persistence through time of the diversity of human communities and ethical ideals of human flourishing, the dynamically balanced development of economic enter-

prise, and the preservation and regeneration of ecological systems and resources that sustain that development. Sustainability intersects other issues in applied ethics, such as environmental ethics, international justice and equity, war and peace, and bioethics. "Sustainability" is sometimes used interchangeably with "sustainable development," a concept given common currency by the Brundtland Commission (World Commission on Environment and Development, p. 8.), and defined as ". . . meeting the needs of the present without compromising the ability of future generations to meet their own needs." In this discussion "sustainability" and "sustainable development" will not necessarily be considered synonyms.

Because the term sustainability appears so frequently in discourse and is used in such varied ways, it is important to isolate salient aspects of the concept. One cluster of ethical concerns addresses issues of equity and justice, conservation, and programs of sustainable development. Discussion of these issues, however, can occur in discourses framed in either economic, ecological, or technological terms. Further complicating the attempts to use the concept of sustainability as a basis for social or political policy are the varied spatio-temporal dimensions of the discussion. Short-term considerations are usually framed in the language of neoclassical economics. Ecological discussions of sustainable ecosystems, however, are more apt to require longer time horizons than are meaningfully dealt with in economic approaches that heavily discount the future. Finally, the increased awareness that human activities can produce global aspects leads to discussions of sustainability in geological time. In addition to varied time horizons, sustainability issues included disparate spatial emphases. Focus may be on local sustainability of a bioregion, a city, or a food or water source. It may take on geopolitical dimensions when identified with a particular nation, subcontinent, or continent. Finally, as was the case with time horizons, the space horizon may be expanded to include the globe itself. Subsequent sections of this discussion will identify the issues involving sustainability that emerge when viewed in these varied ways.

B. Historical Background

Virtually all of the 4 billion years of life on earth was without human beings. With the birth of culture some 65,000 human generations ago, the basic *biometabolism* of all life (inputs . . . of food, water, and oxygen, and the discharge of organic wastes,) was augmented by human technology, what may be termed *technometabol-*

ism (Boyden & Dovers, p. 63). During the vast majority of the following period humans aided by their tools lived of necessity in a state of "aboriginal sustainability" (Ruckelshaus, p. 167.). It should be noted, however, that practices such as fire driving were even then modifying the earth according to human intentions. With development of agriculture about 400 generations ago, human modifications of the land increased. It is of interest that as late as the seventeenth century the northeastern Native Americans while following a variety of hunter-gather and/or agricultural lifestyles, appear to have lived sustainably with their surroundings (Cronon).

While the emergence of cities about 200 generations ago was marked by significant increases in natural resource use, by far the greatest step toward "transitional unsustainability" (Ruckelshaus, p. 168) occurred a mere eight generations ago. The Industrial Revolution comprised the beginning of technological practices powered by hydrocarbon fossil fuels. Energy use increased by a factor of 10,000, a process sometimes described as "the mining of yesterday's sunshine." Accompanying this quantum increase in energy use was an inexorable population increase from less than 0.6 billion 200 generations ago to the current estimate of 5.7 billion, a figure projected to reach 10 billion by the middle of the coming century (World Resources: 1996–1997, p. 173).

Increases in industrialization and energy use and those in population, however, have not occurred uniformly. The fact that the developed countries have high material and energy use and relatively low population growth rates, while the developing countries have the converse, lends urgency to the formulation of social and political practices that are sustainable. The discussion to follow, therefore, bifurcates as to paths to sustainability, with the developed countries requiring policies that emphasize changes in consumption patterns, while the developing countries require empowerment to address root causes of excessive population growth rates and malnutrition, and while all countries are faced with deteriorating environments, loss of flora and fauna, and the possibility of anthropogenic alterations to the life supporting functions of the global biosphere itself.

C. How Ethics Can Help Address Issues of Sustainability

1. Ethical discussion can contribute positively to sustainability discussions by addressing the tradeoffs between intergenerational human interests and intragenerational requirements that human populations are faced with in a world of scarce resources. While ethicists

have long considered issues of international justice and equity within the contemporary context, and while environmental ethicists especially have addressed issues of intergenerational equity, questions of sustainability force both perspectives to be dealt with according to coordinated decision procedures. Of particular note in this regard is the fact that current practices, whether taken out of necessity or choice can irreversibly alter human and natural environments, closing off options for future generations and potentially threatening the viability of the biosphere for human life itself.

2. Ethics can also provide methods of articulating current values reflective of the human/nature interaction. While we may appropriately speak of other species as possessing interests, it is the human species, with culture and language, that can articulate both its own interests and those of other species. It is the task of ethics to systematize the mix of conflicting demands by applying ethical norms to the process of formulating social policy. It is therefore appropriate to speak of this process as anthropocentric even while giving increasing consideration to the interests of nonhuman species.

3. Additionally, ethics can draw attention to unsustainable human practices by formulating systematic sanctions for anthropogenic activities directly implicated in a loss of human cultures, nonhuman flora and fauna, as well as geological processes and cycles. Worldwide currently we are losing 27,000 species a year, 74 per day, one every 20 minutes, due in no small part to the 500,000 trees that are cut each hour in tropical forests (Hawken, p. 29). While some of this deforestation stems from dire impoverishment, the major cause is human greed. Typically, a loss of forest cover carries with it an accompanying human toll as forest tribes, some still living in sustainable cultures, are ejected from their ancestral homes. Additionally, anthropogenic activities, especially the burning of hydrocarbons, are arguably altering the global climate itself. It is facts such as these that give impulse to practices that can achieve greater sustainability. It is the normative contributions of applied ethics that aim to inform such practices.

II. SUSTAINABLE DEVELOPMENT

A. The Constraints

As mentioned, discussions of sustainability engage varied spatial and temporal horizons, disparate disciplines such as ethics, economics and ecology, and a wide range of technological practices. To unpack these approaches it is useful first to look at ethical issues that recur in discussions of sustainable development.

If the term "economics", microeconomics in particular, represents the science of the individual household, "ecology" refers to the larger household, the total environment. The unfettered market is commonly regarded as providing for the efficient regulation of demand of the aggregate of individual households, while at the same time preserving and maximizing individual freedom. The greater household, the global geophysical matrix of human activity, however, cannot operate without limitations on individual freedoms. To attempt to do so is to risk what Hardin has called the "Tragedy of the Commons" (Hardin). Without coercion, and given the impossibility of privatizing every resource necessary to sustain life, the abuser of public resources such as water, air, the hydrologic cycle, even the protective upper atmopshere of the globe, gains short-term benefit to the long-term detriment of all.

In "Development Ethics and Ecological Wisdom," Dennis Goulet notes this persistent tension between development models that focus on the ecological constraints of nature and those that place primary emphasis on greater realization of human freedom. Ecological constraints stress the integrity of nature through conserving resources, preserving species, and protecting nature from human depredations. Discussions of human freedom extend the concepts beyond economic freedom to include ethical ideas of justice, entailing all-out assaults on human poverty, and development of human potential, individually, at the community level and beyond. Goulet believes that the tension between ecology and human development is a matter of emphasis. "The reason is simply that any long-term, sustainable, equity-enhancing combat against poverty requires wisdom in the exploitation of resources, just as the preservation of species cannot be persuasively held out as a priority goal if the human species is threatened with degrading poverty or extinction. Nature itself is diminished or wounded when its human members are kept 'underdeveloped'; those human members cannot become truly 'developed' if their supportive nature is violated" (Goulet, pp. 44).

B. International Initiatives

It is clear from the development literature, however, that this tension does exist. The "Declaration of Principles," of the 1972 United Nations Conference on the Environment, held in Stockholm contained claims of entitlement for "freedom, equality and adequate conditions of life, in an environment of a quality which per-mits a life of dignity and well-being," along with clean environments even if what is required by the industrialized countries includes "the transfer of substantial assistance." (UNCE, Stockholm, Art. 1,9, pp. 179, 180) These principles were emphatically supported by the developing countries. On the other hand, echoing the strong voice of the developed countries, member states claimed by principles of international law that their national sovereignty gives them the right to exploit their own resources "pursuant to their own environmental policies," as long as their actions "... do not cause damage to the environment of other states or of areas beyond the limits of national jurisdiction (art. 21, p. 181).

The contrasting emphases of Articles 1 & 9 and of 21 exemplify the classical dichotomy between positive and negative rights, the former reflecting the claims of the developing countries upon the community of nations to "do good," while the negative rights position, assumed by the developed countries, promised to "do no harm." At the follow-up United Nations conference in Rio de Janeiro in 1992 similar tensions are apparent with Principle One stating "Human beings are at the centre of concerns for sustainable development. They are entitled to a healthy and productive life in harmony with nature." Principle Two reiterated Stockholm, Art. 21, without alteration (UNCED, Rio, p. 208). The United States was particularly vocal at this conference in its advocacy of the negative rights position, relying on free international trade as the primary instrument for addressing issues of entitlement.

C. Our Common Future

Our Common Future, (World Commission on Environment and Development, 1987) or the "Brundtland Report" as it is sometimes called after its Chair, Gro Harlem Brundtland, prime minister of Norway, gave common currency to the phrase "sustainable development." A product of the World Commission on Environment and Development established by the UN General Assembly, it reflects a skillful charting of course between the Scylla of the positive rights position of the members from developing countries on the one hand and the Charybdis of the negative rights advocates of the major industrialized countries. The report proposes policies in six areas: population, food security, the loss of species and genetic resources, energy, industry, and human settlements. Positive successes in international development were noted, including improvements in infant mortality, life expectancy, literacy, percentage of children starting school, and the ratio of food production to population growth. Developmental failures identified were decreases in absolute numbers of persons well-fed, literate, and with access to potable water, sound homes, and adequate fuel. Significant attention was given to global environmental issues, which were called failures of management. These included increases in desertification, deforestation, acidification, global warming, and ozone layer depletion. "Sustainable development" in broadest terms as noted was defined as "meeting the needs of the present without compromising the ability of future generations to meet their own needs" (esp. pp. 43–66).

The report identified five desiderata for sustainable development: (1) economic growth, (2) equity, that is, a new fair allocation of resources to sustain such growth, (3) participatory and more democratic political systems, (4) adoption of life-styles within the planet's ecological means (aimed obviously at the developed countries), and (5) population levels in harmony with the productive potential of ecosystems (aimed at the developing countries.)

D. Alternative Conceptions of Sustainable Development

While *Our Common Future* is a commendable and constructive compromise between conflicting agendas of the developed and less-developed countries, it has received extensive criticism. Even though the term "development" is used in the core phraseology, the policy emphasis is upon economic growth. Noting this, Daly observes "growth" and "development" are far from synonymous. If development is taken to mean "to expand or realize the potentialities of; a qualitative improvement or unfolding of potentialities," then "sustainable development," is an apt characterization. However, if the emphasis is on growth, as it seems to be in *Our Common Future,* "sustainable growth" is an oxymoron, his point being that as long as our race inhabits a finite planet, and a very thin biospheric shell of it at that, both unlimited economic and population growth are unsustainable. (Daly, 1991b).

"Sustainable development" is frequently used with primary emphasis on only one of the two terms of the phrase. Pearce, who has written extensively on the topic of sustainable development, places primary emphasis on sustainability, specifically sustainability of the natural resource base. Environmental quality and environmental inputs have been underappreciated factors in the processes of raising real income and quality of life (Pearce & Warford, p. 8). Engel, on the other hand moves the term "development" beyond strictly eco-

nomic usage to mean "evolution, unfolding, growth, and fulfillment of any and all aspects of life (Engel, J. R., p. 10). Goodland and Ledec echo Brundtland's original definition, while emphasizing economics as the engine of change: ". . . a pattern of social and structural economic transformation (i.e., 'development') which optimizes the economic and societal benefits available in the present, without jeopardizing the likely potential for similar benefits in the future (Goodland & Ledec, p. 36).

Kothari criticizes sustainable development as retaining an economics focus and proposes that it be conceived of as an ethical ideal consisting of four components: ". . . a holistic view of development; equity based on the autonomy and self-reliance of diverse entities instead of on a structure of dependence founded on aid and transfer of technology with a view to 'catching up'; an emphasis on participation; and an accent on the importance of local conditions and the value of diversity" (Kothari, p. 34). Finally, Engel, who supports Kothari's insistence that sustainable development is an issue for applied ethics, proposes a comprehensive social paradigm, consisting of five operational principles: (1) integration of conservation and development (2) satisfaction of basic human needs; (3) achievement of equity and social justice; (4) provision for social self-determination and cultural diversity; and (5) maintenance of ecological integrity (Engel, J. R., pp. 8, 9).

When the concept of sustainable development is given as complete and wide-ranging a treatment as Engel here provides, it becomes apparent that it approaches as the ideal limit the condition of a human sustainability itself. Were such to come close to occurring, the human species would have traveled from Ruckelshaus's "aboriginal sustainability," through the industrial period of "transitional unsustainability," to what he refers, to as a postindustrial era informed by "the consciousness of advanced sustainability" (Ruckelshaus, p. 168).

III. CONCEPTUAL FRAMEWORKS OF SUSTAINABILITY DISCUSSIONS

A. Introduction

Complicating discussions of sustainability is the fact that the issue crosscuts existing disciplines and cultural practices. Traditional neoclassical economists who choose to engage the topic, such as Nobel laureate Robert Solow, consider their discipline adequate to the task. Ecologists and other environmental scientists provide a different disciplinary matrix and selective focus. Each approach utilizes its own specialized vocabulary, making interdisciplinary collaboration difficult. Economists practice a social science, with mathematical rigor that rivals that of the physical sciences. Ecologists are biophysical scientists from the outset.

Increasingly, issues of sustainability are coming under the purview of engineering technologies using rubrics such as "green engineering," engineering for "design and disassembly," or "life-cycle" engineering. The language of technology, and the practices of the various engineering disciplines thus constitute an additional perspective to those of economists and ecologists. It is useful to examine how each of these three approaches attacks the problem of sustainability, and how in the process old disciplinary lines begin to blur and cross-disciplinary, and in the case of ecological economics, truly new interdisciplinary approaches begin to take shape.

B. Economics and Ecology

1. Solow's Approach

Contemporary neoclassical economic theory divides into microeconomics and macroeconomics. Microeconomics focuses on individual firms, their profits/losses, prices/costs, and so on, and on the behavior of individual consumers expressed as preference satisfactions. Macroeconomics deal with aggregate components of the economy, often at the level of a country. Relationships between income and investments, money supply and gross domestic products are tracked and influenced by fiscal and monetary policies. As indicated economic theories are the most rigorous and abstract of all the social sciences.

Robert Solow addresses the topic of sustainability in the following terms. Sustainability, he states, is the obligation to conduct ourselves so that we leave to posterity the option or the capacity to be as well off as we are. "There is," he states, "no *specific* object to the goal of sustainability. What we are transmitting to our heirs is a *generalized* capacity to be as well off as we ourselves are" (Solow, p. 181).

Crucial to Solow's definition is the assumption that all resources, including all minerals, metals as well as ecosystems—the ones we consume and the ones we pass on—are "fungible," or intersubstitutable. That is to say, axiomatic to the economic approach is the assumption that substitutes can always be found for every resource and ecosystem that our technological activities require. Perfect intersubstitutability means that the "bequest package," which is what we pass on to our heirs

(Norton, B. (1995a), p. 116), is unstructured. Monetary capital, labor, natural resources, and ecosystem functions are interchangeable elements of capital. There is no separation of humanly created capital (HCC), those resources generated by technometabolic activity, from so-called natural capital (NC), those functions associated with water courses, forests, ecosystems, and so on. Instead, fungibility solves the problem of intergenerational bequests in as unstructured and varied a set of ways as do humans when they realize their individualized and idiosyncratic preference schedules in their varied patterns of consumer purchases.

The achievement of sustainability along these lines occurs as follows. As the society uses up resources it is able both to meet immediate needs but, if prudent, also to lay aside money for the future in the form of investments. As these investments grow, the bequest package for the future increases. As resources are depleted, money for developing substitutes is thereby available. Solow regards this approach as both ethical and realistic. After all, it is unclear which life-styles and preference schedules future generations will adopt. With complete fungibility of bequest package the freedom of future generations to choose their own lifeplans is enhanced.

Several problems exist with Solow's approach. Given the assumption that resources can be evaluated in money terms there is a problem called "discounting the future." For example, some resource, perhaps a forest or a pool of oil, which might be worth, say, $1000 in 100 years, and assuming a not unreasonable interest rate of interest of 5%, would today in what economists call "net present value" be worth about $7. Under the assumption of complete intersubstitutability one could invest today's profits from the harvest and watch the money grow. But this approach is flawed in several ways.

First, there is no differentiation made between renewable and nonrenewable resources. Depleting the nonrenewable resource means it is gone forever. This may or may not be catastrophic depending on the likelihood that technology can produce substitutes. Depleting the renewable resource, such as the forest, means that something that could under proper management have gone on producing usable resources indefinitely has been permanently stopped.

Second, the consumption of a resource is fraught with uncertainties. It may turn out that what was used was irreplaceable, as perhaps a crucial component of a larger system, such as a regional watershed. Or it may be that an extinction that occurred in the taking of the resource constitutes an irreplaceable loss of genetic material, along with the medicinal potential. The issue of irreversibility of anthropogenic actions will be addressed again.

Third, Solow's approach overemphasizes fungible resources and gives inadequate recognition to whole systems. According to some environmentalist perspectives many of the most critical scarcities are unaccounted for by the economic approach: soil fertility, safe air and water, stable climates, biological nutrient recycling, the assimilative capacity of the environment itself, and critical nutrient cycles of nature for oxygen, carbon, nitrogen, sulfur, and phosphorus. For these processes there are no substitutes (Ayres, p. 195).

2. Ecological Economics

The new field of ecological economics attempts to integrate "... the study and management of 'nature's household (ecology) and 'humankind's household (economics). This integration is necessary because conceptual and professional isolation have led to economic and environmental policies that are mutually destructive rather than reinforcing in the long run" (*Ecological Economics:* Statement of Aims and Scope). Daly, a seminal thinker in the field, advocates disaggregating resources into humanly created capital and natural capital. Humanly created capital (HCC) refers to the human production systems that transform raw materials into finished products or other systems for making products. Natural capital (NC), on the other hand, consists of resources, both renewable and nonrenewable, that supply the inputs into the human productive systems (Daley, 1992, p. 25).

Whereas Solow regards humanly created capital and natural capital as intersubstitutable, Daly argues that they are complements. Natural capital is the stock that yields the flow of natural resources: the forest stock (NC) that yields the flow (HCC) of timber; the petroleum deposits (NC) that yield the flow (HCC) of pumped crude oil; the fish populations (NC) that yield the flow (HCC) of caught fish. Without the natural stock there can be no flow; substitution is not an option other than by locating another natural stock.

In the past, Daly argues, humanly created capital has been the limiting factor on human enterprise. Nature was regarded as unlimited in bounty. Now, however, the roles are reversed. Natural capital is facing limitations as a direct result of anthropogenic actions. Why has this new form of scarcity not been noticed and accommodated to orthodox macroeconomic economic theory? Daly bases his answer in part on a much-quoted paper by Vitousek et al., entitled "Human Appropriation of the Products of Photosynthesis." Nearly 40% of land-based (25% of the total terrestrial) net primary product (NPP), the photosynthetic biomass produced from solar radiation striking the earth, is already being used or coopted by humans, one species among millions, and the fraction is steadily increasing. Included in this estimate are resources used for food, fuel, fiber, and timber. In addition, agricultural and grazing lands, human settlement areas, and cleared lands are included. Finally, the total NPP is adjusted upward because of the deleterious environmental effects of human activity; for example, we see the possible roles of acid deposition and oxidant air pollution in forest decline, the significance of soil erosion in decreasing crop productivity, and reduced estuarine productivity due to desedimentation and toxic pollution (Vitousek, et al., p. 372).

The increase in human appropriation of photosynthetic material has grown at a 2% rate; this means that two doublings have occurred in the past 70 years. When today's senior citizens were born, anthropogenic activity impacted only 10% of the land areas of the earth. "This change," Daly notes, "has been faster than the speed with which fundamental economic paradigms shift" (Daly, 1992, pp. 24, 25). We need to replace "empty earth" economics with "full earth economics."

A concept of sustainability, such as Solow's, which does not differentiate between humanly created and natural capital, nor between renewable and nonrenewable resources, but which assumes that all resources are replaceable, has been designated "weak sustainability" (Daly & Cobb, pp. 72, 73). Economic models, such as those proposed by Daly and other ecological economists, which differentiate between humanly created capital and natural capital and which deal differently with renewable and nonrenewable resources may be designated "strong sustainability."

3. Programmatic Features of Strong Sustainability

Defining "sustainability" requires an entire programmatic approach to the utilization of resources.

A. Management of renewable resources, according to Daly should be guided by the following policies:

(1) Harvest rates should equal regeneration rates (sustained yield);
(2) Waste emission rates should equal the natural assimilative capacities of the ecosystems into which the wastes are emitted;
(3) Regenerative and assimilative capacities must be treated as natural capital;

(4) Failure to maintain these capacities must be treated as capital consumption and thus unsustainable.

B. Management of nonrenewable resources:

(1) Strictly speaking use of nonrenewable resources is necessarily unsustainable;
(2) Proposed quasi-sustainable approach to utilization of nonrenewables would follow two guidelines:
   a. Limit depletion of nonrenewables to the rate of creation of renewable substitutes;
   b. Pair exploitation of nonrenewable resources with compensating investment in a renewable substitute (e.g., oil extraction paired with tree planting for wood alcohol (Daly, 1991b, El Serafy).

C. Design norms of strong sustainability.

(1) Emphasize technologies that increase resource productivity (development), the amount of value extracted per unit of resource, rather than technologies for increasing the resource throughput itself (growth);
(2) Design products and processes to facilitate materials recycling both within the economy and via natural ecosystem cycles (biodegradability, about which more will be mentioned below).

4. Consumption of Resources: Optimal Allocation Versus Optimal Scale

Fully competitive markets, operating under ideal conditions, are said to achieve optimal allocation of the flow of scarce resources. The unfettered market, it is claimed, is self-regulating (recall Adam Smith's metaphor of the "hidden hand."). However, "... optimal allocation of a given scale of resource flow within the economy is one thing (a microeconomic problem). Optimal scale of the whole economy itself relative to the ecosystem is an entirely different problem (a macroeconomic problem) (Daly, 1991a, p. 35).

Within a fully functioning market economy, issues of inequity between members of the community are addressed by means of growth in the economy itself. This expanding-pie approach ensures that the least well-off receive more as the economy grows. A major attraction to this process is that it requires little redistribution of resources. But it assumes that there are no limits on the availability of resources to fuel this growth.

Ecological economics challenges this assumption. "Whole world economics" as Daly terms it, recognizes that human appropriation of natural capital is significantly large (Daly, 1992). Optimal allocation of scarce resources might occur even though the scale of anthropogenic activity is unsustainable. Daly provides a helpful metaphor to underscore this point. Boats carry a painted line on their hull indicating the level at which the boat can safely ride in the water. This is called a Plimsoll line. If the boat is riding with its Plimsoll line submerged, it is overloaded and unsafe. The cargo of the boat may be optimally allocated as to weight fore and aft, port and starboard, but it might still be in danger of sinking. Analogously, an economy may be functioning optimally while using resources at an unsustainable rate. Allocation is optimal, the scale of the enterprise is not.

Considerations of scale are not addressed by the market at the level of macroeconomics. Limiting resource use in a rational way while still dealing with existing inequities requires collective action by the community. But today's communities are mainly national and subnational, whereas economic activity is increasingly international. As free trade is increased, ecological economists worry that environmental protection and conservation standards set at community levels will be overridden at the international level. "Free trade, as a way of erasing the effect of national boundaries, is simultaneously an invitation to the tragedy of the commons" (Daly, 1989, p. 10). "The major task of environmental macroeconomics is to design an economic institution analogous to the Plimsoll mark—to keep the weight, the absolute scale, of the economy from sinking our biospheric ark" (Daly, 1991a, p. 35).

5. Sustainability and Ecosystem Health

Norton provides an extensive body of work demonstrating the differing policies that are generated following the approaches of "weak" and "strong" sustainability. His writings contain discussions of resource use, including significant applications of ecological concepts and categories of questions of environmental policy formation. His approach is philosophical, involving what he calls pragmatic "contextualism," which he applies to issues of resource management, particularly across intergenerational time frames. Norton, along with Haskell and Costanza, provides the following definition of ecosystem health: "An ecological system is healthy and free from 'distress syndrome' if it is stable and sustainable—that is, if it is active and maintains its organization and autonomy over time and is resilient to stress" (Haskell, Norton, Costanza, p. 9). Anthropogenic activity impacts the physical environment in multiple ways. Some alterations to the environment are reversible while others can produce such significant "insults" to an ecological system as to force it to "flip" into a stable but different system entirely. Temporally, human actions involving the physical environment may in some cases be quickly reversible while in others, if reversibility is possible at all, years or even centuries may be involved. Finally, the scale of environmental impact may be local, bioregional, or even global. "How," Norton asks, "should we *measure and compare values that are experienced at different times?* how should we place a value on the *risk of irreverisble loss* of a natural feature or productive ecological process? how should we evaluate changes in the *scale* of an economy vis a vis its ecological and physical context?" (Norton, 1995a, p. 2).

"Weak Sustainability," as Daly & Cobb, and Norton have characterized Solow's conventional economic approach, deals with resource loss as commensurable issues, whether of humanly created capital or natural capital, renewable or nonrenewable resources. We can analyze the predicted changes in money terms, assessing the feasibility of environmental impacts in terms of a "willingness to pay," criterion. Benefit/Cost Analysis (BCA) can provide the model for analysis. The time-discounting of money can deal with impacts that are intergenerational. According to Solow, all forms of capital can be aggregated across generations. Solow adds that this approach "... does not preclude preserving specific resources, [such as National Parks, scenic vistas, etc.] if they have an independent value and no good substitutes. But we shouldn't kid ourselves, that is part of the value of specific resources. It is not a consequence of any interest in sustainability" (Solow, 1993, p. 187).

Norton notes that "... some economists have admitted that significant public goods will be destroyed if all decisions are made on a 'private' discount rate [and] have propounded the concept of a 'social discount rate,' a slower rate that applies to investments in public goods." He criticizes this effort citing Page who has concluded that "searching for the 'correct' social rate of discount is searching for a will o' the wisp (Norton, 1995a, p. 116; Page, 1988). He further criticizes the reductionist approach of conventional economics, for attempting to place a dollar value on entire ecosystems. "Even when environmental managers such as officials at EPA wish to act to protect these whole-system characteristics they are stymied because no accepted means exist by which to measure benefits derived from whole ecosystems, and they have little hope of justifying programs directed to this purpose in terms acceptable to auditors at the Office of Management and Budget. For example, in a recent National Academy of Sciences study, which attempted to weigh the relative costs of prevention versus accommodation to global climate change, zero value was assigned to the damages to natural systems. The panel justified this exclusion by stating that no adequate methods for ecosystem valuation exist" (Norton 1995a, p. 118).

Norton's own approach to "Strong Sustainability," involves a two-tiered decision procedure: an action tier and a metacriterion tier. A risk/decision square is constructed as a flat, square map. For ease of visualization we will refer to the upper left corner of the map as the northwest corner (NW); the upper right corner as the northeast (NE); correspondingly for the SW and SE. Along the upper horizontal axis a spectrum of time reversibility runs from irreversible (NW) eastward, through reversible in indefinite time, then reversible in one lifetime, to quickly reversible (NE). Along the left vertical axis a spectrum of environmental scale runs from local (SW), say the level of a farm, small lake, and so on, northward to ecosystem level, through global level (just below the NW corner.) If we envisage traversing from SE to NW we notice that we are moving from local ecosystems in which human activities are quickly reversible, through ecosystem levels where time reversibility is longer, up to the global level in which reversibilities take indefinite time, if not forever. So, for example, a farm that was losing topsoil from agricultural practices based on petrochemicals could switch to organic farming and reverse the process. This would be activity in the SE corner. On the other hand, the recent Montreal Protocol banning the uses of CFCs because of upper atmosphere ozone depletion, was taken to forestall a global event that would have to be located in the NW region.

What does this way of framing an approach to sustainability achieve? Following Page, (Page, 1977, pp. 190–207) Norton proposes that multiple criteria, stemming from the metacriterion tier, be applied to actions taken. Such actions are located on the risk/decision square. So, for example, at the local level it seems likely that economic criteria, benefit/cost analysis methods, can suffice. In this case it is probable that concepts of "weak sustainability" are adequate.

If we move toward the NW, however, characterized by environmental impacts that are practically irreversible, and that will affect large areas, alternative metacriteria come into play, effectively overriding the "weak sustainability" of the economic approach. This level, the one to which Norton devotes most attention, is the community level. Its temporal horizon is longer; its concerns are historical, cultural, rooted in place; its context is an ecological community populated both by humans and other biota. It is here that we protect, develop, and nurture our cultural identity, decide what kind of community we want to be and give expression to our art, spirituality and political beliefs. The Safe Minimum Standard of conservation, for example, could then be appropriate (Ciriacy-Wantrup; Bishop; Norton, 1987). According to the Safe Minimum Standards (SMS) criterion, when actions are contemplated that would irreversibly alter ecosystems in clearly deleterious ways or would directly lead to the elimination of endangered species, then the preservation of a safe minimum standard of these threatened resources is called for "... unless the social costs of doing so are unacceptably large" (Bishop, p. 10; Ciriacy-Wantrup).

As we approach even nearer the NW corner, action could be dictated by the metacriterion Precautionary Principle, which presents the current generation with a moral obligation to take affordable steps today to avoid catastrophic outcomes in the distant future. Here the risk/decision square indicates the global scale with temporal horizons extending into the indefinite future. Actions taken at this level affect the survival of the human species, war, and international equity and justice issues.

"Strong sustainability," thus, recognizes that not all values are economic values. We are dealing, after all, with potential permanent alteration of landscapes, destruction of cultures, even threatening the viability of human life. Practically speaking, the decision procedure that formerly involved econometric models and technical experts should now be shifted to the public arena. The economics of benefit/cost analysis "... if supplemented with a sense of individual justice and equity, can provide useful decision models" (Norton, 1996, p. 128). Dialogue must reflect ethical, religious, aesthetic, and historical values. At this level, public policies based on economic criteria are unreliable because such criteria undervalue resources in question.

Norton's environmental philosophy continues to develop and deepen. He has recently identified his approach with Peircian pragmatism. Philospher Charles Peirce rejected representational and foundational realism and adopted a constructivist view of science that "... recognizes that the correctibility of scientific inquiry must be fully characterized within human experience, not by reference to 'external objects.'" This stance allows Norton to consider science, especially those sciences that play the largest roles in providing understanding of ecosystems and their components, such as ecology, biology, zoology, in both descriptive and prescriptive ways. Using the analogy to human medical science, which is always both descriptive and norma-

tive, he holds that the sciences, biological, social, and geophysical, have twin objectives: not only to understand the working of ecosystems and their components but also to "... help us to formulate and measure environmental goals effectively and to propose and implement policies to achieve those goals." Science, in this view is not value-free but is applied anthropocentrically: not simply fashioned by humans but given selective focus by human values and interests. "The point is not to purge science of those values, which is both impossible and undesirable; the point is to *understand and justify* those values in specific contexts requiring action, and to attempt to adjust them through public discussion and education when they become maladaptive" (Norton, 1996, pp. 122–126).

In short, Norton focuses on three distinct policy horizons: (1) the local level, reflective of market preferences and short term interests; (2) the ecological community level, where concerns are longer term, cultural, rooted in place and populated both by humans and by other biota; (3) the global level, extending into the indefinite future, concerned with such issues as international equity and justice and the survival of the human species.

We next turn to the third of the approaches to sustainability identified above, the role and embodied values of sustainable technological practices.

C. Technology

Philosopher Joseph Margolis writes extensively about the centrality of technology to human culture and self understanding. "Human engagements involving the real world," he observes, "are inescapably and ineliminably technological . . . . The technological signifies how reality is "disclosed" to humans ... it is through social production and attention to the conditions of survival (both precognitively and through explicit inquiry) that our sense of being in touch with reality is vindicated at all . . . . The technological signifies how the study of the whole of reality—of physical nature, of life, of the social and cultural activities and relations of human existence—is unified in terms of our own investigative interests (Margolis, p. 302).

Technology is much more than a set of evaluatively neutral tools utilized to satisfy human desires. Artifacts and processes both signify and shape our conception of the world, and by their constitution serve as the instruments that render that conception self-fulfilling. Particularly since the beginning of the industrial age our image of that world has been that of a stockpile of resources and a sink for wastes. For two and one-half centuries we have been busily mining the hydrocarbon minerals from the earth at 10,000 times the rate that they were created, and have returned carbon dioxide to the atmosphere at a correspondingly increased rate over preindustrial times. Especially since the middle of this century, with the dramatic increase in use of petrochemical products in all sectors of the industrial economy, our technological practices have amounted to what Commoner calls "... war with the planet" (Commoner, p. 7.). "... [T]he petrochemical industry is unique," he observes. "Not only are its wastes dangerous, but its very products degrade the environment much more than the ones they displace. The petrochemical industry is inherently inimical to environmental quality ... nearly all of the products of the petrochemical industry are substitutes for prefectly serviceable preexisting ones" (Commoner, pp. 54, 55 [exceptions noted: video tape, certain pharmaceuticals, artificial plastic heart]).

The world viewed through the lens of industrial technology is a source of inputs to productive processes and a sink for residue from those processes and from the products of their creation. Unfortunately, the methods of accounting that track these linear processes mislead rather than enlighten, by failing to account for the true cradle-to-grave costs of production, especially as to the toll taken on the natural environment including the global atmosphere. Instead, as Commoner observes "... current environmental practice is a return to the medieval approach to disease, when illness—and death itself—was regarded as a debit on life that must be incurred in payment for Original Sin. Now this philosophy has been recast into a more modern form: some level of pollution and some risk to health are the unavoidable price that must be paid for the material benefits of modern technology" (Commoner, p. 61).

Commoner contrasts the "technosphere," the ensemble of industrial age technologies, with the "ecosphere," the context of human technology throughout the vast history of the species and extending backward to the birth of life itself on the planet. He offers three generalizations that capture the operational principles of the ecosphere: (1) Everything is connected to everything else. Cyclical, rather than linear metaphors capture the cycles of birth, death, regeneration. Complementarity characterizes the co-evolved relations of flora and fauna; (2) Everything has to go somewhere. Natural cycles of the ecosphere contain no waste. By contrast, industrial technologies and the consumer practices they foster create vast amounts of waste. (3) Nature knows best. Commoner claims that for every organic compound found in nature there is an ecosystem enzyme capable of breaking it down. Eons of trial-and-error experimentation on the planet have evolved a chemistry of life involving only 20 amino acids. There are very few chlorinated organic compounds found in nature.

The situation contrasts importantly with the industrial age technosphere. Here, humanly created chlorine is produced in abundance. When it is combined with hydrocarbons, what is formed is known as the organochlorine family of compounds. These chemicals, produced in the hundreds of millions of pounds annually for solvents, fungicides, pesticides, and refrigerants, "... are almost universally poisonous to invertebrates, plants, animals, and humans. ... They cannot be incorporated in the life-cycle of any organism on earth. They are not biologic, but 'toxilogic.'" (Hawken, pp. 40, 41) Thus not only do the practices of industrial technology generate vast amounts of waste, they also inject the vast wastes of the processes into the ecosphere, which has not evolved defenses against them.

Just as ecological economics aims to devise better economic models of accounting for technometabolic activity in order to more accurately measure the true costs of production, there are likewise indications that a "postindustrial technology," is emerging, one that seriously attempts to devise design norms that include considerations of sustainability.

Frosch and Gallopoulos have coined the term "industrial ecology" to describe a comprehensive revision of manufacturing practices that would render them more nearly sustainable. "Recognizing that industrial processes that harm and waste are, by definition, less economic and therefore more costly in the long run, companies and industries are trying to dovetail their material and waste flows, attempting to eliminate pollution by tailoring manufacturing byproducts so that they become the raw materials of subsequent processes. This philosophy goes well beyond the hygiene of curtailing waste; it entails using waste so that it is no longer waste at all" (Frosh and Gallopoulos; Hawken, p. 61). Industrial ecology is so named because it mimics natural processes, their cyclical nature and complementarity between the inputs and outputs of one product or process with those of a linked process.

"Industrial parks" constitute one instance of industrial ecology. In Kalundborg, Denmark, a coal-fired power plant, an oil refinery, a biotech company, a sheetrock plant, producers of concrete and sulfuric acid, along with fish farms, greenhouses, and a municipal heating plant have collaborated to form a complex arrangement of cooperative ventures, obtaining input resources and assimilating wastes from one another. It is noteworthy that while the continguity of the enterprises made such complex mutual ventures possible, the actual impetus for the cooperative was done completely without government prodding (Hawken, p. 63.).

A more radical transformation of technology toward greater sustainability is embodied in what has been termed "regenerative technology." Whereas much of the technology of the industrial era has been characterized by processes that can "overcome" natural obstacles, regenerative technology aims to utilize, not merely mimic, natural processes in the most fundamental sense. A simple example: from antiquity, humans have devised sailing technologies that bend the wind to human intentions. The Chinese are credited with the invention of the lateen or three-sided sail that enabled boats to tack closer to the wind than was possible with the original square sails. Nature, however, still dictated the terms. Industrial technology gave us the steamship. Now nature was not so much bent to human intention as simply overridden (although admittedly not always.) Regenerative technology attempts to bend ecological processes to human aims, not to override them as hydrocarbon energy sources have made possible, while simultaneously directing those aims toward sustainable goals.

Lyle, a seminal figure in the development of regenerative technological systems, provides design norms for regenerative designs. A partial listing includes: (1) Let nature do the work. Virtually all of the human life-support functions dealing with energy, shelter, water, food, and waste are preformed in undisturbed nature by the highly evolved natural processes of conversion, distribution, filtration, assimilation, and storage. Regenerative technology imitates these functions. (2) Consider nature as both model and context—biological processes generally provide more useful models than physical processes. (3) Aggregate, don't isolate. Physical science is impressively analytical. Ecology, on the other hand, does not enjoy the luxury of isolation. As Commoner said, "Everything is connected to everything else." Regenerative technology bases solutions on natural systems. (4) Use information to replace power. Already, independent of regenerative technologies, the age is being dubbed the "information age." Whenever telecommuting replaces auto commuting the environment benefits. Hawken calls this "decarbonization." When human needs are met by a relatively low-energy solution rather than a high-energy one, auto transport, this becomes an instance of "dematerialization" (Hawken, p. 64.) (5) Seek common solutions to disparate problems. Regenerative technologies make use of natural ecosystems to purify water for reuse. As early as the beginning of this century Frederick Olmsted designed the Boston Fens to do just this. His original

successes, however, were overridden by dam builders (Spirn, p. 109.). (6) Manage storage as a key to sustainability. "All natural processes have their storages: groundwater basins for water; the atmosphere for oxygen, nitrogen, and other gases; trees for biomass; and fatty tissue for animal energy. Regenerative systems either draw on these natural storages or incorporate other means of storage for their own use" (Lyle, pp. 37–45).

It is clear that regenerative technologies and other novel approaches to meeting human wants will require implementation strategies capable of matching their creativity. Hawken's *Ecology of Commerce* is an extended discussion of approaches and incentives that can be used in conjunction with the market to change the way technology is practiced. For example, "Because the United States does not have a severance tax on virgin resources, the price of recyclables does not cover the cost of collection" (Hawken, p. 72.). Combinations of government tax policies, such as carbon or green taxes, along with novel approaches to meeting consumer needs, such as lease/buybacks for most appliances, automobiles (retailers of consumer products would become "de-shopping" centers where we would drop off the products we no longer needed and obtain newer ones), along with waste-disposal incentives are but a few of the profusion of ideas he provides.

Two additional points deserve mention regarding the move to technologies that are sustainable. In the first place, the idea that the industrialized countries are about to abandon their current approach based on industrial technologies and growth economics boggles the mind. Winner aptly observes that in the modern industrial order we are presented with a world ". . . of material accomplishments and social adaptations of astounding completeness" (Winner, p. 131). At the least, sustainable technologies will require alterations in the technological practices of the developed countries towards ones that begin to observe the physical limits of resource use and waste disposal. These limits are determined by the earth's regenerative processes, both that of photosynthetic material generation and of sustainable rates of waste disposal. Whereas there are indications that some of the industrialized countries, principally among the European nations and to some extent Japan, have begun to undertake the research and experimentation that could point the way to post industrial models of technology, such a "sustainability consciousness" seems remote to most U.S. manufacturers. Current practices and the economic wisdom that certifies them do appear "astoundingly complete."

Secondly, if as Margolis claims, technology is itself a cultural artifact, it makes no sense to speak of technology, today's or tomorrow's, as moving from one unsustainable technology—today's wrong headed industrial model—to tomorrow's correct and sustainable technology. There are in fact multiple sustainable future scenarios that must be envisaged. Future technological practices, if they are sustainable, are likely to be more localized and culturally diverse. They will share in common an appreciation of the limits of the solar budget and of the capacity of the earth to restore itself. The issue that continues to intrude is that of reconciling sustainability with concerns for equity and justice. The last section of this paper will discuss the topic of intragenerational and intergenerational equity.

D. Intragenerational and Intergenerational Equity Issues

1. Resource Consumption Rates and Population Growth Rates

Whatever the shortcomings of the 1987 Brundtland Report, and as noted they are significant, it must be credited with setting the tone and the terms of contemporary discussions of sustainability. Its dual focus on developing and developed countries underscored vast inequities that continue to prevent progress toward sustainable public policies. The top 1 billion inhabitants of the planet, located in the developed countries live, for the most part, in unprecedented luxury, while the bottom 1 billion are destitute. American children, for example, have more pocket money than the one-half billion poorest people of the globe have for necessities (Durning, p. 57). One writer estimates that the 50 million people that will be born in the United States during the next 40 years will have more of a global impact in terms of resource consumption than the 2 billion projected births in India during the same period. The recent UN Annual Human Development Report finds that the gap between the richest and poorest countries continues to grow; worse still, income levels alone fail adequately to indicate the true dimensions of the disparity. The report devises a "capability poverty measure," which identifies hidden or potential poverty factors such as children under 5 who are underweight, the proportion of unattended births, the number of children in school, and the rates of female illiteracy. These indicators are better predictors than income levels alone of poverty and disadvantage being programmed into coming generations (*New York Times*, July, 15, 1996, p. A3).

In the case of the developed countries, disproportionately large levels of consumption of the earth's re-

sources block progress toward sustainable development. In the case of the less developed countries, it is high rates of population growth that limit such progress, specifically by nipping in the bud productivity increases that might lead to self-sufficiency. Worldwide fertility has declined since the 1960s. The annual growth rate in percent today is 1.7 in the developed countries, and 3.4 among the developing countries. In the most impoverished countries, however, the rate is 5.6 (WRI, p. 174). In her keynote address at the 1994 UN Conference on Population held in Cairo, Norwegian Prime Minister Brundtland observed, "Population growth is one of the most serious obstacles to world prosperity and sustainable development. We may soon be facing new famine, mass migration, destabilization and even armed struggle as peoples compete for ever more scarce land and water resources." She added, "Women's education is the single most important path to higher productivity, lower infant mortality and lower fertility. The economic returns on investment in women's education are generally comparable to those for men, but the social returns in terms of health and fertility by far exceed what we gain from men's education" (Brundtland, 1994).

2. Consequentialist Ethics and Intragenerational Equity

Utility-based welfare economics and commodity-based growth theory view development in utilitarian terms. Increases in utility occur with expansion in the availability of goods and services within the country in question. With increasing command over hunger, ill health, poor shelter and sanitation, all terms of disutility, the freedom to achieve happiness is enhanced. Issues of international justice and equity, in this model, are addressed by developmental loans from outside countries or international development banks, as well as from incomes generated through employment in industries facilitated by outside agencies or multinational corporations. A special case of the commodities approach is known in the literature as the "basic needs" concept, the objective of which is to provide all human beings with the opportunity for a full life (Streeten, p. 21; Sen, 1996, p. 190). Because it focuses on basic needs: nutrition, health, shelter, water, sanitation, education and other essentials, it is more targeted than general utility models. It may, however, be faulted for framing development goals in terms of minimum levels and for emphasizing "needs," a more passive concept than "capability" (Sen, 1996, pp. 190, 191).

Sen, by contrast, provides a consequentialist nonutilitarian approach to international equity policy. His philosophy has been deeply influenced by first-hand experience with famines in India during his childhood. In multiple cases, he observes, the famines were not caused by lack of food. Rather, they occurred because the starving people were incapable of gaining access to the necessary foodstuffs because they were too poor, they were outcasts, or they were victims of corrupt or inefficient food distribution bureaucracies. Within individual families the problems were exacerbated because females in particular were slighted in food distribution (the same was also the case with access to health services) (Sen, 1996, p. 201).

For those families with minimal access to basic needs, Sen was impressed by another fact. In the case of the chronically hopeless, the overworked coolie, or the thoroughly subjugated housewife, the utilitarian calculus is deeply biased. "The absence of present discontent or felt radical desires cannot wipe out the moral significance of this inequality if individual freedom—including the freedom to assess one's situation and the possibilities of changing it—is accepted as a major value" (Sen, 1990). The hedonistic calculus applied to discriminatory social situations such as these would raise no alarms.

Sen's own nonutility based consequentialist approach to economic development calls for an expansion of people's "capabilities." "This approach focuses on what people can *do* or can *be*, and development is seen as a process of emancipation from the enforced necessity to 'live less or be less. ... The essence of the capabilities approach, is to see commodity consumption as no more than a means to generating capabilities..." (Sen, 1996, pp. 187, 192).

The theoretical model that Sen provides can supply the framework for Brundtland's strong emphasis on women's education as the critical factor in addressing world population problems. A recent study bears this out and challenges standard development models that directly link declining birth rates with economic growth. In the case of Sri Lanka, a birth-rate decrease occurred because villages were provided with family planning centers even as the overall economic level of the country remained low. By acquiring the capacity to understand their own reproductive processes, Sri Lankan women were simultaneously empowered to influence and control their patterns of procreation (Robey et al.).

3. Contractarian Ethics and Intragenerational Ethics

Rawls holds that justice is the first virtue of social institutions. Social institutions are characterized as cooperative ventures undertaken for mutual advantage. Because he does not regard separate nations as engaging in cooperative ventures with each other in the way that a community or nation would, he does not apply his full-blown contractarian theory to international relationships. He does, however, recognize issues of international justice, but restricts the set of principles that would be derived in an international original position to matters of self-determination, nonintervention, justifiable self-defense, and principles defining a just war. Beitz believes that Rawls is wrong in so limiting issues of international justice. He extends the Rawlsian model in ways that are directly relevant to issues of sustainability and intragenerational ethics applied internationally.

Beitz argues that Rawls errs in two ways. In the first instance Rawls develops an analogy between natural talents possessed by members of a society and natural resources possessed by nations of the earth. In both cases he assumes initial distributions to be morally arbitrary. Just as the right to develop one's own talents is considered by Rawls to be properly within one's own control, so too does he consider the development of natural resources by any given nation to be a matter to be decided by that nation alone. Beitz (1988) questions this analogy. Development of one's talents does not limit others from developing their talents as well. But development of resources by any given nation, in a world of scarcity, could indeed limit the development plans of other nations. Appropriation of resources by those nations blessed with resources, possibly critical resources, could very well leave others worse off. Accordingly, parties to an international original position "would know that resources are unevenly distributed with respect to population, that adequate access to resources is a prerequisite for successful operation of (domestic) cooperative schemes, and that resources are scarce" (Beitz, p. 34). The result of this awareness "behind the veil of ignorance" would yield consensus that resource redistribution principles should be developed which would enable each society individually to develop just institutions and economies capable of meeting its member's needs. Applying Rawls' difference principle to the resource issue, Beitz further claims that an ideal international consensus would conclude that only those departures from straightforward equalization strategies for resource redistribution are justified which first compensate those countries least endowed in natural resources.

According to Beitz, Rawls errs in a second way in not extending his theory of justice to the international arena. This has to do with Rawls' assumption that nations are not only not engaged in cooperative ventures but are relatively independent of one another. To the contrary, nations today are significantly interdependent. This condition has now been strikingly heightened by recent NAFTA and GATT treaties, implementation of which facilitate the mobility of resources, capital, money, and even waste all around the globe. Outstripping even these trade agreements among nation-states are the actions of the transnational corporations. Their economic heft is staggering. In 1991 the 10 largest multinational corporations had collective revenues of $801 billion, a figure greater than the collective GNPs of the 100 smallest countries in the world. Today the top 500 corporations control 25% of the gross world product and do it while employing 0.01% of the world's population. While the world economy grows at 2 to 3%, the largest transnational corporations enjoy 8 to 10% growth rates (Hawken, p. 91, 92).

There is evidence, already noted, that interdependence leads to a widening of the income gap between rich and poor nations. It has all too frequently exacerbated income inequalities within countries, with profits from foreign-owned corporations going to the already well-off members of the host country. Furthermore, the influence of transnational corporations can have a corrosive effect on democratic processes, such as there may be, within host countries through their inordinate influence in supporting repressive regimes.

Beitz unapologetically defends the ethical principle of international redistribution, even in the face of real world politics. "Ideal theory, then, supplies a set of criteria for the formulation and criticism of strategies of political action in the non-ideal world, at least when the consequences of political action can be predicted with sufficient confidence to establish their relationship to the social ideal" (Beitz, p. 48). By extending Rawls theory to the international arena without substantive criticism of Rawls' model of the just society per se, Beitz aligns himself with Rawls' defense of ideal theory applied to a nonideal world as "...the only basis for the systematic grasp of these more pressing problems" (Rawls, p. 9).

Both Sen and Beitz follow the Enlightenment practice of defining morality in individualistic terms. Such an assumption, while serviceable in discussion of intragenerational equity where moral agents are in principle identifiable, however, causes problems in dealing with issues of intergenerational equity. It is to these problems that we now turn.

4. Intergenerational Equity

a. The Identity Problem

The welfare of future generations can be expressed either as rights *in personam* or *in rem*. The preceding discussion of current equity issues, both consequentialist and contractarian, assumed an *in personam* starting point. That is to say rights are associated with some "specific nameable person persons" (Sterba, p. 116). But this becomes impossible when discussing future peoples that could owe their existence to policies we might implement today in the name of sustainability.

Parfit has famously illustrated the paradoxical nature of present-day policy decisions such as these. Parfit considers two societies, one conserving of resources, the other profligate. It is even possible that the profligacy may extend to unsustainably high procreation rates in one case but lower rates in the other. In either case the options open to future generations will have been affected by today's behaviors and policies. Children that might have been born will not be; others that might not have been born, say, in a low-birthrate culture, will be born. That is to say, individual future persons are in principle unidentifiable. Now Parfit asks, supposing that the lives of those individuals who are, in fact, born are not unbearable, can we expect that they would consider it better had they not been born? Such a response seems highly unlikely. Thus, the paradoxical result appears to be that future generations would have no particular reason to condemn the profligate behavior of their ancestors and no particular reason, on the other hand, to commend those ancestors whose quicky conservatism led them to forgo so many consumer pleasures (Parfit). This puzzling outcome appears both to undermine frugal behavior undertaken by the current generation on behalf of temporally distant peoples, and to render such people individually impossible to identify.

b. The Distance Problem

A related issue in discussion of intergenerational equity has been termed the "distance problem" by Norton (1982, pp. 332–335). Given the uncertainties in dealing with distant peoples, some environmental ethicists have concluded that obligations to the future should be limited to immediately following generations. Passmore (1974), for example, reaches this conclusion because we cannot know what will harm distant peoples. Normally, our intuitions about the next generation, however, do not suffer from such uncertainties. This conclusion is a particularly troubling one for ecologists. The fact is that actions taken today, say, the alteration of a major watershed or technological practices that gradually affect global climate, may have minimal impact on the next generation but might produce conditions inimical to human life a century from now. Again, our intuitions tell us that basing technologies and economic accounting schemes on time horizons one generation in the future is irrational.

c. Alternatives to Individualistic Ethics

Norton argues that both the identity and distance problems can be solved once we abandon the Enlightenment preoccupation with individualistic ethics. An *in rem* rather than *in personam* perspective assigns rights in the future to everyone in a position to exercise them. Recall Edmund Burke's conservative criticism of the individualistic social contract theories of Hobbes, Locke, and Rousseau. He speaks of a partnership "...not only between those who are living, but between those who are living, those who are dead, and those who are to be born. Each contract of each particular state is but a clause in the great primeval contract of eternal society, linking the lower with the higher natures, connecting the visible and the invisible world, according to a fixed compact sanctioned by the inviolable oath which holds all physical and all moral natures, each in their appointed place contract...." Burke's organic theory thus suggests one way that obligations can be expressed to others without explicit individualistic identification.

Consider another nonindividualistic approach to intergenerational obligations. In connection with her scholarship in international and environmental law, Edith Brown Weiss cites what she terms the "common patrimony" of humankind reflected in the great religious traditions of both East and West, as well as African customary law and Marxist socialism. Threading through this vast body of literature is a common idea that there exists for each generation an obligation for "...sustaining the life-support systems of the planet, the ecological processes, environmental conditions, and cultural resources important for the survival and well-being of the human species, and a healthy and decent human environment" (Weiss, p. 23).

Weiss speaks of a "planetary trust," by which the common patrimony is maintained and transmitted (Weiss, pp. 2, 3; Brown, pp. 69–91). She proposes four criteria for guiding the development of principles of intergenerational equity from which three principles follow. The four criteria include (1) encourage equality among generations, neither authorizing overexploitation by one generation nor imposing unreasonable obligations on any generation to protect the future; (2) do not require that one generation predict the values of future generations; (3) choose principles that are reasonably clear in their application to foreseeable situations; and (4) choose values generally shared by different cultural traditions and acceptable to differing economic and social systems. She also notes that intergenerational fairness cannot be pursued without intragenerational fairness—it would be wrong to saddle one segment of present society with the full costs of protecting future generations, for example.

The three principles which follow are: (1) Conservation of options. Each generation should leave to its successors a "robust planet" that will support a variety of life-choices, including such that are not foreseeable at the time; (2) Conservation of quality. Each generation should try to leave the planet in as good a shape as it found it; (3) Conservation of access. This principle "...aims at balancing justice requirements between and within generations. As an example, an environmental conservation programme that would benefit future generations generally but whose burdens weighed mostly on the poorest countries of the present world, would violate the principle. Also, in balancing the interests of successive generations, this principle allows one to steer clear of the two extremes of fanatic preservationism and short-sighted exploitation" (Weiss, pp. 38–45; Mauron).

Weiss's framework provides a strong basis for an ethic of sustainability for two reasons. First, it rests on a common denominator of religious and philosophical ideas shared by a wide variety of human cultures. Second, the emphasis Weiss places on conservation of options moves the discussion of intergenerational equity away from a preoccupation with specific individuals and on to a concern for protection and preservation of the essential features of human habitats.

A sustainability ethic will require multiple conceptions of moral obligation (Norton, 1995b). Individualistic ethics may well continue to govern much of the day-to-day lifeworld. A sustainability consciousness, developed within each of us, will stretch our horizon of concern not only to others of our species spatially and temporally removed, but will enlarge the sense of community, recalling Burke, to the greater biospheric community. Leopold anticipated this development in his proposal for a land ethic. Ethics, he claims, first developed as patterns of behavior between individuals expanding on to relations between the individual and society. The land ethic constitutes the next level of expansion when the individual's horizon of concern is expanded to the land, by which he makes clear he means to include soil, waters, plants, and animals, that is the biotic community itself. "A thing is right," he says "when it tends to preserve the integrity, stability, and beauty of the biotic community. It is wrong when it tends otherwise." The land ethic entails an expanded temporal horizon well beyond the next generation alone, and is beautifully captured in Leopold's essay "Thinking Like a Mountain" (Leopold, pp. 224, 25, 129–136).

Finally, recalling Weiss's emphasis on the "common patrimony," shared by a wide range of religions, personalistic or otherwise, it may not appear extreme to suggest that a sustainability consciousness will involve the emergence of a reoriented consciousness toward the biotic community: a sense of the sacred? While admitting that the scientific/rational mind recoils at the mention of the sacred, Skolimowski, echoing Schweitzer, promotes the ecovalue of reverence for life. He couples reverence for life with responsibility, as exemplified in Leopold's land ethic. Conservation and frugality are the means whereby we express that responsibility. Skolimowski incorporates the sacred in what he calls "reverential development based on ecological values." "In proposing a new form of development, reverential development based on ecological values, I wish simultaneously to bring about sustainability to the planet, dignity to its diverse peoples, and unity to humankind now fractured by inappropriate development." Reverential development addresses four goals: (1) it combines the economic with the ethical and reverential; (2) it combines contemporary ethical imperatives with traditional ethical codes; (3) it attempts to serve all the people of all cultures; and (4) it promises to bring about a peace between humankind and nature" (Skolimowski, p. 103, 104).

IV. CONCLUSION

The sustainability of human populations entails commitments to three goals: ethical treatment of humans and other creatures of the biosphere; enterprise for meeting of human needs based on technologies that are environmentally responsible; and attitudes and policies directed to natural ecosystems and to the earth's regenerative process that are conserving of the capacities of those systems to endure and function indefinitely.

Ethical obligations, it has been suggested, may best be framed in collective categories such as "common patrimony" or "great primal contract," as this approach may avoid problems connected to identity and distance. The point has been stressed that the ethics of sustainability has recognized obligations owed to the less

well-off of the present era as well as to future generations, near as well as distant. Two norms have been mentioned that are bound to be controversial: those of redistribution of resources and frugality of consumption. Concerns for intragenerational equity would appear to require resource redistribution, while the realities of living sustainably within the limits set by the photosynthetic flowrates leads inexorably toward more frugal patterns of consumption. An ethical foundation for a sustainability consciousness can be built on a common patrimony; however, the fact needs to be kept in mind that such commonality will be expressed in many voices, by many cultures, philosophies, and religions. Perhaps, as conjectured, the requisite perspective will not occur without a greater sense of the sanctity of life itself. Even a concept such as "reverential development" may gradually become something other than an oxymoron.

Enterprise for meeting human needs can never return to some Edenic state of aboriginal sustainability. Devising technologies that emphasize durability over disposability, dematerialization over increased consumption of nonrenewables, information flow instead of flow of matter are some of the ways technologies can appropriately contribute to a sustainable future. The policies of ecological economics, characterized as strong sustainability, implemented by technologies that adapt to nature or actually regenerate and restore as part of their normal design, can foster progress toward a postindustrial sustainability. Disaggregating humanly created capital from natural capital with economic accounting models, such as ecological economics, would be a strong first step. Replacement of unreflective commitments to economic growth as a cure-all for poverty with capacity-enhancing models of development can result in human empowerment and the release of full potential.

A conserving attitude toward natural systems, scenic wonders, and the regenerative processes of the planet is difficult when evaluative measures are expressed in terms of utility alone. The two-tier decision procedure that was discussed makes room for concerns other than of short-term economic utility. A land ethic projects a time horizon well beyond what the time-value of money would consider reasonable. Such an ethic, functioning as a second-tier criterion, and applied when loss of the resource in question would be irreversible or would have widespread impact, could trump a benefit/cost analysis ratio by imposing a safe minimum standard of conservation. Anthropogenic activity since the beginning of the industrial period has produced a world of massively unsustainable practices. This discussion has cited some of the important proposals that claim to provide sustainable alternatives to these practices.

Also See the Following Articles

DEVELOPMENT ETHICS • ECOLOGICAL BALANCE • ENVIRONMENTAL ETHICS, OVERVIEW • PRECAUTIONARY PRINCIPLE

Bibliography

Ayres, R. (1993). Cowboys, cornucopians and long-run sustainability. *Ecological Economics* 8, 189–207.

Beitz, C. (1988). International distributive justice. In Luper-Foy, S. (Ed.), *Problems of international justice,* pp. 27–66. Boulder, CO: Westview Press.

Bishop, R. (1978). Endangered species and uncertainty: The economics of a safe minimum standard. *American Journal of Agricultural Economics,* 60, (12 February), 10–18.

Boyden, S., & Dovers, S. (1992). Natural-resource consumption and its environmental impacts in the Western world. Impacts of increasing per capita consumption. *Ambio,* 21, No. 1 (February), 63–69.

Brown, P. (1994). *Restoring the public trust.* Boston: Beacon Press.

Brundtland, G. (1994, 5 September). *Key note address to the international conference on population and development.* Cairo.

Burke, E. (1955). *Reflections on the French revolution.* Indianapolis, IN: Library of Liberal Arts. (Original work published 1790)

Ciriacy-Wantrup, S. (1952). *Resource conservation.* Berkeley: University of California Press.

Commoner, B. (1990). *Making peace with the planet* (p. 7). New York: Pantheon Books.

Costanza, R. (1991). *Ecological economics: The science and management of sustainability.* New York: Columbia University Press.

Costanza, R., Norton, B., & Haskell, B. (Eds.). (1992). *Ecosystem health: New goals for environmental management.* Washington, DC: Island Press.

Cronon, W. (1983). *Changes in the land: Indians, colonists, and the ecology of New England.* New York: Hill and Wang.

Crossette, B. (1996, July 15). U.N. finds world rich-poor gap widening. *New York Times,* p. A3.

Daly, H. (1991a). Elements of environmental macroeconomics. In Costanza, R. (Ed.), *Ecological economics: The science and management of sustainability* (Chapter Three, pp. 32–46). New York: Columbia University Press.

Daly, H. & Cobb, J., Jr. (1989). *For the common good: Redirecting the economy toward community, the environment, and a sustainable future,* Boston: Beacon Press.

Daly, H. (1991a). Elements of environmental macroeconomics. In R. Costanza (Ed.), *Ecological economics: The science and management of sustainability.* (Chapter Three, pp. 32–46) New York: Columbia University Press.

Daly, H. (1991b). Operational principles for sustainable development. *Earth Ethics* (Summer), pp. 6, 7.

Daly, H. (1992). From empty-world economics to full-world economics: Recognizing an historical turning point in economic development. In Goodland, R., Daly, H., El Serafy, S. (Eds.), *Population, technology, and lifestyle: The transition to sustainability* (Chapter 2, pp. 23–37). Washington, DC: Island Press.

Durning, A. (1991). How much is enough? *Technology Review* (May/June), pp. 57–64.

El Serafy, S. (1991). The environment as capital. In Costanza, R. (Ed.), *Ecological economics: The science and management of sustainability.* (pp. 168–75). New York: Columbia University Press.

Engel, J. R. (1990). Introduction: The ethics of sustainable development. In *The ethics of environment and development.* In Engel, J. R., and Engel, J. G. (Eds.) (pp. 1–23). Tucson: University of Arizona Press.

Frosh, R., and Gallopoulos, N. (1989, September). Strategies for manufacturing. *Scientific American,* Special Edition, pp. 144–52.

Goodland, R., and Ledec, G. (1987). Neoclassical economics and principles of sustainable development. *Ecological Modelling* 38, 19–46.

Goulet, D. (1990). Development ethics and ecological wisdom. In Engel, J. R., and Engel, J. G. (Eds.), *Ethics of environment and development: Global challenge, international response* (pp. 36–49). Tucson: University of Arizona Press.

Hardin, G. (1968, December 13). The tragedy of the commons. *Science* 162, 1243–1248.

Haskell, B., Norton, B., and Costanza, R. (1992). What is ecosystem health and why should we worry about it? In Costanza, R., Norton, B., and Haskell, B. (Eds.), *Ecosystem health: New goals for environmental management* (pp. 3–20). Covelo, CA: Island Press.

Hawken, P. (1993). *The ecology of commerce.* New York: HarperCollins.

Kothari, R. (1990). Sustainable development as an ethical ideal: Four primary criteria. In Engel, J. R., and Engel, J. G. (Eds.), *Ethics of environment and development: Global challenge, international response* (pp. 27–35) Tucson: University of Arizona Press.

Leopold, A. (1949). The land ethic, and Thinking like a mountain. *Sand County Almanac,* pp. 201–226 and 129–136.

Lyle, J. (1994). Economics, policy and transition. In *Regenerative Design for Sustainable Development.* New York: John Wiley & Sons, Inc.

Margolis, J. (1983). Pragmatism, transcendental arguments, and the technological. In P. Durbin and F. Rapp (Eds.), *Philosophy and technology* (pp. 291–309). Dordrecht: D. Reidel.

Mauron, A. (1993). Genetics and Intergenerational Concerns. *1993 Yearbook of the Societas Ethica.* Utrecht, NL: (www.,ed.upen.edu/~bioethic/ genetics/ articles/11. mauron.genetic. html).

Norton, B. (1982, Winter). Environmental ethics and the rights of future generations. *Environmental Ethics* (Vol. 4, pp. 319–337).

Norton, B. (1987). *Why preserve natural variety?* Princeton, NJ: Princeton University Press.

Norton, B. (1992a). Sustainability, human welfare, and ecosystem health. *Environmental Values,* 1, 2, (Summer), pp. 97–111.

Norton, B., and Ulanowicz, R. (1992b). Scale and biodiversity policy: A hierarchical approach. *Ambio,* 21, 244–249.

Norton, B. (1995a). Evaluating ecosystem states: Two competing paradigms. *Ecological Economics,* 14, 2 (August) 113–127.

Norton, B. (1995b). Future generations, obligations to. *Encyclopedia of Bioethics* (Vol. 2, pp. 892–899). New York: Macmillan.

Norton, B. (1996). Integration or reduction: Two approaches to environmental values, pp. 105–138. In Light, A., & Katz, E. (Eds.), *Environmental Pragmatism.* London: Routledge.

Norton, B., and Toman, M. (forthcoming). Sustainability: Ecological and economic perspectives. *Journal of Land Economics.*

Page, T. (1977). *Conservation and economic efficiency.* Baltimore: Johns Hopkins Press.

Page, T. (1988). Intergenerational equity and the social rate of discount. In Smith, K. (Ed.), *Environmental resources and ap-*

plied welfare economics. Washington, DC: Resources for the Future.

Parfit, D. (1983). Energy Policy and the Further Future: The Social Discount Rate. In MacLean, D., & Brown, P. (Eds.), *Energy and the Future* (pp. 31–37). Totowa, NJ: Rowman and Littlefield.

Passmore, J. (1974). *Man's responsibility for nature.* New York: Scribners.

Pearce, D., & Warford, J. (1993). *World without end.* Washington, DC: Oxford University Press.

Peirce, C. (1955). *The philosophical writings of Peirce* (esp. pp. 21, 39). New York: Dover.

Rawls, J. (1971). *A theory of justice.* Cambridge, MA: Harvard University Press.

Robey, B., Rutstein, S., & Morris, L. (1993, December). The fertility decline in developing countries. *Scientific American,* pp. 30–37.

Ruckelshaus, W. (1989, September). Toward a sustainable world. *Scientific American,* pp. 166–175.

Sen, A. (1990, June 14). Individual freedom as a social commitment. *New York Review of Books,* pp. 49–53.

Sen, A. (1996). Goods and people. In Aiken, W., & LaFollette, H. (Eds.), *World hunger and morality* (pp. 186–210). Upper Saddle River, NJ: Prentice Hall.

Skolimowski, H. (1990). Reverence for life. In Engel, J. R., & Engel, J. G. (Eds.), *Ethics of environment and development: Global challenge, international response* (pp. 97–103). Tucson: University of Arizona Press.

Solow, R. (1991). Sustainability: An economist's perspective. In Dorfman, R., & Dorfman, N. (Eds.), *Economics of the environment* (3rd edition, pp. 179–87). New York: W. W. Norton & Co.

Spirn, A. (1995). Constructing nature: The legacy of Frederick Law Olmsted. In Cronon, W. (Ed.), *Uncommon ground: Toward reinventing nature.* New York: Norton.

Sterba, J. (1988). The Welfare Rights of Distant Peoples and Future Generations. In Sterba, J. (Ed.), *Morality in practice* (pp. 115–127). Belmont, CA: Wadsworth.

Streeten, P., et al. (1981). *First things first: Meeting basic needs in developing countries.* New York: Oxford.

United Nations Conference on the Environment, Stockholm, "Declaration of Principles," 1972. Reprinted in Gruen, L., and Jamison, D. (1994). *Reflections on nature* (pp. 179–82). New York: Oxford University Press.

United Nations Conference on Environment and Development, Rio de Janeiro, "Declaration on Environment and Development," 1992. Reprinted in Gruen, L., and Jamison, D. (1994). *Reflections on Nature* (pp. 207–211). New York: Oxford University Press.

Vitousek, P., et al. (1986, June). Human appropriation of the products of photosynthesis. *Bioscience* **36**, 6, 368–373.

Weiss, E. (1989). *In fairness to future generations,* Tokyo: UN University and Transnational Publishers. (Find specific location and cite BGN paper where this is cited.)

Winner, L. (1977). The political philosophy of alternative technology: Historical roots and present prospects. In Lovekin, D., and Verene, D. (Eds.), *Essays in humanity and technology* p. 131. Dixon, IL: Sauk Valley College.

World Commission on Environment and Development (1987). *Our Common Future* (p. ix). Oxford: Oxford University Press. (Also referred to as "The Brundtland Report" after the Commission Chair, Gro Brundtland.)

World Resources: 1996–97, WRI, UNEP, UNDP, World Bank. (1996), p. 174. New York: Oxford University Press.

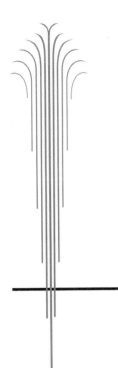

TABLOID JOURNALISM

Seumas Miller
Charles Sturt University

GLOSSARY

autonomous public communicator A person who communicates information and comment to the community via the print and electronic media, and does so wholly on the basis of his or her own judgment. An autonomous communicator is not simply the communicative instrument of someone else. Newsreaders are not autonomous public communicators, while current affairs correspondents are supposed to be.

investigator A newspaper, TV, or radio journalist who unearths, or seeks to unearth, previously unknown—or not widely known—information for the purposes of disseminating it to the public at large.

normative Of, or pertaining to, standards or principles governing what ought to be, as distinct from what in fact is. One category of normative judgments or statements is the moral or ethical.

postmodernism A contemporary intellectual movement associated with the writings of Derrida, Barthes, Lacan, Rorty, and Foucault. Influential in literary and communication studies. Key elements are rejection of the literal–metaphoric distinction, and of rationality and the unitary self, and the tying of knowledge to power.

public forum A meeting place or communicative space in which individuals or representatives can communicate to the community at large.

theoretical Of or pertaining to a theory. A theory is a general account of some type of object or kind of practice, including journalism, which identifies the main features of that object or practice, displays their relationship to one another, and differentiates that object or practice from other sorts of object and practice. A theory enables us to better understand the object or practice in question.

TABLOID JOURNALISM, in the modern sense, refers to the quality of said journalism. "Tabloid" initially referred to the size and layout of a newspaper. Tabloids were distinguished from broadsheets in that they used smaller sheets of paper. Tabloids were more akin to a magazine format than the large, wide broadsheets. However, over time "tabloid" has come to be used to refer to lower quality newspapers and, more recently, certain lower quality TV programs. The *Sun* newspaper published in the United Kingdom is a paradigm of tabloid journalism in this newly established sense.

I. DESCRIPTION OF TABLOID JOURNALISM

A. Content

Taking the *Sun* as our paradigm, let us first look at its overall content. Firstly, there is very little hard news or analysis in the newspaper. Rather it is largely given over to sports, advertising, and so-called human interest stories. Secondly, there is a good deal of space given over to depiction of young female bodies in sexually provocative poses. Most notably there is the page 3 pinup girl. The overall space given to hard news and analysis relative to "trivia" is one indicator of the emphasis of tabloid journalism. Another indicator is the relative lack of prominence of hard news and analysis within the structure of the publication.

Typically, the lead story of the *Sun* is "sensational" and oriented to sex scandal. In short, the lead story is often unimportant news—at least from any perspective other than that of sex scandal. This is not to say, of course, that a sex scandal is always and necessarily unimportant. The Christine Keeler episode, for example, was important and newsworthy.

B. Characteristic Features

Some of the characteristic features of tabloid stories—whether in newspapers or on television—follow.

As already indicated, the lead stories in a tabloid publication are often sensationalist in nature. The private lives of prominent public figures, including politicians, Princess Diana, and the British Royal Family, are a particular obsession of the *Sun*. Other favorite issues for tabloid publications throughout the world are gruesome crimes and exotic and/or bizarre events or conditions. The Yorkshire Ripper and the so-called House of Horrors stories provided the UK tabloids with a feast of headlines and lead stories; as did the woman who took fertility drugs and then decided to try to give birth to all of the resultant eight fetuses.

Second, many of the stories are highly moralistic, the morality in question being popular sentiment. Such moralistic stories include those expressing moral outrage at the (allegedly) light sentences handed out to vicious criminals and those giving vent to nationalistic fervor in the context of war. In this latter connection, consider the jingoism and lack of concern for the lives of Argentina naval personnel on the occasion of the sinking of the *Belgrano* during the Falklands war.

Thirdly, the stories rely heavily on cliches, stereotypes, and even abusive slang. Argentinians become

Argies, and French men and women, Frogs. To take some recent examples from the Australian press, Ivan Milat, the murderer of backpackers in the Belangalo Forest, became the Belangalo Butcher, and Martin Bryant, the murderer of 36 people in Tasmania, a Blonde Blue-Eyed Beast. There is an overrepresentation of young women in sexually provocative poses. There is the tendency to present adherents to the Moslem faith as members of chanting violent crowds. Young black youths are typically represented as the perpetrators and victims of violent crime. And so on and so forth with the portrayal of various ethnic and sexual stereotypes.

Fourthly, there is a blurring of the distinction between drama and actuality. This is partly a result of a lack of concern for the truth. The truth is often hard to obtain. If one is not resolutely striving for it, then one is not likely to arrive at it. Tabloid journalists have no great concern for the truth. Hence their tendency to exaggerate, and their frequent recourse to the tactic of the news story "beat up." Indeed, on occasion the tabloids quite literally forgo any attempt to represent preexisting truths and simply create the news themselves. For example, recently the Australian tabloid TV program "A Current Affair" arranged for the teenage members of the Paxton family in Melbourne to be offered jobs in Queensland and then flew them there; when they refused the jobs, the program "exposed" and castigated them as "welfare cheats."

A lack of concern for truth was dramatically demonstrated recently by the *Sun*. The *Sun*'s publication of alleged pictures of Princess Diana frolicking with her lover turned out to be a hoax. The pictures were of actors pretending to be Princess Diana and her lover. The *Sun* had evidently not taken sufficient trouble to check the authenticity of the pictures.

But the blurring of the distinction between drama and actuality has a more fundamental cause. Tabloids overuse and misuse dramatic forms. Events are not related sequentially, nor are dramatic forms simply used to heighten the sense of reality of newsworthy events. Rather the drama and emotion—whether real or imagined—surrounding an event in effect become the "event" to be communicated to an audience, and communicated for the purpose of triggering an emotive reaction in the audience. The point of the exercise is not to communicate truth, but to capture and keep audiences.

Thus tabloid style TV current affairs programs often provide "reconstructions" of events which are in fact dramatizations. These dramatizations often focus on and exaggerate sensational, scandalous and morally loaded aspects of the events treated. What for? Not for the purpose of informing the audience or assisting in the process of understanding these events. The purpose is rather to trigger and manipulate an emotive response in the audience—whether it be sexual desire, envy, horror, moral outrage, or merely perverse pleasure in the misfortunes or inadequacies of others—and thereby keep it watching.

C. Macro-institutional Context

This description of tabloid journalism would not be complete without some account being offered of the macro-socioinstitutional context in which tabloid journalism is produced. This context includes the large, sometimes transnational, corporations which produce a great amount of tabloid journalism. One such corporation is Rupert Murdoch's News Ltd.

Governments and political leaders are dependent on these media corporations for favorable treatment, for governments and political leaders rely heavily on the media for the presentation of themselves and their policies to the public. Yet the media, including tabloid journalism, are, at least in Australia and the USA, largely owned by these corporations.

Moreover, these large media corporations in part own, and in part are owned by, other nonmedia corporations. This raises the issue of the independence of the media as an institution from nonmedia business corporations.

This general issue of the independence of the media from both business and government has been raised recently in Australia. On the one hand there is an alliance between Murdoch's News Corporation—which owns a majority of Australian newspapers as well as one of the major TV networks—and the government-owned telecommunications provider, Telstra, to create the cable TV operation Foxtel. On the other hand in this overall context, the government is seeking partly to privatize Telstra.

A second element comprises the corporate advertisers whose business is so important to the media in general, and to the producers of tabloid journalism in particular. Indeed the point has been reached where the bulk of the revenue of tabloid newspapers comes not from sales of the newspapers but from fees paid by advertisers. (Tabloid TV is wholly dependent on advertising revenue, and all the points to be made below can equally be made in relation to tabloid TV.) This being so, there are at least three aims the producers of tabloid newspapers have, it being no longer clear which of these is the most important.

The first aim of a tabloid newspaper is to inform or entertain its readership. The second aim is to sell as many newspapers as possible. The third aim is to attract advertising revenue. Obviously these aims are interdependent. If readers are informed and entertained they are more likely to buy a newspaper, and if a newspaper has a large readership then advertisers are more likely to want to buy advertising space. However, the existence of this interdependence does not settle the issue as to the means–end relationship between these three different aims. It might be that the overriding de facto aim of a tabloid newspaper is to make a profit. But advertising is the largest source of revenue. So perhaps the aims of selling large numbers of newspapers and informing/entertaining readers are subsidiary to attracting advertising revenue. In short, perhaps in the overall context of making a profit, tabloid newspapers exist principally in order to sell advertising space rather than to inform/entertain or even to attract a large readership. Certainly the huge amount of space devoted to advertising in tabloids provides some evidence for this view.

A third element comprises the mass audiences or consumers of tabloid journalism. Given the points just made about advertising, we need to conceive of these consumers as consumers not only of the information and entertainment presented in the tabloids, but also, and perhaps most importantly, as consumers of the advertisements. Indeed, given the already-mentioned tendencies of the tabloids to exaggerate, sensationalize, titillate, and run together fact and fiction, perhaps the distinction between tabloid news/entertainment and advertisements has been undermined—scrutiny of the advertisements reveals them to have many of the properties of the nonadvertising material.

Consider in this connection the page 3 pinup girl. Is she there as part of the nonadvertising section or part of the advertising? She is presumably not part of the news stories. Presumably she is there to attract readers to buy the newspaper. But if a reader is attracted by the pinup girl and then simply reads the ads, rather than the news stories, surely the pinup girl has served its purpose. Moreover, in what sense is the pinup girl any different from the picture of Princess Diana allegedly frolicking with her lover? Certainly one posed and the other did not, but from the consumer's point of view, wherein lies the difference? Both pictures titillate. Perhaps the purpose of both is to get the reader to buy the newspaper and then go on to read the ads. Further, the ads themselves involve scantily clad young women. (Unlike the page 3 pinup and Princess Diana, these women are associated with specific products.) At any rate the general point to be made here is that there is a real question about the substantive nature of the distinction between advertising and nonadvertising sections within tabloids.

Perhaps the final element of the macroinstitutional or social context is the new communication technologies and their impact on tabloid journalism, including in particular the capacity of satellite and cable operators to project tabloid journalistic products to larger transnational audiences. This projection to larger, including transnational, audiences relies not simply on technology, but on the existence of relatively homogenous consumer societies, or at least of transnational consumer groups, albeit different ones within any given society.

It would not be unfair to say that this macroinstitutional context of tabloid journalism is one which locates tabloid journalism as a highly successful mass consumer product, albeit a differentiated one. Tabloid journalism not only sells well, it advertises well. Moreover, it appears to do so in part not only by blurring the distinction between information and entertainment, but also by blurring the distinction between information/entertainment and advertisements. The most obvious example of this cocktail of information, entertainment, and advertisement is so-called infotainment.

II. NORMATIVE THEORETICAL ACCOUNT OF THE MEDIA

Having provided a descriptive account of tabloid journalism in the opening section, there is a need to offer a normative theoretical account of the role of the media, and its proper relationship both to other institutions, including government and the business sector, and to individual citizens.

A. Media as Both Industry and Institution

The print and electronic media are at one and the same time an industry and a public institution. As an industry in the private sector the media produces saleable commodities (including advertisements), employs workers and managers, and has investors and owners. It is simply another business, or set of businesses, within the market economy. As such its function is economic; it exists to make profits, provide jobs, and satisfy consumer demand. As a public sector industry funded by government, it also has an economic function; it employs workers and managers and is, to an extent, market oriented, e.g., "consumption" levels are of importance.

The media is also an institution. By "institution" it is here meant that it is an organization, or set of organizations, that has a particular sociopolitical function in respect to public communication. Here a number of points need to be made.

Firstly, in distinguishing between the media as an industry and the media as an institution—between its economic and its sociopolitical function—it is not being maintained that the functions do not overlap and are not linked. Indeed it is commonplace in political and social theory that economic functions intermesh with sociopolitical functions, and that political interests are served by particular economic arrangements and economic interests by political arrangements. This goes as much for the media as for any other major social institution. Notwithstanding their interdependence, there is an important distinction between the economic and the sociopolitical functions of the media. Therefore any conception that seeks to collapse the political and/or the social role of institutions, including the media, into their economic role or vice versa should be resisted.

It follows that crude Marxist views should be rejected, for these views in effect occupy an a priori theoretical position according to which institutions such as governments, universities, and the media must be construed principally as agents of the ascendant economic classes. But equally to be rejected is the view implicit in much of the rational choice theory deployed by "liberal" economists that the social functions of institutions are simply the logical product of the (unexplained) preferences of individual rational agents making choices in a (typically distorted) market economy.

Secondly, we need to distinguish between the de facto function(s) of the media and the function(s) it ought to have. Perhaps the chief function of the mainstream media is to buttress the capitalist system. Whether or not this is so is an empirical question which cannot be addressed here. As far as a normative theory is concerned, we need to ask what the function or functions of the media ought to be. Naturally, a normative conception is not a fanciful conception. A normative conception of an institution is a conception of what realistically could be. Indeed normative issues, far from being the idealist distractions self-styled "real world" advocates proclaim them to be, are in fact central and unavoidable in our common life. When at one level of theorizing neo-Marxists and others dismiss normative claims as ideology, at another level of theorizing the very same theorists appeal—albeit implicitly—to their own unacknowledged set of normative commitments. The point is to argue for and against explicit normative standpoints, whether they be Marxist, Liberal, Postmodernist, or none of these.

Thirdly, as is the case with any organization or institution, the media and the fulfillment of actual and/or legitimate purposes are constrained by the moral rights of individuals. In the case of the media—an institution of public communication—these rights include especially the rights to privacy, to a fair trial, and to not be defamed.

Let us now put forward the following normative theoretical standpoint. In relation to news and comment, the media as an institution—whether it be publicly or privately owned—has the general function of public communication in the public interest. Here the reference to public communication is self-explanatory. The news/comment institution of the media is principally a vehicle for public communication. This is so notwithstanding the emergence of new communications technologies which may well facilitate private interactive communication and do so to some extent at the expense of public and "one way" communication.

The notion of public interest is much more problematic. Suffice it to say here that attempts to explain away the notion of the public interest in terms of sectional or class interests have been unsuccessful. So has the attempted reduction of the notion of the public interest to sets of individual preference or desire. What is in fact in the public interest is not necessarily what the public wants to hear or "consume," and still less what will generate profits for the media industry. Naturally, if the elements of the media in the private sector are to survive they will need to be commercially viable, and this will entail that what is communicated is to an extent what the public will consume. But the point is that if the media is not discharging its obligations as an institution there is no great cause for concern if it does not survive. Normatively speaking, the media—as defined here—is a business, but it is not principally a business; it has other and more important responsibilities than its purely economic ones. It exists to enable public communication in the public interest.

B. Functions of the Media as Institution

Public communication in the public interest involves at least the following subsidiary functions or roles.

Firstly, the media provides a public forum enabling communication by government and other institutions, and by interest groups and individual citizens, to the public at large, and enabling that communication to stand as a public record (media as public forum). Secondly, the media, or at least members of the media, has the task of unearthing and disseminating information of importance to the public (media as investigator). Thirdly, members of the media themselves function as public communicators. In this role members of the media communicate both information and comment (media as autonomous public communicator).

Moreover, these functions, in respect to public communication, are the chief justification for the existence of the (news and comment) media.

1. Media as Public Forum

The media as a public forum enables individual members of the public and representatives of groups and organizations (including the government) to communicate to the public at large. In some of these instances of public communication there is a dispute, and it is in the public interest to be informed about this dispute, for example, the dispute in the United Kingdom in relation to membership of the European Community. These disputes can be about the truth of particular claims, e.g., concerning an alleged "third force" in South Africa, or about the workability or justice of particular policies, e.g., affirmative action policies in relation to Australian Aboriginal education. Here the role of the media is simply to provide a forum for the various disputing parties, and thereby enable them to communicate to the public at large.

Other cases in this category are ones involving basically the communication of information. For example, the government may wish to make known the details of its budget. Here the media provides a mechanism for communication by members of the public (individuals or groups or organizations, including the government) to the public at large.

2. Media as Investigator

The second category of communications involves the media as an investigator. There are cases in which the media investigates matters of public interest and unearths information that is of legitimate interest to the public. For example, consider the role of the journalists Bob Woodward and Carl Bernstein in relation to Watergate, or the sections of the press in South Africa, including, notably, the *Weekly Mail*, who for many years brought to light various covert operations of the South African government and its security agencies.

While this category of cases necessarily involves investigation, it also involves public communication; the journalist investigates in order to communicate his/her discovery to the public. A journalist is not simply a private detective unearthing information for a fee.

In the cases in which the media provides a forum, or finds out and communicates what the public has a right to know, the media is not an autonomous public communicator. Rather in these cases the media exists to ensure that rights to communicate and to know are realized.

3. Media as Autonomous Communicator

The category of cases in which the media acts as an autonomous public communicator comprises such things as editorial comment, and comment and analysis provided by members of the print and electronic media itself, as opposed to comment and analysis in the media provided by academics, community leaders, and others. Political and economic comments are prominent in this category.

In this category the media has an active role as an independent communicator. The media is not simply a mouthpiece or the provider of a forum for other communicators, nor is it simply discharging its obligation to provide information which the public has a right to possess. Rather in these cases the media is a genuinely autonomous communicator.

The general justification for the existence of the media as a public forum is that in a democracy, in respect to certain matters, members of the public and of interest groups—or at least their representatives—have a moral right to address the public at large, and representatives of public institutions have a moral duty to do so. Therefore, there is a need for a forum for public communication, and the media in a modern society is the chief mechanism enabling such public communication. The existence of such a channel or channels of public communication raises important questions of access, particularly given that only limited access is possible.

The general justification for the existence of the media as an investigator/disseminator is the public's right to know in relation to certain matters of public interest and importance.

The general justification for the existence of the media as an autonomous public communicator is more problematic. Suffice it to say here that there are a range of pragmatic reasons why professional journalists and media commentators might be desirable. In the last analysis these reasons come down to the quality of the comment and analysis provided. Note that such reasons do not include the existence of a moral right to exist as an autonomous public communicator.

III. ETHICAL ANALYSIS

In light of the descriptive account of tabloid journalism provided in the first section, and the normative theoretical framework outlined in the second, let me now offer an ethical analysis of tabloid journalism.

Tabloid journalism is ethically problematic on two general counts. Firstly, it is inconsistent with the societal and institutional ethical values which underpin the media as an institution. Secondly, it tends to infringe a number of important individual moral rights, including the rights to privacy, to a fair trial, and to not be defamed.

A. Institutional Ethical Values

As far as the media as an institution is concerned, the following points can be made. In relation to the role of the media as a public forum, we saw in the opening section that tabloid journalism fails to represent important social and economic interest groups; indeed it often misrepresents and stereotypes particular groups, including women and minorities. Moreover, it overemphasizes and focuses attention on individuals and groups who are wealthy and/or glamorous and/or powerful, including not only politicians, but movie actors, sports figures, and members of the Royal Family.

In its role as investigator, the tabloid press pursues the sensationalist and trivial rather than what is important in terms of the public interest. For example, it relentlessly investigates and exposes the sexual lives of politicians and members of the Royal Family, but is not prepared to pursue difficult and expensive investigations of serious public corruption or of internationally significant military conflicts. Moreover, it has scant concern for the truth, preferring rather to provoke and manipulate emotive reactions.

In its role as autonomous communicator, the tabloid press displays little or no objectivity or analytical depth in its comment. It fails absolutely to critically analyze powerful social and institutional interest groups. Indeed ultimately it is at the service of large business corporations, and therefore tends to reproduce and reinforce the consumer ideology.

In short, tabloid journalism is seriously deficient in each of the three roles of public forum, investigator, and autonomous communicator. As such, tabloid journalism—to the extent that it dominates the public communication of news and comment—is ethically problematic. For if most, or even very large numbers, of people rely on the tabloids as their main source of news and comment, then the citizenry will be ill informed and lack understanding of matters of public importance. In short, the dominance of tabloid journalism entails that the media as an institution of public communication has failed in its institutional purposes.

Moreover, tabloid journalism—if it becomes the dominant voice in public communication—will inevitably over time have a corrosive effect on public morality. The point is not that reading about gruesome crime or viewing the page 3 pinup girl pollutes one's mind. The analogy is rather with pornography. Pornography titillates and sexually arouses, but it does not follow that it is an evil that should be eradicated. However, if a person gets to the point where his or her sexual life is principally lived through pornographic images—to the exclusion of sexual relationships with real people—then that person has a moral problem. Similarly, with tabloid journalism.

If a society gets to the point where its principal mode of public communication in relation to news and comment is tabloid journalism, then that society has a moral problem. What is the problem? The problem is that in eschewing important news and quality comment, and in trivializing fundamental moral attitudes by manipulating them for the purposes of sustaining audience attention, the tabloids not only deprive citizens of information and understanding of important events, they ultimately contribute to an undermining of the capacity of audiences to make discerning moral and political judgments on these matters, and thereby to the impoverishment of public morality and a deterioration of the conditions of democratic life.

B. Individual Moral Rights

Tabloid journalism often infringes, or threatens to infringe, individual moral rights, especially the rights to privacy, to a fair trial, and to not be defamed. On occasion it also threatens other moral rights, including the right to life. Consider in this connection the Cangai siege in NSW Australia. Children were being held hostage by armed killers. The tabloid TV journalist Willessee insisted on phoning up the killers and speaking to the children to get a story, notwithstanding the dangers this course of action posed for the safety of the children.

It is obvious that the right to privacy of members of the Royal Family and of Princess Diana is not respected by the tabloid press. As public figures these people can reasonably expect more media attention and scrutiny than persons who are not public figures. Nevertheless, even public figures have a right not to be the objects of what amounts to ongoing intrusive surveillance. Long-range cameras are used by the paparazzi to provide the tabloids with a diet of photographs of Princess Diana at home, in intimate company on holidays, and so on. Another favorite target of tabloid journalists is the grief-stricken. The families of miners were contacted at 3 A.M. by the tabloids for their reactions to the Moura mine disaster in Australia in 1987.

Nor are these infringements of the right to privacy morally insignificant, for the right to privacy is an important moral right. It is not possible to establish and maintain intimate personal relations without a measure of privacy.

Autonomy depends in part on privacy. A measure of privacy is necessary for a person to pursue his or her projects, whatever those projects might be. For one thing reflection is necessary for planning, and reflection requires privacy. For another, knowledge of someone's plans can enable those plans to be thwarted. And there is this further point. Autonomy consists in part of having the capacity to undertake one's public roles. However, certain facts pertaining to a person's public roles and practices are regarded as private in virtue of the potential, should they be disclosed, of undermining the capacity of the person to function in these public roles or to fairly compete in these practices. Evidently, the tabloid press has undermined the potential of many public figures to adequately undertake their public roles, and has therefore undermined their autonomy. For example, the tabloid press in the United Kingdom has clearly undermined the capacity of members of the Royal Family to function in their public roles.

Tabloid journalism frequently violates the individual's right to a fair trial by presenting an accused person as in effect guilty. One method is to ascribe guilt to an individual in the headline, and then qualify this ascription of guilt in the news report itself by making sure terms such as "suspect" and "alleged" are used. This was the case with Martin Bryant. More generally, the possibility of a fair trial can be reduced by saturating the public mind with stories which link the "suspect" with the crime, whether as guilty or innocent. The O. J. Simpson trial is an example.

Another related feature of tabloid journalism is defamation. It feeds on scandal and rumor. The preceding methods of headlines without qualifications and saturation coverage have the effect of defaming someone, even if in technical legal terms that person has not been defamed. Consider, for example, the recent case of the Australian senior diplomat John Holloway. He was named by the tabloids as a suspected pedophile, yet subsequently charges against him were dismissed. He has been found innocent, but his reputation has suffered greatly.

C. Arguments in Support of Tabloid Journalism

Let me now consider some attempts to defend tabloid journalism. Firstly, it is argued, while tabloid press might be uninformative, devoid of analysis, and preoccupied with "girlie pics" and the scandalous lives of show business personalities, it is what the people want and therefore is justified on this basis.

However, on the normative conception outlined above, matters which the public may have a *desire* to know about are to be distinguished from those which they have a *right* to know about, or a legitimate interest in knowing about, and the former are of secondary importance in the following senses.

As indicated, such wants or desires do not of themselves justify the existence of the media as a fundamental sociopolitical institution of modern societies. If the function of the media were merely to satisfy desires for information, comment, and/or entertainment then there would be no pressing reason to establish the media as an institution. Rather it should be viewed as an economic organization, or complex of organizations, and we could have or not have the media depending on whether there was a demand for its products and there was sufficient economic benefit to shareholders, advertisers, managers, journalists, and so on.

Again, matters in respect of which the public only has a desire, but not a right or a legitimate interest, for access ought to exist on the channels of public communication only after the latter have been adequately catered for. Public communication in respect of which the public has a right to or a legitimate interest in must take precedence over public communication whose purpose is simply to entertain or otherwise satisfy a desire.

In this connection it is also worth noting that it is by no means clear that there is some sort of logical connection between being a high-profit-making media organization and satisfying consumers' desires. Profits are a function of the difference between revenue from sales and costs. It may well be that most members of the public would prefer certain kinds of high-quality media products to tabloid products. However, such high-quality newspapers and TV programs for general audiences are very expensive to produce, especially compared to many low-quality tabloid products. For

this reason media organizations driven only by profit might produce tabloids rather than high-quality general audience newspapers and TV programs. However, if so, this would not necessarily reflect a preference on the part of audiences for tabloid products over high-quality general audience media products.

Secondly, it is often argued that the media cannot provide objective communicative content of high quality since the notion of such content is meaningless or hopelessly naive. It is suggested that the reasons for this are manifold and include the views that communicative content always reflects a standpoint, that mechanisms of media communication necessarily mediate and therefore distort, that quality is simply in the eye of the beholder, and so on.

There is not space to deal with all these kinds of arguments in detail, though it is not difficult to show that they do not demonstrate the strong position they are intended to. Suffice it to say here that the notions that one cannot aim at truth, and on occasion approximate it, and that every piece of analysis and comment is as good as every other are self-defeating and, if accepted, would render communication pointless. It is a presupposition of communication in general, including both linguistic communication and visual representation, that there is something to be represented, and that on occasion this is achieved. If this were not so, communication of news would be rendered pointless and cease to take place. Moreover, it is a presupposition of comment and analysis that not every piece of analysis and comment is as good as every other one since there is always as least one which is regarded by the communicator as inferior, namely, that which is the negation of the one put forward.

Thirdly, there is a tendency to try to ground an (alleged) right of the media to communicate what it sees fit, irrespective of objectivity or quality, on the right to property. Roughly, the idea is that if someone wants to use his own money to set up a newspaper or TV station—to set up, that is, a mechanism of public communication—in order to communicate his own views (or the views of his editors or journalists) or to provide low-grade entertainment, or indeed to provide communicative content of whatever sort he likes, then he has a right to do so. After all, it is argued, he owns it.

There are a number of problems with this line of argument. For one thing, it simply does not follow from the fact that a person has a right to set up a mechanism of public communication that the person has a right to use that mechanism to communicate to the public at large any more than it follows from the fact—if it is a fact—that McDonnell-Douglas has a right to build fighter aircraft that the corporation then has a right to establish a military air force and fly sorties against its corporate enemies.

For another thing, everyone, whether he or she is the owner of newspapers or TV stations, has a right to communicate to the public at large. Moreover, this basic right does not derive from, and is not enlarged or extended by, property rights in general, and the right to set up a mechanism for public communication in particular. The right of a citizen to address the public at large is not somehow increased by virtue of the fact that the citizen has the property right (and the money) to set up a newspaper or TV station. Indeed any such extension of the right of owners in particular (or their employees, including editors and journalists) to public communication would constitute an infringement of the equal right of all citizens to communicate to the public at large. This fundamental equality is not undermined by the fact that on particular issues it is more important that certain members of the public be heard than others.

Also See the Following Articles

BROADCAST JOURNALISM • MEDIA OWNERSHIP • OBJECTIVITY IN REPORTING • TRUTH-TELLING AS CONSTITUTIVE OF JOURNALISM

Bibliography

Cohen, E. D. (Ed.) (1992). *Philosophical issues in journalism.* New York: Oxford Univ. Press.

Christians, C. G., Ferre, J. P., & Fackler, P. M. (1993). *Good news: Social ethics and the press.* New York: Oxford Univ. Press.

Dahlgren, P., & Sparks, C. (Eds.) (1991). *Communication and citizenship.* London: Routledge.

Denton, R. E. (1991). *Ethical dimensions of political communication.* New York: Praeger.

Goodwin, G., & Smith, R. F. (1994). *Groping for ethics in journalism* (3rd ed.). Ames, IA: Iowa State Univ. Press.

Patterson, P., & Wilkins, L. (Eds.) (1994). *Media ethics: Issues and cases* (2nd ed.). Madison, WI: Brown and Benchmark.

Taitte, W. L. (Ed.) (1993). *Morality of the mass media.* Austin, TX: Univ. of Texas Press.

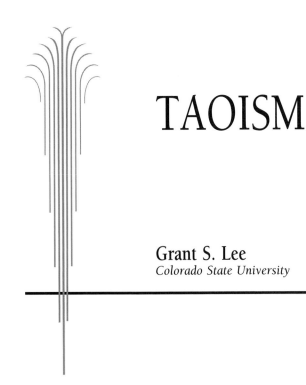

TAOISM

Grant S. Lee
Colorado State University

I. Ultimate Way (Tao), Nonbeing (*wu*),
and Being (*yu*)
II. Virtue (*te*) and Nonaction (*wu wei*)
III. Nature (*tzu jan*) and Simplicity (*p'u*)
IV. True Man (*chen jen*), Fasting One's Mind (*hsin chai*), and Sitting in Forgetfulness (*tso wang*)

Ultimate Way (Tao) Embraces all things in the universe, both visible and invisible.
virtue or power (*te*) Nurtures everything and is the dwelling place of Tao.

GLOSSARY

being (*yu*) All existing realities of the universe.
fasting one's mind (*hsin chai*) Emptying one's mind of any thought at all.
nature (*tzu jan*) Spontaneity and unassuming self-soness.
nonaction (*wu wei*) All action that is aligned with the reality of nonbeing and, hence, nonforcing, nonartificial action going along with the stream of the Tao.
nonbeing (*wu*) A formless matrix that gives birth to being and recycles the dynamic pattern.
parti pris Preconceived opinion or bias
simplicity (*p'u*) Found in the world of nature.
sitting in forgetfulness (tso wang) Associated with *hsin chai* where internal dialogue stops.
sui generis This means its own kind.
summum bonum The supreme or greatest good.
True Man (*chen jen*) One who lives and experiences this world unencumbered by intellectual knowledge.

TAOISM is a system of philosophical and religious beliefs that originated in China approximately 2200 years ago, presented in two books entitled the *Lao Tzu* (or *Tao Te Ching*) and the *Chuang Tzu.*

I. ULTIMATE WAY (TAO), NONBEING (WU), AND BEING (YU)

According to the *Lao Tzu* (or the *Tao Te Ching*) and the *Chuang Tzu,* Tao, which is the Ultimate Way or Reality, has both nonbeing (*wu*) and being (*yu*) aspects. The universe came into being from nonbeing and continually recycles itself through the mysterious power (*te*) of Tao back to nonbeing.

The ideograph Tao has two components, namely, "head" and "go." It came to mean "road" or "way." But the Taoist understanding of Tao is the Ultimate Way or Reality, which is ineffable. The Tao existed without form before Heaven and Earth, and is ineffable and undifferentiated. At the same time, it is the ubiquitous

Copyright © 1998 by Academic Press. All rights of reproduction in any form reserved.

metaphysical reality by which all things are brought into existence, as Chapter 22 of the *Chuang Tzu* implies.

Both nonbeing and being arose from the Tao. Nonbeing is Tao in its negative sense. Like Tao, nonbeing is indescribable and it is invisible, inaudible, untouchable, formless, imageless, vague, and elusive, as stated in Chapter 14 of the *Lao Tzu*. However, "it is not nothing" because all things under Heaven are produced by nonbeing, according to Chapter 40 of the *Lao Tzu*. In this process, *sui generis,* the law of the Tao in nonbeing is spontaneous and natural, and there is no conscious purpose of the Tao. In other words, nonbeing and being are the dyadic complementary opposites when Tao generates "ten thousand things."

In addition to the principle of the Tao that is all-embracing and generating, Taoism asserts the principle of the *te* underlying and rearing each individual thing in the world of being. Heaven and Earth are amoral in the world of being and nature, says Lao Tzu in Chapter 5 of his book. Tao is impersonal, natural, and stable. There are seasons and days and nights. Yet human civilization formulated moral ideas with deliberate intention. As there are days in contrast to nights, so there is good and evil in the human world while nature is indifferent to the weal of all creatures. The recognition of good and evil in the human sphere raises the question: because the idea of morality is tied to the analytic and deliberate human mind that causes the breach between the Tao and us, how did such a moral notion arise in the human sphere and separate itself from the absolute Tao? If the human race aligns itself to the Tao or the natural course of it where all opposites are interdependent, then the possibility of ethics will not emerge. Ethics attempts to eliminate the evil pole by absolutizing the good one and destroying the pristine innocence found in the state of nature. However, when people did not follow the great Tao (*ta-tao*), the concept of "great artifice" such as benevolence (*jen*) and righteousness (*yi*) came into being to control human desires, and benevolence and righteousness took the path of aberration from the Tao because both are fruits of deliberate consciousness of man, according to Chapters 18 and 58 of the *Lao Tzu*. The deliberate mind pursues the endless desires of man, which gives rise to all forms of higher civilization. Therefore, in Chapter 12, Lao Tzu warns his fellow man against man's obsessive sensual desires that go beyond the satisfaction of his basic physical and biological needs, thus creating a more artificial civilization. Lao Tzu tells both rulers as well as those ruled that they must return to the Tao. Such ideas as *wu wei, tzu jan,* and *p'u* are

directed against human desires that lead to obsession for power, wealth, and honor.

Chuang Tzu also takes a value-free attitude that shakes the foundation of our ordinary experiences. According to Chuang Tzu in his second chapter, there is no right or wrong and no good or evil in the absolute Tao. In the final analysis Tao is indifferent to them. This indifference is stressed in moral questions. If human beings follow the flow of the Tao, then it is not necessary to discuss moral issues. Moral issues arise because the human mind has, on the one hand, the capacity to deviate from the path of the Tao and construct conventions that conceal it. On the other hand, as indicated in the example of Wang T'ai according to Chapter 5 of the *Chuang Tzu*, the human mind, through one's knowledge of nonknowledge or nonbeing, may also reach the ultimate mind which is the highest level with the Tao.

II. VIRTUE (*TE*) AND NONACTION (*WU WEI*)

Virtue is the power of the Tao that resides in all that exists. It nurtures individual things. Lao Tzu says in Chapter 21 that the all-embracing expression of virtue proceeds from the Tao alone. Conversely, then the Tao dwells in virtue. The virtuous man is good (*shan*) like water benefiting 10,000 things. He is good for humanity; his word is good; he governs well; he handles his affairs skillfully; and his movements are harmonious, and so on, according to Chapter 8 of the *Lao Tzu*. The principle of good flows from water-nature that proceeds from being, which is the pristine source of all existence. Being comes from nonbeing, and these become in union with the Tao. The virtuous man's goodness, being waterlike is the *summum bonum* of the Taoist ethics. Water is not only a representation of nature-being-nonbeing-Tao, it benefits all things (just like the Tao). The sage loves man universally, as Lao Tzu states in Chapter 49. He treats the good well, and he treats those who are not good well so that in both cases goodness is still attained. To the trustworthy he is trustful and to the untrustworthy, he is also trustful. So trust is attained. The virtuous man does not discriminate against people by our *parti pris* in his action, in his words; and in his faith in people, he is undifferentiating just like the Tao. In his service to the people, because he has the Tao, he provides able assistance, and he is timely in all activities. The virtuous man can do all these because he bases his actions on the three moral principles that are contained in Lao Tzu, Chapter 67. They are: compassion for all, austerity in one's spending, and to not dare to go ahead of the world in competition. While maintaining his mental equilibrium, by bringing his desires or sensual charms under control, he aligns the practices of the three moral principles and himself to higher *te*, as stated in Chapter 38 of the *Lao Tzu*. The man of higher virtue is not even conscious of his virtue. Likewise, for the virtuous ruler (government), people merely know that he is there. The order is attained because people will say that we followed Nature and the order came through. These are some of the fundamental ethical views of the Lao Tzu.

However, the same chapter describes the man of lower virtue. The inferior man has no virtue because he is conscious of his virtue. A deliberate conscious effort to exercise his *te* causes a decline from the higher *te* to the inferior *te*. Chapter 18 of the *Lao Tzu* supports this view. "When the Great Tao declined, the ideas of human-heartedness and righteousness arose. When knowledge and wisdom appear we meet great hypocrisy. When the six family members are in disharmony, there will be the talk of filial piety and compassion. When the country is in disorder, there will be honest subjects." Lower virtues arise through calculating and purposive consciousness that resulted ultimately in the great artifice (*ta-wei*) and decadent civilization. In the political sphere, decadence is expressed in terms of love for the ruler by the people, which is second best because it is in the realm of *yu wei* (action).

Lao Tzu's humanistic concern is further shown in the concept of sage-rulers whom Lao Tzu refers to as one of the four great components of the cosmic realm. They are the Tao, Heaven, Earth, and the universal king, according to Chapter 25. The universal king rules the small state in humility when he relates to the large state and thereby is protected by the large state, as Chapter 61 says. He does not exalt worthy men so as not to encourage competition and avoids war as much as possible, as Chapters 3 and 31 state. Therefore, Lao Tzu's political thought is based on nonaction. What is nonaction?

Nonaction (*wu wei*) is aligned with nonbeing, as the term implies. The meaning of *wei* is to act out, to do, to make, and so on. In a narrow sense, *wu wei* is an action of nonbeing through a human being, but its broader definition is man's life that is united with the Tao. It is the Tao action or the Tao life. Like the Tao, nonaction is spontaneous, nonpurposive,

and holistic. While *yu wei* (deliberate action) is calculating, analytical, and intentional, *wu wei* (nonaction) is unself-conscious action whereby man keeps his pristine, natural, and pure state, free from the lures of the great artifice based on false desire. *Yu wei* leads people away from the Tao stream and establishes its own separate existence in opposition to its pristine Nature. But the man of the Tao helps to restore all things to their natural state and dares not to take any conscious action, as Chapter 64 of the *Lao Tzu* says. The powerful sources affecting human lives, which most people pursue their entire lifetime, include exorbitant wealth, excessive power, insatiable sensual pleasures, and bloated fame.

However, people pay the price with cutthroat and competitive behavior, life-threatening stresses, incessant worries and anxieties, never-ending frustration, and even boredom. Alternative ways to deal with these decadent and alienated paths of life and therapy for them may be found in the primitive yet insightful views expressed by Lao Tzu. Chapter 44 presents a forceful argument by raising questions and giving explanations. "Which one is more important, fame or one's life? Which is more precious, one's life or wealth? Which is more harmful, gain or loss? He who has lavish desires for these pays a higher price. The bigger treasures will suffer heavy loss. One who is contented suffers no shame. One who knows when to stop will not encounter trouble and will enjoy long life." These questions are both diagnostic of the tribulations of our era and prescriptive for our symptoms. The message is that one should lead a life in accordance with the Tao. Chapter 37 says that the Tao never takes action (*wu wei*) yet nothing is undone. Obviously the virtue (*te*) does all. This is why Lao Tzu says in Chapter 57 that "I (the sage) take non-action; people are transformed. I like quietude; people become correct. I do nothing and the people become prosperous." The statement here, deals with principles of government. A universal king trusts the power of the Tao, which so permeates all things that it sustains the social order. The meaning of Chapter 3 expresses the same thing when it says that "by nonacting he governs them all." By leaving people alone, one governs them in the best way. In Chapter 43, Lao Tzu further assures that there is no place where nonbeing cannot penetrate. Therefore, the sage does not use words, and does not credit his achievements, as indicated in Chapter 2. The man of the Tao knows that human nature and destiny are incorrigibly fixed; the Tao is absolute, and the Tao treats us inexorably. Therefore, all human beings are to abide by the Tao naturally, authentically, and in simple ways as much as possible.

III. NATURE (*TZU JAN*) AND SIMPLICITY (*P'U*)

The ideas of naturalness (*tzu jan*) and simplicity (*p'u*) are the natural corollaries of the Taoist behavioral patterns. *Tzu jan* means nature, spontaneity, and self-hood, and the natural world originated in nonbeing. Lao Tzu relates this in Chapter 6, "The valley spirit never dies. It is called profound female. The gate of profound female is the root of Heaven and Earth. It is continuous and always existing. Even if we use it, we can't exhaust it." If female represents yin or nonbeing, then Heaven and Earth were created by nonbeing. The procreative process is based on *tzu jan*. So the Tao principle can be interpreted as what happens with no purpose nor scheme.

In the life cycle, spontaneity governs all. So things arouse spontaneously and reverted to the source. Chapter 40 of the *Lao Tzu* explains this. "The movement of the Tao is reversion. The Tao functions through weakness. All things under Heaven come from being and being comes from non-being." Chapter 42 describes the processes of the generation. "Tao produced the One. The One gave birth to the two. The two gave birth to the three. The three gave birth to the ten thousand things. Ten thousand things carry the yin and receive the yang and by means of breathing force arrive at harmony." Chapter 51 expresses a similar view. "Tao gives birth to them. Virtue nurses them. Matter gives form. The circumstances and usages complete them. Thus the ten thousand things honor Tao and value virtue. Tao is esteemed and virtue is valued without anyone's order. They always come naturally (*tzu jan*)." So Tao and the order of Nature are equal. According to Lao Tzu, in the world of Nature and Tao, Nature is given the highest place, as stated in Chapter 25. "Man models himself after earth. Earth after Heaven. Heaven after Tao. Tao after *tzu jan* (Nature, self-hood, or spontaneity)." If in the world of nature Tao is self-generating by existing through itself—aseity and *tzu jan* is its organic pattern, then the same will be applied to the human realm. It means that Nature guides human behavior, including the moral and ethical dimensions of our lives. Being natural and spontaneous, one is with the Tao going beyond the fixation or finitude of human beings. Thus, enlightenment is attained. A natural man becomes a universal figure in the Taoist tradition. Whatever is natural or spontaneous is good, according to this perspective, because it is the Tao action.

How, then, does one account for calamities nature brings upon us, some of which cause great pains, including untimely deaths? Under the Taoist vision, one who behaves through nonaction in an unassuming or spontaneous way will endure life and its hardships. At this point, Lao Tzu seems ready to accept it with equinimity because the invariable law of nature is to return to where one started. This is human destiny. In this sense, Lao Tzu may be a mystic who bases his life "beyond good and evil." Nature as a principle guiding human behavior has a parallel view, namely, simplicity (*p'u*).

Simplicity, according to Lao Tzu in Chapter 37, is closely related to one's desires. "Simplicity which has no name stilled by simplicity, is free of desires." Chapter 3 traces desire to cunning knowledge. "The sage keeps his people from knowledge (cunning) or desire and weakens the will but strengthens the bones by keeping the people from knowing or wanting, and those who are cunning from daring to act. Thus he governs them all." Simplicity, like Tao, is nameless. Chapter 32 states this. "The Tao has never had a name. Though it is simple and small, no one can master it." If simplicity is named, it will come under the intellectual scrutiny of analysis. Names and definitions eventually lead to decadent civilization because they falsify reality through the means of cunning knowledge. It will go against the metaphor used for simplicity, that is, uncarved wood that is genuine and plain, as expressed in Chapters 15 and 28. One is reminded of the anti-intellectual exhortation given by Lao Tzu in Chapter 48 that said, "Those who pursue learning gain every day, and those who pursue Tao lose every day. They lose and lose until they arrive at non-action." Learning, here, means intellectual pursuit, against which Lao Tzu spoke because it encumbers true enlightenment based on realization of the Tao. Enlightenment frees people from the falsehoods.

This leads one to deal with another component mentioned in Chapter 37, that is, that simplicity is free of desires. So "the sage does not value rare treasures to keep people from stealing. He does not display the objects of desire so the people's heart should not be disturbed ... He keeps their minds empty but fills the stomach," says Chapter 3. Lao Tzu, while rejecting against any excessive wealth and knowledge, which are a part of artificial civilization, allows the simple satisfaction of biological need for survival. A similar message is stressed in Chapter 12. "The five colors blind. The five tones deafen ears. The five flavors numb our mouths. Racing and hunting cause our minds to go insane. Precious goods that are hard to get cause us to break laws. Thus the rule of the sage applies to the stomach and not the eyes." The senses tend toward stimulation and indulgence. People will seek these when knowledge of the luxuries of advanced civilization becomes a part of their lives.

IV. TRUE MAN (CHEN JEN), FASTING ONE'S MIND (HSIN CHAI), AND SITTING IN FORGETFULNESS (TSO WANG)

The central point of Chuang Tzu's book is freedom from conventional values by awakening man from his meaninglessness. Such an awakened man is called a True Man by Chuang Tzu. What is a True Man? Chapter 6 of the Chuang Tzu gives an answer. First, Chuang Tzu asks: Who is a True Man? "The True Man of ancient times did not rebel against want, did not grow proud in plenty, and did not plan his affairs. Leading such a life, he could commit an error and not regret it, could meet with success and not make a show. (Watson, Burton, trans. (1968). *The Complete Works of Chuang Tzu*. New York: Columbia University Press.) The man so described is self-transcending without being distinguished. With the help of knowledge, a True Man can unite himself with the Tao and be free from gain or loss in life—an attitude of equanimity matching inexorable Tao.

Because Chuang Tzu is adamantly opposed to the baggage of conventional values, one wonders whether knowledge that leads a True Man to the Tao is nontraditional and qualitatively different. If it serves as a bridge to link a relative and finite human to the absolute Tao, how is it different from our ordinary sense of knowing? Can this be one of Chuang Tzu's gibbering inanities? Because he mentions that a True Man "could commit an error and not regret it" he probably can apply it to include himself or he meant that knowledge of nonknowledge is a form of knowledge. Chuang Tzu continues, "The True Man of ancient times slept without dreaming and woke without care; he ate without savoring and his breath came from deep within. The True Man breathes with his heel; the mass of men breathe with their throats" (Watson, 1968). These sayings characterize extraordinary ways of sleeping-waking, eating, and breathing, but again a True Man is a Tao Man who shares the absolute power of the Tao. Therefore, the possibility of doing so cannot be denied. A True Man shares all the ordinary people's destinies such as life and death, but he does not become identified with them. Chuang Tzu continues, "The True Man of ancient time knew nothing of loving life, knew nothing of hating death. He emerged without delight; he went back in

without a fuss. He came briskly, he went briskly, and that was all ... This is what I call the True Man" (Watson, 1968).

A True Man is alive but his reaction to human definitions and categories of good and evil do not touch his heart and do not shake his foundation. One sure thing about him is that he is completely identified and attached to the felt reality of Tao. Chuang Tzu gives a vivid example of this unattached life. He tells of a time when Master Ssu visited Master Yü who was ill. When Master Ssu inquired about his health, Master Yü replied, "The Creator is making me all crookedy like this! My back sticks up like a hunchback and my vital organs are on top of me. My chin is hidden in my navel, my shoulders are up above my head, and my pigtail points at the sky" (Watson, 1968). Despite these physical discomforts and abnormalities, he did not resent his condition. He attributed this to the freeing of the bound. "What would I resent? If the process continues, perhaps in time he'll transform my left arm into a rooster. In that case, I'll keep watch on the night ... In ancient times this was called the 'freeing of the bound' " (Watson, 1968). It has to do with the ability to free oneself by not being bound to everything: "There are those who cannot free themselves because they are bound by things. But nothing can ever win against Heaven—that's the way it's always been" (Watson, 1968). How can one reach this transcendent yet imminent stage? Chuang Tzu tells that one way comes from immediate experience as in the story of a Woman Crookback (Watson, 1968). Another case may lead beyond the merely intellectual stage. Chuang Tzu says that "there must be a True Man before there can be true knowledge" (Watson, 1968).

There are two possible ways to becoming a True Man. The first one is to sit down and forget everything (*tso wang*). It is mentioned again in Chapter 6 that "Since he is like this, his mind forgets; his face is calm; his forehead is broad" (Watson, 1968). Another way is the fasting of the mind. Chapter 4 mentions this through a dialogue between Confucius and a disciple. "Don't listen with your ears, listen with your mind. No, don't listen with your mind, but listen with your spirit. Listening stops with the ears, the mind stops with recognition, but spirit is empty and waits on all things.... Emptiness is the fasting of the mind" (Watson, 1968). If one attains the mind of no-mind, stops ongoing internal dialogue, empties all thought, and sits in complete oblivion, then he/she returns to the state of nature and one with the Ultimate Way and he/she goes beyond good and evil. The Taoist ethics start with the metaphysical reality, passes through the protean transformations of nature, and returns to the Ultimate Reality. Both the first and last stages deny the autonomous role of ethics as we know it. Even in the middle stage it is heavily overshadowed by the first and last stages in Lao Tzu. Chuang Tzu amplifies it further to eliminate even the middle stage and eclipses the Taoist ethics by the Ultimate Way. This is apparent in their political philosophy. Lao Tzu's vision favors minimal government as best whereas Chuang Tzu advocates a laissez-faire ideal where nongovernment is the best government. This ideal flows from the *wu wei* notion. Chuang Tzu's True Man requires total freedom from governing and from being governed.

Also See the Following Articles

CONFUCIANISM • RELIGION AND ETHICS

Bibliography

Chan, W. (Trans.). (1963). *The way of Lao Tzu*. Indianapolis: The Bobb-Merrill Company, Inc.

Fung, Y. (1952). *A history of Chinese philosophy*. (D. Bodde, Trans.). Princeton: Princeton University Press.

Giles, H. A. (1961). *Chuang Tzu: Taoist philosopher and Chinese mystic*. London: George Allen & Unwin Ltd.

Hansen, C. (1992). *A Daoist theory of Chinese thought: A philosophical interpretation*. New York: Oxford University Press.

Red Pine (Trans.). (1996). *Lao Tzu's Taoteching*. San Francisco: Mercury House.

Schwartz, B. (1985). *The world of thought in ancient China*. Cambridge, MA: Harvard University Press.

Waley, A. (1965). *The way and its power: A study of the Tao Te Ching and its place in Chinese thought*. London: George Allen & Unwin Ltd.

Watson, B. (Trans.). (1964). *Chuang Tzu: Basic writings*. New York: Columbia University Press.

TERRORISM

Sue Ashford
Murdoch University and The University of Western Australia

GLOSSARY

freedom fighters A relative term used to describe individuals who commit, in the name of freedom or some other political principle, the kinds of acts of violence that others may regard as acts of terrorism.

legitimacy The idea that a government rules by the consent of its peoples.

meliorism The doctrine that over time the world tends to become better, largely through human effort.

political expediency A view that typically advocates some prudent course of action but that may lay claim to notions such as the political good of a society, justice, or the notion of legitimacy to justify that particular course of action. The achievement of these notions—through, for example, the establishing of a new form of government—may not be the true ends of the strategy that has been advocated.

social contract The idea, typically invoked as a metaphor or as a rhetorical device, that at some stage in our history, human beings formally undertook a contract to join together as members of a society.

terrorism A policy that promotes the use of violence to induce fear of death or injury in individuals.

urban guerrilla warfare A term used to describe the kind of violence that others may regard as acts of terrorism; those who use this term believe that the violent acts are actions toward some ultimate good and that those engaged in the warfare (otherwise called terrorists) are involved in a just war.

TERRORISM is the use of violence—as a matter of policy—to cause terror in people, usually so that those individuals will change their beliefs or allegiances. While terrorism is violence that is usually executed against a government or a political system to effect political change, the immediate victims of terrorist acts of violence are typically ordinary citizens, rather than members of government or public property. Terrorism is also a policy used by governments against their citizens, or against the citizens of other states, to intimidate the population or sections of it.

I. ORIGINS OF THE TERM

Terrorism is defined by the *Oxford English Dictionary* as a "system of terror." The *Oxford English Dictionary* is organized on historical basis: hence the dictionary collects chronological illustrations of the uses of a term. Two instances are given of the early uses of the term terror to describe such systems. The first comes from a particular historical illustration that gave rise to the coining of the term terrorism. The example is the government by intimidation as directed and carried out by the party in power in France during the Revolution of 1789–1794, and, in particular, the system of the "Terror" during 1793–1794. More specifically, the period of the Terror is held to have begun in July 1793, the month when the "Committee of Public Safety" was formed under the aegis of Danton and Robespierre. The Terror is usually considered to have ended in July 1794, after the fall and execution of Robespierre, and hence after the abolition of the Commune of Paris.

The second instance given of the use of the term is of a more general conception: that of a policy intended to strike with terror those against whom it is adopted, the employment of methods of intimidation, the fact of terrorizing or the condition of being terrorized.

A. The Ground of Difference

A difference can be seen between the two uses of the term terrorism. The first instance is a case of violence concerning governments: the original use of the term was used to refer both to violence executed against a presiding government and then, after the Revolution, to violence against the people—the citizens of the new government. The second use of the term concerns the psychological and social effects of the use of violence. This ground of difference is significant when arguments in favor of acts of violence against particular governments are considered, acts that are also termed acts of terrorism by those who support the existing regime but which are considered to be legitimate and necessary acts of warfare by those who oppose the acting government.

II. HISTORICAL BACKGROUND

The concern that the very act of revolution undermined the process and nature of government itself, together with illustrations of the types of uses of violence evidenced during the French Revolution, was the basis for the use of the term *terror* to beget the term *terrorism*. Thus, Edmund Burke, in his *Reflections on the Revolution in France,* used the term terror to illustrate his claim that the mob ruled the National Assembly with the result that true government was made impossible. In his *Reflections* Burke draws a picture of the National Assembly in which the individual members of the Assembly and the king have become actors who are constrained to play a role whose nature is determined by the dictates of those whose power lies in physical force rather than in political legitimacy:

> With a compelled appearance of deliberation, they vote under the dominion of a stern necessity. They sit in the heart, as it were, of a foreign republic: they have their residence in a city whose constitution has emanated neither from the charter of their king nor from their legislative power. There they are surrounded by an army not raised either by the authority of their crown or by their command, and which, if they should order to dissolve itself, would instantly dissolve them. There they sit, after a gang of assassins had driven away some hundreds of the members, whilst those who held the same moderate principles, with more patience or better hope, continued every day exposed to outrageous insults and murderous threats. There a majority, sometimes real, sometimes pretended, captive itself, compels a captive king to issue as royal edicts, at third hand, the polluted nonsense of their most licentious and giddy coffeehouses. It is notorious that all their measures are decided before they are debated. It is beyond doubt that, under the terror of the bayonet and the lamppost and torch to their houses, they are obliged to adopt all the crude and desperate measures suggested by clubs composed of a monstrous medley of all conditions, tongues, and nations (pp. 77–78, Edmund Burke *Reflections on the Revolution in France.* ed., with introduction, Thomas H. D. Mahoney (1790; 1955) The Liberal Arts Press Indianapolis, IN: Bobbs-Merrill Co.).

Here, Burke presents two forms of political legitimacy that have been breached by what he calls "the mob": the charter of their king and the legislative power of the National Assembly. The situation that he portrays is thus ironic: those who once held legitimate political power are now puppets whose political actions are dictated by others. As a result, the content of their political actions is really legitimized not by their authority as members of the National Assembly, but by those who are now in a position of what might be thought of as real power—the power that comes from causing an experience of terror, an experience that results from the threat of loss of life and personal property. Burke's irony goes further: in establishing this "foreign republic" in which the members of the National Assembly have become unwilling, even accidental residents, there is a sense in which the puppeteers have forged another kind of constitution—albeit a constitution dictated by and one that prescribes fear.

III. THE COMPLEX NATURE OF TERRORISM

The notion of terrorism is complex and this complexity can be seen in the historical origins of the term, although of course the kinds of behavior that we term terrorism have their origins in human history, not in the French Revolution. On one view the term terrorism was derived from a particular perception of the French Revolution. On this perception the Revolution was to be deplored: the very idea of a revolution against what was hitherto regarded as a legitimate government was regarded as wrong and dangerous. Hence, the action of this Revolution was not an extreme (perhaps justifiable) form of political dissent but rather it was seen as a form of violence that rendered the normal political processes, including legitimate political debate and dissent, impotent. Thus the reason for the perceived danger of the Revolution lay not only in the particular acts of violence that were perpetrated against the institutions of government, against members of the government and ordinary citizens, but also (and what was perhaps more troubling for political theorists) in the concern that the very act of revolution undermined the process and nature of government itself. On this view, revolutions are instruments of social instability and do not simply cause short-term civil strife for a long-term gain of better government; instead, revolutions destroy the very fabric of a society.

There was another form of response to the Revolution. Support for the Revolution (and subsequently for acts of violence regarded by adherents of the first view as acts of terrorism) often came from a reconstruction of the idea that the act of revolution undermined the process and nature of government itself. Reconstruction of the idea that government is undermined by revolution proceeds by affirming both the undesirable nature of the old or existing system of government and the need for change; hence, it is claimed, the current government *must* be undermined. According to this line of thought, the kind or degree of change required can only be achieved by destroying the prevailing form of government. Then, and only in the wake of a revolution, a new and superior form of government or social order

can be instituted. Once given the institution of a new form of government, then, according to this line of thought, the acts of violence perpetrated in the name of the Revolution are in one or another sense acceptable. That is, while the effects of particular acts of violence may not be condoned (although they may—for example, the acts of violence may be seen as punishment or justified retribution), these kinds of acts of violence will be considered at least to be the necessary means to the goal of reestablishing a proper social order. Thus, according to the second response to the Revolution, the very content of a concern about the act of revolution—that the bare act of revolution undermined the process and nature of government itself—was often used as a basis for endorsement of the Revolution. This line of thought is still adopted as a way to sanction acts of violence that are termed acts of terrorism by opponents, opponents who typically uphold the incumbent government.

IV. PROPER SOCIAL ORDERS: ONE MOTIVE FOR TERRORISM

Burke was arguing for the legitimacy of a constitutional monarchy. From our perspective, some 200 years later, it is easy to think that while Burke's sentiments against violence may be appropriate, his support for a form of government that has been largely superseded in the modern world is merely an illustration of Burke's conservatism and a reflection of his place in history. The French Revolution is often regarded as one of the precursors of modern and contemporary political movements. A line of thought that is often encouraged by these contemporary movements is that those governments that are considered not to be directly representative of their peoples are held to be wrong, even immoral, kinds of government. If a government is seen to be unrepresentative of its people, then some may argue that that government has no true basis for power over its people. A government of this kind, the argument goes, does not have a proper basis as a government: hence attempts to overthrow the governing power structure—by means that may include violence—are right-minded political actions.

The style of representative government that is characteristically upheld today as the proper kind of government, and hence the political basis for discriminating between acts of terrorism from other kinds of acts of violence against government, is that of democracy. From this vantage point, those acts of violence that Burke deplored, because they were acts of violence against a legitimate government, can be regarded as politically *necessary* steps toward overthrowing an essentially corrupt form of government. But because this vantage point may change, or may not be held by a theorist, the claim that the acts of violence are *necessary* steps toward political progress is undermined.

Why it matters which kind of government is considered the right form of government is that we need some basis to discriminate those acts of violence against particular governments that are to be rightly regarded as acts of terrorism. For not all acts of violence against governments are acts of terrorism. Acts of banditry, for example, are not necessarily acts of terrorism although they may be directed against governments. Thus we need to distinguish acts of terrorism from those acts of violence against particular governments that are either held to be necessary actions in order to try to destabilize that government (there being good reasons to wish to remove that government and for needing to remove it by force, rather than by peaceful means), or that are believed to be legitimate acts of war (either between nations, or when the acts of violence are regarded as acts of, say, modern urban guerrilla warfare).

We want, then, to be able to distinguish acts of terrorism from acts of violence that may be regarded as actions of a just war. The notion of a just war has a long philosophical and theological history. Medieval philosophers distinguished between two notions, the idea of the *jus ad bellum,* which is the right to make war and the idea of the *jus in bello,* which is a matter of how a war should be waged (of what kinds of actions are permissible ways of conducting a war). Both notions are relevant to the issue of discriminating acts of terrorism from other kinds of acts of violence. From certain vantage points, acts that some of us may describe as acts of terrorism may be held to be strategic actions of a just war: that is, these acts may be authorized, as it were, by the concept of the *jus ad bellum.* But even if this is the case and acts of violence against a government are legitimized in some way, as acts of a just war, we may still want to distinguish between those acts that are appropriate kinds of violence for just warfare and those acts that are impermissible. Not everything is permitted in a just war: some kinds of conduct may be acts of terrorism even within the waging of a just war. However, to determine some sense of when the notion of a just war is applicable, more needs to be said about the basis for discriminating between different kinds of violence in terms of the intention to have a desirable and proper social order (see Sections VI and VII).

V. THE ARGUMENT FROM POLITICAL EXPEDIENCY: A SECOND MOTIVE FOR TERRORISM

The idea that violence may be waged against a government as part of a just war (when some part of the citizenry attempts to bring about a better form of government), must be used with caution. Although the rhetoric of many terrorist organizations relies on the idea of waging a just war, the rhetoric of a just war is often a gloss on the real motives of the combatants who are really terrorists attempting to win support for their actions. (Of course, when the notion of waging a just war is employed, those who carry out violence against the government do not describe themselves as terrorists: the term terrorist is employed by those who condemn the violence.)

The line of thought that terms acts of violence against governments and their citizens as instances of a just war can be also described in terms of an argument from the political expediency of violence. Usually, when this line of thought is adopted, the acts of violence in question are not called acts of terrorism by those who execute the acts or by those who support those actions. Instead the relevant events are redescribed as (say) urban guerrilla warfare (for example, Irish Republican Army bombings of English cities) and those who carry out the violence may be known as freedom fighters (for example, the Tamil Tigers in Sri Lanka).

Expediency is the consideration of what is expedient, of what is conducive to a particular purpose. The idea of political expediency is this: a course of action may be upheld as the right and only political strategy to achieve a certain goal. The strategy is determined as right by means of a notion like justice or representative government or the public good. However, why this strategy is in truth an argument from political expediency and not a full-blooded appeal to political principles such as justice is because it is some other goal that is actually desired by the combatants; and the political principles that are invoked in the name of that goal are relevant in truth only to achieving that end. These political principles are not truly invoked as ends in themselves; the violence is not a means to achieving that which is right (or just, or representative). Because the putative justification for violent political action is spurious (the true goal is, say, the achievement of political power), there is no necessary connection between the espoused political principles and the use of violence to achieve the activists' political ambitions.

When an argument from political expediency is employed, the kinds of justifications brought to the argument often give the impression that a particular kind of government is the goal of the political action: in a sense, the justifications are employed to sanction the use of violence. Given that the kinds of justifications are—in contemporary times—ideas like representative government, justice, equality, and liberty, it is easy to think that again the typical goal of political change is some form of democratic government.

However, the argument from political expediency is not only used to justify violence against a people in order to bring about democracy: this line of thought was, for example, invoked to justify the Russian Revolution (the Bolshevik Revolution of November 1917) and the establishment of a communist state. The justification for the "trials" that marked Stalin's purges was that certain elements of the Soviet population needed to be eliminated for the good of the state. Thus the argument from political expediency regards the loss of human life, or the infliction of pain upon individual citizens of a state, as necessary—perhaps regrettable—stages in a struggle for a better or a just government. The goal of the political good is then used to justify or rationalize the uses of violence.

Thus there is nothing in the argument from the political expediency of violence that enables a theorist, let alone a revolutionary, to claim that the changes in government and society that are sought through violence should be changes toward any one particular kind of government or society. There is nothing in the argument from the political expediency of violence, in itself, to confirm that any one particular style of government is superior to another. While an exponent of the argument from political expediency will typically turn to notions like the political good of a society, to justice or to the notion of legitimacy in order to use these notions to justify a particular employment of the argument, this argument can be used to justify any form of new government that promises to satisfy the desired criterion (whether that is the political good, justice, or legitimacy).

Thus the argument from political expediency gives us two ways to think about terrorism. The first is cautionary: although the invocation of the concept of a just war may be appropriate to argue that particular acts of violence are not, in fact, acts of terrorism, the availability and use of an argument from political expediency warns us that not all appeals to the notion of a just war should be accepted. The second line of thought is that when the idea of a just war is appealed to, there are no clear-cut principles to determine when the concept of a just war is correctly invoked.

VI. HISTORICAL APPRECIATIONS OF REVOLUTIONS

The thrust of Section V was that the idea of a just war could be manipulated for the purposes of political expediency: in such cases the argument for a just war can be reduced to an argument from political expediency. In this section, the theoretical issue is rather that some historical instances of the argument from political expediency may be treated as arguments for a just war.

When theorists evaluate a particular revolution in terms of its political consequences, the argument from the political expediency of violence often gains a foothold insofar as those consequences are determined and evaluated some time after the revolution has occurred. That is, the political consequences need not be immediate and may be, as in the case of the French Revolution, largely symbolic rather than clear and actually realized gains for the citizenry.

There are two problems for the notion of terrorism with this style of retrospective appreciation of political movements such as the French Revolution. The first is a matter of when it is right to call an act of violence an act of political terrorism. The second is the question of when an act of violence aimed at a particular government should be applauded, perhaps to be seen as a step on the path to reforming or overthrowing that government.

A. The Problem of Meliorism

Meliorism is the doctrine that the world tends to become better, or that it may be made better through human effort. According to the meliorist's perspective, the forms of government of the nations of the world are in a continual process of change, and these changes are movements toward an improvement. In a particular version of the meliorist's view, these changes will continue until each nation is represented by, say, a duly elected, democratic government. Thus, in this version of meliorism, the past 300 years of Western civilization can be seen as a model for the transition to proper government, a form of government that will eventually occur across the world. On this account, the dissolution of the Soviet Union, and of other communist states, is a straightforward example of political progress.

B. Meliorism, Styles of Government, and Justifications

One problem is that if we decide that we should approve of the French or some other revolution because that revolution is a step toward transforming the political processes of a country from (say) nondemocratic to democratic (or more democratic) forms of government, then we may commit ourselves to a meliorist view of political history.

However, this view of melioration is self-justifying: there needs to be an argument in order to claim that a democratic political state is the ideal form of human government. Typically an argument to support this claim relies on enunciating the properties of a democratic political state and declaring these properties to be virtues: for example, that it is the form of government that represents the people, that democratic governments are duly elected and legitimized in virtue both of the democratic voting system and a pledge to uphold the rights of the citizens of that state.

But it is not obvious whether the move to expound the properties of a democracy and to declare these properties to be political virtues, is itself an argument for the claim that a democratic government is the best kind of government for human beings. There are two problems here. The first problem—whether the restatement or the proclamation of the properties can be considered an argument for democracies—is that an opponent can claim, with some force, that all the proponent of democracy has done is to describe a democracy and that nothing in that description, per se, demonstrates that democracies are intrinsically superior forms of government. The opponent, then, denies that the acts of violence can be considered events in a just war. As a result, if an opponent of this putative argument for the meliorist view of democratic government wishes to undermine the meliorist's position, the opponent can go on to claim that acts of political violence, perpetrated in the name of furthering democracy, are in fact merely acts of terrorism. The second problem is that the meliorist will also want to be able to recognize some acts of violence—committed in the name of democracy—as acts of terrorism. Here the issues in play rely on the distinction between the concept of *jus ad bellum* (the right to make war) and the idea of the *jus in bello* (how a war should be conducted).

C. From What Style of Government Do We Discriminate Acts of Terrorism?

It is not the case that whether an act of violence against a government is an act of terrorism depends solely on what style of government is in power. There are further aspects of how we discriminate acts of terrorism that will be discussed later. In this section the issues of how

to discriminate acts of terrorism, however, are tied to claims about types of government.

Another problem for the meliorist is more practical. The nations of the world are governed by a variety of political processes. From time to time, a democratic government may act to undermine (explicitly or implicitly) the political processes of a country where that government is deemed to be undemocratic and unjust. A instance of this kind of international intervention is the Gulf War (August 1990 to June 1991) when the United States and a number of largely Western allies attempted to rebuff an Iraqi invasion of Kuwait. Although the war was justified among members of the Western Alliance by the Iraqi incursion into Kuwaiti territory, a widespread hope among the allied leaders was that the government of President Saddam Hussein of Iraq would be undermined, perhaps even weakened to the extent that Iraqi political dissidents might be able to overthrow Hussein. However, criticism of this war often amounted to the claim that the attacks on Iraq were simply acts of terrorism (and, viewed from the perspective of supporters of Hussein's government, such claims seem inevitable: members of a governing class are liable to see attacks on their authority as acts of terrorism). A second kind of criticism that was made is that in attacking Iraq, the United States and its allies were unprincipled, in that while agreement could be found that the Iraqi government was corrupt and unjust, much the same kinds of criticism could and should be leveled at a number of neighboring Arab states, especially Kuwait itself (the government which was being supported, in effect, by the Western alliance).

The problem here, then, is that if acts of terrorism are discriminated according to whether or not the acts are perpetrated against democratic governments, and if democratic government is held to be the just form of government, then any act of violence against a nondemocratic government that is executed with the intention to undermine that government, seems to have the right kind of pedigree for acceptance as justified violence, as an act of war. However, if this pedigree is challenged, then the proponents of change toward democracy appear to lack an argument for their actions. Their acts take on the guise of acts of faith or acts of self-interest.

VII. THE IDEA OF LEGITIMACY

One argument that democratic countries can turn to is to claim that their governments are legitimate, whereas the governments of (say) dictators are not. The notion of legitimacy is a complex one, and the boundaries of its application need to be explored. A notion of legitimacy is technical: this conception of legitimacy rests on the idea that a government's power and role is justified by an act of consent by its people or through a covenant with the people. Discussions of this notion of legitimacy were once framed in terms of an idea called "the state of nature," an idea that directed attention to the first assembly of government—from human kind in a state of nature to human kind in a society (see Section 1, below). This technical conception of legitimacy may be termed a constitutional notion of legitimacy. The idea employed below is related but much looser: it is simply the idea that a government must be able to justify its power in terms of its relation to the peoples it governs, and that this justification must not rest on sheer power over its people alone. Thus the notion of legitimacy is at least related to notions of representational government and the idea of a society.

A. Which Governments Are Legitimate?

Suppose that an act of violence is executed against a nondemocratic government with the intention to undermine that government. Consider, then, the claim that in this case, just because the government that is being resisted is nondemocratic, the acts of violence that precede or accompany the change of government can be considered as acts of justified violence or as an act of war rather than as acts of terrorism. Surely this claim needs clarification and supporting argument. For it is not usually the case that democratic governments—such as those of the United States and many NATO countries—count acts of violence against nondemocratic states as thereby acts of war: more usually the acts are counted as instances of terrorism. International politics is a pragmatic business, and the world's nation-states provide instances of a wide range of kinds of democracies and of kinds of nondemocratic governments. Furthermore, the issue of what kind of state is a democratic state is a matter of contention: while democracies are often thought to be capitalist states with representative governments, the term democracy has even been used to describe communist states, and these states have claimed that their system of government is representative of their peoples.

Yet the problem remains that we are rarely willing to claim that any act of violence against any government is an act of terrorism, simply because it is an act of violence against a prevailing government. Attempts to assassinate Adolf Hitler, at one stage a popular leader who had widespread support among the German people, are not necessarily considered acts of terrorism:

rather, those reflecting on the political state of the Third Reich may well regret that the assassination attempts were unsuccessful.

It is commonplace, in the course of human history, for there to be widespread agreement that a particular government is wrong, unjust, corrupt, insupportable, and that for the sake of those governed by it (as opposed to the sake of nation-states whose affairs are somehow affected by that government) this government should be overthrown.

Situations of this kind may seem to constitute one powerful argument for democracies: the claim is that governments could be changed through the ballot box. However, to make this claim assumes that the democracy in question is a democracy whose government can be changed by the exercise of the will of the people through the ballot box; that the democratic system ensures actual changes of government; and that democracies are the best system of government. Consider what is at stake here: to agree with these assumptions suggests, for example, that were we to think that the government of Germany's Third Reich was wrong, and were we to make this strong claim in favor of the system of democracy, then we should feel assured that Hitler would not have been voted into office by popular election. In particular, to assume that democracies are the best system of government is, in a sense, question begging: for what properties of a democratic government can we appeal to so that we can claim that democracy is the best system of government? (Or, alternatively, what properties of some other system of government might we point to should we wish to claim that this other system of government is a better or the best system of government?)

B. The Claim for Legitimacy

To distinguish acts of violence against governments as acts of terrorism clearly depends, in some way, on the vantage point and interests of those who make the assessment that these are acts of terrorism (as opposed to other kinds of acts of violence, or rather than acts of warfare). There is a certain circularity in definition here: unless we are prepared to accept that decisions to describe such acts of violence as terrorism are simply *relative* to the interests, history, and values of the observers, some property of government must be determined for use as a benchmark to evaluate acts of violence as acts of terrorism. What is needed is a property that may be lacking in certain forms of government or absent in particular governments and which we can claim *must* be present for rightful government. Then, although perhaps the kinds of governments that display this property will vary (and not all will be democracies), the presence or absence of this property can be a mark of good (or just) or bad (or unjust) government. Then assessments of which acts constitute acts of terrorism will not be relativistic (that is, relative to the values, interests, and history of those who make the discriminations). We need, therefore, a more basic criterion than whether a government is a democracy or not to decide when acts of violence against particular governments will be considered acts of terrorism.

One property of government that has been held to constitute a more basic criterion is that of legitimacy, or legitimized or legitimate governments. The notion of legitimacy has its origins in the works of English political theorists of the seventeenth and eighteenth centuries whose thinking was influenced by the civil disturbances of the English Civil War and its complex political and social effects. The theorists include Thomas Hobbes in *The Leviathan*; Robert Filmer, *Patriarcha*; James Tyrrell, *Patriarcha non Monarcha*; and John Locke, *Two Treatises on Government*.

1. Social Contract Theory

The notion of legitimacy was often discussed against an idea that acted as a particular mode of exploration of the basis for society and hence for the existence of governments: this idea was the device of a social contract, the idea that at some stage in our history, human beings formally undertook a contract to join together as members of a society.

While the idea of a social contract was often expressed as if the event of a social contract actually occurred, the use of this idea is typically metaphorical or rhetorical: the idea is used to focus attention on the ingredients for the development of society. The ingredients include self-protection, mutual protection, the protection of property, and the use of language for communication (as a matter of utility or for the pleasure that communication can bring). Use of the device of a social contract also ensures attention to the rights and obligations that come with being a member of a society. Hence the device also focuses attention on the constituents or role of society such as the provision of justice, protection, commerce or livelihood, stability, and fellowship.

2. Consent

Central to discussions of social contract theories is the notion of consent: this is the idea that what justifies or legitimizes a society is that its citizens consent, in some form or manner, to being governed and to being subject to particular rules and obligations in return for the particular rights and privileges that are provided by the society. Quite how the notions of consent, a social contract, and the very idea of a society are developed vary from theorist to theorist. These issues have continued to be debated, although not always through the medium of the notion of a social contract (however, two contemporary political theorists who have made use of this device are John Rawls and Robert Nozick).

C. The Place for Legitimacy

The notion of legitimacy, then, is cashed out in terms of an explication of the role of society and the relation between society and its individual members. In particular, the notion of legitimacy is tied to the idea that members of a society consent, in some sense, to their government—to its laws and demands. If, however, citizens of a society find their government burdensome and withdraw their consent, then—according to the terms of this theory—these citizens may argue that the political systems which governs them is illegitimate.

VIII. WHAT COUNTS AS AN ACT OF TERRORISM?

The discussion so far has taken for granted that we can discern, at some level, acts of violence that are candidates for being described as acts of terrorism (even though some may wish to redescribe these acts as acts of warfare, say). But there is a more fundamental issue for the question of what counts as an act of terrorism. The issue has become more problematic of late because there is a tendency to use the term terrorism outside its more traditional place as a form of violence against governments and their citizens. In some feminist discussions, for example, the notion of terrorism is explored to indicate the kind of power relation that holds between men and women in society: in one version, women may be regarded as terrorized by men. In this view, rape and acts of domestic violence may be viewed as terrorist acts, but regarded likewise may be instances of male verbal abuse of females. Another instance of extended uses of the term terrorism can be found in debates about multiculturalism, racism, and racial vilification: exposure to constant racial insults and threats is sometimes described as a form of violence and as a form of terrorism. Yet another domain in which the term terrorism is used is that of apparently random mass murders. Such events are described as acts of terrorism because an emotion or a cognitive state of terror is engendered in the victims, bystanders, and those who learn of the actions.

There are many kinds of acts of violence that cause feelings of terror in those who witness or who learn of these actions. For example, on March 13, 1996, a lone gunman in Dunblane, Scotland, killed 16 children and one teacher at a primary school. On April 28, 1996, a gunman killed 35 adults and children at Port Arthur, Tasmania, a historic site visited by tourists and picknickers. Both affairs received considerable publicity in the Western world. Typical responses to each massacre, over and beyond sympathy for the victims and their families, were feelings of outrage and fear. In both Britain and Australia, the incidents also provoked debate about gun laws and have led, in both countries, to further restrictions upon gun ownership.

That each incident caused terror, not only among those who were wounded and bystanders but also among members of the wider communities in Britain and Australia, seems clear. A relatively ordinary act—going to school or going on a picnic—took on the possibility of domestic and national tragedy. People's beliefs were changed or galvanized: both incidents caused widespread debate about an aspect of government, namely legislation controlling the ownership of guns, and about the rights of citizens of the state (whether the right to own guns is established by the right to protect one's self and one's family). What is not clear is whether either incident can be regarded as an act of terrorism. Instead, once the immediate emotional effect of the killings has calmed, both events tend to be regarded as horrendous acts of violence committed by an individual who is estranged from his society (which is not to say that the gunmen were necessarily insane).

We do seem to need more than an act of widespread violence in order to term an act of violence an act of terrorism. Certainly we seem to require an intention to cause civil instability or unrest, and these elements appear to be missing in the mass murders at Dunblane and Port Arthur. Yet there are other acts of violence that are often described as acts of terrorism and yet where an express intention to cause civil unrest is absent. Two examples are the explosion of a bomb on Pan Am Flight 103, which destroyed the plane over Lockerbie, Scotland, in December 1988, and the bombing in Centennial Park in Atlanta during the 1996 Olympic Games. Both of these incidents have been termed acts of terrorism and yet neither was acknowledged by a particular terrorist organization (whereas, typically, bombings on the British mainland are owned by, say, the Irish Republican Army). Neither bombing was accompanied by a demand for a political response (say, the release of political prisoners). That these bombings are deemed acts of terrorism seems to rest on their capacity to produce fear, on the willful destruction of civilian life, and on their potential to undermine confidence in an area of life regulated by governments—that is, international travel and a traditional international celebration of sport. And yet, while there seems to be an intuitive basis for distinguishing these bombings from the cases of Dunblane and Port Arthur, all of the characteristic effects of the bombings can be claimed for Dunblane and Port Arthur (going to school and going to a tourist venue that is a historic site are also areas of life that are regulated at some level by governments).

A further ground for distinguishing acts of terrorism from other kinds of acts of violence is the question of sanity: but it is not clear how this criterion works. If we consider, say, the example of the United State's technology terrorist, the Unabomber, we might well question whether sanity is a relevant criterion: in the case of the Unabomber, there appears to be a clear purpose on the part of the bomber. His manifesto against technological change has been widely publicized (for example, by negotiation in the *Washington Post*). While the views he expresses may find sympathy with many individuals, many of these people would abhor and condemn his methods of publicizing these ideas. The example of the Unabomber is interesting for another reason: his attacks were carried out over a period of time, and his choice of targets was not obvious. There is a sense in which we may question whether his actions caused terror in individuals other than those directly affected by his actions. Yet there also seems good reason to call the Unabomber's attacks acts of terrorism.

Perhaps the intuition, whether it is valuable or not—that the cases are different, that only the plane crashes or the bombing attacks may be acts of terrorism—rests more on the sense that to cause a plane to explode probably requires organization by some number of individuals who are all dedicated to that end. The idea that the planning behind the acts of violence is in some way relevant to determining whether the violence is an instance of terrorism, instead of some other kind of violence, seems applicable just because terrorism is typically carried out by organizations, however small their membership. Even this suggestion does not take us very far. Given the illustration of the Unabomber, and the possibility that the Centennial Park bombing was executed by one person, these examples seem to undercut the criterion of membership of an organization; however, that these bombings required considerable organization seems plain.

An alternative appeal to the intentions of those who execute the acts of terrorism is to regard terrorists as socially displaced individuals who enjoy violence. But even if this psychological characterization of (at least some) terrorists is correct, this psychological profile is an inadequate basis to distinguish terrorists from (say) freedom fighters. We cannot be assured that organized terrorist groups such as the IRA or the GIA (the Algerian Armed Islamic Group), who are held responsible for a series of bombings in France during 1995, do not include members who enjoy violence for violence's sake—whose primary motive, perhaps, is not political but psychological.

IX. THE APPEAL TO ABSTRACT PRINCIPLES

If it is the case that acts of terrorism are typically carried out by organizations, however small their membership, perhaps what is important to the members of these organizations is not simply that their acts of violence are planned but that these acts are typically executed under the belief that their actions are acts of war. Furthermore, it is usually the case that terrorist groups are organized on one or other kind of military model (hence they are often described as paramilitary groups).

Thus to distinguish acts of terrorism from other kinds of acts of violence such as mass murder, we seem to need to turn to the idea that the terrorist acts under the belief that she or he is an agent for political change. As such, the terrorist perceives himself to be a member of a group that is waging war against an illegitimate or unjust or corrupt government. Thus the acts of violence are legitimized, in the minds of the terrorist and his supporters, by an appeal to abstract principles.

A caveat needs to be entered here. So far the discussion of acts of violence against the citizens of a state—acts that seem strong candidates to merit the description of terrorism—has been in terms of individuals or organizations who wish to develop an alternative form of government or simply to gain power for power's sake (an example here, perhaps, is the role of the Cosa Nostra in Italian politics). But there are other alternatives: these include some varieties of anarchism and of nihilism. The belief that guides individuals to adopt violence as a tactic here is a belief that government itself is wrong or unjust or contrary to human needs. An abstract prin-

ciple is appealed to here, but the kind of principle that is turned to is radically different from those that have been considered so far. So some extent, this conception of terrorists is the picture familiar in fictional representations of terrorism (for example, in Joseph Conrad's *The Secret Agent* and Doris Lessing's *The Good Terrorist*).

Sometimes an alternative approach is developed to the question of which acts of violence are acts of terrorism, an approach that uses the appeal to abstract principles only in part. On this view what distinguishes acts of terrorism from acts of violence that are executed as part of a "just war" is that the intended targets of acts of terrorism are civilians whereas the intended targets of participants in a just war are combatants whose allegiance is to the enemy—the incumbent government or social order. On this view, then, the loss of civilian life in the plane crash at Lockerbie, the 1995 bombing at Oklahoma City that caused 168 deaths, or the use of the nerve gas Sarin in the Tokyo subway on March 20, 1995, which killed 12 people and injured thousands (allegedly caused by the Aum Shinrikyo cult), are clear cases of terrorism. In contrast, the killings of prominent members of a society—say, the assassination in 1978 of Italian prime minister, Aldo Moro, by the Red Brigade, or the execution of German bankers Alfred Herrhausen and Jürgen Ponto by the Red Army Faction and the Baader-Meinhof group—are held to be instances of carefully targeted violence, the kind of targeted violence that constitutes warfare.

Here, then, are two arguments that appeal to abstract principles in order to discriminate acts of terrorism from other kinds of acts of violence. Both arguments attempt, in particular, to discriminate terrorism from those acts of violence that—by an appeal to their political expediency—can be justified as acts of violence that are believed, by those who execute the violence, to be necessary moves toward a desirable political end.

X. ARGUMENTS AGAINST THE APPEAL TO ABSTRACT PRINCIPLES

But by the very appeal to abstract principles, either kind of argument tends to suggest that acts of violence that may be termed terrorism in an everyday manner should, upon reflection, be redescribed as acts of some kind of warfare, even if it is warfare against the ordinary citizens of a state or nation. However, this method of distinguishing acts of terrorism from other kinds of acts of violence raises a problem. The appeal to abstract principles—for example, that acts of violence against an incumbent government are necessary steps in the engagement of a war for a change of government, a war which is conducted in the name of (say) justice—can be perceived as an instance of the argument from political expediency (see Section V). If the appeal to abstract principles is allowed, then the distinction that has been sought—a basis for discriminating acts of terrorism from other kinds of acts of violence—breaks down.

The types of acts of violence which remain described as acts of terrorism are acts of violence against civilian life: but these acts of violence now become difficult to distinguish from mass murders such as the killings at Dunblane or Port Arthur. Attempts to distinguish the acts of terrorism (violence against civilians) from these kinds of mass murder rely on the intentions of the terrorists (beliefs that they hold in common with agents of terror who chose noncivilian targets) and their preference for civilian (or "soft") targets. Once this move is made, though, it is no longer clear that a distinction between terrorist and, say, pathological, violence can be drawn.

The argument against these appeals to abstract principles can proceed in three ways. The first line of rebuttal is to question the distinction, made above in Section IX, between the idea that terrorism is distinguished by the loss of general civilian life rather than by the deaths of politicians or other individuals who are prominent members of their society.

The second line of rebuttal is to explore a problem raised by the appeal to abstract argument and the appeal to a distinction between civilian and combatant victims. The problem is this: if one accepts the appeal to abstract argument, or the general direction of the argument from political expediency, then how do we describe acts of violence that are perpetrated by governments rather than by a group of individuals working against a particular government. There are two types of cases to consider. The first is acts of violence that a government executes against other states with which it is at war. History repeatedly provides illustrations of governments whose acts of war exceed military targets. Two controversial examples from World War II are the British bombing of Dresden and the U.S. nuclear bombings of Hiroshima and Nagasaki: in both cases, it is arguable that the targets were the civilian populations rather than military and tactical goals, and that the accomplishments of each event was the spreading of terror among the civilian population. If we turn to the terminology of just-war theory, then these cases may be described as cases of *jus in bello,* a matter of how war should or should not be conducted. Yet many who

reflect on incidents of these kinds would wish to go further than the boundaries of just-war theory, and to call these events acts of terrorism not acts of military misconduct.

The second kind of case to consider is that of acts of violence carried out by a government against members of its own civilian population, acts that were designed to cause terror and to subdue the citizens. An example is allegations that leaders of South Africa's former National Party government ordered the 1988 bombing of a Johannesburg trade union building and numerous other attacks on or assassinations of trade union members and other opponents of apartheid. If we accept the appeal to abstract principles and the idea that only the use of civilian targets to destabilize the government distinguishes acts of terrorism from acts of legitimate warfare, then we face a dilemma in how we may describe cases where a government acts against civilian targets: for on what grounds do we draw our distinctions? Yet surely these kinds of cases are instances where we want to apply the term terrorism.

There is a further and fundamental problem with the appeal to abstract principles. The procedure of appealing to abstract principles in order to redescribe acts of violence as something other than acts of terrorism erases or etiolates the very acts and events that are our grounds of evidence for making a judgment at all. It is the act of violence that causes terror that leads us to consider terming that action an act of terrorism. If we appeal to abstract principles to find guidance for our description and classification of that act, we may lose sight of the terror itself and the effects of that fear. To lose sight of the terror that violence brings just seems wrong, for we then ignore the fact that violence is cruel.

Furthermore, to overlook the terror—the effects of violence—should lead us to question why violence is used if terror is not an effective weapon. But terror is a standard result of violence, and the use of violence to achieve subjugation or suffering is often effective: hence terrorism has its uses for those who wish to bring about certain ends, and its efficiency means that its use is thereby justified by those who wish to promote, at almost any cost, certain ends.

Bibliography

Bar On, B. A. (1991). Why terrorism is morally problematic. In C. Card (Ed.), *Feminist ethics,* pp. 107–125. Lawrence KS: University of Kansas Press.

Berlin, I. (1978). *Russian thinkers.* Harmondsworth: Penguin.

Coady, C. A. J. (1985). On the morality of terrorism. *Philosophy* 60, 47–69.

Crenshaw, M. (Ed.). (1983). *Terrorism, legitimacy, and power: The consequences of political violence.* Middletown, CT: Wesleyan University Press.

The Economist (1996, March 2). What is terrorism? Website http://www.economist.com/issue/02-03-96.

Ewin, R. E. (1991). *Virtues and rights: The moral philosophy of Thomas Hobbes.* Boulder, CO: Westview Press.

Hare, R. M. (1979). On terrorism. *Journal of Value Inquiry* **13**, 241–249.

Johnson, J. T. (1975). *Ideology, reason, and the limitation of war.* Princeton, NJ: Princeton University Press.

Johnson, J. T. (1981). *Just war tradition and the restraint of war.* Princeton, NJ: Princeton University Press.

Mandelstam, N. (1976). *Hope abandoned.* (M. Hayward, Trans). Harmondsworth: Penguin.

Plamenatz, J. (1963). *Man and society.* (Vol. 1). London: Longman.

Robb, P. (1996). *Midnight in Sicily.* Potts Point, NSW: Duffy & Snellgrove.

U.S. Department of State (1996, April). Patterns of global terrorism, 1995. ⟨http://www.hri.org/docs/USSD-Terror/95/index.html⟩.

Walzer, M. (1978). *Just and unjust wars.* London: Allen Lane.

Wootton, D. (Ed.). (1993). *John Locke: Political writings.* Harmondsworth: Penguin.

THEORIES OF ETHICS, OVERVIEW

University of Manchester

GLOSSARY

contractarianism An ethical theory that centers ethics on a contract made between moral agents.

emotivism A view of ethics that claims that ethical propositions merely express feelings, and therefore are literally neither true nor false.

ethical naturalism The view that what humans *ought* to be in some sense follows from what they *are*.

intuitionism An ethical theory that claims that the truth of any ethical proposition does not admit of proof or disproof, but is rather to be "perceived" by moral intuition.

Kantianism An ethical theory based on the work of Kant (1724–1804), which says that actions should be chosen not for their consequences (as in utilitarianism) but for their intrinsic features—especially the feature of being part of a policy for action that could be followed on every occasion by an agent who is rational (in a special Kantian sense).

natural law ethics An ethical theory that bases ethics on claims about human nature.

religious ethics An ethical theory grounded on a religious view.

subjectivism The view that no ethical claims are authoritative, because none derive from authoritative viewpoints.

utilitarianism An ethical theory, the central conclusion of which is that agents should always act in a way calculated to bring about the best possible outcomes overall, where the goodness of any outcome depends on the amount of happiness realized in that outcome.

virtue ethics An ethical theory that says that the central concept for ethical theory is that of a virtue, a disposition needed for human excellence or flourishing.

A THEORY OF ETHICS is, in Bernard Williams' words, "A philosophical structure which, together with some degree of empirical fact, will yield a decision procedure for moral reasoning." In this article I shall survey, with reference to their historical development, a number of important examples of the types of moral theory that have been offered.

An important question about all such theories of ethics (and what concerns Williams as just quoted) is the question whether they are even possible. It is certainly a tall order to expect any moral theory to produce a decision procedure that comes anywhere near complete generality or specificity. Again, we do not (it might be said) think it possible to construct philosophical theories about just everything that matters to us. And it can be doubted whether philosophical theories are useful or helpful even where they seem possible. This is a doubt that may have particular resonance in applied ethics. It is not obvious that overworked and harassed doctors or famine relief workers even can make their decisions on the basis of an ethical theory. Still less is it obvious that they should do so. We should bear this sort of doubt in mind throughout what is said here.

Another thing to be borne in mind here is the distinction between an ethical theory's *conclusions* (the actual practical directions to the agent that the theory gives) and its *architecture* (the formal shape or structure of the philosophical view from which the conclusions emerge). In many ethical theories, the conclusions are actually meant to be *logically entailed* by some feature or features of the architecture: that is, in such theories the architecture cannot possibly be as it is *without* yielding the conclusions it does. Of course, weaker relations between a moral theory's architecture and its conclusions than logical entailment may also hold. But the weaker these relations are in a given theory of ethics, the more there arises an important doubt about that theory's coherence. If the theory's architecture does not actually entail its conclusions, then how important is it to accept that architecture? Alternatively, how much pressure can the theory put on us, given that we do approve of its architecture, to accept its conclusions too?

I. RELIGIOUS ETHICS

I begin my survey with the family of positions that bases ethical views upon religious views. These, the oldest ethical theories of all, typically take the form of lists of God-given commands. These commands are (normally) taken to be *laws*: absolute rules, which say to the agent not "Try to ..." or "be reluctant to ...", but "DO ..." or "DON'T ...". They are often of a very complex and specific nature, and often relate closely to ritual (or to what outsiders may consider mere taboos). One such code is summarized in the Ten Commandments shared by Judaism and Christianity, and the "Law" of which, in Judaism, the Ten Commandments are part. Another is the Islamic *shari'a*, which, like the "Law" of Judaism, is both a legal code and a moral system.

Religious theories of ethics may appear to be *just* unstructured and unexplained lists of ad hoc Thou

Shalts and Thou Shalt Nots, designed with nothing but brute practical expediencies in mind, and hence barely *theories* at all. That is, religious theories of ethics may seem strong on conclusions and weak on architecture. (Contrast much modern writing on philosophical ethics, which often has the most elegant and intricate architecture imaginable, but almost no obvious conclusions whatever!)

But of course religious ethical theories do characteristically have at least some architecture. What typically gives them their shape is their rather obvious fundamental requirement that humans should live in a way responsive to the nature of God. "For I am the LORD your God: ye shall therefore sanctify yourselves, and ye shall be holy; for I am holy" (Leviticus 11.44); "Your God is one God; submit then your wills to him" (The Qur'an, Sura 22 verse 34). In such systems the most important reason for "being moral" (as we would call it) is that one cannot be *holy*—acceptable to God—without being moral. A secondary reason, often also stressed, has to do with commemorating what God has done in the past: "the stranger that liveth with you ... thou shalt love him as thyself: for ye were strangers in the land of Egypt" (Leviticus 19.34). Here the Jews are enjoined to treat well the foreigners resident among them, not so much for the sake of the foreigners themselves, as for the sake of a remembrance of their own exile in Egypt, and of how their God delivered them from that exile.

All over the world today, religious ethical theories are vastly influential. Two leading tendencies of such views, which are both very important in applied ethics, are (i) toward invoking absolute rules in ethics, and (ii) toward an insistence on the sanctity or inviolability of human life. (I do not imply that either tendency is the exclusive property of religious ethics, could be justified only on religious grounds, or is even best justified on religious grounds.) However, any such approach faces four central problems.

First, it seems that no religious ethics can be any more credible than the religion it depends upon (although there might also be a converse relation: someone might find, e.g., Catholic ethical views so compelling that they were led to think that perhaps Catholicism itself might be true). At least in the West, many people reject all religions: it follows that they must either find some secular foundation for their ethical views, or else accept Dostoevsky's uncomfortable dictum that "If God does not exist, everything is permitted."

Second, if religious ethics is based upon the revelation of the will of God, then it is always possible for a dissenter from any religious ethical system either to question the sincerity of those who claim to have experienced the revelation, or else to claim—sincerely or otherwise—that *he* has experienced a different revelation, with different ethical consequences. As Locke notes in Book IV of the *Essay,* the notion of basing much ethics (or anything else) on religious experience seems wide open to abuse: "Every conceit that thoroughly warms our fancies must pass for an inspiration, if there be nothing but the strength of our persuasions whereby to judge of our persuasions."

Third, religious views about ethics are widely thought to face the *Euthyphro Dilemma.* This is a question first put by Plato: Is what is ethically good is good because God (or the gods) commands it? Or is it commanded by God because it is good?

The first horn of this dilemma presents an apparent impossibility: evidently, things can no more become good or bad *just because* God commands or prohibits them than odd numbers can become even just because I mistakenly include them on a list of even numbers. The other horn offers us an ethics in which God simply seems an unneeded middle term: if what is good is determined independently of God's commands, then we will not necessarily need God's commands to find out what is good. Moreover, it becomes possible to imagine that obeying God's commands might actually be *bad.*

A religious ethicist need not be stumped by the Euthyphro Dilemma if he believes both that God (a) created everything and (b) is the supreme being. It is significant that few ancient Greeks held both (a) and (b). (E.g., Plato himself believed (a) but not (b), whereas Aristotle believed (b) but not (a).) A religious ethicist who accepts both (a) and (b), as Christians, Jews, and Muslims all do, can get a different picture of the relation of God and ethics from that suggested by the Dilemma. First, he can say that because God is the supreme being, it makes no sense to suppose, as Plato does, that God is answerable to moral standards (or standards of any other sort, e.g., logical) outside and "above" God's own nature. For if there were any such standards, God would not be the supreme being: *they* would. The alleged conflict between "the requirements of morality" and "God's commands" disappears if these are just two names for one and the same thing. Second, he can say that because God made everything, God knows what is best for everything. God's commands are not then arbitrary impositions upon human nature. Rather they are "the maker's instructions," and as such perfectly consonant with what is best for human nature. So even when we have independent methods of getting at the truth about what is good and bad, such as the

appeal to human nature, still God (being infinitely cleverer than us) is infinitely better than we are at deploying that same appeal, and therefore infinitely better than we are at telling us what is good or bad for human nature.

If this reply to the Euthyphro Dilemma succeeds, it complicates the architecture of religious ethics in an interesting way—which brings us to the fourth problem about religious ethics. This is that the appeal to human nature makes it possible for us, for the first time, to question any system of religious ethics "from inside." Given that appeal, we can now question such a system not only by questioning the beliefs about God on which it rests, but also by questioning the connections that the system claims to make between God's commands and human nature. Thus, debate about human nature and what it requires has been central to the development of such highly sophisticated religious theories of ethics as the natural law ethics which has been developed by such Catholic writers as Aquinas and, to name two contemporaries, Finnis and Grisez.

II. NATURAL LAW

But if we have some grip on the notion of human nature, and of what is good for it, quite independently of any religious beliefs we may have, it also seems possible to use appeals to human nature not only to underwrite, but equally to undermine, the authority of any alleged divine command. Indeed, once we have both concepts—divine command and natural law—we may choose simply to drop reference to divine commands, and talk only about the requirements of (human) nature. Hence, the development of more or less thoroughly *nonreligious* accounts of natural law ethics.

Such theories were very popular in the ancient world. There are elements of such thinking in both Aristotle's and Plato's ethical writings, especially evident when they defend the notion of the human "function," which is how humans are by their nature "meant" to live. Again, the injunction to "follow nature" was a commonplace among the Stoics, and also with later writers such as Cicero whom they influenced. Something like an ethics of natural law is discernible, too, in such renaissance and enlightenment writers as Hobbes and Rousseau. A descendant of such views can even be found in Marx's thesis that capitalism is unjust because it entails a society in which most humans live lives that do not allow them to *express their true natures.*

Two central problems faced by any natural law theory of ethics, religious or not, are these: (1) Any natural law ethics rests on an account of human nature. But an account of human nature needs to be shown to be *true* before anything can be rested on it. How might we even begin this task? To establish data about human nature we need (so to speak) an uncontaminated sample of human nature. But where are we to find one of those? At this point the morasses of the "nature/nurture" debate threaten to engulf us. (2) Natural law ethics is a form of ethical naturalism—of the view that what humans *ought* to be in some sense follows from what they *are*. But as Hume famously noted, there is a logical gap between claims about what anything is and what it ought to be—the "Is/Ought gap". Anyone who believes in this gap is likely to think that *any* form of naturalism rests on a simple non sequitur.

I turn to consider two important ways in which a natural law theory can be developed into something else. The first of these is virtue theory.

III. VIRTUE THEORY

What turns natural law theory into virtue theory is the move from an account of human nature to an account of the virtues. This is the move from an account of what counts as a good human life, to an account of what a human character needs to be like to enjoy a good human life. Philippa Foot makes this move when she writes that "Human beings do not get on well without [the virtues]. Nobody can get on well if he lacks courage, and does not have some measure of temperance and wisdom, while communities where justice and charity are lacking are apt to be wretched places to live." Clearly, for Foot, the idea of a virtue is the idea of a character trait—a voluntary disposition that any human needs if he is to live a good life. (The opposite of a virtue is a vice.)

The most important virtues, in Foot's conception, are the five that she mentions in the last quotation. Other catalogues of virtues are found in Plato's and Aristotle's works (which often also include piety and friendship, but never include charity); in St. Paul's famous triad in *1 Corinthians* 13 (faith, hope, and charity); in Aquinas (who combines Aristotle's list with St. Paul's); and in the *Analects* of Confucius (dutifulness, loyalty, reciprocity, respect for parents and siblings, friendship, courtesy, unwillingness to deceive).

Suppose the virtue ethicist knows what the good life is from his account of human nature; and suppose he has an answer ready to the standard objections to any form of ethical naturalism. Still, such lists of virtues as these prompt several further questions. First question: how clear is it that exactly those dispositions on our

list are the ones needed for the good life? Part of the difficulty here is a worry about objectivity. There are obvious differences between the lists just given. Does that not suggest that what counts as the good life varies from one society to another? The other part of the difficulty concerns the causal effects of "other-regarding" virtues such as temperance, courage, charity and, above all, justice. It may be said that it is no help to *me* if *I* am just. What helps *me* to live a good life is *other people's* justice. Conversely, *my* justice helps *them* to live a good life. But then why do *I* have any reason to act justly *myself*? If it is a good life I am after, then what I have reason to do, apparently, is to try and get others to treat me as justly as possible consistently with myself treating them as *unjustly* as possible. But then we might as well call injustice a virtue as justice! This problem— the problem of egoism—was first raised, in different ways, by Plato's characters Thrasymachus (in Plato's *Republic*) and Callicles (in Plato's *Gorgias*). If the virtue ethicist is to answer it, he will have to do what Plato tries to do: give a clearer account of *the different ways* in which different virtues may contribute to a good human life.

Another problem raised by the attempt to catalogue the virtues concerns the virtues' relevance, or lack of it, to action. Suppose we do know, for example, that justice and courage are virtues. Still, how can that ever help us to decide what to *do*? Presumably, if justice and courage are virtues, and if a virtue is something that helps us to live well, then it follows that actions that are just or brave are actions that we have *some* reason to do. But *some* reason may not always be *enough* reason. For one thing, I may simply not *want* to be just or brave, and it is not yet clear why virtue ethics says I *must* be just or brave (or even must want to be). For another, how are we to *know* which actions are just or brave, and which are not? For a third, even if I do want to be just, and do know that some action is just, it may still be unclear that I should do it. Perhaps the action is not only just, but also harsh and uncharitable, as a stern punishment might be. Or perhaps it is not only brave, but also unjust, as a bank robbery might be. What is to stop one and the same action from being an example not only of some virtue, but also of some vice? These questions raise the classic problem of the unity of the virtues—the problem of whether or not we can always avoid acting against some virtue, and if so, how.

One way of answering these problems, first suggested by Plato's *Protagoras*, is to simplify the picture. Perhaps it would be easier to decide what to do in any situation if we said that there were not several virtues, but only one, and if we correspondingly found a single respect in which all possible actions could be compared. That way we would avoid the dilemmas of the agent who finds that of the two options A and B available to him, A is better in one respect (e.g., A is more courageous) but B is better in another respect (e.g., B is more just). For we would then be able to compare all options in the *same* respect; and so we would never be at a loss for a decision about what to do. To take this option would be to take advantage of a second important way in which a natural law theory can be developed into something else. This something else is utilitarianism, to which I therefore turn next.

IV. UTILITARIANISM

John Stuart Mill (1806–1873) is the most famous utilitarian writer, although he is by no means the most hard-line. (Indeed, he regarded himself as something of a revisionist, and his position vis à vis earlier utilitarians such as Bentham has been compared by John Skorupski to that of George Orwell vis à vis more traditional communists.) Mill wrote:

> "The creed which accepts as the foundation of morals, Utility, or the Greatest Happiness Principle, holds that actions are right in proportion as they tend to promote happiness, wrong as they tend to produce the reverse of happiness. By happiness is intended pleasure and the absence of pain; by unhappiness, pain and the privation of pleasure" (Mill: *Utilitarianism*, Chap. 2).

This passage clearly reveals classical utilitarianism's architecture. It consists in the conjunction of three theses: (1) maximalism, the view that it is always wrong to fail to do the best thing available; (2) welfarism, the view that what is good is pleasure, or happiness, or utility, or welfare (as it has variously been called); and (3) consequentialism, the view that the comparative goodness of any option we may consider depends exclusively on the comparative goodness of the *consequences* of choosing that option over others. (There are other ways of using "consequentialism"—but I shall consistently use it in the sense just defined.)

Utilitarianism's ancestral commitment to ethical naturalism comes out most clearly in (2), its welfarism, which I will therefore look at first. Mill famously claimed to prove that "pleasure and freedom from pain," or (equivalently, as he thought) "the general happiness," was the sole good—the only thing desirable in itself. He did this by arguing first that this sole good (which

for ease of reference I shall just call "happiness") was desired, and second that nothing else was desired but happiness. The first move has been criticized as a breach of the Is/Ought gap (cp. Section II), and also an equivocation about "desirable." The premise "Happiness is *desired*" entails the conclusion that "Happiness is *desirable*" only if "desirable" means "capable of being desired," and not if it means "such as *ought to be* desired." But Mill, it is said, wants it to mean the latter. So his argument fails.

However, Mill's argument is not this simple fallacy. Rather, as his much-criticized parallel with "visible" in fact suggests, he needs "desirable" to mean only "capable of being desired." His point is that the notion of happiness, or any good, is centrally the notion of something that people actually do want—just as the notion of a visible thing is centrally the notion of a thing that people actually do see. But people want happiness; therefore, happiness is good. Moreover, because "the ingredients of happiness are very various, and each of them is desirable in itself, [and not merely] as means to a collective something termed happiness," it can also be allowed that the *only* thing desired is happiness (in one form or another). Therefore, happiness is the only good. This establishes the second step of Mill's proof.

It is this second step that ought to attract the criticism, not (as usually happens) the first. Mill's argument for this runs the risk of making (2) a vacuous thesis. It looked at first as if the utilitarian thesis that nothing but happiness is desired was a daringly exclusive thesis—as if Mill was committed to saying that all sorts of things that are *apparently* desired by people, actually are not, and that in fact all people desire is happiness. Certainly (2) had had this exclusive character in earlier formulations, such as Bentham's, which denied that anything was pursued or good except for pleasure in a radically restricted sense—pleasure as meaning only certain sorts of internal sensations. By contrast, in Mill's version it is not clear that *anything* is excluded by claiming that happiness is the only thing that people desire. On Mill's account the ingredients of happiness are *so* various that Mill's version of (2) seems to come only to the thesis that "Happiness is whatever people desire; and people desire whatever they do desire." This claim may be irrefutably true, but it does not give us what, above all, the utilitarian's account of the good was meant to give: namely, one clear, measurable standard of comparison by which to rank the goodness or badness of all options. Contrast again Bentham's version of (2), which evidently does or at least could give us such a standard, but unfortunately suffers from a different defect, that of patent falsity.

Here we see the emergence of a dilemma that continues to haunt writers working in the utilitarian tradition. Many different utilitarian accounts of happiness/utility/welfare have now been offered, many of them far away from the ethical–naturalist roots from which utilitarianism first sprang. The abiding dilemma of such accounts of the good is this: that insofar as they are plausible, they tend not to make the good amenable to measurement, whereas insofar as they make the good amenable to measurement, they tend not to be plausible.

This dilemma suggests that, for the utilitarian, the problem of *measuring* the good is the deepest problem of all. Certainly that problem has a crucial bearing on the other two aspects of utilitarianism identified above, (1) its maximalism, and (3) its consequentialism. If the idea of measuring the good does not make sense, then (3) neither will the idea of measuring the goodness of *consequences* make sense, because this is just a specific way of measuring the good. Again, if the idea of measuring the good does not make sense, then (1) there will not always *be* a "best thing to do"—in which case maximalism too must be not merely false, but senseless.

In any case other problems face both (1) and (3), even if we can deal with the basic difficulty about measurement. Defenders of (1) will still need to define a coherent strategy for maximizing the good. They face two particularly pressing questions. (i) Should we be act utilitarians, and base our choices purely on the direct assessment of utility given by looking at the goodness of the consequences of individual acts? Or rule utilitarians, basing our choices on the indirect assessment of utility given by looking at the cost/benefit balance of there being certain rules that are generally accepted? (ii) Is it our objective to raise people's *average* or *total* happiness? As for (3), its defenders will need to find a coherent way of characterizing the distinction between an option and its consequences, which may be harder to do than it sounds. Again, both (1) and (3) will have to meet the objection that they make impossible or unrealistic demands on agents. It seems natural to think that there are actions that are "above and beyond the call of duty"; but there are not if (unmodified) utilitarianism is correct.

This should give some idea of the architecture of utilitarianism—and of how complex it is, and of how many possible variations there are on the utilitarian theme. It may also help to make apparent how many different sorts of conclusions are possible within a broadly utilitarian framework. It is not too much to say that something like utilitarianism could be used to justify pretty well any conclusion—although in applied ethics, utilitarianism is typically employed to support

revisionist opposition to the typical emphases of religious ethicists and other (relative) conservatives on the sanctity of life and on absolute or near-absolute rules. Whether this use of utilitarianism to support such conclusions is inevitable given utilitarianism's architecture, I leave to the reader for the moment. For now it is time to look at another sort of theory of ethics: Kantianism.

V. KANTIANISM

From earlier theories of ethics such as the natural law theory, classical utilitarianism took over ethical naturalism, but dropped almost everything else. In later formulations, utilitarianism sometimes drops its ethical naturalism too, because, to put it crudely, wants have come to be thought less problematic than needs. Many utilitarians have thought that they are less philosophically exposed if they talk about preferences than about happiness. Partly they have thought this because of the difficulty of deriving an account of happiness that makes it measurable (in contrast, preferences can (usually) at least be *ordered*). Two other reasons for the shift, however, have come from the two general criticisms of any form of ethical naturalism mentioned at the end of Section II—the subjectivist point that we have no "uncontaminated sample" of human nature on which to base our ethical–naturalist ambitions, and the Humean doctrine of the "Is/Ought gap." Both criticisms are taken up by Kant.

Kant is not a subjectivist, although he is a believer in the Is/Ought gap. Indeed, Kant is a believer in that gap precisely because he is not a subjectivist. Kant thinks that there are so many possible ways of moving from claims about nature to claims about ethics that there is no hope of arriving at a naturalism that is both unconfused and untainted by the particularities of our own historical position. Again, Kant believes that his rejection of ethical naturalism entails the rejection of utilitarianism. This is not just because all the forms of utilitarianism that Kant knew of began with some sort of account of human nature. It is also because the commonplace modern utilitarian claim to have avoided giving any such account even implicitly, by talking only about preferences and not also about needs, would have been disputed by Kant. For Kant, to talk about an agent's preferences *is* to make claims about nature.

Kant believes that ethics has to start elsewhere. Where he thinks ethics should start is with his own famous notion of pure reason—that is, with the notion of what reason itself demands, apart from any particular conditions that may be occupied by someone who is open to reason (some rational agent). Thus, Kant construes the basic ethical question "What should we do?" as a question, not so much about what sorts of desires we may have or what sort of consequences we may foresee, as a question about what it would be like for there to be a purely rational agent or a fully rational action. Kant's answer says that any action is fully rational if and only if it is true of the action that the agent can will to do it without necessarily producing an inconsistency in his willing—a contradiction between two things, both of which he wills. Kant takes it that there are some things that any rational agent is bound to will just because he is a rational agent. In particular, he is bound to will that all rational agents, including himself but not especially himself, should have the same opportunities for making choices without being interfered with or dominated by others (autonomous willing). This "egalitarian" requirement on practical rationality is absolutely fundamental for Kant. As Kant himself says, policies for action ("maxims," as Kant calls them) must be chosen "as if they had to hold as universal laws of nature.... [Any] rational being, as by his very nature an end and consequently an end in himself, must serve for every maxim as a condition limiting all merely relative and arbitrary ends" (v. Paton, *The Moral Law* p. 98). But clearly some actions or maxims can be willed that will prevent, or tend to prevent, this equality of opportunity for rational agents from being achieved. In Kant's view, the rational agent who wills actions which tend in this direction of preventing autonomous willing must also, and at the same time, be willing whatever tends in the opposite direction (just because he is a rational agent). Therefore, any such agent is guilty of practical irrationality. For his policy or maxim is not *universalisable*: it contradicts itself.

Kant's ethics of reason in action has a pleasing simplicity and coherence to its architecture. The question of what practical conclusions Kant's ethics leads to is a less simple question, and has received much less coherent answers. This is partly because of a persistent misunderstanding of Kant. As we have just seen, the morally decisive question for Kant is "What can I rationally will?" Again and again, this question has been taken to be equivalent to "What can I rationally *want*?" It has then been objected to Kant, on broadly Humean grounds, that there are no rational limitations on what I can want that could possibly provide us with a fully determinate moral theory. But Kant simply accepts this Humean thesis. (It is a different question whether he should accept it.) Kant also agrees with the critic that Hume's thesis shows that wanting cannot be made the basis of any moral theory that is not hopelessly underde-

termined both in its architecture and its conclusions. But all this proves is that Kant is a nonnaturalist, and that for him *wanting* and *willing* are radically distinct. Only the latter term can be used to describe the operations of pure reason made practical—operations that are of a quite different order from the operations of mere wants and preferences, which need not be rational at all. For Kant, the difference here is a difference between the *objectively* and the *subjectively* motivating. It is a difference between what just happens to motivate some particular agent, and what must necessarily motivate any agent at all, insofar as that agent is rational.

However, even when this persistent misunderstanding is removed, it is still hard to see exactly what conclusions follow from the architecture of Kant's theory. Kant's doctrine of reason in action gives us a "Universalizability Test"—a rule for choosing morally acceptable maxims for action. This rule says that we should not choose to act on maxims that we cannot consistently will should be used by just any rational agent. But which maxims are excluded by this test? Here we face problems about defining two terms in the rule, "maxim" and "consistent."

The problem about "maxim" is just that it is not at all obvious that we will always be able to say what the maxim of a given action is. I said above that Kant's "maxims" are policies for action. In the words of Onora O'Neill: "Maxims are those underlying principles or intentions by which we guide and control our more specific intentions." But then how "underlying" does a principle or intention have to be to count as a maxim? How determinate is it what policy I am acting upon when I, say, accept an offer to write an encyclopedia article on ethics? I do not just mean by this question that others may not know whether I accept the commission (for example) because I want to bring about the flourishing of philosophy, or for the sake of self-aggrandizement. Nor do I just mean that I myself may not be entirely clear about my own underlying motivations. Both of these are certainly points that Kant would have had to accept, given his anti-Cartesian belief that the self is not transparently self-aware of all its own beliefs and volitions. But there is a further and more fundamental problem. The problem is not only that my real maxims may be obscure because we cannot find out what they are. It is also that there may be nothing to find out. It may be that, in truth, my action *has* no determinate maxim: or alternatively, if it has any maxim, it may be equally plausible to say that it has more than one maxim.

The problem about "consistency" is twofold. First, Kant seems to be committed to some rather implausible claims about what an agent *must* will to count as a rational agent. But without these implausible claims, he has (in his own terms) no way of showing that certain sorts of action are immoral, as he believes them to be. For example, Kant wishes to say that suicide is immoral. (In general, the conclusions for applied ethics that Kant draws from his architecture are strikingly conservative, and surprisingly close to what contemporary religious accounts of ethics yielded. It seems to have been a deep concern of his *not* to appear too radical in his ethical conclusions, despite his obviously radical architecture.) But to say that suicide is immoral, Kant has, by his own account, to show that suicide necessarily involves an inconsistency of willing. This apparently leads him to suggest that the inconsistent willing involved in suicide is willing not to will anymore. But for one thing, it is not an inconsistent piece of willing to will not to will anymore—any more than it is an inconsistent piece of typing to type the words "I shall type no more words." For another, if it *was* inconsistent to will not to will anymore, then the consistent agent would always have to will to go on willing. That is, every agent would always have to seek to go on willing as long as possible, on pain of inconsistency. But this would not only mean that no agent could rationally commit suicide. It would also mean that every agent was always obliged to seek to prolong his life as long as possible. Kantian presuppositions aside, it is not at all clear why we should think that agents are obliged to do this.

That point brings us to the second part of the problem about "consistency," which is that Kant's distinction between practical consistency and inconsistency does not always seem to have much to do with the pretheoretical distinction between the moral and the immoral. Offhand it is not obvious that I cannot agree that an action embodies a perfectly consistent piece of rational willing—and yet deny that that action is morally acceptable. Nor, conversely, is it obvious that I cannot agree with Kant that the maxim of some action is nowhere near being universalizable—and yet insist that that action is nonetheless morally permissible or even morally mandatory. For example, if I dropped Kant's special claims about what rational willing necessarily involves, I might see nothing inconsistent in a will that every rational being should commit suicide—and yet still think it a bad thing that that should happen. Or, again, I might agree with Kant's explicit claim that telling lies always means doing something that no one could rationally will everyone to do all the time—and yet deny Kant's claim that this fact gives us sufficient reason never to tell a lie no matter what.

VI. CONTRACTARIANISM

Our story so far is the story of how from the ethics of divine command there have developed two different sorts of ethical naturalism—virtue ethics and classical utilitarianism. I have also noted how the denial of ethical naturalism has led to Kantianism, with its appeal to "pure practical reason" replacing any appeal to "human nature." Again, I have pointed out that a utilitarianism can also be formulated that does not depend, as the classical versions of the theory do, on the truth of naturalism. At this point it is worth noting briefly the possibility of combining a version of (usually) nonnaturalistic utilitarianism with some of the elements of an adapted Kantianism, to give a different kind of theory from traditional versions of either, called contractarianism.

As the name suggests, the central idea of contractarianism is that of a contract. So, for instance, in Rawls's *Theory of Justice,* the big idea is that the institutions of morality, and in particular of justice, can be explained by supposing (or just pretending) that they rest on a society-founding agreement made between all agents about how to live together. These agents' task, therefore, is to arrive at a set of rules for society to which every member of that society shall be able to assent. It is supposed that each agent, presented with this task, will arrive, by neutral reasoning which abstracts away from his or her own particular circumstances (e.g., whether "he" is a he or she), at the same recipe for a society. This society which all such agents arrive at is, therefore, the just society.

In some ways, contractarian theories like Rawls's are obviously reminiscent of Kantianism. In particular, the supposition of ideally rational agents, who are abstracted from and so not influenced by any of their particular circumstances, and who are meant, each of them, to arrive at a set of rules and other social arrangements that any other agent like themselves will be able to accept, is obviously reminiscent of Kant's notion of moral laws as "universalizable," and of rational individuals as makers of "universal moral law." On the other hand, it is worth noting that contractarianism can also be seen as a sort of rule utilitarianism, especially if it is thought (as it is, for instance, by David Gauthier) that the individual agent's *motivation* for accepting the social contract rests upon the fact that the social contract is by definition that set of rules and other social arrangements which maximizes each individual's utility benefit. However, contractarians typically deny that they are utilitarians of any sort; and the contractarian differs from the Kantian because he is not committed to drawing any strong distinction between willing and wanting. Contractarian rationality can, like utilitarian rationality, be purely instrumental—purely concerned with the means to whatever ends one happens to have. Hence, it need have no connection whatever with any objective account of the good. (Thus, Gauthier is explicitly interested only in agents' actual preferences, although Rawls is closer to objectivity and indeed to ethical naturalism.)

If contractarianism really is a sort of halfway house between Kantianism and (rule) utilitarianism, we may expect it to face some of the same problems as both those theories. And so it proves. Like the Kantian, the contractarian has to explain how such ideally rational agents as he posits are even possible. Does it really make sense to talk of abstracting rationality from every particular circumstance of life in the way that contractarians imagine? Again, most contractarians are consequentialists, like utilitarians: they therefore face the problems about consequentialism noted in Section IV, and in particular the problem of defining the good.

Third, all forms of contractarianism face the objection that they deal only with a fragment and not the whole of morality, namely only justice (cp. the title of Rawls's book). And fourth, *consequentialist* contractarianism faces a peculiar difficulty which is all its own (though rule utilitarianism faces a somewhat analogous difficulty, and cp. the problem about justice which has been raised for virtue ethics). Consider the Prisoners' Dilemma. A and B are in prison and under pressure to confess. Both know the following facts. If both confess, both will stay in prison for 5 years; if one confesses and the other does not, the one who confesses will get 30 years and the one who does not will go free; if neither confesses, both will stay in prison for 20 years.

What should either agent, say A, do? A nonconsequentialist contractarian, like Rawls, can give a virtually Kantian answer. A should ask himself "What would I like to happen if I did not know whether I was A or B?" and choose in accordance with his answer to that question (presumably choosing to confess on the assumption that B will choose the same). What about a consequentialist contractarian, like Gauthier? He must say that if A considers only his *own* interest, as consequentialist-contractarian agents are normally supposed to do, A will see that the best outcome for *himself* is that B should confess while A does not. That means that B gets 30 years, but it also means that A goes free. But then, by the same token, it is predictable that B will reason the same way as A. So both will refuse to confess; so both get 20 years. Therefore A would have served his own interests better to make a contract with

B that both shall confess, so that each of them gets only 5 years in prison. So that is the course which *enlightened* self-interest recommends: which goes to show that it really is in our interest to be moral, in just the sense identified by contractarianism.

The trouble is that it is still true that A would have done better yet to get B to confess without confessing himself. And we can now add that a good way for A to achieving this seems to be for A to *pretend* to make a contract with B that both should confess. Of course, once more it may be pointed out that this line of reasoning can also be employed by B, giving us again the result that both A and B spend more time in prison than they would have had they stuck to their contract. But this does not really solve the problem, because it is quite possible for both A and B to go round the little loop of reasoning just described a third time, and a fourth, and a fifth. The essence of the problem posed by the Prisoner's Dilemma is that while I have an incentive to persuade other agents to conform to my own expectations on *every* occasion, there are at least *some* occasions, like the ones just described, on which I have a strong incentive *not* to conform to *their* expectations. Hence, it seems that, for a consequentialist, the mere existence of contracts between agents itself provides those agents with no reason at all to keep those contracts. The fact that I have a contract with you can just as well be a reason for me to break it as keep it: it all depends on my expectations about what *you* will do. This conclusion seems to undermine the claim of consequentialist contractarianism to show that the demands of morality are coextensive with those of enlightened self-interest.

VII. INTUITIONISM

I have considered contractarianism as a kind of hybrid theory developed from utilitarianism and Kantianism. Another interesting line of development from Kant occurred when ethicists abandoned Kant's positive doctrine, his notion that "pure practical rationality" could yield a substantive and meaningful Universalizability Test, but held on to his negative doctrine—the nonnaturalism that made Kant's appeal to pure practical reason seem so cogent (at least to Kantians). It came to seem to many that Kant's apparent failure to establish an ethics of pure practical reason had simply vindicated Hume's insistence on two points. The first Humean claim, which Kant the rationalist did not accept, was that ethics was not based upon anything like rationality. The second, which Kant the nonnaturalist did accept, was that the way in which we understand and appropriate ethical claims is radically different from the way in which we take on board any other sort of claims.

Once this position was reached, the stage was set for the development of a new ethical position—intuitionism. The intuitionist, accepting that ethics is not based upon rationality, bases ethics instead upon a special mode of apprehending moral claims, often referred to in the literature as "intuition." Thus, G. E. Moore, one of the main proponents of intuitionism, speaks in his *Principia Ethica* of "good" as a "simple indefinable quality," or again as a "simple, indefinable, unanalyzable object of thought," which we become aware of in something analogous to the way in which we become aware of yellow—by simple perception of it. Again, W. D. Ross bases ethical thought upon "the apprehension of the self-evident prime facie rightness of an individual act of a particular type" (Ross, *The Right and the Good*). More recently, and with specific reference to medical ethics, Beauchamp and Childress have developed a theory of ethics based upon four basic principles (autonomy, nonmaleficence, beneficence, and justice) that often seem to be regarded by them as both themselves the objects of moral intuition, and themselves the sources of further intuitions.

Notice that, for the intuitionist, ethics has become once more a rather simple business. Indeed, ethics seems a simpler business for the intuitionist than it has been for any ethicist in the history of the development of ethics traced here since the divine command ethicist. For the intuitionist ethics becomes, simply, the business of *seeing* what is good and bad, right and wrong, perhaps under certain further descriptions. Moreover, the intuitionist's focus is clearly on the individual action, not upon action-types. This is patently obvious given Ross's explicit insistence that it is the right- or wrong-making features of individual acts that we have to consider first. (Cp. his remark in *The Foundations of Ethics* that "It will not do to make our perception of particular duties essentially inferences from general principles.") The intuitionist focus on particular acts is also clearly a consequence of Moore's doctrine that "good" is indefinable. If that is so, then even if it is possible to argue that some individual action must be good or bad, right or wrong, just because it belongs to some action-type, this method of argument will still, for the Moorean intuitionist, prove what is more obvious by way of what is less obvious.

It is evident, then, that intuitionism is strong on conclusions but somewhat thin on architecture. This is very obviously true of Moore's ethics, in the application of which, as J. M. Keynes reported in his memoir *My Early Beliefs,* "Moore's disciples . . . would compare alternative possible situations and solemnly inquire in which there was most good, inspecting each in turn . . . and then announcing what they 'saw.' " Less obviously, it is also true of Ross's version of the theory. There is more architecture to Ross's intuitionism than to Moore's, because Ross's theory does not include only "apprehensions" of "self-evident prima facie rightnesses," but also the necessity of arriving at verdicts about *actual* rightnesses and wrongnesses by assessing and comparing our prima facie apprehensions. However, the apparently greater sophistication of Ross's theory at this point in fact only hides a second form of appeal to intuition. For this assessing and comparing of prima facie apprehensions of which he speaks is itself performed by a (second?) sort of intuition.

Moreover, the thinness of intuitionism's architecture leaves it theoretically exposed to an obvious objection, parallel to the second objection we brought against divine command theories of ethics. Anyone can question any alleged revelation of God's will if they find its ethical implications unpalatable. Likewise, it is always possible that anyone who claims to be intuiting the Moorean nonnatural quality of goodness, or experiencing Rossian apprehensions of rightness (whether prima facie or actual), is simply *wrong*—or (worse) insincere. Again, just as alleged revelations of God's will have an unsettling tendency to win their converts by merely rhetorical force (or more bluntly still, by physical force), so likewise there is always a danger in intuitionism of the tendency that Keynes diagnoses among the Mooreans: "In practice, victory was with those who could speak with the greatest appearance of clear, undoubting conviction, and could best use the accents of infallibility."

Neither Moore's intuitionism nor Ross's has any clear answer to the plausible charge that intuitionism elevates the mere expression of its proponents' own preferences or feelings to the status of invincible moral truths. (The same objection has been made to a more recent ethical theory developed from intuitionism by Jonathan Dancy, John McDowell, and others, sometimes called particularism.) Indeed, not only is it, apparently, a matter of fact that intuitionism cannot answer this charge. Intuitionism's own presupposition that there is no more at the basis of moral theory than intuition seems to make that charge *necessarily* unanswerable for the intuitionist. This may be why, historically, intuitionism has so often paved the way for complete scepticism about ethical theory, of the emotivist sort.

Emotivism is the view that any sort of ethical claim has nothing more than an exclamatory or expressive function. To say that "stealing is wrong" is not to pick out a fact, in the way that we pick out a fact if we say that "stealing is a transgression of the laws of England." Rather it is to express our disapproval of stealing, just as if we were to say "Stealing—pah!"

As we have seen, it is not difficult to imagine how emotivism can come to seem plausible if the view of ethics that we are opposing is an intuitionist one. Indeed, there are at least two occasions in the history of ethics where just such a move from intuitionism to something like emotivism has occurred. The first is Hume's critique of writers like Hutcheson in the eighteenth century, and the second is the move from Moore and Ross to Ayer and Stevenson in the twentieth century. But what we should also note about emotivism is the way in which (despite the claims to the contrary of some recent sophisticated proponents of theories significantly like emotivism, e.g., Blackburn and Mackie) it simply abolishes ethical theory as a subject. If all we can do in ethics is to evince or express our feelings about things, that seems to do away with all hope of ethical argument. Ethical debate will be a matter, not of convincing others that they are wrong, but of getting them to feel the same way as we do. If this is the right way to see ethics, then not only is there no room in ethical theory for architecture: there is not really any room for conclusions either, if those are taken to be objective truths which just anyone ought to agree to.

VIII. CONCLUSIONS

I have attempted, in this article, to outline the variety of ethical theories in existence by tracing a historical line of development, from divine command systems of ethics, through natural law ethics, naturalistic ethics such as utilitarianism and virtue theory, and nonnaturalistic ethics such as Kantianis, contractarianism, and intuitionism, to the collapse of ethical theory represented by emotivism. It should not, of course, be thought that the tracing of this line of development in the story I have told is supposed to have any implications about which of these kinds of theory is the most "advanced," or "up-to-date"—and hence (?) the truest. The story I have told does show what philosophical fashion has, at different times, tended to say is the most "advanced" way to do ethical theory. But my story also shows how much philosophical fashion can change—

and hence how unreliable an indicator of philosophical truth it can be.

I have also tried to give some indication of the relationship in all such theories between their architecture and their conclusions; and to keep in the picture a general doubt about whether ethical theories are what we want anyway. One form that that doubt can take is displayed vividly enough by emotivism; another is arrived at by pushing the question of whether *any* ethical theory's architecture can really be sufficient, on its own, to issue in the conclusions that it is supposed to issue in. Other forms of doubt about ethical theory—having to do with such issues as the alleged overdemandingness or inflexibility of ethical theory, its lack of responsiveness to the moral sentiments or "Real Life," or the question whether there are really any such thing as specially *moral* demands on agents—I must, for lack of space, leave to the reader's exploration.

Also See the Following Articles

APPLIED ETHICS, OVERVIEW • RELIGION AND ETHICS

Bibliography

(Unless editions of works are specified, it may be assumed that many editions are available.)

For general introductions to moral philosophy, see
Bernard Williams (1972). *Morality: An introduction to ethics*. Cambridge: Cambridge University Press.
J. L. Mackie (1977). *Ethics: inventing right and wrong*. Penguin.

The Williams quotation with which I begin is from
Williams, *Moral luck* (1981). Cambridge: Cambridge University Press. (Collected essays: harder going than [1], but also a possible way in.)

Three classic sources of religious ethics are
The Bible.
The Qur'an.
Aquinas, *Summa Theologiae*.

For a critique of religious ethics, see
Plato, *Republic*, especially Books 2, 3, and 10.

The Euthyphro Dilemma is first stated in
Plato, *Euthyphro*, pp. 6–11.

Examples of natural law ethics are,
Grisez. (1983/1993). *The way of the Lord Jesus*. Franciscan Herald Press.
Finnis. (1983). *Fundamentals of ethics*. Oxford: Oxford University Press.

For some developments of secularized natural law theories, see
Aristotle, *Nicomachean ethics*.
Cicero, *de Officiis*.

For the examination of this sort of theory there is also much of interest in

Hobbes, *Leviathan.*
Rousseau, *Emile.*

The doctrine of the Is/Ought gap is first propounded in
Hume, *Treatise of human nature,* 3.1.1.

For virtue ethics, see
Foot. (1978). *Virtues and vices.* Blackwell.
Hursthouse.(1991). Virtue theory and abortion. In *Philosophy and public affairs.*
Plato, *Protagoras.*
Plato, *Gorgias.*

The problems that Thrasymachus and Callicles pose for virtue ethics are discussed in
T. D. J. Chappell. (1993). The virtues of Thrasymachus. *Phronesis.*

Classic statements of utilitarianism are found in
Bentham, *Introduction to the principles of morals and legislation,*
Mill, *Utilitarianism.*

For a study of Mill, see
Skorupski. (1989). *The arguments of the philosophers: Mill.* Routledge.

There is a lively discussion of utilitarianism's merits and demerits in
Williams & Smart. (1973). *Utilitarianism: for and against.* Cambridge: Cambridge University Press.

Kant's moral theory is most clearly presented in
Kant (ed. Paton). (1986). *The moral law.* Hutchinson.

It is defended and extended in
O'Neill. (1989). *Constructions of reason.* Cambridge: Cambridge University Press.

Modern contractarianism with a Kantian flavor is clearly expounded by
Rawls. (1972). *A theory of justice.* Oxford: Oxford University Press.

The consequentialist version, with an extended discussion of the Prisoner's Dilemma and related problems, is best seen in
Gauthier. (1986). *Morals by agreement.* Oxford: Oxford University Press.

Intuitionism in its modern form begins with
Moore. (1993). *Principia ethica,* ed. Baldwin. Cambridge: Cambridge University Press.
Ross, (1930). *The right and the good.* Oxford University Press.
Ross, (1939). *The Foundations of Ethics.* Oxford: Oxford University Press.

More recent defences of intuitionism include
McDowell. (1979). Virtue and Reason, *The monist,* and Dancy. (1993). *Moral reasons.* Blackwell.

A sort of intuitionism is applied to medical ethics by
Beauchamp & Childress. (1983). *Principles of Biomedical Ethics* (2nd. ed.). Oxford: Oxford University Press.

Intuitionism of various kinds also flourished in the eighteenth century. See, for example,
Hutcheson. (1969). *A System of moral philosophy.* In Hutcheson's *Collected works.* Hildesheim: George Olms.

Intuitionism has regularly been attacked by emotivists or expressivists such as Mackie and Hume: see also
Ayer. (1936). *Language, truth and logic,* Ch. 6. Gollancz.
Stevenson. (1963). *Facts and values.* New Haven: Yale University Press.
Blackburn. (1984). *Spreading the word* (Chs. 5–6). Oxford: Oxford University Press.

THEORIES OF JUSTICE: HUMAN NEEDS

Clark Wolf
University of Georgia

GLOSSARY

adventitious needs Needs that are not basic. An agent will not be harmed merely because adventitious needs are not satisfied.

basic minimum principle A weaker alternative to Rawls' Difference Principle, which stipulates that a basic minimum of welfare support must be universally provided so that people's basic needs will be satisfied, but that beyond the provision of this minimum, people are responsible for their own welfare.

basic needs (or "course-of-life needs") Those needs satisfaction of which is necessary for the most basic and fundamental activities involved in living a human life. Satisfaction of the basic needs is essential for living or functioning normally such that if a person's basic needs are not satisfied, she or he will consequently suffer harm.

conception of the good A more or less completely articulated account of what is of value.

contractarianism The view that principles of justice are those principles we would choose as the object of a fair agreement or contract.

difference principle A principle in John Rawls' conception of justice as fairness, which stipulates that social and economic inequalities must be arranged so that they are to the greatest benefit of the least advantaged members of society.

needs A necessary requirement for the achievement of some end. An agent A needs a good G if, and only if, possession of G is necessary for the achievement of one of A's ends.

plural specification The condition that for any purportedly universal account of basic need, it must be possible to specify how different goods might be necessary for the satisfaction of these needs in different social or cultural settings.

primary goods John Rawls' list of goods regarded as the necessary requirements for the formulation, critical revision, and pursuit of any reasonable conception of the good.

MANY SOCIAL THEORIES employ a concept of need as one of the central ideas involved in a full account of justice. For some theories of justice, the goal of need satisfaction has highest priority among legitimate social aims, while others place no weight at all on this goal. This article reviews the concept of need and its role in theories of justice. Section I identifies central features that are characteristic of needs, and that serve to distinguish basic needs from merely adventitious needs, desires, values, and preferences. The notion that human needs are universal, and that appeal to common needs might undermine ethical relativism is explored in Section II. Section III examines a collection of theories of need, and Section IV reviews the role played by "need" in some of the most important contemporary theories of justice.

I. ANALYZING THE CONCEPT OF NEED

A. The General Concept of Need

The concept of "need" is essentially instrumental: in general, an agent A needs a good G just in case possession of G is a necessary condition for the achievement of some end that is desired by A or would in some sense be good for A. Thus, when something is needed, it should be possible to say what end it is needed for, or what goal cannot be achieved without it. In this general and rather weak sense of need, people's needs are many and some are trivial: in this sense, one person may need heroin to satisfy an addiction, another may need 6 million dollars to purchase a palatial resort in the tropics, and yet another may need cleverness and stealth to commit a heinous murder. No special moral priority is associated with this general sense of the term need, for some projects are extravagant and some aims are not worth achieving.

B. Basic Needs

If aims can be ranked according to their relative importance, some general needs may be judged more significant than others. For example, a child's need for education, adequate nutrition, and shelter should clearly be considered to have greater moral urgency than a bored suburbanite's need for amusement. A ranking of general needs depends on a ranking of projects and aims in terms of their significance, their moral permissibility, their urgency, and perhaps other properties as well. The *basic needs,* or *course-of-life* needs are the things that are necessary for the most fundamental projects involved in living a human life, and which are essential to living or to functioning normally. This is what distinguishes needs that are *basic* from nonbasic needs, desires, values, and preferences, which need not be associated with normal functioning in the same way. In addition, it is often regarded as essential or criteriological of the concept of basic need that it is associated with the concept of harm, such that if one's basic needs are not satisfied, one will be harmed in some crucial or fundamental way. Less urgent needs, which are not

associated with harm in this way are often called "adventitious needs." If, as seems likely, some circumstances and misfortunes are universally harmful or catastrophic for those who experience them, there will be corresponding universality in the theory of basic needs. If there are some projects and aims that are universally urgent, then perhaps the needs associated with them are also basic and universal.

C. A Criterion for Identifying the Basic Needs

Virtually all theories of basic needs identify the necessary conditions for life and health as basic. But other needs are also thought to have the high priority of basic needs. In his well-known work on meeting needs, David Braybrooke offers a richer criterion for the identification of basic needs as follows:

> Basic needs are those things that are "indispensable to mind or body in performing the tasks assigned a given person under a combination of basic social roles, namely, the roles of parent, householder, worker, and citizen." Braybrooke further stipulates that "If what is thus indispensable is not supplied, the person's functioning in these tasks is deranged," where derangement is understood to include sheer incapacity (for want, say, of strength or skill). Something is "indispensable" in the relevant sense just in case every member of the population in question will find it indispensable (at least in the way of a rebuttable presumption) at some time in the course of life (Braybrooke, D. (1987). *Meeting Needs,* p. 48. Princeton: Princeton University Press).

Even given a rigorous criterion like Braybrooke's, it is difficult to explain just which needs are basic, and even to justify the claim that basic needs should always take precedence over adventitious needs, or over mere preferences and desires. If a crippled musician needs a wheelchair, but would prefer a new violin instead, who are we to tell her that her need has priority over her "mere preference?" Further, most of the fundamental projects involved in human lives are in some measure *social* projects, and the things people need to achieve the aims associated with these projects are quite different depending on the culture in which they live. For example, if the opportunity for sexual reproduction is fundamental to the role of "parent," the indispensable requirements for achieving and performing this role will obviously be quite different in different social circumstances, and will essentially depend on the free participation of other people. For example, the things needed to attract a mate will differ greatly between one person in New York City and another in the Ituri Forest in central Africa.

It is sometimes argued that no human needs are truly universal, and that any attempt to give an account of what other people need will be potentially oppressive because such an account could be used as ground for criticizing the practices of other cultures. Those who defend the notion that some needs are universal have usually made this case on the basis of one of three kinds of argument: (i). It is sometimes argued that the common limitations of human nature imply that we have some basic needs in common. (ii). Others argue that some *goods* are necessary for the pursuit of a wide variety of human projects or the achievement of any conception (or any reasonable conception) of the good. (iii). Still others argue that some capabilities and functions are essential features of a human life, or of a good human life, and that there are universal basic needs for whatever is necessary for the expression of these capabilities and functions. The following section examines the problems associated with the social variability of needs, and the prospects for a universal standard.

II. THE UNIVERSALITY OF NEEDS, AND THE PROBLEM OF RELATIVISM

A. Are Some Needs Universal?

It might be argued that all needs are culturally relative, and that any purportedly universal list or theory of basic needs will actually describe things that are necessary in the culture and social circumstances of the theorist. Even the most basic needs have a social component: for example, the need for adequate protein in one's diet may be adequately met by cooked meat in some social circumstances, but not in cultures that regard animals as holy and meat eating as morally reprehensible. Because the claim to know the needs of others better than they know their own needs has often been taken as license for various forms of oppression, some theorists resist any move to articulate a universal standard of need, claiming that such a standard must be culturally bound and potentially dangerous. Because standards of basic need are often used to criticize the practices of other cultures, concern for the potential misuse of a need standard must be a central issue for any theory that purports to be universal. For example, when cultural practices such as polygamy, purdah, or asceticism are sometimes condemned on grounds that they involve systematic oppression and deprivation with respect to

basic needs, it may be argued in return that such criticism reflects a misunderstanding of the role that these practices play in a wider cultural setting. Cultural practices that seem harmful to an outsider may be perceived quite differently by those for whom these practices are part of, or constitutive of, a comprehensive way of life. There is serious concern that universal standards of need may neglect historical and cultural differences, or that they may fail to respect people's right to choose a plan of life according to their own lights. Even if a theory of need *were* universal, concern would remain that it could be applied in a parochial or prejudiced way that might marginalize or exclude those whose lifestyles or cultural practices fail to conform.

Defenders of the idea that there may be universal standards of basic need must be responsive to these serious concerns, but need not regard them as decisive. In what sense, after all, can it reasonably be regarded as "dangerous" or "culturally bound" to claim that all people have a need for potable water? Some have urged in response to need skepticism that *failure* to articulate such a universal standard is often to blind oneself to yet *other* forms of traditional oppression. Thus in a 1992 article, Martha Nussbaum argues that to give up on the notion that some human needs and functional capacities are universal is "to turn things over to the free play of forces in a world situation in which the social forces affecting the lives of women, minorities, and the poor are rarely benign" (Nussbaum, M. (1992). Human functioning and social justice. *Political Theory*, 2, p. 212). Those who have tried to articulate a universal needs standard have often done so in order to find a normative basis for identifying common characteristics of oppression and deprivation as they operate in a wide range of social and cultural circumstances. One important aim of those who have articulated standards of basic need is to find a basis for such a theory that avoids prejudice and parochialism, and to articulate conditions for the use and application of such a theory that avoids inappropriate marginalization of persons, cultures, and practices that harmlessly diverge from the theoretical norm. There is no current agreement on whether this is an achievable theoretical goal.

B. Human Nature

It can be argued that common characteristics of human beings and common features of the human condition imply that there are some things that we all need regardless of cultural and social differences. The common limitations of the human body imply that we all require food, clothing, shelter, and medical resources. Critics point out that even nutritional needs, often considered the most basic of all needs, are culturally informed. But it may still be possible to identify commonalities that explain the degree to which such needs are universal and to specify those needs in terms broad enough to accommodate cultural differences. People *do* all need adequate nutrition, even though cultural differences may importantly determine what specific goods would satisfy that need. People *do* all need shelter and access to medical care, although different forms of shelter, and different arrangements for health-care distribution will be appropriate in different circumstances. The two accounts discussed below, one focusing on all purpose goods, the other on essential human capabilities, are both attempts to specify such commonalities at an appropriate level of abstraction.

C. All-Purpose Goods

Some theories propose a list of multipurpose goods or "primary goods," thought to be requirements for the pursuit of any conception of a good life. John Rawls, whose work introduced this term, explains that primary goods are the things every rational person must be presumed to want, because they are necessary for the pursuit of any conception of a good life. Another way to understand the Primary Goods is as those things that constitute the necessary conditions for autonomy, or for adoption, critical revision, and pursuit of a conception of the good. The items Rawls lists among the primary goods are identified at a level of abstraction sufficient to accommodate wide cultural and social differences, perhaps without losing their normative applicability. For example, Rawls lists "the social bases of self-respect" and "income and wealth," among the primary goods, rather than listing individually the things people might choose to do with their wealth, and without attempting to specify precisely what is socially necessary for self-respect.

D. Universal Capabilities

Some theorists have argued that it is inappropriate to focus on goods rather than focusing on what people can do or become, given the circumstances of their lives. Thus, David Braybrooke argues that a useful account of human needs must include elements that have to do with "the functioning of human beings," and not merely with the material means for subsistence. In a similar vein, Amartya Sen and Martha Nussbaum have argued that standards of well-being and need should depend on an account of people's capabilities, not their posses-

sion of some set of goods. Instead of a list of *needs,* Nussbaum offers a list of basic human functional *capabilities* that she hopes can be used as a normative criterion for evaluating human well-being over a wide range of circumstances.

Such approaches to the problem of relativism raise serious questions concerning the degree to which needs are socially determined. All hold that it is possible and desirable to articulate common needs at some level of abstraction from concrete social circumstances, and that we may be able to evaluate the welfare of others using a standard of basic needs. Such standards must be open to what Martha Nussbaum calls *"plural specification"*: that is, they must articulate needs at an appropriate level of abstraction, leaving latitude for individuals to articulate more specifically what would be adequate to meet them under different social and cultural circumstances.

III. PROPOSED ACCOUNTS OF BASIC NEEDS: A COLLECTION OF LISTS

In considering various accounts of human needs, it is important to distinguish the question "What do people need?" from the question "How should we measure whether people's needs are being met?" It may not always be possible to devise an index for precise measurement of needs-satisfaction, and most of the instruments employed by economists and development theorists are quite coarse: for example, the Physical Quality of Life Index (PQLI) ranks countries on the basis of infant mortality, life expectancy, and illiteracy rates alone, while the Human Development Index (HDI) restricts consideration to per-capita income, literacy, and life expectancy at birth. No one would claim that these measures are adequate to determine whether people's basic needs are satisfied, but many regard the PQLI and HDI as important indicators of needs satisfaction nonetheless. Hicks and Streeten formulate the following minimal list of basic needs: (a) health, (b) education, (c) food and clothing, (d) water supply, (e) sanitation, drinking water, and social security, (f) housing, and (g) participation in government activities. As indicators of progress with respect to needs provision, they recommend looking to such measurable phenomena as life expectancy, literacy, primary school enrollment, calorie intake, infant mortality, percentage of population with access to potable water, and percentage of population with access to sanitation facilities. (Hicks, Norman, &

TABLE 1

Course-of-Life Needs

Drenowski (UN)	Mandel	Terleckyij	OECD
Nutrition	Food	Health and safety	Health
Shelter	Clothing and shelter (and warmth	Education skills, and income	Individual development through
Health	in some climates)	Human habitat	learning
Education	Protection against animals, climates	Finer things	Employment and quality of
Leisure	Desire to decorate	Freedom, justice, and	working life
Security	Sex	harmony	Time and leisure
(Personal safety, economic	Reproduction		Command over goods and ser-
security)	Hygiene		vices
Environment	Health care		Physical environment
(Cultural, social, and	To increase one's knowledge (ex-		Personal safety and the adminis-
physical)	tending into enriching one's		tration of justice
	leisure)		Social opportunity for partici-
			pation

From D. Braybrooke, *Meeting Needs.* Princeton NJ: Princeton University Press, 1987. p. 34. Sources: Jan F. Drenowski, "The Level of Living Index—New Version (A Revision of United Nations Research Institute for Social Development Report No. 4, Parts 1–2, September 1966)," in *Studies in the Measurement of Levels of Living and Welfare,* UNRISD report no. 73 (Geneva, 1970). Ernest Mandel, *Marxist Economic Theory,* tr. Brian Pearce, vol. 2. (London: Merlin Press, 1968), vol. 2, p. 660. Nestor E. Terleckyj, "Measuring Progress Towards Social Goals: Some Possibilities at National and Local Levels," *Management Science,* 16(12), August 1970. pp. B-765–B-778. "List of Social Concerns Common to Most OECD Countries," (Paris: Organization for Economic Cooperation and Development, 1973), pp. 14–17.

Streeten, P. (1979). Indicators of development: The search for a basic needs yardstick. World Development, 7, pp. 568–579.) Still, it is difficult to construct an index that reduces these indicators to a single scale and that allows comparison and evaluation of need satisfaction and human development.

A. Course-of-Life Needs

Any proposed list of basic needs will be controversial and must be taken as provisional, open to later discussion and revision. But if the aim to satisfy basic needs is to be used as a measure for the success or failure of economic development or social policy, we must have some idea what the basic needs are, even if the account we use is clearly understood to be provisional and revisable. Table 1 shows four different accounts of basic course-of-life needs as articulated in different sources and as collected by David Braybrooke. These lists are sufficiently different that it is not at all clear that their authors intended them as answers to the same question. As Braybrooke notes, many of the items listed could not sensibly be substituted in an open sentence like "People have a need for X." Some listed elements (nutrition, clothing, and shelter) focus on physical necessities and bodily needs, while others (desire to decorate, "finer things," education) focus on specifically human charac-

teristics and on the requirements of sociality. As many theorists insist, the use of such lists to evaluate human well-being will require consideration not only of what *goods* people possess, but also whether the circumstances of their lives allow expression of essential human capabilities.

B. Braybrooke's Two-Part List of Matters of Need

The most comprehensive philosophical examination of human needs and their relevance to social and development policy has been done by David Braybrooke, who proposes a method for arriving at a minimally controversial set of needs based on the judgment of a representative decision-making body and relativized to a given reference population. He emphasizes that no such list can ever be definitively completed, "for how could it be completed without setting a limit to the categories that are to be used and the distinctions drawn in describing human beings, their environment, and the relationship between them and their environment?" But even though Braybrooke's subtle theory cannot be reduced to a simple list, he does offer a provisional "List of Matters of Need," developed from the similar lists identified in Table 1. Braybrooke divides this list into two parts, the first being "strongly colored by" notions about physical functioning, while the second "has more to do with functioning as a human being."

First part:

1. The need to have a life-supporting relationship to the environment.
2. The need for food and water.
3. The need to excrete.
4. The need for exercise.
5. The need for periodic rest, including sleep.
6. The need (beyond what is covered under the preceding needs) for whatever is indispensable to preserving the body intact in important respects.

Second Part:

7. The need for companionship.
8. The need for education.
9. The need for social acceptance and recognition.
10. The need for sexual activity.
11. The need to be free from harassment, including not being continually frightened.
12. The need for recreation. (Braybrooke, D. (1987). *Meeting Needs,* pp. 36–37. Princeton: Princeton University Press.)

Clearly Braybrooke's list describes a richer conception of human well-being than the PQLI, and the other indices discussed above. Braybrooke includes some *goods* as basic needs (for example food and water), but his account of the basic needs places great emphasis not only on the goods that people need, but also on what people can do with the goods they command.

C. Rawls' Primary Goods

John Rawls identifies a set of "Primary Goods," understood as all-purpose goods, possession of which (to some minimum degree) is necessary for the pursuit of any reasonable conception of the good life, and as the necessary prerequisites for the formation and rational revision of such an evaluative conception. Thus, people are understood to have reason to want these goods no matter what individual or social projects they want to pursue, and no matter what the social circumstances of their lives. Within Rawls' broader theory of justice, all social primary goods—liberty and opportunity, income and wealth, and the bases of self respect—are to be distributed equally unless an unequal distribution of any or all of these goods is to the advantage of the least-favored members of society. Rawls offers the following (provisional) list of primary goods:

1. Basic rights and liberties (political liberty, freedom of speech and assembly, liberty of conscience, freedom of thought, freedom of the person, along with the right to hold personal property, freedom from arbitrary arrest and seizure as defined by the Rule of Law.)
2. Freedom of movement and free choice of occupation against a background of diverse opportunities.
3. Powers and prerogatives of offices and positions of responsibility in the political and economic institutions of the basic structure of society.
4. Income and wealth.
5. The social bases of self-respect.

The list of *primary goods* is intended to describe what Rawls calls a *"thin theory of the good."* A theory of the good is to be understood as a more or less complete account of what is of value in a human life. Liberal theorists like Rawls strive to show that some liberal principles for the structure of society's basic institutions are consistent with a wide variety of different conceptions of the good (all *reasonable* conceptions, Rawls claims). A *thin* theory of the good is an account of the good that is less completely specified, and that includes only what would be needed for the pursuit of any of the more richly described accounts of value accepted by different members of a pluralist liberal society. In this sense, Rawls list of primary goods functions as an account of universal general necessities or basic needs.

Some of the items on Rawls list have been called into question as parochial concerns that people might not have under alternate social circumstances. For example, Marxian critics have argued that the value of "income and wealth" applies to persons in capitalist societies but not in socialist societies that seek to eliminate or minimize the influence of market institutions. Defenders of the Rawlsian conception argue that the items listed can be specified in a way that makes such objections moot. For example, Rawls explains that "wealth" should be taken to include "virtually any socially recognized form of access to goods and services, including wealth in 'non-individualistic' forms, such as access to public facilities such as libraries."

D. The Capabilities Approach

A number of contemporary theorists including Amartya Sen and Martha Nussbaum have argued that theories of justice and needs have focused excessively on *goods* and *things* as the objects of need, and that a more adequate theory would focus instead on *what can be done* with the goods a person can command. According to Nussbaum, the "thin theory of the good" described by Rawls's primary goods is more limited than necessary, because a richer account can be given of the essential elements of a good human life. She claims that it is both possible and desirable to provide a more complete account of the human good, and that such an account will provide a better specification of human needs. Both Nussbaum and Sen urge that different goods enable people to function normally in different circumstances, so it will be important to provide local specification of the way in which people are enabled to exercise their characteristic human functions. However, the account of human functioning and the accompanying list of essential capabilities is intended to identify functions that are cross-culturally valuable.

Nussbaum argues that the list of functions she identifies constitutes a "thick, vague conception of the good," in contrast to Rawls' thin theory of the good. Initially she specifies a "first approximation" by noting what she takes to be broad and uncontroversial human characteristics, including mortality, the limitations of the human body, the capacity of pleasure and pain, cognitive abilities to perceive, imagine, and think, beginning life in infancy, practical reason, affiliation with other human beings, relatedness to other species and to nature, the ability to laugh and play, and "separateness." She notes that these characteristics include both limits (like mortality) and capabilities (like cognitive capacity). From this basic list, she goes on to describe a more specific account of the functional capacities exercise of which she takes to be necessary for a good human life. These basic human functional capabilities include:

1. Being able to live to the end of a complete human life, as far as possible; not dying prematurely, or before one's life is so reduced as to be not worth living.

2. Being able to have good health; to be adequately nourished; to have adequate shelter; having opportunities for sexual satisfaction, and for choice in matters of reproduction; being able to move from place to place.

3. Being able to avoid unnecessary and nonbeneficial pain, so far as possible, and to have pleasurable experiences.

4. Being able to use the five senses; being able to imagine, to think, and to reason—and to do these things in a way informed and cultivated by an adequate education, including, but by no means limited to literacy and basic mathematical and scientific training. Being able to use imagination and thought in connection with experiencing and producing spiritually enriching materials and events of one's own choice; religious, literary,

musical, and so forth. Nussbaum asserts that protection of this capability requires not only education, but also legal guarantees of freedom of expression with respect to both political and artistic speech, and freedom of religious exercise.

5. Being able to have attachments to things and persons outside ourselves; to love those who love and care for us, to grieve at their absence, in general, to love, grieve, to feel longing and gratitude.

6. Being able to form a conception of the good and to engage in critical reflection about the planning of one's own life. This includes, asserts Nussbaum, being able to seek employment outside the home, and to participate in political life.

7. Being able to live for and with others, to recognize and show concern for other human beings, to engage in various forms of social interaction; to be able to imagine the situation of another and to have compassion for that situation; to have the capability for both justice and friendship.

8. Being able to live with concern for and in relation to animals, plants, and the world of nature.

9. Being able to laugh, to play, to enjoy recreational activities.

10. Being able to live one's own life and nobody else's; being able to live one's own life in one's very own surroundings and context. (Nussbaum, M. (1995). Human Capabilities, Female Human Beings. In M. Nussbaum & J. Glover (Eds.), *Women, culture, and development*, pp. 83–85. New York: Oxford University Press.

Clearly Nussbaum's account of "essential human functions" articulates a far richer and more detailed conception of human well-being than Rawls' primary goods or Braybrooke's list of matters of need. Such richly described accounts raise problems of their own: one may wonder how we could use this list to evaluate policies or choices unless we knew more about how these essential functions relate to one another, and whether some have priority over others. The account of basic needs given by Streeten and Hicks above, and the lists of "course of life needs" presented in Table 1 are generally more restricted than the accounts given by Braybrooke, Rawls, and Nussbaum. The richer an account of human needs, the greater the risk that the conception articulated will reflect the parochial concerns of the theorist: indeed, it may seem unlikely that any one could effectively exercise the capacities identified by Nussbaum except under a liberal constitutional regime like that in Britain or the United States. The sparer an account of human needs, the greater the risk that crucial human capacities or projects will be left out and that fundamental needs may go unmet when a given standard is used to frame social policy. An appropriate needs standard must avoid both the potential oppressiveness of parochialism while providing a standard rich enough to identify deprivation where it exists.

IV. NEEDS IN CONTEMPORARY THEORIES OF JUSTICE

A. Needs and Rights

The requirements of justice are distinguished, in part, by the fact that they can be claimed and enforced as a matter of right. If need-satisfaction is itself a requirement of justice, then those in need can reasonably argue that they have a right to whatever is necessary for the satisfaction of their needs. But few believe that the connection between needs and rights is quite as simple as this. For to claim something as a matter of right, one must show that no one else has a competing claim of similar weight or priority. Even in the case of claims based on the most fundamental human needs, this is not always the case. For example, many needs theorists list "sexual satisfaction" as a basic human need. But recognition of such a need does not automatically imply that other people have a duty to satisfy the sexual needs of the needy.

Still, while needs do not automatically create rights, they may provide the ground for prima facie moral claims. Unless these claims are rebutted or overridden by the competing claims of others, they will indeed constitute rights. Because claims of basic need typically have high priority and moral urgency, it can be argued that people often have a right that at least their most basic needs should be met, and that those who possess more than they need have a corresponding obligation to see to it that the basic needs of others are met. At least, it is argued, people possess such a right in sufficiently wealthy societies, providing that the claims of those who possess surplus resources are not of overriding significance. However, the success of such an argument will depend, in part, on the role played by needs within a broader theory of justice, because such theories will have implications concerning the relative strength of competing claims.

B. Needs and Exploitation

The notion that one crucial function of government is to prevent the oppression and exploitation of the weak (or the poor) by the strong (or the wealthy) has been defended by political theorists as diverse as Adam Smith and Karl Marx, and is common to many theories of justice. It is plausible to think that the satisfaction of basic needs is necessary for the avoidance of such evils, because it is when people are needy that they are subject to the most egregious forms of exploitation and oppression. It has often been argued that the only way effectively to protect people from such exploitation is to guarantee that basic needs will be met. It would follow that any conception of justice that condemns oppression and exploitation must also regard the satisfaction of needs as a primary concern of justice. The success of this argument depends on the theorists ability to articulate an account of exploitation or oppression—a promising project, but much more difficult than might initially be expected.

C. Libertarianism

Libertarians hold that political institutions should protect property rights, enforce people's purely negative rights, and rectify the injustice that results when these rights are violated, but that they should otherwise leave people free to do as they choose. On such views, "negative rights" are understood to be rights against interference, while "positive rights" embody positive claims on the goods or the charity of others. According to libertarians, justice has nothing to do with welfare, the satisfaction of needs, or the protection of the poor and vulnerable. In fact, the libertarian conception of justice forbids the taxation of the better off for the benefit of those who are worse off, because such taxation, it is argued, would violate people's property rights. It is an obvious consequence of this view that the satisfaction of needs is not a matter of justice, and that people have no general right that their needs should be satisfied. However, many libertarians acknowledge duties of charity that imply a weighty *imperfect* obligation to respond to the needs of others. Because these obligations are imperfect, however, those in need cannot claim satisfaction of basic needs as a matter of right.

The challenge for libertarians is to articulate grounds for placing such high moral priority on negative rights and rights to private property. Typically property rights are grounded in antecedent rights of self-preservation, and the benefits for planning and welfare afforded by a stable property rights regime. But inasmuch as these reasons are based on human well-being and the ability of a stable property regime to satisfy people's *needs,* they provide no ground for the claim that protection of property rights will always trump needs satisfaction when the two aims conflict.

D. Contractarianism

Contractarian theories hold that just principles for social organization are those that would be accepted as the terms of a mutual agreement or contract, and that political institutions are just to the extent that they fulfill the terms of such a contract. What justifies the state to its individual members, in this view, is that they are better off than they would have been in the absence of the state, or in the presence of the likely alternative states that might have existed instead. Thus, contractarians argue that political institutions are justified only if their terms could be the object of a free agreement by all who live under them. Some contractarians have argued that the terms of agreement would include welfare institutions that would provide for at least the basic needs of all. It can be argued that people whose needs are unmet have no reason to abide by the social contract, and that the terms of agreement cannot be justified to them. If the state is justified by what it can do for us, as contractarians suppose, then when it fails to provide for basic needs, it looses its claim to citizens' allegiance. On the other hand, those who are antecedently wealthy and powerful might be worse off under a regime that taxed them for the benefit of the needy than they would have been in the absence of such a regime, or in the presence of an alternative (perhaps a libertarian) regime. This would undermine the claim that the *wealthy* have adequate self-interested reasons to accept such a social contract, because the terms of cooperation might not be justifiable to *them*. If we stipulate that the principles of justice are those that literally everyone could actually agree upon, regardless of their antecedent power or wealth, then we may find that there are no such principles. This problem, among others, has led many contractarians to argue that the terms of the social contract must exclude such morally arbitrary influences as wealth and power, and to move from simple contractarianism to *ideal* contractarian theories.

E. Ideal Contractarianism

While simple contractarian theories hold that the state is justified only if we would actually agree to the terms of cooperation it involves, *ideal contractarians* argue that the principles of justice are those we would agree to under certain restrictive conditions that are intended to guarantee that the agreement arrived at will be *fair*. To insure fairness, ideal contractarians strive to exclude or minimize the influence of threats and partial interests on the terms of the social contract. Thus, John Rawls

and John Harsanyi have both argued that we should consider the terms of social cooperation we would agree upon if we were denied information about our particular station or situation in society, because such information might lead us to choose rules that would be biased toward our own parochial interests. Rawls calls this mental constraint the "veil of ignorance." Parties to the contractual agreement (or choice) behind this veil know facts about society: they know that people have religious beliefs, that they have different conceptions of the good, different wants, different needs, but they do not know their own condition in life. From behind this veil, not knowing whether or not one will be a woman or a man, Asian or Caucasian, Muslim or Jew, one will be careful to avoid choosing principles that would arbitrarily disadvantage the members of any such group. Rawls believes that parties to such a choice would choose (among others) a difference principle requiring that social and economic inequalities must be arranged so that they are to the greatest benefit of the least advantaged members of society. More specifically, Rawls' difference principle requires equal distribution of primary goods except where an unequal distribution would improve the condition of the worst off, as measured by their possession of primary goods. As long as the minimal provision of primary goods guaranteed by the difference principle is adequate to satisfy basic needs, Rawls principles of justice will require that these needs must be met. But Amartya Sen has objected that some people may need *more* than others if their basic needs are to be met: for example, some people require wheelchairs to meet their need for mobility, while others do not. It is for this reason, among others, that Sen advocates a "capabilities" standard rather than a "goods" standard for measuring the well-being of the worse off members of society.

Other advocates of ideal contractarianism have argued that a somewhat weaker principle would be chosen from behind the veil of ignorance: a *basic minimum principle*, stipulating that a basic minimum of welfare support must be universally provided, but that beyond the provision of this minimum, people are responsible for themselves. This weaker principle prescribes that basic needs must be satisfied, but requires somewhat less than Rawls' difference principle. In his more recent 1993 work, Rawls articulates a similar "needs principle," stipulating that the goal of meeting basic need is prior to all other principles of justice, because these needs must be met if citizens are to be able to understand and exercize the rights and liberties justice is supposed to guarantee (John Rawls, J. (1993). *Political liberalism*, p. 7. New York: Columbia University Press). The success of any such ideal contractarian argument depends on the claim that just principles are those that would be chosen from behind the veil of ignorance, and the claim that the *difference principle* or *basic minimum principle* would be chosen as the object of a fair agreement behind the veil.

F. Communitarianism

Communitarians emphasize the social needs associated with community membership and belonging, and have condemned the individualism of liberal and libertarian theories. Some communitarians have argued that such theories place too much emphasis on individual rights, and have failed to recognize that these rights may damage the social ties that bind communities together. Because communitarians also argue that community ties are necessary for well-being and for the living of a good human life, this constitutes an important objection. Another strain of communitarian thought insists that all normative standards are "relative to social meanings" and that a society should be considered just as long as "its substantive life is lived in a certain way ... that is faithful to the shared understandings of the members. To override those understandings is (always) to act unjustly" (Walzer, M. (1983). *Spheres of Justice*, pp. 312–314. New York Basic Books). This strand of the communitarian view is closely associated with the critique of universality and the concern that universal standards may be misused to justify the condemnation of difference. The contrary worry is that such communitarian views may be unable to recognize, and may lack the theoretical resources necessary to criticize certain forms of culturally embedded oppression and deprivation, for if all needs are relative to "social meanings," what are we to say about traditional, socially embedded sexism, racism, and classism? When forms of deprivation are culturally embedded, those who suffer them may be unable to desire or even to articulate what they need. People raised in a culture of slavery may be unable to imagine or hope for freedom and autonomy, but this would be a poor reason for us to accept that their circumstances are just and their needs adequately met.

G. Perfectionism

Another tradition in the theory of justice might be considered a version of perfectionism. Aristotle argued that the function of the state should be better when they accomplish this function more effectively. Martha Nussbaum, whose theory was described in Section III, recommends that social policy should be framed with the aim that no one should be prevented or prohibited from having the ability to exercise these functions and capabilities, and that the ability to live a human life, and a good human life, ideally should be available for all. How are these capabilities to be used in evaluating human well-being or social welfare? Nussbaum argues that a life that lacks any one of these capabilities, whatever else it has, will fall short of being a good human life. Policy makers and development theorists should thus guide their choices with two thresholds mind: First, claims Nussbaum, some lives are so characterized by deprivation with respect to the fundamental human capabilities that they are not recognizable as human lives at all. The first priority should be to see that the circumstances of every person's life is above this minimal threshold. But a second, also important priority, is articulated by a somewhat higher threshold of functional capability, beneath which people cannot live good human lives. The second aim of policy is to see that the circumstances everyone's life bring them above this second threshold, such that they have at least the possibility of living a *good* human life. This will not guarantee, of course, that everyone's life will *be* good, but only that people will not be arbitrarily excluded from the opportunity to live a good life.

Like other theories, the capabilities approach has been subject to serious criticism. Some have argued that Nussbaum's version of this approach suffers from parochialism: if capabilities identified inappropriately reflect the author's own Western liberal outlook, this would undermine the claim that they reflect truly universal standards. Others note that Nussbaum's list of essential functions is ambiguous, since there may often be practical conflicts that arise when policies promise to promote some capabilities over others. The aim of the capabilities approach is, in part, to provide an account of human flourishing that is specific enough to identify deprivation and oppression where they exist, but general enough to be applied across widely different social and cultural circumstances. The success of this approach will depend on the plausibility of the claim that there is an identifiable list of essential human functions, and that the evaluative standard defined by such a list can be used in a way that is culturally sensitive. Like other theories described in this article, this is an evolving project, and a final, definitive evaluation is surely a long way off.

Also See the Following Articles

HUMAN NATURE, VIEWS OF • RIGHTS THEORY • THEORIES OF ETHICS, OVERVIEW

Bibliography

Braybrooke, D. (1987). *Meeting needs*. Princeton, NJ: Princeton University Press.

Copp, D. (1995). *Morality, normativity, and society*. New York: Oxford University Press.

Frankfurt, H. (1988). Necessity and desire. In *The importance of what we care about*. New York: Cambridge University Press.

Goodin, R. (1985). The priority of needs. *Philosophy and Phenomenological Research*, 45(2), 615–625.

Nussbaum, M., & Glover, J. (1995). *Women, culture, and development*. New York: Oxford University Press.

Rawls, J. (1971). *A theory of justice*. Cambridge: Harvard University Press.

Sen, A. (1992). *Inequality reexamined*. Oxford: Clarendon Press.

Streeten, P., and Burki, S. J., Ul Haq, M., Hicks, N., & Stewart, F. (1981). *First things first: Meeting basic human needs in developing countries*. New York: Oxford University Press.

Wiggins, D. (1987). *Needs, values, truth*. Oxford: Oxford University Press.

THEORIES OF JUSTICE: RAWLS

Andros Loizou
University of Central Lancashire

I. Introduction
II. The Original Position
III. Rawls's Two Principles of Justice
IV. Some Critical Perspectives on the Theory

GLOSSARY

difference principle A principle according to which social and economic inequalities are to be arranged so as to be of maximum benefit to the least advantaged socioeconomic sector. This is the most distinctive part of Rawls's theory of justice.

justice as fairness A conception of justice that would be agreed upon in an initial situation of equality, between persons as moral equals. Rawls uses this phrase as the most general name for his theory of justice.

lexical ordering of principles An order of priority among principles, in which the prior principles define the constraints within which principles further down the line may operate.

original position Rawls's adaptation of *social contract* theory [see below], in the form of a thought experiment designed to model an initial position of equality between prospective citizens who, as "free and rational persons," are to engage in a reasoned debate over principles of justice in order to arrive at a final and binding consensus.

social contract The idea that society under government, or the coming together of individual persons to constitute community, is to be explained in terms of a contract made between separate, self-determining individuals. Whether to exist under the government or within the community in question is thus construed as a voluntary choice on the part of the individual.

social primary goods A set of fundamental goods that, according to Rawls, all rational persons want. They comprise the following: liberty, income, wealth, social position, and the bases of self-respect.

veil of ignorance A constraint introduced by Rawls into the original position [see above] designed to promote equality between the contracting parties by depriving them of certain kinds of knowledge about themselves, for example, their level of wealth and social position.

well-ordered society A society ordered by a public conception of justice, constituted by principles that free and rational persons would agree to in an initial position of equality.

WHAT PRINCIPLES OF JUSTICE—principles according to which the benefits and burdens of social cooperation are to be distributed—should we opt for if we had the choice? What if we wanted these principles to be definitive and final, so that they regulated all further agreements we entered into? Is there a particular set of principles that we all ought, and in appropriate conditions *would in fact*, all agree to? Is it possible to attain some impartial perspective or standpoint from which such principles might be advocated and defended, with some real hope of arriving at an agreement?

I. INTRODUCTION

A. Justice as Fairness: The Main Idea

John Rawls, in his seminal work *A Theory of Justice* (Rawls, 1971—hereafter T.J.), answers yes to the last two questions; and in that book he gives us an account of the principles of justice that would constitute the rational choice, and also of the impartial perspective from which these principles are chosen and defended. By "justice as fairness" Rawls means a conception of justice that is agreed to in an initial situation of equality (i.e., between persons as moral equals) and that regulates all further agreements about how institutions are to be set up or reformed.

The parties to the agreement, in agreeing to a set of principles definitive of a conception of justice, are *ipso facto* autonomous. In thus reaching an agreement, therefore, they see the resulting obligations as self-imposed. The idea of *self-imposed* obligations is, of course, reminiscent of Rousseau and Kant, and this is no accident. For Rawls sees himself as presenting "a conception of justice which generalises and carries to a higher level of abstraction the familiar theory of the social contract as found, say, in Locke, Rousseau, and Kant" (T.J., p. 11).

What, then, are the principles that (according to Rawls) would be chosen? There are two. The first has to do with basic rights and liberties, and requires strict equality in their distribution. The second holds (roughly speaking) that social and economic inequalities can be justified only if they can be shown to be of benefit to everyone, and in particular to the least advantaged members of society.

In the sections that follow, we explore the theory in detail, and conclude with some critical perspectives. But first, we need to look in a more general way at the philosophical basis of the theory.

B. The Philosophical Basis of Rawls's Theory

The circumstances in which we find ourselves include the existence of vastly different, often competing, theories or definitions of justice, each with exponents deploying characteristic ways of promoting their preferred theory over its rivals. For example, Robert Nozick's "entitlement theory of justice" has as its basis a strong notion of individual property rights. Clearly, therefore, any uses by the state of revenues raised in taxation for redistributive purposes are going to come out on Nozick's theory as individual rights violations. Now clearly some debate must be possible between rival theories of justice. But how? Rawls's answer is that we all must share the *concept* of justice, despite having rival *conceptions* of justice (T.J., pp. 5–6). We may all disagree as to what justice *is*, what precisely it consists in, but we all—necessarily—agree that our institutions and social arrangements should be just. (No one says "I prefer *un*just social arrangements").

This suggests that the different conceptions of justice, albeit that they are so different, nonetheless share something. But even a cursory look at different definitions of justice shows this to be impossible, if by "sharing something" we mean "having elements or features in common." The answer lies in the *role* the concept of justice plays. Justice is, for Rawls, "the first virtue of social institutions, as truth is of systems of thought" (T.J., p. 3). In other words, justice stands to social institutions in the same way as truth stands to systems of thought. We demand of our institutions that they be just, *whatever* we mean by "just," analogously to the way in which we seek among theories or systems of thought the one which is *true*. So it is possible for there to be reasoned agreement or disagreement over "what justice is," and at the same time an inescapable consensus *that* the outcome should be just.

But Rawls makes a stronger claim. Among all these possible *conceptions* of justice, there is *just one* that it would be rational to choose in preference to all others. In this subsection, we take an overview of the basic philosophical intuitions—more specifically, the *ethical* intuitions—underlying this claim, and examine it in more detail later.

A number of ideas are presented early on in *Theory of Justice*, within the first 15 pages. Some of these we have noted already: the notion of reaching an agreement over principles of justice in a way that is expressive of autonomy and moral equality (and the presumption that such an agreement is *possible*), the idea of the social contract with particular reference to Rousseau and Kant, and the idea of justice as the first virtue of social institutions. In addition to these are notions that find expression in three key phrases: first, "a sense of justice," second "considered judgments" (or "considered convictions"), and third "a well-ordered society."

For Rawls, all persons capable of rational choice must also be capable of "a sense of justice," and so must have a set of intuitions or "considered convictions" about justice. A *theory* of justice must therefore address these intuitions, allow itself to be modified or rejected in the face of them—or if found acceptable, perhaps it might actually *refine* them. But what such a theory *cannot* do is reject these intuitions out of hand. The way these ideas come together makes it clear that Rawls owes a great debt to Kant. For Kant saw his own ethical theory—about autonomy, the good will, the categorical imperative and so on—as providing a philosophical explanation of what the ordinary man or woman innocent of philosophy understands by morality. The purpose of this complex theory was merely to explain, for example, the ordinary person's understanding of the difference between the shopkeeper who refrains from cheating his customers because it is bad for business, and the shopkeeper who refrains because it is wrong to cheat one's customers. All that Kant's theory can give the ordinary person is a greater clarity of reasoning—it cannot give him the capacity to exercise the good will, the capacity to assent to the moral law. In the same way for Rawls, no amount of theorising about justice can—or should be allowed to—undermine one's basic moral intuitions.

A "well-ordered society" in Rawls's sense is one where an agreement about principles of justice has been reached, the basic institutions of the society satisfy and are known to satisfy these principles, and each person knows that everyone else accepts the principles. Here again it is possible to see the Kantian parallel. Just as for Rawls the principles of justice are "the principles that free and rational persons concerned to further their own interests would accept in an initial position of equality as defining the fundamental terms of their association" (T.J., p. 11), so the moral law can be seen as defining what Kant calls "the kingdom of ends," that is, an ideal of community in which individual moral ends form a systematic harmony.

Rawls conceives himself, as we have seen, as an inheritor of the social contract tradition. The upshot of this, and of the foregoing considerations, is that the theory of justice is viewed as the end result of a social contract made between contracting parties, all of whom share a sense of justice, and all of whom are committed to arriving at some rational consensus about a conception of justice that will then constitute the foundational charter of their association. In order to take his readers through to such a consensual result, Rawls involves them in an extended thought experiment that places his contracting parties in an initial situation of equality. From this vantage point, his contracting parties are to agree upon principles of justice that will regulate all

further agreements about forms of government, and so on, and more specifically, will define once and for all the basic structures through which the benefits and burdens of social cooperation are to be distributed. To this way of conceiving the principles of justice Rawls gives the name "justice as fairness," and to the initial situation of equality he gives the name "the original position."

Accordingly, Rawls's theory of justice divides into two parts: the specification and detailed description of the original position, and the principles of justice themselves that this contractual situation generates. We deal with these in turn in the two sections that follow.

II. THE ORIGINAL POSITION

A. The Real-World Circumstances of Justice

Why engage in the aforementioned thought experiment at all? The answer, for Rawls, lies in the conspicuous facts of *inequality* that we find in the real world. We need the vantage point of the original position in order to distance ourselves from these facts and to arrive at a conception of justice that meets the requirements of "justice as fairness." The original position, while being an idealized situation, must be sufficiently distanced from these facts of inequality—of wealth, social position, and so on—to exclude their influence on the choice of principles; and yet not *so* distanced from ordinary experience that it fails to throw light on that experience. We deal with these matters in subsections B to D below. In this subsection we focus on the real-world circumstances that for Rawls give rise to the need for constructing the original position.

These are, for Rawls, of two kinds—"objective" and "subjective" circumstances. The objective circumstances are what make cooperation both possible and necessary, chief among these being the existence of large numbers of people in a given geographical territory. This fact involves further constituent facts: that these people are roughly similar in mental and physical capacity, that they are vulnerable to attack, that their individual plans and aspirations can be thwarted by the actions of others, and that a situation of "moderate scarcity" prevails. This latter condition, of moderate scarcity of resources, ensures both the necessity and the fruitfulness of human cooperation. For on the one hand, resources are not so plentiful as to render cooperation superfluous, while at the same time they are not so scarce that cooperative ventures are doomed to failure.

Among the subjective circumstances is counted the fact that each of the parties will have his or her own plans of life, aspirations, and conception of the good. Their claims on the available resources, natural and social, will therefore inevitably conflict much of the time. Typically, this will reflect preoccupation with one's own interests to the exclusion of the interests of others, and in many cases this will be due to moral failings—selfishness, laziness, negligence—whereas in other cases it will be merely down to different yet equally legitimate aims and aspirations having their origin in, say, different religious beliefs, philosophical outlooks, or political convictions. The existence of these religious, philosophical, and political differences is, for Rawls, just a fact of life, and constitutes a large part of what he calls "the circumstances of justice."

The circumstances of justice obtain "whenever mutually disinterested persons put forward conflicting claims to the division of advantages under conditions of moderate scarcity" (T.J., p. 128). Rawls stresses mutual disinterest not because he accepts *a priori* some metaphysical thesis about egoism (e.g., that necessarily we are all egoists, our "altruistic" behavior being merely a more sophisticated variant of egoism) but simply to avoid what he calls "strong assumptions" (T.J., p. 129). His theory is not inconsistent with the possibility that the life plans and aspirations of some members of society *may* be directed toward promoting the good of others—but they do not *have* to be so directed. To have argued otherwise would have required precisely those "strong assumptions" Rawls wants to avoid. The original position corresponds, for Rawls, to the "state of nature" in the seventeenth and eighteenth century social contract tradition, and the avoidance of strong assumptions is therefore essential.

The original position is accordingly set up in the following way. The contracting parties are denied the possibility of "strong assumptions" because Rawls places them behind what he calls "the veil of ignorance." It is assumed that they are in a state of ignorance, or amnesia, about the central contingencies of their own particular situation—they do not know, for example, anything at all about their own wealth and social position. They have no reason therefore to choose principles on a basis that favors one degree of wealth or social position over another. There are factors in addition to wealth and social position whose influence, Rawls maintains, needs to be similarly excluded, and these are examined in subsection C. In the next subsection, we look at some moral constraints on what are to count as principles between which the contracting parties are to make their choice.

B. Some Moral Constraints on Principles of Justice

What are the basic conditions for what is to be allowed on the list of principles which are presented to the parties in the original position? (This theme is dealt with by Rawls in T.J. section 23, pp. 130–136). Rawls outlines five conditions: generality, universality, publicity, capacity for deciding between conflicting demands, and finality. In what follows we take each of these in turn and then view them as a whole.

Generality and universality must be distinguished. The generality condition ensures that no definitely described individuals are favored by the principle. What is clearly ruled out by the generality condition is, for example, "what is right is what Hitler commands." The universality condition, on the other hand, holds that the principle should apply to all, by virtue of the fact that they are moral persons. The universality condition carries further entailments: for example, it rules out principles that would be self-defeating if everyone acted on them, such as "everyone should to pursue his/her own interests whatever the consequences." Clearly, a principle can meet the generality condition but not that of universality, and vice versa. For example, "what is right is what Hitler commands" meets the generality condition but not the universality condition, whereas "White men have the right of dominion over the earth" meets the universality condition but not that of generality.

Publicity, the third condition, would ensure that the principles would be known to all, and that their universal acceptance would be known to all. Clearly this condition presupposes that of universality. Rawls's example is that formula of Kant's categorical imperative which enjoins us to act on principles that we would be willing as rational beings to see embodied as law in a kingdom of ends (T.J., p. 133). Rawls refers also here to Kant's general thesis that the constitution should be a matter of public knowledge without secret clauses—for example, if there were a right of rebellion in the constitution, this would have to be a matter of public knowledge (see T.J., p. 133, footnote 8).

The fourth condition is put in place to ensure that principles of justice should be capable of ordering competing social arrangements in a way that demonstrates clearly which set of social arrangements would be more just, and which less just, without having to appeal to such considerations as who has the greater power to coerce and intimidate.

The fifth condition, finality, is clearly allied to the fourth, and requires that principles of justice should override considerations of self-interest and prudence. Because competing claims and interests have already been given appropriate weighting as part of the structure prescribed by the principle, it would be wrong to count them again as exceptions. The principles of justice would therefore have to be, by this condition, the final court of appeal in any disagreements and so on.

The five conditions come together to give us, in Rawls's words, "a set of principles, general in form and universal in application, that is to be publicly recognised as a final court of appeal for ordering the conflicting claims of moral persons" (T.J., p. 135). The conditions do not rule out any of the traditional main conceptions of justice, but they do rule out singular or first-person egoism, the free rider, personal dictatorship, and the idea of a class or caste that has a right to enjoy supremacy. In other words they rule out, or aim to rule out, principles that are based on distinctions which are irrelevant from a moral point of view.

C. The Veil of Ignorance

The veil of ignorance defines the initial situation of equality in two ways: by what the contracting parties *do not* know, and by what they *do* know. As we have seen, one category of facts they do not know about is their wealth and social position. Rawls adds to this two further categories: first, their talents, abilities, intelligence, or other natural assets—so that they do not know whether their talents would be those of a laborer, or a skilled craftsman, or an entrepreneur, or a professional, or any combination of these; second, they do not know their political and/or religious convictions, nor their own conception of the good as this is embedded in their psychological makeup. There are thus three levels of facts about themselves of which they are made ignorant. They also do not know the particular circumstances of their society. such as its level of culture and civilization, its political and economic situation, and so on. They also do not know to which generation they belong. By contrast, they *do* know, first, the one particular fact that their society is subject to the circumstances of justice as these are described in subsection A above, and whatever follows from this knowledge; and secondly, the general facts about human society such as form the subject matter of political science, economic theory, and human psychology.

We now address the question: Why does Rawls set up the original position in this way? The answer *in general terms* is: In order to ensure that the contracting parties remain uninfluenced in their choice of principles by the particular contingent circumstances in which people normally find themselves, and yet leave them with sufficient knowledge about the human situation in general for them to be able to make informed choices between different principles of justice. But Rawls gives a more detailed answer.

Ignorance of their level of wealth and social position ensures that they do not choose principles of justice that favor one socioeconomic sector over another—the least well-off over the most favored, or vice versa. This much is clear so far. But there are two further levels of ignorance of their personal circumstances, and these need explaining. Ignorance of their talents and abilities, level of intelligence, and so on, ensures that principles of justice that favor a particular talent, or a particular level of intelligence, are excluded. Ignorance of their psychological characteristics and conceptions of the good ensures that they do not choose on a basis that favors one type of character, or set of values, over another—for example, risk takers over more cautious types, religious over atheists, one political persuasion over another, or one set of ethical virtues over another. (Ancient Sparta would be an example of a state that favored above all else a certain set of ethical virtues, namely, the soldierly virtues of courage, loyalty, fierceness in battle, and so on.)

But what is the purpose of denying the contracting parties knowledge of the society to which they belong? The purpose of this does not become really clear until part 2 of the book (T.J., Section 31). The purpose is to ensure that the contracting parties can arrive at principles of justice that are untainted by their knowledge of existing political institutions. In section 31, Rawls adds a refinement to his theory according to which the veil of ignorance is partially lifted, in distinct stages. The first stage comes once the principles of justice have been chosen: the veil of ignorance is then partially lifted, giving the parties knowledge of their particular society, its economic and political nature, and so on. The parties are then in a position to modify these factors in a way that accords with the principles of justice chosen—in short, they are able to rewrite their political constitution if necessary in order to make it reflect the principles of justice, which are both more fundamental and more abstract than any constitution could be. The reason for denying the parties knowledge of which generation they belong to is precisely in order to ensure justice between generations, and in particular the preservation of the heritage of both capital and natural resources.

The parties are now in the required initial situation of equality, or the original position. Rawls's central thesis regarding the original position—and more specifically, the veil of ignorance—is that it provides the starting point from which rational deliberation will lead to the choice of a certain conception of justice. It is not therefore to be thought of, says Rawls, as in any way representing an actual historical gathering of persons alive at a particular time. Rather, it provides a standpoint that we can take up, as an aid to arriving at a conception of justice. It is Rawls's main thesis in the book that rational persons placed in the original position, behind the veil of ignorance, would choose his two principles of justice. But how are we to understand "rationality" in this context? We address this in the brief subsection that follows.

D. The Rationality of the Contracting Parties

Rawls claims that his conception of rationality is "with the exception of one essential feature, the standard one familiar in social theory" (T.J., p. 143). By this conception, rational persons will want more rather than less liberty, opportunities for realizing their chosen ends, wealth, and so on. The "exception" to which Rawls refers is that for him rational persons do not suffer from envy. Such a person for Rawls will not be persuaded by the thought that it is alright for him to accept less, provided everyone else does, if it is at all *possible* for him (and indeed others) to have more. It is rational for him/her to want the most that it is possible to have. Behind the veil of ignorance, this is generalized: it is rational for one (*whoever* one is) to prefer more rather than less in *absolute* terms, not more in relation to others. The irrational nature of envy is made the more clear in the original position precisely because the basis of envy in ordinary life circumstances—namely, knowledge of one's wealth, social position, and so on—is made unavailable in that position. It would therefore be rational for the contracting parties in the original position, behind the veil of ignorance, to choose those principles of justice that would maximally realize, in absolute and not relative terms, the chosen ends of everyone and anyone.

Accordingly, Rawls has to show that his two principles of justice are the principles that meet this requirement. In the next section, we examine these principles as well as Rawls's arguments aimed at establishing that they constitute the rational choice.

III. RAWLS'S TWO PRINCIPLES OF JUSTICE

A. Statement of the Principles

Rawls's starting point is that the most obvious choice for the contracting parties, placed in an initial situation of equality in the original position behind the veil of ignorance, would be strict equality. The only reason for which it would be justifiable to distribute any of these unequally would be if it were to *everyone's* advantage. So much is stated in what Rawls calls "the *general* conception of justice as fairness," first stated on page 62 of *Theory of Justice* thus: "All social values—liberty and opportunity, income and wealth, and the bases of self-respect—are to be distributed equally *unless an unequal distribution of any, or all, of these values is to everyone's advantage*" (our italics). The two principles of justice, which Rawls refers to as "the special conception of justice as fairness," receive their first statement on pp. 61–62 and their final statement on p. 302. The first statement of the first principle is that each person has an equal right to the most extensive basic liberty compatible with the same liberty for others. The first statement of the second principle is that social and economic inequalities should be arranged so as to be both (a) to everyone's advantage, and (b) attached to positions and offices open to all. The final statement of the first principle is more specific than the first, in that it includes the phrase "the most extensive total system of equal basic liberties" in place of "the most extensive liberty." Subsequent statements of the second principle, including the final version on p. 302, include the phrase "to the greatest benefit of the least advantaged" in place of "to everyone's advantage." This first part of the second principle Rawls refers to as "the difference principle." Part (b) of the second principle has the added phrase "under conditions of fair equality of opportunity."

Rawls's final statement of the two principles reads thus:

First Principle
Each person has an equal right to the most extensive total system of equal basic liberties compatible with a similar system of liberty for all.
Second Principle
Social and economic inequalities are to be arranged so that they are both: (a) to the greatest benefit of the least advantaged, consistent with the just savings principle, and (b) attached to offices and positions open to all under conditions of fair equality of opportunity.

(The term "just savings principle" concerns justice between generations, the preservation of the environment, etc.) Taken in conjunction with "the general conception," the overall thrust of Rawls's theory is that there must be a presumption in favor of equality, and any deviation from this in the direction of inequality requires special justification. Initially, inequalities are justified only if they are to *everyone's* advantage. As Rawls's argument procedes, they are justified only if they are of *greatest* benefit to the *least* advantaged. Yet the "general" and "special" conceptions are deemed to be consistent. If they are, then it must surely be to *everyone's* benefit, in some sense of "benefit," that any social or economic inequalities are to the greatest benefit ("benefit" in *the same* sense?) of the least advantaged. This may appear paradoxical, or even contradictory. It is perhaps a useful expository device to measure his attempt to show that the two principles constitute the rational choice by the yardstick of how far he succeeds in overcoming this air of paradox, real or apparent. Perhaps whether this paradoxical air disappears or not depends on how convincing one finds Rawls's defense of the two principles. This forms the theme of subsection B. To conclude this subsection, we turn to how Rawls conceives the relation between the two principles, that is, his system of priority rules or "lexical ordering."

There is an ordering of the principles. The first, equal liberty principle always has priority, in that liberty cannot be traded off for opportunities, wealth, social position, and so on. Within the constraints defined by the first principle, part (b) of the second principle ensures that fair equality of opportunity prevails. Equality of opportunity too cannot be traded off for wealth, social position, and so on. Third, within these constraints—and in that order—the difference principle comes into play. The upshot is, then, that within the constraints defined by equal liberty and fair equality of opportunity, social and economic inequalities can be arranged so as to be of greatest benefit to the least advantaged.

B. Rawls's Main Arguments for the Two Principles

1. The Priority of Liberty

It is relatively easy from the standpoint of the original position to defend the *general* conception of justice as fairness, given its presumption in favor of equality and the proposition that inequalities of any kind can only be justified if they are to everyone's advantage. The

special conception, namely, the conception that includes the two principles, does not permit inequality of *liberty*, but it *does* permit social and economic inequalities. Furthermore, as we saw at the end of the last subsection, economic inequalities are permitted to arise only when the requirements of liberty (the first principle) and of equality of opportunity (the second part of the second principle) have been met, and in that order. What are Rawls's arguments for this overall position, and why are social and economic inequalities permitted, but not inequalities of liberty? What is special about liberty for Rawls?

The main argument for the priority of liberty has to do with determining one's own plan of life. *Less* than equal liberty would mean that some persons would be required to sacrifice choice over their own life plans in a trade-off for some other social good such as greater income. But the priority of liberty ensures that justifiable inequalities in terms of the difference principle are precluded from compromising that liberty. *Social and economic* inequalities are to be arranged so as to be to everyone's benefit, especially the least advantaged, but only within a context in which it has been decided in advance that there can be no sacrifice of liberty (namely, liberties such as freedom of speech, thought, association, etc.). The veil of ignorance ensures that no one life plan is more important than another, and thus the contracting parties are forced to abstract from their particular life plans and prioritize liberty.

The denial of equal liberty only makes sense, Rawls claims, in a society that has not yet attained a level where basic liberties can be exercised—that is, effectively prior to the attainment of a basic standard of material well-being. It is for this reason that the general conception of justice as fairness must be presupposed. But it is important to notice that even the general conception does not enjoin running roughshod over liberty. For any deviation from equality—equality of liberty, equality of wealth, equality of the bases of self-respect—has to receive a special *justification*. And the justification for departure from equal liberty is that the society in question is *not yet* ready for it, but is on the way. So even here, liberty is restricted only for the sake of greater liberty (albeit in the future).

In conclusion, we draw the reader's attention to Rawls's distinction between liberty itself and the worth of liberty. The purpose of the distinction is to rule out such constraints as poverty, ignorance, lack of the means to achieve one's goals, and so on, from being counted as among the constraints definitive of lack of liberty. By "liberty" Rawls means the system of equal citizenship liberties, whereas the worth of liberty is the capacity for individuals to advance their ends through the legitimate channels. There is no question of *compensating* for lesser liberty, because there is no lesser liberty. However, some will have less *worth* of liberty than others. Where this is so, it will be compensated for by the difference principle. This distinction, expressed in different terms, marks a long-standing dispute between Marxists and liberals (see, for example, the writings of Isaiah Berlin and C. B. Macpherson). It is discussed in section IV.A.2.

2. Why the Difference Principle?

In a situation where equal liberty—or more precisely, a set of equal basic liberties—is assured, the question arises: How should wealth and social position be distributed? The presumption is, as we have seen, in favor of equality, unless *unequal* distribution is to *everyone's* benefit (and of maximum benefit to the *least* advantaged). *Unequal* distribution of wealth in accordance with the difference principle is viewed as a deviation from the general conception of justice as fairness, and needs special justification. That special justification is what constitutes the reasoning behind the difference principle. To this we now turn.

First, and in light of the circumstances of justice, entrepreneurs are likely to have greater expectations than unskilled laborers. What, Rawls asks, is the *morality* of this situation? How, if at all, can such inequalities in levels of expectation be justified? Rawls's answer is: only if these inequalities are arranged in conformity with the difference principle. Rawls introduces the discussion and justification of the difference principle through a comparison with the notion of economic efficiency. An economy is 100% efficient, or "Pareto optimal," if no further *total* economic gain is possible—or, to put it another way, no one can *gain* economically unless someone else *loses*. Clearly, economic efficiency thus defined is consistent with any number of possible distributions, including extremes of wealth and poverty. The question therefore arises, which of these distributions would be *just* as well as efficient? How must the principle of efficiency be supplemented to yield an arrangement which is *just* as well as efficient?

Rawls approaches this question through considering three possible accounts of how a distribution might be to everyone's benefit. He calls these, respectively, "natural liberty," "liberal equality," and "democratic equality." In a system of natural liberty, there is a background of equal liberty as prescribed by the first principle of justice, and a free market regulated by purely *formal* equality of opportunity in the competition for advantaged social positions, and so on. Those who succeed will be those whose talents and abilities are both high and *sufficiently developed*. This means that those with the more advantaged upbringing will succeed over those without these advantages, irrespective of whether the latter equal the former in natural talent and ability. Rawls's comment here is that "intuitively, the most obvious injustice of the system of natural liberty is that it permits distributive shares to be improperly influenced by these factors so arbitrary from a moral point of view" (T.J., Section 12, p. 72). Liberal equality tries to correct for this deficiency by adding the notion of *fairness*: positions should not be open in merely a formal sense, but all should be given a fair chance to attain them. Those with similar abilities should not be held back for lack of education. This requires that those born into a lower income class should have the same opportunities to develop their talents as those with the more advantaged background. This in turn requires that institutions should be specifically designed to overcome barriers of race, class and so on.

However, even the system of liberal equality is for Rawls deficient. True enough, it overcomes the influence of social contingencies. But it still leaves those who are more talented in a more advantaged position, and for Rawls this is still arbitrary from a moral point of view. "There is no more reason," he claims, "to permit the distribution of income and wealth to be settled by the distribution of natural assets than by historical and social fortune" (T.J., p. 74). Clearly for Rawls the distribution of talents and abilities is just as arbitrary from a moral point of view as are the contingencies of social circumstance, and accordingly he speaks of the former as "the natural lottery" (T.J., p. 75).

The *democratic* interpretation of what is to everyone's advantage must therefore take a more radical stance toward equality. How can the benefits and burdens of social cooperation be distributed fairly, given Rawls's understanding of the moral equality of persons? The constraints are these: they cannot be distributed in a way that favors the contingencies of social circumstance, or "the natural lottery" of talents and abilities. What is left? At this point, *strict* equality may seem the only way of honoring the presumption in favor of equality. But Rawls does not take this route. Instead, he chooses allowing inequality of distribution, but only if it benefits the less advantaged. What follows constitutes some of the reasoning behind this choice.

It is clear that the entrepreneurial class in a modern democratic state, who are the most likely to own property, have higher expectations, higher income, and better life prospects than (say) the class of unskilled laborers. This is, arguably, an inescapable fact of life. Rawls asks, what can possibly *justify* such differences from a moral point of view, given that, from that point of view, they must appear *arbitrary*? Rawls's answer is that such inequalities in income, life prospects, and so on, can only be justified morally if they work to the greatest benefit of the least advantaged socioeconomic group, namely, the class of unskilled laborers. "Greatest benefit" is given a clear meaning: the inequality arising from this difference in income, and so on, is justified only if decreasing the inequality, for example, by greater taxation of the entrepreneur's income, would lower the level of well-being of the unskilled laborer still further. This is to work in such a way that the differential in income level encourages the entrepreneur to do things that promote the long term well-being of the unskilled laborer. Redistribution through taxation operates at a high enough level to confer the maximal benefit possible on the least advantaged socioeconomic sector, but not at *so* high a level that the most advantaged sector loses the incentive to make the economic system more efficient and hence create more wealth.

Rawls explains the difference principle through Figure 1 (see T.J., pp. 75–82). The graph represents the level of well-being of the least advantaged man along the vertical [the y] axis plotted against the level of well-being of the most advantaged man along the horizontal [the x] axis. The nearer we are to O, the lower are x's expectations allowed to rise, for example, through less entrepreneurial activity consequent upon too high taxation—and therefore y's expectations are lower. As the level of expectation of the entrepreneur rises, so does that of the unskilled laborer, as a direct result of the developing economy and the contributions made by x to y's well-being in terms of taxation for educational provision, redistribution, and so on. But there is a limit to how far the expectations of x can be allowed to rise on the difference principle—to be exact, no further than

the point D on the graph. In illustrating the difference principle, Rawls contrasts two cases. The first is the *perfectly* just situation represented by point D, where the expectations of the worst off (the unskilled workers) are maximized. No further increase in the expectations of the most advantaged, that is, the entrepreneurs, could further improve the expectations of the worst off—instead it would lower those expectations. The second case is represented by the point P on the graph. Here the entrepreneur is allowed to keep less of what he has earned, and he is correspondingly less motivated to engage in further entrepreneurial activity. Hence the economy remains inefficient. Such a situation, regulated by the difference principle, would be *just* according to Rawls, but not the *best* just arrangement as represented by point D. The reason why D is the best just arrangement is because although all points on the curve from D to O are just, D is both just *and efficient*. The least well-off y are better off than they could be under any other arrangement. Any point to the right of D on the curve is *efficient* but not *fair*. No one gains unless someone else loses; the gains of x (the most advantaged) are at the expense of y (the least advantaged). It follows (somewhat surprisingly, perhaps) that a third case, represented by Q on the graph, would be for Rawls *unjust*, despite the fact that in absolute terms the level of well-being of the least advantaged would be the same (i.e., P and Q have the same value along the vertical axis). The crucial fact for Rawls is, however, that the well-off *gain at the expense of* the worst-off, and this violates the principle of mutual advantage.

The central question about the difference principle is this: In what sense does it embody an ideal *of equality*, given that it advocates inequality under specified conditions? We begin with Rawls's discussion of the principle of redress for undeserved inequalities (T.J., section 17). The difference principle, Rawls argues, goes beyond this principle of redress, and yet it incorporates something of its intent. It goes beyond notions of efficiency, and technocratic values generally, to view the distribution of natural talents among individuals as a common or collective asset; the difference principle is for Rawls an agreement to share the benefits of this common pool of assets. This amounts to *some* kind of redress for those less fortunate in the natural lottery—those more fortunate are allowed to benefit from their natural talents only on terms which improve the lot of the less fortunate. We as rational beings can *determine* that this should be so—we do not have to acquiesce in the injustice that would result from such differences in talent in the same way as we are forced to acquiesce in the inevitability of death. It is not the distribution of natural

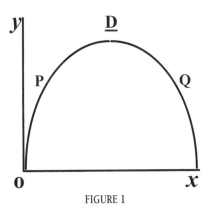

FIGURE 1

talents *itself* that is just or unjust—this distribution is morally neutral—but rather it is how institutions *deal* with it that is just or unjust.

The difference principle is a principle of mutual benefit. It is rational for the less favored man to accept the greater wealth of the most favored, if the former knows that were it not for the latter's more advantaged position he would be worse off. The former therefore has no cause for complaint once the difference principle is in operation. But Rawls wants to show that the man in the *most* advantaged position has no cause for complaint either. As more talented, or more skilled, does he not *deserve* the greater fruits that his labors bring, whether or not they benefit others? Rawls maintains that the notion of desert is one that presupposes a set of rules and conventions within which desert is determined, and that therefore one cannot be said to deserve one's talents, abilities, and so on. If one does not deserve these talents, one cannot be said to have a right to benefit from them exclusively, that is, in a way that does not contribute at all to the welfare of others. In terms of the diagram, mutual benefit characterizes the left-hand part of the curve up to and including the point D, but not the right-hand part.

While it is easy to see why it it would be rational for the least advantaged to accept the difference principle, Rawls insists it would be rational for the most advantaged to accept it as well. In the original position, behind the veil of ignorance, it would be rational for the contracting parties to choose principles of justice that ensure both that the least advantaged are better off than they would be under any other scheme, and that the most favored, that is, those with leadership and entrepreneurial abilities, would be free to realize their potential and get sufficient reward for it. Crucial to persuading the most favored to accept the rationality of the outcome once the veil of ignorance is lifted, and they *know* about their advantaged position, is the notion of a well-ordered society (see section I, subsection B). The most favored will accept the situation because they know that they are members of a well-ordered society, so they know that their advantaged position is not resented by those less favored. By being rationally persuaded to forego what they might have had under a pure system of *laissez-faire* capitalism, they have *ipso facto* assented to a well-ordered society in which there is a consensual, public conception of justice shared by all. But they also know that they stand to gain enough in wealth via the difference principle to motivate them to maintain their productive activity.

On the difference principle, then, it is to *everyone's* benefit that social and economic inequalities should be arranged so as to benefit maximally the *least* advantaged. If we were to sum up the difference principle in a single phrase or slogan, it might well be this: "as much by way of equality as it would be rational to hope for."

3. The Rejection of Utilitarianism

How attractive would utilitarianism be, from the standpoint of the contracting parties in the original position behind the veil of ignorance? Rawls considers two forms of utilitarianism: "classical utilitarianism" as espoused by, for example, Henry Sidgewick, and "average utilitarianism." Neither version fares well in Rawls's hands. His main argument against classical utilitarianism is a highly original restatement of of a well-known criticism of that position, and we examine this first. Then we turn to average utility.

A standard "textbook" objection to classical utilitarianism goes as follows. In seeking to maximize the greatest good or welfare of the greatest number, the utilitarian may be forced to impose on some a series of burdens that are unacceptable from almost any other moral standpoint, *morally* unacceptable to the ordinary man or woman. But, claims the utilitarian, these burdens on a few are justified if they are outweighed by greater gains, greater benefits, to the majority. The objection is: they are not justified, despite this disclaimer.

Rawls takes as his starting point the thesis that a society is just when its major institutions are arranged to achieve the greatest aggregate amount of satisfaction, obtained by adding together the satisfactions of its individual members, and subtracting the dissatisfactions. The aim is to achieve the highest aggregate; and if this means that some individuals have to lose out, so be it. The loss is justified by the greater gains of the rest. Rawls next makes explicit an analogy between individual and society that he claims is implicit in the utilitarian position, and then draws out its consequences. Starting with the fact that an individual has a set of aims, desires, aspirations, and so on, that, over the span of a life, he endeavors to meet and satisfy, Rawls notes the familiar fact of life that sometimes the individual has to prioritise among these aims, desires etc., and this often means that he has to sacrifice some in order to realize others that are more important to him. This principle is then extended to the society as a whole, so that the society advances *its* interests by harmonizing into a coherent scheme the various desires, projects, interests, and so on residing in its individual members. By analogy with the individual case, the society prioritizes among these—hence, some desires and projects have to be sacrificed for the sake of others considered more important. Just as the individual balances present losses against future gains, so the society balances satisfactions and dissatisfactions between different individuals. Hence, just as particular *desires* are sacrificed for the *individual's* greater good, so particular *individuals* are sacrificed for *society's* greater good.

This, says Rawls, is further legitimized by the way utilitarianism defines the good independently of the right, and then defines the right as that which maximizes the good. Those acts are right, therefore, that produce the most good, that is, in this case the largest total system of desire-satisfactions it is possible to produce. Thus, it may be necessary sometimes to sacrifice the rights and liberties of a few in order to attain the greater good as so defined. In this conception, it is not only rational but *right* to violate the liberty of a few for the greater good of the many. And the whole basis of this conception is "to adopt for society as a whole the principle of rational choice for one man" (T.J., pp. 26–27). It is as if there were an impartial spectator who imaginatively identifies with the desires and aspirations of each member of the society as if they were his own, weighs and balances them against each other, then seeks to maximize their realization (given scarce resources, etc.). He then assigns rights and duties accordingly. Some individuals will lose out; but the society as a whole, viewed as some kind of superindividual, inevitably gains. Rawls ends this initial account with the now famous words, "utilitarianism does not take seriously the distinction between persons" (T.J., p. 27).

The lexical priority of Rawls's first principle ensures that individual rights and liberties cannot be traded off for some greater good; and so in this way at least, Rawls's theory is the very antithesis of classical utilitarianism, and this presents no serious challenge to the theory. It is clear that the principle of average utility would be more appealing than classical utility, and in the original position it would be ranked higher. For classical utilitarianism is concerned with maximizing *total* welfare irrespective of distribution, so that in a situation of expanding population, greater total utility may be bought at the price of falling *average* utility; and the greatest total utility may be achieved with a very low final figure for average utility. Average utilitarianism, on the other hand, would pursue average utility at the expense of total utility if necessary, and from the standpoint of the original position there would be a greater probability that the interests of the contracting parties would be served, and so it would constitute a more rational choice than the classical principle. But even this would be found wanting in the original position, for the reasons that follow.

Rawls assesses the principle of average utility from the standpoint of one who has ranged before him a number of possible alternative societies he might join. In the first such thought experiment, he knows his own interests and abilities, and also has enough detailed knowledge about the various alternative societies to know how he would fit into them. There is no problem for him, he can choose with certainty *which* of these societies would best serve his interests. But now Rawls modifies the picture, in two stages. In the first, the hypothetical joiner knows nothing of his own abilities or the place he might occupy in any of the alternative societies, but he *does* know that he has the same preferences as the members of these societies. In the second stage, the latter assumption is dropped. He does not know whether his preferences match those of the societies ranged before him, or indeed anything at all about the structures of these societies. His situation is now indistinguishable from the veil of ignorance. But the veil of ignorance robs him *precisely* of what he needs to know in order to make the kind of choice which makes the principle of average utility meaningful. Hence, from the standpoint of the original position, the principle of average utility cannot but seem meaningless and empty.

In the section that follows, we turn to some critical perspectives on Rawls's theory of justice. Necessarily, we have to be selective. The secondary literature generated by the theory is vast, and it is no exaggeration to say that it has played a major part in setting the agenda for the subject areas of ethics and political philosophy for the foreseeable future.

IV. SOME CRITICAL PERSPECTIVES ON THE THEORY

A. Earlier Critiques of Rawls's Theory

1. Problems of the Original Position

Responses to Rawls's original position have been, roughly, of three kinds. First, the question is asked: How can Rawls base so much substantive theory, namely, his two principles of justice and their implications for recognizably contemporary political institutions, on the deliberations of such radically disengaged, gender neutral Cartesian egos as his contracting parties in effect become, once they are placed behind the veil of ignorance? Second, some critics have claimed that Rawls's original position is not as neutral as he would have us believe. On the one hand, it has been claimed that it is inherently biased in a way that privileges a particular conception of justice and the polity, namely liberal individualism; while on the other, it has been claimed that its bias consists in the fact that it *excludes* certain conceptions (e.g., classical Marxism, Nozick's entitlement conception of justice). In some cases both versions of the second claim are maintained, and in others both the first and the second claims are maintained. Third, there is the view that there are some deeply buried, inexplicit presuppositions in the original position—presuppositions that some critics claim to have unearthed. The three are not mutually exclusive. Perhaps most critics would own to the first; and it is anyway the least interesting as it stands, without further qualification. In what follows, we focus on the second. The critiques we refer to here are to be found in Norman Daniels, *Reading Rawls*. Under this heading we examine one: Thomas Nagel's paper, "Rawls on Justice."

The focus of Nagel's criticism is Rawls's exclusion of substantive conceptions of the good from the original position. It is perfectly understandable, he says, to exclude information on "morally irrelevant grounds like race, sex, parentage or natural endowments" (Daniels, p. 8), but not conceptions *of the good*—which are, as he says, just that and not mere tastes and preferences. The weakness of the argument here lies in treating different conceptions of the good on a par with differences in wealth, social position, and so on. One can be seeking special advantages for oneself in one's choice of principles through knowledge of one's level of wealth and social position; but it makes no sense to speak in this way about a genuinely held conception of the good. Through a conception of the good, one seeks the advantage of all, not merely oneself. Nagel faults Rawls for thinking it unfair that one should seek to promote one's conception of the good in the choice of principles of justice, in just the same way as it is unfair that one should allow one's wealth and social position to influence one's choice. Particular *substantive* conceptions of the good are excluded by the veil of ignorance, but not the premise that the contracting parties unanimously want "the social primary goods," namely, rights and liberties, powers and opportunities, income and wealth, and (later in the book) self-respect. Rawls, as we have seen, wants to avoid "strong assumptions"—people *may* be motivated by considerations other than rational self-interest, such as concern for their fellow humans, the poor, the disenchanted, and so on, but they do not *have* to be. In fact, what their *real* projects and concerns are, in real life, is irrelevant from the point of view of justice as fairness. The primary goods, which *everyone* is presumed to want, provide a kind of common denominator. But the supposed neutrality between conceptions of the good is illusory for Nagel, because it prioritizes those values of liberal individualism that allow mutually disinterested persons to pursue their chosen ends so long as those ends do not interfere with each other. The supposed "weak assumptions" are, Nagel claims, strong, because they are to carry the weight of a public conception of justice whch is intended to permeate the society *despite* the plurality of conceptions of the good. And in so far as it is achieved, it will be *unfair* to all those whose particular conceptions of the good are not advanced by Rawls's primary goods. (The examples Nagel has in mind here are: societies involving a well-defined social structure, societies dedicated to realizing certain higher human capacities, etc.).

2. The Consistency of the Two Principles

A number of critics have claimed that Rawls's two principles are inconsistent. In what follows, we consider *one* such criticism. It occurs in Norman Daniels' paper, "Equal liberty and unequal worth of liberty," and draws on Rawls's distinction between liberty itself and the worth of liberty which was outlined in Section III.B.2 above. The main thrust of Daniels' argument is that it would be rational in the original position to choose equal *worth* of liberty rather than merely equal liberty itself. Daniels takes Rawls's arguments for equal citizenship liberties and uses them to construct an argument for equal worth of liberty. Daniels picks out three claims in Rawls's argument for equal liberties of citizenship: first, public affirmation of equal liberties acts as a social basis for self-respect; second, because the liberties thus affirmed are equal, self-respect will be equally enhanced among all citizens; and third, viewed from behind the veil of ignorance, the risk of low self-respect is minimized. He next constructs parallel claims to these for equal worth of liberty. First, Daniels claims that public knowledge of unequal *worth* of liberty will undermine self-respect just as much as public recognition of unequal *liberties* would. Those with less worth of liberty would know, and others in turn would know about them, that they were *less* able to command the attention of lawyers, the mass media, and so on, than their better-off peers. Second, it is hard to see how Rawls's well-ordered society could guarantee that public affirmation of equal liberties would provide a basis for self-respect, but prevent knowledge of unequal worth of liberty from undermining that self-respect. And third, the contracting parties in the original position, once alerted to the distinction, would consider it to be as rational to guarantee equal *worth* of liberty as to guarantee the equal liberties themselves.

As a result of this argument, Daniels thinks that

the two principles do not form a consistent whole, and that it is Rawls's first principle that contains what he calls "the egalitarian punch," once the constraints definitive of liberty are widened to include the worth of liberty.

3. Nozick's Libertarian Critique

Robert Nozick's own theory of justice, 'the entitlement theory' as he calls it, is proposed and defended vigorously in Chapter 7 of *Anarchy, State and Utopia*. The first part of that chapter consists of an account of his theory, and the second part comprises a critique of Rawls's theory. Having read the first part of the chapter, the reader might be forgiven for wondering whether the second part was necessary—for it is clear at once how *different* the two theories are. In many ways it is clear what Nozick's criticisms are from reading *only* the first part of the chapter, certainly at the level of "principles of justice." Without going into too much detail, Nozick's entitlement theory of justice is based on a strong notion of individual property right, according to which no one has a right to anything unless he or she has obtained it by gift or transfer from someone else who legitimately owns it, or unless he or she has been the first legitimate owner. The first of these is "the principle of justice in transfer," the second the "principle of justice in acquisition," which is meant to determine when a first acquisition of something previously unowned is just. Coupled with the claim that any state more extensive than the minimal state violates individual rights, and therefore that any taxes levied for purposes beyond financing the minimal state are illegitimate, clearly there is no place for *redistributive* social policies involving welfare benefits, and so on— whether directly, or at the level of the basic structure of society according to the difference principle. Indeed, on Nozick's theory, operating the difference principle would violate individual rights.

So much is clear from the first part of Nozick's Chapter 7. But Nozick is not content with this. He wants to show that the way in which the original position is set up *actually excludes* Nozick's theory. He does this by appeal to the distinction between *historical, entitlement principles* and *patterned, end-state principles*. He claims that the original position is capable of generating the latter, but not the former. Before leaving Nozick's critique of Rawls, we mention one final point. Nozick claims that the nearest Rawls comes to discussing anything resembling the entitlement theory is when he speaks of "the system of natural liberty" (see Section III.B.ii above), and he takes issue with Rawls's assertion that differences in talent, circumstances etc. are 'arbi-

trary from a moral point of view' (see Nozick, pp. 213–231).

B. The Communitarian Critique: Michael Sandel

There are four contemporary philosophers who are considered to be the major communitarian critics of liberalism: Michael Sandel, Alasdair MacIntyre, Charles Taylor and Michael Walzer. In what follows, we examine Michael Sandel's critique, which appears in his book, *Liberalism and the Limits of Justice*, for the reason that it is closely focused on Rawls. Central to Sandel's critique is the claim that at the heart of Rawls's theory there is a certain conception of the self. It is a conception of the self such that it is given prior to its actions, values, purposes, and qualities of character. If we take seriously Rawls's veil of ignorance, then (arguably) what is left behind the veil after the various "encumbrances" and "externalities" have been removed is, surely, the real self as Rawls conceives it. This has important implications for Rawls's theory, and especially as regards the primacy of justice.

It is Sandel's claim that the notion of the self he finds in Rawls is central to the thesis that justice is the first virtue of social institutions. However, as Sandel points out, the idea that justice has some kind of moral primacy is not new. Sandel cites Locke's claim that man's natural rights are stronger than any commonwealth can override, as well as J.S. Mill's claim that justice is the chief, most sacred, and most binding part of morality. But Rawls's understanding of the primacy of justice, Sandel claims, has another and a deeper source—and it is here that Kant is first mentioned, as the originator of a kind of liberalism for which Sandel coins the name "deontological liberalism." The chief feature of this variant of liberalism is that it elevates the primacy of justice to a higher level of abstraction and gives it, Sandel claims, a deeper justification.

This deeper justification consists of the notion of the primacy of the right over the good, coupled with a prior and independent definition or construal of the right. We are now firmly in Kantian territory. The principles of the right are independently derived, and are expressive of autonomy understood in its Kantian sense; namely, rational nature as an end in itself, having not merely "worth" but also "dignity." The primacy of justice thus acquires a strong metaphysical basis. *Justice is then an end in itself, regulating all other ends.* The reader should notice at this point how far *this* understanding of Rawls is from those earlier understandings that view Rawls's assertion of the primacy of justice as an attempt to fudge up some diluted virtue that the diverse full conceptions of the good, excluded by the veil of ignorance, might perchance have in common. Sandel's Rawls is elevated to a higher plane. Famously—or notoriously, depending on one's view—Rawls himself gives enough fuel to this understanding of his theory to make Sandel's critique worthy of serious attention. This is so particularly in *Theory of Justice*, Section 40, where he speaks of the two principles of justice as categorical imperatives in Kant's sense, and as *expressing our nature as free and equal rational beings.*

However, Sandel comes not to praise Caesar but to bury him. This very strength of "deontological liberalism" is, according to Sandel, also its downfall. This is most clearly seen in Sandel's construal of the Rawlsian self, and in the understanding of community that it bespeaks. The very elevation of the self to the higher realms of Kantian autonomy at the same time distances it from its projects, its ends, its character, its settled and communally embodied convictions about the good. *Discovering* oneself, *discovering* one's ends, are replaced by *choosing.* (Kant himself perhaps unwittingly fuels this understanding, when he claims at the start of the *Groundwork of the Metaphysic of Morals* that the only thing good without qualification is "a good will," and that in effect one's character with its virtues, powers, and abilities is secondary and *external* to the good will or true self).

At this point, Sandel's critique of Rawls begins to parallel Hegel's critique of Kant. Because the self is given prior to its ends, or what Sandel calls its "constitutive attachments," one's projects and attachments can only be understood as something this distanced self *has*, something the self *owns*, and thus not what the self *is*. Parallel to this, my relations to others in the polity—in which (as Rawls puts it) we are all mutually disinterested rational self-interest maximizers (albeit with an intrinsic sense of justice)—also become distanced. Communitarian aims can at best be professed as ideals, and can never attain that solidary embodiment that requires another conception of self and community—a conception in which my ends, my character, my relations with others, constitute what I *am*, something I might *discover* and bring to awareness from the prereflective depths in which the self in community with others is, for Sandel, truly located.

Rawls, aware perhaps of these metaphysical difficulties that his theory in its more Kantian formulations might appear to generate, has moved away from these wider issues about the nature of the self, the nature of community, and so on. This is the emphasis to be found in Rawls's *Political Liberalism*—a way of thinking that possibly began with "Justice as Fairness: Political not Metaphysical." In this paper, in a footnote (note 21 on p. 239), Rawls specifically repudiates the picture of the self Sandel attributes to him. But *can* this picture of the self be repudiated and yet leave the theory of justice intact? This and similar questions the reader will have to seek his or her own answer to. (Useful here is Stephen Mulhall and Adam Swift. *Liberals and Communitarians.*) In the next subsection, we deal briefly with how Rawls sees the relation between his new book *Political Liberalism* and the theory of justice in *Theory of Justice* that we have examined hitherto.

C. *Political Liberalism* and Justice as Fairness

Although it may appear that *Political Liberalism* and the works that led up to it constitute Rawls's response to communitarian critiques, Rawls himself disavows this motive. He claims that the new work seeks to preserve and strengthen the theory of justice as fairness by freeing it from possible interpretations he is now at pains to disavow, and that the theory as presented in *Theory of Justice* may appear to legitimize. He claims that the theory of justice can be defended without taking sides on any metaphysical disputes over the nature of the self. This is clearly at variance with the more Kantian formulations of the theory of justice—and in particular, with *Theory of Justice* section 40, "the Kantian interpretation of justice as fairness," where Rawls views the original position as incorporating a standpoint similar to that of Kant's noumenal self. More generally, Rawls claims that justice as fairness does not rest on any *particular* conception of liberalism, but is rather compatible with *any* form of it.

Rawls still wishes to assert the primacy of justice, but *without* the metaphysical underpinnings that Sandel ascribes to him regarding the nature of the self and the nature of liberalism. It will go some way toward explaining what Rawls *means* by a "political not metaphysical" conception of liberalism, and of justice as fairness, if we can come to see how he claims to be able to do this. Let us first notice the reference he makes to a certain historical fact: the large fact of the modern world, owing its origin to the rise of Protestantism and to the consequent emergence of the need for religious toleration, that no citizen of a modern liberal democratic state expects to live in his or her society under a single, universally accepted, all-embracing conception of the *summum bonum* or highest good of the kind that was common in medieval Europe. We are at home with the idea that self-esteem and mutual respect can be workable ideals among citizens whose worldviews are vastly different. Pluralism is thus an inescapable fact—a requirement—of modern life. But not just *any* pluralism. Conceptions of the good that deny equality and liberty as these are understood in a modern liberal democracy would be excluded in *any* conception of liberalism. Rawls accordingly speaks of this fact as "the fact of *reasonable* pluralism" (P.L., p. xvi—our italics). What this means is that within a liberal democratic framework, there will always be room for *reasoned* debate over different understandings of such notions as liberty, equality and justice. By "reasoned debate" we mean proper attention to argument to the exclusion of such factors as prejudice, narrow self-interest, and *merely* rhetorical disputation—the point being that it is both conceivable and common for rational persons, in all good faith, to arrive at different understandings of justice, equality, liberty, and so on, in a situation where there is public avowal of the mutual respect enjoined by the liberal ideal.

Crucial to understanding Rawls's later position is the term "overlapping consensus." This is meant to express the idea that persons with radically different *worldviews*—for example, a religious believer, a thinker who takes a Kantian view of individual autonomy, and a humanist liberal—may nonetheless, despite their differences, have shared *political* values. They may think that the basic structure of their society (i.e., the basic institutions concerned with the primary goods of income, wealth, social position, and the bases of self-respect) should conform to a particular conception of justice that, upon reflection, they find themselves reaching a consensus over. Thus, persons with radically *different* ultimate beliefs and conceptions of the good may come to hold identical *political* beliefs, despite the fact that they may hold these beliefs for different reasons. Hence, "*overlapping* (rather than identical) consensus": the religious believer respecting his fellow citizen as equal because (say) he sees God as loving all persons equally, the Kantian because he sees persons as equally ends in themselves, the humanist liberal because he has certain overriding, purely political values concerned with rights, liberty, equality, and so on.

Given this notion of an "overlapping consensus," we need to focus on Rawls's claim that the political values (and hence justice as fairness) have priority over ultimate belief systems or conceptions of the highest good. What is implied here is the possibility of a "political, not metaphysical" affirmation of a set of values, sustainable in the public sphere, that is the result of a genuine consensus between citizens who may, as individuals or as members of constituent communities, have vastly different conceptions of the good. But the priority of this set of values, while absolute, is nonetheless restricted to what properly belongs in the public political sphere: those institutions of society that are concerned with the distribution of the social primary goods.

Rawls's intention is that the public political sphere as thus outlined should be understood as constituting a genuine sphere of value that makes *moral* demands on citizens. What this excludes, for Rawls, is a purely *instrumental* conception of the public sphere, that is, one that serves only the narrowest self-interest of individuals, and therefore a purely instrumental conception of social cooperation and of community itself. In *Theory of Justice* he explicitly rejects this conception (see Section 79, "The Idea of Social Union"). Briefly, the essence of this discarded conception is that there is no cooperative social value *per se*—there are only individual aims and aspirations, and the institutions of society exist merely as the means, the instrument, by which these aims and aspirations are realized. In contrast to this, Rawls claims that justice as fairness constitutes a consensual agreement to regard society as regulated by shared, public values in the form of a conception of justice, which itself means that one wills not only one's own good but the collective public good. Essentially the same conception is carried over into *Political Liberalism,* where Rawls—in the context of his discussion of the overlapping consensus—extols "the virtues of political cooperation," including among their number tolerance, reasonableness and a sense of fairness (P.L., p. 157).

Let us take at its face value Rawls's claim that his later work does not constitute replies to critics (communitarian or otherwise), but rather represents his own rethinking, his own shift of emphasis. It is then easy to see what is *left out* by the later work: the metaphysical infrastructure that Sandel finds in *Theory of Justice*, and that Rawls himself lends weight to in Section 40 and elsewhere in the book. But what is *added* by the later work? This is not an easy question to answer. Clearly he is trying to free his conception of justice from the metaphysical baggage that—rightly or wrongly— Sandel considers inseparable from it, and also from too specific a conception of liberalism. In the process, many themes familiar to readers of *Theory of Justice* recur: a well-ordered society, equality between (moral) persons, the original position, the exclusion of strong assumptions, among others. In brief: you do not have to be a specific *kind* of liberal to be persuaded about justice as fairness—you can be *any* kind of liberal—and you do not have to endorse any particular metaphysical thesis about the nature of selves or persons.

The later work is written in full awareness of "the fact of reasonable pluralism." In accordance with this fact, it is *not unreasonable* for one to disagree with justice as fairness, and to have good arguments and conscientious reasons for doing so. Espousing a *different* conception of justice, within certain limits, is not therefore to be viewed as *inevitably* either an expression of mere self-interest, or of class-interest, or simply narrow-mindedness, or a failure of logical reasoning. Were a "metaphysical" construal of justice as fairness possible (and more generally, of a particular conception of liberal theory), then the failure to espouse that conception of justice, together with its liberal underpinning, could be viewed as a failure of logic, or ideological bias, or mere perversity, or the like. These considerations perhaps serve to explain what the shift from the metaphysical to the political essentially is. To clarify it further, we need to note another crucial element in the later work, namely, Rawls's notion of an underlying political culture shared by all who assent to the values of constitutional democracy. The ideas lying submerged within this political culture can be regarded as shared in this way—a kind of common property of all who are committed to democratic institutions. Justice as fairness is then represented by Rawls as *one* reasonable interpretation or articulation of this implicitly shared political culture. Others are possible within the constraints of "reasonable pluralism," and the arguments supporting them will appear reasonable. Justice as fairness is, however, Rawls's own preferred interpretation of the underlying political culture, and for this he is prepared to argue. But he argues for it as a *political* conception, distinguishing it from (a) a metaphysical theory, and (b) a total, all-embracing *moral* theory.

D. Concluding Remarks

The foregoing subsection constitutes a summary, albeit brief, of how Rawls sees his theory of justice in the light of his later work. We shall not take issue with Rawls on this; we shall merely point out some alternatives. We may accept Rawls's own account of the relation between the earlier and the later work, or we may not. If we are impressed by Sandel's critique, Rawls must convince us either that the metaphysical presuppositions Sandel claims to find are not really there, or that the later work finally banishes them. If we are not so convinced, the project of a political but not metaphysical account of justice as fairness must fail. If, on the other hand, we accept Rawls's claim that a purely political account is possible, then Sandel's critique no longer stands.

Of the other critiques of Rawls we have considered, it seems that two would fall readily within the category of alternative conceptions under "reasonable pluralism." Nozick's critique, and his own rival theory of justice, share with Rawls's theory a commitment to the priority of liberty, but construe equality differently—but not *so* differently that no discussion is possible. Norman Daniels also prioritizes liberty; but in counting economic constraints as among those definitive of lack of liberty, he makes the "worth" of liberty a part of liberty itself. This is something many liberals would hesitate over. The debate over economic constraints and liberty is a familiar battleground between liberals and Marxists—but it can just as easily be viewed as a debate *within* liberalism, between socialists (or social democrats) and libertarians. If this is so, then clearly Daniels's "worth of liberty" argument represents just one more option within "reasonable pluralism."

Nagel's criticisms are perhaps less easy to accommodate. We close with some remarks about these criticisms. Nagel makes essentially two points: that it is wrong to treat conceptions of the highest good as if they were factors comparable to race, sex, level of wealth, and so on, from the standpoint of the original position; and that Rawls's supposedly weak assumptions are really quite strong. The presumption that everyone, whatever his or her ultimate beliefs or conceptions may be, will place the same weight on the social primary goods may be simply wrong. As we have seen, in his later work Rawls extols the value of social cooperation under a liberal system as a value in its own right. Such a value may well come into conflict with some conscientiously held beliefs, particularly beliefs that require patently *anti*liberal interventions in liberal institutions. *Can* liberalism sustain a polity with a mixture of strong subcommunities (humanist, Roman Catholic, Islamic, Buddhist, Hindu, etc.) without the spectre of secession—or worse, civil war—perpetually hanging over it? This would be the scenario if Rawls's "weak assumptions" turned out to be *too* weak. If, on the other hand, they are as strong as Nagel claims they are, might they not have the outcome, on the historical scale, of weakening the various belief systems, and substituting in their place some bland relativism? Or is there some greater imaginative leap of which humanity may one day prove itself capable, in relation to which liberalism is only a preparatory stage?

Perhaps there is. There again, perhaps not. In this we are hostages to history—and "political liberalism," unsustained by any metaphysical "grand narratives," perhaps throws us all the more forcibly against this inescapable condition.

Also See the Following Articles

COMMUNITARIANISM • CONTRACTARIAN ETHICS • HUMANISM • KANTIANISM • LIBERALISM • THEORIES OF JUSTICE: HUMAN NEEDS • UTILITARIANISM

Bibliography

Daniels, N. (Ed.). (1975). *Reading Rawls.* Oxford: Basil Blackwell
MacIntyre, A. (1988). *Whose justice? Which rationality?* London: Duckworth.
Miller, D., & Walzer, M. (eds.). (1995). *Pluralism, justice and equality.* Oxford: Oxford University Press.
Mulhall, S., & Swift, A. (1996). *Liberals and communitarians* (2nd ed.). Oxford and Cambridge, MA: Basil Blackwell.
Nozick, R. (1974). *Anarchy, state and utopia.* Oxford: Basil Blackwell.
Pogge, T. W. (1988). *Realizing Rawls.* Ithaca and London: Cornell University Press.
Rawls, J. (1971). *A theory of justice.* Cambridge, MA: Harvard University Press.
Rawls, J. (1993). *Political liberalism.* New York: Columbia University Press.
Rawls, J. (1985). Justice as fairness: Political not metaphysical. *Philosophy and Public Affairs,* 14, 3.
Sandel, M. (1982). *Liberalism and the limits of justice.* Cambridge: Cambridge University Press.

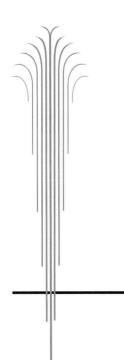

THOMISM

Jude P. Dougherty
The Catholic University of America

GLOSSARY

beatific vision After death, man's union with God, in which the human intellect is brought into direct contact with the divine mind itself and in knowing that mind achieves its contemplative good.

common good The good of the community or polis considered in its totality; the locus of personal self-fulfillment. In the interest of communal goals individuals may be required partially to subordinate their autonomy and personal goals. The concept implies that social life is fundamentally communal, not, as Hobbes would have it, based on a discordant group requiring a sovereign to guarantee one's long-term preservation.

Enlightenment A seventeenth- and eighteenth-century philosophical movement that self-consciously contrasted itself to the medieval period or to the dark ages in which belief in the existence of God and the immortality of the human soul were taken for granted. The Anglo-French Enlightenment is often contrasted with the German. Both emphasize the value of reason over faith, the natural over the supernatural; both challenge the inherited or the traditional as symbolized by mitre and crown. Man is considered to be the measure of all.

epistemology The theory of knowledge, including the philosophy of science.

essence The fundamental characteristic or quiddity of the thing under consideration as opposed to properties and other accidental features that it may or may not have. Considered as a source of the activity of a thing, it is a synonym for "nature."

final cause The purpose, reason, or end on account of which an entity is either brought into being or acts. The principle of finality is sometimes stated as "Every agent acts on account of a preconceived end." For Aquinas, this is true even of the material and sentient orders, which are thought to be purposive as a result of the divine creative act.

metaphysics The most general account of being, focusing on the common features of the material and immaterial orders of reality. For Aquinas, metaphysics consists of a philosophy of being, a philosophy of God, and a philosophy of knowledge.

natural law Refers to laws of nature as uncovered in the natural sciences and to laws discovered by philosophical reflection on human nature. Natural law is contrasted with positive or man-made law.

transcendental As applied to Thomism, it indicates a willingness to place the epistemological problem first, that is, prior to metaphysics as one attempts to intellectually grasp that which is beyond sensory experience, namely, God and an immaterial order.

THOMISM takes its name from Thomas Aquinas (1224/25–1274) whose philosophy inspired a following in his lifetime and whose work has generated an interest in every century since his death. The "Thomism" to which the term is most often applied is a movement of the late nineteenth century, a movement generated in part by the endorsement of Aquinas's thought by Pope Leo XIII. Leo's endorsement was largely a defensive move on the part of a religious leader. Western Christianity had been intellectually challenged by the Enlightenment, Anglo/French and German, an eighteenth- and early nineteenth-century philosophical movement that set about to replace an inherited, largely Christian, way of interpreting nature, man, and society.

Ecclesiastical leaders were not alone in their assessment of the task. Of the same generation as Leo XIII, the American philosopher Josiah Royce addressed the need for a philosophy which could serve as a rational preamble to the Christian faith. Royce attempted to provide one with his own version of an Hegelian inspired idealism; Leo XIII, in his 1879 encyclical *Aeterni Patris*, recommended not Hegel, but the philosophy of St. Thomas. St. Thomas was recommended, Leo XIII said, because of the value of his philosophy in meeting "the critical state of the times in which we live." In Leo XIII's judgment, the regnant philosophies of his day not only undercut Christian faith, but because of their moral implications were beginning to have negative effects on personal and communal life. Succinctly he wrote, "Erroneous theories respecting our duty to God and our responsibilities as men, originally propounded in philosophical schools, have gradually permeated all ranks of society and secured acceptance among the majority of men."

The problem for Leo XIII was not limited to the philosophical arena. The philosophers also tutored the architects of the new biblical criticism, the *Redaktionsgeschichte* movement. Many German scholars under the influence of the *Aufklärung* examined the Gospels and the life of Jesus from the standpoint of the higher criticism and concluded that Christ was not God but a supremely good man whose moral imperatives deserved to be followed. This conclusion Leo XIII could not accept; there was no philosophically compelling reason to embrace a purely naturalistic interpretation of the sacred scriptures. With Royce, he affirmed that philosophy must be fought by philosophy.

I. MEDIEVAL RECEPTION OF AQUINAS

While "Thomism" is identified with a nineteenth- and twentieth-century movement, it should be realized that Thomas was widely studied in his own lifetime. His philosophy was endorsed and disputed by members of his own Dominican order, by members of the rival Franciscan order and by the secular masters of the University of Paris. Well-known opponents of Thomas included the Dominican Robert Kilwardby (d. 1279), the Franciscan John Peckham (d. 1292), and the Parisian master Henry of Ghent (ca. 1217–1293). In spite of initial opposition, appreciation of Aquinas grew steadily as time went on. His basic metaphysical positions were adopted by such masters as Ulric of Strassburg (d. ca. 1278), Giles of Rome (ca. 1243–1316), Peter of Auvergne (ca. 1240/1250–1304), Godfrey of Fontaines (ca. 1250–1306), and Vincent of Beauvais (d. 1264). Dante (1265–1321) may be counted as an early disciple. Thomas's Franciscan opponents were to find their champions in St. Bonaventure (ca. 1221–1274) and John Duns Scotus (1266–1308). The philosophy of Scotus has remained a viable system to this day as one of a number of philosophical options compatible with the Catholic faith.

II. NINETEENTH- AND TWENTIETH-CENTURY THOMISTIC MOVEMENT

It is always hazardous to write about a movement. The difficulty is compounded when the movement is contemporary and therefore fluid. There is the risk not only of attributing to the whole movement what is true of only some individuals within it, but of neglecting that personal philosophical growth that may have removed a thinker from the movement altogether, or that may have radically changed its direction. Despite these difficulties, this article endeavors to survey the scene of contemporary Thomism as a philosophical movement. In one form or another it is a worldwide movement that is as distinguishable as the phenomenological movement in Europe or the analytic movement in the United Kingdom and the United States.

Any attempt to characterize a movement encounters the difficulty of selectivity. Obviously not everyone who may be called a Thomist can fall under this study or need be taken into account. By selecting the thought of a few representatives of the different currents within the movement, we can attempt to give a picture of the whole.

Thomism as a philosophy is characterized by the conviction that philosophy is a science with conclusions that are valid and can be passed from generation to generation. Possessing a methodology consequent upon its understanding of science, it employs a dictionary-length set of distinctions and definitions that makes concerted work possible. Thus, its worldwide adherents, despite cultural and linguistic differences, can immediately enter into discourse, advancing insight, correcting failures and responding to criticism. Thomistic institutes, conferences, textbooks, and monographs are to be found from Lublin to Washington to Kyoto, and in Nairobi, Buenos Aires and Santiago.

III. PROMINENT SCHOLARS

The revived interest in Aquinas sparked by Leo XIII gave rise not only to systematic textual studies but to an interest in medieval philosophy as a whole. Programs in medieval philosophy arose and historians of medieval philosophy multiplied throughout the Catholic world and beyond. Interest was not confined to the thought of Aquinas. Bonaventure, Scotus, and Ockham, among others, received their share of attention. The Thomistic revival led to new colleges and institutes named in honor of Aquinas. From the late nineteenth and early twentieth centuries, one must acknowledge the seminal contributions of Désiré Mercier (1851–1926), Ambroise Gardeil (1859–1931), Joseph Gredt (1863–1940), Réginald Garrigou-Lagrange (1877–1964), and Antonin D. Sertillanges (1863–1948), to mention only a few.

Two French scholars, Jacques Maritain (1882–1973) and Etienne Gilson (1884–1978) were to exercise considerable influence in North America. Gilson founded the Pontifical Institute of Medieval Studies, affiliated with St. Michael's College, University of Toronto, and that graduate faculty, which included prominent Thomists such as A. C. Pegis and G. B. Phelan, was to train like-minded scholars who were to occupy professorial positions throughout the United States, prominently at Marquette University, Notre Dame University, St. Louis University and Loyola University of Chicago. Another major center of Thomistic studies was The Catholic University of America, one of the earliest graduate faculties in the United States. Under the direction of Edward

A. Pace, its School of Philosophy awarded its first Ph.D. in 1894 upon the submission of a dissertation investigating the thought of Herbert Spencer. Many of its early dissertations not only explored the thought of St. Thomas but critically evaluated contemporary philosophers and movements, "ad mentem divi Thomae." Among its prominent alumni were Leo Ward and Vincent Smith, who taught at Notre Dame University; James Collins, who became a respected historian at St. Louis University; and John Noonan, a Federal appellate judge, who, before appointment to the bench from a professorship at the University of California, Berkeley, produced important studies in moral philosophy, notably on usury, abortion, bribes, and judicial responsibility. Allan Wolter, although trained in the Thomistic tradition, became a prominent translator and interpreter of the philosophy of Duns Scotus.

Gerard Smith (Marquette University), Norris Clarke (Fordham University), Yves Simon (University of Notre Dame), and James Weisheipl (University of Toronto) must be mentioned as prominent Thomists who wrote and taught through the middle decades of this century. Nicholas Rescher, reviewing the status of American philosophy, has noted that the Catholic "big five" (Boston College, The Catholic University of America, Fordham University, Georgetown University, and The University of Notre Dame) in the period 1986–1991 outproduced five major Ivy League schools (Harvard, Yale, Princeton, Columbia, and The University of Pennsylvania) in awarding Ph.D.'s in the field of philosophy. Few of those dissertations were on Aquinas per se, but the spirit of Thomism was not absent in the topics and philosophers selected for study and in the method of inquiry employed.

IV. ARISTOTELIAN CHARACTER

Thomism is a realism in the spirit of Aristotle and for that reason many speak of an Aristolian/Thomistic tradition. Thomas himself commented on most of the major works of Aristotle, and the common scholastic method of commenting on classical works is still followed in the Thomistic school. Thomism is a realism with a metaphysics at its core. It is confident both in the intelligibility of nature and in the human intellect's ability to ferret out the secrets of nature. Science, it holds, is the intellectual habit of seeking explanations, not simply one of describing and predicting. Thomists in common accept Aristotle's distinction between potency and act, his doctrine of the four causes, and his distinctions between matter and form, substance and accident, power and activity. With Thomas they acknowledge a real distinction between essence and existence, a distinction not found in Aristotle. God is conceived as self-existent being, the source of the existence of things. He is named by way of analogy, in which the limited perfections found in things are affirmed of God but in an unlimited way. The basis for all affirmations is the principle of efficient causality, namely, that what is not intelligible in terms of itself must be rendered intelligible in terms of another. In common with Aristotle and Thomas, Thomists affirm the principle of finality, expressed as "every agent acts on account of a preconceived end" or "being in act is intelligible." From considerations of human knowing and conation, Thomists reason to an immaterial intellect and will, faculties of an immaterial soul which in principle is capable of survival after death. That the separated soul does continue in existence, they maintain, is not known from reason but from divine revelation.

Aquinas's major work is the *Summa Theologiae*. Starting with experience, he argues to the existence of God and to affirmations about His nature. The treatise on God (*Summa Theologiae* I, QQ. 2–26) includes a defense of the thesis that faith is a completion of natural insight, a criticism of a priori demonstrations of the existence of God, and summary statements of the arguments then commonly employed to establish "what every one calls God." God is conceived as absolutely simple, perfect, infinite, eternal, omnipotent, and omniscient. He possesses intellect and will and has created the world ex nihilo by an act of free choice. Drawing upon Aristotle, Thomas expands the Stagirite's analysis of being and the transcendentals, treating of substance and the categories, causation and change. His treatise on man (*Summa Theologiae* I, QQ. 75–88) is a carefully developed interpretation of Aristotle's *De Anima*. In the second part of the *Summa* his moral philosophy contains an illuminating and detailed interpretation of Aristotle's *Nicomachean Ethics*.

Portions of Aquinas's work may be marred for the contemporary reader by the use of astronomical and physiological views that have long been discarded in the natural sciences. The intelligent reader, however, will have little difficulty in separating Aquinas's philosophical arguments from their medieval scientific contexts.

V. ETHICAL THEORY

In the field of ethics Thomism is associated with the theory of natural law. The concept of "natural law" is acknowledged to be an ancient one. It is found in the Greek poets, in the Athenian philosophers Plato and Aristotle, and in the Roman Stoics Cicero and Seneca. The notion is rather simple. There are laws of nature, some of which we have discovered and have articulated for ourselves and for others. A law of nature is simply a report on what is. It is a description of an act or process that under specified conditions remains invariant through time and place. A law of nature is opposed to an accidental generality, for example, all the senators from the southern provinces have deep brown eyes. Examples of natural laws known to antiquity might include: copper expands when heated, silver is malleable, wine loosens the tongue, to be fruitful the vines must have at least 85 days of sun, creditability follows a habit of speaking the truth, and a well-ordered household permits leisure.

These homey, prescientific laws are analogous to the modern laws of physics, chemistry, biology, and those laws that govern music, painting, architecture, corporate management, and personal fulfillment. They can be stated flatly as declarative sentences, for example, bodily health is contingent upon a proper diet; or they may take the form of admonitions: "One should observe a healthful diet," "Desiring other people's property will make you miserable," or "Thou shall not covet thy neighbor's goods." Some of the laws that deal with personal self-fulfillment are "moral laws" as distinct from rules that promote good manners. The Fulbright Scholars Program, for example, is promoting good manners when it suggests to American youths going abroad to bring flowers to the hostess when invited to a dinner party.

To be moral, one must be prudent, temperate, just, and courageous. To be just, one must pay homage to God, honor one's father and mother, remain faithful to one's spouse, and respect the terms of any contract to which one has agreed. The list goes on and on. Experience teaches that the cardinal virtues, prudence, temperance, justice, and fortitude, must be cultivated early in life if one is to lead a successful life.

In providing a theory about the determination of moral norms, Thomism speaks to topics such as ethical reasoning, the movement from descriptive to normative assertions, the use of science in ethics, the extralegal grounds for judicial decision, and the societal basis of law. In this respect Thomism may be regarded as a meta-ethic because it is more like advice about how to proceed than a set of firm conclusions.

The confidence that nature is intelligible was a distinctive feature of the Greek mind that gave birth to the concept of natural law. Intelligibility, for the Greek, owed itself to design, and was explained variously by an ultimate final cause drawing all things to itself or in terms of a demiurgos, a divine-like artificer. For Aquinas, and for the Thomists who follow him, nature is conceived as the handiwork of God. Things are as they are because of a divine plan. Both Aristotle and Aquinas affirm that things have natures that disclose tendencies and that both are the product of intelligence. Aristotle, for example, maintained that from a consideration of what a thing is in its tendential aspects one can determine what is suitable for it—namely, its good. From a consideration of what man is, one can determine what ends he ought to pursue. For Aristotle, the supreme end of man is happiness, which consists primarily in intellectual activity, all other pursuits being subordinate or instrumental to that one. In practice, to use a contemporary example, this means that one should not spend all of one's leisure on the golf course; one needs to spend some time in one's library as well. Aquinas's principal addition is that ultimate fulfillment consists of an eternal beatitude, that is, in union with the divine, in which man's intellectual and appetitive faculties will find complete satisfaction. For Aquinas, ultimate beatitude is possible even if temporal beatitude of the Aristotelian sort escapes one by reason of chance or the poverty of the human organism. The concept "eternal beatitude" is, of course, a theological one and, while plausible from a philosophical point of view, is beyond demonstration.

In these considerations we can observe the foundation of a natural law methodology. It consists of advice to look to man's nature to determine what is good for him. No conclusions are ready-made. This is evident in both Aristotle and Aquinas, although there is a difference in starting points and emphases. Aristotle's ethical quest begins with a man already in society with a given set of mores. The culture that has already formed him will play an important role as he systematically works out a moral code. Aquinas's beginning is different but compatible. He begins with the confidence that nature is the handiwork of the divine, with the conviction that the divine intellect is the root of an order that the human intellect is able to perceive. What this order is remains, as it did for Aristotle, to be discovered. Hence Aquinas's emphasis on reason. In his famous "Treatise on Law," he tacitly identifies law with reason; elsewhere he develops a methodology for reason to follow.

It is significant that Aquinas does not attempt to deduce from general principles the content of natural law. It is also significant that he draws no clear-cut distinction between natural and civil law. His famous definition of law, summarized as "an ordinance of reason promulgated by one who has authority in the community," while formulated to be predicated of all law, is primarily a definition of civil law. Most Thomists recognize that there is no hard and fast line where so-called natural law leaves off and civil law begins. True, there is this difference: civil law is articulated in some fashion by the state, whereas natural law is not, yet the difference is not determinative. Natural law may be articulated by a church or by an academic community and may be reflected in the ordinances of a community; by whom it is articulated is not significant. Nor is it significant that the state does not articulate all that is affirmed by the community of scholars, call them rabbis, bishops, or professors. Deserving of emphasis is the fact that law, natural or civil, is the product of reason figuring out what is good for the race, men taken as individuals or as members of a community, a community designed to serve their common interest. This suggests that the principal difference between natural law and civil law is the difference between an intellectually articulated norm and a promulgated statute.

Thomists, like anyone in the natural law tradition, recognize that there are certain constants in man, and that these can be discerned. These constants are the grounds for those normative enunciations that will remain the same from generation to generation, whenever and wherever man is found. The variables are cultural, economic, and topographical. The proportion between the constant and the variable is not worked out; Aquinas himself is not generous in mentioning constants. The assertion that the natural law is immutable can easily misrepresent Aquinas's position. As he presents his views in the "Treatise on Law," most of the content of the natural law is variable. For example, a contemporary Thomist might say that in home construction, safety is promoted through building codes, but building codes vary from climate to climate. The enduring principle pertains to safety; the variables are topographical. Similarly, in any profession, accepted standards may change as matters become more intricate. In the field of accounting, for example, the enduring principle of fairness or justice will dictate changes in reporting as complexity requires. In the delivery of health care extraordinary means may become normal care through technological innovation. Thus, the availability of the CAT scan, having ceased to be prohibitively expensive as a medical diagnostic device, may render morally culpable a physician who fails to employ it.

Aquinas, in his treatise on law, affirms principally that law is rooted in something other than the will of the legislator. Where he distinguishes between the immutable and temporal aspects of law, he is recognizing that in certain basic features man is everywhere alike. But his emphasis is on reason as the proper way of discovering what is good for man. In stressing reason Aquinas is more concerned with inquiry than he is with the content of laws discovered.

It should be clear that not everything that is legislated or deemed to be law by a lawmaking court is to be treated as law. Aquinas will not give the force of law to those enactments that clearly fly in the face of reason and experience. One may assume, however, that when lawmaking bodies are interested in determining the equitable, and conditions are propitious, they will in a large measure, perhaps as far as humanly possible, succeed. This is not to ignore the fact that much legislation is a tissue of compromise, often reflecting conflicting and contradictory insights and principles. Free intelligence and goodwill will produce good law, not inevitably but for the most part. Good positive law is continuous with the dictates of nature, or natural law if you will.

VI. METAPHYSICAL AND EPISTEMOLOGICAL PRESUPPOSITIONS

The foregoing concept of natural law rests upon two ontological pillars: (1) the conviction that there are natural structures, and (2) the conviction that the processes of nature are orderly; in the language of Aristotle, upon the principles of substance and final causality, and upon the related notions of potency and act.

In an attempt to understand change, Aristotle distinguishes between the relatively permanent nature (essence) and its modifications (accidents). Becoming is understood as the gaining of further actuality. Through its activity a substance emerges from isolation and enters into relation with other substances, either by passively receiving their influence to which it is actively open, or by actively acting in ways ultimately determined by its essence. Each entity tends toward further actuality beyond what it already has. For Thomists, following the lead of Aristotle, the whole of reality is shot through with the distinction between potentiality and actuality, between what that entity can become and what it actually is. The potential is related to the actual as the imperfect to the perfect, the incomplete to the complete.

Equipped with these insights Aquinas could understand not only what a thing is when viewed statically, but also when viewed dynamically—that is, as subject to change. Change is rendered intelligible in terms of its end. That toward which a thing is essentially tending is judged to be its proper good; there is a relation of fitness. The proper good is not to be identified with any goal; it is a fulfillment and thus is founded on a being's essence and its tendencies. By "good" is meant what is fit for a thing, what is due its nature, the further existence that will complete its basic tendencies, and its incidental tendencies as well, so far as these do not conflict with the former. Thus, the valid ground for desire is that the thing desired is prescriptively required by the nature that desires it.

For Thomists a teleological concept of nature supported by a realistic epistemology is therefore the basis of the unity of "being" and "ought," of "fact" and "value," of "nature" and "goodness." The ontological and moral orders are ultimately one. A basis for values exists only in the tendency of something incomplete to complete itself. In apprehending a tendency, the viewer grasps something of what the entity is tending toward. The essence of a thing implies the goal of becoming.

Here Thomists will insist that essence is not something that we first understand by itself and from which we infer tendency. We experience beings and infer something of their natures by observing them in the process of fulfilling their basic tendencies. Things are always in a state of becoming or development. Thus, essence is not to be thought of as an immutable substrate, nor is it to be thought of as created subjectively by interest; nor does it represent a kind of shorthand by which we keep in mind properties or observations that we cannot now conveniently articulate.

Rather, essence is given in experience and discovered upon reflection. It controls our endeavor to distinguish between the peripheral and the central, to discover the order and cause of the properties that the sciences catalogue. In our attempt to answer the question "What is it?" essence marks the thing off from other entities. And most importantly for value theory, essence in its tendential aspect implies what is suitable to it.

In these considerations we can observe the groundwork of a Thomistic theory of the good. It consists of advice (1) to look to man's nature to determine what is good for him, and (2) to look to political and social structures, given both through experience and through history, to determine which of them are conducive to man's communal well-being. No conclusions are ready-made.

VII. IMPLICATIONS FOR COMMUNITY

From a Thomistic point of view, the compatibility of individual and community interests is taken for granted; each is regarded as contributing to the vitality of the other. Community does not imply the holding of goods in common, but community does depend on the common recognition that certain goods are to be preferred and that some goods are more important than others. Acknowledgment of a hierarchy of communal goods does not conflict with the recognition that individuality is the wellspring of initiative, enterprise, and responsibility. An individual's autonomy is seen as a condition for the cultivation of such goods as study, reflection, recreation, and intimacy, all of which are important. Thomists will insist that a community is not diminished because its members cordon off certain areas of their lives. A group is strengthened by the goods that its members return to it as a result of their individual pursuits and by their participation in heterogeneous but noncontradictory communities. Community is not a total unity, but rather a harmony of complementary interests under the umbrella of shared values.

A communal interest that Thomists recognize may be called the "spiritual common good." The state, it is argued, has a stake in the success of those structures which contribute to man's well-being as a thinking and choosing agent. Conversely, the state must be careful not to aid and abet social forces inimical to the pursuit of personal moral virtue. The state is finally accountable to a natural moral order. Thomists tend to be defenders of rectitude, virtue, and conservative customs. They also recognize the indispensable role that religion plays in fostering these values. The perpetuation of civil liberty cannot depend on a Hobbesian procedural democracy, but upon the cultivation of good manners and morals in the people.

In contemporary discussions of human rights Thomists are likely to recognize only a short list of universal rights, for example, the right to life, the right to sustenance, the right to an education in the basic laws governing self-preservation, and those other rights that in principle the child may secure as claims on its parents. Following Aristotle, the Thomist is likely to assert that most of the rights that today are called "human rights" are part of the generic category "political rights." These rights presuppose society and depend on the presence of established social structures. Thus, rights cannot be discussed in the abstract or most rights be presumed to be unchangeable. For Thomists rights are grounded in an anthropocentric teleology, an order the polis is created to promote. A universally valid hierarchy of ends is assumed even though there are no universally valid rules of action. Although the proper ends of government may be known, one does not know how and to what extent those ends can be realized here and now under these circumstances. Recognized is the difference between acknowledging a norm and the prudential decision of acting in the light of that norm. A willingness to honor one's father and mother does not decide the issue of whether an aged parent should remain in one's home or be placed in a nursing home.

VIII. EVOLVING CHARACTERISTICS

Since its resurgence in the past century Thomism has not remained static. Josiah Royce, writing in the late nineteenth century was convinced that the neoscholastic movement endorsed by Leo XIII was an important one "for the general intellectual progress of our time." The use of St. Thomas, he said, entails growth, development and change. "Pope Leo, after all, 'let loose a thinker' amongst his people—a thinker to be sure of unquestioned orthodoxy, but after all a thinker whom the textbooks had long tried, as it were to keep lifeless, and who once revived, proves to be full of suggestions of new problems, and of an effort towards new solutions." But Royce was also fearful that a resurgent Thomism might give way to the Kantian legions and their demand that the epistemological issue be settled first. The temptation that Royce feared, was experienced by Pierre Rousselot (1878–1915) and Joseph Maréchal (1878–1944) and precipitated the movement known as transcendental Thomism, one that was to have considerable influence in theological circles, notably through the teaching of Karl Rahner (1904–1984) and Bernard Lonergan (1904–1984).

As Gerald McCool has observed, the widespread enthusiasm for Thomas declined somewhat in the aftermath of the Second Vatican Council as theologians in an ecumenical spirit sought common ground with other religions by adopting certain contemporary philosophical outlooks. The process philosophy of Alfred North Whitehead and various continental philosophies were favored. In the curriculum of many Catholic colleges the social sciences, valued for their empirical character, were allowed to replace philosophy where it theretofore had commanded a significant portion of the humanities core curriculum. In theological circles recognition of the role of philosophy as a rational preamble to Christian faith faded under the spell of Kant and Kierkegaard. Thomism in the late 1990s has become merely an option in the curriculum of many Catholic colleges; yet its intrinsic merit has never lost favor with those steeped in classical learning or with those who value it as an important preamble to the Catholic Faith itself.

From any vantage point, Aquinas himself may be regarded as an all-time worthy commentator on Aristotle and a common sense appropriator of Stoic moral philosophy. Most Thomists do not stop with the texts of Aquinas. They do not regard Thomism as a system analogous to the systems of Kant and Hegel. Rather, they regard it as an open-ended inquiry that appropriates the best the past has to offer in an attempt to address contemporary issues. As the positivism of the late nineteenth and early twentieth centuries is found inadequate when confronted with actual practice in the natural sciences, Thomism fosters a growing realist interpretation of contemporary science. Presenting itself as simultaneously compatible with common sense and the natural sciences, it retains its claim as a *philosophia perennis*.

Also See the Following Articles

ARISTOTELIAN ETHICS • CHRISTIAN ETHICS, ROMAN CATHOLIC • GREEK ETHICS, OVERVIEW • KANTIANISM • RELIGION AND ETHICS

Bibliography

Aquinas, St. Thomas. (1995). *De Malo.* (Jean Oesterle, Trans.). Notre Dame: University of Notre Dame Press.

Aquinas, St. Thomas. (1957). *Summa Contra Gentiles* (Four vols.). (Charles J. O'Neil, Trans.) Notre Dame: University of Notre Dame Press.

Aquinas, St. Thomas. (1964). *Summa Theologiae.* (Latin text with English trans.). (61 vols.) Blackfriars in conjunction with London: Eyre & Spottiswoode.

Brezik, V. B. (Ed.) (1981). *One hundred years of Thomism.* Houston: University of St. Thomas.

Collins, J. (1962). *Three paths in philosophy.* Chicago: Regnery.

Crenet, P. (1967). *Thomism: An introduction.* (J. F. Ross, Trans.). New York: Harper and Row.

Fabro, C. (1960). *Breve introduzione al Tomismo.* Rome: Desclée.

Fortin, Ernest L. (1987). St. Thomas Aquinas. In *History of political philosophy* (3rd Ed.). (L. Strauss and J. Cropsey, Eds.). Chicago: University of Chicago Press.

Foucher, L. (1955). *La philosophie catholique en France au xixe siècle avant la renaissance thomiste et dans son rapport avec elle (1880–1880).* Paris: J. Urin.

Gilson, E. (1956). *The Christian philosophy of St. Thomas Aquinas* (L. K. Shook, Trans.). New York: Random House.

Gilson, E. (1964). *The spirit of Thomism.* New York: Kennedy.

Gilson, E. (1939). *Réalisme Thomiste et critique de la connaissance.* Paris: J. Vrin, pp. 130–155; in English, *Thomistic realism and the critique of knowledge* (Mark A. Wauck, Trans.) San Francisco: Ignatius Press, 1986, pp. 129–148.

Hartley, T. J. A. (1971). *Thomistic revival and the modernist era.* Toronto: Institute of Christian Thought.

Hart, C. A. (1959). *Thomistic metaphysics.* Englewood Cliffs, NJ: Prentice Hall.

Lonergan, B. (1957). *Insight: A study of human understanding.* London: Longmans, Green and Co.

McCool, G. A. (1989). *Nineteenth-century scholasticism: The search for a unitary method.* New York: Fordham University Press.

McCool, G. A. (1989). *From unity to pluralism: The internal evolution of Thomism.* New York: Fordham University Press.

McInerny, R. (1966). *Thomism in an age of renewal.* Garden City, NY: Doubleday.

McInerny, R. (1982). *Ethica Thomistica.* Washington, DC: The Catholic University of America Press.

McInerny, R. (1986). *Being and predication: Thomistic interpretations.* Washington, DC: The Catholic University of America Press.

Maritain, J. (1931). *The angelic doctor: The life and thought of Saint Thomas Aquinas.* (Trans. J. F. Scanlan.). New York: Dial.

Maritan, J. (1951). *Man and the state.* Chicago: The University of Chicago Press.

Maritan, J. (1964). *Moral philosophy: An historical and critical survey of the great systems.* New York: Scribner's.

Roensch, F. J. (1964). *Early Thomistic school.* Dubuque, IA: The Priory Press.

Shook, L. K. (1984). *Etienne Gilson.* Toronto: The Pontifical Institute of Mediaeval Studies.

Steenberghen, F. van. (1966). *La philosophie au XII siècle.* Louvain: Nauwelaerts.

Torrell, J.-P. (1996). *St. Thomas Aquinas. Volume I: The Person and His Work.* (Trans. Robert Royal.). Washington, DC: The Catholic University of America Press.

van Riet, G. (1946). *L'Epistémologie thomiste.* Louvain: Institut upérieur de Philosphie, 495–517; in English, *Thomistic epistemology* (two vols.). (Gabriel Franks, Trans.). St. Louis: B. Herder, vol. 2, pp. 153–74.

Veatch, H. (1971). *For an ontology of morals: A critique of contemporary ethical theory.* Evanston: Northwestern University Press.

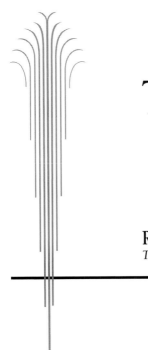

TOURISM

Robert Prosser
The University of Birmingham

GLOSSARY

import substitution The replacement of imported goods by home-produced goods.

market segmentation The subdivision of the total tourism market into segments, each of which possesses a distinctive set of attributes and toward which specific tourism products can be marketed.

multipliers Numerical coefficients that measure the total effect (direct, indirect, induced) of initial tourist expenditure as a result of its subsequent diffusion through the economy of a destination region.

product differentiation The process by which a tourism opportunity is made distinctive and identifiable in terms of product, price, promotion, place, and hence targeted market segment.

sustainable development Development that meets the needs of the present without compromising the ability of future generations to meet their own needs.

TOURISM has been conceptualized and defined in a number of ways: as a phenomenon, an industry, an experience, a system, a subset of leisure. As movement is an essential element of the concept, many sources and agencies use the combined title of travel and tourism. For example, in the United States, the 1981 National Tourism Policy Act established the United States Travel and Tourism Administration. Whichever title or conceptualization is used, there is no doubt that during the second half of the twentieth century, it has emerged as a major component of the global system in economic, social, political, and environmental terms.

It is perhaps inevitable therefore, that tourism is generating an increasingly intense ethical debate, focusing around several key issues. For instance, is it by nature elitist, based on selfish, hedonistic motives and hence is it degrading rather than enhancing to the human character? From a global stewardship perspective, tourism may be perceived as dangerous, in that it "actively seeks out the earth's treasures—the most wondrous, but also sensitive natural and cultural environments—as the basis for the experiences it provides."

I. DEFINITIONS OF TOURISM AND TOURISTS

A. Tourism

The definition of tourism currently adopted by the World Tourism Organisation (WTO) emerged from their 1991 International Conference on Travel and Tourism Statistics: "The activities of a person travelling outside his or her usual environment for less than a specified period of time and whose main purpose of travel is other than exercise of an activity remunerated from the place visited" (WTO (1991). Conference resolutions, international conference on travel and tourism statistics, Ottawa. Madrid: World Tourism Organization).

A second useful definition includes the reality that tourism involves the provision of facilities during the travel and stay components of the trip: "The temporary movement of people to destinations outside their normal places of work and residence, the activities undertaken during their stay in those destinations, and the facilities created to cater for their needs" (Mathieson, A., & Wall, G. (1982). *Tourism: Economic, physical and social impacts,* p. 1. London: Longman).

Neither of the above definitions specifies a dimension crucial to any discussion of the ethics of tourism, namely, its impacts. This omission is remedied in the following: Tourism is " a study of man [sic] away from his usual habitat, of the industry which responds to his needs, and the impacts that both he and the industry have for the host socio-cultural, economic, and physical environments" (Jafari, J. (1981). Editor's page. *Annals of Tourism Research,* 8 (1)).

The central components are therefore, movement, non-permanent stay, activities and experiences during the travel and stay, resources and facilities required, and impacts resulting from the travel and stay.

B. Tourists

Definitions of a tourist are, naturally, based upon the concept of tourism, and include the elements of travel and stay. Thus, a tourist is a visitor who spends at least one night in the destination to which he or she has traveled. This distinguishes a tourist from an excursionist, who is someone who visits and leaves without spending a night in the destination. Many sources, such as W. Theobald, today combine the two categories by using the single term "visitor": "Any person traveling to a place other than that of his/her usual environment for less than twelve months and whose main purpose of trip is other than the exercise of an activity remunerated from within the place visited."

The classification of a tourist as someone whose visit lasts two days to a year, emphasizes the nonpermanent character of the travel. It is worth noting that some classification systems apply a time limit of six months. Most definitions and usages by countries and agencies

regard stays of more than one year as "residence" or "migration." Refugees are a special category of nonresidents distinguished by primary motives which are not voluntary.

Distance traveled is a further parameter used to define a "trip," and this too, varies from country to country. For example, from 1992 the U.S. Travel Data Center has reported on all trips with a one-way distance of 100 miles, while the Canadian Travel Survey uses a lower one-way limit of 50 miles. The Australian Bureau of Industry Economics uses a one-way distance of 25 miles.

II. DIMENSIONS OF TOURISM

Because tourism is such a huge and complex phenomenon, it is multidimensional and can be compartmentalized in a variety of ways. The two fundamental variables applied are the origin-destination relationship, and trip purpose. Using origin–destination characteristics, the following standard categories are used:

1. International tourism: trips involving the crossing of at least one national border.
   a. Inbound: visits to a country by nonresidents.
   b. Outbound: residents of a country visiting another country.
2. Internal tourism: residents of a country visiting places away from their normal environment within their own country.
3. Domestic tourism: internal tourism plus inbound tourism, that is, the total tourism market within a country.
4. National tourism: internal tourism plus outbound tourism, that is, the total tourism market generated by the residents of a country.

The varied motivations for and purposes of travel are categorized in several ways. Chadwick suggests the following:

1. Pleasure: leisure, culture, active sports, visits to friends and relatives (VFR), etc.
2. Professional: meetings, mission, business, etc.
3. Other purposes: study, health, transit, etc.

The annual International Passenger Survey carried out by the British Tourist Authority distinguishes five types of visit: holiday independent; holiday inclusive; business; VFR; miscellaneous. The classification system used may depend upon the agency collecting the data,

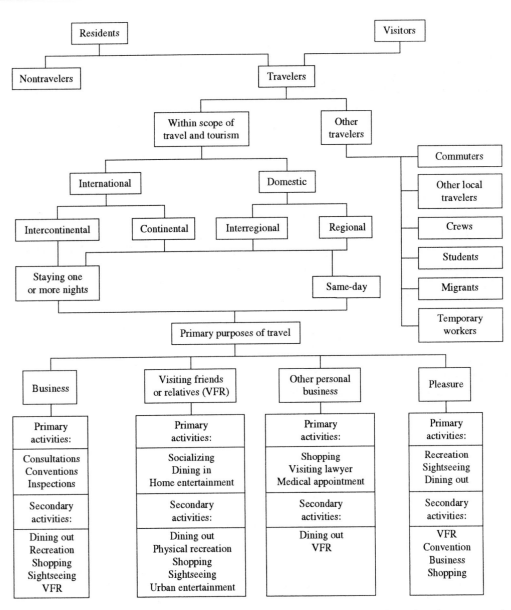

FIGURE 1   A Classification of Travelers and Tourists. (Source: Brent Ritchie and Goeldner. (1994). Fig 1. p. 68.)

and the purpose for which the data is to be used. For example, the tourism industry—tour operators, hotel chains, airlines, and so on—needs to be able to disaggregate different types of visitor. This is why the VFR component is distinguished, as in many destinations it provides a significant proportion of the total and has distinctive spending patterns, for example, up to 20% of visitors to Australia. Thus, Prosser suggests three general categories: pleasure; business; VFR.

Other variables used include duration, mode of transportation, accommodation type, and activities. It must be remembered, too, that many trips have multiple purposes, involve different transport modes, accommodation types, and so on, thus limiting the usefulness of any single classification system. With this proviso in mind, Fig. 1 provides a practical, comprehensive framework.

III. THE SCALE OF TOURISM

David Lodge in his novel *Paradise News* describes tourism as "the new world religion. Catholics, Protestants, Hindus, Muslims, Buddhists, atheists—the only

FIGURE 2 Tourism is about education as well as enjoyment: Visitors listening to an ecological talk by a ranger in the Everglades National Park, Florida.

thing they have in common is that they all believe in seeing the Parthenon. Or the Sistine Chapel, or the Eiffel Tower." (Lodge, D. (1992). *Paradise News.* London: Collins). This is more than a fictional flight of fancy, for respected researchers claim that "travel and tourism have become an institutionalised way of life for most of the world's middle class population." A range of statistics support such claims: By 1995, the tourism industry's gross output was approaching $4 trillion, more than 12% of all consumer spending, generating 132 million jobs, and producing more than 6% of global GNP. By such macromeasures, travel and tourism has become the world's largest industry (Fig. 2).

A. Global Growth

Accurate figures are notoriously difficult to obtain but generalized data tells a vivid story. In 1950, the global total for international travel was only 25 million international arrivals. By 1995, the figure exceeded 500 mil-

lion, up from 440 million in 1990 (Table I). Internal tourism totals are thought to be of the order of five times as great (Table II).

This phenomenal growth, averaging 7% a year over the period from 1970 through 1990, has been energized by the complex interaction of socioeconomic change, entrepreneurial effort, and technological innovation.

TABLE I

The Growth of International Arrivals

Year	Number (million)
1950	25
1960	70
1970	160
1980	290
1990	440
1995 (est.)	500

(Source: WTO, 1993).

TABLE II

International Tourism in the United Kingdom,
1991–1994 (million)

Year	Total	Market area		
		North America	Western Europe	Rest of world
1991	17.1	2.9	11.1	3.1
1992	18.5	3.4	11.7	3.4
1993	19.4	3.4	12.4	3.6
1994	21.0	3.5	13.3	4.2

(Source: British Tourism Authority, *Insights* January 1996)

TABLE III

World's Top 10 International Tourist Flows, 1993

Flow	Million arrivals
Canada → U.S.	17.4
U.S. → Canada	12.4
Germany → France	12.3
Germany → Italy	11.0
Switzerland → Italy	10.5
Portugal → Spain	10.3
France → Italy	9.5
Mexico → U.S.	7.6
U.K. → France	7.5
Belgium → France	7.3

(Source: WTO. 1993)

Throughout the industrialized world and increasingly in newly industrializing countries, for example, the "tiger" economies of Southeast Asia, enhanced holiday entitlements, greater disposable income, increasing car ownership, improved education, and media exposure creating greater awareness and interest, and growing acceptance of travel across broadening components of the social spectrum, have provided powerful stimuli to pleasure travel. An increasingly sophisticated travel and tourism industry, from local individuals, for example, "Mom and Pop" bed and breakfast operations, to transnational corporations, such as Hyatt Hotels and United Airlines, have both responded to and generated the expanded demand. They have been aided in this by technological breakthroughs, in particular jet aircraft, for example, the first commercial passenger jet service began in 1950, and more recently by the application of computer technology to administrative and logistics systems.

Two vivid manifestations illustrate the combined power of these three forces. First there is the all-inclusive "package" holiday that has made international travel accessible far beyond a wealthy elite. Second, the enhanced capability for business travel has accelerated the globalization of commerce and industry, hence the targeting of this lucrative business market by all major airlines with air mile schemes and executive lounges.

The second dimension of growth has been geographical. More than 60% of all international travel is still between countries of the developed North (Table III), but the most rapid growth rates are being experienced in newly industrializing countries (NICs) and in economically developing countries (EDCs) (Fig. 3). This growth applies both as destinations for tourists and, especially in the case of NICs, origins of tourists:

Drawn by Asia's exotic appeal, its history, dynamism and new-found wealth, West Europeans, Australians and North Americans are flocking there in record numbers... The biggest surge, however, come from Asians. .... No one else in Asia has had more impact than the Japanese.... The fastest growing segment of the Japanese tourist crowd consists of young women. (Beyer, L. (1995, October 23). Destination Asia: The hottest ticket in travel. *Time,* 36–38).

Nonetheless one indicator of continuing global inequalities is the persistent low volume of travel from most EDCs.

B. Geographical Growth

The inexorable spread of tourists across the world over time has been expressed in model form as "The Pleasure Periphery" (Fig. 4). In this model, a bow wave or leading edge of tourist presence ripples progressively outward from a major generating source of tourists. As expressed in Figure 4, the origins are Western Europe and the Northeast United States, still the largest sources of tourists. Today's reality, of course, sees a growing number of sources, like pebbles thrown into the water and sending ripples outwards, for example, the emergence of Japan as a major source of business travelers and pleasure tourists since 1980.

Each source spreads its own pattern of ripples, that is, each country of origin generates a distinctive pattern of destinations. Factors that influence this pattern include geographical proximity: the United

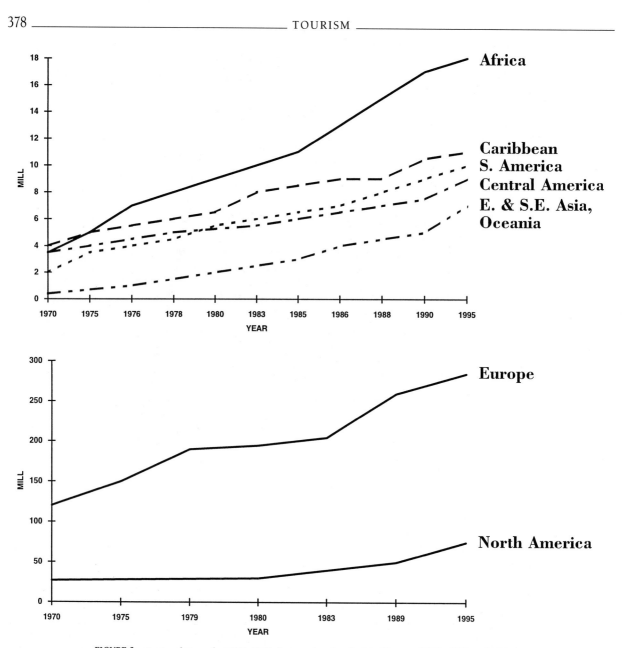

FIGURE 3   Regional Growth: 1970–1995 (international arrivals). (Source: WTO, 1993 and 1995.)

States dominates Mexico and Bermuda arrivals; colonial history: France's contribution to Mauritius tourism; cultural heritage: Iceland's links with Scandinavia; business interests: the Japan–Hong Kong attraction; and tour operator policies: German and British operators have marketed aggressively in Greece. It is important to note that destinations vary in their dependence: some, such as the United States or Spain are affected by a number of "ripples," that is, they attract tourists from several main sources; others, such as

Bermuda, are heavily dependent upon arrivals from a single country.

There is no question that one of the most important characteristics of tourism today is its penetration to all parts of the world, including some of the most remote and environmentally sensitive environments. For example, in 1995, at least 9000 tourists visited Antarctica; expedition permits to the great Himalayan peaks are fully taken for up to 10 years in the future. There are even plans for space tourism! This degree of penetration

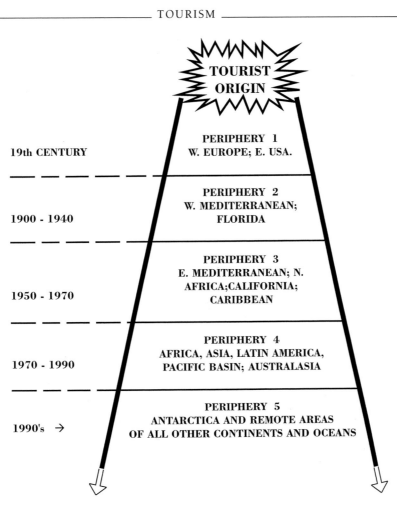

FIGURE 4   The Tidal Wave of the Pleasure Periphery.

and the apparently unending growth of demand has major ethical and environmental implications, including the questioning of the assumed rights of the tourist to impose such an intrusion.

C. Data Constraints

The principal difficulty in measuring the volume of tourism is the inconsistency and incomparability of the figures collected. This holds true for all scales of aggregation, international, national, and internal. For example, the WTO Yearbook of Tourism Statistics gives figures by country for "international arrivals," but the reliability of the data collection process varies, and the geographical makeup of a continent or cluster of countries has considerable influence upon the totals. Thus, although U.S. citizens are highly mobile, a much higher proportion of their total travel is internal. European citizens, on the other hand, cross international boundaries much more frequently.

Within countries, collection criteria may vary. Theobald for example, notes that in the U.S. state of Alaska, a tourist is "a non-resident traveling to Alaska for pleasure or culture and for no other purpose," while in Florida a tourist is "an out-of-state resident who stays at least one night in the state for reasons other than necessary layover for transportation connections or for strictly business transactions."

As a result of these imperfections, great care must be taken in interpreting available data. As Middleton summarizes:

In practice the technicalities of achieving statistical precision in measuring visitors are extremely complex and, despite various international guidelines, no uniformity yet exists in the measurement methods used around the world.

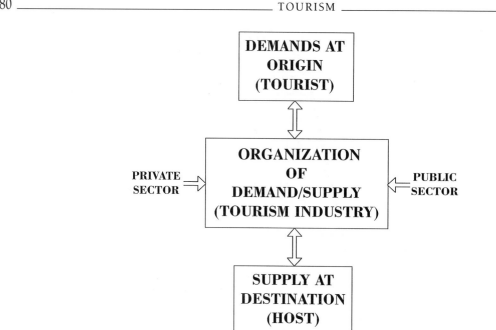

FIGURE 5   The Tourism System.

IV. THE TOURISM SYSTEM

One popular way of encapsulating the complexity of the tourism phenomenon is to adopt the systems concept, that, is an operational structure built of a set of interacting components. For example, Figure 5 is a construct of tourism as an organizational system. The industry provides the logistical and promotional energy that fuels the system, operationalizing and integ-

rating demand and supply. The system of Figure 6 is a geographical conceptualization presenting a three-component framework: a tourist-generating region, a destination region, and a transit route region, bound together by tourist flows. Such models may be criticized for their overgeneralization, and as a result, attempts have been made to construct systems that represent more effectively the inner complexities of the tourism environment (Fig. 7).

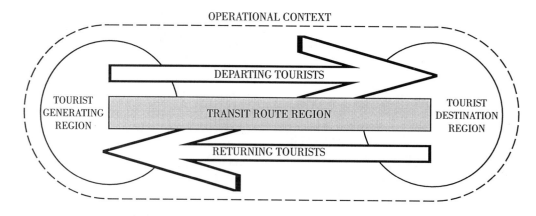

FIGURE 6   The Tourism System: A Spatial Construct. (Adapted from Leiper, 1990.)

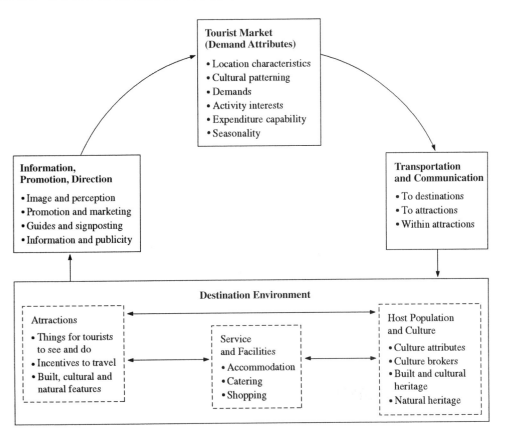

FIGURE 7   The Tourism Environment.

A. Tourism as an Industry

The tourism industry has been defined as "the range of businesses and organizations involved in delivering the tourism product." It functions as "a broad network of commercial and noncommercial organisations, linked together by the common objective of servicing the needs of travelers and tourists." Yet Mill has argued that "tourism is not an industry, although tourism gives rise to a variety of industries." It is the breadth and diversity of tourism that has led to such views as that of Theobald:

> Defining tourism as an industry is incorrect.... Tourism is a social/economic phenomenon that acts both as an engine of economic progress and as a social force. Tourism is much more than an industry. Tourism is more like a "sector" that impacts a wide range of industries."

Nonetheless, for most purposes, it is convenient to regard travel and tourism as an industry which can be divided into a number of sectors (Fig. 8).

This multifaceted industry has a number of distinctive characteristics. It is a service industry delivering a wide range of products and services that are consumed at the point of production (Fig. 9). Organizationally it is dominated by a small number of transnational corporations, but operationally it is articulated via the efforts of large numbers of small enterprises. This fragmentation makes the coordination of policies and control difficult, a problem accentuated by the geographical dispersal of tourism destinations and enterprises. For instance, policies for impact control and sustainability in a destination region are difficult to implement because of the diversity of interests and "stakeholders" involved, and also because of the economic power and political influence of the large corporations.

Tourism is a labor-intensive industry, although the demands in number and type vary over time and space. For example, during the development stage of a project, male employment predominates, while at the operational stage, there are more job opportunities for women. At the shorter time scale, many tourism jobs are seasonal, and involve part-time and shift working. The type of tourism introduced influences

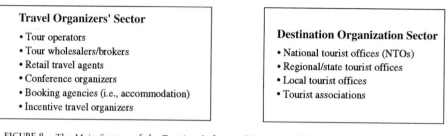

FIGURE 8   The Main Sectors of the Tourism Industry. (Source: Middleton, V. 1994. Fig. 1.1, p. 4.)

employment structures. For example, "exclusive" beach resorts create different job patterns from mountain and jungle trekking centers. Destinations vary, too, in the extent to which they provide job opportunities for local people or to which labor is imported. Until recently, management level staff at many large hotels in African safari destinations have been European, American, or Australian expatriates. In the Maldives, service level staff in the resorts are mainly non-Maldiveans.

B. Tourism and The Destination Life-Cycle

Two characteristics commonly attributed to tourism are first that it is an exploitative industry, and second, that it is a fashion industry. Thus, the tourism industry exploits an attractive resource, that is, destination, while supply lasts and demand exists, then moves on

to exploit the resources of another destination. This process is encouraged because tourism demand is driven by the concepts of fashion, image, and status as well as the search for novelty, challenge, escape, and so on. When we go on vacation, the "ego-boosting" motive is ever strong: flaunting a suntan is a powerful visual sign and status symbol that we have been on vacation. However, it is not simply displaying a tan that is crucial, but proclaiming where we got it—never wear a T-shirt from Coney Island; even one admitting that "I got laid back in California" is losing its image rating; but a shirt advertising the Cook Islands is definitely "cool"!

One result of these processes is that a particular type of tourism product has a finite life cycle, and is, over time, displaced by new products. Thus, when a destination offers and retains an identifiable product it is likely to experience a finite life cycle of growth, popularity and decline. Figure 10 presents this destination life cycle in model form.

FIGURE 9   Cultural tourism: Visitors enjoying the temples of Bangkok, Thailand.

V. TOURISM IMPACTS

Any touristic presence has some impact upon a destination. Impact implies change, which may be positive or negative, and can be assessed along economic, sociocultural, and environmental dimensions. Thus, analysis of the impacts of tourism may take the form of a balance sheet based on these dimensions (Fig. 11). Remember, however, that classification as "positive" or "negative" may involve value-laden judgments. For instance, a young woman getting a job in a hotel may be an economic benefit, but may bring negative social impacts through increased family tensions.

The final balance will be determined by the carrying capacity of the destination, definable as "that level of tourist presence which creates impacts on the host community, environment and economy that are acceptable to both tourists and hosts, sustainable over future time periods." Three important attributes of this definition should be noted: first, the notion of sustainability over time; second, the overall balance is a sum of the 'budgets' of all three dimensions, for example, strong negative environmental impacts (costs) may outweigh positive economic impacts (benefits) when accounted over time; third, the term "tourist presence" is preferred to "tourist numbers," as volume alone is an inadequate

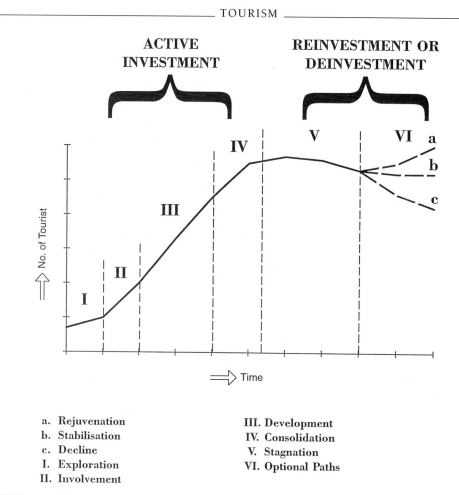

ACTIVE INVESTMENT

REINVESTMENT OR DEINVESTMENT

a. **Rejuvenation**
b. **Stabilisation**
c. **Decline**
I. **Exploration**
II. **Involvement**

III. **Development**
IV. **Consolidation**
V. **Stagnation**
VI. **Optional Paths**

FIGURE 10   A Model of the Destination Life Cycle. (Adapted from: Butler, R. (1990). *Canadian Geographer,* 24, 5–12.)

measure, because type of tourist and their preferred activities, their length of stay, their degree of concentration or dispersion, and the extent of seasonality all influence impact and hence carrying capacity.

A further characteristic of the carrying capacity concept is that for a specific destination, it may change over time, as the character of the tourism and resulting impacts change. Figure 12 summarizes these dynamic processes.

A. Economic Impacts

Anticipated economic benefit is the primary reason why a country, a locality, or an individual decides to encourage tourists. Governments are attracted to tourism because it is believed to create jobs, increase income and spending levels, bring in foreign currency, enlarge the tax potential, and encourage regional development and diversification of the economy, that will improve political and social stability and enhance national image. This is then expected to lead to increased foreign and internal investment. International tourism acts as an invisible export industry, attracting foreign currency, and hence improving a country's balance of payments. There is no doubting the huge sums involved, nor that benefits

Dimension	Benefits (positive impacts)	Costs (negative impacts)
Economic		
Sociocultural		
Environmental		

FIGURE 11   A Matrix for Tourism Impact Analysis.

Type	**Explorers** discover a destination	**Off-beat Adventurer** penetrates a region	**Elite** wealthy status conscious groups arrive on expensive tours	**Early mass** middle income groups on organized hotel or villa rental packages and tours	**Mass package** tourists on fully standarized packages
Number	Very few	Small numbers	Limited numbers	Steady flow	Massive numbers
Expectation and Impacts	Accept local conditions	Revel in local conditions	<u>Either</u> demand Western amenities or "rough it in comfort"	Look for Western amenities	Expect Western amenities
Example	Scientists and travel writers	Student backpackers	Social elites	Professional families	Wide range of social groups

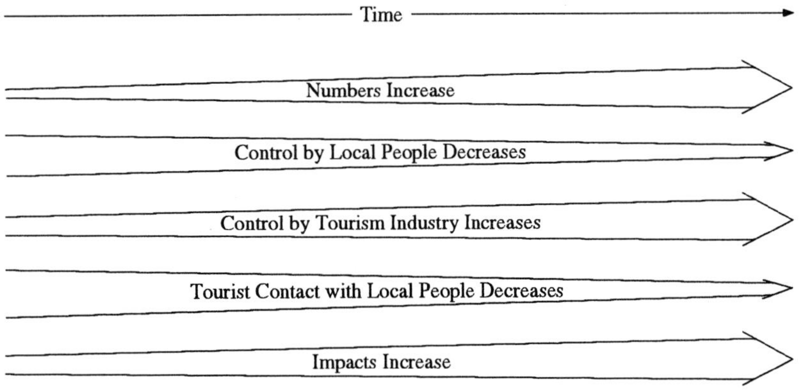

————————————— Time —————————————→

Numbers Increase ⟩

Control by Local People Decreases ⟩

Control by Tourism Industry Increases ⟩

Tourist Contact with Local People Decreases ⟩

Impacts Increase ⟩

FIGURE 12   Touristic Dynamics in a Destination Region. (Source: Adapted from Prosser. (1994). p. 116.)

have accrued to many destination regions in both the developed and less developed worlds (Fig. 13).

Introducing tourism as part of the economic development process seems straightforward—make sun, sea, sand, exotic cultures, forests, wild animals, and so on available, provide some transport and accommodation, and the tourists will flock in. Especially to countries in the less-developed world, it has seemed a low tech, labor-intensive opportunity. However, it is very evident today that economic reality is far more complicated, and severe questions hover over the economic balance sheet of tourism.

1. Major Global Flow Patterns

By the early 1990s, global international tourism receipts and expenditure were each approaching $300 billion a year, with every nation-state contributing to some degree. Yet the flows of these huge sums remain predominantly between countries of the developed world (Table IV). In 1992, the five top-ranking countries accounted for 52% of the total expenditure and 44% of total re-

In 1994, 21 million foreign visitors arrived in the United Kingdom (population 55 million) an increase of 8% on 1993. This total included 3 million from the United States, 2.8 million from France, and 2.5 million from Germany. Analyzed by main purpose of visit, 44% were on holiday, 24% on business, 21% were visiting friends and relatives, and 12% came for "other" reasons. The average length of stay was 9.2 days, and an average of £50.5 was spent per person per day, ranging from £82.3 per day for Japanese to £29.4 for New Zealanders. The gross receipts totaled £9.9 billion.

Once in the United Kingdom, 64% spent time in the capital city, London, and the neighboring Southeast region, where they spent more than 60% of the total expenditure. This may be compared with the whole of Scotland, a renowned and well-publicized tourist region, with 8.4% of the visits and 7.8% of the spending.

These impressive figures must be balanced against the expenditure by U.K. citizens while abroad. The 1994 outbound flow was 39.8 million visits, an increase of 12% from 1993. Some 80% of these visits were to countries of Western Europe. The total expenditure was £14.5 billion, which, when set against the £9.9 billion income, left a travel account deficit for the United Kingdom of £4.6 billion.

FIGURE 13   United Kingdom: The Economic Impact of Foreign Tourism, 1994.

TABLE IV
Tourism Expenditure and Receipts, 1991 ($ billions)

Rank	Country	Expenditure	Rank	Country	Receipts
1	U.S.A.	$39.4	1	U.S.A.	$45.6
2	Germany	31.6	2	France	21.3
3	Japan	24.0	3	Italy	19.7
4	U.K.	18.9	4	Spain	19.0
5	Italy	13.3	5	Austria	14.0
6	France	12.3	6	U.K.	12.6
7	Canada	10.5	7	Germany	10.9
8	Netherlands	7.9	8	Switzerland	7.1
9	Austria	7.4	9	Canada	5.5
10	Sweden	6.1	10	Hong Kong	51

(Source: WTO, *Yearbook of Tourism Statistics*, 45th Edition, vol 2, 1993, WTO, Madrid.)

ceipts. Cooper raises a question mark over the frequently made claim in support of tourism that it assists the global redistribution of wealth from the developed North to the less developed South: "Tourism does not appear to perform a great role as a global redistributor of income in the same way that it is claimed to do for regional redistribution."

At the national level too, the benefit-cost balance sheet varies widely, some countries being net gainers and others, losers. In Table IV, Spain, for instance, has a huge tourism budget surplus, with tourism yielding over 20% of export earnings. In contrast, spending abroad by Japanese nationals greatly exceeds receipts from foreign visitors to Japan (cf., U.K. in Fig. 13). The United States has a distinctive balance sheet: it ranks first in both expenditure and receipts, and although it recorded a net surplus of over $6 billion in 1991, during the 1980s, spending roughly balanced receipts. (In 1991, spending abroad by U.S. citizens was reduced by the effects of the Gulf War and an economic recession.)

Using GDP as a measure puts the economic significance of tourism into further perspective. Among OECD countries, only Austria and Portugal record travel account receipts above 5% of GDP. In countries of the developing world on the other hand, figures may exceed 20%. In the Cook Islands, for example, receipts were 22% in 1990. This means that although in money volume terms, tourism in such countries is smaller than in many developed countries, their economies are more dependent upon it. In turn, they are more vulnerable to shifts in tourism fashion and changes in tour operator

or airline policy. For example, more than 40% of Kenya's foreign exchange earnings come from tourism.

2. Distribution of Expenditure

As the global tourism system is controlled by institutions based in the developed North, for example, the 10 leading hotel chains are all based in and capitalized from the United States or Japan, the distribution of the tourist revenue is crucial in determining economic impact. Investment policies by financial institutions, destination marketing strategies by international tour operators, routing and pricing policies by airlines, financial and staffing guidelines by hotel companies, all originating in developed countries, have been so strong that tourism in the less-developed world has become known as a form of "economic colonialism." Recently, independent nations have found that economic dependence has replaced political dependence; for example, at least 40% of the hotels in Fiji are foreign-owned. Ryan found that only 33% of the total cost of a foreign inclusive "package" holiday from the United Kingdom actually reached the destination region, including hotels and other services, although there would be additional spending by the tourist once there (Ryan, C. (1991). *Recreational Tourism*. London: Routledge).

Problems of obtaining and retaining control of the tourist industry and hence of tourist revenue are not confined to LEDCs. For instance, Queensland, Australia, faces the development puzzle: in an effort to diversify the state economy beyond primary agricultural, forestry, and mining products, there is clearly enormous tourism potential in the attractive resources of tropical beaches, rainforests and, of course, the Great Barrier Reef (Fig. 14). Japanese and Hong Kong investors in particular have shown great interest, and Queensland's dilemma is how to maximize the benefit to the state without becoming too dependent upon foreign capital and institutions. There is concern, too, over the environmental impact of large-scale developments.

Beyond the issue of how much of tourist revenue enters the destination region, is that of how much *stays* there. This loss of income is known as "leakage": the proportion of receipts from tourism that are lost without direct benefit to the destination economy. This leakage may be payment of interest on foreign loans, payments and profits to foreign companies, such as hotel companies and airlines, the portion of wages and salaries sent home by expatriate workers, payments for imported goods consumed by the tourists, including food, drink, cameras, gifts, and so on, and local business people investing their tourism earnings abroad.

FIGURE 14   Port Douglas, Queensland, Australia. Large-scale tourism projects destroy valuable expanses of coastal mangrove forest.

The leakage levels can be disturbingly high. For the Caribbean region, the proportion that leaks is around two-thirds. In Fiji, while more than 75 cents of every dollar of tourist revenue enters the foreign exchange account, a further 32 cents leaks via induced import payments, leaving a net impact of 43 cents from every dollar (Table V).

Clearly, a primary aim of a destination country or region is to minimize leakage. An allied aim is to reduce the import requirements for tourists and the induced

spending on imported goods by local people (import substitution), thereby improving the circulation of tourist revenue through the destination economy, so improving the multiplier effect. For instance, there is much evidence that as tourism grows, local agriculture and fishing suffer from land loss and population migration to work in resorts. Thus, on many Caribbean islands, for example, a high proportion of food for hotels has been imported, while farming has declined.

B. Socio-Cultural Impact

Consideration of the sociocultural effects of tourism must include both hosts and guests, that is destination societies and tourists. Supporters of tourism claim that it improves international understanding by creating interactions between people of different cultures, thereby broadening minds, enhancing understanding, and encouraging empathy and tolerance. For the tourist a vacation becomes a life-enhancing experience involving recreation, recuperation, happiness, escape, self-realization and so on.

Critics argue that the inequalities and inequities exposed by the experience heighten antipathy, and rein-

TABLE V

Leakage and the Economic Impact of Tourism Expenditure in Fiji, 1991 (in $U.S.)

Tourist expenditure (+)		$1000
Import requirements (−)		
Direct	120.8	
Indirect	115.3	236.1
Net effect on balance of payments		763.9
Induced imports (−)	326.3	326.3
Net impact after induced effects		437.6

(Source: Ryan, 1991, Table 11.10, p. 125.)

force stereotyping and bigotry, thus narrowing or closing the minds of both hosts and guests. For example, the only contact many tourists have with their "hosts" is as servants, waiters, or shop assistants. On the reverse side of the interaction, local people meet visitors only in this subservient formal role and also see those visitors only in "holiday mode." Given such contexts and perspectives, misconceptions readily take root.

One factor that obscures the debate is that measurable and quantifiable indicators of the sociocultural impact of tourism prove difficult to identify. For example, one oft-quoted manifestation is "the demonstration effect": the host community observes alien forms of behavior, mores, dress, and spending. This in turn influences their values, expectations, and life-styles. The impact varies among different sections of the population. Older, more traditional groups may find the overt physical contact in public among the tourists with their scanty clothing offensive. There is much evidence of this in the eastern Mediterranean, the Muslim world, and on the Pacific Islands. In contrast, many young people are attracted to the liberal, materialistic, hedonistic, and even narcissistic life-styles they see "demonstrated" by the tourists. They become dissatisfied and disaffected, and they adopt the values and styles of the visitors. The outcome is increased intergenerational tensions within families and communities.

This is a plausible but simplistic scenario. All societies are dynamic and contain internal tensions associated with such change. All but the most remote communities possess increasing levels of literacy and exposure to media that introduce them to the wider world. These processes generate forces which accelerate change. Furthermore, cultures vary in their internal strength and hence susceptibility to external inputs. Thus, tourism must not be seen in isolation and it must not be given sole praise or blame for sociocultural dynamics.

1. The Sociocultural Budget

The "impact balance sheet" depends upon the complex interaction of several factors, including rate, scale, and character of tourism development, seasonality, nature of the host society, and character and behaviour of the visitors. There are three crucial relationships: first, the ratio of visitors to locals; second, the "cultural distance" between hosts and guests; and third, the speed at which tourism is introduced in relation to the scale and nature of the local population. In general, the higher the visitor-to-local ratio, the greater the guest-host cultural distances, the smaller the scale of the destination society, and the more rapid the speed of

tourism development, the more severe is likely to be the sociocultural impact.

Studies in the eastern Mediterranean have shown that the sizeable and comparatively complex societies of larger islands such as Rhodes and Corfu are resilient and possess adaptability to the coming of even mass tourism. The small-scale, less variegated societies of smaller islands have proved fragile and less adaptive. On the other hand, the tourism developments have stemmed the serious out-migration from a number of these smaller, remote islands, especially by younger people.

Impacts may change, too, as communities adopt coping strategies and modified perceptions. Doxey has codified this shift in an "Irritation Index" in which host community attitudes follow the succession: a. euphoria; b. apathy; c. annoyance; d. antagonism as they endure the passage of the tourism development cycle. This model is now accepted as simplistic and overgeneralized. Yet it does illustrate that attitudinal change among a host population may be deep-seated. In the words of a native Hawaiian at a 1987 conference: "We don't want tourism. We don't want you. We don't want to be degraded as servants and dancers. That is cultural prostitution."

Such views should give the tourism industry and tourists considerable cause for reflection.

2. Cultural Regeneration or Cultural Degradation?

The ethics and impact of the use of cultural attributes such as ritual, art forms, and artifacts as elements in the tourism product and experience arouse strong controversy. One perspective sees the commercialization and commodification of religious ceremony, traditional dance, music, painting, sculpture, carving, pottery, or any other manifestations bearing spiritual meaning as degrading and unacceptably intrusive. The opposing viewpoint is that societies and their culture can be strengthened by involvement with tourism. The production and display of their culture and skills, and the fact that people are willing to travel great distances and pay large sums to experience these things can be a source of pride. There is little doubt, too, that in many societies, the rituals associated with traditional beliefs and the skills required for crafts were in decline. They have been revitalized by their integration into the tourism product.

At the heart of the debate lie the ideas of meaning and ownership. So, do cultural attributes and manifestations belong to the society within which they have evolved, and should it remain within the power of that society to decide on their role and use? There is general agreement among academics and societies themselves that culture that is commodified for tourist consumption acquires a different meaning and, indeed, form. This is often a conscious adaptation. Societies have been resourceful and pragmatic in adapting their crafts to tourist tastes and needs. For example, Pacific islanders make their bark paintings and masks to fit cruise ship tourists' luggage! Balinese dance today has two distinct forms— one that retains its spiritual context and meaning; the other that is adapted and abbreviated for tourist consumption and commercial gain. Among a number of North American First Peoples, one of the energies driving the revival of ethnic and cultural pride is ceremony, music, and dance. There is a subtle symbiotic relationship between the internal meaning and the external display of these cultural forms. The outcome ranges across the spectrum between sacred, secret enactment, through "Pow Wows," to which visitors are accepted, and the commercial display for tourists.

3. The Authenticity Issue

Any discussion of meaning and ownership leads to consideration of authenticity. In the words of the Oxford English Dictionary it means "of undisputed origin; genuine; trustworthy"; in marketing-speak, it is "The Real Thing." It encapsulates the experience of the visitor, the articulation of the experience by the producer or manager, and the host–guest relationship. Yet it can be argued that authenticity is a socially constructed concept attributed to the world "out there" by Western societies.

From the tourist's perspective, there has always been the "adventurer" or "explorer" who has sought total immersion in the destination environment, human and ecological. Today, however, this search has been institutionalized and marketed by the tourism industry. Specialist tour operators offering "unspoiled islands," "undiscovered peoples," "the real Africa," "the secret Spain," and so on, have proliferated. They proclaim an "authentic" experience, to allow the tourist inside the life of the destination society. Critics argue that such tourism is intrusive and ethically unacceptable in terms of the host society. Furthermore, it is dishonest in that any so-called authenticity is, at best, "staged", that is, a show put on for the tourists.

The staging is presented across a continuum from the "Hawaiian Evening" in a Waikiki hotel, which is a Las Vegas-style floor show that few would claim is an "authentic" experience of Hawaiian culture, to a stay in a Punan longhouse on Papua New Guinea. The debate revolves around questions of honesty, respect, and con-

trol. Is the tour operator being honest in marketing the product as offering an "authentic" experience? Does the tourist really believe that the experience is not "staged"? One argument is that authenticity lies in the mind of the consumer, that is the tourist. Are the local people and their culture being held in respect by allowing exposure to the tourist gaze, and by the accompanying commercialization and commodification?

The search for answers returns once more to the issue of cultural ownership—whose culture is it, anyway? One popular criterion for evaluating acceptability is the extent to which the local community and what sections of it have control over the decisions. The argument runs that as the culture is community property, then they have the right to determine how that property shall be used. The counterargument is that ownership brings with it responsibilities as well as rights, and that the present-day community is custodian of a heritage to be passed on to future generations. Furthermore, this task of cultural transmission is constrained by a loss of control over the local development of tourism, or its control by an entrepreneurial coterie.

The problems can be illustrated vividly where the attractive tourism resource is a culture of past times, or one that is receding. This heritage tourism is catered for by a thriving heritage industry, known disparagingly as the "nostalgia industry," wherein aspects of cultural, political, and economic history are restored and presented for the education and enjoyment of tourists. Claims are made for this process in terms of reviving local and national pride, and of the importance of cultural transmission. Examples range from Charlestown in the United States, through the ancient temples of Southeast Asia, to the industrial towns of western Europe. Several studies of industrial heritage sites in Britain have found that local people, whose cultural heritage the developments purport to conserve and present, have been very little involved in the projects, and feel alienated from them. So, the question remains—whose culture is it?

4. Whose Land Is It? The Ethics of Ownership

The land on which a community lives provides the spatial domain within which the society and culture have evolved. Yet all too often, these ancestral lands have come under threat from tourism. The following extract illustrates a central ethical dilemma surrounding conservation and tourism development:

Two leaders of the last tribal people of the Kalahari desert arrived in London yesterday to call for

British support in their fight against the Botswana government.... The 3000 Khwe in the game reserve are the last of their people to live mainly by traditional means of hunting animals and gathering plants.

Now the government wants to encourage tourism, Botswana's fastest growing industry, in the Kalahari, and ... the tribal people are considered unsightly and in the way.... [A tribal leader] claims the Khwe are to be loaded onto trucks in May and taken to towns where they are to be integrated with the rest of the population (*The Guardian* (1996) 5 April, p. 12).

The Khwe are being pushed from their ancestral homelands by their own national government, who proclaim that the reserves are "for wildlife." The primary motive however, is economic profit from nature-based tourism, with the secondary aim of social engineering, that is, to force the assimilation of the nomadic Khwe into mainstream society.

This is a conflict repeated across the world, from the Masai, removed from Kenya's Masai Mara Reserve, the tribal bands excluded from hunting and gathering in Korup National Park, Cameroon, to the Native Americans constrained in their traditional practices inside U.S. National Parks. Yet there are signs that such rights are being legitimized and incorporated into conservation and tourism policies. It is an acknowledgement by governments not only that indigenous peoples have rights of ownership and stewardship, but also that conservation goals can be achieved by "selling" wildlife, wildlands and their cultures to these peoples as possessing economic potential through tourism. In other words, conservation can be worth their while. In Australia, after long-continued oppression and neglect, Aboriginal bands are today encouraged to run tourism enterprises, such as accommodations and guided walks. In Zimbabwe, the Campfire project in 22 districts aims to give communities power over the use of wildlife and the revenue from safaris.

5. Sex Tourism

The promotion of eroticism and sex as part of the tourism product and experience spans the globe. This ranges from the prurience of London's Soho clubs, through the long-established "red light" district of Amsterdam, to the well-publicized package tours to Thailand for Japanese businessmen, the "beach boy" trade of African resorts, and the "rent boy" agencies of California.

The debate is founded upon the moral philosophy of prostitution and has intensified with the growing threat of communicable disease, especially AIDS. Not all societies condemn concubines and prostitution as immoral or illegal. In other societies, traditional, conservative taboos are facing more liberal challenges. Thus, ethical discussions within tourism cannot be dissociated from the cultural context of a destination region. The multifaceted controversy may be summarized in three broad perspectives. The first states that there is a demand for sex tourism, destination societies should retain the right to supply the "product," and the tourism industry should be permitted to respond to these market forces. From a second, and opposing perspective, prostitution is immoral, it degrades human dignity, it violates human rights, it indulges humans' baser cravings, and it has no place within the tourism system. A third perspective, increasingly adopted, accepts that sex tourism is inevitable, so legalizing it will facilitate control, especially over extreme forms, leading to improved health, hygiene, and "working conditions." This third perspective is the proclaimed official policy in Thailand.

6. Gender Issues

Feminist perspectives and platforms, in particular, have given high profile to prostitution as an illustration of unequal male–female power relationships at work within tourism. First, there is concern over young women entering prostitution independently as a means of economic survival, but being controlled by male "pimps" and degraded by male clients. Second, at a more focused level, there is growing concern over young women being forced into prostitution. Evidence is available from Latin America, Africa, and Southeast Asia of fathers selling daughters to male pimps in tourist towns. Third, and perhaps most disturbingly, there is the increasing abuse of female children in countries such as Cambodia, where male clients prefer, and are willing to pay higher prices for virgins. The growing intensity of concern is illustrated in the organization of a major international conference on child exploitation in Stockholm in 1996. It needs to be remembered, however, that one line of argument assigns blame not solely to male domination, but to the absence of effective rural development strategies.

Within the legitimate realm of tourism, there is the continuing issue of the role of women as "sex objects", from Las Vegas floor-shows, through "belly dancing" in the Middle East, to the stylized cultural dancing of Southeast Asia and the Geisha experience of Japan. This issue surfaces too in the images of women projected in tourism marketing and promotion, for example, in the "welcoming" female imagery in airline advertising.

Throughout the tourism industry there has been much criticism of the employment of women in predominantly menial jobs, while senior management is dominated by men. While such discrimination is declining in Western societies, there are a number of cultures where equal opportunity policies create problems, for example, in Muslim societies. In the broader context of tourism development, women are underrepresented in the decision-making process within many destination societies, especially in EDCs. Yet, there are instances where women do play decisive roles, for example, in Western Samoa, and there are circumstances in which women choose to remain in lower echelon jobs. For instance, a study in Looe, a small resort town in Southwest England, found that most women working in tourism held jobs that were "low skilled" and "part-time, seasonal, or short-term." For many, however, this was their choice, as it provided supplementary income, while being compatible with their other commitments.

C. Environmental Impacts

1. Concentration or Dispersion?

Mass resort tourism inevitably generates extreme environmental change. For example, the huge beach resort of Cancun, Mexico, has long lines of large apartment blocks and hotels where continuous mangroves once grew. The growth of resorts along the North Queensland coast is threatening the delicate relationships between the rainforest, coastal mangrove and coral reef ecosystems, which are the very resources on which sustainable tourism depends. In the European Alps, forest clearance associated with the building of large ski resorts is increasing slope erosion and river flood hazards.

The environmental impacts of such developments are severe, but they are concentrated. One argument is that as mass tourism is inevitable, then large-scale enclave developments are environmentally the best option. By circumscribing their extent, and by adopting firm planning, and management and monitoring strategies, impact control can be achieved. For a number of years there have been calls to extend visitor access and facilities in Grand Canyon National Park, to take pressures off the South Rim "honeypot." The park managers have resisted this option in order to protect the other 99% of the park and to use the South Rim capacity as their key management control valve. A similar policy has been adopted in Yellowstone National Park, where extensive environmental modification has been ac-

cepted at the Old Faithful geyser site, to increase its carrying capacity and to conserve the rest of the park ecosystem.

Thus, while dispersal of tourism and tourists might at first seem preferable, this may not be environmentally sound. Clearly, for certain forms of tourism experience, movement and dispersal is essential. For example, safaris, wilderness canoeing, and other penetrative tourism uses fragile and beautiful settings, with low carrying capacities. But management of low density, dispersed tourist activity is not easy to monitor and control, especially in sensitive environments where widespread damage can gradually occur unchecked (Fig. 15). Managers may use high-density enclaves as protection for sensitive and highly valued environmental resources, such as the use of the Recreation Opportunities Spectrum (ROS) to introduce a system of recreational zones from wilderness to developed. These zoning systems are popular among managers of North America's national parks. But they are people-control mechanisms as well as environmental management tools, while leisure experiences are built around the idea of freedom. All recreational and touristic activity involves environmental impact, so the ethical debate is concerned with the question of who decides, whose environment it is, and what level of environmental change is "acceptable" and to whom (Fig. 16).

2. The Issue of Carrying Capacity

As tourism's popularity and the attraction of beautiful natural and built environments continue to grow, governments, conservationists, local communities, and tourists are crying "Enough is enough!" They are expressing the view that the carrying capacity of particular environments is being exceeded. The essence of carrying capacity is simple—the amount of use a destination can take without deteriorating, but in reality it is a relative and site-specific concept subject to a set of interacting variables (Fig. 17).

The Victoria Falls, on the Zambezi River along the Zambia-Zimbabwe border, is one of the world's great natural attractions. Yet a 1996 study cites evidence of serious environmental damage. Resources around the falls are being exhausted, with demand for housing, water, and waste disposal infrastructure at critical levels. Sightseeing flights have pushed noise pollution beyond acceptable levels, and the increasing number of tourist boats require the limiting of licenses. (Similar problems concerning pleasure flights and river rafting capacities have a protracted history in the Grand Canyon National Park.) Environmentalists want a moratorium on further expansion of hotel

FIGURE 15   Denali National Park, Alaska, U.S. A ranger talk emphasizes the fragility of the tundra ecosystem and the danger from growing tourism numbers.

capacity around the falls, but tourism is a major source of foreign currency for Zambia and Zimbabwe, and the governments are reluctant to restrict growth. This is a classic case of the central dilemma—short-term economic gain, or long-term environmental sustainability? It can be argued, of course, that environmental sustainability is the only way to economic sustainability.

Equally powerful pressures push against carrying capacity limits at built-environment sites. Venice is said to be sinking literally and metaphorically beneath a tourist tide. Economic, environmental, and social decline act together, resulting in a 50% decline in the resident population between 1975 and 1995. There are fears that the city is becoming a "museum" or even a "theme park." Florence, another Italian city on the global cultural tourism circuit, has become one of the world's most congested tourist destinations. During high season in 1995, the city received 50,000 visitors a day, and had to absorb 500 tourist buses in an urban fabric of narrow streets and piazzas lined by historic buildings. In response, city authorities in 1996 introduced a plan to reduce bus numbers by 70% and to require visitors to make advance reservations for entry to the central area and the key galleries, museums, and churches. In Britain, cities such as Oxford, Stratford-on-Avon, and Edinburgh are seasonally swamped by tourist hordes, and are struggling to establish sensible carrying capacities, which ensure economic benefit while accommodating the preferred life-styles of local people, maintaining environmental attributes and the quality of visitor experience.

In natural, human, and built environments, therefore, there is the potential to utilize economic revenue to upgrade infrastructures and the quality of life. Yet concern remains over the motivations of those in decision-making positions. Short-term economic gain is a powerful motivator. In Cyprus, village communities within the designated area have opposed the new Akamas National Park because it prevents them from developing mass beach tourism, which they see as having brought wealth to nearby villages such as Ayia Napa. Yet the prevention of environmental damage comparable to that created by such resorts is one of the main reasons environmentalists have fought so hard for the park.

FIGURE 16 Tropical rainforest, Sabah, Malaysia. A forest canopy walkway attempts to balance visitor pleasure with conservation values.

3. Local Empowerment

Much is made of the need to empower local communities to take control of decisions. Once more, a "responsible" argument that may lead to developments that may not be environmentally sound, or even economically sustainable. Yet whose views and perspectives should prevail—external elites and interest groups, or local people?

One approach to achieving this conservation–community development symbiosis has emerged from the 1992 United Nations Conference on Environment and Development (UNCED), held in Rio de Janeiro.

This is the establishment of the Global Environmental Facility (GEF), to be funded by wealthier nations "to provide finance for poorer countries to protect rather than over-exploit their fragile environments." The GEF has been used to establish protected areas, such as parks and reserves, with the dual goals of ecological conservation and local community development, to be achieved through integrated conservation–development projects (ICDPs).

Nature-based tourism is a popular component of the projects whose origins may predate the GEF, within and outside formally protected areas. For example, the

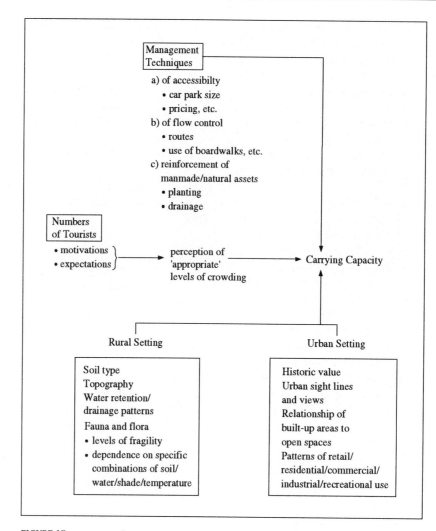

FIGURE 17   Factors Influencing Ecological Impacts. (Source: Ryan, C. (1991). Fig 6.3. 130)

Community Baboon Sanctuary in Belize has been running since 1982. In order to sustain a healthy, viable population of howler monkeys (known locally as "baboons") the farmers of Bermudian Landing village were persuaded by advice from the WWF, to conserve corridors of forest habitat along streams, and to encourage tourists to enjoy the forest and the resident monkeys. By the mid-1990s, the howler population had doubled to 1900 animals, and eight villages had joined the project. About 6000 visitors a year came for the guided walks led by young local people, and to browse and buy souvenirs at the visitor center. About 25% of the visitors stay overnight in local houses, eating local foods. A community committee runs the project, and tourism, conservation, and agriculture coexist sustainably.

D. Freedom and Human Rights

A quality often ascribed to tourism is the opportunity it provides for the expression of choice and freedom. This applies to the freedom of an individual to choose a destination, and to the tourism industry to satisfy these demands. However, this refreshingly simple idea obscures significant ethical and moral issues concerning human rights and responsibilities. Two questions serve to illustrate this complex and sensitive area. First, should tourism be encouraged and should tourists visit destinations where there is evidence of persistent violation of human rights? Second, is ability to pay the sole criterion by which a tourist is allowed to purchase the product?

By the criteria set out in the United Nations Convention on Human Rights, there is recurrent evidence of persistent violations scattered across the world. The debate over how the tourism industry and tourists should respond to such abuses produces a variety of value stances. Three main positions summarize the alternatives: first, that tourism should not be judgmental, and so should not interfere; second, that the offending country should be boycotted; third, that tourism should be encouraged in order to expose conditions to international scrutiny. The aim of the second and third options is to engender change.

The issues and options have been debated over a period of years and destinations; for example, South Africa during apartheid and China and the former USSR during repressive episodes. During the mid 1990s, Burma (Myanmar) was the focus of strong debate following the plans by a few operators to promote tours into this hitherto closed country. The brochure for one British company proclaimed that "the happiness and serenity of the Burmese people radiates from within and this is Burma's greatest gift to visitors." Other tour companies and human rights organizations protested that Burma's military regime was repressive, and in particular that forced labor was being employed to build tourist facilities. The U.S. and British governments considered calling for a world boycott. One company promoting the tours responded: "We are aware of some people's opinion of the Burmese government but we believe everyone has the right to choose whether to visit the country. Tourism is all about opening up countries and is one way of changing them."

The issues of freedom and responsibility were brought into tragic focus in May 1996, when nine people died on the slopes of Mt. Everest during an extreme storm. Those killed were leaders and clients on commercial expeditions. The clients (tourists) had paid up to $65,000 for the opportunity to climb the world's highest mountain. The leaders of such expeditions are highly experienced, the logistics are well organized, and the health and climbing competence of the clients are claimed to be thoroughly scrutinized. Inevitably, perhaps, concerns are growing that commercial pressures and increasing competitiveness in the expanding adventure business are resulting in a lowering of standards, and that risk levels are rising. One party leader described the 1996 situation on Everest:

Its weird scene. There's hundreds and hundreds of climbers here, with varying degrees of experience; some of the best climbers in the world and some people who don't even know how to put crampons on. There are a lot of people here who shouldn't

be; people who wouldn't have the experience, but have the money (quoted in *The Observer*, London, 12 May 1996).

The ethical issues center around the client–leader relationship. Companies make it clear they have the right and responsibility to reject a prospective client, and to control the behavior and actions of a client; in other words, the leader decides. On the other hand, clients who are able and willing to pay large sums to fulfill what may be a lifetime's dream, may perceive the commercial transaction differently, that is, the payer decides.

VI. ALTERNATIVE TOURISM AND SUSTAINABILITY

A. Concepts and Principles

Alternative tourism is a term commonly applied to forms of tourism that promise "tourists something 'different': a social experience, a relief from the crowds of mega-resorts and, for some, an opportunity to learn first-hand about lifestyles different from their own" (Smith, V. L. (1994). Boracay, Philippines: A Case Study in "Alternative Tourism." In V. L. Smith and W. R. Eadington (Eds.), *Tourism Alternatives*, p. 135. Chichester: Wiley). It is then, Wanderlust tourism rather than Sunlust tourism. It has been defined too, in terms of social equity and justice: ". . . a process which promotes a just form of travel between members of different communities. It seeks to achieve mutual understanding, solidarity and equality amongst participants" (Holden, P. (Ed.). (1994). Alternative Tourism: Report on the Workshop on Alternative Tourism with a Focus on Asia, p. 15. Bangkok). It claims to offer therefore, a distinctive experience based upon psychological as well as physical immersion in the cultural and natural destination environment. It is penetrative tourism, in which a core expectation is authenticity.

For instance, one distinctive characteristic is the opportunity to stay in local homes. Studies in Senegal and St. Vincent have found that indigenous accommodation was seen not only as a way by which the local people could become involved in tourism, but also as a means of offering a more authentic, meaningful and satisfying experience for both the visitor and the visited.

Alternative tourism has become today an umbrella term subsuming a variety of touristic forms, including ecotourism, green tourism, soft tourism, nature tourism, responsible tourism, and adventure tourism. All claim to be founded upon the core principles of conservation, stewardship, respect, responsibility, community empowerment, sustainability and authenticity, although there is vigorous discussion within the academic and business communities over the realism and honesty of these principles. Cater and Lowman's book, *Ecotourism: A Sustainable Option?* is an indicative title.

Smith sees green tourism as "tourism in the context of man's stewardship with nature . . . . . and with the need to develop responsible tourism policies." Mowforth introduces an atmosphere of uncertainty in claiming that "one of the most sought after and hoped for qualities of ecotourism is its sensitivity to local communities and the participation of the local population in all aspects of the planning and management of ecotourist activities." Wheeler is more firmly critical, and even cynical of the realities: "For eco-tourism, read egotourism. We are more concerned with maintaining our status, massaging our own egos and appeasing our guilt than with addressing the actual issues involved" (Wheeller, B. (1993). Sustaining the Ego. *Journal of Sustainable Tourism,* **1**(2), 22).

B. Factors Influencing the Growth of Alternative Tourism

Because tourism thrives on fashion, status, image, and conspicuous consumption, tourists seek new experiences and the industry promotes new products. Thus, constant change in demand and supply is inevitable. In attempting to account for the movement toward alternative tourism since the early 1980s, four broad energizing forces can be identified.

First, there has been a rising swell of dissatisfaction among tourists with standardized, homogenized mass package products. As tourists become more experienced and discerning, they seek wider choice, variety, and individuality in the opportunities offered. This has been interpreted within the context of the societal shift from Fordism to post-Fordism, from choice control by the producer to choice control by the consumer. One consequence is greater market segmentation and product differentiation, with the broadening range of alternative tourism products serving rapidly expanding market segments. In terms of tourist perceptions and expectations, this represents a shift from the "collective gaze" to the "romantic gaze."

Second, the growth of the environmental and conservation movements has heightened awareness of the impacts and implications of increasing and often careless use of global resources, both natural and human. This is generating a greater reflectiveness within the tourism

system, focusing around the issues of responsibility, stewardship and sustainability.

Third, the governments and peoples of potential and existing tourist destinations are responding to the abundant evidence of the negative impacts as well as the benefits of mass tourism. In the words of one Hawaiian:

> I have seen the oppression and the exploitation of an "out-of-control" global industry that has no understanding of limits or responsibility or concern for the host people of a land. . . . All is not well in paradise.

Destinations realize that if tourism and the quality of their own lives are to be sustained, then their natural and human resource base must be conserved.

Fourth, the tourism industry itself is acknowledging the need to change attitudes, products, and performance. It is unclear whether this shift is genuine or whether it is driven by external influences such as demand change and stronger environmental policies and legislation in destination regions. Certainly, operators of all types, from mass package corporations to small specialist businesses, claim to have environmentally responsible policies. For instance, Thomson, the largest British tour operator, has a "Holiday Code," which is published in its brochures and displayed in hotels it uses:

> Thomson are committed to caring for the environment and the communities in which we operate. . . . . We actively encourage our staff, at home and abroad, to become involved with local issues to support environmental protection.

C. Seeking Sustainability

There is general agreement of the need for tourism to change from an essentially exploitative to a sustainable way of thinking and acting. The difficulties lie in the practicalities: What changes are needed? Who is to make the decisions and implement them? Who is to pay for the changes? How can the changes be monitored and enforced? What is a realistic timescale? Such questions must be addressed by all components of the tourism system—tourists, destinations, industry—with the added complication that the responses require coordination.

1. Ways and Means

The responses range from guidelines and voluntary codes of conduct and practice through policy statements to legislation. Produced and promoted by individuals, special interest groups, business organizations, world institutions, and government agencies, they target tourists, destination populations, and the tourism industry. These statements and methodologies are developed upon alternative tourism principles, but are intended for application to the mainstream tourism system—to Hilton and Hawaii as well as Audubon and Alaska! Some are destination specific, but their approach is frequently transferable, and based upon a common set of principles and concepts: responsibility, sensitivity, respect, stewardship, sustainability and community involvement.

The values and principles being promoted are exemplified in the Minimum Impact Code developed by the managers of the Annapurna Conservation Area Project (ACAP) (Fig. 18). It is directed at the growing number of trekkers visiting the Nepalese Himalayas, where there is alarming evidence of accelerating negative impacts. The problem with all such codes and sets of guidelines is that they are advisory only, and so are not enforceable, even when promoted by official agencies.

Advisory and mandatory statements and documents are increasingly directed toward the tourism industry, either from within the industry itself or by outside groups and organizations. This reflects the recognition or perception that "in many well-documented cases ..... the supply side of the industry has been shown to be the guilty party in environmental degradation, cultural abuse or disregard, economic leakage, and the development of patronising attitudes." The World Tourism Organization (WTO) has produced sets of guidelines for a number of tourism-related themes, but it is unclear what effects they are having upon the industry. The industry's own global organization, the World Travel and Tourism Council (WTTC) has issued its exhortation to all member organizations and governments (Fig. 19). Advice from outside the industry varies from the succinct admonition from the Center for World Development Education (CWDE) to "Sell more selectively; plan more sensitively," to the strongly prescriptive advisory statement of the Germany-based international organization, Tourism with Insight:

"We shall not organize travel, trip or expeditions to ethnic groups who live apart from our western civilisation. We shall not promise our clients 'contact with untouched peoples', because we know they are vulnerable and must be protected" (Tourisme mit Einsicht. (1987). Code for the Travel Business. Starnberg, Germany).

ACAP: MINIMUM IMPACT CODE

As visitors and friends, we invite you to help conserve the sanctity and beauty of the Annapurna region for generations to come. Here's how to "step gently" in this fragile area, and make your visit a positively memorable one for all or to step gently in this fragile area, we ask that you:

• CONSERVE FIREWOOD. Be self-sufficient in your fuel supply and make sure your trekking staff uses kerosene and has enough warm clothing. Make no open fires. Limit hot showers, If possible, stay at lodges that use kerosene or fuel efficient wood stoves and space heaters. Kerosene is available in Chhomrong village near the Annapurna Sanctuary.

• STOP POLLUTION. Dispose of all trash properly: Paper products, cigarette butts, toilet paper, food scraps etc. should be burned or buried. Bottles, plastics and other non-biodegradable items should be packed out or deposited in rubbish pits if available. Use toilet facilities provided–if none exist, make sure you are 20 metres from any water source and carry a small shovel to bury wastes. Don't use soap or shampoo in any stream or hot spring. Supervise trekking staff to make sure they cover toilet pits and dispose of garbage properly.

• BE A GUEST. Do not damage, disturb or remove any plants, animals, animal products or religious artifacts. Respect Nepali customs in your dress and behaviour – women should not wear shorts or revealing blouses and men should always wear a shirt. Avoid outward displays of physical affection. Ask permission to take photos and respect people's right to privacy. Begging is a negative interaction that was started by well-meaning tourists–please do not give ANYTHING to beggars. Don't barter for food or lodging–many areas have lodge management committees that have set standard rates to ensure a more equal return for their efforts.

Encourage young Nepalis to be proud of their culture.

Above all, remember that your vaction has a great impact on the natural environment and people who live off its resources. By assisting in these small ways, you will help the land and people of Nepal enormously. THANK YOU!

NEPAL IS HERE TO CHANGE YOU NOT FOR YOU TO CHANGE NEPAL.

FIGURE 18   ACAP: Minimum Impact Code.

WTTC Environmental Guidelines

Travel & Tourism is the world's largest industry. A clean, healthy and safe environment is essential to further growth. The WTTC commends these Guidelines to companies and governments to take them into account in policy formulation.

Travel & Tourism Companies
Should State Their Commitment
to Environmentally
Compatible Growth

Targets for Improvements
Should Be Established
and Monitored

The Environment Commitment
Should Be Company Wide

Education and Research into
Improved Environmental
Programs Should
Be Encouraged

Travel & Tourism Companies
Should Seek to Implement Sound
Environment Principles Through
Self-Regulation, Recognizing
that National and International
Regulation May Be Inevitable and
that Preparation Is Vital

Environmental Improvement
Programs Should Be
Systematic and
Comprehensive

They should aim to:

1. **Identify and minimize** product and operation environmental problems, paying particular attention to new projects;
2. **Pay due regard** to environmental concerns in design, planning, construction and implimentation;
3. **Be sensitive** to conservation of environmentally protected or threatened areas, species and scenic aesthetics, achieving landscape enhancement where possible;
4. **Practice** energy conservation;
5. **Reduce** and recycle waste;
6. **Practice** fresh-water management and control sewage disposal;
7. **Control and diminish** air emissions and pollutants;
8. **Monitor**, control and reduce noise levels;
9. **Control, reduce and eliminate** environmentally unfriendly products, such as asbestos, CFCs, pesticides and toxic, corrosive, infectious, explosive or flammable materials;
10. **Respect and support** historic or religious objects and sites;
11. **Exercise due regard** for the interests of local populations, including their history, traditions and culture and future development;
12. **Consider environmental issues** as a key factor in the overall development of Travel & Tourism destinations.

These Guidelines have been prepared taking into account the International Chamber of Commerce (ICC) Business Charter for Sustainable Development.

FIGURE 19   WTTC Environmental Guidelines.

2. Is Sustainability Feasible? The Cases of the Galapagos Islands and Antarctica

The Galapagos Islands are part of Ecuador and are on every "conservation top ten" list because of their unique ecosystems and species assemblages, which were the inspiration for Darwin in his theory of evolution. These attributes make the islands a highly attractive ecotourist destination.

The islands have been designated as a national park and a World Heritage Area. The conservation and tourism policies are largely implemented by the national park staff. In 1990 the national tourism plan set an annual limit of 25,000 visitors, and severely restricted on-shore accommodations. By 1995, visitor numbers exceeded 40,000, which conservationists believe is sig-

nificantly beyond the carrying capacity of the fragile ecosystems, and hence is nonsustainable.

Ecuador desperately needs to maximize income from tourism, and the island population is increasing rapidly as people arrive to seek tourism-related jobs. The national park is insufficiently funded and equipped to control the number of tourist ships and their movements. Many local people are antagonistic to the national park because they perceive it as restricting tourism, thereby reducing job opportunities. International environmental groups express their alarm strongly but, with some justification, Ecuador objects to any intrusion upon its national sovereignty.

The ethical debate focuses upon whether the environmental resources of the Galapagos are of sufficient value to be part of "the global commons" and not exclusively "owned," and who should determine what touristic role the resources should play. A second and related dilemma centers upon the issue of short-term economic benefit versus longer term sustainability: people who need food and clothing today may find it difficult to give priority to the rights of future iguanas and whether a rich tourist should be able to take photos of them.

Issues surrounding the ownership–stewardship debate and the conservation–tourism tightrope are even more strongly highlighted in Antarctica. This continent is unique in that it is not "owned" by individual nation-states, nor is it the ancestral homeland of an indigenous human population. It is "governed" through the Antarctic Treaty System (ATS), ratified in 1961, and to which in 1990, 25 nations belonged, membership being based on territorial claims and substantive scientific interests. Approximately 98% is covered by ice, and the exposed fragments are extremely fragile: "With low rates of weathering and flora and fauna at the extremes of their environmental tolerance, disturbance is rapid, and recovery of land surface, vegetation and wildlife very slow."

Ecotourism is expanding rapidly. Antarctica is decreasingly protected by its inaccessibility in terms of time, cost or distance. In 1995 at least 9000 visitors arrived, a 50% increase since 1990. They travel and stay on cruise ships, mostly small, but increasing in size each year, and take trips ashore by Zodiac inflatables.

The principal attractions, in addition to the spectacular scenery are wildlife congregations, scientific bases, and historic sites such as explorers' huts and old whaling stations.

Because of the low carrying capacity of this sensitive environment, scientists and environmental groups claim evidence of the intrusiveness of tourism. For instance, the tourist season is from December through February, which is breeding season for penguins and seals, and the increasing tourist presence is causing stress in some of the colonies. Furthermore, tour operators are pressing to establish on-shore facilities, including accommodation and the use of the historic buildings as "heritage sites," with the ensuing effluents and pollution.

In response to these concerns, in 1991 the tour operators formed the International Association of Antarctic Tour Operators (IAATO) as a self-regulatory body, and have adopted an "Antarctic Travellers Code" (Fig. 20). Principal problems arise from the confusion over responsibility for and feasibility of control, and upon the ethics of resource use. This is one disadvantage of the absence of jurisdictional sovereignty and ownership: "There is no polar police force."

Scientists differ in their stance. Some welcome tourists, others believe them to be intrusive and detrimental to the scientific programs and conceive Antarctica as a "global laboratory." Few feel that it is their responsibility to control tourist behavior except where there is

---

Antarctic Traveler's Code

Antarctic visitors

- MUST *NOT* leave footprints in fragile mosses, lichens or grasses.
- MUST *NOT* dump plastic or other non-biodegradable garbage overboard or onto the Continent.
- MUST *NOT* violate the seals', penguins', or seabirds' *Personal Space*.
  - start with a 'baseline' distance of 15 ft (5 m) from penguins, seabirds, and true seals and 60 ft (18 m) from fur seals
  - give animals the right-of-way
  - stay on the edge of, and don't walk through, animal groups
  - back-off if necessary
  - never touch the animals
- MUST *NOT* interfere with protected areas or scientific research.
- MUST *NOT* take souvenirs.

Antarctic tour companies

- SHOULD apply the Antarctic Traveler's Code to all officers, crew, staff and passengers.
- SHOULD utilize one (1) guide or leader for every twenty (20) passengers.
- SHOULD employ experienced and sensitive on-board leadership.
- SHOULD use vessels that are safe for Antarctic ice conditions.
- SHOULD adopt a shipwide anti-dumping pledge.

FIGURE 20   Antarctic Traveler's Code.

direct impact upon the scientific work. Environmental groups are divided on the role of historic structures as tourist attractions, that is, as resources for heritage tourism. To some, they should remain untouched; to others, they can be renovated and displayed with respect, although few support the pressures for development as tourist accommodations.

Tourism is, therefore, one element in a broader debate. There is an awareness that this may be the last chance to prove whether humankind possesses the will to shift perspective from "it's mine" to "it's ours." In sum—"If we cannot succeed in Antarctica we have little chance of succeeding elsewhere."

VII. CONCLUSION

There is a growing number of examples of good practice, where genuine efforts to achieve and retain the principles of sustainability are being made, such as Zimbabwe's Campfire project, Belize's Community Baboon Sanctuary (Fig. 21). Individual countries now

have tourism strategies founded upon sound environmental and ethical principles. For example, Costa Rica has developed a code of conduct for government departments and personnel, which includes the concept of "proper stewardship of nature with all that this implies." Effective implementation of such good intentions is unlikely to be easy, and it will be interesting to see how far and how well the Costa Rican government can put such principles onto the statute book and into practice.

One problem that the various proposals and policies for alternative tourism fail to address is that of sheer numbers. The "holiday code" initiated by the mass tourism operator, Thomson is a well intentioned wish list only. The impact of escalating visitor numbers in America's national parks illustrates the difficulties of sustaining environmental integrity even in areas whose designated purpose is sustainability. It seems inevitable that tourist numbers will continue to increase and that they will assume the right to penetrate planet earth ever more comprehensively. It must be remembered too, that large numbers of people prefer "mass" destinations,

FIGURE 21 Ecotourism lodge, Rio Negro, near Manaus, Brazil. This floating lodge has a capacity of 30, employs 14 people, mostly locals, uses solar energy, and collects wastes in a tank for removal. It is owned by a Portugese company.

with the full range of comforts and facilities, and will continue to do so.

There is also the issue of whether alternative tourism projects, generally low key and relatively small scale, can by themselves "survive in developing countries, or elsewhere, without having some other form of tourism to be an 'alternative' to." From this perspective, even though such projects may be environmentally and ethically sound, they may not be economically sustainable.

It may well be, therefore, that the most effective strategy is to absorb the growth in demand through development of carefully located, planned, and developed large-scale destination enclaves. Such developments concentrate the impacts and environmental modifications, while facilitating the opportunities for monitoring and control. The "product consumption" takes place within the resort, and is thus demand based, not resource based: local dance groups perform and craftspeople sell their artifacts in the hotels or in a "cultural center." In parallel, dispersed alternative tourism projects would be under less pressure and yet would remain economically sustainable within the broader tourism system of the destination region or nation. From the demand side, the tourism industry would be offering a range of opportunities and experiences, from the synthetic to the authentic, or at least the staged authentic.

Also See the Following Articles

ENVIRONMENTAL IMPACT ASSESSMENT • INDIGENOUS RIGHTS • SUSTAINABILITY • STEWARDSHIP • ZOOS AND ZOOLOGICAL PARKS

Bibliography

Brent Ritchie, J. R., & Goeldner, C. R. (Eds.). (1994). *Travel, tourism and hospitality research: A handbook for managers and researchers.* New York: Wiley.

Cater, E., & Lowman, G. (Eds.). (1994). *Ecotourism: A sustainable option?* Chichester: Wiley.

Cooper, C., Fletcher, J., Gilbert, D., & Wanhill, S. (1993). *Tourism: Principles and Practice.* London: Pitman.

Doxey, G. V. (1975). A causation theory of visitor-resident irritants: methodology and research influence. Proceedings of the Travel Research Associates, 6th Annual Conference, pp. 195–198. San Diego, CA.

Middleton, V. T. C. (1994). *Marketing in travel and tourism* (2nd ed.). Oxford: Butterworth-Heinemann.

Mill, R. C. (1990). *Tourism: The international business.* Englewood Cliffs, NJ: Prentice-Hall.

Mowforth, M. (1993). Eco-tourism: Terminology and definitions. Research Report No. 1. Department of Geographical Sciences, University of Plymouth.

Prosser, R. (1994). *Leisure, recreation and tourism.* London: Collins.

Ryan, C. (1991). *Recreational tourism.* London: Routledge.

Smith, V. L., & Eadington, W. R. (Eds.). (1994). *Tourism alternatives.* Chichester: Wiley.

Theobald, W. (Ed.). (1994). *Global Tourism: The Next Decade.* Oxford: Butterworth-Heinemann.

TRADE SECRETS AND PROPRIETARY INFORMATION

John Snapper
Illinois Institute of Technology

GLOSSARY

common law Rules derived from custom, including a tradition of legal decisions, in contrast to statutory or legislated law.

copyright An exclusive right to reproduce, publicly distribute, display, perform, or make derivative works based upon a written work for a set period, on condition that the written work satisfies standards for copyrightable subject matter.

GATT The international General Agreement on Tariffs and Trade, which includes the Agreement on Trade Related Aspects of Intellectual Property, and which establishes the World Trade Organization.

intellectual property An informal classification of property under proprietary rights granted by several interrelated legal and social policies, including patent, copyright, trademark, and trade secrecy policy. Intellectual property is typically contrasted with "tangible" property.

patent An exclusive right to make, use, sell, or to authorize the making, use, and sale of an invention for a set period, on condition that the invention satisfies standards for patentable subject matter.

reverse engineering The discovery of engineering technology through the study of an existing, engineered product.

theft The unlawful taking of property.

trade secret Information that has economic value, that is not easily discoverable by independent means, and that has been subject to measures to keep it secret.

unfair trade practice An informal classification of business practices that are forbidden under several interrelated legal and social policies, including policy providing remedies for those who have been the victims of industrial espionage, interference with contractual relations, use of a misleading business identification, unfair pricing strategies, and improper means of discovery.

A TRADE SECRET, in the traditional definition, is information that (a) has economic value, (b) is not easily discovered by independent means, and (c) has been subject to measures to keep it secret. Examples range from customer lists, to the recipes of gourmet chefs, to technological innovations. When such information becomes known through "improper means," such as industrial espionage or breach of confidence, the persons who lose secrets may have legal remedies against those who discover them. These remedies include injunctions against the use of the information, recompense for the loss of economic advantages, and in some cases punitive damages.

Encyclopedia of Applied Ethics, Volume 4
Copyright © 1998 by Academic Press. All rights of reproduction in any form reserved.

I. LEGAL FOUNDATION FOR RECOGNITION OF TRADE SECRETS

In contrast to other forms of "intangible" or "intellectual" property (such as patent, copyright, and trademark rights), there is no general agreement on how or whether trade secrets should be recognized. The United States has a notably strong tradition in the protection of trade secrets, although most of its policies are based in state rather than federal law. Before 1985, trade secrecy in the United States was recognized in a mishmash of legal statutes, common law, and a classic definition in the 1939 *Restatement of Torts*. More recently, however, the basic principles of trade secrecy have been codified in the *Uniform Trade Secrets Act*, which has been enacted in most of the states. In contrast, the United Kingdom and most of the former British colonies have traditionally opposed the recognition of trade secrecy ownership as an independent legal right, and most trade secrecy is dealt with under a number of more or less separate legal principles, including a civil tort of breach of confidence.

Given a history of disagreement on even the most basic principles of trade secrecy, it is no surprise that the study of trade secrecy becomes more confused as we look to a broader international picture. Japan, for instance, agrees more or less with the United States on the need for strong protections of trade secrets, while Brazil would like to weaken those protections to a very limited recognition of some explicit licensing agreements. The 1995 GATT TRIPs (Agreement on Trade Related Aspects of Intellectual Property Rights of the General Agreement on Tariffs and Trade) may, however, prefigure a more uniform international picture. The TRIPs (Article 39) demand that governments and their agencies protect "undisclosed information," and recognizes the rights of individuals and businesses against the disclosure of secrets in "a manner contrary to honest commercial practices." Although the TRIPs make no attempt to specify remedies against the loss of secrets, the mere existence of a discussion of "undisclosed information" in the agreement that established the World Trade Organization might suggest that trade secrecy is about to acquire greater international significance with at least a modicum of unity.

II. TRADE SECRETS VIEWED AS INTELLECTUAL PROPERTY

The very notion of a trade secret is replete with philosophical and ethical controversy. Even the identification of trade secrets as "proprietary information" is controversial. In one view, trade secrets are property and their misappropriation is theft. In an alternative view, the tort is the reprehensible means of discovery, such as the bribery of a disloyal employee, in which case there is no need to think of the tort as a violation of a property right. Each view has its merits and its problems.

One advantage of the view that secrets are property (at least to those who wish to claim ownership of information) is that it extends to information those protections that are given to more traditional forms of property. Thus in western Europe, for instance, it would extend to information the same protections that a business has against the government appropriation of real property. Moreover, the view that trade secrets are property permits their loss to be viewed as a form of "theft." This is clearly the dominant view in the United States, where the majority of the states impose criminal punishment for theft of trade secrets. Moreover, in 1996 the U.S. federal government made this approach federal policy in the Economic Espionage Act (18 USCA 18.31), which imposes criminal penalties for passing "stolen" trade secrets to foreign corporations. Recognizing this view of trade secrets, Roger Milgrim begins his influential study of U.S. trade secrecy law with the remark that the view of trade secrets as property is "the basic conceptual step" that is needed to understand American trade secrecy law (Milgrim, 1967. *Milgrim on Trade Secrets*, at 1.01. Bender).

In contrast to the U.S. treatment of trade secrecy loss as theft, the standard approach in Canada is to treat the loss of trade secrets as a breach of confidence, which leaves only civil remedies that are generally weaker than criminal penalties. The U.S. approach has the apparent advantage of simplifying our analysis of trade secrecy by applying to it the same sort of categories that we use for other forms of "property." This approach has consequences for taxation (is the transfer of information to be treated as a sale or a service?), for inheritance, and for a myriad of other areas of property law. In contrast, treating the loss of secrets as an improper business practice fragments trade secrecy policy into a variety of torts, depending on how the secret was compromised. This very fragmentation, however, has been seen as a positive feature, particularly by British commentators who in the common law tradition prefer narrow decisions, without the far-reaching (and perhaps unintended) consequences for business practice that would follow from a general policy on proprietary information.

The outstanding philosophical problem with the treatment of trade secrets as proprietary information is that it violates the legal commonplace (codified into both copyright and patent law) that no one may own "ideas." Under copyright law, for instance, this policy entails that, although the owner of a copyright on a manuscript controls the production of "copies" of the manuscript, a copyright may not be used to prevent the dissemination of the "ideas expressed" in that manuscript. And when there are few alternative ways to express ideas (as happens, for instance, when ideas are expressed in standard mathematical notation), then there is said to be a "merger of idea and expression" and no copyrights are recognized. But this standard policy for most forms of intellectual property is explicitly rejected by trade secrecy policies that focus on the "ownership of information." The American *Uniform Trade Secrets Act* states, for instance, that "trade secret means information . . ." and the "owner" of a trade secret may enjoin the "thief" from further dissemination of that information in any form.

This dispute over the "ownership of ideas" in intellectual property policy must be understood in the context of a general theory about the ideals of those policies— that is, a sense of what those policies are designed to achieve. Although there is general agreement that most intellectual property policies (especially patent and copyright policy) should promote progress in science and technology, there is disagreement over how the policies function to achieve that end. One common claim is that intellectual property policy promotes progress in technology by encouraging the open access to ideas that is essential for a lively and efficient research community. Taking this view, for instance, it is frequently stated (both in the critical literature and in legal dicta) that a patent monopoly is given to inventors in "exchange" for their disclosure of their technology. In this theory, intellectual property policy functions by encouraging disclosure. And because the legal recognition of trade secrets provides legal assistance to those who have taken measures to preserve secrecy, trade secrecy policy functions in this theory in a manner contrary to the function of "other" intellectual property policies. We would, then, need to seek a justification for the legal recognition of trade secrets in a distinct legal theory that distinguishes trade secrecy, patent, and copyright policies, with their independent and conflicting legal aims. Trade secrecy policy, in contrast to the other forms of intellectual property policy, might for instance recognize a basic right to do independent research in secret, regardless of its inhibiting effect on openness in science and technology.

But there are alternative economic theories on how intellectual property policies function to achieve the aim of promoting progress in science and technology. Some of these theories make no appeal to the notion of openness in science, and can accommodate both trade secrecy and patent policy in a coherent theory of intellectual property. E. W. Kitch has argued, for instance, that patents promote progress in science and technology by enriching research corporations that have a good, prior record of successful invention (Kitch, 1977. The Nature and Function of the Patent System. *Journal of Law and Economics*, 20). In this influential theory, a patent monopoly thereby puts economic resources in the hands of those most likely to continue to produce new technology. Extending the theory, trade secrecy can complement the economic effect of patent policy by providing strong research corporations with additional economic advantages in their research industries, which translates into additional resources to carry forth their research programs. In such a theory, it is possible to give a consistent treatment of how patent and trade secrecy policy both promote progress in technology. In contrast to the view that patent policies are intended to encourage openness, this view permits a coherent notion of intellectual property including both patent and trade secrecy policy. (It should be noted that Kitch has also suggested that a property analysis may not be the best approach to trade secrecy in Kitch (1980). The Law and Economics of Rights in Valuable Information. *Journal of Legal Information.*)

A much cited case in U.S. law that reflects on the legal relation of trade secrecy to other intellectual property policy is *Kewanee Oil Co v Bicron Corp* (416 US 470 (1974)). At issue was whether federal patent policy preempts state trade secrecy policy. If federal patent law is designed to encourage the disclosure of secret technology, while state trade secrecy law provides legal assistance to those who keep technology secret, then there is a potential for a conflict and (in U.S. policy) the federal law should preempt when state trade secrecy policy interfers with the goals of federal policy. In *Kewanee*, however, patent and trade secrecy policies were viewed as protecting distinct interests, with separate policy justifications that do not conflict. Whereas trade secrecy provides for the immediate ownership of ideas or information, patent policy grants control over the commercial use of an invention and (like copyright policy) explicitly does not grant proprietary control over underlying ideas or information. The Court held therefore that trade secrecy and patent policy have separate areas of concern and that there is no direct conflict. The Court also noted that, whereas patent policy is designed to protect significant innovation, trade secrecy policy protects technological details. Although *Kewanee* itself put the lie to this argument (because Kewanee had an interesting method for producing a synthetic crystal that it opted to protect as a trade secret rather than patent), this position is generally sensible. Although some trade secrets have scientific or technological value, typical examples of a trade secrets include customer lists, plans for advertising campaigns, and investment policies. And when trade secrets govern technology, it is often such things as the details of the formulas for the production of ink used in ball point pens, which are of little interest for basic research. There certainly are trade secrets with basic research significance, but a debate over "proprietary information" that focuses on these cases may miss the main point of trade secrecy policy.

III. TRADE SECRETS VIEWED AS A FAIR TRADE PRACTICE

The obvious alternative to the view of trade secrets as proprietary information is the view of trade secrets policy as bars against improper means of discovery. This is the main traditional in British law. Thus, in *Boardman v Phillips* (2 AC 46 (1967)), the court remarked that trade secrecy law is a matter of proper business practice and that trade secrets are "not property in any normal sense." This feature of trade secrecy is not ignored in U.S. law. Thus, the U.S. Supreme Court recognized in *Kewanee* that the policy behind trade secrecy law is "the maintenance of commercial ethics" (along with "the encouragement of invention").

This approach to trade secrecy will obviously raise questions concerning which means of discovery are improper and what are standard business practices. The development of trade secrecy law, then, both recognizes current ethical standards and influences the development of changing standards. In a U.S. case, *E.I. duPont deNemours v Christopher* (431 F.2d 1012 (1970)), the issue was whether it is proper to photograph a factory construction site from an airplane circling the area. With the photographs it was possible to interpret the pipe runs, vat structures, and so on, of a factory under construction and to discover the process that was to be performed in that factory. There was simply no business standard for this sort of practice prior to the court decision in *Christopher*. The court decided that to permit the photography would require businesses to shield their construction sites. Given the financial strain and waste of financial resources that this would demand of businesses trying to preserve trade secrets, the court

established that such photography is improper. In this case, the court established a new standard for business ethics where there had been no prior standard. In British law, which tries to avoid a unified trade secrecy policy, each such decision is a matter of the recognition of an independent business standard. In *Shelley Films Ltd v Rex Features Ltd* (1993), the issue was the use of photographs made by a visitor to a film studio that had as yet not released its image of the Frankenstein monster. The British court here recognized a tort of unauthorized photography in a private area, without direct appeal to the general notion of a trade secret.

The majority of trade secrecy infringements involve a breach of an agreement (either implied or explicit) to preserve confidential information. (Although as *Christopher* clearly illustrates, not all infringements fall into this category.) Therefore, a large portion of trade secrecy has focused on when agreements (explicit or implied) are to be recognized as binding. It is, for instance, standard engineering practice to "reverse engineer" a competitor's products. A properly acquired machine (for example a machine purchased on the open market, but not a machine stolen from the competitor's research laboratory) is taken apart to discover the "secrets" that make it work. Most engineers and most courts would strongly object to any trade secrecy policy that interfered with this standard practice. In some cases, however, machines are leased with trade secrecy contracts that forbid reverse engineering. Although that practice seems acceptable when the machines are individually customized items, the practice becomes more controversial as the machines have wider distribution. In the extreme, there has been an attempt to use "shrink-wrap contracts" to preclude the practice of reverse compilation in the software industry. Software is "sold" in a package that announces to the buyer that to open the package is to "agree" to certain conditions on use, including an agreement not to reverse engineer by reverse compiling, which is a severe limitation on reverse engineering. At issue, then, is whether engineers should be permitted to reverse engineer the software without regard to the shrink-wrap statements that attempt to impinge on a standard engineering practice. It is an issue of what constitutes a binding agreement.

As we shift the discussion of trade secrecy away from "intellectual property" and toward a notion of "fair trade practice," there is a shift in the legal theory that justify the policies. Whereas intellectual property policy is typically seen as promoting progress in science and technology, policies on "fair trade" are typically seen as a means to encourage fair business competition and economic progress. A classic example with direct bearing on trade secrecy is the contractual limitation on a former employee's opportunities to work for a competitor. Because any restriction on the mobility of skilled or knowledgeable workers has an obvious negative impact on workplace competition, there is a prima facie opposition to the enforcement of agreements that restrict the employment opportunities of ex-employees. (In English common law, this tradition dates from the "Dyer's Case" in 1414, when a master dyer tried and failed to persuade the local magistrate to enforce an agreement barring an ex-apprentice from establishing a competing practice.) On the other hand, restrictive employment agreements can also encourage business investment by making it possible for employers to invest in the training of skilled workers in a trade secret technology without risk of losing the investment to competitors who offer higher pay. The common law on covenants that restrict employment is largely a matter of balancing these two concerns, both of which focus on how to encourage a lively and competitive business environment without undue concern for whether the information or training is "proprietary."

In judging whether a trade secrecy employment agreement is binding, the courts had traditionally tried to find a "reasonable" balance between what encourages a competitive workplace and what encourages investment in the training of employees in new technology. In outline, there is agreement between U.K., U.S., and Commonwealth traditions on what passes as a reasonable limitation on employment opportunities. It might be reasonable, for instance, for a genetic engineering firm that is developing new varieties of corn to bar its trainees for 1 year from taking employment in another genetic engineering firm that also works on corn. But it would certainly be unreasonable to prevent those trainees from ever taking alternative employment in the genetic engineering industry. When the legal notion of reasonableness draws on a notion of trade secrecy or proprietary information, however, the issues become much more controversial, and there is little hope for a unified common law tradition. Broadly speaking, it seems reasonable that only minimal limitations be placed on employees who wish to sell their technical skills to the highest bidder in the industry, but that permanent bans be placed on the sale of detailed knowledge of trade secrets (or, at least, until the "secrets" become common knowledge through independent means). Although this approach makes sense on a theoretic level, its application depends on distinctions between a skill, generalized knowledge, know-how, specific information, and a trade secret that are at best strained or blurred. In any event, a policy on trade secrecy agreements demands that some such distinctions be made while assessing the reasonableness and enforceability of those contracts.

Also See the Following Articles

CONFIDENTIALITY, GENERAL ISSUES OF • FREEDOM OF SPEECH • PATENTS • PRIVACY

Bibliography

The works by McManus (1993) and Miller (1990) in the Nutshell Series give an excellent introduction to the legal issues. The standard comprehensive study is Milgrim (1967). The most important legal statutes are included in Goldstein (1995). The *European Intellectual Property Review* offers a good overview of current international issues.

Goldstein, P., Kitch, E. W., & Perlman, H. S. (1995). *Selected statutes and international agreements on unfair competition, trademark, copyright, and patent.* Foundation Press.

Kitch, E. W. (1980). The law and economics of rights in valuable information. *Journal of Legal Studies.*

McManis, C. R. (1993). *Unfair Trade Practices in a Nutshell.* St. Paul, MN: West Publishing.

Miller, A. R., & Davis, M. H. (1990). *Intellectual property: Patents trademark and copyright in a nutshell.* St. Paul, MN: West Publishing.

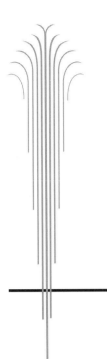

TRANSSEXUALISM

Dahlian Kirby
University of Wales, College of Cardiff

GLOSSARY

cross-dressing Wearing clothes usually associated with the other gender according to cultural norms.

hermaphrodite From the Greek Aphrodite and Hermes, the goddess and god of love. A person who is difficult to label as one sex or another according to biological criteria. The individual may have male and female sexual organs. A less offensive term is intersex.

intersex An alternative term for hermaphrodite. Considered more culturally acceptable.

sexual realignment A form of medical treatment used on transsexuals involving hormone therapy and surgery. This gives the transsexual the physical appearance of the gender they believe themselves to be.

third sex A recent term used by some transsexuals to describe themselves and also by people who consider themselves neither female nor male.

transsexing The medical processes used to change the body of a transsexual. See also sexual realignment.

transsexual A person who believes he or she was born in the wrong body and requires transsexing. The term can be used for both pre- and postoperative individuals.

transvestite A person who dresses in clothes usually associated with the other sex. The term is almost exclusively used to describe men who wear clothes that parody female fashion. Many transvestites dress in women's clothes in private. It has been suggested that transvestites exist because the clothes of Western men are in general drab.

TRANSSEXUALISM is the condition of crossing over to live permanently as the opposite sex from that designated at birth. The term also implies a method of treatment rather than a diagnosis.

I. A BRIEF HISTORY OF TRANSSEXUALISM

Although transsexualism has roots in ancient times and across many cultures, the term was not recognized by the American Psychiatric Association until 1980. Without medical assistance transsexing cannot take place and therefore transsexuals could not have existed as they are presented now before surgery was developed. However, the urge to live as the other sex is not unusual, especially where there is a wide division

Encyclopedia of Applied Ethics, Volume 4
Copyright © 1998 by Academic Press. All rights of reproduction in any form reserved.

between the expected behavior of men and that of women.

In the Middle Ages hermaphrodites were permitted to choose their own gender when they were old enough to marry. Once they made their choice they had to adhere to it. In this century many children who are hermaphroditic are given surgery to remove one set of sexual organs to enable them to be reared as the other sex. It appears that social expectation will allow them to fit comfortably into their designated sex in most cases. At puberty they will be given further treatment to "masculinize" or "feminize" their appearance.

In some cultures it is acceptable to act as a member of the other sex. The Hijras of India are one example of a cultural acceptance of something similar to transsexualism. The Hijras are castrated males who form a privileged community. Some of them are born with ambiguous genitalia and are considered to have special powers; others are men who's behavior is considered "feminine." Once a person becomes a Hijra he cannot go back to acting like a man. Women who have cross-dressed and pretended to be men have usually done so to escape violence or poverty. There are many well-documented cases of women living as men in order to serve in the armed forces during wars. These women were often decorated for bravery, their true sex not being discovered until they died.

The earliest known case of surgical "sex changing" was made on Sophie Hedwig in 1882, although there are few details of the case. In 1886 Krafft-Ebing created the term "gynandry" to describe what is now considered the condition of female-to-male transsexuality. In 1949 Cauldwell reported a case of a woman who wanted to be a man and labeled the case "psychopathia transsexualis," introducing the term transsexualism into clinical literature. In the 1950s Benjamin used the term "transsexuality" to describe the condition of the patients he was treating with hormones to relieve their distress and in 1966 published the first textbook on transsexualism.

The first U.S. medical institution to devote itself to transsexual surgery was the Johns Hopkins Hospital. Before it opened Americans had traveled abroad in order to be transsexed, often in clinics with poor hygiene and little or no aftercare. In 1980 transsexualism was officially recognized as an illness in the American Psychiatric Association's *Diagnostic and Statistical Manual of Mental Disorders* (DSM). The definition was revised in 1987. Transsexual activists are now lobbying for the depathologizing of transsexualism within the Association and also from the DSM.

II. THE TRANSSEXING PROCESS

Transsexuals requiring realignment will have hormone therapy and surgery. Treatment will give an approximation of the body of the sex they wish to be. For male-to-female transsexuals this will involve hormonal "feminization" with estrogen or estrogen combined with progestin which will induce breast enlargement and reduce muscle mass. The penis is reformed into a vagina by inverting it into a newly opened cavity. Many male-to-female transsexuals also have elective cosmetic surgery and lessons in deportment and social skills.

Postsurgery female-to-male transsexuals usually have deepened voices and an increase in body hair induced by hormone treatment. They will also have an increase in muscle mass. They sometimes have their wombs removed as well as their breasts. Some have an artificially constructed penis (phalloplasty), although surgery for this is still often unsuccessful or only partially successful. A phalloplasty typically costs $200,000. Postoperative transsexuals will be incapable of reproducing.

III. REASONS FOR TRANSSEXING

The classic explanation for requesting transsexing is that the person is "a woman trapped in a man's body" or vice versa. For the transsexual who requires realignment, their present physical state is unacceptable; they feel they will never be able to be truly who they are until they are given the body of the sex they believe they are. Not all transsexuals require realignment, and the emphasis is on identity rather than sexuality. Many transsexuals express a hatred of their genitalia and have a strong urge to have them removed. There have been many cases where transsexuals have either been refused realignment or been unable to wait for surgery and have removed their own genitalia.

Living as the other sex and cross-dressing are usually unsatisfactory solutions for transsexuals. They want to be accepted as the sex they believe they are, rather than living in a situation where they need to deceive others about their body and legal status. Recently some people have relabeled themselves as being members of the third sex. They consider themselves neither male or female, and do not always require surgery. They are concerned about the deceit that transsexuals are encouraged to engage in, and intend to be open about their gender and sex.

There is no one full acceptable medical explanation for transsexualism. Some doctors have suggested biological explanations, while others, most notably Stoller, consider that transsexualism has a social and therefore psychological basis. Montgomery, working with transsexuals in Britain, has suggested that there is no psychological, biological, or sociological theory which fits every patient and that each has a unique pattern to their gender identity.

IV. CRITERIA FOR TRANSSEXING

In order to be accepted for realignment each transsexual must fulfill the criteria for the American Psychiatric Association's official diagnosis. It is as follows:

1. Sense of discomfort and inappropriateness about one's anatomic sex
2. Wish to be rid of one's genitals and live as the other sex
3. That the disturbance has been continuous, not limited to periods of stress, for at least two years
4. Absence of physical intersex or genetic abnormality
5. Not due to another mental disorder, such as schizophrenia

Not all transsexuals who fulfill the criteria will go on to have realignment; the majority respond to a psychotherapeutic approach by choosing not to have surgery. Not all transsexuals will approach doctors in search of medical assistance. It is therefore impossible to say how many transsexuals there are in this country.

V. ETHICAL OBJECTIONS TO TRANSSEXUALISM

There are many ethical objections to transsexualism and include:

1. Surgically altering a healthy body
2. Using valuable resources in a nontherapeutic situation
3. Interfering with nature
4. Altering a God-given body
5. Colluding with a mentally ill person
6. Encouraging and expecting deception
7. Reinforcing gender stereotypes
8. Financial gain from an individual's self-hatred

Transsexualism works on the principle that something is wrong with a person and that he can only be put right through surgery and hormone treatment. As there is no definite evidence that transsexualism is a medical condition, doctors work on the theory that those seeking transsexing appear to have similar problems and desires.

Those calling themselves transsexuals must conform to the criteria in order to gain that which they desire, i.e., to be transsexed.

Transsexing is a medical response. It involves taking away and changing flesh and altering a person's hormones. Individuals become infertile. Transsexing causes a lot of physical pain and surgery, especially for female-to-males, and may result in artificially created body parts which do not function properly. It may be thought unethical to damage a healthy body while using money and expertise which would be better employed helping the sick.

Another objection to transsexing is that it interferes with nature, presuming we can alter what we do not like or feel uncomfortable with. As we have moved so far from what may be thought of as "natural humans" this objection may be considered to have little foundation. It can be said that all medical treatment is interfering with nature. It would, however, be reasonable for people who feel that they are transsexuals to refuse the offer of medical intervention because they feel it is unnatural to change their body, no matter how uncomfortable they feel with it.

The objections in terms of altering a God-given body are similar to interfering with nature and in the same way object to an arrogance that human beings can improve upon what was already there. The original objection by theologians to transsexing is that it involves mutilating the body. Mutilation violates humanity's custodianship of the body and is immoral because it ignores supreme ownership. If it is believed that the body is made in God's image it may be considered sinful to alter it.

It may be considered immoral to collude with a mentally ill person by pretending that we believe that they are "trapped in the wrong body." As many transsexuals receive other forms of treatment which appear to relieve their suffering, it may be considered that transsexing is unnecessary. Further objections can be made to the profit gained by those colluding.

Transsexualism involves a lot of deceit. Transsexing appears to be the only treatment which encourages people to lie about their past. In order to be accepted for realignment transsexuals must fit the criteria and are therefore often in situations where they will distort any feelings about their past for fear they will fail to be diagnosed as transsexual.

A further objection comes from many feminists. They consider that transsexing reinforces gender stereotypes. This appears to be mostly the case with male-to-female transsexuals who pay for expensive elective cosmetic surgery so that they can be beautiful and desirable women. Transsexualism suggests that each individual must dress and act strictly according to a rigid gender code. There is a possibility that transsexuality would be unnecessary if individuals were allowed to act as individuals and not have to conform to precise social expectations. People who self-define as the third sex are attempting to address this dilemma.

The central moral question concerned with transsexualism is whether anybody should be allowed to have transsexing? In order to address this question we need to consider all the objections stated above, then ask whether the agent should be allowed to pursue their desired goal, and finally whether we should ever interfere in a person's actions because we wish to prevent them from harming themselves.

In order to help decide on an ethical position as regards transsexualism it is useful to consider whether John Stuart Mill was correct when he said, "Over himself, over his own body and mind, the individual is sovereign" (1991 [1859]. *On liberty and other essays*. London: Oxford Univ. Press).

VI. THE LEGAL POSITION OF TRANSSEXUALS

Sex is defined biologically at birth (or shortly after) and is legally unalterable, despite cases of ambiguity. Although gender does not always correspond to the named sex at birth, legally a person cannot alter from male to female or from female to male. In the United States married people must first be divorced before they are allowed realignment. Transsexual activists are working toward recognition of the difficulties caused by inflexible laws and also the prejudice faced by transsexuals.

Also See the Following Articles

GENDER ROLES • SEXUAL ORIENTATION

Bibliography

Bornstein, K. (1994). *Gender outlaw*. London: Routledge.
Millot, C. (1990). *Horsexe: Essay on transsexuality*. Brooklyn, NY: Autonmedia.
Morris, J. (1974). *Conundrum*. London: Faber & Faber.
Money, J. (1968). *Sex errors of the body: Dilemmas, Education, Counseling*. Baltimore, MD: Johns Hopkins Univ. Press.
Nathaf, Z. I. (1996). *Lesbians talk transgender*. London: Scarlet Press.
Raymond, J. (1979). *The transsexual empire*. Boston, MA: Beacon Press.
Thompson, R. (1995). *What took you so long? A girl's journey into manhood*. Baltimore, MD: Penguin.

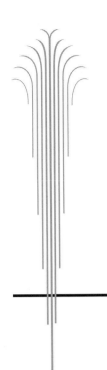

TRUST

Olli Lagerspetz
Åbo Academy and The University of Wales at Swansea

GLOSSARY

evidence Facts which, in the circumstances, rightly incline us to believe that certain other facts obtain.

first-person description An agent's description of her own motives or dispositions, constituting part of her practical deliberation in the situation at hand. Compare to third-person description.

Pascal's wager The suggestion that it is advisable to hold certain beliefs even in the absence of relevant evidence, provided sufficiently beneficial effects will result.

Prisoner's Dilemma Game played by two parties, A and B, with the options of cooperation and defection. The possible outcomes for A are, in descending order of desirability, A defects, B cooperates; A cooperates, B cooperates; A defects, B defects; and A cooperates, B defects.

reliance Dependence on another agent's actions based on an explicit or implicit judgment of relevant risks and relevant possible benefits.

risk A form of harm perceived as the possible outcome of some adopted course of action.

testimony A truth claim accepted on the authority of the person making the claim.

third-person description The description of an agent's motives or dispositions typically made by someone else than herself. Compare to first-person description.

THE NOTION OF TRUST is connected with central issues in epistemology, philosophical psychology, moral and political philosophy, economics, and religion. Yet it has only recently become a topic in its own right in mainstream academic philosophy.

Trust entails a belief in another agent's goodwill or veracity; a belief which, in some sense, goes beyond or against available evidence. Hence the rationality of trusting is often seen as posing a *prima facie* problem.

A distinction can be made between trust and reliance. To rely on another person (or agency) is to exercise judgment concerning the reasonableness of depending on them for a particular purpose. We consider the evidence concerning the other's competence and dispositions and weigh it against the stakes involved. Trusting, on the contrary, is characterized by the fact that we do not *consider* whether it is reasonable to depend on the other's goodwill. If we refuse to trust a person more than she has demonstrably "earned" we are not properly speaking of trusting her. When we trust a person, we do recognize that she may, in an unexpected situation, be unable to fulfill our expectations; however, we do

Encyclopedia of Applied Ethics, Volume 4
Copyright © 1998 by Academic Press. All rights of reproduction in any form reserved.

not consider the possibility that she might deliberately let us down.

The claim that trusting involves accepting the other's trustworthiness to a degree that goes beyond or against available evidence must be qualified if we distinguish between first- and third-person descriptions. While a third party can describe the truster's actions in this way, the truster herself will typically not find that serious reasons exist for doubting the other's trustworthiness. Thus, from her own point of view, she is not engaging in anything that particularly needs justification.

Trust can be characterized as a moral relation. A breach of trust can be said to injure us quite independently of any harm done to our interests.

I. TRUST AND RATIONAL JUSTIFICATION

A. The Problem of Insufficient Evidence

Questions of predictability have been a central topic in many recent discussions of trust. Trust is typically taken to involve the belief that the probability that the other will act in ways that are beneficial (or not detrimental) to us is high enough for us to consider engaging in cooperation with her. On this view, trust is either equated with a belief in the other's goodwill or veracity, or seen as the individual's cooperative disposition based on such beliefs.

On this approach, the relevant beliefs occupy the middle of a continuum stretching from rationally tested and approved beliefs to guesses or wishful thinking. Thus trust involves, by definition, an element of uncertainty.

This creates an obvious *prima facie* problem of rationality. Rationally, we should try to support our beliefs with evidence. However, our trust is frequently expressed in the fact that we are happy with what (to others) looks like a lack of crucial information. Even worse, trust seems resistant to evidence that runs counter to it. If a friend is suspected of a crime we may naturally trust her word in the face of what may, to others, appear to be incriminating evidence. We not only see such trust as natural but often expect it of our friends and think favorably of those who exhibit it.

Therefore, many authors have looked for some way of justifying trusting as rational—despite the lack of the sort of evidence that we would normally accept as proving the other party's trustworthiness.

B. Trust and Risk Taking

One answer to the problem of insufficient evidence is to construe trust as a form of risk taking. Even in the absence of "sufficient" guarantees of the other's trustworthiness, the willingness to take certain risks may produce long-term benefits for the individual. Many philosophers, psychologists, and social scientists have utilized game theory—such as the Prisoner's Dilemma—to demonstrate this.

According to a standard interpretation of the Prisoner's Dilemma, the player's lack of mutual trust will prevent cooperation and consequently result in a suboptimal outcome for both players. While it is good on the whole that the players should trust each other, it does not lie in the individual player's interests to be trustful.

The point has important economic applications. Different national and regional cultures exhibit different patterns of trusting. It has been noted that these cultural variations result in far-reaching differences in patterns of economic development (F. Fukuyama, 1995. *Trust. The social virtue and the creation of prosperity*. New York: Free Press). For instance, in regions where entrepreneurs are reluctant to trust nonfamily members as partners, businesses rarely grow beyond a certain size. Generally, it seems that all economic activities require a certain atmosphere of trust in order to fluorish.

Some research suggests that patterns of cooperation might spontaneously arise under certain conditions. Robert Axelrod demonstrates in *The Evolution of Cooperation* (1984) that in iterated Prisoner's Dilemma, a strategy of tit-for-tat with a cooperative first move will yield a better individual outcome than that produced by a purely "egoistic" strategy.

It has been concluded that a general *prima facie* trustfulness might in some conditions be adopted as a rational strategy also by moderately forward-looking egoists. Even in the absence of conclusive evidence of the others' trustworthiness, it may be rewarding for the individual to behave *as if* she trusted them even in unpromising situations. Consequently, many writers—both game theorists and others—converge in recommending a form of "Pascal's wager." Despite our inability to establish the trustworthiness of others, the belief itself has outcomes of great utility.

In this way, trust can be seen as justified in terms of the individual's rational pursuit of interests. The argument may be thought of as providing either a local or a global justification of trusting (or both).

A local justification of trusting in these terms would imply that the individual decision whether or not to trust the other party may in principle be assessed by balancing the available evidence against the value of what is at stake. When the costs of disappointment are tolerable the agent may justifiably rely on the other's goodwill even if the available evidence falls significantly short of warranting certainty. For instance, a tourist asking for directions in a foreign city will not typically seek advance confirmation of his informant's veracity.

A global justification of trusting would not imply committing oneself to the view that justifications of this type are applicable to individual cases of trusting. However, it would involve the claim that a general preparedness to trust others contributes significantly to human well-being.

1. Critique of the Local Justification

One may object, however, that Pascal's wager can only give us reasons to act as if we believed that the other party is trustworthy. It does not provide grounds for actually holding the belief.

Another way to take Pascal's wager would be to say that trusting is acting as if you believed, and to think that the argument gives you reason to do that. But this seems misleading. Most writers discussed here recognize that genuine trusting implies genuine belief in the other's trustworthiness. Pascal's wager, as a purely pragmatic solution, cannot yield a sufficient justification of those cases.

On the whole, it seems that considerations about risk taking can only motivate risk taking, not trusting. The construal of trusting as a form of risk taking blurs the difference between trust and a risky reliance on the other's good behavior. Trusting implies not thinking that a risk exists. The truster may run a risk (if the risk of betrayal is bigger than she realizes). However, she is not, from her own point of view, deciding to take a risk—even if she might agree that someone else could see a similar situation as involving a risk.

But to justify a course of action is to point to considerations which, in some circumstances, could make someone embark on the relevant course of action. And the considerations discussed here could not make a person trust another (as opposed to only relying on them) since they are based on a form of reasoning that would not be taken seriously by a person trusting the other.

2. Critique of the Global Justification

The Global Justification view can be criticized on two counts. First, it may be argued that a global justification is redundant if it can never be applied to individual cases. Hence any acceptable global justification would be vulnerable to the same objections as the local justification.

Secondly, it may be suggested that trusting is too integral a part of human life to be justified in this way. The alternative—i.e., a life that involves no trusting relationships—would be impossible for us to assess. Virtually all social life will involve some preparedness to trust. The rational justification of trusting would amount to no less than a justification of the fact that we are social beings. Whether such a justification would be possible is a question of dispute.

Someone might suggest that the global justification can, at any rate, give us reasons to be slightly more trusting than we tend to be, provided we live approximately the sort of lives we now do. But this brings in difficulties about the subjective assessment of risks. Negligent and overcautious persons will perceive the relevant risks differently. Which assessment is the correct one can, however, only be appreciated once we know whether betrayal in fact has taken place. Thus even if it was established that we should, on the whole, avoid being overcautious, we are left to our own judgment to decide what counts as exaggerated caution.

C. Trust and Evidence

1. General Points

Another response to the problem of insufficient evidence is to reconsider the notion of evidence. A fact's being a piece of evidence is not a quality of it in the sense in which shape and color are qualities of objects. The notion of evidence derives its intelligibility from situations where practical reasoning of a certain kind takes place.

By "evidence" we mean facts that, in the circumstances, rightly incline us to believe that certain other facts obtain. Calling a fact a piece of evidence implies (1) that there exists a serious disagreement to which the piece of evidence suggests an answer, and (2) that the answer suggested by it is the correct one.

Thus (from (1)) newspapers from 1945 cannot today be cited by scholars as evidence that World War II took place, as that would imply that there might be a serious disagreement about the question. And (from (2)) a circumstance cannot correctly be called evidence of a defendant's guilt by anyone who suspects or knows that the evidence is forged.

This calls for a revision of the claim that trusting involves going beyond or against the available evidence. What constitutes evidence for us is dependent on what kinds of question we can take seriously in the circumstances.

For example, suppose my friend is accused of a serious crime. I ask her about it, she denies the charges, and I trust her. Hence (from (1)) I will not treat the facts in question as evidence against (or in support of) my friend. I will think that some other explanation can be given to what others cite as evidence against her. For me, the would-be evidence constitutes problematic facts calling for investigation. I am disputing their status as evidence.

Here (from (2)) the question whether the available facts really constitute evidence against my friend cannot be divorced from the question of my friend's guilt. My stand may increasingly place me at odds with authorities or the public opinion. Admittedly, this may take irrational forms. But there is no *prima facie* reason why my view would always stand more in need of a justification than the views of those who distrust my friend. Besides, their distrust implies trust in other directions, e.g., the prosecution.

The general point is that our willingness to interpret certain facts as pieces of evidence will always, in one way or another, reflect our relations to others. On this view, trust is not a new element outweighing or obscuring the judgments we "ought to" make. The fact that we trust certain people is an aspect of our judgments, part of judging.

And the fact that our epistemic situations differ, while perhaps deplorable, is a natural consequence of the fact that we are different individuals, differently placed in the world.

2. The Role of Induction

It seems that trustful relations cannot be viewed, in any important sense, as inductively based. This is so for three reasons.

First of all, we frequently trust strangers without stopping to consider whether they are trustworthy. Sometimes we do justify our trust of strangers, e.g., by the fact that they look trustworthy. But this is obviously not a neutral description. By not describing the stranger as, say, a cunning actor, we already express some trust.

Secondly, the suggestion that the trust involved, e.g., in a long-standing friendship, is inductively based would invite the question which of our friend's earlier actions are instances of the same behavior as we are now expecting of her. They might all be part of a prolonged plan to deceive us. A paranoiac could see every new act of benevolence as a new attempt to lull him into false confidence.

Finally, our trust in a friend does not always imply that we expect her to perform any specific action. We may trust that whatever our friend does will be right

in the circumstances. A disappointment may give us reason to consider whether our own expectations were justified. Thus the question whether our trust was violated is not always settled by the facts alone.

II. EPISTEMOLOGICAL CONSIDERATIONS

Traditionally, knowledge based on testimony is seen as less certain than that based on perception. If I accept someone else's testimony I must assume both the accuracy of her perception and her veracity. Admittedly, there may be good pragmatic reasons for doing so despite the lack of certainty involved. Still, knowledge based on perception would always be rationally preferable.

But the traditional view may be said to distort what we usually mean by rationality. In many cases it is, on the contrary, rational of us to believe someone else's account and distrust our own perception. This may be true, for instance, of situations where competing eyewitnesses' accounts are presented by a number of people. Our standard way of establishing the accuracy of our perceptions and memories is to compare them with the accounts of others. The idea that there can be objective accounts of an event requires us to recognize the fallibility of our own perception and memory. Consequently, a certain preparedness to take other people's testimonies on trust is constitutive of what we mean by rationality.

Similar views are suggested by Ludwig Wittgenstein's discussion of the idea of certainty (1972. *On certainty*. New York: Harper & Row). He discusses the fact that we take perhaps most of our beliefs for granted without asking for evidence. For instance, I do not seriously doubt the fact that I have never been to China.

My certainty in believing this is necessarily based on the acceptance of a great deal of what I have been told by others about geography. Furthermore, the possible methods I could use for checking the relevant information also presuppose that I take for granted some information I have received from other people.

Wittgenstein's discussion suggests that the very intelligibility of rationally motivated doubt is dependent on the fact that we have starting points which we do not subject to doubt. Most of these things we simply accept on human authority.

Putting the point nontemporally, our preparedness to rely on what other people tell us is an aspect of our exercise of reason. To put it temporally, if we are to learn to make rational judgments we must *start* by depending on others (such as our parents and educators), and in doing so we will not question their trustworthiness. Such dependence on others is not, however, only characteristic of children but of any normal adult. It does not imply a residual child-like innocence; rather, as we grow more independent we learn to make more use of such sources of knowledge.

The discussion in this section, however, does not suggest a rational justification of reliance on testimony. Rather, it suggests that it may be misguided to ask for a justification. Such reliance is already an aspect of rationality as we know it.

III. NORMATIVE CONSIDERATIONS

A. The Expressibility Test

Annette Baier (1986. Trust and antitrust. *Ethics*, 96, 231–260) criticizes the tendency of modern moral and political philosophy to treat human relations on the model of hypothetical contracts between minimally trusting and minimally trustworthy adults. The model throws no light on the dependence of children on their parents, the parents' duty to take care of them, or a wife's dependence on the husband-cum-breadwinner. These relations are (or should be) based on trust. Baier's discussion has an obvious relevance to feminist approaches to ethics.

Baier wants to work out criteria for when such non-contractual dependence on others can be morally acceptable. According to Baier, a trusting relation is unacceptable "to the extent that either party relies on qualities in the other which would be weakened by the knowledge that the other relies on them" (p. 256). Morally acceptable trust should be able to survive the explicit expression of the attitudes and considerations informing it. For instance, a relation based on either party's gullibility will be unlikely to survive the expressibility test. The exploited party will terminate the relation once he realizes its character.

It may be objected, however, that the expressibility test cannot be applied to an important range of (morally acceptable) relations to which the word "trust" is applicable. In many cases, a certain lack of reflection and explicitness is constitutive of the trustful relation.

For example, if I invite a friend over for dinner I will not be making sure he is not pocketing valuables from the house. Someone might describe me as relying on my friend's honesty. But this description would imply that a serious question can be raised about my

friend's honesty in the circumstances. I might protest against the suggestion and reject any articulation of our relation in such terms. Alternatively, if I do accept the new description, by doing so I would change my view of the relation. Consequently, the relation itself would be changed by the application of the expressibility test.

B. Trust as a Moral Relation

Another approach would involve a discussion of the distinction between trust and reliance. Trust can sometimes be replaced by reliance or vice versa, as they can be said to constitute alternative ways of coming to terms with other people's freedom of decision. For instance, a paranoiac characteristically acts on the basis of theories about what others are likely to do. In this way he substitutes reliance for trust.

While reliance can be characterized as cognitively based, trust can be described as a moral relation. Speaking of a moral relation implies that certain ways of behaving toward the other party are *ipso facto* morally appropriate or inappropriate in the context. Speaking of trust creates a conceptual room where notions like betrayal, sincerity, and conscientiousness make sense.

We may hold a theory about the behavior of a person who does not know of our existence. However, strictly speaking we cannot be said to trust a person unless she in some way knows about it. The appropriate moral ties between us would be missing.

The distinction between moral and cognitively based relations can best be appreciated in cases of disappointment. The failure of a theory always implies some shortcoming of the theory itself. A psychologist cannot correctly admonish his subjects for failing to conform to his theory about human behavior. On the other hand, when a person betrays someone else's trust the blame lies with him, not with the injured party (whereas facts cannot be said to "betray" a theory when they fail to conform to it).

On this view, to describe someone else's relation to us as one of trust (rather than, say, an expression of naiveté) is to claim that her expectations of goodwill from us are to be respected. By going along with the description we accept the truster's claim to our respect as justified. To describe a relation as one of trust is to make a claim about what a person has right to expect, even demand, from another.

On this view, the natural analogy of trust should not be sought in predictive beliefs but rather in morally significant relations such as friendship or religious faith.

IV. PSYCHOLOGICAL CONSIDERATIONS

A. Difficulties of Classification

The notion of trust is difficult to define in terms of the traditional categories employed by philosophy of the mind. Trust cannot simply be a behavioral disposition since a person who only pretends to trust another might also exhibit the relevant behavior. Nor can trust be a belief since (1) we might hold the relevant belief without trusting the other (as in the case of reliance) and (2) trusting does not always involve any specific belief about what the other is likely to do (as in the case of the nonspecific trust between friends or family members). Finally, trust is obviously not an emotion since no particular feeling of trust can be identified in many, probably most, cases where the word "trust" is applicable. Psychologically, trust rather seems to be characterized by the fact that certain beliefs and emotions—such as certain suspicions and fears—fail to appear.

Some scholars suggest that trust should be seen as some sort of combination of the elements mentioned, e.g., a belief of the other's trustworthiness combined with a cooperative disposition and an emotive attitude. This involves the idea that trust is a specific psychological state which could be discovered in the individual whenever the word "trust" is applicable.

B. Trust as "Posthumous"

Typically, we are made aware of the existence of a trustful relation posthumously, only after the relation has been violated or questioned in some way. For the most part, for instance, we rely on what others tell us without stopping to consider their trustworthiness. We say we trusted them only if it subsequently turns ont that they lied to us or might have been expected to do so. Similarly, the behavior of a friend who steals from us can be characterized as a breach of trust despite the fact that we would not normally, before the event, think, feel, or say we trust our friends not to steal from us.

Thus in most cases it is impossible to identify a specific psychological state of trusting in the agent before the relationship has been violated or questioned.

One way of accounting for this fact would be by suggesting that the psychological states involved in trusting are for the most part unconscious, consisting chiefly of unconscious expectations. The agent's reac-

tion to disappointment would be a proof of the existence of the previously unconscious state.

The problem with this is that it is impossible in principle for a person to produce a list of all the different possible actions which, at a given moment, would qualify as violations of his trust. Thus if one wants to construe every case where the possibility of such a violation exists, as a case of unconscious psychological states, one will be forced to attribute an unending list of such states to the agent.

One would then have to say, e.g., that a typical mother entertains the unconscious expectation or feeling that her children will not put out her eyes when asleep, since the action undoubtedly would involve a breach of her trust. This does not look like a helpful approach.

Another way to account for the facts is to focus on the circumstances in which we can meaningfully attribute trust to ourselves and others.

C. First- and Third-Person Perspectives

It seems that a certain disparity between first- and third-person descriptions is constitutive of the meaningfulness of speaking of trust. Analogous points apply to the way we speak of generosity, modesty, innocence, and other traits of human character.

Speaking of me as trusting my friend does not make sense except in connection with a suggestion of possible betrayal. At the same time, my trust in a friend is expressed in the very fact that I do not think there is a possibility of betrayal. The observer will see my behavior as trustful because he sees that there is conceivable room for suspicion. But the suspicion itself is not part of the behavior, state of mind, or attitude that he is characterizing as trust.

This means that we need not commit ourselves to thinking that trusting involves any specific psychological state. The intelligibility of attributing trust to a person depends, instead, on the overall situation.

This discussion may invoke the question of how it is possible at all for me to say I trust my friend. To speak of trust is to invoke a suspicion which, by definition, I am not entertaining. The answer is that by saying, "I trust X," I am responding to a suspicion that I do not hold myself but which I understand to be possibly entertained by others.

The discussion also implies that, since we cannot freely choose our beliefs about the relevant risks, there will be important limits to our ability to choose whether or not to trust someone else.

D. Basic Trust

Several psychologists, such as E. H. Erikson, focus on the importance of trust in personal development. The child will need a sense of "basic trust" if it is to gain a firm sense of reality and personal identity. Personality disorders such as autism can be seen as expressions of a lack of basic trust. The preceding discussion suggests that, while the idea of a basic trust may be illuminating, it may not be helpful to interpret basic trust unproblematically as an emotional or cognitive state of the individual.

The previous discussion also suggests that the question of whether our ability to trust is innate or learned may be misplaced, roughly in the same way as it would be confused to ask whether our ability to hold a bank account is innate. The possibility of being included in human relationships for which the word "trust" is applicable is not a faculty in the sense in which, e.g., the ability to keep one's balance is a faculty.

V. TRUST AND SOCIAL LIFE

Some scholars, e.g., N. Luhmann, suggest that trust is a necessary condition of participation in social life. By trusting, the agent subjectively reduces the overwhelming complexity of social reality.

Social life involves, by definition, dependence on others and some anticipation of their future behavior. Therefore, social life will necessarily involve relations to which, in certain circumstances, the word "trust" will be applicable. But the point obviously cuts both ways: we cannot imagine a social life without trust, but the relations to which the word "trust" is applicable are themselves instances of social life. Therefore the suggestion that social life is based on trust, or explained by the fact that we trust each other, seems misleading. Rather, the existence of certain types of mutual dependence is a constitutive feature of what we call social life.

Apparently, in all legitimate systems of political representation, i.e., systems in which rulers are said to be acting on behalf of the population, some form of trust must obtain between the rulers and the ruled.

John Locke describes this trust as instrumentally motivated (1980. In P. Laslett, Ed., *Two treatises on government*. Cambridge: Cambridge Univ. Press). Citizens entrust their ruler with sovereign power on the condition that it shall be used for the protection of their interests. The legitimacy of a government is essentially a function of its ability to live up to this commitment. On the other hand, a sovereign may be permitted to overstep his legal powers if such a breach of legality serves this overall goal.

There will, however, be a problem about what one would say of an exiled government which *ipso facto* cannot fulfil its commitments but which nevertheless may be perceived by the citizens as their legitimate government.

The Lockean, predominantly liberal view can be contrasted with a suggestion that political trust consists of some form of community of values between the rulers and the ruled. The fact that such a community of values exists is seen as desirable as such, not only for instrumental reasons.

VI. TRUST AND RELIGIOUS FAITH

The distinction between holding a belief and trusting is theologically central, particularly in Protestant countries. It is possible to believe in the historical truth of the Gospel story while lacking genuine faith. Even devils are said to believe in the existence of God.

Genuine faith, on the other hand, is viewed as a form of trust (*fiducia*) or joyous confidence in God's mercy. The classical statement of this position is included in Luther's "Preface to St. Paul's Epistle to the Romans" where the author expands on the doctrine of justification by faith alone (M. Luther, 1956. *Reformation writings of Martin Luther* (pp. 284–300). London: Lutterworth). Due to this view on religious faith, the philosophical emphasis is shifted from questions about the existence of God to questions about the nature of faith.

Important analogies can be drawn between religious faith and the sort of ungrounded certainty that can be said to be the accompaniment of most of our everyday dealings with people and physical objects. In both cases, the guiding principles of our actions may possibly be stated in terms of certain propositional beliefs (such as belief in God's existence and belief in the constancy of material objects). However, the propositional belief can be seen as a secondary formulation of ungrounded basic attitudes informing our lives.

Some philosophers observe the analogy between trust and religious faith but leave it on one side as unfit for elucidating relations between mature adults. The religious believer's trust in God obviously cannot be a relation between equals.

But all forms of religious faith certainly cannot be

depicted just as instances of nostalgic regression to childhood naiveté. To have faith is to resign oneself to the will of God—to acknowledge one's helplessness. That itself, however, may indeed be taken as a sign of maturity. Many religious writers see the life of faith as a continuous task that the believer must consciously undertake.

The fact that the religious believer trusts God informs his trust in a crucial way. There is an internal connection between the identity of the object of trust and the fact that trust is the appropriate attitude toward him. The empirical question of whether God is trustworthy cannot arise. Unlike the case in most human relations, it makes sense for trust in God to show itself in the believer's preparedness to accept everything—in an extreme case, his own physical destruction—as the will of God.

Also See the Following Articles

FAMILY, THE • FRIENDSHIP • PERSONAL RELATIONSHIPS

Bibliography

Baier, A. (1994). *Moral prejudices.* Cambridge, MA: Harvard Univ. Press.

Baker, J. (1987). Trust and rationality. *Pacific Philosophical Quarterly, 68,* 1–13.

Coady, C. A. J. (1992). *Testimony: A philosophical study.* New York: Oxford Univ. Press.

Gambetta, D. (Ed.) (1988). *Trust—Making and breaking cooperative relations.* Oxford: Blackwell.

Govier, T. (1993). Trust and testimony: Nine arguments for testimonial knowledge. *International Journal of Moral and Social Studies, 8,* 21–39.

Hertzberg, L. (1988). On the attitude of trust. *Inquiry,* **31,** 307–322. Reprinted in Hertzberg, L. (1994). The limits of experience. *Acta Philosophica Fennica,* **56,** 113–130.

Kurtén, T. (1994). Basic trust—The hidden presence of God. *Studia Theologica,* **48,** 110–124.

Lagerspetz, O. (1992). Legitimacy and trust. *Philosophical Investigations,* **15,** 1–21. [The author's name is misspelled as "Lagenspetz"]

Pannenberg, W. (1983). *Anthropologie in theologischer Perspektive.* Göttingen: Vandenhoeck & Ruprecht.

Winch, P. (1991). Certainty and authority. In A. P. Griffiths, Ed., *Wittgenstein Centenary Essays* (pp. 223–237). Cambridge: Cambridge Univ. Press.

TRUTH TELLING AS CONSTITUTIVE OF JOURNALISM

John O'Neill
Lancaster University

I. The Practice of Journalism
II. The Virtues of the Journalist
III. Corruption, Virtues, and Institutions

GLOSSARY

practice A complex human activity that has internal ends that are partially constitutive of that activity.
professional virtues Those excellences of character and technique that enable a person to realize the internal goods of the practice a profession sustains.

CERTAIN HUMAN PRACTICES, such as medicine, have internal ends that are constitutive of the kind of activity they are. Journalism is among such practices. Truth telling is an internal and constitutive end of journalism. This is not to say that journalism necessarily delivers truth, but where it fails to do so it fails in a special way: it points to an internal failure in the journalistic enterprise. Truth telling as a constitutive end of journalism also defines qualities that are characteristic of a good practitioner of the professions— particular virtues and excellences of a journalist as journalist. These include both technical excellences and broader ethical excellences such as honesty and integrity. Even contested virtues such as "objectivity" are contested in terms of the relation to the internal end of truth telling.

I. THE PRACTICE OF JOURNALISM

Journalism is a practice. I use the term practice in the Aristotelian sense to refer to human activities that have internal ends that are partially constitutive of the kind of activity they are. The concept has been elaborated thus by MacIntyre:

> By a "practice" I am going to mean any coherent and complex form of socially established cooperative human activity through which goods internal to that form of activity are realized in the course of trying to achieve those standards of excellence which are appropriate to, and partially definitive of, that form of activity ... (MacIntyre (1985). *After virtue* (2nd Ed.). London: Duckworth, p. 187).

Medicine is for example a practice in the Aristotelian sense. Medicine is an activity that has a particular point for which it is done, causing individuals to be healthy, which defines the nature of the activity and the excellences of activity and practitioner that are characteristic of the activity. Journalism is a practice in this sense. Just as health is an internal and constitutive end of medicine, so truth telling about significant contemporary public events is an internal and constitutive end of journalism. As an end truth telling distinguishes journalism from other practices akin to it, but distinct from it—for example, those of pure entertainment. The object of the journalistic enterprise—significant, con-

Encyclopedia of Applied Ethics, Volume 4
Copyright © 1998 by Academic Press. All rights of reproduction in any form reserved.

temporary public events—distinguishes journalism from other truth-oriented practices such as science and history.

Truth telling in the context of journalism involves more than simply the presentation of accurate information. Two points are of particular significance here. First, the journalist works within certain norms of communication. Some of these are particular to the practice, for example, those governing that very particular genre, the newspaper headline. Others are general norms of communication that have particular relevance in the journalistic context. Thus, something like Gricean conversational implicatures set up inferences among readers between what is strictly said in a story and what is meant. Hence, Gricean principles of quantity and relevance assumed in standard conversation—that one supplies all relevant information—can convert partial truths into falsehoods. (Grice, H. (1975). Logic and conversation. In P. Cole & J. L. Morgan (Eds.). *Syntax and semantics 3: Speech acts.* New York: Academic Press.). For example, reports of wars are often slotted into a narrative structure in which they are solely a conflict with a particular tyrant. Now, this may in part be true but it sets up implicatures that this is all they are, which is rarely if ever true. One can depart from truth telling through the presentation of true propositions that set up implicatures that are false. For similar reasons, the selection of stories matters in virtue of the implicatures set up by what is not reported.

A second feature of the journalist's art that raises special issues of truth lies in the very fact that journalists standardly write a story. Events are presented within narrative structures. That this is the case does not entail the radical constructivist conclusion that the concepts of truth and falsity no longer apply, that we merely have different constructions of social reality. It does however raise special and difficult issues about what it is for a story to be "a true story." A story can be false in fairly straightforward ways. The particular events it describes never happened as the story says. Its descriptions are inaccurate. However, it can also depart from truthfulness through the choice of narrative structure for connecting the events. Thus, problems of truthfulness are often a question of the genre in which a story is placed, and this turns on normative appraisal of events and their structure that goes beyond "mere" reportage. The choice of narrative genres involves the normative appraisal of the actors, their relationships to each other, and the social order to which they belong: a strike might be presented either as a struggle of the powerless and exploited workers against rich and powerful employers or as unreasonable demands of produc-

ers who despite good living standards are willing to "hold the public to ransom." The story will have structure, as Aristotle has it, a "beginning, middle, and end," and the genre to which the story belongs, epic, tragic, or whatever, depends upon its ending, and again the appraisal one makes of it: the story of a strike can be presented as success or failure, and as such, as a sad defeat or as a splendid victory.

These features of the news story raise two distinct problems about truthfulness. First, given that the genre depends upon normative appraisal, if the concept of truth is to apply, it must be possible to have criteria to distinguish true and false normative characterizations of events: for example, it must be possible to assess the truth or falsity of the claim that workers are exploited and powerless. Truthfulness applied to narratives presupposes some form of cognitivism about norms. Second, it must be possible to assert that sequences of events have a narrative structure that we capture in our descriptions more or less adequately and are not merely contingently related to each other. It must not be true that, as Mink has it, "Stories are not lived but told. Life has no beginnings, middles or ends ..." (Mink, L. (1970). History and fiction as modes of comprehension. *New literary history* 1, pp. 541–558, 557). If Mink is right, then we merely project stories upon a world; we do not make assertions about the world. Truthfulness assumes some form of narrative realism. I believe that both normative cognitivism and narrative realism should be accepted. The most plausible versions of the denial of cognitivism about norms and the denial of narrative realism share a deep scientism: all that is true of the world is that which can be captured by a true physical theory; because reference to norms and narrative structure make no appearance in physical theory, they are not part of the furniture of the world to be captured by truth claims. This scientism should be rejected. As far as journalism goes we should argue the other way. Because we can make perfect sense of the distinction between true and false narratives about historical and contemporary events, scientism should be rejected. This philosophical worry should, however, be distinguished from a different and more important worry about the actual narratives that appear in newspapers. It is true that much popular journalism appeals to a narrow range of narrative structures and it forces stories into them. The result often is a failure of truth telling.

To assert that truth telling is constitutive of journalism is not to say that journalism always delivers the truth any more than it is true to say that medicine always delivers health because health is the constitutive end of medicine. Rather, it is to say that where these practices do fail to deliver such goods they fail in a special way. To criticize a doctor or medical institution for failing to provide adequate health care for patients is to make an internal criticism. It is to criticize them for failing to realize the very ends that the practice of medicine aims to serve. Likewise, to criticize a journalist, a newspaper, or radio or T.V. news programs for failing to report significant events truthfully is to accuse them of failing to perform that function constitutive of the very practice of journalism. Thus, while it is true that some doctors are bad doctors or that medical institutions may systematically fail to solve health problems—and may perhaps even create them—it remains true that health as an end is constitutive of medicine. Likewise, although some journalists may cease to report truthfully, and some newspaper may systematically distort the truth, it remains true that truth telling is constitutive of journalism.

Indeed, that truth is constitutive of the practice is perhaps most apparent where the journalist is under pressure to depart from it. Consider for example the pressure both from the state and self-censorship on truth telling in time of war. Arguments about the justifiability of the failure to report truthfully presuppose that the journalistic activity itself has that end. Hence, the remark of one war correspondent for World War II: "We were a propaganda arm of our governments. At the start the censors enforced that, but by the end we were our own censors. We were cheerleaders. I suppose there wasn't an alternative at the time. It was total war. But, for God's sake let's not glorify our role. It wasn't good journalism at all" (C. Lynch, cited in Knightley, P. (1982). *The first casualty: The war correspondent as hero, propagandist and myth maker,* p. 317. London: Quartet). It failed as good journalism because truth telling is suspended. The failure is justified because, it is claimed, journalism here has to be subordinate to more pressing ends: as Hopkinson, the wartime editor of the *Picture Post* puts it, "in wartime there is something more important than truth" (cited in Williams, K. (1992). Something More Important Than Truth: Ethical Issues in War Reporting. In A. Belsey & R. Chadwick (Eds.). *Ethical issues in journalism and the media,* p. 154. London: Routledge). This claim that the constitutive ends of journalism should be thus abandoned is clearly open to dispute. The central arguments to that dispute point not just to its implications for the practice of journalism as such but to the relation of the internal goods of journalism and wider public goods.

The internal end of journalism in truth telling about events of public interest has a general social and political significance in modern society: it forms a central component of debate in the public sphere. The internal end is sometimes stated in professional codes as a duty to inform a public correlative to a right of the public to be informed: "The public's right to know of events of public importance and interest is the overriding mission of the mass media" (Society of Professional Journalists *Code of Ethics* adopted 1926, revised 1973). It is in virtue of that informing role that journalism has traditionally been held to have a special role within democracies, where it is understood as a forum. Thus, for example, the third Press Commission defined press freedom in terms of such democratic responsibilities:

We define the freedom of the press as that freedom from restraint which is essential to enable proprietors, editors and journalists to advance the public interest by publishing facts and opinions without which a democratic electorate cannot make responsible judgements (Royal Commission on the Press Cmnd 6810 (1977), Chapter 2, paragraph 3).

There are two components to the view that free journalism is a necessary condition for democracy. The first is that the media acts as a watchdog in government. Even where the press gains immense independent powers, it acts as a "fourth estate" that provides a check on the other estates of government. The second is that the press is a necessary condition for an informed and critical citizenship. It provides information on major issues without which the public would not be able to make intelligent judgments. Ideally, it functions as a forum for public debate about such issues, serving to ensure that a diversity of opinions is heard. It is clear that there is a necessary relationship between the internal goods of journalism and the functions that journalism is assumed to perform. Because truth telling about significant contemporary public events is constitutive of journalistic practice, where excellence in journalism exists, journalism will serve the creation of an informed and critical political citizenry. The deliberative institutions in democracy rely on a "public sphere" in which debate can be conducted, and the role of the media in representing the issues and different perspectives is critical both to the possibility and to the quality of that sphere. Hence, not just the direction suspension of the practice of journalism as a truth-seeking activity, but also its corrosion by political and commercial institutions (see Section III, below) disrupt a central component of democratic life.

To say that truth telling is a constitutive end of journalism is not to say that all truths come within its domain nor that their are no ethical limits upon its investigative activities. Standardly, the contemporary events that form a legitimate object of journalistic inquiry are taken to be those in which a "public interest" exists. Those facts about the "private lives" of individuals that have no bearing on the interests of the public do not form proper objects of scrutiny. In modern societies there is taken to be a sphere, central to a person's identity and a condition for her autonomy, that is not a permissable object for the public gaze. While this limitation standardly finds itself into journalistic codes, it leaves open considerable room for argument, for example, over what counts as an object of public interest and what criteria demarcate the "private" sphere.

II. THE VIRTUES OF THE JOURNALIST

The constitutive ends of journalism define specific virtues of the profession, those qualities characteristic of a good practitioner—the particular excellences of a journalist as journalist. Among these are those technical skills that are part of the journalist's craft—the ability to construct a story, to tell it well. However, they also include broader ethical virtues that are associated with truth telling—with the recognition and discovery of important truths and a willingness and courage to report them. Thus, typical virtues used by journalists to describe their peers are "honest," "perceptive," "truthful." Closely associated with these virtues of honesty and truthfulness is that of integrity—for example, the subeditor who insists on rewriting a front-page story to eliminate systematic bias in it. Another, more contested, virtue that is often raised here is that of "objectivity." The virtue of "objectivity" is often rejected by some of the best journalists of our day. Thus, James Cameron writes that:

> I do not see how a reporter attempting to define a situation involving some kind of ethical conflict can do it with sufficiently demonstrable neutrality to fulfil some arbitrary concept of "objectivity." It never occurred to me, in such a situation, to be other than subjective, and as obviously so as I could manage to be. I may not always have been satisfactorily balanced; I always tended to argue that objectivity was of less importance than the truth, and that the reporter whose technique was informed by no opinion lacked a very serious

dimension. (Cameron, J. (1969). *Point of departure,* p. 74. London: Grafton Books.)

Two comments are in order. First, Cameron's rejection of objectivity stays within the circle of values of journalism. Objectivity is rejected in terms of a contrast with "truth" and, later with the need to present an account that can be "examined and criticized" such that it will: "encourage an attitude of mind that will challenge and criticise automatically, thus to destroy the built in advantages of all propaganda and special pleading—even the journalist's own" (Cameron (1969), pp. 74–75). The criticism of objectivity stays within the particular set of virtues associated with truth telling. Secondly, and relatedly, the rejection of objectivity in journalism appeals to an argument that is accepted by traditional defenders of objectivity in the social sciences—notably by Weber—that if values are to enter in to the reportage of empirical matters of fact, it is better that they do so explicitly rather than implicitly (see Weber, M. (1949). *The methodology of the social sciences* (E. Shils & H. Finch, Trans.). New York: Free Press.). This has particular importance in journalism: given the degree to which the selection and presentation of news is value-laden, the critical faculties of the audience are better served by making those values explicit. "Objectivity" in the sense of reportage that best allows the audience to appreciate the complexities of a situation may be better served by the nonobjective presentation of events. Journalism, then, is a practice constituted by its own goods and a set of virtues among its practitioners that are necessary for the realization of such goods.

III. CORRUPTION, VIRTUES, AND INSTITUTIONS

Practices are open to corruption from the institutional settings in which they occur, for such settings may involve the pursuit of external ends that are distinct from the internal ends of a practice and are potentially in competition with them. Hence, Aristotle's comments on the corrupting effects of markets upon practices: it is not the internal end of medicine to make money, but within a market setting it can be pursued for that end. Similarly, it is not the end of philosophy to make money, but within the market it can be pursued with that end. The pursuit of external ends can corrupt a practice: where a practitioner has been so corrupted, he or she takes the pursuit of the external ends to have priority over the internal ends. Hence, sophism is a corrupt form of philosophy: "the art of the sophist is the semblance of wisdom without the reality, and the art of the sophist is one who makes money from apparent but unreal wisdom" (*De Sophisticis Elenchis,* I (1928). (Trans. W. Pickard-Cambridge). London: Oxford University Press). The virtues required for the pursuit of a practice are then not just those excellences that enable an individual to perform a function well, but also those that enable a practitioner to resist the temptations of putting aside the internal goals of the practice for external goods: the virtues of courage and integrity are of particular significance in this regard.

These general Aristotelian observations about practices have particular relevance to journalism, which exists in the world of commerce or is subsidized by political institutions as a public organ. Both are potentially corrosive of the internal ends of journalism. That political power is potentially corrosive of the internal ends of journalism is widely recognized. Where the press has no independence of political power, then both positive powers of patronage and negative powers of coercion entail that the journalist's pursuit of the end of truth telling may depart radically from the ends of personal advancement or even survival. Hence, the virtues of personal courage and integrity are particularly evident.

The same virtues are also required by the journalist in the commercial press, for the reasons that Aristotle notes: the semblance of truth may sell better than truth itself. A press within a market setting has to satisfy the preferences of its consumers. As De Tocqueville puts it: "A newspaper can survive only on the condition of publishing sentiments or principles common to a large number of men" (De Tocqueville, A. (1945). *Democracy in America* (Vol. II), p. 113. New York: Knopf); or as Balzac more cynically puts it: "Every newspaper is ... a shop which sells to the public whatever shades of opinion it wants" (de Balzac, H. (1971). *Lost illusions*, p. 314 (H. Hunt, Trans.). Harmondsworth: Penguin). This market imperative is potentially corrosive of the internal goods of journalism. Save where there already exists a self-critical audience, the end of giving apparent truth that satisfies the desires of an audience can take precedence over the internal aims of the practice. The marketplace encourages the producer to present news in a way that is congruent with the preexisting values and beliefs of its audience. It does not pay to present news that is outside of the dominant cultural framework of the audiences addressed. Hence, mass journalism will tend to work within the confines of the dominant culture in which it operates. Relatedly, the value of truth telling becomes at best subsidiary in the presentation of

news, for it is not always the case that the truth about significant public events is what the consumer prefers to hear or read. What is portrayed in the press, how it is portrayed, and how much it is portrayed is, within a free market, shaped by consumer preference. What ought to be portrayed, how it ought to be portrayed, and how much it ought to be portrayed might be quite odds with such preferences. Hence, while truth telling might be constitutive of journalism as a practice, the institutional setting of the market can be corrosive of that end. The "news value" of a story is rarely a function of its truth value. It is, rather, a function of the perceived market at which the story is aimed. At its worst this leads to the abandonment of the internal ends of journalism so that media become mere vehicles for entertainment produced by entertainers employing traditional journalistic skills. Consider Murdoch's telling comment during the Hitler diary hoax: "we are in the entertainment business" (Evans (1983). *Good times, bad times,* p. 404. London; Weidenfield and Nicolson). Some newspapers are no longer vehicles for the practice of journalism and are not perceived to be so. There is evidence, for example, that readers of many popular newspapers are sceptical of the accuracy of what they read, while in the United Kingdom papers like *The Sunday Sport* are explicitly unconcerned with the truth value of what they "report" such that the entertaining hoax becomes the object of paper. This distancing of newspaper production from the values of truth telling and its recharacterisation as entertainment allows the easy relativism that identifies "quality" with "satisfaction of market preferences." None of this is to deny the value of entertainment: it is rather to contest the claim that the practice of journalism can be treated purely as entertainment and to criticize the increasing tendency for the traditional vehicles of journalism to be thus subverted.

Even where entertainment values are not pursued to the exclusion of journalism's constitutive values, the demands of the market systematically shape what is reported in a news story. The consequence of this is not so much the reporting of falsehoods in the media—although this occurs—but the failure to report what is of significance and to simplify the presentation of events. Hence, the standard complaints about modern mass journalism are that it decontextualizes events, it prefers news that fits standard narrative structures and it presents it in these terms, it personalizes domestic and international politics, it has a systematic bias towards European and American issues, and so on. The consequence is not so much a departure from truth telling as such, but from truthfulness. This is exhibited in the failure to report significant events—and most censor-ship is a suppression of truth rather than the statement of falsehood—and the presentation of partial truths that, while not false in themselves, depart from what in a court of law might be called the "whole truth." For reasons noted earlier such failures matter in that they virtually create implicatures among readers that are false. These biases are often compounded by economic pressures on the supply of information. Gathering infor-mation is costly, and there are pressures on newspapers to accept ready-made news stories from potential sup-pliers. Those with a particular viewpoint to present will effectively subsidize the media in the costs of gathering news; hence, the growth of press agents and public relations officers. In doing so they are forced to present the press with versions of events that will sell within a particular market niche.

These pressures point to those virtues in the journal-ist that are required for the pursuit of the internal ends of the practice. The journalist exists in two worlds: he or she enters a practice that is characterized by a commitment to truth telling, and at the same time he or she is an employee who works for a wage and is expected to produce a story of the kind demanded by his or her newspaper, magazine or television station. The nature of such stories is determined by political and commercial pressures that can clearly conflict with the internal ends of journalism. Conflicting demands are placed upon the journalist. Where this occurs, the journalist exhibits vices and virtues that are characteris-tic of the trade. Of the vices perhaps the most character-istic is that of cynicism concerning the values constitu-tive of journalism and the divorce between the journalist's written word and his or her own beliefs and temperament. To be a cynical journalist is to believe that truth telling in journalism is a sham and that the practice is universally pursued for narrow, self-inter-ested aims. However, while the cynic does not believe that the goods of journalism are anywhere realized, either in his or her own work or that of others, the attitude presupposes a view of what the constitutive goods of journalism are supposed to be. The cynicism is parasitic on the acceptance of a shared view that the end of journalism is truth telling. The virtues that the journalist exhibits are those familiar in biographies of particular journalists: mention of the virtues of integrity and courage are common. Such virtue is required not

only in the performance of a practice, but in resisting those external pressures that undermine its goods. The history of journalism is full of examples of principled resignation by editors and journalists. The tension be-tween the practice of journalism and the market frame-work in which it operates then produces characteristic virtues and vices. This is not to say that journalists fall into two classes—villains and heroes. Many may find themselves forced to compromise the constitutive val-ues of journalism, while at the same time insisting that some of the standards be enforced. The copy editor may still have reservations about the final form of a story he or she has rewritten, yet be able in the process of rewriting to remove some of the bias, simplification, and falsehood. That the constitutive values of journal-ism are still realized in the modern world is in part a consequence of the resistance of journalists to the pressures of both marketplace and state power.

Also See the Following Articles

FREEDOM OF THE PRESS IN THE USA • OBJECTIVITY IN REPORTING • TABLOID JOURNALISM

Bibliography

Belsey, A., & Chadwick, R. (Eds.). (1992). *Ethical issues in journalism and the media.* London: Routledge.
Bennet, W. L. (1988). *News: The politics of illusion* (2nd ed.). New York: Longman.
Bok, S. (1983). *Secrets.* New York: Random House.
Cohen, S., & Young, J. (Eds.). (1981). *The manufacture of news* (2nd ed.). London: Constable.
Curran, J., & Gurevitch, M. (Eds.). (1991). *Mass media and society.* London: Edward Arnold.
Curran, J., & Seaton, J. (1991). *Power without responsibility* (4th ed.). London: Routledge.
Entman, R. (1989). *Democracy without citizens.* Oxford: Oxford Uni-versity Press.
Evans, H. (1983). *Good times, bad times.* London: Weidenfield and Nicolson.
Jones, J. C. (1980). *Mass media codes of ethics and councils: A compara-tive international study on professional standards.* Paris: Unesco.
Keane, J. (1991). *The media and democracy.* Cambridge: Polity Press.
Klaidman, S., & Beauchamp, T. (1987). *The virtuous journalist.* New York: Oxford University Press.
Lichtenberg, J. (Ed.). (1990). *Democracy and the mass media.* Cam-bridge: Cambridge University Press.
McQuail, D., & Siune, K. (Eds.). (1986). *New media politics.* London: Sage.

UNDERCOVER INVESTIGATIONS, ETHICS OF

Gary T. Marx
Massachussetts Institute of Technology

I. Changes in Law Enforcement
II. Arguments for and against Undercover Actions
III. Some Questions and Criteria to Guide Ethical Assessment of Undercover Tactics

GLOSSARY

anticrime decoys An undercover tactic in which officers present themselves as potential victims of a crime (e.g., a "drunk" with an exposed wallet) while a hidden backup team watches and waits to intervene.

informer A person, often involved in criminal activities, who secretly provides information or operational support to police.

moral dilemma A situation in which whatever action is taken will produce moral costs, as well as moral benefits.

property crime stings An undercover tactic in which authorities pretend to be fences interested in buying stolen goods or thieves interested in selling them.

undercover A crime-control strategy in which the police identity of the participants is hidden.

UNDERCOVER INVESTIGATIONS are a common, although not dominant feature of law enforcement in the United States. A popular cartoon nicely illustrates the central features of one type of investigation. Next to a sign reading "Do not feed the bears," a park ranger wearing a bear's costume gives a ticket to a couple who have just fed the "bear," not realizing that it was a trick. This is a facilitative operation in which authorities provide the opportunity for the rule to be broken. This contrasts with intelligence operations in which the goal is to find out information about a crime that has already occurred. An example of the latter is an officer in plainclothes who befriends a suspect in a bar in an effort to learn about a particular crime. These in turn contrast with preventive operations in which authorities believe that a crime is to be committed and then take actions to stop it, for example, posing as clerks in a targeted jewelry store.

While our discussion here focuses on law enforcement, secrecy and deception are fundamental social processes found in all organizations from the corporation to the family. Deception, temptation, and informers are ancient and virtually universal forms. Undercover practices are more characteristic of federal police than of local; of detective units than of patrol; and of private police than of public. They are most likely to be used for offenses that are consensual (e.g., vice); that involve a recurring organized set of exchanges; where victims or witnesses are lacking because they are unaware of the crime (e.g., consumer fraud) or fail to come forward because they are intimidated, fearful, rewarded, or indifferent. Undercover activities are believed to have many advantages—they may offer clear evidence of the violation (especially if it is videotaped), they may serve as a deterrent in creating uncertainty in the minds of potential violators about whether a tempting situation is really a police trap, their interventions may stop a crime from being committed or from doing as much harm, they may substitute a police victim for a citizen victim, they need not rely on coercion for obtaining information, they are sometimes the only means of gathering information. Yet they raise other troubling questions. There is the issue of entrapment. Can we be sure that the crime would have occurred absent the state's providing an opportunity for it to occur? Should the state be an official sponsor of lying and deception? What of unknowing third parties who may be harmed by the deception? What is the impact of playing an undercover role on the identity and social life of those who play undercover roles? Undercover activities offer us a moral dilemma. When the state sponsors deception there are clear costs and other risks. Yet for the state to never use the tactic involves other costs. There is no easy answer to the question of whether such activities are ethical. To answer that we need to agree on criteria for judgment and on the specific type of undercover actions in question.

I. CHANGES IN LAW ENFORCEMENT

Undercover work has changed significantly in the United States in recent decades, expanding in scale and appearing in new forms. Covert tactics have been adopted by new users and directed at new targets and offenses. Law enforcement agents have penetrated criminal and sometimes noncriminal milieus to an extraordinary degree. The lone undercover worker making isolated arrests has been supplemented by highly coordinated team activities involving complex technology, organizational fronts, and multiple arrests. What was traditionally a relatively marginal and insignificant tactic used only by vice and "red" squads has become more significant. The traditional "buy-bust" tactic in which undercover agents seek to purchase contraband has been joined by the "sell-bust" tactic in which, for example, undercover agents offer to sell drugs and then arrest purchasers.

The spread of undercover tactics is one element in the new surveillance that also includes video cameras, computer dossiers, drug testing, and electronic location monitoring devices. This is related to urbanization and industrialization and reflects a subtle and deep-lying shift in social control, which has become more special-

ized and technical and in many ways more penetrating and intrusive.

II. ARGUMENTS FOR AND AGAINST UNDERCOVER ACTIONS

The legality of undercover means has been well established in American history, even though there will always be gray areas and unresolved issues. There is disagreement about the effectiveness and comparative costs of such covert means as stings and anticrime decoys. But, assuming undercover means are both legal and often effective, that is not sufficient to make them ethical or desirable as public policy. Consider, for example, an investigation of vice activities at "Tina's Leisure Spa" in New York City. Undercover investigators engaged in (and paid for) sexual relations with employees of the spa, developing clear evidence of illegality. Affidavits were subsequently filed as part of an effort to close the spa, but the district attorney refused to take action. He stated, "It's unseemly. There is a limit on how far you go to make cases. All sorts of evils flow from going too far."

What judgments underlay a conclusion that even if "legal" and "effective" some tactics are nevertheless "unseemly" and "go too far," or that some clearly illegal actions nevertheless may seem appropriate? What are the ethical justifications for and arguments against undercover tactics? By what criteria should they be judged?

Conflicts over the ethics of undercover means are often resolved by feelings about a particular enforcement goal rather than by consideration of more general criteria. Both liberals and conservatives tend to base the acceptability of covert means on the ends for which they are used, although they differ on which ends create legitimacy. Thus, although some conservatives may support the tactic when used against drugs, prostitution, and radicals, they are less enthusiastic when it is used against corporate executives. Liberals may oppose the tactic when directed against civil rights and peace groups, and the sexual activities of adults, but welcome its use against racist groups. Many police strongly defend covert tactics, except when used by internal affairs units investigating wrongdoing within their own department. It is important to consider ethical criteria that go beyond specific ends.

Some philosophers would reach conclusions about this by starting with an abstract system of values from which they would deduce conclusions, stressing, for example, values such as justice, equality, truth, or dignity. But as a social scientist my approach is rather to listen to the debate and to describe the terms of argument others put forth. I can then ask whether arguments are based on empirical or normative claims and if there are ways of integrating conflicting views, at least partially.

The following list of justifications and objections regarding the ethical aspects of covert means do not carry equal weight, but they reflect the range of ideas heard in current debate. Any decision or resolution about using or not using undercover tactics must come to terms with these arguments.

For:

1. Citizens grant to government the right to use exceptional means.
2. Undercover work is ethical when used for a good and important end.
3. Enforce the law equally.
4. Convict the guilty.
5. An investigation should be as nonintrusive and noncoercive as possible.
6. When citizens use questionable means, government agents are justified in using equivalent means.
7. Undercover work is ethical when there are reasonable grounds for suspicion.
8. Special risks justify special precautions.
9. Undercover work is ethical when the decision to use it has been democratically reached and publicly announced.
10. Undercover work is ethical when done by persons of upright character in accountable organizations.
11. Undercover work is ethical when it is undertaken with the intention of eventually being made public and judged in court.

Against:

1. Truth telling is moral; lying is immoral.
2. The government should neither participate in, nor be a party to, crime nor break the law in order to enforce it.
3. The government should not make deals with criminals.
4. The government should not offer unrealistic temptations or tempt the weak.
5. Do no harm to the innocent.
6. Respect the sanctity of private places.
7. Respect the sanctity of intimate relationships.
8. Respect the right to freedom of expression and action.
9. It is wrong to discriminate in target selection.
10. The government should not do by stealth what it is prohibited from doing openly.

A. Ethical Deception

There are some principles that would render undercover tactics categorically or contingently ethical: the broadest justification lies in the "social contract" view of the world, which holds that undercover work is ethical because citizens grant to government the right to use exceptional means, such as coercion and deception, in order to be protected.

Consistent with this view is the traditional belief that the end justifies the means, making undercover work ethical when used for a good and important end—protecting society from crime, apprehending criminals, preventing crime, substituting a police victim for a citizen victim, gathering intelligence and contraband, and even protecting the potential offender. If the intent is noble, then the action is justified, even if it has some bad effects.

According to these arguments, the ethical acceptability of means is contingent on ends. Thus, Thomas Jefferson felt that should "the public preservation" require the leader to go beyond the "strict line of the law ... his motives will be his justification." Abraham Lincoln suspended habeas corpus during the Civil War, explaining that sometimes one had to amputate a foot to save a body. The granting of "wartime power" to governments, for example, is comparable to the resort to covert means to combat a crisis in crime control. Such a "state of siege" mentality can be seen in former Alabama Governor George Wallace's suggestion during the 1968 presidential campaign to "let the police run the country, but just for a few years until the mess gets cleaned up." A related argument holds that, even if no crisis exists, exceptional means may be justified on the grounds of prevention, and that the failure to use them may lead to a government's loss of legitimacy, the possibility of a more repressive government, or the rise of vigilante groups using far worse techniques.

This justification may even apply to perpetrators. When undercover means result in the prevention of a serious crime, offenders may be spared paying as full a price as they would if they were successfully to complete the crime. For vice offenses, the belief that enforcement "is for your own good" would also apply here (e.g., saving someone from possible drug addiction). It may be believed that government has the obligation to prevent us from harming ourselves, as well as others. "We may have saved their lives," states a customs official about an undercover operation that led to the arrest of 13 people in Louisiana who planned to invade the country of Surinam.

The principle that there should be equal enforcement of the law commonly refers to equal treatment for rich and poor, men and women, minorities and nonminorities. But equity can also be considered with respect to types of offense. The failure to use undercover tactics for white-collar, consensual, or conspiratorial offenses, while actively carrying out a war on street crime using conventional means, is inequitable. Undercover tactics offer an important means for dealing with the crimes of higher-status offenders who may otherwise be virtually immune from prosecution.

Undercover tactics may be seen as ethical because they are consistent with the principle: convict the guilty. Advocates argue that covert means offer greater certainty of guilt and provide evidence that goes beyond the standard of "no reasonable doubt" required to convict. Taking a wallet from a decoy, being in possession of the contraband, or going along with an undercover scheme is thought to offer clear evidence of guilt.

Undercover means permit police to literally catch offenders in the act, avoiding problems of confessions (whether coerced or otherwise), perjury, mistaken identity, and intimidated witnesses. When police themselves play the undercover role, the need to depend on informers or witnesses with questionable reputations is reduced. With other tactics (lie detectors, voice stress, handwriting analysis, or after-the-fact testimony of witnesses), there may be a greater risk of convicting an innocent person. Conversely, because the evidence from an undercover investigation may involve a video and/or audio tape or testimony of a participating officer, there is less likelihood that the guilty will be found innocent.

In addition, undercover work may be seen as ethically preferable to other means because an investigation should be as nonintrusive and noncoercive as possible. Covert investigations can be more directly targeted than a wiretap or room bug that is indiscriminate. Undercover means often avoid elaborate dossiers, extensive documentation, and long, drawn-out investigations. They permit rapid determination of guilt or innocence, because a person either goes along with or refuses the illegal opportunity. When an investigation involves overt methods, such as searches, subpoenas of records, or the interrogation of witnesses, the reputation of subjects later found innocent is often damaged. The identity of the subject of an undercover investigation ideally is

kept secret; when no evidence of guilt is found, the fact that an investigation occurred need not be made public.

Searches, electronic surveillance, grand jury subpoenas, and compelled testimony are usually carried out against the subject's will. Information from informers is often obtained by coercively "twisting" or "leaning" on them. In contrast, undercover operations structured to permit self-selection involve voluntary actions on the part of the subject. Even with targeted subjects, coercion is lacking in the sense that the tempted person is always free to refuse the opportunity. Deception replaces coercion.

Running through the two principles above is a "lesser of evils" or "least drastic alternative" morality, wherein a less than perfect means may be nonetheless ethically preferable to no means, or an even worse means. The assumption is made that, whatever harm may lie in using undercover tactics, even worse harm would appear were other means to be used or were nothing to be done. Tyranny is seen as less of a threat than anarchy.

Another principle espoused by advocates is based on the norm of reciprocity: "Do unto others." Although violence and deception on the part of the state are normally undesirable, proponents of covert means argue that when citizens use questionable means, control agents are justified in using equivalent means. It is the idea of "fighting fire with fire," the morality of "An eye for an eye." News headline writers often play on the implicit irony and morality here ("Con Man Conned," "Police Fool Thieves") in stories describing undercover operations. As poetic justice, although offenders are not quite hoist with their own petards, they are at least beaten at their own game. The principle serves to legitimate, or at least soften, the moral bite of many con games. The moral appeal of the movie *The Sting* lies here, as a swindler is swindled. In rare contrast, the film *Absence of Malice* receives its moral power when a suspect uses deception against the government agents who initially misuse deception against him.

Another justification is that undercover work is ethical when there are reasonable grounds for suspicion. The grounds may involve persons or situations, and suspicion may be created by victims, witnesses, audits, paper trails, threats, informers, or surveillance. The stronger the grounds, the greater the justification. At a minimum, the nature of the offense must be specified, and some information limiting it to particular locations, categories of suspect, or victims must be provided.

The specific identity of a suspect, however, need not (and often will not) be known in advance. Targeted street decoy operations are a good example. Were undercover operations to be restricted to known suspects, this would work to the advantage of experienced offenders who are skilled at avoiding arrest and suspicion, as well as first-time offenders who are not known to police. Through a catch-22 logic, they would escape arrest via undercover means. However, by targeting an undercover operation toward a given milieu where a pattern of crime occurs and by structuring it to permit self-selection rather than preselection of particular suspects, the operation becomes consistent with Fourth Amendment values that preclude government from intervening in the private affairs of its citizens without grounds for suspicion.

Implicit in the justifications that involve broad social goals is the justification of self-defense. If undercover agents are asked to take risks on society's behalf, society must recognize that special risks justify special protections. The well-being of the agent justifies deception in the search for evidence, after an investigation has begun, prior to arrests, and in the creation of new identities as with witness protection programs that relocate government witnesses.

Some proponents of undercover operations argue that forewarning equals justification: undercover work is ethical when the decision to use it has been publicly announced. People are given notice, and the players then attempt to outwit each other. The basic repertoire of potential moves and consequences is known, and those used by police have been arrived at demoncratically. This concept of playing by the rules holds even from the perspective of many criminals. When arrested, some are docile and almost philosophical, feeling "this time the breaks went against me and the cops won."

Announcing the rules beforehand may also permit a degree of self-selection, when people choose to participate in activities where they know they may be deceived by control agents. Persons in certain high-risk occupational roles, for example, cashiers in contexts where dishonesty is easily hidden, where undercover practices are likely, may actually consent to their use. Agreement to be tested becomes a condition of employment. Assuming one has the option to refuse, consenting to surveillance is regarded as making it more ethical.

Undercover work is ethical when it is undertaken with the intention of eventually being made public and judged in court. This principle applies the test of publicity after the fact. Lying in undercover operations (assuming the truth will eventually come out) is thus different from lying in perjured testimony.

This justification assumes that the need to make a case for the deception before a judge and in cross-examination from a skeptical defense attorney will hold police accountable for deception. Presentation of the evidence requires disclosing the facts of the undercover investigation. Where these are distorted or withheld, the adversary system offers a means of discovery. The increased use of video and audio tapes in the courtroom is thought to enhance the accuracy of police testimony.

Undercover work is ethical when it is carried out by persons of upright character in accountable organizations. According to this assumption, deeds become ethical through the character of those who carry them out and the context in which they are used. Undercover work is legitimate when it is done by trained professionals sworn to uphold the law. Proponents argue that state practitioners of the covert arts are not "rogue elephants on a rampage" (a phrase used by Senator Frank Church to describe the CIA during a government inquiry), but carefully chosen, monitored, supervised, and subjected to restrictive departmental, judicial, and legislative standards and oversight, not to mention their own consciences.

Most of the justifications for undercover work are not categorical assertions but involve contingencies (the objective, the kind of people involved, proper procedures) that make the operations ethical. Even so, most people experience at least some unease in the face of such tactics. Why should this be the case?

B. Deceptive Ethics

Those who justify undercover work argue that it represents ethical deception, but, to others, the effort to justify it represents deceptive ethics and involves logically irreconcilable elements. One police leader, when asked about the ethics of undercover work, shook his head and said, "that's like trying to invent dry water or fireproof coal."

The central (though not the only) ethical objection to undercover work is its very dependence on deception. A fundamental tenet of our culture is that, other factors being equal, truth telling is moral, and lying is immoral. Deception represents a form of lying.

The morally undesirable character of deception can be seen in widely scattered places, such as the Ninth Commandment, Immanuel Kant's absolutist position that truth telling is an unconditional duty, legal judgments against fraud, false representation and perjury, and various aspects of popular culture—for example, George Washington and the cherry tree. A literal application of the Law Enforcement Code of Ethics would even preclude undercover practices because it calls on an officer to be "honest in thought and deed in both my personal and official life."

Lying is wrong because it violates the trust that is central to human relationships and a civil society. It also must be avoided because of its tendency to expand. In Augustine's words, "little by little and bit by bit [it will] grow and by gradual accessions will slowly increase until it becomes such a mass of wicked lies that it will be utterly impossible to find any means of resisting such a plague grown to huge proportions through small additions." All lying has long-range consequences.

Deception is likely to increase because it is required to protect the original deception and because it has a morally numbing, contagious quality. Pinocchio's ever-extending nose symbolizes this. The acceptance of deception at the investigative stage eases the way for its use at the stage of interrogation after arrest and in courtroom testimony (where it is clearly prohibited). To accept questionable means for good ends allows that they are also available for bad ends. Those against whom it is directed may use deception as self-defense or in retaliation.

The government should neither participate in, nor be a party to, crime nor break the law in order to enforce it. The state should not teach bad moral lessons or engage in "conduct that shocks the conscience." In the important 1928 Olmstead Supreme Court case Justice Holmes wrote: "For my part I think it less evil that some criminals should escape than that the government should play an ignoble part." For government agents to behave as criminals negates the difference between them. For agents to participate in or facilitate crime tarnishes the government's image. Law enforcement agents must set a moral tone and example. When they fail to do so, citizens may act in equivalent ways, and suspicion, mistrust, and lack of respect for, and cooperation with, government increase.

An August 1984 editorial in *Hawk Chalk* (the journal of the North American Falconry Association) captures the essence of these objections. The editorial was written in response to the U.S. Fish and Wildlife Service's "Operation Falcon":

> Three years of running a sting; three years of instigating illegal activities; three years of nonenforcement of falconry regulations; three years of some part of the falconry community watching someone "get away with" and try to persuade others into illegal activities; three years of watching authorities ignore reports that he was doing so—this is not the way to inspire respect for the USFWS or obedience to falconry regulations.

George Bernard Shaw once remarked that "just because God and the devil are on different sides of the fence doesn't mean they can't be friends." A former commissioner of narcotics, Harry J. Anslinger, stated in praise of a famous undercover agent that the individual would "grow a tail and dance with the devil" if necessary to make a case. These statements highlight an important aspect of much undercover work: the need for cooperation with criminals and persons of questionable character who are uniquely situated to catch other criminals.

Such cooperation is anathema to those who believe that the government should not make deals with criminals. As the Law Enforcement Code of Ethics holds, the police officer should act "with no compromise for crime and with relentless prosecution of criminals." Persons who violate laws should be punished, not rewarded. They should be officially shunned, not made allies. It is a mockery to let evildoers profit from their wrongdoing. Dependence on such persons has a negative symbolism: it is unseemly for government to enter into such alliances.

It can also be unwise, given the belief that one cannot make deals with the devil without becoming tainted. A Southern folk saying catches this: "If you lie with dogs, you get fleas." This is the converse of the belief that covert action is ethical when it is carried out by ethical persons. Instead, it is unethical because it involves dealings with unethical persons. Both views presume a spin-off of either contamination or purification by association.

The expression "virtue's greatest ally is a lack of opportunity" suggests a principle involving temptation. The government should not offer temptations to those who would otherwise be unlikely to encounter them, or offer unrealistically attractive temptations, or tempt the weak. Religious texts are rich in directives about this—Lead us not into temptation; Do not offer wine to a Nazarite, or put a stumbling block before the blind. In Proverbs 28:10 one reads: "Who so causeth the righteous to go astray in an evil way, he shall fall himself into his own pit." The righteous may be led astray because they are tempted, tricked, cajoled, coaxed, or unaware that a crime is involved.

There are some offenses that certain undercover tactics can turn up a good proportion of the time, on the part of noncriminals as well as criminals. It is wrong to use extremely attractive temptations that go beyond what is found in the real world or temptations that are not normally available. It is also wrong to induce crime on the part of the weak or vulnerable (addicts, alcoholics, juveniles, mentally limited, or ill persons).

Critics derisively refer to certain forms of undercover activity as "cheap shots," "whore's tricks," "taking candy from a baby," "shooting sitting ducks," "stealing from a blind man," "letting a wolf herd the sheep," or "putting Dracula in charge of the blood bank." Certain arrests were either "too easy" or unrelated to important law enforcement goals. Some covert activities were considered beneath the dignity of, and degrading to, the professional officer, for example, deceiving addicts in search of drugs (or worse, experiencing withdrawal) to engage in some criminal act in return for drugs; the use of scantily clad, attractive policewomen to pose as prostitutes; the use of undercover officers dressed in outlandish costumes at gay bars; and the arrest of juveniles for purchasing small amounts of marijuana from undercover agents.

There is a profound difference between carrying out an investigation against someone when there are grounds for suspicion and carrying it out against someone to see if they can be induced to break the law. It is wrong to carry out an investigation merely to determine if a person can be corrupted. Law enforcement should devote its energies to actual wrongdoers and not to those who may under certain conditions be susceptible to temptation.

It is wrong for government to artificially create criminals and victims. Justice Brandeis wrote in the Olmstead case in 1928 that "the government may set decoys to entrap criminals. But it may not provoke or create a crime, and then punish the criminal, its creature." The principle of fairness, as well as efficient resource use, underlies this principle.

The ancient medical proverb, *Primate non nocer*—"First of all, do no harm"—is the source of the principle: Do no harm to the innocent. The Law Enforcement Code of Ethics obligates the officer "to protect the innocent against deception," but undercover operations may victimize the innocent. The secret and open-ended nature of the tactic prevents many of the controls found with conventional means and greatly increases the risk of collateral harm. Innocent "third parties" may be victimized by undercover crimes committed by others; as targets of an investigation, they may reject "the bait" but nevertheless suffer reputational damage and embarrassment.

Opponents of undercover operations further point to the surreptitious and unwarranted intrusiveness of covert tactics with respect to private places, personal relationships, and protected activities. Such operations are seen to violate spatial and social boundaries and values of privacy and liberty, including the right not to be spied on in these special domains. The dangers from intrusion are much greater with undercover means than with electronic surveillance; the actions of a decoy and the creation of a tempting opportunity can affect conversation and behavior in ways that a hidden recording device never can. Human bugs are not only ambulatory, they can ask leading questions and direct or deflect conversations.

Respect the sanctity of private places is best captured in the immortal eighteenth-century words of William Pitt: "The poorest man may in his cottage bid defiance to all the forces of the Crown. It may be frail—its roof may shake—the wind may blow through it—the storm may enter—the rain may enter—but the King of England cannot enter—all his force dare not cross the threshold of the ruined tenement."

Undercover agents often violate this sanctity when they gain access to a person's home or workplace without a warrant. They may be invited in, but only because of deception—under the guise of friendship, a business partnership, or through the access granted a phony housing inspector or meter reader. It is sophistry to argue that such searches are voluntary. A person may give consent to a meter reader, but only to have the meter read, not to have the house searched. Consent is highly circumscribed; if the target was not duped, access would be denied. When the public–private boundary can be transgressed at will, whether through deception or coercion and force, liberty is impossible. Liberty exists partly because there are private and personal spaces that are beyond official reach.

Respect for the sanctity of intimate relations is another cornerstone of our concept of freedom and dignity. The duplicity and betrayal inherent in covert operations trades in and debases the trust that is essential to, and characterizes, primary relations. Their essence is the openness in communication that is characteristic of relationships where persons can be truly themselves. The common-law privilege precluding spousal testimony reflects a similar concern.

Sometimes both personal trust and professional confidentiality are violated by an undercover operation. For example, the undercover drug agent who enrolled as a student at the University of Texas and took a job as resident assistant in his dorm had, among his duties, drug counseling. But, even in more professional relationships, such as between doctors and patients or lawyers and clients, trust is enhanced and protected by nondisclosure rules. In return for a promise of confidentiality, persons in need of help feel freer to confide. When authorities pose as trusted professionals or surreptitiously use them as agents, this promise is obviously violated.

The right to freedom of action and expression is based on the First Amendment and includes the right to communicate ideas freely, to organize, to demonstrate, and to otherwise enjoy the projections of our political system. Undercover actions in some cases may only seek to creat a "myth" of surveillance. The suspiciousness and paranoia generated by the myth may far transcend their actual use, but, by creating uncertainty, they may have a far greater repressive impact (at a much lower cost) than overt forms of surveillance.

Although generalized deterrence as a goal with respect to conventional criminal activities may be appropriate, it chills basic rights when directed against political groups. As a nineteenth-century English observer notes:

> Men may be without restraints upon their liberty: they may pass to and fro at pleasure but if their steps are tracked by spies and informers, their works noted down for crimination, their associates watched as conspirators—who shall say they are free? Nothing is more revolting to Englishmen than the espionage which forms part of the administrative system of continental despotism . . . the freedom of a country may be measured by its immunity from this baleful agency.

However, the threat to political action is rarely of such a general nature. Only certain categories of people are likely to be objects of surveillance. This compounds the problem, as the method is then applied unequally. Rather than seeing undercover tactics as a means of equal law enforcement, it is seen to offer a dangerous potential for unequal law enforcement. As Paul Chevigny (1980) observes: "The power to offer a temptation to crime is the power to decide who shall be tempted. It can and often has been used as way for the government to eliminate its enemies or for one faction in government to get rid of another." This leads to the ethical principle of not discriminating in target selection.

Wherever there is discretion in law enforcement, however, there may be discrimination. But what lends the issue particular strength in the application of undercover means is the secrecy and absence of a complainant. Police can take the initiative on whatever grounds they choose. Ideally, the grounds should be universal (based on the seriousness of the offense) rather than personal and political (to get one's enemies). Undercover means permit disguising the latter as the former.

Discrimination in target selection can be seen in two contexts. In the first, a pattern of illegality is widespread (speeding, tax violations). Rather than deciding who to target as a result of citizen complaints, seriousness, or a random process, illegitimate criteria, such as the politics or life-style of the offender, are used. Enforcement of the law is discriminatory, but the person caught is presumably guilty of the offense. In the second, more troubling pattern, politics or life-style are used to determine whose morality will be tested. Although those who succumb to the bait are legally guilty, this guilt is a function of the initial targeting decision. Regardless of whether the context involves an overabundance of violations or a decision about whose morality will be tested, the discrimination permitted by undercover means is troubling.

Twentieth-century technical and social developments have radically altered the nature of law enforcement. The founders of the country could not have foreseen the many imaginative ways that have been devised to alter or evade constitutional projections. Nor have contemporary courts and legislatures usually chosen to get involved in providing concrete regulations for law enforcement.

With respect to undercover work, this suggests that it is unethical for the government to do by stealth what it is prohibited from doing openly. This principle recognizes the use/misuse of undercover tactics as a form of displacement or as an alternative to prohibited means.

Undercover tactics can be an effective means for getting around restrictions on interrogation (the right to remain silent, to have a lawyer, protection against self-incrimination), testimonial privilege, electronic surveillance, search and seizure, and even entrapment when an unwitting informant is used. Where grounds for judicial warrant are lacking, it is wrong to use undercover methods to accomplish the same end.

III. SOME QUESTIONS AND CRITERIA TO GUIDE THE ETHICAL ASSESSMENT OF UNDERCOVER TACTICS

G. K. Chesterton has noted that morality is like art—the line has to be drawn somewhere. What should we conclude from these opposing arguments? We might conclude that no conclusion is possible because there can be no consensus on how the principles should be weighed or, given the nature of the issue, even what the facts really are. Or we might decide that a conclusion about ethics and undercover work is unimportant. Police will do what they feel they have to do, regardless of what outside observers may say. Concerns over innocence, moral purity, logical consistency, and conceptual distinctions are fine for academic analysts but are unlikely to count for much on the late shift in an impoverished high-crime area on Saturday night.

I don't think the situation is quite so hopeless. A degree of reconciliation, integration, and compromise is possible. Logical and empirical analysis can take us far toward reaching conclusions. Policy guidelines and even the law do in fact reflect ethical concerns and help shape work environments, though they are far from the only factors.

Much of the conflict between arguments for and against undercover work is more apparent than real. Many seemingly "conflicting" principles can be reconciled for at least five reasons.

They are contingent rather than categorical, and permissive or restrictive only under given conditions. Unlike the categorical prohibition "thou shalt not lie," many undercover issues deal with different and nonconflicting questions. Only in a few cases are they necessarily opposed. Thus, "respect the sanctity of private places" permits undercover means in public places.

To justify the tactic when there are grounds for suspicion means prohibiting it when such grounds are absent. To permit using it when the agent is the victim, as with anticrime decoys, does not justify making deals with criminals. Concerns about temptation do not preclude operations where the government agent plays a more passive observational role or comes to participate in an ongoing criminal plan. Most principles implicitly call for logical or empirical analysis and contain the qualifying phrase, "if, when, or to the extent that undercover tactics involve [whatever the claim] they are/are not justified."

They may state different aspects of a general principle, for example, "convict the guilty" and "do no harm to the innocent"; "enforce the law equally" and "do not discriminate in the selection of targets"; or "an investigation should be as nonintrusive and noncoercive as possible" and "respect the sanctity of intimate relations."

They can sometimes be weighed with respect to importance. Cultures may differ in how they weigh values, but within a culture there is often a broad-based consensus on the relative importance of competing values. Thus, although most persons would agree that "truth telling is moral and lying is immoral," they would also agree that the end may justify the means, for example, when protection from serious crime comes about as a result of official lying. When values or principles conflict, the less important value may have to be sacrificed. As court decisions often suggest, conflicting values

can be balanced through compromise, so that no value is fully realized or fully violated. Thus, a requirement that limits, though still permits, temptation may mean fewer arrests and less deterrence but greater protection of the weak and less entrapment.

Even when principles are logically inconsistent, empirical research may suggest directives for action. A considerable amount of disagreement about undercover tactics lies not with principles, but with conflicting beliefs about what the facts are. For example, if research suggests that a large majority of those arrested as a result of street decoy operations show no evidence of previous criminal activity (and turn out to be simply weak or vulnerable persons), many observers would feel that the tactic is inappropriate. The grounds for this would be drawn from the principles stated earlier—convict the guilty; Don't harm the innocent. Although we may agree that it is immoral to harm the innocent and for the government to increase crime, if research suggests that undercover work (or more properly, particular types under given circumstances) does not do this, then we can simply ignore these principles. Although they remain sound principles, they do not apply here.

Furthermore, some of the arguments between supporters and opponents of the tactic are misplaced because both sides are not responding to the same questions. Failing to differentiate among the following four issues can be a source of confusion. First, can undercover practices be ethical? I think the answer to this is a qualified "Yes." This leads to a second and a third question: under what conditions are they ethical? As a broad strategy or as tactically implemented? If we can resolve these matters, there is still a fourth question: in any given case, to what extent do the conditions for ethical use hold?

Some of the disagreement over particularly controversial cases such as Abscam (in which an FBI agent posing as an Arab sheik sought to buy favors from members of congress) for example, stems from antagonists responding to different questions. Supporters often respond to the first and second questions, arguing that undercover practices are ethical, but critics respond to the third and fourth questions, arguing that in some, if not all, of the Abscam cases, the tactic was used in an unethical way.

As suggested earlier, one solution to the problem of conflicting principles is to weigh them. In the criminal justice system, effectiveness often conflicts with humaneness, decency, or fairness. A democratic society gives significant weight to fairness and, thus, formally rejects the notion that the end justifies the means. Ethics attach to means as well as to ends, and some means are just too abhorrent to use. Police are prohibited from torturing people, pumping their stomachs to discover drugs, or harming innocent friends or relatives of the accused. These tactics are seen as so unethical that they are categorically rejected. The moral distinction between crime and criminal justice is maintained only by such restrictions.

However, few persons would argue that undercover means ought to be categorically prohibited or that they should be used indiscriminately without restrictions and guidelines. Given an intermediate position, where and how should the lines be drawn?

It is one thing to suggest why the reconciliation of conflicting ethical arguments is possible, and quite another to reconcile them. What should we answer to the question: is undercover work ethical? We can learn from the response of a wizened old stationmaster who, when asked whether or not the train would be on time, looked down at his watch, hesitated and then said, "That depends." When asked "What does it depend on?" he hesitated again and replied, "That depends too." So it is with undercover work. Whether or not it is ethical "depends." I think much of what it depends on is revealed by answers to the following questions.

Seriousness: is the use of undercover work proposed for crimes of a seriously harmful nature?

Alternatives: are alternative nondeceptive means unavailable for obtaining the same end?

Democratic decision-making: has granting police the option to use undercover means been subject to a degree of democratic decision making, however indirect, and has it been publicly announced that such means will be used?

Spirit of the law: is use of the strategy consistent with the spirit, as well as the letter, of the law?

Prosecution: is the goal of the strategy eventually to invoke criminal justice processing and hence make the deception publicly subject to judgment, rather than to gather intelligence indiscriminately, to harass, or to coerce cooperation from an informer?

Clarity of definition: is its use proposed for crimes that are clearly defined, or, if not, can a tactic be devised that ensures the target is well aware of the criminal nature of the behavior?

Crime occurrence: are there reasonable grounds for concluding that the crime that occurs as a result of the undercover operation is not an artifact of the method of intervention?

Grounds for suspicion: are there reasonable grounds for concluding that the particular target of an undercover operation has already committed or is likely to commit an equivalent offense, regardless of the government's undercover effort?

Prevention: are there reasonable grounds for concluding that the undercover operation will prevent a serious crime from occurring?

The greater the number and strength of affirmative answers, the more ethically defensible a general undercover strategy is. Questions must also be raised about the ethics of particular activities within the investigation. (It may be ethical as a broad strategy, even when specific aspects are unethical.) The following questions deal with the actual organization and dynamics of the operation.

Autonomy: does the tactic permit a high degree of self-selection and/or autonomy on the part of the suspect in breaking the law?

Degree of deception: does use of the tactic involve minimal or extensive deception, and is the degree of deception involved only that which is necessary to carry out the investigation?

Bad lessons: how far does the tactic go in casting the state in the role of teaching a bad moral lesson?

Privacy and expression: will use of the tactic sufficiently respect the sanctity of private places, intimate and professional relations, and the right to freedom of expression and action?

Collateral harm: how great is the potential for exploitation, corruption, perjury, or abuses and harm to police, informers, and unwitting third parties? Can these be adequately controlled or compensated for?

Equitable target selection: are the criteria for target selection equitable?

Realism: does the undercover scene stay reasonably close to real-world settings and opportunities?

Relevance of charges: are the charges brought against a person directly connected with criminal harm, or do they reflect mere procedural violations?

Actors: does the undercover investigation involve sworn agents playing central roles rather than informers?

Asking such questions is important if one accepts Sissela Bok's (1978) position that lying is not neutral and that there should be a presumption against it. To use undercover tactics will require greater justification than is the case for more conventional police methods. The situation is analogous to the greater justification required for, and stricter controls around, the use of force. The greater the extent of the affirmative or "harm-avoiding" answers to the above questions, the more justified an undercover operation is.

The two sets of questions presented above should be seen as navigational aids and not as a flight plan. They are skill-honing devices that can increase the sensitivity of the judgments made by agents, police supervisors, criminal justice officials, and concerned citizens. In noting that some resolution of the disagreements around secret police tactics is possible, our optimism (for both the resolution and the tactic) must remain qualified and guarded.

This article is influenced in part by Edward Shils's observation that "civil politics requires an understanding of the complexity of virtue, that no virtue stands alone, that every virtuous act costs something in terms of other virtuous acts, that virtues are intertwined with evil." The contradiction involved in calling something a necessary evil alerts us to the fact that principles do not cease to conflict, even when an operational solution is found. The hallmark of a moral dilemma, of course, is that there is no way out. This is part of the topic's fascination and why persons of good will may strenuously disagree. We cannot reach a general conclusion about whether undercover tactics should be prohibited or justified on ethical grounds. Paradoxically, no matter what action is taken, there are moral costs. There are clear costs whenever the government uses deceit, and still other costs are at risk. But not to use the tactic can have costs to—whether inaction and inequality in law enforcement in the face of serious crime, or the greater costs that may accompany use of some other tactic.

In dealing with such moral dilemmas, the problem is not only whether we can find an acceptable utilitarian calculus, but that the choice always involves competing wrongs or rights. The danger of automatically applied technical, bureaucratic, or occupational subcultural formulas lies in their potential for generating the self-deluding and morally numbing conclusion that a cost-free solution is possible.

Also See the Following Articles

CRIME AND SOCIETY • INFORMED CONSENT • POLICE ACCOUNTABILITY • VICTIMLESS CRIMES

Bibliography

Bok, C. (1978). *Lying: Moral choice in public and private life.* New York: Pantheon.

Caplan, G. (1983). *Abscam ethics: Moral issues and deception in law enforcement.* Cambridge: Ballinger.

Chevigny, P. (1980, February 23) A rejoinder. *Nation.*

Crime, Law and Social Change. (1992, September). Special issue: Issues and theories on covert policing.

Fijnaut, C., & Marx, G. T. (1995). *Undercover: Police surveillance in comparative perspective.* The Hague: Kluwer Law International.

Journal of Social Issues, 3. (1987). Special issue devoted to the covert facilitation of crime.

Marx, G. T. (1988). *Undercover: Police Surveillance in America.* Berkeley: University of California Press.

Marx, G. T. (1992, Spring) Under-the-covers-undercover investigations: Some reflections on the state's use of deception in intimate relations. *Journal of Criminal Justice Ethics.*

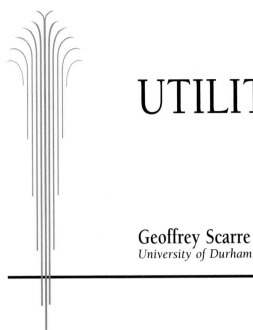

UTILITARIANISM

Geoffrey Scarre
University of Durham

I. The Main Features of the Theory
II. Historical Development
III. Problems and Prospects

GLOSSARY

calculus of utility (sometimes "felicific calculus") A method, associated particularly with Jeremy Bentham, of reducing moral judgment of actions to the computation of their utility yield (measured in "units" of pleasure or satisfaction).

consequentialism The view that actions should be judged right or wrong solely according to the value of their (intended) consequences.

deontological ethics Theories that regard certain actions as being right or wrong in themselves, regardless of the value of their consequences.

greatest happiness principle The injunction to act always so as to produce the greatest quantity of happiness for the largest number of people.

hedonism The view that pleasure is the chief human good.

maximization, idea of The notion that utility should always be promoted as fully as possible.

utility Equated by traditional utilitarian theories with pleasure or happiness, by many twentieth-century writers with the satisfaction of preferences; more generally definable as welfare or well-being.

UTILITARIANISM names an extended family of ethical theories that take as the yardstick of moral appraisal the propensity of actions to promote or diminish human well-being (or, more broadly, the well-being of all sentient creatures). In its simplest classical form, it holds that "actions are right in proportion as they tend to promote happiness, wrong as they tend to produce the reverse of happiness," "happiness" being explained as "pleasure, and the absence of pain" (J. S. Mill). A popular alternative tradition, influenced by welfare economics, considers utility as "correlative to Desire or Want" (Alfred Marshall), and defines right actions as those that most fully satisfy people's desires or preferences. All utilitarians reject the view that some things simply ought, or ought not, to be done irrespective of the results to be expected from doing or omitting to do them. Kantian moral theorists would hold, for instance, that breaking a promise is intrinsically wrong even where keeping the promise can be predicted to have calamitous effects. In contrast a utilitarian would consider that *not* breaking the promise would be wrong in such circumstances, given the serious disutility of keeping it.

The term "utilitarian," introduced by Bentham in 1781, has its ancestry in Hume's remark in the *Enquiry Concerning the Principles of Morals* that "the circumstance of *utility*, in all subjects . . . is constantly appealed to in all moral decisions concerning the merit and demerit of actions." It has been well said of utilitarianism that it is not so much a theory as a movement, and in the later eighteenth and nineteenth centuries it was, particularly in Britain, a powerful engine of social and political reform. Coming to prominence in the Enlightenment era, utilitarianism has continued to appeal to many as a down-to-earth and liberating approach to morals that treats everyone's welfare as equally important and refuses to accept the tyranny of questionable moral conventions; although it has long attracted the criticism that in its concern for the general good (classically expressed in the greatest happiness principle) it can be cavalier in its attitudes to the rights and interests of individuals.

I. THE MAIN FEATURES OF THE THEORY

Most versions of utilitarianism have been *welfarist*, *consequentialist*, *aggregative*, and *maximizing*. We shall look at these features in turn.

A. Welfarist

The "utility" of which utilitarians speak is usually identified with welfare, but views of welfare vary widely. The earlier utilitarians tended to construe it, as Bentham did, in terms of pleasure and pain: a life was held to be going well to the extent that it contained a balance of pleasurable over painful sensations. These early writers mostly disregarded an older tradition going back to Aristotle whereby pleasure was to be distinguished from happiness (Greek *eudaimonia*), the state of a person engaged in satisfying and worthwhile activity displaying excellences of mind and character. For Bentham the value of a pleasure is determined solely by its quantity, whereas in the subtler work of J. S. Mill a distinction is drawn between qualitatively "higher" and "lower" pleasures according to the worth of the activities that produce them (intellectual pleasures, for example, score higher and are more worth promoting than those of "mere sensation"). In a further echo of Aristotle, Mill holds the truly happy person to be someone who pays close attention to his self-development, and desires "for its own sake, the conformity of his own character to his standard of excellence."

Some contemporary utilitarians, in a tradition that might reasonably be described as Millian or "eudaimonist," affirm that the holding of certain objective facts about a person's condition is more salient than the history of his subjective states to judgments about how well his life is going. Thus David Brink writes that a plausible theory of welfare "counts reflective pursuit

and realization of agents' reasonable projects and certain personal and social relationships as the primary components of valuable lives." Yet objectivist accounts of welfare are controversial because they imply the existence of standards for judging the quality of lives which their subjects might not themselves share. Some philosophers (e.g., Sen, Harsanyi) therefore argue for a more subjectivist account of individual utility in terms of a person's own conception of his well-being. Such conceptions receive expression in the preferences people display, and promoting their welfare consists in satisfying their preferences. Preference-satisfaction utilitarians usually acknowledge, however, that we are not required to satisfy a person's foolish or self-harming preferences: although whether a distinction between sensible and foolish preferences can be drawn without the tacit invocation of an objectivist criterion of well-being may be open to doubt. (Harsanyi proposes that we should take into account only the "true" preferences a person would retain after careful reflection and in full possession of all relevant facts: but how do we determine what Tom, who is feckless and silly, would have chosen had he been sensible? And in what sense would an inferred preference be a "true" one if it were one that Tom would never actually have had?)

B. Consequentialist

Act-utilitarianism (the simplest form) holds that an action is right if it can reasonably be expected to produce at least as much utility as any alternative feasible act. (Note the reference here to the effects that may "reasonably be expected" from an action: an agent would merit no additional praise or blame if the consequences of his action were better or worse than he could reasonably have foreseen.) But some utilitarians have favored more indirect criteria of right action, which appraise actions not by their individual propensity to increase utility but by reference to their conformity with utility-enhancing rules, motives, or virtues. Thus, rule-utilitarians hold that an action is right if it conforms to a rule whose general observance could reasonably be expected to promote utility at least as effectively as any alternative feasible rule. (For further discussion of rule-utilitarianism see Section II.)

It is sometimes mistakenly thought that for consequentialists it is not actions themselves but only their "consequences," in the sense of their further effects, that are morally significant. But it would be a highly eccentric theory that held that when a robber shoots a bank guard dead, he is culpable not for killing the guard but only for the bad effects that follow from the killing, such as the grief of the guard's wife and the anxiety generated among bank staff. In fact, utilitarians do not concern themselves with where the line between an "action" and its "consequences" is drawn, but count the utility of both.

The real point of the term "consequentialist" is to signal the difference between theories like utilitarianism that judge actions according to their consequences for the promotion of a particular conception of the good, and deontological theories that grade actions by reference to a scheme of moral laws, rules, rights or duties. While in practice both approaches commonly lead to the same moral judgments, the rationales they offer for them differ. For instance, some deontologists assert that theft is morally wrong because it infringes a person's right to hold private property; the utilitarian's condemnation refers rather to the unhappiness or inconvenience suffered by the victim who loses his goods. In some cases, however, utilitarian and deontological prescriptions may diverge. Bernard Williams has imagined a scenario in which a visitor to a South American town is given the choice of shooting one of 20 innocent hostages whereupon the others will be released, or standing by while government soldiers shoot all 20. Utilitarians would say he should kill the one to save the rest, as one death, although bad, is less bad than 20; deontologists who believe in an exceptionless law against killing human beings, or in an absolute human right to life, will say he should not. From a strict deontological perspective, comparison of utilities is always beside the point: some acts should simply not be done, *whatever* the consequences. (It is sometimes suggested that the most satisfactory theory would be a hybrid composed of both deontological and consequentialist elements; the problem, however, with this irenic proposal is that it is hard to draw together in a coherent manner considerations drawn from such conceptually disparate bases.)

It is clear that utilitarianism is a consequentialist theory of *moral justification*, concerned to lay down conditions of right and wrong actions. But should it also be seen as a theory of *moral deliberation*, informing us how to decide which actions to perform and which to avoid? Some utilitarians think not, on the ground that engaging in long and complicated calculations of utility may make one ineffectual and overhesitant as an agent (one reaches one's decision about what to do when the moment for action has passed); thus human welfare may on the whole be better promoted by people who act habitually on simple moral rules like "Keep your promises" or "Be charitable to the needy." (However, even act-utilitarians can allow a role in delibera-

tion for "rules of thumb" like these, provided that we are ready to drop them in circumstances where conforming to them is plainly disutilitarian). Other utilitarians have suggested that utility is most effectively maximized by agents who do not calculate consequences (even with the help of rules of thumb) but try instead to become more loving, more virtuous or more noble of soul (see, e.g., Adams 1976). It is important to grasp that the status of utilitarianism as a theory of moral justification is not threatened by the recognition that the most efficient utility producers may not always be those whose main preoccupation is to promote utility.

C. Aggregative

It is a standard assumption of utilitarian theory that utility comes in greater and lesser amounts. Many utilitarians have accordingly been tantalised by the prospect of a "calculus of utility"—a method of reducing moral judgment to mathematical calculation. For outcomes to be evaluated mathematically, it is necessary, first, to have a way of calibrating individual utility. The trouble is that the philosophical sophistication of a concept of utility and its susceptibility to quantitative treatment are generally in inverse proportion to one another. It is not easy to see how we could calibrate utility in the sense of Aristotelian *eudaimonia*, or even in Sen's more subjectivist sense of "a person's conception of his own well-being."

Nevertheless, progress has been made in providing a mathematical theory of utility capable at least of application in such a limited domain as welfare economics. Economic utilitarians have laid stress on the fact that measurement of utility is attainable provided that some standard of comparison can be determined. Richard Brandt has shown how such an approach can be applied in a wider context, assuming that we are content to work with a simple hedonistic notion of utility. We start by selecting a pair of experiences A and B such that A is very slightly more enjoyable than B. Unit value is arbitrarily assigned to the degree of enjoyment by which A exceeds B. We then give the same number to other cases of equal increments, and the number 2 to any increments "just equal to that of the joint increments of two elements already assigned the number 1" (Brandt (1979). *A Theory of the Good and the Right*, p. 255. Oxford: Oxford University Press). Brandt shows how to develop this basis so that experiences can be plotted on an enjoyment graph, whose two axes represent the pleasantness of an experience and its duration. Two experiences plotted on the graph can now be compared in respect of utility by computing the areas under their curves. The method can then be extended to the many-persons case, provided that we can devise a sound way of making interpersonal comparisons of utility.

Utilitarians assume that it is possible to sum everyone's utility to yield an overall utility total. This assumption has been viewed with scepticism by critics who point to the difficulty of knowing just what is going on in other minds and the great variety of personal tastes and aspirations. But even conceding the variation in human desires, it is reasonable to ascribe to all rational persons an interest in such "primary goods" (Rawls) as political freedoms and social opportunities, adequate income and a basis for self-respect, while as for the more individual goods that help to make lives go well or badly we can listen to people's reports of their likes and dislikes and note what they choose or avoid. Even if interpersonal utility comparisons can rarely be made with the quantitative precision looked for by constructors of calculuses, utilitarians point out that any of us with some knowledge of life and a modicum of imaginative empathy (the ability to put ourselves in other people's shoes) are capable of rough and ready ones. Doubtless some of our judgments of others' utility are wrong, but that is a fact with which we must live. Harsanyi remarks that utilitarianism makes no assumption that people are good at making interpersonal comparisons, but only that such comparisons are the necessary basis of rational moral judgment about social policies and arrangements.

D. Maximizing

Although some recent utilitarians have suggested that it is sufficient for an action to count as right that it should produce *enough* on-balance utility even if some alternative action might have produced more (a view termed by Slote "satisficing utilitarianism"), most have held the maximizing doctrine that human welfare should be promoted as fully as possible. Utilitarians standardly believe that social welfare is some function of the utilities of individuals. But it is not easy to define this function, and it is certainly false that any increase in the utility of an individual must also increase the social utility. Not only does one person's gain often depend upon another's loss, as when the poor benefit from the taxes paid by the rich, but interpersonal differences in values and tastes create conflicting desires regarding such public issues as the allocation of scarce resources, the educational, cultural, and recreational priorities of the community, and the management of the shared environment. Social-policy makers must recognize the impossibility of pleasing all of the people

all of the time. Individual utilities are assumed to be aggregative; the task is to determine how best to aggregate them. That our intuitions are unreliable guides in this area has been shown by the "Impossibility Theorem" of Kenneth Arrow, which demonstrates that no social-welfare function can satisfy all of a number of prima-facie highly reasonable assumptions which we might antecedently have made about such a function.

Despite these theoretical worries, we often have little difficulty in deciding which of a number of alternative feasible actions is likely to yield the most utility. Donating $20 to save the life of a starving peasant in a drought-stricken country will obviously produce a larger increase in the general utility than spending the same sum on some unnecessary luxury for oneself. The problem of defining an acceptable social-welfare function is an acute one chiefly at the level of public policy decisions. Much of the morally significant behavior of individuals affects fewer people, and affects them in more limited ways, than the actions of governments and institutions, and ranking the feasible options open to us in respect of their likely utility yield is often an easier task than critics of the theory allow.

Classical utilitarian theories hold that it is the *total* utility that should be maximized; some twentieth-century theorists (e.g., Harsanyi) have proposed that the *average per capita* utility is a more plausible maximand, on the ground that a self-interested individual who was asked to choose between two social policies without knowing what his own position would be in the resulting social system would reasonably prefer the policy that yielded the higher average utility. There is, however, no operational difference between these alternatives given a population of constant size. But it is a nice question for debate among utilitarians whether a crowded world with a higher total but lower average utility would be preferable to a less heavily populated world with a lower total but higher mean utility. The claim that average utilitarianism is a more rational choice for someone concerned to maximize his own expected utility needs to be set against the thought that from the point of view of an impartial ideal observer who delights in every increase in the amount of human good, total utilitarianism might seem to be the more attractive option.

The maximizing component of utilitarianism draws its support from an apparently compelling principle of practical reason: that if something is a good, it is irrational to choose to produce a smaller amount of it where one could produce a greater. Under the maximizing conception, one set of individual utilities is as good as another if, and only if, it has at least as large a sum total. But this formula implies an indifference to *how* the utilities are distributed. Traditionally, many utilitarians have been inspired by a supplementary *universalist* idea (expressed in the greatest happiness principle) that utility should be spread as widely as possible—that we should strive not only to create the largest amount of happiness, but create it for the greatest possible number of people. Behind this idea is the familiar ethical principle that there are no moral second-class citizens. But the problem is that we cannot coherently pursue the double maximand of the greatest happiness of the greatest number, for we sometimes have to choose between an action that will provide a lesser utility for a larger number of people and another that will produce a larger utility for a smaller number. In such circumstances it is impossible simultaneously to produce the greatest happiness *and* to benefit the greatest number. Utilitarians who have recognized this have generally preferred to drop the universalist element.

II. HISTORICAL DEVELOPMENT

The earliest known thinker who can fairly be described as a utilitarian was the Chinese sage Mo Tzu (fifth century B.C.E.), who preached an ethic with two central themes: the all-embracing love of mankind and the evaluation of all actions by their fruitfulness. In the Greek world utilitarianism was most closely approached by Epicurus (341–271 B.C.E.), who combined a hedonistic theory of value with a consequentialist account of right action. Epicurus taught that the happiest life is that of the philosopher who restrains his physical appetites and pursues the things of the mind, thus anticipating the later distinction between higher and lower pleasures; but the self-centered focus of the Epicurean agent on his own well-being is alien to the utilitarian concern with the general good.

While utilitarian arguments are sometimes encountered in medieval writers, it was not until the Enlightenment that utilitarianism came into its own as a major school of thought. Rooted in the scientific study of human nature, equipped with empirical theories of sensation, motivation, and the intellectual operations, socially progressive and secular, utilitarianism appealed to many who looked for an ethic unindebted to Jerusalem, Rome, or Geneva. Writers like Helvétius, Condorcet, and Chastellux in France, Hutcheson, Priestley, Godwin, and Bentham in Britain, argued that the general happiness should be the determining principle of the actions both of states and of individuals, and the test of all national institutions and laws. In the light of the utilitarian critique, many features of public life were found to be sadly wanting even in the most advanced European countries, where wealth and privilege existed alongside want, misery, and ignorance. Hence, utilitarianism became a major reforming philosophy, dedicated to the practical improvement of the living conditions of the masses, the overhaul of legal systems and the instruments of government, and (particularly in the nineteenth century) the extension of political rights.

Most radical of the British utilitarians was William Godwin (1756–1836), who pursued to its furthest logical conclusion the principle that "Morality is that system of conduct which is determined by a consideration of the greatest general good." In Godwin's rigorously maximizing view, justice requires that we should do everything in our power to increase public utility—even if this means dying for it: "We have in reality nothing that is strictly speaking our own. We have nothing that has not a destination prescribed to it by the immutable voice of reason and justice."

Jeremy Bentham (1748–1832) has been characterized by Sir Leslie Stephen as posing the question "What is the use of you?" to every institution and to every law. Less interested in abstract philosophy than in the practical work of legal reform, Bentham was nevertheless immensely important in bringing utilitarian ideas to the notice of a wider public. According to Bentham, human motivation may be reduced to the promptings of the "two sovereign masters" pleasure and pain, and actions are morally praiseworthy insofar as they tend to increase our pleasures and decrease our pains. Bentham thought that numerical values could in principle be attached to the "circumstances" productive of pleasure and pain, enabling moral judgments to be reached by mathematical calculation; although he conceded the impossibility in practice of settling all moral questions by reference to a "felicific calculus." Bentham is also noteworthy for his acute and often witty criticisms of nonutilitarian moral theories. These, he claimed, either rested on nothing more substantial than their authors' say-so, or involved a tacit and unacknowledged appeal to the utility principle. Rights-based theories attracted his particular scorn, and he roundly condemned the language of rights then popular with apologists of the French and American revolutions as "rhetorical nonsense—nonsense upon stilts." He was also one of the first major thinkers to ascribe a significant moral status to animals, arguing that although animals lacked rationality, their capacity for suffering entitled them to moral consideration. Since Bentham's day a concern for the welfare of animals has remained an important strand in the utilitarian tradition.

John Stuart Mill (1806–1873) was the greatest of all utilitarian writers. Son of Bentham's most fervent ally, the philosopher and historian James Mill, John Stuart was groomed in youth for the role of standard-bearer of Benthamism, but at 20 reacted against the narrowness of its view of human life. Inspired by his reading of Romantic authors and the Greek classics to give more weight than his predecessors had done to the culture of the feelings and the development of character, Mill greatly refined the utilitarian theory of value. His *Utilitarianism* of 1861 begins with a simple statement of Bentham's view that happiness consists in the acquisition of pleasures and the avoidance of pains, but Mill emphasised that pleasures are not all of equal worth, and that fulfilled lives manifest also "spiritual perfection" and self-respect, and the love of external objects like beauty, order, and truth. The central place that Mill accorded to self-development and autonomy among the "parts of happiness" is further apparent in the famous thesis of his essay *On Liberty* (1859), that "the sole end for which mankind are warranted, individually or collectively, in interfering with the liberty of action of any of their number, is self-protection." Ideal utilitarian states, Mill explained, avoid heavy-handed paternalist interventions in the lives of individuals, but empower their citizens to lead their lives according to their own conceptions of the good.

Mill believed that the truth of the principle of utility could be proved by the simple fact that everyone desires happiness. Yet it is not really possible to justify an impartial concern for the happiness of all on the basis of the partial concern of each individual for his own happiness, a point clearly noted by Henry Sidgwick (1838–1900), the subtlest psychologist of the utilitarian school. Sidgwick's book *The Methods of Ethics* attempted instead to justify utilitarianism by means of rational intuitions. Sidgwick thought it self-evident both that no single individual's happiness was more important than any other's "from the point of view of the Universe," and that "as a rational being I am bound to aim at good generally": from which it appeared to follow that "each one is morally bound to regard the good of any other individual as much as his own." But Sidgwick candidly confessed that from a more subjective standpoint each individual has reason to prefer his own good above the good of others. His reluctant conclusion was that there was "an ultimate and fundamental contradiction in our apparent intuitions of what is reasonable in conduct." More conservative in outlook than many other utilitarians, Sidgwick was a firm supporter of the conventional moral values of Victorian Britain, which he thought well warranted by the principle of utility.

In Sidgwick's view, the masses should be encouraged to obey the standard moral rules in a spirit of blind and respectful obedience, leaving the intricacies of utilitarian moral reflection to the rational elite.

Twentieth-century work in utilitarianism has proceeded on a number of fronts, some of which have been indicated in Section I. A fringe development was the "Ideal Utilitarianism" of G. E. Moore, which broadened the meaning of "utility" to include, besides human welfare, certain objective features of the universe, in particular the beauty of its constituents. More important has been rule-utilitarianism, which, although foreshadowed by some earlier writers, received its first systematic defence in R. F. Harrod's 1936 paper "Utilitarianism Revised." Harrod attempted to give a utilitarian sanction to common moral convictions that "certain types of act are obligations." He argued that while, for example, a single lie might do little harm, widespread lying would undermine the useful practices and institutions that rely on telling the truth; hence, we should always tell the truth, because general mendacity would be intolerable. Act-utilitarians have objected that there can be no good utilitarian ground to obey a rule in circumstances where obeying that rule does not enhance utility, and that those who think otherwise are succumbing to a quasi-Kantian "rule-worship." Against this it has been pointed out that some utility-promoting practices will only operate effectively if people agree to abide in all but the most exceptional circumstances by their constitutive rules. For instance, promising functions as a useful practice only if people desist from thinking about the advantage to be gained or lost by keeping particular promises. Rule-utilitarianism seems therefore to have a clear advantage over act-utilitarianism in regard to practices devised by human ingenuity to promote mutual advantage by means of common consent to constitutive rules; it is less clear, on the other hand, that any reference to rules is needed to explain, from a utilitarian point of view, the wrongness of murder, cruelty, or rape.

Other contemporary utilitarians, such as R. M. Hare, have argued in a way reminiscent of Sidgwick that none of us can reasonably hope to do without prima facie moral rules in practical day-to-day decision-making. Lacking the calculative intelligence and foresight of archangels (Hare's paradigms of rational beings), we have no real alternative but to abide for the most part by principles that experience has shown to increase human welfare. But Hare stresses that "critical thinking" about our principles is not beyond our capacities, and that when we engage in such critical thinking we should do so as utilitarians. Hare's dual-level account of the moral life, presented most forcefully in his *Moral Think-*

ing of 1981, has been one of the chief foci of utilitarian debate in recent years. Other topics of major concern in the contemporary discussion of utilitarianism will be explored in the next section.

III. PROBLEMS AND PROSPECTS

A. Utilitarianism and Its Values

Utilitarianism is committed to treating the good as an aggregative commodity, something that comes in greater or lesser amounts. But how persuasive is the theory's identification of the proper goal of action with happiness, or the satisfaction of preferences, in the light of our common disposition to regard good lives as directed on a great variety of valuable objectives and ideals? Can there really be a common currency of value, in terms of which the worth of the various value-giving components of flourishing lives can be expressed and compared? And does a synoptic theory like utilitarianism, which imposes a single covering conception ("utility") on those components, take sufficiently seriously the fact that many of our ends are pursued, as Mill himself admitted, "disinterestedly," for the sake of their own merits?

Many utilitarians regard the provision of a satisfactory account of value as the most urgent task facing the theory today (see Griffin, 1986, Hardin, 1988). Preference-satisfaction models are specially problematic because there seems to be no necessary connection between having one's preferences satisfied and having one's welfare promoted, and because individuals' preferences fluctuate over time, making it difficult to know how to satisfy them maximally in the long term. Happiness accounts are perhaps more promising, and Brandt has noted that we tend to care about people getting what they want or prefer *just because* we care about their being happy rather than miserable.

Mill proposed to square the claim that happiness is the ultimate good with the recognition that there are many things in life that we pursue for their own sake (excellence, love, wealth, health, artistic and literary achievement, etc.), by representing the latter objectives as "parts of happiness." Happiness is thus, for Mill, an *inclusive end* that incorporates a set of individual goals pursued for their own sake, and not as it was for Bentham a *dominant end* (to be identified with pleasure) for the sake of which everything else is pursued. Mill further thought, like Aristotle, that the happy life was a life with a certain kind of shape and unity to it, whose parts fit together in a rationally ordered manner.

But if happiness has many parts, the utilitarian goal appears to defy precise specification. What detailed content can be given to the injunction to maximize happiness, if happiness is multiform and happy lives can be lived in a large variety of ways? Can we have a sufficiently nuanced understanding of another's particular needs and wants to ensure that our interventions in his life will always be helpful? Yet these questions may rest on a misunderstanding of the proper role of the utilitarian agent. Mill rejected the idea of the utilitarian as a do-gooding busybody who constantly pokes his nose into other people's affairs seeking for opportunities to increase their utility. Such an agent would need to be able to make very precise judgments of others' utility in order to make his interventions effective, and most of us know few people well enough for that; many of his well-meant attentions would, moreover, be highly unwelcome. People may occasionally have to be prevented from doing foolish or self-damaging things which will make them unhappy. But Mill thought that many of the positive "parts of happiness" are things that individuals can only attain for themselves. An aspirant to qualities like excellence of character, spiritual perfection, or eminence in some field of scientific or artistic endeavor will look to other people mainly for moral support and encouragement. In general the most fruitful happiness-enhancing service that utilitarians can render is to facilitate individuals' own efforts to create fulfilling lives for themselves, by ensuring that they have political rights and liberties, free access to information, economic independence, and a minimum standard of material well-being. Particularly important, Mill believed, was the provision of a sensitive and enlightened education that would expand people's cultural horizons, introduce them to the higher pleasures, and increase their awareness of life's possibilities.

Doubts may remain, however, whether even an inclusive-end view of happiness can do full justice to our ordinary conviction that many ends are worth pursuing for their own sake, *irrespective* of the contribution they make to our happiness. In fact, it is hard to see how the pursuit of many of our political, religious, domestic, social, artistic, and other goals could contribute to happiness unless we ascribed to those goals an intrinsic value independent of their capacity to make us happy. The achievement of goals is normally satisfying precisely because of the value we place on achieving them. So, to be maximally happy, it looks as if we must care about, and strive for, much else besides being happy; we need to have a range of objectives that we value for their own sake. But if this is right, then utilitarianism fails to do justice to the mode in which many of our ends actually matter to us when it attempts to impose a covering conception ("happiness") to justify them. Whether some form of Ideal Utilitarianism, which broadens the conception of utility to include a larger range of ends, could do any better than this is an issue worth further study.

B. Does Utilitarianism Tolerate Unfairness?

Utilitarians are concerned to maximize the net utility of the members of society. But critics allege that as a maximization policy is inherently indifferent to the pattern of distribution of gains and losses, utilitarians must be prepared to tolerate grossly unfair things being done to individuals or groups when the utility sums require them. Caiaphas's sentiment that "It is better that one man should die for the good of the people" is closely echoed in Godwin's view that we may "put a man to death for the common good, either because he is infected with a pestilential disease, or because some oracle has declared it essential to the public safety." Even milder versions of utilitarianism seem committed to allowing some people to suffer pain or loss, as the price of increasing net social utility. Thus in the eyes of many of its opponents, utilitarianism fails to erect sufficiently strong protective boundaries around individuals and minorities: differently put, it is too neglectful of their moral rights.

Utilitarians have responded vigorously to accusations like these. They have pointed out that in practice playing fast and loose with individual liberty, goods, or lifestyle, far from enhancing the public utility, is likely to destroy the social fabric and produce a set of discontented and neurotic human beings. Without relations of mutual respect and the sense of belonging to a community that cares for the interests of each constituent member, people might muddle along in some sort of social nexus, but scarcely very happily. Rule-utilitarians emphasise the utility value of rules and laws to limit the sacrifices that may be demanded of individuals in the name of the general good; but even act-utilitarians who take a wide view of the consequences of such sacrifices will condemn them as normally causing more harm than good. (There is no point, say, in cannibalizing one healthy person in order to give his kidneys to two other sick people who would otherwise die, if everyone is made fearful that they may be next on the list of unwilling organ donors.) Utilitarians will concede that on rare occasions it may be better for one person to suffer serious harm than for many to suffer it: as in Williams' hostage story, where

one life is the purchase price of many. But such acts are not incompatible with most people's moral intuitions of fairness; they are deeply regrettable deeds rather than wrong ones. By permitting, in extraordinary circumstances, some relaxation of the usual conventions of behavior, utilitarianism is really closer to common sense than those rigid deontological outlooks that forbid any exceptions even *in extremis*.

By refining their accounts of human welfare and the nature of the good life, utilitarians can do much to defend themselves against the stock charge that they are prepared to tolerate, in the name of utility, all sorts of dreadful things to be done to people. It is sometimes said, for instance, that utilitarianism has difficulty in condemning the pleasures of the sadist, who delights in seeing others suffer. No utilitarian thinks suffering to be a good, but if pleasure (or the satisfaction of preferences) is a positive quantity in the utilitarian balance sheet, then the enjoyment that sadists take in the pain of their victims should offset some of their evil! However, the move to a more sophisticated theory of value makes it easier for the utilitarian to avoid this disturbing conclusion and to say what is wrong with sadistic pleasures. Although sadists may gain a lot of pleasure from other people's pain, they can also be held to be seriously damaging themselves, by undermining the basis of their self-respect as human beings. Self-respect is needed to provide a sense that one's life is worth living, and utilitarians may reasonably regard it as one of the primary "parts of happiness." Sadists and others who fail to respect humanity in others, by refusing to treat them as ends in themselves, cannot consistently respect *their own* humanity and see *themselves* as ends. To regard other people as mere objects of sport is incompatible with regarding humanity in one's own person as of value. Of course, someone brought up in an environment where cruelty to others is the norm may remain blind to the deficiencies of his outlook. Yet if cruelty and maltreatment of others subvert a person's ability to respect himself for his own most valuable properties—those basic human qualities he shares with the rest of humanity—then they prevent his maximizing his own utility, whether he knows it or not.

For many critics, however, utilitarianism's Achilles' heel remains the consequentialist nature of its moral judgments. From a deontological point of view, no amount of refinement of utilitarian value theory will alter the fact that utilitarians objectionably refuse to allow that some things are intrinsically wrong and should not be done, irrespective of consequences. Yet utilitarians have reasonably countered that the deontological viewpoint is itself difficult to defend. As Samuel

Scheffler has pointed out in his important book *The Rejection of Consequentialism* (1982), it is one thing to assert that certain actions that enhance utility are wrong but quite another to give a rational explanation of that wrongness. Scheffler thinks that it is particularly hard for deontologists to justify forbidding agents to breach moral constraints where breaching them will avert a greater number of infractions of those same constraints by others. Should not even deontologists actively seek to minimize wrongdoing? If one act of killing is wrong, then even an anticonsequentialist can scarcely deny that two acts of killing are worse. So why not kill one person where, as in the hostages case, this prevents a larger number of people from being killed? The deontologist's rejection of "moralizing by numbers" seems very dubiously coherent when the evils to be weighed in the balance are not amounts of misery or other disutility but quantities of *wrongful acts*.

It is possible that some intuitively cogent deontological rules and side constraints have a causal basis in psychological traits and inhibitions that have been selected in the course of human evolution and passed down to us as part of our genetic inheritance. If an inhibition against taking the life of another human being is an element of this native endowment, small wonder that we find "Thou shalt not kill" a prima facie compelling principle. Yet the rational agent can look beyond the moral color of his immediate action to that of its consequences; and arguably he should make an effort to overcome his deep-seated inhibitions against doing instrumental evil where consequentialist reasoning warrants it. Utilitarians, at least, will continue to argue that he should.

C. Utilitarianism and Personality

Some philosophers think that however justifiable utilitarian morality may be in the cold light of reason, it is a psychologically unsuitable morality for human beings. The complaint has been made by Williams and others that utilitarianism constrains people to subordinate their private ideals, projects, interests, and tastes—in short, all that makes their lives worth living—to the goal of becoming maximally efficient promoters of the general good. Utilitarianism is committed to maximizing human well-being regardless of the identities of individuals; therefore, it seems, there are no limits on what any of us can be asked to sacrifice, when public utility requires it. The utilitarian agent is (or aspires to be) a moral saint who never gives any special thought to himself; his perspective is a strictly person-neutral one from which everyone's interests, including his own,

count equally. Williams claims not only that such agents must inevitably become depersonalized, but that by making such demands utilitarianism renders itself incoherent: for unless people were permitted to have first-order projects, the "general project of bringing about maximally desirable outcomes" would "have nothing to work on, and would be vacuous"—because no one would have any personal desires to satisfy.

Hare has riposted to Williams that while moral sainthood may be beyond the power of all but a few, most of us could afford to become much less self-centered than we are without any danger of losing our character; the effort to care more for others would indeed be self-improving, making us more energetic and resourceful persons, and increasing our self-respect. Because "ought" implies "can," we cannot reasonably be blamed for a genuine incapacity to meet the highest standards of utilitarian self-denial. But we should resist the temptation to claim the psychological impossibility of sainthood as an excuse for self-indulgence. Only by trying do we know how good we can be.

Yet Hare's line seems to permit us to give a special weighting to our individual projects and interests only as a concession to human weakness. Some utilitarians have preferred a different strategy that permits individuals considerable space to pursue their own projects and concerns, but justifies the permission on the ground that not granting it would impede the maximization of the general happiness. They point out that, because abandoning one's particular concerns is painful, it is reasonable to take such hardships into account when doing the utility sums (cf. Scheffler, 1982: ch. 3). To insist that people relinquish these concerns and become full-time optimizers is a self-defeating tactic, because, in Mill's words, "the notion of a happiness for all, procured by the self-sacrifice of each, if the abnegation is really felt to be a sacrifice, is a contradiction." By developing their individual talents and interests and by pursuing (within reasonable bounds) their personal aims and ambitions, people will not only lead richer lives themselves but will have more distinctive contributions to make to the lives of their communities. In this view, Williams' claim that unless people are permitted to have first-order projects there will be nothing for the general project of bringing about maximally desirable outcomes to work on is seen not as an objection to utilitarianism, but simply as a reminder that the theory needs to leave scope for such projects.

The strategy can be used to justify our doing more for the welfare of people we care about (our parents, partners, children, and friends) than for complete strangers. Sidgwick argued that there was no real contradition between "the commonly received view of special claims and duties arising out of special relations" and the "impartial universality of the Utilitarian principle"; for not only are we naturally prepared to work harder on behalf of people with whom we have close connections, but we usually have a better knowledge of their character and situation and can direct our benevolent efforts to more telling effect. People to whom we are not related by ties of affection or comradeship will often resent our efforts, however well-meaning, to improve the quality of their lives. It contributes considerably to our self-respect to be the primary satisfiers of our own wants, and we normally resent the sidelining of our own efforts to achieve our goals; still more do we resent other people's attempting to define those goals for us.

But may a person pursue an object he cares about only when he sees nothing else to do that would promote utility more effectively? Some philosophers think that an agent who seeks to warrant his pursuit of private ends by exclusive reference to how well their pursuit promotes the general utility is in danger of losing sight of the special importance those ends have *for him*; he runs the risk of becoming, in a significant way, *alienated* from his own projects. And someone who is thus alienated from his projects may come, in time, to be alienated from himself. Agents who feel entitled to take their private interests seriously only insofar as doing so conduces to the general utility seem to be viewing their own lives from a fundamentally *impersonal* perspective. Seen in this light, utilitarianism remains a threat to the integrity of the personality in Williams' sense, despite making room for private projects: for while it allows people to have such projects, it forbids them to think about them in the psychologically appropriate way, as ends in themselves.

This problem has been discussed with considerable subtlety in recent years (e.g., in some of the papers in Scheffler, 1988). While the details of the debate are too complex to be summarized here, two observations may be made. The first is that the appearance of a substantial difficulty for utilitarianism may stem in some measure from misconstruing the impersonal point of view as permitting us to value our individual projects only *instrumentally* for their capacity to contribute to the public good. But this means-ends model of the relation between private and public good is misleading. Utilitarianism allows an individual to value the promotion of his own utility not merely as a causally efficacious method of promoting utility generally, but as a *constitutive part* of that utility. An agent should look on his own good not as an intermediate end whose promotion

brings the final end closer, but as a proper component of that end. Taking the impersonal point of view means seeing one's own utility as subordinate to the general utility only in the sense that it involves considering one's own good alongside other people's; it is fully compatible with ascribing ultimate value to the fulfilment of one's own interests. The impersonal viewpoint sometimes reveals that our private projects are too costly to others for their pursuit to be justified. But we can assume the impersonal viewpoint without ceasing to value our projects from a personal point of view, and without being forced to think that the only good reason to increase our own utility is that doing so swells the aggregate utility.

The second observation is that worries over the extent to which utilitarianism can permit agents to leave reasonable scope for their personally important interests and projects arise much more in regard to the morality of individual life than that of social and economic policy. No one thinks that politicians, public officials, and other servants of the people should use their positions to advance their personally significant projects. Goodin remarks that people in authority, like other agents, bring to their roles "a whole raft of baggage of personal attachments, commitments, principles and prejudices"; but we reasonably insist that when they act in their public capacities "they should stow that baggage as best they can." The utility of the makers and executors of public policy can be accorded little weight in comparison with that of the thousands or millions of people whom their policies affect.

Although utilitarianism leaves more room for self-regard than some of its critics have acknowledged, there is no denying that it is a more demanding philosophy than some. The theory must grant us sufficient space to lead personally fulfilling lives, or become self-defeating. But this space is liable to be squeezed when general utility levels are low. When some people in the world are starving, utilitarian morality finds it hard to justify much spending on luxuries by the affluent. Yet while utilitarianism is not an easy philosophy to live by, its defenders deny that it is as costly to the agent as the morally indolent contend. They point out that there is nothing to prevent a care for the general welfare figuring among an individual's most deeply felt concerns. One does not have to be a saint to include among one's *personal* projects a commitment to aiding people who are worse off than oneself. Utilitarians have, in fact, always laid special stress on the pleasure to be found in benevolent activity. Serving others' needs is a source of intense satisfaction to an agent with normal human

Box 1	Utilitarianism: A Selection of Major Works[a]
Mo Tzu:	*The Mo Tzu Book* (Fifth Century B.C.E.)
Francis Hutcheson:	*An Inquiry into the Original of Our Ideas of Beauty and Virtue* (1725)
David Hume:	*An Enquiry Concerning the Principles of Morals* (1748)
Joseph Priestley:	*Essay on the First Principles of Government* (1768)
Jean François de Chastellux:	*An Essay on Public Happiness* (1768)
Jeremy Bentham:	*An Introduction to the Principles of Morals and Legislation* (1789)
William Godwin:	*Enquiry Concerning Political Justice* (1793)
John Stuart Mill:	*Utilitarianism* (1861)
Henry Sidgwick:	*The Methods of Ethics* (1874)
R. F. Harrod:	Utilitarianism Revised, *Mind* (1936)
David Lyons:	*Forms and Limits of Utilitarianism* (1965)
J. J. C. Smart and Bernard Williams:	*Utilitarianism For and Against* (1973)

[a] For some more recent works, consult the Bibliography.

sympathies. "When people," thought Mill, "who are tolerably fortunate in their outward lot do not find in life sufficient enjoyment to make it valuable to them, the cause generally is, caring for nobody but themselves." In the utilitarian view, caring for others is a very good way of caring for yourself, and self-fulfilled people are rarely selfish ones.

Also See the Following Articles

CODES OF ETHICS • CONSEQUENTIALISM AND DEONTOLOGY • EPICUREANISM • HEDONISM • KANTIANISM

Bibliography

Adams, R. M. (1976). Motive utilitarianism. *The Journal of Philosophy,* 73, 467–481.

Brandt, R. B. (1979). *A theory of the good and the right,* p. 255. Oxford: Oxford University Press.

Brink, D. O. (1989). *Moral realism and the foundations of ethics,* p. 231. Cambridge: Cambridge University Press.

Goodin, R. E. (1995). *Utilitarianism as a public philosophy.* Cambridge: Cambridge University Press.

Griffin, J. (1986). *Well-being.* Oxford: Clarendon Press.

Hardin, R. (1988). *Morality within the limits of reason.* Chicago and London: University of Chicago Press.

Hare, R. M. (1981). *Moral thinking.* Oxford: Clarendon Press.

Harsanyi, J. C. (1976). *Essays on ethics, social behavior, and scientific explanation* pp. 50–51. Dordrecht: Reidel.

Scarre, G. (1996). *Utilitarianism.* London: Routledge.

Scheffler, S. (1982). *The rejection of consequentialism.* Oxford: Clarendon Press.

Scheffler, S. (Ed.). (1988). *Consequentialism and its critics.* Oxford: Oxford University Press.

Sen, A. & Williams, B. (Eds.) (1982). *Utilitarianism and Beyond.* Cambridge: Cambridge University Press.

Slote, M. (1984). Satisficing consequentialism. *Proceedings of the Aristotelian Society.* Supplementary volume 58, 139–163.

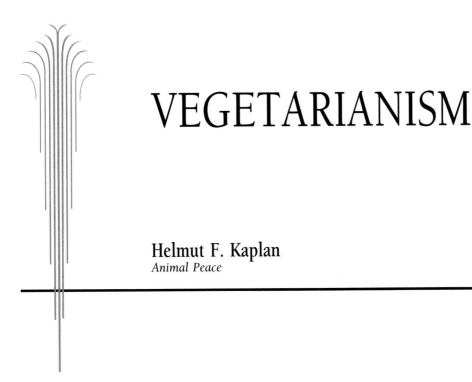

VEGETARIANISM

Helmut F. Kaplan
Animal Peace

GLOSSARY

greenhouse effect A contemporary phenomenon in which the warming of the earth's surface and lower atmosphere is intensified by the presence of increased levels of carbon dioxide; associated with the burning of fossil fuels and with the loss of areas of vegetation; e.g., rainforests.

metabolism The sum of all the physiological and chemical processes necessary to sustain life within an organism.

organic farming A nontechnical term for methods of plant growing and stock raising that employ only organic materials and methods, or at least a minimum of inorganic materials, for fertilizers, feed, weed and pest controls, and so on.

VEGETARIANISM consists of excluding meat from one's diet. Until just a few decades ago meat eating was considered a matter of course with no serious moral implications. Since the 1970s, however, attention has increasingly focused on the moral problems arising from meat eating: world hunger, destruction of the environment, disease, and animal suffering.

I. HUNGER

One argument often used against excluding meat from the diet, i.e., against vegetarianism, is that if we ate no meat then we would be unable to feed the steadily growing world population. Biological factors indicate quite the opposite, however; meat eating causes hunger.

The relevant fact here is that the animals whose meat we eat require some 90% of the feed we give them to sustain their own metabolism. This means that, of the earth's food resources which are used in the production of meat, 90% is lost. In other words, if we ate the plants ourselves, i.e., adhered to a vegetarian diet, instead of feeding the plants to animals in order to eat their meat, then we could feed 10 times as many people.

In the Third World large tracts of agricultural land are not available to provide for the needs of the local population because they are used instead to cultivate feed for meat production in rich countries. "The livestock of the rich eats the bread of the poor" illustrates this disastrous correlation.

II. DESTRUCTION OF
THE ENVIRONMENT

The inefficiency of meat production means that demands for fertile soil become ever greater. Achieved using massive amounts of chemicals, e.g., artificial fertilizers and pesticides, this has devastating consequences for the environment (for example, contamination of groundwater) and poses serious health risks for people (for example, increased incidence of cancer).

In order to produce the large amounts of meat which are consumed today, large numbers of animals are required. And large numbers of animals produce large amounts of excrement, which in turn has a negative ecological impact: poisoning groundwater and damaging forests as a result of emissions of ammonia gases.

The reclamation of land for cattle farming is one of the main reasons for the destruction of the tropical rainforest. This in turn causes flooding and drought and exacerbates the greenhouse effect. Other alarming ecological consequences include the immense waste of energy and water (for example, in heating stalls, storing meat, and cleaning slaughterhouses).

III. DISEASE

The negative ecological implications of meat production pose considerable health risks for people. Moreover, the consumption of meat itself represents a health problem. Numerous dietary studies carried out around the world conclude unanimously that the less meat you eat, the healthier you live.

Diseases which are significantly more common among meat eaters than vegetarians include gall stones, colonic cancer, breast cancer, gout, and kidney failure. The dramatic increase in susceptibility to coronary heart disease is particularly conspicuous. Against the background of such research results, the U.S. Committee for Responsible Medicine has now classified meat a luxury food instead of a staple.

IV. ANIMAL SUFFERING

Those most immediately affected by our meat eating are, of course, the animals which lose their lives. It is consistent, therefore, that moral considerations regarding meat eating concentrate on its impact on animals. In the philosophical approaches of Tom Regan and Peter Singer, meat eating is described in terms of a disregard for animal rights and a violation of the principle of equality.

In the rearing, transporting, and slaughtering of animals, their basic rights, such as the right to life and freedom from injury, are culpably neglected. In contravention of the principle of equality, interests shared by humankind and animals are not considered to be of equal moral importance. Instead, animal interests are either deemed markedly less important or not taken into account at all: practically all animal interests are sacrificed for the sake of a single human interest, namely, that of enjoying a particular culinary experience.

The suffering of animals stands out in the work of both Singer and Regan. Richard Ryder makes suffering the central concept of his philosophy. But the issue of suffering has also come to the fore in the wider public discussion of the moral admissibility of meat eating. There is increasing consensus that the conditions prevalent in intensive factory farming, which cause suffering among animals, are morally questionable and worthy of practical improvement.

However, in recognizing this, people usually overlook the fact that this realization does not resolve the moral issue raised by meat eating in itself. Since, as Peter Singer emphasizes, the decisive factor is not how animals *could* be treated, but how they are *in fact* treated.

In this context attention is often drawn to organic farming, which sets out to guarantee more natural treatment of animals according to their species. Firstly, it is important to realize that nowhere in the world is organic farming a decisive factor in overall farming practices. Above all, when compared with conventional farming, it represents a diminution, but by no means an elimination, of animal suffering.

On the one hand, organic stock raising is not pursued primarily out of any moral consideration for animals, but for practical reasons concerned with people: the production of more flavorsome, healthier, "organic" meat. Most importantly, however, people usually forget that these animals also have to be slaughtered before their meat lands on our plates. As a rule, this certainly does not take place "organically"—whatever that might mean in this context—but "normally"; as the name indicates, organic stock raising differs from conventional stock raising mainly as regards the rearing of the livestock, not its slaughter. This is in keeping with its primary objective as already mentioned, the production of quality meat for the human consumer.

At this point, people often raise the objection that at least these animals have a good life until they are slaughtered. A strange and hardly consistent moral argument: viewed logically, it corresponds with the defense offered by the mass murderer who attempts to justify his crimes by insisting, "In selecting my victims, I always made sure that they had had a good life!"

The question remains as to whether it is in principle possible to produce meat free of suffering. Helmut F. Kaplan points out that, ultimately and for psychological reasons, such an undertaking seems doomed to failure. Even if all the technical and organizational conditions for meat production free of suffering were fulfilled (sufficient staff, truly "free ranging" animals, facilities for a quick and surprising death, etc.), such "ideal" meat production could only be realized by "true human monsters": those who looked after the animals would have to do so lovingly while knowing that this loving treatment will eventually end in the—objectively completely unnecessary—slaughter of their charges. This would be moral and psychological schizophrenia, a state which hardly anyone would be able to bear, comparable with stroking a cat affectionately one minute, and then wringing its neck the next.

V. CONCLUSION

The facts, issues, and points of discussion raised here prove that meat eating does in fact represent a moral problem. The global trend toward a vegetarian lifestyle shows that meat eating is increasingly considered problematic. It would be wrong, however, to see this height-ened awareness exclusively as an achievement of our times. The Greek philosopher Plutarch recognized the core of the problem some 2000 years ago: But for the sake of some little mouthful of flesh we deprive an animal of the sun and light, and of that proportion of life and time it was born into the world to enjoy.

Also See the Following Articles

AGRICULTURAL ETHICS • ANIMAL RIGHTS • BIOCENTRISM • ENVIRONMENTAL JUSTICE • LAND-USE ISSUES • PAINISM • SPECIESISM

Acknowledgment

Translated from the German by Bernadette Boyle.

Bibliography

Akers, K. (1989). *A vegetarian sourcebook: The nutrition, ecology and ethics of a natural food diet.* Denver: Vegetarian Press.

Kaplan, H. F. (1993). *Leichenschaus. Ethische Gründe für eine vegetarische Ernährung.* Reinbek bei Hamburg: Rowohlt Taschenbuch Verlag.

Regan, T. (1983). *The case for animal rights.* Berkeley: Univ. of California Press.

Robbins, J. (1992). *May all be fed: Diet for a new world.* New York: William Morrow.

Ryder, R. D. (1992). *Painism: Ethics, animal rights and environmentalism.* Cardiff: Univ. of Wales College.

Sapontzis, S. F. (1987). *Morals, reason and animals.* Philadelphia: Temple Univ. Press.

Singer, P. (1990). *Animal liberation* (2nd ed.). New York: Random House.

VETERINARY ETHICS

Bernard E. Rollin

Colorado State University

GLOSSARY

companion animal Politically correct term for "pet animal."

confinement agriculture High-technology agriculture that essentially replaces labor with capital, and applies industrial methods to agriculture.

consensus ethic The views of right and wrong, good and bad, accepted (and enforced) in society.

ethical relativism The view that there is no absolute right and wrong or good and bad, and that these values vary from society to society or even person to person.

ethics Beliefs about right and wrong, good and bad, justice and injustice (ethics₁). Also, a rational critique of such beliefs (ethics₂).

extra-label drug use The use of a drug in a manner, or for a species, not specified by the manufacturer.

food animal An animal raised for human consumption.

husbandry agriculture Traditional agriculture, in which animals are raised in open spaces and conditions that suit their biological needs and natures.

laboratory animal An animal used in research or testing.

VETERINARY ETHICS is arguably the most interesting branch of professional ethics, a field including medical ethics, legal ethics, research ethics, and indeed the ethics of all fields performing a specialized function in society and demanding specialized knowledge.

Veterinarians, like human medical practitioners, have special privileges in society, such as prescribing drugs and doing surgery, and also, they thereby incur special ethical obligations in virtue of their social role. Veterinary ethics is the study of these ethical obligations. In addition to obligations to clients, society, peers and the profession, and self, all of which veterinarians share with physicians, veterinarians also have obligations to animals. Given that society has only recently begun to pay attention to the moral status of animals and has not yet articulated a full ethic for animal treatment, the latter obligation is the most problematic and difficult aspect of veterinary ethics.

I. SOCIAL, PERSONAL, AND PROFESSIONAL ETHICS

Veterinary ethics is arguably the most interesting branch of professional ethics, a field including medical ethics, legal ethics, research ethics, and indeed the ethics of all fields performing a specialized function in society and demanding specialized knowledge and special privileges. What makes veterinary ethics especially interesting is the prominence therein of the issue of human obligations to animals, an issue society has only recently begun to engage. Before focusing on these unique features of veterinary medical ethics, it is important to remind ourselves of some generic features of ethics. Understanding these key notions will help to place veterinary ethics into the proper context of ethics in general.

In the first place, it is important to distinguish two different senses of the term "ethics" that are, unfortunately, often confused. To help avoid confusion, we shall draw a distinction between ethics$_1$ and ethics$_2$. Ethics$_1$, or morals, is the set of principles that governs our views of right and wrong, good and bad, just and unjust, fair and unfair. We learn ethics$_1$ from a variety of sources, from the time we are children—parents and other family members, peers, teachers, church, books, magazines, films, radio, and television, friends, and so on.

Ethics$_2$, on the other hand, is the study of these principles. This activity can and does include ferreting out inconsistencies among the principles, drawing out unnoticed implications that can logically be deduced from ethics$_1$ principles, and attempting to provide a justification for why we should adhere to some, or indeed *any,* ethics$_1$ principles. Ethics$_2$ is therefore a branch of philosophy. What we are doing in this article is in fact ethics$_2$, or philosophy of ethics. In such an activity, we look at the logic of ethics. We will shortly provide examples of how ethics$_2$ operates in a number of different areas of ethics$_1$.

First, however, one must distinguish three major areas of ethics$_1$—social ethics, personal ethics, and professional ethics. *Social ethics,* or social consensus ethics, are the consensus principles adopted by or accepted by society at large, taught to the young, and codified in laws and regulations. Laws, ranging from laws against murder and rape, to laws against discrimination, to local zoning ordinances that prohibit bars or pornographic book stores in school zones, reflect (and help teach) the social ethical consensus "written large," in Plato's lovely phrase. There obviously must be a good deal of social consensus ethics in a society, or there would be chaos and anarchy. No one would know what to expect from anyone else; we could not adjust our behavior to one another; and above all there would be no "glue" of accepted mutual expectations to hold society together.

Personal ethics is what is left to the discretion of the individual by society, or more accurately, what is left to his or her own set of principles of right and wrong. Personal ethics begins where social ethics is silent. For example, such matters as whether and to whom one gives charity, how many children one has, or whether or not one adheres to a religious tradition, are all left to an individual's personal ethic in our society, although not in all societies.

Over the course of time, areas may move from the purview of social ethics to that of personal ethics or vice versa. Excellent examples of such movement are readily available. Beginning in the 1960s in the United States, sexual behavior began to move out of the area of social control into the realm of personal ethics—laws against homosexuality, adultery, cohabitation, oral sex, and the like began to disappear. In contrast, in a social change highly relevant to veterinary medicine, beginning during roughly the same period issues of animal treatment, animal pain and suffering, and animal husbandry, which were traditionally left to one's personal ethic (except for deliberate cruelty), increasingly entered the purview of the social ethic; hence the new federal laws regulating the treatment of animals in scientific research that were passed in 1985.

Generally, something is taken over by the social ethic from personal ethics when leaving it to the latter seems to be leading to injustice and unfairness. During the 1950s, to whom one rented or sold one's own property, or who one hired in one's business, were paradigmatic examples of personal choice. But when society saw that this resulted in major unfairness for Blacks and others, it took control of these areas.

What, then, is *professional ethics*? Members of a profession are first and foremost members of society, and thus are bound by the consensus social ethic not to steal, murder, and so on. However, veterinarians, like physicians, attorneys, and other professionals, perform a special and vital function in society. This function involves special situations that ordinary people do not face, and it warrants special privileges, for example, dispensing medicines and performing surgery. Democratic societies assume that professionals understand the ethical issues that they confront better than society does as a whole, and thus generally leave it to such professionals to set up their own rules of conduct. In other words, the social ethic gives general rules, whereas the subclasses of society comprising professionals are asked to develop their own ethic to cover the special situations they deal with daily. As a result of this situation, professional ethics stands midway between social and personal ethics, because it neither applies to all members of society nor are its main components left strictly to individuals. It is, for example, a general rule of medical ethics but not a law for psychiatrists not to have sex with their patients.

Professionals do need freedom from external regulation by society to do their job. But with the privilege of autonomy comes an onerous responsibility for professionals to keep their own house in order in a way that accords with the consensus social ethic. Failure to do this results in society making rules for professionals without fully understanding the area in question. Veterinarians, for example, came very close to losing the indispensable privilege of extra-label drug use when society questioned whether they were abusing it. The human health care profession may well be regulated because many in society see its behavior as out of step with the social ethic; for example, when hospitals turn patients away if they do not have insurance.

These are the main subdivisions of ethics. Each can be rationally criticized by an ethics$_2$ activity.

Consider the social: Those of us who are over 40 have lived through a period of social-ethical self-examination regarding our treatment of Blacks. We were taught from the time that we were children that all humans should be treated equally regardless of race, creed, or color. Yet we also knew that Black people were treated quite differently, most clearly in the segregated states. The society, at the instigation of rational critics, reasoned that separate was inherently unequal, and thus that segregation, however widely practiced, was incompatible with our consensus ethic. Indeed, if the social ethic could not be rationally criticized, we could make no social progress.

By the same token, one can criticize personal ethics. As I said earlier, what one believes religiously is a matter of personal ethics. Yet one can still rationally criticize the content of another's beliefs. For example, I often ask my audiences how many of them are Christians and, if they are, to hold up their right hands. I also ask the same audiences how many of them are ethical relativists, explaining that an ethical relativist is a person who believes that there are no objective ethical truths; that everyone's opinion is equally valid. I ask the relativists to hold up their left hands. Many people end up holding up both hands. But this is *logically* impossible. One cannot be a Christian and a relativist at the same time, because a Christian must believe that certain things are absolutely right and wrong, for example, the Ten Commandments, whereas a relativist asserts that nothing is absolutely right and wrong.

Finally, one can rationally criticize professional ethics in many ways. Two examples come to mind. In the mid-1970s I wrote some articles criticizing veterinary ethics, as embodied in the AVMA Code of Ethics, for failing to deal with many of the issues society expected veterinary ethics to deal with, for example, whether one should euthanize a healthy animal for owner convenience, when one should control pain in animals, and whether veterinarians had a social obligation to lead in changing practices that hurt animals, and instead devoting much attention to questions of intraprofessional etiquette—how big one's sign could be, what form one's yellow pages advertisement could take, whether or not one could advertise, and so on. Eventually, society got tired of the bickering about advertising, and the decision as to its acceptability was made by the courts, not by veterinarians.

A second example concerns the treatment of animals in veterinary teaching. Also beginning in the 1970s, I attempted to persuade veterinary educators that, although how they treated animals had essentially been left by society to the discretion of their professional and personal ethics, their behavior was not in accord with emerging social ethics on animal treatment, but was in fact at odds with it. If society knew about some of the practices that were rife in veterinary education, such as the multiple use of animals for surgery teaching, (up to 20 operative procedures on the same animal in some schools), or the failure to provide these animals with proper postoperative care or analgesia, then society would appropriate the treatment of animals in teaching into the social ethic, no longer leaving it to the professionals. Sure enough, that is what occurred, and what needed to occur. Furthermore, it was easy to get veterinary educators to realize that there were no morally relevant differences between client-owned animals and the pound animals with which they taught practice surgery. Both were capable of pain and suffering, which mattered equally to *them*. In addition, they came to realize that such use of teaching animals was brutalizing to students, creating cynicism and callousness, not the sensitivity educators wished to instill.

Now that we have seen that ethics$_1$ is subject to rational criticism at all levels—social, personal, and professional—we can flag major concerns pertaining to veterinary ethics in particular.

II. ANALYZING ETHICAL ISSUES IN VETERINARY MEDICINE

In interesting ways, dealing with ethical issues is analogous to dealing with medical problems. To diagnose a disease, one must be sure that one has taken cognizance of all relevant symptoms. And one must diagnose before one can treat. By the same token, to deal with ethical issues, one must take cognizance of all morally relevant components of the situation. Failure to do so can lead to a very distorted view of the case, and to an inappropriate moral decision.

In my experience "misdiagnosing" the ethical components of a situation is among the greatest impediments to resolving ethical issues in veterinary medicine. This in turn occurs because we perceive with our expectations, beliefs, prejudices, theories, and training as well as our five senses. It is easy to prove this to veterinary students. I ask the class for a four letter word for a funny story which word begins with "J". They say "joke." I then ask them what one does with a cigarette. They say "smoke." I follow this with a request for the name of a cola drink in a red can. They say "Coke." I then ask for a word for what one does when one puts dirty laundry in a tub, and they say "soak." Finally, I ask them to give me another word for the white of an egg. They invariably say "yolk" instead of "albumen."

A human physician has provided an excellent example of how perceiving with one's expectations leads to mistakes in medicine. As a young intern in the 1940s in a big city hospital, he did emergency room duty. Senior clinicians from all areas of medicine would serve as advisors to the young physicians on weekends. One Saturday night, a patient came in complaining of severe thoracic pain. The clinician, a cardiologist, immediately began an elaborate differential diagnostic regimen for various heart problems. As he ordered test after test, the young physician struggled to get his attention and, when he finally succeeded, meekly pointed out that the patient was showing all of the classical signs of appendicitis!

The way this phenomenon works to the detriment of identifying ethical issues is tellingly revealed in the following case which occurred at my own veterinary school. A man brought a small comatose dog with a head injury into a veterinary school clinic. He freely admitted, and even boasted, that he had struck the dog in the head with a frying pan because it barked too much. When the dog did not regain consciousness, and the man's wife became upset, he took the dog to his regular practitioner. The veterinarian advised him to take the dog to the veterinary school hospital. The dog died there, and the animal's body was brought to necropsy and presented as a case to a group of students by a pathology instructor. Coincidentally, one of the veterinary students in that class was an animal control officer, among whose duties was investigating cruelty

complaints. With the instructor's permission, the student took the client's name from the file and began to investigate the case, phoning the client's home and speaking with his wife. The client became irate and complained to both the referring veterinarian, and the veterinary school clinician who had taken his case, that his right to privacy had been violated. The private practitioner and the veterinary school referral clinician in turn were furious with the student. The student was frightened, worried about the effect of the incident on his academic and subsequent career, and sought help.

What moral conflicts and problems does this case raise? Initially, the referring practitioner, the veterinary school clinician, and some administrators saw only one issue—the betrayal of client confidentiality by the student. As the case evolved, administrators were also troubled by the involvement of the pathologist who had "betrayed" the identity of the client. Only after much dialogue with an ethicist, the pathologist, and the student did the parties begin to realize that there were many other concurrent issues.

First, there was an animal welfare issue: The client should not be allowed to fatally beat an animal with impunity. In addition, there was a social or moral obligation to report the occurrence of a crime and, particularly, the same sort of moral obligation (now also a legal one in human medicine) as exists for health care professionals to report suspected child abuse. The pathologist argued that veterinarians ought to treat cases of suspected animal abuse the same as other health care professionals do cases of suspected child abuse. Furthermore, there was the moral (and legal) question of whether one could invoke confidentiality in a public teaching hospital, where it is implicit that cases will be discussed with students as part of their learning process. Finally, the pathologist argued that, as a veterinary teaching institution, the school had a high moral obligation not to condone that which society as a whole has recognized as immoral and illegal.

Some veterinarians argued that the pathologist was within his rights to reveal the name, but that the student ought not to have acted upon the information. To this point, the student replied that, as a law officer, he had a sworn duty (moral obligation) to enforce the law. Some veterinarians hypothesized that if confidentiality were not strictly observed, abusers of animals would not bring animals in for treatment. A controversy also arose over the fact that the school clinician had at least obliquely threatened the student with recriminations when he came to the clinic. Others worried that the information about the case and these issues had not been sent back to the referring veterinarian for that party to handle. The issue of a conflict of interest between being a veterinary student and serving with animal control was also raised.

Ultimately, the situation was resolved, at least for the future, by the university's drafting a formal policy that suspected abuse cases of this sort would automatically be reported to the school and government authorities. One of the valuable features of the case was its dramatic teaching value in demonstrating just how complex a single ethical problem or case can be.

III. FIVE TYPES OF ETHICAL OBLIGATIONS IN VETERINARY MEDICINE

The best way to assure that one is seeing all aspects of a case is to engage in dialogue about it with a wide variety of people with differing perspectives. Unfortunately, like many other professionals, veterinarians are trained to be most comfortable, socially and intellectually, with others of their own profession. Veterinary education isolates veterinary students from the university at large, and works to create a predictable corps of "professionals." As a result many veterinarians seek counsel from other veterinarians of similar age and background, thereby minimizing the chances of getting radically new perspectives on issues and cases.

In the absence of the opportunity for dialogue, there is a procedure for maximizing the likelihood of identifying unnoticed ethical components of a veterinary situation. Whenever one encounters a situation that one senses has ethical nuances, one should proceed to examine the case in terms of each of the following five types of ethical "pulls" that veterinarians experience:

A. Obligations to the Client

Obviously, veterinarians owe an obligation to clients who hire them. This obligation does not, of course, always trump all others, but is usually a major component in ethical decision making.

B. Moral Obligations to Peers and the Profession

This, too, is obvious and important, so important, in fact, that for many years it constituted the bulk of what veterinarians thought of as veterinary ethics: Does one advertise? Does one criticize a colleague?

C. Moral Obligations to Society in General

These include such duties as protecting public health, being expected by society to lead in animal welfare matters, and so on.

D. Moral Obligations to Self

This is an extremely neglected but nonetheless significant moral vector. Clearly, veterinarians have an obligation to themselves and their families to spend time at home, allow for recreation, not live under constant stress, and so on.

E. Moral Obligations to the Animal

This is the most difficult and most interesting branch of veterinary medical ethics, in virtue of the fact that social and professional ethics has, until very recently, been silent on articulating these obligations. Thus most veterinarians loathe euthanizing an animal merely for owner convenience, yet the consensus social ethic as hitherto embodied in law sees animals as property. Until very recently, the social ethic was silent on moral obligations to animals except for a prohibition on deliberate cruelty.

Obviously, any combination of such conflicting obligations can arise in ethically charged cases. An excellent representative sample can be found in the columns on veterinary medical ethics I have written monthly for the *Canadian Veterinary Journal* since 1991. In this column, all cases are real cases encountered by veterinarians, who send them in to be analyzed and discussed by readers and myself. The situations described run the gamut from food animal to laboratory animal to companion animal, and include such issues as clients demanding euthanasia for a cat who sprays in the house; a farmer who leaves a pregnant sow with a broken leg untreated because he cannot afford the labor to treat her; a veterinarian who recommends animal heartworm injections in an area free of heartworms; the validity of alternative surgical training; the proper response to a colleague using homeopathic therapy, and so on. In each column, the cases are presented, analyzed, and a resolution is suggested. Readers also provide comment.

IV. TWO MODELS FOR VETERINARY OBLIGATIONS TO ANIMALS

In any case, the issue of a veterinarian's obligation to the animal itself is clearly the most problematic aspect of veterinary ethics, because the social ethic has traditionally virtually ignored that issue. In veterinarians' personal ethics, there were two possible guiding ideals according to which veterinarians could articulate their obligation to the animal. At one end of the spectrum, one could see oneself as analogous to a garage mechanic. If a person brings a car into a garage mechanic, the mechanic does strictly what the owner decrees, and is morally bound to do no more. If the owner does not wish to spend money to repair, the mechanic's responsibility ends. On the other end of the spectrum, the veterinarian may see his or her role as more analogous to that of a pediatrician. If a pediatrician tells a parent "It will cost $2000 to cure your child," the parent cannot say, "So what, let the kid die, I'll make another one." The pediatrician recognizes the moral status of the child as independent of the parent's desire, and pediatricians in fact historically worked assiduously to raise the status of children in the social consensus ethic and in the laws mirroring it.

Most veterinarians in my experience lean more toward the pediatrician model. With the society recognizing little moral status for animals, this personal ethical predilection clashed with the social ethic. In the last two decades, however, society has become increasingly concerned with elevating the moral status of animals.

V. VETERINARIANS AND THE NEW SOCIAL ETHIC FOR ANIMALS

Recall from what we have said thus far that professions should constantly monitor the social consensus ethic, and adjust to accord with the social ethic as it changes, ideally in an anticipatory way, so that the profession can lead in responsible ethical change related to its activities, and not be caught unawares. In this way, the profession can not only preserve its autonomy, but it can also deploy its special expertise to assure that ethical change occurs in a rational, informed fashion.

Western societies are dramatically changing their consensus ethic for animal treatment. Plainly, veterinarians should be leaders in this area, because they understand both the needs and interests of those who use animals, and the needs and interests of animals. It is also clear that society expects veterinarians to lead—U.S. federal laws for research animals put the responsibility for proper animal care and use on the shoulders of laboratory animal veterinarians, as does British law. One veterinary school dean in an agricultural state with a good deal of its economy tied up in confinement

animal agriculture related a very enlightening anecdote to me. On assuming the deanship, he immediately sent letters to all major users of veterinary school services asking where the school was doing well and where improvement was needed. The response from the agricultural community was telling. The farmers felt that the school was doing an excellent job in strictly scientific and medical areas, but had failed to monitor changing social ethics regarding animal treatment. "We expect veterinarians to tell us when we are pushing the animals harder than society will accept," said the producers, "yet veterinarians have simply uncritically accepted all of our production methods, and then we are blind-sided by social change." By the same token, laboratory animal veterinarians were reluctant to support the very legislation that empowered them to do their job.

In the same vein, over the past decade Congress has asked organized veterinary medicine to define the emerging social ethical issues pertaining to genetic engineering of animals as well as the ethical and practical issues pertaining to animal pain and suffering and their control. Given that organized veterinary medicine was taken by surprise by both of these requests, it responded very well. The point is, it should not have been taken by surprise. After all, the task of defining ethically acceptable euthanasia has fallen to veterinary medicine for many years.

In sum, veterinary medicine must become a leader, not a follower, in developing and applying the emerging social ethic for animal treatment. This ethic has become necessary because, in essence, the nature of animal use has changed significantly. The major use of animals in society was and is, of course, agricultural. Before the mid-twentieth century, the essence of agriculture was husbandry. People who used animals put those animals into environments for which they were evolved and adapted and then augmented their natural ability to cope with additional food, shelter, protection from predators, and so on. The Biblical shepherd who leads the animals to green pastures is the lovely paradigm case of this approach. Producers did well if and only if animals did well. No producer could, for example, have attempted to raise 10,000 egg-laying chickens in one building—he would have had all his animals succumb to disease in weeks. Self-interest guaranteed proper animal treatment. The only explicit ethic needed in society was a prohibition against willful, intentional, sadistic infliction of unnecessary pain and suffering on animals—the anticruelty ethic.

In contrast, when "animal husbandry" departments symbolically became "animal science" departments in the 1940s and 1950s, industry replaced husbandry, and the values of efficiency and productivity above all else entered agricultural thinking and practice. Whereas traditional agriculture was about putting square pegs in square holes, round pegs in round holes, and creating as little friction as possible while doing so, "technological sanders" such as antibiotics and vaccines allowed us to produce animals in environments that did not suit their natures but were convenient for us. For example, we could now raise 10,000 chickens in one building.

Similarly, the rise of significant amounts of research and toxicity testing on animals in the mid-twentieth century also differs from the fairness of husbandry agriculture—we inflict disease on animals, wound, burn, and poison them for our benefit, with no benefit to them. Although both confinement agriculture and animal research generate significant amounts of animal suffering, they do not fall under the traditional ethic of anticruelty, and thus society seeks a new ethic to control animal suffering arising from nonsadistic motives.

This social concern has in turn been reflected in increasing demands for new laws regulating many areas of animal treatment, including hunting, trapping, entertainment, and most important animal research. Whereas the treatment of animals in animal research was traditionally left to researchers, in 1985 two new federal laws designed to minimize animal suffering were passed, in essence demonstrating society's desire to change the social ethic to protect animals. Numerous new laws based on this new concern are regularly being proposed and it is affecting animal husbandry without being legislated; the extensive efforts over the past decade to create zoos that respect animal natures give testimony to the spread of the new ethic. Furthermore, it appears that society is actually willing to give up certain animal uses and conveniences for the sake of the animals; the abandonment of the Canadian seal hunt, the massive social rejection of furs, and the rejection of cosmetic testing on animals by many companies, all without legislation, attest to the growing hold of the new ethic.

The new laboratory animals laws are especially relevant to veterinary medicine, for these laws charged laboratory animal veterinarians with being the people responsible for implementing the laws. Correlatively, the remuneration (and job satisfaction) of veterinarians in this area rose precipitously. This is a model for what is likely to happen in all areas of animal use. Society will demand more and more legalized protection for animals. It also sees veterinarians as the natural animal advocates. And as the status of animals rises in society, so too will that of the veterinarians who care for them. Thus the changing social ethic can enable veterinarians both to do good and to do well, provided they forthrightly embrace it and utilize their expertise to help define and implement its application.

Also See the Following Articles

AGRICULTURAL ETHICS • ANIMAL RIGHTS • MEDICAL ETHICS, HISTORY OF • RESEARCH ETHICS

Bibliography

Kesel, M. L. (1995). Veterinary ethics. In *The encyclopedia of bioethics*, pp. 2520–2525. New York: Macmillan.

Rollin, B. E. (1978). Updating veterinary medical ethics. *Journal of the American Veterinary Medical Association* 173, 8, 1015–1018.

Rollin, B. E. (1988). Veterinary and animal ethics. In J. E. Wilson (Ed.). *Law and Ethics of the veterinary profession*, pp. 24–48. Yardley, PA: Priority Press.

Rollin, B. E. (1991 ff). Veterinary Medical Ethics. A monthly column in *The Canadian Veterinary Journal*, analyzing real ethically problematic cases sent to the journal by veterinarians.

Rollin, B. E. (1993). *Animal rights and human morality* (2nd ed.). Buffalo, NY: Prometheus Books.

Tannenbaum, J. (1989). *Veterinary ethics*. Baltimore, MD: Williams and Wilkins.

VICTIMLESS CRIMES

Eric Heinze
Queen Mary and Westfield College, University of London

GLOSSARY

alienable rights Rights, such as certain rights in property or contract, that the possessor is free to transfer or to relinquish.

civil law The law governing relationships or transactions between private persons in areas such as property, contract, personal injury, or domestic relations.

consent Agreement given, either expressly or by implication, to assume, exercise, forego, or modify one's rights, liberties, or obligations. As to legal rights and obligations, invalid, that is, without legal effect, if given under duress or fraud, without mental competence, or without legal competence (e.g., by a minor).

criminal law The law governing public obligations and prohibitions placed upon persons by the state on behalf of society as a whole, and typically prescribing punitive sanctions for violations.

harm Any injury or wrongdoing of a physical, psychological, or moral nature.

inalienable rights Rights that cannot be transferred or relinquished by their possessor. In classical liberalism, these include so-called fundamental human rights, for example, in life, liberty, or property, which can be abridged by the state only with some appropriate rationale and with procedural safeguards.

NEMO PUNITUR SINE INJURIA, no one is punished except for wrongdoing. It would seem that a just society should punish only those acts that cause harm. Yet many acts have, at one time or another, met with penal sanctions despite the speculative nature of the harm they cause. Drug or alcohol consumption, loitering, gambling, cockfighting, hate speech, blasphemy, possession of weapons, euthanasia, flag burning, smoking, spitting, contraception, abortion, nudity, indecent exposure, erotic art, obscenity, pornography, prostitution, adultery, polygamy, homosexual as well as heterosexual "sodomy" (oral or anal intercourse), sexual sadomasochism or bestiality all provide vivid examples. If nontherapeutic consumption of drugs is harmful for some people but harmless for others, when, if ever, should it be prohibited? If greater incidence of death or bodily injury results from boxing than from public nudity, should the latter be legal and the former illegal? If eating sweets causes more overall damage to health than failure to wear seat belts, which should government punish? The distinction between "victimizing" and "victimless" acts raises questions as to (1) the definition of harm, (2) the persons or entities who are harmed, (3) the gravity of various harms, and (4) the appropriate forms of redress. These issues cannot be resolved by purely objective or empirical criteria. Any resolution assumes some broader legal, ethical, political, economic, or social theory. A number of standard theories have long competed with each other. These include liberalism, utilitarianism, communitarianism, paternalism, and republicanism. Each school provides cogent possibilities for delimiting the legitimate reach of criminal law. Yet each is subject to ambiguities and contradictions.

I. PROBLEMS OF DEFINITION

A. Harm as a Basis for Legal Prohibitions

The concept of crime presupposes a concept of harm. Throughout history, however, jurists have avoided explaining exactly what constitutes harm for purposes of defining the elements of a crime. Does harm necessarily mean bodily injury or pain? Clearly not. Theft is a classic crime. Does harm necessarily entail emotional distress? Psychological harm can indeed suffice as a component of the crime, as with crimes of extortion or stalking, for which the mere threat of force or intimidation suffices to constitute the act. Yet most crimes are subject to identical penalties whether their victims react with agony or apathy (although, for some crimes, emotional impact on the victim or the victim's relatives or dependents can affect sentencing or can augment liability in civil law). If neither physical nor emotional pain are necessary ingredients of harm, then what is? What is the least harmful ingredient necessary to constitute harm? Offense to the sensibilities of a civilized society? Yet *Ulysses* and *Les Fleurs du mal* have caused such offense, incurring prohibitions in one generation that were ridiculed by the next.

In addition to the problem of defining harm, there are questions about who suffers it. Should harm incurred by someone with informed and willing consent, as may be the case with boxing or assisted suicide, nevertheless justify criminal liability for the person who caused or assisted in it? What if the two are the same person, as in the case with unassisted suicide or drug use? What if there is disagreement about whether a given entity, such as a fetus, can be a person, hence a victim, at all? Moreover, should harm only justify criminal proscription when incurred by some specifically identifiable person, or should some acts, such as loitering or gambling, be penalized for the harm they do to society on the whole, regardless of whether harm is caused to some specific individual? If society as a whole can count as a victim, then must the harm caused to it be mate-

rial—based, for example, on the statistical likelihood of other criminal activity ensuing from acts such as loitering or gambling? Or does society's moral outrage, such as that still caused in some countries by private, adult, consensual homosexual sex, provide an equally valid basis for a criminal proscription?

B. Standard Definitions of Crime

Standard definitions of crime barely advance the inquiry. *Black's Law Dictionary* (5th Ed., 1979) offers two. One defines a crime as "an act committed or omitted in violation of a law forbidding or commanding it." Yet that description is circular: a crime is an act that violates the criminal law, and the criminal law is the sum total of recognized crimes. Another defines a crime as "any act done in violation of those duties which an individual owes to the community." Such a definition does not, however, explain what those duties are. If they are duties not to cause harm, then the question as to the nature of harm remains. If they are duties to obey the law, then this definition is as circular as the first. The American Law Institute Model Penal Code Official Draft (1962), although eager to define such ingredients of crime as "act," "action," "actor," "omission," or "conduct," avoids defining the term "crime" itself. Legal doctrine has resisted formulating some *sine qua non* of criminal acts, which would distinguish, in self-evident fashion, those acts that do properly constitute crimes from those that do not, either on the basis of harm or of any other element. Law offers no algorithm by which, for any "truly just" legal system, one would know a priori which acts would and would not properly constitute crimes. Throughout most of history crime has largely been whatever those in power have said it is. Yet that "might makes right" principle has never sat comfortably with post-Enlightenment liberal democracies. Fundamental to liberal democracy is that laws should be made by deliberative government and should not be arbitrary or capricious. They should have some rational basis. It is this need for a rational basis that brings the concept of harm to the forefront of the problem of victimless crimes.

II. THEORETICAL PROBLEMS

A. Classical Liberalism and Utilitarianism

Where law equivocates often philosophy ventures. The most famous philosopher to attempt a theory of criminal acts based on notions of those acts' specific, demonstrable harmfulness was John Stuart Mill. In his essay, *On Liberty* (1859), Mill observed that, throughout history, nations were largely in agreement in punishing at least some forms of clearly harmful acts, such as murder or assault. "[B]ut if we except a few of the most obvious cases," he continued, acts that do not so clearly entail some specific, demonstrable harm create a dilemma "which least progress has been made in resolving. No two ages, and scarcely any two countries, have decided it alike; and the decision of one age or country is a wonder to another."

Mill proposed a solution to the problem of victimless crimes consisting of "one very simple principle" to which he nevertheless lent two different formulations. The first echoes the philosophy for which Mill is most noted, utilitarianism: "the sole end for which mankind are warranted, individually or collectively, in interfering with the liberty of action of any of their number is self-protection." The second, on the other hand, stresses the language of classical liberalism: "the only purpose for which power can be rightfully exercised over any member of a civilized community, against his will, is to prevent harm to others."

The first formulation has suffered the fate of utilitarianism generally. It introduces a concept not only of individual but also of collective self-protection on which consensus would be difficult to achieve. Does collective self-protection entail only that which is necessary to the organic survival of a group, or does it extend to that group's sense of identity, to its sense of spiritual well-being? Under sufficiently precarious circumstances, for example, a work such as Salman Rushdie's *Satanic Verses* could sow such discord as to threaten the spiritual self-protection of a local, national, or even international collectivity. The criterion of collective self-protection suggests a "greatest good for the greatest number," despite inevitable disagreement about what that is.

In most contemporary debate the utilitarian formulation generally cedes to the classical liberal formulation. Contemporary inquiry emphasises harm rather than self-protection, in accordance with Mill's second formulation, although such a formulation is by no means unique to Mill. Article 2 of the French *Déclaration des droits de l'homme et du citoyen* (1789), another landmark document of classical liberalism, had already proclaimed, "Liberty consists in being able to do anything that does not harm others: thus, the exercise of the natural rights of every man has no bounds other than those that ensure to the other members of society the enjoyment of these same rights."

B. Varieties of Harm

If Mill's theory were to end here it would add little to the indeterminate or circular concepts of crime offered by the standard legal texts. In the second formulation of his general principle, Mill does not simply speak of acts that cause harm. He speaks of acts that cause harm *to others*. According to Mill, a harmful act may be perfectly lawful, as long as the "right" person is harmed, namely, someone who was willing to incur the harm. The issue of victimless crimes thus involves two distinct questions. The first question concerns the persons harmed: Assuming that an act does cause harm, should it nevertheless be lawful if it harms someone who has validly consented to it? The second question concerns the actual acts that cause harm: Assuming that an act does not cause harm, are there nevertheless grounds for making it unlawful?

The first question simply assumes that a given act causes harm. The second question, however, must be further subdivided. There are different kinds of harm, as is suggested by contrasting two simple examples. On the one hand, the physical, psychological, or material harms caused by acts such as murder, assault or theft are generally acknowledged; any disputes center largely around such issues as the frame of mind of the accused, permissible defenses or the appropriate form of punishment. On the other hand, acts such as failing to act with courtesy toward a neighbor or to show respect to one's parents can also cause harm, if only through an affront to another's status or dignity, as is acknowledged by age-old moral injunctions governing such situations. Although these kinds of harm would not generally be considered to be as grave as the former kinds, that does not mean that they cause no harm at all. The question is whether the difference between these two classes of harm is a difference in degree or a difference in kind. Is harm the same whenever it is caused, varying only in degrees of intensity? Or, despite the use of the word "harm" for both, do these two classes actually correspond to categorically different kinds of effects of the acts that cause them, such that all acts, once the context be known, would fall self-evidently either under one or under the other category?

Any suggestion that the difference is merely subjective, merely a matter of personal opinion, is belied by what law actually does. As a general matter, the legal systems of contemporary liberal-democratic societies punish murder and theft, but not lack of courtesy toward a neighbor or of respect toward one's parents ("courtesy" and "respect" understood, here, in the ordinary sense, and not encompassing special duties or so-called culpable omissions). Thus the two types of harm merit at least a rugged, approximate distinction, even if a transcendental principle that would distinguish them in all cases, for any "just" legal system, remains elusive. We can call the harm caused by the former acts *palpable harm,* which would consist of at least minimally significant physical, psychological, or material damage. We can call the harm caused by the latter acts *putative harm,* which would essentially encompass outrage or disapproval, including offense to deeply held values.

The terms "palpable" and "putative" are formulated here only for convenience. They are not current in traditional debate about victimless crimes. (Various writers, such as Kadish, Packer, Kaplan, Feinberg, von Hirsch, and Jareborg, have developed their own conceptual schemes.) Even a cursory inspection of these two categories suggests possible ambiguities. As to the definition of palpable harm, for example, it is not indicated when damage becomes "significant," let alone "minimally significant." Differences between "psychological damage" and "moral outrage" may also become nebulous, particularly in light of different persons' varying levels of sensitivity. Even more troubling, as examined in Part III *infra,* is the question of the link required between the act and the harm caused. Rules requiring the wearing of seat belts, for example, envisage only a probable, cumulative harm, and not individual harm in every instance of breach. The same holds true for rules governing environmental pollution, the cumulative effect of which may be very much in dispute. Yet once a concept of cumulative palpable harm is admitted, certain applications might dissolve any practical distinction between palpable and putative harms. Adultery or fornication, for example, might be proscribed for purposes of preventing venereal diseases. Indeed, such arguments have been proffered for maintaining bans or limits on homosexuality, particularly with reference to AIDS, precisely where there was some doubt about the cogency of arguments based only on putative harms. Acts such as blasphemy offer an extreme example. These might be banned merely because of the uproar, hence the prospect of violence and thus of palpable harm, that might occur, despite the fact that such reactions would be ensuing from a harm that originally was only putative.

Nevertheless, these potential ambiguities have not prevented voices in the debate from assuming some distinction between these two types of harms. Classical liberalism follows it closely, generally endorsing the proscription of acts causing palpable harm and rejecting the proscription of acts causing only putative harm. As a basic rule (some exceptions are noted below), classical liberalism would recognize only palpable harm, not putative harm, as harm at all for purposes of criminal prohibitions. Meanwhile theories that do advocate proscriptions on victimless acts do not necessarily attempt to contrive palpable harms out of putative ones. They may freely acknowledge that some acts do not cause any harm aside from moral outrage, but would nevertheless deem putative harm to count as legally actionable, moral outrage supplying sufficient grounds for punishment. Thus they, too, implicitly acknowledge the validity of some distinction between palpable and putative harms. Opponents of pornography or homosexuality, for example, may well offer empirical evidence of palpable harm to bolster their claims, but are also likely to cite ethical principles—principles that would govern even if no palpable harm could be adduced.

C. Law and Morality

Assuming that palpable harm justifies criminal sanction, the question then becomes whether putative harm does so. This formulation of the question restates one of the classic problems of law, namely, the relationship between law and morality. Briefly, the problem can be stated as follows. On the one hand, law and morality are not one and the same. Again, some widely held moral values, such as the opprobrium of murder, are generally subsumed by law while others, such as courtesy to neighbors, are not. On the other hand, law and morality are not utterly distinct. All rules of law, even "technical" rules governing, for example, time limitations on bringing law suits or filing rebuttals to the submissions of other parties, are, presumably, chosen on the basis of their desirability in contrast to alternatives. Such choices can be called moral if only because they are normative—because they assume some political order, even some minute aspect thereof, to be preferable to alternatives. The relationship between law and morality might be envisioned as two partially overlapping spheres. But then the question arises which elements lie within the overlap and which outside. Or the relationship could be envisioned as hierarchical, morality taking a number of forms of which law would be only one. But then the question arises which elements fall within, and which outside, of law as a subset of morality, and what relationships law maintains with other such subsets, such as politics or religion. (Indeed, whether religion is merely a "subset" of morality is itself subject to dispute, with important consequences for law.)

The relationship between substantive criminal law and morality has always been of special interest to the broader inquiry into the relationship between law and morals. The classification of crimes in terms of varieties of harm does not solve, but does formalize the problem. As the harmfulness of palpable harms is not generally in dispute, it generally becomes a sufficient justification for legal proscriptions; no further inquiry into the independent immorality of the corresponding acts becomes necessary. Those acts are immoral *because* they are, by common consensus, harmful. The loss of life caused by the act of murder, for example, generally provides sufficient grounds for penalizing murder, obviating further inquiry into whether the overall detrimental effect of that murder, or of murder generally, in society provides independent justification for the proscription. What characterizes putative harms, on the other hand, is the impossibility of separating harm from morals in this way. Unlike palpable harms, they do not, on the basis of harm caused, provide justification of criminal proscriptions independent of a distinct assessment of the morality of the acts at issue. An ascription of putative harm is *nothing but* an ascription of immorality.

The observation that the problem of victimless crimes involves the more general question of the relationship between law and morals has become a focal point of the contemporary debate. Barely a hundred years after Mill's philosophical excursus, the debate was taken up, impeccably intact, by two renowned jurists of Mill's own soil, Professor H. L. A. Hart and Sir Patrick Devlin. In the wake of a 1959 British government report (*The Wolfenden Report*) urging that private, adult, consensual homosexual conduct no longer be prohibited, the two men took opposing positions on how the government should respond. Although the debate took place in the legal literature over a period of several years, with occasional third voices joining in, full expositions can be found in Devlin's *The Enforcement of Morals* (1961) and Hart's *Law, Liberty and Morality* (1963). Each has become a classic statement of its respective position in the modern debate. Hart, following in the steps of Mill, generally denounced the use of the criminal law to prevent activities that cause no harm other than moral outrage. Devlin, on the other hand, attributed to law the vital role of maintaining values so deeply held as to form the fundamental moral fiber of society.

D. Communitarianism and Paternalism

Mill's liberalism, then, is not the only theory to inform the debate. Indeed, historically it is rather an aberration. In most cultures and at most times, lack of palpable harm to a specific, ascertainable victim has not sufficed

to shield from the criminal law acts otherwise deemed detrimental to society. Preliberal and antiliberal theories play an important and, historically, by far the dominant role. These include communitarianism and paternalism. Both offer justifications for penalizing at least some acts causing only putative harm.

Communitarianism challenges certain assumptions of classical liberalism as adequate bases for a just social and political order. It rejects the notion that civil society serves as nothing more than a well-ordered arena in which individuals may freely pursue their own interests as long as they do not harm others; in which persons may do positively evil things as long as no specific, palpable harm to others can be demonstrated. It rejects what it sees as a world of moral relativism, where "anything goes" and all individuals' ideas of good and evil are equally valid, where good and evil are nothing but matters of personal choice and preference. Liberalism's ostensible neutrality toward victimless crimes, from gambling to loitering to homosexuality, is seen as acquiescence, and acquiescence implies approval. With Hobbes's *Leviathan* (1651), the state purports to triumph over the *bellum omnium contra omnes*, the war of all against all in the brutal state of nature. Yet, in an unrestricted marketplace of morals as well as goods, it is, on the moral plane, that same brutal condition that reemerges. There is no moral order, only the moral chaos—the immorality—of countless private morals antagonistic to each other. Liberalism's relativism ensues from its individualism. We all become Cain, never our brothers' keepers.

For communitarian theories, the mission of civil society is not simply to keep people from injuring each other, but also positively to undertake to eliminate evil, private as well as public. The private *is* public. It is the mission of civil society to induce people to cooperate in realizing certain general human needs and goods that only can be achieved collectively. While the liberal asserts that, by definition, an act is not evil unless others unwillingly suffer some palpable harm, communitarians point to obscenity, pornography, promiscuity, hate speech, or drug use as harms to society as a whole, in the long run, even if discrete acts of palpable harm cannot be adduced.

Liberalism, however, insists that the good that emerges from such a social order is not necessarily the goodness of gambling or loitering per se, but rather the goodness of personal freedom to choose whether one wants to pursue such activities. Even if such acts are evil, the goodness of permitting them lies in the goodness of allowing the individual to come to the knowledge of their evil, rather than having it dictated within a legal order that obliges all to accept it on faith. The liberal ideal is the Enlightenment ideal. In the words of Milton, "though all the winds of doctrine were let loose to play upon the earth, so Truth be in the field, we do injuriously, by licensing and prohibiting to misdoubt her strength. Let her and Falsehood grapple: who ever knew Truth put to the worst, in a free and open encounter." Liberalism does not deny the existence of good and evil. It rejects only dictatorial means of reaching such judgments. In a wondrous clash of "isms," just as communitarianism would accuse liberalism of relativism and egoism, so would liberalism accuse communitarianism of absolutism and authoritarianism. Liberalism would condemn any impulse to decree good and evil beyond the bounds of palpable harm, imposing judgments of good and evil on others.

Paternalism is equally motivated by a critique of liberalism's shortcomings, but tends to emphasize more of a corrective of liberalism's defects than a fundamental rejection of liberalism. Paternalism assumes that ignorance, poverty, or some other incapacity can cause people to act contrary to their best interests, and thus recognizes a duty on the state to, as the standard formulation runs, protect persons from themselves. In civil law, for example, this means that persons may be relieved from contractual obligations to which they have given otherwise valid consent, as in the case of usury, if those obligations would entail excessive hardship. In areas of health, education, or social welfare, it generally connotes tax and transfer plans for the benefit of the materially disadvantaged. In criminal law, it means that the state may legitimately prohibit, say, drugs, gambling, or possession of certain firearms, not because these necessarily entail harm to persons involved with them, but simply because they may entail such harm if abused—a rationale that ostensibly, avoids the question of harm to society as a whole. To its friends, this is a welfare state, elevating our quality of life, caring about its citizens. To its foes, it is a nanny state, wagging its finger, telling us what to eat and drink, butting into every detail of our lives, refusing to let people make their own choices about their lives.

E. Left and Right

Liberalism and communitarianism are umbrella concepts. Each includes a variety of perspectives on the left as well as the right. Not all liberal theories are mutually compatible, nor are all communitarian theories. Nowhere are the mutual incompatibilities of theories under each umbrella more apparent than in those theories' approaches to victimless crimes.

Certainly, liberal ideas motivated the—in the context of their time—progressive politics of the Enlightenment, politics of antimonarchism, constitutionalism, disestablishment, free trade, and free transfer and development of property. Since that time, however, adherence to such ideas to the exclusion of tempering concepts of the paternalist, welfare state have come to represent a leading strand of conservatism, often known in our era as "libertarian," in contradistinction to the contemporary English-language notion of "liberalism," particularly in the United States, as left wing. On the other hand, theories that have attempted a reconciliation of classical liberal ideas with the welfare state have been represented in the social-democratic policies that have dominated most of the post-World War II government policies of Sweden, Denmark, Norway, and the Netherlands, and, to a greater or lesser extent, the social democratic movements of Britain, Germany, France, Italy, or Spain.

Attitudes toward victimless crimes reflect this division. Extreme libertarians would lift prohibitions on any activity, right up to suicide, Russian roulette or dueling, that does not cause palpable harm to persons who have not given valid consent. Nor would they recognize crimes of homosexuality, sexual sadomasochism, prostitution, contraception, polygamy, or flag burning. What makes them "conservative" is the purity of their liberalism, which, applied with equal zeal to the marketplace, results in little more than survival of the fittest. Those unable to help themselves are, at best, consigned to charity of strictly voluntary origin. Even taxation for goods or services aside from those, such as an army, absolutely necessary to the survival of the state is seen as punitive—punitive of the victimless act of earning and spending one's money as one sees fit—and would be abolished for the same reasons that punishments of homosexuality or dueling are abolished. Social democrats, on the other hand, have sometimes favored policies deemed progressive across the board, in social as well as economic areas. A number of social-democratic governments have thus lifted prohibitions of homosexuality, sexual sadomasochism, prostitution, pornography, or soft drugs, while maintaining prohibitions on gambling, cockfighting, or hate speech.

Some issues do not clearly appear as either "left-wing" or "right-wing." Libertarianism, for example, however pure, assumes no particular stance on what constitutes a legal person. It only characterizes the freedoms rightly accruing to legal persons once these have been ascertained. Accordingly, it would entail no particular view on whether a fetus can count as a person, hence a victim, of an act such as abortion, and, if so, whether such personhood starts at conception or only at a later stage of pregnancy. Equally "pure" libertarians could disagree on these issues, and could thus create internal contradictions within libertarianism about whether, or at what stage, abortion is a victimless crime. Similar contradictions are to be found in social-democratic liberalism.

Communitarianism, too, comes in different hues, from traditional-values conservatism or religious fundamentalism to Marxism or certain schools of feminism. Distinctions between left and right are even hazier than in the case of liberalism. Again, all forms of liberalism aim for the greatest possible individual freedom: libertarianism in an absolute sense, social democracy through the greatest possible personal liberty that a balancing against social welfare will allow. Communitarianism, on the other hand, does not necessarily seek even that individual freedom that might be balanced against social welfare. Individual freedom is never a priority in the first instance. It is at best residual, to be enjoyed only after more important collective goals have been achieved. Nevertheless, some distinctions between more left-wing or right-wing theories of communitarianism can be made. Enlightened, as opposed to Stalinist or Maoist, Marxism, along with communitarian feminist ethics, can properly be characterized as progressive or left-wing. Such theories have, for example, generally favored individual freedom to practice contraception or to engage in homosexual acts. Nevertheless, prostitution, pornography, sexual sadomasochism, polygamy, or hate speech are more readily frowned upon. These are seen to perpetuate, if only symbolically, misogyny, exploitation, or racism. Right-wing communitarianism, such as religious fundamentalism or traditional-values conservatism, is even less disposed to concede to individual interests. In the first instance, everything must, so to speak, cede to the word of God or to time-honored values of families and communities, however harmless by other measures. God or community are always judges of evil, always sufficient "victims" of evil acts.

It is the extreme views, then, on the left and the right, that offer more uniform but perhaps more simplistic theories of victimless crimes. For these theories take only one principle into account. Libertarianism places the value of individual liberty above all others, and is thus hostile to any use of the criminal law that would deprive persons of individual liberty absent a showing that the exercise thereof would palpably harm the person or liberty of another. Right-wing communitarianism places a vision of the collectivity above all others, and thus invokes the criminal law to advance that vi-

sion, regardless of the abridgement of individual liberties. It is the more moderate theories, attempting to find some status for individual liberty within a broader collective good, that run into graver contradictions. In the United States, for example, the American Civil Liberties Union (ACLU), traditionally, self-avowedly, associated with the political left and with progressive politics, also remains strongly committed to classical liberal ideas of free expression. It has thus found itself uncomfortably allied with Nazi, racist, and male-supremacist causes against Holocaust victims, racial minorities, and feminists. Meanwhile, in pursuit of progressive communitarian aims, a number of feminists have found common cause with the religious right in campaigns against pornography.

F. Republicanism and Fundamental Rights

The foregoing discussion should not be construed as implying a necessary correlation between, on the one hand, liberalism and democracy, and, on the other, communitarianism and authoritarianism. Some versions of communitarianism approach a pure, popular democracy more closely than do some versions of liberalism, which would expressly renounce pure democracy. If a society is to be governed by a principle of collective welfare, and if notions of collective welfare are to be ascertained by consensus, then majority rule provides sufficient justification for deciding which acts should be penalized. No additional justification, with reference to the specific harm that would be caused by penalized acts, would be required. If the majority wishes to penalize gambling, alcohol consumption, flag burning, contraception, or homosexuality, then it may do so with no greater notion of harm than the sentiment that individuals and society would be better off without such things.

It was precisely this power of the majority—to its foes, "tyranny of the majority"—that motivated Enlightenment thinkers to temper democracy not only with notions of constitutional republicanism, by which government, albeit largely through democratic elections, would enjoy certain insulation from direct democratic pressures, but also with notions of fundamental, inalienable, or "human" rights, interests of vital importance to human life, such as expression or association, which would enjoy special protections from popular or state interference. Classical liberalism purports to incorporate these antidemocratic buffers for the sake of strengthening democratic society overall. Yet antidemocratic they are. Liberal democracies tend to resolve the problem of victimless crimes through appeal to fundamental rights. If a victimless act, such as gambling, does not entail a discrete, legally cognizable, fundamental right, then it may more easily be penalized by government. If, on the other hand, such an act, such as production and distribution of atheist literature, does involve such a right, then government must present a stronger case against the purported harm. A special sphere of protection thus becomes reserved for acts performed in the exercise of fundamental rights where such exercise does not cause palpable harm. These relationships can be depicted as follows:

	Ordinary right	Fundamental right
	I.	II.
Palpable harm caused by exercise of right	Exercise of right may be penalized without special justification	Exercise of right may be penalized without special justification
	III.	IV.
Putative harm caused by exercise of right	Exercise of right may be penalized without special justification	Exercise of right may *not* be penalized without special justification

Such a scheme envisages a balance between liberal and communitarian ideals, although adherents of a strong liberalism or communitarianism would still find it inadequate. Acts not performed in the exercise of fundamental rights, or acts causing palpable harm (fields I, II, and III), are left to normal democratic consensus for determinations as to their legality or illegality. Acts performed in the exercise of fundamental rights and causing no palpable harm (field IV) enjoy greater protection from those forces. Field I would comprise most acts that have traditionally and uncontroversially fallen under the criminal law. Murder, assault, or rape, for example, are palpably harmful exercises of freedoms of bodily mobility that are not generally supported by fundamental rights. Although some civil or human rights instruments recognize specific rights of travel or movement, these rights are not conceived so broadly as to create general rights of bodily mobility. Field II would comprise acts within the sphere of fundamental rights, but constituting abuse of these. Rights of free speech, for example, tend to be rather broadly conceived in liberal democracies, but preclude such palpably harmful exercise as, for example, treason or incitement to imminent violent activity. It is in the remaining areas that problems of victimless crimes more readily arise, and in which liberal democracies are likely to draw distinctions between ordinary rights (field III) and fundamental rights (field IV). Field III

would comprise acts, such as drug use, gambling, loitering, or possession of firearms, not causing palpable harm, but not supported by fundamental rights. Liberal democracies have maintained some margin of discretion on the part of government to regulate or prohibit such activities, despite their possibly victimless nature. It is only acts that are committed in the exercise of fundamental rights and cause no palpable harm (field IV), such as religious dissent or use of contraceptive devices, that most liberal democracies have increasingly recognized as meriting greater protection, and requiring special, perhaps compelling, justification on the part of government before criminal punishment of them will be allowed.

Such a regime, however, still leaves numerous questions unanswered. What, for example, properly counts as a fundamental right? The first 10 amendments to the United States Constitution, for example, known as the Bill of Rights (1791), were one of the earliest attempts to enumerate fundamental rights that might not be abridged by government without special justification. These include, inter alia, rights governing free speech, free assembly, and free exercise of religion. They do not, however, include, as such, a fundamental right to privacy—a concept of more recent vintage. In a landmark case, the Supreme Court nevertheless deduced the implied presence of such a right, overturning a state prohibition on the use of contraceptive devices, and in subsequent cases, held that the right protects individual autonomy in such areas as abortion, marriage, and child rearing. Yet in a later case the Court declined to overturn a state prohibition on private, adult, consensual acts of "sodomy" as applied to homosexuals. The United Kingdom, maintaining a tradition of constitutionalism rather than a single and unified written constitution, has no instrument of constitutional stature enumerating fundamental rights, which, as a result, tend to be promulgated and ascertained ad hoc. Newer efforts, such as the European Convention on Human Rights (1950), although by no means free of problems of interpretation, are more comprehensive and more specific as to the content and limits of fundamental rights, and have produced a jurisprudence less ambiguous in the elaboration of the relationships depicted in this schema. Although differences of opinion will invariably arise about the boundaries between fields I, II and III, it is the boundaries between these and field IV that pose the most difficult problems concerning victimless crimes. Finally, an additional question arises as to the "special" justification that would be required for the state validly to punish field IV acts. If that justification is not based on some palpable harm, there is likely to be some question about how "special" or urgent it is.

III. SPECIFIC APPLICATIONS

A. The Problem of Casuistry

Absolute doctrines of liberalism or communitarianism provide easy answers to the question of victimless crimes. Yet the question persists precisely because absolute doctrines of liberalism or communitarianism are difficult to maintain. More moderate doctrines, such as paternalism or republicanism, tend to be preferred. The more moderate, however, the more subject a position is to contradictions. Such are the dilemmas of casuistry, the application of general principles to specific problems. Even Mill, in the later portions of *On Liberty,* attempting to apply his principle to specific cases, ultimately cedes ground to a communitarian impulse. He concedes, for example, that "taxation for fiscal purposes is absolutely inevitable." Similarly, while Hart and Devlin represent, respectively, liberal and communitarian views, neither's position is absolute. Devlin hardly sets out to abolish the liberal state. Hart grants a doctrine of "limited paternalism." Where Mill was surely correct was in his observation that no two jurisdictions, nor even the same jurisdiction at different periods of time, resolve the problem of victimless crimes in the same way.

B. Persons Harmed

Various entities can be harmed by various acts. These include legal persons, such as oneself, another person, members of society as a whole, even a corporation (in its capacity as a legal person), but can also, depending on one's philosophy of harm, include entities not generally deemed in contemporary, liberal democracies to be legal persons. These may be either material, such as animals, or immaterial, such as deities or spirits. Any view about who can suffer from harmful acts raises its own set of questions. (1) As to oneself or some specific, ascertainable person, the question arises whether willingness to incur palpable harm removes legitimate grounds for punishment. Putative harm does not raise such an issue, as grounds for punishing it are based either on harm to a specific, ascertainable person who has not consented, or to society as a whole, or to an intangible entity such as God. (2) As to members of society as a whole, the question arises whether the desire (be it popular or on the part of state officials)

that they not incur putative harm creates legitimate grounds for punishment. Palpable harm does not raise such an issue, as it, by definition, is incurred by oneself or by specific, ascertainable persons, even if only on a cumulative scale. (3) As to entities other than legal persons, such as animals or deities, the question arises whether they can be harmed, either palpably or putatively, in a way that would justify criminal punishment.

1. Harm to Oneself or to Specific, Ascertainable Persons

What if the persons palpably harmed have consented to the harm? Despite regular occurrences of grievous bodily harm and even death, boxing, for example, remains a lawful sport. There is no question about the harmfulness of the acts involved. A swift punch to the jawbone in the barroom might well send the author to jail; placed in the ring with the lawful consent of both parties, that same punch will shower the author in glory.

Consent is not a green light to cause harm to whomever consents. Ironically, criminal law has often prohibited suicide, which entails only harm, albeit consensual, to oneself, while harms caused to someone else, albeit consensual, in the form of boxing, may be rewarded with a world championship and film contracts. Of course, suicide is an act that intends death as its purpose. Acts with that same purpose, directed toward someone else, have also met with criminal sanctions, hence prohibitions against mutual suicide pacts, dueling, Russian roulette, and euthanasia. On the other hand, given the statistically certain knowledge that a significant number of deaths and grievous injuries will result every year from boxing, quaere whether such a teleological distinction truly explains the different legal treatment of the respective acts. Another explanation might lie in the state's desire not so much to punish those who would commit suicide or euthanasia as to help them. Yet it remains unclear why the state would "help" people out of these kinds of acts, but not out of boxing. Particularly as contrasted with euthanasia, the implication would almost be that it is more desirable to die accidentally by boxing than deliberately by euthanasia, despite the questionable medical ethics of promoting the death of healthy boxers while frustrating the wishes of those whose health may be terminally impaired. The difference might also be thought to lie in the private, concealed practice of suicide, euthanasia, dueling, or Russian roulette, as opposed to the public, supervised practice of boxing. If, however, the latter does not preclude regular and foreseeable death and grievous injury, the cogency of this distinction is equally dubious. As a practical matter, prohibitions of boxing might be seen as useless, as they would merely push the sport underground, rendering it even less susceptible to open scrutiny. However, the same is true of such consensual activities as drug use or gambling.

The disparity is more likely rooted in the popular affection for certain dangerous activities, such as sports, as opposed to popular repugnance toward others. This view would seem to ensue, for example, from a comparison between boxing and sexual sadomasochism. Whether sexual sadomasochism is, as a general matter, dangerous at all is questionable. There is no evidence that it approaches the number of fatalities and grievous injuries caused by boxing, taking into account respective proportions of accidents with respect to the probable number of participants in each activity. Yet sexual sadomasochism involves fears and taboos without parallel in conventional athletics. In the United Kingdom, for example, legal boxing has culminated in well-publicized deaths while persons have been prosecuted for engaging in acts of adult, private, consensual sadomasochism that had not resulted in death or grievous bodily injury. The result is a legal regime in which certain acts causing palpable harms may be committed with impunity, while acts that appear, for the most part, to cause only the putative harm of moral disapproval are proscribed.

The element of consent is muddled not only by the problem of consistent application but also by the assumption of individual rational choice. Prostitution has traditionally been regulated or prohibited on the grounds that it poses dangers to public morals—again, a justification difficult to reconcile with liberal ideals of privacy or individual autonomy. A number of feminists, however, see no contradiction between the two interests, as they challenge the notion of effective consent to, hence individual autonomy within, such an act. They argue that women do not choose prostitution in pursuit of their own well-being, but rather are coerced into it through entrenched pressures of economic, political, social, and psychological inferiority. Feminists of more classical-liberal persuasion, however, argue that the empowerment of women lies precisely in their insistence on making their own choices regarding sexual, and economic, conduct.

Like palpable harm, putative harm, too, can be caused by a specific, ascertainable person. For example, an unsuspecting passerby in a park late at night may inadvertently happen upon persons engaging in sexual acts, and may thus feel a sense of outrage not immediately shared by others. However, prohibitions of such sexual acts in public are not based merely on individual moral outrage, but on a collective sentiment of offence to community values. They are thus properly understood as harm to society as a whole.

2. Harm to Society as a Whole

Many people may gamble, loiter, take drugs, purchase guns, burn flags, and practice sodomy their whole lives without harming anyone—or, at least, anyone in particular. The question is whether these acts may nevertheless legitimately be proscribed on the basis of their intrinsic evil or their overall harm to society. Such acts are not identical, however, with respect to the harm they cause. Acts such as smoking, gambling, loitering, arms possession, or drug consumption, although they may be conducted without evidence of palpable harm to some specific, ascertainable other person, are widely believed to entail broader, more long-term, but nevertheless equally material harms. Gambling is widely believed to prey on the poor or to attract organized crime. Loitering, particularly among juveniles, is widely believed to promote delinquency and possibly social disorder or petty damage to property. Drug use is also believed to cause socially disruptive, and possibly dangerous, behavior. Gun ownership, if innocuous on a small scale, becomes daunting when proliferation of firearms numbers in the millions, unforeseen or accidental harms becoming inevitable. Other acts, on the contrary, such as blasphemy, are only evil insofar as they violate deeply held moral beliefs.

Ostensibly, such a distinction might appear welcome in a liberal democracy as a basis for distinguishing among putative harms, by promising an objective, value-neutral, empirical standard. Those putative harms for which a sufficiently strong empirical correlation to material harms can be documented would legitimately be subject to proscription, whereas those lacking any such correlation would not be. For several reasons, however, such a hope is inevitably frustrated.

First, empiricism does not necessarily imply objectivity. A "battle of the experts" is the norm in most areas of pressing social concern. Different researchers produce different data and disagree about what constitutes proper method, results, and interpretation.

Second, empiricism does not necessarily imply value neutrality. Until recently there was a widespread consensus that homosexuality did not simply entail moral opprobrium but also psychiatric and sociopathological illness. Respected, purportedly empirical studies suggested significant correlations between homosexuality and delinquency or criminality. Similar "empirical" claims have been made regarding ethnicity, class, and gender. What purports to be neutral science has often proven to be the mere translation of prevailing values into a discourse of scientific objectivity.

Third, empiricism does not necessarily imply amenability to quantification. Some harms resist measurement. Prohibitions on hate speech, for example, envisage not only the general moral outrage of society, but also some meaningful correlation between hate speech and more material, criminal acts of racism. It is unclear, however, whether societies maintaining extensive prohibitions on hate speech, such as Germany, enjoy lower levels of criminal racist activity than societies, like the United States, lacking such prohibitions. Some would argue that such prohibitions aggravate, rather than alleviate, racism by pushing it underground, prompting racists to devise ever more insidious means to pursue their aims, whereas freedom in such areas would keep racism in view and thus easier to monitor. Others, in the classical liberal tradition, would follow Milton's ideal of truth grappling with falsehood. They would argue, in the famous formulation of United States Supreme Court Justice Louis Brandeis, that "the fitting remedy for evil counsels is good ones." Similarly, some feminists advocate prohibitions on pornography in order to combat long-term harm to women. Here again, however, even if the inferior status of women can be measured in innumerable ways, any demonstrable correlation to pornography is difficult to establish. Violent television programs raise similar concerns, although the specific causal relationship between exposure to violent programs and violent behavior among children may more readily be submitted to standard methods of scientific analysis.

Fourth, even putative harms, such as that caused by blasphemy, might be said to pose the danger of more serious harm in the long run, for example by leading to social unrest, violence, and thus to palpable harms. Even if such harm can have ensued only from reactions to a putative harm, once the prospect of palpable harm arises, the reason for it might be considered secondary to the desire to prevent it.

Fifth, such a standard already presupposes a strong liberalism that many would reject on its face. Many communitarians would advocate proscriptions of certain acts regardless of, and even willingly conceding, the absence of any empirical correlation to material harm to society, harm to morals being as pernicious as harm to a community's physical, psychological, or economic health.

Once harm to society in general is admitted as a grounds for criminal sanctions, practical problems of enforcement also arise. Whereas societies may uphold the ideal of punishing every possible murderer, rapist, armed robber, or drunk driver, the punishment of every drug user, pornography consumer, or "sodomite" seems to be of questionable desirability not only in practice but even in principle. As controversy surrounding the U.S. Supreme Court case of *Bowers v. Hardwick* suggested, the enforcement of sodomy laws would either require punishing enormous segments of the population, or must be so random as to be utterly arbitrary. A similar observation can be made of drug consumption, particularly with regard to cannabis or hashish. Effective enforcement is unlikely without the deployment of massive resources. Many would challenge the commitment of valuable resources to crimes arguably of minor significance. The experiment with prohibition of alcohol in the United States failed because, far from ameliorating social problems, it exacerbated them by removing alcohol production from public view and encouraging organized crime.

3. Harm to Nonlegal Persons

To define palpable harm as possible only to legal persons, and to define these, in turn, as consisting only of human beings or human institutions, is already to presuppose a liberal, secular state. Blasphemy, for example, can be said to cause merely putative harm on the assumption that only those legal persons defined by the liberal state as such are capable of suffering real, effective harm. Other worldviews would not categorically distinguish harm to humans from harm to other entities. Nonsecular worldviews would typically characterize offense to deities, spirits, or other nonhuman entities to be of equal or greater moment, as suggested by the Rushdie affair and by the harsh, often lethal punishments of homosexuals or adulterers in a number of Islamic states. Even if such Draconian sanctions are, in some states, more politically than religiously motivated, popular support generally invokes religious beliefs.

A similar problem is posed by the concept of animal rights. If the assumption of rationality as the distinguishing feature of homo sapiens is in doubt, then the legal privilege accruing to the human being as an object of legal protections, as the only possible victim of harm, becomes equally doubtful. In Western law, animals have traditionally been regarded only as chattels, that is, as articles of personal property, not unlike women, children, and slaves in earlier times. As such, the law governing the possession, transfer, and use of animals traditionally imposed only duties applicable to the disposition of personal property generally, for example, that it not be used so as to create a nuisance or injury to other legal persons. No other restrictions applied. Acts of cruelty or neglect were not actionable. They were legally meaningless, hence victimless, on the theory that only homo sapiens, as a rational animal, could constitute a proper subject of law and of rights. Some, however, would not distinguish humans from animals on a principle of rationality, but would instead reconcile them on a principle of sentience, which, moreover, might appear to be the more relevant principle where specific issues of pain and suffering are at hand.

By the nineteenth century, activists protesting unrestricted rights over animals demanded law reform, which was eventually achieved in many countries. Such reforms often envisaged human as much as animal welfare, for example, in the case of laws governing the safe and hygienic processing of animals for food. Still, elimination of needless suffering in animals was at least partially recognized as a good in itself. Understandings of "needless" suffering, however, tend to diverge. Animal research for cosmetics, for example, causes great suffering, but is still lawful in most countries, despite the questionable need for new cosmetics, although initiatives have begun at least to reduce, if not eliminate, such experimentation. Vegetarianism, on the other hand, remains the exception rather than the norm, thus the slaughter of animals for food continues to be considered essential, despite the often harsh conditions in which livestock are maintained. Accordingly, even where law reform regarding the protection of animals has occurred, it in no way elevates palpable harm to animals to the status of palpable harm to humans. The desire to reduce animal suffering might also be attributed to human sensibilities vis-à-vis the pain of defenseless animals, but not to any recognition of full or partial parity of animals with human beings, comparable to a desire to keep the streets clean without thereby attributing legal personality to them. On this view, animals would simply be beneficiaries of human largesse, rather than holders of rights or, concomitantly, victims of harmful acts. Whether animals have rights, and can be victims at all, thus remains questionable. Still, some schools of environmental ethics would extend parity not only to animals but to the natural world generally, or to elements thereof, such as oceans or rain forests, as part of an effort to combat environmental destruction. Under such theories, the victimlessness of all industrial and technological development, even barring demonstrable harm to others, would come into question.

As already noted, an entity with a stronger, yet still highly debated claim to legal personhood is the fetus. To the extent that a fetus is ascribed some measure of legal personhood, harm to it may be culpable, although the harmful act may be treated differently in different circumstances. Abortion, at least up to a certain point in the pregnancy, is legal in much of the world, whereas harm caused through the act of some outside party, as in the case of medical malpractice, or, in some cases, even harm induced through maternal neglect, may give rise to criminal or civil liability.

C. Degrees of Harm

Acts are rarely discrete. Most can in some sense be divided into component acts, and most can in some sense be seen as components of larger acts. There thus arises the question of delimiting acts for purposes of determining criminal culpability. Problems related to alcohol consumption, for example, are generally addressed only in close proximity to some locus of specific, palpable harm, such as on the highways or in schools. Despite the many deaths resulting each year from driving under the influence of alcohol, or the problems of teenage alcoholism, liberal democracies have not, in recent years, responded with outright prohibitions on the manufacture, distribution or consumption of alcohol. Drug abuse, on the other hand, is assailed not only in close proximity to situations of heightened danger, but on all fronts, from small farmers in less industrialized countries through to Los Angeles street gangs. It is often argued that, given the devastating consequences of drug abuse, not only supply but also demand must be combated. The validity of this distinction between alcohol abuse and drug abuse has been challenged. The result, however, is that some problems are seen as sufficiently urgent to warrant criminal penalties on every act that somehow constitutes a link in the causal chain—at the "illness," "cause," "root," or "demand" links as well as the "symptom," "effect," "surface," or "supply" links. Other problems are confronted only at the stages most proximate to specific, harmful results.

Laws against child pornography offer another "every-link-in-the-chain" example, albeit a more difficult one, as fundamental rights of expression are at stake. Popular and official opinion in democratic societies overwhelmingly approves of all possible means of eradicating the sexual exploitation of children. The palpable harms involved easily justify punishment of explicit material, such as photographs of children engaged in sexual acts with each other or with adults. Yet these hard-core materials are only part of a continuum. As with drugs, if the desire to eliminate sexual exploitation of children is earnest, even softer materials may be viewed as justifiable objects of criminal sanctions. Questions then arise as to how explicit material must be before it qualifies for criminal liability. These are age-old questions, but urgent ones, as those who produce or distribute such materials may seek to push the law to the limits of what it will allow. What is to be the status of children in "suggestive" poses but not engaged in sexual acts? What counts as sexual? Nudity? Touching? Kissing? Artwork created from the artist's imagination rather than from child models? Or pornographic ("blue") novels using no illustrations at all?

Further questions arise as to the links of production, distribution, possession, and consumption. In the case of drugs, punishment can be attached to every link, even private possession. Given the comparable or greater urgency of sexual exploitation of children, should punishment attach to every link as well? Can one legitimately be punished for taking "suggestive" photographs of one's own children? Or one's friends' children? Or strangers' children running naked on the beach? And if one may take such photographs for personal use, may one show them to others? Sell them to others? Display them in an art exhibition? And, again, what if the pictures are not photographs of live models but artistic images drawn from the imagination, perhaps even doodled on a scrap of paper, yet possibly depicting explicit sexual acts? Rights of free expression under the United States Constitution, for example, have been construed go protect private possession of much pornography that might be punished at the stages of production or distribution, yet recent jurisprudence suggests that some sexually suggestive materials involving children may justify punishment even for purely private possession.

IV. FURTHER RESEARCH

Although there is an abundance of published work on particular victimless crimes, there have been, since the Hart-Devlin debates, few attempts to develop an integrated, systematic theory of victimless crimes as part of a theory of criminal law. Such a theory is no easy task. It cannot avoid established debates between liberalism and communitarianism, law and morals, ethics and politics, rationalism, and empiricism, ideals and pragmatics, or left and right. These categories are themselves subject to ambiguities and internal contradictions. The task is further complicated by the fact that, due to the speculative nature of the issues raised, the law strongly diverges from one jurisdiction or time period to another. It is unlikely that further research can remain committed to any one of the standard theoretical positions. The limits of the standard theories must be further explored if subtler approaches are to be developed.

Also See the Following Articles

CRIME AND SOCIETY • DRUGS: MORAL AND LEGAL ISSUES • FREEDOM OF SPEECH • GAMBLING • GUN CONTROL • HOMOSEXUALITY, SOCIETAL ATTITUDES TOWARD • PORNOGRAPHY • PROSTITUTION • SAFETY LAWS • SUICIDE • VIOLENCE IN FILMS AND TELEVISION

Bibliography

Barnett, H. (1996). *Sourcebook on feminist jurisprudence.* London: Sweet & Maxwell.

Fish, S. (1994). *There's no such thing as free speech.* New York: Oxford University Press.

Heinze, E. (forthcoming). The jurisprudence of morals in the European convention on human rights.

Heinze, E. (1995). *Sexual orientation: A human right.* Dordrecht and London: Martinus Nijhoff.

MacKinnon, C. (1993). *Only words.* London: HarperCollins.

Matsuda, M., Lawrence, C., Delgado, R., & Crenshaw, K. (Eds.). (1993). *Words that wound.* Boulder, CO. Westview Press.

Morrison, W. (1995).*Theoretical criminology: From modernity to postmodernism.* London: Cavendish.

Norrie, A. W. (1993). *Crime, reason and history.* London: Weidenfeld & Nicolson.

Von Hirsch, A. & Jareborg, N. (1991). Gauging criminal harm: A living standard analysis. *Oxford Journal of Legal Studies* **11**, 1.

VIOLENCE IN FILMS AND TELEVISION

Marian I. Tulloch and John C. Tulloch
Charles Sturt University

GLOSSARY

arousal A nonspecific physiological response.
catharsis A discharge of hostile feeling in response to watching violence.
correlational research Relation of individuals' measured characteristics and behaviors.
cultivation effects The way television cultivates a distorted view of social reality in the minds of viewers.
desensitization Reduced emotional arousal to aversive stimuli.
disinhibition Reduction in the constraints against behaving in a socially undesirable way.
effects research Research into the direct behavioral consequences of television viewing on individuals.
experimental research Research undertaken in controlled conditions with relevant variables manipulated by the experimenter.
longitudinal panel studies Studies undertaken with the same subjects being measured at intervals over a period of time.

meta-analysis A statistical procedure for combining the results of multiple research studies.

VIOLENCE IN FILMS AND TELEVISION has been a subject of wide public concern since the inception of these media forms. Although a range of issues have been raised by the conjuncture of new media forms and the mass reception of representations of violence (associating violence with subcultural categories of gender, class, and ethnicity), it is the category of age, particularly children, that has attracted most attention. Extensive research has been conducted into the possible negative effects, particularly on children, of exposure to the frequent portrayal of acts of violence, but there has been disagreement as to the conclusiveness of these findings and the appropriate policy implications. Cultural differences in legal and constitutional frameworks, the organization of the communications industry, and the sociopolitical climate have led to countries finding different approaches and solutions to issues of media violence. More recently research has extended both to public perceptions of media violence and its influence on the way audiences view their world and to a study of public attitudes toward portrayals of media violence and appropriate policy interventions. In addition to concern about the extensive portrayal of fictional violence are the particular issues raised by violence in factual television. The media plays a role in shaping public attitudes to violent national and international events as well as impacting directly on those involved in violence, especially victims. This survey will focus primarily on ethical and methodological considerations in the policy, media, and research debate surrounding children and violence in films and television. Having overviewed the historical and institutional context within which research and policy are formed, the article will examine the psychological effects approach to film and television violence, and will then consider a range of research and policy traditions which have in recent years moved away from or critiqued that tradition.

I. CULTURAL CONTEXT

A. Historical Overview

1. Mass Entertainment and the Fear of Violence

Fear of the potential harmful consequences of mass entertainment preceded the moving image. Continuities have been drawn between the avowed dangers of music halls, "penny dreadfuls," or "dime comics" in promoting crime and violence and reducing traditional authority, and subsequent anxieties, sometimes termed "moral panics," at each new technological development: film, television, video, cable and satellite TV, and the Internet. The advent of film led to claims that the moving image bypasses the thinking areas of the brain to impact directly on the subconscious, and therefore unprotected, mind.

> Before these children's greedy eyes with heartless indiscrimination horrors unimaginable are . . . presented night after night. . . . Terrific massacres, horrible catastrophes, motor-car smashes, public hangings, lynchings. All who care for the moral well being and education of the child will set their faces like flint against this new form of excitement. (April 12, 1913. Cinematography and the Child, *The Times*, London)

Because moral panics have been so clearly associated with the relationship between media violence and mass audiences, they have sometimes been dismissed as an attack on popular culture by a middle-class elite. Yet the ubiquitous nature of the TV violence debate suggests an ongoing and widespread concern with possible links between a diet of screen violence and problems of social aggression.

2. Early Research into Film Violence

Of all the potential harmful effects of film and television, by far the greatest emphasis has been on the consequences, particularly for the young, of excessive portrayals of violence. The first major study of this issue was established by the National Committee for the Study of Social Values in Motion Pictures and financed by a private philanthropic foundation, the Payne Fund (1928–1933). Despite their negligible effect on public policy, these studies represent an important breakthrough in establishing the role of social scientific research in policy debates, raising issues of public concern, and causing some disquiet in the motion-picture industry. The notion of powerful direct communication effects underlying the research was a simplistic one, later characterized as the "hypodermic model" because it neglected the possible mediating role of viewer characteristics. Although effects models have increased in theoretical and methodological sophistication, they have remained guided by a search for a causal connection between on-screen and real world violence, with the individual viewer as the unit for analysis.

B. Structural and Industry Contexts

Despite the important role assigned to psychological principles in explaining the effects of media violence, the impact of television and indeed public concern about that impact are extensively mediated by specific cultural contexts. The amount and type of violence in the media vary greatly between cultures. In the multiple-channel deregulated U.S. market, the level of violence is much higher than that in many other cultures where less violence is presented or is contextualized quite differently. Japanese television has a heavy diet of television violence, but heroes themselves are more frequently subjected to violence with a greater focus on their resultant pain and suffering. The role of the United States as the major exporter of film and television, however, means that American shows are a standard part of the viewing offerings in very diverse societies.

C. Changing Communication Technology

Changes in communication technology have also altered the availability of violent material. Cable and satellite technology has vastly increased the range of available products, and in the many countries where television can be accessed from neighboring states there are limited governmental powers of control. For instance, Canadian attempts to reduce violence on television affects Canadian stations but not the cable and satellite programs from the United States available in the majority of Canadian homes. Britain has not imposed the same regulatory regimes on satellite as terrestrial services. The advent of the videocassette recorder means that systems of regulation relying on the exclusion of underage cinema patrons from certain film screenings no longer ensure the restriction of material to adult viewers. Children's access to violent materials through video or pay channels has become an important focus of current public concern.

II. PSYCHOLOGICAL STUDIES OF TV VIOLENCE AND AGGRESSION

A. Psychological Processes

A variety of psychological processes have been posited as mechanisms by which the viewing of violence on film or television can influence behavior. The focus of this research paradigm is on explaining individual differences in aggressive behavior and tolerance for aggression as a function of differential exposure to violent programs.

1. Desensitization

One hypothesized effect of viewing violence is a gradual emotional desensitization, not only to screen violence but to real life violence. For instance, R. S. Drabman and M. H. Thomas asked children to monitor by video the behavior of some younger children. Those who had watched a violent program were found to be less likely to intervene to prevent a fight among younger children in their charge than children who had not seen the film. A subsequent study in which the physiological and emotional responses of the children were monitored found that those who had previously watched violent programming were subsequently less aroused by what was purported to be real life violence (1974. *Developmental Psychology*, 17, 399–407).

Desensitization, at the physiological level, has been demonstrated in the lower arousal to violent scenes among heavy vs light television viewers. Repeated viewing of extremely violent videos has been frequently presented as an explanation for the blunted sensibilities of those who perpetrate acts of extreme violence. A concern with the regular portrayal even of factual violence is that it serves to blunt the public's sensitivities and the power to shock or feel.

2. Imitation

Social learning theorists who emphasize children's ability to learn by observing the behavior of others see television as a prime source of aggressive models. Experimental studies have investigated a range of variables that influence the level of imitative aggression. In A. Bandura's classic studies, children watched a live or filmed model performing aggressive acts against a large plastic Bobo doll. When left alone to play in a room containing the doll, children who had witnessed the aggression produced similar actions to a much greater extent than children who had not. If the model was rewarded rather than punished for their aggression the level of imitation increased, a finding relevant to the tendency of television to portray the final triumph of the forces of good (e.g., in crime series or war movies), by means often as violent as those of their enemies (1973. *Aggression: A Social Learning Analysis*. Prentice-Hall, Englewood Cliffs, NJ).

Several studies have investigated direct imitative effects via fluctuations in suicide rates following television coverage of a suicide—whether actual, as in the case of Marilyn Monroe, or of a major fictional character.

3. Disinhibition

Portrayals of media violence may lower social inhibitions against violent behavior, making aggression appear permitted or even approved. Frequent viewing of violence can make it appear more socially acceptable; violent behaviors are seen to benefit the aggressor or to be judged situationally appropriate. Such lowering of inhibitions can facilitate the enactment of learned behavioral responses.

4. Arousal

One difficulty in research on the consequences of screen violence is in determining whether the effects could be the product not of violence specifically but of emotional arousal in general. The impact of material that is exciting or inspires strong feelings may depend on the viewer's prior mood and the way that arousal is perceived. For instance, arousal in a frustrated viewer witnessing violent action is more likely to be self-perceived as anger. Young children have become more restless and aggressive after watching very fast-paced, fragmented material, whether or not it contains violence. It is possible that what has been interpreted as an effect of violence may sometimes be a more generalized arousal effect.

5. Catharsis

It has been suggested, applying the traditional Aristotelian notion of catharsis, that viewing violence is a harmless way of draining off aggressive energies. While a few studies have found evidence of lowered aggression after violent viewing, support for the catharsis hypothesis from researchers within the effects paradigm has been generally very low.

6. Cognitive Approaches

As psychological theories have shifted from stimulus response to cognitive models, processes of social learning of aggression have been reformulated in cognitive terms. The child is seen to internalize patterns of social action organized into narrative scripts. Scripts contain both images and conceptual representations, providing guides to behavior in specific contexts. Television can play a role in the encoding of violent scripts and the maintenance and rehearsal of scripts by repeated exposure, and may cue the enactment of scripts in everyday contexts, a process that may be fostered by the child's identification with aggressive characters. Such a model can incorporate various psychological processes: social learning, arousal, disinhibition, and the triggering effect of specific cues. One such source of cues can be the "antisocial" toys that are marketed in conjunction with certain violent cartoons, a possibility that has been specifically studied. The way aggressive scripts may be learned and then cued and reenacted has been investigated in a study of preschool children by A. Sanson and C. Di Muccio. They found that children who watched a violent cartoon and then had "spin-off" toys to play with behaved more aggressively than other children who watched a neutral cartoon and/or received neutral toys. (1993. *Australian Psychologist*, 28, 93–99.)

With psychologists conceptualizing the TV violence–aggression relationship increasingly in cognitive terms, the gap between psychological and cultural theorists has diminished. The psychologist Leonard Berkowitz terms his approach "cognitive neoassociationism," and although presenting his theories in terms of memory networks and associative pathways, he considers the audience members' response to a communication as contingent on their prior ideas and the way these shape their interpretation. These ideas and interpretations may determine whether thoughts about violence activated by a program lead to overt aggressive behavior.

G. Comstock, in a review of a large number of experiments, has endeavored to conceptualize the multiplicity of factors that have been found to relate to differences in audience responses to televised acts of violence. Four conceptual dimensions have been identified to make sense of the range of factors affecting program impact: efficacy of violence, normativeness (the morality of violent acts), pertinence (their relevance to the viewer), and viewer susceptibility. Although recognizing that the first three dimensions can depend on viewer perception, effects researchers continue to operate from the position that the properties of the program (for instance, the justifiability of violence) can be determined by the researcher rather than identified by a study of audience readings.

B. Types of Effects Research

1. Laboratory Experiments

Numerous studies on the effects of viewing violence under carefully controlled experimental conditions have been conducted within a psychological paradigm. The significant differences in subsequent aggression found in most of these studies between groups that have viewed violent and nonviolent excerpts have been taken as strong evidence that violence on screen can affect viewers' behavior. The strength of laboratory studies lies in an ability to study the consequence of very specific manipulations under carefully controlled conditions. They have been criticized, however, for the artificial nature of the viewing context and the measures of aggression that are employed, and for the demand characteristics operating in a laboratory setting, including the lack of social prohibitions or apparent negative consequences for perpetrators or victims of aggression. A study by W. A. Collins and S. K. Getz, with its use of a button to measure aggressive responses, is typical of traditional laboratory studies. Collins and Getz presented children with an episode of "Mod Squad" that had been edited in two ways. The protagonist responded to interpersonal provocation either constructively or aggressively. Children who viewed the aggressive behavior were less likely to demonstrate a desire to cooperate when given an opportunity to assist a peer by pressing a "help" button and more likely instead to press a "hurt" button. (1976. *Journal of Personality*, 44, 488–500). Questions have been raised as to the generalizability of the findings to a natural viewing context and also whether a cumulative impact of violent viewing can be inferred from short-term effects.

2. Field Studies

Field experiments can offer opportunities to study behavior within natural social contexts over longer time periods. However, the real life environment often comes at the expense of the stringent controls operating in the laboratory, possibly leaving findings open to plausible alternative explanations. If preexisting groups are studied they may well differ in initial characteristics. Moreover, while purporting to use the individual as the unit of analysis, ongoing groups are inevitably affected by group processes, reflecting the social reality that aggression is an interactive social behavior, not a unidirectional personal response. It may also be hard to keep those who rate the children's behavior unaware as to which TV programs a given individual is being shown. Even the imposition of particular viewing regimes within a naturalistic environment may be difficult; subjects may be bored by their programming diet or object to the absence of regular favorite programs, suggesting that real life experiments, despite their appeal, can be difficult to implement effectively.

Some of the ethical issues posed by researchers' manipulation of viewing have been overcome in what have been termed naturally occurring experiments. A comparative study of three similar communities in British Colombia in which, for technical reasons, television was introduced at different times found an overall increase in children's playground aggression with the introduction of television, but not a specific relation between quantity of viewing and aggressive behavior. Moreover, the levels of children's aggression in the town that received television during the study became higher than those of children in the towns which already had access to television. The shift appeared in part to reflect overall changes in community social life, suggesting the need for a broad consideration of the impact of television on a community (In T. M. Williams, Ed., 1986. *The Impact of Television: A Natural Experiment in Three Communities*. Academic Press, New York).

The gradual introduction of television on a national level can also be viewed as a natural experiment. A comparison of U.S. cities receiving television before or after the 1949–1952 licensing freeze found television associated with increases in larceny but not with crimes of violence. The introduction of television to a whole country was studied by South African psychologists. Levels of television viewing were found to relate to increased aggressiveness in children in the white community.

3. Correlational Research

Another approach to demonstrating the effects of screen violence on viewer aggression is to relate individual differences in viewing levels to measures of naturally occurring aggressive behavior. Self or parental reports of viewing habits or program preferences, viewing logs, clinical interviews, peer or teacher nominations of be-

havioral aggression, and records of criminal convictions have all been employed in correlational research and have a variety of potential sources of measurement error. Although these weaknesses can be seen to limit the validity of research conclusions, an alternative view is that it produces an underestimation of the effects of viewing violence. While it has been clearly shown that the frequency of television viewing is associated with higher levels of aggressive behavior, demonstrating a causal linkage is difficult. Studies have attempted to control factors likely to contribute to the association, such as socioeconomic status, educational performance, parenting practices, intelligence, and personality. Studies of preschoolers have found TV viewing and everyday aggressive behavior to be related when a set of other factors are controlled.

One of the most complex attempts to control a range of over 200 variables was made by W. A. Belson in a study of adolescent boys in London. When heavy and light viewers of violence were statistically equated on these possible explanatory variables, heavy viewers were still significantly higher on a set of indices of aggression, particularly seriously harmful acts. This data gave little support to the alternative hypothesis that more aggressive boys sought out more violent entertainment (1978. *Television and the Adolescent Boy*. Teakfield, Farnborough).

4. Longitudinal Research

The problem of inferring causality from association in nonexperimental research can be addressed by studying the same group of children over an extended period of time, although longitudinal studies tend to be plagued by high attrition rates. Cross-lagged correlations that measure the association between two variables at two points in time test specific hypotheses about the direction of relationships. Work by Eron, Huesmann, and colleagues in which the same individuals were studied at ages 9 and 19, and again one and two decades later, did find some support for a bidirectional model: preference for violent TV predicted later aggression even when the level of earlier aggression was controlled, and aggressive children later chose to view more violent programs. For some commentators on these studies, the stability of aggression over time and the importance of child-rearing variables in predicting aggressive behavior are seen as more substantial findings than the relatively small long-term effects of violent viewing. The evidence points to any contribution of violent viewing to aggressiveness being most influential in the elementary school years, with attitudes and patterns of behavior established then having the potential to act cumulatively on aggression in adolescence and adulthood. Eron, L. D. Leftkowitz, M. M. Huesmann, L. R. & Walder, L. O. (1972. *American Psychologist*, 27, 253–263).

Because of the technical statistical complexity of such analyses, there is great scope for varying interpretation. A notable example is Milavsky's study sponsored by the NBC network which claimed negligible evidence of long-term effects. While the reinterpretation of the statistical analysis in this study has led many experts in the United States to present the data as supporting the viewing–violence link, several overseas reviews have cited it as more convincing than other American studies, focusing in particular on Milavsky's concern about the inaccuracies evident in some respondents' viewing reports.

5. Cross-Cultural Studies

Cross-cultural research in which the same techniques and measures are used in different countries is a powerful way to test the generalizability of psychological explanations across cultures. A major cross-cultural project included studies in countries as diverse as Australia, Finland, Israel, the Netherlands, Poland, and the United States. Again interpretations diverge, with some reviewers claiming a consistent pattern of support for the hypothesis that TV violence causes aggression, while others find the data patchy and inconclusive, with demonstrable effects so small as to lack practical import (L. R. Huesmann and L. D. Eron, Eds., 1986. *Television and the Aggressive Child: A Cross-National Comparison.* Erlbaum, Hillsdale, NJ).

6. Meta-analysis

Meta-analysis is a statistical technique which combines the findings from a large number of studies. A recent analysis by Paik and Comstock combined findings from 217 studies dating from between 1957 and 1990 and demonstrated moderate positive effects of screen violence on aggressive behavior. Their analysis aimed to answer some of the perennial criticisms of effects research by comparing the size of measured differences in aggression according to the ecological and design validity of the studies. They found no evidence that substantial effects were produced only in studies characterized by the artificiality of their setting and of the aggression measures employed. As a summary of a large number of effects studies, the meta-analysis supports the link between greater viewing of film and television violence and increased aggressive behavior.

However, for those who reject this paradigm the aggregation of studies serves only to confuse rather than

clarify the complex questions of definition, measurement, and process raised in relation to individual studies. It reflects a broader dispute between those who believe that when looked at separately none of the various types of studies can stand alone and the alternative position that the similarity of conclusions from different types of research together support claims for effects of television violence.

III. ALTERNATIVE PARADIGMS: PERCEPTIONS OF VIOLENCE

A. Content Analysis of TV Violence

Violence on television has the potential to influence not just viewers' behavior but their perceptions—how they understand violence and its place in the world. Content analysis attempts to quantify the extent of this violence. In 1992 the American Psychological Association estimated that the average American child has viewed 8000 dramatized murders and 100,000 acts of televized violence before leaving elementary school. With the advent of unrestricted cable TV, these numbers are likely to increase. Saturday morning television, with its diet of cartoons aimed at children, has violence in over 90% of programs with cartoons having an average of 32 violent acts an hour. The most extensive attempt to quantify television violence has been made by George Gerbner and his colleagues.

Gerbner has attempted to measure and monitor violence on television with a Violence Index. He has defined violence as "the overt expression of physical force (with or without weapon) against self or other, compelling action against one's will on pain of being hurt or killed or actually hurting or killing" (G. A. Comstock et al., 1978. Television and Human Behavior. Columbia University Press, New York, p. 64), a definition that has guided much content analysis but omits notions of intentionality generally central to the meaning of aggression. The Violence Index provides a formula for quantifying fictional violence, taking account of its type, its duration, and the role of the protagonists within the program. The Violence Index is calculated by adding together %P, the percentage of programs in which there is violence; 2(R/P), twice the number of violent episodes per program; 2(R/H), twice the number of violent episodes per hour; %V, percentage of leading characters involved in violence, either as victim or perpetrator; and %K, percentage of leading characters involved in an actual killing, either as victim or perpetrator. But, as many culturally oriented commentators have pointed out, content analysis suffers from taking little account of narrative encoding, genre, and audience decoding.

B. Cultivation Effects

Instead of concern with the direct behavioral effects of screen violence, Gerbner's cultivation analysis asserts that television has affected the way viewers perceive their world; the diet of television drama is a "message system" with a relatively simple myth structure for modern society. For Gerbner, messages about violence are messages about power and authority, creating a symbolic cultural environment that protects dominant forces within society and legitimizes their social control, while conveying to their audience messages of vulnerability and insecurity. "Risk ratios," which measure the relative likelihood of different demographic groups being represented as aggressors or victims in television drama, define a social pecking order that affects the way in which particular groups in society, women, the elderly, and racial minorities are perceived and view themselves. Their underrepresentation and victimization represent a symbolic annihilation, weakening their sense of identity and esteem while legitimizing the status quo that relegates them to positions of powerlessness.

One aspect of the construction of social reality through television is the claim that heavy viewing makes people more fearful, coming to see the world as a meaner place. Although high viewing levels have been associated with greater fear of crime, the limitations of correlational evidence make the causal role of television questionable, with the association reduced by control for demographic characteristics. Gerbner has accepted that residents of high-crime neighborhoods have a greater fear of crime and violence but has argued for a resonance effect whereby television reinforces and amplifies fear among heavy viewers in these areas. Research outside the United States has produced mixed findings, although differences in the nature of television programming and viewing patterns may alter the relevance of the cultivation model. In assessing violent incidents on television, viewers have proved capable of fine discriminations; British viewers react differently in rating the perceived realism and disturbance felt at police violence in American and British drama. The level of TV viewing in Swedish adolescents was found not to be related to fear of violence, but higher levels of viewer involvement and identification were linked to exaggerated perceptions of societal violence. As stable individual differences in the way people perceive their

world have been associated with fear of victimization, perceptions of danger and threat may be better viewed as part of an individual's more global sense of lacking environmental control rather than being contingent on viewing crime and violence on television. It is possible that fearful viewers retreat to the security of their home and television set; reassuring themselves with crime and action drama which, despite its level of violence, frequently portrays the ultimate triumph of law and order.

An underlying assumption of both the cultivation model and the behavioral effect approaches is that the impact of television is gradual and cumulative. An alternative position is that critical images may affect a viewer more dramatically than the continual repetition of predictable violence. One narratively justified moment of aggression by an heroic sheriff or law enforcement officer in a Western may have more ideological "effect" in supporting the status quo than numerous deaths and mutilations in cartoons, news, etc. Under this "drench hypothesis" innovative and challenging portrayals may make a substantial impact on audience perspectives, an approach particularly important to those concerned with the potential of film and television to contest accepted realities.

C. Viewers' Perceptions of Violence

While body counts and violence indices deproblematize the measurement of violence, research into how viewers perceive violence indicates the importance of factors other than the number and severity of injuries. Larry Gelbart, creator of "M*A*S*H," claimed people can tolerate 5000 killings on TV shows, but not one meaningful death of a character they love. The realism of the genre, features of the setting, gender of protagonists, and age, gender, and personality characteristics of the viewer all affect the extent to which an incident is deemed violent. The distinction is particularly marked in responses to cartoons. Both adults and child viewers themselves judge many cartoons, because of their unreality and humor, as low in violence, and quite young children demonstrate clear understanding of modality cues. Ratings based on content analysis of the frequency of violent incidents, however, place cartoons among the most violent forms of programming. What disturbs viewers relates strongly to a show's relevance to their own personal concerns.

A study by Tulloch and Tulloch of children's responses to depictions of violence indicated that the seriousness with which young people responded to violence was a function of context, not the extent of injury inflicted (J. C. Tulloch and M. I. Tulloch, 1993. In *Nation, Culture and Technology: Australian Media and Cultural Studies* (G. Turner, Ed.). Routledge, London). Thus the slaughter of a group of villagers in a war movie or actual injury on the sporting field was rated less disturbing than a fictional depiction of offscreen violence by a husband against his wife despite an absence of serious injury. Perceptions of violence can interact in a complex way with gender and developmental processes; younger children are more accepting of violence by authority figures, though generally violence is more disturbing to younger and female viewers. Specific social understanding may increase the impact of violence. Although older children are often less disturbed than younger children by portrayals of violence, they have been found to be more disturbed by depictions of nuclear war.

D. Understanding Violence: Qualitative Studies

Additional insights into how viewers perceive violence have been gained from qualitative studies. Researchers exploring the media literacy of children through qualitative techniques reveal how their understanding and responses are mediated by a sophisticated knowledge of generic conventions which are too often ignored in quantitative research. Qualitative research is particularly valuable in exploring the meaning of violent viewing for particular subcultural groupings. For instance, young males may use the viewing of excessively violent material to demonstrate their toughness and masculinity, while first nationals in one country may applaud the violent screen exploits of another first national group (e.g., Native Americans).

One research technique that has uncovered valuable insights into viewers' responses to violence that even qualitative interviews often miss requires participants to identify how they would edit a tape for broadcast. This task elicits strong emotional reactions to very specific details. A key factor in the decision-making processes demanded by the editing task is the extent to which portrayals of violence challenge and threaten an individual's view of the world. When the level of viewer engagement was shallow, violence could be deemed entertaining or merely personally distasteful, but violence that threatened individuals' views of their world provoked more intense though varied responses. Some viewers felt that scenes of disturbingly graphic aggression portrayed important social issues that should be broadcast uncut, while other viewers saw a shocking undermining of established values that was quite unac-ceptable as television fare (D. Docherty, 1992, *Violence in Television Fiction: Public Opinion and Broadcasting Standards*. Libbey, London).

Such depth of involvement is not confined to nonfictional material. The complexity of viewers' responses to fiction is dramatically demonstrated in an Australian study where female viewers' tense responses to what they were aware of as a fictional portrayal of rape were diffused when they discovered that, within the narrative, the rape was staged, not genuine. In some instances screen violence can provoke intense emotional responses which can mobilize attempts to diminish violence, not to emulate it.

IV. NONFICTIONAL VIOLENCE

A range of quite specific ethical issues emerge if we apply cultural considerations to nonfictional representations of violence.

A. Reporting of Violent Crime

1. Values in News Reporting

A television producer's primary concern in reporting violent crime is with newsworthiness. Accuracy may be sacrificed to the constraints of timing in highly competitive markets that demand an appealing and, most importantly, a current product. Reporting is often accused of sensationalism: pandering to an audience's perceived bloodthirsty enjoyment of violence, with graphic, often gruesome images of blood, injuries, body bags, and distraught victims or relatives. On the other hand, the representation of official violence, as in police attacks on picketers or public marches, can be weakened, effaced, or even suppressed. In either case, the focus in television news on the dramatic moment results in a virtual ignoring of underlying explanations of both violent crime and "official" victimization. Official perspectives on violence remain unchallenged and are frequently further cemented by a close cooperative relationship between journalists and authorities which promotes the flow of violent images, not analysis. Instead reports of violence tend to promote stereotypes and a scapegoating of minorities and outsiders.

2. Media and Victims Rights

The handling of victims of violence by the media involves a balance of rights between the public right to know and the victim's right to privacy. While recent constitutional interpretation has favored media freedom, ethical concerns about the treatment of victims has led to calls for a media code of ethics on dealing with victims. Because of the immediacy of TV news coverage, victims of violence are particularly vulnerable to intrusive, insensitive treatment, and the search for a voyeuristic or prurient angle can lead to victims feeling further victimized and blamed. Australian research found the practice of interviewing victims of violence or their relatives to be the most objectionable aspect of news coverage of violent incidents, eliciting greater public concern than close-ups, bodies, or blood. On the other hand, some parents argued at the hearing on the Dunblane massacre that, in order to strengthen support for antigun legislation, the public should be fully acquainted with the graphic details of the physical damage that modern weaponry inflicted on their children.

B. War, Terrorism, and Public Disorder

Although public concern with violence on television has often focused on the effects of fictional violence or personalized aggression, an important component of violence on television is the news coverage of public acts of violence, whether perpetrated against the state, as in terrorism or civil unrest, or by the state, as in war. Defining these distinctions is itself part of the role of television; the labeling of terrorists as distinct from resistance fighters implies not only the value attached to their violent actions but to those of the government which they oppose, with the potential to justify repression and terror by security forces. Discourses about riots can range from a stigmatizing of rioters as the "younger generation" out of control or of the structurally unemployed as a "race riot," to a critique of state-imposed economic and social repression. Frequently, the positioning of television cameras behind police lines presents a "natural" view of protesters or picketers as aggressors. A remarkably different view of police and strikers was presented by Ken Loach's film *Which Side Are You On?*, a documentary on the 1984 British Miners' strike where cameras and vox pop interviews presented the police themselves as violent aggressors. For Loach, the film was designed to both critique the "common-sense" status quo and to mobilize support for the miners.

Television images of demonstrators attacked with fire hoses and the brutal treatment of freedom riders have also been important in mobilizing support for the civil rights cause. Powerful images of social disorder can be feared by people positioned differently in the social hierarchy as promoting copycat violence, encour-aging support or criticism of forces of law and order, or serving as a stimulus to social change.

Despite frequent claims that television sensationalizes violence, the horrors of real violence are often too graphic to present in viewers' lounge rooms. News reporters have been put at risk attempting to film scenes of carnage in a form sufficiently sanitized to be acceptable for public broadcast. A British survey of viewers' responses to violence in factual television indicated that viewers are more upset when the incident is closer either geographically or through perceived similarity, when they are unaware of the eventual outcome, and when the victim is seen as innocent rather than provoking or deserving the attack. Viewers recognize that although the reality of factual violence makes it more disturbing, it is also the reason why the public needs to be informed. Graphic depictions, however, are often viewed as unnecessary to the provision of adequate information.

Particular violent images, such as the summary execution of a Vietcong collaborator in the streets of Saigon or the beating of Rodney King, can also become iconic, playing an important role in the mobilization of public opinion. Aware that nightly images of violence eroded public support for American intervention in Vietnam, state control of media coverage in wartime has become a very sophisticated process. As a result the Gulf War was largely seen through images of high-tech "smart" weaponry and pyrotechnics. It is no coincidence that a study of young British viewers found the most frequently mentioned distressing image of that war was of struggling sea birds drenched in oil. At the same time, militarily and politically controlled "sanitized" imagery of this kind can be used to support continued massive funding of smart weaponry, whereas later evidence cast considerable doubt on its effectiveness.

V. PUBLIC ATTITUDES TO VIOLENCE ON TELEVISION

A. Extent of Public Concern

Opinion polls have suggested widespread American anxiety about media violence, with the majority favoring more regulation to control it. The extent of public concern depends a great deal on the type of questions asked. In both the United States and Britain, audiences endorse statements that there is too much violence on television but are less likely to be critical of specific violent television shows. Nearly 80% of British respondents felt people are justified in being concerned about the impact of TV violence on children, and 60% agreed there was too much violence on TV. Yet viewers generally accepted that violence was part of television as it was part of life, favoring warnings, late scheduling, and parental vigilance rather than censorship. An ABC study found that around half of a national sample of television viewers felt there was too much violence on television, yet having rated the "The A-Team" as one of the most violent shows, respondents indicated that the level of violence was acceptable. Much greater concern was expressed about the violence available on cable services. Frequently excessive media presentation of both sex and violence was perceived as the cause of social ills, with 67% of American adults surveyed attributing increases in teenage violence to this cause, and 73% then favoring greater controls on television portrayal of sex and violence.

VI. CENSORSHIP AND PUBLIC POLICY

Responsibility for the regulation and control of film and television in different countries can be examined as a continuum from individual to state control. The model of individual regulation with philosophic roots in the work of Thomas Paine espouses a belief in an informed citizenry capable of protecting themselves and their families from harm. Any intervention by the state is deemed an unwarranted infringement of civil liberties. The United States' deregulated approach to media control most clearly typifies this approach. At the other end of the spectrum are authoritarian systems with tightly controlled, state-run media where public opinion on media products is unsolicited and unwelcome. Somewhere between an investiture of responsibility solely with either the individual viewer or the state lie the mixed systems operating in Australia, Canada, Britain, and other countries in Western Europe. Here an important regulatory and control role is delegated to expert bodies who exercise a degree of responsibility for television content. The rhetoric of threats to democratic freedoms have been far less often voiced in countries of Western Europe. Initiatives such as the British 9:00 P.M. watershed are generally perceived by their audience as a realistic compromise, enhancing parental control without depriving the public of adult programs. A degree of regulation has been accepted as responsible, and the possible threat of license losses encourages greater industry self-regulation. In such mixed systems, the existence of clear, informative labeling of products and accessible viewer complaint procedures are part of the combination of individual and delegated responsi-

bility. In the United States, where the level of violence on TV is greater and concern among researchers much more intense, there is great resistance, even from many of these same researchers, to regulatory powers that smack of censorship or restriction of individual freedoms. The lack of complaint from citizens of European democracies in response to greater controls has itself been presented as evidence of the dangers inherent in such a direction.

A. Regulation and Censorship in the U.S. Context

1. Public Inquiries, Regulation, and Policy Issues

a. Regulatory Role of the Federal Communications Commission (FCC)

The Broadcasting Act of 1934 established the FCC as the governing agency responsible for the granting licenses and the oversight of the radio and television industries. Properties of the broadcast spectrum which limit access have permitted a degree of regulation and extensive investigatory powers. Despite the requirement that broadcasters "serve the public interest," this test has never been used to refuse a license. Historically the FCC has not concerned itself with program content so it has not served the same role as regulatory bodies in many other countries which restrict the level of violence on television.

b. The Surgeon General's Report and Beyond

The emphasis on the effects of media violence on children has led to major government-funded research in this field. The 1972 Surgeon General's Report (by the Surgeon General's Scientific Advisory Committee on Television and Social Behavior) was a major attempt to resolve the issue of television violence effects by the accumulation of scientific evidence, including the commissioning of a series of studies as part of the investigation. Parallels were drawn explicitly with the way scientific research established a link between smoking and lung cancer. Preference was given to researchers within a quantitative social scientific paradigm, particularly from the psychology discipline where support for the demonstrability of violence effects has been greatest. Causal effects of television violence on aggression were accepted, although in a qualified way, in the report, a view reiterated over a decade later by the National Institute of Mental Health (1982), the U.S. Attorney General's Task Force on

Family Violence (1984), and the American Psychological Association (1985).

2. First Amendment and Libertarian Concerns

Debate in the United States about regulation and censorship has been fought in the context of the freedom of speech rights granted in the First Amendment. Even a voluntary network agreement not to broadcast violent programs between 7 and 9 P.M. was ruled unconstitutional. The history of U.S. broadcasting has been replete with investigation into the potential psychologically harmful effects of television violence, with a minimum of legislative control. More federal dollars have been spent researching the effects of televized violence than any other social effects of the commercial media. Yet any attempt at government regulation or censorship has been forcefully resisted by civil libertarians and commercial interests.

a. Creativity and the Suppression of Ideas

Any attempt to address the issue of screen violence by censorship can be seen as an attack on individual freedom of speech and creativity. Violence plays a dramatic role in many artistic products. It has been argued that the condemnation of screen violence relates to its mass consumption, thereby demonstrating an elitist distrust of popular art forms. Because of the complex links between political issues and violence, codes to restrict violence can serve also to control critical and subversive challenges to the state. Inasmuch as violence is a reality, not just a representation, any attempt to define unacceptable portrayals of violence potentially restricts the use of graphic depictions of violence in morally or politically challenging ways.

At the heart of legal analysis of the First Amendment is the notion of the free marketplace of ideas, yet within America supporters of diversity in television have identified the commercial pressure of ratings as stifling creativity and diversity. They argue that nowhere is this more evident than in the homogeneity and violence of children's programs. More generally, the sovereignty of the mass audience is seen to limit the forms in which violence is presented. Institutional imperatives work to pull experimentation, at least on network television and mainstream cinema, back toward the safe and acceptable. By contrast the ideology of authorship made possible within the combined public and commercial broadcasting structure of a country like Britain has allowed a wider range of drama and documentaries, promoting within mainstream broadcasting greater variety in the organizing of discourses about violence.

b. The Linking of Sex and Violence

Consideration of screen violence cannot be separated from issues of pornography and sexual violence. Responses in this area involve a complex of political and ideological positions from conservative moralists, to feminists concerned about the impact of demeaning portrayals of women, and to libertarians concerned that threats of sexual violence are being used to countenance tighter control on nonviolent erotica. Research on the impact of sexual violence poses particular dilemmas; experimental study of the effects of portrayals of sexual violence on adolescents has been deemed unethical in a way that studies involving nonerotic physical violence have not. Studies using college students have found that viewing sexual violence has increased male endorsement of rape myths, diminished sympathy for victims of sexual assault, and decreased the length of sentences deemed appropriate for such crimes. While the Attorney General's Commission in 1986 recognized that research findings identified violence, not sex, as the crucial variable in creating antisocial effects, their legislative recommendations were related more to the strengthening of the obscenity laws than to controlling sexually violent material.

3. Lobbying and Citizen Action

The power of citizens to influence what is broadcast can be applied by pressuring for regulations and more directly by commercial pressure on broadcasters. The latter strategy has been particularly prominent in the United States where reluctance to regulate is greater than that in Europe or other English-speaking countries. Such pressure can take the form of direct approaches to networks to modify the content of particular programs, or by organizing boycotts of companies whose advertising is linked to excessively violent shows. Such strategies have been quite effective in encouraging withdrawal of sponsorship and changing programming schedules.

An alternative strategy is lobbying for direct action accompanied by orchestrating public opinion through media campaigns. Such campaigns, viewed by their opponents as "moral panics," may spring out of specific incidents as in the case in England where child murderers were supposed to have viewed a particular violent video. These media campaigns are frequently characterized by sweeping claims, including simplified or distorted presentation of research findings and generalizations from individual cases, often on the basis of misreported information.

B. Children, Violence, and Public Policy

1. Protecting Children: The Vulnerable Child/The Active Child

Underlying much of the TV violence debate have been assumptions about the nature of the child viewer. The idea that children are uniquely vulnerable and in need of protection has been central to demands for a reduction in screen violence. Children, it is argued, are unable to differentiate fact from fantasy and lack an understanding of the constructed nature of fictional portrayals or, at an older age, of the atypicality of the events and solutions portrayed in TV drama. By contrast, a more robust view of children sees them as active viewers. Hodge, working within a cultural studies tradition, has shown how children possess quite sophisticated media decoding abilities and a range of resistant practices through which they actively reframe the programs that they watch. From this perspective, regulatory practices serve to exert control over children and to define children's needs and interests from an adult perspective (R. Hodge, 1989. In *Australian Television: Programs, Pleasures and Politics* (J. Tulloch and G. Turner, Eds.). Allen & Unwin, Sydney).

The active audience perspective has, however, been criticized for ignoring the role of economic and institutional forces in shaping children's television, overemphasizing individual agency, and ignoring any possible role for the media in shaping children's attitudes or behavior. There are signs that a "third generation" audience analysis is developing within cultural studies which will focus equally on structural, textual, and active audience determination of meanings received from the media.

In countries concerned with development of quality children's television, the focus at the professional media level has been as much on the encouragement of diversity and creativity in children's programming as on the removal of violence. For instance, the Australian Children's Television Foundation was funded in order to foster the development of "high-quality" children's programs. Attempts to sanitize children's viewing by censorship of violent programs may simply produce a bland, uncritical, unvaried diet.

2. Educational and Informational Alternatives

An alternative strategy to censorship or regulation of violence lies in informing and educating the viewing public.

a. Ratings

Many countries implement a system of ratings for cinema and television which can have a regulatory or purely informational purpose. The complexity of U.S. rating systems has been criticized, and the need for public education to clarify the meaning of rating codes has been advocated. Ratings can reflect the presence of profanities, explicit sexuality, or violent content and thus lack clear informational value. Moreover, such systems are often driven by notions of what is offensive rather than what is harmful. Introducing programs with warnings that specifically identify levels of coarse language, sex, or violence has the potential to provide the viewer or parent with much clearer guidance as to program content. While ratings serve to inform parents, they can also serve as a guide to young people seeking material that has been defined as "forbidden fruit." A current subject of debate is the technological extension of the ratings system via electronic blocking devices that respond to program classification signals, with the aim of enabling parents to establish controls over the channels or types of content they deem appropriate.

b. Educational Programs

The possibility of lessening the impact of violence by educational programs that promote nonviolent values and emphasize the fictional and unrealistic nature of much violence on television has been supported by specific research showing their effectiveness in reducing the link between viewing and aggressive behavior. The extension of educational interventions to mitigate the effects of exposure to portrayals of sexual violence have been canvassed after some preliminary work conducted on college students. Both in studies with children focusing on general television violence and with adults focusing on sexual violence, the strategy of requiring participants to produce antiviolence messages has been found to impact subsequent beliefs and attitudes. Programs of media education in schools can promote children's awareness of the processes of media construction, and this construction–deconstruction approach to media education has developed in a number of Western countries.

Dutch researchers developed a curriculum to increase the awareness of elementary school students of the consequences of real violence both physically and psychologically for victims and for the police involved in shooting suspects. In addition to gaining novel information from credible sources, students were encouraged to use their newfound knowledge analytically in response to violent incidents in crime series. A demonstrable impact of this program lasted over a period of 2 years, with children more ready to perceive acts as violent, less accepting of violence by good characters, and with lowered perceptions of televized violence as being realistic. This study did not aim to reduce child aggression but to encourage children to assess depictions of violent scenes in crime drama more critically (M. W. Vooijs and T. H. A. van der Voort, 1993. *Journal of Research and Development in Education*, 26, 133–142).

The potential educational role of the media in promoting antiviolence messages has become increasingly recognized. The film *Schindler's List* is an instance of a high-profile film aimed at raising public awareness of the Holocaust. A growing genre of dramatized documentaries have explored a range of issues concerning violence: rape, wife battering, child abuse, police abuse, and terrorism.

C. Investigation and Regulation: Comparative Perspectives

Government initiated investigations into screen violence have been a recurring response to public concerns, although their nature, findings, and policy implications have varied with the temporal and cultural contexts in which they occurred. It is an irony of the particular constitutional and socioeconomic culture of the United States that in the country where violence on television is very high and the scientific community most united in its belief in the harmful effects of television violence, regulation has been so resisted. By contrast the very different relationship of public and commercial broadcasting in Britain, with its greater diversity of programming within a much smaller set of broadcast options, presents a very different climate for policy development in the television violence area. The Broadcasting Standards Council was set up in 1988 to "consider the portrayal of violence, of sex, and matters of taste and decency in broadcast and video works," both monitoring and researching in the area of broadcasting standards. The publications produced by this body have not generally taken an effects approach, the very title of a monograph on mass media effects, *A Measure of Uncertainty*, indicating a more questioning appraisal of

effects research. Concern with the portrayal of violence has led to an exploration of viewer responses in order to assess public concerns in both fictional and factual violence.

A similar shift was evident in the approach of the Australian Broadcasting Tribunal (1990) investigation of violence on television which was part of a much broader investigation into violence in Australia prompted by community concern following a spate of multiple killings. Research commissioned as part of this study moved away from the concerns of the effects tradition and used both quantitative and qualitative methods to look at viewers' perceptions of television violence, what disturbed them, and what they believed should be controlled. This represents a paradigm shift from a scientific determination of what is harmful to an examination of community perceptions and concerns.

Epistemological issues are at stake here, since the paradigm shift also involves a move from positivist notions of effects measured objectively by scientific "experts" to hermeneutic, constructivist, and even relativist notions of "the real," as constructed through the language, discourse, and theoretical assumptions of the contextualized observer. This survey of ethical concerns relating to violence in film and television has itself been structured by this epistemological debate, as it has traversed a path from single-nation (U.S.) focused "scientific" assumptions about the effects of media violence to more comparative, relative, and cultural approaches to this field.

Also See the Following Articles

CENSORSHIP • FREEDOM OF SPEECH • PORNOGRAPHY • SEXUAL CONTENT IN FILMS AND TELEVISION • TABLOID JOURNALISM

Bibliography

Comstock, G. (1991). "Television and the American Child." Academic Press, San Diego.

Gauntlett, D. (1995). "Moving Experiences: Understanding Television's Influences and Effects." Libbey, London.

Gerbner, G. (1994). The politics of media violence: Some reflections. In "Mass Communications Research: On Problems and Policies" (C. J. Hamelink and O. Linné, Eds.). Ablex, Norwood, NJ.

Hargrave, A. M. (1993). "Violence in Factual Television, Vol. 4, Broadcasting Standards Council Public Opinion and Broadcasting Standards." Libbey, London.

Paik, H., and Comstock, G. (1994). The effects of television violence on anti-social behavior: A meta-analysis. *Communication Research*, 21, 516–546.

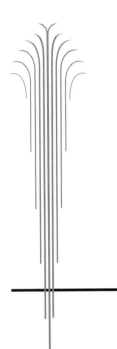

VIRTUE ETHICS

Robert B. Louden
University of Southern Maine

GLOSSARY

agent-based ethics A radical type of virtue ethics in which all moral evaluation concepts (including evaluations of acts and consequences) are either based on or derived from judgments about inner states of agents.

deontology Any type of ethical theory which denies what teleology asserts. Holds that certain acts or types of act exhibit intrinsically right-making virtues in themselves, regardless of the consequences that may come after them.

Kantianism The most influential example of deontological theory in modern and contemporary ethics. Named after the German philosopher Immanuel Kant (1724–1804), who held that all genuine moral duties are instances of categorical imperatives which bind unconditionally.

teleology Any type of ethical theory which holds that morally right actions are defined as those which produce good consequences.

utilitarianism The most influential example of teleological theory in modern and contemporary ethics, according to which "good consequences" are understood in terms of "happiness."

virtue ethics An approach to the study of ethics which puts the virtues first, before analyses of acts or consequences.

virtues Traits of character which are judged to be morally valuable.

VIRTUE ETHICS is a theoretical perspective within ethics which holds that judgments about the inner lives of individuals (their traits, motives, dispositions, and character), rather than judgments about the rightness or wrongness of external acts and/or consequences of acts, are of the greatest moral importance. An approach to ethics that has become increasingly popular in recent years, virtue ethics was first articulated as an explicit project within Anglo-American philosophy in the late 1950s, and was developed in explicit opposition to modern deontological and teleological approaches that did not grant sufficient weight to the importance of character judgments in ethics. At the same time, it is also true that a general virtue ethics perspective represented the dominant outlook in both western and eastern schools of moral thought until the Enlightenment.

One major criticism levied against virtue ethics is that its strong agent perspective prevents it from giving us sufficiently specific advice about what we ought to do. If true, a virtue ethics perspective would not seem to have much to offer applied ethics and casuistry. Nevertheless, within the past 10 years a number of studies have appeared which attempt to incorporate

Encyclopedia of Applied Ethics, Volume 4
Copyright © 1998 by Academic Press. All rights of reproduction in any form reserved.

virtue ethics into applied and professional ethics. While practitioners of virtue ethics do not usually aim to "solve problems" or resolve quandaries in difficult situations, it is also the case that new questions and perspectives are being introduced in applied ethics as a result of the recent infusion of a virtue ethics perspective.

I. VIRTUE ETHICS AS A THEORY

In 1930 the Cambridge philosopher C. D. Broad first proposed to divide ethical theories into two classes, teleological and deontological, thereby introducing a dichotomy that quickly became standard in ethics. Teleological theories were defined as ones that hold that the moral rightness of an action is always determined by its tendency to promote certain consequences deemed intrinsically good; deontological theories, denying this claim, held that certain acts exhibit intrinsically right-making features in themselves, regardless of the consequences that may come after them (C. D. Broad, 1930. *Five Types of Ethical Theory*, pp. 206–207. Routledge & Kegan Paul, London). Broad's dichotomy was widely accepted as being exhaustive, but in fact there are two fundamental classes of normative moral judgments that do not fit easily into it. First, it focuses on rightness or obligation, excluding moral judgments concerning what is admirable, good, excellent, or ideal. Second, it concerns only actions and their consequences, saying nothing about moral judgments concerning persons, character, character traits, or motives.

The contemporary movement known as virtue ethics is usually said to have begun in 1958 with Elizabeth Anscombe's advice to do ethics without the notion of a "moral ought." Although her own critique of moral obligation concepts (viz., that they have meaning only within religious frameworks that include the notion of a divine lawgiver) did not gain widespread acceptance among secular ethicists, her constructive proposal to look for moral norms not in duty concepts but within the virtues or traits of character that one needs to flourish as a human being quickly caught on (G. E. M. Anscombe, 1958. *Philosophy* 33, 1–19. Reprinted, 1981. *Collected Philosophical Papers*, Vol. 3. Univ of Minnesota Press, Minneapolis). Soon thereafter, philosophers such as Alasdair MacIntyre, Philippa Foot, Edmund Pincoffs, and many others began to articulate and defend a third option in normative ethics, one whose chief concern was not a theory of morally right action but rather those traits of character that define the morally good or admirable person.

Phrases such as "revival of" or "return to" often precede mention of virtue ethics in contemporary discussions, and it is generally true that questions about the virtues occupy a much more prominent place in ancient and medieval moral philosophy than in western moral theories developed since the Enlightenment. But it is important to note that the conscious articulation of virtue ethics as a distinct way of theorizing about ethics arose from within contemporary Anglo-American ethical theory. Virtue ethics took root as a reaction against the underlying common assumptions of both teleological and deontological ethical theories and has achieved its greatest critical success as a protest against these accepted ways of doing normative ethics. Accordingly, one can view virtue ethics as having two complementary aspects: a critical program that presents a critique of the prevailing assumptions, methods, and aspirations of normative teleological and deontological moral theories, and a constructive program in which an alternative virtue-oriented normative moral conception is developed and defended.

A. The Critical Program

At this level virtue theorists are not necessarily committed to defending a full-scale alternative to existing ethical theory programs, but rather to showing why such approaches are systematically unable to satisfactorily account for moral experience. Major criticisms made by virtue theorists against their opponents include the following:

Overreliance on rule models of moral choice. Utilitarians and Kantians (the two most influential contemporary versions of teleological and deontological theories, respectively), it is held, both mistakenly view universal and invariable principles and laws as being exhaustive of ethics. But real-life moral exemplars do not simply deduce what to do from a hierarchy of timeless, universal principles and rules. They possess sound judgment skills that enable them to respond appropriately to the nuances of each particular situation in ways that go beyond mere mechanical applications of rules.

Strictly speaking, the rule-bashing tone of much virtue ethics literature does not necessarily distinguish it from its teleological and deontological competitors. For some members of the latter camps (tagged variously as "act deontologists," "act-utilitarians," "intuitionists," or "particularists") have also argued that agents do not determine morally right actions by consulting rules and principles. Again, the clearest difference between virtue theorists and their opponents lies in the former's strong commitment to an agent perspective as opposed to an act- (or consequences of act) perspective. But it is true that the dominant tone within both modern deontology and modern teleology has been strongly rule oriented.

Overly rationalistic accounts of moral agency. Teleologists and deontologists, it is held, too often assign a merely negative role in the moral life for desires and emotions. However, the people we most admire morally are not simply those who do their duty and act on the correct principles, but those who do so with the right kinds of desires and emotions. (In this respect, virtue ethics also shares certain affinities with ideas developed in feminist ethics concerning the importance of, e.g., care and sympathy in the moral life. Both approaches emphasize the positive roles of feelings and desires in ethics.) Additionally, though many teleologists and deontologists do acknowledge the importance of motives in ethics, they typically mislocate them in abstractions such as "the greatest happiness principle" or "the moral law" rather than in particular persons and our relationships to them. The person who visits an ill friend in the hospital strictly because it is the morally right thing to do does not seem to be as morally admirable as the person who visits an ill friend in the hospital out of direct concern for the friend's well-being.

Formalism. Mainstream teleological and deontological theorists tend to focus exclusively on conceptual analyses of their favored duty concepts and then on formal, logical arguments based on such analyses. Additionally, they tend to view moral questions as arising only when an individual agent is trying to decide what to do in rarely occurring, problematic situations. These methodological commitments result in a view of morality that is impoverished, overly restrictive, and insensitive to the necessary content of ethics. Virtue theorists, on the other hand, are much more open to drawing connections between morality and other areas of life such as psychology, anthropology, history, art, and culture. Their long-term agent perspective also enables them to correctly view moral deliberation and choice as involving much more than discrete decisions made in moments of uncertainty.

B. The Constructive Program

In offering their alternative, virtue theorists face the fundamental task of showing how and why a virtue-oriented conception of ethics is superior to its act- and duty-based competitors. In what ways is moral experience better understood once virtue concepts become the primary tools of analysis? Here one may distinguish two general tendencies: radical or pure agent-based virtue ethics attempts to interpret moral experience and

judgment without employing act and duty concepts at all (or at least claiming that such concepts are always derivable from more fundamental ones concerning good people—e.g., "morally right" acts might be defined simply as those acts performed by moral exemplars); moderate virtue ethics seeks to supplement standard act approaches with an account of the virtues. The former approach tends to view teleological and deontological ethical theories as totally misguided; the latter sees them merely as incomplete. Major issues confronting constructive virtue ethics programs include the following:

Defining moral virtue. What counts as a moral virtue and why? Is there any plausible way to distinguish between moral and nonmoral virtues? How exactly do virtues relate to actions, reasons, beliefs, principles, rules, desires, and emotions? Are virtues beneficial to their possessors, and, if so, are they too self-centered to count as moral traits?

Justifying the virtues. How can we establish the validity of those character traits defined as moral virtues, once the option of appealing to the value of the acts and/or consequences that the virtues tend to encourage is ruled out as a justificatory strategy? On the traditional Aristotelian model, which still today remains the chief inspiration for most contemporary virtue ethics programs, moral virtues are defined as traits that human beings need in order to live well or flourish. But does the idea of flourishing provide solid enough ground on which to base the moral virtues? Is it still possible to speak accurately of *one* single human function, or is human life more variously textured than the classical picture allows? How and why is evidence of flourishing necessarily evidence of moral virtuousness? Is it necessarily the case that all moral virtues contribute to flourishing (and all vices to withering)? On the other hand, if one declines to issue pronouncements about "the human *telos*" and instead opts for a softer, more pluralistic functionalism that seeks to define virtues in terms of different kinds of human purposes or practices, can one still arrive at a substantive notion of the virtues that holds that they are more than merely local cultural products?

Relations among the virtues. How do the virtues relate to one another in real life? Is there anything to the ancient "unity of virtues" thesis (which, on the Aristotelian model, views *phronêsis* or practical wisdom as generating and uniting all of the moral virtues), or does it make more sense to hold that a person might possess one moral virtue such as courage and nevertheless lack others? How many different moral virtues are there? Are some more fundamental than others? Can they be ranked in order of importance? Do virtues ever conflict with one another? What kinds of specific practical guidance do we get from the virtues, especially in cases where they appear to conflict with one another (e.g., honesty vs. kindness, love vs. fidelity)?

It should come as no surprise that radical or pure agent-based virtue ethics approaches have attracted far fewer followers than more moderate versions, and that the critical program has had a much stronger influence on contemporary ethical theory discussions than has the constructive program. Those who turn to recent work in virtue ethics in hopes of finding greater consensus on either conceptual or normative issues than exists among ethical theorists elsewhere are bound to be disappointed. Still, it is no small sign of virtue ethics' success that contemporary ethical theorists of all persuasions are addressing questions of character, agency, and motivation as never before—and that there now exist greater realism and humility among contemporary philosophers concerning how ethical theory should proceed and what it might reasonably accomplish.

II. THE APPLICATION PROBLEM

A central criticism of virtue ethics is that due to its primary focus on moral character and the inner states of agents it is structurally unable to tell us much about what we ought to do or not do in specific situations. If this criticism is sound, virtue ethics would seem to be of little use in applied ethics and casuistry. It is therefore important to examine the precise nature of the criticism and to assess it in some detail.

A. Misinterpretations of the Application Problem

1. Moral Education

Critics who claim that virtue ethics does not tell us how to act do not deny that the virtues are necessary and important ingredients in everyone's moral education. Obviously, the world would be a better place if more lawyers were taught the virtue of honesty; politicians integrity; physicians beneficence; professors humility; etc. Professional ethics is not simply a matter of making one's publicly observable behavior adhere to the rules laid out in the relevant code of ethics, just as ordinary morality is not exhausted by calculative rule-following. Professionals (like everyone else) need to develop good moral character in order to act morally, and the development of good character should be a fundamental part of everyone's moral education. However, all of these claims are straightforward, simple truths of moral education to which all competing schools of ethical theory consent. Virtue ethicists cannot claim a monopoly on the common insight that proper character development is vital for all areas of ethical life.

2. The Need for Judgment

The criticism should also not be identified with the objection that virtue ethics, in its opposition to rule models of moral choice, declines to offer moral agents a precise algorithm or step-by-step decision procedure that will tell them exactly what to do for each moral problem they encounter. No moral theory worth taking seriously aims to produce such a simplistic "package deal" or total algorithm for life. All traditional schools of moral theory recognize that informed judgment and practical wisdom are needed to apply rules and principles correctly, and that such rules and principles cannot be applied efficaciously in difficult or novel situations by people who lack moral experience, insight, and imagination. Virtue ethics also cannot claim a monopoly on the common insight that human beings need practical judgment in order to navigate successfully through the waters of life.

3. Moral Dilemmas and Incommensurable Values

Similarly, the criticism that virtue ethics is of little use in applied ethics and casuistry does not merely come down to the objection that its adherents often leave specific cases unresolved, admitting that there are genuine moral dilemmas in human life and that our values are not always commensurable. For here, too, some moral theorists outside of the virtue ethics movement have also argued that a proper analysis of moral experience reveals the existence of an irreducible plurality of moral values as well as a recognition that agents are sometimes faced with tragic choices where no morally right decision is possible. Furthermore, a proper understanding of value pluralism and of moral dilemmas would itself seem to entail a recognition that such problems do not stem from the personalities of moral agents but are due rather to facts of life and with the specific nature of the situation at hand. At any rate, it is not just friends of the virtues who have acknowledged value pluralism and moral dilemmas.

In sum, though proponents of virtue ethics rightly emphasize the need for moral education and judgment, as well as the reality of moral dilemmas and incommensurable values, such criticisms are not necessarily exclusive to virtue ethics alone. Some ethical theorists outside of the virtue ethics movement also stress these same points.

B. What the Application Problem Is

What then does the criticism that virtue ethics cannot tell us what to do come down to? Is the criticism justified? How have virtue theorists responded to it?

1. Agent-Based Virtue Ethics

First of all, the criticism is directed solely against what were earlier called radical or pure agent-based forms of virtue ethics in which act-evaluation concepts such as "morally wrong" and "morally obligatory" are either dispensed with entirely or else treated as being derivable from more fundamental agent-, motive-, or trait-evaluation concepts. More moderate versions of virtue ethics which seek merely to supplement rather than replace act ethics are not objects of the criticism. If the agent-based route is taken, talk about what the "morally right" thing to do consists of is usually cashed out in terms of what the morally good person would do. Certain inner states of agents are first identified and evaluated morally, and actions and consequences are then evaluated in terms of their relationships to these inner states.

Historically, two of the clearest and most influential proponents of this approach are Plato and, closer to our own time, James Martineau (1805–1900). Plato, in the *Republic* (ca. 380 B.C.), argues that justice (*dikaiosune*) is properly understood not in terms of external conduct but rather in terms of a certain harmonious relationship between the parts of a man's soul: justice is concerned "with what is inside him, with what is truly himself and his own" (443c–d). All other virtues are in effect analyzed analogously by Plato, with this same strong focus on the inner state of one's soul. Similarly, Martineau, in *Types of Ethical Theory* (1885 [1898], 3rd ed. Clarendon Press, Oxford), argues that the inner motives of agents rather than their outwardly observable acts are always the fundamental objects of moral evaluation. What we judge in ethics, he writes, "is always the *inner spring* of an action, as distinguished from its outward operation" (Vol. 2, p. 24). On this view, the moral value of the inner motives of the agent is what determines whether he or she is a morally good person, and right action is then defined in terms of the choices a morally good person would make. Both Plato and Martineau are thus in effect early followers of Elizabeth Anscombe's advice to do ethics without act-evaluation concepts such as "moral ought," assessing action instead in terms of trait concepts such as "untruthful" and "unjust." And it is the heeding of this particular

counsel, as noted earlier in Section I, which is usually said to mark the beginning of the contemporary revival of virtue ethics. At the same time, as the example of Anscombe herself indicates, the pure agent-based approach is not merely a historical curiosity—it is being pursued in earnest by numerous contemporary theorists.

2. Casuistry

Secondly, the application criticism is directed solely at the possible contributions virtue ethics might make to the specific subfield or domain of applied ethics traditionally known as casuistry. This area of ethics concerns attempts to resolve specific moral problems that arise in real-life situations. Other dimensions of applied ethics which are of possible interest to theorists (e.g., the moral education of professionals, conflicting role responsibilities, institutional arrangements, and methodological disputes of one sort or another) are not effected by the criticism.

3. Agent-Independent Assessments

In the area of applied ethics traditionally known as casuistry, our foremost concern is not always the state of people's souls or the condition of their moral characters. For a multitude of reasons, we are often primarily concerned not with the motives and inner states of agents but rather with determining the rightness of acts in some manner which is not derivative on the inner states of agents. To start with, good people occasionally do bad things, and once in a while bad people surprise us by doing something good. These two truisms alone should suffice to make us aware of the need to at least occasionally assess the morality of action in an agent-independent manner.

Second, in analyzing specific moral problems it is often the case that our most fundamental concern is a rock-bottom one of whether or not certain acts should be viewed as morally permissible. We recognize that admirable as well as not-so-admirable people may in certain circumstances be forced to consider, say, abortion, euthanasia, or suicide. But in reflecting on such dilemmas our chief moral concern is not whether those involved are fundamentally admirable or not-so-admirable people, or even how committing the acts in question might affect the condition of their characters, but rather whether we as a society are prepared to call such acts morally permissible, and if so, why and in what precise circumstances. It is not that judgments of character are a high-end luxury item which applied ethics cannot afford, but simply that there are times when such judgments are not what is most important, morally speaking.

Third (and relatedly), there is often an important difference of temporal perspective between virtue ethics and the art of resolving perplexing moral cases. Since our moral characters are acquired only over a very long period of time, virtue ethics necessarily takes a long-term perspective. In applied ethics and casuistry, our perspective is sometimes much more temporally limited: what should I do here and now? The issue of one's character is not always the most important thing to consider in making such decisions.

Finally, it should also be noted that the connection between moral virtues and action is not at all a simple one. A just person will normally act justly, a generous person generously, etc. (Important exceptions include acts done out of character, and people sometimes *do* act out of character when faced with morally perplexing cases. Here we find yet another reason for developing the conceptual resources to make agent-independent assessments of action.) But our knowledge that someone is a just person cannot always be translated into an accurate prediction of how that person will perform in a given situation—particularly a situation involving a morally perplexing case. All people of good character will hopefully agree that murder, torture, and rape are morally intolerable. But it is the hard cases which rightfully attract attention in applied ethics, and to insist that all people of good character must take exactly the same line on, say, abortion or client confidentiality is highly implausible. Also, some important moral virtues are not tied to action in any obvious way at all. Integrity is viewed as an important moral virtue in nearly all moral traditions. But how exactly does the person of integrity act?

In sum, there are many, many reasons why knowledge about the virtues is not always helpful when our concern is specific acts and choices.

III. APPLIED VIRTUE ETHICS

Nevertheless, as virtue ethics gains a deserved hearing in contemporary discussions, and as more and more writers come to view it as a third alternative to the limited perspectives of deontology and teleology, it is perhaps inevitable that the impact of virtue ethics will begin to be felt within applied ethics circles. Admittedly, the earlier work in the revival of virtue ethics literature was often heavily theoretical and metaethical in tone. However, this is understandable, for its authors were concerned primarily with putting forward a different conception of morality itself and of what is most important in moral evaluation. And they did this within an academic climate of opinion which was often unreceptive to their outlook. But more recently articles have begun to appear in a variety of journals and anthologies which attempt to apply virtue ethics to, e.g., euthanasia and abortion, as well as to select issues within environmental ethics, business ethics, biomedical ethics, population policy, social justice, and other areas. Numerous attempts have also been made to incorporate a virtue ethics perspective into professional ethics.

How have recent advocates of virtue ethics replied to the application problem? What kinds of work does the perspective of virtue ethics actually perform in their analyses of issues in applied ethics? More generally, in what ways might virtue ethics transform background assumptions, premises, arguments, and conclusions within applied ethics in the future?

A. From Acts to Agents

As one might expect, there is a marked shift of perspective in these writings away from the familiar (and often interminable) debates concerning the rights and obligations of competing parties and toward the character of the agents involved in the decisions. People who exercise their rights are often selfish, callous, and inconsiderate; those who do their duty can be cold and unsympathetic toward others. Establishing the relevant rights and duties in the case at hand (again, no easy task in itself) does not take us very far in resolving the deeper moral issues.

It is also of interest to note that this shift from an act- to an agent perspective has been carried out not only in discussions of problems which arise in the moral lives of individuals (euthanasia, abortion, etc.) where the virtues are normally associated, but also in addressing large-scale matters of social justice. At what might be called the larger macro as opposed to micro level of morality, some virtue theorists working in applied ethics have advocated that social policies, institutional arrangements, and societies themselves should be evaluated and critiqued by asking what kinds of people they produce (Slote, 1993). Are the moral characters of citizens living within a given society or under a specified set of institutions and policies morally admirable or not, and to what extent can we causally track their characters back to the social and political environments in which they live?

Usually the shift toward traits and persons looks at specific virtues. But occasionally interesting analyses of vices are also prominent. For instance, in environmental ethics authors have asked, What traits of character does a despoiler of nature exhibit, and how do our reactions to these traits help us to understand what is morally objectionable about such behavior even when we cannot produce a knockdown argument which demonstrates that the destructive acts issuing from such traits are clearly wrong (Hill, 1983; Frasz, 1993)?

B. Responses to the Application Problem

However, such shifts to an agent perspective within applied ethics discussions do not usually involve attempts to resolve specific moral problems by means of the virtues. To this extent, the application problem discussed earlier remains untouched. Nevertheless, there have been several specific responses to the application problem. The following three are of note.

We are all in the same boat. Perhaps the most common response is simply to assert that the myriad versions of deontology and teleology fare equally poorly when it comes to offering clear and uncontested guidance in specific situations. Theorists of nearly every persuasion talk and (mostly) write a lot about applying their pet theories to concrete moral issues, but the results of such efforts are often highly contested (particularly by other theorists). However, this charge of collective guilt, while perhaps not lacking in substance, does not in itself further the debate.

Positive instructions for action. Second, it has been asserted that all of the virtues do in fact generate positive instructions for action (Hursthouse, 1991; 1995. In *Virtues and Reasons: Philippa Foot and Moral Theory.* R. Hursthouse, G. Lawrence, and W. Quinn, Eds. Clarendon Press, Oxford). Given the virtue of justice, we obtain the instruction to act justly; from the virtue of courage we generate the imperative to act courageously; etc. Similarly, each vice generates its own prohibition on action. Do not act cruelly, selfishly, deceitfully, etc. So the virtues and vices are not as silent about action as critics assume. This is true enough, but there still remains the important issue of the degree of specificity contained in such instructions. And as noted earlier, the degree of specificity contained in injunctions such as "act justly" is, for various reasons, often very slim. Again, what exactly does the just person do in morally problematic situations? Even if virtue theorists could agree on a priority ranking for the virtues to use in cases where virtues conflict with one another (a big if), the degree of specific practical guidance for resolving hard cases that one gets from the virtues will necessarily often remain slim.

Contextualism. Third, several authors have claimed that virtue ethics, precisely because it eschews the abstract rule-approach, formalism, and overly rationalist accounts of moral agency of its competitors, is in fact closer to real life and thus naturally better equipped to deal with concrete moral problems than more familiar deontological and teleological versions of moral theory. Utilitarian and Kantian theories, it is alleged, try to transcend context and end up with vacuity, whereas virtue ethics remains firmly rooted in the context of human life (Solomon, 1992; Vitek, 1993). Here too, a virtues approach to ethics would not seem to be as distant from the practical issues of real life as its critics allege. However, while it is the case that virtue ethics analyses of morality generally are less abstract, less formalist, and less rationalistic than those of deontologists and utilitarians, its own contextualist analyses do not necessarily translate into specific advice about what to do. Agents who lack the requisite virtues will often not act rightly, but offering them a contextualist story about what is morally lacking in their characters (even when the story is true) unfortunately does not always tell them what to do.

C. Virtue Ethics and Antitheory

A survey of recent attempts to do applied ethics from a virtues perspective reveals that most of them do not in fact try to "solve problems" in the straightforward way that many people traditionally have assumed an applied moral theory was supposed to do. But one should not necessarily infer from this that the application problem discussed earlier constitutes a conclusive argument against the relevance of a virtues approach in applied ethics. Rather, it more plausibly suggests a deeper skepticism among practitioners of virtue ethics concerning the nature of moral theory itself. If by "moral theory" is meant an ordered set of abstract, universal principles which is to be applied deductively to solve any and all particular problems which are thrown at it, then virtue ethics does not qualify as a moral theory. Indeed, it has been argued by some that virtue ethics represents yet another articulation of the general antitheory mood that one finds expressed in so many areas of the humanities and social sciences at present. But a careful reading of the evidence here suggests rather that virtue ethics itself constitutes more a critique of many traditional assumptions concerning the nature and aims of moral theory rather than a flat-out rejection of theory per se. Virtue ethics is not competing for quite the same turf as modern deontological and utilitarian theories but is rather an attempt to return moral theory to more realistic possibilities. While it is not possible at present to state in detail the precise ways and manners in which this rethinking of theory will play itself out in applied and professional ethics, it is clear that the basic orientation will be much more "front-loaded." More emphasis will be placed on the development of character and on acquiring requisite experiential skills of judgment and perception, and less on intellectualistic efforts to resolve quandaries which confront adults after their characters are set.

IV. CONCLUSION

Thus far, most of the existing work on applied virtue ethics has been rather programmatic and exploratory in tone. However, this is understandable, since its authors have primarily been concerned with introducing the general notion that, contrary to what critics have claimed, a virtue ethics perspective can indeed inform one or another region of applied ethics. It is hoped that this first wave of research will be followed by a second one which includes more fine-grained analyses and specific examples of how virtue ethics can enrich our understanding of the problems of applied ethics.

The history of the working relationship between traditional ethical theory and applied ethics has not been a comfortable one. More and more practitioners and even researchers in applied ethics have grown increasingly skeptical as to whether the traditional grand-scale theories of normative ethics have anything useful at all to offer applied ethics. Clearly, it is time to give new theoretical perspectives their day. At the same time, practitioners and researchers alike need to reexamine their own assumptions concerning what exactly a theory of ethics can and should provide. And part of this reexamination must also include greater scrutiny concerning the nature of moral problems themselves, their place in human life, and the extent to which they do (or do not) even admit of solutions.

Also See the Following Articles

CONSEQUENTIALISM AND DEONTOLOGY • KANTIANISM • MORAL DEVELOPMENT • PLATONISM • UTILITARIANISM

Acknowledgment

Portions of section I of this contribution are borrowed, with some modifications, from the author's previously published entry on "Virtue Ethics" in *The Encyclopedia of Philosophy Supplement* (1996. Macmillan, New York).

Bibliography

Foot, P. (1977). Euthanasia. *Philosophy and Public Affairs* 6, 85–112. Reprinted, 1978. "Virtues and Vices and Other Essays in Moral Philosophy." Univ. of California Press, Berkeley.

Frasz, G. B. (1993). Environmental virtue ethics: A new direction for environmental ethics. *Environmental Ethics,* 15, 259–274.

Hill, T. E., Jr. (1983). Ideals of human excellence and preserving natural environments. *Environmental Ethics,* 5, 211–224.

Hursthouse, R. (1991). Virtue theory and abortion. *Philos. Public Affairs,* 20, 223–246.

Hursthouse, R. (1995). Applying virtue ethics. In "Virtues and Reasons: Philippa Foot and Moral Theory" (R. Hursthouse, G. Lawrence, and W. Quinn, Eds.). Clarendon Press, Oxford.

Jordan, A. E., and Meara, N. M. (1991). Ethics and the professional practice of psychologists: The role of virtues and principles. *Professional Psychology: Research and Practice,* 21, 107–114.

Shelp, E. A. (Ed.) (1985). "Virtue and Medicine: Explorations in the Character of Medicine." Reidel, Dordrecht.

Slote, M. (1993). Virtue ethics and democratic values. *Journal of Social Philosophy,* 24, 5–37.

Solomon, R. C. (1992). Corporate roles, personal virtues: An Aristotelian approach to business ethics. *Business Ethics Quarterly,* 2, 317–339.

Statman, D. (1995). Virtue ethics and psychology. *International Journal of Applied Philosophy,* 9, 43–49.

Vitek, W. (1993). Virtue ethics and mandatory birth control. In "Biomedical Ethics Reviews 1992" (J. M. Humber and R. F. Almeder, Eds.). Humana, Totowa, NJ.

WARFARE, CODES OF

Judith Wagner DeCew
Clark University

I. Conditions of Justified Warfare
II. Permissible Conduct in War
III. Challenges to Codes of Warfare
IV. A Contemporary Defense: Walzer on Just and Unjust Wars

GLOSSARY

aggression An unprovoked attack or invasion, initiation of hostilities.

discrimination principle A basis for distinguishing who and what may be a legitimate target of military action; it generally prohibits intentional attack on noncombatants.

doctrine of double effect The proposition that it may be permissible to bring about a result as the foreseen but unintended byproduct of an action that it would not be permissible to bring about as the direct and intended result of the same action.

jus ad bellum Justice of war. Criteria that establish a right to go to war; just cause.

jus in bello Justice in war. Criteria that determine legitimate conduct in war; just means.

obliteration bombing Aerial bombing of a large area that may include killing innocent civilians along with soldiers and support personnel at military installations.

pacifism The view that war cannot be justified, because violence is morally unjustified. Sometimes also the view that it is morally wrong to use force to resist, punish, or prevent violence, implying a duty not to use force to resist or prevent violence.

proportionality principle The principle that force used must be proportional to the end sought.

self-defense Defense of oneself or of one's property, security, rights, and reputation, or the right to preserve oneself with whatever force is reasonably necessary against actual violence or the threat of violence.

war A period of open hostilities or the threat of such. More commonly, hostilities and combat.

CODES OF WARFARE have been developed for a variety of issues concerning morality and warfare. In ancient times and thereafter, mass killing was practiced in most societies, often with little worry about its morality. A warrior or soldier or officer was often viewed as a hero. Since the Middle Ages, however, philosophers have attempted to address three central issues on morality and war. First, they have examined what circumstances, if any, justify a country in going to war. In classical theory, this has been called the issue of *jus ad bellum* (justice of war), or just cause. Second, they have asked what conduct is permissible or prohibited in conducting a war, the issue of *jus in bello* (justice in war), or just means. Third, theorists have reflected on who can and should be held responsible for wrongful conduct in going to war or fighting a war.

Classical theory tended to ignore this third issue,

taking the view that people are not normally to be held accountable for wrongful conduct relating to war. In part this may have been because the conduct often involves mass killing, and it is complicated to assign moral responsibility for large scale, concerted acts of violence. The twentieth century trials of war criminals at the end of World War II and of soldiers following the Vietnam War, however, have made the issue of responsibility more visible and more important. Nonetheless, codes of warfare generally apply more strictly to the first two issues. Taken together, theories of just cause and just means make up just war theories, which attempt to specify the moral limits of military strategy and defense. Codes of warfare focus, then, on questions about conditions of justified warfare and permissible conduct in war, as well as on amendments to and critiques of these theories of just cause and just means.

I. CONDITIONS OF JUSTIFIED WARFARE

A. Aquinas' Three Conditions for Just War

Conditions of justified warfare address the circumstances, if any, that can justify waging and fighting a war. Classical just war theory derives from St. Thomas Aquinas. Aquinas defended three conditions for a just war. The first two are known as conditions for *jus ad bellum*.

1. Declaration by Legitimate Authority

First, Aquinas argued war must be declared not by a private individual but through the decision of a ruler or rulers with legitimate public authority. Historically, this condition was invoked to limit the military activities of lesser feudal lords. Today it continues to emphasize the importance of fighting for a cause that is related to the welfare of a large community, rather than an individual. It also emphasizes the importance of a formal declaration rather than ambiguous ongoing participation in warfare. A formal declaration of war gives clear notice to the enemy of military action, serves as an ultimatum that may be a last means of persuasion short of force itself, and may heighten accountability by minimizing large-scale covert governmental action. Assuming that one can distinguish legitimate group authorities from private citizens, this condition is reasonably straightfoward.

2. Just Cause

Second, Aquinas held that war must be fought for a "just cause," for example, that those attacked must deserve it. One way of understanding when an attack is deserved focuses on war waged defensively, that is, in response to aggression seriously endangering the lives and well-being of targeted citizens, or as a preemptive strike against imminent aggression of this type. Offensive warfare has been taken to be justified in certain circumstances as well. Two moral justifications that have been suggested to distinguish offensive warfare with a just cause include war undertaken to reestablish a social order that will promote justice and war undertaken to bring about peace.

3. Just Means

Third, Aquinas argued that war must be waged using "moderate means," that is, the war must not be waged by means more savage than necessary to ensure victory. This last condition will be discussed in more detail in Section II.

B. Criticisms of Aquinas' Conditions

Note that both the second and third of Aquinas' conditions are problematic. Waging war as a defense against aggression may seem reasonable, but self-defense is not an absolute right. It may only be appropriate when urgent action is needed and no other remedy is available. Moreover, we may well wonder how to evaluate just causes that have been claimed to justify offensive warfare. For example, a commonly cited justification for going to war is to rectify or end injustice in another territory or country. But the intrusiveness associated with this approach, and the moral assessments required to determine which behavior is outrageous enough to fight for, make this justification more controversial than self-defense. Aquinas' third condition, that the means must be "moderate"—that is, that the savagery of the war must be in some sense only what is necessary to accomplish the goals of the war—is extremely vague. It is difficult to lay down criteria for weighing means and ends and hence the condition apparently leaves room for widely divergent appraisals of just means.

Moreover, Aquinas' three conditions are certainly not sufficient. That is, all the conditions may be satisfied yet a war not be justified. Suppose, for example, that a war is declared by a legitimate authority, fought for a "just cause" and waged using "moderate means." Nevertheless, if warfare is not necessary for achieving the just cause—if, for example, diplomacy could have brought about the just cause as well—then the war is not necessary and hence is not justified. Clearly Aquinas' conditions must be revised and expanded to provide an adequate theory of just war.

C. Supplements to Aquinas' Conditions

1. Last Resort

Several conditions have been proposed as supplements to traditional just war theory as described in Aquinas' three conditions. Most important, in response to the objection presented above, it has been claimed that a just war is one in which hostilities have been initiated only as a "last resort." In this view, a war is unjust if its ends can be attained by nonbelligerent means. It has been claimed, therefore, that negotiation, mediation, arbitration, and judicial settlement must be utilized first, assuming such correctives are neither too hopeless nor too costly. Diplomatic alternatives might be effective in avoiding war, or might at least clarify doubts about the facts of the situation and divergent assessments of culpability.

2. Real and Certain Danger

Second, some theorists have suggested that speculative and remote danger such as the possibility of an invasion on foreign soil, can never justify warfare. In this view, the injury the war is intended to prevent must be real and certain. This condition apparently rules out the justifiability of preemptive strikes. It is problematic in other ways as well. Unfortunately, data to safisfy this condition may not always be available, and there are obvious difficulties in determining whether human knowledge can ever lead to certainty.

3. Reasonable Hope of Success

Third, it has been urged that war cannot be justified unless there is a reasonable hope of success. If defeat is inevitable, hostilities will only impose costs with no hope of gain, aggravating the situation without accomplishing the just cause or rectifying injustice. Nevertheless, more needs to be said about how to assess when the chance of success is reasonable.

4. Right Intention

Fourth, drawing on Aquinas' own discussion, it has been claimed that a war may be justified only when the responsible agents have a good intention. Aquinas apparently endorsed the general principle that there must be a right intention to achieve a good or avoid an evil. His idea can be illustrated by example: a country may not justifiably use some wrong as a pretext for acquiring territory. An important effect of this condition is that it challenges authorities repeatedly to confront and appraise their purposes in fighting. As Joseph McKenna has observed, "A war which is otherwise just becomes immoral if it is waged out of hatred. A war of self-defense becomes immoral if, in its course, it becomes an instrument of expansion. A war to vindicate justice becomes immoral if, as it goes on, it becomes a means of aggrandizement. The facility with which nations rationalize their resort to war is a commonplace of diplomatic history" (1960. Ethics and War: A Catholic View. *American Political Science Review,* 54 647–658). Aquinas apparently believed that the requirement of right intention could not only prevent rash initiation of war but could also minimize vengeful dispositions that might prolong hostilities and fighting. Others, however, have been more disparagingly cynical about the genuine inhibitory influence of conscience. Moreover, reliance on intentions can be problematic given the ambiguity of intentions and the fact that aims can change during a war. And we might well wonder whether the right intention requirement is always reasonable. Would a war that ended the torture of innocents truly be immoral if it were waged out of hatred?

II. PERMISSIBLE CONDUCT IN WAR

Aquinas' third condition of just war addresses *jus in bello,* the means used in waging war, and raises the question concerning what conduct is permissible or prohibited in combat. Several principles regarding the morality of conduct in war, including proportionality, discrimination, and double effect, appear to have their roots in natural law theory.

A. The Principle of Proportionality

The principle of proportionality holds that even in cases where the use of force is justified, there are limits to the legitimate magnitude of force. If war is waged to correct injustice, for example, it cannot be justified if the level of force used creates new and greater injustices. Thus, proportionality demands that the quantity of force employed or threatened always be proportionate to the end being sought in war.

While the principle seems intuitive and highly plausible in theory, there are several difficulties associated with it. First, the end considered might include both the immediate military aim as well as the general political aim of the war, and the importance or magnitude of these two goals may be quite different, making it difficult to determine proportional means. Second, as noted above, it is highly debatable how to distinguish means that are sufficient to accomplish the goals of war but not more savage than necessary. The malleability of the proportionality principle may allow multiple appraisals. Third, the proportionality principle can be expected to lead to the evaluation of the type of damage rendered by alternative weapons systems; for example, there has been considerable debate about weapons such as napalm bombs. But in practice it has been extremely uncommon for any existing weapons systems, especially those that are highly effective, to have been viewed as disproportionate. It would be surprising to find widespread condemnation of weapons commonly found in arsenals across the globe. If the significance of portionality is dependent on whatever weapons happen to exist at a given time, however, the principle may become vacuous.

B. The Principle of Discrimination

The principle of discrimination focuses on who and what can be legitimate targets of military action. It begins with the assumption that not every target is properly the object of military force. If there is to be a distinction between killing in war and murder, there must be a prior conception of the relevant differences between potential targets. A central theme in discussions of conduct in war has concerned the treatment of noncombatants. The principle of discrimination usually prohibits intentional attack on noncombatants, or, more generally, prohibits attack on nonmilitary targets. Discrimination thus restricts appropriate targets in war to combatants and military installations.

One problem with the principle of discrimination is the difficulty of distinguishing between combatants and noncombatants. It is not obvious, for example, whether or not nonuniformed support personnel should be viewed as combatants. Second, even if noncombatants can be distinguished in some adequate way in the context of traditional warfare, it has been suggested that Aquinas' third condition of just war theory as exemplified in the principle of discrimination is irrelevant or at least no longer fully applicable in the context of modern warfare techniques. For example, the practice of obliteration bombing—that is, aerial bombing of a large area that may include killing innocent civilians along with soldiers and support personnel at military installations—was not even possible with traditional methods of warfare. Nuclear warfare and obliteration bombing, as well as chemical and biological warfare,

erode attempts to rely on a distinction between combatants and noncombatants. Third, as will become clear in the next section, the emphasis on intention as a defining feature of justified actions in warfare, as it is utilized in the principle of discrimination, raises further questions.

C. The Doctrine of Double Effect

General considerations regarding the discriminating use of force in warfare have been refined by appeal to the principle of double effect. The doctrine of double effect is one of the most well-known arguments invoked to allow exceptions from absolute prohibitions against killing in order to justify any warfare at all. The doctrine is also invoked to allow exceptions from absolute prohibitions against killing innocents in order to justify modern warfare techniques that inevitably involve such killing.

The doctrine of double effect originates from a more general criterion of moral judgment enunciated by Aquinas: "now moral acts take their species according to what is intended and not according to what is beside the intention, since this is accidental" (*Summa Theologica* 2.2, q. 64, art. 7). Presumably, Aquinas was not arguing that effects of an action are morally irrelevant, but rather that in addressing issues about the morality of action, one must inevitably make reference to the agent's intentions. He apparently used the term "accidental" to mean not only unforeseen effects, but also foreseen yet unintended consequences.

The doctrine of double effect begins with the supposition that the use of force can have multiple actual or probable effects or consequences, those that are intended and those that are unintended, whether foreseen or unforeseen. According to the double effect doctrine, it may be permissible to bring about a result as the foreseen but unintended byproduct of an action that it would not be permissible to bring about as the direct and intended result of the same action. Therefore, a normally unjustified effect can be tolerated or allowed if it is the unintended consequence of an action positively intended to produce morally good consequences.

In this way, an act that harms innocents can be judged to be moral if the damage is adventitious in restraining the guilty. For example, bombardment of a strategic fortress is legitimate even if noncombatants are killed, and unfortunate civilian casualties from bombing explosions can be tolerated, if the agent only intends the military destruction. The objective can be sufficiently important to outweigh unintended noncombatant deaths. Consequently, conduct in warfare that harms the innocent can be justified. Many philosophers have appeared to endorse application of the doctrine of double effect in warfare contexts.

Nevertheless, there are serious questions raised by the doctrine of double effect. Consider first whether one can seriously not intend the means or additional effects of one's acts if one knows that those extra effects are inevitable consequences of these acts. If obliteration bombing to stop an injustice must necessarily lead to the deaths of many innocents in the area, is it plausible to believe that one only intends to stop injustice and does not intend to kill any innocents, especially if one is fully aware that the former entails the latter? Can it really be possible to separate intentions from actions in the way the principle of double effect requires? Second, if an intention is an interior act of the mind, it appears one can merely direct one's intention in the suitable way to justify any killing. If so, then the doctrine of double effect can be used perversely as an excuse, in which case it becomes difficult to see how the principle can avoid being completely elastic and malleable.

D. Natural Rights Considerations and Kant's Principles

1. Natural Rights

Natural rights considerations may also be viewed as placing restrictions on conduct in war. It is difficult to defend the view that war cannot violate any rights, because it seems that killing in war would violate one's natural right to life. One could argue in response, however, that combatants forfeit their right to life. Then nonviolation of individual rights might focus on concerns raised in "traditional" rules of war from international agreements after World War I, including rules against murder or ill-treatment of prisoners of war, taking noncombatants as hostages, and indiscriminate destruction of property unrelated to military requirements. There will, of course, be disagreement concerning what constitutes ill-treatment of prisoners of war and when destruction of property is indiscriminate, but general rules of this type have been codified in formal treaties such as the articles adopted at the Hague and Geneva Conventions.

2. Kant's Principles

Kant's categorical imperative generates further methods for evaluating conduct in war. Focus on his categorical imperative instructs authorities to ask themselves what methods of warfare could be willed as a universal law

of nature, and what methods treat people as ends only, and not merely as means to ends. The latter might be used to justify killing combatants on the grounds that they have chosen to participate in war and hence are not being used as means. Kant defended an additional principle in his essay "Perpetual Peace," namely that war must always be conducted so as not to preclude a future peace. Kant thought the actions prohibited by such a principle included the use of assassins, prisoners, killing by ambush, and even spies. Given the wide disagreement on his more particular conclusions, it seems best to say that Kant has defended principles that are important to keep in mind, but that these principles are so general that they are unlikely to yield uncontroversial substantive details about acceptable conduct in war.

E. Social Contract and Utilitarian Considerations

1. Social Contract Ideals

It is not obvious what a contractarian approach to conduct in warfare would imply. It is likely, however, that it would endorse some version of a principle of proportionality. Limitations on killing and injury based on choice behind a veil of ignorance and Rawls' maximin principle, for example, would likely focus on limiting killing of innocents as well as minimizing killing and injury to combatants as far as possible.

2. Utilitarianism

General utilitarian guidelines to morality in war were developed by Henry Sidgwick. He urged strict limitations on harm not contributing to the ends of war as well as on major harm that contributes only slightly to the war effort. Both of these are straightforward applications of the principle of utility, and reflect the ideals of the principle of proportionality. Note, however, that utilitarian theory stresses the avoidance of suffering and hence death that does not sufficently enhance the goals of war, but makes no reference to whether or not death is intended or foreseen. Moreover, alternative versions of utilitarianism may defend restrictions in different forms. An act utilitarian would not be likely to endorse general prohibitions but would advocate evaluation of particular situations on a case-by-case basis. Rule utilitarians would presumably advocate rules of conduct in war that maximize utility, such as rules protecting noncombatants and prohibiting the use of weapons causing unnecessary harm.

An interesting question is whether or not some rule utilitarians would defend exceptions based on military necessity. Richard Brandt allows one exception to a utilitarian theory of rules of war, according to which a nation has the right to "use all force necessary to overcome the enemy" (1972. Utilitarianism and the Rules of War. *Philosophy and Public Affairs,* 1, (2) 145–165). Unfortunately this exception appears to undercut his arguments for limited warfare.

III. CHALLENGES TO CODES OF WARFARE

A. Why Not Pacifism?

Some would argue that there can not be an acceptable theory of the justification of warfare because war can never be justified. The pacifist challenge to just war theory is that there are no just causes. Pacifism is often taken to be the view that war cannot be justified because it involves violence, which is morally unjustified. Sometimes pacifism also includes the stronger view that it is morally wrong to use force to resist, punish, or prevent violence, implying a duty not to use force to resist or prevent violence. Given the difficulties associated with provisions included in the codes of warfare discussed above, it is reasonable to ask whether warfare can be justified at all, and whether pacifism is a preferable alternative.

Numerous philosophers have taken the option of pacifism seriously, but have rejected it nonetheless. Jan Narveson has leveled a serious charge against pacifism. He has argued that pacifism is internally inconsistent and self-contradictory. Narveson argues first that if we have any rights at all, then we have a right to use force in defense of our rights at least on some occasions. Moreover, he argues that the pacifist principle that everyone has a duty not to oppose violence with force— that is, a duty to avoid violence—implies that pacifists must believe we do have some rights, namely the right not to have violence done to us. But then the pacifist position is self-contradictory because it says both that violence is wrong, yet at the same time that people have a right to prevent violence by force if necessary.

Cheyney Ryan has pointed out, however, that Narveson's argument only works against a version of pacifism that prohibits any use of force. It is ineffective against what Ryan believes is a more defensible form of pacifism prohibiting any lethal use of force.

G.E.M. Anscombe has presented two additional criticisms of pacifism. She argues that pacifism is a false moral ideal because it denies that individuals have the right to self-defense. She argues, in addition, that pacifism is pernicious because it encourages people to believe that all killing is equally wrong. This leads people to neglect the distinction between killing in wartime for a justified cause and unjustified atrocities. The result is that war becomes more murderous rather than moderated.

B. Political Duty to Nation versus Moral Duty to Preserve Life

Thomas Nagel has focused on the conflict between one's political duty to nation or party and the moral duty to preserve life. The former justifies means necessary to achieve the results of one's political cause, whereas the latter places absolute limits on what may be done to achieve even the most worthy goals. Nagel is unable to reconcile these rival claims on individuals. He is willing to accept killing enemy soldiers in self-defense, yet he argues that indiscriminate conduct in war such as bombardment of cities and massacre of prisoners must be condemned because it is impersonal killing that is degrading to human beings. Maintaining that modern warfare techniques unavoidably allow such indiscriminate killing, Nagel concludes that all modern wars are morally unjustified. Nagel's attack need not entail rejection of all codes of warfare, however. His critique poses a challenge for others to respond by differentiating those causes and means that can be justified.

C. The Feminist Challenge

For years, many women and feminists have been identified with antiwar and antimilitarist efforts. But it is worth keeping in mind that there is no single feminist position on the role of women in the military. There are common themes, however, that can be abstracted from writings by scholars who have examined the relationship between gender, violence, and war. These themes emphasize the association between male sexuality and virility with violence, between manhood and male superiority with combat, and between coercive control of unequally valued human beings with the competition and authoritarianism of warfare. According to the feminist challenge to codes of warfare, sexism and militarism are inextricably linked in society. Militarism is a policy of excessive military preparedness and eagerness to go to war, rooted in a view of human nature based on masculine characteristics such as being competitive, aggressive, and adverse to cooperation. Thus, participation in the institution of the military as it exists is viewed as incompatible with ideals of women's equality and a commitment to peace.

Even if sexism and militarism are inextricably linked in the ways these feminists have suggested, however, this fact alone does not entail the rejection of theories of just war and just cause. It is possible that feminists can endorse the need for military establishments for peacekeeping efforts, to prevent atrocities and violations of human rights such as those that have occurred in Bosnia, and to provide aid in crises like Rwanda. If so, then codes of warfare, far from being irrelevant, may be crucial for determining when and where such intervention can be justified.

IV. A CONTEMPORARY DEFENSE: WALZER ON JUST AND UNJUST WARS

Michael Walzer has attempted to differentiate just and unjust wars by analyzing the testimony of participants, both decision-makers and victims, to examine the moral issues of warfare. He takes seriously the arguments presented by participants to justify conduct in warfare and to judge the conduct of others that reveal "a comprehensive view of war as a human activity and a more or less systematic moral doctrine" (1977. *Just and Unjust Wars: A Moral Argument With Historical Illustrations,* p. xiii. New York: Basic Books). His goal is to recapture the just war for political and moral theory. Although deeply committed to human rights, Walzer believes an absolute rule of nonintervention will be ignored and hence useless. Thus he defends invasion to assist secessionist movements, to balance prior interventions of other powers, and to rescue people threatened with massacre as examples of *jus ad bellum*. These causes are just because they uphold the values of individual life and communal liberty. Nevertheless, in Walzer's view, requirements of just intervention must be seriously constrained.

Similarly, for *jus in bello,* Walzer argues that we can and must distinguish just and unjust means. He attempts to make the combatant/noncombatant distinction plausible in terms of a detailed account of the history of individual rights under conditions of warfare and battle. Walzer passionately defends the principle of noncombatant immunity, leading to particular judgments, for example, that nuclear warfare is morally unacceptable. In sum, Walzer provides a contemporary defense of the view that we must insist on defending rules of war that protect human rights as a restraint on military struggle that can only be overridden in the face of an imminent catastrophe. For, he concludes, "the restraint of war is the beginning of peace" (Walzer, 335).

Also See the Following Articles

CIVILIAN POPULATION IN WAR, TARGETING OF • NATIONAL SECURITY ISSUES • PACIFISM • WARFARE, STRATEGIES AND TACTICS

Bibliography

Anscombe, G. E. M. (1962). War and murder. In W. Steen (Ed.), *Nuclear weapons: A Catholic response* (pp. 43–62). New York: Sheed & Ward.

DeCew, J. W. (1995). The combat exclusion and the role of women in the military. *Hypatia* 10, 1, 56–73.

Held, V. (1993). *Feminist morality.* Chicago: University of Chicago Press.

Nagel, T. (1972). War and massacre. *Philosophy and Public Affairs* 1, 123–144.

Narveson, J. (1965). Pacifism: A philosophical analysis. *Ethics* 75, 259–271.

Ryan, C. (1985). Self-defense and pacifism. In Sterba, (Ed.), *The ethics of war and nuclear deterrence* (pp. 45–49). Belmont: Wadsworth.

WARFARE, STRATEGIES AND TACTICS

John D. Becker
United States Air Force Academy

GLOSSARY

continuum of national security The range of national security issues that includes war, Operations Other Than War (OOTW), and peacetime concerns.

operational art Serves as the connecting link between strategy and tactics. Operational art concerns itself with employment of larger military units, usually echelons above the corps level, and it focuses on campaigns or a series of battles.

Operations Other Than War (OOTW) Those operations that involve the employment of military and nonmilitary resources, but without the intention of using violent force as a primary means to achieve a specific end or set of ends. OOTW include such actions as peacekeeping, counterdrug operations, and disaster relief.

peacetime concerns The important political and economic concerns that nations normally conduct with each other, when not at war or in hostile conflict. These include both defense and deterrence, as well as diplomacy, trade actions, and economic concerns.

spectrum of morality The range of ethical positions that deal with war. These positions include nihilism, just warism, and pacifism.

strategy In general, a plan of action, using available resources, to obtain certain goals over time. Strategy is often considered both an art and a science, in that it requires both intuition and rationality. There are different types of strategy including national strategies, grand strategies, and military strategies.

tactics The employment of military units in combat operations. This employment includes the ordered arrangement and maneuver of those units in relationship to each other to maximize their full potentiality and defeat enemy forces. The units are usually divisions or smaller in size and are concentrated on battles.

war A state of open armed conflict between states (or coalitions of states), or between parties in a state, carried on by force of arms for various reasons. There are various types of wars, ranging from attacks or raids, low-intensity conflicts, limited wars, general wars, and nuclear war.

WAR is the state of open armed conflict between states (or coalitions of states), or between parties in a state, carried on by force of arms for various reasons. There are various types of wars, ranging from attacks or raids, low-intensity conflicts, limited wars, general wars, and nuclear war. War is considered the most serious of a state's national security issues and one that receives the most attention.

I. OVERVIEW

War is only one piece of the continuum of national security. There are also nontraditional operations, Operations Other Than War (OOTW) and peacetime concerns. OOTW are those operations that involve the employment of military and nonmilitary resources, but without the intention of using violent force as a primary means to achieve a specific end or set of ends. OOTW include such actions as peacekeeping, counterdrug operations, and disaster relief. Peacetime concerns are the important political and economic concerns that nations normally conduct with each other, when not at war or in hostile conflict. These include both defense and deterrence, as well as diplomacy, trade actions, and economic concerns.

Warfare is traditionally broken into two parts—strategy and tactics. Strategy is a plan of action, using available resources, to obtain certain goals over time. Strategy is often considered both an art and a science, in that it requires both intuition and rationality. There are different types of strategy, including national strategies, grand strategies, and military strategies. Tactics, on the other hand, is the employment of military units in combat operations. It includes the ordered arrangement and maneuver of those units in relationship to each other to maximize their full potentiality and defeat enemy forces. The units are usually corps level and below, and they concentrate on battles.

There is also a third part, called operational art. It serves as the connection between strategy and tactics. Operational art concerns itself with employment of larger military units, usually echelons above corps, and it focuses on campaigns or a series of battles.

In addition, as part of war, applied ethical issues are raised and considered. These issues include traditional just war concerns which are often broken into two types—*jus ad bellum* (justice of war) and *jus in bello* (justice in war). They also include questions about nontraditional issues, such as OOTW and future war forms, such as information warfare, space warfare, and virtual warfare.

II. STRATEGIES

A strategy is simply a plan of action, using available resources, to obtain certain goals over time. Strategy is often considered both an art and a science, in that it requires both intuition and rationality. There are different types of strategy, including national strategies, grand strategies, and military strategies. At the national level, strategy is a state's plan to attain its interests and objectives, which is done by fusing all of its available resources. A national security strategy will normally include two other strategies—a grand strategy and a military strategy. A grand strategy involves employing national power under all circumstances to exert desired degrees and types of control over a state's enemies or opponents. Threats, force, indirect pressure, diplomacy, subterfuge, and other imaginative means are all employed in grand strategy.

For example, the United States developed and employed a grand strategy for the war in Panama in 1989. This strategy included the administration's use of media in establishing the basis for intervention; the use of various forms of diplomatic and economic sanctions against Panama and its leader Manuel Noriega; the establishment of a political support from neighboring countries in attacking Panama; statements of support by both the Congress and the United Nations; and the integration of special operations forces and psychological warfare forces in the strategy. These parts were woven together into a single, integrated plan—a grand strategy for going to war with Panama.

Military strategy, an element of grand strategy, is predicated on physical violence or the threat of violence. It seeks to support national security interests and objectives through the use of arms and the attainment of military objectives. It involves, as General Karl von Clausewitz noted, the use of engagements to attain the object of war. There is a variety of approaches to military strategy, including sequential and cumulative, direct and indirect, deterrent and combative, and counterforce and countervalue.

In the example of Panama, the U.S. military strategy was to use multiple attacks at varied targets throughout the country. Joint military forces, including ground, sea, and air elements, conducted a synchronized attack on key installations and Panamanian forces.

The difference between grand strategy and military strategy is a simple one: grand strategy is the purview of political leaders while the military strategy is the territory of generals. Moreover, military strategy should be understood as a subset of the larger, grand strategy.

III. TACTICS

As mentioned before, tactics is the employment of military units in combat operations. It stresses the ordered arrangement and maneuver of those units in relationship to each other to maximize their potential and to defeat enemy forces. Tactics include numerous factors, such as maneuver, firepower, protection, sustainment, and leadership. For example, maneuver allows friendly forces to gain the positional advantage over the opposing forces while firepower provides destructive bombardment to exploit that advantage. Simultaneously, friendly force must be protected during the fight and sustained before, during, and after the battle. Leadership is the glue that holds these factors together.

Tactics, like strategy, is both an art and a science, but it employs all available military means to win battles and engagements. Tactics is also thought of as a battlefield problem-solving method—one that is usually rapid and dynamic in its very nature.

There are two types of operations that tactics support—offensive and defensive. Offensive operations are aggressive, forward movements to close with and destroy enemy forces. They are distinguished by rapid momentum, taking advantage of opportunities provided by the enemy, and the destruction of that enemy. Surprise, concentration, tempo, and audacity are important offensive characteristics. Defensive operations are meant to stop and defeat an enemy attack. They are often used to buy time, hold key terrain, or erode enemy resources. Key defensive characteristics include prepared positions, security, disruption, mass and concentration, and flexibility.

In planning and conducting tactical operations, both offensive and defensive, careful consideration is given to the elements of METT-T. This acronym refers to mission, enemy, terrain and weather, troops, and time available. Various plans, including operations orders, make use of these elements.

IV. APPLIED ETHICAL ISSUES

In warfare, there are a number of applied ethical issues raised and discussed. These issues fall into two general categories—*jus ad bellum* and *jus in bello*. The first category, *jus ad bellum* (or justice of war) focuses on whether a state is justified in starting or engaging in a war. Consideration is given to criteria like just cause, right intention, proportionality of ends, last resort, reasonable chance of success, and the aim of peace. If a state can satisfy these criteria, then the war is most likely a just one, rather than an unjust one. *Jus ad bellum* has traditionally been seen as an issue for statesmen and political leaders.

The second category, *jus in bello* (justice in war), focuses on the conduct of the war itself. These issues generally concern soldiers and their leadership and the manner in which they are waging the war. Questions include whether the use of certain weapons and tactics is ethical, what is the proper proportionality of means in the war, and who is a legitimate combatant in the war. These questions are raised on a continuous basis throughout the war.

Similar questions are raised and discussed about both OOTW and peacetime concerns. Their limited use of force requires some modifications of both of those questions and their answers. Nonetheless, the ethical element of warfare often finds itself manifest even in these operations, in things like the names of conflicts, such as Provide Hope and Provide Comfort (recent U.S. OOTW).

In sum, warfare is often thought of as having a dual nature—both practical and ethical. On one side is the strategic and tactical element; the "how to" approach, while on the other side is the ethical element, asking "when should" it be used approach. Both must be addressed in this most serious of a state's endeavors.

Also See the Following Articles

CIVILIAN POPULATIONS IN WAR, TARGETING OF • MILITARY CODES OF BEHAVIOR • NUCLEAR WARFARE • WARFARE, CODES OF

Bibliography

Field Manual 100-5, *Operations,* Headquarters, Department of the Army, 1993 Edition, Washington, DC.
Fotion, N. & Elfstrom, G. (1986). *Military ethics.* Boston: Routledge & Kegan Paul, Boston, MA.
Lykke, A. F., Jr. (1989). *Military strategy: Theory and application.* Carlisle Barracks, PA: U.S. Army War College.
Summers, H. G., Jr. (1992). *On strategy II: A critical analysis of the Gulf War.* New York: Dell Books.
Walzer, M. (1992). *Just and unjust wars* (2nd ed.). New York: Basic Books.

WELFARE POLICIES

Norman Barry
University of Buckingham

GLOSSARY

adverse selection A condition that occurs in insurance markets when those most vulnerable are most likely to insure. In relation to unemployment and health insurance, it could make the private market unviable.

altruism The moral belief that personal interests should be sacrificed to satisfy the needs of others.

collective good A wanted good (or service) that is provided for the general population and financed by taxation or compulsory contributions.

institutional welfare state A state that meets welfare needs by providing a wide range of social services, for example, health care, pensions, education, and unemployment insurance.

market failure The private enterprise system's inadequate supply of (or failure to provide at all) wanted goods and services.

moral hazard The danger that a too-generous welfare policy may encourage more people to become its beneficiaries.

need The lack of certain elements, for example, food, shelter, and health care, that are essential for persons to lead reasonable lives. These required things are objective and are identifiable by an outside observer.

residual welfare state Public arrangement to meet the needs of deprived people by means-tested income transfers, or by minimal public services for which the user does not have to pay.

social insurance Contributions levied compulsorily on citizens to provide for non-means-tested welfare goods and services, for example, unemployment and health insurance.

subjectivism The belief that all value is a product of individual choice in the market. This doctrine holds that there are no objectively valuable goods and services.

underclass A class of citizens that tends not to work, to consist of broken or single parent families, to live entirely on benefits, and to be apart from the mainstream of society.

WELFARE POLICY has become the most important feature of domestic politics in all Western democracies in the past 20 years. The rising expenditures of the various welfare schemes have concerned governments, and considerable doubts are now expressed as to whether the programs are sustainable. There is also uncertainty about the meaning of welfare. Radical subjectivists maintain that a person's welfare is simply a function of the choices she makes for goods and ser-

Encyclopedia of Applied Ethics, Volume 4
Copyright © 1998 by Academic Press. All rights of reproduction in any form reserved.

vices. The policy implication of this is that government should encourage the market supply of wanted things. At most, government should maximize opportunities for individualistic welfare improvement through cash aid to the poor. The direct provision of welfare goods is objectionable because it is paternalistic.

Others doubt the capacity of individuals to behave rationally; people's preferences may not always be well informed so that they do not constitute evidence of their real *choices*. Some writers therefore favor direct supply of welfare goods, for example, health care, education, unemployment insurance, and so on. Without some element of compulsion here people's welfare in the long run will be lowered. Collective supply is also thought to increase social equality and to advance community values. The role of the welfare state is to compensate individuals for any misfortune that might befall them.

Conservative critics are not worried so much by the cost of the welfare state, they are more concerned about its effect on character. In the United States especially it is argued that cash payments unaccompanied by social duties produce family breakdown, voluntary unemployment, and other social dysfunctions. Defenders of the welfare system deny that there is a causal connection between the size of welfare payments and the breakdown of traditional standards of behavior. Poverty is curable by appropriate government action in the labor market and by aid to the deprived, which in the United States is not costly. European countries have more comprehensive and costly welfare states and theorists argue that the common consumption of welfare goods generates valuable social integration. However, there is some disquiet at the reduction in free choice that such systems involve and their ever-rising cost.

I. THE MEANING OF WELFARE

To describe someone's welfare is to say something about her well-being. Economists might measure welfare purely in subjectivist terms: an individual's capacity to buy wanted goods in the market. Each person is the best judge of her own welfare, and free choice is the only indication of satisfaction. They might want to say that the choice should be *informed*, that is, what is preferred should be decided upon with full knowledge of available alternatives and with complete information about likely consequences, but we reveal our choices through our preferences. If a person prefers not to spend income on what are regarded as welfare goods, even though she is fully informed of the possible adverse consequences of so acting, from a subjectivist's position no government can increase that person's welfare by dictating certain choices. Although economists might wish to increase people's opportunities for maximizing subjective welfare by income redistribution this, strictly speaking, would not increase *social* welfare, because some would be made worse off. But most observers of welfare policy are not prepared to adopt such a rigorous notion of welfare and approve of the redistribution it inevitably involves. There is, however, great disagreement about the form that welfare policy should take.

The Western world is characterized by a vast array of welfare services and redistributive policies; all designed to increase people's sense of well-being. The relief of poverty has always been a prime social goal: and although it is not the only object of welfare policy it is recognized that access to the market depends on income. Originally, inadequate opportunity to acquire goods and services was dealt with by voluntary methods, often originating with the churches, and public intervention was minimal and mainly local. The centralized state has largely replaced these methods in contemporary society.

The rationale for welfare policies normally derives from a notion of need. Even those who do not want welfare redistribution to bring about a contestable notion of equality and social justice recognize that people can be in need through no fault of their own: although it might be difficult to determine an objective measure of need because the concept itself seems controversial. Is there an agreed measure of medical need, or nutritional requirements, or are criteria that are used here condemned to irresolvable dispute? Is there a hierarchy of needs that enables legislators to determine priorities in a world of scarcity? In addition, is need not irredeemably relativistic in that it will depend on the particular stage of economic development of a country?

Despite these problems, policymakers, within specified countries at least, have produced workable criteria of need. Needs are normally distinguished from mere wants. They are in a sense acquired involuntarily, and must be satisfied for human flourishing. In contrast, wants, for example, for many consumer goods, are purely subjective and are not compelling enough to warrant immediate satisfaction. Furthermore, a person may be in need of something and may not be aware of it. Medicine is the best example here. These considerations indicate that there is a certain objectivity about needs and this implies that there is a duty on government and other social agencies to satisfy them. This is a necessary, although by no means sufficient, condition for a satisfactory welfare policy.

Even subjectivists have considerable sympathy for action to deal with uncontroversial cases of need; although they might doubt their true objectivity, and question the extent of agreement about what are pressing cases of need. For subjectivists, one justification for remedial action in cases of deprivation would be that the utility of the better off is increased when distress is alleviated. Throughout history there has been an altruistic sentiment that, although it may not validate contemporary welfare states, has provided a rationale for various welfare policies. Of course, advocates of extensive welfare policies would invoke social justice for their justification rather than rely on the probably weak altruistic sentiment.

In England policies for the satisfaction of need began with the Elizabethan Poor Law, which introduced collective measures to deal with various categories of the poor (similar measures were adopted in other countries). This, and later Poor Law legislation, attempted to cope with problems that occur to this day. Thus the early social welfare measures were designed to limit relief to those who met a rigorous criterion of need. Aid should not go to those who could take care of themselves and must not be generous.

Modern welfare policies that involve means-testing continue this tradition. There is an additional point about welfare policies that derives from the early Poor Law experience and exercises policymakers just as much today. It is the phenomenon of "moral hazard." This means that measures taken to aid a deprived group encourage the size of that group to grow; our moral efforts are, in effect, exploited by individuals who behave, from a subjectivist's point of view, in a perfectly rational manner. The early Poor Law legislators devised harsh "eligibility" rules to discourage able-bodied people from opting for welfare. The permanent, and insoluble, problem for welfare policymakers is that measures designed to counteract moral hazard are likely to make the conditions of the really needy worse than most would like them to be. They become the victims of attempts to discipline the indolent.

However, welfare policies today are by no means confined to poor relief, and many theorists regard this as far too modest a goal for policymakers. Since the last century (beginning with Bismarck's Germany), most Western countries have provided *social* insurance against unemployment and ill health, and saving for old age has been made compulsory. Such welfare goods and services are provided not for the poor and indigent alone but are available to all citizens regardless of their means. There are various justifications for this strategy. One is clearly antisubjectivist. It depends on the assumption that people are unwise in their choices: they will not insure against ill health, they cannot be relied on to save for their retirement, and they are unlikely to insure against unemployment. Therefore, to save the community from being burdened with an excessive welfare bill for these categories the welfare state developed through a mild form of coercion.

This paternalistic rationale is not the only justification for extensive social policy. A more cogent rationale derives from the problem of "adverse selection" in private insurance markets. This occurs because only those vulnerable to unemployment, or likely to be victims of ill health, will insure against these contingencies. The private insurance market cannot cope with this so the state has to organize compulsory social insurance to spread the risk. The "nationalization" of certain parts of the insurance market can be seen as a response to market failure and is not necessarily connected to the paternalistic justification for the welfare state, or to income redistribution.

Even if the problem of adverse selection could be solved, purely private insurance markets obviously will not offer cover to certain categories of people because the risks would be too high. Insurance companies have to work on the basis of the records of their clients and the market test here would leave certain people, for example, the chronically ill, uninsurable. No society would leave these to rely on private charity. In fact, modern theories of the welfare state derive from a theory of citizenship that extends beyond the traditional definition in terms of civil liberties, legal protection, and voting rights, to include entitlements to welfare. These claims do not necessarily depend on contributions to a fund but are legitimately made by members of an inclusive community.

This theory of welfare policy depends on a concept of social justice. Economic inequalities are justified only to the extent that they increase the well-being of the least advantaged. A comprehensive range of welfare goods should exist to aid the potentially underprivileged (a fate that could befall anyone) and redistribution from the better off to these recipients is a form of compensation for their misfortunes. It would eliminate means-testing as far as possible. This is a quite different approach to that welfare policy that understands it merely as aid to the deprived, who are assessed in purely income terms.

II. THE RESIDUAL WELFARE STATE

An important distinction in welfare theorizing is that between the "residual" and the "institutional" welfare states. In the former, welfare policy is focused on people who temporarily, or perhaps permanently, find themselves in distress. They are normally a minority who can easily be identified and made the target of welfare policy. Everybody else can make their own way in the world and can be relied on to purchase whatever welfare goods and services they desire. Thus it is not the whole population that ought to be the object of social action, and no collective, publicly delivered policies are thought to be necessary to integrate people into the community. Socialized medicine or collectivized pension arrangements are said to be inefficient and unresponsive to people's choices.

Of course, in the residual welfare state people in receipt of benefits are to an extent stigmatized and subjected to serious means-testing. However, this is thought to be the only way of reducing the demands made on the system. It also claimed that the poor actually benefit from such an arrangement because welfare is not expended on those who do not need it and it can be targeted to the deprived. The theory of the residual welfare state does not exclude some collective provision, for example, zero-priced health care and a minimal state pension for the poor, but it is assumed that these arrangements will only be used by the minority who cannot afford private provision.

The believers in the residual welfare state would actually like its compulsory features to be a supplement to private charity. However, although eleemosynary activity has a long history (especially in the U.S.) very few theorists, even most free marketeers, take the austere view that it could replace all welfare policy. Most advocates of limited government concede that there is a welfare role for the state.

Some writers even suggest that there can be welfare policy without redistribution. If there are altruistic sentiments then these might require some state intervention for them to be realized. It would happen because individuals might feel that the difference any one person's contribution would make to the relief of poverty would be so infinitesimally small that it is not worth her making it. Also, if a person knew that others were making a donation then suffering is alleviated anyway, so the incentive to give is again reduced. For a combination of these reasons people would not give voluntarily even though they would prefer distress to be alleviated and would not object to paying for it. They would approve then of some social cooperation to aid the deprived. Thus taxation would not be regarded as coercive if it is spent on what the better off actually want, that is, the relief of suffering. It is difficult, though, to argue that welfare policy can ever be anything but redistributive (despite the claims of some writers in this tradition) but individualists say that it does to some extent reflect our altruistic sentiments.

Theorists who take this line often argue for some kind of guaranteed minimum income or negative income tax. In its purest form this policy would entail the elimination of all in-kind welfare services. Individuals would be free to spend their income on whatever welfare goods they desired: markets would provide health, unemployment insurance, education, pensions, and so on. The theory is an extreme subjectivist's position because it is assumed that each individual is the best judge of her own welfare and the state's involvement in the direct supply of welfare goods constitutes an unjust infringement of the person's right to choose. Also, such cash payments are usually accompanied by no social obligations on the part of the recipients. After all, the welfare of the donor is increased merely by the fact money has been allocated for the relief of suffering. It would also be thought to be coercive if individuals were compelled to spend their welfare payments in a way determined by the state.

It is rare for such an extreme individualist's policy to be pursued consistently. All modern democracies have some publicly provided welfare goods and services from which it is impossible for individuals to withdraw. The United States has had Social Security since 1935 and Medicare (and Medicaid) since 1965. The range of collective welfare goods is much wider in Britain and Europe.

However, some form of cash supplement to income (or income replacement) is common to most countries. Indeed, Congress got close to passing the Family Assistance Plan, which was a version of a Guaranteed Minimum Income, in the late 1970s. It is admitted to be a form of redistribution but it is justified morally on the utilitarian ground that the loss in pleasure experienced by those compelled to contribute to it is less than the gains to the recipients. The familiar form in the United States is Aid to Families with Dependent Children (AFDC), inaugurated in 1935, but Britain has had, since the postwar Labour government's restructuring of the welfare states, various forms of cash payments to those not covered by social insurance schemes. On mainland Europe there are fewer direct cash payments to the needy because the range of social insurance tends to be wider there.

There are a number of difficulties with cash payments of the type above that have been recognized by social theorists. All of them are subject to means-tests, which involve a loss in dignity to the recipient and sometimes lead to low takeup. For example, in the United States it was not until the 1970s that takeup of AFDC reached most of those entitled. This would not be a problem under a pure negative income tax where payment is made automatically as soon as income falls below a certain level, or under most versions of the guaranteed minimum income.

However, simple cash payments have turned out to be the most controversial of welfare policies. This is not solely because of their cost (in the U.S. the cost of direct welfare is scarcely 2% of all public spending) but it has more to do with certain behavioral traits that they are said to encourage. They are thought to cause moral hazard in the form of defection from work, and to encourage the breakdown of marriage and the family. In fact, the most socially undesirable phenomenon is the incentive not to marry at all, which cash welfare tends to produce. Thus, the illegitimacy rate in the African-American community is now over 60%; in certain inner-city areas it is above 80%. The same phenomenon is beginning to be observed in the white community.

In the United States, welfare policy since President Roosevelt's New Deal was aimed at encouraging people to get work, to stay in work, and remain off the welfare rolls. Because of the Depression, government, especially the federal government, was active in both economic and welfare policy. However, all observers agree that the extension to welfare brought about by President Johnson's Great Society reforms of the 1960s have not been successful in the pursuit of the original welfare aims.

At the time of the implementation of these reforms (the "war against poverty") far too many Americans were below the official poverty line. While it is true that fewer Americans are poor these days it would appear that this is so, not because there has been an increase in employment for the deprived, especially minorities, but because for many people the attractions of the mainly cash welfare benefits proved irresistible. Using a measure of "latent poverty," that is, those who would be poor but for the cash payments, Charles Murray ((1994). *Losing Ground*. Tenth Anniversary Edition. New York: Basic Books) found that this poverty gradually increased from the early 1970s as the welfare policies began to take effect. He also traced the breakdown of the family and the rise of illegitimacy to the same cause. Christopher Jencks, who challenges some of Murray's analysis concedes, nevertheless, that the con-

ditions of the poor improved faster from 1950 through 1965 than from 1965 through 1980.

In Murray's somewhat mechanistic view there is a direct relationship between not merely the value of welfare benefits but the ease with which they can be claimed (the eligibility requirements were considerably relaxed in the 1970s through two important Supreme Court decisions) *and* deprivation. Many writers noted that the welfare policies turned out to be to the benefit not of the working poor (many of whom remained below the poverty line) but to the nonworking poor. The very worst results, in terms of defection from work and breakdown of marriage (Murray, 1994, pp. 147–153), occurred in two cities that had experimented with versions of the negative income tax (although they were not perfect examples because federal welfare policies, e.g., Social Security, remained). Murray blames the emergence of an "underclass" of drug users and petty criminals in the inner cities on the welfare policies that were initiated by the Great Society programs.

However, writers have challenged Murray's assumptions of a correlation between the availability of welfare and the social pathologies he describes. Although there is some evidence of moral hazard, the imperfect correlation between, say, illegitimacy and AFDC, seems to suggest that a serious reduction in its value would make little difference to behavior. Indeed, male African-American unemployment fell sharply when welfare benefits were at their most generous (in the early 1970s) but rose in the late 1970s when they were considerably reduced in real value.

Welfare payments would have to go to a morally unacceptably low level to induce a return to work at the optimal level. Although the phenomenon of people remaining on AFDC for long periods of time has disturbed observers, many of the recipients are unmarried mothers who find it difficult to work and bring up children at the same time. They would be unfairly punished by serious attempts to overcome the moral hazard problem.

Other, more conservative critics of the American welfare system argue that its main effect has been to render a class of people "incompetent," and that the simple withdrawal of benefits would not make any difference to their capacity to cope. From his extensive enquiries, Lawrence Mead ((1992). *The new politics of poverty*. New York: Basic Books) claims that the main reason for the decline in civic responsibility and the emergence of social dysfunctioning has been the fact that the welfare system has been superimposed on the traditional American liberties. The welfare policies of the Great Society gave people too much freedom. The receipt of cash payments without corresponding social obligations encouraged the growth of an incompetent underclass. His argument, then, is that it is not the size of the welfare state that is important but its *form*. For Mead, that form should be one that reintegrates hitherto incompetent persons into the mainstream of the community.

In common with other critics, from the Left as well as the Right, of the American welfare system Mead believes that work is the solution to the problem of a growing underclass. Unlike the original poor, the members of this class have never worked and they survive entirely on welfare benefits. Because unmarried mothers comprise a large part of this class there is a fear that it will reproduce itself throughout the generations. However, the withdrawal of benefits is not the answer because in his view people do not respond to incentives in the mechanical way stressed by the economists (and by Murray). A cutback in payments would merely increase the size of the underclass and probably lead to an increase in crime. What is required is a more active role for government in welfare policy. It should make the receipt of welfare benefits conditional on taking a job, even though it is low paid; and if private sector employment is unavailable then people should be compelled to work on community projects (that may have no specific economic rationale). In fact, various states in the United States had workfare schemes before a modest version of the policy became part of federal law in the Family Support Act (1988).

A more stringent version of workfare features in the welfare reform law (The Personal Responsibility and Work Opportunity Act) passed in Congress in 1996. The law has also abolished the main form of cash payments, AFDC, and replaced this, and other federal payments, with block grants to the states. Within certain limits, and subject to important guidelines, they are free to spend this money as they wish. What is important in this legislation is its rigorous effort to enforce work on the recipients of welfare. It is a welfare policy that reflects the major concerns of critics of the prevailing system. Indeed, it is not necessarily a conservative policy because many on the Left have stressed that ideally people should be in work rather than on welfare, although they have doubted that suitable work is regularly available.

However, the traditional problem with attempts to make welfare conditional on such things as work is that it penalizes the deserving poor in order to encourage good behavior in others. The removal of AFDC might produce many victims, especially children. It is a problem that goes back to the nineteenth-century Poor Law.

There are other disincentives to work in the United States that could be explained with the economist's model. One problem is that in the absence of a nationalized and universal health system access to care is limited to those qualified for Medicaid, zero-priced treatment designed only for the poor; a category that obviously includes welfare recipients. However, if they go into even low-paid work they may lose this and might not be able to afford health insurance premiums. If their employer, as is quite likely, does not provide medical coverage they are in a worse position than while on welfare. Hence, many reformers have recommended an extension of Medicaid, or even drastic reform of the whole medical system in the United States, in order to overcome this further disincentive to work.

What is implicit in the analyses of reformers, like Mead, of the American social welfare system is a clear move away from the model of welfare "rights"; entitlements that require no corresponding duties on the part of beneficiaries. The trend of conservative thinking on welfare is to recommend a more active role for the state in inculcating in the poor appropriate social values. Indeed, this philosophy is likely to lead to a mild authoritarian state that is antithetical to traditional liberal values.

There is, however, one important criticism of the above theories, and of those American public policies that increasingly seem to derive from them. It is a new and sophisticated version of the argument that the economy does not create enough jobs to absorb the current welfare beneficiaries.

This claim would, superficially, have more resonance in Europe than in the United States. The latter country has had an enviable record in job creation over the last few decades, whereas unemployment in Europe is much higher, and individuals are out of work there for long periods of time. It is argued that, although jobs in the United States might be poorly paid, they are crucially important for the development of independence and self-reliance. Almost all welfare theorists regard that the cultivation of these dispositions as essential if welfare policies are to be effective.

But it might be the case that a particular form of employment has declined in recent years and that this has not been replaced by equivalent jobs for the working class in certain parts of the United States. There might then be a role, in welfare policy, for government action of the conventional, progressive, type. Thus it is argued by William Julius Wilson that traditional manufacturing jobs in the inner city have declined dramatically and the new technologically based industries tend to be located in the suburbs. Thus, travel costs, or the expenses involved in uprooting a familiar life-style and residence, are powerful discentives to take up whatever new employment opportunities are created. Thus, according to Wilson, the reason for the resort to welfare in the inner city areas is not simply explained by the existence of favorable incentives (indeed, cash payments were never high and have declined significantly in real terms since the late 1970s) but by the unavailability of work.

Furthermore, there has been a social implication of all this. It is that the original employment structures in the inner cities provided integrated communities with social values that encouraged the traditional work ethic and produced community leaders who enforced (informally) good behavior. However, with the change in employment prospects potential community leaders and appropriate role models moved out of these areas, leaving them prey to the criminal classes, and to the drug culture. According to Wilson, then, welfare policy has to be reintegrated into an active government-led economic strategy to reinvigorate the inner cities. The traditional mobility of American labor is apparently inadequate to cope with the problems that arise in the inner cities.

An additional interesting side issue is Wilson's claim that the decline in opportunities for minorities is not caused by discrimination (a traditional explanation for the plight of, especially, African Americans); in his view this has declined significantly as a consequence of federal law and Supreme Court decisions. Therefore, welfare policy should be almost organically linked to economic policy with little role for further antidiscrimination measures, or for the more conservative policy that derives from an understanding of social deprivation primarily in behavioral and moral terms.

Still, critics of American welfare policy argue that these economic changes are quite normal in American economic history; but they did not produce similar dysfunctioning in the prewelfare past. When there have been periods of industrial relocation people simply moved to the areas where the new jobs were. Also, it is claimed that employment has moved out of the inner cities because normal civic life there has been disrupted by crime and other antisocial behavior, caused by generous welfare policies.

III. WELFARE POLICIES IN EUROPE

Welfare policies in Britain and in most countries in Europe share a few similarities with the United States. However, they have a different history and much of the ideological background to their formation is relevant to issues today. Europe pioneered the institutional welfare state that delivers universal services in unemployment insurance, health care, pensions, education and training, and so on to all citizens irrespective of their income. There are elements of the residual welfare state, in Britain and Germany especially, but the European social welfare tradition is extremely reluctant to divide society into groups according to whether or not they are in receipt in welfare. Payments for the wide range of services offered is supposed to be by contribution in order to preserve a sense of entitlement.

Social insurance was pioneered in Bismarck's Germany in the nineteenth century and this became the model for the European welfare state. It also ended all incentives for the voluntary provision of welfare arrangements, which had been developing via the trade union movement in most European countries. Britain was an early follower of the Bismarck system but it was Sweden, and other Scandinavian countries, which developed the most comprehensive welfare systems. The role of voluntary organizations in the relief of deprivation, and for the provision of private insurance, is correspondingly very low in most of Europe. Debate in the last 20 years has concentrated almost exclusively on the escalating cost of what are now primarily tax-financed services. There is little discussion (unlike in the U.S.) of the social pathologies that welfare allegedly produces, although it should be pointed out that Sweden has always had schemes equivalent to workfare to discourage indolence in youth. There is no automatic right to cash aid there.

The distinctive features of European welfare policies may be explained by the continent's ideological tradition (outside of that in Britain, which is slightly more akin to America's). It has always been more statist and skeptical of the market system. It is a social philosophy that predates Marx and begins with Claude Henri de Saint-Simon (1760–1825). He specifically rejected supply and demand as proper determinants of income, pioneered the idea that need should be decisive as the criterion for reward and was responsible for the strategy of organizing society so that problems could be solved by centralist planners. This is obliquely reflected in the uniformity of most European welfare programs.

There is, however, a competing tradition, which derives from the Roman Catholic Church. Its social philosophy stresses "subsidiarity": in application to welfare this means that services should be provided at the lowest possible level of government, with central authority playing a supervisory role and providing an ultimate financial guarantee. Subsidiarity is best ememplified in the postwar German welfare state. Still, the range of welfare policies pursued does not vary much whatever the religious predilections of European welfare states and whatever institutional form they take. In all these countries the debate in the last two decades has been over whether "civil society" that is, the range of autonomous social institutions that exist alongside the state, has lost too much to the formal institutions of government in the delivery of welfare.

Sweden is perhaps the most advanced welfare state and has a range of services (dating from the early part of the twentieth century and covering old-age pensions, health care, child allowances, income maintenance, unemployment benefits) available to all citizens. The share of government spending on social policy has risen from 1.4% in 1930 to 35.8% in 1990. The state has authority to interfere with many aspects of family life, especially with the care of children. Despite the wide range of services supplied by the state the Swedish tradition is individualistic in that the family, neighborhood, and community groups have a very small role in meeting welfare needs. Furthermore, the range of welfare services is so wide and of such high quality that there is little need for private provision.

Although it is costly for the taxpayer the Swedish welfare system enjoyed wide support until very recently. It was developed to its present form by social democratic governments but on the rare occasions when more conservative governments have been in power they have done very little to stem its growth. There is, however, evidence that the consensus that once dominated Swedish welfare policy is now breaking down, mainly as a result of the fear that its cost will impose excessive burdens on future generations. But Sweden also seems to be experiencing the same sort of moral hazard that tends to characterize many welfare policies. There is a declining workforce because of generous disability and sickness benefits, and increased employment in the public sector, especially in the welfare departments

The German welfare state is nearly as extensive as Sweden's but welfare policies there are subtly different. Although the foundations in social insurance date back to Bismarck, the post war arrangements were designed to make welfare consistent with the market economy (the idea of the *Sozialemarktwirtschaft*, or social market economy). There was also an attempt at the beginning to avoid the type of dependency that German social theorists thought that the Swedish system produced. Still, the dominant party, the Christian Democrats, has always been divided between those who stress the social

element and those who emphasize free market economics in German social policy.

The German welfare state is organized on the subsidiarity principle with the Länder (the component states in the German federal union) being responsible for the major policies having to do with sickness, unemployment, children's allowances, and so on. The local authorities administer and partly fund social assistance (which is means-tested) given to those not covered by insurance schemes. The latter are semiautonomous organizations that operate under guidelines ultimately validated by the federal government. The payments that it makes for unemployment benefits, pensions, and health care are nominally based on contributions. The whole system is underwritten by the ideas of "social solidarity" and partnership between the participants. But the federal government provides about 12% of the cost of social insurance.

The system is generous. For example, the "equivalence" principle guarantees that the unemployed should get a wage not too much the lower than that which they received when in work and the system of children's allowance has gradually been extended and improved. German social spending (which has increased unavoidably since the reunification of the country) has been as high (with the possible exception of the Scandinavian countries) as any in the European Union. It now absorbs about a third of GDP. The original ideals of the social market economy, which were to restrict welfare spending and to preserve individual and family autonomy, have not been realized. Despite criticisms, primarily having to do with its rising costs, the system enjoys considerable social support. Although Christian Democratic governments since the early 1980s have promised to make economies they spend no less on welfare than other conservative governments in the European Union. It is very much an insurance-based system and the more radical Social Democrats argue that it does little for the really poor, who have to rely on means-tested benefits.

Although European countries have different welfare states from that of the United States there are similar comments made about the effects of welfare policies whenever they take the income supplement form. Britain (which generally follows the European model, although it is less generous) does have features of the residual welfare state—notably its Income Support Scheme. This is a means-tested benefit that in its original form was intended for those who fell outside the normal social insurance arrangements (which were introduced in 1911 but extended in 1946). The original recipients were widows, divorced women with children, and the elderly who could not live on the meager old-age pension. However, the cost (and the extent) has shifted upward considerably over the past two decades. Now a significant recipient group consists of unmarried mothers who have never worked. Observers of the British scene have noted similar phenomena to those that afflict the United States. Once again there would appear to be a problem of moral hazard. Policymakers have been reluctant to take action to solve the problem of the exploitation of the system that would have an adverse effect on those really in need.

In addition to social dysfunctioning there is evidence that over the years income inequality and poverty in Britain have worsened relative to other industrialized countries and that the benefit system has failed to compensate individuals sufficiently for the growing market-generated wage differentials. As in other countries, there has been a decline in the incomes of traditional manufacturing workers and indeed a loss of these sorts of job opportunities. It might be the case that not enough investment is made in human capital to equip individuals for the new technologically based jobs. It could be seen as a disabling feature of some welfare policies that they are designed to supplement (or replace) incomes rather than to equip persons with essential skills. The latter is more associated with the institutional welfare state.

A particular policy, which has aroused as much controversy as Income Support, is universal Child Benefit. This is a cash payment (made directly to the mother) for children. It is by no means unique to Britain but is a feature of all European welfare states; it is a real difference between them and the United States. The complaint is not about the dysfunctioning that it might cause but the fact that it is not means-tested. Thus, the rich get exactly the same cash as the poor if they have children and critics argue that if it were targeted to those in need poor mothers would gain significantly and there would only be a minor loss to the rich.

Here the debate is between rival philosophies of welfare policy. One side holds to the view that cash should be redistributed so that all people in need (subject to a means test) are brought up to an acceptable level of income, while its rival maintains that certain social roles, such as being a parent, or being old or disabled are themselves morally deserving of special treatment by the state. The benefit (or compensation) should be allocated to a person who has this position or status and should not be made dependent on whatever income she may have. If Child Benefit is means-tested then the average-income mothers are made worse off in comparison to people who are childless and remain in work. From this perspective the point of welfare policy is not

to supplement income but to guarantee a standard of living that would otherwise be lowered by child rearing. Certain universal payments of the Child Benefit type remove any taint of stigma and therefore fulfill, their advocates say, the valuable function of integrating all citizens into the welfare community.

It is the case that features of the European welfare state seem not to generate the kind of social disorders that American welfare policies are alleged to have caused. Only in Britain and Scandinavia do illegitimacy rates approach those experienced in certain parts of the United States. In Sweden, Denmark, and Norway they appear not to be accompanied by the same type of dependency as occurs in the United States (although this is now disputed). Italy has remarkably low rates of unmarried motherhood (although the welfare payments to this category are ungenerous) and this may be a consequence of the Catholic social culture. Obviously, cultural conditions interrelate subtly with welfare policies so that it is difficult to isolate the causal factors, if there are any, in the production of various social consequences. Certainly, there is not as much criticism of welfare policies in Europe as there is in the United States.

IV. WELFARE AND THE LOGIC OF THE INSTITUTIONAL WELFARE STATE

The major difference between the United States and Europe is the wide range of collectively delivered welfare goods and services that is available in the latter. These cover unemployment insurance, health care, pensions, and education (including higher education). The United States has some of these things. Social Security (inaugurated in 1935) provides mainly old-age pensions but it also includes unemployment insurance (a responsibility that, unlike old-age pensions, is shared with the states). However, it is noticeable that in the United States "welfare policy" in political discussion refers almost entirely to the features of the residual welfare state, it does not include Social Security or Medicare, which constitute a large part of the federal government's budget. In Britain and Europe such a distinction is not made.

The institutional welfare state is not supposed to be redistributive. Its designers based it on the principle of social insurance. The recipients of health care, unemployment benefits, and old age pensions were meant to receive something for which they had, in effect, paid. They had contributed to a fund on which they were drawing in times of need. Certain difficulties involved in the private insurance market, not only adverse selection but also the unpredictable nature of employment and health prospects, meant that these phenomena had to be handled collectively. The state should "smooth out" the rough patches in people's lives. As it turned out, no publicly provided institutional welfare state scheme has been properly self-financing and they tend to be partially, and sometimes mainly, dependent on taxation.

Despite the aims of their founders, the policies of the institutional welfare state are effectively redistributive. But unlike the redistributive effect of the residual welfare state, which is from the better off to the deprived, the redistribution in the institutional welfare state is between various groups in society. Thus, it is from the employed to the (temporarily) unemployed, from the healthy to the sick and the young to the old. This redistribution takes place whatever the existing levels of income of the participants in the schemes. As the institutional welfare state is based on quasi-insurance principles, its beneficiaries are not subject to means tests. A major disadvantage of means-tested benefits is that they produce "poverty traps"—people have a disincentive to work because they will then lose welfare payments. There is also a tendency for fraud to occur in means-tested systems.

The justification for the institutional welfare states derives in part from market failure but the major moral justification for its particular policies depends on a view of social justice, that is, that everyone should be equally entitled to essential goods and services without attracting stigma. A further claim is that the common consumption of such goods is less socially divisive than purely private arrangements. The institutional welfare state does not normally forbid private consumption, say, of pensions or health care, but it makes opting out cumbersome and expensive (the Canadian nationalized health service does not formally forbid private medicine but it does de facto).

Critics of the institutional welfare state normally focus on what they see as its inefficiency in dealing with questions of need. Because everybody consumes its services, whatever their income, it does not fully discriminate between the deserving and the undeserving poor. Thus, although social justice decrees that certain services in the institutional welfare state remain free at the point of consumption and equally available to all, recent research has demonstrated that there is unequal consumption. Britain has a fairly advanced institutional welfare state and it has been shown that the better off classes consume a disproportionate amount of, for example, health care and (especially) more or less zero-priced higher education. It occurs because the opportunity cost to them, what they have to give up to take advantage of the benefits, is much less than for poorer people. For example, the families of the rich do not expect their children to leave school early to take paid employment so they can easily consume almost free university education. Also, they can afford to take time off work to attend a doctor's surgery.

However, one answer to this problem, that the better off should go private, has an unfortunate but likely consequence. That is, the standard of the institutional welfare state would fall if the better off withdrew from it because it would then only be provided for the poor, who are a minority. However, without pressure from the electorate, governments would have little incentive to maintain high standards. With widespread privatization the institutional welfare state would rapidly become the residual welfare state.

A feature of the institutional welfare state that is often criticized is the reduction in choice that it is said to produce. Because the market in welfare goods has been seriously curtailed consumers do not normally choose between competing suppliers but have to accept what welfare policies are offered by government. Also, the amount spent on the various services will depend on political decisions; and the voting mechanism may not accurately reflect people's preferences for various goods and services. For example, in Britain, the proportion of GDP spent on health is no more than 7%, which is much less than either the mainly private systems, such as that in the United States, or those that involve some combination of public and private principles, as in mainland Europe. Similar observations are made about the educational features of the institutional welfare state; they tend to reduce the influence parents have over their children's schooling.

V. HEALTH CARE AND PENSIONS

The major problems with welfare policies of the institutional welfare state concern cost rather than social dysfunctioning. In Europe especially, disquiet is constantly expressed at the ever-rising share of GDP absorbed by health care and pensions. Certain problems arise out of structural features intrinsic to these goods but others emerge from the way that the public sector delivers them. Despite being mainly a residual welfare state, the United States has a very large public sector in pensions and a growing one in health (Medicare and Medicaid, established in 1965).

The disagreements in health policy arise out of the nature of the health care service and a major debate concerns the respective merits of the market and the state. The rationale for the state's involvement in health policy arises out of market failure (as well as morality). The patient is normally ignorant of her health needs and is, therefore, potentially vulnerable to opportunism by the the doctor. The conventional feature of market competition, the consumer shopping around for the best deal, is not applicable to phenomena where information is asymmetric, as it is said to be between doctor and patient.

The problem worsens when we consider the peculiar nature of the insurance market for health care. Once a patient has brought an insurance policy the marginal cost of treatment for her is zero; so there is every reason to expect that the demand for (possibly) unnecessary health care will rise. And the medical profession has every incentive to supply it. This leads to an inexorable rise in the cost of medical insurance and the consequent pricing of poorer people out of the market (that is an important reason why more than 30 million Americans do not have health insurance). The market fails in a technical sense because no one person has any incentive to economize on health consumption, even though everybody is made worse off in the long run by excess demand.

All this goes to explain the remarkable level of expenditure on health in the United States. Although costs are beginning to be constrained with the development of health maintenance organizations (a system by which the person purchases a set amount of health care in advance, which cannot increase in cost) and better monitoring of costs by insurance companies, there is still a problem of oversupply in the United States. Interestingly, Germany, which has a social insurance-based health care system, seems to suffer from a mild version of this phenomenon: for although patients pay a small part of the costs of their treatment the complaint is that there is oversupply and that too much is spent on "luxury" (or less than urgent) health care.

However, publicly supplied health care has its own problems. They arise out of the fact that politicians decide how much is spent and administrators determine how the service is delivered. Nationalized health systems are not monopolies, because in most welfare states it is possible to buy the service privately, but many people, probably a majority, cannot afford to pay twice. They do, in effect, face a mononpoly supplier with all the problems of lack of choice which that produces. Thus, although the evidence is that most people in Britain are generally happy with the health system, there are complaints mainly about undersupply of the service (especially of nonemergency care), the phenomenon of long waiting times for surgery, the arbitrariness of the (nonprice) rationing of costly treatment, and the poor quality of ancillary facilities. Because the delivery is at zero-price, demand for health care is theoretically infinite. The rationing problem will worsen with the rapid development of medical technology.

These considerations relate to health care as an individually consumed good. But a justification for treating it as a subject suitable for welfare policy derives from the argument that it generates positive externalities. Thus a healthy population advances the well-being of everyone, not just those who consume medicine. Workers are more productive and children are more amenable to education and therefore benefit from school.

Because it is unlikely that, in a free market, individual consumers will take these features into account in their own calculations regarding the purchase of health care, this is an additional reason for the state's involvement. It can be seen, therefore, as a mechanism for making the market economy work better. Such reasoning was no doubt behind the original European development of the institutional welfare state, even though private and voluntary associations for the delivery of health care to the poor have a long history.

Health policy interacts with what is likely to prove to be the most serious welfare problem in all Western democracies in the very near future—the provision of old-age pensions. Increasing longevity (brought about mainly by improved medical care) and a declining birthrate are combining to produce serious funding problems for the care of the retired. The future costs of pensions raise not only issues of economic policy but also questions of intergenerational justice. What obligations are owed by one generation to another? Can one generation be bound by a "promise" (which it did not voluntarily undertake) to pay the old-age pensions of the present retirees on the vague understanding that a later generation of workers will honor the "promise" to it?

In nonindustrialized societies there is much less of a problem because the closer family ties that they maintain produce a natural sense of reciprocal duty between parents and children. But in communities that are more anonymous, that have weaker family ties and higher rates of social and geographical mobility there are certain to be serious economic and moral questions concerning the aged. The United States, Germany, Japan, Britain, and the rest of Europe are all experiencing the same phenomenon of increasingly unsustainable future pensions burdens. It is an aspect of the costs of the institutional welfare state because there are clearly no behavioral difficulties associated with the state's involvement in the supply of pensions.

Theoretically, there need not be a serious problem. Pensions are simply deferred wages and in a well-functioning market individuals save for their old age. Their saving will depend on their time preferences—the rate at which they discount the future—and if these are normal then people will take care of their old age. If there is a problem of poverty among the elderly, which was at one time the case, then it will be dealt with by conventional welfare policies designed to deal with distress. There should be nothing *special* about pensions.

Apart from the fact that at one time being old did mean being poor (it is less so now) the original rationale for the state's involvement in pensions presumably was that people had time preferences that were too high and they would not save. This leaves a big welfare bill for society. The knowledge that they would be taken care of would presumably lead to a further raising of time preferences (a form of moral hazard) and ever-greater welfare costs. Thus the state, in its pensions policy, forces people to save.

Throughout the second half of this century the state's welfare policy has inexorably been bound up with the pensions problem, especially with the emergence of unfunded, or not properly funded, arrangements. Although they are nominally part of social insurance systems, and are therefore supposed to be dependent on contributions, pensions tend to be organized as "pay as you go" systems (PAYG); they are not financed from an accumulated fund of savings but by the transfers of part of the earnings of current workers to the old. It might be the case that pensioners would actually get more if their "tax investments" had been put into the stock and bond markets but, leaving this question aside, PAYG systems would only be stable if the facts about population growth and death rates were fully predictable and not subject to much change. Then governments could plan a pension system on the assumption that there would always be sufficient income from contributions and taxes to honor the intergenerational promise.

However, these data are rarely exactly predictable. What has happened in Western countries is an unanticipated decline in the birthrate and an increase in longevity. Under PAYG systems no funds, or insufficient funds, are accumulated to cover the increase in costs. In the United States the trust funds that have been built up are simply paper assets that will have to be redeemed one day, that is, paid for by taxation. Pensions are also costly because they tend to be earnings related, which

has the additional ethical problem of reproducing in old age inequalities that are established in a working life.

The European welfare state is by no means immune to these problems. Germany is facing a very serious crisis because it has had an exceptionally low birthrate in the last 30 years. It has been estimated that by the year 2030 pension fund contributions will have to be doubled if entitlements are to be honored. It is unlikely that the ethics of solidarity and partnership will extend through the generations. Sweden has similar problems, which are compounded by the remarkable phenomenon of early retirement.

As in other schemes, there is considerable variation in ultimate payments because Germany's system is earnings related. Furthermore, there is no national minimum pension (as in Britain) and those not covered by insurance have to rely on social assistance.

All nationalized pension systems, then, face the same problem: as the numbers of the retired rise additional social insurance contributions have to be levied (or additonal taxes raised), otherwise reduced payments must be made to the elderly (a breach of the intergenerational contract). The "support ratio," the ratio of workers to retirees, has declined in the United States from about 5 to 1 in the 1950s to a predicted below 3 to 1 in the early part of the next century. Britain is in a slightly better position because in 1986 it significantly reduced the generosity of its PAYG earnings related scheme (established in 1975 as an addition to a basic, and extremely meager, old-age pension) and it gave financial inducements for people to go private. Chile is exceptional in completely privatizing its state pensions scheme. There, people are compelled to save a portion of their earnings but have considerable freedom in their choice of pension scheme.

The problem with pensions being part of welfare policy is that there is no guarantee that governments have lower time preferences than those of individuals. In fact, the reverse is likely to be the case because their concern for the future is likely to be bounded by the date of the next election. Thus, debt is loaded onto the future generations. And the longer this goes on the more difficult it is for the sytem to be modified without one generation being harmed by having their pensions reduced (or their contributions dramatically increased).

VI. CONCLUSION

It is clear that even within the Western world there is considerable variety in welfare policies. But all of them face special problems as economic conditions change, population alters, and increased longevity places extra burdens on the taxpayer. But the problems vary in accordance with the type of welfare policy pursued. Americans seem especially concerned with behavioral problems associated with cash payments. In the future these are much less likely to be "open ended." Furthermore, lower tiers of government will be involved in their delivery (which is an important feature of the German system). Whether this is because politicians hope to reduce federal spending or because they expect the states and the localities to exercise closer control over the behavior of beneficiaries is difficult to say but it is clear that welfare policy will in the next century be different from the middle and later years of this one.

With regard to the institutional welfare state two factors are already dominating the debate. First, individual taxpayers will continue to express dissatisfaction with the compulsory nature of the services, even though, paradoxically, the better off do comparatively well out of them. The growing influence of individualistic, subjective choice will eventually have a decisive effect on welfare policy. Thus, there will be increased pressure to privatize services even though there will be considerable transitional difficulties. The fact that generations have paid into collectively delivered welfare goods and services means that obligations of government have been accumulated that cannot be abrogated.

Whichever aspect of welfare policy is analyzed it is clear that the concensus that may have once obtained on the subject no longer exists. Most Western countries are in the early stages of reform of their conventional welfare policies, but a process is beginning that could eventually revolutionize what have become familiar arrangements.

Also See the Following Articles

HEALTH CARE FINANCING • PATERNALISM • RESOURCE ALLOCATION • SOCIAL SECURITY • SOCIAL WELFARE, PROVISION AND FINANCE

Bibliography

Atkinson, A. (1996). *Incomes and the welfare state: Essays on Britain and Europe.* Cambridge: Cambridge University Press.
Barry, N. (1990). *Welfare.* Open University Press, Buckingham.
Braybrooke, D. (1987). *Meeting needs.* Princeton: Princeton University Press.
Brittan, S., & Webb, S. (1990). *Beyond the welfare state.* Aberdeen: Aberdeen University Press.
Ellwood, D. (1988). *Poor support.* New York: Basic Books.
Friedman, M. (1962). *Capitalism and freedom.* Chicago: University of Chicago Press.
Goodin, R., & Le Grand, J. (1987). *Not only the poor.* London: Allen and Unwin.
Hamlin, A. (1993). Welfare. In R. Goodin and P. Pettit (Eds.), *A companion to contemporary political philosophy.* pp. 651–662. Oxford: Blackwell.
Jencks, C. (1992). *Rethinking social policy.* Cambridge: Harvard University Press.
Kaus, M. (1992). *The end of equality.* New York: Basic Books.
Mangen, S. (1991). The German social state: A selective critique. In E. Kolinsky (Ed.), *The Federal Republic of Germany.* Oxford: Berg.
Robinson, R. (1990). *Competition and health care: A comparative analysis of UK plans and US experience.* London: King's Fund Institute.
Wilson, W. (1991). The truly disadvantaged revisited. *Ethics,* 101, 593–609.
Zetterberg, Hans L. (1995). *Before and beyond the welfare state.* Stockholm: City University Press.

WHISTLE-BLOWING

Geoffrey Hunt
University of East London

I. Presumptions
II. Perceiving Wrongdoing
III. Disclosing Wrongdoing
IV. Conclusions

GLOSSARY

accountability The preparedness to explain and justify one's acts and omissions to relevant others.

confidentiality The requirement that information is not to be disclosed to a third party.

constructive dismissal An employee's resignation on the ground that the employer has breached contract by making the work impossible in some respect.

disclosure The communication of information to a third party.

employee One who is contractually bound to provide labor in exchange for remuneration.

freedom of information The citizen's right to know what the government has in its files.

presumption in favor The assumption that something is to be generally accepted unless it can be shown otherwise under special conditions.

stakeholder Any group that has an interest or stake in the activities of some other group.

Whistle-Blower Protection Act A statute designed to protect legitimate whistle-blowers from victimization.

WHISTLE-BLOWING is the public disclosure, by a person working within an organization, of acts, omissions, practices, or policies perceived as morally wrong by that person and is a disclosure regarded as wrongful by that organization's authorities.

Here is a simple illustration: a civil engineer believes that a certain building practice is unsafe and reports this to his employer. The employer does not act on the report so the engineer takes it to his professional body. This body also does not act to the satisfaction of the engineer so he then decides to take his report to the media. The employer dismisses the engineer for gross misconduct in breaching confidentiality.

The term probably arises by analogy with the referee or umpire who draws public attention to a foul in a game by blowing a whistle, as in soccer.

Whistle-blowing thus has three essential elements: (1) the perception by someone within an organization that something is morally amiss within that organization; (2) the communication of that perception to parties outside the organization; and (3) the perception by at least some of those in authority in that organization that such a communication ought not to have been made.

Conceptual and ethical difficulties arise over such questions as the rightness of the perception of wrongdoing; the justifiability of "going public"; the nature and scope of corporate, managerial, professional, and employee responsibility; the conflicting claims of confidentiality and freedom of speech and of loyalty and honesty; and the openness and accountability of organizations.

I. PRESUMPTIONS

Any systematic treatment of these questions immediately encounters the methodological problem of how to adopt an impartial point of departure between the viewpoint of the employer and that of the whistleblower. One form this takes is the fundamental question of whether there is a presumption in favor of freedom of speech in the workplace or a presumption in favor of confidentiality. This has to be dealt with first, because any characterization of whistle-blowing tends to introduce a bias in favor of the whistle-blowing employee or the authority.

A. Impartiality and the Inequality of Employment

Whistle-blowers are most often nonmanagerial employees, but others such as clients, customers, suppliers and subcontractors, workers on various kinds of nonemployee arrangements, and managers also blow the whistle. We shall mainly discuss employees since these are typical.

A problem of impartiality arises here because the traditional workplace culture rests on the historically quite recent concept of the employer–employee relationship and, indeed, still carries traces of the older concept of the master–servant relationship. The employment relationship is unequal in respect of power since in general the employer's "hire and fire" capacity has far greater consequences for the life of the employee than the employee's capacity to "choose or lose" a workplace has for the life of the employer.

The employment relationship is defined by a contract of exchange of services (labor) for remuneration, and the employer is generally in the position of determining the nature and terms of the services required on a "take it or leave it" basis; implicit in this is the loyalty and fidelity (confidence) of the employee to the employer. A *mutual* loyalty and confidence is rarely assumed in practice. Thus the relationship is intrinsically one in

which the employee's voice regarding any aspect of the service being delivered is much weaker than the employer's. There is a potential for disagreement and conflict since the employer's principal objectives (e.g., to obtain or maintain competitive advantage) is, in current social arrangements, unlikely to be identical with the employee's principal objectives (e.g., personal and family security).

B. Some Manifestations of the Inequality

This situation facilitates the employer raising a voice about the conduct of the employee and deters the employee from raising a voice about the conduct of the employer. Thus the employer who has an ethical concern about the employee may ultimately dismiss them for "gross misconduct," but the employee who has an ethical, or other, concern about the employer may ultimately only resign and claim constructive dismissal. Thus the very term "whistle-blowing" tends to put the onus on the individual employee concerned to justify her action rather than on the party which regards the action as wrongful to justify that perception and any counteraction based upon it.

The cultural bias against unauthorized public disclosure is manifested in the labeling of those who disclose with a wide range of epithets in all countries, such as informer, dobber, snitcher, squealer, tell-tale, grass, Judas, tittle tattle, and stool pigeon. There is no word in general currency corresponding to "whistle-blower" to identify the employing individual (corporate executive or manager) who attempts to prevent legitimate disclosure, and therefore no corresponding literature and research program dedicated to comprehending the nature of what we might call disclosure prevention (gagging, muzzling, secrecy, victimization, etc.).

The polarized and unbalanced employment situation described entails contrary views about the rightness or wrongness of the subject matter of the whistle-blowing, about the justifiability of public disclosure, and the rightness or wrongness of the authority's counteractions.

C. Why Is Whistle-Blowing a Contemporary Issue?

The reason that whistle-blowing has become a contemporary social and ethical issue, largely unrecognized before the 1960s, is of philosophical as well as sociological interest. As is the case with many issues in applied ethics, it is probably another indication of a generally recognized extension of the liberal-rationalistic cultural framework under the impact of the marketization of social relations, marked in academic ethics discourse by the central concept of "autonomy." In this case a problematic social relation—employment—is cast as the problem of the autonomous individual in a new guise: the whistle-blower. Organizations, public and private, have not always caught up with the general movement to greater autonomy.

Several historical forces have combined to bring about a new awareness and controversy on the philosophical and ethical plane:

- The demand for greater equality and "political correctness"
- The undermining of the professional role, especially in the public sector, where private sector commercial values are either well established or more recently on the increase since the decline of the welfare state in the 1980s and 1990s
- The growth of citizenship and "stakeholder" notions, in connection with social concerns and corporate responsibility, e.g., for the environment
- The extension of the consumer rights movement
- The growing recognition of human rights, particularly freedom of speech and freedom of information
- The growing recognition of employment rights

II. PERCEIVING WRONGDOING

A. The Content of Whistle-Blowing

The employee may blow the whistle on any matter of moral concern in the workplace which is of general public interest. An employee's unhappiness about his salary, for example, does not, on the face of it, fit into this category.

One may group the majority in terms of danger or detriment to the workforce and/or the public, e.g., pollution, explosion, or fraud; threats to professional integrity and autonomy, e.g., managerial overriding of professional judgment, scientific fraud, or negligent treatment of clients; and unfairness or injustice in the workplace, e.g., sex, race, or disability discrimination.

Any one act of whistle-blowing may fall into more than one category. What unifies them is the perception that the public interest, the good of society, is at stake. However, in some cases what is perceived as a matter of public concern by the employee may not be so perceived by the employer. For example, an employee may perceive a particular act as one of sexual harassment,

and therefore a matter of public policy, while an employer perceives it as a purely personal matter which should be dealt with as such.

B. Levels of Whistle-Blowing

The content of the whistle-blowing act is not always on the same level of generality. It is convenient to distinguish, at an increasing level of generality, the single act or omission, the practice or procedure, the policy, and the organizational culture. While any level does not entail the level above it, it does entail any level below it. Thus a one-time act of moral wrongdoing does not entail a morally wrong practice or procedure, but a morally wrong practice or procedure entails morally wrong acts, at least potentially. Of course, real situations are not always so clear since there are usually uncertainties, indeterminacies, and differences in moral perception.

There may be a tendency for the whistle-blower to see a particular wrongness as an instance of a higher level wrongness while the employer tends to see the same wrongness as limited to a lower level.

1. The Act or Omission

A worker may witness a single act or omission that is morally troubling. For example, a student nurse witnessed a surgeon allowing his teenage son to put in two stitches during an operation on an anesthetized patient. Although the anesthetist lodged an internal complaint, nothing was done, so the nurse decided to go public. As a result the surgeon was disciplined and suspended from duty for two weeks. If this is a unique incident, then it has no implications for practices and policies in the hospital as a whole. It may not even be typical of this surgeon's behavior. Perhaps it was a lapse or an aberration. It is generally accepted that it is a responsibility of management to satisfy themselves that such an incident is not a symptom of wider failures. A criticism sometimes made is that managers may privately admit there is a wider problem while publicly presenting the incident as an aberration in order to protect the reputation of the organization.

2. The Practice or Procedure

An employee may be concerned about a practice or procedure that is routinely followed in their place of work, or about the lack or inadequacy of a practice or procedure. For example, a railway technician is concerned that no one appears to be following the official manual in dealing with checks on the signaling systems. The practice has developed of ignoring one of the fail-safe systems recommended because it is too costly and time consuming to check and maintain. First-level managers have informally (verbally) sanctioned this omission and the other technicians comply because it lightens their workload and they do not wish "to rock the boat." The technician raises the concern with managers repeatedly and each time they say that they will deal with it later.

After one year of inaction the technician tells a union official who then leaks it to the press. Colleagues ostracize the whistle-blower for "making us look bad." There is an inquiry, at which the technician is the principal witness, and the employer is fined for breach of safety regulations. Managers are ordered to implement the fail-safe system even if it means reallocating resources.

In this scenario it is not a one-time omission but a pattern of omissions that troubles the employee. At the same time it cannot be said that there is any policy to ignore the fail-safe; indeed, the policy states the opposite: all signaling systems must have fully operational fail-safe mechanisms.

The employers may be clearly negligent. However, the employer may see the wrongness of ignoring the fail-safe but, in a situation of scarce resources, may have given higher priority to other items of expenditure, for example, punctuality in departures and arrivals. They may have already faced public criticism for poor punctuality, and fearing loss of customer revenue, may have, perhaps unwittingly, caused a shortfall in resources for fail-safe maintenance.

3. The Policy

An employee may believe that a policy which has been, or will be, implemented at work is detrimental to the public either directly or indirectly by putting the employees under stress or restriction. For example, the head of a university department adopts an "open door" and "self-directed learning" policy for professional people taking the department's courses. This policy is very successful in bringing fee-paying students into the institution. The professors teaching the courses repeatedly raise with the head concerns about the policy's effect on academic standards. They are worried that applicants are not screened with sufficient stringency, so that many do not have the ability for a course with this status. They are also worried that "self-directed learning" has reduced professor–student contact hours to a point at which students are not able to benefit sufficiently from academic knowledge and skills.

Following the examinations, one of the academics, Professor P., complains to the university authorities that the department's examining board has passed several students who have learned too little to qualify. The authorities disagree with P., and a few months later P. is one of a number of staff chosen for removal, while the staff who passed the students keep their jobs. Professor P. feels victimized and goes public, resulting in a public debate about standards at the university department. As a result of this controversy, student applications to the department fall off dramatically. Some of the students threaten P. with legal action for having damaged their job opportunities, while others support P.

While the university authorities, and the head of department, regard the new policy as a bold innovation which takes advantage of changed market opportunities and requiring new methods of educational delivery, Professor P. (and his now silent colleagues) regard it as a matter of putting profits before intellectual discipline and educational excellence.

4. The Culture

In cases similar to that of the railway technician (II.B.2.), we may suspect that the failure of practice has a much wider dimension. Sometimes, where no one has blown the whistle or the whistle-blower has been ignored, the first public sign that something is *systemically* wrong in an organization is an accident or disaster of some kind. In this case a train might sooner or later crash into another with great loss of life. An inquiry into that incident might then reveal a systemic problem, a defect in the organizational or workplace culture. Such defects typically take a number of forms (see III.C.2.).

In this particular case there appears to be a laissez-faire culture in which no one cares very much about his work or the organization, and everyone adopts a minimalist, or even a "corner-cutting," approach to his responsibilities and duties. There may be an implicit collusion between nearly everyone in the organization. Naturally this affects the perception of wrongdoing, for a typical employee or manager in a certain workplace culture may fail to see as "wrong" what a typical member of the public would see as wrong. In this scenario the whistle-blower is often the new recruit, or the older professional attached to "traditional values," who has not been fully socialized into this culture.

Very often at official inquiries following some human-made disaster the public will be puzzled, even shocked, to hear one member of staff after another, both managers and workers, say, "That is the way we have always done things. We didn't think there was anything wrong with it."

C. Value Foundations

The values appealed to by the whistle-blower and other parties often have different, if related, foundations. It is useful to distinguish between three foundations: morality, professional ethics, and the law.

These will overlap, and there is a strong argument for regarding professional ethics and law as resting ultimately on moral foundations. However, parties to a dispute about public disclosure may be at cross purposes because, for example, one is attaching prime importance to a infringement of the law while another is attaching it to a matter of moral conscience.

1. Morality

Putting aside possibilities of ulterior motive and malice, an employee may make a public disclosure on moral grounds. This may go beyond the weak sense of that which underlies any objection to something which is "wrong" to the strong sense of that which underlies individual conscientious objection, often situated in a religious framework.

A health care worker, H., with strong "sanctity of life" views may refuse to conform with a hospital ward's tacit policy of not responding with resuscitation attempts in the case of certain severely ill patients (the so-called "slow code"). Although the management and staff are willing to discuss the issue and draw up explicit guidance on resuscitation, H. appears to wish to push resuscitation to limits which the rest of the team find unacceptable. H. tells her church group of her concern and a local newspaper finds out. The headline appears, "Hospital Staff Accused of Manslaughter Policy." The disagreement here may be so strong that while H. sees wrongness in many cases of the omission (not resuscitating certain patients), the rest of the team see wrongness in the corresponding act (resuscitating certain patients).

In some cases the personal values of the individual are pitted against the ethical values of the organization. For example, the employee may put honesty above the organization's demand for loyalty.

2. Professional Ethics and Regulation

Many professionals in the public sector subscribe to a "public service ethic" and a notion of "professional autonomy" to which they may appeal in defending a decision to make a public disclosure. Management does not necessarily share these professional values and may have a framework of values drawn from a commercial background. Doctors may feel that the decision when to discharge a patient is a purely clinical one, while managers may feel it is also determined by efficient allocation of resources and will try to prevent "bed blocking." In a dispute doctors might refer to their professional code of conduct which may state that patients must always be put first. Professionals are inclined to refer disputes and complaints to a self-regulatory body for resolution, but management may choose not to attach prime importance, or any importance, to the findings of such a body.

3. The Law

Many whistle-blowers have drawn attention to illegal acts or omissions in their organization, such as criminal fraud, breaches of environmental regulation, and civil negligence. But the law is by no means always the basis for a public disclosure. In some cases the whistle-blower may put the morality and professional ethics of the matter at the forefront, even if the incident is also illegal. In the example of the student nurse (II.B.1.), the surgeon's act was illegal as well as being one which was unethical from a professional point of view and simply immoral as a manifestation of one human being's lack of consideration for another (the patient).

A great deal could be morally and ethically objectionable in an organization which strictly involves no legal transgression. Indeed, an employee may feel that precisely what is wrong with the organization is that it is "minimalist." In our opening example of the civil engineer, it might be that this person is applying rigorous professional standards taught in a first-rate university, whereas the employer is content with the minimal standards prescribed by law.

III. DISCLOSING WRONGDOING

A. What Constitutes Disclosure?

What is it to disclose information? What does disclosure consist of? Is there a right and a wrong way of disclosing? Are intention and motive important? Is the character of the whistle-blower relevant, or only the truth of what is being disclosed?

1. Disclosure of What?

Not everything which an employee may disclose could count as a whistle-blowing item. When a person mentions at a social club event that the coffee machine in the office gives black coffee when the "white coffee" button is pressed it is hardly likely to be regarded as an act of whistle-blowing by anyone. If the same person mentions at the same event that there is massive fraud occurring in the office this is likely to be seen as whistle-blowing by everyone. While one item is clearly more important than the other it is not so easy to say what constitutes importance.

Not infrequently an employee will disclose something thinking it of no particular importance while the employer attaches great significance to it. While one can say that one item is likely to be sensitive and another is unlikely to be so, any particular item generally comes to be seen as a whistle-blowing one only in a particular context. Without the context it is hard to predict with any certainty what will generally be regarded as a non-disclosable item.

It is because of this, and the inequality in the employment relation (I.B), that many employees will err on the side of safety and be quite reluctant to publicly disclose very much about their workplace. After all, it is usually the employer that defines what is and what is not a sensitive item and it may not be clear what this is until a disclosure is made. This is not to forget that some items are defined as nondisclosable by statute, e.g., those protecting patients' medical information and those protecting state security.

2. Disclosure by Whom?

Since whistle-blowing is unauthorized public disclosure, it follows that a public announcement by the chief executive of an organization that massive fraud has been uncovered is unlikely to be an act of whistle-blowing. The very same announcement by an employee is probably a whistle-blowing act. What is important here perhaps is not who makes the disclosure but whether that person is authorized to do so. The chief executive just as much as the employee is a whistle-blower if the announcement is unauthorized. Presumably chief executives are also accountable, for example, to the board of directors, and should seek authorization. A lot depends on the system of authorization at work in an organization. Workplace cultures differ, within countries and across countries, and even the size of the organization may be important.

Some whistle-blowers have rather tenuous connections with an organization, e.g., as a supplier or subcontractor, so that the question of authorization is controversial. Presumably it is possible for someone to be identified as a whistle-blower, for example, a customer or client of an organization, even though this person cannot be said to have made an unauthorized disclosure because they are not subject to the organization's authority. At the other extreme certain employees, such as internal auditors or intelligence officers, may have strong restrictions and sanctions attached to unauthorized disclosure even for apparently quite trivial matters.

3. Disclosure to Whom?

Does it matter to whom one discloses the information? There are often disagreements between employee and employer as to whether authority exists for making disclosure to a particular party or kind of party. The question of onus arises again. While the employer may make a case that employees should presume that certain information is not disclosable to a particular party unless that party has been approved by the authorities, the employees may argue that all information is disclosable to certain parties unless the employer provides an overriding reason for nondisclosure. Parties which are often controversial as proper recipients of such information are regulatory bodies, outside inspectors, electoral representatives (members of parliament, congressmen, senators, etc.), the police, and trade union representatives. Generally a very strong case has to be made for the immediate disclosure to the media of organizational information. National cultures vary and a stronger case would probably have to be made in the United Kingdom than in the USA.

What is at stake here may be whether the disclosure counts as a *public* disclosure or not, and whether the informer and/or recipient in some sense straddles the boundaries of the organization. Without a clear idea of where the boundaries of the organization are it is hard to say whether an individual has gone "outside" with the piece of information at issue. It is perhaps not surprising if employers tend to have a more exclusive notion of these boundaries than the disclosing employee.

B. When Is Disclosure Justifiable?

When is an unauthorized public disclosure justifiable and when is it unjustifiable? Although perceptions will differ in a particular case there are some clarificatory rules. (Note that "justifiable" means that an act or omission in principle has a justification, that is, that it is possible to justify it, not that it has in fact been justified; "unjustifiable" means that there could be no justification in principle.)

1. Criteria of Justifiability

The justifiability of a whistle-blowing act revolves around issues such as the manner of the disclosure, the reasons for it, and the motives which lie behind it. Extreme positions are that whistle-blowing is always justifiable and that it is never justifiable. In the former, sometimes associated with advocates of unlimited freedom of speech, the argument depends on a narrow and positive understanding of whistle-blowing. In the latter, sometimes associated with advocates of organizational confidentiality, the argument depends on a narrow and negative understanding of whistle-blowing. A broadening of this understanding brings both extremes into a more balanced and fruitful debate in which whistle-blowing is sometimes justifiable and sometimes not.

It would appear reasonable to claim that whistle-blowing is only justifiable where certain minimal conditions have been met. A justifiable disclosure is arguably one which does more good than harm; serves some purpose in correcting or preventing the wrongdoing concerned; is made in a responsible manner; and follows upon the exhaustion of internal channels of complaint and redress.

Even when these conditions are met it is possible that, for someone, there is some other reason which makes the disclosure unjustifiable. There may be disagreement about whether this is a good reason or, indeed, whether it counts as a reason at all. Thus one may argue for including the legality of the disclosure as a condition. But, while an illegal disclosure probably needs a stronger justification (especially if it is criminal, as opposed to contestable in a civil court), it is the ethics of the disclosure that is at issue here. In a liberal democracy in which civil disobedience is regarded as acceptable under some conditions, most would agree that an illegal disclosure may be morally justifiable. (Indeed, whistle-blowing and civil disobedience may be regarded as conceptually related.) Of course, the position that it is never morally justifiable to disobey the law is not indefensible.

Furthermore, each of the *prima facie* conditions given is contestable in any particular case, since every case is open to interpretation, within a reasonable range, depending on the interests and values of the parties involved.

2. Good and Harm

A whistle-blower may find it difficult, or impossible, to ascertain whether a disclosure will do more good than harm. All the well-rehearsed arguments for and against utilitarian calculation could be invoked at this point. Some would take the view that it is not unreasonable to make a disclosure simply and only because "it is the right thing to do" even if harmful consequences are known to be more likely than beneficial ones. A whistle-blower in this position might feel, for example, that they are ultimately answerable to a god who will judge them only for being virtuous or following moral principles and not for the consequences of the right act. In real situations a potential whistle-blower is very unlikely to be able to assess all, or even most, of the consequences of disclosure. Even if one could, it would always be *her* interpretation of harms and benefits rather than, say, the employer's.

It must be admitted that it would give rise to legitimate suspicion about motives if a whistle-blower was not disappointed or regretful if their disclosure clearly did more harm than good. But even this is problematic since there need be no inconsistency in the whistle-blower being in a minority of one regarding the rightness of their act. Conversely, a whistle-blower may not be comforted in the knowledge that most (or even all) people believe the disclosure was, on balance, the right thing to do when the whistle-blower now perceives harmful consequences which would have been sufficient to make them refrain from disclosing had they predicted them.

All that can be said with certainty is that potential whistle-blowers are well advised to give thought, together with supporters and well-informed parties, to the consequences of the disclosure before making it. If they fail to do this there may be a widespread opinion that their disclosure was unjustified, even if it was justifiable.

A disclosure which could not possibly do anything to rectify the wrongdoing or prevent future wrongdoing may be regarded as unjustifiable. After all, it may be asked, what is the point of making the disclosure? In all the examples we have already given there is the possibility of rectifying the matter which is perceived as wrong and preventing reoccurrence. Quite often, however, people disagree about what is possible and what is not. Optimistic and courageous whistle-blowers sometimes find themselves isolated by their well-meaning colleagues on the grounds that "there is no point, the system *cannot* be changed."

Furthermore, the rectification criterion is itself contestable. The whistle-blower, as we have seen, may not be concerned so much with the consequences of the disclosure as with simply making the truth known, because it is the truth. Even the most pessimistic person may blow the whistle without ill motivation. Some may blow the whistle primarily, or only, to redeem themselves for years of complicity or collusion in organizational wrongdoing. No doubt it remains the case that most whistle-blowers would appeal to rectification to justify their act, at least in part.

Potential whistle-blowers are also well advised to make their disclosure in a responsible manner if only for the pragmatic reason that those who object may be inclined to make an issue of the manner, thereby drawing attention away from examining the matter which is being disclosed. This is one aspect of "shooting the messenger." Then there is the additional point that disinterested people will tend to treat the level of responsibility manifested in the whistle-blower's behavior as a test of the truth and importance of the matter being disclosed. Someone who is clearly irresponsible in handling a matter is usually less likely to be listened to and believed than someone who handles it with great care.

Putting prudential considerations aside, responsible disclosure is surely a moral requirement, and it is here that it may be considered as a condition of justifiability. In concrete terms, responsible disclosure might include:

- Making sure one has one's facts right
- Refraining from exaggeration and distortion
- Consulting colleagues
- Avoiding hurt to innocent parties
- Putting aside any inclination to personalize or act vindictively
- Choosing the proper time
- Disclosing to the most appropriate party (someone who is also responsible)

None of these can be regarded as a necessary requirement, regardless of context, however. Indeed, "responsible manner," like the other criteria, can serve only as a general guide to justifiable disclosure, for it is always possible, if exceptional, that a particular disclosure is justifiable even where the manner was quite irresponsible. Thus it is arguable that a cleaner at a child care institution who blows the whistle on serious child abuse has acted justifiably and was justified even though, in their ignorance, they made it in an irresponsible manner—perhaps publicly revealing to a newspaper the names of the children.

3. Exhaust Internal Channels?

Again, it is judicious to exhaust all channels of complaint and concern internal to the organization, and to be seen to do so, before blowing the whistle. Public sympathy may not be very strong for someone who is seen to have acted hastily or impulsively. A preparedness to exhaust internal channels may be regarded as a test of the whistle-blower's sincerity and professionalism.

But it is more importantly a moral matter. To fail to give an organization a chance to deal with the wrongdoing, or even consider whether it is a wrongdoing, is to act unfairly. An organization and its executives and managers, and even its employees and clients, may suf-

fer extensive collateral damage from a disclosure about a serious wrongdoing which the organization would have been prepared to rectify with less damage had it been informed in a timely and helpful way.

Difficulties may arise with attempting to use such channels, however, and again these show that this condition cannot be a necessary one, although it is consideration potential whistle-blowers should always keep in mind. One difficulty is that the organization may not have adequate channels for staff to raise concerns. Whether the channels which do exist are adequate or not will sometimes become part of the controversy around a public disclosure, for there is often a difference between management and staff about what constitutes adequacy here. Channels such as complaints, grievance, and disciplinary procedures may have fallen into disuse or may be biased or perceived to be biased in favor of management. That is, such channels appear to be better designed to deal with managerial complaints against staff rather than the other way round.

If an organization suffers from systemic maladministration, mismanagement, or corruption, then it may be very dangerous for the conscientious employee to raise a concern internally. It might be tantamount to taking a concern for adjudication to the very people who are implicated in the matter of concern. More radically, even where such channels do function well, they are almost entirely negative in form. That is, they are designed to deal with complaints about what is going, or has gone, wrong, rather than with preventing wrong (see III.C.3.).

C. The Organization

1. Confidentiality, Gagging, and Freedom of Speech

Our analysis of possible conditions for justifiable disclosure (III.B.) may have given the impression that it is right to put the onus on the potential whistle-blower. If we speak of the "conscientious employee" rather than the "whistle-blower" this may invite us to reverse the onus. To restore balance we should also ask, what are the conditions under which it is justifiable to prevent public disclosure of organizational information?

We might suggest "gagger" (or "muffler" or "muzzler") as the negative correlate for whistle-blower on the employer side of the employment relation. But it is perhaps more useful to think of both employers and employees as having rights and duties which have more in common than has been traditionally understood. It is true that the employer, in the shape of executives and senior managers, has traditionally been more concerned with protecting the organization as a whole—its competitiveness, cohesion, and reputation. This might be regarded as a managerial duty. It follows that the employer will tend to put a stronger emphasis on confidentiality. However, while the employee has a duty to keep disclosure within certain bounds, the employer has a duty to keep confidentiality within certain bounds and stop it from spreading into managerial secrecy, deafness, and victimization.

Since the Western liberal tradition accepts the existence of a human right to freedom of speech, one may argue that there is also a presumption in favor of this right in the workplace. Unfortunately there are some unresolved inconsistencies between a number of human and civil rights and the usual provisions of the contract of employment, without much clarity as to which takes precedence. The historical trend would appear to be to carry these rights into the workplace, and this would include freedom of speech. In that case there is a general onus on the employer to justify workplace exemptions to this right and make them explicit for the benefit of the workforce and society at large. Such exemptions might include:

- Professionally privileged information, e.g., medical information obtained by doctor from patient
- Commercially confidential information, as defined by various statutes
- Information which arises in connection with national or public security (intelligence, policing)
- Other information which is exempt by statute
- Information which is potentially damaging in terms of civil action

Since the government is always a major employer, the question of public sector whistle-blowing needs special treatment. Accepted democratic principles would require that no government extend national security legislation beyond certain limits, and that every government legislate for freedom of information to allow citizens access to government-held information. The absence of a Freedom of Information Act (in 1997 the United Kingdom still did not have one) and overextended official secrecy laws tend to create whistle-blowers by default.

2. The Whistlegenic Organization?

There is a temptation to undertake psychological studies of whistle-blowers to determine what they have in common. It might be thought that this research could encourage employers to take on psychologists in a risk management program to eliminate certain character types from their organizations. This would not deal with the ethical issues at stake, and may be regarded as an unethical corporate strategy. In any case there does not appear to be hard evidence that whistle-blowers have anything in common other than having blown the whistle. Furthermore, this approach overlooks the fact that many people in an organization may wish to raise a public concern but are afraid to do so, and many others may have been socialized into a kind of blindness to public concerns.

Another object of study is the organization itself. Organizational change, in response to wider cultural changes or economic exigencies, may often lead to a rash of whistle-blowing cases. A dislocation may occur between, for example, traditional professional values and new managerial values. In the example of the university department (II.B.3.), Professor P. understands the need for sustaining, or even increasing, university income, but believes that traditional academic standards are of great importance to society's cultural level. He also thinks that long-term reputation may be sacrificed for short-term gains. But the authorities disagree, maintaining that the policy is innovative and creates new opportunities for students and the organization. Many public sector professionals blew the whistle in the 1980s and 1990s as their professional autonomy and judgment were undermined by a new managerialism.

One should also consider whether there is what might be called a "whistlegenic" organization; that is, one which generates a potential for whistle-blowing. The essential feature of such an organization might be general arrangements which fail to deter and rectify wrongdoing and fail to encourage ethical values and behavior. One would not expect whistle-blowing situations to arise very often, if at all, in organizations which take account of all stakeholders (employees, shareholders, executives, clients and customers, suppliers, local community, the general public, etc.) and arrange their activities in an open and accountable fashion. The experience of whistle-blowers has demonstrated some common cultural patterns in the unethical organization:

- A laissez-faire culture. Proper procedures and practices are not followed rigorously and nearly everyone acquiesces. This is often sustained by a kind of collective collusion: "I won't inform on you, if you don't inform on me."
- A climate of fear. There is an autocratic managerial style, usually in a closed institution such as a prison,

which allows systemic prejudice and intimidation to flourish.

• A culture of corruption. Significant power centers in the organization are involved in conspiracy and secrecy to serve their own interests at the expenses of the organization and its clients.

• A culture of hypocrisy. There are two codes of behavior: the formal and official one for the public and the informal one that operates in practice. Lip service will be paid to proper procedure, and staff take a cynical view of communications from management.

Such organizations will generally have a gamut of internal failures, such as poor communication, low participation in decision making, dissonance in the values held by the stakeholders and by the organization in practice, and low morale. It is possible for such an organization to maintain a high, if false, public reputation by gagging staff by sustaining a climate of insecurity or fear. Sometimes this situation appears normal to those who have worked long term in the organization, even if it appears highly abnormal or even bizarre to those on the outside or to new recruits.

3. Protecting and Preventing

All organizations are subject to change and may improve or deteriorate from an ethical point of view. In those which have not deteriorated too far (implicating senior executives and management) there is always the possibility of managerial initiative to engender openness and internal and external accountability. Staff concerns, which may lead to whistle-blowing if ignored, may be treated under certain guiding ethical principles of management. These might include:

• Above all, to consider the concern impartially and establish whether it is true, wholly or in part

• Not to penalize the conscientious employee for raising a concern even if it is false or misguided

• To act on a presumption in favor of genuineness on the part of the employee; even if malice or ulterior motive should emerge, the truth of the whistle-blowers' claims remain paramount

• To create *positive* channels for the expression of concern, such as participatory meetings, exit interviews, rewards for employee vigilance, periodical ethical audits, and open door management

• A readiness to explain and justify to all stakeholders, in a consensus-building spirit, their decisions and actions, for example, around resource allocation

While from the managerial point of view whistle-blowing may be seen as a problem and a threat, from the employee and public point of view it may be unethical and secretive management which is the problem and the threat. For example, environmental dangers created by corporate disregard for public opinion, industrial regulation, and law cannot await the emergence of more whistle-blowing martyrs.

Furthermore, in the long term the promotion of ethical management is more likely to deal with the kinds of issues raised by whistle-blowers, on the level of practice, procedure, policy, and culture, than legislation which punishes employers for victimizing whistle-blowers. Such "whistle-blower protection" legislation, which is now to be found, for example, at the state level in the USA and Australia, may play its part in a wider program of cultural change.

However, much of this legislation needs to be amended to shift the onus from the whistle-blower, who currently has to justify disclosure from a presumption in favor of commercial or government confidentiality, to the employer, who should have to justify gagging from a presumption in favor of freedom of speech and freedom of information.

IV. CONCLUSIONS

An understanding of whistle-blowing must start from a recognition of assumptions of partiality and onus in the employer–employee relation.

Such a starting point indicates a need to clarify this relation, manifesting inconsistencies and conflicts among rights, for example, between the generally recognized human right to freedom of speech and the contractual right of employers to confidentiality in the workplace. The general recognition of a human right to nondiscrimination in the workplace for public interest disclosure may be on the horizon. In 1997 the whistle-blower organizations Freedom to Care (UK) and Whistleblowers Australia jointly proposed an amendment to the Convention of the International Labour Organisation to effect such a right.

It also indicates the need for a reappraisal of employer and employee duties and thus their practices. For example, while executives and senior managers think of the protection of the organization as their special duty, employees who are valued and listened to are more likely to think of this as a duty of theirs too.

Also See the Following Articles

ACTS AND OMISSIONS • CIVIL DISOBEDIENCE • CONSUMER RIGHTS • CORPORATIONS, ETHICS IN •

CORPORATE RESPONSIBILITY • PRIVACY VERSUS PUBLIC
RIGHT TO KNOW • TRADE SECRETS AND PROPRIETARY
INFORMATION

Bibliography

Freedom to Care (1995). A whistleblower protection act: Would it work? *The Whistle*, 3 (8/9).

Glazer, M. P., & Glazer, P. M. (1989). *The whistleblowers*. New York: Basic Books.

Hunt, G. (1995). *Whistleblowing in the health services*. London: Arnold.

Hunt, G. (1997). *Whistleblowing in the social services*. London: Arnold.

Miceli, M. P., & Near, J. P. (1992). *Blowing the whistle*. New York: Lexington Books.

Sheppard, B. H., Lewicki, J., & Minton, J. W. (1992). *Organizational justice*. New York: Lexington Books.

WILDLIFE CONSERVATION

Clive L. Spash and Jonathan Aldred
University of Cambridge

I. The Need for Conservation
II. Whose Life Is to Be Conserved and on What Grounds?
III. Utilitarian Arguments
IV. Rights and Wild Things
V. Conclusions

GLOSSARY

biodiversity The biological diversity of life described in terms of the range and type of genes, species, and ecosystems on the planet Earth.

conservation The act of preserving, guarding, or protecting from loss, decay, injury, or violation.

contingent valuation A survey method used by economists to place a monetary value on non-market goods such as wildlife and aesthetics.

species A biological grouping that shares a common pool of genes, the basic units of heredity, thus allowing successful interbreeding for organisms capable of reproduction.

wildlife Life found in an original undisturbed state, without domestication, cultivation, or taming; commonly used with implicit reference to vertebrates.

WILDLIFE CONSERVATION is a reaction to the increasing loss of species, the rate of which has accelerated dramatically this century. Species loss has been highlighted by some notable cases of extinction and near extinction in recent centuries, such as the dodo and the American buffalo. In this century large mammals and predatory birds have tended to be a focus for popular attention, with nongovernmental organizations trying to protect whales, lions, tigers, pandas, and eagles. However, this has tended to treat wildlife conservation from a narrow vertebrate species perspective which risks neglecting the growing concern over ecosystem structure. Given the underlying concern for preserving life in a wild state, restricting attention to large readily identifiable species will clearly be inadequate, but is a result of a consequentialist tendency. That is, reference to the preferences of the general public for guidance on how wildlife conservation is to proceed tends to lead to the neglect of plants, reptiles, insects, and microorganisms. The conservation of such wild, untamed life requires the recognition of the interdependence of plant and animal species mix in determining the ecological resilience of wildlife. Thus, wildlife conservation has moved from the idea that key species could be preserved in zoos to the protection of ecosystems, while the nongovernmental organizations involved in the area have transformed from passive clubs for the study of natural history to active lobby groups for the environment and the maintenance of biodiversity.

Along with this dawning recognition of the breadth of trying to conserve wildlife has been a growing concern for the treatment of the wilder side of Earth by humans. As long as the losses driving the conservation

Encyclopedia of Applied Ethics, Volume 4
Copyright © 1998 by Academic Press. All rights of reproduction in any form reserved.

movement were infrequent and localized they could be regarded as having limited and estimable consequences for humans. A general lack of concern is then a reflection of the relative weight given to species loss over other goals in human society and the low priority of the resulting loss. Today this has been refined to a high degree in the application by some economists of monetary valuation of the costs and benefits of species extinction. However, an alternative underlying motivation for wildlife conservation has been the protection of animal rights. While conservation of objects for identifiable ends is the central theme in the consequentialist approach, under a rights-based system more turns upon the rights of nonhuman life-forms to be wild and have self-determination. The relative dominance of these two motivations is particularly relevant to the way in which wildlife conservation develops in the future.

I. THE NEED FOR CONSERVATION

A. Historical Roots of Concern

1. Creation

About two millennia ago the Roman poet Lucretius wrote about the changing world he saw around him, and in particular mentioned ideas akin to those of Charles Darwin. That is, he recognized features in the species he saw which had allowed them to survive, e.g., the cunning of the fox, the prowess of the lion, and the speed of the stag in flight. Some species survived under human protection because of their usefulness to humanity. Others were theorized to have perished. Today this is unremarkable.

However, in the intervening period the dominance of Christian theology meant the suppression of such ideas as extinction. In the story interpreted from biblical texts God had given all creatures to man for his stewardship at the time of the creation and they had all been aboard Noah's Ark. There was an absence of the notion that species might become, or had become, extinct. This perspective became strong in the medieval period.

Despite the Protestant movement, weakening the central authority of the Pope, little change in the official story occurred. In fact Martin Luther reinforced the line that all animals and fish appeared at once upon the word of God. The date of this creation was estimated a hundred years later by Archbishop James Ussher of Armagh, Ireland, as 4004 B.C. This date persisted as a defense of the theory of creation and was employed by the English naturalist Philip Gosse in his book of 1857 on the subject.

However, the repeated discovery of dinosaur bones and skeletons cast doubt on the creation theory from the 18th century onward. In the 19th century the theories of evolutionists such as Darwin took hold. Thus, no longer could the mysterious skeletons be regarded as animals that missed the boat (Noah's Ark) from the antediluvian era. The importance of this change in thinking was that now causes of extinction became a topic for discussion and soon concern.

2. Extinction

While extinction is regarded to be a normal evolutionary process, the rate of extinction induced by humans is of concern. Over geological time several causes of species loss have been postulated, including climate change, ice ages, interspecies competition, and catastrophic events such as the impact of a giant meteorite. Fossil records show about nine mass cases of extinction in the past.

About 1500 million years ago the trilobite was the dominant life-form. This crab-like creature took on a variety of forms and sizes but largely died out about 500 million years ago, taking a million years to do so. Around 250 million years ago an extinction took place in which 50% of all species are estimated to have become extinct with 96% marine, 75% amphibian, and 80% of reptilian life-forms disappearing. The dinosaurs were dominant for around 150 million years, becoming extinct 65 to 70 million years ago. Mammals have been the most recent dominant species group arising over the last 25 million years or so, with the rise of mankind slowly in the last million years.

Mankind as a hunter may have aided in the destruction of species over the last 50,000 years or more. For example, the first human migration in to the New World (North America) is estimated to have occurred about 35,000 years ago. Large mammal species which had disappeared elsewhere but survived there then disappeared, probably aided by a warming climate. Similar cases of mass extinction are found in relation to the arrival of mankind in Australia and New Guinea 50,000 years before present, and in New Zealand less than a millennia ago with the extinction of large species of bird (e.g., the giant moa), lizards, frogs, and fur seals.

The reason for concern over extinction today is the rapid growth in its rate. By the middle of the 20th century two species of animal were being lost every year and plant species were disappearing at similar or higher rates. Other wild life-forms such as insects and microorganisms have been neglected in this regard so their losses are unrecorded.

B. Conservation and Causes of Species Loss

1. Diversity and Species Interdependence

About 1.7 million organisms have been identified and named; their distribution is 6% in boreal and polar latitudes, 59% in temperate zones, and 35% in the tropics. However, there is a great ignorance as to the global diversity of species, and attempting to account for the undescribed organisms thought to exist places the tropics as holding 86% of global species. Species are interdependent in such a way as to make insects and invertebrates the building blocks and glue in existing habitat structure. Wildlife conservation projects often concentrate upon large vertebrates or admired plants while neglecting these other life-forms. For example, in tropical forests insects are important because they are the primary food for most small carnivores, are predators of seeds influencing species composition, and influence the structure and functioning of the ecosystem.

2. Extinction and Extermination

Extinction can have nonhuman causes such as random catastrophic events, biological interactions (e.g., competition, disease, and predation), physical stress, and frequent disturbance. The process of extinction prior to the dominance of mankind was a gradual one requiring millennia. Human-induced extinction is therefore in a different class as the process can be extremely rapid, requiring a few decades. Thus, some distinguish this anthropocentric extinction process by terming it extermination. This term applies aptly to the dodo, the North American passenger pigeon, the great auk (the penguin of the northern hemisphere), and the giant moa of New Zealand. Some of these stories of extermination are apocryphal, while others are so well documented that the names of the hunters who killed the last live individuals of the species is known.

In general, human-induced extinction was historically due to hunting beyond the natural growth rates of species. However, the rapid rate of species extinction this century has been due to the increasingly widespread impact of human activities. The introduction of foreign species has been foremost among causes of extermination, e.g., introducing terrestrial mammals to New Zealand. Destruction of and encroachment upon habitat are now of great concern and form the focus of attention in tropical forest conservation.

Chemical and organic pollutants, acidic deposition, and general reductions in environmental quality all stress species if they are able to survive in the altered environment. The highlighting of this pollutant cause

of extinction occurred most forcefully in the 1960s with the focus upon what was seen as the indiscriminate use of pesticides and insecticides by the agrochemical industry. In particular, the scare over the use of DDT and the publication of *Silent Spring* by Rachel Carson in 1962 led to legislation in the United States. These are persistent and widespread problems which go far beyond the agricultural sector. The build up of heavy metals, nitrates, and acidic deposition has altered entire regions. Persistent pollutants have been released in to the environment so that damage to the genes of wild species has been and is occurring, leading to infertility and deformed and/or dead young.

3. Concern for Conservation

Wildlife conservation can be regarded as being based on one or more of three fundamental reasons. First is the primarily economic argument. Humans are part of a larger environment with which they interact. This means wildlife provides a source of human welfare from food and clothing to aesthetic and spiritual enrichment. In this way wildlife conservation is seen to preserve the potential for future human happiness via the uses which can be made of that wildlife in order to create improvements in utility. Wildlife loss is then primarily of concern because it removes the ability of humans to benefit by exploiting biochemical, ecological, and other wildlife properties.

Second is the related consequentialist but ecological concern over the role wildlife plays in ecosystem functioning, stability, and resilience. The emphasis here is upon the interdependencies of species and the potential for ecosystems and their functions to be destroyed to the ultimate detriment of humanity. Because the ecological importance of any given species, in nutrient cycles, ecosystem productivity, and structure, is largely unknown, precaution is suggested by this justification for wildlife conservation. Third, the concern is raised that wildlife extermination is a violation of species and other rights which humans have a duty to respect. However, before these viewpoints can be explored, the issue of which life-forms are to be given moral consideration must be addressed.

II. WHOSE LIFE IS TO BE CONSERVED AND ON WHAT GROUNDS?

A. Species and Individuals

Two preliminary distinctions are required. The first is between ethics which focus on conservation of a whole species and ethics which attend directly to individual members of that species. The concerns of wildlife conservationists have increasingly centered around entire species, on the basis of the consequences of species extinction—and thus the depletion of global biodiversity—for the planet. The question then arises of whether "the health of the planet" is taken to matter in and of itself, or because this would adversely affect human quality of life.

The second, related, distinction is between the view that extinction of species (or individuals) is bad in itself, no matter what the consequences, and the view that the negativity of such an outcome derives from its consequences, which violate some other ethical principle. The possible consequences and principles will depend on the range of entities which enter into direct moral consideration.

Consider some endangered species of elephant. The extinction of each individual elephant may be held to be of moral concern, or only the extinction of the entire species, but our answer to this question tends to depend on a prior one—whether the elephants matter only insofar as their survival affects the interests of humans, or whether the interests of the elephants themselves are held to be worth considering. That is, are humans the only morally considerable creatures or are elephants also morally considerable?

B. Five Accounts of Moral Considerability

There are at least five basic accounts of the range of moral considerability: it can be limited to humans alone or extended to all vertebrates, all living creatures, non-living things, or even whole ecosystems. The account adopted will have implications for the way in which wildlife conservation is put into effect.

1. Only Human Interests Count

In theory human interests could be the sole concern in a variety of moral philosophies, e.g., only human rights count. However, in wildlife conservation this ethic tends to be reflected as a variant of utilitarianism where the interest of humans alone is involved in the maximization of happiness as the goal of society. An endangered species, such as the elephant, matters only insofar as its survival affects the sum total of happiness and unhappiness among humans in the society. Logically the next step for wildlife conservation policy is to obtain information about the effects on human happiness of the extinction of the threatened species, and this is discussed in the section on utilitarianism.

2. Including All Vertebrates

This ethic implies that all vertebrates (mammal, bird, reptile, amphibian, fish) are morally considerable, so that the direct consequences for the well-being of the affected animals should be taken into account when formulating wildlife conservation policies. Adversely affecting the interests of vertebrates is to be taken into account, even if the demise of the individual or species is judged to be of no importance to present or future generations of humans.

Note that the center of attention here is the individual animal rather than the species as a whole. Since vertebrates are held to enter into the moral calculus in their own right, they count as individuals for their own sake, rather than merely as a means to the end of conserving their species. Thus, perhaps contrary to expectations, this animal-centered ethic only provides indirect justification for wildlife conservation. Avoiding arbitrariness entails that equal interests are treated equally, so that, for instance, all adult elephants of a particular species will be granted equal moral considerability regardless of whether the species is threatened with extinction. In contrast, the wildlife conservation perspective makes species conservation the fundamental objective, implying that individuals in the set of elephants, which together form a viable population to maintain the species, count for more than "marginal" elephants which may be added to this set.

Vertebrate-centered ethics may be subdivided further according to the categories of animals which are granted moral considerability. This may be limited to only those higher mammals which have some form of self consciousness (e.g., apes, dolphins), or include all mammals, or be extended to include fish as well. Although the notion of wildlife conservation typically brings to mind images of furred creatures, most animals do not conform to this picture. In fact, in terms of numbers, the biologist Robert May has noted, "as a rough approximation, every living thing on Earth is an insect," which raises the next ethic.

3. Every Living Thing Has Standing

Ethics of this form aim to represent the interests of all living things, including invertebrates, plants, single-celled organisms, and perhaps even viruses. Usually such arguments reject the claim that all living things are of *equal* moral significance, even if they all possess moral considerability. Judgments of the relative goodness of protecting an endangered species of mammal, as opposed to an endangered species of tree, will finally depend on a detailed evaluation of the consequences of these two preservation options. Such evaluation takes place on a case-by-case basis; nothing in general can be said about the relative moral significance of, say, mammals as opposed to other living things. An exception to this is the form of life-centered ethic sometimes known as biotic egalitarianism where all living things count equally, as discussed by Arnae Naess in his book, *Ecology, Community and Lifestyle: Outline of an Eco-sophy*.

A problem with such an approach, in the current context, is that it seems highly unlikely to be able to inform wildlife conservation decision making. Biotic egalitarianism would allow only quantitative comparisons—that two living things count for more than one—and hence almost all forms of human management of the natural environment would be ruled out because they make trade-offs in terms of one living thing for another.

4. Consider All Natural Entities

Despite this last point, some go even further in widening the scope of moral considerability. Nonliving entities such as mountains or rocks might be granted consideration "for their own sake." Such ethics have met with a considerable degree of skepticism, so it is important to emphasize that they make no attempt to discern a consciousness among rocks, or establish that a rock is striving unconsciously to achieve certain goals and therefore can be said to have interests. Rather, these ethics aim to provide support for the idea that certain activities such as mining might be wrong simply because of the damage they do to the fabric of the natural world, even though no living things might be affected.

5. Ecological Holism

Ecological holism represents the culmination of the view that humans have certain duties toward preservation of the natural world; nature *itself* should be preserved as far as possible rather than any particular component entities. Thus, ecological holism counts whole ecosystems and the wider biosphere as morally considerable. It is particularly associated with Aldo Leopold's Land Ethic, which has been elaborated in J. Baird Callicott's *In Defense of the Land Ethic*.

The distinctive feature of this position is the shift of emphasis from part to whole—from individual to community. According to this view, the extinction of some species of wildlife would not matter because it entailed the demise of individual members of the species, nor would it matter for its own sake. Instead it matters only insofar as it undermines the sustainability of the ecosystem as a whole. For example, the land

ethic is concerned more with endangered species, and largely indifferent to the plight of domestic animals. More starkly, the violence of the predator-prey relationship cannot be said to serve the interests of the prey and hence will be regretted by some animal-centered ethics, but it is a relationship Leopold respects and would leave undisturbed. Clearly, an ethic of ecological holism directly supports the shift toward biodiversity maintenance rather than species conservation.

C. Implications of Moral Considerability

1. Contrasts between Different Approaches

The different environmental ethics outlined briefly here have a number of implications for wildlife conservation. If only humans are morally considerable, then specific species should be preserved only to the extent that a desire for this is reflected in human preferences. As noted above, moral considerability for vertebrates gives individual animals standing, which may conflict with the aim of wildlife conservation to maximize the number of species preserved. This is particularly so when the specific form of animal ethic in question limits moral considerability to a number of key species, such as "representative" higher mammals. A situation might arise where the dominance of such key species in their habitat threatens to lead to the extinction of another species which is ignored according to the ethic. Alternatively, the limited culling of members of a key species could be sanctioned in order to ensure the survival of the other threatened species, but this would violate the vertebrate-centered ethic.

A similar problem arises when the domain of moral considerability, according to an ethic, is wider than that implicit in traditional wildlife conservation policy. Increasingly vertebrate-centered ethics extend moral consideration beyond a limited number of higher mammals to include all those creatures which, in some meaningful sense, have the capacity to suffer. In contrast, the traditional wildlife conservation approach seeks to preserve key species at the expense of others.

Ethics which consider all living organisms as valuable for their own sake obviously make much stronger claims on us than the wildlife conservation perspective. However, the latter may sanction similar environmental policies to these broader ethics because the objective of species preservation demands that a balanced, fully functioning habitat for the species is maintained, which in many cases will ensure the flourishing of plants and other organisms just as readily as attending to them for their own sake. On the other hand, the preservation of species in zoos and plants in seed banks is equally valid under the wildlife conservation approach, but is often not supported by broader ethics. As noted, ecological holism supports biodiversity maintenance rather than species conservation, but when combined with other ethics it may yield a position much closer to the practice of wildlife conservation. For instance, ecological holism and an animal-centered ethic taken together imply that policy measures should focus on the preservation of those animal species which support biodiversity and other aspects of the flourishing of the ecosystem.

2. Human-Centered versus Animal-Centered Ethics

The differences between a narrow anthropocentric viewpoint and the wider views previously outlined have been dominant in policy debate. In sum, a human-centered ethic depends on individual preferences for conservation while an animal-centered ethic offers at least the possibility of supporting wildlife conservation measures directly. However, in practice this difference is more apparent than real because of the impossibility of directly measuring the interests of animals. Policy makers will often rely on human value judgments to determine the extent to which a given conservation proposal serves the interests of the animals. Yet human value judgments which are made to justify wildlife conservation may depart from case-specific preference-based concepts .

In particular, the ethics of wildlife conservation have become inextricably interlinked with contemporary debates over "animal rights," with most ethical questions being couched in animal rights language. This is partially due to the dominance of rights-based discourse throughout ethical debate, particularly in the United States. Such rights are seen to facilitate clear and readily understood "rules-of-thumb" concerning which actions are sanctioned and which are prohibited, rather than requiring lengthy debate on a case-by-case basis. The extent to which the animal rights perspective supports wildlife conservation can be examined and contrasted with a utilitarian basis for policy.

III. UTILITARIAN ARGUMENTS

A. The Case for Concern

The utilitarian argument for wildlife conservation recognizes mankind as the cause of the deliberate destruction of large numbers of species. The question is whether some species are more useful than others and therefore deserve to be saved, i.e., whether scarce resources should be used to save them. This in turn implies prioritizing species in order of destruction potential. Norman Myers supports this argument in his book, *The Sinking Ark*, where he rejects saving species "come what may." For him and others the issue is whose needs are served by the conservation of species, and how does saving a species enhance the long-term welfare of humans.

B. Ethical Basis of Consequential Conservation

The consequentialist rationale for wildlife conservation is forced to address ethical concerns despite the tendency of economists valuing wildlife to avoid these issues. Similarly, wildlife conservation on the grounds of the scientific value of biodiversity still ultimately rests on how much "better" a future world in which that value is preserved would be compared to alternative futures. No matter how "better" is defined, an ethical claim is being made.

A consequentialist view of the value of animals adopts a different account of moral considerability from the rights-based approach: The moral significance of preserving different animals will depend explicitly on the consequences of the action taken. Moreover, unlike the animal rights account which necessarily assumes an animal-centered ethic, a consequentialist view of the value of animals may either be couched in terms of the animal-centered ethic or be limited to a human-centered ethic alone. Put another way, the consequentialist account may consider only those consequences which affect humans (including the adverse effects on human well-being which arise from the implications for animals of some action), or extend to consequences which affect the interests of animals directly, regardless of whether these consequences have any effect on human well-being.

Historically the most influential version of consequentialism has been utilitarianism. Utilitarianism is egalitarian in the sense that it considers equally the interests of all beings affected by an action. In particular, it considers equally the abilities of all beings to suffer. As Jeremy Bentham wrote in *The Principles of Morals and Legislation* (1789 [1996] Oxford: Clarendon p. 273), "The day may come when the rest of the animal creation may acquire those rights which never could have been withholden from them but by the hand of tyranny.... The question is not, Can they reason? nor Can they talk? but Can they suffer?"

In modern times, Peter Singer, in *Practical Ethics*, has perhaps been the most influential of those offering a more sophisticated utilitarian defense of the value of animals. Singer's approach, as a version of consequentialism, evaluates consequences in terms of the extent to which they satisfy the preferences of the agents granted moral considerability. Following Bentham, this is defined to be all creatures with the capacity to suffer. This evaluation of preference satisfaction can become quite complicated.

Some of the ethical problems with this approach can be illustrated by the following example. Five survivors are in a lifeboat, which only has the capacity to support four. All weigh approximately the same and would take up approximately the same amount of capacity. Four of the five are normal adult human beings, while the fifth is a dog. If one must be thrown over board to prevent all five perishing, whom shall it be? For instance, throwing any one of the humans overboard will not only fail to satisfy the presumed preference of the individual for continued existence, but cause great suffering to that individual's family and friends. In addition, the argument is made that although both dogs and humans have the capacity to suffer, the total amount of suffering experienced by a human during the course of anything other than an instantaneous death exceeds that of a dog. By contrast, all such consequential considerations are irrelevant if all individuals have the right to life. The nonconsequentialist approach to the lifeboat example will be discussed further on, but first the extent to which this consequentialist reasoning has been taken is summarized.

C. Monetary Valuation of Wildlife

Here the influence of modern market economics is felt, with its emphasis on the sovereignty of the consumer, whose decisions about his or her purchases—or sources of happiness—are to be respected rather than overruled by the moral philosopher. Thus, in seeking information about the consequences of some potential species extinction for human happiness, policy makers increasingly turn to environmental economists, who in turn refer to individual preference information. As with items of food, clothing, and other commodities, a market for conservation of, say, elephants is envisaged. The extent of consumer demand for elephant conservation in that market is then taken as a proxy measure of how much human happiness is affected. As no such elephant conservation market actually exists, consumer preferences are measured in hypothetical markets where monetary valuations are gained on the basis of contingent factors; a process termed the contingent valuation method.

The contingent valuation method (CVM) involves the direct questioning of individuals by means of a survey, typically to obtain how much the individual would be willing to pay to ensure the protection of some endangered species of wildlife, or, far less commonly, how much they would be willing to accept in compensation if the species were exterminated. Three elements can then be identified: (i) a description of the species and habitat to be valued, which may be detailed enough to include a schedule giving the probabilities that various numbers of the species will survive if preservation is attempted; (ii) a method by which payment or compensation will be made; and (iii) a method of eliciting the monetary values. In a survey of 20 U.S. studies, covering 18 rare, threatened, and endangered species, per household preservation costs fell well below the benefits revealed in the hypothetical contingent market, even for the most expensive project. Annual willingness to pay ranged from a low of $6 per household for fish such as the striped shiner to $95 for the northern spotted owl and its old growth habitat.

Noneconomists are often surprised by the apparent crudeness of contingent valuation, but the U.S. District Court of Appeals has upheld the values obtained, a "blue-ribbon" panel (including three Nobel Laureate economists) assembled by the U.S. National Oceanic and Atmospheric Administration has endorsed the method, and test–retest reliability studies confirm internal validity. The result of refinement has been to achieve statutory requirement in the United States whenever compensation following industrial accidents is to be determined. More importantly for wildlife conservation, the U.S. Congress, in reauthorizing the Endangered Species Act, may determine that a cost–benefit analysis, and by implication contingent valuation, is required to support a listing decision.

There are many economic criticisms and corresponding refinements in the literature on contingent valuation, and more generally cost–benefit analysis (see N. Hanley & C. L. Spash, 1993. *Cost–benefit analysis and the environment.* Cheltenham: Elgar). Ethical criticisms have been much more fundamental, including claims that: (i) the procedure treats species preservation as a good which is "consumed" merely for the uses and facilities it provides; (ii) environmental species cannot be itemized as commodities of monetary value; and (iii) respondents are neither willing nor able to make trade-offs between species preservation and monetary alternatives. Environmental economists have largely ignored objections (ii) and (iii). Their response to (i) has been to try to capture "existence value" in their surveys, meaning the value to an individual of some species quite apart from that associated with any actual or potential use of it by that individual. This derives from the satisfaction of knowing that a particular species simply continues to *exist*, that is, with a sustainable population in its native habitat.

Existence value appears to admit the possibility of an animal-centered ethic, albeit one where, by default, the judgments of individuals are relied upon to determine the interests of the animals. Certainly the many definitions of existence value in the literature reflect an attempt to capture a value which goes beyond the direct interests of humans in species preservation. Humans may recognize values which are unrelated to either human interests or those of an extended moral community including animals. Examples involve the language of awe, reverence, and respect rather than benefit and cost. They include our wonder at the marvel of a setting sun, or the sense of raw nature in a wilderness area. The danger here is that CVM, in focusing on the narrow consequences for humans of a wildlife conservation proposal, will overlook altogether the broader ways in which we value nature. Bernard Williams concludes, "the human concern for other, non-human and non-animal, effects is misrepresented if one tries to reduce it simply to a kind of human self-concern" (1995. *Making sense of humanity* (p. 235). Cambridge: Cambridge Univ. Press).

IV. RIGHTS AND WILD THINGS

A. The Animal Rights Case

Attributing rights to animals is a particular form of animal-centered ethic rather than upholding a more general view that animals deserve moral consideration. Rights-based approaches to ethics are nonconsequentialist and thus often associated with Kant, although a position which treats rights rather than obligations as fundamental can only be loosely described as Kantian. Kant in *Lectures on Ethics* (1930 London: Methuen p. 239), was nevertheless one of the first philosophers to show concern for animals: "The more we come in contact with animals the more we love them, for we see how great is their concern for their young. It is then difficult for us to be cruel in thought even to a wolf."

A classic modern defense of animal rights is Tom Regan's *Case for Animal Rights*. Regan essentially holds that only beings with inherent value have rights. Inherent value is the value that the being possesses independently of its value to others. For the purposes of the discussion here, this may be understood as equivalent to a creature being morally considerable. Only self-conscious beings, deliberate actors capable of having beliefs, desires, and goals for the future, can have inherent value. Regan holds that all mammals over a year of age, if not mentally defective, can have inherent value on this definition, and thus possess rights. Animal rights are universal moral rights, rather than legal rights, so they remain the same as we move from one human society to another. What then is the difference between the animal rights ethic and the argument, already discussed, that "all animals" are morally considerable?

B. Rights and Moral Considerability

Crucially, on most rights-based approaches, all beings with inherent value have it equally; thus rights are not possessed to differing degrees by rights bearers. Although this position has the virtue of being egalitarian, it faces difficulties when there are conflicts between rights. In contrast, the notion of moral considerability makes no claim about the relative moral significance of different creatures, and allows for variations in the degree of consideration attributed to different agents. Thus, the animal rights approach represents a particular account of moral considerability.

We can return to the lifeboat example to analyze the conflicts between rights in that situation. Regan argues that the dog must be sacrificed, because the harm done to the dog, if thrown overboard, is less than that done to a human, in throwing one of them overboard. Indeed, Regan goes further by maintaining that, in general, sacrificing any number of dogs would be better than the death of four humans. Animal rights activists might reject this approach because of the downgrading of the animals' relative position and the weighing up of consequences. In this case, making a choice between conflicting rights results in an appeal to welfare consequences. Human capacity for suffering is then judged greater than that of dogs; therefore humans are to be preserved in preference to dogs. For wildlife conservation policy, this account leaves open the possibility that, for instance, some species of elephant should be exterminated if it threatens the survival of some species of higher primate.

C. Animal Rights versus Consequentialism

1. Similarities

The preference utilitarian may reach the same conclusions in the lifeboat example as Regan does with his rights-based account. This is surprising given the traditional antagonism between consequentialist and nonconsequentialist rights-based ethics. Certainly in principle the positions of Regan and Singer are capable of reaching very different conclusions. However, in practice (e.g., wildlife conservation) the two theoretical approaches in their more plausible formulations will often lead to convergent policy recommendations.

Consider a species of elephant which is threatened with extinction by a development proposal which would destroy its habitat. Singer's interpretation of preference utilitarianism would almost certainly rule out this proposal because of the adverse consequences of the species' extinction for: (a) the elephants themselves, (b) animals in their ecological community dependent on the elephants' continued existence, and (c) human welfare. These considerations might weigh so heavily in the utilitarian scales that it would be almost impossible to outweigh them. This problem is easy to resolve in terms of Regan's position: saving the elephants does not, it is assumed, involve the sacrifice of any other species, so the utmost must be done to save them.

2. Problems and Differences

The language of rights may be an unpromising expression of our concern for animals, because that language is designed with "normal" adult humans in mind. For example, rights of ownership can only have meaning in a community of agents who recognize that they owe to each other, and are owed by each other, certain forms of behavior. How animals are to become full members of such a moral community is unresolved because they lack certain capacities of the archetypal rights bearer, such as the ability to negotiate conflicts of interest and to plan, choose, and accept responsibility for actions. However, this criticism of animal rights is easily extended to rule out rights for young children and mentally defective adult humans. This leaves the critique valid, but requires an explanation of the wider implications and, for example, how a line can be drawn between animals and humans lacking some key capacities of a rights bearer.

Perhaps more worrying for Regan's animal rights account is its apparent tendency to contradict itself. The rights-based account grants by definition equal moral significance to those creatures treated as morally considerable, yet, in adjudicating between competing rights claims in the lifeboat example, some animals are to be regarded as more equal than others. Moreover, in deciding that the dog should be thrown overboard, Regan appears to justify this decision on consequentialist grounds—in terms of relative harms. These difficulties will be sidestepped by a rights-based account which denies the eventual trade-offs in terms of relative

harms which Regan admits when determining which creatures should be sacrificed. But such an approach still needs to determine how a decision is to be made when there are conflicting rights.

Regan's account will be equally powerless when neither of the conflicting rights is a right to life. In the earlier example, a proposed development might significantly increase the nutritional intake of numbers of humans living at subsistence level, but erode the habitat of the elephant, perhaps leading to greater competition for food among elephants. The rights-based account appears unable to resolve this dilemma without some appeal to consequences.

If the rights-based justification for wildlife conservation must in practice perform some, albeit constrained, evaluation of consequences, then the evaluation procedure will be crucial. Granting that all animals are morally considerable is inadequate. One debate here revolves around the efficacy of using scientific experts to determine animal interests. If, as with humans, these interests lack a specific, "correct" form, and sympathy with the animals' way of life is mainly required, then the judgment of experts would be unnecessarily privileged over that of laypeople. Despite adopting an animal-centered ethic, the justification for wildlife conservation may still come to turn on human preferences. The danger here is that this preference information may be too impoverished, or too unreliable, to capture certain aspects of our concern for wildlife. Thus, for wildlife conservation policy in practice, the relevance of preference information, and the means by which consequences are measured more generally, may matter more than whether the underlying conservation ethic is rights-based or consequentialist.

V. CONCLUSIONS

Wildlife has formed a focus for environmental concern with considerable emphasis placed upon protecting specific species of vertebrates, e.g., the lions of *Born Free*. The arguments for this conservation can be viewed as partially related to the expression of individual human preferences, which have seen the rise of conservation organizations such as the World Wildlife Fund (WWF). Economists were quick to recognize the role of these human preferences as an indicator which might be useful for policy purposes. This lead to the development of conservation arguments based upon consequentialist reasoning. The most refined example is the use of the contingent valuation method to estimate the value of endangered species and suggest the extent to which resources should be used to prevent their extinction or reduce their rate of decline, e.g., elephants, whales, the corn crake, and other birds. These studies are important in the debate over wildlife conservation because of the way in which they characterize the expression of concern. This consequentialist motive differs from ecological and nonconsequentialist ethical motives.

In the latter regard, this economic viewpoint contrasts with an alternative expression of the need to conserve wildlife as found in animal rights. Animal rights also imply a position which falls far less comfortably under the title of conservation. Conservation and consequentialism in essence allow for trade-offs in terms of species' freedoms and allow for individual animals to be treated as expendable. Even when the consequences for all species are to be taken into account, a hierarchy of importance is normally imposed so that human welfare comes out on top. The expression of moral considerability under an animal rights perspective tends to deny what is regarded as an inequitable treatment of different species. However, when rights conflict, a consequentialist approach may be invoked. Thus, the current concern for the rate of human-induced species extinction centers the ethical debate on the conflict between human welfare and other species needs.

The complexity of determining consequences, and an appeal to public preferences for guidance, has tended to lead wildlife conservation into focusing on key species to the neglect of wider concerns. Thus, the framing of the issue of wildlife conservation as species preservation can be contrasted both with the wider concern for biodiversity maintenance and with more narrow individual moral considerability. Concentration on biodiversity maintenance emphasizes both genetic and ecosystem diversity but neglects the individual. This can be seen as consistent with the underlying driving force behind the emphasis of 1950s conservationists on specific species more as a means of avoiding reductions in ecosystem diversity. Extinction of the wild lion and tiger is then only a symptom of the loss of entire ecosystems and a tool for their preservation.

The modern environmental concern is more directly focused upon the less tangible aspects of wildlife conservation and less so on key species. In addition, ecological conservation is dynamic because it requires room for ecosystems and their components to change and adapt. In this way the ability of reflection upon supposedly static individual human preferences to inform public policy appears limited; a point some economists have been reluctant to admit. Wildlife conservation viewed

as economically rational behavior is far removed from modern wild land preservation with its emphasis on ecosystem functions and resilience where species come and go. Wildlife conservation as traditionally understood is then only a small part of that modern movement for environmental preservation, and this can help explain why, for example, WWF has become the World Wide Fund for Nature.

The traditional wildlife conservation perspective may also conflict with some of the most deep-rooted concerns for the environment. For many the genesis of nature conservation lies in a desire to preserve a nature which is neither controlled nor fashioned by humans but is simply *natural*. But wildlife conservation as species preservation already implies an intervention in nature which degrades this ideal. Preserving a "wilderness" means preserving a definite, delimited wilderness. Most starkly, the disappearance of a species can be a natural process of ecological evolution, and human attempts to counter that process seem to imply unnatural intervention. Rights for ecosystems to evolve and individual species to compete successfully may express the ecological perspective. This returns us to Leopold's land ethic, which seeks to preserve the diversity, integrity, beauty, and authenticity of the natural environment, rather than having some form of humanitarian concern with individual animals. Reconciling wildlife conservation in terms of species preservation with this genuinely ecological approach to nature may be impossible. Of course the immediate and pressing concern is over the rate of species extermination and its moral implications, but the wider meaning of conserving life which is wild also confronts conservationists on a daily basis.

Also See the Following Articles

ANIMAL RIGHTS • BIODIVERSITY • ECOLOGICAL BALANCE • GAIA HYPOTHESIS • SPECIESISM • STEWARDSHIP • ZOOS AND ZOOLOGICAL PARKS

Bibliography

Hanley, N., & Spash, C. L. (1993). *Cost-benefit analysis and the environment*. Cheltenham: Elgar.

Jakobsson, K. M., & Dragun, A. K. (1996). *Contingent valuation and endangered species: Methodological issues and applications*. Cheltenham: Elgar.

Loomis, J., & White, D. (1996). Economic benefits of rare and endangered species. *Ecological Economics*, 18, 197–206.

Williams, B. (1995). *Making sense of humanity*. Cambridge: Cambridge Univ. Press.

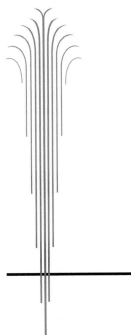

WOMEN'S RIGHTS

Xiaorong Li
University of Maryland

GLOSSARY

human rights As stated in the 1948 UN Universal Declaration of Human Rights, "a common standard of achievement" by which social, economic, and political arrangements can be criticized and reformed. Human rights are the moral rights of all human beings by virtue of being human, irrespective of their citizenship, nationality, race, ethnicity, language, sex, sexuality, or abilities. These rights are inviolable and they demand protection. Human rights include political, civil, social, and economic rights.

natural rights As understood by political philosophers in the Western classical liberal tradition, certain rights that all persons possess equally and that are in some sense inalienable and indefeasible. They include the rights to life, libery, and property. Classical liberal political philosophers such as John Locke use "natural rights" to set limits to legitimate governmental interference.

sex and gender In the discourse of gender analysis and feminism, "sex" is often used in contrast to "gender." Whereas "sex" refers to males and females in terms of their physiological or biological differences, "gender" refers to socially and culturally constructed perceptions of the behavioral differences between men and women, and to the socially and culturally assigned roles of males and females.

WOMEN'S RIGHTS, as this concept is used today in feminist philosophy, in the discourse of feminism, and in the women's rights movement in general, is not exclusively a philosophers' brainchild. It has been forged in intellectual reflections responding to the social reality of female subordination and to relatively recent political demands for change. It should thus be understood within the context of modern political as well as philosophical debates.

"Women's rights" refers to those human rights, the violation of which is suffered by women because of their sex or gender. It is true that many violations of the human rights of women (political persecution, for example) are similar to those suffered by men. But the category of women's rights addresses those abuses that are directed specifically against females. It seeks to protect the rights of girls to be free from infanticide and malnutrition in societies where sons are favored over daughters; the right of women not to be subject to forced marriage, domestic violence, sexual exploitation and harassment, or to sex-based discrimination in education, employment, and political participation; and the right to adequate reproductive health care. The protection of women's rights is essential for women to pursue their well-being on a basis of sex and gender equality.

I. NATURE AND GROUNDS

If human rights are universal and already acknowledge the claims of all human beings, male or female, why is there any need for a distinct category of women's rights? The identification of women's rights as a separate category of human rights is based on the recognition that the UN Declaration of Human Rights was developed in a male-oriented world. Although the various human rights instruments insist that all human beings, irrespective of their sex, have human rights by virtue of being human beings, feminist scholars argue that men have taken advantage of their dominance in social and political power to shape the human rights reality. The paradigm of human rights violations is the violation of men's human rights and is based on men's experiences. Thus, these scholars argue that human rights should be restated to take account of gender, in order to respond to women's particular experiences of injustice. They point out that the concept of human being, upon which the notion of "human rights" has rested, has long excluded women, and that women's human rights are violated in many ways that men's rarely are, particularly in the sexual and reproductive realm. In Catharine MacKinnon's words, "what happens to women escapes the human rights net." "Women's rights" serves therefore as a distinct category though still under the general rubric of human rights. It stresses "man's inhumanity to women" (MacKinnon, 1993. Crimes of War, Crimes of Peace. In *On Human Rights: The Oxford Amnesty Lectures 1993*. New York: Basic Books). "Women's rights" thus reflects a gender analysis of human rights violations as well as a political strategy of feminists to fight gender-specific social injustice.

The inadequacy of "human rights" to address gender-specific injustice also stems from the complex philosophical arguments that shaped the theoretical foundations of human rights in the Western liberal tradition.

A. The "Rights of Man"

"Women's rights" as a separate category of human rights has clearly expanded the classical liberal concept of rights as limited to individual rights. Women's rights, for instance, address sexual and reproductive exploitation in the private sphere, and economic and political discrimination in the public sphere. In both spheres, women as a group are victims of collective male patriarchal subordination. Women's rights seek the liberation of women as a group; in this sense, they are collective as well as individual rights, which women have by virtue of being members of the female "group." The classical liberal concept in the Western tradition of the "rights of man" proves an inadequate basis for conceptualizing women's rights.

The "rights of man" had its foundation in the European Enlightenment of the seventeenth and eighteenth centuries. During the period of capitalist accumulation and early industrialization, the Enlightenment represented a cultural/intellectual movement promoting knowledge, reason, and secularization, as well as liberation from the predominance of the church and feudal lords. Such notions as "an Englishman's birthright" or "natural right" began to compete with the notion of duties men owed to the lord, the king, the church, or God. Political philosophers, such as Rousseau, Locke, and Hobbes articulated the concept of men as free and equal and rational beings, modeling this concept on the bourgeois males who possessed the rights to life, liberty, and property. The proper role of the state and law, these philosophers believed, was to safeguard these "natural rights" of man. The American Bill of Rights and the French Declaration of the Rights of Man invoked these rights as sources of guidance for, and limits on, governments.

The classical notion of man in the discourse of natural rights, the basis for the liberal conception of a human being, virtually excluded women. Human beings own property and are free to make rational decisions in public affairs. But women did not own property and were often owned by men as property; they had no social reality and were thus not free to participate in public affairs. The legal holders of full citizenship rights were at that time male property owners in European and North American societies. The moral persons who have interests and not merely instrumental functions for others were thus conceived, in the philosophy of "natural rights," as men. The revolutions in France and in the United States, inspired by the natural rights of man, occurred alongside slavery and the owning of women as property through marriage, and these practices continued long after the revolutions. White males who owned property thus had a monopoly on the newly achieved rights of equality, opportunity, and political participation. The intellectual legacy of the Enlightenment left untouched the subjugation of women and the enslavement of non-Whites, and to some extent even perpetuated these groups' lack of freedom. If the concept of human rights is understood as natural rights-based, this concept would be biased and narrow.

After the industrial revolutions, women in European and North American societies, like women similarly situated in many developing societies today, continued to be considered their husbands' legal property. The liberated "man" continued to be used as a synonym for "human being," thus sustaining the perception that, as MacKinnon put it, being a woman does not count as one way of being human. Social, political and legal institutions did not count women as independent legal/ moral persons and made them ineligible to own or inherit property, sign contracts, seek a divorce or obtain legal custody of their children.

B. Other Theoretical Failures for Securing Women's "Human Rights"

Contemporary philosophers have developed alternative theories to ground human rights. It has been argued, for instance, that the protection of human rights is justified because it gives human beings the opportunity to carry out their "life projects," or because it secures respect for human "dignity." Another theory holds that it is "rational" for people to respect others' rights. But these arguments are not much of help in addressing the inadequacy of "human rights" as a response to gender injustice. In the reality that women face, their "life projects" have often been restricted by their gender role in society; they have not been permitted to have any choice. Women are expected to find "dignity" and "self-respect" in living out obediently their social roles. The justification for such "social division" often rests on the perception of women's irrationality—by nature, they act only on the basis of irrational emotions or sentiments. Consequently, the violations of women's human rights do not count as "human rights violations," because such violations often constitute the only "life projects" and "dignity" that are permitted to them.

The institutionalization of international human rights after World War II was largely a reaction to state-sponsored atrocities, particularly the crimes against humanity committed by the Nazis. Thus, international human rights law recognizes only states as violators and at the same time demands state accountability and action to redress violations. From the point of view of male-dominated state power, the violations of women's rights by men have often not counted as human rights violations. As a result, international human rights instruments not only left the power to act against violations in the hands of states—which in most cases have themselves committed the violations—but also neglected "private" (and thus considered "natural" or culturally justifiable) acts by men against women. Challenges to state violations of women's rights, or to the failure of states to protect women from human rights violations by men, have often met with arguments for respecting culture and against state intervention in citizens' "private" lives.

A human rights regime that excludes women has been therefore perpetuated by a web of ideas and practices, including (1) a classical concept of the human being as the free and rational man, upon which "human rights" has been constructed, (2) international human rights norms that ignored male dominance in the "domestic" quarters such as the family, and (3) women's continued dependent status and subjugation, "privately" and worldwide, which deprived them of influence at the time when "human rights" were first defined and proclaimed by state-parties at the UN.

II. THE SCOPE

A. Should All Women's Rights Be Human Rights?

It is controversial whether women's rights should be included in or covered by the general category of human rights. One could argue that violations of women's rights should count as human rights violations and should be addressed by available human rights instruments. Such an argument would demand for women no rights beyond those that have already been confirmed by the international human rights instruments. Women's rights only demand that human rights be reinterpreted so as to recognize women as human beings entitled to the same mainstream rights. For example, rape would be considered an instance of torture.

This view may not be shared by everyone, however. Some feminists have argued that women's liberation demands the creation of a new set of rights, exclusively for women, expanding the existing range of internationally recognized human rights. Some point out that certain rights, such as reproductive rights, are for women only because women alone bear children. Given the unique reproductive needs of women, granting women special rights such as pregnancy benefits does not constitute unfairness or injustice to men.

Feminists who defined women's rights as human rights warn against the risks of introducing special rights for women that are not universal human rights. They argue that such an expansion may trivialize women's rights and may provide a new rationale for gender discrimination. Moreover, advocates for women's rights as human rights believe that creating exclusive rights for women is unnecessary. They argue that the right to reproductive health care, for example, is already included in the universal human right to "a standard of living adequate for the health and well-being . . ." of every person (UN Declaration, article 25). This reading assumes an understanding of "health" based upon individual human needs. Health is not simply defined by the standard health needs of men but by the needs that have to be met in order to enable different human beings (of either sex and at various stages of development, with or without disability, and so on) to live to their fullest potentials. Each human being's health needs will not be the same, but all human beings should have the right to live a life with their different basic health needs adequately met. Understood in such a way, women's special reproductive health needs, as well as children's needs for special care and nurture, are already addressed by the human right to a standard of living adequate for every person's health. It is thus redundant to introduce an additional right just for women. Equal but need-based treatments of women and men are not discriminatory so long as there is a genuine difference that explains and justifies the treatments.

B. Women's Rights within the Family

As suggested by the definition of human rights as the "common standard of achievement" in social justice, women's rights as human rights are closely tied to social and political justice or injustice. Yet one implicitly shared assumption of current mainstream theories of justice is that the head of the family is a benevolent male acting rationally to promote the interest of all family members, all of whose interests are harmonious, with female members performing unpaid domestic and reproductive work. These theories tacitly assume that family relationships belong to a "private" realm where natural instinct or sentiments govern.

Some communitarian philosophers and legal scholars such as Michael Sandel and Roberto Unger have argued that justice as a virtue appropriate for public institutions does not govern private spheres of life in the family. Family life embodies and is governed by higher virtues such as love and generosity. What goes on within the family is, according to this view, in some sense beyond the reach of justice or judgments of fairness. This view implicitly repudiates any efforts to raise rights concerns within the family, even though domestic violence, household discrimination and unequal distribution, and the imposition of unfair burdens of child care and housework on women, continue to occur within the family in many societies.

Feminist critics of this view respond that the idea of a love beyond justice has frequently served the interests of men as lovers, husbands, and fathers. True love

and generosity, as Martha Nussbaum argues, should at least be just; and the virtues of love and generosity are not incompatible with concern about injustice. Thus the family should not be exempt from the demand of justice, even when it is at its best pursuing love and other high virtues.

In the liberatl contractarian model, justice has to do with the "public" sphere, where male heads of families deal with each other according to mutually accepted rational contracts. This model has eluded the reality of injustice within the family. John Rawls' theory of justice as fairness stipulates that the representative persons who deliberate and choose principles of justice are "heads of households" who act on behalf of the interests of their households as a whole.

The need to open up the "private" sphere for scrutiny comes from the sheltering of injustice within this sphere: unpaid domestic labor, social and cultural devaluation of "women's work," women's economic dependency, and unequal power between men and women within marriage. Because of these injustices, the family is an important site of the struggle for women's rights. And women's rights should therefore go beyond protections against discrimination in the "public" domain.

The relevance of justice and women's rights to the family can also be defended by highlighting the value of bringing up children in a just and fair domestic setting. As Susan M. Okin argues, taking up Rawls's brief discussion, the family is the school of justice for the larger society. It is where children are exposed early on to fairness and unfairness in family relationships, conditions that will have an impact on their moral sentiments and their sense of justice. Family in this sense is part of the basic structure of society and public life. It should not be exempt from the scrutiny of justice and human rights. To be true to their principles, liberal (male) theorists of justice should give as much attention to the lives of women and children within the family as they have given to the "public" relationships between male heads of households.

Some feminists, however, have not been satisfied with these internal criticisms of liberalism. They are far from complete, they point out. Because of its view of the family as the center of "private" life and its commitment to a public–private distinction, liberalism is unable to allow interference in the family to advance women's autonomy and equal opportunity. Any outside interference in the family—for example, state intervention to protect women from abuse, or official recognition of domestic labor—might be argued by some liberals as a violation of privacy. The liberal right to privacy is incompatible with applying the liberal principle of autonomy and equal opportunity to family life; it hinders reform in those areas of life where women suffer domestic oppression (Jaggar A. 1983. *Feminist Politics and Human Nature.* Totowa, NJ: Rowman and Allanfeld). This assessment, as we shall see, may underestimate the role of constructive feminist criticisms within liberalism.

III. FEMINIST CRITIQUES

A. A Critique of the Rights-Based Approach

The language of rights has come under attack for its inappropriateness in dealing with women's oppression. Some feminists, especially those in the Marxist–socialist tradition, stress that the significance of the rights of women as a group should not be overstated. Instead, attention should be paid to the differences among women and between the sources of their oppression. Women's liberation cannot be achieved, these critics argue, until women are protected against all forms of discrimination—class, racial, ethnic, sexual, and political. Some of these critics are willing to abandon the language of "women's rights" altogether. They contend that the liberal "rights" idea is too individualistic. Liberalism assumes a kind of "political solipsism" (Jaggar), centering itself on the claims of the individual and slighting the values attached to collective social entities such as families, groups, and classes—values that the feminist movement tries to preserve. What liberalism forgets is that individuals could not exist outside a social context and are not self-sufficient.

This charge may not be completely fair to the liberal rights tradition. Mainstream liberal philosophers who support the language of rights, such as Mill, Kant, and Rawls, have indeed emphasized the separateness of human beings, and have argued that persons must not be treated as mere means. But these philosophers have also defended an other-regarding ethic that urges concern and respect for, and the provision of assistance to, individuals in distress. For them, individuals cannot pursue their own happiness independently of community and human connectedness. These liberal thinkers may not have been consistent in applying their principles to the situation of women—a flaw that justifies internal criticisms. But the tradition of liberal individual rights has proven to be a powerful resource in women's struggle for equality, because women have too often been treated as means to others' ends and their individual well-being has rarely counted in political and economic decisions. The dignity and worth of individual women

has far too rarely been recognized and respected in societies in general.

B. A Critique of the Gender-Neutral Approach

Some feminists have rejected the view of women's rights as a call for equal rights between men and women. They question the notion of equality understood as "gender neutrality." This notion is said to be insensitive to women's disadvantage in competing by gender-neutral rules for positions or roles in traditionally male-dominated institutions. For example, women in our society continue to be expected to care for children, and most jobs are designed for men with wives at home who can assume this responsibility. Women have been excluded from the workplace and public positions for so long that these activities or institutions have developed in a way suited only to their exclusively male participants. Thus, these critics demand, as we consider whether gender should be taken into account, we need to know to what extent gender bias has historically been built into important roles and rewarding positions. A gender-neutral approach would disadvantage women in their efforts to gain access to the social goods that come with these roles and positions, because these roles and positions are not gender-neutral—they have been systematically defined by men and in favor of men.

The notion of gender equality as an objective of women's rights thus needs to be reconceptualized. Gender inequality is not so much a problem of arbitrary discrimination against women as a problem of society's systematic domination over women, critics point out. A struggle for gender equality in gender-biased institutions would be for women to emulate or imitate men. Its goal would be limited to the achievement of an absolute sameness in the treatment of men and women. An equal opportunity to enter male-defined games is not enough and tends only to perpetuate the gendered status quo.

According to this approach, women's rights should aim at abolishing not only discrimination but also men's domination, and at recognizing women's differences and special needs—such as maternal needs that are not met by socially constructed institutions suitable for men only. An understanding of women's rights is thus a call for resistance to systematic social domination over women because they are female. It is a critique of socially organized power and societal subordination of women. Conceivably, this critique would not be relevant if men had not been systematically dominant in society.

The argument that the struggle for women's rights

should be construed as an equal rights movement presupposes an ideal condition in which male dominance is abolished and women are no longer required to compete for positions, credentials, and benefits adapted to the needs of men. Under conditions of prevalent female subordination in the real world, however, women's rights as human rights should rather be understood as a demand for the abolition of such structural social dominance and a demand for empowering women to achieve autonomy. The difference between women's rights as aiming for "equality" and for "autonomy" is put by Elizabeth Gross in this way: "Autonomy implies the right to see oneself in whatever terms one chooses. . . . Equality, on the other hand, implies a measurement according to a given standard. . . . Struggle for equality . . . impl[ies] an acceptance of given standards and a conformity to their expectations and requirements. Struggle for autonomy, on the other hand, impl[ies] the rights to reject such standards and create new ones." (Gross E. 1986. What Is Feminist Theory? In C. Pateman & E. Gross (Eds.), *Feminist Challenges, Social and Political Theory*, p. 193. Boston: Northeastern University Press). This approach reflects a rationale for a political strategy by the contemporary women's rights movement rather than merely normative principles of equal rights and justice.

IV. THE GLOBAL APPEAL

With abuses and violence against women continuing today in many parts of the world, women's rights have appealed to feminists and women in many countries. International feminist activists and theorists have argued in support of and utilized the language of women's rights as human rights. They have insisted that international human rights already affirmed by the UN be consistently and systematically applied to women. They have also demanded that major human rights documents specify the right of women to be free from gender-specific abuses and violence against women.

Of course, "women's rights" sometimes has different emphases and implications depending on the social context. The trend is certainly to push women's issues on the regional, international, intergovernmental, and multinational levels. The international discourse on women's rights has placed new issues in the forefront of public discussion—issues concerning the interrelationship of women's well-being and economic development, global peace and security, international economic inequality and sustainable development. These issues are reflected in the Convention on the Elimination of All Forms of Discrimination Against Women (1981), which urges state parties take actions "to modify the social and cultural patterns of conduct of men and women, with a view to achieving the elimination of prejudices and customary and all other practices which are based on the idea of the inferiority or the superiority of either of the sexes or on stereotyped roles for men and women" (Article 5). At recent UN world conferences, governmental and nongovernmental organizations have continued the debates about the international norm of women's rights protection. The United Nations World Conference on Human Rights in Vienna in 1993 called attention to the persistence of widespread violence against women. Nongovernmental organizations raised concerns about reproductive health and freedom at the World Population Conference in Cairo in 1994. Disputes and productive discussions over the nature, scope and specification of women's rights gained unprecedented publicity in and around the Fourth World Conference on Women in Beijing in 1995.

V. CONCLUSIONS

Women's rights are conceived as those human rights, or norms and standards of achievements in social justice, the violations of which are committed against women because they are female. The protection of these rights is essential if women are to pursue their well-being.

Given the dominance of men in formulating universal standards of human rights, and given that women's human rights have been violated in many ways that men's rarely are, these standards should be restated with a sensitivity to gender so as to respond to women's particular experiences of injustice.

The classical liberal concept of the "rights of man" provides an inadequate basis for a human rights standard embracing women's rights. The classical notion of "man" in the discourse of natural rights, and thus its conception of the human being, excluded women. This "man" was modeled on the bourgeois men who owned property and were free to make decisions in public affairs. But women did not own property and were often owned by men as property, with no social reality of their own.

The international human rights regime created after World War II had little bearing on women. This was true in part because of the influence of the classical tradition of "natural rights," and in part because the modern human rights norms, created in response to state-sponsored atrocity, neglected male dominance.

Women's dependent status and subjugation at the time when international human rights were first defined and proclaimed prevented them from having a voice in the formulation of those rights.

Feminists have debated whether universal human rights encompass all women's rights, or whether there are any rights held exclusively by women. Some have argued that there is a need to create a special set of women's rights, such as reproductive rights. Opponents worry that introducing women's special rights may trivialize these rights and make them redundant. They argue that women's reproductive rights have already been included in the human right to a standard of living adequate for the health and well-being of every person. Their argument assumes an understanding of "health" based on individual human needs.

Mainstream theories of justice have assumed that the heads of families are benevolent, rational males and that family relationships belong to a "private" realm where natural instinct or sentiments govern. State protections of women's rights or the rights of female children would, according to these theories, constitute an intrusion into individual privacy. Internal critiques of liberalism point to the failure of liberal theories of justice to apply principles of equal opportunity and autonomy wherever inequality and oppression exist. Outside critics have urged abandoning the individual right to privacy and the liberal "rights" language altogether. This radical approach may risk jettisoning a powerful intellectual legacy favorable to women's struggle for justice, discounting the possibility of constructive feminist criticism within liberalism.

Finally, some feminists have criticized taking gender neutrality as the appropriate goal for the struggle for women's rights. Given our gender-structured social reality, women's rights should, in their view, aspire to the elimination of male dominance, not to the achievement of gender-neutral "equality" in a male-dominated world.

Continued debates over the nature, foundation, and scope of women's rights have engaged feminists and activists worldwide, who have joined forces to press for international recognition of women's rights in the international feminist discourses and at various UN conferences in recent decades.

Also See the Following Articles

AUTONOMY • FEMINIST ETHICS • FEMINIST JURISPRUDENCE • GENDER ROLES • HUMAN NATURE, VIEWS OF • LIBERALISM • SEX EQUALITY

Bibliography

Cook, R. (1994). *Human rights of women: National and international perspectives.* Philadelphia: University of Pennsylvania Press.

Hart, H. L. A. (1955). Are there any natural rights? *Philosophical Review* 64, 175–191.

Kymlicka, W. (1990). Feminism. In *Contemporary political philosophy: An introduction.* Oxford: Clarendon Press.

Macpherson, C. B. (1962). *The political theory of possessive individualism: Hobbes to Locke.* Oxford: Oxford University Press.

Nussbaum, M. (1992, October 8). Justice for Women. *New York Review of Books.*

Nussbaum, M. (1996). The Feminist Critique of Liberalism. Forthcoming in M. Forey & J. Gardner (eds.), *Women's Voices, Women's Lives: The Amnesty Lectures 1996.* London: Oxford University Press.

Okin, S. M. (1989). *Justice, gender, and the family.* New York: Basic Books.

Peters, J. & Wolper, A. (1995). *Women's rights/human rights: International feminist perspectives.* New York: Routledge.

Rawls, J. (1971). *A theory of justice.* Cambridge, MA: Harvard University Press.

Sandel, M. (1982). *Liberalism and the limits of justice.* Cambridge: Cambridge University Press.

Unger, R. (1987). *Politics: A work in constructive social theory.* Cambridge: Cambridge University Press.

WORKPLACE ETHICS: ISSUES FOR HUMAN SERVICE PROFESSIONALS

Paul A. Kurzman
Hunter College, City University of New York

I. Conceptual Framework
II. Practice Issues
III. The Common Good
IV. Conclusions

GLOSSARY

common good The intended outcome of the application of the theory of distributive justice emphasizing principles of equity and of fairness.

distributive justice The fair allocation of scarce resources in the context of pervasive inequality in order to achieve a common good.

employee assistance program (EAP) A confidential counseling program voluntarily sponsored by labor and management as a human service entitlement for their workers.

equity A principle which focuses not necessarily on the equal distribution of resources, but rather on a fair and a just distribution.

human service professionals Practitioners in the human services who, by dint of their function and training, provide social and health services to patients or clients.

relative confidentiality An acknowledgment that the principle of confidentiality is not absolute, in common law or in statute.

HUMAN SERVICE PROFESSIONALS often are asked to address questions of knowledge and skill as components of expertise. However, seldom are they requested to concentrate on the value dimension of practice, perhaps because such an endeavor is somewhat more difficult and is open to challenge by friend and foe. Yet the task must be accepted. In the postindustrial era, no time could be more appropriate than the present to undertake such a challenge. The ethical dilemmas in an increasingly conservative Western world compel us to focus not just on the formation of new knowledge and the further deployment of skill, but also on how both are shaped and conditioned by the dominant values of contemporary society. Our clients, our professions, ourselves, and the organizations for which we work all are affected by the pushes and pulls of a conservative capitalistic system, whose rewards and constraints may conflict, both in theory and in practice, with the values and goals of the human services.

This entry addresses and defines the ethical issues that pertain to the practice of the human services at the workplace. Simply put, this concept refers to professional practice under the auspices of organized labor or employing organizations (generally companies or trade unions), or in formal contractual relationship with such institutions. What is important is that employment in this area involves practice not merely in a host environment (such as a school or hospital) but practice in a nontraditional, nonhuman service host setting. The somewhat alien nature of the host environment poses new ethical issues for the helping professions. These issues pertain more to value dilemmas than to the adequacy of knowledge and skills.

I. CONCEPTUAL FRAMEWORK

In their 1976 study of the ethics of medical care, Albert Jonsen and Andre Hellegers noted that ethics is more than a body of prescriptions and prohibitions; it is a comprehensive theory of human morality. In this respect, they noted that an adequate study of ethics would consist of the exploration of at least three principal theories: the theory of virtue, the theory of duty, and the theory of the common good. At the risk of oversimplification, the theory of virtue refers to such traits as honesty, probity, and respect for others. Duty analyzes the relationship between intentions and consequences, and between motivations and circumstances. A theory of duties therefore suggests prescriptions and prohibitions, and contractual permissions and obligations. Human service professionals have a duty to refrain from prohibited interventions, on the one hand, and on the other an obligation to engage in certain areas of prescribed activity which represent the social responsibility of their profession.

Jonsen and Hellegers suggest that the most complex and vexing dimension of professional ethics involves the theory of the common good. This theory is concerned with two essential questions: the definitional (that is, what the common good or goods might be) and the distributive (that is, how benefits and resources are allocated when the need or demand is greater than the supply). Simply put, the theory of the common good addresses the issue of social justice.

In his classic development of a comprehensive theory of justice, John Rawls reminds us that institutions, not just individuals, are the vehicles for the distribution of the benefits and burdens of social life, and a theory of social justice therefore does not merely address the personal characteristics of individuals, but the virtue of social institutions as well. The fair and equitable assignment of rights and duties and the parallel distribution of benefits and burdens place the issue of social justice in an appropriately social and organizational context. While the individual practitioner is still bound by the concepts of virtue and duty, the theory of the common good, as a dimension of professional ethics, inevitably points toward the systemic dimension and the institutional context in which one may practice.

There are, of course, many approaches toward the institutionally bound concept of the common good.

Egalitarian philosophers, for example, would say that everyone should have equal access to resources—that the limited pool should be evenly divided. Proponents of a meritocracy view (such as veterans' organizations) would recommend that resources be distributed primarily to the most deserving—those who have merited the rewards. Advocates of a triage concept (frequently deployed in medical and rehabilitation settings) suggest that benefits should accrue first to those who can make best use of them. The utilitarians, such as John Stuart Mill, advocate the distribution of scarce resources so that they do the greatest good for the greatest number.

Rawls, however, proposes a theory of distributive justice. To achieve the common good, he suggests that the greatest resources should go to the most disadvantaged in the social system. In a compelling discourse, he offers a theory of equity rather than a theory of equality. In a society that places certain portions of the population at a competitive disadvantage for no reason or fault of their own, such a theory underscores the need to ensure fair and equitable distribution of scarce resources in the context of pervasive social inequality. If one accepts Rawls' proposition, one must look at human services practice in the workplace not only through the lens of its professional practitioners, but in the context of the institutional arrangements in which they are employed. The virtue of the organization becomes as significant as the virtue of the individual, since a person inevitably is an agent of the institution by which she or he is formally engaged.

Do labor and industrial organizations generally promote the common good in our society? In a relative framework, do they do so as frequently as primary and host human service organizations such as hospitals, schools, mental health clinics, and child welfare agencies. If one is not a free agent (except perhaps to some extent in private practice), then is there a significant difference between the constraints and supports for practice in a human service setting and those in settings where the primary goals are *different* from the human service mission? To what extent can one meet the ethical obligation to pursue the common good, not merely to evidence duty and virtue, under the auspices of a company or trade union?

II. PRACTICE ISSUES

A. Overview

One may appropriately pose the question of the fundamental conflict between a profession's commitment to people's well-being and industry's dedication to productivity and profit. The firm thread binding the diverse settings in which human service workers traditionally practice is a humanistic philosophy that underlines the inherent dignity and worth of people. The common thread in a capitalistic economic system which binds industry, however, is the priority of production and profits. Individuals in industry—the workers—have an instrumental value in the context of a larger goal: they are a means toward an end or central purpose. How does one, philosophically and pragmatically, reconcile this apparent dichotomy between commitments when placed on the payroll of an industrial organization? Above all, how will one address the systemic issues inherent in the mandate to be a humanistic agent of social change as well as an instrument for human service?

Lest these issues appear directed only toward the management side of the industrial equation, we are reminded of parallel dilemmas as an agent of organized labor. Leo Perlis, long-term director of the Department of Community Services of the United States AFL-CIO, advocated for the concept of a "human contract" to build services at the workplace to meet the needs of labor force participants.

However, Perlis felt that the sole responsibility of the human services worker is to help clients solve their personal and family problems. He felt that it would be pure fantasy to suggest that there is a role for such workers in setting policy or proposing organizational change. However, ignoring labor or industrial injustice—such as hazardous working conditions, worker dehumanization, and violations of affirmative action—may negate human service professionals' contributions through a failure to fulfill their social change obligation. Even if such workers are dutiful, virtuous, knowledgeable, and skillful in meeting their ethical commitments to social service, would the ethical imperative to promote the common good in part be sacrificed by failing to be agents of change, by being careful not to "bite the hand that feeds them"?

The U.S. First National Conference on Practice in Labor and Industrial Settings noted additional examples of this dilemma posed by its participants. If an employing organization is about to lay off 500 workers, is it the human service function to defuse the situation? If the employer institutes a speed-up on the production line, does the practitioner treat workers who respond negatively to the stress as failures or as victims? If an approaching union election brings a flurry of directives to set aside program goals to assist in promoting the survival needs of the leadership

(the practitioner's employers), how does one appropriately and ethically respond? And finally, as an employee assistance counselor in the corporation's personnel department, what does one do when a senior member of management requests confidential data (regarding an employee you are seeing) as a condition of future cooperation with and organizational support for your program?

There are few simple answers, yet one must be willing to wrestle with these issues. One should recognize, too, that these dilemmas are not uncommon in most traditional agencies in which human service providers work. Such are the strains between organizational role and professional preference, and knowledge of administrative theory reminds us that these conflicts pervade all organizational life. The issue is in part one of extent and degree, not of mere presence or absence of organizational demands.

B. Whose Agent Are We?

From an ethical perspective, the fundamental question here is, "Whose agent are we?" At times, organizational goals—in this situation, productivity and profit maximization—are not entirely congruent with client needs. Yet neither can exist without the other: workers need jobs and organizations need a workforce. The professional challenge is to recognize the symbiotic relationship and discover the equilibrium that optimizes the common interest of both parties.

External demands of the organization sometimes conflict with clients' best interests. When this occurs, following the theory of virtue, the dilemma must be shared openly so that clients may select the route or set of options which they feel are in their best interests. Such situations are not frequent, but when they occur the human service worker must advocate for the maximum options for clients and preserve their right to self-determination. Since the human services mandate comes in part from the organizational subsystem (for example, personnel, medical, human resources) which is the home base for the service, professional practitioners often are protected within the organization in view of their special human service role within the larger institution.

Finally, an added point of reference is their profession. Its value system, formalized through a commitment to a code of ethics, not only gives human service professionals a common external frame of reference, but constitutes clout within the organization in support of ethical positions. Ultimately, as professionals, human service workers must retain the right to leave, however personally difficult this might be, if they frequently are unable to reconcile client and organizational interest.

What becomes most important, from the outset, is the nature of the contract with the employer in labor and industrial settings. If occupational practitioners suggest that they may bring greater productivity or profit to the company, for example, people (employees) quickly will become a means, not an end. If one defines the function, however, as helping the corporation fulfill its social obligations and its commitment to improving the quality of life for its workforce, the practitioner's role is more likely to become an ethical one.

Human service expertise is not in promoting profit maximization but in helping organizations meet the needs of individuals, groups, and communities in the world of work—and, reciprocally, in recognizing unions' and managements' obligation and vested interest in doing so. They are specialists in the human dimension of the workplace and in increasing labor and industrial sponsors' commitment of both human and fiscal resources in this arena. Such clarity around role and function is essential to ensure that people will be a central focus of attention; that a goal will be to enhance the quality of life for work force participants; and that the commitment will be both to the provision of social services and to the creation of humanistic forms of organizational change.

C. Confidentiality

The issue of confidentiality frequently is brought forward as a principal ethical dilemma in the area of the theory of virtues and duties. The concept often is bound by absolute and inviolable notions akin to a military or diplomatic classification of "top secret." What exactly do occupational human service practitioners promise when they pledge confidentiality? Do they actually promise that what the client tells them will be known to no one but themself? If they do, it is unethical because it is not true.

What the client (i.e., worker) tells them will be known to the typist who transcribes the record, to the supervisor who reviews it, and to the practitioners who follow; all one can promise is that what is shared will be used responsibly and will be scrupulously guarded against misuse. Confidentiality is relative, not absolute. Even privileged communication statutes for the professions and government privacy acts note explicit areas of exception to confidentiality and privilege.

D. Examples

For example, in hospital-based employee assistance programs, practitioners sometimes find themselves working with a medical staff person who is actively abusing drugs (e.g., heroin or cocaine) while on duty. Despite the fact that an emergency room nurse may be a voluntary client (e.g., self-referral), the employee assistance program's (EAP) policy of confidentiality must be weighed against the legitimate needs of the (hospital) organization and the patients it serves.

Leon Warshaw, a prominent occupational physician opines that by design, EAP counselors serve as the agents of the employee even against the immediate interests of the organization, and that staff therefore should reveal no more than the employee wishes to have divulged. However, Sheila Akabas, an expert in the EAP field, suggests that the issues here, when conceptualized in the ethical context of duties and virtues, are somewhat more complex than Warshaw might portray.

There is a tension, she correctly notes, between an individual's right to privacy and society's right to know—so that it can protect its members and ensure the accountability of its institutions. The concept of relative confidentiality shall govern in this situation, because the hospital (as the EAP's sponsoring institution) has rights and obligations too. One of a medical center's central commitments is to responsible patient care, and therefore knowledge it may have (even if voluntarily provided) that a staff nurse is seriously impaired and hence may place an emergency room patient's life at risk must take precedence over a general policy of client confidentiality.

Furthermore, in a corporate setting, especially in the "smokestack industries" of the Midwest, large-scale layoffs, retrenchment, and plant closings are increasingly common. For the professional human service practitioner, who may be a staff member of the company's Employee Assistance Program, Community Affairs Division, or Human Resources Department, such an event may trigger an understandable crisis regarding appropriate professional role and function. Feeling helpless in reversing an economically based corporate decision, and even guilty to be on board when others are facing employment termination, such staff may wonder whether—by omission or commission—they themselves are agents of the event.

The principal ethical mandate in this situation is for such staff to assume a commitment both to service delivery *and* to advocacy on behalf of those displaced. In so doing, they must follow the admonition not to "blame the victim," but rather to serve and empower workers through individual and family counseling, aid in the formation of self-help and mutual support groups, and advocate collectively for and with these workers as a constituency in the community. While few EAP staff are in positions to prevent massive layoffs, corporate relocation, or capital flight, they generally can and should mobilize community services, promote self-help groups, advocate for entitlements, and initiate referrals to other employers in the community who are hiring.

III. THE COMMON GOOD

The core ethical question returns to the theory of the common good. The issue is whether practice in the workplace offers opportunities for promoting distributive justice.

If developing new service delivery systems to meet the needs of currently underserviced portions of the population can be considered a proactive ethical mandate, then an example is in order. Working-class people often are caught in the well-known bind of not having access to scarce publicly funded mental health services and unable to afford to pay for such services in the marketplace. Therefore, their mental health needs often go unmet. In addition, they frequently have no idea of where to go for such help since the public and private agencies usually are not located where they live or work, and are not open during the hours when they would be free. Employee assistance programs—free, onsite, available as needed, and responsive to working-class style and needs—frequently become an oasis in a desert, without which little professional intervention on behalf of this population ever would occur.

Opportunities for creative program development that promote the principle of distributive justice also are available in labor and industrial organizations. For this reason, it is essential that occupational practitioners in these settings not see themselves merely as providers of service, but also as agents of program innovation. By documenting unmet needs in a direct practice unit, human service workers in one U.S. trade union became the pivotal force in demonstrating workers' need for legal services. They translated this evidence into a preliminary program design and advocated for its approval by senior union officials. As a result, an innovative legal services program was implemented to fill a critical gap in services and now

is available in that setting to more than 100,000 union members and their families.

Other management-based occupational service professionals, through their training and consultation function with line managers around the social and mental health needs of the workforce, identified the necessity for job accommodation options, such as job sharing and fleximtime. As a result, opportunities opened up for whole new sectors of the community, such as older workers, working mothers, and the mentally and physically disabled. Such innovations promote a more equitable distribution of opportunity to portions of the population who would not otherwise be able to compete for some of the tangible rewards of workforce participation.

In the world of work, moreover, a focus on advocacy is essential. Within the framework of their employing agency's function, and in the context of their ethical obligations to society, occupational human service providers must impact on the institutional and social conditions which disadvantage portions of the work population. As the expert from within, for example, they can identify what Harold Lewis termed "the cause in function, the ends in means," and move with force and authenticity toward new and more equitable provisions. Not only is this mandate important to mitigate against the counterpull of organizational cooptation, the opportunity to achieve these goals is uncommonly good because the occupational human service practitioner is working under the auspices of exceptionally influential institutions in the society.

IV. CONCLUSIONS

Although there are risks for the professions through engagement in the labor and industrial arena, there is the promise of rewards as well—such as promoting the common good. However, the need exists for a consciousness raising for prospective occupational practitioners around substantive ethical imperatives. Human service professionals are venturing, perhaps to a somewhat greater degree in this than in other host settings, into alien terrain. Clearly, ethical quandries are involved, but there are unique opportunities as well. The dangers are posed primarily by the potential for compromise of our virtues, and to a lesser extent by the possibility of inattention to our duties. The new 1996 National Association of Social Workers' code of ethics, for example, with its explicit delineation of ethical responsibilities to clients, colleagues, and employers—as well as to society and one's profession—should be helpful in this regard.

The ethical challenge we feel is ultimately joined around the theory of the common good as a critical component of an adequate ethics. We speak here of the fair or equitable distribution of the benefits and burdens of social life in an institutional rather than individual context. Although the issues are never simple, the public and private institutions for which human service professionals traditionally work are seldom well positioned within the economic system to impact on issues of distributive justice. To the extent that one can maintain a sense of duty and virtue, and at the same time recommit to the social change component of professional practice, new opportunities may be envisioned.

The enormous potential of the occupational arena must be weighed against the risks and the unknown. If labor and industrial organizations, for example, even modestly can be moved to accomodate to new populations and to new communal needs, the contribution of the human service professions in this regard will be warranted. In this context, it is the judgment of most participants and observers that the risk is worth taking. In the end, what will be essential and critical will be a willingness to bind oneself to a normative discipline of morality that underscores the notions of advocacy and equity. One's conceptual clarity around these ethical issues, professional readiness to discuss them, and personal commitment to honor them in practice will serve as the best protection—for one's clients, oneself, and the human service professions.

Acknowledgment

This entry is adapted in part from the author's "Ethical Issues in Industrial Social Work Practice" (1983. *Social Casework* (pp. 105–111). February) and "Ethical Base for Social Work in the Workplace" (1988. In *Social Work in the Workplace* (pp. 17–27). New York: Springer).

Also See the Following Articles

DISTRIBUTIVE JUSTICE, THEORIES OF • MEDICAL CODES AND OATHS • PROFESSIONAL ETHICS • NURSES' ETHICS • WHISTLE-BLOWING

Bibliography

Abramson, M. (1996). Reflections on knowing oneself ethically. *Families in Society,* 77(4), 195–202.
Anderson, G. R., & Glesnes-Anderson, V. A. (Eds.) (1987). *Health care ethics: A guide for decision makers.* Rockville, MD: Aspen.
Clark, B., & Abeles, N. (1994). Ethical issues and dilemmas in the mental health organization. *Administration and Policy in Mental Health,* 22(1), 7–17.
Corey, G., et al. (1993). *Issues and ethics in the helping professions* (4th ed.). Belmont, CA: Brooks-Cole.
Finkle, A. L. (1995). Ethics at work: Mediator in the middle. *Employee Assistance Quarterly,* 11(1), 55–79.
Kurzman, P. A. (1991). Managing risk in the workplace. In R. L. Edwards and J. A. Yankey, Eds., *Skills for effective human services management.* Silver Spring, MD: NASW Press.
National Association of Social Workers (1996). *Code of ethics.* Washington, DC: NASW Press.
Reamer, F. G. (1993). *Ethical dilemmas in social service* (2nd ed.). New York: Columbia Univ. Press.
Stein, R. H. (1990). *Ethical issues in counseling.* Buffalo, NY: Prometheus.

WORLD ETHICS

Nigel Dower
University of Aberdeen

GLOSSARY

communitarianism Any ethical theory which sees moral values and identities as arising out of established community and shared traditions.

cosmopolitanism Any ethical theory which asserts that all human beings belong to one "society of humankind" within which there are some universal values and global responsibilities.

internationalism The claim within international relations theory that states are the dominant actors in world affairs and that there is a "morality of states."

realism A term used in international relations theory to indicate either the stronger thesis that ethical norms do not apply to international relations or the weaker thesis that they only apply to the extent that they are part of the reality of international discourse and practice.

WORLD ETHICS is the philosophical exploration of ethical issues in world affairs. A world ethic is a set of values which are universal and responsibilities which are global in scope. Three broad approaches in international relations theory are identified: realism, internationalism, and cosmopolitanism (see glossary). Cosmopolitanism is also contrasted to communitarianism, a theory of the social origin of morality which reduces or, linked to relativism, denies the significance of universal values and global obligations.

I. WHAT IS WORLD ETHICS?

World Ethics is the philosophical inquiry into the ethical issues which arise both in respect to the relations between nation-states themselves and in respect to relations between all human beings in what may be called the society of humankind. The area of inquiry may also be referred to as "global ethics" or "international ethics" (though international can be used either in a broad sense, as just implied, or in a narrower sense to refer specifically to relations between states).

World ethics, as an area of philosophical inquiry, covers three interrelated areas of thought: (i) theoretical considerations about the nature of morality (in order to answer such questions as what an ethic must be like to account for our intuitions that the rich in the North ought to help the poor in the South or, to take the position of a skeptical realist, what it is about relationships between states which make moral relations between them impossible); (ii) normative considerations, including the justification of the norms adopted, concerning the content of the values and principles adopted; (iii) applications of these norms, including, as in other areas of applied ethics, the comparison of different normative approaches to specific areas of concern at a global level such as private and government aid, care for the environment, protection of human rights, refugees, secession, nuclear weapons, terrorism, and respecting cultural diversity.

A. World Ethics and World Ethic Distinguished

It is useful to distinguish between world "ethics" and a world "ethic." Although the distinction may be a little stipulative so far as actual usage is concerned, it does pick out a substantive difference between world ethics as an area of philosophical inquiry and a world ethic (or a "global/international ethic") which can refer to the particular set of norms accepted by an individual or a group (such as the body of international diplomats). (See Box 1.)

At the extreme, it is possible for a skeptic (whose position is expanded upon later) to engage in world ethics as an area of inquiry of academic interest, but actually argue that there is no such thing as a world ethic—the idea of a world ethic is either unintelligible or does not have application. What is it that some reject but most will assert? A world or global ethic will have two components: (i) a claim that there are some values (elements of the good, duties, rights, etc., where different thinkers will stress different elements) which are universal, that is, they apply to all human beings anywhere in the world; and (ii) a claim that there are certain responsibilities (duties, obligations) which are global in scope, that is, actors anywhere, either individ-

uals or institutional actors such as states, have moral responsibilities, in principle, toward human beings anywhere in the world—duties not to harm, to respect rights and autonomy, to help, etc. Lying behind these two claims, which cover great differences of form and content, are generally also theoretical normative positions justifying them.

Such a normative ethic may or may not be accepted after or through self-conscious ethical reflection, and indeed for many moral agents, past and present, it may not have been identified as such as a global or world ethic. Nevertheless both the content of these ethics and the nature of their value systems shows that they have in effect a global ethic—for instance, a Kantian in recognizing that all humans qua rational agents are objects of moral respect, or a Christian who believes in the brotherhood of humankind, is essentially accepting a world or global ethic, though he or she may never have considered these values in these terms. Likewise someone who believes in democratic values or in the values of the liberal free market, sees these as appropriate for other countries in the world, and sees it as right to promote their spread elsewhere is in effect assuming a set of universal values and global responsibilities, which together constitute a global ethic, even if it is not presented as such.

B. Is World Ethics New?

Is world ethics a relatively new arrival onto the intellectual stage? The answer is yes and no. In one sense intellectual speculation on both how ethically humans are related to one another as a whole and how human associations such as nation-states relate to one another goes right back to the origins of philosophical thought, as have particular world ethics as systems of value.

The Stoics from the 4th century B.C. conceived of the idea of "cosmopolis" ("the city of the cosmos") and thus the idea of being citizens of the cosmos, with identities and loyalties going beyond the particular and contingent political communities men happen to live in. In the late medieval and early modern period, thinkers such as Aquinas, Grotius, and Vittoria assumed that human beings constituted a *civitas maxima*—the greatest city/community—living under the same natural law (discoverable by reason), so that living in particular political groupings, though necessary for order because of human frailties, was ultimately justified in term of the ends of human life given by natural law.

Since the commencement of the modern nation-state system, conventionally dated with the Peace of Westphalia (1648), there have been two developments—on

---

Box 1

World ethics is the philosophical exploration of ethical issues arising from:

1. The relations between nation-states
2. The relations between all human beings in the world

A *world ethic* is a set of:

1. Values which are universal
2. Responsibilities which are global in scope

the one hand a complex body of thought on the working of the international system, concerning the development of international law and international norms (which many see as moral norms), and on the other hand, alongside this, the more theoretical speculation about international relations from thinkers such as Hobbes, Locke, Kant, Rousseau, Hegel, Clausewitz, and so on.

In a second sense, world ethics as an area of academic inquiry is in many ways a relatively new development. To some extent this is due to various processes occurring in the world, particularly since the second world war, which have increasingly disturbed the assumptions lying behind the two dominant (and mutually competing) approaches within international relations theory itself—the one being a skeptical realism (which assumes that international relations is an arena of power and national interests in which moral considerations have little or no place), and the other being the internationalist tradition already noted (which assumes that there is a fairly conservative "morality of states" dominated by the value of respecting sovereignty).

The development of nuclear weapons raised ethical challenges since it seemed to violate traditional "just war" principles. The Nuremberg Trials (for crimes against humanity during the second world war) together with the Declaration of Human Rights (1948) focused critically on the rights and duties of individual human beings. The gap between the wealth of developed countries and the poverty of developing countries together with the existence of absolute poverty on a large scale raised ethical challenges about the nature of the world economic system.

The phenomenon of globalization, as the process has now come to be called in the last few years because of its increasing momentum, has, through greater interdependence, communication, and ease of transportation, created a "global village" in which what happens in distant lands has a greater immediacy for practical action than it did before. Secessionist movements and resorts to terrorist violence have shaken conventional assumptions about how order is to be maintained in the world (or even whether order is always the overriding value). Last but not least, the threats to the environment have a strongly global dimension, requiring responses conceived of in global terms, and challenging assumptions about development and the good life.

All these challenges, and many others, would certainly have made world ethics as an area of active engagement with ethical issues something that was intellectually required, even if the latter had not occurred. But gradually it has emerged through the efforts of

thinkers from various disciplines, from within international relations itself, from philosophy and theology, etc. While some thinkers have focused on the ethical standing of international relations itself, both on the general theory and on various areas of key interest such as nuclear weapons, terrorism, international trade, and international cooperation to protect the environment, others have focused on what responsible individuals ought to be doing as "world/global citizens" (though the phrase may not always be used) in response to global poverty, environmental damage, threats to peace, violations of human rights, and so on. Overall though, all these concerns are part of one domain of ethical enquiry. In any case, for most thinkers what is to be said about states and what is to be said about individuals stems from the same intellectual foundations.

II. THE ETHICS OF INTERNATIONAL RELATIONS: INITIAL DISTINCTIONS

If we look first at different approaches to ethics and international relations we will quickly see how it is possible to adopt many different approaches. Nardin and Mapel identified as many as 12 approaches, while Donelan discussed six basic approaches. For the purpose of this exposition, I shall limit the exploration to two ways of contrasting approaches to ethics and international relations.

The first way of setting out contrasts is found in many textbooks and is partly associated with the way writers such as Martin Wight and Hedley Bull (H. Bull, 1977. *The anarchical society*, London: Macmillan), in the so-called English School of Realists, put it (see Box 2). (This is "realism" in a broader sense of being

---

Box 2

Three Approaches to Ethics in International Relations

(a) Ethical norms do not apply to international relations (*skeptical realism*)

(b) Ethical norms do apply to international relations:

    (b1) they are the norms of the "morality of states" (*internationalism*)

    (b2) They are norms which apply to all human beings in the society of humankind (*cosmopolitanism*)

grounded in the realities of international practice, as contrasted with (skeptical) realism.) A division is drawn between three positions, each identified by a confusingly large number of labels:

(a) (Skeptical) realism, Hobbesianism, (international) skepticism, anarchism, nihilism
(b) Internationalism, Grotianism, rationalism, "morality of states," legalist paradigm
(c) Cosmopolitanism, universalism, Kantianism, idealism, revolutionism

A number of different contrasts are in fact wrapped up in these labels. Nevertheless the following discussion does represent some of the key points often intended to be conveyed by the contrasts. I identify two elements to each general position, one descriptive, i.e., factual, and the other normative/theoretical.

A. Skeptical Realism

1. Descriptive

Relations between states are determined by power and calculation of national interest. International relations is largely a competitive game. War, in Hobbes' sense of not merely actual fighting but a period of time in which there is insecurity because of the known disposition to resort to violence, is a dominant feature of international relations. Such norms as develop in international relations are not really moral norms, but maxims of prudence, abandoned whenever prudence dictates. If moral language is used in foreign policy pronouncements, this is hypocritical and merely another way of promoting foreign policy. (Machiavelli has been seen as an inspiration for the realist approach. Prominent among more recent writers was Hans Morgenthau.)

2. Normative/Theoretical

Because of various arguments, ethical norms do not apply to international relations. It is not merely the weaker claim above that, though applicable, they are systematically ignored. International relations is basically an ethical vacuum. Such arguments include the famous argument drawn from Hobbes that because of a lack of a "common power," i.e., world government, to enforce and hence render sufficiently predictable the observance of norms, norms do not apply and states are in "a state of nature" vis-à-vis each other, exercising their "right of nature" to do whatever is conducive to their survival without moral restraint.

Other arguments include the claims that governments, acting in a trustee role, always have an overarching duty to their citizens or subjects to promote the national interest; that the very idea of sovereignty entails that there is no higher authority to which a state is answerable; that because of the facts adduced by the cultural relativist about the diversity of values in the world, there is no universal moral standard which can be used to construct a normative framework; and finally, through considerations concerning the conditions necessary for a moral community/society to exist (such as conventions, shared traditions, and sense of community), that all these conditions apply to societies within nation-state boundaries but do not apply, or only apply in a marginal way, to relations between states or between individuals on a global scale.

B. Internationalism

1. Descriptive

Although relations between states are to a large extent dominated by considerations of national interest, there is an ethical framework within which state actors do generally operate—namely, that set of norms which has come to be established in the "society of states." The key features of this ethic are duties of nonaggression and noninterference toward other sovereign states; the observance of the principles of the just war (*ius ad bellum* and *ius in bello*); the keeping of agreements and treaties (i.e., *pacta sunt servanda*); and a code for the treatment of ambassadors. States and the international system which they constitute are the dominant reality of the world. Relations between states are a mixture of cooperation and conflict, as is shown in extensive economic interdependence.

2. Normative/Theoretical

The norms that actually operate in international relations are in fact to be accepted; that is, from the point of view of the theorist, these norms are the right norms for the relations of states. Various kinds of justification are given for the defense of the status quo. On the one hand, there are various considerations which are somewhat detached from considerations about ordinary human well-being, such as appeals to convention or established practice (i.e., it is their being established and serving the goal of preserving the international order of states itself which is important), as Bull himself suggests, or appeals are made to the inherent rights of states, qua artificial persons, in a way somewhat analogous to the appeal to inherent rights of natural persons.

On the other hand, the norms of the international order may be defended on the grounds that, from the perspective of the defender of it, they are what is needed to promote human values in the best possible way. Thus, it may be said, as Grotius (1583–1645), the key intellectual founder of the international system, recognized, that peace and order among states is the best way of promoting human values (so that going against peace on the grounds of justice or human rights is generally dangerous); that the right to live in one's own political community is so important that the international order is sacrosanct (M. Walzer, 1977. *Just and unjust wars*. New York: Basic Books); or, as a Hegelian variant of this developed by Mervyn Frost, that one's very identity is constituted by free citizenship of a political community, itself acknowledged as a free member of a community of states.

C. Cosmopolitanism

1. Descriptive

Despite the dominance of the international order, i.e., the division of peoples into separately controlled areas of the world, there is already, even if in undeveloped form, a community of all human beings in the world. There are many ways in which human cooperation is of benefit, and generally perceived to be of benefit, to all human beings. Various values are already widely shared, as evidenced in the core values of each society, in international agreements like the Universal Declaration of Human Rights of 1948 (which can be seen as having moral force as well as legal status), in the shared values in religious groups (which cross national boundaries), and more recently but very significantly in international NGOs (nongovernmental organizations). Obligations to help those in need (e.g., international responses to disasters) and to play one's part to combat common threats, e.g., to the environment, are widely accepted. Many do have some sense of their being "world citizens" (as well as citizens of their own states).

2. Normative/Theoretical

What, however, is generally the case about the cosmopolitan position is not an appeal to what has as a matter of fact already been accepted. It may well be recognized that global community is not well established (especially if a sense of it in most people is required). What is important for the cosmopolitan is a theory about what ought to be the case, not what is the case (where what is the case includes what ethical norms are as a matter of fact accepted). On this theory, we are global citizens and have duties—to give aid, change our ways vis-à-vis the environment, work for peace, or show tolerance toward other cultures (if these are the things one's cosmopolitan theory requires)—whether most of us accept this now or not. National boundaries do not, on this approach, have any ultimate moral significance.

There are two consequences of cosmopolitan thinking which are usually stressed. First, that the relations between states have to be assessed, and assessed critically, in the light of the overall theory. What states do, what rules they follow, and what institutions they set up are to be judged by the theory: do they express the values which the theory asserts as well as other policies, rules, or institutions would do? If not, there is an argument for change—including possibly change in the very nature of the international system itself toward, for instance, a world federal system or world government (see articles in S. Luper-Foy, Ed., 1988. *Problems of international justice*. London: Westview).

Second, individual human beings need to take seriously their identity as global citizens; there is a layer of obligation in them which may well require of them actions which go beyond, and even in some cases, be in conflict with, what is required of them as citizens of their own political communities. There is therefore, either explicitly or implicitly, a challenge to the idea of absolute loyalty to one's own state. While most cosmopolitans are not revolutionaries in the sense of advocating disruptive or violent social change (though some have been, including some Marxists), they are revolutionary in this more modest sense.

There are at least two sets of polarities in terms of what cosmopolitans will actually advocate as practical priorities, partly determined by the basic norms which the theories support, and partly determined by the theorist's reading of the world, e.g., how much potential there is for real change without damaging or endangering what is also valuable and already achieved. Thus opposing human rights violations may be desirable in terms of the theory but be ill advised in situations where other rights are thereby endangered. There is one continuum in which at one pole there are theories which assert a very specific conception of the "right moral order" which needs to be accepted by the rest of the world (and advanced by various forms of imposition, proselytising, and even crusades), and at the other pole an emphasis on recognizing and even celebrating cultural diversity, but still within a framework of some broadly identified universal core values and responsibilities of mutual support—as illustrated by Hans Kung's approach emphasizing dialogue among religions for world peace (1990. *Global responsibility—In search of a new world ethic*. London: SCM Press).

There is another continuum in which at one end there are theories which require radical positive action to improve the world (to pursue global social justice by positive intervention, etc.), and at the other end theories which stress the value of nonintervention and autonomy. There is no space to pursue these important contrasts here. What needs to be identified here are the various intellectual sources for the cosmopolitan approach.

III. VARIETIES OF COSMOPOLITAN THEORIES

A. Kantianism

As noted earlier, the label "Kantian" is often used as a way of describing this general approach. The general ethical conception of the 18th century German philosopher Immanuel Kant, already noted at the beginning, was one of a global ethical order or a "kingdom of ends." His essay on cosmopolitan world history was one of the key essays to bring the idea back into modern discourse, and it is certainly true that, for his time, his proposals for "Perpetual Peace" (the title of a short but important work on international relations theory) were revolutionary in the sense that the rules he proposed for peace went well beyond anything accepted in his day. On the other hand his theory is hardly revolutionary in the sense of advocating change to the international order as such; he firmly believed in the "society of states" idea himself, and he restricted cosmopolitan duty to the duty of "hospitality" to foreigners.

Later Kantians, such as Onora O'Neill, have been less cautious and have shown how the essential vision that Kant had of human beings respecting one another's rational autonomy, both in individual actions and in the arrangements of institutions, can translate into quite radical changes, at least under the conditions of the modern world. (See O. O'Neill, 1986. *The faces of hunger*. London: Allen & Unwin.)

B. Natural Law

The idea that there is a law concerning what is to be pursued and shunned inherent in our nature as human beings, and discoverable by the use of our natural reason, has been a very powerful theory ever since the middle ages (and indeed before, having its origins in the Stoic thought of Cicero), and provided a very clear basis for a universal morality and the idea of a community of all humankind. It also has modern adherents such as John Finnis and provides one basis, among others, for the advocacy of human rights doctrines.

C. Human Rights

The idea that all human beings have certain rights qua human beings, and not qua members of this or that community, is certainly a very influential modern theory of a cosmopolitan kind. Its "global scope" character is brought out by the claim generally made by human rights theories, following Henry Shue, that the correlative duties (to avoid depriving, to protect from standard threats of deprivation, and to aid those deprived) are duties which, in principle, extend to all other human beings; that is, basic rights (e.g., to subsistence, security, and liberty) are the minimum claims we can all make on the rest of humanity.

D. Utilitarianism

One of the most attractive features of utilitarianism is its global reach. If actions (rules, institutions, etc.) are to be judged by their effects on human well-being, it is the well-being of all human beings, and indeed in Bentham's view all sentient beings, who might be affected by actions which needs to enter the moral calculus. Bentham himself was very interested in this dimension and his great advocacy of international law was premised on his view that its strengthening would lead to greater human felicity. More recently, Gerald Elfstrom has developed a utilitarian form of international ethic.

E. Contract Theory

Several recent writers, including Beitz and Thomas Pogge, have used the contractarian method, adapting Rawls' approach in *A Theory of Justice*, to argue that if we regard the whole world (as the facts require us to do) as one society, then Rawls' "original position" method should apply, and the principles of social justice should apply to the world as a whole. This is an example of how a global ethic could be constructed (rather than simply discovered as an objective truth).

F. Religious Theories

It is worth noting here that many theories emanating from religious belief will also assume a cosmopolitan dimension. But there will be a wide range of such theories, advocating very different normative positions, even within each major religious tradition. On the one hand there is the deeply pessimistic position of Reinhold Niebuhr who saw state action as necessarily immoral by the private standards of love, or the defense of economic liberty among right wing evangelical Christians in the USA, and on the other hand there is the commitment to major social change, in liberation theology or commitment to social justice. Religious convictions may lead to challenges to state authority, one example being pacifist conscientious objection, but there are many others.

G. Environmental Theories

Finally, in this necessarily restricted survey of cosmopolitan theories I need to note that the advocacy of environmental ethics is either implicitly or explicitly cosmopolitan in character. Many environmental problems are global in scope and require for their solution cooperation between many countries and citizens acting in appropriate ways. While it is conceivable that a country (or its citizens) could advocate action by other countries to achieve an agreed upon goal only from the motive that that country would benefit from its share of the improved global change, it is unlikely.

Environmental ethics comes in two forms: human-centered and nature-centered. Briefly, an ethical theory based on long-term human interests is at heart one that takes seriously the consequences (usually unintended) of human activity, and therefore the effects on others, irrespective of whether they live here or elsewhere, now or in the future. It will either be a theory such as Kantianism, utilitarianism, or human rights theories, or be one very like them in terms of its commitment to human well-being generally.

If, on the other hand, one adopts a biocentric perspective according to which either nonhuman living things or whole ecosystems, or both, have a value, one is likely again to accept an ethical theory which puts emphasis upon the effects of activity on any being or thing affected by it (and not to accept a moral theory which tries to limit the domain of responsibility to membership of one's own society or whatever, as communitarian thinking, which is discussed later, does).

IV. ASSESSMENT OF THE THREE APPROACHES

The three approaches—realist, internationalist, and cosmopolitan—have each been presented as having two

parts, a descriptive claim and a normative/theoretical claim. Though both halves may well be put forward by a thinker about international relations, they do not have to go together. It may well be the case that one thinker is more interested in the descriptive claim and another thinker interested in the normative/theoretical claim. This point may help to throw light on the following features of the "debate" about ethics and international relations.

A. Alternative Descriptive Claims

Insofar as thinkers in the three camps are presenting alternative descriptive claims about the presence of or efficacy of moral norms in international relations, there is a sense in which, while one position could be completely right and the other two completely wrong, the likelihood is that they are all right to some degree. Indeed that is precisely the position adopted by one writer advocating this kind of analysis, namely, Hedley Bull. It is probably the case that a very large number of actions of international actors (statesmen, diplomats, etc.) are in fact governed by self-interest (even though they may say they are not, and even though our own theory may judge that they ought not to have been); that to a considerable extent the norms of international conduct are followed by such actors (when one might have wished more radical principles to be followed); and that to some extent common values and acceptance of humanitarian responsibility are in place.

B. Alternative Normative/ Theoretical Claims

However, what is more interesting theoretically is the relationship between the three normative/theoretical claims, for these claims are not such that each might partly be right. They are presented as claims which mutually exclude each other. If there are no ethical norms in international relations, then both the internationalist and the cosmopolitan are wrong in claiming that there are. If the internationalist is right that there are norms constituting a morality of states, which is either self-justifying or is clearly the way to promote human values in an ordered world, then the realist is wrong, and so is the cosmopolitan who thinks there is a valid moral theory which is both the ultimate source of validation for a morality of states and the basis for a critique of what states do, where what states do fails to promote human values as well as they might. If the cosmopolitan is right, then both realism and internationalism are inadequate ethical theories (though they may describe the realities of practice and the acceptance of norms quite well).

C. Mixed Claims and Failure to Engage

On the other hand there can be, as is evidenced by the experience of teaching international relations students and philosophy students together, a kind of "missing each other in the dark," where one thinker is presenting what is basically a descriptive thesis, but the other is presenting her thesis as a normative theory. Thus, a realist or internationalist may only be asserting something that the cosmopolitan is willing (albeit with regret) to concede—namely, that as a matter of fact foreign policy is largely determined by interest or a rather limited morality of states—whereas the cosmopolitan is asserting moral claims about how we ought to be ordering our global affairs, the truth or validity of which is not in the least bit affected by what the realist or internationalist asserts by way of descriptive observation.

D. Assessment as Utopian

If, however, the realist or internationalist dismissed the cosmopolitan claim by saying it is idealist or utopian, i.e., not really applicable to the real world, this would show that it is not a matter of missing each other. For by saying it is utopian, the thinker is saying that the values which international actors really ought to follow are different, so he is not just reporting a descriptive claim about what is done or accepted but endorsing it—i.e., giving normative endorsement to it. And this is what a cosmopolitan is challenging. What he says ought to be done is meant to apply here and now.

As a cosmopolitan writer, Beitz says a cosmopolitan theory (such as his own theory of global social justice, already outlined) has to distinguish between what ideal theory might require and what is practically possible in the real world. A cosmopolitan thinker who did not take into account the reality constraints would indeed be utopian. But it remains important that cosmopolitan thought is likely to be progressive in just this sense, that it will put moral pressure on governments, corporate bodies (such as multinational companies), and individuals to do more to advance the values specified in the theory than they would do in the absence of such a framework being accepted.

E. World Ethic as Theory and World Ethic as Social Reality: Importance of Both

In this sense it is a truism, an important if neglected one, that a cosmopolitan ethic, like any other ethical code, is more likely to be realized the more people accept it. Therefore the development of a public ethical culture which embodies the values in question is clearly crucial to the more effective realization of the values involved. For instance, if one's theory says that the rich ought to be generous toward reducing extreme poverty, then the more people who believe this, the more individuals will be motivated ethically to do, the more such behavior will be strengthened by the perception of like behavior, and the more governments are likely to reflect such electoral preferences in aid programs. So while a cosmopolitan may actually be more interested in the normative/theoretical part of his claim, it is clearly important that the descriptive claim becomes more fully representative of the global social reality.

V. A SECOND WAY OF MAKING A CONTRAST: THE COSMOPOLITAN– COMMUNITARIAN DIVISION

Several writers in recent years, such as Chris Brown and Janna Thompson, have set out the terms of the ethical debate in a somewhat different way. Here the contrast is between two styles of thought, one cosmopolitan and the other communitarian. The cosmopolitan position is essentially the same as that already indicated; what is significant is what it is contrasted with, namely, a way of thinking about how values arise in or from established community. If the nature and scope of ethical values and norms depend upon certain contingent facts about the community in which one lives, then clearly whatever ethical norms apply to one's relations outside that community will depend upon other contingent facts—how much or how little in the way of social bonds and relationships one may have to others, to what extent there is a parallel community of states with it own traditions, and so on. If one's identity is shaped by the particularities of the society one lives in rather than by any universal features associated with humanness (which may be denied or seen as less important), then this identity and the loyalties that come from it are of central importance, in a way that being a human being or a citizen of the world is not.

It should be noted that while communitarianism has in recent years become a distinctive social philosophy, associated with writers such as Sandel, Walzer, and MacIntyre, the contrast here to cosmopolitanism is a broader band of approaches which stress for one reason or another the idea that there is within organized societies, usually seen as falling within nation-state boundaries, a layer of obligation, social identity, and moral relationships which is both centrally important and at the heart of the basic theory, and in comparison to which obligations and identities associated with the rest of humanity are secondary or nonexistent. These approaches then include various theories in the idealist tradition, Hegelian thinking (as in Frost), convention theories (such as Hume's theory of social obligations), and some versions of contractarianism.

A. Communitarian Conceptions of Morality

The contrast here, then, is one drawn primarily from social/political philosophy. It concerns the fundamental question of the nature of morality. Whereas cosmopolitan thinking tends to see ethical relations as based on certain general facts about human nature and to see the scope of obligations as extending in principle as far as the capacity for effective action extends, communitarian thinking stresses the idea that ethical relations are embedded in social practices and traditions; that conceptions of well-being and identity are not given in the abstract but are grounded in concrete cultural particularities of time and place; and that the relations which a person has with the community as a whole or to the "nation" or the "state" (often seen as the same in the internationalist tradition, though they are in fact distinct, as witnessed in the rationale for much secessionist movement in recent years) are of central significance.

Conversely when one looks at the position of government, the idea that a government has a special responsibility to foster the well-being of the community it has charge of is central, whether this is understood in contractarian terms or in terms of any other political theory which stresses the special "trustee" role which a government has vis-à-vis its nationals.

B. A Stronger Thesis

Communitarianism can come in a stronger form, with links to relativism, postmodernism, and international skepticism—for if its story about the basis of morality in established community is right, and it is also accepted that no such social bonds exist between societies, then indeed it is a real possibility that values in different communities are just radically different, that there is no universal vantage point of reason claimed by the Enlightenment from which to construct or discern universal values, or that the structure of international relations does not permit the existence of moral norms within it. In this case the communitarian approach, coupled with these further background analyses, is not merely in tension with cosmopolitanism but directly in opposition to it.

C. A Weaker Thesis

Communitarianism theories, though, are primarily theories about the nature of society and how moral norms arise from it. They are not as such theories about international relations, or more generally global relations between individuals, though they may have powerful consequences for the latter. At the very least they give some credence to the conviction which most people have that their primary responsibilities and loyalties (beyond immediate family and special relations based on friendship and promise) are to their own society or nation-state, rather than to the world as a whole, and that correspondingly governments have powerful and often overriding obligations to promote the national interest.

In this moderate form, it is quite consistent with acknowledging some universal values and global obligations, though the latter may not be very pressing. These values and duties might be recognized either by combining the theory with a form of moderate cosmopolitanism (which stresses as one of its universal values the value of community and loyalty to particular communities) or by accepting that some community already exists at the global level, albeit in a less developed form.

Again, the theory allows for the possibility of the existence of a community of nations-states as well, with its own set of norms established over time and sanctioned by tradition, i.e., essentially the internationalist tradition. (So governments are in effect pulled in two directions, having to weigh obligations owed to citizens against obligations owed to other states.) Thus cosmopolitanism and communitarianism need not be in mutually exclusive opposition, but in tension with each other, each picking out different themes in a complex moral picture.

In this connection one of the interesting and important debates which has been raised has been over the practical importance of developing identities as world citizens through "cosmopolitan education." How far can such identities and loyalties be developed in harmony with a legitimate sense of national loyalty and pride, and how far are they in tension? Martha Nussbaum, a prominent cosmopolitan in the Aristotelian tradition, started a lively and ongoing debate on this issue in a lead article, "Patriotism and Cosmopolitanism" in the *Boston Review* (1994).

VI. CONCLUSION

In this entry I have mapped out the main approaches which can be adopted over the question of whether there are moral relations between states and between individuals in the world as a whole, and if so, what are the main types of normative positions adopted and what are the kinds of justification given? The field of inquiry which I have called world ethics or global ethics would not have come into focus, of course, but for the need to think adequately in ethical terms over a range of more specific issues to do with nuclear weapons, terrorism, refugees, foreign aid, sustainable development, human rights, and so on, which have come onto the public agenda. Many of these, and other topics which are actually explorations of world ethics issues (whether or not highlighted as such), are of course covered in other entries in this encyclopedia. What is provided here is a framework for the more penetrating exploration of those issues.

Bibliography

Beitz, C. R. (1979). *Political theory and international relations.* Princeton: Princeton Univ. Press.

Frost, M. (1996). *Ethics in international relations: A constitutive theory.* Cambridge: Cambridge Univ. Press.

Graham, G. (1996). *Ethics and international relations.* Oxford: Blackwell.

Nardin, T., & Mapel, D. (1992). *Traditions of international ethics.* Cambridge: Cambridge Univ. Press.

Shue, H. (1996). *Basic rights: Subsistence, affluence and US foreign policy* (2nd ed.). Princeton: Princeton Univ. Press.

Wright, M. (Ed.) (1996). *Morality and international relations—concepts and issues.* Aldershot: Avebury.

ZOOS AND ZOOLOGICAL PARKS

Stephen St. C. Bostock
Glasgow Zoo and University of Glasgow

GLOSSARY

animals Humans are animals, but for convenience, "animals" in this article normally means "non-human animals," and usually mammals or other vertebrates.

ARKS Animal Records Keeping System; computer software package used by zoos participating in ISIS.

conspecific A member of the same species.

domestic/domesticated animal A member of the 16 or so mammal species selectively bred for millennia, or (more questionably) a member of any other species regularly kept and bred.

ISIS International Species Information System; a scheme (founded in the USA in 1975) for a central computerized database of animal records, enabling zoo animals (of any particular species) to be managed as single populations in which much genetic diversity (as in a wild population) is retained.

WZCS World Zoo Conservation Strategy, established in 1993.

wild animal One living independently of humans and whose ancestors (normally) have always done so. Animals in zoos are not fully wild but they are in varying degrees relatively wild; if reintroduced to their wild habitat, they may become fully wild.

zoo Collection of (mainly) wild animals, usually kept at least partly for exhibition. (A popular contraction, common from 1867, of "The Zoological Gardens" of the Zoological Society of London, founded 1826.) Zoos include general collections, bird gardens, aquaria, dolphinaria, butterfly houses, and others.

zoological gardens/zoological park Today, alternative and more formal terms for "zoo," often used of large and scientifically reputable zoos.

ZOOS raise various ethical questions. They may be regarded as cruel or unjust in keeping animals (particularly wild animals) captive. Discussion of this involves not only the question of animals' moral status, but also the meaning and significance of "wild animals" and freedom, and an examination of how far animals can be kept satisfactorily. Zoos' aspirations today toward serving conservation, education, and science provide possible justifications for the existence of zoos, but also raise problems of their own, such as whether saving endangered species justifies culling animals surplus to requirements, or whether it is right, even if possible, to save species for habitats which may not exist.

I. GENERAL ACCOUNT OF ZOOS

Collections of wild animals have been kept almost throughout recorded history and in very different civilizations, such as China and Aztec Mexico. The earliest collections were probably in Egypt. Lions were probably kept first in Sumer about 2000 B.C. It was not unknown for lions to be tame and be walked on leashes like dogs (a report of this is known from the Roman period in Egypt), but they were probably kept usually in pits or barred cages. The great stone sealing the entrance of the lions' den in the Old Testament Book of Daniel sounds remarkably impractical. A famous "Intelligence Park" in ancient China was remembered for its peacefulness, and the Greeks also seem to have enjoyed peacefully the company of exotic animals. In contrast, the Assyrians' lions and other impressive beasts most likely served as symbols of their rulers' domination; Assyrian kings showed their valor by fighting with captive lions. Fighting with animals, or just massacring them, for entertainment, reached its lowest depths in ancient Rome, though even Roman emperors sometimes showed affection to their animals (talking birds, for example).

In medieval and renaissance Europe exotic animals were often kept by kings, even by popes. The Tower of London housed the British royal menagerie for some 6 centuries. The animal accommodation there must have been almost literally prison cells, and no doubt it was similar enough in other royal courts, though there were variations. Monkeys in French palaces, for example, were often "free" to wander, restrained by a ball and chain like a human prisoner. Concern for animals from their human owners was certainly not unknown; a notable example would be Pope Leo X's clear affection for an elephant and sadness at the animal's death. On the other hand animal fights for entertainment were often arranged; James I of England enjoyed lion fights at the Tower. Not all animals had restricted conditions. Deer and other herbivores sometimes had the relative freedom of very large enclosures or "deer-parks." These were hunting parks, yet many outlasted their use for hunting, so the animals clearly had some further appeal. A deer-park at Lowther Castle in England still continues after 7 centuries. A notable Chinese example of a deer-park was Kubla Khan's, described by Marco Polo, and later in Coleridge's poem. A striking example of a zoo in a civilization entirely independent of Europe and Asia is that of Montezuma, the Aztec emperor of Mexico. His collection included large numbers of birds of prey, waterbirds, large cats, and poisonous snakes, as well as deformed humans (kept humanely, it seems).

Ordinary people enjoyed viewing strange beasts too. In Britain, for example, there were traveling menageries in the 18th century, and a famous permanently housed menagerie in the late 18th and early 19th centuries in the Strand, London, called Exeter Change. It must have kept its animals in appallingly cramped conditions. Menageries often claimed to be educational, which in a way, before the film and television age, they clearly were.

The first zoo founded as a scientific institution was "London Zoo," opened to members of the Zoological Society of London and their friends (not the general public) in 1826. It had fine gardens, but there were still plenty of cramped cages, and plenty of critics (for example the writer Leigh Hunt) of the poor conditions. Possibly the first real advances in the technique of keeping and displaying wild animals were made by the German animal trader and trainer Carl Hagenbeck at his famous Stellingen Zoo near Hamburg, founded in 1907. He introduced moated enclosures to replace bars, and elaborate habitat-like settings. He also showed that tropical animals kept in temperate Europe did not require (as previously supposed) to be perpetually in overheated houses but had far better health with outside enclosures provided, an approach introduced (in the light of Hagenbeck's experience) at London Zoo.

In recent years zoos have continued to develop, though often claimed by their critics to have long outlived their usefulness, if any. In America especially major zoos have perfected remarkable naturalistic displays, such as simulations of the tropical rain forest. Far from their past position as consumers of wildlife, reputable zoos have come to see themselves (with some justification) as potential or actual guardians of endangered species. This conservational role is encouraged in America by the American Zoo and Aquarium Association (AZA), and in Britain by the Federation of Zoos. It has become much more of a reality thanks to the starting in Minnesota in 1975 of a scheme called ISIS which is enabling zoos, with the aid of computerized animal records, to manage their animals more and more as total captive populations. However, while the world's reputable zoos now take very few mammals from the wild, this is probably far less the case with, for example, reptiles and amphibians. A recent official zoo statement of their conservational aims—the World Zoo Conservation Strategy—enjoins reputable zoos to take no animals from the wild, except where this is done as a serious conservation measure in consultation with such conservation bodies as the World Conservation Union (IUCN).

Other great advances in recent decades have been in veterinary medicine available for zoos' animals, in the quality of their feeding, and in innumerable improvements in enlightened zoos in the general standard of animal care. But it is also the case that many of the thousands of zoos in the world would probably be found to have advanced very little from past centuries. There is a great range in the standard of animal care between the many poor zoos on the one hand and the reputable and highly responsible zoos on the other. Some countries, such as Britain, have legislation to control zoos, and thus ban the worst ones. But many countries, including the USA, have no such legislation; America has many very poor zoos as well as several of the world's finest.

II. ETHICAL STANDPOINTS FOR ASSESSING ZOOS

How we judge zoos and approach the moral predicaments zoos themselves face depends in some degree on our ethical standpoint and how this relates to animals. There are at least five possible positions.

A. The View That Animals Do Not Matter

The first possible standpoint is the view that animals have either no or else very little moral status. The strongest version of this would be the view that they have no feelings or inner lives, a view proposed by Descartes and held by some scientists, at least as a working hypothesis, until recently. A less extreme version would be that animals, while they do have experiences, have none really comparable to our own. We are marked off by our possession of language as rational beings, unlike all other animals (M. P. T. Leahy, 1991. *Against Liberation*. Routledge, London). Animals, lacking language, have no long-term aims, and their experiences, as they can never formulate them in language, must remain inchoate and insignificant compared to human experience. From this position, there might be aesthetic objections to zoos, or conservational objections, if one thought zoos were damaging natural populations of animals. But concern for the welfare of their individual animals would be misplaced.

B. The View That Animal Welfare Is Important

Much closer to the assumptions of most of us, who probably care considerably about our dogs or cats even

if we ignore the welfare of other animals, is the second possible moral position which recognizes animals as at least having feelings and the ability to suffer, and indeed interests. It is important on this view that animals should not be ill-treated, and in Britain animals' need of consideration is established in law. All domestic and captive vertebrates in Britain arguably have certain legal rights; certainly cruelty to any of them is an offense in law, though this legal protection is not extended to wild (i.e., noncaptive) animals. Clearly keeping animals well depends not only on benevolent intentions toward them, but on understanding their actual needs. These needs are today studied by veterinarians and some ethologists. There is a science of animal welfare (see M. S. Dawkins, 1980. *Animal Suffering: the Science of Animal Welfare*. Chapman & Hall, London), so the view that animals should be treated in such a way as to ensure their welfare may be regarded as having scientific backing. There is a developing body of scientific findings concerning how different species of animals, including wild animals, should be kept (see D. M. Broom and K. G. Johnson, 1993. *Stress and Animal Welfare*. Chapman & Hall, London). This is then a basic moral position from which zoos can be assessed and from which any zoo might be judged to be an unjustifiable institution if there were clear evidence that the animals kept in it suffered from being there. Most past zoos, if they could be assessed by modern scientific standards of animal welfare, would probably fail dismally, due both to lack of knowledge of their animals' requirements and to failure to see their animals as mattering morally.

C. Utilitarianism

A third possible position is utilitarianism; this, unlike a concern for animal welfare, is a full moral theory, offering an analysis of what makes courses of action good or bad: roughly, the extent to which they increase the pleasure or well-being of all those affected by them, which could well include animals affected as well as humans. So utilitarianism provides a philosophical underpinning for our concern for animal welfare. One problem is its need, in assessing the moral worth of any particular course of action, to balance against each other the advantages it would bring to different persons or animals. In theory, the gains for the many thousands of human visitors to a zoo could be regarded as outweighing the losses of the much smaller number of animals kept in the zoo. It is unlikely though that a utilitarian would argue in this way; certainly Peter Singer, for example, an opponent of zoos on utilitarian grounds, does not.

Singer does, however, consider that a course of action bringing great advantage to many people or animals could be justified even if it involved suffering for a few (P. Singer, 1979. *Practical Ethics*, p. 58. Cambridge Univ. Press, Cambridge), so perhaps on utilitarian grounds the saving of a species (and thus the securing of the future happiness of its many members) would justify the suffering of the few species members being saved in a zoo. However, a utilitarian would not argue thus unless there was at least clear evidence that this was the only way the species could be saved, so that the suffering of the animals involved was unavoidable. The mere possibility that zoos' policies would be successful conservationally would not be enough.

D. Animal Rights

A fourth possible moral position is the assertion of animal rights. However, we need to note that animal rights may be opposed in two quite different ways, and also supported in at least two rather different ways.

1. Animals Lack Moral Status

Animal rights may firstly be opposed on the same grounds on which animals may be regarded as being of no moral concern, i.e., a claim that animals do not have experiences, or the claim that their experiences, while real, are so inferior to ours as not to count morally. On this position zoos would pose no problem.

2. Rights Are an Unhelpful Concept

A second position which also opposes the view that animals have rights is quite different. This is the position of someone who recognizes that animals are of moral concern but regards animal rights as an unhelpful concept or inappropriate language. Such a person may be a utilitarian; they may hold that the concept of natural or moral rights (as contrasted with legal rights) is unhelpful even in regard to people; or they may consider that people can be said to have rights but that animals cannot, perhaps because they cannot have any corresponding duties. Somebody who holds views of this kind may be greatly concerned about ill-treatment of animals, and may object to zoos. (See, for example, L. Brown, 1988. *Cruelty to Animals*. Macmillan, London.)

3. "Full Animal Rights"

The first of the two positions which support animal rights is that associated with Tom Regan, who holds that any animal which appears to be a "subject of a life" should be regarded as having inherent value and

as possessing moral rights as absolute as those we normally regard other people as possessing—rights not to be, for example, killed, imprisoned (except by due process of law), or physically hurt. This might perhaps be called the "full animal rights view." On this view zoos appear to be unjustifiable because of their infringement of animals' right to freedom, except perhaps in cases where a zoo is clearly acting as a sanctuary, i.e. providing the best "home" possible for an animal which, because of either injury or some other reason, cannot be released to the wild with any prospect of its surviving. Regan does, however, seem in practice to limit rights possession to "higher mammals," so an "insect zoo" or a reptile collection could presumably be acceptable to him.

4. "Qualified Animal Rights"

The second of the two positions favoring animal rights is one well presented by Mary Anne Warren (M. A. Warren, 1983. In *Environmental Philosophy* (R. Elliot and A. Gare, Eds.), pp. 109–133. Open Univ. Press, Milton Keynes). This view would accept some of the points made by those who would accord animals no moral status at all, such as the facts (as it appears to us) that animals do not have the kind of long-term aims that we often have, and cannot formulate their thoughts or feelings in language. Animals (mammals and other vertebrates at least) are regarded as having rights, but rights less strong than those of people. This might perhaps be called the "qualified animal rights" view. The use of the term "rights" here would be a way of emphasizing that animals' moral claims upon us are a matter of justice—that cruelty to them is reprehensible, not merely something we may dislike. On this view, animals will probably be regarded, as on the previous view, as having rights to life, freedom, and freedom from being hurt. Zoos are challenged on this view, but may be regarded as acceptable if they can show that their animals are being kept in good conditions and for serious reasons. Our relationships with our companion or domestic animals may be acceptable on this view of rights, but seem difficult to justify on the previous view of rights. Their only defense on the "full rights view" could be that, being so altered by our selective breeding, domestic animals cannot now survive on their own, so that a regrettable situation must be accepted. On the "qualified animal rights" view, our relationships with well-treated companion animals, and some other domestic animals (such as well-treated horses), may be regarded as valuable. (On rights, see also S. R. L. Clark, 1977. *The Moral Status of Animals*. Clarendon Press, Oxford.)

E. Environmental Holism

The fifth possible moral position to be noted is that sometimes called environmental holism and often associated with the American conservationist Aldo Leopold (who called it the "land ethic"). According to this view, there is value in all natural things, but in them as a whole rather than individually. A follower of Leopold would not be concerned about killing animals; he might well hunt. But he would regard damaging the land and its constituent ecosystems as morally wrong, and a course of action which sought to maintain natural ecosystems as morally right. Most of us today are conservationists in that we believe that endangered species should be protected. We are not arguing as holists, however, if we justify our concern for endangered species and the environment in terms of their usefulness to mankind. In fact many of us probably would agree that the natural world should not be regarded as valuable only because of its usefulness to humans. If we think the natural world should be regarded as valuable for its own sake, then to that extent we are sharing the position of the environmental holist. Zoos often claim that their final aim is to reintroduce endangered species to the wild; where this is genuinely so, and if they believe this should be their purpose because of the inherent value of the natural world, then they are arguing holistically. So holism could provide a philosophical underpinning of zoos' conservational aims. It seems unreasonable to regard an environmental position on the one hand and those of animal welfare, utilitarianism, or animal rights on the other as exclusive alternatives. It seems more reasonable to recognize ourselves as drawn more than one way here, and having to make difficult compromises (see Warren, 1983).

III. ARE ZOOS WRONG IN PRINCIPLE?

A. Should Wild Animals Be Kept?

Many people regard it as appropriate for domesticated animals to be kept, but feel that it is quite inappropriate or wrong in principle to keep wild animals, as zoos do. Mullan and Marvin note this contrast in human perceptions, but seem to regard the terms "wild" and "domesticated" as merely "cultural" (B. Mullan and G. Marvin, 1987. *Zoo Culture*. Weidenfeld & Nicolson, London). In fact, the terms point to real biological differences.

A wild animal is basically an animal living its natural life in its natural habitat. A fully wild animal would be one wholly uninterfered with by humans. What makes a wild animal less wild is various kinds of human interference, such as being moved about (or "translocated"), kept in an enclosure or cage, tamed, or selectively bred. (This last is of course a treatment which can only be applied to members of a species through the generations, not to an individual animal.)

Thus there are different ways of becoming less wild and there are degrees of wildness. An animal in a zoo will be in various respects and to varying degrees different from a wild conspecific. It will be in some degree used or habituated to humans and to its captive conditions; it may be tame in some degree, may have been bred in captivity, and be one generation or several generations away from the wild. It may be the product of some degree of selective breeding, perhaps unintentionally so. The zoo animal will still be relatively a wild animal, by comparison with a fully domesticated one.

"Domesticated" could be defined as "changed by selective breeding so as to be easy to keep and useful to humans." This definition will exclude taming within a generation. There will be degrees of domestication as of wildness, but "full domestication" (not a very precise term) happens over many generations. Man's unquestionably domesticated animals, such as dogs, sheep, and horses, are considerably more than 2000 years from the wild state.

Such animals as these are clearly suited in some respects to being kept by humans: they have been bred for docility; they are unlikely to be disturbed by being close to humans; they will probably be tame or easily tameable; and they can probably be handled or managed, perhaps given "work" to do, which will help to provide exercise. Obviously this will apply much less to relatively wild animals. But it still will apply, in varying degrees, for the zoo animals may be tame (in some degree), must at least be habituated to human nearness, and may be slightly domesticated.

As it happens, long domesticated animals (pigs, horses, and so on) still show some wild (i.e., natural) behavior; they still are likely to have natural needs, and should therefore have conditions which allow or, better, encourage them to express their natural behavior. (This makes intensive farming conditions particularly oppressive.) In fact, therefore, good conditions for long-domesticated animals are likely to be at least fairly suitable also for relatively wild animals.

Zoos may seem in a cleft stick in as much as the most humane approach to the keeping of their animals might be to tame and to domesticate them (if possible; e.g., selectively breed them for docility), but at the same time zoos are duty bound by their conservational responsibilities to change their animals as little as possible from being wild. i.e., not to tame them and not to domesticate them. Again, it is as if zoos should avoid that situation which seems, when it occurs, to be the most positive aspect of zoos: the coming about of a kind of community or partnership between the animals and their keepers (or other involved people) so that each enjoys the company of the other.

But perhaps zoos need not worry about taming their animals (i.e., as individuals), so far as this is possible, or about letting them become tame, or about a sort of animal–human partnership developing, if it does. This is because it is unlikely that any particular individual animals in a zoo are going to be reintroduced themselves to the wild. When any particular reintroduction program is decided upon, it may well be the young of any individuals actually in the zoo, rather than those individuals themselves, which will be reintroduced. In any case, special training, perhaps a special environment, may well be necessary for the individuals to be-reintroduced. But it will not be required for other individuals not due for reintroduction.

The matter is quite different with selective breeding, for here what is being avoided, so far as possible, is the genetic changes involved in domestication, which will be nonreversible, as it were—certainly not by the special training to be provided for individual animals to be reintroduced.

Perhaps a zoo will still want to restrict any taming process; perhaps it will feel that educational or welfare considerations make desirable even the avoidance of taming. But this should be carefully considered. It looks as if the animal's own interests could best be served by not rigorously trying to avoid taming. Perhaps even the training of certain animals might be desirable for welfare reasons, such as providing therapeutic activity (M. Kiley-Worthington, 1990. *Animals in Circuses and Zoos: Chiron's World*. Little Eco-Farms Publishing, Basildon, UK). This, for the same reasons that applied in the case of taming, would not be objectionable on conservational grounds.

What of the taking of animals from the wild? Ought this not to be regarded as particularly objectionable? Here an important point is that animal collection or capture from the wild is already regarded by reputable zoos as undesirable except in those special circumstances when there are serious conservational reasons for the removal of certain animals from the wild. Clearly, such animals should be captured and transported with the utmost care and expertise; the operation should not be carried out by unskilled locals or commercial collectors. The ideal of not taking animals from the wild except for very serious reasons is far yet from being realized. But that is

what zoos should work toward as quickly as possible. They should distance themselves utterly from the appalling commercial and often illegal trade in wild-caught animals which still continues.

B. Freedom

To put a wild animal, or any animal, in a zoo may seem cruel and unjust because of its loss of freedom, except perhaps where it is obvious that an animal is being rescued for its own sake because there are threats to its habitat or there is great danger from hunting. This would have applied, for example, in the case of the taking of Arabian oryxes from the wild in the 1960s when there was no chance of saving the species except by captive breeding. In this particular case many oryxes have already been returned to their natural habitat. Even a "full animals rights" supporter such as Tom Regan might feel that this was not unwarranted interference in the lives of free individuals.

But what of less exceptional cases? Hediger argued that the deprivation of freedom in a zoo is illusory, because animals are in reality not free in the wild, being so hedged about by territorial restrictions and dangers. His detailed view is worth serious consideration (H. Hediger, 1964. *Wild Animals in Captivity*. Dover, New York). But the contrast of the captive state with the freedom of the wild seems unavoidable. An animal's being fully free can hardly not mean its being able to live its natural life, whatever the drawbacks of that state. The obvious sense of the words "set free" supports this. (See J. Rachels, 1976. In *Animal Rights and Human Obligations* (P. Singer and T. Regan, Eds.), p.209. Prentice-Hall, Englewood Cliffs, NJ.)

So it seems we must be depriving a captive animal of its true freedom, almost by definition. But perhaps this deprivation is not a great wrong, if it is justified by a serious, conservational aim, and there is a concern to do all possible to lessen any suffering or deprivation. A "strong animal rights" supporter will not regard this as a satisfactory justification; for him the right to freedom is absolute. But perhaps his position is too dogmatic. We are pulled by respect for different values, and may feel it is a reasonable compromise to protect the wild even at the cost of an individual animal's freedom, provided that the animal is treated in other respects as well as possible.

It may seem self-contradictory to speak of an animal's losing its freedom and being treated properly. But freedom is never absolute. The wild animal is indeed restricted in various natural ways. "Free" is a complex concept. It can be used of the animal's natural state, but also in measuring its area for locomotion, and for exploring and foraging, and how much it can express its natural behavior. An animal can be given a good deal of freedom in these respects in a zoo, and may not then be seriously deprived.

A zoo animal may be better off in some respects than in the wild, as the "five freedoms" concept reminds us; it is important to be free of starvation, cold, injury, and fear, as well as free to wander and express one's natural behavior. A good zoo should provide a high level of the other four freedoms, and this, plus as much as possible of the fifth freedom—freedom "itself" as it were—could mean that the animal was in a state of well-being.

IV. CAN ANIMALS BE KEPT SATISFACTORILY?

At worst the situation of a captive animal is indeed imprisonment: a deprived state in barren, unchanging surroundings. But conditions were sometimes better even in the past, and certainly can and should be far better now.

Herbivores were often luckier than carnivores (and still are sometimes today) in being in open enclosures, with grazing and the opportunity for social relations with conspecifics. Sometimes both carnivores and herbivores had something of great importance, a friendly relationship with humans. In traveling menageries, some animals (e.g., elephants and camels) had work to do. Some might be trained to perform, in itself probably therapeutic. Training methods have often been cruel, but do not need to be, a point Carl Hagenbeck emphasized.

How do we decide an animal's requirements? We can use various criteria to guide us, which will also be criteria for assessing the suitability of the way different species, and different individual animals, are kept in zoos. One fairly uncontroversial one is physical health, which in certain respects should be far better in captivity than in the wild, with the availability of veterinary care, though it is also arguable that in some ways an animal not living its natural life cannot be enjoying the fullest health. The question here is whether it is possible to provide the captive animal with a full life simulating or substituting for its natural life.

Another criterion, reproduction, must be used with caution. Reproducing is no proof of good conditions. One thinks, for example, of captive lions which were breeding 200 years ago, even in the miserable condi-

tions in the Change menagerie in London. Yet many wild animals are not easy to breed in captivity, such as cheetahs. These do reproduce quite often now in zoos, thanks to modern understanding of how the female comes into breeding condition on the sudden arrival of the male, but their breeding is still far from routine. So success in breeding may be a good indicator of the suitability of conditions.

The occurrence of natural behavior is perhaps the most important criterion for judging and for improving an animal's well-being, and the quality of its conditions. The more of its total behavioral repertoire that we see, the more confidence we can feel in its well-being. By providing actual stimuli as they would occur in the wild, or a simulation of them, it is often possible to induce a natural response. Chimpanzees can be provided with artificial termite mounds from which to extract an award (honey probably, rather than termites) with a stick; bears can be encouraged to climb a tree for honey artificially concealed but at least naturally located by smell; and servals can be stimulated to leap into the air for flying meatballs as they would in the wild for a passing bird. (This last is an example of Markowitz's behavioral engineering approach, which is sometime criticized for its artificiality.)

The application of criteria is not always straightforward. For example, it is usually thought better not to provide stressful stimuli. But is it better? To live a stress-free existence is not natural, and would be boring for us. Humans sometimes choose stressful situations, such as rock-climbing. There is evidence in the wild of herbivores apparently going dangerously near their predators as if they enjoyed the risk. The best arrangement in the zoo might be if the animal had the opportunity to choose a (moderately) stressful situation when it wanted to.

Another important criterion is the degree of occurrence of abnormal behavior. Abnormal behavior is not straightforward to define. We are referring not merely to behavior which does not occur in the wild, but behavior which in addition seems harmful, or can be demonstrated perhaps physiologically or psychologically to be so. It may even be that, in a zoo's restricted conditions, abnormal behavior is actually beneficial to the animal; but clearly no animal should be in circumstances where it can only, perhaps, retain its sanity by disturbing stereotyped behavior, or by manipulating or eating feces, or even mutilating itself, these being documented examples of abnormal behavior only too well known from the restricted conditions of the past, and far from unknown today. (On the whole problem of providing the right conditions, see M. F. Stevenson, 1983. In

Exploration in Animals and Humans (J. Archer and L. Birke, Eds.). Van Nostrand–Reinhold, Wokingham, UK.)

If we decided an animal was not in a state of well-being, and its conditions unimprovable, we should find that animal a better home, release it to the wild, or at the least decide against keeping any more animals of that kind. An example would be where a zoo decides not to keep polar bears, whose welfare in zoos has been sharply criticized in recent years. Some of their stereotyped behavior such as body and head swaying (or "weaving," also well known in stabled horses) or repeated patterns of walking are good examples of abnormal behavior. Here the criteria for captive animal welfare could well lead to a decision not to keep the animal at all.

Suppose, however, it was found that providing polar bears with trees and logs made them more exploratory and generally more active. It could be argued that polar bears should not have trees because this is not naturalistic. But in this case, apparently unnatural behavior (in that we would not see it in the wild) is likely to be perfectly acceptable. (A case in terms of the bears' closeness to brown bears and their only recent moves—recent in evolutionary terms—into Arctic regions could be argued.)

Naturalistic purists insist that anything provided for zoo animals, preferably the whole enclosure, should be as naturalistic as possible. This makes for fine displays, which may be best for the animals also. But we should not reject what the animals like just because it looks untidy or unnaturalistic. Sometimes naturalistic displays are only apparently for the animals' benefit. Fine trees may be fiberglass imitations; not that this matters as long as there is other real vegetation, but sometimes even this is pseudo-provision of real plants which appear to be in the enclosure but actually merely surround it.

Zoos are never going to achieve perfection in the captive environments they provide for all their animals, because every species is in some degree unique and may have its own specialized requirements. But by careful observation of the animals' behavior, both in captivity and still more importantly in the wild, and by ingenuity and creativeness, it should be possible to get nearer and nearer to ideal conditions. Zoo-keeping should be a perpetually continuing attempt to improve conditions. But often it will not be, because some zoos and zoo staff will not be motivated to make such efforts; they may not have the skill, time, or money. Clearly whatever can be done to raise standards should be, perhaps by seeking to fix specific minimum standards (which

should be as high as possible) for particular groups of animals. There are now plenty of ways of improving conditions (or providing enrichment, as it is often called), and they should be routinely put into practice. Where a zoo has problems, solutions could include keeping fewer carnivores, so as to provide really good conditions for those it does have, or moving out large ungulates, if it does not have enough space—perhaps in a city zoo where space is limited—to concentrate on smaller mammals. But perhaps a major problem with zoo-keeping is the likelihood that much of it always will be substandard because of human failings.

V. ZOOS AND CONSERVATION

A. Can Zoos Save Endangered Animals?

Reputable zoos have now a conservational superstructure and a grand strategy to reintroduce endangered species to restored habitats a century or two in the future after humans have come to their senses and limited their own population, a vision of the zoos of the world as lifeboats or arks, backed by computer technology and rapidly advancing genetic knowledge. There is perhaps a clear need for captive breeding as an insurance policy against extinction in the wild when, for example, the last few thousand wild tigers and black rhinoceroses are being poached so that money may be made out of the supply of various parts of their bodies for traditional oriental medicine markets. Reintroduction as such is in fact only one option; there are various possible strategies, but one point of the whole policy is to keep options open. This kind of approach may be the only way of saving many species, especially larger vertebrates, from extinction.

Or it may be an elaborate scheme to give zoos a moral justification, now that an environmentally minded public is expressing doubts about them. Or more reasonably, zoos may be simply mistaken in their worthy ambitions. It is an irony, as John Robinson notes, to attempt to save wild animals—by definition independent of us—by making them our dependents. It is a rank impossibility in the view of Dale Jamieson. (But see Section III.A.) According to Robert Loftin we cannot restore the wild, though it may be worthwhile to reconstruct it with facsimile animals. But captive breeding, in its concentration on single species divorced from their ecosystems, may inculcate wrong attitudes. And despite zoos' elaborate conservational machinery, links with IUCN, and no doubt genuine intentions, captive breeding projects can become an excuse for exhibiting endangered animals instead of protecting the wild population. This has happened with pandas, according to George Schaller. Some zoos may even use underhand methods to procure gorillas, though if this is so, it is a serious breach of the policies of WZCS.

B. Reintroductions

One unquestionably successful reintroduction has been that of the Arabian oryx, where the original threat, motorized shooting of the last remnants of the wild population, has ended and been replaced by excellent support from local people. Yet some other reintroductions, Loftin argues, such as the golden lion tamarin and black-footed ferret projects are less succesful than often claimed. And whether or not they actually work, a welfare problem with reintroductions is the high losses among the animals reintroduced, and the pressures on them of the necessary training in zoos beforehand. Zoos here have to depart from their animal welfare attitude, for high motives, indeed, but for our interests rather than those of the individual animals, who would probably prefer to continue as protected captives.

Reintroductions in the distant future face another all but insoluble problem: what likelihood is there of suitable habitat being available? Could the much hailed ark be on an endless voyage, with lifelong passengers (as noted by Jamieson)?

C. Culling

Space on arks is limited. Breeding in conservationally committed zoos must be managed. Zoos have already many surplus or unusable animals. For example, there are nearly 90 hybrid orangutans in American zoos. There are two subspecies of orang, and zoos now recognize that crossbreeding should be avoided in the interests of successful reintroduction. Much crossbreeding took place before the importance of avoiding it was realized. Sometimes zoos may be at fault for letting this come about, but surplus animals are probably often unavoidable. One solution would be humanely to kill the surplus animals (that is, cull them).

This poses a moral dilemma. Zoo conservationists tend probably to be explicit or implicit environmental holists. There should be no moral problem for them over the killing of surplus animals, the seat of value being in their view not individual animals but their species and ecosystems. Animal rights supporters would also support the conservation of wild species, species being made up of individuals, each of value in themselves. But for rights thinkers, the species' value

is the sum total of the individuals' values, so they cannot justify killing any of those individuals for the sake of the whole. Thus "full animal rights" supporters would oppose any culling of zoo animals, and neither "qualified animal rights" supporters nor welfarists will feel happy with it. The fact that zoo conservationists find an ethical, not just a public relations, problem here suggests that their holism is tempered by or combined with not only a concern for animal welfare, but perhaps some degree of animal rights concern. Should we not respect the value of species and also of individuals? Bryan Norton argues for a moral pluralism—a recognition that we are drawn by different, and partly incompatible, values.

Some zoo conservationists argue strongly for the necessity of culling, if zoos are to carry out their professed conservational aims and responsibilities. Both Michael Brambell and Robert Lacy consider that there is no escape from the unpleasant duty of culling; otherwise (as Lacy argues) at a future date other animals will have to be killed or births of conservationally needed animals prevented—because space in zoos is limited. Money is short too, and, as saving species is a serious moral purpose, to spend precious resources on maintaining surplus individual animals is irresponsible. Norton, recognizing the difficulty for zoos in culling animals even for the highest motives, suggests an interesting solution: that we recognize how individual wild animals can be altruistic and sacrifice themselves for their fellows. We, in culling for the good of the species, may reasonably feel that the individuals concerned, could they know our motive, would accept our decision.

Others reject the culling option, however seemingly unavoidable. Donald Lindburg notes that no one has yet started the culling of the hybrid orangs, that zoo conservationists' own feelings are involved, and that in any case there is no way the public would accept it. Some argue that all that is needed, in public relations terms, is honesty. But Lindburg does not believe the public will accept zoos' conservational and animal welfare intentions if these go hand in hand with extensive culling. He and Linda Lindburg examine other solutions to the surplus problem, such as the setting up of retirement homes.

The many problems with zoos as conservational breeding centers may be solvable, but even if zoos are able to save substantial numbers of larger mammals and other vertebrates, there is no way they could save by captive breeding the mass of species, especially invertebrates, of the rainforests. However, as zoos see it, their conservational role extends further than captive breeding of endangered species; it involves their educational and scientific roles also.

VI. ZOOS AND EDUCATION

A fine display in a zoo can bring home to us what the loss of the rainforest would mean. For example, the sight of a hornbill in a richly planted enclosure in the Wildlife Conservation Park in New York worked like this for me, and probably works like that for many other visitors. Thus the best zoos at least may have considerable effect in motivating people toward conserving the natural world.

Good exhibits can stimulate our appreciation of the beauty and "otherness" of animals, and convey an animal welfare message (an animal should be kept, if at all, in the best conditions you can provide) and information about their animals' natural habitats. But poor exhibits may instead demonstrate human domination over animals, which many people have suggested is the main message conveyed by an animal exhibited in a zoo. And animals' poor conditions may convey a very contrary message to one of animal welfare.

How much children or the public actually learn in zoos is uncertain. There are some research indications that they learn little. Jamieson emphasizes that we rely too much on anecdotes, and that research and data are needed. But at least good exhibits in zoos must be excellent starting points for learning because of the interest of the animals they contain. The public goes by choice, so must get something out of it. That teachers bring schoolchildren in large numbers is some indication that the experience appears valuable to them. Zoo education officers' own work of endeavoring to make visits to zoos educationally worthwhile (there are many different approaches to this), and investigating their effectiveness, are supported by the International Association of Zoo Educators (and their journal), as well as by, for example, the British Association of Zoo Educators.

But then again some animals in zoos are kept appallingly, and even in good enclosures or cages the interests of display can clash with the interests of the animals. Snakes by choice often disappear from view, and small mammals do not normally sit around waiting to be looked at, though there is a possible solution to this: to provide places for the animals to hide, but try to attract them out by suitable enrichment, such as a comfortable spot for basking or something interesting to dig for.

Any possibility of ill-treating animals could be avoided by replacing zoos by virtual reality centers, where computer simulations might even provide the visitor with, for example, the apparent experience of walking through a rainforest and observing different creatures. Such technology must have great potential as an educational tool. But many people like the attraction of real animals, and surely find a special value in the contact (in some degree) with a living creature rather than a technological experience. A "Visitors Report" in a country park near Glasgow found that its children's zoo was far more popular with its visitors than its expensive visitors' center. One pensioner came in every day just to visit a particular donkey. While this is no argument for the keeping of wild or exotic animals, for donkeys or hens will provide this contact, it does show the special appeal of actual animals. If the animals in a zoo are assisting conservational breeding programs, and provided they are in good conditions, then their educational role seems to remain valid as a further justification for them.

It may seem that wildlife films leave no educational need for zoos, now often the poor relation besides dazzling displays of animals in their natural habitats. However, zoos do still have, besides the sizes and smells of real (by contrast with filmed) animals, the fact that whatever is seen is not edited. Behavioral studies are possible in zoos, but not necessarily from films because of editing. Films need action, and cannot, for example, show animals doing nothing for hours and hours, even if some animals, such as lions, do just this sometimes in the wild as in zoos. The best zoo exhibits, such as the rainforest displays at the National Zoo in Washington or the Wildlife Conservation Park, are not of course poor relations of wildlife films. (Occasionally, too, film sequences are shot in zoos, often so skillfully that their not being shot in the wild would never be suspected.)

Good accommodations for animals like big cats are very expensive. One wonders why more zoos do not follow the example of David Hancocks' Sonora-Desert Museum in concentrating on small (and local) animals. Rodents are the most numerous mammals, and often most active, and can be displayed for a fraction of the cost of large mammals. Zoos also tend to ignore 99% of the animal kingdom, the enormously diverse invertebrates, which can be displayed far more cheaply than large mammals, and without most of the ethical questions raised by many vertebrate displays.

VII. ZOOS AND SCIENCE

How far are today's zoos scientific, and how valuable is their research? Major zoos have long assisted many biological sciences—taxonomy, physiology, animal behavior, and originally mainly anatomy—but the focus of zoo science has in recent years become more and more various aspects of conservation. Michael Hutchins of the AZA makes clear in an impressive list of the kinds of science practiced in zoos that though much assists better animal care, much (genetics and veterinary science particularly) is also aimed at conservation in the wild.

Skeptics of conservational captive breeding may also dismiss zoo-based science as unimportant. Some field biologists oppose the need for management in the wild that some zoo conservationists recommend, and Regan would agree. But as Hutchins sees it, not to manage some natural habitats is to court disaster. His case is impressive. He also rebuts Jamieson's dismissal (D. Jamieson, 1985. In *In Defence of Animals* (P. Singer, Ed.), p. 112. Blackwell, Oxford) of zoo science as restricted to studies in behavior or anatomy and pathology.

Jamieson was right, though, that most zoos are not scientific. But there still are many serious, scientific zoos, especially in the United States. And there are degrees of being scientific. Many zoos, including the 56 or so members of the British Federation of Zoos, at least keep systematic records, often on ARKS, and encourage student and professional research projects, often with results useful to their own animal care. Keepers at smaller zoos often make some contribution to science, especially recording details of reproductive behavior and requirements.

Zoo research may be seen as posing new problems in itself—as a liability so far as justifying zoos ethically is concerned. Regan, consistently, approves no interference with animals. However, he would no doubt concede that, if animals are being kept, it does them no further harm to observe them systematically, which is all zoo behavioral studies usually involve. Veterinary research in zoos is also usually noninvasive.

An exception is a case mentioned by Hutchins of research into the development of predatory behavior in zoo-bred lions and cheetahs, involving live domestic goats as prey. Concern for the welfare of these goats, or recognition of their rights, can be no less than that in the case of the zoo's own animals. This particular work would probably be legally unacceptable in Britain. But it is clearly relevant to carnivore reintroduction. Without such knowledge, how can the necessary assistance be given to carnivores that are to be reintroduced to enable them to hunt effectively? There is a direct clash between the interests of the beneficiaries and those of the victims. And zoo researchers might here balance the pain and death of the prey animals not with the interests of the released individuals, but with the benefit to wild populations or species, to the conservation of which the reintroductions are of course dedicated. But can the interests of individuals, who can suffer, be properly overruled in favor of a species, which cannot, though its constituent individuals can? Would great benefits (for populations) be seen as justifying great suffering to even one individual animal? This could be regarded as justifiable by a utilitarian appraisal, and even more so by one in terms of environmental holism. It seems to emphasize the need to recognize at least a "qualified animal rights" position, which would include an absolute right not to be caused severe pain. This would rule out the predator research, so we are faced here as elsewhere with conflict between the values of conservation and those of individual animals' rights.

VIII. CONCLUSIONS

All those concerned about zoos, including responsible zoo directors and staff, are likely to agree that zoos vary greatly in quality, that much of zoos' accommodation for their animals is nothing like good enough, and that much knowledge and expertise is available to improve zoos' provision for their animals. Such may be agreed by welfarists, utilitarians, and "full" as well as "qualified" animal rights supporters. Some of these, such as the full animal rights supporters, will believe that zoos, either in principle or because many of them are in practice so poor, would be better swept away. But they run up against the consideration that zoos may now have the ability to save certain species which are not going to be saved otherwise, and also that zoos, at their best, may provide not only appreciative contact but even community with our fellow creatures, perhaps feeding an awareness from which concern for animals' welfare and conservation may come. So they may grant that it is probably best to support the work of the better zoos, because the need for active conservational measures appears urgent, and zoos can probably help considerably. Some (like Jamieson and Loftin) are unconvinced. Jamieson, though, does not, like Regan, regard the claims zoos make as irrelevant; he challenges their accuracy (about zoos' meeting animals' welfare needs and about their serving education as well as conservation), and demands factual evidence, with the implication that zoos, if they are doing or can do what they claim, can be justified. The need for conservational management, including captive breeding and conservational work by zoos, is in fact made convincingly by Hutchins among others.

Perhaps there is need for compromise, and to recognize a moral pluralism: there are conflicting moral demands on us. We are pulled to some extent different ways by the demands to conserve species and to respect individual animals' rights or interests.

Disagreements about how far zoos can help in conservation are difficult to resolve because they involve the future, in particular predictions about the situation in the world in the next century and beyond. This may be good reason to give responsible zoos the benefit of the doubt: if it is confirmed in the year 2050 that the conservational work of zoos is necessary, it will be already too late if that work was not under way back in 1996.

Those interested are recommended particularly to consult *Ethics on the Ark* (B. G. Norton *et al.,* Eds., 1995. Smithsonian Institution Press, Washington/London), the papers in which cover almost all possible viewpoints, and *Wildlife Conservation, Zoos, and Animal Protection* (A. N. Rowan, Ed., 1995. Tufts Center for Animals and Public Policy, Boston), not least for the long discussions following each paper.

Also See the Following Articles

ANIMAL RIGHTS • SPECIESISM • STEWARDSHIP

Bibliography

Bostock, S. St. C. (1993). "Zoos and Animal Rights: The Ethics of Keeping Animals." Routledge, London/New York.

Brambell, M. (1993). "The Evolution of the Modern Zoo." Federation of Zoos, London.

Cavalieri, P., and Singer, P. (1993). "The Great Ape Project." Fourth Estate, London.

IUDZG/CBSG (IUCN/SSC) (1993). "The World Zoo Conservation Strategy: The Role of the Zoos and Aquaria of the World in Global Conservation." Chicago Zoological Society, Brookfield, IL.

Norton, B. G., Hutchins, M., Stevens, E. F., and Maple, T. L. (Eds.) (1995). "Ethics on the Ark: Zoos, Animal Welfare and Wildlife Conservation." Smithsonian Institution Press, Washington, DC/London.

Rowan, A. N. (Ed.) (1995). "Wildlife Conservation, Zoos and Animal Protection." Tufts Center for Animals and Public Policy, Boston.

Tudge, C. (1992). "Last Animals at the Zoo." Oxford Univ. Press, Oxford.

REVIEWERS

DOUGLAS ADENEY University of Melbourne

GEORGE J. AGICH Cleveland Clinic Foundation

WILLIAM H. AIKEN, JR. Chatham College

TIMO AIRAKSINEN University of Helsinki

NANCY J. ALEXANDER National Institute of Child Health and Human Development, National Institutes of Health

BRENDA ALMOND University of Hull

RON AMUNDSON University of Hawaii at Hilo

ALBERT A. ANDERSON Babson College

DAVID ARDAGH Charles Sturt University

SUSAN ARMSTRONG Humboldt State University

RICHARD ASHCROFT University of Bristol

ROBIN ATTFIELD Cardiff University of Wales

PATRICIA AUFDERHEIDE American University

ROBERT D. BAIRD University of Iowa

ROBERT M. BAIRD Baylor University

STEVE BALDWIN Edith Cowan University

TERENCE BALL University of Minnesota

LINDA BARCLAY Australian National University

HILAIRE BARNETT Queen Mary and Westfield College, University of London

FRANCOISE BAYLIS Dalhousie University

R. W. BEARDSMORE University College of Swansea

JOHN BECKER United States Air Force Academy

LAWRENCE BECKER College of William and Mary

MARC BEKOFF University of Colorado at Boulder

HERMAN BELZ University of Maryland at College Park

JACQUES BERLEUR University of Namur, Belgium

FLOYD BLOOM Scripps Research Institute

ANDREA BONNICKSEN Northern Illinois University

RICHARD BONNIE University of Virginia School of Law

STEPHEN BOSTOCK Glasgow Zoo

KENNETH BOYD University of Edinburgh Royal Infirmary

JOHN BRAITHWAITE Australian National University

DAVID BRAYBROOKE University of Texas at Austin

ANDREW BRENNAN University of Oslo

SUSAN J. BRISON Dartmouth College

DAN W. BROCK Brown University

JEAN PAUL BRODEUR University of Montreal

MICHAEL BURGESS University of British Columbia

ROBB BURLAGE Columbia School of Public Health

GEORGE BUTTERWORTH University of Sussex

TERRY BYNUM Southern Connecticut State University

STEVEN CAHN The City University of New York

JOAN C. CALLAHAN University of Kentucky

J. BAIRD CALLICOTT University of Wisconsin, Stevens Point

R. CAMPBELL Bolton Institute, Bolton, England

NORMAN CANTOR Rutgers University

PAUL CAPETZ United Theological Seminary

ARTHUR L. CAPLAN University of Pennsylvania

JOHN D. CAPUTO Villanova University

TOD CHAMBERS Northwestern University Medical School

ANDREW CHITTY University of Sussex at Brighton

STEPHEN R. L. CLARK University of Liverpool

C. A. J. COADY University of Melbourne

LORRAINE B. CODE York University

DONALD COHEN Yale Child Study Center

583

DANIEL COHN-SHERBOK University of Kent

VANESSA COLIN University of Luneburg

GARY COLWELL Concordia University College of Alberta

GARY COMSTOCK Iowa State University

JAY CONGER University of Southern California

DANIEL CONWAY Pennsylvania State University

WILLIAM N. COONEY Briar Cliff College

CHRISTOPHER COOPE University of Leeds

NEIL COOPER University of Dundee

DAVID COPP University of California, Davis

C. J. COWTON University of Huddersfield

MARTIN COYLE Cardiff University of Wales

BETTE-JANE CRIGGER The Hastings Center

ROGER CRISP St. Anne's College

MANUEL DAVENPORT Texas A & M University

SCOTT A. DAVISON Morehead State University

I. D. DEBEAUFORT Erasmus Universiteit, Rotterdam

JOHN DEIGH Northwestern University

WIM DEKKERS Catholic University of Nijmegen Medical School

DOUGLAS DEN UYL Bellarmine College

RALPH DOLGOFF University of Maryland

JOHN DOMBRINK University of California, Irvine

ANNE DONCHIN London, England

ELLIOT DORFF University of Judaism, Los Angeles

MARY S. DOUCET Bowling Green State University

DAVID JOHN DOUKAS Ann Arbor, Michigan

HEATHER DRAPER University of Birmingham

ANTONY DUFF University of Stirling

PAUL T. DURBIN University of Delaware

DENIS DUTTON University of Canterbury

SUSAN L. EBBS St. John's University, Jamaica, New York

ANDREW EDGAR Cardiff University of Wales

JOSEPH ELLIN Michigan State University

MICHAEL R. EMERSON United States Air Force Academy

RICHARD A. EPSTEIN University of Chicago Law School

CHARLES ERIN University of Manchester

PAUL J. ERMAK Briar Cliff College

PAUL FARBER Oregon State University

WALTER FEINBERG University of Illinois at Champaign

FREDERICK FERRÉ University of Georgia

STANLEY FISH Duke University

ANTONY FLEW Reading, England

GAVIN FLOOD University of Wales

DANIEL H. FRANK University of Kentucky

MARK S. FRANKEL American Association for the Advancement of Science

BENJAMIN FREEDMAN McGill University

R. G. FREY Bowling Green State University

LUCY FRITH University of Liverpool

STEPHEN FULDER Consultancy and Research on Biomedicine, Israel

K. W. M. FULFORD University of Warwick

RICHARD GALVIN Texas Christian University

JORGE GARCIA Rutgers University

ROBERT E. GOODIN Australian National University

LAWRENCE O. GOOTIN Georgetown University Law Center

DENIS GOULET University of Notre Dame

GORDON GRAHAM University of Aberdeen

MARK GRANQUIST St. Olaf College

YRJO HAILA University of Tampere, Finland

J. J. HALDANE University of St. Andrews

EUGENE HARGROVE University of North Texas

CHARLES EDWIN HARRIS, JR. Texas A & M University

ANTHONY HARTLE United States Military Academy

PETER HARVEY University of Sunderland

JOCELYN HATTAB Eitanim Mental Health Center, Jerusalem

STANLEY HAUERWAS Duke University

HETA HAYRY University of Helsinki

MATTI HAYRY University of Helsinki

TIM HAYWARD University of Edinburgh

LARS HERTZBERG Abo Academy

LARRY HICKMAN Southern Illinois University

JOHN HITTINGER United States Air Force Academy

ROBERT L. HOLMES University of Rochester

SARAH W. HOLTMAN University of Minnesota

NILS HOLTUG University of Copenhagen

TONY HOPE University of Oxford

CHARLES HUDLIN United States Air Force Academy

RICHARD HUGMAN Curtin University of Technology

DALE JAMIESON University of Colorado at Boulder

MERC JEANNEROD Institut National de la Santé et de la Recherche Médicale

KATHIE JENNI University of Redlands

KAREN JONES Cornell University

STEPHEN KAPLAN Manhattan College

JOSEPHINE KARAVASIL The International Labour Organization

SHYLI KARIN-FRANK Herzelia, Israel

MICHAEL KEARNEY Our Lady's Hospice, Dublin

NUALA P. KENNY Dalhousie University

MATTHEW KIERAN University of Leeds

DONALD KIRBY LeMoyne College

STEVEN M. KIRSH Indianapolis, Indiana

PATRICIA KITCHER University of California at San Diego

STEPHEN KLAIDMAN Washington, DC

JOHN KLEINIG John Jay College of Criminal Justice

GEORGE KLOSKO University of Virginia

DUDLEY KNOWLES Glasgow University

BEVERLY J. KRACHER Creighton University

FRIEDRICH KRATOCHWIL Ludwig Maximillians Universitat, München

S. KRIMSKY Tufts University

HAROLD W. KUHN Princeton University

PAUL A. KURZMAN Hunter College

WILL KYMLICKA University of Ottawa

DOUGLAS LACKEY Baruch College, City University of New York

ROSALIND LADD Wheaton College

ROBERT F. LADENSON Illinois Institute of Technology

MARCEL C. LAFOLLETTE George Washington University

DAVID LAMB University of Birmingham

SHELLEY LANE Queen Mary and Westfield College, University of London

HAROLD Q. LANGENDERFER University of North Carolina, Chapel Hill

DUNCAN LANGFORD University of Kent

BRUCE LANGTRY University of Melbourne

DAVID W. LANKSHEAR Board of Education, The Church of England

GERALD A. LARUE University of Southern California

RÜDIGER LAUTMANN Universität Bremen

DOMINIQUE LECOURT Association Diderot, Paris, France

STEVEN LEE Hobart and William Smith Colleges

TOM LEE University of Alabama

HUGH LEHMAN University of Guelph

SALLY LERNER University of Waterloo

HARRY LESSER University of Manchester

MICHAEL LESSNOFF Glasgow University

ANDRÉ LIEBICH Institut Universitaire des Hautes

IAN LOADER Keele University

ANDREW LOCKYER University of Glasgow

JANE LUTZ University of Birmingham

NEIL MACDONALD Clinical Research Institute of Montreal

DARRYL MACER University of Tsubuka

TIBOR R. MACHAN Auburn University

CATRIONA MACKENZIE Macquarie University

THOMAS MAGNELL Drew University

MARTIN H. MALIN Chicago-Kent College of Law

JEFF MALPAS Murdoch University

TOM MANDEL Walter & Eliza Hall Institute of Medical Research

IAN MARKHAM Liverpool Hope University College

SANDRA MARSHALL University of Stirling

PETER MASON Massey University

RICHARD O. MASON Southern Methodist University

LARRY MAY Washington University

TOM MAYER University of Colorado at Boulder

SEAN MCCONVILLE Queen Mary and Westfield College

TERENCE H. MCLAUGHLIN University of Cambridge

SARA MEADOWS University of Bristol

VICENTE MEDINA Seton Hall University

SCOTT MEIKLE Glasgow University

GILBERT MEILAENDER Valparaiso University

CURT MEINE International Crane Foundation, Baraboo, Wisconsin

GREG MELLEMA Calvin College

BEN MEPHAM University of Nottingham

FRED D. MILLER Bowling Green State University

RICHARD B. MILLER Indiana University

STEVEN MINTZ California State University

JOHN MONAHAN University of Virginia

PATRICK MOONEY John Carroll University

EMILIO MORDINI Psychoanalytic Institute for Social Research, Rome

WILLIAM J. MORGAN University of Tennessee, Knoxville

MAURIZIO MORI Center for Research in Politics and Ethics, Milan, Italy

ADAM MORTON University of Bristol

JOHN C. MOSKOP East Carolina University School of Medicine

ERIC MOUNT Centre College

STEPHEN R. MUNZER University of California, Los Angeles Law School

THOMAS H. MURRAY Case Western Reserve University

CHARLES R. MYERS United States Air Force Academy

ETHAN NADELMANN Lindesmith Center, New York

NGAIRE NAFFINE University of Adelaide

JAN NARVESON University of Waterloo

STEPHEN NATHANSON Northeastern University

FREDERICK L. NEUMANN University of Illinois at Champaign

GEORGE NEWLANDS Glasgow University

RICHARD NORMAN University of Kent at Canterbury

ALAN NORRIE Queen Mary and Westfield College, University of London

BRYAN G. NORTON Georgia Institute of Technology

REED F. NOSS The Wildlands Project, Corvallis, Oregon

JAMES O'CONNOR University of California, Santa Cruz

JOHN F. O'NEILL University of Lancaster

TIMOTHY O'RIORDAN University of East Anglia

SUSAN M. OKIN Stanford University

FREDERICK OLAFSON University of California at San Diego

NORMAN OLCH John Jay College of Criminal Justice

EMILY CAROTA ORNE University of Pennsylvania College of Medicine

DAVID OWEN Southampton University

ROBERT PAEHLKE Trent University

JOY A. PALMER University of Durham

DIANE B. PAUL University of Massachusetts at Boston

JOYCE MAGUIRE PAVAO Center for Family Connections, Inc., Cambridge, Massachusetts

ROBERT ALLAN PEARLMAN Veteran Affairs Medical Center, Seattle, Washington

ROSALIND PETCHESKY Hunter College

BRUCE PIASECKI Rensselaer Polytechnic Institute

NEIL PICKERING University of Wales, Swansea

DAVID PIMENTEL Cornell University

THOMAS PLATT West Chester University

EVELYN B. PLUHAR Pennsylvania State University

TREVOR B. POOLE Animal Welfare Scientist, Essex, England

PHILLIP POPPLE Western Michigan University

CHARLES S. PREBISH Pennsylvania State University

T. E. QUILL University of Rochester

JAMES RACHELS University of Alabama at Birmingham

HAYDEN RAMSAY LaTrobe University

ALBERT RANDALL Austin Paey State University

FREDERIC G. REAMER Rhode Island College

TOM REGAN North Carolina State University

ROBERT REINER London School of Economics

WILLIAM RHODES United States Air Force Academy

GENEVRA RICHARDSON Queen Mary and Westfield College, University of London

MELINDA A. ROBERTS The College of New Jersey, Trenton

K. ROBINSON Australian National University

SIMON ROGERSON DeMontfort University

EUGENE ROSA Washington State University

STUART ROSENBAUM Baylor University

PETER ROSSEL University of Copenhagen

HOLMES ROSTON, III Colorado State University

ANDREW ROWAN Tufts University School of Veterinary Medicine

WILLIAM RUDDICK New York University

CHARLES SABATINO Daeman College

DONALD SABO D'Youville College

MARK SAGOFF University of Maryland

DAVID P. ST. GEORGE Royal Free Hospital School of Medicine, London

EDWARD P. ST. JOHN University of Dayton

SAM SALEK Welsh School of Pharmacy, Cardiff, Wales

MIGUEL A. SANCHEZ-GONZALEZ Complutense University, Madrid

PAUL C. SANTILLI Siena College

STEVE F. SAPONTZIS California State University, Hayward

DEBRA SATZ Stanford University

DORY SCALTSAS University of Edinburgh

GEOFFREY F. SCARRE University of Durham

WALTER SCHALLER Texas Technical University

FREDERICK SCHAUER Harvard University

JONATHAN SCHONSHECK LeMoyne College

PETER SCHOULS Massey University

PETER SCHREINER Comenius Institute, Münster

UDO SCHÜKLENK Centre for Professional Ethics, University of Central Lancashire

DOUGLAS SCHUURMAN St. Olaf College

JOHN R. SEARLE University of California, Berkeley

ANNE SELLER University of Kent at Canterbury

STAN SHAPIRO McGill University

ROBERT SHARPE University of Wales at Lampeter

SUSAN SHERWIN Dalhousie University

CHARLES SHIREMAN Portland State University

LAURENCE SHUTE California State Polytechnic University, Pomona

A. J. SIMMONS University of Virginia

PETER SINGER Monash University

ANTHONY SKILLEN University of Kent at Canterbury

DAVID B. SMITH Lancaster University

DAVID C. SMITH Council for Ethics in Economics, Columbus, Ohio

DAVID J. SMITH University of Edinburgh

R. A. MCCALL SMITH University of Edinburgh

ALLEN K. SNYDER University of Tennessee, Knoxville

JEFFREY SPINNER University of Nebraska

JOSEPH S. SPOERL Saint Anselm College

ODED STARK University of Oslo

DANIEL STATMAN Bar-Ilan University, Ramat-Gan, Israel

EDWARD STEIN Yale University

JAMES P. STERBA University of Notre Dame

RICHARD H. STERN Washington, DC

ELAINE STERNBERG University of Leeds

MICHAEL STINGL University of Lethbridge

KENNETH A. STRIKE Cornell University

CARSON M. STRONG University of Tennessee, Memphis

WAYNE SUMNER University of Toronto

CARL TALBOT Cardiff University of Wales

C. L. TEN Monash University

BERNARD TEO Victoria, Australia

MARGARET THORNTON LaTrobe University

TERRY THREADGOLD Monash University

ROSEMARIE TONG Davidson College

SUZANNE UNIAEKE University of Wollongong

JOHN VEIT-WILSON University of Newcastle-Upon-Tyne

MALHAM M. WAKIN United States Air Force Academy

PAUL WARREN Florida International University

STEVEN WASSERMAN John Jay College of Criminal Justice

PETER WEBSTER Victoria University, Wellington, New Zealand

VIVIAN WEIL Illinois Institute of Technology

JOS V. M. WELIE Creighton University

N. A. WELLMAN Oxford University & Warneford Hospital

ALAN WERTHEIMER University of Vermont

CAROLINE WEST Macquarie University

JOHN P. WHITE University of London

RICHARD C. WHITFIELD University of Aston

ROY WILKIE University of Strathclyde

KEVIN WILLIAMS Cardiff University of Wales

PETER WILLIAMS State University of New York, Stony Brook

DAVID WILLIS Yarra Theological Union

PETER WILSON New Zealand

MICHAEL WREEN Marquette University

GEORGE WYMAN Durham, North Carolina

ROBERT YOUNG LaTrobe University

SUSAN KHIN ZHAW The Open University

INDEX

G